ANNUAL EDITION

2015 ALMANAC OF BUSINESS AND INDUSTRIAL FINANCIAL RATIOS

Leo Troy, Ph.D.
Philip Wilson

Wolters Kluwer

EDITORIAL STAFF
Production .... Christopher Zwirek
Design .... Craig Arritola

This publication is designed to provide accurate and authoritative information in regard to the subject matter covered. It is sold with the understanding that the publisher is not engaged in rendering legal, accounting, or other professional service and that the author is not offering such advice in this publication. If legal advice or other professional assistance is required, the services of a competent professional person should be sought.

ISBN: 978-0-8080-3829-0

4025 W. Peterson Avenue
Chicago, IL 60646-6085
800 248 3248
CCHGroup.com

Printed in the United States of America

DEDICATED

Professor Leo Troy, the author of The *Almanac of Business and Financial Ratios*, passed away on November 2, 2013. The *Almanac*, now in its 46th edition, is the product of our beloved father's vision. He recognized early on that the raw data collected by the IRS could be used to sharpen one's understanding of the true value of a business or industry. Dad painstakingly set about creating the Almanac out of that data so that its users could make more informed decisions. The *Almanac* thus reflects his passion for truth, his devotion to education, his curiosity and intellect, his diligence, and his relentless drive to provide a better life for his family. Dad appreciated the work of his colleagues **Ka-Neng Au** and **Phil Wilson**, and we thank them for their invaluable contributions to the *Almanac*. All of us, Dad's children and grandchildren, his relatives, friends and colleagues, seek to follow the example he set for us.

The memory of the righteous is for blessing.

Alexander Troy & Suzannah B. Troy

PREFACE

Now in its 46th Edition, the *Almanac of Business and Industrial Financial Ratios* provides a precise benchmark for evaluating an individual company's financial performance. The performance data is derived from the latest available IRS figures on U.S. and international companies, and tracks 50 operating and financial factors in nearly 200 industries. The *Almanac* provides competitive norms in actual dollar amounts for revenue and capital factors, as well as important average operating costs in percent of net sales. It also provides other critical financial factors in percentage, including debt ratio, return on assets, return on equity, profit margin, and more. Beyond its reliable insights into corporate behavior, the *Almanac* can be used by other countries looking to model their economies on American performance.

Also included with the text, in a special pocket provided in the inside cover of the book, is a CD-ROM that contains all the materials found in the book including the explanatory discussion, the data tables, and the supporting index. Also included on the CD, but not in the book itself, is a special template that allows the reader to add individual company data of interest to compare and contrast with data from the book.

2015 Edition Highlights

The 2015 Edition of the *Almanac of Business and Industrial Financial Ratios* has been updated to include the following:

- **Broad scope:** *2015 Almanac* features the North American Industry Classification System (NAICS), so you can benchmark or analyze results consistently with corporations in the United States, Canada, and Mexico.

- **Most industry types:** *2015 Almanac* highlights most industry types, including industries with advanced technologies and newly emerging industries such as paging and wireless communications.

- **A truer picture** of corporate financial performance, since the data isn't based on a mixed bag of averages that might include partnerships or sole proprietors. *2015 Almanac* features a homogeneous universe of American corporate financial performance.

- **Many classifications:** *2015 Almanac* analyzes 195 industries with 50 financial performance items.

- **Benchmarks:** *2015 Almanac* provides 13 benchmarks, including such critical measures as Receipts to Cash Flow, Debt to Total Assets, and Return on Equity both before and after taxes.

- **Analytical tables:** *Table I, Corporations with and without Net Income (All Corporations), and Table II, Corporations with Net Income.*
- **Easier apples-to-apples comparisons:** Each table is divided into 13 asset sizes.
- **More comprehensive:** Total receipts of all corporations covered by *2015 Almanac* is $28.3 trillion, making the *Almanac* the Anatomy of American Corporate Capitalism.

Philip Wilson

July 2014

INTRODUCTION

QUESTIONS, ANSWERS AND COMMENTS ON THE *ALMANAC*

Some users have requested further information on the use of the *Almanac's* ratios and statistics. This Q & A addition to the *Almanac* is in response to that demand.

1. What are the general purposes of the Almanac?

The goal of the *Almanac* is to provide users with a reliable and comprehensive source of standard financial ratios and financial statistics on all corporations, public and private, including those filing 1120S returns in the United States. Excluded are all individual proprietorships and partnerships. The *Almanac* makes available key business and financial statistics, which are consistent and neutral (unbiased by any commercial publisher or trade association).

2. What is the source and reliability of the Almanac's results?

The *Almanac's* results are computed from the Department of the Treasury, Internal Revenue Service's statistical sampling of the tax returns of all corporations. Dividends received from foreign corporations are included in total receipts of those corporations affected. The statistics apply to the company rather than the establishment.

3. Are international comparisons available?

Yes. Because of the adoption of a common system of industrial classification by the U.S., Canada and Mexico, known as the North American Industrial Classification System of industries (NAICS), under the North American Free Trade Agreement, users in Canada and Mexico can compare and contrast their results with those corporations in the United States.

4. What about comparisons within the U.S?

These are the most important applications of the *Almanac*. Results are available for each and every corporation within the U.S., whether public or private, and include small business corporations, those which file the 1120S tax return. Therefore, users can compare their corporate performance with that of their industry and asset size group of corporate enterprise in the United States.

5. How many corporations are covered in the Almanac?

The *Almanac's* results are derived from more than 5.8 million corporation tax returns. Furthermore, the user can easily determine the number of enterprises for the total of each industry and by each of the 12 asset size groups. This makes for a total of 13 asset size comparisons.

6. What about differences in the size of corporations?

In addition to the results for each industry, the *Almanac* displays 12 columns of performance by the size of assets. Again, this makes for a total of 13 asset size comparisons.

7. Does the Almanac distinguish between the profitability of corporations?

In a word, yes. Each industry is divided between two tables: Table I reports the results of all corporations in an industry, that is, those with and without net income. It is followed by a second table for the same industry, Table II, which reports only those corporations with net income.

8. How many items of information are there for each industry?

There are 50 indicators of corporate performance in each table and each industry and for all asset size groups, except where the IRS' data sample is too small, or it does not supply the necessary information.

9. Who are the users of the Almanac?

Accountants, corporate managers, business consultants, investors evaluating a corporate takeover, entrepreneurs considering new businesses, lawyers, and students of accounting, business, and management.

10. What accounting time period is covered?

The Internal Revenue Service provides the most recent statistics publicly available for the *Almanac*. For the 2015 *Almanac*, these statistics apply to the accounting period from July 2011 through June 2012.

WHAT'S NEW IN THIS EDITION

Beginning with the year 2002, the *Almanac of Business and Industrial Financial Ratios* began using the North American Industry Classification System (NAICS). NAICS replaces the Internal Revenue Service's own system, which it had used for many years, an adaptation of Standard Industrial Classification (SIC); all previous *Almanacs* had used that adaptation.

The new industrial classification system is the product of the North American Free Trade Agreement (NAFTA), and it replaces the existing classification systems not only of the United States but also of Canada and Mexico. Hence, the new system applies uniformly to the three countries, and users of the *Almanac 2015*, utilizing the new international industrial classification system, can now compare their results with corporations in all three nations.

In the United States, the new manual was created by the Office of Management and Budget (OMB). The NAICS system gives special attention to industries producing and furnishing advanced technologies, new and emerging industries, as well as service industries in general. NAICS divides the economy into 21 sectors, five in the predominantly goods-producing area, and 16 in the service producing area.

INDUSTRY SECTORS

In 2007, NAICS was revised and reorganized; several of those changes apply to the *Almanac 2015*. The Real Estate Investment Trust category (525930) was deleted. In its place, Mortgage REIT's were reclassified to Other Financial Vehicles (525995) while Equity REIT's were reclassified either to Lessors of Buildings (531115) or Lessors of Miniwarehouses, Self-Storage Units and other Real Estate (531135), depending on the content of the REIT portfolio.

The other major changes were in the information sector. The Internet Publishing and Broadcasting category (516100) was deleted and reclassified with Other Information Services (519100). Internet Service Providers (518115) were reclassified to Telecommunications (517000). Web Search Portals (also part of 518115) were reclassified to the expanded category, Other Information Services

(519100). The remainder of the 518115 category was reorganized as Data processing, Hosting and Related Services (518210).

The source of the IRS's data are the tax returns of all *active* public and private corporations. Because the *Almanac's* data are derived only from corporate tax returns, there is a mixture of corporate with the financial performance of partnerships and individual proprietorships; the *Almanac's* information constitutes a **homogeneous universe**. The tax returns are classified by the IRS on the basis of the business activity which accounts for a corporation's largest percentage of total receipts. Large corporations with dissimilar business activities are included in only one industry, despite operations that are unrelated to the industry in which they are grouped.

The data developed by the IRS are derived from a stratified probability sample of corporation income tax returns. Where the sample data from the sample are small and should those numbers be used in a denominator, the result is reported as a dot (•) in the *Almanac*. Returns of the largest corporations are generally in the sample from year to year, but comparability can be affected by consolidations and mergers, changes in the law and the tax forms, and changes in the industrial classification system used over the years.

REPRESENTATIVE INDUSTRIES

The *Almanac* reports on nearly 200 industries. Minor industries are denoted by a six-digit code; major industries are designated by a three-digit industry code; industrial sectors by a two-digit code; and industrial divisions by a two-digit code. When the data are the same for minor, major, sector, and industrial division, the IRS reports only the industrial division, and similarly for other identities applicable to the major and sectoral industries; the *Almanac* follows this procedure.

Almanac 2015 continues the previous coverage of reporting information: for all industries, **Table I, Corporations with and without Net Income** (that is, the entire universe of active reporting corporations), and **Table II, Corporations with Net Income**, a subset of the universe. In the *Almanac 2015*, Table I covers over 5.8 million enterprises (corporations), and Table II covers 3.4 million corporations with net income. This implies that 2.4 million corporations reported deficits. The IRS defines net income (or deficit) as the companies' net profit or loss from taxable sources of income reduced by allowable deductions. Total receipts of the 5.8 million corporations reported in *Almanac 2015* was $28.3 trillion, up by $2.1 trillion.

The *Almanac* continues to report performance results not only by the total for each industry, but by 12 other asset size groups (a total of 13 asset size groups), providing 50 items of data and/or ratios on corporate performance:

TOTAL
Zero
$1 to $500,000
$500,001 to $1,000,000
$1,000,001 to $5,000,000
$5,000,001 to $10,000,000
$10,000,001 to $25,000,000
$25,000,001 to $50,000,000
$50,000,001 to $100,000,000
$100,000,001 to $250,000,000
$250,000,001 to $500,000,000
$500,000,001 to $2,500,000,000
$2,500,000,001 or more

All data in Tables I and II cover an accounting period identified on all tables and are the most recent information available from the IRS. For the *Almanac 2015*, the accounting period is July 2011 through June 2012. The dating of the data is counterbalanced by the most extensive industrial coverage available in any report on financial performance, the number of items of corporate performance, and their availability in thirteen asset size groups. Moreover, the timing of the data are also counterbalanced by the stability of the *Almanac's* values as past trends have indicated. Therefore, the *Almanac's* financial results are reliable in assessing current corporate performance.

Beyond its reliable insights into corporate behavior on a micro basis, its comprehensive and detailed coverage make the *Almanac* the **Anatomy of American Corporate Capitalism**. In this macro sense, it constitutes **the** example to those countries desirous of modeling their economies on the American performance.

HOW TO USE THE ALMANAC

On the micro level, the *Almanac* multiplies manyfold the power of financial analysis to evaluate an individual company's financial performance: In contrast to many standard reports, the *Almanac* gives management, and analysts independent of any company, more of the fundamental analytical tools needed to compare their company with companies in the same industry and of the same asset size. The *Almanac* can enhance the value of any company's annual report because it affords the analyst and the stockholder detailed background of financial information for comparison.

All items and ratios are listed in Both Table I and Table II. No figures are reported in the *Almanac* when the IRS has either suppressed the underlying data, or the sample size, or other reasons affecting a calculated result, and where the ratio/item was not applicable to an industry. The 50 tax-based items that provide that financial analysis are as follows:

1. Number of Enterprises

These are the count of corporate tax returns filed by active corporations on one of the Form 1120-series returns.

> **SPECIAL NOTE:** Net Sales is used to compute the percentage of items 3 to 7 to Net Sales for all industries, except Finance, Insurance, and Real Estate (FIRE). For the FIRE industries, Total Receipts are used to compute the percentage of items 3 to 7.

REVENUES ($ IN THOUSANDS), ITEMS 2 TO 9

2. Operating Income (Net Sales)

This is the IRS item Business Receipts, the gross operating receipts reduced by the cost of returned goods and allowances.

3. Interest

Taxable interest includes interest on U.S. Government obligations, loans, notes, mortgages, arbitrage bonds, nonexempt private activity bonds, corporate bonds, bank deposits, and tax refunds; interest received from tax-exempt state or local municipal bonds and ESOP loans are not included in this item.

4. Rents

These are the gross amounts received from the use or occupancy of property by corporations whose principal activities did not involve operating rental properties.

5. Royalties

These are gross payments received for the use of property rights before taking deductions.

6. Other Portfolio Income

These consist of cash, notes, and accounts receivable, less allowance for bad debts and inventories.

7. Other Receipts

These receipts include such items as income from minor operations, cash discounts, claims, license rights, judgments, and joint ventures.

8. Total Receipts

Total receipts are the sum of ten items: 1. Business receipts; 2. Interest; 3. Interest on government obligations: state and local; 4. Rents; 5. Royalties; 6. Net capital gains (excluding long-term gains from regulated investment companies); 7. Net gain, noncapital assets; 8. Dividends received from domestic corporations; 9. Dividends received from foreign corporations; 10. Other receipts.

9. Average Total Receipts

Total receipts divided by the number of enterprises.

OPERATING COSTS/OPERATING INCOME, ITEMS 10 TO 22

10. Cost of Operations

This is the IRS's Costs of Goods Sold; it consists of the costs incurred in producing the goods or furnishing the services that generated the corporations' business receipts.

11. Salaries and Wages

These include the amount of salaries and wages paid as well as bonuses and director's fees, but no contributions to pension plans (see item 16) nor compensation of officers (see item 20).

12. Taxes Paid

Excludes Federal Income Taxes; they are the amounts paid for ordinary state and local taxes, social security, payroll taxes, unemployment insurance taxes, excise taxes, import and tariff duties, and business license and privilege taxes.

13. Interest Paid

These amounts consist of interest paid on all business indebtedness.

14. Depreciation

The charges allowed are governed principally by the IRS rules in effect in 1997, basically enacted in 1986, but also include other modifications. Hence, depreciation could represent amounts computed by different sets of rules.

15. Amortization and Depletion

Most amortization is calculated on a straight-line basis. Depletion is allowed for the exhaustion of natural deposits and timber.

16. Pensions, Profit-Sharing, Stock Bonus, and Annuity Plans

These are amounts deducted during the current year for qualified pension, profit-sharing, or other funded deferred compensation plans.

17. Employee Benefits

These are employer contributions to death benefit, insurance, health, accident, and sickness, and other welfare plans.

18. Advertising

Amounts include promotion and publicity expenses.

19. Other Expenses

These include expenses for repairs, bad debts, rent paid on business property, domestic production activities, contributions and gifts, and expenses not allocable to specific deductible items.

20. Officers' Compensation

Salaries, wages, stock bonuses, bonds, and other forms of compensation are included in this item.

21. Operating Margin

This is the net income after all operating costs have been deducted.

22. Operating Margin Before Officers' Compensation

This measure takes into account the effect of Officers' Compensation on the operating margin.

SELECTED AVERAGE BALANCE SHEET ITEMS ($ IN THOUSANDS) ITEMS 23 TO 29

23. Average Net Receivables

The total of Notes and Accounts Receivable, less Allowance for Bad Debts, divided by the number of enterprises. Notes and Accounts Receivable are the gross amounts arising from business sales or services to customers on credit in the course of ordinary trade or business. This includes commercial paper, charge accounts, current intercompany receivables, property investment loans, and trade acceptances.

24. Average Inventories

Total inventories are divided by the number of enterprises. Inventories include finished goods, partially finished goods, new materials and supplies acquired for sale, merchandise on hand or in transit, and growing crops reported as assets by agricultural enterprises.

25. Average Net Property, Plant and Equipment

This includes depreciable assets less accumulated depreciation, depletable assets less accumulated depletion, and land; the sum is divided by the number of enterprises. Depreciable assets consist of end-of-year balance sheet tangible property, such as buildings and equipment used in trade or business, or held for the production of income, and that has a useful life of one year or more. The amount of accumulated depreciation represents the portion written off in the current year, as well as in prior years. Depletable assets represent the end-of-year value of mineral property, oil and gas wells, and other natural resources; standing timber; intangible development and drilling costs capitalized; and leases and leaseholds, subject to depletion. Accumulated depletion represents the cumulative adjustment of these assets.

26. Average Total Assets

Total Assets (and Total Liabilities) are amounts reported in the end-of-year balance sheet. Total Assets are net amounts after reduction from accumulated depreciation, accumulated amortization, accumulated depletion, and the reserve for bad debts. Total Liabilities include the claims of creditors and stockholders' equity, and were net after reduction by the cost of treasury stock. The average of total assets was obtained by dividing it by the number of enterprises.

27. Average of Notes and Loans Payable, and Mortgages

These liabilities were separated on the balance sheet according to the time to maturity of the obligations. Time to maturity was based on the date of the balance sheet, rather than the date of issue of the obligations. The total was divided by the number of enterprises.

28. Average of All Other Liabilities

These included accounts payable, and other liabilities including other current liabilities. The total was divided by the number of enterprises.

29. Average Net Worth

Net Worth represents the stockholders' equity in the corporation (total assets minus the claims of creditors). It consists of Capital Stock, Paid-In Capital Surplus, Retained Earnings Appropriated, Retained Earnings Unappropriated, less cost of treasury stock.

SELECTED FINANCIAL RATIOS, NUMBER OF TIMES TO ONE, RATIOS 30 TO 44

30. CURRENT RATIO

The items that used Current Assets for this ratio are Cash; Notes and Accounts Receivable, Less: Allowance for Bad Debts; Inventories; Government Obligations; Tax-Exempt Securities; and Other Current Assets. For Current Liabilities, the following items were included: Accounts Payable; Mortgages and Notes Maturing in Less than 1 Year; and Other Current Liabilities.

This ratio, rated highest by CPAs as a measure of liquidity, gauges the ability of a company to meet its short-term financial obligations should it be compelled to liquidate its assets. However, it is not an absolute measure of the company's ability to meet its obligations. It is obtained by dividing current assets by current liabilities. The standard guideline has been a ratio of 2 to 1; however, some companies have found that in their experience, a ratio less than 2 to 1 is adequate, while others consider a larger one to be necessary. The ratio is affected by the method of valuation of inventory (LIFO or FIFO) and by inflation. The *Almanac* provides measures that can be treated as standards by size of asset.

31. Quick Ratio

This ratio is also known as the "Acid Test Ratio" because it is often used to estimate a company's general liquidity. There is some disagreement about the inclusion of inventory in the numerator because it may be slow moving, obsolete, or pledged to specific creditors, and, therefore, not be readily convertible into cash. The *Almanac* adopts a conservative approach and does not include the item in calculating the ratio. Excluding inventories and other current assets, the numerator is the same as that used in determining current assets. The denominator, current liabilities, is unchanged. The ratio of 1 to 1 has been considered a reasonable standard, but it is jeopardized because accounts and notes receivable may not be convertible into cash at face value and at short notice. The *Almanac* provides measures that can be treated as standards by size of asset.

32. Net Sales to Working Capital

This is an efficiency, or turnover, ratio that measures the rate at which current assets less current liabilities (Working Capital) is used in making sales. (In industries in Finance, Insurance, and Real Estate, total receipts rather than net sales is used.) A low ratio indicates a less efficient (profitable) use of working capital in making sales. The *Almanac* provides measures that can be treated as standards by size of asset. Working Capital is the difference between current assets and current liabilities.

33. Coverage Ratio

This ratio measures the number of times all interest paid by the company is covered by earnings before interest charges and taxes (EBIT). For that reason, the ratio is also known as the "times interest earned ratio." The ratio indicates the company's ability to service its debt based on its income.

34. Total Asset Turnover

The ratio is an efficiency ratio because it indicates the effectiveness of the company's use of its total assets in generating sales. It is measured by dividing net sales by total assets.

35. Inventory Turnover

Inventory turnover measures the liquidity of the inventory. It is computed by dividing the cost of goods sold by the average inventory. The result shows the number of times that the average inventory can be converted into receivables or cash. The ratio reflects both on the quality of the inventory and the efficiency of management. Typically, the higher the turnover rate, the more likely profits will be higher.

> **SPECIAL NOTE:** Inventory turnover is not computed for industries in Finance, Insurance, and Real Estate.

36. Receivables Turnover

This ratio measures the liquidity of accounts receivable. It indicates the average collection period throughout the year. It is obtained by dividing sales average by net receivables. It is not computed in the Finance, Insurance, and Real Estate industries (although it is calculated for all other industries even though conventional analysis typically omits it) for many of the industries in the *Almanac.*

37. Total Liabilities to Net Worth

This ratio indicates the extent to which the company's funds are supplied by short- and long-term creditors compared to its owners. It is an indicator of the company's long-term debt paying ability. The ratio is one of the most important bearing on the company's capital structure. Net worth is defined in ratio 29.

38. Current Assets to Working Capital

The dependence of Working Capital in part on current assets is important to understanding this part of the source of Working Capital. Current Assets are defined in ratio 30 and Working Capital is defined in ratio 32.

39. Current Liabilities to Working Capital

The dependence of Working Capital in part on current liabilities is important to understanding this part of the source of Working Capital. Current Liabilities are defined in ratio 30 and Working Capital is defined in ratio 32.

40. Working Capital to Net Sales or Total Receipts

The purpose of this ratio is to determine the working capital needed in relation to projected sales or receipts. Working Capital is defined in ratio 32.

41. Inventory to Working Capital

This ratio, by showing the proportion of Working Capital invested in Inventory, indicates the part of Current Assets that are least liquid. Inventories which exceed working capital indicate that current liabilities exceed liquid current assets. Working Capital is defined in ratio 32.

42. Total Receipts to Cash Flow

Cash Flow is the difference between cash receipts and cash disbursements. The ratio of total receipts to cash flow could suggest steps which management might take to improve the company's cash position.

43. Cost of Goods to Cash Flow

This ratio can be the basis for projections of cash requirements needed to fund projected costs of production. Cash flow is defined in ratio 42.

44. Cash Flow to Total Debt

This ratio indicates the extent to which a company could service its total debt from cash flow. It is analogous to the coverage ratio; refer to ratio 33. Cash flow is defined in ratio 42.

SELECTED FINANCIAL FACTORS (IN PERCENTAGES), ITEMS 45 TO 50

45. Debt Ratio (Total Liabilities to Total Assets)

This ratio indicates the company's ability to pay all its debts. It measures the creditors' and owners' of the company's ability to withstand losses. It is an indicator of the long-run solvency of the firm.

46. Return on Total Assets

The ratio combines the turnover and profit ratios (Sales/Total Assets x [times] Profit/Sales) and yields the return on investment (Total Assets). The result is the end product of the DuPont System of financial analysis. The system takes into account both operating income and operating assets. In Table I of each industry, the Return on Investment (ROI) is net income less deficit before income taxes divided by total assets. In Table II of each industry, the ROI is net income before income taxes divided by Total Assets. Total Assets are used because management has discretion in the investment of the resources provided by both the creditors and owners.

47. Return on Equity Before Income Taxes

This ratio measures the profitability of the company's operations to owners, before income taxes. For Table I this is net income, less deficit before income taxes and before credits. For Table II this is net income minus income tax before credits.

48. Return on Equity After Income Taxes

This ratio measures the profitability of the company's operations to owners, after income taxes. For Table I this is net income, less deficit and minus income tax before credits. For Table II this is net income minus income tax and before credits.

49. Profit Margin (Before Income Tax)

This is net income before income tax divided by net sales (or total receipts) and indicates the contribution of sales to the profitability of the company. Competition, capital structure, and operating characteristics cause the margin to vary within and among industries. For Table I, net income less deficit and before income taxes is the numerator; for Table II it is net income before tax.

50. Profit Margin (After Income Tax)

This ratio is the same as ratio 49 except that income taxes are taken into account.

TABLE OF CONTENTS

Page references to tables for industries with net income are in italic

PRINCIPAL BUSINESS ACTIVITY (BASED ON NAICS)

11 *Agriculture, Forestry, Fishing and Hunting*

111005	Agricultural Production	1, *2*
113005	Forestry and Logging	3, *4*
114005	Support Activities and Fishing, Hunting and Trapping	5, *6*

21 *Mining*

211110	Oil and Gas Extraction	*7, 8*
212110	Coal Mining	*9, 10*
212200	Metal Ore Mining	11, *12*
212315	Nonmetallic Mineral Mining and Quarrying	13, *14*
213110	Support Activities for Mining	15, *16*

22 *Utilities*

221100	Electric Power Generation, Transmission and Distribution	17, *18*
221210	Natural Gas Distribution	19, *20*
221300	Water, Sewage, and Other Systems	21, *22*
221500	Combination Gas and Electric	23, *24*

23 *Construction*

236115	Construction of Buildings	25, *26*
237105	Heavy and Civil Engineering Construction	27, *28*
237210	Land Subdivision	29, *30*
238	Special trade contractors	
238210	Electrical Contractors	31, *32*
238220	Plumbing, Heating, and Air-Conditioning Contractors	*33, 34*
238905	Other Specialty Trade Contractors	*35, 36*

31 *Manufacturing*

311	Food manufacturing	
311115	Animal Food and Grain and Oilseed Milling	*37, 38*
311300	Sugar and Confectionery Product	39, *40*
311400	Fruit and Vegetable Preserving and Specialty Food	41, *42*
311500	Dairy Product	43, *44*
311615	Meat and Seafood Processing	45, *46*
311800	Bakeries and Tortilla	47, *48*
311900	Other Food	49, *50*
312	Beverage and Tobacco Product Manufacturing	
312110	Soft Drink and Ice	51, *52*
312120	Breweries	53, *54*

312135	Wineries and Distilleries	55, *56*
312200	Tobacco Manufacturing	57, *58*
313	Textile Mills and Textile Product Mills	
313000	Textile Mills	59, *60*
314000	Textile Product Mills	61, *62*
315	Apparel Manufacturing	
315100	Apparel Knitting Mills	63, *64*
315215	Cut and Sew Apparel Contractors and Mfrs.	65, *66*
315990	Apparel Accessories and Other Apparel	67, *68*
316115	Leather and Allied Product Manufacturing	69, *70*
321115	Wood Product Manufacturing	71, *72*
322	Paper Manufacturing	
322100	Pulp, Paper, and Paperboard Mills	73, *74*
322200	Converted Paper Product	75, *76*
323	Printing and Related Support Activities	
323100	Printing and Related Support Activities	77, *78*
324	Petroleum and Coal Products Manufacturing	
324110	Petroleum Refineries (Including Integrated)	79, *80*
324125	Asphalt Paving, Roofing, Other Petroleum and Coal Products	81, *82*
325	Chemical Manufacturing	
325100	Basic Chemical	83, *84*
325200	Resin, Synthetic Rubber and Fibers and Filaments	85, *86*
325410	Pharmaceutical and Medicine	87, *88*
325500	Paint, Coating, and Adhesive	89, *90*
325600	Soap, Cleaning Compound, and Toilet Preparation	91, *92*
325905	Chemical Product and Preparation	93, *94*
326	Plastics and Rubber Product Manufacturing	
326100	Plastics Product	95, *96*
326200	Rubber Product	97, *98*
327	Nonmetallic Mineral Product Manufacturing	
327105	Clay, Refractory and Other Nonmetallic Mineral Product	99, *100*
327210	Glass and Glass Product	101, *102*
327305	Cement, Concrete, Lime and Gypsum Product	103, *104*
331	Primary Metal Manufacturing	
331115	Iron, Steel Mills and Steel Product	105, *106*
331315	Nonferrous Metal Production and Processing	107, *108*
331500	Foundries	109, *110*
332	Fabricated Metal Product Manufacturing	
332110	Forging and Stamping	111, *112*
332215	Cutlery, Hardware, Spring and Wire Machine Shops, Nut, Bolt	113, *114*
332300	Architectural and Structural Metals	115, *116*
332400	Boiler, Tank, and Shipping Container	117, *118*
332810	Coating, Engraving, Heat Treating, and Allied Activities	119, *120*
332900	Other Fabricated Metal Product	121, *122*

333	Machinery Manufacturing	
333100	Agriculture, Construction, and Mining Machinery	123, *124*
333200	Industrial Machinery	125, *126*
333310	Commercial and Service Industry Machinery	127, *128*
333410	Ventilation, Heating, A.C. & Commercial Refrigeration Equip.	129, *130*
333510	Metalworking Machinery	131, *132*
333610	Engine, Turbine and Power Transmission Equipment	133, *134*
333900	Other General Purpose Machinery	135, *136*
334	Computer and Electronic Product Manufacturing	
334110	Computer and Peripheral Equipment	137, *138*
334200	Communications Equipment	139, *140*
334315	Audio and Video Equip., Reproducing Magnetic & Optical Media	141, *142*
334410	Semiconductor and Other Electronic Component	143, *144*
334500	Navigational, Measuring, Electromedical, and Control	145, *146*
335	Electrical Equipment, Appliance, and Component Manufacturing	
335105	Electrical Lighting Equipment and Household Appliance	147, *148*
335310	Electrical Equipment	149, *150*
335900	Other Electrical Equipment and Component	151, *152*
336	Transportation Equipment Manufacturing	
336105	Motor Vehicle and Parts	153, *154*
336410	Aerospace Product and Parts	155, *156*
336610	Ship and Boat Building	157, *158*
336995	Other Transportation Equipment and Railroad Rolling Stock	159, *160*
337000	Furniture and Related Product Manufacturing	161, *162*
339	Miscellaneous Manufacturing	
339110	Medical Equipment and Supplies	163, *164*
339900	Other Miscellaneous Manufacturing	165, *166*

42 *Wholesale Trade*

423	Wholesale Trade, Durable Goods	
423100	Motor Vehicle and Motor Vehicle Parts and Supplies	167, *168*
423300	Lumber and Other Construction Materials	169, *170*
423400	Professional and Commercial Equipment and Supplies	171, *172*
423500	Metal and Mineral (except Petroleum)	173, *174*
423600	Electrical Goods	175, *176*
423700	Hardware, Plumbing, Heating Equipment, and Supplies	177, *178*
423800	Machinery, Equipment, and Supplies	179, *180*
423905	Furniture, Sports, Toys, Jewelry, Other Durable Goods	181, *182*
424	Wholesale Trade, Nondurable Goods	
424100	Paper and Paper Product	183, *184*
424210	Drugs and Druggists' Sundries	185, *186*
424300	Apparel, Piece Goods, and Notions	187, *188*
424400	Grocery and Related Product	189, *190*
424500	Farm Product Raw Material	191, *192*
424600	Chemical and Allied Products	193, *194*
424700	Petroleum and Petroleum Products	195, *196*
424800	Beer, Wine, and Distilled Alcoholic Beverage	197, *198*
424915	Miscellaneous Nondurable Goods	199, *200*
425115	Wholesale Electronic Markets and Agents and Brokers	201, *202*

44 *Retail Trade*

441 Motor Vehicle Dealers and Parts Dealers
441115 New and Used Car Dealers 203, *204*
441215 Other Motor Vehicle and Parts Dealers 205, *206*
442115 Furniture and Home Furnishings Stores 207, *208*
443115 Electronics and Appliance Stores 209, *210*

444 *Building Material and Garden Equipment and Supplies Dealers*

444115 Home Centers; Paint and Wallpaper Stores 211, *212*
444130 Hardware Stores 213, *214*
444190 Other Building Material Dealers 215, *216*
444200 Lawn and Garden Equipment and Supplies Stores 217, *218*

445 *Food, Beverage, and Liquor Stores*

445115 Food and Beverage Stores 219, *220*
445310 Beer, Wine, and Liquor Stores 221, *222*

446115 Health and Personal Care Stores 223, *224*

447100 Gasoline Stations 225, *226*

448115 Clothing and Clothing Accessories Stores 227, *228*

451115 Sporting Goods, Hobby, Book, and Music Stores 229, *230*

452115 General Merchandise Stores 231, *232*

453115 Miscellaneous Store Retailers 233, *234*

454115 Nonstore Retailers 235, *236*

48 *Transportation and Warehousing*

481 Air, Rail, and Water Transportation
481000 Air Transportation 237, *238*
482110 Rail Transportation 239, *240*
483000 Water Transportation 241, *242*

484115 Truck Transportation 243, *244*

485115 Transit and Ground Passenger Transportation 245, *246*

486000 Pipeline Transportation 247, *248*

487005 Other Transportation and Support Activities 249, *250*

493100 Warehousing and Storage 251, *252*

51 *Information*

511 Publishing Industries
511110 Newspaper Publishers 253, *254*
511120 Periodical Publishers 255, *256*
511130 Book Publishers 257, *258*
511145 Database, Directory, and Other Publishers 259, *260*
511210 Software Publishers 261, *262*

512 *Motion Picture and Sound Recording Industries*

512100	Motion Picture and Video Industries (except Video Rental)	263, *264*
512200	Sound Recording Industries	265, *266*
515105	Broadcasting (except Internet)	267, *268*
517000	Telecommunications (wired, wireless, satellite, internet providers)	269, *270*
518210	Data Processing, Hosting, and Related Services	271, *272*
519100	Other Information Services, Internet Publishing, Web Portals	273, *274*

52 *Finance and Insurance*

520000	Credit Intermediation	275, *276*
5221	Depository Credit Intermediation	
522110	Commercial Banking	277, *278*
522125	Savings Institutions and Other Depository Credit	279, *280*
5222	Nondepository Credit Intermediation	
522215	Credit Card Issuing and Other Consumer Credit	281, *282*
522292	Real Estate Credit Incl. Mortgage Bankers and Originators	283, *284*
522295	Intl. Trade, Secondary Financing, Other Nondepository Credit	285, *286*
522300	Activities Related to Credit Intermediation	287, *288*
523	Securities, Commodity Contracts, and Other Financial Investments	
523110	Investment Banking and Securities Dealing	289, *290*
523120	Securities Brokerage	291, *292*
523135	Commodity Contracts Dealing and Brokerage	293, *294*
523905	Security & Commodity Exchanges, Other Financial Investment	295, *296*
524	Insurance Carriers and Related Activities	
524140	Life Insurance	297, *298*
524142	Life Insurance, Stock Companies (Form 1120L)	299, *300*
524143	Life Insurance, Mutual Companies (Form 1120L)	301, *302*
524156	Mutual Property and Casualty Companies (Form 1120-PC)	303, *304*
524159	Stock Property and Casualty Companies (Form 1120-PC)	305, *306*
524210	Insurance Agencies and Brokerages	307, *308*
524290	Other Insurance Related Activities	309, *310*
525	Other Financial Vehicles and Other Investment Companies	
525910	Open-End Investment Funds (Form 1120-RIC)	311, *312*
525995	Other Financial Vehicles	313, *314*

53 *Real Estate and Rental and Leasing*

531	Real Estate	
531115	Lessors of Buildings	315, *316*
531135	Lessors of Miniwarehouses, Self-Storage, Other Real Estate	317, *318*
531210	Offices of Real Estate Agents and Brokers	319, *320*
531315	Other Real Estate Activities	321, *322*
532	Rental and Leasing Services	
532100	Automotive Equipment Rental and Leasing	323, *324*
532215	Other Consumer Goods and General Rental Centers	325, *326*
532400	Commercial and Industrial Machinery and Equipment Rental	327, *328*
533110	Lessors of Nonfinan. Intangible Assets (ex. copyrighted works)	329, *330*

54 *Professional, Scientific, and Technical Services*

541115	Legal Services	331, *332*
541215	Accounting, Tax Preparation, Bookkeeping, and Payroll Services	333, *334*
541315	Architectural, Engineering, and Related Services	335, *336*
541400	Specialized Design Services	337, *338*
541515	Computer Systems Design and Related Services	339, *340*
541600	Management, Scientific, and Technical Consulting Services	341, *342*
541700	Scientific Research and Development Services	343, *344*
541800	Advertising and Related Services	345, *346*
541915	Other Professional, Scientific, and Technical Services	347, *348*

55 *Management of Companies (Holding Companies)*

551111	Offices of Bank Holding Companies	349, *350*
551112	Offices of Other Holding Companies	351, *352*

56 *Administrative and Support and Waste Management and Remediation Services*

561	Administrative and Support Services	
561300	Employment Services	353, *354*
561500	Travel Arrangement and Reservation Services	355, *356*
561905	Other Administrative and Support Services	357, *358*
562000	Waste Management and Remediation Services	359, *360*

61 *Educational Services*

611000	Educational Services	361, *362*

62 *Health Care and Social Assistance*

621115	Offices of Physicians	363, *364*
621210	Offices of Dentists	365, *366*
621315	Offices of Other Health Practitioners	367, *368*
621415	Outpatient Care Centers	369, *370*
621515	Misc. Health Care and Social Assistance	371, *372*
622005	Hospitals, Nursing, and Residential Care Facilities	373, *374*

71 *Arts, Entertainment, and Recreation*

711105	Other Arts, Entertainment, and Recreation	375, *376*
713105	Amusement, Gambling, and Recreation Industries	377, *378*

72 *Accommodation and Food Services*

721115	Accommodation	379, *380*
722115	Food Services and Drinking Places	381, *382*

81 *Other Services*

811	Repair and Maintenance	
811115	Automotive Repair and Maintenance	383, *384*
811215	Other Repair and Maintenance	385, *386*
812115	Personal and Laundry Services	387, *388*
813000	Religious, Grantmaking, Civic and Professional Organizations	389, *390*

Appendix — NAICS to Published Industry Codes 393

Index 461

46TH

ANNUAL EDITION

2015 ALMANAC OF

BUSINESS AND INDUSTRIAL FINANCIAL RATIOS

Table I

Corporations with and without Net Income

AGRICULTURAL PRODUCTION

MONEY AMOUNTS AND SIZE OF ASSETS IN THOUSANDS OF DOLLARS

Item Description for Accounting Period 7/11 Through 6/12		Total	Zero Assets	Under 500	500 to 1,000	1,000 to 5,000	5,000 to 10,000	10,000 to 25,000	25,000 to 50,000	50,000 to 100,000	100,000 to 250,000	250,000 to 500,000	500,000 to 2,500,000	2,500,000 and over
Number of Enterprises	1	100754	9576	55958	16008	17066	1194	579	184	92	•	•	•	0
Revenues ($ in Thousands)														
Net Sales	2	120888381	881736	13574619	14912423	28859455	6839157	9411319	4907866	7274877	•	•	•	0
Interest	3	176180	5347	14766	18024	58056	15112	10323	9986	6122	•	•	•	0
Rents	4	927047	16610	160173	175323	365147	78418	19894	19663	11070	•	•	•	0
Royalties	5	281411	628	18735	13168	63215	3011	9337	22666	2548	•	•	•	0
Other Portfolio Income	6	1702716	100146	227927	198527	663415	73319	148212	56695	38730	•	•	•	0
Other Receipts	7	21091308	231545	4735616	3839761	7194264	3566913	526104	427894	172749	•	•	•	0
Total Receipts	8	145067043	1236012	18731836	19157226	37203552	10575930	10125189	5444770	7506096	•	•	•	0
Average Total Receipts	9	1440	129	335	1197	2180	8858	17487	29591	81588	•	•	•	•
Operating Costs/Operating Income (%)														
Cost of Operations	10	53.9	27.5	16.3	57.8	35.6	43.9	58.8	64.7	67.9	•	•	•	•
Salaries and Wages	11	7.9	6.3	11.4	5.1	13.5	13.0	6.9	7.4	5.9	•	•	•	•
Taxes Paid	12	2.1	3.2	3.1	2.2	3.0	2.8	1.6	1.7	1.3	•	•	•	•
Interest Paid	13	1.9	3.9	2.3	1.8	2.5	2.2	1.6	1.9	1.1	•	•	•	•
Depreciation	14	7.2	3.2	10.3	8.8	10.1	9.2	5.6	4.8	4.6	•	•	•	•
Amortization and Depletion	15	0.4	0.1	0.6	0.1	0.1	0.1	0.1	0.3	0.4	•	•	•	•
Pensions and Other Deferred Comp.	16	0.2	0.0	0.1	0.1	0.1	0.1	0.2	0.2	0.2	•	•	•	•
Employee Benefits	17	0.8	0.6	1.3	0.8	0.8	0.8	0.8	0.7	0.8	•	•	•	•
Advertising	18	0.3	0.1	0.4	0.1	0.2	0.2	0.3	0.3	0.2	•	•	•	•
Other Expenses	19	41.3	69.0	84.0	46.6	56.6	75.3	29.5	25.4	20.1	•	•	•	•
Officers' Compensation	20	1.8	2.5	4.2	2.2	2.8	1.3	1.2	1.2	1.0	•	•	•	•
Operating Margin	21	•	•	•	•	•	•	•	•	•	•	•	•	•
Operating Margin Before Officers' Comp.	22	•	•	•	•	•	•	•	•	•	•	•	•	•

Selected Average Balance Sheet ($ in Thousands)													
Net Receivables **23**	103	0	4	29	81	556	1822	5620	10971	•	•	•	•
Inventories **24**	132	0	12	40	159	778	2605	3806	12335	•	•	•	•
Net Property, Plant and Equipment **25**	498	0	84	360	1007	3246	6148	13406	28383	•	•	•	•
Total Assets **26**	1148	0	176	714	1930	6851	15705	34708	71631	•	•	•	•
Notes and Loans Payable **27**	616	0	173	524	1122	3535	7824	14111	28158	•	•	•	•
All Other Liabilities **28**	173	0	13	57	195	952	2547	5255	11012	•	•	•	•
Net Worth **29**	359	0	-10	133	614	2364	5334	15343	32462	•	•	•	•
Selected Financial Ratios (Times to 1)													
Current Ratio **30**	1.6	•	1.5	1.7	1.6	1.5	1.5	1.6	1.7	•	•	•	•
Quick Ratio **31**	0.8	•	1.0	1.1	0.9	0.6	0.7	1.0	0.8	•	•	•	•
Net Sales to Working Capital **32**	8.1	•	13.2	12.0	8.6	7.4	8.1	5.0	6.3	•	•	•	•
Coverage Ratio **33**	2.2	7.0	2.8	2.6	2.5	3.7	1.9	2.2	0.7	•	•	•	•
Total Asset Turnover **34**	1.0	•	1.4	1.3	0.9	0.8	1.0	0.8	1.1	•	•	•	•
Inventory Turnover **35**	4.9	•	3.3	13.3	3.8	3.2	3.7	4.5	4.4	•	•	•	•
Receivables Turnover **36**	11.9	•	73.0	32.6	20.7	10.6	8.8	5.1	7.2	•	•	•	•
Total Liabilities to Net Worth **37**	2.2	•	•	4.4	2.1	1.9	1.9	1.3	1.2	•	•	•	•
Current Assets to Working Capital **38**	2.7	•	3.1	2.5	2.7	3.1	3.1	2.7	2.4	•	•	•	•
Current Liabilities to Working Capital **39**	1.7	•	2.1	1.5	1.7	2.1	2.1	1.7	1.4	•	•	•	•
Working Capital to Net Sales **40**	0.1	•	0.1	0.1	0.1	0.1	0.1	0.2	0.2	•	•	•	•
Inventory to Working Capital **41**	0.9	•	0.6	0.5	0.8	1.2	1.3	0.8	1.0	•	•	•	•
Total Receipts to Cash Flow **42**	2.9	1.4	1.5	2.8	2.1	1.4	4.2	4.3	5.9	•	•	•	•
Cost of Goods to Cash Flow **43**	1.6	0.4	0.2	1.6	0.8	0.6	2.5	2.8	4.0	•	•	•	•
Cash Flow to Total Debt **44**	0.5	•	0.9	0.6	0.6	0.9	0.4	0.3	0.3	•	•	•	•
Selected Financial Factors (in Percentages)													
Debt Ratio **45**	68.7	•	105.7	81.4	68.2	65.5	66.0	55.8	54.7	•	•	•	•
Return on Total Assets **46**	4.4	•	8.7	6.1	5.4	6.7	3.1	3.2	0.9	•	•	•	•
Return on Equity Before Income Taxes **47**	7.7	•	•	20.2	10.1	14.3	4.5	3.9	•	•	•	•	•
Return on Equity After Income Taxes **48**	6.1	•	•	17.2	8.9	13.2	3.5	3.0	•	•	•	•	•
Profit Margin (Before Income Tax) **49**	2.3	23.6	4.0	2.9	3.6	5.9	1.5	2.3	•	•	•	•	•
Profit Margin (After Income Tax) **50**	1.8	22.4	3.7	2.4	3.2	5.5	1.1	1.7	•	•	•	•	•

Table II

Corporations with Net Income

AGRICULTURAL PRODUCTION

MONEY AMOUNTS AND SIZE OF ASSETS IN THOUSANDS OF DOLLARS

Item Description for Accounting Period 7/11 Through 6/12		Total	Zero Assets	Under 500	500 to 1000	1,000 to 5,000	5,000 to 10,000	10,000 to 25,000	25,000 to 50,000	50,000 to 100,000	100,000 to 250,000	250,000 to 500,000	500,000 to 2,500,000	2,500,000 and over
Number of Enterprises	1	56389	4923	27984	10981	11226	758	308	103	50	•	15	•	0
Revenues ($ in Thousands)														
Net Sales	2	72136262	640550	9436666	5849954	19616775	5550834	7131033	3298217	4769001	•	7346461	•	0
Interest	3	145856	3295	11186	15676	51424	12991	9520	8518	3255	•	8198	•	0
Rents	4	762650	14477	88794	163369	325833	70813	10851	9700	9061	•	18891	•	0
Royalties	5	259598	0	6009	13168	63215	3011	9333	18409	0	•	15817	•	0
Other Portfolio Income	6	1174256	99733	181604	181293	323034	70220	122802	34889	10996	•	29812	•	0
Other Receipts	7	16109964	224236	3293918	3049400	5555643	2842177	430421	300948	66988	•	-2015	•	0
Total Receipts	8	90588586	982291	13018177	9272860	25935924	8550046	7713960	3670681	4859301	•	7417164	•	0
Average Total Receipts	9	1606	200	465	844	2310	11280	25045	35638	97186	•	494478	•	•
Operating Costs/Operating Income (%)														
Cost of Operations	10	45.0	8.4	16.6	20.1	33.4	35.9	65.7	60.9	63.4	•	68.6	•	•
Salaries and Wages	11	8.1	5.6	10.4	9.0	10.2	14.6	5.3	6.7	5.8	•	4.7	•	•
Taxes Paid	12	2.2	3.9	3.1	3.5	2.4	2.8	1.3	1.7	1.1	•	1.2	•	•
Interest Paid	13	1.7	2.6	1.8	3.0	2.1	1.4	1.2	1.0	1.0	•	1.0	•	•
Depreciation	14	7.4	2.5	9.1	14.8	9.7	9.5	4.1	4.2	3.7	•	2.3	•	•
Amortization and Depletion	15	0.3	0.1	0.7	0.1	0.1	0.1	0.1	0.1	0.3	•	0.3	•	•
Pensions and Other Deferred Comp.	16	0.1	•	0.1	0.1	0.1	0.1	0.2	0.3	0.2	•	0.2	•	•
Employee Benefits	17	0.8	0.5	1.2	1.6	0.8	0.7	0.6	0.6	0.8	•	0.5	•	•
Advertising	18	0.2	0.1	0.2	0.2	0.1	0.1	0.3	0.2	0.1	•	0.3	•	•
Other Expenses	19	46.2	75.3	73.0	83.5	58.4	76.9	22.0	24.1	18.9	•	17.0	•	•
Officers' Compensation	20	2.2	3.0	4.2	4.6	2.7	1.3	1.1	1.4	0.8	•	0.4	•	•
Operating Margin	21	•	•	•	•	•	•	•	•	3.9	•	3.4	•	•
Operating Margin Before Officers' Comp.	22	•	1.0	•	•	•	•	•	0.1	4.7	•	3.8	•	•

Selected Average Balance Sheet ($ in Thousands)

Net Receivables 23	97	0	6	23	67	700	2274	5644	13333	•	45433	•	•
Inventories 24	150	0	12	38	152	953	2992	3553	13444	•	76151	•	•
Net Property, Plant and Equipment 25	490	0	97	327	951	2673	5561	10765	25732	•	98901	•	•
Total Assets 26	1192	0	211	721	1870	6876	16205	34102	72758	•	321906	•	•
Notes and Loans Payable 27	493	0	114	320	900	2886	6663	10054	24344	•	110068	•	•
All Other Liabilities 28	152	0	14	47	177	704	3007	5801	12899	•	58088	•	•
Net Worth 29	548	0	83	355	793	3286	6535	18248	35515	•	153751	•	•

Selected Financial Ratios (Times to 1)

Current Ratio 30	1.8	•	1.9	2.2	1.6	1.6	1.4	1.8	1.8	•	1.8	•	•
Quick Ratio 31	0.9	•	1.4	1.6	0.9	0.7	0.6	1.1	0.9	•	0.8	•	•
Net Sales to Working Capital 32	6.6	•	9.7	4.8	9.2	6.9	10.0	4.6	6.4	•	6.1	•	•
Coverage Ratio 33	7.6	21.0	10.9	7.0	6.6	8.5	6.5	10.7	6.8	•	5.1	•	•
Total Asset Turnover 34	1.1	•	1.6	0.7	0.9	1.1	1.4	0.9	1.3	•	1.5	•	•
Inventory Turnover 35	3.8	•	4.7	2.8	3.8	2.8	5.1	5.5	4.5	•	4.4	•	•
Receivables Turnover 36	11.5	•	62.2	19.2	25.6	11.9	11.1	5.4	6.7	•	11.0	•	•
Total Liabilities to Net Worth 37	1.2	•	1.5	1.0	1.4	1.1	1.5	0.9	1.0	•	1.1	•	•
Current Assets to Working Capital 38	2.3	•	2.1	1.8	2.6	2.7	3.3	2.2	2.3	•	2.2	•	•
Current Liabilities to Working Capital 39	1.3	•	1.1	0.8	1.6	1.7	2.3	1.2	1.3	•	1.2	•	•
Working Capital to Net Sales 40	0.2	•	0.1	0.2	0.1	0.1	0.1	0.2	0.2	•	0.2	•	•
Inventory to Working Capital 41	0.8	•	0.4	0.3	0.9	1.0	1.5	0.6	0.9	•	1.0	•	•
Total Receipts to Cash Flow 42	2.1	1.0	1.4	1.3	1.8	1.3	4.7	3.4	4.6	•	5.1	•	•
Cost of Goods to Cash Flow 43	1.0	0.1	0.2	0.3	0.6	0.5	3.1	2.1	2.9	•	3.5	•	•
Cash Flow to Total Debt 44	0.9	•	1.9	1.1	0.9	1.5	0.5	0.6	0.6	•	0.6	•	•

Selected Financial Factors (in Percentages)

Debt Ratio 45	54.0	•	60.5	50.8	57.6	52.2	59.7	46.5	51.2	•	52.2	•	•
Return on Total Assets 46	14.0	•	30.8	15.5	13.2	12.9	11.3	10.2	9.0	•	8.0	•	•
Return on Equity Before Income Taxes 47	26.5	•	71.0	26.9	26.4	23.8	23.7	17.4	15.7	•	13.5	•	•
Return on Equity After Income Taxes 48	24.5	•	68.8	25.2	25.0	22.6	22.2	16.0	15.1	•	12.1	•	•
Profit Margin (Before Income Tax) 49	11.3	51.4	17.6	17.9	12.0	10.7	6.7	9.9	5.8	•	4.3	•	•
Profit Margin (After Income Tax) 50	10.5	49.7	17.0	16.8	11.4	10.2	6.3	9.1	5.6	•	3.8	•	•

Table I

Corporations with and without Net Income

FORESTRY AND LOGGING

MONEY AMOUNTS AND SIZE OF ASSETS IN THOUSANDS OF DOLLARS

Item Description for Accounting Period 7/11 Through 6/12		Total	Zero Assets	Under 500	500 to 1,000	1,000 to 5,000	5,000 to 10,000	10,000 to 25,000	25,000 to 50,000	50,000 to 100,000	100,000 to 250,000	250,000 to 500,000	500,000 to 2,500,000	2,500,000 and over
Number of Enterprises	1	8168	1894	4397	938	767	57	68	31	11	0	5	0	0
Revenues ($ in Thousands)														
Net Sales	2	11473288	761415	2120991	1663541	2772192	460929	1181721	1005121	450858	0	1056518	0	0
Interest	3	41087	2	837	68	2395	170	973	109	5466	0	31068	0	0
Rents	4	34214	57	7	30	24033	60	2858	880	232	0	6057	0	0
Royalties	5	32311	0	0	0	1682	19840	211	6146	0	0	4431	0	0
Other Portfolio Income	6	235278	2864	18402	65559	60242	9685	53061	988	1919	0	22561	0	0
Other Receipts	7	67446	4375	2281	13842	39749	2494	11239	-3052	261	0	-3743	0	0
Total Receipts	8	11883624	768713	2142518	1743040	2900293	493178	1250063	1010192	458736	0	1116892	0	0
Average Total Receipts	9	1455	406	487	1858	3781	8652	18383	32587	41703	•	223378	•	•
Operating Costs/Operating Income (%)														
Cost of Operations	10	54.7	0.1	24.1	42.2	58.8	83.0	82.1	90.9	71.4	•	79.4	•	•
Salaries and Wages	11	8.9	0.2	12.5	11.6	12.8	8.9	4.4	1.7	1.1	•	8.7	•	•
Taxes Paid	12	2.8	1.5	3.6	2.7	3.5	4.3	1.5	1.6	1.2	•	2.7	•	•
Interest Paid	13	1.4	0.9	1.0	2.8	1.0	1.1	1.1	0.9	3.3	•	1.4	•	•
Depreciation	14	6.5	0.1	14.9	10.3	5.7	10.4	0.9	0.8	2.0	•	1.8	•	•
Amortization and Depletion	15	0.6	0.0	0.0	•	0.0	0.7	0.4	1.1	2.5	•	3.6	•	•
Pensions and Other Deferred Comp.	16	0.1	•	•	0.0	0.2	0.0	0.2	0.1	0.1	•	0.2	•	•
Employee Benefits	17	1.0	•	0.4	1.3	1.4	0.3	0.7	0.4	0.4	•	2.4	•	•
Advertising	18	0.1	0.0	0.0	0.1	0.1	0.0	0.0	0.0	0.0	•	0.1	•	•
Other Expenses	19	24.9	94.0	43.5	28.5	16.8	4.8	7.9	4.7	7.6	•	7.8	•	•
Officers' Compensation	20	2.0	0.2	2.9	4.0	2.1	1.8	1.9	0.5	0.7	•	0.4	•	•
Operating Margin	21	•	3.0	•	•	•	•	•	•	9.5	•	•	•	•
Operating Margin Before Officers' Comp.	22	•	3.2	•	0.6	•	•	0.7	•	10.2	•	•	•	•

Selected Average Balance Sheet ($ in Thousands)													
Net Receivables 23	104	0	4	25	173	81	1194	2739	2485	•	95723	•	•
Inventories 24	54	0	2	13	67	333	4119	1521	1075	•	2732	•	•
Net Property, Plant and Equipment 25	468	0	54	405	993	4637	4941	20842	34628	•	163813	•	•
Total Assets 26	1143	0	90	687	1919	6181	16133	38957	75254	•	668788	•	•
Notes and Loans Payable 27	591	0	130	656	1471	1795	3503	11778	18533	•	321643	•	•
All Other Liabilities 28	83	0	2	14	203	1540	1057	2353	2518	•	48094	•	•
Net Worth 29	469	0	-42	17	244	2845	11573	24826	54204	•	299051	•	•
Selected Financial Ratios (Times to 1)													
Current Ratio 30	2.2	•	1.6	1.4	1.4	0.4	5.2	2.6	5.3	•	3.1	•	•
Quick Ratio 31	1.5	•	1.6	0.4	0.9	0.4	1.8	1.9	3.9	•	2.9	•	•
Net Sales to Working Capital 32	8.3	•	38.5	22.0	22.0	•	3.2	5.9	2.5	•	2.2	•	•
Coverage Ratio 33	1.5	5.2	•	1.5	3.1	•	5.3	•	4.4	•	•	•	•
Total Asset Turnover 34	1.2	•	5.4	2.6	1.9	1.3	1.1	0.8	0.5	•	0.3	•	•
Inventory Turnover 35	14.2	•	77.2	56.1	31.6	20.1	3.5	19.4	27.2	•	61.4	•	•
Receivables Turnover 36	16.0	•	161.6	56.4	29.2	53.3	16.1	15.8	13.0	•	2.6	•	•
Total Liabilities to Net Worth 37	1.4	•	•	39.2	6.9	1.2	0.4	0.6	0.4	•	1.2	•	•
Current Assets to Working Capital 38	1.8	•	2.6	3.3	3.3	•	1.2	1.6	1.2	•	1.5	•	•
Current Liabilities to Working Capital 39	0.8	•	1.6	2.3	2.3	•	0.2	0.6	0.2	•	0.5	•	•
Working Capital to Net Sales 40	0.1	•	0.0	0.0	0.0	•	0.3	0.2	0.4	•	0.5	•	•
Inventory to Working Capital 41	0.3	•	0.1	0.1	0.4	•	0.8	0.3	0.1	•	0.0	•	•
Total Receipts to Cash Flow 42	4.8	1.0	2.8	4.3	7.6	•	14.1	57.5	6.2	•	51.7	•	•
Cost of Goods to Cash Flow 43	2.6	0.0	0.7	1.8	4.5	•	11.6	52.3	4.4	•	41.0	•	•
Cash Flow to Total Debt 44	0.4	•	1.3	0.6	0.3	•	0.3	0.0	0.3	•	0.0	•	•
Selected Financial Factors (in Percentages)													
Debt Ratio 45	59.0	•	146.5	97.5	87.3	54.0	28.3	36.3	28.0	•	55.3	•	•
Return on Total Assets 46	2.6	•	•	10.6	5.9	•	6.2	•	7.9	•	•	•	•
Return on Equity Before Income Taxes 47	2.2	•	22.6	137.5	31.3	•	7.0	•	8.5	•	•	•	•
Return on Equity After Income Taxes 48	0.0	•	23.0	126.7	22.5	•	6.0	•	3.5	•	•	•	•
Profit Margin (Before Income Tax) 49	0.7	4.0	•	1.3	2.1	•	4.6	•	11.3	•	•	•	•
Profit Margin (After Income Tax) 50	0.0	3.9	•	1.2	1.5	•	4.0	•	4.6	•	•	•	•

Table II

Corporations with Net Income

FORESTRY AND LOGGING

MONEY AMOUNTS AND SIZE OF ASSETS IN THOUSANDS OF DOLLARS

Item Description for Accounting Period 7/11 Through 6/12		Total	Zero Assets	Under 500	500 to 1,000	1,000 to 5,000	5,000 to 10,000	10,000 to 25,000	25,000 to 50,000	50,000 to 100,000	100,000 to 250,000	250,000 to 500,000	500,000 to 2,500,000	2,500,000 and over
Number of Enterprises	1	4497	1212	2354	512	354	5	47	•	•	•	•	•	0
Revenues ($ in Thousands)														
Net Sales	2	8318679	759273	1947175	1202113	1579948	10961	1004805	•	•	•	•	•	0
Interest	3	37734	2	809	26	1198	155	973	•	•	•	•	•	0
Rents	4	29398	57	0	0	21135	0	2858	•	•	•	•	•	0
Royalties	5	32311	0	0	0	1682	19840	211	•	•	•	•	•	0
Other Portfolio Income	6	127954	2864	16691	2160	36527	75	52496	•	•	•	•	•	0
Other Receipts	7	78481	795	2027	13648	34255	752	7774	•	•	•	•	•	0
Total Receipts	8	8624557	762991	1966702	1217947	1674745	31783	1069117	•	•	•	•	•	0
Average Total Receipts	9	1918	630	835	2379	4731	6357	22747	•	•	•	•	•	•
Operating Costs/Operating Income (%)														
Cost of Operations	10	51.7	0.0	21.1	41.7	66.8	87.7	85.6	•	•	•	•	•	•
Salaries and Wages	11	7.5	0.2	13.3	13.3	5.0	12.6	2.9	•	•	•	•	•	•
Taxes Paid	12	2.5	1.2	3.5	2.6	3.0	15.3	1.5	•	•	•	•	•	•
Interest Paid	13	1.0	0.9	0.6	1.4	0.8	1.1	0.7	•	•	•	•	•	•
Depreciation	14	6.2	0.1	14.8	8.7	6.2	1.5	0.5	•	•	•	•	•	•
Amortization and Depletion	15	0.2	0.0	•	•	0.0	27.2	0.4	•	•	•	•	•	•
Pensions and Other Deferred Comp.	16	0.1	•	•	0.0	0.0	•	0.2	•	•	•	•	•	•
Employee Benefits	17	1.0	•	0.4	1.7	1.9	2.4	0.5	•	•	•	•	•	•
Advertising	18	0.1	•	0.0	0.1	0.1	0.1	0.0	•	•	•	•	•	•
Other Expenses	19	26.4	93.1	42.0	26.6	13.7	27.4	6.1	•	•	•	•	•	•
Officers' Compensation	20	1.7	0.2	2.1	2.4	2.7	20.4	1.9	•	•	•	•	•	•
Operating Margin	21	1.7	4.3	2.1	1.4	•	•	•	•	•	•	•	•	•
Operating Margin Before Officers' Comp.	22	3.4	4.5	4.2	3.9	2.4	•	1.6	•	•	•	•	•	•

Selected Average Balance Sheet ($ in Thousands)													
Net Receivables 23	84	0	8	44	223	69	1552	•	•	•	•	•	•
Inventories 24	47	0	2	24	75	3401	1966	•	•	•	•	•	•
Net Property, Plant and Equipment 25	301	0	71	336	654	1519	5008	•	•	•	•	•	•
Total Assets 26	1078	0	126	716	1764	7035	16404	•	•	•	•	•	•
Notes and Loans Payable 27	610	0	141	587	1016	125	2473	•	•	•	•	•	•
All Other Liabilities 28	94	0	3	19	302	624	1389	•	•	•	•	•	•
Net Worth 29	373	0	-19	110	446	6285	12543	•	•	•	•	•	•

Selected Financial Ratios (Times to 1)													
Current Ratio 30	2.1	•	1.4	1.1	2.5	17.8	4.0	•	•	•	•	•	•
Quick Ratio 31	1.4	•	1.4	0.3	1.5	17.0	1.7	•	•	•	•	•	•
Net Sales to Working Capital 32	10.7	•	55.8	73.4	9.2	0.4	4.2	•	•	•	•	•	•
Coverage Ratio 33	6.5	6.1	5.9	3.0	8.0	83.7	9.5	•	•	•	•	•	•
Total Asset Turnover 34	1.7	•	6.6	3.3	2.5	0.3	1.3	•	•	•	•	•	•
Inventory Turnover 35	20.2	•	92.1	40.7	39.8	0.6	9.3	•	•	•	•	•	•
Receivables Turnover 36	28.0	•	170.8	50.7	31.0	3.2	19.6	•	•	•	•	•	•
Total Liabilities to Net Worth 37	1.9	•	•	5.5	3.0	0.1	0.3	•	•	•	•	•	•
Current Assets to Working Capital 38	1.9	•	3.4	11.3	1.7	1.1	1.3	•	•	•	•	•	•
Current Liabilities to Working Capital 39	0.9	•	2.4	10.3	0.7	0.1	0.3	•	•	•	•	•	•
Working Capital to Net Sales 40	0.1	•	0.0	0.0	0.1	2.3	0.2	•	•	•	•	•	•
Inventory to Working Capital 41	0.4	•	0.1	0.6	0.2	•	0.7	•	•	•	•	•	•
Total Receipts to Cash Flow 42	3.6	1.0	2.5	4.1	6.9	0.9	14.6	•	•	•	•	•	•
Cost of Goods to Cash Flow 43	1.9	0.0	0.5	1.7	4.6	0.8	12.5	•	•	•	•	•	•
Cash Flow to Total Debt 44	0.7	•	2.3	1.0	0.5	3.2	0.4	•	•	•	•	•	•

Selected Financial Factors (in Percentages)													
Debt Ratio 45	65.4	•	115.0	84.7	74.7	10.7	23.5	•	•	•	•	•	•
Return on Total Assets 46	10.9	•	24.8	13.4	16.4	29.8	9.0	•	•	•	•	•	•
Return on Equity Before Income Taxes 47	26.7	•	•	58.8	57.0	32.9	10.5	•	•	•	•	•	•
Return on Equity After Income Taxes 48	21.7	•	•	55.7	46.5	19.3	9.3	•	•	•	•	•	•
Profit Margin (Before Income Tax) 49	5.4	4.8	3.1	2.7	5.7	94.4	6.2	•	•	•	•	•	•
Profit Margin (After Income Tax) 50	4.4	4.8	3.1	2.6	4.6	55.4	5.4	•	•	•	•	•	•

Table I

Corporations with and without Net Income

SUPPORT ACTIVITIES AND FISHING, HUNTING AND TRAPPING

MONEY AMOUNTS AND SIZE OF ASSETS IN THOUSANDS OF DOLLARS

Item Description for Accounting Period 7/11 Through 6/12		Total	Zero Assets	Under 500	500 to 1,000	1,000 to 5,000	5,000 to 10,000	10,000 to 25,000	25,000 to 50,000	50,000 to 100,000	100,000 to 250,000	250,000 to 500,000	500,000 to 2,500,000	2,500,000 and over
Number of Enterprises	1	26726	6865	15520	1743	1975	416	141	43	14	•	•	•	0
Revenues ($ in Thousands)														
Net Sales	2	33432846	280045	5470122	2607082	10438386	4519594	4435569	2000284	1003413	•	•	•	0
Interest	3	18498	619	738	495	5592	685	6119	2724	1020	•	•	•	0
Rents	4	13553	490	87	2208	3789	3345	3283	337	9	•	•	•	0
Royalties	5	6016	0	0	0	755	4565	125	0	0	•	•	•	0
Other Portfolio Income	6	136109	24758	10154	20060	18941	7591	39219	11214	1085	•	•	•	0
Other Receipts	7	1186197	751	519908	162911	212392	95834	89609	36655	20298	•	•	•	0
Total Receipts	8	34793219	306663	6001009	2792756	10679855	4631614	4573924	2051214	1025825	•	•	•	0
Average Total Receipts	9	1302	45	387	1602	5408	11134	32439	47703	73273	•	•	•	•
Operating Costs/Operating Income (%)														
Cost of Operations	10	68.9	17.8	46.4	51.3	77.7	76.8	75.0	75.4	64.6	•	•	•	•
Salaries and Wages	11	7.2	10.9	7.2	8.2	6.7	6.3	9.4	4.3	9.4	•	•	•	•
Taxes Paid	12	1.6	2.5	2.2	1.2	1.4	1.4	1.7	0.9	2.2	•	•	•	•
Interest Paid	13	0.6	0.4	0.6	0.4	0.4	0.9	0.7	0.8	0.7	•	•	•	•
Depreciation	14	2.9	2.0	4.3	2.8	2.1	2.3	3.3	2.4	4.6	•	•	•	•
Amortization and Depletion	15	0.1	0.0	0.1	0.0	0.1	0.2	0.0	0.0	0.3	•	•	•	•
Pensions and Other Deferred Comp.	16	0.1	•	0.1	0.3	0.1	0.0	0.2	0.2	0.1	•	•	•	•
Employee Benefits	17	0.6	0.0	0.4	0.6	0.3	0.5	0.8	0.7	1.8	•	•	•	•
Advertising	18	0.2	0.3	0.3	0.1	0.1	0.2	0.1	0.1	0.6	•	•	•	•
Other Expenses	19	15.1	45.5	33.9	29.1	10.1	10.6	7.8	10.4	6.5	•	•	•	•
Officers' Compensation	20	2.0	11.8	5.4	2.4	1.3	1.1	1.2	0.5	1.1	•	•	•	•
Operating Margin	21	0.7	8.8	•	3.7	•	•	•	4.1	8.1	•	•	•	•
Operating Margin Before Officers' Comp.	22	2.7	20.6	4.4	6.1	1.0	0.9	0.8	4.6	9.1	•	•	•	•

Selected Average Balance Sheet ($ in Thousands)

Net Receivables	23	105	0	5	71	313	1405	2960	7599	12352	•	•	•	•
Inventories	24	79	0	7	33	192	429	3433	4028	9926	•	•	•	•
Net Property, Plant and Equipment	25	187	0	43	151	672	2149	4772	9696	15893	•	•	•	•
Total Assets	26	647	0	114	715	2049	6865	16107	36032	74605	•	•	•	•
Notes and Loans Payable	27	208	0	55	308	523	2080	6604	11111	16182	•	•	•	•
All Other Liabilities	28	145	0	16	76	471	1528	4950	7828	22576	•	•	•	•
Net Worth	29	293	0	43	331	1055	3257	4552	17093	35848	•	•	•	•

Selected Financial Ratios (Times to 1)

Current Ratio	30	1.8	•	2.2	2.4	1.9	1.7	1.6	1.6	1.5	•	•	•	•
Quick Ratio	31	1.1	•	1.4	1.7	1.3	1.2	0.8	1.1	0.9	•	•	•	•
Net Sales to Working Capital	32	8.3	•	14.0	6.4	10.9	7.4	8.2	7.3	5.3	•	•	•	•
Coverage Ratio	33	8.7	50.0	15.4	29.7	5.8	3.4	4.7	9.2	15.7	•	•	•	•
Total Asset Turnover	34	1.9	•	3.1	2.1	2.6	1.6	2.0	1.3	1.0	•	•	•	•
Inventory Turnover	35	10.9	•	24.1	23.5	21.4	19.4	6.9	8.7	4.7	•	•	•	•
Receivables Turnover	36	12.5	•	54.2	20.6	17.0	8.3	10.3	5.9	5.5	•	•	•	•
Total Liabilities to Net Worth	37	1.2	•	1.7	1.2	0.9	1.1	2.5	1.1	1.1	•	•	•	•
Current Assets to Working Capital	38	2.3	•	1.9	1.7	2.1	2.5	2.6	2.8	3.0	•	•	•	•
Current Liabilities to Working Capital	39	1.3	•	0.9	0.7	1.1	1.5	1.6	1.8	2.0	•	•	•	•
Working Capital to Net Sales	40	0.1	•	0.1	0.2	0.1	0.1	0.1	0.1	0.2	•	•	•	•
Inventory to Working Capital	41	0.6	•	0.3	0.2	0.3	0.4	1.1	0.5	0.7	•	•	•	•
Total Receipts to Cash Flow	42	6.1	2.2	3.0	2.8	10.0	9.2	12.4	6.4	6.7	•	•	•	•
Cost of Goods to Cash Flow	43	4.2	0.4	1.4	1.4	7.8	7.1	9.3	4.8	4.3	•	•	•	•
Cash Flow to Total Debt	44	0.6	•	1.7	1.4	0.5	0.3	0.2	0.4	0.3	•	•	•	•

Selected Financial Factors (in Percentages)

Debt Ratio	45	54.7	•	62.4	53.7	48.5	52.6	71.7	52.6	51.9	•	•	•	•
Return on Total Assets	46	10.4	•	29.0	23.3	6.2	4.8	6.8	9.6	10.5	•	•	•	•
Return on Equity Before Income Taxes	47	20.2	•	72.1	48.7	10.0	7.2	18.9	18.1	20.4	•	•	•	•
Return on Equity After Income Taxes	48	19.1	•	71.5	47.7	9.3	7.1	15.5	16.8	17.5	•	•	•	•
Profit Margin (Before Income Tax)	49	4.7	18.3	8.8	10.8	2.0	2.2	2.7	6.6	10.2	•	•	•	•
Profit Margin (After Income Tax)	50	4.5	15.4	8.7	10.6	1.9	2.1	2.3	6.2	8.8	•	•	•	•

Table II

Corporations with Net Income

SUPPORT ACTIVITIES AND FISHING, HUNTING AND TRAPPING

MONEY AMOUNTS AND SIZE OF ASSETS IN THOUSANDS OF DOLLARS

Item Description for Accounting Period 7/11 Through 6/12		Total	Zero Assets	Under 500	500 to 1,000	1,000 to 5,000	5,000 to 10,000	10,000 to 25,000	25,000 to 50,000	50,000 to 100,000	100,000 to 250,000	250,000 to 500,000	500,000 to 2,500,000	2,500,000 and over
Number of Enterprises	1	14799	2057	9361	1447	1520	243	118	•	•	•	•	•	0
Revenues ($ in Thousands)														
Net Sales	2	28844574	146060	4386988	2418541	9457271	2896630	4121731	•	•	•	•	•	0
Interest	3	16217	594	429	125	4352	647	5896	•	•	•	•	•	0
Rents	4	11188	490	85	2208	1441	3335	3282	•	•	•	•	•	0
Royalties	5	6016	0	0	0	755	4565	125	•	•	•	•	•	0
Other Portfolio Income	6	118378	24529	9744	19527	3733	7457	38173	•	•	•	•	•	0
Other Receipts	7	947335	613	456388	159447	100936	45413	78702	•	•	•	•	•	0
Total Receipts	8	29943708	172286	4853634	2599848	9568488	2958047	4247909	•	•	•	•	•	0
Average Total Receipts	9	2023	84	518	1797	6295	12173	35999	•	•	•	•	•	•
Operating Costs/Operating Income (%)														
Cost of Operations	10	69.0	11.8	42.8	52.7	79.2	72.6	75.5	•	•	•	•	•	•
Salaries and Wages	11	6.4	6.1	7.1	7.5	5.1	6.0	9.1	•	•	•	•	•	•
Taxes Paid	12	1.5	2.6	2.1	1.0	1.1	1.9	1.6	•	•	•	•	•	•
Interest Paid	13	0.5	0.3	0.6	0.3	0.3	0.5	0.7	•	•	•	•	•	•
Depreciation	14	2.5	2.4	3.1	2.4	1.6	2.1	3.2	•	•	•	•	•	•
Amortization and Depletion	15	0.1	•	0.1	0.0	0.1	0.0	0.0	•	•	•	•	•	•
Pensions and Other Deferred Comp.	16	0.1	•	0.1	0.1	0.1	0.1	0.1	•	•	•	•	•	•
Employee Benefits	17	0.6	0.0	0.5	0.6	0.2	0.5	0.7	•	•	•	•	•	•
Advertising	18	0.1	•	0.3	0.1	0.1	0.1	0.1	•	•	•	•	•	•
Other Expenses	19	13.5	36.6	32.0	27.6	8.7	9.4	7.3	•	•	•	•	•	•
Officers' Compensation	20	2.0	12.8	6.4	2.0	1.3	1.0	1.2	•	•	•	•	•	•
Operating Margin	21	3.6	27.4	4.9	5.7	2.2	5.9	0.4	•	•	•	•	•	•
Operating Margin Before Officers' Comp.	22	5.7	40.3	11.3	7.6	3.5	6.9	1.7	•	•	•	•	•	•

Selected Average Balance Sheet ($ in Thousands)														
Net Receivables	23	144	0	7	84	349	1377	2902	•	•	•	•	•	•
Inventories	24	119	0	6	39	199	404	3640	•	•	•	•	•	•
Net Property, Plant and Equipment	25	212	0	23	134	535	1739	4231	•	•	•	•	•	•
Total Assets	26	872	0	118	710	2038	6674	16183	•	•	•	•	•	•
Notes and Loans Payable	27	226	0	39	213	437	1166	4795	•	•	•	•	•	•
All Other Liabilities	28	223	0	17	90	556	1801	5257	•	•	•	•	•	•
Net Worth	29	423	0	63	407	1045	3707	6131	•	•	•	•	•	•

Selected Financial Ratios (Times to 1)														
Current Ratio	30	1.8	•	2.7	2.7	1.8	1.9	1.6	•	•	•	•	•	•
Quick Ratio	31	1.1	•	2.1	1.9	1.3	1.5	0.7	•	•	•	•	•	•
Net Sales to Working Capital	32	8.5	•	12.3	5.7	12.3	6.5	8.4	•	•	•	•	•	•
Coverage Ratio	33	15.7	145.4	26.3	48.6	12.9	15.9	6.4	•	•	•	•	•	•
Total Asset Turnover	34	2.2	•	4.0	2.4	3.1	1.8	2.2	•	•	•	•	•	•
Inventory Turnover	35	11.3	•	35.7	22.9	24.8	21.4	7.2	•	•	•	•	•	•
Receivables Turnover	36	13.2	•	56.0	19.2	18.4	7.0	12.1	•	•	•	•	•	•
Total Liabilities to Net Worth	37	1.1	•	0.9	0.7	1.0	0.8	1.6	•	•	•	•	•	•
Current Assets to Working Capital	38	2.2	•	1.6	1.6	2.2	2.1	2.6	•	•	•	•	•	•
Current Liabilities to Working Capital	39	1.2	•	0.6	0.6	1.2	1.1	1.6	•	•	•	•	•	•
Working Capital to Net Sales	40	0.1	•	0.1	0.2	0.1	0.2	0.1	•	•	•	•	•	•
Inventory to Working Capital	41	0.6	•	0.2	0.2	0.3	0.2	1.2	•	•	•	•	•	•
Total Receipts to Cash Flow	42	5.6	1.7	2.5	2.6	9.9	6.8	12.0	•	•	•	•	•	•
Cost of Goods to Cash Flow	43	3.9	0.2	1.1	1.4	7.8	4.9	9.1	•	•	•	•	•	•
Cash Flow to Total Debt	44	0.8	•	3.3	2.1	0.6	0.6	0.3	•	•	•	•	•	•

Selected Financial Factors (in Percentages)														
Debt Ratio	45	51.5	•	47.1	42.7	48.7	44.4	62.1	•	•	•	•	•	•
Return on Total Assets	46	17.7	•	63.9	31.6	11.0	14.9	8.9	•	•	•	•	•	•
Return on Equity Before Income Taxes	47	34.2	•	116.3	54.1	19.9	25.2	19.9	•	•	•	•	•	•
Return on Equity After Income Taxes	48	32.8	•	115.6	53.2	19.0	24.9	16.9	•	•	•	•	•	•
Profit Margin (Before Income Tax)	49	7.4	45.4	15.5	13.2	3.3	7.8	3.5	•	•	•	•	•	•
Profit Margin (After Income Tax)	50	7.1	39.8	15.4	12.9	3.2	7.8	3.0	•	•	•	•	•	•

Table I

Corporations with and without Net Income

OIL AND GAS EXTRACTION

MONEY AMOUNTS AND SIZE OF ASSETS IN THOUSANDS OF DOLLARS

Item Description for Accounting Period 7/11 Through 6/12		Total	Zero Assets	Under 500	500 to 1,000	1,000 to 5,000	5,000 to 10,000	10,000 to 25,000	25,000 to 50,000	50,000 to 100,000	100,000 to 250,000	250,000 to 500,000	500,000 to 2,500,000	2,500,000 and over
Number of Enterprises	1	21955	3549	13891	1191	1596	737	434	182	127	84	57	62	43
Revenues ($ in Thousands)														
Net Sales	2	215268864	3064175	4578100	896852	2647534	2793145	3687126	2476553	2272596	6587322	4273669	21007387	160984406
Interest	3	1777557	3306	434	3707	7895	5044	10207	20885	9524	16488	22523	47959	1629586
Rents	4	494263	3189	11270	1007	9771	7646	5775	4880	12145	10371	1875	5029	421306
Royalties	5	646297	17081	43928	4213	34549	38533	94995	41910	56537	17074	3143	35565	258768
Other Portfolio Income	6	21522433	1608325	12517	19425	148875	56726	177348	193067	294614	224387	469183	904782	17413182
Other Receipts	7	12465394	97250	240711	218037	319811	262827	250389	316297	391525	697973	204973	1347839	8117762
Total Receipts	8	252174808	4793326	4886960	1143241	3168435	3163921	4225840	3053592	3036941	7553615	4975366	23348561	188825010
Average Total Receipts	9	11486	1351	352	960	1985	4293	9737	16778	23913	89924	87287	376590	4391279
Operating Costs/Operating Income (%)														
Cost of Operations	10	52.0	30.1	28.5	47.2	16.6	28.5	33.4	31.3	25.1	48.3	28.7	40.4	57.6
Salaries and Wages	11	4.7	10.0	7.3	17.1	10.6	13.0	9.3	9.4	10.5	7.0	8.2	4.4	3.8
Taxes Paid	12	2.8	4.3	2.4	3.9	6.0	3.6	3.9	3.9	5.2	2.1	3.9	2.8	2.6
Interest Paid	13	4.8	10.2	0.6	2.9	1.4	1.2	1.9	3.8	3.1	2.5	6.1	5.6	5.1
Depreciation	14	11.5	10.4	4.6	6.8	7.8	7.0	9.4	11.8	19.9	10.1	14.1	13.1	11.6
Amortization and Depletion	15	7.7	7.3	0.7	1.9	3.4	3.9	5.0	6.8	14.4	8.1	21.3	15.1	6.7
Pensions and Other Deferred Comp.	16	0.4	0.2	1.4	0.3	0.1	0.4	0.4	0.4	0.5	0.6	1.0	0.3	0.4
Employee Benefits	17	0.6	0.4	0.7	0.9	1.2	0.6	0.7	1.0	1.2	0.4	0.9	0.4	0.6
Advertising	18	0.0	0.0	0.1	0.1	0.2	0.1	0.2	0.1	0.0	0.0	0.0	0.0	0.0
Other Expenses	19	30.0	81.5	37.1	26.0	37.3	30.0	32.5	37.8	46.0	21.4	59.9	30.6	27.8
Officers' Compensation	20	1.2	8.1	8.5	8.8	5.0	4.0	2.4	5.2	2.8	1.3	2.1	1.3	0.5
Operating Margin	21	•	•	7.9	•	10.4	7.7	0.7	•	•	•	•	•	•
Operating Margin Before Officers' Comp.	22	•	•	16.5	•	15.4	11.7	3.1	•	•	•	•	•	•

Selected Average Balance Sheet ($ in Thousands)

Net Receivables 23	2171	0	23	55	375	1066	1871	3075	5519	14281	31693	57041	867159
Inventories 24	235	0	1	26	29	51	145	323	415	2538	3098	8894	91390
Net Property, Plant and Equipment 25	16142	0	22	250	502	1550	5272	12516	31671	74325	165084	720501	6579900
Total Assets 26	26504	0	120	755	2182	7040	16396	34869	71426	161155	338249	1119822	10369283
Notes and Loans Payable 27	7030	0	63	668	668	937	4969	9566	17080	33296	87623	327374	2715437
All Other Liabilities 28	7769	0	10	259	739	2083	3583	7915	15477	37604	58965	265930	3242859
Net Worth 29	11704	0	46	-173	775	4021	7843	17387	38868	90255	191661	526519	4410987

Selected Financial Ratios (Times to 1)

Current Ratio 30	1.0	•	5.3	1.1	1.2	1.8	1.4	1.4	1.7	1.6	2.1	1.3	0.8
Quick Ratio 31	0.7	•	4.9	0.6	1.0	1.3	1.1	1.0	1.4	1.2	1.7	0.9	0.6
Net Sales to Working Capital 32	•	•	5.3	19.6	9.3	2.2	4.1	4.0	2.1	4.6	1.6	7.0	•
Coverage Ratio 33	1.8	0.4	24.6	5.0	21.7	18.7	8.8	4.1	2.7	6.2	•	0.5	1.7
Total Asset Turnover 34	0.4	•	2.8	1.0	0.8	0.5	0.5	0.4	0.3	0.5	0.2	0.3	0.4
Inventory Turnover 35	21.7	•	150.6	13.8	9.5	21.1	19.5	13.2	10.8	14.9	6.9	15.4	23.6
Receivables Turnover 36	4.9	•	15.1	12.9	3.8	3.8	5.1	4.0	3.7	5.0	2.5	6.3	4.7
Total Liabilities to Net Worth 37	1.3	•	1.6	•	1.8	0.8	1.1	1.0	0.8	0.8	0.8	1.1	1.4
Current Assets to Working Capital 38	•	•	1.2	8.0	5.7	2.3	3.2	3.6	2.4	2.5	1.9	3.9	•
Current Liabilities to Working Capital 39	•	•	0.2	7.0	4.7	1.3	2.2	2.6	1.4	1.5	0.9	2.9	•
Working Capital to Net Sales 40	•	•	0.2	0.1	0.1	0.4	0.2	0.2	0.5	0.2	0.6	0.1	•
Inventory to Working Capital 41	•	•	0.0	0.7	0.1	0.0	0.1	0.1	0.0	0.1	0.1	0.2	•
Total Receipts to Cash Flow 42	3.9	3.4	2.3	3.2	1.7	2.2	2.4	2.4	2.2	3.3	5.5	4.6	4.2
Cost of Goods to Cash Flow 43	2.0	1.0	0.6	1.5	0.3	0.6	0.8	0.8	0.6	1.6	1.6	1.9	2.4
Cash Flow to Total Debt 44	0.2	•	2.0	0.3	0.7	0.6	0.4	0.3	0.2	0.3	0.1	0.1	0.1

Selected Financial Factors (in Percentages)

Debt Ratio 45	55.8	•	61.5	122.9	64.5	42.9	52.2	50.1	45.6	44.0	43.3	53.0	57.5
Return on Total Assets 46	3.2	•	42.1	14.4	23.9	11.9	8.9	6.1	2.1	7.5	•	0.8	3.2
Return on Equity Before Income Taxes 47	3.1	•	104.8	•	64.1	19.8	16.4	9.2	2.4	11.2	•	•	3.2
Return on Equity After Income Taxes 48	0.3	•	103.8	•	61.8	18.8	15.2	7.1	1.7	8.3	•	•	•
Profit Margin (Before Income Tax) 49	3.7	•	14.7	11.5	30.0	21.0	15.1	11.7	5.3	12.9	•	•	3.8
Profit Margin (After Income Tax) 50	0.3	•	14.5	11.4	28.9	19.9	14.0	9.1	3.6	9.6	•	•	•

Table II

Corporations with Net Income

OIL AND GAS EXTRACTION

MONEY AMOUNTS AND SIZE OF ASSETS IN THOUSANDS OF DOLLARS

Item Description for Accounting Period 7/11 Through 6/12		Total	Zero Assets	Under 500	500 to 1,000	1,000 to 5,000	5,000 to 10,000	10,000 to 25,000	25,000 to 50,000	50,000 to 100,000	100,000 to 250,000	250,000 to 500,000	500,000 to 2,500,000	2,500,000 and over
Number of Enterprises	1	14145	1565	9719	680	1108	496	296	106	68	50	22	22	13
Revenues ($ in Thousands)														
Net Sales	2	127195004	281251	2817131	434908	2277227	2267756	3021786	1998952	1527113	4895802	2563741	11982493	93126843
Interest	3	1256939	128	342	3631	7328	3407	7061	18979	6111	11937	9203	28103	1160709
Rents	4	58616	189	0	0	8636	7200	4590	2175	8528	3869	1218	264	21947
Royalties	5	341782	8952	31978	4159	22624	22701	94820	40693	42501	9101	4	14215	50035
Other Portfolio Income	6	12566057	424887	11660	18359	102843	50988	161963	188588	262002	196486	376634	762781	10008867
Other Receipts	7	7861537	108911	119865	209149	221087	212716	259567	286317	365116	680361	69156	624193	4705098
Total Receipts	8	149279935	824318	2980976	670206	2639745	2564768	3549787	2535704	2211371	5797556	3019956	13412049	109073499
Average Total Receipts	9	10554	527	307	986	2382	5171	11993	23922	32520	115951	137271	609639	8390269
Operating Costs/Operating Income (%)														
Cost of Operations	10	60.9	14.9	19.5	22.0	14.8	32.7	33.3	31.1	20.3	42.6	34.9	53.2	69.1
Salaries and Wages	11	3.4	24.6	2.4	19.4	5.9	8.3	7.3	8.2	10.6	8.2	5.2	2.8	2.6
Taxes Paid	12	2.3	11.1	2.5	4.2	5.5	3.2	4.1	3.9	5.1	2.1	3.2	1.7	2.1
Interest Paid	13	2.8	1.7	0.4	0.8	0.9	0.8	0.8	1.3	1.6	1.8	1.3	1.8	3.4
Depreciation	14	7.0	5.7	3.5	8.7	5.6	6.3	8.0	8.6	13.4	8.8	8.0	7.5	6.9
Amortization and Depletion	15	4.5	1.7	0.9	3.1	2.9	2.4	3.9	5.0	6.5	6.3	5.7	5.1	4.5
Pensions and Other Deferred Comp.	16	0.5	0.6	2.3	0.0	0.1	0.2	0.4	0.4	0.6	0.6	1.6	0.2	0.4
Employee Benefits	17	0.6	1.2	0.6	0.8	1.2	0.4	0.5	0.9	1.3	0.4	0.6	0.4	0.7
Advertising	18	0.0	0.1	0.1	0.1	0.1	0.1	0.2	0.1	0.0	0.0	0.0	0.0	0.0
Other Expenses	19	16.5	74.8	29.8	29.6	27.1	23.3	22.1	24.3	33.1	18.7	19.5	20.8	14.0
Officers' Compensation	20	1.0	2.1	10.8	9.2	4.4	2.6	2.4	4.6	2.0	1.1	1.6	0.4	0.5
Operating Margin	21	0.4	•	27.3	2.1	31.6	19.6	17.2	11.6	5.5	9.4	18.5	5.9	•
Operating Margin Before Officers' Comp.	22	1.4	•	38.1	11.2	36.0	22.3	19.6	16.2	7.5	10.5	20.1	6.3	•

Selected Average Balance Sheet ($ in Thousands)													
Net Receivables 23	1378	0	27	56	447	975	1986	3125	5397	18238	58956	82552	992482
Inventories 24	208	0	1	39	32	20	106	500	588	3758	3704	17005	161236
Net Property, Plant and Equipment 25	9261	0	17	105	419	1455	4246	10451	24138	64273	102361	632152	8169055
Total Assets 26	17788	0	113	696	2089	6983	16499	35412	70838	160491	340024	1179398	14565130
Notes and Loans Payable 27	3590	0	47	187	249	688	2732	4027	10601	31718	31452	273082	3025480
All Other Liabilities 28	4173	0	9	269	354	2000	3037	6555	11553	40692	71439	293544	3455549
Net Worth 29	10025	0	57	240	1486	4294	10730	24830	48684	88081	237132	612772	8084100

Selected Financial Ratios (Times to 1)													
Current Ratio 30	1.3	•	6.3	1.4	3.6	1.9	2.6	2.7	2.8	1.8	2.7	1.6	0.9
Quick Ratio 31	1.0	•	5.7	0.5	3.0	1.4	2.0	2.0	2.2	1.3	2.2	1.0	0.7
Net Sales to Working Capital 32	13.6	•	4.1	5.9	2.4	2.5	2.1	2.1	1.5	4.1	1.1	5.0	•
Coverage Ratio 33	8.7	94.6	92.1	70.1	54.7	42.0	42.1	31.4	32.0	16.4	28.8	10.7	6.5
Total Asset Turnover 34	0.5	•	2.6	0.9	1.0	0.7	0.6	0.5	0.3	0.6	0.3	0.5	0.5
Inventory Turnover 35	26.3	•	63.4	3.6	9.5	76.2	32.1	11.7	7.8	11.1	11.0	17.1	30.7
Receivables Turnover 36	5.3	•	10.5	9.6	4.1	5.6	6.1	5.4	4.6	5.6	2.0	5.8	5.4
Total Liabilities to Net Worth 37	0.8	•	1.0	1.9	0.4	0.6	0.5	0.4	0.5	0.8	0.4	0.9	0.8
Current Assets to Working Capital 38	4.7	•	1.2	3.8	1.4	2.1	1.6	1.6	1.6	2.2	1.6	2.6	•
Current Liabilities to Working Capital 39	3.7	•	0.2	2.8	0.4	1.1	0.6	0.6	0.6	1.2	0.6	1.6	•
Working Capital to Net Sales 40	0.1	•	0.2	0.2	0.4	0.4	0.5	0.5	0.7	0.2	0.9	0.2	•
Inventory to Working Capital 41	0.2	•	0.0	0.4	0.0	0.0	0.0	0.0	0.0	0.2	0.0	0.1	•
Total Receipts to Cash Flow 42	3.2	1.4	1.7	1.3	1.5	1.9	1.9	1.8	1.3	2.4	2.3	3.1	4.0
Cost of Goods to Cash Flow 43	2.0	0.2	0.3	0.3	0.2	0.6	0.6	0.6	0.3	1.0	0.8	1.7	2.8
Cash Flow to Total Debt 44	0.4	•	3.1	1.1	2.3	0.9	0.9	1.0	0.8	0.6	0.5	0.3	0.3

Selected Financial Factors (in Percentages)													
Debt Ratio 45	43.6	•	49.8	65.5	28.9	38.5	35.0	29.9	31.3	45.1	30.3	48.0	44.5
Return on Total Assets 46	12.4	•	85.5	52.3	47.5	21.9	21.8	21.1	16.5	18.1	12.8	9.1	10.7
Return on Equity Before Income Taxes 47	19.5	•	168.2	149.5	65.5	34.8	32.8	29.1	23.3	30.9	17.8	15.8	16.4
Return on Equity After Income Taxes 48	14.5	•	167.2	148.6	63.8	33.5	31.5	26.6	22.1	26.0	13.4	13.5	10.6
Profit Margin (Before Income Tax) 49	21.7	154.8	33.1	56.2	47.4	32.7	34.5	38.3	50.6	27.8	36.2	17.8	18.5
Profit Margin (After Income Tax) 50	16.2	153.0	32.9	55.8	46.1	31.4	33.1	35.1	48.0	23.4	27.3	15.2	12.0

Table I

Corporations with and without Net Income

COAL MINING

MONEY AMOUNTS AND SIZE OF ASSETS IN THOUSANDS OF DOLLARS

Item Description for Accounting Period 7/11 Through 6/12		Total	Zero Assets	Under 500	500 to 1,000	1,000 to 5,000	5,000 to 10,000	10,000 to 25,000	25,000 to 50,000	50,000 to 100,000	100,000 to 250,000	250,000 to 500,000	500,000 to 2,500,000	2,500,000 and over
Number of Enterprises	1	1074	•	•	•	65	64	60	18	15	6	6	9	6
Revenues ($ in Thousands)														
Net Sales	2	36039781	•	•	•	864186	498616	1060024	617889	1023611	703971	2060361	6401565	21801636
Interest	3	102726	•	•	•	937	272	629	22	494	132	950	15903	79081
Rents	4	19554	•	•	•	8	33	0	0	0	13956	4	398	5156
Royalties	5	209165	•	•	•	18629	892	0	0	10000	3	25	1299	165142
Other Portfolio Income	6	382893	•	•	•	794	135	43641	3537	48913	841	28792	20221	223048
Other Receipts	7	1323312	•	•	•	10926	9711	15247	28999	9469	20583	10547	245190	961331
Total Receipts	8	38077431	•	•	•	895480	509659	1119541	650447	1092487	739486	2100679	6684576	23235394
Average Total Receipts	9	35454	•	•	•	13777	7963	18659	36136	72832	123248	350113	742731	3872566
Operating Costs/Operating Income (%)														
Cost of Operations	10	58.0	•	•	•	80.0	50.0	82.8	57.5	83.4	70.7	66.3	60.9	52.2
Salaries and Wages	11	5.4	•	•	•	1.4	•	1.7	5.7	3.6	1.1	0.9	4.1	7.1
Taxes Paid	12	5.4	•	•	•	6.7	7.1	3.3	2.7	2.6	4.5	3.5	4.3	6.3
Interest Paid	13	4.1	•	•	•	0.0	0.5	0.4	1.5	1.6	0.7	3.9	3.4	5.2
Depreciation	14	8.0	•	•	•	1.3	5.2	3.9	10.3	6.0	9.4	7.1	13.4	7.3
Amortization and Depletion	15	5.5	•	•	•	0.0	1.8	1.9	2.8	3.9	5.2	7.5	5.1	6.2
Pensions and Other Deferred Comp.	16	0.7	•	•	•	•	0.4	0.1	0.1	0.3	0.3	0.2	0.6	0.9
Employee Benefits	17	4.4	•	•	•	0.2	1.4	1.4	1.5	1.2	1.6	2.7	4.0	5.5
Advertising	18	0.0	•	•	•	0.0	0.0	0.0	0.0	0.0	0.0	0.0	0.0	0.1
Other Expenses	19	12.2	•	•	•	12.6	37.5	10.2	26.5	4.0	6.4	12.1	6.4	13.5
Officers' Compensation	20	0.4	•	•	•	0.2	1.8	0.4	2.4	0.5	0.7	0.4	0.4	0.3
Operating Margin	21	•	•	•	•	•	•	•	•	•	•	•	•	•
Operating Margin Before Officers' Comp.	22	•	•	•	•	•	•	•	•	•	•	•	•	•

Selected Average Balance Sheet ($ in Thousands)													
Net Receivables **23**	8759	•	•	•	538	932	1685	10002	5394	13992	88615	53771	1295510
Inventories **24**	1774	•	•	•	0	141	645	1100	2663	10902	21371	51699	200519
Net Property, Plant and Equipment **25**	37317	•	•	•	698	1350	4013	13938	30031	69011	129613	440876	5640248
Total Assets **26**	74959	•	•	•	1985	6848	15779	33518	71937	148236	334475	1046915	10804688
Notes and Loans Payable **27**	25059	•	•	•	3278	2336	4116	14240	19466	23864	168125	349871	3570813
All Other Liabilities **28**	24267	•	•	•	1374	1144	4697	9718	14559	53769	85206	396747	3442182
Net Worth **29**	25633	•	•	•	-2667	3368	6967	9561	37912	70604	81144	300297	3791693
Selected Financial Ratios (Times to 1)													
Current Ratio **30**	1.5	•	•	•	0.5	2.3	2.0	2.0	1.1	0.9	1.1	0.8	1.9
Quick Ratio **31**	1.2	•	•	•	0.5	2.2	1.8	1.8	0.8	0.7	0.8	0.6	1.4
Net Sales to Working Capital **32**	6.2	•	•	•	•	4.3	5.6	4.4	44.3	•	42.3	•	3.7
Coverage Ratio **33**	1.4	•	•	•	32.9	•	•	•	0.6	6.9	0.3	1.6	1.4
Total Asset Turnover **34**	0.4	•	•	•	6.7	1.1	1.1	1.0	0.9	0.8	1.0	0.7	0.3
Inventory Turnover **35**	11.0	•	•	•	•	27.7	22.7	18.0	21.4	7.6	10.7	8.4	9.5
Receivables Turnover **36**	1.6	•	•	•	17.4	8.9	6.5	3.6	14.1	3.4	7.8	10.8	1.1
Total Liabilities to Net Worth **37**	1.9	•	•	•	•	1.0	1.3	2.5	0.9	1.1	3.1	2.5	1.8
Current Assets to Working Capital **38**	2.9	•	•	•	•	1.8	2.0	2.0	8.4	•	18.7	•	2.1
Current Liabilities to Working Capital **39**	1.9	•	•	•	•	0.8	1.0	1.0	7.4	•	17.7	•	1.1
Working Capital to Net Sales **40**	0.2	•	•	•	•	0.2	0.2	0.2	0.0	•	0.0	•	0.3
Inventory to Working Capital **41**	0.3	•	•	•	•	0.1	0.1	0.1	2.0	•	2.6	•	0.2
Total Receipts to Cash Flow **42**	9.7	•	•	•	13.7	4.5	13.7	7.4	42.1	11.6	18.4	15.6	8.5
Cost of Goods to Cash Flow **43**	5.6	•	•	•	11.0	2.3	11.3	4.3	35.1	8.2	12.2	9.5	4.4
Cash Flow to Total Debt **44**	0.1	•	•	•	0.2	0.5	0.1	0.2	0.0	0.1	0.1	0.1	0.1
Selected Financial Factors (in Percentages)													
Debt Ratio **45**	65.8	•	•	•	234.4	50.8	55.8	71.5	47.3	52.4	75.7	71.3	64.9
Return on Total Assets **46**	2.6	•	•	•	9.3	•	•	•	1.0	4.0	1.2	3.6	2.4
Return on Equity Before Income Taxes **47**	2.1	•	•	•	•	•	•	•	•	7.1	•	4.5	2.0
Return on Equity After Income Taxes **48**	0.5	•	•	•	•	•	•	•	•	6.3	•	4.5	0.1
Profit Margin (Before Income Tax) **49**	1.6	•	•	•	1.3	•	•	•	•	4.3	•	1.9	2.1
Profit Margin (After Income Tax) **50**	0.4	•	•	•	0.7	•	•	•	•	3.8	•	1.9	0.1

Table II

Corporations with Net Income

COAL MINING

Item Description for Accounting Period 7/11 Through 6/12		Total	Zero Assets	Under 500	500 to 1,000	1,000 to 5,000	5,000 to 10,000	10,000 to 25,000	25,000 to 50,000	50,000 to 100,000	100,000 to 250,000	250,000 to 500,000	500,000 to 2,500,000	2,500,000 and over
		MONEY AMOUNTS AND SIZE OF ASSETS IN THOUSANDS OF DOLLARS												
Number of Enterprises	1	530	•	•	•	32	41	27	5	10	0	3	0	3
Revenues ($ in Thousands)														
Net Sales	2	18577270	•	•	•	796551	351525	319439	266846	972465	0	3014486	0	11893000
Interest	3	70373	•	•	•	61	0	619	9	495	0	535	0	64348
Rents	4	15198	•	•	•	8	0	0	0	13956	0	0	0	1235
Royalties	5	52107	•	•	•	18629	0	0	0	9901	0	25	0	10377
Other Portfolio Income	6	259520	•	•	•	133	135	42171	2785	49512	0	15692	0	136121
Other Receipts	7	936974	•	•	•	10774	7769	13262	8609	17116	0	120684	0	751847
Total Receipts	8	19911442	•	•	•	826156	359429	375491	278249	1063445	0	3151422	0	12856928
Average Total Receipts	9	37569	•	•	•	25817	8767	13907	55650	106344	•	1050474	•	4285643
Operating Costs/Operating Income (%)														
Cost of Operations	10	42.8	•	•	•	86.8	43.8	67.8	25.2	67.8	•	52.0	•	32.6
Salaries and Wages	11	8.5	•	•	•	0.0	•	3.0	6.9	3.5	•	2.7	•	12.1
Taxes Paid	12	5.3	•	•	•	6.9	5.2	3.6	2.8	3.4	•	1.9	•	6.6
Interest Paid	13	3.6	•	•	•	•	•	0.2	1.4	0.5	•	2.1	•	5.0
Depreciation	14	7.0	•	•	•	1.1	4.9	3.3	6.0	8.5	•	8.9	•	7.5
Amortization and Depletion	15	5.7	•	•	•	0.0	2.6	1.5	3.5	7.0	•	7.5	•	6.3
Pensions and Other Deferred Comp.	16	0.8	•	•	•	•	0.4	0.2	0.0	0.2	•	0.4	•	1.0
Employee Benefits	17	4.2	•	•	•	0.0	•	0.6	1.3	1.3	•	3.0	•	5.7
Advertising	18	0.1	•	•	•	0.0	0.0	0.0	0.0	0.0	•	0.0	•	0.1
Other Expenses	19	17.5	•	•	•	5.4	42.5	21.5	45.6	3.5	•	3.8	•	22.0
Officers' Compensation	20	0.4	•	•	•	0.0	1.9	1.1	4.0	0.6	•	0.1	•	0.3
Operating Margin	21	4.1	•	•	•	•	•	•	3.1	3.5	•	17.6	•	0.9
Operating Margin Before Officers' Comp.	22	4.4	•	•	•	•	0.6	•	7.1	4.2	•	17.8	•	1.2

Selected Average Balance Sheet ($ in Thousands)													
Net Receivables 23	12802	•	•	•	415	308	1600	8440	6843	•	87838	•	2087880
Inventories 24	1629	•	•	•	0	98	941	1648	2109	•	40154	•	202452
Net Property, Plant and Equipment 25	30399	•	•	•	1274	1045	994	18915	38080	•	228685	•	4945292
Total Assets 26	73721	•	•	•	1894	6302	16879	36625	90189	•	1168554	•	11190202
Notes and Loans Payable 27	24377	•	•	•	0	54	244	27037	12603	•	19017	•	4189583
All Other Liabilities 28	21825	•	•	•	1343	1024	6337	6814	17702	•	385558	•	3262934
Net Worth 29	27520	•	•	•	551	5224	10298	2774	59885	•	763978	•	3737685
Selected Financial Ratios (Times to 1)													
Current Ratio 30	2.8	•	•	•	0.5	3.5	4.7	1.8	1.8	•	2.1	•	3.0
Quick Ratio 31	2.2	•	•	•	0.5	3.4	4.3	1.6	1.6	•	1.7	•	2.3
Net Sales to Working Capital 32	2.7	•	•	•	•	3.4	1.4	11.2	9.8	•	6.6	•	2.0
Coverage Ratio 33	4.1	•	•	•	•	•	95.1	6.2	25.7	•	11.6	•	2.8
Total Asset Turnover 34	0.5	•	•	•	13.1	1.4	0.7	1.5	1.1	•	0.9	•	0.4
Inventory Turnover 35	9.2	•	•	•	•	38.5	8.5	8.2	31.3	•	13.0	•	6.4
Receivables Turnover 36	4.4	•	•	•	29.8	•	5.3	5.7	15.7	•	22.9	•	•
Total Liabilities to Net Worth 37	1.7	•	•	•	2.4	0.2	0.6	12.2	0.5	•	0.5	•	2.0
Current Assets to Working Capital 38	1.6	•	•	•	•	1.4	1.3	2.3	2.2	•	1.9	•	1.5
Current Liabilities to Working Capital 39	0.6	•	•	•	•	0.4	0.3	1.3	1.2	•	0.9	•	0.5
Working Capital to Net Sales 40	0.4	•	•	•	•	0.3	0.7	0.1	0.1	•	0.2	•	0.5
Inventory to Working Capital 41	0.1	•	•	•	•	0.0	0.1	0.1	0.2	•	0.3	•	0.1
Total Receipts to Cash Flow 42	4.1	•	•	•	11.3	3.5	2.8	2.4	6.4	•	4.3	•	3.8
Cost of Goods to Cash Flow 43	1.7	•	•	•	9.8	1.5	1.9	0.6	4.3	•	2.2	•	1.3
Cash Flow to Total Debt 44	0.2	•	•	•	1.6	2.3	0.6	0.7	0.5	•	0.6	•	0.1
Selected Financial Factors (in Percentages)													
Debt Ratio 45	62.7	•	•	•	70.9	17.1	39.0	92.4	33.6	•	34.6	•	66.6
Return on Total Assets 46	7.1	•	•	•	45.6	1.3	10.6	12.7	14.5	•	20.9	•	5.0
Return on Equity Before Income Taxes 47	14.4	•	•	•	156.7	1.5	17.2	140.9	20.9	•	29.2	•	9.7
Return on Equity After Income Taxes 48	11.4	•	•	•	123.9	1.5	15.9	129.3	20.3	•	29.1	•	5.9
Profit Margin (Before Income Tax) 49	11.3	•	•	•	3.5	0.9	14.9	7.3	12.9	•	22.2	•	9.2
Profit Margin (After Income Tax) 50	9.0	•	•	•	2.7	0.9	13.9	6.7	12.5	•	22.1	•	5.6

Table I

Corporations with and without Net Income

METAL ORE MINING

MONEY AMOUNTS AND SIZE OF ASSETS IN THOUSANDS OF DOLLARS

Item Description for Accounting Period 7/11 Through 6/12		Total	Zero Assets	Under 500	500 to 1,000	1,000 to 5,000	5,000 to 10,000	10,000 to 25,000	25,000 to 50,000	50,000 to 100,000	100,000 to 250,000	250,000 to 500,000	500,000 to 2,500,000	2,500,000 and over
Number of Enterprises	1	1363	•	•	•	113	42	57	37	14	14	9	15	10
Revenues ($ in Thousands)														
Net Sales	2	61220044	•	•	•	1414	5205	264817	127236	631625	293712	1378046	6034354	52428517
Interest	3	587309	•	•	•	348	3905	235	508	1091	2740	4600	48140	525716
Rents	4	45471	•	•	•	1057	1835	553	5	99	5	147	1	34986
Royalties	5	412939	•	•	•	5396	0	0	8013	6323	0	0	226159	167048
Other Portfolio Income	6	1972467	•	•	•	36270	0	22232	1109	37776	677	159357	111063	1599974
Other Receipts	7	2343356	•	•	•	7688	12041	15283	9866	11540	9739	7680	320713	1935701
Total Receipts	8	66581586	•	•	•	52173	22986	303120	146737	688454	306873	1549830	6740430	56691942
Average Total Receipts	9	48849	•	•	•	462	547	5318	3966	49175	21920	172203	449362	5669194
Operating Costs/Operating Income (%)														
Cost of Operations	10	52.6	•	•	•	17.9	55.0	91.7	73.4	31.2	78.4	52.8	63.3	51.2
Salaries and Wages	11	1.5	•	•	•	1317.3	333.7	11.3	11.2	12.3	7.9	1.4	1.3	1.2
Taxes Paid	12	1.4	•	•	•	140.7	7.7	0.9	1.4	2.6	0.9	1.5	1.3	1.4
Interest Paid	13	2.7	•	•	•	416.1	77.9	1.3	2.8	1.1	5.1	1.1	0.8	3.0
Depreciation	14	5.9	•	•	•	268.2	29.6	3.6	9.7	5.7	18.4	17.5	7.6	5.3
Amortization and Depletion	15	11.6	•	•	•	1216.3	122.6	4.1	16.1	10.0	27.6	10.5	12.5	11.5
Pensions and Other Deferred Comp.	16	0.5	•	•	•	42.5	•	0.1	0.2	0.5	0.1	•	0.1	0.5
Employee Benefits	17	0.8	•	•	•	•	0.9	0.5	1.3	2.4	1.0	2.6	0.1	0.8
Advertising	18	0.0	•	•	•	16.9	0.1	0.2	0.3	0.0	0.1	0.0	0.0	0.0
Other Expenses	19	9.9	•	•	•	6461.9	1845.8	36.1	55.3	26.6	26.8	13.9	12.2	8.5
Officers' Compensation	20	0.5	•	•	•	117.5	53.1	0.6	6.2	1.1	4.6	0.4	0.7	0.4
Operating Margin	21	12.8	•	•	•	•	•	•	•	6.5	•	•	0.1	16.3
Operating Margin Before Officers' Comp.	22	13.2	•	•	•	•	•	•	•	7.6	•	•	0.8	16.6

Selected Average Balance Sheet ($ in Thousands)

Net Receivables 23	21663	•	•	•	113	18	2041	1597	9048	1980	4222	48472	2841894
Inventories 24	6445	•	•	•	154	56	14	1388	4472	6901	18973	80137	718072
Net Property, Plant and Equipment 25	33095	•	•	•	376	1422	4395	14310	22588	30599	191684	513883	3401222
Total Assets 26	138347	•	•	•	2715	7505	14516	35218	73691	165479	340287	1209711	16110021
Notes and Loans Payable 27	19908	•	•	•	1090	5109	3542	13805	29538	72037	60436	147174	2185770
All Other Liabilities 28	42979	•	•	•	2619	7132	5317	11827	16648	52688	81458	200261	5251192
Net Worth 29	75459	•	•	•	-994	-4736	5657	9586	27505	40754	198394	862276	8673059

Selected Financial Ratios (Times to 1)

Current Ratio 30	1.8	•	•	•	0.6	0.2	2.2	1.1	2.0	1.6	2.2	2.4	1.7
Quick Ratio 31	1.3	•	•	•	0.2	0.0	2.1	0.4	1.5	0.9	1.3	1.4	1.3
Net Sales to Working Capital 32	2.6	•	•	•	•	•	2.2	4.7	3.5	1.4	2.4	2.4	2.5
Coverage Ratio 33	9.3	•	•	•	•	•	•	•	14.9	•	11.2	18.2	9.5
Total Asset Turnover 34	0.3	•	•	•	0.0	0.0	0.3	0.1	0.6	0.1	0.4	0.3	0.3
Inventory Turnover 35	3.7	•	•	•	0.0	1.2	295.1	1.8	3.1	2.4	4.3	3.2	3.7
Receivables Turnover 36	2.3	•	•	•	0.2	8.2	2.8	2.9	4.1	3.5	25.4	9.5	2.0
Total Liabilities to Net Worth 37	0.8	•	•	•	•	•	1.6	2.7	1.7	3.1	0.7	0.4	0.9
Current Assets to Working Capital 38	2.3	•	•	•	•	•	1.8	12.3	2.0	2.7	1.8	1.7	2.3
Current Liabilities to Working Capital 39	1.3	•	•	•	•	•	0.8	11.3	1.0	1.7	0.8	0.7	1.3
Working Capital to Net Sales 40	0.4	•	•	•	•	•	0.4	0.2	0.3	0.7	0.4	0.4	0.4
Inventory to Working Capital 41	0.4	•	•	•	•	•	0.0	1.3	0.4	0.4	0.4	0.5	0.4
Total Receipts to Cash Flow 42	3.4	•	•	•	•	•	•	•	3.3	•	8.2	4.4	3.2
Cost of Goods to Cash Flow 43	1.8	•	•	•	•	•	•	•	1.0	•	4.3	2.8	1.7
Cash Flow to Total Debt 44	0.2	•	•	•	•	•	•	•	0.3	•	0.1	0.3	0.2

Selected Financial Factors (in Percentages)

Debt Ratio 45	45.5	•	•	•	136.6	163.1	61.0	72.8	62.7	75.4	41.7	28.7	46.2
Return on Total Assets 46	8.1	•	•	•	•	•	•	•	10.2	•	5.4	4.8	9.1
Return on Equity Before Income Taxes 47	13.3	•	•	•	79.6	54.5	•	•	25.4	•	8.4	6.3	15.2
Return on Equity After Income Taxes 48	8.3	•	•	•	79.6	54.5	•	•	22.3	•	3.8	3.7	9.8
Profit Margin (Before Income Tax) 49	22.3	•	•	•	•	•	•	•	15.5	•	10.8	13.5	25.1
Profit Margin (After Income Tax) 50	14.0	•	•	•	•	•	•	•	13.6	•	5.0	8.0	16.2

Table II

Corporations with Net Income

METAL ORE MINING

MONEY AMOUNTS AND SIZE OF ASSETS IN THOUSANDS OF DOLLARS

Item Description for Accounting Period 7/11 Through 6/12		Total	Zero Assets	Under 500	500 to 1,000	1,000 to 5,000	5,000 to 10,000	10,000 to 25,000	25,000 to 50,000	50,000 to 100,000	100,000 to 250,000	250,000 to 500,000	500,000 to 2,500,000	2,500,000 and over
Number of Enterprises	1	924	•	•	•	9	4	3	6	7	0	4	8	10
Revenues ($ in Thousands)														
Net Sales	2	57074258	•	•	•	730	5030	141520	118598	475861	0	947087	2901798	52428517
Interest	3	561300	•	•	•	3	0	0	5	243	0	2634	32699	525716
Rents	4	35734	•	•	•	0	0	549	0	99	0	100	0	34986
Royalties	5	406865	•	•	•	0	0	0	8002	5794	0	0	226021	167048
Other Portfolio Income	6	1919140	•	•	•	22015	0	19891	0	36735	0	138625	99782	1599974
Other Receipts	7	2294117	•	•	•	182	0	2835	4211	5697	0	5546	326849	1935701
Total Receipts	8	62291414	•	•	•	22930	5030	164795	130816	524429	0	1093992	3587149	56691942
Average Total Receipts	9	67415	•	•	•	2548	1258	54932	21803	74918	•	273498	448394	5669194
Operating Costs/Operating Income (%)														
Cost of Operations	10	50.9	•	•	•	•	56.6	86.1	76.0	31.3	•	43.8	47.9	51.2
Salaries and Wages	11	1.3	•	•	•	1.5	•	1.9	1.3	9.1	•	1.4	1.4	1.2
Taxes Paid	12	1.5	•	•	•	78.1	0.1	0.5	0.7	2.6	•	2.0	2.6	1.4
Interest Paid	13	2.8	•	•	•	24.4	•	•	0.6	1.3	•	0.4	0.8	3.0
Depreciation	14	5.3	•	•	•	•	•	0.3	3.5	4.9	•	7.6	5.9	5.3
Amortization and Depletion	15	11.8	•	•	•	0.1	•	•	0.4	12.4	•	14.1	19.0	11.5
Pensions and Other Deferred Comp.	16	0.5	•	•	•	•	•	•	0.1	0.1	•	•	0.0	0.5
Employee Benefits	17	0.8	•	•	•	•	•	•	0.6	0.9	•	3.6	0.1	0.8
Advertising	18	0.0	•	•	•	•	•	0.0	0.0	0.0	•	•	0.0	0.0
Other Expenses	19	8.9	•	•	•	442.9	19.7	3.6	8.2	17.3	•	14.1	13.5	8.5
Officers' Compensation	20	0.4	•	•	•	•	•	•	0.5	0.6	•	0.4	0.7	0.4
Operating Margin	21	15.8	•	•	•	•	23.6	7.6	8.0	19.5	•	12.5	8.1	16.3
Operating Margin Before Officers' Comp.	22	16.2	•	•	•	•	23.6	7.6	8.5	20.1	•	12.9	8.8	16.6

Selected Average Balance Sheet ($ in Thousands)

Net Receivables	23	31198	•	•	•	0	9	9907	3199	13030	•	5386	30818	2841894
Inventories	24	8930	•	•	•	0	0	0	6380	6529	•	45402	125198	779706
Net Property, Plant and Equipment	25	41578	•	•	•	96	3727	1527	2748	31784	•	116416	456337	3401222
Total Assets	26	186947	•	•	•	4318	9056	17554	36763	76238	•	339695	1166020	16110021
Notes and Loans Payable	27	26031	•	•	•	94	0	1305	17297	57503	•	18185	199930	2185770
All Other Liabilities	28	59554	•	•	•	847	0	2920	24632	22118	•	112430	218351	5251192
Net Worth	29	101362	•	•	•	3377	9056	13328	-5166	-3382	•	209079	747740	8673059

Selected Financial Ratios (Times to 1)

Current Ratio	30	1.8	•	•	•	0.2	•	4.2	1.9	1.5	•	2.7	2.6	1.7
Quick Ratio	31	1.3	•	•	•	0.2	•	4.0	0.3	1.1	•	1.9	1.3	1.3
Net Sales to Working Capital	32	2.5	•	•	•	•	86.7	4.7	1.2	7.0	•	2.2	1.8	2.5
Coverage Ratio	33	10.3	•	•	•	107.4	•	•	29.7	24.0	•	65.8	45.5	9.5
Total Asset Turnover	34	0.3	•	•	•	0.0	0.1	2.7	0.5	0.9	•	0.7	0.3	0.3
Inventory Turnover	35	3.5	•	•	•	•	•	•	2.4	3.3	•	2.3	1.4	3.4
Receivables Turnover	36	2.4	•	•	•	•	287.4	3.7	5.2	3.5	•	•	12.6	•
Total Liabilities to Net Worth	37	0.8	•	•	•	0.3	•	0.3	•	•	•	0.6	0.6	0.9
Current Assets to Working Capital	38	2.3	•	•	•	•	1.0	1.3	2.1	3.2	•	1.6	1.6	2.3
Current Liabilities to Working Capital	39	1.3	•	•	•	•	•	0.3	1.1	2.2	•	0.6	0.6	1.3
Working Capital to Net Sales	40	0.4	•	•	•	•	0.0	0.2	0.8	0.1	•	0.4	0.5	0.4
Inventory to Working Capital	41	0.4	•	•	•	•	•	•	0.2	0.7	•	0.4	0.6	0.4
Total Receipts to Cash Flow	42	3.2	•	•	•	•	2.3	3.7	3.9	3.1	•	3.8	2.3	3.2
Cost of Goods to Cash Flow	43	1.6	•	•	•	•	1.3	3.2	3.0	1.0	•	1.7	1.1	1.7
Cash Flow to Total Debt	44	0.2	•	•	•	•	•	3.0	0.1	0.3	•	0.5	0.4	0.2

Selected Financial Factors (in Percentages)

Debt Ratio	45	45.8	•	•	•	21.8	•	24.1	114.1	104.4	•	38.5	35.9	46.2
Return on Total Assets	46	9.4	•	•	•	49.2	3.3	80.4	10.2	27.6	•	19.8	11.2	9.1
Return on Equity Before Income Taxes	47	15.7	•	•	•	62.3	3.3	105.9	•	•	•	31.7	17.1	15.2
Return on Equity After Income Taxes	48	10.3	•	•	•	62.3	3.3	69.2	•	•	•	22.0	11.5	9.8
Profit Margin (Before Income Tax)	49	25.8	•	•	•	2594.1	23.6	29.9	18.3	29.7	•	28.0	35.1	25.1
Profit Margin (After Income Tax)	50	16.8	•	•	•	2594.1	23.6	19.6	15.0	27.1	•	19.4	23.8	16.2

Table I

Corporations with and without Net Income

NONMETALLIC MINERAL MINING AND QUARRYING

MONEY AMOUNTS AND SIZE OF ASSETS IN THOUSANDS OF DOLLARS

Item Description for Accounting Period 7/11 Through 6/12		Total	Zero Assets	Under 500	500 to 1,000	1,000 to 5,000	5,000 to 10,000	10,000 to 25,000	25,000 to 50,000	50,000 to 100,000	100,000 to 250,000	250,000 to 500,000	500,000 to 2,500,000	2,500,000 and over
Number of Enterprises	1	4380	273	2687	321	707	157	99	60	33	24	7	12	0
Revenues ($ in Thousands)														
Net Sales	2	25127612	82055	1012802	598426	2193051	1282835	1408694	1522124	1478006	2812689	2018044	10718884	0
Interest	3	31637	2	48	1187	715	80	1724	1580	1420	2495	1023	21363	0
Rents	4	40345	0	0	0	3083	187	580	1340	1235	1857	210	31855	0
Royalties	5	31578	0	361	0	0	0	0	182	191	119	42	30683	0
Other Portfolio Income	6	297554	18176	3649	6954	9889	10886	7222	42847	6693	9977	24634	156626	0
Other Receipts	7	405034	1107	10671	172	13436	9375	41745	24016	4559	6996	25390	267567	0
Total Receipts	8	25933760	101340	1027531	606739	2220174	1303363	1459965	1592089	1492104	2834133	2069343	11226978	0
Average Total Receipts	9	5921	371	382	1890	3140	8302	14747	26535	45215	118089	295620	935582	•
Operating Costs/Operating Income (%)														
Cost of Operations	10	64.3	82.4	30.2	79.2	58.7	64.8	70.4	68.1	64.6	68.5	68.2	64.4	•
Salaries and Wages	11	4.9	1.0	19.8	1.7	3.0	3.3	5.6	4.0	6.6	3.4	4.1	4.5	•
Taxes Paid	12	2.5	0.7	3.0	3.8	4.2	2.7	3.0	1.9	1.5	1.6	1.1	2.6	•
Interest Paid	13	3.0	1.4	1.6	1.4	1.2	2.5	1.3	1.7	1.1	1.9	1.2	5.0	•
Depreciation	14	9.1	4.3	6.7	4.9	5.8	7.7	7.5	10.8	6.9	9.7	10.6	10.4	•
Amortization and Depletion	15	3.2	0.5	1.5	0.2	1.8	0.9	2.4	2.5	1.4	2.2	3.0	4.8	•
Pensions and Other Deferred Comp.	16	0.8	•	•	0.0	0.6	0.3	0.5	0.5	0.5	0.7	1.7	1.1	•
Employee Benefits	17	2.0	0.3	1.8	2.6	2.1	1.8	2.5	1.6	2.4	2.2	1.1	2.2	•
Advertising	18	0.2	0.0	0.2	0.2	0.6	0.2	0.2	0.2	0.2	0.1	0.1	0.3	•
Other Expenses	19	10.5	28.7	37.9	5.6	17.2	10.8	9.0	8.9	15.3	9.8	6.4	7.3	•
Officers' Compensation	20	1.3	1.1	1.4	3.2	2.9	1.9	2.4	1.8	1.6	1.5	0.9	0.6	•
Operating Margin	21	•	•	•	•	2.0	3.0	•	•	•	•	1.6	•	•
Operating Margin Before Officers' Comp.	22	•	•	•	0.5	4.9	4.9	•	•	•	•	2.5	•	•

Selected Average Balance Sheet ($ in Thousands)

Net Receivables 23	747	0	0	208	335	1102	2592	3665	7293	18984	33457	115704	•
Inventories 24	681	0	0	27	192	520	2281	2674	6524	15170	33586	129756	•
Net Property, Plant and Equipment 25	3513	0	44	280	1116	4272	5695	14292	28677	66667	176064	709722	•
Total Assets 26	8667	0	70	711	2567	7089	15953	32328	65345	161242	357404	1880720	•
Notes and Loans Payable 27	2797	0	30	355	935	3727	2855	10679	17640	33817	80792	660692	•
All Other Liabilities 28	1926	0	26	92	231	919	3241	4734	10977	37814	73259	469932	•
Net Worth 29	3944	0	14	264	1402	2443	9857	16915	36729	89611	203352	750096	•

Selected Financial Ratios (Times to 1)

Current Ratio 30	2.1	•	1.4	4.0	4.6	1.6	2.1	2.2	2.4	2.3	2.0	1.8	•
Quick Ratio 31	1.2	•	1.0	3.5	3.9	1.2	1.3	1.3	1.6	1.3	1.2	0.8	•
Net Sales to Working Capital 32	4.9	•	66.3	6.4	3.2	10.0	3.6	4.3	3.2	3.6	5.2	5.7	•
Coverage Ratio 33	1.4	3.2	•	0.0	3.7	2.8	0.3	2.5	0.1	0.5	4.5	1.3	•
Total Asset Turnover 34	0.7	•	5.4	2.6	1.2	1.2	0.9	0.8	0.7	0.7	0.8	0.5	•
Inventory Turnover 35	5.4	•	•	54.1	9.5	10.2	4.4	6.5	4.4	5.3	5.9	4.4	•
Receivables Turnover 36	8.0	•	1012802.0	16.1	9.4	7.2	6.0	7.0	6.8	7.0	6.8	8.1	•
Total Liabilities to Net Worth 37	1.2	•	4.0	1.7	0.8	1.9	0.6	0.9	0.8	0.8	0.8	1.5	•
Current Assets to Working Capital 38	1.9	•	3.6	1.3	1.3	2.7	1.9	1.8	1.7	1.8	2.0	2.2	•
Current Liabilities to Working Capital 39	0.9	•	2.6	0.3	0.3	1.7	0.9	0.8	0.7	0.8	1.0	1.2	•
Working Capital to Net Sales 40	0.2	•	0.0	0.2	0.3	0.1	0.3	0.2	0.3	0.3	0.2	0.2	•
Inventory to Working Capital 41	0.6	•	•	0.1	0.1	0.5	0.6	0.4	0.5	0.5	0.5	0.9	•
Total Receipts to Cash Flow 42	13.7	3.2	4.1	31.1	7.7	8.9	17.7	19.0	9.0	18.0	13.6	22.3	•
Cost of Goods to Cash Flow 43	8.8	2.6	1.2	24.6	4.5	5.8	12.5	13.0	5.8	12.4	9.3	14.4	•
Cash Flow to Total Debt 44	0.1	•	1.7	0.1	0.3	0.2	0.1	0.1	0.2	0.1	0.1	0.0	•

Selected Financial Factors (in Percentages)

Debt Ratio 45	54.5	•	79.9	62.9	45.4	65.5	38.2	47.7	43.8	44.4	43.1	60.1	•
Return on Total Assets 46	2.9	•	•	0.2	5.4	8.2	0.3	3.3	0.1	0.7	4.3	3.1	•
Return on Equity Before Income Taxes 47	1.9	•	•	•	7.2	15.3	•	3.9	•	•	5.8	1.7	•
Return on Equity After Income Taxes 48	0.6	•	•	•	7.1	15.0	•	2.2	•	•	3.1	0.3	•
Profit Margin (Before Income Tax) 49	1.3	3.1	•	•	3.2	4.6	•	2.6	•	•	4.1	1.4	•
Profit Margin (After Income Tax) 50	0.4	3.1	•	•	3.2	4.5	•	1.5	•	•	2.2	0.3	•

Table II

Corporations with Net Income

NONMETALLIC MINERAL MINING AND QUARRYING

MONEY AMOUNTS AND SIZE OF ASSETS IN THOUSANDS OF DOLLARS

Item Description for Accounting Period 7/11 Through 6/12		Total	Zero Assets	Under 500	500 to 1,000	1,000 to 5,000	5,000 to 10,000	10,000 to 25,000	25,000 to 50,000	50,000 to 100,000	100,000 to 250,000	250,000 to 500,000	500,000 to 2,500,000	2,500,000 and over
Number of Enterprises	1	2232	3	1480	83	471	66	51	40	14	14	3	7	0
Revenues ($ in Thousands)														
Net Sales	2	14553391	82055	998484	144890	1857813	623103	772437	1054872	648009	1586388	1037667	5747672	0
Interest	3	23195	0	0	290	272	0	529	1462	507	2136	585	17415	0
Rents	4	25213	0	0	0	1095	0	344	604	875	558	74	21664	0
Royalties	5	30160	0	361	0	0	0	0	47	191	117	0	29443	0
Other Portfolio Income	6	168773	18176	2548	0	3852	8309	5621	41589	3515	5339	18545	61280	0
Other Receipts	7	308922	1107	5868	0	7361	1213	33207	21033	4363	13448	20434	200887	0
Total Receipts	8	15109654	101338	1007261	145180	1870393	632625	812138	1119607	657460	1607986	1077305	6078361	0
Average Total Receipts	9	6770	33779	681	1749	3971	9585	15924	27990	46961	114856	359102	868337	•
Operating Costs/Operating Income (%)														
Cost of Operations	10	59.7	82.4	30.6	80.6	58.3	53.3	65.8	64.0	54.8	64.6	64.6	61.7	•
Salaries and Wages	11	5.2	0.6	19.9	4.8	2.7	3.7	6.7	3.4	8.3	2.9	3.0	4.6	•
Taxes Paid	12	2.1	0.7	2.9	3.4	4.3	2.2	3.0	2.0	1.9	1.3	0.9	1.7	•
Interest Paid	13	1.9	1.4	1.3	0.4	0.3	2.6	1.1	0.8	0.9	2.3	0.4	3.0	•
Depreciation	14	9.1	4.1	6.6	0.4	4.0	10.7	7.1	11.0	8.4	7.9	8.3	11.8	•
Amortization and Depletion	15	3.7	0.0	1.5	0.5	1.6	1.5	2.7	2.4	1.3	3.0	3.6	6.0	•
Pensions and Other Deferred Comp.	16	0.8	•	•	•	0.7	0.3	0.4	0.6	0.3	1.1	1.3	1.1	•
Employee Benefits	17	1.7	0.2	1.8	1.2	2.1	0.6	1.7	1.6	2.8	2.1	1.1	1.4	•
Advertising	18	0.2	•	0.2	0.3	0.5	0.1	0.2	0.2	0.1	0.1	0.0	0.2	•
Other Expenses	19	10.2	4.1	32.2	5.0	15.0	11.5	7.2	6.9	14.4	9.6	8.1	6.0	•
Officers' Compensation	20	1.5	0.8	1.3	3.3	2.9	1.9	2.6	2.3	1.2	1.4	0.4	1.1	•
Operating Margin	21	3.9	5.6	1.8	0.3	7.6	11.6	1.5	4.7	5.4	3.7	8.3	1.6	•
Operating Margin Before Officers' Comp.	22	5.4	6.4	3.1	3.6	10.4	13.5	4.1	7.0	6.6	5.0	8.8	2.6	•

Selected Average Balance Sheet ($ in Thousands)													
Net Receivables 23	840	0	0	87	426	1680	2299	4296	9416	14575	36573	117348	•
Inventories 24	731	0	0	47	235	390	2490	2789	8064	19048	29438	105989	•
Net Property, Plant and Equipment 25	3428	0	58	393	1052	3971	6347	15443	23129	70938	173697	571075	•
Total Assets 26	8254	0	73	571	2897	7696	16730	30743	60207	165414	407387	1418653	•
Notes and Loans Payable 27	2208	0	14	247	460	4088	2799	7291	14415	31354	67386	446305	•
All Other Liabilities 28	1855	0	3	60	240	976	2681	5023	12366	39902	67152	383199	•
Net Worth 29	4190	0	56	265	2197	2632	11250	18428	33426	94158	272850	589149	•

Selected Financial Ratios (Times to 1)													
Current Ratio 30	2.3	•	2.8	2.0	5.5	1.5	2.6	2.7	2.2	3.6	1.7	1.8	•
Quick Ratio 31	1.4	•	2.8	1.9	4.8	1.1	1.5	1.6	1.6	2.0	1.3	0.9	•
Net Sales to Working Capital 32	4.5	•	67.8	20.7	2.9	12.6	3.2	3.7	3.4	2.6	6.1	5.6	•
Coverage Ratio 33	5.1	22.1	3.1	2.1	26.0	6.0	7.0	14.5	8.4	3.1	31.3	3.5	•
Total Asset Turnover 34	0.8	•	9.3	3.1	1.4	1.2	0.9	0.9	0.8	0.7	0.8	0.6	•
Inventory Turnover 35	5.3	•	•	30.0	9.8	12.9	4.0	6.1	3.1	3.8	7.6	4.8	•
Receivables Turnover 36	7.7	•	•	19.7	10.2	•	6.5	7.1	4.9	6.1	•	7.7	•
Total Liabilities to Net Worth 37	1.0	•	0.3	1.2	0.3	1.9	0.5	0.7	0.8	0.8	0.5	1.4	•
Current Assets to Working Capital 38	1.8	•	1.5	2.0	1.2	3.2	1.6	1.6	1.8	1.4	2.5	2.3	•
Current Liabilities to Working Capital 39	0.8	•	0.5	1.0	0.2	2.2	0.6	0.6	0.8	0.4	1.5	1.3	•
Working Capital to Net Sales 40	0.2	•	0.0	0.0	0.3	0.1	0.3	0.3	0.3	0.4	0.2	0.2	•
Inventory to Working Capital 41	0.5	•	•	•	0.1	0.5	0.6	0.3	0.5	0.5	0.5	0.8	•
Total Receipts to Cash Flow 42	7.6	3.1	4.1	27.6	6.1	4.7	8.8	9.3	5.7	8.8	6.4	10.3	•
Cost of Goods to Cash Flow 43	4.5	2.5	1.3	22.2	3.6	2.5	5.8	6.0	3.1	5.7	4.1	6.4	•
Cash Flow to Total Debt 44	0.2	•	9.8	0.2	0.9	0.4	0.3	0.2	0.3	0.2	0.4	0.1	•

Selected Financial Factors (in Percentages)													
Debt Ratio 45	49.2	•	23.1	53.7	24.2	65.8	32.8	40.1	44.5	43.1	33.0	58.5	•
Return on Total Assets 46	7.6	•	36.1	2.6	11.7	19.3	7.1	10.0	6.0	5.0	10.6	6.0	•
Return on Equity Before Income Taxes 47	12.0	•	31.8	3.0	14.8	47.0	9.0	15.5	9.5	6.0	15.4	10.3	•
Return on Equity After Income Taxes 48	9.8	•	31.8	2.6	14.8	46.4	8.6	13.2	8.5	4.6	10.7	7.3	•
Profit Margin (Before Income Tax) 49	7.7	29.1	2.6	0.5	8.2	13.1	6.7	10.8	6.8	5.0	12.1	7.4	•
Profit Margin (After Income Tax) 50	6.3	29.1	2.6	0.4	8.2	12.9	6.4	9.2	6.1	3.8	8.5	5.3	•

Table I

Corporations with and without Net Income

SUPPORT ACTIVITIES FOR MINING

Item Description for Accounting Period 7/11 Through 6/12		MONEY AMOUNTS AND SIZE OF ASSETS IN THOUSANDS OF DOLLARS												
		Total	Zero Assets	Under 500	500 to 1,000	1,000 to 5,000	5,000 to 10,000	10,000 to 25,000	25,000 to 50,000	50,000 to 100,000	100,000 to 250,000	250,000 to 500,000	500,000 to 2,500,000	2,500,000 and over
Number of Enterprises	1	12940	2861	7030	1050	1406	244	165	58	41	30	14	23	18
Revenues ($ in Thousands)														
Net Sales	2	99225998	2103522	4377690	2925148	7015883	3126945	3962743	4170754	3133051	3890147	1992208	14091771	48436137
Interest	3	729000	2877	238	333	1806	2027	1838	1198	3169	1040	4596	36122	673755
Rents	4	1384095	1245	0	57	7332	5895	4598	324	70	67635	5670	93034	1198235
Royalties	5	352157	0	0	0	204	57744	13945	297	1963	454	627	12607	264317
Other Portfolio Income	6	2689110	105622	15129	38669	44934	38334	33229	45324	15444	25138	88348	336638	1902297
Other Receipts	7	1824237	110574	8965	4991	516587	16131	55214	12452	163320	97203	142485	139170	557148
Total Receipts	8	106204597	2323840	4402022	2969198	7586746	3247076	4071567	4230349	3317017	4081617	2233934	14709342	53031889
Average Total Receipts	9	8207	812	626	2828	5396	13308	24676	72937	80903	136054	159567	639537	2946216
Operating Costs/Operating Income (%)														
Cost of Operations	10	50.9	58.2	16.0	33.1	45.7	50.7	53.3	67.2	57.7	53.9	55.4	54.5	52.0
Salaries and Wages	11	8.8	11.6	26.6	15.6	12.5	10.8	12.7	7.5	10.0	12.3	10.5	7.8	5.7
Taxes Paid	12	2.2	2.0	3.7	3.6	2.0	3.5	2.5	1.7	3.1	1.9	3.4	2.0	2.0
Interest Paid	13	3.5	2.1	0.6	0.6	0.4	0.3	1.0	1.1	1.3	2.5	4.5	4.6	5.0
Depreciation	14	14.1	12.8	3.4	5.6	7.1	9.4	8.6	5.9	10.8	12.5	16.9	20.9	16.4
Amortization and Depletion	15	0.9	0.4	0.3	0.0	0.1	0.0	0.2	0.3	0.5	1.2	0.6	1.8	1.0
Pensions and Other Deferred Comp.	16	0.4	0.2	0.8	0.1	0.2	0.2	0.2	0.3	0.2	0.1	0.4	0.2	0.5
Employee Benefits	17	1.5	1.2	1.5	1.4	0.6	0.8	0.8	1.1	1.3	1.3	1.3	1.4	1.8
Advertising	18	0.1	0.1	0.4	0.2	0.2	0.2	0.2	0.2	0.2	0.1	0.2	0.1	0.1
Other Expenses	19	16.5	21.4	29.2	25.1	24.5	19.8	15.4	9.4	16.7	17.0	14.1	11.5	15.5
Officers' Compensation	20	1.6	5.1	9.1	5.8	3.9	2.4	1.7	0.8	1.0	0.9	2.0	0.8	0.6
Operating Margin	21	•	•	8.3	9.0	2.8	1.7	3.5	4.4	•	•	•	•	•
Operating Margin Before Officers' Comp.	22	1.1	•	17.4	14.7	6.7	4.1	5.2	5.2	•	•	•	•	0.1

Selected Average Balance Sheet ($ in Thousands)

Net Receivables	23	2105	0	12	127	251	1823	5074	10005	15713	35071	62059	196574	983986
Inventories	24	412	0	1	33	82	177	484	1633	1999	4775	41338	24254	199772
Net Property, Plant and Equipment	25	4538	0	41	211	387	1406	4050	10063	24737	58486	85623	499934	2255479
Total Assets	26	12319	0	131	750	1884	6264	16016	35762	73135	155104	363820	1096453	6158028
Notes and Loans Payable	27	3886	0	68	339	586	1251	5641	8986	22715	46356	71835	280044	2061305
All Other Liabilities	28	3368	0	27	180	471	966	4407	8661	21499	47667	104172	305014	1682714
Net Worth	29	5065	0	36	231	827	4047	5968	18115	28922	61081	187812	511395	2414009

Selected Financial Ratios (Times to 1)

Current Ratio	30	2.1	•	1.6	1.4	2.2	3.0	2.0	1.9	1.7	1.2	1.9	1.8	2.4
Quick Ratio	31	1.6	•	1.6	1.1	1.5	2.6	1.7	1.4	1.3	1.0	1.2	1.4	1.8
Net Sales to Working Capital	32	3.9	•	21.2	20.9	8.4	5.7	5.1	8.9	6.1	11.6	2.2	5.0	2.7
Coverage Ratio	33	2.9	•	15.8	19.7	27.3	17.5	7.2	6.1	3.5	1.4	1.6	0.8	2.9
Total Asset Turnover	34	0.6	•	4.8	3.7	2.6	2.0	1.5	2.0	1.0	0.8	0.4	0.6	0.4
Inventory Turnover	35	9.5	•	157.0	27.7	27.8	36.7	26.4	29.6	22.1	14.6	1.9	13.8	7.0
Receivables Turnover	36	3.9	•	43.0	22.2	21.7	8.2	5.4	7.5	5.0	4.1	3.2	3.6	2.8
Total Liabilities to Net Worth	37	1.4	•	2.7	2.2	1.3	0.5	1.7	1.0	1.5	1.5	0.9	1.1	1.6
Current Assets to Working Capital	38	1.9	•	2.5	3.8	1.9	1.5	2.0	2.1	2.4	5.3	2.1	2.3	1.7
Current Liabilities to Working Capital	39	0.9	•	1.5	2.8	0.9	0.5	1.0	1.1	1.4	4.3	1.1	1.3	0.7
Working Capital to Net Sales	40	0.3	•	0.0	0.0	0.1	0.2	0.2	0.1	0.2	0.1	0.4	0.2	0.4
Inventory to Working Capital	41	0.2	•	•	0.5	0.2	0.0	0.1	0.3	0.2	0.5	0.6	0.2	0.2
Total Receipts to Cash Flow	42	6.1	9.7	3.0	3.2	3.6	5.5	6.0	8.1	6.4	8.2	9.6	22.9	6.0
Cost of Goods to Cash Flow	43	3.1	5.6	0.5	1.1	1.7	2.8	3.2	5.5	3.7	4.4	5.3	12.5	3.1
Cash Flow to Total Debt	44	0.2	•	2.2	1.7	1.3	1.1	0.4	0.5	0.3	0.2	0.1	0.0	0.1

Selected Financial Factors (in Percentages)

Debt Ratio	45	58.9	•	72.6	69.2	56.1	35.4	62.7	49.3	60.5	60.6	48.4	53.4	60.8
Return on Total Assets	46	6.4	•	45.0	41.0	30.0	12.1	10.8	14.0	4.7	3.1	2.8	2.0	6.4
Return on Equity Before Income Taxes	47	10.3	•	154.2	126.4	65.9	17.6	25.0	23.2	8.6	2.4	2.1	•	10.8
Return on Equity After Income Taxes	48	6.9	•	152.2	125.7	63.4	14.6	21.1	20.9	4.7	0.7	0.8	•	6.8
Profit Margin (Before Income Tax)	49	6.8	•	8.8	10.5	10.9	5.6	6.2	5.8	3.3	1.1	2.8	•	9.6
Profit Margin (After Income Tax)	50	4.6	•	8.7	10.4	10.5	4.6	5.2	5.3	1.8	0.3	1.0	•	6.1

Table II

Corporations with Net Income

SUPPORT ACTIVITIES FOR MINING

MONEY AMOUNTS AND SIZE OF ASSETS IN THOUSANDS OF DOLLARS

Item Description for Accounting Period 7/11 Through 6/12		Total	Zero Assets	Under 500	500 to 1,000	1,000 to 5,000	5,000 to 10,000	10,000 to 25,000	25,000 to 50,000	50,000 to 100,000	100,000 to 250,000	250,000 to 500,000	500,000 to 2,500,000	2,500,000 and over
Number of Enterprises	1	9152	2017	4939	781	1060	150	104	42	22	11	5	8	13
Revenues ($ in Thousands)														
Net Sales	2	72043858	1580806	3470806	2657168	5899401	1960483	3062414	2426811	2191979	1664036	1169947	7274303	38685704
Interest	3	647287	184	208	26	1669	1582	1053	421	1880	463	2146	27900	609754
Rents	4	1217621	1245	0	57	1862	5895	3710	190	0	33793	2464	11018	1157386
Royalties	5	300219	0	0	0	204	17391	6692	0	0	0	0	12607	263326
Other Portfolio Income	6	2306529	73374	15104	38669	44285	17942	32411	44062	4824	15585	31207	218822	1770242
Other Receipts	7	1532242	106278	8965	4991	511330	7876	56535	9908	159897	4482	99916	91784	470282
Total Receipts	8	78047756	1761887	3495083	2700911	6458751	2011169	3162815	2481392	2358580	1718359	1305680	7636434	42956694
Average Total Receipts	9	8528	874	708	3458	6093	13408	30412	59081	107208	156214	261136	954554	3304361
Operating Costs/Operating Income (%)														
Cost of Operations	10	50.1	59.5	15.7	34.0	51.6	44.0	59.8	53.6	60.4	44.4	57.2	48.4	52.8
Salaries and Wages	11	8.2	8.9	20.4	15.5	12.3	13.2	10.2	10.3	6.8	10.3	5.8	10.1	5.0
Taxes Paid	12	2.2	2.0	3.7	3.5	1.8	2.5	2.2	2.4	3.1	2.0	3.2	2.2	1.9
Interest Paid	13	3.0	0.9	0.3	0.4	0.3	0.4	0.5	1.2	0.7	2.5	4.7	2.2	4.7
Depreciation	14	10.6	5.2	3.1	5.1	5.2	7.9	4.0	7.3	4.9	9.7	10.4	17.3	12.7
Amortization and Depletion	15	0.7	0.1	0.4	0.0	0.1	0.1	0.2	0.2	0.3	0.6	0.8	0.8	1.0
Pensions and Other Deferred Comp.	16	0.5	0.3	1.0	0.1	0.2	0.2	0.2	0.4	0.2	0.2	0.4	0.2	0.6
Employee Benefits	17	1.5	1.4	1.8	1.5	0.6	0.8	0.5	1.7	1.1	0.9	0.4	1.1	1.9
Advertising	18	0.1	0.1	0.4	0.2	0.1	0.2	0.2	0.2	0.2	0.1	0.2	0.1	0.1
Other Expenses	19	16.3	13.8	29.9	23.3	18.6	18.5	12.9	10.9	15.3	16.9	12.5	11.9	15.9
Officers' Compensation	20	1.8	3.6	10.6	5.2	4.2	3.1	1.2	1.2	1.0	1.2	2.5	0.9	0.6
Operating Margin	21	4.9	4.2	12.8	11.3	4.9	9.1	8.3	10.6	6.1	11.2	2.0	4.9	2.7
Operating Margin Before Officers' Comp.	22	6.7	7.8	23.4	16.4	9.1	12.2	9.5	11.8	7.1	12.4	4.5	5.8	3.4

Selected Average Balance Sheet ($ in Thousands)

Net Receivables	23	2355	0	3	157	259	2238	5914	11153	20899	45423	62544	343828	1207992
Inventories	24	425	0	0	15	78	268	634	1566	2067	5118	12783	58783	229571
Net Property, Plant and Equipment	25	3693	0	35	186	340	1557	2385	10328	11057	41429	74006	395951	2151405
Total Assets	26	11838	0	134	763	1811	6690	15607	36031	73610	150581	341773	1190026	6655345
Notes and Loans Payable	27	3414	0	34	193	525	918	3727	7951	19079	47215	95961	219166	2025705
All Other Liabilities	28	3030	0	26	230	492	1028	4869	7519	19847	27181	58703	452179	1636539
Net Worth	29	5395	0	73	340	794	4745	7011	20561	34684	76186	187108	518681	2993101

Selected Financial Ratios (Times to 1)

Current Ratio	30	2.5	•	2.4	2.0	2.1	3.5	2.1	2.6	2.2	1.8	2.2	2.2	2.6
Quick Ratio	31	1.9	•	2.3	1.9	1.5	3.2	1.8	2.0	1.7	1.5	1.7	1.7	2.0
Net Sales to Working Capital	32	3.1	•	14.6	12.5	9.3	4.3	5.5	4.8	4.6	4.5	3.9	3.4	2.3
Coverage Ratio	33	5.5	18.5	52.1	31.6	44.0	33.8	26.7	11.8	20.5	6.8	3.9	5.7	4.1
Total Asset Turnover	34	0.7	•	5.3	4.5	3.1	2.0	1.9	1.6	1.4	1.0	0.7	0.8	0.4
Inventory Turnover	35	9.3	•	•	78.1	37.0	21.4	27.8	19.8	29.1	13.1	10.5	7.5	6.9
Receivables Turnover	36	3.6	•	62.8	22.1	26.0	6.3	5.4	5.6	5.4	3.8	4.7	2.9	2.7
Total Liabilities to Net Worth	37	1.2	•	0.8	1.2	1.3	0.4	1.2	0.8	1.1	1.0	0.8	1.3	1.2
Current Assets to Working Capital	38	1.7	•	1.7	2.0	1.9	1.4	1.9	1.6	1.8	2.3	1.8	1.9	1.6
Current Liabilities to Working Capital	39	0.7	•	0.7	1.0	0.9	0.4	0.9	0.6	0.8	1.3	0.8	0.9	0.6
Working Capital to Net Sales	40	0.3	•	0.1	0.1	0.1	0.2	0.2	0.2	0.2	0.2	0.3	0.3	0.4
Inventory to Working Capital	41	0.2	•	•	0.1	0.2	0.0	0.1	0.2	0.2	0.2	0.1	0.2	0.2
Total Receipts to Cash Flow	42	4.5	3.7	2.5	3.2	3.5	4.2	5.0	5.0	3.8	4.6	4.7	6.8	4.9
Cost of Goods to Cash Flow	43	2.2	2.2	0.4	1.1	1.8	1.9	3.0	2.7	2.3	2.0	2.7	3.3	2.6
Cash Flow to Total Debt	44	0.3	•	4.6	2.5	1.6	1.6	0.7	0.7	0.7	0.4	0.3	0.2	0.2

Selected Financial Factors (in Percentages)

Debt Ratio	45	54.4	•	45.0	55.4	56.1	29.1	55.1	42.9	52.9	49.4	45.3	56.4	55.0
Return on Total Assets	46	11.1	•	72.2	59.5	45.1	23.5	22.6	22.5	19.6	17.1	12.5	9.5	8.5
Return on Equity Before Income Taxes	47	19.9	•	128.8	129.3	100.5	32.2	48.5	36.1	39.5	28.7	17.0	18.0	14.3
Return on Equity After Income Taxes	48	15.4	•	127.4	128.6	97.1	28.0	43.2	33.3	33.4	25.0	13.3	12.5	9.9
Profit Margin (Before Income Tax)	49	13.6	15.6	13.5	12.9	14.3	11.7	11.6	12.8	13.7	14.5	13.6	10.3	14.4
Profit Margin (After Income Tax)	50	10.5	13.8	13.3	12.9	13.9	10.2	10.3	11.8	11.6	12.6	10.6	7.1	9.9

Table I

Corporations with and without Net Income

ELECTRIC POWER GENERATION, TRANSMISSION AND DISTRIBUTION

MONEY AMOUNTS AND SIZE OF ASSETS IN THOUSANDS OF DOLLARS

Item Description for Accounting Period 7/11 Through 6/12		Total	Zero Assets	Under 500	500 to 1,000	1,000 to 5,000	5,000 to 10,000	10,000 to 25,000	25,000 to 50,000	50,000 to 100,000	100,000 to 250,000	250,000 to 500,000	500,000 to 2,500,000	2,500,000 and over
Number of Enterprises	1	1503	56	749	318	82	59	50	29	27	35	20	35	43
Revenues ($ in Thousands)														
Net Sales	2	300588034	2925355	9669	70906	131259	119992	321481	1927624	892940	2779661	1659018	12120692	277629436
Interest	3	3308931	20513	229849	744	780	826	2354	4711	15635	69935	23138	181992	2758454
Rents	4	1405960	1149	0	0	0	1621	77	0	865	588	10654	11156	1379851
Royalties	5	20276	0	0	0	0	0	0	1347	198	0	0	121	18611
Other Portfolio Income	6	2766332	29776	0	0	0	10959	1491	4724	1396	32503	140593	361039	2183849
Other Receipts	7	10420495	52801	57569	75	2129	15153	10069	43210	43411	-30982	255178	329160	9642723
Total Receipts	8	318510028	3029594	297087	71725	134168	148551	335472	1981616	954445	2851705	2088581	13004160	293612924
Average Total Receipts	9	211916	54100	397	226	1636	2518	6709	68332	35350	81477	104429	371547	6828208
Operating Costs/Operating Income (%)														
Cost of Operations	10	56.0	65.4	18.9	14.4	18.4	43.2	60.8	80.8	45.5	79.7	57.0	56.0	55.6
Salaries and Wages	11	3.7	3.2	67.0	24.7	25.3	23.9	9.7	6.1	3.2	3.9	4.3	5.1	3.5
Taxes Paid	12	3.8	5.7	4.9	11.7	4.6	4.5	2.3	0.9	2.3	0.8	2.8	2.7	3.9
Interest Paid	13	7.2	6.2	2149.9	1.5	0.7	2.4	2.1	1.0	3.7	2.9	18.3	7.3	7.2
Depreciation	14	16.7	13.6	16.0	3.3	5.5	28.2	7.9	0.8	12.7	6.4	15.2	14.5	17.0
Amortization and Depletion	15	1.8	2.0	10.6	0.3	1.1	2.1	0.5	1.6	0.7	0.7	1.8	1.8	1.8
Pensions and Other Deferred Comp.	16	1.4	0.8	•	•	0.0	0.6	1.2	0.5	0.3	0.2	0.6	1.0	1.4
Employee Benefits	17	1.3	0.4	14.8	0.6	2.3	2.6	1.4	2.2	1.7	0.3	1.3	1.0	1.3
Advertising	18	0.1	0.0	•	0.5	0.1	0.0	0.2	0.1	0.1	0.1	0.1	0.1	0.1
Other Expenses	19	20.1	11.0	1040.9	98.6	46.9	32.7	41.0	6.9	46.5	14.9	30.8	30.6	19.6
Officers' Compensation	20	0.4	0.4	•	32.6	17.8	12.4	2.9	0.9	1.0	0.3	0.9	0.6	0.3
Operating Margin	21	•	•	•	•	•	•	•	•	•	•	•	•	•
Operating Margin Before Officers' Comp.	22	•	•	•	•	•	•	•	•	•	•	•	•	•

Selected Average Balance Sheet ($ in Thousands)

Net Receivables	23	29478	0	0	25	236	948	3877	5059	6551	18475	9501	75858	935184
Inventories	24	9981	0	0	4	41	125	435	153	1540	1123	8824	31358	316488
Net Property, Plant and Equipment	25	369630	0	2	110	970	1947	4579	8952	25824	61251	145315	688854	12208783
Total Assets	26	628498	0	59	732	2942	6313	16357	33742	69030	148433	372500	1218747	20576294
Notes and Loans Payable	27	246999	0	102	57	534	1889	4964	13525	27861	59126	190653	547454	8012858
All Other Liabilities	28	221735	0	7	174	3383	714	4962	31848	32439	33726	91567	284482	7392357
Net Worth	29	159765	0	-50	501	-975	3710	6431	-11630	8729	55581	90280	386811	5171079

Selected Financial Ratios (Times to 1)

Current Ratio	30	1.1	•	0.4	3.3	3.8	4.4	2.6	0.5	0.6	1.3	1.1	1.3	1.1
Quick Ratio	31	0.6	•	0.3	2.8	3.3	4.0	2.0	0.3	0.4	1.1	0.6	1.0	0.5
Net Sales to Working Capital	32	33.4	•	•	0.6	2.1	1.2	1.4	•	•	10.0	21.8	5.3	41.8
Coverage Ratio	33	0.1	0.2	0.9	•	•	•	•	2.1	•	•	0.6	•	0.2
Total Asset Turnover	34	0.3	•	0.2	0.3	0.5	0.3	0.4	2.0	0.5	0.5	0.2	0.3	0.3
Inventory Turnover	35	11.2	•	•	8.5	7.2	7.0	9.0	352.2	9.8	56.4	5.4	6.2	11.3
Receivables Turnover	36	6.1	•	203.6	10.5	13.1	2.9	2.5	9.5	2.3	6.0	7.3	4.7	6.1
Total Liabilities to Net Worth	37	2.9	•	•	0.5	•	0.7	1.5	•	6.9	1.7	3.1	2.2	3.0
Current Assets to Working Capital	38	14.7	•	•	1.4	1.4	1.3	1.6	•	•	4.3	14.7	3.9	18.0
Current Liabilities to Working Capital	39	13.7	•	•	0.4	0.4	0.3	0.6	•	•	3.3	13.7	2.9	17.0
Working Capital to Net Sales	40	0.0	•	•	1.7	0.5	0.8	0.7	•	•	0.1	0.0	0.2	0.0
Inventory to Working Capital	41	1.7	•	•	0.0	•	0.1	0.2	•	•	0.2	3.4	0.4	2.1
Total Receipts to Cash Flow	42	13.4	37.3	0.1	•	4.6	•	10.7	13.5	3.6	24.5	9.2	8.6	13.8
Cost of Goods to Cash Flow	43	7.5	24.4	0.0	•	0.9	•	6.5	10.9	1.6	19.5	5.3	4.8	7.6
Cash Flow to Total Debt	44	0.0	•	0.8	•	0.1	•	0.1	0.1	0.2	0.0	0.0	0.0	0.0

Selected Financial Factors (in Percentages)

Debt Ratio	45	74.6	•	184.4	31.5	133.1	41.2	60.7	134.5	87.4	62.6	75.8	68.3	74.9
Return on Total Assets	46	0.3	•	413.6	•	•	•	•	4.0	•	•	2.4	•	0.4
Return on Equity Before Income Taxes	47	•	•	64.6	•	33.7	•	•	•	•	•	•	•	•
Return on Equity After Income Taxes	48	•	•	65.1	•	33.7	•	•	•	•	•	•	•	•
Profit Margin (Before Income Tax)	49	•	•	•	•	•	•	•	1.1	•	•	•	•	•
Profit Margin (After Income Tax)	50	•	•	•	•	•	•	•	0.2	•	•	•	•	•

Table II

Corporations with Net Income

ELECTRIC POWER GENERATION, TRANSMISSION AND DISTRIBUTION

MONEY AMOUNTS AND SIZE OF ASSETS IN THOUSANDS OF DOLLARS

Item Description for Accounting Period 7/11 Through 6/12		Total	Zero Assets	Under 500	500 to 1,000	1,000 to 5,000	5,000 to 10,000	10,000 to 25,000	25,000 to 50,000	50,000 to 100,000	100,000 to 250,000	250,000 to 500,000	500,000 to 2,500,000	2,500,000 and over
Number of Enterprises	1	746	22	434	177	23	23	5	15	10	14	8	10	6
Revenues ($ in Thousands)														
Net Sales	2	45491516	2297581	9665	60068	116933	83008	2386	744127	312260	2161052	665216	4282846	34756373
Interest	3	355314	1963	229849	0	33	677	248	344	500	15250	9595	25669	71187
Rents	4	192131	1149	0	0	0	1621	0	0	575	340	102	6671	181673
Royalties	5	12222	0	0	0	0	0	0	1347	0	0	0	121	10754
Other Portfolio Income	6	212373	29776	0	0	0	5358	0	4724	509	32304	6399	56794	76511
Other Receipts	7	4651155	21131	158	76	1913	14538	9610	39065	20485	28698	191281	249031	4075167
Total Receipts	8	50914711	2351600	239672	60144	118879	105202	12244	789607	334329	2237644	872593	4621132	39171665
Average Total Receipts	9	68250	106891	552	340	5169	4574	2449	52640	33433	159832	109074	462113	6528611
Operating Costs/Operating Income (%)														
Cost of Operations	10	55.5	65.1	18.9	•	17.6	43.6	•	51.5	49.0	85.5	64.1	51.5	53.7
Salaries and Wages	11	4.0	1.8	•	3.0	25.8	10.7	36.4	14.1	3.7	2.4	3.7	8.5	3.4
Taxes Paid	12	3.9	6.0	•	9.4	3.9	4.6	5.1	2.1	4.1	0.4	3.5	2.3	4.2
Interest Paid	13	11.7	5.4	2141.4	•	0.2	2.0	57.2	2.2	3.0	1.7	11.6	5.7	13.2
Depreciation	14	15.0	9.0	•	0.8	3.2	18.8	•	1.0	5.6	2.0	7.8	9.3	17.5
Amortization and Depletion	15	2.3	1.7	•	•	1.2	•	2.5	4.2	0.4	0.3	1.5	1.1	2.7
Pensions and Other Deferred Comp.	16	0.7	0.7	•	•	0.0	0.8	•	1.3	0.3	0.2	0.2	1.1	0.6
Employee Benefits	17	1.0	0.2	•	•	2.5	1.8	0.6	5.4	4.1	0.3	1.6	0.9	1.0
Advertising	18	0.1	0.0	•	•	0.1	•	•	0.0	0.1	0.0	0.1	0.1	0.1
Other Expenses	19	13.1	7.1	3.0	38.2	17.8	14.9	269.2	12.8	22.3	5.4	13.4	24.6	12.3
Officers' Compensation	20	0.6	0.3	•	32.4	17.9	4.5	44.3	2.1	1.1	0.2	0.7	0.6	0.5
Operating Margin	21	•	2.6	•	16.2	9.9	•	•	3.4	6.3	1.6	•	•	•
Operating Margin Before Officers' Comp.	22	•	2.9	•	48.6	27.8	2.8	•	5.5	7.4	1.7	•	•	•

Selected Average Balance Sheet ($ in Thousands)													
Net Receivables 23	7099	0	0	0	758	2344	21325	4015	5559	13067	12419	75143	661392
Inventories 24	9049	0	0	0	0	175	848	25	1634	1468	8837	44824	1031043
Net Property, Plant and Equipment 25	112972	0	0	165	339	2004	2	8474	29717	37363	133786	560958	12761085
Total Assets 26	190301	0	5	781	2562	5386	17707	37461	70073	146934	349412	1138982	20674691
Notes and Loans Payable 27	98153	0	0	0	130	1268	20736	21991	20578	49420	109532	394428	11173055
All Other Liabilities 28	63856	0	0	179	8855	906	400	45149	21473	53466	142873	402736	6761190
Net Worth 29	28292	0	5	602	-6424	3211	-3429	-29679	28021	44047	97007	341818	2740446
Selected Financial Ratios (Times to 1)													
Current Ratio 30	1.2	•	20.1	3.4	6.6	6.8	32.9	0.4	1.0	0.9	1.2	1.2	1.2
Quick Ratio 31	0.5	•	18.1	3.4	6.4	6.4	32.9	0.2	0.7	0.7	0.7	0.9	0.5
Net Sales to Working Capital 32	12.7	•	4.6	0.8	2.7	1.3	0.0	•	39.3	•	11.2	9.4	10.9
Coverage Ratio 33	1.4	1.9	1.1	•	52.9	13.7	2.7	5.3	5.5	4.1	2.9	1.4	1.3
Total Asset Turnover 34	0.3	•	4.4	0.4	2.0	0.7	0.0	1.3	0.4	1.1	0.2	0.4	0.3
Inventory Turnover 35	3.7	•	•	•	•	9.0	•	1041.3	9.4	89.9	6.0	4.9	3.0
Receivables Turnover 36	3.0	•	•	•	13.4	2.5	0.0	23.3	3.1	10.0	5.7	6.1	2.5
Total Liabilities to Net Worth 37	5.7	•	0.1	0.3	•	0.7	•	•	1.5	2.3	2.6	2.3	6.5
Current Assets to Working Capital 38	6.7	•	1.1	1.4	1.2	1.2	1.0	•	21.3	•	5.1	7.4	6.0
Current Liabilities to Working Capital 39	5.7	•	0.1	0.4	0.2	0.2	0.0	•	20.3	•	4.1	6.4	5.0
Working Capital to Net Sales 40	0.1	•	0.2	1.3	0.4	0.7	43.8	•	0.0	•	0.1	0.1	0.1
Inventory to Working Capital 41	0.9	•	•	•	•	0.0	•	•	2.3	•	1.3	0.5	0.9
Total Receipts to Cash Flow 42	6.6	8.7	0.3	2.3	4.0	3.2	0.3	4.6	3.3	13.2	3.0	4.6	7.1
Cost of Goods to Cash Flow 43	3.7	5.7	0.1	•	0.7	1.4	•	2.4	1.6	11.3	2.0	2.4	3.8
Cash Flow to Total Debt 44	0.1	•	280.8	0.8	0.1	0.5	0.1	0.2	0.2	0.1	0.1	0.1	0.0
Selected Financial Factors (in Percentages)													
Debt Ratio 45	85.1	•	5.0	23.0	350.8	40.4	119.4	179.2	60.0	70.0	72.2	70.0	86.7
Return on Total Assets 46	5.1	•	10725.1	7.1	23.3	18.1	4.2	15.5	7.3	7.1	8.1	3.0	4.7
Return on Equity Before Income Taxes 47	9.0	•	1453.5	9.2	•	28.1	•	•	14.9	17.9	19.2	2.8	7.5
Return on Equity After Income Taxes 48	7.6	•	1443.2	9.2	•	21.9	•	•	12.5	14.0	13.8	2.5	6.5
Profit Margin (Before Income Tax) 49	4.2	5.0	316.6	16.3	11.5	25.0	97.9	9.5	13.4	5.1	22.4	2.2	3.6
Profit Margin (After Income Tax) 50	3.5	3.9	314.3	16.3	11.5	19.5	96.1	7.3	11.2	4.0	16.1	2.0	3.1

Table I

Corporations with and without Net Income

NATURAL GAS DISTRIBUTION

MONEY AMOUNTS AND SIZE OF ASSETS IN THOUSANDS OF DOLLARS

Item Description for Accounting Period 7/11 Through 6/12		Total	Zero Assets	Under 500	500 to 1,000	1,000 to 5,000	5,000 to 10,000	10,000 to 25,000	25,000 to 50,000	50,000 to 100,000	100,000 to 250,000	250,000 to 500,000	500,000 to 2,500,000	2,500,000 and over
Number of Enterprises	1	799	•	•	30	39	34	9	•	•	•	3	12	15
Revenues ($ in Thousands)														
Net Sales	2	89136546	•	•	74488	359591	342921	588107	•	•	•	3311941	29783971	44197394
Interest	3	764764	•	•	43	268	351	96	•	•	•	2871	22203	733995
Rents	4	49509	•	•	0	0	243	0	•	•	•	1747	2117	42289
Royalties	5	658	•	•	0	0	0	0	•	•	•	0	332	312
Other Portfolio Income	6	773467	•	•	0	117	1541	12	•	•	•	6	165514	594011
Other Receipts	7	3698729	•	•	84	3928	3399	576	•	•	•	7896	129441	3320338
Total Receipts	8	94423673	•	•	74615	363904	348455	588791	•	•	•	3324461	30103578	48888339
Average Total Receipts	9	118177	•	•	2487	9331	10249	65421	•	•	•	1108154	2508632	3259223
Operating Costs/Operating Income (%)														
Cost of Operations	10	78.4	•	•	62.0	84.0	76.3	88.4	•	•	•	94.1	93.6	65.1
Salaries and Wages	11	2.9	•	•	12.9	2.5	0.5	3.8	•	•	•	0.6	1.0	4.4
Taxes Paid	12	1.9	•	•	1.7	0.2	1.3	0.6	•	•	•	0.7	0.5	3.0
Interest Paid	13	2.9	•	•	0.0	0.4	0.5	0.1	•	•	•	0.5	0.8	5.2
Depreciation	14	7.2	•	•	2.4	0.7	4.7	0.5	•	•	•	1.1	2.0	12.2
Amortization and Depletion	15	0.8	•	•	•	0.0	0.2	0.0	•	•	•	0.0	0.2	1.4
Pensions and Other Deferred Comp.	16	0.6	•	•	5.1	0.5	0.5	0.1	•	•	•	0.1	0.3	1.0
Employee Benefits	17	0.9	•	•	•	0.2	1.2	0.4	•	•	•	0.3	0.3	1.4
Advertising	18	0.1	•	•	0.2	0.0	0.3	0.0	•	•	•	0.0	0.1	0.1
Other Expenses	19	12.6	•	•	11.5	2.8	4.8	1.6	•	•	•	2.3	4.6	21.0
Officers' Compensation	20	0.4	•	•	6.9	0.8	2.2	0.8	•	•	•	0.0	0.3	0.4
Operating Margin	21	•	•	•	•	8.0	7.4	3.8	•	•	•	0.2	•	•
Operating Margin Before Officers' Comp.	22	•	•	•	4.2	8.8	9.6	4.6	•	•	•	0.2	•	•

Selected Average Balance Sheet ($ in Thousands)													
Net Receivables 23	15236	•	•	118	734	203	7344	•	•	•	49327	168672	621485
Inventories 24	4583	•	•	43	33	263	1640	•	•	•	33273	92577	155162
Net Property, Plant and Equipment 25	96833	•	•	244	171	4507	3999	•	•	•	114393	415060	4722774
Total Assets 26	219342	•	•	879	2153	8860	19386	•	•	•	310407	1269046	10399961
Notes and Loans Payable 27	103138	•	•	28	194	563	61	•	•	•	88991	492701	5050740
All Other Liabilities 28	88036	•	•	640	874	1635	6210	•	•	•	144601	485233	3239386
Net Worth 29	28168	•	•	211	1084	6662	13115	•	•	•	76815	291112	2109836
Selected Financial Ratios (Times to 1)													
Current Ratio 30	1.0	•	•	0.9	1.7	3.6	2.4	•	•	•	0.9	1.1	1.0
Quick Ratio 31	0.5	•	•	0.8	1.7	3.0	2.0	•	•	•	0.3	0.6	0.4
Net Sales to Working Capital 32	•	•	•	•	14.6	4.5	7.4	•	•	•	•	55.2	•
Coverage Ratio 33	0.0	•	•	•	24.7	17.4	64.5	•	•	•	2.1	•	0.1
Total Asset Turnover 34	0.5	•	•	2.8	4.3	1.1	3.4	•	•	•	3.6	2.0	0.3
Inventory Turnover 35	19.1	•	•	35.5	237.3	29.3	35.2	•	•	•	31.2	25.1	12.4
Receivables Turnover 36	7.3	•	•	42.0	10.2	35.3	•	•	•	•	23.8	13.9	4.8
Total Liabilities to Net Worth 37	6.8	•	•	3.2	1.0	0.3	0.5	•	•	•	3.0	3.4	3.9
Current Assets to Working Capital 38	•	•	•	•	2.4	1.4	1.7	•	•	•	•	10.2	•
Current Liabilities to Working Capital 39	•	•	•	•	1.4	0.4	0.7	•	•	•	•	9.2	•
Working Capital to Net Sales 40	•	•	•	•	0.1	0.2	0.1	•	•	•	•	0.0	•
Inventory to Working Capital 41	•	•	•	•	•	0.1	0.2	•	•	•	•	2.0	•
Total Receipts to Cash Flow 42	12.8	•	•	17.6	8.7	7.9	18.6	•	•	•	40.1	56.5	7.8
Cost of Goods to Cash Flow 43	10.0	•	•	10.9	7.3	6.0	16.4	•	•	•	37.8	52.9	5.1
Cash Flow to Total Debt 44	0.0	•	•	0.2	1.0	0.6	0.6	•	•	•	0.1	0.0	0.0
Selected Financial Factors (in Percentages)													
Debt Ratio 45	87.2	•	•	76.0	49.6	24.8	32.4	•	•	•	75.3	77.1	79.7
Return on Total Assets 46	0.1	•	•	•	41.1	10.6	13.6	•	•	•	3.6	•	0.2
Return on Equity Before Income Taxes 47	•	•	•	•	78.2	13.2	19.7	•	•	•	7.7	•	•
Return on Equity After Income Taxes 48	•	•	•	•	63.2	11.4	18.5	•	•	•	7.0	•	•
Profit Margin (Before Income Tax) 49	•	•	•	•	9.2	8.7	4.0	•	•	•	0.5	•	•
Profit Margin (After Income Tax) 50	•	•	•	•	7.4	7.6	3.7	•	•	•	0.5	•	•

Table II

Corporations with Net Income

NATURAL GAS DISTRIBUTION

MONEY AMOUNTS AND SIZE OF ASSETS IN THOUSANDS OF DOLLARS

Item Description for Accounting Period 7/11 Through 6/12		Total	Zero Assets	Under 500	500 to 1,000	1,000 to 5,000	5,000 to 10,000	10,000 to 25,000	25,000 to 50,000	50,000 to 100,000	100,000 to 250,000	250,000 to 500,000	500,000 to 2,500,000	2,500,000 and over
Number of Enterprises	1	385	•	265	0	39	34	5	6	•	•	0	6	5
Revenues ($ in Thousands)														
Net Sales	2	48826122	•	40595	0	359591	342921	579884	95121	•	•	0	24795072	9903771
Interest	3	115620	•	0	0	268	351	83	14	•	•	0	5255	102780
Rents	4	29685	•	0	0	0	243	0	0	•	•	0	75	24651
Royalties	5	300	•	0	0	0	0	0	0	•	•	0	0	286
Other Portfolio Income	6	179879	•	0	0	117	1541	12	0	•	•	0	160901	5233
Other Receipts	7	781239	•	0	0	3928	3399	575	148295	•	•	0	91937	483006
Total Receipts	8	49932845	•	40595	0	363904	348455	580554	243430	•	•	0	25053240	10519727
Average Total Receipts	9	129696	•	153	•	9331	10249	116111	40572	•	•	•	4175540	2103945
Operating Costs/Operating Income (%)														
Cost of Operations	10	86.1	•	•	•	84.0	76.3	89.2	23.0	•	•	•	96.1	56.9
Salaries and Wages	11	1.4	•	61.7	•	2.5	0.5	3.7	23.2	•	•	•	0.6	2.5
Taxes Paid	12	1.5	•	27.0	•	0.2	1.3	0.5	5.9	•	•	•	0.4	4.2
Interest Paid	13	1.3	•	•	•	0.4	0.5	0.1	0.9	•	•	•	0.3	5.0
Depreciation	14	3.8	•	•	•	0.7	4.7	0.1	4.4	•	•	•	0.6	14.1
Amortization and Depletion	15	0.1	•	•	•	0.0	0.2	0.0	0.2	•	•	•	0.1	0.2
Pensions and Other Deferred Comp.	16	0.3	•	•	•	0.5	0.5	0.0	1.3	•	•	•	0.2	0.8
Employee Benefits	17	0.4	•	•	•	0.2	1.2	0.3	2.8	•	•	•	0.2	1.1
Advertising	18	0.1	•	•	•	0.0	0.3	•	0.0	•	•	•	0.0	0.2
Other Expenses	19	5.6	•	0.8	•	2.8	4.8	1.3	108.5	•	•	•	1.4	19.8
Officers' Compensation	20	0.2	•	•	•	0.8	2.2	0.8	8.8	•	•	•	0.2	0.4
Operating Margin	21	•	•	10.5	•	8.0	7.4	4.0	•	•	•	•	•	•
Operating Margin Before Officers' Comp.	22	•	•	10.5	•	8.8	9.6	4.8	•	•	•	•	0.2	•

Selected Average Balance Sheet ($ in Thousands)													
Net Receivables 23	8892	•	0	•	734	203	13163	15754	•	•	•	232596	274415
Inventories 24	5037	•	0	•	33	263	1549	1385	•	•	•	146384	219784
Net Property, Plant and Equipment 25	75926	•	0	•	171	4507	839	8820	•	•	•	310371	5307546
Total Assets 26	131311	•	0	•	2153	8860	26133	39680	•	•	•	1225315	8100840
Notes and Loans Payable 27	45810	•	0	•	194	563	110	3697	•	•	•	390304	2974963
All Other Liabilities 28	80335	•	0	•	874	1635	10792	2414636	•	•	•	412096	2601499
Net Worth 29	5166	•	0	•	1084	6662	15231	-2378654	•	•	•	422916	2524378
Selected Financial Ratios (Times to 1)													
Current Ratio 30	1.0	•	•	•	1.7	3.6	2.3	1.3	•	•	•	1.3	0.7
Quick Ratio 31	0.5	•	•	•	1.7	3.0	1.9	1.2	•	•	•	0.6	0.3
Net Sales to Working Capital 32	•	•	•	•	14.6	4.5	8.4	2.6	•	•	•	31.6	•
Coverage Ratio 33	2.1	•	•	•	24.7	17.4	65.8	85.7	•	•	•	4.8	1.2
Total Asset Turnover 34	1.0	•	•	•	4.3	1.1	4.4	0.4	•	•	•	3.4	0.2
Inventory Turnover 35	21.7	•	•	•	237.3	29.3	66.8	2.6	•	•	•	27.1	5.1
Receivables Turnover 36	8.0	•	1.8	•	10.2	35.3	17.5	1.0	•	•	•	•	2.4
Total Liabilities to Net Worth 37	24.4	•	•	•	1.0	0.3	0.7	•	•	•	•	1.9	2.2
Current Assets to Working Capital 38	•	•	•	•	2.4	1.4	1.8	4.2	•	•	•	4.6	•
Current Liabilities to Working Capital 39	•	•	•	•	1.4	0.4	0.8	3.2	•	•	•	3.6	•
Working Capital to Net Sales 40	•	•	•	•	0.1	0.2	0.1	0.4	•	•	•	0.0	•
Inventory to Working Capital 41	•	•	•	•	•	0.1	0.2	0.0	•	•	•	1.1	•
Total Receipts to Cash Flow 42	15.7	•	8.8	•	8.7	7.9	18.9	0.6	•	•	•	44.6	5.4
Cost of Goods to Cash Flow 43	13.5	•	•	•	7.3	6.0	16.8	0.1	•	•	•	42.8	3.1
Cash Flow to Total Debt 44	0.1	•	•	•	1.0	0.6	0.6	0.0	•	•	•	0.1	0.1
Selected Financial Factors (in Percentages)													
Debt Ratio 45	96.1	•	•	•	49.6	24.8	41.7	6094.7	•	•	•	65.5	68.8
Return on Total Assets 46	2.6	•	•	•	41.1	10.6	18.5	31.1	•	•	•	4.4	1.4
Return on Equity Before Income Taxes 47	34.1	•	•	•	78.2	13.2	31.2	•	•	•	•	10.0	0.7
Return on Equity After Income Taxes 48	27.8	•	•	•	63.2	11.4	29.4	•	•	•	•	8.4	0.5
Profit Margin (Before Income Tax) 49	1.4	•	10.5	•	9.2	8.7	4.1	76.9	•	•	•	1.0	0.9
Profit Margin (After Income Tax) 50	1.1	•	10.5	•	7.4	7.6	3.9	76.6	•	•	•	0.9	0.6

Table I

Corporations with and without Net Income

WATER, SEWAGE AND OTHER SYSTEMS

MONEY AMOUNTS AND SIZE OF ASSETS IN THOUSANDS OF DOLLARS

Item Description for Accounting Period 7/11 Through 6/12		Total	Zero Assets	Under 500	500 to 1,000	1,000 to 5,000	5,000 to 10,000	10,000 to 25,000	25,000 to 50,000	50,000 to 100,000	100,000 to 250,000	250,000 to 500,000	500,000 to 2,500,000	2,500,000 and over
Number of Enterprises	1	4670	267	3425	281	385	184	65	27	10	10	5	8	3
Revenues ($ in Thousands)														
Net Sales	2	9511983	26218	773530	194648	246405	583651	588867	244417	118217	245444	216096	1902209	4372280
Interest	3	28117	8	502	101	1021	96	271	1300	322	1047	871	5636	16943
Rents	4	23640	0	388	0	1443	8087	417	2537	162	738	1069	8671	130
Royalties	5	75	0	0	0	0	0	0	75	0	0	0	0	0
Other Portfolio Income	6	29354	1692	1799	0	461	1667	1379	3638	35	927	113	12295	5348
Other Receipts	7	131237	0	163	2084	8638	8162	5403	8178	8412	20661	4708	7928	56898
Total Receipts	8	9724406	27918	776382	196833	257968	601663	596337	260145	127148	268817	222857	1936739	4451599
Average Total Receipts	9	2082	105	227	700	670	3270	9174	9635	12715	26882	44571	242092	1483866
Operating Costs/Operating Income (%)														
Cost of Operations	10	26.8	•	21.2	15.4	10.6	36.9	37.3	37.0	37.5	35.5	17.2	35.8	21.8
Salaries and Wages	11	9.1	•	5.4	17.1	5.2	6.1	23.1	6.6	12.2	9.6	9.6	6.8	9.2
Taxes Paid	12	6.5	0.2	2.4	6.6	5.4	5.9	3.4	10.2	4.9	8.2	6.8	6.0	7.9
Interest Paid	13	8.5	•	0.7	0.9	5.1	4.1	2.3	5.5	13.1	8.1	12.3	11.3	10.5
Depreciation	14	17.4	•	3.8	9.2	15.6	7.2	8.7	14.1	30.5	31.2	27.4	21.2	19.8
Amortization and Depletion	15	1.1	•	0.3	•	0.0	0.1	0.5	2.7	13.4	6.8	0.2	0.4	1.2
Pensions and Other Deferred Comp.	16	2.9	•	0.6	0.6	0.1	0.3	1.8	0.6	0.3	2.3	1.6	3.0	4.3
Employee Benefits	17	2.7	•	1.7	2.8	0.9	3.1	3.4	4.1	1.6	2.8	2.2	3.1	2.8
Advertising	18	0.2	•	0.3	0.5	0.1	0.0	0.2	0.6	0.1	0.3	0.3	0.1	0.2
Other Expenses	19	24.0	134.2	37.6	41.1	57.9	26.5	13.7	23.1	36.2	22.9	17.2	13.3	24.1
Officers' Compensation	20	3.1	•	19.8	5.2	1.8	3.6	7.4	5.0	1.9	3.8	2.8	1.0	0.3
Operating Margin	21	•	•	6.1	0.5	•	6.1	•	•	•	•	2.4	•	•
Operating Margin Before Officers' Comp.	22	0.7	•	26.0	5.8	•	9.7	5.6	•	•	•	5.2	•	•

Selected Average Balance Sheet ($ in Thousands)

Net Receivables 23	330	0	5	75	56	221	1117	681	1559	3578	5096	30917	341734
Inventories 24	94	0	7	7	13	5	31	424	41	4238	6360	6732	93170
Net Property, Plant and Equipment 25	6108	0	63	551	1366	3311	9548	18078	35869	122867	256535	722490	5752253
Total Assets 26	8605	0	129	771	2504	6128	16681	32961	70178	174746	347577	1024461	7693407
Notes and Loans Payable 27	3253	0	51	186	920	3059	4683	10579	23341	85348	107687	354887	2998402
All Other Liabilities 28	2777	0	26	42	160	1419	7099	8545	24750	46160	151556	376189	2458402
Net Worth 29	2575	0	51	544	1425	1650	4898	13836	22087	43238	88334	293385	2236603

Selected Financial Ratios (Times to 1)

Current Ratio 30	1.0	•	1.5	14.7	1.2	1.6	1.5	0.9	1.9	0.8	1.7	1.1	0.7
Quick Ratio 31	0.6	•	1.3	10.4	1.0	1.1	0.9	0.5	0.6	0.5	0.6	0.6	0.5
Net Sales to Working Capital 32	•	•	12.9	3.4	12.3	4.2	5.9	•	2.3	•	3.2	32.3	•
Coverage Ratio 33	1.0	•	10.1	2.8	1.4	3.3	0.7	0.4	•	•	1.4	1.0	1.0
Total Asset Turnover 34	0.2	•	1.8	0.9	0.3	0.5	0.5	0.3	0.2	0.1	0.1	0.2	0.2
Inventory Turnover 35	5.8	•	6.8	14.9	5.3	240.1	107.5	7.9	109.0	2.1	1.2	12.6	3.4
Receivables Turnover 36	7.3	•	41.9	7.7	12.1	13.2	6.4	12.6	8.2	7.2	4.6	7.8	5.8
Total Liabilities to Net Worth 37	2.3	•	1.5	0.4	0.8	2.7	2.4	1.4	2.2	3.0	2.9	2.5	2.4
Current Assets to Working Capital 38	•	•	2.9	1.1	6.4	2.6	2.8	•	2.1	•	2.5	10.5	•
Current Liabilities to Working Capital 39	•	•	1.9	0.1	5.4	1.6	1.8	•	1.1	•	1.5	9.5	•
Working Capital to Net Sales 40	•	•	0.1	0.3	0.1	0.2	0.2	•	0.4	•	0.3	0.0	•
Inventory to Working Capital 41	•	•	0.4	0.1	0.3	0.0	0.0	•	0.0	•	0.9	0.1	•
Total Receipts to Cash Flow 42	5.9	1.0	2.8	2.7	1.9	3.9	11.4	6.3	•	•	5.1	12.3	6.4
Cost of Goods to Cash Flow 43	1.6	•	0.6	0.4	0.2	1.4	4.3	2.3	•	•	0.9	4.4	1.4
Cash Flow to Total Debt 44	0.1	•	1.0	1.1	0.3	0.2	0.1	0.1	•	•	0.0	0.0	0.0

Selected Financial Factors (in Percentages)

Debt Ratio 45	70.1	•	60.1	29.5	43.1	73.1	70.6	58.0	68.5	75.3	74.6	71.4	70.9
Return on Total Assets 46	2.0	•	12.7	2.3	1.8	6.9	0.9	0.7	•	•	2.2	2.6	1.9
Return on Equity Before Income Taxes 47	•	•	28.7	2.1	0.9	17.7	•	•	•	•	2.7	•	•
Return on Equity After Income Taxes 48	•	•	28.3	2.1	0.6	17.7	•	•	•	•	1.3	•	•
Profit Margin (Before Income Tax) 49	•	•	6.5	1.7	2.0	9.2	•	•	•	•	5.4	•	•
Profit Margin (After Income Tax) 50	•	•	6.4	1.6	1.4	9.2	•	•	•	•	2.6	•	•

Table II

Corporations with Net Income

WATER, SEWAGE AND OTHER SYSTEMS

Item Description for Accounting Period 7/11 Through 6/12		Total	Zero Assets	Under 500	500 to 1,000	1,000 to 5,000	5,000 to 10,000	10,000 to 25,000	25,000 to 50,000	50,000 to 100,000	100,000 to 250,000	250,000 to 500,000	500,000 to 2,500,000	2,500,000 and over
		MONEY AMOUNTS AND SIZE OF ASSETS IN THOUSANDS OF DOLLARS												
Number of Enterprises	1	2763	•	•	223	204	112	37	17	0	•	0	•	0
Revenues ($ in Thousands)														
Net Sales	2	6165118	•	•	153153	131967	472629	381021	157477	0	•	0	•	0
Interest	3	17976	•	•	95	962	58	165	1176	0	•	0	•	0
Rents	4	5894	•	•	0	0	0	89	2403	0	•	0	•	0
Royalties	5	0	•	•	0	0	0	0	0	0	•	0	•	0
Other Portfolio Income	6	18818	•	•	0	461	1636	338	2334	0	•	0	•	0
Other Receipts	7	31447	•	•	2074	2782	1763	4686	5403	0	•	0	•	0
Total Receipts	8	6239253	•	•	155322	136172	476086	386299	168793	0	•	0	•	0
Average Total Receipts	9	2258	•	•	697	668	4251	10441	9929	•	•	•	•	•
Operating Costs/Operating Income (%)														
Cost of Operations	10	23.8	•	•	19.6	6.7	38.3	33.7	28.1	•	•	•	•	•
Salaries and Wages	11	9.3	•	•	21.7	8.7	5.7	30.0	3.4	•	•	•	•	•
Taxes Paid	12	6.3	•	•	5.1	4.7	5.6	3.1	14.9	•	•	•	•	•
Interest Paid	13	7.4	•	•	1.1	7.2	2.2	1.8	5.0	•	•	•	•	•
Depreciation	14	12.3	•	•	7.7	20.7	5.4	3.3	12.7	•	•	•	•	•
Amortization and Depletion	15	0.5	•	•	•	0.0	0.1	0.3	0.3	•	•	•	•	•
Pensions and Other Deferred Comp.	16	3.4	•	•	0.8	0.1	0.4	1.7	0.8	•	•	•	•	•
Employee Benefits	17	2.6	•	•	3.6	1.6	1.6	4.4	4.0	•	•	•	•	•
Advertising	18	0.2	•	•	0.6	0.0	0.0	0.0	•	•	•	•	•	•
Other Expenses	19	25.4	•	•	32.4	42.4	20.1	9.8	25.0	•	•	•	•	•
Officers' Compensation	20	3.6	•	•	6.7	3.3	3.9	10.0	5.2	•	•	•	•	•
Operating Margin	21	5.3	•	•	0.7	4.5	16.6	2.0	0.4	•	•	•	•	•
Operating Margin Before Officers' Comp.	22	8.9	•	•	7.4	7.9	20.5	12.0	5.6	•	•	•	•	•

Selected Average Balance Sheet ($ in Thousands)													
Net Receivables 23	379	•	•	95	52	297	1442	822	•	•	•	•	•
Inventories 24	119	•	•	9	19	0	13	103	•	•	•	•	•
Net Property, Plant and Equipment 25	6249	•	•	566	1796	2201	9190	26230	•	•	•	•	•
Total Assets 26	8366	•	•	789	2350	6054	15177	38685	•	•	•	•	•
Notes and Loans Payable 27	3092	•	•	233	982	3113	3331	11366	•	•	•	•	•
All Other Liabilities 28	2790	•	•	14	284	1293	7679	14473	•	•	•	•	•
Net Worth 29	2484	•	•	542	1083	1648	4168	12845	•	•	•	•	•
Selected Financial Ratios (Times to 1)													
Current Ratio 30	1.3	•	•	13.8	1.3	2.5	1.6	0.8	•	•	•	•	•
Quick Ratio 31	0.8	•	•	11.9	1.1	1.7	1.0	0.4	•	•	•	•	•
Net Sales to Working Capital 32	10.8	•	•	3.4	5.8	2.4	5.8	•	•	•	•	•	•
Coverage Ratio 33	1.9	•	•	3.0	2.1	9.0	2.9	2.5	•	•	•	•	•
Total Asset Turnover 34	0.3	•	•	0.9	0.3	0.7	0.7	0.2	•	•	•	•	•
Inventory Turnover 35	4.4	•	•	14.9	2.2	•	269.2	25.3	•	•	•	•	•
Receivables Turnover 36	7.7	•	•	12.4	14.5	11.8	9.9	11.2	•	•	•	•	•
Total Liabilities to Net Worth 37	2.4	•	•	0.5	1.2	2.7	2.6	2.0	•	•	•	•	•
Current Assets to Working Capital 38	4.6	•	•	1.1	4.1	1.7	2.7	•	•	•	•	•	•
Current Liabilities to Working Capital 39	3.6	•	•	0.1	3.1	0.7	1.7	•	•	•	•	•	•
Working Capital to Net Sales 40	0.1	•	•	0.3	0.2	0.4	0.2	•	•	•	•	•	•
Inventory to Working Capital 41	0.9	•	•	0.1	0.2	•	0.0	•	•	•	•	•	•
Total Receipts to Cash Flow 42	4.3	•	•	3.2	2.2	3.6	8.9	3.5	•	•	•	•	•
Cost of Goods to Cash Flow 43	1.0	•	•	0.6	0.1	1.4	3.0	1.0	•	•	•	•	•
Cash Flow to Total Debt 44	0.1	•	•	0.9	0.2	0.3	0.1	0.1	•	•	•	•	•
Selected Financial Factors (in Percentages)													
Debt Ratio 45	70.3	•	•	31.3	53.9	72.8	72.5	66.8	•	•	•	•	•
Return on Total Assets 46	3.7	•	•	2.8	4.1	13.6	3.5	3.0	•	•	•	•	•
Return on Equity Before Income Taxes 47	5.8	•	•	2.7	4.6	44.3	8.3	5.5	•	•	•	•	•
Return on Equity After Income Taxes 48	5.3	•	•	2.7	3.9	44.3	7.2	3.7	•	•	•	•	•
Profit Margin (Before Income Tax) 49	6.5	•	•	2.1	7.7	17.3	3.3	7.6	•	•	•	•	•
Profit Margin (After Income Tax) 50	5.9	•	•	2.1	6.5	17.3	2.9	5.2	•	•	•	•	•

Table I

Corporations with and without Net Income

COMBINATION GAS AND ELECTRIC

MONEY AMOUNTS AND SIZE OF ASSETS IN THOUSANDS OF DOLLARS

Item Description for Accounting Period 7/11 Through 6/12		Total	Zero Assets	Under 500	500 to 1,000	1,000 to 5,000	5,000 to 10,000	10,000 to 25,000	25,000 to 50,000	50,000 to 100,000	100,000 to 250,000	250,000 to 500,000	500,000 to 2,500,000	2,500,000 and over
Number of Enterprises	1	458	•	•	0	0	0	5	•	•	•	0	4	27
Revenues ($ in Thousands)														
Net Sales	2	180897466	•	•	0	0	0	75746	•	•	•	0	1872109	174389115
Interest	3	642158	•	•	0	0	0	5	•	•	•	0	4172	633126
Rents	4	763251	•	•	0	0	0	0	•	•	•	0	8645	751447
Royalties	5	15267	•	•	0	0	0	0	•	•	•	0	0	15267
Other Portfolio Income	6	753718	•	•	0	0	0	0	•	•	•	0	4961	747543
Other Receipts	7	3859728	•	•	0	0	0	2770	•	•	•	0	42534	3757251
Total Receipts	8	186931588	•	•	0	0	0	78521	•	•	•	0	1932421	180293749
Average Total Receipts	9	408148	•	•	•	•	•	15704	•	•	•	•	483105	6677546
Operating Costs/Operating Income (%)														
Cost of Operations	10	50.2	•	•	•	•	•	50.9	•	•	•	•	61.3	49.6
Salaries and Wages	11	7.3	•	•	•	•	•	7.8	•	•	•	•	2.6	7.3
Taxes Paid	12	4.2	•	•	•	•	•	1.0	•	•	•	•	2.8	4.3
Interest Paid	13	4.6	•	•	•	•	•	6.7	•	•	•	•	5.0	4.7
Depreciation	14	16.6	•	•	•	•	•	11.0	•	•	•	•	13.9	16.9
Amortization and Depletion	15	0.8	•	•	•	•	•	•	•	•	•	•	0.3	0.8
Pensions and Other Deferred Comp.	16	2.0	•	•	•	•	•	•	•	•	•	•	1.7	2.0
Employee Benefits	17	1.7	•	•	•	•	•	0.7	•	•	•	•	0.5	1.8
Advertising	18	0.2	•	•	•	•	•	0.0	•	•	•	•	0.4	0.2
Other Expenses	19	19.4	•	•	•	•	•	41.5	•	•	•	•	19.6	19.7
Officers' Compensation	20	0.3	•	•	•	•	•	0.0	•	•	•	•	0.6	0.3
Operating Margin	21	•	•	•	•	•	•	•	•	•	•	•	•	•
Operating Margin Before Officers' Comp.	22	•	•	•	•	•	•	•	•	•	•	•	•	•

Selected Average Balance Sheet ($ in Thousands)													
Net Receivables 23	50763	•	•	•	•	•	1398	•	•	•	•	46089	850499
Inventories 24	22084	•	•	•	•	•	1342	•	•	•	•	14861	371790
Net Property, Plant and Equipment 25	616357	•	•	•	•	•	1852	•	•	•	•	620468	10362911
Total Assets 26	1018076	•	•	•	•	•	14444	•	•	•	•	1060940	17100313
Notes and Loans Payable 27	353168	•	•	•	•	•	1082	•	•	•	•	417798	5925885
All Other Liabilities 28	387479	•	•	•	•	•	3172	•	•	•	•	306525	6522473
Net Worth 29	277428	•	•	•	•	•	10190	•	•	•	•	336616	4651955
Selected Financial Ratios (Times to 1)													
Current Ratio 30	0.8	•	•	•	•	•	2.2	•	•	•	•	1.0	0.8
Quick Ratio 31	0.4	•	•	•	•	•	0.5	•	•	•	•	0.5	0.4
Net Sales to Working Capital 32	•	•	•	•	•	•	3.8	•	•	•	•	191.5	•
Coverage Ratio 33	0.1	•	•	•	•	•	•	•	•	•	•	•	0.1
Total Asset Turnover 34	0.4	•	•	•	•	•	1.0	•	•	•	•	0.4	0.4
Inventory Turnover 35	9.0	•	•	•	•	•	5.8	•	•	•	•	19.3	8.6
Receivables Turnover 36	7.4	•	•	•	•	•	•	•	•	•	•	10.0	7.3
Total Liabilities to Net Worth 37	2.7	•	•	•	•	•	0.4	•	•	•	•	2.2	2.7
Current Assets to Working Capital 38	•	•	•	•	•	•	1.8	•	•	•	•	53.5	•
Current Liabilities to Working Capital 39	•	•	•	•	•	•	0.8	•	•	•	•	52.5	•
Working Capital to Net Sales 40	•	•	•	•	•	•	0.3	•	•	•	•	0.0	•
Inventory to Working Capital 41	•	•	•	•	•	•	0.3	•	•	•	•	6.1	•
Total Receipts to Cash Flow 42	10.2	•	•	•	•	•	4.4	•	•	•	•	10.9	10.1
Cost of Goods to Cash Flow 43	5.1	•	•	•	•	•	2.2	•	•	•	•	6.7	5.0
Cash Flow to Total Debt 44	0.1	•	•	•	•	•	0.8	•	•	•	•	0.1	0.1
Selected Financial Factors (in Percentages)													
Debt Ratio 45	72.7	•	•	•	•	•	29.5	•	•	•	•	68.3	72.8
Return on Total Assets 46	0.3	•	•	•	•	•	•	•	•	•	•	•	0.2
Return on Equity Before Income Taxes 47	•	•	•	•	•	•	•	•	•	•	•	•	•
Return on Equity After Income Taxes 48	•	•	•	•	•	•	•	•	•	•	•	•	•
Profit Margin (Before Income Tax) 49	•	•	•	•	•	•	•	•	•	•	•	•	•
Profit Margin (After Income Tax) 50	•	•	•	•	•	•	•	•	•	•	•	•	•

Table II

Corporations with Net Income

COMBINATION GAS AND ELECTRIC

MONEY AMOUNTS AND SIZE OF ASSETS IN THOUSANDS OF DOLLARS

Item Description for Accounting Period 7/11 Through 6/12		Total	Zero Assets	Under 500	500 to 1,000	1,000 to 5,000	5,000 to 10,000	10,000 to 25,000	25,000 to 50,000	50,000 to 100,000	100,000 to 250,000	250,000 to 500,000	500,000 to 2,500,000	2,500,000 and over
Number of Enterprises	1	431	•	•	0	0	0	0	0	•	0	0	•	11
Revenues ($ in Thousands)														
Net Sales	2	70718729	•	•	0	0	0	0	0	•	0	0	•	68635533
Interest	3	137336	•	•	0	0	0	0	0	•	0	0	•	135489
Rents	4	474248	•	•	0	0	0	0	0	•	0	0	•	471089
Royalties	5	228	•	•	0	0	0	0	0	•	0	0	•	228
Other Portfolio Income	6	556481	•	•	0	0	0	0	0	•	0	0	•	553358
Other Receipts	7	1440347	•	•	0	0	0	0	0	•	0	0	•	1405596
Total Receipts	8	73327369	•	•	0	0	0	0	0	•	0	0	•	71201293
Average Total Receipts	9	170133	•	•	•	•	•	•	•	•	•	•	•	6472845
Operating Costs/Operating Income (%)														
Cost of Operations	10	50.6	•	•	•	•	•	•	•	•	•	•	•	50.0
Salaries and Wages	11	5.5	•	•	•	•	•	•	•	•	•	•	•	5.6
Taxes Paid	12	3.6	•	•	•	•	•	•	•	•	•	•	•	3.6
Interest Paid	13	3.7	•	•	•	•	•	•	•	•	•	•	•	3.7
Depreciation	14	13.2	•	•	•	•	•	•	•	•	•	•	•	13.4
Amortization and Depletion	15	0.7	•	•	•	•	•	•	•	•	•	•	•	0.7
Pensions and Other Deferred Comp.	16	1.5	•	•	•	•	•	•	•	•	•	•	•	1.5
Employee Benefits	17	1.5	•	•	•	•	•	•	•	•	•	•	•	1.5
Advertising	18	0.2	•	•	•	•	•	•	•	•	•	•	•	0.2
Other Expenses	19	19.6	•	•	•	•	•	•	•	•	•	•	•	19.8
Officers' Compensation	20	0.3	•	•	•	•	•	•	•	•	•	•	•	0.3
Operating Margin	21	•	•	•	•	•	•	•	•	•	•	•	•	•
Operating Margin Before Officers' Comp.	22	•	•	•	•	•	•	•	•	•	•	•	•	•

Selected Average Balance Sheet ($ in Thousands)												
Net Receivables 23	18291	•	•	•	•	•	•	•	•	•	•	706882
Inventories 24	9079	•	•	•	•	•	•	•	•	•	•	351938
Net Property, Plant and Equipment 25	220164	•	•	•	•	•	•	•	•	•	•	8573157
Total Assets 26	385759	•	•	•	•	•	•	•	•	•	•	15021506
Notes and Loans Payable 27	121537	•	•	•	•	•	•	•	•	•	•	4715722
All Other Liabilities 28	152879	•	•	•	•	•	•	•	•	•	•	5975615
Net Worth 29	111343	•	•	•	•	•	•	•	•	•	•	4330169

Selected Financial Ratios (Times to 1)												
Current Ratio 30	1.1	•	•	•	•	•	•	•	•	•	•	1.1
Quick Ratio 31	0.5	•	•	•	•	•	•	•	•	•	•	0.5
Net Sales to Working Capital 32	45.0	•	•	•	•	•	•	•	•	•	•	46.0
Coverage Ratio 33	1.9	•	•	•	•	•	•	•	•	•	•	1.9
Total Asset Turnover 34	0.4	•	•	•	•	•	•	•	•	•	•	0.4
Inventory Turnover 35	9.1	•	•	•	•	•	•	•	•	•	•	8.9
Receivables Turnover 36	6.2	•	•	•	•	•	•	•	•	•	•	6.0
Total Liabilities to Net Worth 37	2.5	•	•	•	•	•	•	•	•	•	•	2.5
Current Assets to Working Capital 38	12.4	•	•	•	•	•	•	•	•	•	•	12.9
Current Liabilities to Working Capital 39	11.4	•	•	•	•	•	•	•	•	•	•	11.9
Working Capital to Net Sales 40	0.0	•	•	•	•	•	•	•	•	•	•	0.0
Inventory to Working Capital 41	1.5	•	•	•	•	•	•	•	•	•	•	1.6
Total Receipts to Cash Flow 42	5.5	•	•	•	•	•	•	•	•	•	•	5.5
Cost of Goods to Cash Flow 43	2.8	•	•	•	•	•	•	•	•	•	•	2.7
Cash Flow to Total Debt 44	0.1	•	•	•	•	•	•	•	•	•	•	0.1

Selected Financial Factors (in Percentages)												
Debt Ratio 45	71.1	•	•	•	•	•	•	•	•	•	•	71.2
Return on Total Assets 46	3.0	•	•	•	•	•	•	•	•	•	•	2.9
Return on Equity Before Income Taxes 47	4.9	•	•	•	•	•	•	•	•	•	•	4.8
Return on Equity After Income Taxes 48	3.2	•	•	•	•	•	•	•	•	•	•	3.1
Profit Margin (Before Income Tax) 49	3.3	•	•	•	•	•	•	•	•	•	•	3.3
Profit Margin (After Income Tax) 50	2.2	•	•	•	•	•	•	•	•	•	•	2.2

Table I

Corporations with and without Net Income

CONSTRUCTION OF BUILDINGS

MONEY AMOUNTS AND SIZE OF ASSETS IN THOUSANDS OF DOLLARS

Item Description for Accounting Period 7/11 Through 6/12		Total	Zero Assets	Under 500	500 to 1,000	1,000 to 5,000	5,000 to 10,000	10,000 to 25,000	25,000 to 50,000	50,000 to 100,000	100,000 to 250,000	250,000 to 500,000	500,000 to 2,500,000	2,500,000 and over
Number of Enterprises	1	207364	45356	122832	15549	18311	2917	1654	389	168	115	31	•	•
Revenues ($ in Thousands)														
Net Sales	2	404258891	6701473	53453220	23854434	80768720	32344014	45598882	24975726	22359124	28219357	15968366	•	•
Interest	3	697391	621	8672	9387	35500	10925	18025	17040	4790	24092	57786	•	•
Rents	4	472453	6852	32696	40039	74191	39592	50538	22410	11194	57500	53805	•	•
Royalties	5	12507	0	0	0	1	868	70	6	0	10631	418	•	•
Other Portfolio Income	6	1260911	89754	66682	25671	108118	35933	46038	42346	21453	51683	20435	•	•
Other Receipts	7	4564350	39534	310512	371768	680399	195087	244473	109444	210859	351742	306668	•	•
Total Receipts	8	411266503	6838234	53871782	24301299	81666929	32626419	45958026	25166972	22607420	28715005	16407478	•	•
Average Total Receipts	9	1983	151	439	1563	4460	11185	27786	64697	134568	249696	529273	•	•
Operating Costs/Operating Income (%)														
Cost of Operations	10	85.3	67.0	70.9	77.3	84.9	88.1	88.7	91.2	91.7	90.2	91.2	•	•
Salaries and Wages	11	3.8	3.3	5.2	4.7	3.9	2.8	2.6	2.5	2.5	3.0	3.0	•	•
Taxes Paid	12	1.1	1.3	1.9	1.7	1.1	0.9	0.9	0.6	0.7	0.8	0.9	•	•
Interest Paid	13	0.7	0.7	0.5	1.0	0.5	0.3	0.3	0.5	0.4	0.4	1.1	•	•
Depreciation	14	0.7	1.3	1.0	1.1	0.7	0.5	0.5	0.5	0.6	0.8	0.6	•	•
Amortization and Depletion	15	0.1	0.0	0.0	0.0	0.0	0.0	0.0	0.0	0.0	0.2	0.2	•	•
Pensions and Other Deferred Comp.	16	0.2	0.0	0.1	0.2	0.1	0.2	0.2	0.2	0.2	0.2	0.1	•	•
Employee Benefits	17	0.7	0.6	0.7	1.2	0.6	0.6	0.8	0.4	0.5	0.6	1.0	•	•
Advertising	18	0.3	0.3	0.5	0.2	0.3	0.1	0.2	0.2	0.2	0.2	0.1	•	•
Other Expenses	19	6.0	25.6	12.8	8.0	5.5	3.8	3.6	3.0	2.4	3.2	4.0	•	•
Officers' Compensation	20	2.1	3.7	4.8	4.3	2.6	1.8	1.5	1.1	1.1	0.7	0.8	•	•
Operating Margin	21	•	•	1.5	0.3	•	0.8	0.6	•	•	•	•	•	•
Operating Margin Before Officers' Comp.	22	1.2	•	6.4	4.7	2.4	2.7	2.1	0.9	0.9	0.4	•	•	•

Selected Average Balance Sheet ($ in Thousands)

Net Receivables 23	270	0	11	122	554	1770	4950	11248	24583	45900	106564	•	•
Inventories 24	215	0	14	135	365	1255	2212	4521	8446	14903	35233	•	•
Net Property, Plant and Equipment 25	139	0	24	179	306	782	1858	3297	6509	19332	37308	•	•
Total Assets 26	1190	0	95	725	2088	6954	15412	34670	68168	147743	360684	•	•
Notes and Loans Payable 27	397	0	69	439	732	2521	4480	8047	17983	27734	144190	•	•
All Other Liabilities 28	476	0	29	208	811	2642	6693	16664	34331	68902	149545	•	•
Net Worth 29	317	0	-3	78	546	1791	4239	9959	15854	51107	66949	•	•

Selected Financial Ratios (Times to 1)

Current Ratio 30	1.6	•	1.7	1.6	1.6	1.6	1.5	1.4	1.4	1.5	1.6	•	•
Quick Ratio 31	0.9	•	1.1	0.8	0.9	0.9	1.0	1.0	1.0	1.0	1.1	•	•
Net Sales to Working Capital 32	6.1	•	17.8	8.7	7.5	5.3	7.3	7.8	8.3	7.7	6.1	•	•
Coverage Ratio 33	2.1	•	5.8	3.2	2.8	6.0	5.0	2.1	3.1	4.4	0.7	•	•
Total Asset Turnover 34	1.6	•	4.6	2.1	2.1	1.6	1.8	1.9	2.0	1.7	1.4	•	•
Inventory Turnover 35	7.8	•	22.1	8.8	10.3	7.8	11.1	13.0	14.4	14.9	13.3	•	•
Receivables Turnover 36	7.3	•	40.3	12.3	8.7	6.1	5.7	6.2	5.2	5.7	6.4	•	•
Total Liabilities to Net Worth 37	2.8	•	•	8.3	2.8	2.9	2.6	2.5	3.3	1.9	4.4	•	•
Current Assets to Working Capital 38	2.6	•	2.4	2.7	2.6	2.6	3.0	3.2	3.4	3.2	2.7	•	•
Current Liabilities to Working Capital 39	1.6	•	1.4	1.7	1.6	1.6	2.0	2.2	2.4	2.2	1.7	•	•
Working Capital to Net Sales 40	0.2	•	0.1	0.1	0.1	0.2	0.1	0.1	0.1	0.1	0.2	•	•
Inventory to Working Capital 41	0.7	•	0.5	0.7	0.5	0.6	0.6	0.5	0.5	0.4	0.4	•	•
Total Receipts to Cash Flow 42	19.0	4.7	7.7	11.7	20.0	22.5	26.0	40.1	42.9	27.0	36.1	•	•
Cost of Goods to Cash Flow 43	16.2	3.2	5.5	9.0	17.0	19.9	23.1	36.5	39.3	24.3	33.0	•	•
Cash Flow to Total Debt 44	0.1	•	0.6	0.2	0.1	0.1	0.1	0.1	0.1	0.1	0.0	•	•

Selected Financial Factors (in Percentages)

Debt Ratio 45	73.3	•	103.2	89.3	73.9	74.2	72.5	71.3	76.7	65.4	81.4	•	•
Return on Total Assets 46	2.5	•	12.8	6.8	2.8	3.3	3.1	1.7	2.5	2.9	1.1	•	•
Return on Equity Before Income Taxes 47	4.8	•	•	43.7	7.0	10.6	8.9	3.1	7.3	6.5	•	•	•
Return on Equity After Income Taxes 48	4.1	•	•	42.7	6.2	9.8	8.7	2.6	7.0	5.9	•	•	•
Profit Margin (Before Income Tax) 49	0.8	•	2.3	2.2	0.9	1.7	1.4	0.5	0.9	1.4	•	•	•
Profit Margin (After Income Tax) 50	0.7	•	2.3	2.2	0.8	1.6	1.3	0.4	0.8	1.2	•	•	•

Table II

Corporations with Net Income

CONSTRUCTION OF BUILDINGS

MONEY AMOUNTS AND SIZE OF ASSETS IN THOUSANDS OF DOLLARS

Item Description for Accounting Period 7/11 Through 6/12		Total	Zero Assets	Under 500	500 to 1,000	1,000 to 5,000	5,000 to 10,000	10,000 to 25,000	25,000 to 50,000	50,000 to 100,000	100,000 to 250,000	250,000 to 500,000	500,000 to 2,500,000	2,500,000 and over
Number of Enterprises	1	116813	23484	70793	8308	11153	1613	994	252	111	67	•	20	•
Revenues ($ in Thousands)														
Net Sales	2	288827388	4115625	40343153	18023572	58005530	25693219	35888493	19283207	17568181	21651469	•	37027002	•
Interest	3	165278	10	4445	3224	22968	8401	13463	11253	2863	17773	•	59421	•
Rents	4	212101	0	13214	21787	35673	27646	19671	20301	9051	17246	•	16961	•
Royalties	5	11564	0	0	0	1	868	70	6	0	10617	•	1	•
Other Portfolio Income	6	983878	81545	48962	11546	81407	22216	28505	28263	11995	27541	•	624911	•
Other Receipts	7	2645893	60516	295471	309289	352070	132743	179077	77696	114915	273889	•	700528	•
Total Receipts	8	292846102	4257696	40705245	18369418	58497649	25885093	36129279	19420726	17707005	21998535	•	38428824	•
Average Total Receipts	9	2507	181	575	2211	5245	16048	36347	77066	159523	328336	•	1921441	•
Operating Costs/Operating Income (%)														
Cost of Operations	10	83.9	52.4	69.1	77.3	82.8	86.7	88.2	90.1	90.7	90.1	•	89.7	•
Salaries and Wages	11	3.2	4.1	4.8	3.5	3.7	2.7	2.3	2.3	2.3	2.5	•	3.5	•
Taxes Paid	12	1.0	1.1	1.8	1.5	1.1	0.7	0.7	0.6	0.7	0.7	•	0.8	•
Interest Paid	13	0.3	0.4	0.4	0.8	0.3	0.2	0.2	0.2	0.2	0.2	•	0.2	•
Depreciation	14	0.6	1.0	0.8	0.8	0.7	0.4	0.4	0.4	0.4	0.7	•	0.7	•
Amortization and Depletion	15	0.0	0.0	0.0	0.0	0.0	0.0	0.0	0.0	0.0	0.0	•	0.1	•
Pensions and Other Deferred Comp.	16	0.2	0.1	0.1	0.2	0.2	0.2	0.2	0.2	0.2	0.2	•	0.4	•
Employee Benefits	17	0.6	0.2	0.7	1.2	0.6	0.5	0.6	0.4	0.5	0.5	•	0.5	•
Advertising	18	0.2	0.3	0.6	0.2	0.3	0.1	0.2	0.1	0.1	0.1	•	0.1	•
Other Expenses	19	5.0	29.0	11.4	6.5	4.9	3.3	3.2	2.5	1.8	2.6	•	3.0	•
Officers' Compensation	20	2.2	2.9	4.4	4.6	2.6	1.9	1.5	1.2	1.1	0.8	•	0.8	•
Operating Margin	21	2.8	8.6	6.0	3.4	3.0	3.2	2.5	1.9	2.0	1.7	•	0.3	•
Operating Margin Before Officers' Comp.	22	5.0	11.5	10.4	8.0	5.5	5.1	4.0	3.0	3.2	2.4	•	1.1	•

Selected Average Balance Sheet ($ in Thousands)													
Net Receivables 23	333	0	14	162	641	2369	6069	13163	28952	58874	•	350352	•
Inventories 24	92	0	11	88	318	1085	1287	3129	4338	4144	•	43689	•
Net Property, Plant and Equipment 25	105	0	23	141	258	502	853	2573	5108	14429	•	109188	•
Total Assets 26	1044	0	97	730	2081	7154	15538	33929	68871	151617	•	1315551	•
Notes and Loans Payable 27	205	0	57	301	503	1186	2797	4462	9079	15968	•	133247	•
All Other Liabilities 28	483	0	24	232	886	3195	7851	18698	38452	82165	•	637136	•
Net Worth 29	356	0	16	198	692	2772	4890	10769	21340	53484	•	545168	•

Selected Financial Ratios (Times to 1)													
Current Ratio 30	1.5	•	2.1	1.8	1.7	1.7	1.5	1.5	1.4	1.3	•	1.3	•
Quick Ratio 31	1.1	•	1.4	1.1	1.0	1.1	1.1	1.1	1.1	1.1	•	0.9	•
Net Sales to Working Capital 32	9.7	•	17.9	9.2	8.0	6.6	8.7	8.5	9.5	11.5	•	10.8	•
Coverage Ratio 33	14.9	30.5	18.7	7.8	13.3	19.5	17.1	13.7	19.2	15.4	•	18.6	•
Total Asset Turnover 34	2.4	•	5.9	3.0	2.5	2.2	2.3	2.3	2.3	2.1	•	1.4	•
Inventory Turnover 35	22.6	•	36.6	19.0	13.5	12.7	24.8	22.0	33.1	70.2	•	38.0	•
Receivables Turnover 36	7.6	•	47.3	15.5	9.6	6.8	6.1	6.2	5.1	5.5	•	•	•
Total Liabilities to Net Worth 37	1.9	•	5.0	2.7	2.0	1.6	2.2	2.2	2.2	1.8	•	1.4	•
Current Assets to Working Capital 38	3.0	•	1.9	2.3	2.5	2.5	3.1	3.1	3.4	3.9	•	4.5	•
Current Liabilities to Working Capital 39	2.0	•	0.9	1.3	1.5	1.5	2.1	2.1	2.4	2.9	•	3.5	•
Working Capital to Net Sales 40	0.1	•	0.1	0.1	0.1	0.2	0.1	0.1	0.1	0.1	•	0.1	•
Inventory to Working Capital 41	0.4	•	0.4	0.4	0.5	0.4	0.3	0.3	0.3	0.2	•	0.3	•
Total Receipts to Cash Flow 42	12.7	2.6	6.1	9.7	13.4	15.7	18.2	23.6	26.6	20.1	•	21.0	•
Cost of Goods to Cash Flow 43	10.7	1.4	4.2	7.5	11.1	13.7	16.1	21.3	24.2	18.1	•	18.8	•
Cash Flow to Total Debt 44	0.3	•	1.1	0.4	0.3	0.2	0.2	0.1	0.1	0.2	•	0.1	•

Selected Financial Factors (in Percentages)													
Debt Ratio 45	65.9	•	83.3	72.9	66.7	61.2	68.5	68.3	69.0	64.7	•	58.6	•
Return on Total Assets 46	10.6	•	42.4	18.2	10.3	9.3	7.9	6.2	6.8	7.3	•	6.0	•
Return on Equity Before Income Taxes 47	28.9	•	240.6	58.6	28.7	22.8	23.5	18.2	20.7	19.5	•	13.7	•
Return on Equity After Income Taxes 48	27.7	•	239.4	57.9	27.7	21.9	23.1	17.6	20.4	18.5	•	12.0	•
Profit Margin (Before Income Tax) 49	4.2	12.1	6.9	5.3	3.8	4.0	3.2	2.6	2.8	3.2	•	4.0	•
Profit Margin (After Income Tax) 50	4.0	12.0	6.8	5.3	3.7	3.8	3.1	2.5	2.8	3.1	•	3.5	•

Table I

Corporations with and without Net Income

HEAVY AND CIVIL ENGINEERING CONSTRUCTION

MONEY AMOUNTS AND SIZE OF ASSETS IN THOUSANDS OF DOLLARS

Item Description for Accounting Period 7/11 Through 6/12		Total	Zero Assets	Under 500	500 to 1,000	1,000 to 5,000	5,000 to 10,000	10,000 to 25,000	25,000 to 50,000	50,000 to 100,000	100,000 to 250,000	250,000 to 500,000	500,000 to 2,500,000	2,500,000 and over
Number of Enterprises	1	23649	2475	11175	3171	3928	1649	678	324	139	63	21	20	5
Revenues ($ in Thousands)														
Net Sales	2	189736310	981748	8830845	6009359	19396446	24605884	20084357	20444434	15071576	13367568	7207168	22453882	31283045
Interest	3	210904	15	1100	3964	10011	7030	25119	6896	33736	5065	12174	19094	86700
Rents	4	107160	0	369	11669	9621	3416	10641	27792	8153	15149	4177	9519	6653
Royalties	5	67732	0	0	0	0	34	1542	688	175	99	944	12711	51540
Other Portfolio Income	6	1336425	73659	66821	44460	306692	148933	105579	104080	113463	94427	49875	92694	135737
Other Receipts	7	3248217	76873	17355	13450	100559	129507	156380	123886	254434	254741	445314	233284	1442437
Total Receipts	8	194706748	1132295	8916490	6082902	19823329	24894804	20383618	20707776	15481537	13737049	7719652	22821184	33006112
Average Total Receipts	9	8233	457	798	1918	5047	15097	30064	63913	111378	218048	367602	1141059	6601222
Operating Costs/Operating Income (%)														
Cost of Operations	10	78.4	61.3	50.7	73.5	67.9	78.7	81.3	83.2	81.8	80.0	87.1	82.8	81.8
Salaries and Wages	11	3.9	3.1	8.1	3.5	6.3	3.8	3.6	2.7	3.1	3.7	3.1	3.9	2.8
Taxes Paid	12	1.7	1.8	2.9	2.6	2.3	2.0	1.6	1.3	1.4	1.7	1.1	1.6	1.0
Interest Paid	13	0.6	2.4	0.8	0.9	0.6	0.5	0.4	0.5	0.4	0.4	0.7	0.8	0.7
Depreciation	14	3.5	5.5	2.9	2.8	4.6	2.7	3.4	3.5	4.0	3.5	5.2	3.8	2.6
Amortization and Depletion	15	0.2	0.1	0.0	0.1	0.0	0.0	0.1	0.2	0.1	0.2	0.5	0.7	0.5
Pensions and Other Deferred Comp.	16	0.3	0.3	0.0	0.3	0.2	0.4	0.5	0.3	0.5	0.6	0.2	0.1	0.3
Employee Benefits	17	1.1	1.0	1.0	1.2	1.1	1.7	1.2	0.7	1.6	0.9	0.8	1.3	0.5
Advertising	18	0.1	0.1	0.5	0.1	0.2	0.1	0.1	0.1	0.1	0.1	0.1	0.4	0.0
Other Expenses	19	7.6	34.0	24.2	11.5	12.4	5.9	5.4	6.6	5.5	7.2	5.4	4.9	5.2
Officers' Compensation	20	2.0	3.9	6.1	3.3	3.2	2.9	1.7	1.3	1.3	1.0	1.6	0.8	1.5
Operating Margin	21	0.6	•	2.8	0.3	1.2	1.4	0.8	•	0.2	0.6	•	•	3.0
Operating Margin Before Officers' Comp.	22	2.6	•	9.0	3.5	4.4	4.3	2.5	0.9	1.5	1.6	•	•	4.5

Selected Average Balance Sheet ($ in Thousands)														
Net Receivables	23	1214	0	29	104	584	2489	4802	10298	19185	35983	53433	183338	1067477
Inventories	24	150	0	1	17	79	243	405	1055	2531	7351	13212	32327	80088
Net Property, Plant and Equipment	25	1334	0	57	273	749	1512	3829	8282	18768	35025	107410	213945	1595392
Total Assets	26	5145	0	148	674	2381	6914	15100	33617	71404	153434	319071	844035	6563244
Notes and Loans Payable	27	934	0	123	233	645	1287	2825	6618	12759	24508	50527	167790	702317
All Other Liabilities	28	1958	0	23	136	532	2802	4794	11060	23080	49931	92339	312171	3509243
Net Worth	29	2253	0	3	305	1204	2825	7481	15940	35564	78995	176206	364074	2351685
Selected Financial Ratios (Times to 1)														
Current Ratio	30	1.4	•	1.1	1.6	2.0	1.7	1.8	1.8	1.8	1.9	1.9	1.4	0.7
Quick Ratio	31	1.0	•	0.9	1.2	1.5	1.3	1.4	1.4	1.4	1.4	1.4	0.9	0.5
Net Sales to Working Capital	32	11.6	•	213.6	14.2	7.1	7.5	7.0	6.7	5.9	5.2	4.4	9.2	•
Coverage Ratio	33	6.5	1.8	6.0	2.7	7.1	6.5	6.3	2.5	8.1	8.5	2.4	1.6	14.5
Total Asset Turnover	34	1.6	•	5.3	2.8	2.1	2.2	2.0	1.9	1.5	1.4	1.1	1.3	1.0
Inventory Turnover	35	42.1	•	276.6	79.8	42.4	48.4	59.5	49.7	35.0	23.1	22.6	28.7	63.9
Receivables Turnover	36	6.9	•	27.4	23.9	7.9	6.5	6.0	6.5	6.2	6.1	5.4	7.3	6.3
Total Liabilities to Net Worth	37	1.3	•	52.5	1.2	1.0	1.4	1.0	1.1	1.0	0.9	0.8	1.3	1.8
Current Assets to Working Capital	38	3.7	•	20.6	2.5	2.0	2.4	2.3	2.3	2.3	2.1	2.1	3.2	•
Current Liabilities to Working Capital	39	2.7	•	19.6	1.5	1.0	1.4	1.3	1.3	1.3	1.1	1.1	2.2	•
Working Capital to Net Sales	40	0.1	•	0.0	0.1	0.1	0.1	0.1	0.1	0.2	0.2	0.2	0.1	•
Inventory to Working Capital	41	0.2	•	0.2	0.1	0.2	0.1	0.1	0.1	0.1	0.2	0.1	0.3	•
Total Receipts to Cash Flow	42	12.7	3.6	4.5	12.7	8.9	17.8	20.4	24.1	18.4	13.8	18.5	33.7	7.8
Cost of Goods to Cash Flow	43	9.9	2.2	2.3	9.3	6.0	14.0	16.5	20.1	15.0	11.0	16.1	27.9	6.4
Cash Flow to Total Debt	44	0.2	•	1.2	0.4	0.5	0.2	0.2	0.1	0.2	0.2	0.1	0.1	0.2
Selected Financial Factors (in Percentages)														
Debt Ratio	45	56.2	•	98.1	54.8	49.4	59.1	50.5	52.6	50.2	48.5	44.8	56.9	64.2
Return on Total Assets	46	6.0	•	24.4	6.7	8.3	6.5	5.2	2.6	5.0	5.2	1.9	1.7	9.1
Return on Equity Before Income Taxes	47	11.6	•	1088.1	9.3	14.0	13.5	8.9	3.2	8.8	8.8	1.9	1.5	23.7
Return on Equity After Income Taxes	48	10.2	•	1084.7	8.7	13.3	12.6	8.1	2.4	8.1	7.8	0.5	0.0	20.7
Profit Margin (Before Income Tax)	49	3.3	1.9	3.8	1.5	3.4	2.5	2.2	0.8	2.9	3.3	1.0	0.5	8.9
Profit Margin (After Income Tax)	50	2.9	0.5	3.8	1.4	3.2	2.4	2.0	0.6	2.6	2.9	0.3	0.0	7.8

Table II

Corporations with Net Income

HEAVY AND CIVIL ENGINEERING CONSTRUCTION

MONEY AMOUNTS AND SIZE OF ASSETS IN THOUSANDS OF DOLLARS

Item Description for Accounting Period 7/11 Through 6/12		Total	Zero Assets	Under 500	500 to 1,000	1,000 to 5,000	5,000 to 10,000	10,000 to 25,000	25,000 to 50,000	50,000 to 100,000	100,000 to 250,000	250,000 to 500,000	500,000 to 2,500,000	2,500,000 and over
Number of Enterprises	1	14958	1523	6673	2004	2747	1207	449	193	92	41	•	12	•
Revenues ($ in Thousands)														
Net Sales	2	145752614	344809	6560156	4825108	14617827	19494477	13523073	12718670	10588589	9659969	•	18565457	•
Interest	3	168805	13	327	3245	4952	4529	21677	2597	29992	3216	•	15223	•
Rents	4	84824	0	369	11669	4094	2585	984	24916	6964	14849	•	9482	•
Royalties	5	66870	0	0	0	0	14	864	662	175	99	•	12711	•
Other Portfolio Income	6	1084585	73502	61167	33031	259541	129491	75219	59383	88154	72467	•	63263	•
Other Receipts	7	3035898	75956	15952	12507	89398	126266	130282	80640	246247	234858	•	182192	•
Total Receipts	8	150193596	494280	6637971	4885560	14975812	19757362	13752099	12886868	10960121	9985458	•	18848328	•
Average Total Receipts	9	10041	325	995	2438	5452	16369	30628	66771	119132	243548	•	1570694	•
Operating Costs/Operating Income (%)														
Cost of Operations	10	77.3	70.0	45.8	72.5	65.6	76.8	77.2	81.6	80.1	80.3	•	82.7	•
Salaries and Wages	11	3.7	3.1	7.3	2.7	6.9	3.9	3.7	2.6	2.8	3.3	•	3.3	•
Taxes Paid	12	1.6	2.7	2.4	2.5	2.4	1.9	1.7	1.1	1.5	1.9	•	1.6	•
Interest Paid	13	0.5	1.6	0.8	0.8	0.5	0.4	0.4	0.3	0.3	0.4	•	0.6	•
Depreciation	14	2.9	6.1	2.7	1.9	3.8	2.5	3.1	2.8	3.3	3.1	•	3.1	•
Amortization and Depletion	15	0.2	0.2	0.0	•	0.0	0.0	0.1	0.0	0.1	0.2	•	0.8	•
Pensions and Other Deferred Comp.	16	0.3	0.7	0.1	0.2	0.2	0.5	0.4	0.2	0.6	0.7	•	0.1	•
Employee Benefits	17	1.0	1.7	0.8	0.9	0.9	1.6	1.0	0.6	1.6	1.0	•	1.3	•
Advertising	18	0.2	0.1	0.4	0.1	0.2	0.1	0.2	0.1	0.1	0.1	•	0.5	•
Other Expenses	19	7.2	30.8	26.2	10.7	11.6	5.6	6.3	6.0	5.6	5.3	•	4.9	•
Officers' Compensation	20	2.0	5.4	5.5	2.9	3.0	3.0	1.9	1.3	1.4	0.9	•	0.6	•
Operating Margin	21	3.2	•	8.1	4.8	4.8	3.7	4.1	3.2	2.6	2.7	•	0.4	•
Operating Margin Before Officers' Comp.	22	5.1	•	13.6	7.6	7.8	6.6	6.0	4.5	4.0	3.6	•	1.1	•

Selected Average Balance Sheet ($ in Thousands)													
Net Receivables **23**	1439	0	32	118	577	2594	4798	10459	20260	38214	•	225870	•
Inventories **24**	167	0	1	20	96	223	393	1036	2325	9483	•	37348	•
Net Property, Plant and Equipment **25**	1326	0	66	260	725	1572	3477	7262	16852	32086	•	225885	•
Total Assets **26**	5915	0	165	649	2350	6983	15132	33212	71913	152111	•	976843	•
Notes and Loans Payable **27**	811	0	124	175	612	1240	2522	5310	9753	21750	•	155846	•
All Other Liabilities **28**	2342	0	15	170	504	2591	4832	10643	22721	43799	•	348117	•
Net Worth **29**	2762	0	27	304	1233	3152	7777	17259	39439	86562	•	472880	•
Selected Financial Ratios (Times to 1)													
Current Ratio **30**	1.3	•	1.0	1.5	2.0	1.9	1.9	2.0	1.9	2.1	•	1.6	•
Quick Ratio **31**	1.0	•	0.9	1.2	1.6	1.4	1.6	1.6	1.5	1.6	•	1.0	•
Net Sales to Working Capital **32**	12.5	•	•	22.8	7.7	6.9	6.2	5.9	5.3	4.9	•	8.9	•
Coverage Ratio **33**	13.5	14.1	12.6	8.5	14.7	12.2	17.1	14.6	23.7	16.9	•	4.1	•
Total Asset Turnover **34**	1.6	•	5.9	3.7	2.3	2.3	2.0	2.0	1.6	1.5	•	1.6	•
Inventory Turnover **35**	45.2	•	382.8	87.2	36.3	55.6	59.1	51.9	39.7	20.0	•	34.3	•
Receivables Turnover **36**	7.0	•	41.9	33.2	9.0	6.8	5.6	6.2	5.7	5.9	•	8.7	•
Total Liabilities to Net Worth **37**	1.1	•	5.1	1.1	0.9	1.2	0.9	0.9	0.8	0.8	•	1.1	•
Current Assets to Working Capital **38**	3.9	•	•	3.1	2.0	2.1	2.1	2.0	2.1	1.9	•	2.7	•
Current Liabilities to Working Capital **39**	2.9	•	•	2.1	1.0	1.1	1.1	1.0	1.1	0.9	•	1.7	•
Working Capital to Net Sales **40**	0.1	•	•	0.0	0.1	0.1	0.2	0.2	0.2	0.2	•	0.1	•
Inventory to Working Capital **41**	0.2	•	•	0.2	0.2	0.1	0.1	0.1	0.1	0.2	•	0.3	•
Total Receipts to Cash Flow **42**	9.5	2.5	3.4	8.5	6.9	12.9	11.0	12.8	11.7	12.7	•	23.5	•
Cost of Goods to Cash Flow **43**	7.3	1.7	1.5	6.1	4.5	9.9	8.5	10.5	9.4	10.2	•	19.5	•
Cash Flow to Total Debt **44**	0.3	•	2.1	0.8	0.7	0.3	0.4	0.3	0.3	0.3	•	0.1	•
Selected Financial Factors (in Percentages)													
Debt Ratio **45**	53.3	•	83.7	53.2	47.5	54.9	48.6	48.0	45.2	43.1	•	51.6	•
Return on Total Assets **46**	11.2	•	60.0	25.3	17.7	12.6	12.3	9.5	10.2	10.0	•	4.1	•
Return on Equity Before Income Taxes **47**	22.1	•	338.3	47.6	31.4	25.6	22.5	17.1	17.8	16.6	•	6.4	•
Return on Equity After Income Taxes **48**	20.2	•	337.7	46.7	30.3	24.6	21.3	15.8	16.8	15.1	•	4.4	•
Profit Margin (Before Income Tax) **49**	6.3	20.7	9.3	6.0	7.3	5.0	5.8	4.5	6.1	6.1	•	1.9	•
Profit Margin (After Income Tax) **50**	5.7	16.5	9.3	5.9	7.0	4.8	5.5	4.1	5.8	5.6	•	1.3	•

Table I

Corporations with and without Net Income

LAND SUBDIVISION

Item Description for Accounting Period 7/11 Through 6/12		Total	Zero Assets	Under 500	500 to 1,000	1,000 to 5,000	5,000 to 10,000	10,000 to 25,000	25,000 to 50,000	50,000 to 100,000	100,000 to 250,000	250,000 to 500,000	500,000 to 2,500,000	2,500,000 and over
		Money Amounts and Size of Assets in Thousands of Dollars												
Number of Enterprises	1	32889	3275	16993	3221	7475	1067	562	178	60	36	16	6	0
Revenues ($ in Thousands)														
Net Sales	2	18009991	631623	5115203	467237	2709392	3668714	1043831	1284300	560089	1233952	927458	368193	0
Interest	3	91327	365	4796	1741	4289	2724	4596	7133	4008	12425	32501	16749	0
Rents	4	313314	223	16288	324	7036	19246	38719	9504	28707	31998	60125	101143	0
Royalties	5	26453	0	0	0	774	0	4157	170	0	231	0	21121	0
Other Portfolio Income	6	191746	2409	0	5083	8781	8613	5833	12308	6589	2961	58972	80198	0
Other Receipts	7	580713	5373	-60658	27015	139550	89899	23318	24997	35923	94006	71846	129444	0
Total Receipts	8	19213544	639993	5075629	501400	2869822	3789196	1120454	1338412	635316	1375573	1150902	716848	0
Average Total Receipts	9	584	195	299	156	384	3551	1994	7519	10589	38210	71931	119475	•
Operating Costs/Operating Income (%)														
Cost of Operations	10	86.1	133.4	88.2	104.0	75.7	88.2	80.9	89.5	68.5	74.1	94.2	59.8	•
Salaries and Wages	11	6.0	6.9	4.5	4.0	7.1	2.4	7.9	5.9	9.1	10.0	10.8	21.1	•
Taxes Paid	12	2.1	1.0	1.1	2.1	2.5	1.4	3.7	2.2	4.1	3.1	2.9	8.7	•
Interest Paid	13	4.0	1.7	2.0	3.6	4.0	1.3	11.5	6.1	10.1	5.4	8.4	8.7	•
Depreciation	14	2.1	0.0	0.9	1.6	1.4	1.4	3.9	2.7	3.3	3.0	5.2	14.1	•
Amortization and Depletion	15	0.1	•	0.0	0.0	0.1	0.0	0.3	0.1	0.8	0.4	0.3	1.7	•
Pensions and Other Deferred Comp.	16	0.3	•	0.0	•	0.2	0.0	0.2	0.1	0.4	1.0	1.0	2.3	•
Employee Benefits	17	1.1	0.0	0.8	0.3	1.5	1.8	0.6	0.5	0.8	1.6	1.1	3.3	•
Advertising	18	0.5	0.1	0.1	0.1	0.7	0.4	0.7	0.5	1.3	0.7	0.8	3.7	•
Other Expenses	19	14.5	19.6	8.7	10.1	18.2	5.2	18.6	12.1	26.4	18.6	36.4	67.8	•
Officers' Compensation	20	2.2	0.3	1.2	0.6	4.4	1.6	2.9	1.9	3.6	3.4	1.6	6.0	•
Operating Margin	21	•	•	•	•	•	•	•	•	•	•	•	•	•
Operating Margin Before Officers' Comp.	22	•	•	•	•	•	•	•	•	•	•	•	•	•

Selected Average Balance Sheet ($ in Thousands)

Net Receivables	23	136	0	2	13	143	506	860	2918	4068	11793	53925	44136	•
Inventories	24	521	0	35	283	548	2674	4543	8754	20963	34028	76571	141315	•
Net Property, Plant and Equipment	25	599	0	42	106	649	1296	5224	10158	14020	44872	93114	619914	•
Total Assets	26	1925	0	141	693	1908	6753	15236	33552	68989	157356	373431	1149950	•
Notes and Loans Payable	27	1159	0	204	362	1274	3771	10748	18694	44617	91290	190792	259090	•
All Other Liabilities	28	258	0	15	114	145	888	1467	6084	8090	31151	86270	157114	•
Net Worth	29	508	0	-78	217	490	2094	3021	8774	16282	34915	96369	733746	•

Selected Financial Ratios (Times to 1)

Current Ratio	30	2.7	•	2.9	1.8	3.4	3.2	2.5	2.2	3.4	1.8	2.7	2.5	•
Quick Ratio	31	0.7	•	0.5	0.3	0.8	0.6	0.5	0.7	0.8	0.6	1.0	1.3	•
Net Sales to Working Capital	32	1.0	•	5.7	0.7	0.6	1.2	0.4	0.9	0.4	1.3	0.5	0.5	•
Coverage Ratio	33	•	•	•	•	•	0.7	•	•	•	•	•	0.7	•
Total Asset Turnover	34	0.3	•	2.1	0.2	0.2	0.5	0.1	0.2	0.1	0.2	0.2	0.1	•
Inventory Turnover	35	0.9	•	7.6	0.5	0.5	1.1	0.3	0.7	0.3	0.7	0.7	0.3	•
Receivables Turnover	36	3.9	•	134.4	11.1	2.2	11.2	1.9	2.2	1.9	3.0	1.1	1.3	•
Total Liabilities to Net Worth	37	2.8	•	•	2.2	2.9	2.2	4.0	2.8	3.2	3.5	2.9	0.6	•
Current Assets to Working Capital	38	1.6	•	1.5	2.2	1.4	1.5	1.7	1.8	1.4	2.2	1.6	1.7	•
Current Liabilities to Working Capital	39	0.6	•	0.5	1.2	0.4	0.5	0.7	0.8	0.4	1.2	0.6	0.7	•
Working Capital to Net Sales	40	1.0	•	0.2	1.4	1.7	0.9	2.5	1.2	2.6	0.8	1.9	1.9	•
Inventory to Working Capital	41	0.8	•	0.8	1.6	0.7	1.0	0.8	1.0	0.8	1.2	0.8	0.6	•
Total Receipts to Cash Flow	42	•	•	•	•	20.5	24.5	•	•	17.0	15.3	•	3.2	•
Cost of Goods to Cash Flow	43	•	•	•	•	15.6	21.6	•	•	11.7	11.3	•	1.9	•
Cash Flow to Total Debt	44	•	•	•	•	0.0	0.0	•	•	0.0	0.0	•	0.0	•

Selected Financial Factors (in Percentages)

Debt Ratio	45	73.6	•	155.4	68.7	74.3	69.0	80.2	73.8	76.4	77.8	74.2	36.2	•
Return on Total Assets	46	•	•	•	•	•	0.4	•	•	•	•	•	0.3	•
Return on Equity Before Income Taxes	47	•	•	31.7	•	•	•	•	•	•	•	•	•	•
Return on Equity After Income Taxes	48	•	•	31.7	•	•	•	•	•	•	•	•	•	•
Profit Margin (Before Income Tax)	49	•	•	•	•	•	•	•	•	•	•	•	•	•
Profit Margin (After Income Tax)	50	•	•	•	•	•	•	•	•	•	•	•	•	•

Table II

Corporations with Net Income

LAND SUBDIVISION

MONEY AMOUNTS AND SIZE OF ASSETS IN THOUSANDS OF DOLLARS

Item Description for Accounting Period 7/11 Through 6/12		Total	Zero Assets	Under 500	500 to 1,000	1,000 to 5,000	5,000 to 10,000	10,000 to 25,000	25,000 to 50,000	50,000 to 100,000	100,000 to 250,000	250,000 to 500,000	500,000 to 2,500,000	2,500,000 and over
Number of Enterprises	1	5245	26	1793	557	2223	476	100	48	14	4	5	0	0
Revenues ($ in Thousands)														
Net Sales	2	7279687	83925	209575	187170	1340895	3419506	280698	846982	295865	293989	321082	0	0
Interest	3	50327	0	4553	109	1692	1491	582	1146	305	3139	37310	0	0
Rents	4	114407	0	2150	0	3172	11572	36450	1702	4758	0	54604	0	0
Royalties	5	26041	0	0	0	763	0	4157	0	0	0	21121	0	0
Other Portfolio Income	6	102815	0	0	0	61	7630	5221	3176	1321	0	85408	0	0
Other Receipts	7	487834	56514	18838	25917	146502	121565	22918	17880	16694	5406	55598	0	0
Total Receipts	8	8061111	140439	235116	213196	1493085	3561764	350026	870886	318943	302534	575123	0	0
Average Total Receipts	9	1537	5402	131	383	672	7483	3500	18143	22782	75634	115025	•	•
Operating Costs/Operating Income (%)														
Cost of Operations	10	77.2	137.8	53.2	65.1	62.0	86.2	58.7	85.5	55.2	95.6	50.8	•	•
Salaries and Wages	11	4.3	•	•	2.0	8.5	2.4	7.1	2.3	5.5	1.0	18.7	•	•
Taxes Paid	12	1.6	0.0	2.2	1.4	2.0	1.1	4.3	1.0	2.8	0.2	5.6	•	•
Interest Paid	13	1.9	•	1.6	2.4	1.9	0.4	7.0	1.9	2.6	1.2	12.6	•	•
Depreciation	14	1.7	•	2.0	0.0	1.3	1.4	4.0	1.2	1.7	0.0	9.4	•	•
Amortization and Depletion	15	0.1	•	•	•	0.1	0.0	0.5	0.0	0.3	0.1	1.1	•	•
Pensions and Other Deferred Comp.	16	0.2	•	•	•	0.0	0.0	0.2	0.2	0.1	0.2	2.9	•	•
Employee Benefits	17	1.1	•	•	•	0.9	1.9	0.6	0.1	0.2	•	0.7	•	•
Advertising	18	0.3	•	0.1	0.1	0.6	0.2	0.6	0.3	0.9	0.0	1.4	•	•
Other Expenses	19	6.8	0.1	10.5	8.0	8.4	3.0	14.9	4.4	14.5	0.6	37.2	•	•
Officers' Compensation	20	2.0	•	1.0	1.5	3.3	1.6	3.9	0.8	3.4	0.7	4.3	•	•
Operating Margin	21	2.6	•	29.5	19.5	11.0	1.8	•	2.2	12.8	0.3	•	•	•
Operating Margin Before Officers' Comp.	22	4.6	•	30.5	21.0	14.3	3.4	2.3	3.1	16.3	1.0	•	•	•

Selected Average Balance Sheet ($ in Thousands)

Net Receivables 23	277	0	6	0	125	1040	1216	4449	5357	18572	37214	•	•
Inventories 24	603	0	24	348	411	2253	2732	4841	12592	42060	70586	•	•
Net Property, Plant and Equipment 25	849	0	15	87	617	1461	5903	10426	14655	32660	176306	•	•
Total Assets 26	2792	0	102	718	1821	6459	16317	32462	74140	144578	426454	•	•
Notes and Loans Payable 27	1362	0	56	428	1005	3067	8299	10034	46992	88849	157548	•	•
All Other Liabilities 28	364	0	-0	164	135	1188	1262	7301	4672	28204	58935	•	•
Net Worth 29	1066	0	46	126	680	2204	6756	15127	22475	27524	209970	•	•

Selected Financial Ratios (Times to 1)

Current Ratio 30	2.3	•	6.7	0.9	2.3	2.6	4.8	2.1	3.0	0.6	3.1	•	•
Quick Ratio 31	0.9	•	4.5	0.2	0.8	1.0	2.1	1.1	1.1	0.5	1.3	•	•
Net Sales to Working Capital 32	1.9	•	2.2	•	1.4	3.0	0.6	2.3	0.8	•	0.7	•	•
Coverage Ratio 33	8.1	•	27.9	15.1	12.5	15.2	4.3	3.5	8.8	3.7	3.7	•	•
Total Asset Turnover 34	0.5	•	1.2	0.5	0.3	1.1	0.2	0.5	0.3	0.5	0.2	•	•
Inventory Turnover 35	1.8	•	2.5	0.6	0.9	2.7	0.6	3.1	0.9	1.7	0.5	•	•
Receivables Turnover 36	5.1	•	22.3	10.4	4.1	13.1	2.5	3.2	3.1	1.3	3.5	•	•
Total Liabilities to Net Worth 37	1.6	•	1.2	4.7	1.7	1.9	1.4	1.1	2.3	4.3	1.0	•	•
Current Assets to Working Capital 38	1.8	•	1.2	•	1.8	1.6	1.3	1.9	1.5	•	1.5	•	•
Current Liabilities to Working Capital 39	0.8	•	0.2	•	0.8	0.6	0.3	0.9	0.5	•	0.5	•	•
Working Capital to Net Sales 40	0.5	•	0.4	•	0.7	0.3	1.7	0.4	1.3	•	1.4	•	•
Inventory to Working Capital 41	0.7	•	0.4	•	0.6	0.8	0.3	0.7	0.6	•	0.8	•	•
Total Receipts to Cash Flow 42	5.7	3.4	2.0	2.4	3.4	11.9	3.0	11.5	3.0	27.1	2.6	•	•
Cost of Goods to Cash Flow 43	4.4	4.7	1.0	1.6	2.1	10.2	1.8	9.8	1.7	25.9	1.3	•	•
Cash Flow to Total Debt 44	0.1	•	1.1	0.2	0.2	0.1	0.1	0.1	0.1	0.0	0.1	•	•

Selected Financial Factors (in Percentages)

Debt Ratio 45	61.8	•	55.0	82.4	62.6	65.9	58.6	53.4	69.7	81.0	50.8	•	•
Return on Total Assets 46	7.5	•	49.7	16.7	8.1	7.1	5.2	3.6	6.6	2.3	7.1	•	•
Return on Equity Before Income Taxes 47	17.3	•	106.5	88.6	19.8	19.5	9.6	5.6	19.3	8.6	10.5	•	•
Return on Equity After Income Taxes 48	16.5	•	106.3	88.5	19.5	19.4	9.0	5.5	19.3	8.5	7.4	•	•
Profit Margin (Before Income Tax) 49	13.2	29.4	41.7	33.4	22.4	6.0	23.0	4.8	20.5	3.2	34.4	•	•
Profit Margin (After Income Tax) 50	12.6	29.4	41.6	33.3	22.0	5.9	21.7	4.7	20.5	3.2	24.2	•	•

Table I

Corporations with and without Net Income

ELECTRICAL CONTRACTORS

Item Description for Accounting Period 7/11 Through 6/12		MONEY AMOUNTS AND SIZE OF ASSETS IN THOUSANDS OF DOLLARS												
		Total	Zero Assets	Under 500	500 to 1,000	1,000 to 5,000	5,000 to 10,000	10,000 to 25,000	25,000 to 50,000	50,000 to 100,000	100,000 to 250,000	250,000 to 500,000	500,000 to 2,500,000	2,500,000 and over
Number of Enterprises	1	58484	10497	39818	3516	3552	708	265	70	40	10	•	•	•
Revenues ($ in Thousands)														
Net Sales	2	85708406	1938226	16443809	6685215	18792352	13682830	9499093	5171804	6722598	3267278	•	•	•
Interest	3	40475	2777	1597	2657	8519	3644	2385	2069	2913	908	•	•	•
Rents	4	8327	0	334	3	2402	1144	2357	1501	310	277	•	•	•
Royalties	5	3	0	0	0	0	3	0	0	0	0	•	•	•
Other Portfolio Income	6	156948	32359	17684	12624	18606	12670	8051	1231	9519	5103	•	•	•
Other Receipts	7	1088626	14134	32151	75594	47881	53257	42047	42722	17986	33423	•	•	•
Total Receipts	8	87002785	1987496	16495575	6776093	18869760	13753548	9553933	5219327	6753326	3306989	•	•	•
Average Total Receipts	9	1488	189	414	1927	5312	19426	36053	74562	168833	330699	•	•	•
Operating Costs/Operating Income (%)														
Cost of Operations	10	70.7	56.6	51.2	65.6	72.8	78.0	76.4	82.8	80.7	81.3	•	•	•
Salaries and Wages	11	6.7	4.7	8.6	6.5	7.4	5.8	5.4	3.9	5.8	5.7	•	•	•
Taxes Paid	12	2.6	1.5	3.6	2.8	3.0	2.0	2.5	1.4	1.9	3.0	•	•	•
Interest Paid	13	0.4	0.6	0.4	0.4	0.4	0.3	0.3	0.1	0.3	0.3	•	•	•
Depreciation	14	1.6	1.1	1.6	2.3	1.0	0.9	0.7	1.3	1.3	1.8	•	•	•
Amortization and Depletion	15	0.2	0.2	0.0	0.1	0.1	0.0	0.0	0.0	0.2	0.4	•	•	•
Pensions and Other Deferred Comp.	16	0.4	0.0	0.3	1.0	0.5	0.4	0.3	0.2	0.5	0.2	•	•	•
Employee Benefits	17	2.3	3.9	0.7	1.8	3.4	1.8	4.1	2.0	1.9	0.4	•	•	•
Advertising	18	0.2	0.2	0.6	0.2	0.1	0.1	0.1	0.1	0.1	0.1	•	•	•
Other Expenses	19	9.1	25.3	19.3	11.5	6.5	5.8	5.2	3.0	3.8	6.0	•	•	•
Officers' Compensation	20	4.2	3.5	8.7	5.5	3.6	2.4	3.3	2.8	1.1	1.8	•	•	•
Operating Margin	21	1.7	2.4	5.1	2.4	1.3	2.5	1.7	2.4	2.5	•	•	•	•
Operating Margin Before Officers' Comp.	22	5.8	5.9	13.7	7.9	4.9	4.9	4.9	5.2	3.6	0.9	•	•	•

Selected Average Balance Sheet ($ in Thousands)													
Net Receivables 23	245	0	14	219	989	3860	8119	15644	37428	67733	•	•	•
Inventories 24	23	0	9	60	73	144	735	477	1196	9291	•	•	•
Net Property, Plant and Equipment 25	85	0	20	130	211	663	1286	4502	6431	19276	•	•	•
Total Assets 26	615	0	80	710	2104	7382	15337	33401	71123	157466	•	•	•
Notes and Loans Payable 27	102	0	42	139	361	1161	2188	2422	8837	19688	•	•	•
All Other Liabilities 28	237	0	23	197	832	3296	6576	15579	33605	71796	•	•	•
Net Worth 29	275	0	15	373	911	2925	6573	15399	28682	65982	•	•	•

Selected Financial Ratios (Times to 1)													
Current Ratio 30	1.8	•	1.7	2.2	1.8	1.8	1.8	1.9	1.6	1.6	•	•	•
Quick Ratio 31	1.4	•	1.3	1.7	1.5	1.5	1.5	1.6	1.3	1.1	•	•	•
Net Sales to Working Capital 32	7.7	•	22.0	6.9	7.3	7.1	6.0	6.2	7.5	8.0	•	•	•
Coverage Ratio 33	10.0	9.8	13.9	11.5	5.7	12.0	9.5	24.9	11.4	2.3	•	•	•
Total Asset Turnover 34	2.4	•	5.2	2.7	2.5	2.6	2.3	2.2	2.4	2.1	•	•	•
Inventory Turnover 35	44.4	•	24.1	20.7	53.0	104.9	37.3	128.1	113.5	28.6	•	•	•
Receivables Turnover 36	6.4	•	27.8	7.6	5.9	5.5	4.9	5.0	5.0	5.1	•	•	•
Total Liabilities to Net Worth 37	1.2	•	4.4	0.9	1.3	1.5	1.3	1.2	1.5	1.4	•	•	•
Current Assets to Working Capital 38	2.3	•	2.5	1.8	2.3	2.3	2.2	2.1	2.6	2.6	•	•	•
Current Liabilities to Working Capital 39	1.3	•	1.5	0.8	1.3	1.3	1.2	1.1	1.6	1.6	•	•	•
Working Capital to Net Sales 40	0.1	•	0.0	0.1	0.1	0.1	0.2	0.2	0.1	0.1	•	•	•
Inventory to Working Capital 41	0.1	•	0.4	0.2	0.1	0.1	0.1	0.1	0.1	0.2	•	•	•
Total Receipts to Cash Flow 42	9.9	3.8	4.6	8.0	16.0	13.8	17.6	20.3	19.1	26.8	•	•	•
Cost of Goods to Cash Flow 43	7.0	2.1	2.4	5.3	11.7	10.8	13.4	16.8	15.4	21.8	•	•	•
Cash Flow to Total Debt 44	0.4	•	1.4	0.7	0.3	0.3	0.2	0.2	0.2	0.1	•	•	•

Selected Financial Factors (in Percentages)													
Debt Ratio 45	55.2	•	81.5	47.4	56.7	60.4	57.1	53.9	59.7	58.1	•	•	•
Return on Total Assets 46	8.4	•	29.9	11.0	5.1	8.7	5.8	7.6	7.6	1.2	•	•	•
Return on Equity Before Income Taxes 47	16.8	•	149.7	19.1	9.7	20.0	12.1	15.8	17.1	1.7	•	•	•
Return on Equity After Income Taxes 48	15.7	•	148.3	19.0	8.4	19.0	11.3	14.8	16.6	•	•	•	•
Profit Margin (Before Income Tax) 49	3.2	5.0	5.4	3.8	1.7	3.0	2.2	3.3	2.9	0.3	•	•	•
Profit Margin (After Income Tax) 50	2.9	4.8	5.3	3.7	1.4	2.9	2.1	3.1	2.8	•	•	•	•

Table II

Corporations with Net Income

ELECTRICAL CONTRACTORS

MONEY AMOUNTS AND SIZE OF ASSETS IN THOUSANDS OF DOLLARS

Item Description for Accounting Period 7/11 Through 6/12		Total	Zero Assets	Under 500	500 to 1,000	1,000 to 5,000	5,000 to 10,000	10,000 to 25,000	25,000 to 50,000	50,000 to 100,000	100,000 to 250,000	250,000 to 500,000	500,000 to 2,500,000	2,500,000 and over
Number of Enterprises	1	37054	5597	26013	2369	2210	556	201	64	30	•	•	0	•
Revenues ($ in Thousands)														
Net Sales	2	66302893	1312070	13394331	4768794	12904786	11231421	7408169	4693280	5031366	•	•	0	•
Interest	3	26564	203	564	2581	3631	1578	2006	1801	583	•	•	0	•
Rents	4	7342	0	61	3	1846	1138	2287	1501	310	•	•	0	•
Royalties	5	3	0	0	0	0	3	0	0	0	•	•	0	•
Other Portfolio Income	6	134335	32178	13811	12127	11342	12218	3218	1065	8291	•	•	0	•
Other Receipts	7	1003132	4613	23553	63256	30978	49332	18510	43148	13077	•	•	0	•
Total Receipts	8	67474269	1349064	13432320	4846761	12952583	11295690	7434190	4740795	5053627	•	•	0	•
Average Total Receipts	9	1821	241	516	2046	5861	20316	36986	74075	168454	•	•	•	•
Operating Costs/Operating Income (%)														
Cost of Operations	10	70.3	49.2	52.2	64.0	72.5	77.0	74.4	82.6	81.1	•	•	•	•
Salaries and Wages	11	6.0	2.2	7.8	6.1	5.5	5.7	5.2	3.7	5.2	•	•	•	•
Taxes Paid	12	2.6	1.4	3.2	2.8	3.1	2.1	2.4	1.4	1.9	•	•	•	•
Interest Paid	13	0.3	0.5	0.3	0.3	0.3	0.3	0.2	0.1	0.1	•	•	•	•
Depreciation	14	1.4	1.0	1.3	2.7	0.9	0.9	0.6	1.3	0.8	•	•	•	•
Amortization and Depletion	15	0.1	0.2	0.0	0.1	0.1	0.1	0.0	0.0	0.1	•	•	•	•
Pensions and Other Deferred Comp.	16	0.4	0.0	0.3	1.2	0.4	0.3	0.4	0.3	0.3	•	•	•	•
Employee Benefits	17	2.0	0.7	0.6	1.6	2.8	1.8	4.5	1.6	1.6	•	•	•	•
Advertising	18	0.2	0.2	0.6	0.2	0.1	0.1	0.1	0.1	0.1	•	•	•	•
Other Expenses	19	8.5	30.7	17.0	10.7	6.1	5.5	4.7	3.2	3.5	•	•	•	•
Officers' Compensation	20	4.0	3.9	8.2	4.0	3.6	2.2	3.7	2.7	1.2	•	•	•	•
Operating Margin	21	4.1	9.8	8.6	6.4	4.5	4.1	3.7	3.1	4.1	•	•	•	•
Operating Margin Before Officers' Comp.	22	8.1	13.7	16.8	10.4	8.1	6.3	7.4	5.8	5.3	•	•	•	•

Selected Average Balance Sheet ($ in Thousands)													
Net Receivables **23**	297	0	14	213	1040	3994	8402	15321	37378	•	•	•	•
Inventories **24**	26	0	8	63	76	128	704	457	880	•	•	•	•
Net Property, Plant and Equipment **25**	98	0	22	134	211	704	1018	4576	5524	•	•	•	•
Total Assets **26**	740	0	91	726	2174	7466	15192	32956	71188	•	•	•	•
Notes and Loans Payable **27**	99	0	39	127	302	1082	2095	2292	6689	•	•	•	•
All Other Liabilities **28**	288	0	22	148	963	3453	6748	15623	32620	•	•	•	•
Net Worth **29**	352	0	30	451	909	2931	6349	15040	31878	•	•	•	•
Selected Financial Ratios (Times to 1)													
Current Ratio **30**	1.8	•	1.8	3.2	1.8	1.8	1.8	1.9	1.7	•	•	•	•
Quick Ratio **31**	1.5	•	1.5	2.4	1.5	1.5	1.5	1.6	1.4	•	•	•	•
Net Sales to Working Capital **32**	7.5	•	21.0	5.7	7.5	7.4	6.1	6.3	6.8	•	•	•	•
Coverage Ratio **33**	21.8	26.5	26.5	25.9	16.7	18.4	19.3	32.8	48.3	•	•	•	•
Total Asset Turnover **34**	2.4	•	5.7	2.8	2.7	2.7	2.4	2.2	2.4	•	•	•	•
Inventory Turnover **35**	49.3	•	31.6	20.4	55.4	121.1	38.9	132.5	154.5	•	•	•	•
Receivables Turnover **36**	6.7	•	37.6	9.1	6.4	6.2	4.6	5.2	4.7	•	•	•	•
Total Liabilities to Net Worth **37**	1.1	•	2.0	0.6	1.4	1.5	1.4	1.2	1.2	•	•	•	•
Current Assets to Working Capital **38**	2.2	•	2.2	1.5	2.3	2.3	2.2	2.2	2.5	•	•	•	•
Current Liabilities to Working Capital **39**	1.2	•	1.2	0.5	1.3	1.3	1.2	1.2	1.5	•	•	•	•
Working Capital to Net Sales **40**	0.1	•	0.0	0.2	0.1	0.1	0.2	0.2	0.1	•	•	•	•
Inventory to Working Capital **41**	0.1	•	0.3	0.2	0.1	0.1	0.1	0.1	0.0	•	•	•	•
Total Receipts to Cash Flow **42**	8.1	2.6	4.3	6.2	10.9	11.7	13.9	16.8	15.2	•	•	•	•
Cost of Goods to Cash Flow **43**	5.7	1.3	2.2	4.0	7.9	9.0	10.3	13.9	12.3	•	•	•	•
Cash Flow to Total Debt **44**	0.6	•	2.0	1.2	0.4	0.4	0.3	0.2	0.3	•	•	•	•
Selected Financial Factors (in Percentages)													
Debt Ratio **45**	52.4	•	67.1	37.9	58.2	60.7	58.2	54.4	55.2	•	•	•	•
Return on Total Assets **46**	14.9	•	52.3	23.2	13.9	13.3	10.4	9.4	10.9	•	•	•	•
Return on Equity Before Income Taxes **47**	29.8	•	153.2	35.8	31.3	32.0	23.5	19.9	23.8	•	•	•	•
Return on Equity After Income Taxes **48**	28.4	•	152.1	35.7	29.2	30.7	22.4	18.8	23.2	•	•	•	•
Profit Margin (Before Income Tax) **49**	5.9	12.6	8.9	8.0	4.9	4.6	4.0	4.1	4.5	•	•	•	•
Profit Margin (After Income Tax) **50**	5.6	12.3	8.8	8.0	4.5	4.5	3.9	3.9	4.4	•	•	•	•

Table I

Corporations with and without Net Income

PLUMBING, HEATING, AND AIR-CONDITIONING CONTRACTORS

Item Description for Accounting Period 7/11 Through 6/12		MONEY AMOUNTS AND SIZE OF ASSETS IN THOUSANDS OF DOLLARS												
		Total	Zero Assets	Under 500	500 to 1,000	1,000 to 5,000	5,000 to 10,000	10,000 to 25,000	25,000 to 50,000	50,000 to 100,000	100,000 to 250,000	250,000 to 500,000	500,000 to 2,500,000	2,500,000 and over
Number of Enterprises	1	78940	10472	59876	3721	3559	833	361	79	•	7	•	•	•
Revenues ($ in Thousands)														
Net Sales	2	115369564	1014961	34618436	8652089	23325649	15377032	12823431	6345265	•	2103326	•	•	•
Interest	3	26247	339	4705	1381	6049	2294	8162	921	•	495	•	•	•
Rents	4	14096	0	1140	0	1369	684	10547	16	•	0	•	•	•
Royalties	5	0	0	0	0	0	0	0	0	•	0	•	•	•
Other Portfolio Income	6	153676	6464	83717	3408	15857	8677	5689	3546	•	954	•	•	•
Other Receipts	7	383188	9411	79970	12667	100946	94186	37298	9868	•	9320	•	•	•
Total Receipts	8	115946771	1031175	34787968	8669545	23449870	15482873	12885127	6359616	•	2114095	•	•	•
Average Total Receipts	9	1469	98	581	2330	6589	18587	35693	80501	•	302014	•	•	•
Operating Costs/Operating Income (%)														
Cost of Operations	10	67.0	50.3	49.8	60.4	71.5	75.8	78.2	82.3	•	81.3	•	•	•
Salaries and Wages	11	8.1	6.9	12.0	9.9	6.9	7.0	5.1	4.9	•	5.1	•	•	•
Taxes Paid	12	2.7	2.3	3.3	3.2	2.9	2.3	2.0	2.1	•	1.4	•	•	•
Interest Paid	13	0.4	0.3	0.5	0.4	0.3	0.3	0.3	0.2	•	0.6	•	•	•
Depreciation	14	1.1	0.4	1.5	1.8	0.9	0.9	0.8	0.7	•	0.7	•	•	•
Amortization and Depletion	15	0.1	1.1	0.0	0.0	0.0	0.1	0.1	0.1	•	0.4	•	•	•
Pensions and Other Deferred Comp.	16	0.5	0.1	0.2	0.4	0.8	0.5	0.5	0.6	•	0.4	•	•	•
Employee Benefits	17	1.8	1.9	1.6	2.2	1.8	1.4	3.4	0.9	•	0.7	•	•	•
Advertising	18	0.7	1.9	1.0	1.6	0.9	0.5	0.1	0.1	•	0.1	•	•	•
Other Expenses	19	10.2	34.1	17.5	11.2	8.4	7.2	5.0	3.6	•	2.3	•	•	•
Officers' Compensation	20	4.9	5.4	9.0	5.5	3.9	2.6	2.5	1.9	•	2.6	•	•	•
Operating Margin	21	2.4	•	3.5	3.3	1.7	1.6	1.9	2.6	•	4.5	•	•	•
Operating Margin Before Officers' Comp.	22	7.3	0.6	12.4	8.8	5.6	4.1	4.3	4.5	•	7.0	•	•	•

Selected Average Balance Sheet ($ in Thousands)														
Net Receivables	23	198	0	20	242	1023	3330	8040	17698	•	52994	•	•	•
Inventories	24	22	0	6	51	183	212	497	652	•	894	•	•	•
Net Property, Plant and Equipment	25	55	0	23	104	203	737	1350	2465	•	9804	•	•	•
Total Assets	26	466	0	93	676	2266	6938	14986	33415	•	127466	•	•	•
Notes and Loans Payable	27	97	0	51	173	390	912	2208	2758	•	9902	•	•	•
All Other Liabilities	28	198	0	29	192	945	2818	7310	17871	•	81863	•	•	•
Net Worth	29	171	0	13	311	931	3208	5467	12786	•	35701	•	•	•

Selected Financial Ratios (Times to 1)														
Current Ratio	30	1.7	•	1.6	2.2	1.9	1.9	1.6	1.5	•	1.2	•	•	•
Quick Ratio	31	1.4	•	1.3	1.9	1.5	1.6	1.3	1.3	•	1.0	•	•	•
Net Sales to Working Capital	32	10.2	•	28.6	8.9	7.5	7.0	7.6	8.8	•	20.9	•	•	•
Coverage Ratio	33	8.4	•	8.2	9.2	7.5	9.2	8.2	18.8	•	8.6	•	•	•
Total Asset Turnover	34	3.1	•	6.2	3.4	2.9	2.7	2.4	2.4	•	2.4	•	•	•
Inventory Turnover	35	44.4	•	45.9	27.4	25.6	65.9	55.9	101.4	•	273.2	•	•	•
Receivables Turnover	36	7.8	•	26.9	10.1	6.8	6.0	5.0	4.8	•	6.1	•	•	•
Total Liabilities to Net Worth	37	1.7	•	6.2	1.2	1.4	1.2	1.7	1.6	•	2.6	•	•	•
Current Assets to Working Capital	38	2.5	•	2.8	1.8	2.2	2.1	2.7	3.1	•	6.9	•	•	•
Current Liabilities to Working Capital	39	1.5	•	1.8	0.8	1.2	1.1	1.7	2.1	•	5.9	•	•	•
Working Capital to Net Sales	40	0.1	•	0.0	0.1	0.1	0.1	0.1	0.1	•	0.0	•	•	•
Inventory to Working Capital	41	0.2	•	0.3	0.2	0.2	0.1	0.1	0.1	•	0.1	•	•	•
Total Receipts to Cash Flow	42	9.1	3.9	5.4	8.1	11.8	13.2	17.2	19.1	•	16.5	•	•	•
Cost of Goods to Cash Flow	43	6.1	1.9	2.7	4.9	8.4	10.0	13.4	15.7	•	13.4	•	•	•
Cash Flow to Total Debt	44	0.5	•	1.3	0.8	0.4	0.4	0.2	0.2	•	0.2	•	•	•

Selected Financial Factors (in Percentages)														
Debt Ratio	45	63.3	•	86.1	54.0	58.9	53.8	63.5	61.7	•	72.0	•	•	•
Return on Total Assets	46	10.5	•	27.9	13.4	7.3	6.7	6.3	7.1	•	13.1	•	•	•
Return on Equity Before Income Taxes	47	25.1	•	176.5	25.9	15.4	12.8	15.2	17.5	•	41.5	•	•	•
Return on Equity After Income Taxes	48	24.0	•	173.7	25.5	14.7	12.2	14.4	16.9	•	41.5	•	•	•
Profit Margin (Before Income Tax)	49	2.9	•	3.9	3.5	2.2	2.2	2.3	2.8	•	4.9	•	•	•
Profit Margin (After Income Tax)	50	2.8	•	3.9	3.4	2.1	2.1	2.2	2.7	•	4.9	•	•	•

Table II

Corporations with Net Income

PLUMBING, HEATING, AND AIR-CONDITIONING CONTRACTORS

MONEY AMOUNTS AND SIZE OF ASSETS IN THOUSANDS OF DOLLARS

Item Description for Accounting Period 7/11 Through 6/12		Total	Zero Assets	Under 500	500 to 1,000	1,000 to 5,000	5,000 to 10,000	10,000 to 25,000	25,000 to 50,000	50,000 to 100,000	100,000 to 250,000	250,000 to 500,000	500,000 to 2,500,000	2,500,000 and over
Number of Enterprises	1	50436	4926	39152	2314	2966	683	292	69	25	•	•	0	•
Revenues ($ in Thousands)														
Net Sales	2	91561443	509843	24352297	6287977	20056610	13239472	10860841	5221225	3585337	•	•	0	•
Interest	3	12419	339	1695	566	4001	1523	1628	918	426	•	•	0	•
Rents	4	2881	0	1019	0	44	541	922	16	276	•	•	0	•
Royalties	5	0	0	0	0	0	0	0	0	0	•	•	0	•
Other Portfolio Income	6	63915	1536	9459	818	11203	6563	5399	2969	1402	•	•	0	•
Other Receipts	7	344455	3518	73761	12886	88079	86491	34998	8166	10663	•	•	0	•
Total Receipts	8	91985113	515236	24438231	6302247	20159937	13334590	10903788	5233294	3598104	•	•	0	•
Average Total Receipts	9	1824	105	624	2724	6797	19524	37342	75845	143924	•	•	•	•
Operating Costs/Operating Income (%)														
Cost of Operations	10	67.6	33.1	49.8	59.3	71.4	75.1	77.7	80.3	81.5	•	•	•	•
Salaries and Wages	11	7.5	7.8	10.8	9.3	7.0	7.2	4.9	4.8	4.0	•	•	•	•
Taxes Paid	12	2.7	2.1	3.2	2.8	2.9	2.2	2.0	2.4	2.3	•	•	•	•
Interest Paid	13	0.3	0.5	0.4	0.4	0.3	0.2	0.2	0.1	0.1	•	•	•	•
Depreciation	14	1.1	0.6	1.6	1.8	0.9	0.8	0.7	0.7	0.8	•	•	•	•
Amortization and Depletion	15	0.1	•	0.0	0.1	0.0	0.0	0.1	0.1	0.1	•	•	•	•
Pensions and Other Deferred Comp.	16	0.5	0.0	0.3	0.4	0.8	0.5	0.5	0.7	0.6	•	•	•	•
Employee Benefits	17	1.6	2.3	1.4	1.2	1.7	1.4	3.1	1.1	1.9	•	•	•	•
Advertising	18	0.7	1.9	1.0	1.9	0.9	0.5	0.1	0.1	0.1	•	•	•	•
Other Expenses	19	9.0	30.2	15.5	11.0	7.8	7.0	5.0	3.5	2.8	•	•	•	•
Officers' Compensation	20	4.6	4.2	8.8	5.6	3.8	2.5	2.6	2.2	1.4	•	•	•	•
Operating Margin	21	4.4	17.3	7.2	6.2	2.5	2.5	3.0	3.9	4.5	•	•	•	•
Operating Margin Before Officers' Comp.	22	9.0	21.5	16.0	11.9	6.3	5.0	5.6	6.1	5.9	•	•	•	•

	Selected Average Balance Sheet ($ in Thousands)													
Net Receivables	23	253	0	19	249	1024	3436	8420	17202	29828	•	•	•	•
Inventories	24	25	0	6	49	174	213	431	569	2015	•	•	•	•
Net Property, Plant and Equipment	25	62	0	25	68	208	655	1109	2522	7711	•	•	•	•
Total Assets	26	582	0	100	659	2285	7037	14935	32685	66918	•	•	•	•
Notes and Loans Payable	27	96	0	40	168	360	591	1951	2557	7689	•	•	•	•
All Other Liabilities	28	244	0	25	142	969	2871	7312	17536	28063	•	•	•	•
Net Worth	29	242	0	35	349	955	3575	5672	12591	31167	•	•	•	•
	Selected Financial Ratios (Times to 1)													
Current Ratio	30	1.8	•	2.0	3.1	1.9	2.0	1.6	1.5	1.7	•	•	•	•
Quick Ratio	31	1.5	•	1.7	2.7	1.5	1.7	1.4	1.3	1.4	•	•	•	•
Net Sales to Working Capital	32	9.0	•	20.4	7.6	7.6	6.5	7.3	7.9	7.0	•	•	•	•
Coverage Ratio	33	16.6	37.0	18.0	18.2	10.7	19.9	15.6	31.4	33.4	•	•	•	•
Total Asset Turnover	34	3.1	•	6.2	4.1	3.0	2.8	2.5	2.3	2.1	•	•	•	•
Inventory Turnover	35	48.6	•	51.9	33.0	27.7	68.4	67.0	106.8	58.0	•	•	•	•
Receivables Turnover	36	7.7	•	29.0	10.7	7.7	6.1	5.2	4.5	5.0	•	•	•	•
Total Liabilities to Net Worth	37	1.4	•	1.8	0.9	1.4	1.0	1.6	1.6	1.1	•	•	•	•
Current Assets to Working Capital	38	2.3	•	2.0	1.5	2.2	2.0	2.5	2.9	2.5	•	•	•	•
Current Liabilities to Working Capital	39	1.3	•	1.0	0.5	1.2	1.0	1.5	1.9	1.5	•	•	•	•
Working Capital to Net Sales	40	0.1	•	0.0	0.1	0.1	0.2	0.1	0.1	0.1	•	•	•	•
Inventory to Working Capital	41	0.1	•	0.2	0.2	0.2	0.1	0.1	0.1	0.1	•	•	•	•
Total Receipts to Cash Flow	42	8.5	2.1	4.9	6.6	11.3	11.9	14.7	15.6	15.4	•	•	•	•
Cost of Goods to Cash Flow	43	5.7	0.7	2.4	3.9	8.1	8.9	11.4	12.5	12.5	•	•	•	•
Cash Flow to Total Debt	44	0.6	•	2.0	1.3	0.4	0.5	0.3	0.2	0.3	•	•	•	•
	Selected Financial Factors (in Percentages)													
Debt Ratio	45	58.4	•	64.6	47.0	58.2	49.2	62.0	61.5	53.4	•	•	•	•
Return on Total Assets	46	16.0	•	49.8	28.2	9.9	9.3	8.9	9.8	10.7	•	•	•	•
Return on Equity Before Income Taxes	47	36.1	•	132.9	50.3	21.4	17.4	22.0	24.6	22.2	•	•	•	•
Return on Equity After Income Taxes	48	34.9	•	131.3	49.8	20.6	16.7	21.1	24.0	21.9	•	•	•	•
Profit Margin (Before Income Tax)	49	4.8	18.3	7.6	6.5	3.0	3.2	3.4	4.1	4.8	•	•	•	•
Profit Margin (After Income Tax)	50	4.7	18.3	7.5	6.4	2.9	3.1	3.2	4.0	4.8	•	•	•	•

Table I

Corporations with and without Net Income

OTHER SPECIALTY TRADE CONTRACTORS

MONEY AMOUNTS AND SIZE OF ASSETS IN THOUSANDS OF DOLLARS

Item Description for Accounting Period 7/11 Through 6/12		Total	Zero Assets	Under 500	500 to 1,000	1,000 to 5,000	5,000 to 10,000	10,000 to 25,000	25,000 to 50,000	50,000 to 100,000	100,000 to 250,000	250,000 to 500,000	500,000 to 2,500,000	2,500,000 and over
Number of Enterprises	1	307111	57308	219885	13415	13318	1879	949	226	•	29	12	•	0
Revenues ($ in Thousands)														
Net Sales	2	308837525	5574848	107541695	29110019	66535189	28376395	29406322	13966416	•	6646065	6092075	•	0
Interest	3	82864	606	7911	7381	20638	7789	8931	4578	•	10221	1997	•	0
Rents	4	190625	0	10948	8346	18386	18982	7161	5964	•	1864	114	•	0
Royalties	5	7425	1017	0	0	0	788	0	3529	•	2	71	•	0
Other Portfolio Income	6	1320031	229373	308454	199683	136090	81775	92637	58193	•	18520	9300	•	0
Other Receipts	7	1217053	28528	385593	80164	257272	99293	159579	64574	•	24831	34738	•	0
Total Receipts	8	311655523	5834372	108254601	29405593	66967575	28585022	29674630	14103254	•	6701503	6138295	•	0
Average Total Receipts	9	1015	102	492	2192	5028	15213	31269	62404	•	231086	511525	•	•
Operating Costs/Operating Income (%)														
Cost of Operations	10	65.2	43.3	53.0	61.5	68.9	77.2	78.3	77.2	•	75.9	79.3	•	•
Salaries and Wages	11	7.6	10.2	9.5	11.6	6.6	5.0	4.3	5.3	•	4.7	5.0	•	•
Taxes Paid	12	2.4	2.7	2.9	2.9	2.3	1.9	2.1	2.0	•	1.4	0.9	•	•
Interest Paid	13	0.6	0.8	0.5	0.5	0.5	0.5	0.4	0.6	•	0.8	1.5	•	•
Depreciation	14	2.1	2.1	1.8	2.1	2.0	2.3	2.4	2.9	•	2.7	2.4	•	•
Amortization and Depletion	15	0.1	0.0	0.0	0.1	0.0	0.0	0.1	0.1	•	0.3	0.4	•	•
Pensions and Other Deferred Comp.	16	0.3	0.0	0.2	0.1	0.4	0.3	0.7	0.5	•	0.2	0.4	•	•
Employee Benefits	17	1.6	0.8	1.4	1.4	1.8	1.7	1.9	1.8	•	0.9	0.8	•	•
Advertising	18	0.4	0.6	0.7	0.6	0.2	0.2	0.2	0.2	•	0.1	0.1	•	•
Other Expenses	19	13.6	33.7	20.1	14.5	10.9	7.3	6.5	6.7	•	10.2	6.4	•	•
Officers' Compensation	20	4.3	6.6	6.6	4.5	3.8	2.7	1.9	1.5	•	1.4	0.7	•	•
Operating Margin	21	1.8	•	3.1	0.1	2.6	0.9	1.2	1.4	•	1.3	2.0	•	•
Operating Margin Before Officers' Comp.	22	6.1	5.8	9.7	4.6	6.4	3.6	3.1	2.9	•	2.7	2.7	•	•

Selected Average Balance Sheet ($ in Thousands)													
Net Receivables 23	118	0	11	190	745	3123	6266	13057	•	56948	96610	•	•
Inventories 24	16	0	4	45	99	284	366	1186	•	4422	12090	•	•
Net Property, Plant and Equipment 25	77	0	24	151	428	1113	2722	7123	•	27545	57400	•	•
Total Assets 26	357	0	77	706	2063	7027	14868	33835	•	156234	316762	•	•
Notes and Loans Payable 27	117	0	49	218	581	1653	2961	8387	•	30434	92010	•	•
All Other Liabilities 28	112	0	20	184	574	2697	5473	12468	•	60029	105458	•	•
Net Worth 29	128	0	7	304	908	2678	6434	12980	•	65771	119295	•	•

Selected Financial Ratios (Times to 1)													
Current Ratio 30	1.7	•	1.4	2.0	2.0	1.5	1.8	1.6	•	1.7	1.6	•	•
Quick Ratio 31	1.3	•	1.1	1.6	1.6	1.3	1.4	1.3	•	1.4	1.2	•	•
Net Sales to Working Capital 32	10.7	•	40.4	9.2	6.9	8.4	6.8	7.4	•	6.0	7.9	•	•
Coverage Ratio 33	5.8	5.6	8.8	3.2	7.2	4.5	6.2	5.2	•	3.5	2.9	•	•
Total Asset Turnover 34	2.8	•	6.4	3.1	2.4	2.1	2.1	1.8	•	1.5	1.6	•	•
Inventory Turnover 35	41.5	•	59.8	29.8	34.8	41.0	66.3	40.2	•	39.4	33.3	•	•
Receivables Turnover 36	8.6	•	40.3	12.1	6.7	4.7	5.0	5.2	•	4.2	•	•	•
Total Liabilities to Net Worth 37	1.8	•	9.5	1.3	1.3	1.6	1.3	1.6	•	1.4	1.7	•	•
Current Assets to Working Capital 38	2.4	•	3.3	2.0	2.0	2.8	2.3	2.7	•	2.5	2.8	•	•
Current Liabilities to Working Capital 39	1.4	•	2.3	1.0	1.0	1.8	1.3	1.7	•	1.5	1.8	•	•
Working Capital to Net Sales 40	0.1	•	0.0	0.1	0.1	0.1	0.1	0.1	•	0.2	0.1	•	•
Inventory to Working Capital 41	0.2	•	0.3	0.2	0.1	0.2	0.1	0.2	•	0.1	0.2	•	•
Total Receipts to Cash Flow 42	7.7	3.0	4.9	8.1	9.5	17.3	17.2	16.6	•	11.1	17.5	•	•
Cost of Goods to Cash Flow 43	5.0	1.3	2.6	5.0	6.6	13.3	13.4	12.8	•	8.5	13.9	•	•
Cash Flow to Total Debt 44	0.6	•	1.4	0.7	0.5	0.2	0.2	0.2	•	0.2	0.1	•	•

Selected Financial Factors (in Percentages)													
Debt Ratio 45	64.1	•	90.5	57.0	56.0	61.9	56.7	61.6	•	57.9	62.3	•	•
Return on Total Assets 46	9.3	•	27.3	4.9	9.1	4.4	5.1	5.4	•	4.3	6.9	•	•
Return on Equity Before Income Taxes 47	21.4	•	254.9	7.9	17.7	9.0	10.0	11.4	•	7.3	11.9	•	•
Return on Equity After Income Taxes 48	20.4	•	251.6	7.4	17.0	8.0	9.2	10.1	•	6.4	10.3	•	•
Profit Margin (Before Income Tax) 49	2.7	3.8	3.8	1.1	3.2	1.6	2.1	2.4	•	2.1	2.8	•	•
Profit Margin (After Income Tax) 50	2.6	3.5	3.7	1.0	3.1	1.4	1.9	2.1	•	1.8	2.4	•	•

Table II

Corporations with Net Income

OTHER SPECIALTY TRADE CONTRACTORS

MONEY AMOUNTS AND SIZE OF ASSETS IN THOUSANDS OF DOLLARS

Item Description for Accounting Period 7/11 Through 6/12		Total	Zero Assets	Under 500	500 to 1,000	1,000 to 5,000	5,000 to 10,000	10,000 to 25,000	25,000 to 50,000	50,000 to 100,000	100,000 to 250,000	250,000 to 500,000	500,000 to 2,500,000	2,500,000 and over
Number of Enterprises	1	197029	32365	145892	7849	8802	1216	661	161	53	18	9	3	0
Revenues ($ in Thousands)														
Net Sales	2	221420125	3510592	79215575	19340320	48657859	19671814	21794549	10778110	6381266	4649253	4385239	3035547	0
Interest	3	43951	245	3326	3422	12997	5404	3229	2662	1981	9510	381	794	0
Rents	4	40545	0	2103	2001	11999	16508	5542	1876	384	121	10	0	0
Royalties	5	7416	1017	0	0	0	788	0	3529	0	2	71	2009	0
Other Portfolio Income	6	779888	118525	118490	184216	85193	72196	53724	49873	75900	14858	5391	1523	0
Other Receipts	7	956027	34144	274321	63034	257845	40689	114233	53322	45280	18666	34791	19703	0
Total Receipts	8	223247952	3664523	79613815	19592993	49025893	19807399	21971277	10889372	6504811	4692410	4425883	3059576	0
Average Total Receipts	9	1133	113	546	2496	5570	16289	33239	67636	122732	260689	491765	1019859	•
Operating Costs/Operating Income (%)														
Cost of Operations	10	62.9	30.5	50.0	61.0	67.2	75.1	76.8	76.8	78.1	73.8	80.8	75.2	•
Salaries and Wages	11	7.3	9.2	9.2	11.0	6.3	5.0	4.2	4.7	4.3	4.1	4.6	6.0	•
Taxes Paid	12	2.2	1.9	2.7	2.6	2.1	1.6	2.0	1.8	1.6	1.4	1.0	1.2	•
Interest Paid	13	0.4	0.7	0.4	0.4	0.4	0.3	0.3	0.4	0.3	0.4	0.3	1.2	•
Depreciation	14	1.8	1.8	1.6	1.6	1.9	1.4	1.9	2.7	2.6	2.1	2.2	2.5	•
Amortization and Depletion	15	0.0	0.0	0.0	0.0	0.0	0.0	0.0	0.0	0.1	0.1	0.1	1.4	•
Pensions and Other Deferred Comp.	16	0.3	0.0	0.2	0.2	0.4	0.3	0.7	0.6	0.2	0.2	0.4	0.3	•
Employee Benefits	17	1.5	0.8	1.4	1.4	1.2	1.7	1.9	1.7	3.0	1.1	0.9	1.0	•
Advertising	18	0.4	0.6	0.7	0.6	0.3	0.2	0.2	0.2	0.2	0.1	0.1	0.1	•
Other Expenses	19	13.2	33.9	20.1	13.0	10.4	6.8	6.1	5.8	4.8	11.3	4.6	6.7	•
Officers' Compensation	20	4.2	6.1	6.4	4.2	3.7	2.9	2.0	1.6	1.9	1.6	0.8	1.2	•
Operating Margin	21	5.7	14.3	7.2	3.9	6.1	4.6	4.0	3.6	3.0	3.8	4.3	3.2	•
Operating Margin Before Officers' Comp.	22	10.0	20.4	13.6	8.1	9.7	7.5	6.1	5.2	4.9	5.4	5.1	4.4	•

Selected Average Balance Sheet ($ in Thousands)													
Net Receivables 23	121	0	11	177	751	3148	6580	13549	26951	56321	90334	199523	•
Inventories 24	15	0	4	53	95	291	404	1005	1788	4401	5795	62296	•
Net Property, Plant and Equipment 25	67	0	23	147	398	890	2121	6605	11112	20605	46412	73803	•
Total Assets 26	358	0	79	728	2084	7061	14609	34461	71643	154581	294821	603248	•
Notes and Loans Payable 27	84	0	38	171	452	1159	2152	7141	9120	23612	37217	180812	•
All Other Liabilities 28	113	0	17	167	567	2940	5542	13168	29669	59458	95644	223973	•
Net Worth 29	161	0	25	389	1066	2962	6915	14151	32854	71510	161960	198463	•
Selected Financial Ratios (Times to 1)													
Current Ratio 30	1.9	•	2.0	2.7	2.2	1.6	1.9	1.6	1.7	1.8	1.5	0.9	•
Quick Ratio 31	1.5	•	1.6	2.2	1.7	1.3	1.5	1.3	1.4	1.5	1.2	0.7	•
Net Sales to Working Capital 32	9.9	•	26.1	7.6	6.7	8.4	6.3	7.5	6.2	5.4	8.1	•	•
Coverage Ratio 33	17.0	26.1	18.5	13.1	17.8	16.6	19.4	11.6	17.0	13.7	17.7	4.4	•
Total Asset Turnover 34	3.1	•	6.9	3.4	2.7	2.3	2.3	1.9	1.7	1.7	1.7	1.7	•
Inventory Turnover 35	45.9	•	68.1	28.2	39.0	41.8	62.7	51.2	52.6	43.3	67.9	12.2	•
Receivables Turnover 36	9.2	•	46.7	13.3	7.4	5.0	5.0	5.6	4.7	4.3	6.3	2.9	•
Total Liabilities to Net Worth 37	1.2	•	2.2	0.9	1.0	1.4	1.1	1.4	1.2	1.2	0.8	2.0	•
Current Assets to Working Capital 38	2.2	•	2.0	1.6	1.8	2.7	2.2	2.7	2.5	2.2	2.9	•	•
Current Liabilities to Working Capital 39	1.2	•	1.0	0.6	0.8	1.7	1.2	1.7	1.5	1.2	1.9	•	•
Working Capital to Net Sales 40	0.1	•	0.0	0.1	0.2	0.1	0.2	0.1	0.2	0.2	0.1	•	•
Inventory to Working Capital 41	0.1	•	0.2	0.2	0.1	0.1	0.1	0.1	0.1	0.1	0.2	•	•
Total Receipts to Cash Flow 42	6.0	2.1	4.1	6.5	7.1	10.9	12.1	12.9	13.5	7.9	13.7	13.0	•
Cost of Goods to Cash Flow 43	3.8	0.6	2.0	4.0	4.8	8.2	9.3	9.9	10.5	5.8	11.0	9.8	•
Cash Flow to Total Debt 44	1.0	•	2.4	1.1	0.8	0.4	0.4	0.3	0.2	0.4	0.3	0.2	•
Selected Financial Factors (in Percentages)													
Debt Ratio 45	55.1	•	68.3	46.5	48.9	58.1	52.7	58.9	54.1	53.7	45.1	67.1	•
Return on Total Assets 46	21.9	•	55.7	19.0	19.2	12.9	11.5	9.7	8.7	8.5	9.1	8.6	•
Return on Equity Before Income Taxes 47	45.9	•	166.1	32.8	35.4	28.8	23.1	21.7	17.9	17.1	15.6	20.3	•
Return on Equity After Income Taxes 48	44.7	•	164.7	32.2	34.4	27.4	22.0	20.0	17.1	15.8	14.0	16.4	•
Profit Margin (Before Income Tax) 49	6.6	18.7	7.7	5.2	6.8	5.3	4.8	4.6	4.9	4.7	5.2	4.0	•
Profit Margin (After Income Tax) 50	6.4	18.1	7.6	5.1	6.6	5.0	4.6	4.2	4.7	4.4	4.7	3.2	•

Table I

Corporations with and without Net Income

ANIMAL FOOD AND GRAIN AND OILSEED MILLING

MONEY AMOUNTS AND SIZE OF ASSETS IN THOUSANDS OF DOLLARS

Item Description for Accounting Period 7/11 Through 6/12		Total	Zero Assets	Under 500	500 to 1,000	1,000 to 5,000	5,000 to 10,000	10,000 to 25,000	25,000 to 50,000	50,000 to 100,000	100,000 to 250,000	250,000 to 500,000	500,000 to 2,500,000	2,500,000 and over
Number of Enterprises	1	2130	653	843	0	301	137	75	40	34	28	9	7	4
Revenues ($ in Thousands)														
Net Sales	2	145519277	1260253	151151	0	3478352	3050319	3427386	2787346	6052980	9905136	3298580	8456977	103650797
Interest	3	221563	901	179	0	790	493	1212	1380	472	3108	15911	7403	189714
Rents	4	181582	10	0	0	366	446	101	909	58	994	1059	899	176739
Royalties	5	499636	0	0	0	0	0	0	0	0	205	2932	3667	492832
Other Portfolio Income	6	315732	12010	1	0	479	1797	851	7553	1375	12231	33227	9447	236760
Other Receipts	7	2207738	11306	1	0	2536	7493	21526	9614	52807	91707	17718	76449	1916582
Total Receipts	8	148945528	1284480	151332	0	3482523	3060548	3451076	2806802	6107692	10013381	3369427	8554842	106663424
Average Total Receipts	9	69927	1967	180	•	11570	22340	46014	70170	179638	357621	374381	1222120	26665856
Operating Costs/Operating Income (%)														
Cost of Operations	10	83.1	81.0	70.8	•	81.4	91.4	85.6	80.1	82.6	83.5	79.4	79.5	83.4
Salaries and Wages	11	2.4	3.2	5.2	•	5.1	1.3	3.7	4.0	3.5	2.7	3.9	3.2	2.0
Taxes Paid	12	0.6	0.6	9.9	•	0.9	0.5	0.5	0.7	0.8	0.6	0.9	0.7	0.5
Interest Paid	13	1.3	1.1	0.3	•	0.3	0.3	0.4	0.4	0.4	0.6	2.9	2.7	1.4
Depreciation	14	2.4	2.7	1.6	•	2.6	1.9	1.7	2.2	2.6	2.9	3.8	4.8	2.1
Amortization and Depletion	15	0.2	0.4	•	•	0.1	0.0	0.0	0.1	0.1	0.1	0.7	1.0	0.1
Pensions and Other Deferred Comp.	16	0.5	0.2	•	•	0.0	0.0	0.1	0.3	0.3	0.3	0.4	1.0	0.6
Employee Benefits	17	0.6	1.0	3.5	•	0.7	0.2	0.4	1.0	0.6	0.7	0.5	0.9	0.6
Advertising	18	4.5	0.3	0.1	•	2.0	0.1	0.6	0.8	0.9	0.3	0.5	0.8	6.0
Other Expenses	19	3.9	6.0	16.2	•	4.4	2.6	5.0	5.1	4.7	5.0	6.1	6.4	3.4
Officers' Compensation	20	0.3	0.7	10.4	•	1.7	0.5	0.8	0.9	0.6	0.6	1.3	0.3	0.2
Operating Margin	21	0.3	2.8	•	•	0.8	1.0	1.4	4.2	3.0	2.6	•	•	•
Operating Margin Before Officers' Comp.	22	0.6	3.4	•	•	2.4	1.5	2.1	5.1	3.6	3.2	0.9	•	0.1

Selected Average Balance Sheet ($ in Thousands)														
Net Receivables	23	3915	0	4	•	960	1992	3833	5910	17151	30668	43325	120711	1143044
Inventories	24	6150	0	14	•	1013	1040	3997	8287	15290	36986	47222	116807	2302723
Net Property, Plant and Equipment	25	8703	0	13	•	846	1547	4358	11437	19294	52361	93446	378513	2915783
Total Assets	26	43336	0	39	•	3137	6439	14932	32744	70963	169912	362201	1131267	17417002
Notes and Loans Payable	27	18534	0	252	•	2809	912	3511	9119	17515	35882	162245	601682	7598756
All Other Liabilities	28	12157	0	32	•	891	3251	3294	9356	19340	38313	88847	410631	4781996
Net Worth	29	12644	0	-246	•	-563	2276	8127	14268	34108	95717	111109	118954	5036250
Selected Financial Ratios (Times to 1)														
Current Ratio	30	1.5	•	0.7	•	1.0	1.4	1.9	1.7	2.2	1.9	1.8	1.6	1.4
Quick Ratio	31	0.6	•	0.2	•	0.5	0.9	1.1	0.8	1.1	0.9	0.9	0.6	0.5
Net Sales to Working Capital	32	15.1	•	•	•	•	17.8	11.2	9.4	7.6	9.3	7.6	8.8	18.4
Coverage Ratio	33	3.2	6.1	•	•	3.7	5.0	6.7	14.0	10.4	7.4	1.8	0.9	3.3
Total Asset Turnover	34	1.6	•	4.6	•	3.7	3.5	3.1	2.1	2.5	2.1	1.0	1.1	1.5
Inventory Turnover	35	9.2	•	9.2	•	9.3	19.6	9.8	6.7	9.6	8.0	6.2	8.2	9.4
Receivables Turnover	36	18.0	•	40.0	•	13.3	13.8	10.3	11.0	12.6	11.4	6.9	13.8	22.7
Total Liabilities to Net Worth	37	2.4	•	•	•	•	1.8	0.8	1.3	1.1	0.8	2.3	8.5	2.5
Current Assets to Working Capital	38	3.1	•	•	•	•	3.7	2.1	2.4	1.9	2.1	2.3	2.8	3.5
Current Liabilities to Working Capital	39	2.1	•	•	•	•	2.7	1.1	1.4	0.9	1.1	1.3	1.8	2.5
Working Capital to Net Sales	40	0.1	•	•	•	•	0.1	0.1	0.1	0.1	0.1	0.1	0.1	0.1
Inventory to Working Capital	41	1.3	•	•	•	•	1.2	0.8	1.1	0.8	0.9	1.0	1.1	1.5
Total Receipts to Cash Flow	42	19.2	11.6	•	•	25.4	29.7	16.1	11.3	13.5	13.3	15.4	23.2	20.8
Cost of Goods to Cash Flow	43	16.0	9.4	•	•	20.7	27.1	13.8	9.0	11.2	11.1	12.2	18.4	17.3
Cash Flow to Total Debt	44	0.1	•	•	•	0.1	0.2	0.4	0.3	0.4	0.4	0.1	0.1	0.1
Selected Financial Factors (in Percentages)														
Debt Ratio	45	70.8	•	735.7	•	118.0	64.7	45.6	56.4	51.9	43.7	69.3	89.5	71.1
Return on Total Assets	46	6.6	•	•	•	4.6	5.9	7.4	11.2	10.9	9.2	5.2	2.6	6.6
Return on Equity Before Income Taxes	47	15.6	•	12.9	•	•	13.3	11.6	23.9	20.4	14.0	7.4	•	15.9
Return on Equity After Income Taxes	48	10.6	•	12.9	•	•	12.6	11.3	23.0	17.2	11.2	3.5	•	10.3
Profit Margin (Before Income Tax)	49	2.9	5.6	•	•	0.9	1.4	2.1	4.9	3.9	3.8	2.3	•	3.1
Profit Margin (After Income Tax)	50	2.0	3.9	•	•	0.9	1.3	2.0	4.7	3.3	3.0	1.1	•	2.0

Table II

Corporations with Net Income

ANIMAL FOOD AND GRAIN AND OILSEED MILLING

MONEY AMOUNTS AND SIZE OF ASSETS IN THOUSANDS OF DOLLARS

Item Description for Accounting Period 7/11 Through 6/12		Total	Zero Assets	Under 500	500 to 1,000	1,000 to 5,000	5,000 to 10,000	10,000 to 25,000	25,000 to 50,000	50,000 to 100,000	100,000 to 250,000	250,000 to 500,000	500,000 to 2,500,000	2,500,000 and over
Number of Enterprises	1	699	258	•	0	186	112	52	•	27	23	6	•	4
Revenues ($ in Thousands)														
Net Sales	2	131029052	857232	•	0	1577446	2334076	2654248	•	5219695	8512345	2119352	•	103650797
Interest	3	211077	901	•	0	426	297	1117	•	437	2999	10482	•	189714
Rents	4	180765	10	•	0	366	9	5	•	58	960	1058	•	176739
Royalties	5	496158	0	•	0	0	0	0	•	0	205	2810	•	492832
Other Portfolio Income	6	303631	12008	•	0	112	716	722	•	1321	11962	32528	•	236760
Other Receipts	7	2106605	10751	•	0	1582	1785	18346	•	47367	87810	8431	•	1916582
Total Receipts	8	134327288	880902	•	0	1579932	2336883	2674438	•	5268878	8616281	2174661	•	106663424
Average Total Receipts	9	192171	3414	•	•	8494	20865	51432	•	195144	374621	362444	•	26665856
Operating Costs/Operating Income (%)														
Cost of Operations	10	83.1	79.7	•	•	72.7	92.2	87.1	•	81.6	84.1	77.0	•	83.4
Salaries and Wages	11	2.2	2.6	•	•	6.1	0.7	2.6	•	3.6	2.3	4.5	•	2.0
Taxes Paid	12	0.5	0.8	•	•	0.9	0.4	0.4	•	0.8	0.6	1.0	•	0.5
Interest Paid	13	1.2	1.0	•	•	0.6	0.3	0.2	•	0.4	0.6	1.4	•	1.4
Depreciation	14	2.1	1.0	•	•	2.4	1.6	1.7	•	1.9	2.6	3.1	•	2.1
Amortization and Depletion	15	0.1	0.6	•	•	•	0.0	0.0	•	0.1	0.1	0.7	•	0.1
Pensions and Other Deferred Comp.	16	0.5	0.1	•	•	0.1	0.0	0.2	•	0.2	0.3	0.4	•	0.6
Employee Benefits	17	0.6	1.0	•	•	1.1	0.2	0.4	•	0.6	0.7	0.5	•	0.6
Advertising	18	4.9	0.4	•	•	3.5	0.1	0.1	•	0.9	0.3	0.6	•	6.0
Other Expenses	19	3.6	6.9	•	•	5.4	2.1	3.1	•	4.5	4.5	6.6	•	3.4
Officers' Compensation	20	0.3	1.0	•	•	2.8	0.5	0.6	•	0.6	0.6	1.7	•	0.2
Operating Margin	21	0.7	4.8	•	•	4.4	1.9	3.7	•	4.7	3.5	2.5	•	•
Operating Margin Before Officers' Comp.	22	1.0	5.8	•	•	7.2	2.4	4.2	•	5.3	4.0	4.2	•	0.1

Selected Average Balance Sheet ($ in Thousands)

Net Receivables 23	10066	0	•	•	1101	2251	4136	•	18989	31465	42547	•	1143044
Inventories 24	16745	0	•	•	978	1025	4634	•	15467	36916	46363	•	2168305
Net Property, Plant and Equipment 25	21968	0	•	•	526	1274	4679	•	16939	48671	82690	•	2915783
Total Assets 26	118593	0	•	•	3007	6318	15237	•	71676	166895	341889	•	17417002
Notes and Loans Payable 27	48348	0	•	•	1223	992	2385	•	17499	35390	113060	•	7598756
All Other Liabilities 28	31750	0	•	•	995	2632	2975	•	19077	35596	79051	•	4781996
Net Worth 29	38495	0	•	•	788	2694	9877	•	35100	95910	149778	•	5036250

Selected Financial Ratios (Times to 1)

Current Ratio 30	1.5	•	•	•	2.5	1.8	2.4	•	2.3	2.1	2.1	•	1.4
Quick Ratio 31	0.6	•	•	•	1.4	1.2	1.5	•	1.1	1.0	1.1	•	0.5
Net Sales to Working Capital 32	14.7	•	•	•	5.8	9.7	10.0	•	7.4	8.8	6.2	•	18.4
Coverage Ratio 33	3.9	10.1	•	•	8.2	8.4	19.9	•	14.3	9.5	5.2	•	3.3
Total Asset Turnover 34	1.6	•	•	•	2.8	3.3	3.3	•	2.7	2.2	1.0	•	1.5
Inventory Turnover 35	9.3	•	•	•	6.3	18.7	9.6	•	10.2	8.4	5.9	•	10.0
Receivables Turnover 36	18.4	•	•	•	•	11.1	9.2	•	12.6	11.1	6.2	•	•
Total Liabilities to Net Worth 37	2.1	•	•	•	2.8	1.3	0.5	•	1.0	0.7	1.3	•	2.5
Current Assets to Working Capital 38	2.9	•	•	•	1.7	2.3	1.7	•	1.8	1.9	1.9	•	3.5
Current Liabilities to Working Capital 39	1.9	•	•	•	0.7	1.3	0.7	•	0.8	0.9	0.9	•	2.5
Working Capital to Net Sales 40	0.1	•	•	•	0.2	0.1	0.1	•	0.1	0.1	0.2	•	0.1
Inventory to Working Capital 41	1.3	•	•	•	0.7	0.6	0.6	•	0.7	0.8	0.8	•	1.5
Total Receipts to Cash Flow 42	18.0	8.3	•	•	11.7	27.0	14.7	•	11.3	12.6	9.5	•	20.8
Cost of Goods to Cash Flow 43	14.9	6.6	•	•	8.5	24.8	12.8	•	9.2	10.6	7.3	•	17.3
Cash Flow to Total Debt 44	0.1	•	•	•	0.3	0.2	0.6	•	0.5	0.4	0.2	•	0.1

Selected Financial Factors (in Percentages)

Debt Ratio 45	67.5	•	•	•	73.8	57.4	35.2	•	51.0	42.5	56.2	•	71.1
Return on Total Assets 46	7.4	•	•	•	14.5	7.7	15.6	•	16.2	11.8	7.4	•	6.6
Return on Equity Before Income Taxes 47	17.0	•	•	•	48.6	15.9	22.9	•	30.8	18.3	13.6	•	15.9
Return on Equity After Income Taxes 48	12.0	•	•	•	47.8	15.3	22.5	•	26.8	14.9	9.2	•	10.3
Profit Margin (Before Income Tax) 49	3.5	9.0	•	•	4.5	2.1	4.4	•	5.6	4.7	5.8	•	3.1
Profit Margin (After Income Tax) 50	2.5	6.4	•	•	4.4	2.0	4.4	•	4.9	3.9	3.9	•	2.0

Table I

Corporations with and without Net Income

SUGAR AND CONFECTIONERY PRODUCT

MONEY AMOUNTS AND SIZE OF ASSETS IN THOUSANDS OF DOLLARS

Item Description for Accounting Period 7/11 Through 6/12		Total	Zero Assets	Under 500	500 to 1,000	1,000 to 5,000	5,000 to 10,000	10,000 to 25,000	25,000 to 50,000	50,000 to 100,000	100,000 to 250,000	250,000 to 500,000	500,000 to 2,500,000	2,500,000 and over
Number of Enterprises	1	1212	•	•	165	•	33	34	19	12	6	3	7	3
Revenues ($ in Thousands)														
Net Sales	2	63916344	•	•	256089	•	478449	1213141	1680911	1874387	1183425	1627433	6978101	46640947
Interest	3	112629	•	•	0	•	351	209	63	139	189	8	7390	104223
Rents	4	34552	•	•	0	•	347	83	381	0	4181	98	16469	12947
Royalties	5	316421	•	•	0	•	0	10895	56	3	736	2483	4958	297291
Other Portfolio Income	6	2079297	•	•	0	•	0	55	1485	284	1142	194	8552	2067545
Other Receipts	7	343221	•	•	1567	•	401	2934	9638	8619	12202	4625	40181	260036
Total Receipts	8	66802464	•	•	257656	•	479548	1227317	1692534	1883432	1201875	1634841	7055651	49382989
Average Total Receipts	9	55118	•	•	1562	•	14532	36098	89081	156953	200312	544947	1007950	16460996
Operating Costs/Operating Income (%)														
Cost of Operations	10	54.8	•	•	63.9	•	67.9	75.8	79.0	69.4	66.5	58.5	80.1	48.2
Salaries and Wages	11	5.4	•	•	14.8	•	6.4	5.5	2.4	7.0	5.3	8.0	1.7	5.6
Taxes Paid	12	1.0	•	•	1.4	•	2.1	1.2	0.9	1.1	1.2	1.3	0.4	1.0
Interest Paid	13	3.2	•	•	0.8	•	1.2	0.9	0.5	0.9	1.5	2.6	0.9	3.9
Depreciation	14	3.3	•	•	2.0	•	2.5	1.8	2.4	2.0	3.2	3.5	3.8	3.5
Amortization and Depletion	15	1.1	•	•	•	•	0.0	0.2	0.2	0.3	1.0	0.3	0.8	1.4
Pensions and Other Deferred Comp.	16	0.6	•	•	2.5	•	0.6	0.4	0.2	0.5	0.5	0.2	1.3	0.6
Employee Benefits	17	1.4	•	•	•	•	0.9	1.2	0.5	1.8	1.7	0.9	0.9	1.5
Advertising	18	6.3	•	•	0.3	•	1.4	0.7	0.4	3.9	1.9	6.1	0.5	8.1
Other Expenses	19	19.4	•	•	10.8	•	12.7	10.3	5.8	9.3	11.7	15.3	7.7	22.9
Officers' Compensation	20	0.9	•	•	2.9	•	3.9	1.7	3.8	1.2	1.1	1.1	1.1	0.5
Operating Margin	21	2.6	•	•	0.6	•	0.3	0.2	3.8	2.5	4.3	2.2	0.8	2.9
Operating Margin Before Officers' Comp.	22	3.5	•	•	3.5	•	4.2	1.9	7.7	3.7	5.5	3.3	1.9	3.4

Selected Average Balance Sheet ($ in Thousands)													
Net Receivables	23	5112	•	•	243	•	1447	2319	7204	16270	28720	78978	73696	1559498
Inventories	24	4456	•	•	381	•	1302	5200	7031	21975	30850	124016	143935	1024441
Net Property, Plant and Equipment	25	9818	•	•	189	•	2570	4371	8770	17151	42043	151224	269245	2855807
Total Assets	26	74130	•	•	816	•	7939	14444	32644	72580	141311	379425	939073	26165907
Notes and Loans Payable	27	33815	•	•	460	•	2607	5051	6554	25273	31064	168266	206968	12630951
All Other Liabilities	28	19714	•	•	192	•	1290	4086	7546	22752	74140	100734	262314	6854286
Net Worth	29	20601	•	•	164	•	4043	5308	18544	24556	36107	110425	469790	6680671
Selected Financial Ratios (Times to 1)													
Current Ratio	30	0.7	•	•	2.4	•	5.0	2.0	2.7	2.0	0.9	2.0	1.2	0.6
Quick Ratio	31	0.3	•	•	1.0	•	3.4	0.8	1.6	0.9	0.4	1.0	0.3	0.3
Net Sales to Working Capital	32	•	•	•	4.4	•	4.5	7.7	7.1	6.6	•	5.7	20.2	•
Coverage Ratio	33	3.7	•	•	2.5	•	1.5	2.5	10.3	4.2	6.4	2.0	3.2	3.7
Total Asset Turnover	34	0.7	•	•	1.9	•	1.8	2.5	2.7	2.2	1.4	1.4	1.1	0.6
Inventory Turnover	35	6.5	•	•	2.6	•	7.6	5.2	9.9	4.9	4.2	2.6	5.5	7.3
Receivables Turnover	36	8.0	•	•	6.7	•	8.4	14.5	13.1	10.4	8.1	6.1	15.2	7.1
Total Liabilities to Net Worth	37	2.6	•	•	4.0	•	1.0	1.7	0.8	2.0	2.9	2.4	1.0	2.9
Current Assets to Working Capital	38	•	•	•	1.7	•	1.3	2.0	1.6	2.0	•	2.0	7.3	•
Current Liabilities to Working Capital	39	•	•	•	0.7	•	0.3	1.0	0.6	1.0	•	1.0	6.3	•
Working Capital to Net Sales	40	•	•	•	0.2	•	0.2	0.1	0.1	0.2	•	0.2	0.0	•
Inventory to Working Capital	41	•	•	•	1.0	•	0.4	1.1	0.6	1.0	•	0.9	3.7	•
Total Receipts to Cash Flow	42	4.0	•	•	11.1	•	10.5	10.4	10.9	9.3	6.6	6.2	13.1	3.3
Cost of Goods to Cash Flow	43	2.2	•	•	7.1	•	7.1	7.9	8.6	6.5	4.4	3.6	10.5	1.6
Cash Flow to Total Debt	44	0.2	•	•	0.2	•	0.4	0.4	0.6	0.3	0.3	0.3	0.2	0.2
Selected Financial Factors (in Percentages)													
Debt Ratio	45	72.2	•	•	79.9	•	49.1	63.3	43.2	66.2	74.4	70.9	50.0	74.5
Return on Total Assets	46	8.4	•	•	3.9	•	3.2	5.7	13.6	8.5	13.8	7.5	3.1	8.7
Return on Equity Before Income Taxes	47	22.1	•	•	11.8	•	2.1	9.4	21.6	19.0	45.5	13.1	4.3	25.1
Return on Equity After Income Taxes	48	14.7	•	•	11.8	•	•	7.0	21.0	16.0	40.3	13.1	2.3	16.4
Profit Margin (Before Income Tax)	49	8.6	•	•	1.2	•	0.6	1.4	4.5	3.0	8.3	2.7	2.0	10.8
Profit Margin (After Income Tax)	50	5.7	•	•	1.2	•	•	1.0	4.4	2.5	7.4	2.7	1.1	7.1

Table II

Corporations with Net Income

SUGAR AND CONFECTIONERY PRODUCT

MONEY AMOUNTS AND SIZE OF ASSETS IN THOUSANDS OF DOLLARS

Item Description for Accounting Period 7/11 Through 6/12		Total	Zero Assets	Under 500	500 to 1,000	1,000 to 5,000	5,000 to 10,000	10,000 to 25,000	25,000 to 50,000	50,000 to 100,000	100,000 to 250,000	250,000 to 500,000	500,000 to 2,500,000	2,500,000 and over
Number of Enterprises	1	747	•	400	165	96	19	23	•	•	•	0	4	3
Revenues ($ in Thousands)														
Net Sales	2	59353805	•	1011227	256089	553376	233118	970224	•	•	•	0	4558255	46640947
Interest	3	111638	•	0	0	0	168	209	•	•	•	0	6675	104223
Rents	4	34102	•	0	0	0	0	83	•	•	•	0	16464	12947
Royalties	5	311398	•	0	0	0	0	10895	•	•	•	0	2417	297291
Other Portfolio Income	6	2079296	•	0	0	0	0	55	•	•	•	0	8552	2067545
Other Receipts	7	322710	•	0	1567	0	9	717	•	•	•	0	31017	260036
Total Receipts	8	62212949	•	1011227	257656	553376	233295	982183	•	•	•	0	4623380	49382989
Average Total Receipts	9	83284	•	2528	1562	5764	12279	42704	•	•	•	•	1155845	16460996
Operating Costs/Operating Income (%)														
Cost of Operations	10	53.3	•	51.2	63.9	73.5	58.3	77.7	•	•	•	•	77.7	48.2
Salaries and Wages	11	5.4	•	16.0	14.8	4.8	7.5	4.3	•	•	•	•	1.1	5.6
Taxes Paid	12	1.0	•	6.2	1.4	1.9	2.2	0.9	•	•	•	•	0.3	1.0
Interest Paid	13	3.3	•	0.2	0.8	1.4	1.1	0.4	•	•	•	•	0.8	3.9
Depreciation	14	3.4	•	•	2.0	2.1	3.8	1.5	•	•	•	•	4.9	3.5
Amortization and Depletion	15	1.1	•	•	•	0.0	0.0	0.0	•	•	•	•	0.5	1.4
Pensions and Other Deferred Comp.	16	0.6	•	•	2.5	•	0.5	0.2	•	•	•	•	1.5	0.6
Employee Benefits	17	1.4	•	•	•	1.3	0.9	0.9	•	•	•	•	0.8	1.5
Advertising	18	6.5	•	1.0	0.3	•	2.0	0.8	•	•	•	•	0.1	8.1
Other Expenses	19	20.0	•	16.5	10.8	7.4	12.9	8.3	•	•	•	•	8.3	22.9
Officers' Compensation	20	0.9	•	8.8	2.9	1.2	2.9	1.7	•	•	•	•	1.3	0.5
Operating Margin	21	3.0	•	0.1	0.6	6.3	8.1	3.3	•	•	•	•	2.6	2.9
Operating Margin Before Officers' Comp.	22	3.9	•	8.9	3.5	7.5	10.9	5.0	•	•	•	•	4.0	3.4

Selected Average Balance Sheet ($ in Thousands)													
Net Receivables **23**	7749	•	65	243	667	1233	2911	•	•	•	•	83242	1559498
Inventories **24**	6137	•	86	333	426	1742	4625	•	•	•	•	155100	1024441
Net Property, Plant and Equipment **25**	14951	•	5	189	1002	2727	4005	•	•	•	•	398393	2855807
Total Assets **26**	116220	•	243	816	2919	7903	14827	•	•	•	•	1198478	26165907
Notes and Loans Payable **27**	53343	•	0	460	1970	2430	3215	•	•	•	•	228937	12630951
All Other Liabilities **28**	30628	•	150	192	581	1449	3693	•	•	•	•	289093	6854286
Net Worth **29**	32249	•	93	164	369	4023	7919	•	•	•	•	680448	6680671
Selected Financial Ratios (Times to 1)													
Current Ratio **30**	0.7	•	1.6	2.4	1.9	5.8	2.8	•	•	•	•	1.2	0.6
Quick Ratio **31**	0.3	•	1.0	1.0	0.8	3.8	1.2	•	•	•	•	0.3	0.3
Net Sales to Working Capital **32**	•	•	29.5	4.4	6.8	4.9	6.7	•	•	•	•	21.0	•
Coverage Ratio **33**	3.9	•	1.8	2.5	5.4	8.2	13.0	•	•	•	•	6.0	3.7
Total Asset Turnover **34**	0.7	•	10.4	1.9	2.0	1.6	2.8	•	•	•	•	1.0	0.6
Inventory Turnover **35**	6.9	•	15.1	3.0	10.0	4.1	7.1	•	•	•	•	5.7	7.3
Receivables Turnover **36**	7.7	•	51.8	7.5	14.0	6.0	16.9	•	•	•	•	•	7.1
Total Liabilities to Net Worth **37**	2.6	•	1.6	4.0	6.9	1.0	0.9	•	•	•	•	0.8	2.9
Current Assets to Working Capital **38**	•	•	2.8	1.7	2.1	1.2	1.6	•	•	•	•	7.6	•
Current Liabilities to Working Capital **39**	•	•	1.8	0.7	1.1	0.2	0.6	•	•	•	•	6.6	•
Working Capital to Net Sales **40**	•	•	0.0	0.2	0.1	0.2	0.1	•	•	•	•	0.0	•
Inventory to Working Capital **41**	•	•	0.8	1.0	0.8	0.4	0.8	•	•	•	•	2.9	•
Total Receipts to Cash Flow **42**	3.8	•	9.3	11.1	7.9	6.0	8.8	•	•	•	•	9.7	3.3
Cost of Goods to Cash Flow **43**	2.0	•	4.7	7.1	5.8	3.5	6.8	•	•	•	•	7.6	1.6
Cash Flow to Total Debt **44**	0.2	•	1.8	0.2	0.3	0.5	0.7	•	•	•	•	0.2	0.2
Selected Financial Factors (in Percentages)													
Debt Ratio **45**	72.3	•	61.7	79.9	87.4	49.1	46.6	•	•	•	•	43.2	74.5
Return on Total Assets **46**	8.7	•	3.3	3.9	15.3	14.4	13.8	•	•	•	•	4.8	8.7
Return on Equity Before Income Taxes **47**	23.3	•	3.9	11.8	98.5	24.8	23.9	•	•	•	•	7.1	25.1
Return on Equity After Income Taxes **48**	15.7	•	3.9	11.8	96.3	16.4	21.5	•	•	•	•	4.6	16.4
Profit Margin (Before Income Tax) **49**	9.5	•	0.1	1.2	6.3	8.1	4.5	•	•	•	•	4.2	10.8
Profit Margin (After Income Tax) **50**	6.4	•	0.1	1.2	6.2	5.4	4.0	•	•	•	•	2.8	7.1

Table I

Corporations with and without Net Income

FRUIT AND VEGETABLE PRESERVING AND SPECIALTY FOOD

MONEY AMOUNTS AND SIZE OF ASSETS IN THOUSANDS OF DOLLARS

Item Description for Accounting Period 7/11 Through 6/12		Total	Zero Assets	Under 500	500 to 1,000	1,000 to 5,000	5,000 to 10,000	10,000 to 25,000	25,000 to 50,000	50,000 to 100,000	100,000 to 250,000	250,000 to 500,000	500,000 to 2,500,000	2,500,000 and over
Number of Enterprises	1	592	13	4	0	270	85	96	51	29	22	9	6	6
Revenues ($ in Thousands)														
Net Sales	2	52491331	526663	3312	0	1702363	1690038	2760270	2979559	2826436	5644802	4297446	9476028	20584414
Interest	3	143657	4	0	0	335	1	458	1482	1299	1850	28780	2949	106499
Rents	4	12925	29	0	0	1574	0	94	9	3275	2198	949	248	4550
Royalties	5	275520	0	0	0	0	0	0	0	0	0	0	0	275520
Other Portfolio Income	6	499260	25249	0	0	6756	215	9364	1666	5679	377	25346	610	423994
Other Receipts	7	1187177	2919	1	0	9265	82126	42815	20483	31223	8761	3596	55507	930483
Total Receipts	8	54609870	554864	3313	0	1720293	1772380	2813001	3003199	2867912	5657988	4356117	9535342	22325460
Average Total Receipts	9	92246	42682	828	•	6371	20852	29302	58886	98894	257181	484013	1589224	3720910
Operating Costs/Operating Income (%)														
Cost of Operations	10	69.9	74.8	137.3	•	84.4	81.1	75.2	74.5	80.3	78.6	77.8	61.9	64.5
Salaries and Wages	11	4.7	10.1	4.8	•	1.0	2.6	4.5	4.7	3.0	3.2	2.2	7.4	5.1
Taxes Paid	12	1.2	1.2	3.2	•	2.8	1.2	1.4	1.1	1.2	1.2	1.5	1.4	0.9
Interest Paid	13	2.4	0.9	1.9	•	0.8	0.3	0.9	1.1	1.2	0.9	2.4	1.6	4.1
Depreciation	14	3.7	6.1	28.0	•	4.1	1.0	3.1	5.3	4.6	3.5	4.0	3.4	3.5
Amortization and Depletion	15	0.9	0.3	•	•	0.4	0.4	0.1	0.2	0.3	0.1	0.4	1.2	1.5
Pensions and Other Deferred Comp.	16	0.6	0.0	•	•	0.2	•	0.2	0.2	0.2	0.3	0.1	0.4	1.1
Employee Benefits	17	1.2	1.1	•	•	0.6	2.3	1.0	0.8	0.9	1.1	0.8	2.1	1.1
Advertising	18	2.6	0.2	0.1	•	0.2	0.0	1.2	2.0	0.8	0.3	1.5	6.9	2.4
Other Expenses	19	10.7	10.8	438.0	•	4.3	11.6	8.7	7.1	7.5	7.3	7.2	11.7	13.5
Officers' Compensation	20	0.6	0.7	0.5	•	2.7	0.3	1.1	1.0	0.7	0.6	0.3	0.8	0.4
Operating Margin	21	1.4	•	•	•	•	•	2.5	1.9	•	3.0	1.8	1.1	1.9
Operating Margin Before Officers' Comp.	22	2.1	•	•	•	1.3	•	3.6	2.9	•	3.6	2.1	1.9	2.2

Selected Average Balance Sheet ($ in Thousands)													
Net Receivables 23	11365	0	12	•	1016	865	3710	6507	8852	24597	36791	85569	674987
Inventories 24	14475	0	22	•	556	1433	5751	10925	19005	65439	89595	173904	558112
Net Property, Plant and Equipment 25	17888	0	57	•	1035	1163	4669	12298	20642	45586	109635	305179	786039
Total Assets 26	124198	0	164	•	3342	8741	16332	38009	68353	154352	393402	1224113	8685002
Notes and Loans Payable 27	37106	0	110	•	939	396	5199	16572	22614	44670	108286	446180	2507414
All Other Liabilities 28	25523	0	2111	•	978	1327	5906	6500	16967	41825	129617	277729	1596806
Net Worth 29	61570	0	-2058	•	1425	7018	5227	14938	28772	67856	155499	500205	4580783

Selected Financial Ratios (Times to 1)													
Current Ratio 30	1.7	•	3.2	•	1.2	2.4	1.8	2.0	1.7	1.7	1.8	2.2	1.6
Quick Ratio 31	0.8	•	2.1	•	0.8	0.9	0.9	0.7	0.6	0.5	0.6	0.8	1.0
Net Sales to Working Capital 32	6.6	•	18.7	•	19.9	9.2	6.1	5.4	6.3	6.5	6.2	7.6	6.0
Coverage Ratio 33	3.4	0.0	•	•	0.6	17.6	6.0	3.4	1.6	4.5	2.3	2.1	3.7
Total Asset Turnover 34	0.7	•	5.0	•	1.9	2.3	1.8	1.5	1.4	1.7	1.2	1.3	0.4
Inventory Turnover 35	4.3	•	52.3	•	9.6	11.2	3.8	4.0	4.1	3.1	4.1	5.6	4.0
Receivables Turnover 36	7.3	•	•	•	•	20.9	7.5	10.6	10.7	10.2	13.7	21.9	4.4
Total Liabilities to Net Worth 37	1.0	•	•	•	1.3	0.2	2.1	1.5	1.4	1.3	1.5	1.4	0.9
Current Assets to Working Capital 38	2.3	•	1.5	•	5.8	1.7	2.2	2.0	2.4	2.4	2.3	1.9	2.5
Current Liabilities to Working Capital 39	1.3	•	0.5	•	4.8	0.7	1.2	1.0	1.4	1.4	1.3	0.9	1.5
Working Capital to Net Sales 40	0.2	•	0.1	•	0.1	0.1	0.2	0.2	0.2	0.2	0.2	0.1	0.2
Inventory to Working Capital 41	1.0	•	0.5	•	1.8	0.7	1.1	1.1	1.4	1.6	1.1	1.0	0.8
Total Receipts to Cash Flow 42	7.3	14.3	•	•	36.1	7.2	8.8	13.5	15.4	12.1	12.4	9.2	4.7
Cost of Goods to Cash Flow 43	5.1	10.7	•	•	30.5	5.9	6.6	10.1	12.4	9.5	9.6	5.7	3.0
Cash Flow to Total Debt 44	0.2	•	•	•	0.1	1.6	0.3	0.2	0.2	0.2	0.2	0.2	0.2

Selected Financial Factors (in Percentages)													
Debt Ratio 45	50.4	•	1352.7	•	57.4	19.7	68.0	60.7	57.9	56.0	60.5	59.1	47.3
Return on Total Assets 46	5.8	•	•	•	0.9	10.1	9.4	5.8	2.7	6.8	6.7	4.4	6.0
Return on Equity Before Income Taxes 47	8.3	•	206.8	•	•	11.9	24.5	10.4	2.4	12.0	9.7	5.7	8.3
Return on Equity After Income Taxes 48	5.7	•	206.8	•	•	11.9	22.5	9.1	0.1	10.8	5.8	4.2	5.4
Profit Margin (Before Income Tax) 49	5.8	•	•	•	•	4.2	4.4	2.7	0.7	3.2	3.1	1.8	11.1
Profit Margin (After Income Tax) 50	4.0	•	•	•	•	4.2	4.1	2.3	0.0	2.9	1.9	1.3	7.3

Table II

Corporations with Net Income

FRUIT AND VEGETABLE PRESERVING AND SPECIALTY FOOD

MONEY AMOUNTS AND SIZE OF ASSETS IN THOUSANDS OF DOLLARS

Item Description for Accounting Period 7/11 Through 6/12		Total	Zero Assets	Under 500	500 to 1,000	1,000 to 5,000	5,000 to 10,000	10,000 to 25,000	25,000 to 50,000	50,000 to 100,000	100,000 to 250,000	250,000 to 500,000	500,000 to 2,500,000	2,500,000 and over
Number of Enterprises	1	435	•	•	0	180	82	70	36	20	17	•	6	•
Revenues ($ in Thousands)														
Net Sales	2	45354100	•	•	0	1439455	1636032	2065295	2045786	1917885	4624242	•	9476028	•
Interest	3	137243	•	•	0	122	0	344	820	803	1044	•	2949	•
Rents	4	12632	•	•	0	1574	0	63	9	3177	2198	•	248	•
Royalties	5	271899	•	•	0	0	0	0	0	0	0	•	0	•
Other Portfolio Income	6	490892	•	•	0	0	215	9327	506	5618	374	•	610	•
Other Receipts	7	1145117	•	•	0	6726	82125	25135	15025	21951	7713	•	55507	•
Total Receipts	8	47411883	•	•	0	1447877	1718372	2100164	2062146	1949434	4635571	•	9535342	•
Average Total Receipts	9	108993	•	•	•	8044	20956	30002	57282	97472	272681	•	1589224	•
Operating Costs/Operating Income (%)														
Cost of Operations	10	68.4	•	•	•	83.4	80.7	70.6	74.3	77.9	77.7	•	61.9	•
Salaries and Wages	11	5.0	•	•	•	0.4	2.5	5.3	3.6	2.8	3.1	•	7.4	•
Taxes Paid	12	1.2	•	•	•	2.0	1.2	1.5	1.1	1.4	1.3	•	1.4	•
Interest Paid	13	2.1	•	•	•	0.8	0.0	0.7	0.8	0.8	0.8	•	1.6	•
Depreciation	14	3.4	•	•	•	4.1	1.0	2.7	3.7	3.3	3.4	•	3.4	•
Amortization and Depletion	15	0.7	•	•	•	0.4	0.4	0.1	0.1	0.2	0.1	•	1.2	•
Pensions and Other Deferred Comp.	16	0.7	•	•	•	0.2	•	0.3	0.1	0.2	0.3	•	0.4	•
Employee Benefits	17	1.3	•	•	•	0.5	2.4	1.1	0.6	1.0	1.0	•	2.1	•
Advertising	18	2.8	•	•	•	0.1	•	1.5	1.7	0.8	0.3	•	6.9	•
Other Expenses	19	11.3	•	•	•	3.1	11.5	9.0	7.8	7.6	7.4	•	11.7	•
Officers' Compensation	20	0.7	•	•	•	2.9	0.3	1.2	1.2	0.7	0.7	•	0.8	•
Operating Margin	21	2.5	•	•	•	2.2	0.1	5.8	4.9	3.1	3.9	•	1.1	•
Operating Margin Before Officers' Comp.	22	3.2	•	•	•	5.0	0.4	7.1	6.2	3.9	4.6	•	1.9	•

Selected Average Balance Sheet ($ in Thousands)														
Net Receivables	23	13534	•	•	•	607	831	2826	5792	8701	26595	•	85569	•
Inventories	24	14960	•	•	•	676	1360	6657	11567	18860	70606	•	173904	•
Net Property, Plant and Equipment	25	20904	•	•	•	1345	1162	4743	11392	19928	48733	•	305179	•
Total Assets	26	150924	•	•	•	3580	8816	16076	36809	69917	163736	•	1224113	•
Notes and Loans Payable	27	40284	•	•	•	1219	0	4268	13393	20528	43873	•	446180	•
All Other Liabilities	28	30685	•	•	•	787	1235	5186	6406	16808	43815	•	277729	•
Net Worth	29	79954	•	•	•	1574	7581	6622	17010	32581	76048	•	500205	•
Selected Financial Ratios (Times to 1)														
Current Ratio	30	1.8	•	•	•	1.1	3.0	2.1	2.3	1.9	1.8	•	2.2	•
Quick Ratio	31	0.8	•	•	•	0.6	1.1	0.9	0.8	0.7	0.5	•	0.8	•
Net Sales to Working Capital	32	6.4	•	•	•	67.2	8.2	5.5	4.4	5.0	5.8	•	7.6	•
Coverage Ratio	33	4.5	•	•	•	4.6	233.3	11.6	8.2	6.8	6.0	•	2.1	•
Total Asset Turnover	34	0.7	•	•	•	2.2	2.3	1.8	1.5	1.4	1.7	•	1.3	•
Inventory Turnover	35	4.8	•	•	•	9.9	11.8	3.1	3.6	4.0	3.0	•	5.6	•
Receivables Turnover	36	7.3	•	•	•	•	21.9	8.4	10.3	11.1	10.6	•	21.9	•
Total Liabilities to Net Worth	37	0.9	•	•	•	1.3	0.2	1.4	1.2	1.1	1.2	•	1.4	•
Current Assets to Working Capital	38	2.3	•	•	•	13.5	1.5	1.9	1.7	2.1	2.2	•	1.9	•
Current Liabilities to Working Capital	39	1.3	•	•	•	12.5	0.5	0.9	0.7	1.1	1.2	•	0.9	•
Working Capital to Net Sales	40	0.2	•	•	•	0.0	0.1	0.2	0.2	0.2	0.2	•	0.1	•
Inventory to Working Capital	41	1.0	•	•	•	5.7	0.6	0.9	1.0	1.2	1.5	•	1.0	•
Total Receipts to Cash Flow	42	6.3	•	•	•	19.8	6.9	6.7	8.6	9.5	10.9	•	9.2	•
Cost of Goods to Cash Flow	43	4.3	•	•	•	16.5	5.5	4.8	6.4	7.4	8.4	•	5.7	•
Cash Flow to Total Debt	44	0.2	•	•	•	0.2	2.4	0.5	0.3	0.3	0.3	•	0.2	•
Selected Financial Factors (in Percentages)														
Debt Ratio	45	47.0	•	•	•	56.0	14.0	58.8	53.8	53.4	53.6	•	59.1	•
Return on Total Assets	46	6.6	•	•	•	7.8	11.7	15.1	10.1	7.8	8.3	•	4.4	•
Return on Equity Before Income Taxes	47	9.6	•	•	•	13.9	13.6	33.5	19.2	14.3	14.9	•	5.7	•
Return on Equity After Income Taxes	48	6.9	•	•	•	13.8	13.6	31.3	17.5	11.5	13.4	•	4.2	•
Profit Margin (Before Income Tax)	49	7.4	•	•	•	2.7	5.2	7.5	5.7	4.9	4.2	•	1.8	•
Profit Margin (After Income Tax)	50	5.3	•	•	•	2.7	5.2	7.0	5.2	3.9	3.8	•	1.3	•

Table I

Corporations with and without Net Income

DAIRY PRODUCT

Item Description for Accounting Period 7/11 Through 6/12		MONEY AMOUNTS AND SIZE OF ASSETS IN THOUSANDS OF DOLLARS												
		Total	Zero Assets	Under 500	500 to 1,000	1,000 to 5,000	5,000 to 10,000	10,000 to 25,000	25,000 to 50,000	50,000 to 100,000	100,000 to 250,000	250,000 to 500,000	500,000 to 2,500,000	2,500,000 and over
Number of Enterprises	1	1341	•	•	0	•	93	36	42	14	21	6	11	0
Revenues ($ in Thousands)														
Net Sales	2	55614810	•	•	0	•	1953710	1616486	4180635	2465070	5677616	5399180	32443204	0
Interest	3	33280	•	•	0	•	219	537	2340	1566	2378	316	25636	0
Rents	4	10165	•	•	0	•	0	2024	161	3542	1775	245	2418	0
Royalties	5	144678	•	•	0	•	0	0	910	3107	16	0	140645	0
Other Portfolio Income	6	263924	•	•	0	•	22	12564	1395	13640	1710	201	234222	0
Other Receipts	7	424858	•	•	0	•	4367	874	5313	9998	17776	26411	310808	0
Total Receipts	8	56491715	•	•	0	•	1958318	1632485	4190754	2496923	5701271	5426353	33156933	0
Average Total Receipts	9	42127	•	•	•	•	21057	45347	99780	178352	271489	904392	3014267	•
Operating Costs/Operating Income (%)														
Cost of Operations	10	78.5	•	•	•	•	84.9	87.5	79.4	77.6	79.1	77.0	77.9	•
Salaries and Wages	11	4.1	•	•	•	•	2.7	2.6	4.5	4.8	3.6	3.4	4.3	•
Taxes Paid	12	1.0	•	•	•	•	1.2	0.7	1.0	0.9	0.8	0.8	0.9	•
Interest Paid	13	1.2	•	•	•	•	0.6	0.4	0.4	0.8	1.0	0.3	1.6	•
Depreciation	14	3.4	•	•	•	•	1.6	2.3	2.2	2.8	4.5	4.6	3.5	•
Amortization and Depletion	15	0.4	•	•	•	•	0.0	0.1	0.1	0.2	0.2	0.0	0.7	•
Pensions and Other Deferred Comp.	16	0.4	•	•	•	•	0.1	0.3	0.4	0.3	0.3	0.4	0.5	•
Employee Benefits	17	0.8	•	•	•	•	0.5	0.6	0.8	0.9	0.9	1.0	0.8	•
Advertising	18	1.4	•	•	•	•	0.4	1.0	0.4	0.5	1.6	1.9	1.7	•
Other Expenses	19	7.9	•	•	•	•	5.9	4.5	7.5	10.3	5.7	5.9	8.6	•
Officers' Compensation	20	0.6	•	•	•	•	1.8	0.4	1.3	0.7	0.5	0.4	0.4	•
Operating Margin	21	0.2	•	•	•	•	0.1	•	2.0	0.3	1.9	4.2	•	•
Operating Margin Before Officers' Comp.	22	0.8	•	•	•	•	1.9	0.0	3.4	0.9	2.4	4.6	•	•

Selected Average Balance Sheet ($ in Thousands)

Net Receivables 23	3046	•	•	•	•	1650	5311	9531	15891	20098	63422	200142	•
Inventories 24	2601	•	•	•	•	1954	3297	3972	13583	23529	74392	155424	•
Net Property, Plant and Equipment 25	7313	•	•	•	•	2241	4952	11775	24314	52531	143886	586089	•
Total Assets 26	20152	•	•	•	•	7087	15536	33675	72114	161505	366482	1559730	•
Notes and Loans Payable 27	8549	•	•	•	•	2349	4144	8462	21012	55922	88210	767479	•
All Other Liabilities 28	6539	•	•	•	•	2416	4397	11013	21757	32370	106695	555498	•
Net Worth 29	5063	•	•	•	•	2323	6996	14200	29344	73214	171577	236753	•

Selected Financial Ratios (Times to 1)

Current Ratio 30	1.4	•	•	•	•	1.3	1.6	1.4	1.3	2.3	1.6	1.3	•
Quick Ratio 31	0.7	•	•	•	•	0.6	1.2	0.9	0.8	1.2	0.8	0.7	•
Net Sales to Working Capital 32	17.7	•	•	•	•	21.8	14.0	18.8	25.2	7.5	13.1	23.7	•
Coverage Ratio 33	2.7	•	•	•	•	1.6	2.5	6.9	3.0	3.5	14.9	2.1	•
Total Asset Turnover 34	2.1	•	•	•	•	3.0	2.9	3.0	2.4	1.7	2.5	1.9	•
Inventory Turnover 35	12.5	•	•	•	•	9.1	11.9	19.9	10.1	9.1	9.3	14.8	•
Receivables Turnover 36	14.2	•	•	•	•	13.8	7.0	11.9	10.0	15.2	16.7	15.4	•
Total Liabilities to Net Worth 37	3.0	•	•	•	•	2.1	1.2	1.4	1.5	1.2	1.1	5.6	•
Current Assets to Working Capital 38	3.4	•	•	•	•	4.7	2.7	3.4	4.9	1.8	2.5	4.3	•
Current Liabilities to Working Capital 39	2.4	•	•	•	•	3.7	1.7	2.4	3.9	0.8	1.5	3.3	•
Working Capital to Net Sales 40	0.1	•	•	•	•	0.0	0.1	0.1	0.0	0.1	0.1	0.0	•
Inventory to Working Capital 41	1.2	•	•	•	•	2.4	0.7	0.8	1.3	0.8	1.2	1.3	•
Total Receipts to Cash Flow 42	12.2	•	•	•	•	21.9	28.2	12.1	9.8	13.6	10.4	12.0	•
Cost of Goods to Cash Flow 43	9.6	•	•	•	•	18.6	24.7	9.6	7.6	10.8	8.0	9.3	•
Cash Flow to Total Debt 44	0.2	•	•	•	•	0.2	0.2	0.4	0.4	0.2	0.4	0.2	•

Selected Financial Factors (in Percentages)

Debt Ratio 45	74.9	•	•	•	•	67.2	55.0	57.8	59.3	54.7	53.2	84.8	•
Return on Total Assets 46	6.5	•	•	•	•	2.9	2.9	7.8	5.7	5.5	12.4	6.4	•
Return on Equity Before Income Taxes 47	16.4	•	•	•	•	3.2	3.9	15.9	9.5	8.6	24.8	22.3	•
Return on Equity After Income Taxes 48	11.9	•	•	•	•	2.2	1.8	14.4	5.8	7.6	23.3	13.5	•
Profit Margin (Before Income Tax) 49	2.0	•	•	•	•	0.4	0.6	2.3	1.6	2.3	4.7	1.8	•
Profit Margin (After Income Tax) 50	1.5	•	•	•	•	0.2	0.3	2.1	1.0	2.1	4.4	1.1	•

Table II

Corporations with Net Income

DAIRY PRODUCT

MONEY AMOUNTS AND SIZE OF ASSETS IN THOUSANDS OF DOLLARS

Item Description for Accounting Period 7/11 Through 6/12		Total	Zero Assets	Under 500	500 to 1,000	1,000 to 5,000	5,000 to 10,000	10,000 to 25,000	25,000 to 50,000	50,000 to 100,000	100,000 to 250,000	250,000 to 500,000	500,000 to 2,500,000	2,500,000 and over
Number of Enterprises	1	216	•	0	0	55	69	21	32	•	18	•	6	0
Revenues ($ in Thousands)														
Net Sales	2	32165006	•	0	0	453422	1521249	891675	2760627	•	5127314	•	15080339	0
Interest	3	22551	•	0	0	180	199	532	1078	•	1867	•	17038	0
Rents	4	7991	•	0	0	0	0	2024	60	•	1620	•	861	0
Royalties	5	135003	•	0	0	0	0	0	0	•	0	•	131897	0
Other Portfolio Income	6	141779	•	0	0	8	0	12564	657	•	1638	•	117815	0
Other Receipts	7	292832	•	0	0	16514	3185	836	1875	•	4766	•	231124	0
Total Receipts	8	32765162	•	0	0	470124	1524633	907631	2764297	•	5137205	•	15579074	0
Average Total Receipts	9	151691	•	•	•	8548	22096	43221	86384	•	285400	•	2596512	•
Operating Costs/Operating Income (%)														
Cost of Operations	10	80.1	•	•	•	66.9	83.2	85.1	80.3	•	78.5	•	82.9	•
Salaries and Wages	11	2.9	•	•	•	4.6	2.5	3.0	3.4	•	3.7	•	2.0	•
Taxes Paid	12	0.7	•	•	•	1.6	1.2	1.0	0.9	•	0.8	•	0.5	•
Interest Paid	13	0.7	•	•	•	0.4	0.6	0.5	0.4	•	1.0	•	0.8	•
Depreciation	14	3.3	•	•	•	2.9	1.6	1.6	2.2	•	4.0	•	3.3	•
Amortization and Depletion	15	0.2	•	•	•	0.0	•	0.0	0.1	•	0.2	•	0.3	•
Pensions and Other Deferred Comp.	16	0.5	•	•	•	0.2	0.1	0.5	0.4	•	0.3	•	0.6	•
Employee Benefits	17	0.6	•	•	•	0.5	0.6	0.7	0.4	•	0.8	•	0.4	•
Advertising	18	1.3	•	•	•	0.5	0.4	0.2	0.3	•	1.8	•	1.3	•
Other Expenses	19	6.5	•	•	•	8.4	6.3	5.7	5.8	•	5.8	•	6.0	•
Officers' Compensation	20	0.9	•	•	•	4.2	2.1	0.5	1.9	•	0.5	•	0.8	•
Operating Margin	21	2.3	•	•	•	9.7	1.4	1.2	3.8	•	2.7	•	1.1	•
Operating Margin Before Officers' Comp.	22	3.2	•	•	•	13.8	3.5	1.7	5.7	•	3.1	•	1.8	•

Selected Average Balance Sheet ($ in Thousands)													
Net Receivables 23	11772	•	•	•	742	1753	6181	10429	•	21306	•	174752	•
Inventories 24	12820	•	•	•	1545	1958	3864	4192	•	25805	•	216629	•
Net Property, Plant and Equipment 25	27276	•	•	•	304	2282	4983	10815	•	53441	•	554872	•
Total Assets 26	77572	•	•	•	3552	7071	15752	32698	•	157966	•	1538485	•
Notes and Loans Payable 27	24484	•	•	•	530	2366	3575	8360	•	59248	•	517520	•
All Other Liabilities 28	24048	•	•	•	761	2478	4831	9553	•	32951	•	527094	•
Net Worth 29	29041	•	•	•	2261	2227	7345	14786	•	65767	•	493871	•

Selected Financial Ratios (Times to 1)													
Current Ratio 30	1.7	•	•	•	3.1	1.2	1.7	1.6	•	2.2	•	1.7	•
Quick Ratio 31	0.9	•	•	•	1.8	0.6	1.2	1.1	•	1.1	•	0.8	•
Net Sales to Working Capital 32	10.3	•	•	•	4.1	29.7	9.7	12.4	•	8.1	•	9.6	•
Coverage Ratio 33	7.5	•	•	•	33.9	3.7	6.5	11.2	•	4.0	•	7.1	•
Total Asset Turnover 34	1.9	•	•	•	2.3	3.1	2.7	2.6	•	1.8	•	1.6	•
Inventory Turnover 35	9.3	•	•	•	3.6	9.4	9.3	16.5	•	8.7	•	9.6	•
Receivables Turnover 36	11.4	•	•	•	5.1	12.8	5.7	9.7	•	14.6	•	10.9	•
Total Liabilities to Net Worth 37	1.7	•	•	•	0.6	2.2	1.1	1.2	•	1.4	•	2.1	•
Current Assets to Working Capital 38	2.4	•	•	•	1.5	5.9	2.4	2.6	•	1.8	•	2.4	•
Current Liabilities to Working Capital 39	1.4	•	•	•	0.5	4.9	1.4	1.6	•	0.8	•	1.4	•
Working Capital to Net Sales 40	0.1	•	•	•	0.2	0.0	0.1	0.1	•	0.1	•	0.1	•
Inventory to Working Capital 41	0.9	•	•	•	0.6	2.9	0.7	0.6	•	0.8	•	0.8	•
Total Receipts to Cash Flow 42	10.6	•	•	•	5.5	17.0	16.7	11.9	•	12.5	•	10.8	•
Cost of Goods to Cash Flow 43	8.5	•	•	•	3.7	14.1	14.2	9.6	•	9.8	•	9.0	•
Cash Flow to Total Debt 44	0.3	•	•	•	1.2	0.3	0.3	0.4	•	0.2	•	0.2	•

Selected Financial Factors (in Percentages)													
Debt Ratio 45	62.6	•	•	•	36.3	68.5	53.4	54.8	•	58.4	•	67.9	•
Return on Total Assets 46	10.0	•	•	•	32.0	6.7	9.6	11.5	•	6.9	•	9.7	•
Return on Equity Before Income Taxes 47	23.2	•	•	•	48.8	15.7	17.4	23.1	•	12.4	•	26.1	•
Return on Equity After Income Taxes 48	18.5	•	•	•	41.5	14.2	13.9	21.2	•	11.1	•	18.4	•
Profit Margin (Before Income Tax) 49	4.5	•	•	•	13.4	1.6	3.0	4.0	•	2.9	•	5.1	•
Profit Margin (After Income Tax) 50	3.6	•	•	•	11.4	1.4	2.4	3.6	•	2.6	•	3.6	•

Table I

Corporations with and without Net Income

MEAT AND SEAFOOD PROCESSING

MONEY AMOUNTS AND SIZE OF ASSETS IN THOUSANDS OF DOLLARS

Item Description for Accounting Period 7/11 Through 6/12		Total	Zero Assets	Under 500	500 to 1,000	1,000 to 5,000	5,000 to 10,000	10,000 to 25,000	25,000 to 50,000	50,000 to 100,000	100,000 to 250,000	250,000 to 500,000	500,000 to 2,500,000	2,500,000 and over
Number of Enterprises	1	2909	9	1922	153	513	41	119	59	38	23	15	12	5
Revenues ($ in Thousands)														
Net Sales	2	137879001	142895	1200540	1768309	5191330	587229	8189995	5953754	7866654	7639709	11648426	18699041	68991117
Interest	3	132473	186	3	268	311	2	1727	1627	512	1344	7577	8799	110117
Rents	4	27434	0	0	77	2280	216	836	910	478	861	8277	2704	10796
Royalties	5	14142	0	0	0	60	0	0	39	100	0	0	196	13746
Other Portfolio Income	6	215493	508	8660	12716	233	73	914	40574	3169	7430	5504	15393	120319
Other Receipts	7	1275541	1384	427	4382	23081	17106	24689	9989	32794	34574	154711	75029	897376
Total Receipts	8	139544084	144973	1209630	1785752	5217295	604626	8218161	6006893	7903707	7683918	11824495	18801162	70143471
Average Total Receipts	9	47970	16108	629	11672	10170	14747	69060	101812	207992	334083	788300	1566764	14028694
Operating Costs/Operating Income (%)														
Cost of Operations	10	86.1	87.9	74.6	81.7	79.0	82.9	87.2	84.5	85.4	88.7	85.1	83.4	87.6
Salaries and Wages	11	2.5	3.5	7.4	5.1	4.1	3.6	2.5	4.3	2.4	1.9	2.5	3.8	1.9
Taxes Paid	12	0.8	0.9	1.4	1.0	1.4	0.8	0.7	1.1	0.8	0.7	0.9	0.8	0.7
Interest Paid	13	0.8	0.2	0.1	0.3	0.4	1.3	0.3	0.5	0.6	0.5	0.7	1.5	0.8
Depreciation	14	2.2	2.9	0.3	1.0	1.5	2.5	1.4	1.9	2.7	2.4	2.0	3.4	2.0
Amortization and Depletion	15	0.3	0.3	0.7	0.2	0.1	0.7	0.0	0.1	0.1	0.1	0.3	1.1	0.2
Pensions and Other Deferred Comp.	16	0.2	0.1	0.0	0.1	0.4	0.1	0.1	0.1	0.1	0.2	0.2	0.3	0.2
Employee Benefits	17	0.8	0.3	0.0	0.4	1.0	0.4	0.5	0.4	0.9	0.6	0.7	1.7	0.6
Advertising	18	0.4	0.7	0.9	0.2	0.2	0.3	0.4	0.5	1.0	0.5	1.1	0.5	0.2
Other Expenses	19	4.5	6.1	10.6	11.8	8.1	3.6	5.2	5.2	4.6	4.1	4.8	5.8	3.5
Officers' Compensation	20	0.5	5.8	3.7	0.6	2.5	0.8	0.9	0.6	0.5	0.3	0.3	0.5	0.2
Operating Margin	21	0.9	•	0.2	•	1.4	3.1	0.7	0.7	0.9	0.1	1.3	•	2.0
Operating Margin Before Officers' Comp.	22	1.4	•	4.0	•	3.9	3.9	1.6	1.3	1.4	0.4	1.6	•	2.2

Selected Average Balance Sheet ($ in Thousands)

Net Receivables 23	2674	0	15	89	795	1273	3885	7443	14934	24315	59017	107902	613575
Inventories 24	4128	0	6	72	424	1468	2604	10236	15645	34180	88988	188465	1163476
Net Property, Plant and Equipment 25	5533	0	2	70	1099	2652	4404	9852	25718	49694	106936	252105	1510314
Total Assets 26	20481	0	82	762	3288	7438	15158	34805	69175	144413	354108	1018249	5995111
Notes and Loans Payable 27	6563	0	21	136	1796	3450	4789	12508	21242	45889	158036	425187	1465202
All Other Liabilities 28	5077	0	1	210	687	2421	3063	8837	14479	39140	74122	246088	1576760
Net Worth 29	8841	0	61	416	805	1567	7306	13461	33454	59384	121951	346974	2953149

Selected Financial Ratios (Times to 1)

Current Ratio 30	1.6	•	22.0	1.4	2.2	0.8	2.0	1.8	1.8	1.5	1.8	1.5	1.6
Quick Ratio 31	0.7	•	16.3	1.1	1.3	0.5	1.1	0.8	0.9	0.8	0.7	0.6	0.6
Net Sales to Working Capital 32	13.6	•	19.6	99.8	10.5	•	15.5	11.0	12.5	15.3	9.5	11.6	15.2
Coverage Ratio 33	3.7	•	9.9	•	6.0	5.8	4.1	4.0	3.4	2.3	5.3	•	5.5
Total Asset Turnover 34	2.3	•	7.6	15.2	3.1	1.9	4.5	2.9	3.0	2.3	2.2	1.5	2.3
Inventory Turnover 35	9.9	•	84.1	130.5	18.8	8.1	23.1	8.3	11.3	8.6	7.4	6.9	10.4
Receivables Turnover 36	18.0	•	38.1	133.3	13.3	5.7	17.9	12.5	14.7	11.2	13.8	17.2	22.8
Total Liabilities to Net Worth 37	1.3	•	0.3	0.8	3.1	3.7	1.1	1.6	1.1	1.4	1.9	1.9	1.0
Current Assets to Working Capital 38	2.5	•	1.0	3.4	1.8	•	2.0	2.3	2.3	3.0	2.3	2.9	2.6
Current Liabilities to Working Capital 39	1.5	•	0.0	2.4	0.8	•	1.0	1.3	1.3	2.0	1.3	1.9	1.6
Working Capital to Net Sales 40	0.1	•	0.1	0.0	0.1	•	0.1	0.1	0.1	0.1	0.1	0.1	0.1
Inventory to Working Capital 41	1.3	•	0.3	0.7	0.4	•	0.6	1.1	1.0	1.3	1.2	1.5	1.4
Total Receipts to Cash Flow 42	17.7	•	11.6	23.1	12.6	11.9	19.9	17.8	19.3	27.1	15.0	43.3	15.4
Cost of Goods to Cash Flow 43	15.3	•	8.7	18.9	10.0	9.9	17.3	15.0	16.4	24.0	12.8	36.1	13.5
Cash Flow to Total Debt 44	0.2	•	2.5	1.4	0.3	0.2	0.4	0.3	0.3	0.1	0.2	0.1	0.3

Selected Financial Factors (in Percentages)

Debt Ratio 45	56.8	•	25.9	45.5	75.5	78.9	51.8	61.3	51.6	58.9	65.6	65.9	50.7
Return on Total Assets 46	6.9	•	8.4	•	7.1	14.0	6.2	6.4	5.7	2.5	7.7	•	10.6
Return on Equity Before Income Taxes 47	11.6	•	10.2	•	24.1	55.0	9.7	12.5	8.3	3.5	18.2	•	17.6
Return on Equity After Income Taxes 48	7.4	•	10.2	•	24.0	44.8	8.7	11.6	7.1	1.1	15.4	•	11.4
Profit Margin (Before Income Tax) 49	2.2	•	1.0	•	1.9	6.0	1.0	1.7	1.3	0.6	2.9	•	3.8
Profit Margin (After Income Tax) 50	1.4	•	1.0	•	1.9	4.9	0.9	1.5	1.2	0.2	2.4	•	2.4

Table II

Corporations with Net Income

MEAT AND SEAFOOD PROCESSING

Item Description for Accounting Period 7/11 Through 6/12		MONEY AMOUNTS AND SIZE OF ASSETS IN THOUSANDS OF DOLLARS												
		Total	Zero Assets	Under 500	500 to 1,000	1,000 to 5,000	5,000 to 10,000	10,000 to 25,000	25,000 to 50,000	50,000 to 100,000	100,000 to 250,000	250,000 to 500,000	500,000 to 2,500,000	2,500,000 and over
Number of Enterprises	1	1717	•	•	•	422	36	83	42	25	16	10	4	5
Revenues ($ in Thousands)														
Net Sales	2	107719420	•	•	•	4253907	359559	5611326	4552955	4868310	5353849	7175745	3763926	68991117
Interest	3	122434	•	•	•	311	2	1703	610	326	1263	4735	3093	110117
Rents	4	24549	•	•	•	2024	216	836	903	466	777	8277	176	10796
Royalties	5	13846	•	•	•	60	0	0	39	0	0	0	0	13746
Other Portfolio Income	6	197419	•	•	•	191	73	687	39936	2189	7105	5504	38	120319
Other Receipts	7	1127893	•	•	•	18599	17105	19661	4589	17380	15860	110765	24840	897376
Total Receipts	8	109205561	•	•	•	4275092	376955	5634213	4599032	4888671	5378854	7305026	3792073	70143471
Average Total Receipts	9	63603	•	•	•	10131	10471	67882	109501	195547	336178	730503	948018	14028694
Operating Costs/Operating Income (%)														
Cost of Operations	10	85.8	•	•	•	79.1	76.1	86.4	85.3	82.4	87.0	81.7	74.7	87.6
Salaries and Wages	11	2.3	•	•	•	3.6	4.4	2.6	3.7	2.7	2.0	3.1	2.9	1.9
Taxes Paid	12	0.8	•	•	•	1.4	1.2	0.7	0.9	0.8	0.6	1.1	1.0	0.7
Interest Paid	13	0.7	•	•	•	0.3	1.7	0.3	0.4	0.4	0.4	0.6	1.2	0.8
Depreciation	14	2.1	•	•	•	1.5	3.6	1.3	1.7	2.6	2.4	2.4	4.0	2.0
Amortization and Depletion	15	0.2	•	•	•	0.0	1.1	0.0	0.0	0.1	0.0	0.1	1.4	0.2
Pensions and Other Deferred Comp.	16	0.2	•	•	•	0.4	0.1	0.1	0.2	0.2	0.2	0.2	0.3	0.2
Employee Benefits	17	0.6	•	•	•	1.2	0.5	0.6	0.4	0.8	0.7	0.6	0.7	0.6
Advertising	18	0.4	•	•	•	0.2	0.4	0.5	0.4	1.2	0.5	1.1	0.1	0.2
Other Expenses	19	4.2	•	•	•	6.6	3.4	4.1	4.1	5.2	3.4	5.0	7.9	3.5
Officers' Compensation	20	0.4	•	•	•	2.8	1.3	0.8	0.6	0.5	0.3	0.3	0.7	0.2
Operating Margin	21	2.4	•	•	•	2.9	6.1	2.5	2.1	3.2	2.4	3.7	5.0	2.0
Operating Margin Before Officers' Comp.	22	2.8	•	•	•	5.7	7.4	3.3	2.7	3.7	2.7	4.0	5.6	2.2

Selected Average Balance Sheet ($ in Thousands)														
Net Receivables	23	3428	•	•	•	839	1104	3755	8696	15771	27160	53456	85680	613575
Inventories	24	5360	•	•	•	428	1259	2714	10403	16160	27418	79681	136704	1254147
Net Property, Plant and Equipment	25	7197	•	•	•	1117	2559	4394	9473	24778	46629	118323	230117	1510314
Total Assets	26	26301	•	•	•	3307	7146	14981	35747	70684	139550	325755	820551	5995111
Notes and Loans Payable	27	6931	•	•	•	1762	3159	2717	12582	18522	32353	107176	220910	1465202
All Other Liabilities	28	6525	•	•	•	631	2257	3061	8205	12370	29718	64561	228341	1576760
Net Worth	29	12846	•	•	•	913	1730	9203	14959	39791	77479	154018	371300	2953149
Selected Financial Ratios (Times to 1)														
Current Ratio	30	1.7	•	•	•	2.6	0.7	2.7	2.0	2.1	2.0	2.0	1.1	1.6
Quick Ratio	31	0.7	•	•	•	1.6	0.4	1.6	1.0	1.1	1.0	0.9	0.6	0.6
Net Sales to Working Capital	32	13.5	•	•	•	8.8	•	12.1	9.1	9.4	9.9	8.9	38.8	15.2
Coverage Ratio	33	6.3	•	•	•	11.7	7.3	9.7	8.4	10.4	8.5	10.1	5.7	5.5
Total Asset Turnover	34	2.4	•	•	•	3.0	1.4	4.5	3.0	2.8	2.4	2.2	1.1	2.3
Inventory Turnover	35	10.0	•	•	•	18.6	6.0	21.5	8.9	9.9	10.6	7.4	5.1	9.6
Receivables Turnover	36	17.6	•	•	•	12.3	4.1	16.6	13.2	12.5	•	•	9.5	•
Total Liabilities to Net Worth	37	1.0	•	•	•	2.6	3.1	0.6	1.4	0.8	0.8	1.1	1.2	1.0
Current Assets to Working Capital	38	2.4	•	•	•	1.6	•	1.6	2.0	1.9	2.0	2.0	10.5	2.6
Current Liabilities to Working Capital	39	1.4	•	•	•	0.6	•	0.6	1.0	0.9	1.0	1.0	9.5	1.6
Working Capital to Net Sales	40	0.1	•	•	•	0.1	•	0.1	0.1	0.1	0.1	0.1	0.0	0.1
Inventory to Working Capital	41	1.2	•	•	•	0.3	•	0.5	0.9	0.8	0.8	1.0	4.2	1.4
Total Receipts to Cash Flow	42	14.4	•	•	•	13.0	7.6	16.8	16.3	12.4	18.8	10.8	7.9	15.4
Cost of Goods to Cash Flow	43	12.3	•	•	•	10.3	5.8	14.5	13.9	10.2	16.4	8.8	5.9	13.5
Cash Flow to Total Debt	44	0.3	•	•	•	0.3	0.2	0.7	0.3	0.5	0.3	0.4	0.3	0.3
Selected Financial Factors (in Percentages)														
Debt Ratio	45	51.2	•	•	•	72.4	75.8	38.6	58.2	43.7	44.5	52.7	54.7	50.7
Return on Total Assets	46	10.8	•	•	•	11.2	17.8	14.5	10.7	11.1	7.9	13.5	8.0	10.6
Return on Equity Before Income Taxes	47	18.6	•	•	•	37.0	63.3	21.2	22.5	17.8	12.5	25.8	14.5	17.6
Return on Equity After Income Taxes	48	13.6	•	•	•	36.8	52.7	20.0	21.3	16.4	9.9	22.6	10.5	11.4
Profit Margin (Before Income Tax)	49	3.8	•	•	•	3.4	11.0	2.9	3.1	3.6	2.9	5.5	5.7	3.8
Profit Margin (After Income Tax)	50	2.8	•	•	•	3.3	9.1	2.7	2.9	3.3	2.3	4.8	4.2	2.4

Table I

Corporations with and without Net Income

BAKERIES AND TORTILLA

Item Description for Accounting Period 7/11 Through 6/12		Total	Zero Assets	Under 500	500 to 1,000	1,000 to 5,000	5,000 to 10,000	10,000 to 25,000	25,000 to 50,000	50,000 to 100,000	100,000 to 250,000	250,000 to 500,000	500,000 to 2,500,000	2,500,000 and over
		MONEY AMOUNTS AND SIZE OF ASSETS IN THOUSANDS OF DOLLARS												
Number of Enterprises	1	3561	402	2354	110	316	192	94	40	22	15	0	15	0
Revenues ($ in Thousands)														
Net Sales	2	47218333	85173	722603	224513	1709457	3892542	3093576	2452649	2995666	3488896	0	28553257	0
Interest	3	61618	0	3	0	459	57	1122	189	107	2891	0	56790	0
Rents	4	12745	0	14	0	39	273	0	552	8	543	0	11315	0
Royalties	5	58102	0	0	0	0	0	0	4769	0	30978	0	22355	0
Other Portfolio Income	6	355005	35545	72	1	2246	1048	1281	620	1926	12884	0	299382	0
Other Receipts	7	403692	-1	771	3368	8255	5280	8240	7976	12609	30784	0	326412	0
Total Receipts	8	48109495	120717	723463	227882	1720456	3899200	3104219	2466755	3010316	3566976	0	29269511	0
Average Total Receipts	9	13510	300	307	2072	5444	20308	33024	61669	136833	237798	•	1951301	•
Operating Costs/Operating Income (%)														
Cost of Operations	10	63.6	64.0	41.6	80.0	68.1	73.4	70.9	69.5	63.2	64.2	•	61.0	•
Salaries and Wages	11	8.9	6.5	15.3	1.6	5.3	7.5	5.3	6.3	10.1	7.6	•	9.8	•
Taxes Paid	12	1.9	0.8	5.3	0.7	1.6	2.1	1.7	2.0	1.8	1.7	•	1.9	•
Interest Paid	13	1.5	0.8	0.0	0.6	0.3	0.5	0.7	1.3	0.6	0.9	•	2.0	•
Depreciation	14	3.5	1.5	1.9	2.6	2.0	3.4	4.5	5.2	4.7	5.3	•	3.1	•
Amortization and Depletion	15	0.6	•	0.2	0.2	0.3	0.0	0.0	0.7	0.5	0.7	•	0.8	•
Pensions and Other Deferred Comp.	16	0.8	•	0.0	0.0	0.3	0.1	0.2	0.6	1.4	1.4	•	0.9	•
Employee Benefits	17	3.0	0.1	0.0	0.3	0.6	2.3	1.3	2.1	2.9	2.4	•	3.6	•
Advertising	18	1.9	0.1	0.5	1.4	1.2	0.2	0.2	0.5	1.4	3.5	•	2.3	•
Other Expenses	19	12.1	49.8	23.3	13.7	10.8	6.5	8.4	8.7	11.5	12.8	•	13.3	•
Officers' Compensation	20	1.2	2.6	11.3	0.0	3.4	2.6	2.6	2.3	1.4	1.1	•	0.3	•
Operating Margin	21	1.0	•	0.6	•	6.1	1.4	4.2	0.9	0.5	•	•	0.8	•
Operating Margin Before Officers' Comp.	22	2.2	•	12.0	•	9.5	3.9	6.8	3.1	2.0	•	•	1.2	•

Selected Average Balance Sheet ($ in Thousands)													
Net Receivables 23	982	0	5	21	373	1322	2544	4612	11443	26137	•	136186	•
Inventories 24	689	0	14	28	229	872	1901	3438	6010	10386	•	71123	•
Net Property, Plant and Equipment 25	2670	0	10	323	648	4008	6222	13840	30925	60569	•	383314	•
Total Assets 26	9863	0	68	562	2016	8210	15128	34869	72252	181687	•	1703664	•
Notes and Loans Payable 27	3162	0	83	449	711	2630	5147	17736	17739	36781	•	543402	•
All Other Liabilities 28	3044	0	15	168	272	3206	3355	6056	18975	46031	•	561439	•
Net Worth 29	3656	0	-29	-55	1033	2373	6626	11077	35539	98875	•	598823	•
Selected Financial Ratios (Times to 1)													
Current Ratio 30	1.0	•	2.7	0.3	3.8	1.0	1.8	1.4	1.4	1.6	•	0.8	•
Quick Ratio 31	0.6	•	1.3	0.2	1.8	0.5	1.1	0.9	1.0	1.1	•	0.5	•
Net Sales to Working Capital 32	11499.8	•	12.0	•	6.2	•	10.0	17.6	17.5	9.8	•	•	•
Coverage Ratio 33	3.1	19.6	83.8	1.4	24.6	4.2	7.3	2.1	2.7	1.8	•	2.8	•
Total Asset Turnover 34	1.3	•	4.5	3.6	2.7	2.5	2.2	1.8	1.9	1.3	•	1.1	•
Inventory Turnover 35	12.2	•	9.4	57.9	16.1	17.1	12.3	12.4	14.3	14.4	•	16.3	•
Receivables Turnover 36	11.7	•	44.8	172.8	17.5	16.8	14.1	14.1	13.2	9.7	•	13.8	•
Total Liabilities to Net Worth 37	1.7	•	•	•	1.0	2.5	1.3	2.1	1.0	0.8	•	1.8	•
Current Assets to Working Capital 38	2292.8	•	1.6	•	1.4	•	2.2	3.5	3.2	2.6	•	•	•
Current Liabilities to Working Capital 39	2291.8	•	0.6	•	0.4	•	1.2	2.5	2.2	1.6	•	•	•
Working Capital to Net Sales 40	0.0	•	0.1	•	0.2	•	0.1	0.1	0.1	0.1	•	•	•
Inventory to Working Capital 41	608.4	•	0.5	•	0.3	•	0.6	0.9	0.8	0.5	•	•	•
Total Receipts to Cash Flow 42	8.2	3.1	8.1	9.9	6.6	18.6	9.1	11.9	10.6	8.7	•	7.3	•
Cost of Goods to Cash Flow 43	5.2	2.0	3.4	7.9	4.5	13.7	6.5	8.2	6.7	5.6	•	4.4	•
Cash Flow to Total Debt 44	0.3	•	0.4	0.3	0.8	0.2	0.4	0.2	0.4	0.3	•	0.2	•
Selected Financial Factors (in Percentages)													
Debt Ratio 45	62.9	•	143.4	109.8	48.7	71.1	56.2	68.2	50.8	45.6	•	64.9	•
Return on Total Assets 46	6.2	•	3.5	3.3	18.9	5.0	11.4	4.9	3.1	2.0	•	6.4	•
Return on Equity Before Income Taxes 47	11.3	•	•	•	35.4	13.1	22.4	8.1	4.0	1.6	•	11.7	•
Return on Equity After Income Taxes 48	8.3	•	•	•	33.9	13.1	21.0	6.8	3.2	1.5	•	7.6	•
Profit Margin (Before Income Tax) 49	3.1	15.4	0.8	0.3	6.8	1.5	4.5	1.5	1.0	0.7	•	3.7	•
Profit Margin (After Income Tax) 50	2.3	15.4	0.3	0.2	6.5	1.5	4.2	1.2	0.8	0.6	•	2.4	•

Table II

Corporations with Net Income

BAKERIES AND TORTILLA

MONEY AMOUNTS AND SIZE OF ASSETS IN THOUSANDS OF DOLLARS

Item Description for Accounting Period 7/11 Through 6/12		Total	Zero Assets	Under 500	500 to 1,000	1,000 to 5,000	5,000 to 10,000	10,000 to 25,000	25,000 to 50,000	50,000 to 100,000	100,000 to 250,000	250,000 to 500,000	500,000 to 2,500,000	2,500,000 and over
Number of Enterprises	1	1749	402	949	55	115	109	63	22	12	8	0	12	0
Revenues ($ in Thousands)														
Net Sales	2	35452141	85173	433698	56662	1052132	1857064	2312063	1127807	1759990	2431950	0	24335602	0
Interest	3	55438	0	0	0	28	57	956	31	18	2157	0	52191	0
Rents	4	9433	0	0	0	19	273	0	138	8	433	0	8563	0
Royalties	5	42850	0	0	0	0	0	0	342	0	30935	0	11573	0
Other Portfolio Income	6	334140	35545	0	1	4	1048	570	2	1260	1445	0	294266	0
Other Receipts	7	377276	-1	0	3367	7680	2165	2734	6498	11224	21078	0	322529	0
Total Receipts	8	36271278	120717	433698	60030	1059863	1860607	2316323	1134818	1772500	2487998	0	25024724	0
Average Total Receipts	9	20738	300	457	1091	9216	17070	36767	51583	147708	311000	•	2085394	•
Operating Costs/Operating Income (%)														
Cost of Operations	10	61.6	64.0	37.2	52.3	64.3	67.1	69.3	70.2	65.3	57.1	•	60.5	•
Salaries and Wages	11	8.0	6.5	13.4	0.0	5.2	6.1	4.7	4.8	7.5	9.5	•	8.6	•
Taxes Paid	12	1.8	0.8	2.4	2.5	1.3	2.2	1.6	2.0	1.5	1.7	•	1.8	•
Interest Paid	13	1.4	0.8	0.0	0.0	0.3	0.3	0.4	0.7	0.3	0.4	•	1.9	•
Depreciation	14	3.5	1.5	2.7	3.3	1.7	2.6	2.9	5.1	4.9	4.0	•	3.4	•
Amortization and Depletion	15	0.7	•	0.0	1.0	0.1	0.1	0.0	0.4	0.2	0.6	•	0.9	•
Pensions and Other Deferred Comp.	16	0.9	•	•	0.0	0.2	0.2	0.2	0.2	0.9	1.7	•	1.0	•
Employee Benefits	17	2.6	0.1	•	1.2	0.4	2.0	1.5	0.6	2.4	2.8	•	3.0	•
Advertising	18	2.2	0.1	0.6	4.9	1.3	0.2	0.2	0.3	1.6	4.1	•	2.6	•
Other Expenses	19	13.5	49.8	20.5	36.0	11.0	10.7	7.9	7.1	10.3	15.1	•	14.4	•
Officers' Compensation	20	1.0	2.6	18.1	0.1	2.4	0.8	3.1	1.7	1.4	1.2	•	0.3	•
Operating Margin	21	2.9	•	5.2	•	11.8	7.7	8.2	7.0	3.7	1.9	•	1.6	•
Operating Margin Before Officers' Comp.	22	3.9	•	23.3	•	14.2	8.5	11.3	8.7	5.1	3.1	•	1.9	•

Selected Average Balance Sheet ($ in Thousands)

Net Receivables	23	1531	0	0	5	626	1312	2685	4099	13579	29315	•	150425	•
Inventories	24	1126	0	21	5	487	732	2011	3956	8011	12656	•	74465	•
Net Property, Plant and Equipment	25	4175	0	6	324	929	3125	5266	14794	33228	65718	•	437416	•
Total Assets	26	15691	0	85	620	2699	7663	14790	34607	73079	196467	•	1836754	•
Notes and Loans Payable	27	4271	0	30	661	932	1421	2951	7346	11573	34112	•	532009	•
All Other Liabilities	28	4627	0	1	42	392	3745	3533	3536	18026	45515	•	562906	•
Net Worth	29	6793	0	53	-83	1375	2497	8307	23725	43480	116840	•	741839	•

Selected Financial Ratios (Times to 1)

Current Ratio	30	1.1	•	22.8	0.2	3.9	0.8	2.1	2.2	1.7	1.8	•	1.0	•
Quick Ratio	31	0.6	•	12.5	0.2	2.5	0.4	1.3	1.5	1.2	1.1	•	0.5	•
Net Sales to Working Capital	32	46.7	•	8.5	•	7.8	•	8.6	6.9	11.7	9.3	•	•	•
Coverage Ratio	33	4.9	19.6	707.6	366.3	37.5	26.4	20.0	12.5	14.4	10.6	•	3.6	•
Total Asset Turnover	34	1.3	•	5.4	1.7	3.4	2.2	2.5	1.5	2.0	1.5	•	1.1	•
Inventory Turnover	35	11.1	•	7.9	100.4	12.1	15.6	12.6	9.1	12.0	13.7	•	16.5	•
Receivables Turnover	36	13.0	•	53.2	343.4	16.4	11.8	15.2	11.3	10.7	10.8	•	20.1	•
Total Liabilities to Net Worth	37	1.3	•	0.6	•	1.0	2.1	0.8	0.5	0.7	0.7	•	1.5	•
Current Assets to Working Capital	38	9.4	•	1.0	•	1.3	•	1.9	1.8	2.4	2.2	•	•	•
Current Liabilities to Working Capital	39	8.4	•	0.0	•	0.3	•	0.9	0.8	1.4	1.2	•	•	•
Working Capital to Net Sales	40	0.0	•	0.1	•	0.1	•	0.1	0.1	0.1	0.1	•	•	•
Inventory to Working Capital	41	2.6	•	0.5	•	0.5	•	0.5	0.5	0.6	0.5	•	•	•
Total Receipts to Cash Flow	42	6.4	3.1	7.7	3.4	4.7	6.2	6.9	7.4	8.5	5.9	•	6.3	•
Cost of Goods to Cash Flow	43	3.9	2.0	2.9	1.8	3.0	4.2	4.7	5.2	5.6	3.4	•	3.8	•
Cash Flow to Total Debt	44	0.4	•	1.9	0.4	1.5	0.5	0.8	0.6	0.6	0.6	•	0.3	•

Selected Financial Factors (in Percentages)

Debt Ratio	45	56.7	•	37.2	113.3	49.1	67.4	43.8	31.4	40.5	40.5	•	59.6	•
Return on Total Assets	46	8.9	•	28.1	7.5	43.5	18.2	21.9	12.2	9.4	7.2	•	7.4	•
Return on Equity Before Income Taxes	47	16.4	•	44.7	•	83.1	53.7	37.0	16.4	14.7	11.0	•	13.2	•
Return on Equity After Income Taxes	48	13.1	•	38.3	•	80.0	53.6	35.4	15.3	13.5	10.8	•	9.1	•
Profit Margin (Before Income Tax)	49	5.5	15.4	5.2	4.5	12.5	7.9	8.4	7.6	4.4	4.2	•	4.8	•
Profit Margin (After Income Tax)	50	4.4	15.4	4.5	4.4	12.0	7.9	8.0	7.1	4.0	4.2	•	3.3	•

Table I

Corporations with and without Net Income

OTHER FOOD

Item Description for Accounting Period 7/11 Through 6/12		MONEY AMOUNTS AND SIZE OF ASSETS IN THOUSANDS OF DOLLARS												
		Total	Zero Assets	Under 500	500 to 1,000	1,000 to 5,000	5,000 to 10,000	10,000 to 25,000	25,000 to 50,000	50,000 to 100,000	100,000 to 250,000	250,000 to 500,000	500,000 to 2,500,000	2,500,000 and over
Number of Enterprises	1	2929	794	684	266	704	147	167	61	39	37	13	11	4
Revenues ($ in Thousands)														
Net Sales	2	125670372	483706	36160	560966	3363927	2255557	5284173	5330870	4793405	9134112	5566406	15265399	73595691
Interest	3	2289242	0	1	4	830	716	445	503	1176	4713	3654	36034	2241167
Rents	4	145405	0	0	0	5	90	680	155	4118	7781	10201	2817	119559
Royalties	5	1162214	0	0	0	0	0	226	135	293	15129	736	714	1144980
Other Portfolio Income	6	235833	22973	0	0	12231	11602	44864	21297	5019	16515	55469	24255	21608
Other Receipts	7	4913394	6043	87	19	14673	6672	37254	8729	13006	66140	9440	369789	4381540
Total Receipts	8	134416460	512722	36248	560989	3391666	2274637	5367642	5361689	4817017	9244390	5645906	15699008	81504545
Average Total Receipts	9	45892	646	53	2109	4818	15474	32142	87897	123513	249848	434300	1427183	20376136
Operating Costs/Operating Income (%)														
Cost of Operations	10	70.6	57.8	45.1	75.9	67.0	74.2	72.7	80.7	75.5	68.6	67.7	75.9	68.8
Salaries and Wages	11	5.8	13.5	10.6	4.1	10.4	7.2	6.8	4.7	4.0	7.6	7.3	4.0	5.6
Taxes Paid	12	1.0	0.9	4.2	2.1	2.0	2.1	1.4	0.8	1.0	1.4	1.3	0.9	0.9
Interest Paid	13	4.3	2.4	0.4	0.2	0.5	0.5	0.5	0.5	1.0	1.0	1.1	2.9	6.3
Depreciation	14	2.8	7.1	0.8	1.4	1.3	1.4	3.1	1.6	3.2	3.4	3.1	2.7	2.9
Amortization and Depletion	15	0.5	0.8	0.2	0.0	0.1	0.0	0.2	0.1	0.5	0.4	0.6	1.0	0.5
Pensions and Other Deferred Comp.	16	1.0	0.2	•	0.1	0.2	0.2	0.6	0.4	0.2	0.4	0.5	0.3	1.4
Employee Benefits	17	1.8	3.0	4.2	0.3	0.9	0.5	1.2	0.7	0.9	1.6	1.1	1.3	2.2
Advertising	18	2.7	0.3	0.6	0.6	1.1	0.4	0.9	0.9	1.9	1.7	5.3	0.6	3.6
Other Expenses	19	13.0	11.4	27.0	12.1	11.6	8.9	7.6	5.8	7.6	11.7	7.5	10.2	15.6
Officers' Compensation	20	0.6	2.6	0.0	3.1	3.5	2.1	2.1	1.0	1.1	1.1	0.6	0.4	0.1
Operating Margin	21	•	0.1	6.9	0.1	1.6	2.5	2.9	2.7	3.1	1.3	3.9	•	•
Operating Margin Before Officers' Comp.	22	•	2.6	6.9	3.3	5.1	4.6	5.0	3.8	4.2	2.4	4.6	0.3	•

Selected Average Balance Sheet ($ in Thousands)														
Net Receivables	23	102562	0	3	100	359	1528	2867	7132	12403	19800	44134	148222	73891289
Inventories	24	3570	0	8	21	396	1877	4024	9804	15677	31476	46627	160690	1117515
Net Property, Plant and Equipment	25	6964	0	6	83	452	1518	4402	8247	19152	45488	83764	264187	3041373
Total Assets	26	181202	0	23	711	1911	6813	16331	33983	70693	153953	309613	1221926	124367002
Notes and Loans Payable	27	26947	0	19	432	583	2459	3931	7998	20563	45235	58188	564838	16859519
All Other Liabilities	28	117008	0	6	158	498	1916	3712	11553	19963	47324	95105	292610	83432156
Net Worth	29	37247	0	-3	121	831	2438	8687	14432	30166	61394	156320	364478	24075326

Selected Financial Ratios (Times to 1)														
Current Ratio	30	1.0	•	1.7	1.6	2.4	3.0	2.5	1.5	1.7	1.6	1.8	2.0	1.0
Quick Ratio	31	1.0	•	0.8	1.4	1.2	1.5	1.4	0.7	0.9	0.7	1.1	0.9	1.0
Net Sales to Working Capital	32	•	•	8.6	22.5	6.9	5.8	5.3	12.6	8.6	9.3	7.0	6.5	•
Coverage Ratio	33	1.8	3.5	21.0	1.7	6.4	7.8	10.8	8.1	4.6	3.6	5.9	2.0	1.5
Total Asset Turnover	34	0.2	•	2.3	3.0	2.5	2.3	1.9	2.6	1.7	1.6	1.4	1.1	0.1
Inventory Turnover	35	8.5	•	3.1	77.0	8.1	6.1	5.7	7.2	5.9	5.4	6.2	6.6	11.3
Receivables Turnover	36	0.4	•	37.0	38.8	14.3	8.2	10.0	11.2	9.8	13.0	9.5	9.2	0.2
Total Liabilities to Net Worth	37	3.9	•	•	4.9	1.3	1.8	0.9	1.4	1.3	1.5	1.0	2.4	4.2
Current Assets to Working Capital	38	•	•	2.5	2.7	1.7	1.5	1.7	3.0	2.5	2.7	2.2	2.0	•
Current Liabilities to Working Capital	39	•	•	1.5	1.7	0.7	0.5	0.7	2.0	1.5	1.7	1.2	1.0	•
Working Capital to Net Sales	40	•	•	0.1	0.0	0.1	0.2	0.2	0.1	0.1	0.1	0.1	0.2	•
Inventory to Working Capital	41	•	•	0.9	0.2	0.6	0.6	0.6	1.4	1.1	1.3	0.7	0.7	•
Total Receipts to Cash Flow	42	7.1	6.8	3.3	11.2	9.7	9.6	10.0	12.8	10.4	8.2	8.9	9.0	6.0
Cost of Goods to Cash Flow	43	5.0	3.9	1.5	8.5	6.5	7.2	7.3	10.3	7.9	5.6	6.0	6.9	4.1
Cash Flow to Total Debt	44	0.0	•	0.6	0.3	0.5	0.4	0.4	0.3	0.3	0.3	0.3	0.2	0.0

Selected Financial Factors (in Percentages)														
Debt Ratio	45	79.4	•	111.9	83.0	56.5	64.2	46.8	57.5	57.3	60.1	49.5	70.2	80.6
Return on Total Assets	46	1.8	•	17.4	1.1	7.2	8.7	9.6	9.8	8.0	5.8	8.9	6.3	1.4
Return on Equity Before Income Taxes	47	3.9	•	•	2.5	14.0	21.1	16.4	20.1	14.5	10.4	14.7	10.4	2.6
Return on Equity After Income Taxes	48	2.8	•	•	•	12.5	18.9	16.0	17.7	13.2	8.5	11.1	6.0	1.8
Profit Margin (Before Income Tax)	49	3.4	6.1	7.1	0.1	2.4	3.4	4.5	3.3	3.6	2.6	5.3	2.7	3.4
Profit Margin (After Income Tax)	50	2.4	5.9	7.1	•	2.2	3.0	4.4	2.9	3.2	2.1	4.1	1.6	2.3

Table II

Corporations with Net Income

OTHER FOOD

Item Description for Accounting Period 7/11 Through 6/12		Total	Zero Assets	Under 500	500 to 1,000	1,000 to 5,000	5,000 to 10,000	10,000 to 25,000	25,000 to 50,000	50,000 to 100,000	100,000 to 250,000	250,000 to 500,000	500,000 to 2,500,000	2,500,000 and over
		MONEY AMOUNTS AND SIZE OF ASSETS IN THOUSANDS OF DOLLARS												
Number of Enterprises	1	1642	4	395	•	660	101	122	49	26	25	10	•	4
		Revenues ($ in Thousands)												
Net Sales	2	114558891	179439	7378	•	3030362	1803708	4215659	4316594	3681110	6534954	4489069	•	73595691
Interest	3	2286617	0	0	•	749	654	262	357	786	4331	2968	•	2241167
Rents	4	136200	0	0	•	5	87	521	155	1889	1085	10083	•	119559
Royalties	5	1160981	0	0	•	0	0	0	0	175	14376	736	•	1144980
Other Portfolio Income	6	216516	22449	0	•	12231	277	44001	21282	4726	15710	49977	•	21608
Other Receipts	7	4801835	5849	0	•	14308	2249	33904	10016	7213	30808	7201	•	4381540
Total Receipts	8	123161040	207737	7378	•	3057655	1806975	4294347	4348404	3695899	6601264	4560034	•	81504545
Average Total Receipts	9	75007	51934	19	•	4633	17891	35200	88743	142150	264051	456003	•	20376136
		Operating Costs/Operating Income (%)												
Cost of Operations	10	70.1	63.2	7.3	•	64.5	74.9	72.2	79.7	75.0	67.4	68.8	•	68.8
Salaries and Wages	11	5.6	6.2	0.3	•	10.5	5.2	6.1	4.7	4.2	7.3	5.5	•	5.6
Taxes Paid	12	1.0	1.9	5.4	•	2.0	2.2	1.4	0.9	0.9	1.4	1.3	•	0.9
Interest Paid	13	4.5	0.6	0.1	•	0.4	0.4	0.3	0.4	0.6	0.6	0.8	•	6.3
Depreciation	14	2.7	7.4	0.1	•	1.3	1.1	2.8	1.4	2.2	3.3	2.7	•	2.9
Amortization and Depletion	15	0.5	0.1	•	•	0.1	0.0	0.1	0.1	0.2	0.2	0.3	•	0.5
Pensions and Other Deferred Comp.	16	1.0	0.6	•	•	0.2	0.2	0.6	0.2	0.3	0.5	0.3	•	1.4
Employee Benefits	17	1.8	4.5	•	•	0.8	0.5	1.0	0.7	0.6	1.6	0.7	•	2.2
Advertising	18	2.8	0.5	0.0	•	1.0	0.4	0.4	0.8	1.8	1.2	6.3	•	3.6
Other Expenses	19	13.2	11.8	11.2	•	11.2	6.1	6.9	5.3	7.3	12.1	6.8	•	15.6
Officers' Compensation	20	0.5	0.7	0.1	•	3.5	2.0	2.1	1.1	1.1	1.2	0.6	•	0.1
Operating Margin	21	•	2.5	75.4	•	4.4	7.1	6.0	4.8	5.7	3.2	6.0	•	•
Operating Margin Before Officers' Comp.	22	•	3.2	75.5	•	7.9	9.1	8.0	5.9	6.9	4.4	6.6	•	•

Selected Average Balance Sheet ($ in Thousands)													
Net Receivables 23	182412	0	0	•	371	1647	3156	7279	13124	23076	48253	•	73891289
Inventories 24	5604	0	9	•	324	1849	4325	10559	17869	40055	49739	•	1117515
Net Property, Plant and Equipment 25	11045	0	0	•	434	1816	4731	7710	17792	41769	84879	•	3041373
Total Assets 26	318324	0	2	•	1872	6550	16728	34091	71205	158890	315439	•	124367002
Notes and Loans Payable 27	45520	0	5	•	515	1601	3040	6777	14109	36377	48473	•	16859519
All Other Liabilities 28	207200	0	1	•	472	1032	3411	11709	19993	52446	86494	•	83432156
Net Worth 29	65604	0	-4	•	885	3916	10277	15605	37103	70067	180471	•	24075326
Selected Financial Ratios (Times to 1)													
Current Ratio 30	1.0	•	0.3	•	2.7	3.0	2.5	1.6	1.9	1.7	1.9	•	1.0
Quick Ratio 31	1.0	•	0.3	•	1.3	1.8	1.5	0.8	1.0	0.7	1.2	•	1.0
Net Sales to Working Capital 32	•	•	•	•	6.3	7.2	5.6	10.7	7.6	7.5	6.2	•	•
Coverage Ratio 33	1.9	32.7	928.2	•	14.2	21.3	23.8	15.9	11.9	8.5	10.7	•	1.5
Total Asset Turnover 34	0.2	•	8.7	•	2.5	2.7	2.1	2.6	2.0	1.6	1.4	•	0.1
Inventory Turnover 35	8.7	•	0.2	•	9.1	7.2	5.8	6.6	5.9	4.4	6.2	•	11.3
Receivables Turnover 36	0.4	•	245.9	•	14.5	8.7	9.6	10.2	10.0	10.6	9.1	•	0.2
Total Liabilities to Net Worth 37	3.9	•	•	•	1.1	0.7	0.6	1.2	0.9	1.3	0.7	•	4.2
Current Assets to Working Capital 38	•	•	•	•	1.6	1.5	1.7	2.6	2.1	2.4	2.1	•	•
Current Liabilities to Working Capital 39	•	•	•	•	0.6	0.5	0.7	1.6	1.1	1.4	1.1	•	•
Working Capital to Net Sales 40	•	•	•	•	0.2	0.1	0.2	0.1	0.1	0.1	0.2	•	•
Inventory to Working Capital 41	•	•	•	•	0.5	0.6	0.6	1.3	0.9	1.2	0.7	•	•
Total Receipts to Cash Flow 42	6.6	3.7	1.2	•	7.7	8.4	7.8	10.7	8.4	6.9	7.8	•	6.0
Cost of Goods to Cash Flow 43	4.6	2.3	0.1	•	5.0	6.3	5.6	8.6	6.3	4.6	5.4	•	4.1
Cash Flow to Total Debt 44	0.0	•	2.8	•	0.6	0.8	0.7	0.4	0.5	0.4	0.4	•	0.0
Selected Financial Factors (in Percentages)													
Debt Ratio 45	79.4	•	271.6	•	52.7	40.2	38.6	54.2	47.9	55.9	42.8	•	80.6
Return on Total Assets 46	1.9	•	655.9	•	14.0	20.8	16.9	15.2	13.3	8.0	11.8	•	1.4
Return on Equity Before Income Taxes 47	4.4	•	•	•	27.5	33.2	26.4	31.1	23.4	16.0	18.7	•	2.6
Return on Equity After Income Taxes 48	3.4	•	•	•	25.9	31.2	25.9	28.4	21.7	13.5	14.7	•	1.8
Profit Margin (Before Income Tax) 49	4.2	18.3	75.4	•	5.3	7.3	7.8	5.5	6.1	4.3	7.5	•	3.4
Profit Margin (After Income Tax) 50	3.2	18.0	75.3	•	5.0	6.8	7.7	5.0	5.7	3.6	5.9	•	2.3

Table I

Corporations with and without Net Income

SOFT DRINK AND ICE

MONEY AMOUNTS AND SIZE OF ASSETS IN THOUSANDS OF DOLLARS

Item Description for Accounting Period 7/11 Through 6/12		Total	Zero Assets	Under 500	500 to 1,000	1,000 to 5,000	5,000 to 10,000	10,000 to 25,000	25,000 to 50,000	50,000 to 100,000	100,000 to 250,000	250,000 to 500,000	500,000 to 2,500,000	2,500,000 and over
Number of Enterprises	1	961	420	279	137	35	9	18	22	13	13	8	4	3
Revenues ($ in Thousands)														
Net Sales	2	46597158	151	95313	294206	172774	134592	784437	1773569	1281144	4097955	3056163	4645804	30261051
Interest	3	82365	0	0	19	568	1	6	467	1986	584	1341	919	76474
Rents	4	40690	0	0	0	0	0	148	0	71	196	8094	7	32174
Royalties	5	2805661	0	0	0	0	0	0	0	0	0	9	0	2805652
Other Portfolio Income	6	1959869	7461	0	8315	26	3710	1063	965	943	52742	21593	861	1862189
Other Receipts	7	2344232	3728	0	-6	314	29875	13914	4408	4798	39673	40955	100615	2105958
Total Receipts	8	53829975	11340	95313	302534	173682	168178	799568	1779409	1288942	4191150	3128155	4748206	37143498
Average Total Receipts	9	56015	27	342	2208	4962	18686	44420	80882	99149	322396	391019	1187052	12381166
Operating Costs/Operating Income (%)														
Cost of Operations	10	50.3	21.2	79.2	70.8	52.1	69.9	73.7	71.2	67.5	67.2	61.9	60.6	42.3
Salaries and Wages	11	13.4	34.4	•	1.6	5.5	14.6	5.4	6.5	11.3	6.5	12.4	14.1	15.3
Taxes Paid	12	2.1	32.5	0.1	2.9	2.9	2.1	1.2	1.4	2.0	1.1	2.3	2.1	2.3
Interest Paid	13	3.2	9.9	•	1.0	0.9	0.0	0.4	0.5	1.0	0.5	3.6	4.0	3.8
Depreciation	14	6.0	5.3	0.1	3.4	5.2	2.5	1.5	3.1	5.3	2.9	5.5	5.6	6.8
Amortization and Depletion	15	1.3	•	•	0.9	•	•	0.6	0.0	0.4	0.6	1.5	1.2	1.5
Pensions and Other Deferred Comp.	16	1.6	•	•	1.0	0.1	1.2	0.1	0.5	0.3	0.4	0.5	0.4	2.2
Employee Benefits	17	3.6	5.3	•	0.9	0.3	3.1	0.7	1.9	2.4	1.6	2.1	2.6	4.5
Advertising	18	3.9	•	0.0	1.5	2.3	0.9	2.6	7.2	0.8	2.6	1.5	0.7	4.9
Other Expenses	19	18.4	914.6	0.4	26.6	20.5	24.9	8.1	5.3	7.5	11.0	10.4	11.5	22.7
Officers' Compensation	20	0.4	•	•	3.6	2.5	0.3	1.6	1.8	0.7	0.8	0.4	0.7	0.2
Operating Margin	21	•	•	20.2	•	7.6	•	4.1	0.5	0.7	4.7	•	•	•
Operating Margin Before Officers' Comp.	22	•	•	20.2	•	10.1	•	5.6	2.4	1.5	5.6	•	•	•

Selected Average Balance Sheet ($ in Thousands)

Net Receivables 23	4408	0	0	122	318	1703	3159	7869	11814	23289	26716	123563	932722
Inventories 24	2752	0	7	210	296	990	2242	6124	6885	16033	20501	69764	560352
Net Property, Plant and Equipment 25	13655	0	3	62	2324	1147	3423	9249	27098	54966	98700	310374	3219426
Total Assets 26	69262	0	35	648	4110	5615	17391	35171	63709	151679	319545	931084	18700256
Notes and Loans Payable 27	36229	0	0	310	1131	0	3243	17604	20818	37775	133482	565772	10065242
All Other Liabilities 28	19380	0	8	215	817	762	3424	16262	14302	48063	100608	348636	5042445
Net Worth 29	13654	0	27	123	2162	4853	10724	1304	28588	65842	85455	16676	3592569

Selected Financial Ratios (Times to 1)

Current Ratio 30	0.5	•	4.1	1.4	0.5	3.9	2.3	1.1	2.1	1.5	0.8	0.7	0.4
Quick Ratio 31	0.3	•	3.1	0.8	0.4	2.7	1.5	0.7	1.4	0.9	0.5	0.4	0.2
Net Sales to Working Capital 32	•	•	14.1	14.4	•	6.7	10.3	44.1	7.6	19.7	•	•	•
Coverage Ratio 33	5.7	654.0	•	•	9.5	3714.0	14.8	2.9	2.4	14.3	1.0	0.7	6.8
Total Asset Turnover 34	0.7	•	9.8	3.3	1.2	2.7	2.5	2.3	1.5	2.1	1.2	1.2	0.5
Inventory Turnover 35	8.9	•	37.9	7.3	8.7	10.6	14.3	9.4	9.7	13.2	11.5	10.1	7.6
Receivables Turnover 36	10.5	•	•	•	13.0	9.7	15.2	10.3	7.1	11.3	14.4	9.0	10.5
Total Liabilities to Net Worth 37	4.1	•	0.3	4.3	0.9	0.2	0.6	26.0	1.2	1.3	2.7	54.8	4.2
Current Assets to Working Capital 38	•	•	1.3	3.7	•	1.3	1.8	8.8	1.9	3.1	•	•	•
Current Liabilities to Working Capital 39	•	•	0.3	2.7	•	0.3	0.8	7.8	0.9	2.1	•	•	•
Working Capital to Net Sales 40	•	•	0.1	0.1	•	0.1	0.1	0.0	0.1	0.1	•	•	•
Inventory to Working Capital 41	•	•	0.3	1.4	•	0.4	0.5	2.7	0.5	1.1	•	•	•
Total Receipts to Cash Flow 42	3.7	0.0	4.9	16.7	4.1	6.4	7.5	22.3	14.6	6.0	15.3	14.3	2.7
Cost of Goods to Cash Flow 43	1.9	0.0	3.9	11.8	2.2	4.5	5.5	15.9	9.9	4.1	9.4	8.7	1.2
Cash Flow to Total Debt 44	0.2	•	9.1	0.2	0.6	3.0	0.9	0.1	0.2	0.6	0.1	0.1	0.2

Selected Financial Factors (in Percentages)

Debt Ratio 45	80.3	•	22.0	81.0	47.4	13.6	38.3	96.3	55.1	56.6	73.3	98.2	80.8
Return on Total Assets 46	12.9	•	198.1	•	10.9	14.7	16.1	3.0	3.6	15.7	4.5	3.3	14.1
Return on Equity Before Income Taxes 47	53.9	•	254.1	•	18.5	17.0	24.3	53.3	4.6	33.6	0.6	•	62.5
Return on Equity After Income Taxes 48	35.3	•	254.1	•	18.3	13.2	23.2	40.2	3.9	30.5	•	•	40.7
Profit Margin (Before Income Tax) 49	15.2	6486.8	20.2	•	8.1	5.5	6.0	0.9	1.3	7.0	0.1	•	22.3
Profit Margin (After Income Tax) 50	10.0	6353.6	20.2	•	8.0	4.3	5.7	0.7	1.1	6.4	•	•	14.5

SOFT DRINK AND ICE

MONEY AMOUNTS AND SIZE OF ASSETS IN THOUSANDS OF DOLLARS

Item Description for Accounting Period 7/11 Through 6/12		Total	Zero Assets	Under 500	500 to 1000	1,000 to 5,000	5,000 to 10,000	10,000 to 25,000	25,000 to 50,000	50,000 to 100,000	100,000 to 250,000	250,000 to 500,000	500,000 to 2,500,000	2,500,000 and over
Number of Enterprises	1	152	•	•	60	18	9	18	16	10	9	•	0	3
Revenues ($ in Thousands)														
Net Sales	2	41574218	•	•	209432	128814	134592	784437	1126698	1029170	3344549	•	0	30261051
Interest	3	81099	•	•	6	568	1	6	467	1757	399	•	0	76474
Rents	4	39539	•	•	0	0	0	148	0	71	0	•	0	32174
Royalties	5	2805652	•	•	0	0	0	0	0	0	0	•	0	2805652
Other Portfolio Income	6	1928208	•	•	0	26	3710	1063	648	851	47881	•	0	1862189
Other Receipts	7	2322865	•	•	9	315	29875	13914	4076	3336	34068	•	0	2105958
Total Receipts	8	48751581	•	•	209447	129723	168178	799568	1131889	1035185	3426897	•	0	37143498
Average Total Receipts	9	320734	•	•	3491	7207	18686	44420	70743	103518	380766	•	•	12381166
Operating Costs/Operating Income (%)														
Cost of Operations	10	47.8	•	•	65.6	47.4	69.9	73.7	58.0	67.5	66.6	•	•	42.3
Salaries and Wages	11	14.0	•	•	0.5	5.2	14.6	5.4	9.6	11.4	6.0	•	•	15.3
Taxes Paid	12	2.1	•	•	2.8	1.9	2.1	1.2	1.7	1.9	0.9	•	•	2.3
Interest Paid	13	3.0	•	•	0.3	•	0.0	0.4	0.5	0.9	0.3	•	•	3.8
Depreciation	14	5.8	•	•	1.7	2.6	2.5	1.5	3.1	4.5	1.9	•	•	6.8
Amortization and Depletion	15	1.2	•	•	0.2	•	•	0.6	0.0	0.3	0.5	•	•	1.5
Pensions and Other Deferred Comp.	16	1.7	•	•	1.5	0.1	1.2	0.1	0.7	0.3	0.3	•	•	2.2
Employee Benefits	17	3.9	•	•	0.5	•	3.1	0.7	2.7	2.6	1.5	•	•	4.5
Advertising	18	4.3	•	•	1.4	3.1	0.9	2.6	10.8	0.9	3.0	•	•	4.9
Other Expenses	19	19.6	•	•	20.8	19.0	24.9	8.1	6.3	7.3	11.1	•	•	22.7
Officers' Compensation	20	0.4	•	•	2.6	3.3	0.3	1.6	2.9	0.7	0.8	•	•	0.2
Operating Margin	21	•	•	•	2.1	17.5	•	4.1	3.7	1.6	7.2	•	•	•
Operating Margin Before Officers' Comp.	22	•	•	•	4.7	20.8	•	5.6	6.6	2.3	8.0	•	•	•

	Selected Average Balance Sheet ($ in Thousands)												
Net Receivables 23	24829	•	•	120	534	1703	3159	5032	13032	26666	•	•	932722
Inventories 24	15454	•	•	369	77	990	1310	5371	6730	17360	•	•	560352
Net Property, Plant and Equipment 25	75672	•	•	74	1390	1147	3423	8314	22591	42115	•	•	3219426
Total Assets 26	411897	•	•	620	4244	5615	17391	35087	59654	151970	•	•	18700256
Notes and Loans Payable 27	209132	•	•	157	0	0	3243	7642	12775	27247	•	•	10065242
All Other Liabilities 28	115744	•	•	59	471	762	3424	11790	13742	49706	•	•	5042445
Net Worth 29	87020	•	•	404	3774	4853	10724	15655	33136	75016	•	•	3592569
	Selected Financial Ratios (Times to 1)												
Current Ratio 30	0.5	•	•	9.0	2.8	3.9	2.3	1.9	2.6	1.5	•	•	0.4
Quick Ratio 31	0.3	•	•	3.4	2.1	2.7	1.5	1.1	1.8	1.0	•	•	0.2
Net Sales to Working Capital 32	•	•	•	7.3	8.6	6.7	10.3	10.7	5.9	18.0	•	•	•
Coverage Ratio 33	6.9	•	•	8.7	•	3714.0	14.8	9.3	3.4	32.8	•	•	6.8
Total Asset Turnover 34	0.7	•	•	5.6	1.7	2.7	2.5	2.0	1.7	2.4	•	•	0.5
Inventory Turnover 35	8.5	•	•	6.2	43.9	10.6	24.5	7.6	10.3	14.3	•	•	7.6
Receivables Turnover 36	10.5	•	•	22.1	13.6	9.7	21.4	•	6.6	12.4	•	•	10.5
Total Liabilities to Net Worth 37	3.7	•	•	0.5	0.1	0.2	0.6	1.2	0.8	1.0	•	•	4.2
Current Assets to Working Capital 38	•	•	•	1.1	1.6	1.3	1.8	2.1	1.6	2.8	•	•	•
Current Liabilities to Working Capital 39	•	•	•	0.1	0.6	0.3	0.8	1.1	0.6	1.8	•	•	•
Working Capital to Net Sales 40	•	•	•	0.1	0.1	0.1	0.1	0.1	0.2	0.1	•	•	•
Inventory to Working Capital 41	•	•	•	0.7	0.1	0.4	0.5	0.8	0.3	0.9	•	•	•
Total Receipts to Cash Flow 42	3.3	•	•	5.8	3.1	6.4	7.5	11.7	13.6	5.1	•	•	2.7
Cost of Goods to Cash Flow 43	1.6	•	•	3.8	1.5	4.5	5.5	6.8	9.1	3.4	•	•	1.2
Cash Flow to Total Debt 44	0.3	•	•	2.8	4.9	3.0	0.9	0.3	0.3	0.9	•	•	0.2
	Selected Financial Factors (in Percentages)												
Debt Ratio 45	78.9	•	•	34.9	11.1	13.6	38.3	55.4	44.5	50.6	•	•	80.8
Return on Total Assets 46	13.8	•	•	13.4	30.6	14.7	16.1	9.4	5.2	24.4	•	•	14.1
Return on Equity Before Income Taxes 47	55.9	•	•	18.2	34.4	17.0	24.3	18.7	6.7	48.0	•	•	62.5
Return on Equity After Income Taxes 48	37.5	•	•	14.9	34.1	13.2	23.2	17.2	5.9	44.0	•	•	40.7
Profit Margin (Before Income Tax) 49	17.8	•	•	2.1	18.1	5.5	6.0	4.2	2.1	9.7	•	•	22.3
Profit Margin (After Income Tax) 50	11.9	•	•	1.7	18.0	4.3	5.7	3.8	1.9	8.9	•	•	14.5

Table I

Corporations with and without Net Income

BREWERIES

MONEY AMOUNTS AND SIZE OF ASSETS IN THOUSANDS OF DOLLARS

Item Description for Accounting Period 7/11 Through 6/12		Total	Zero Assets	Under 500	500 to 1,000	1,000 to 5,000	5,000 to 10,000	10,000 to 25,000	25,000 to 50,000	50,000 to 100,000	100,000 to 250,000	250,000 to 500,000	500,000 to 2,500,000	2,500,000 and over
Number of Enterprises	1	370	0	164	6	147	15	12	19	0	4	4	0	0
Revenues ($ in Thousands)														
Net Sales	2	20276742	0	78685	20734	486749	170038	229435	1246941	0	951501	17092658	0	0
Interest	3	76012	0	0	0	0	33	27	125	0	5	75822	0	0
Rents	4	2689	0	0	0	0	0	0	11	0	0	2678	0	0
Royalties	5	230482	0	0	0	0	0	46	0	0	0	230436	0	0
Other Portfolio Income	6	36946	0	4	0	298	266	245	160	0	12816	23155	0	0
Other Receipts	7	508598	0	145	1565	4332	29	1114	7959	0	6154	487303	0	0
Total Receipts	8	21131469	0	78834	22299	491379	170366	230867	1255196	0	970476	17912052	0	0
Average Total Receipts	9	57112	•	481	3716	3343	11358	19239	66063	•	242619	4478013	•	•
Operating Costs/Operating Income (%)														
Cost of Operations	10	40.3	•	43.9	•	36.3	59.3	62.5	59.2	•	55.2	37.7	•	•
Salaries and Wages	11	6.8	•	5.5	•	7.0	2.7	6.4	6.6	•	5.2	6.9	•	•
Taxes Paid	12	12.5	•	3.5	0.0	3.9	1.3	4.8	4.7	•	10.0	13.7	•	•
Interest Paid	13	13.4	•	2.2	•	2.0	0.0	1.4	1.0	•	1.2	15.6	•	•
Depreciation	14	3.4	•	18.8	•	7.7	8.5	6.7	6.9	•	4.6	2.8	•	•
Amortization and Depletion	15	1.5	•	0.2	•	•	0.1	0.1	0.1	•	0.7	1.7	•	•
Pensions and Other Deferred Comp.	16	2.0	•	0.6	•	0.2	1.7	0.2	0.4	•	0.3	2.2	•	•
Employee Benefits	17	1.4	•	0.4	•	0.8	1.8	1.9	1.2	•	1.4	1.4	•	•
Advertising	18	3.8	•	1.8	•	1.0	0.3	3.6	2.5	•	2.2	4.2	•	•
Other Expenses	19	9.8	•	12.4	3.2	10.3	7.8	6.3	7.8	•	13.0	9.8	•	•
Officers' Compensation	20	0.4	•	2.1	•	3.0	2.6	3.4	1.4	•	0.7	0.2	•	•
Operating Margin	21	4.8	•	8.6	96.8	27.9	14.0	2.8	8.4	•	5.5	3.6	•	•
Operating Margin Before Officers' Comp.	22	5.2	•	10.7	96.8	30.9	16.6	6.1	9.8	•	6.2	3.8	•	•

Selected Average Balance Sheet ($ in Thousands)													
Net Receivables **23**	6456	•	47	631	46	1432	1700	8577	•	40476	500936	•	•
Inventories **24**	1946	•	15	0	461	1383	2391	3329	•	13718	122492	•	•
Net Property, Plant and Equipment **25**	19813	•	101	0	1512	2428	9483	25212	•	73126	1542544	•	•
Total Assets **26**	237747	•	186	734	3208	8566	15130	44324	•	188631	21388254	•	•
Notes and Loans Payable **27**	130546	•	240	0	1105	2406	5300	11159	•	36860	11910217	•	•
All Other Liabilities **28**	52283	•	-19	0	470	1718	7975	9012	•	46530	4699991	•	•
Net Worth **29**	54918	•	-35	734	1633	4442	1855	24154	•	105240	4778047	•	•
Selected Financial Ratios (Times to 1)													
Current Ratio **30**	1.2	•	1.1	•	2.8	4.0	1.7	1.7	•	1.9	1.1	•	•
Quick Ratio **31**	0.9	•	0.8	•	1.8	2.4	1.0	1.2	•	1.4	0.9	•	•
Net Sales to Working Capital **32**	13.7	•	127.3	4.7	3.5	2.9	8.8	10.0	•	8.5	16.9	•	•
Coverage Ratio **33**	1.7	•	5.1	•	15.8	365.1	3.4	10.5	•	7.5	1.5	•	•
Total Asset Turnover **34**	0.2	•	2.6	4.7	1.0	1.3	1.3	1.5	•	1.3	0.2	•	•
Inventory Turnover **35**	11.3	•	14.5	•	2.6	4.9	5.0	11.7	•	9.6	13.2	•	•
Receivables Turnover **36**	5.5	•	6.9	11.0	59.8	12.8	8.2	10.8	•	6.0	17.1	•	•
Total Liabilities to Net Worth **37**	3.3	•	•	•	1.0	0.9	7.2	0.8	•	0.8	3.5	•	•
Current Assets to Working Capital **38**	6.8	•	19.5	1.0	1.6	1.3	2.4	2.4	•	2.1	9.1	•	•
Current Liabilities to Working Capital **39**	5.8	•	18.5	•	0.6	0.3	1.4	1.4	•	1.1	8.1	•	•
Working Capital to Net Sales **40**	0.1	•	0.0	0.2	0.3	0.3	0.1	0.1	•	0.1	0.1	•	•
Inventory to Working Capital **41**	0.5	•	4.4	•	0.4	0.5	0.8	0.6	•	0.4	0.5	•	•
Total Receipts to Cash Flow **42**	6.1	•	6.1	0.9	3.0	5.0	12.2	6.5	•	5.6	6.3	•	•
Cost of Goods to Cash Flow **43**	2.5	•	2.7	•	1.1	3.0	7.6	3.9	•	3.1	2.4	•	•
Cash Flow to Total Debt **44**	0.0	•	0.4	•	0.7	0.6	0.1	0.5	•	0.5	0.0	•	•
Selected Financial Factors (in Percentages)													
Debt Ratio **45**	76.9	•	118.9	•	49.1	48.1	87.7	45.5	•	44.2	77.7	•	•
Return on Total Assets **46**	5.2	•	28.2	491.3	31.8	18.8	6.1	14.8	•	10.9	4.8	•	•
Return on Equity Before Income Taxes **47**	9.0	•	•	491.3	58.5	36.1	35.1	24.6	•	16.9	7.5	•	•
Return on Equity After Income Taxes **48**	6.5	•	•	491.3	58.5	35.1	26.1	23.7	•	16.6	5.0	•	•
Profit Margin (Before Income Tax) **49**	9.0	•	8.8	104.3	28.9	14.1	3.4	9.0	•	7.5	8.4	•	•
Profit Margin (After Income Tax) **50**	6.5	•	2.5	104.3	28.9	13.8	2.5	8.7	•	7.4	5.6	•	•

Table II

Corporations with Net Income

BREWERIES

MONEY AMOUNTS AND SIZE OF ASSETS IN THOUSANDS OF DOLLARS

Item Description for Accounting Period 7/11 Through 6/12		Total	Zero Assets	Under 500	500 to 1,000	1,000 to 5,000	5,000 to 10,000	10,000 to 25,000	25,000 to 50,000	50,000 to 100,000	100,000 to 250,000	250,000 to 500,000	500,000 to 2,500,000	2,500,000 and over
Number of Enterprises	1	262	0	•	6	147	15	8	14	0	4	•	0	0
Revenues ($ in Thousands)														
Net Sales	2	19992316	0	•	20734	486749	170038	153300	1042312	0	951501	•	0	0
Interest	3	76010	0	•	0	0	33	27	123	0	5	•	0	0
Rents	4	2689	0	•	0	0	0	0	11	0	0	•	0	0
Royalties	5	230482	0	•	0	0	0	46	0	0	0	•	0	0
Other Portfolio Income	6	36946	0	•	0	298	266	245	160	0	12816	•	0	0
Other Receipts	7	507677	0	•	1565	4332	29	634	7518	0	6154	•	0	0
Total Receipts	8	20846120	0	•	22299	491379	170366	154252	1050124	0	970476	•	0	0
Average Total Receipts	9	79565	•	•	3716	3343	11358	19282	75009	•	242619	•	•	•
Operating Costs/Operating Income (%)														
Cost of Operations	10	39.9	•	•	•	36.3	59.3	68.9	57.2	•	55.2	•	•	•
Salaries and Wages	11	6.8	•	•	•	7.0	2.7	6.3	7.0	•	5.2	•	•	•
Taxes Paid	12	12.6	•	•	0.0	3.9	1.3	2.1	4.6	•	10.0	•	•	•
Interest Paid	13	13.5	•	•	•	2.0	0.0	1.6	0.5	•	1.2	•	•	•
Depreciation	14	3.2	•	•	•	7.7	8.5	3.5	6.4	•	4.6	•	•	•
Amortization and Depletion	15	1.5	•	•	•	•	0.1	0.0	0.0	•	0.7	•	•	•
Pensions and Other Deferred Comp.	16	2.0	•	•	•	0.2	1.7	0.3	0.4	•	0.3	•	•	•
Employee Benefits	17	1.4	•	•	•	0.8	1.8	2.6	1.2	•	1.4	•	•	•
Advertising	18	3.8	•	•	•	1.0	0.3	1.7	2.8	•	2.2	•	•	•
Other Expenses	19	9.8	•	•	3.2	10.3	7.8	5.9	7.8	•	13.0	•	•	•
Officers' Compensation	20	0.4	•	•	•	3.0	2.6	2.5	1.4	•	0.7	•	•	•
Operating Margin	21	5.0	•	•	96.8	27.9	14.0	4.5	10.7	•	5.5	•	•	•
Operating Margin Before Officers' Comp.	22	5.4	•	•	96.8	30.9	16.6	7.1	12.0	•	6.2	•	•	•

Selected Average Balance Sheet ($ in Thousands)

Net Receivables 23	9034	•	•	631	46	1432	1938	10441	•	40476	•	•	•
Inventories 24	2638	•	•	0	379	1383	1894	4218	•	13718	•	•	•
Net Property, Plant and Equipment 25	27447	•	•	0	1512	2428	9062	28320	•	73126	•	•	•
Total Assets 26	334845	•	•	734	3208	8566	15721	48673	•	188631	•	•	•
Notes and Loans Payable 27	183871	•	•	0	1105	2406	6165	9860	•	36860	•	•	•
All Other Liabilities 28	73550	•	•	0	470	1718	9810	8530	•	46530	•	•	•
Net Worth 29	77424	•	•	734	1633	4442	-254	30283	•	105240	•	•	•

Selected Financial Ratios (Times to 1)

Current Ratio 30	1.2	•	•	•	2.8	4.0	2.2	2.1	•	1.9	•	•	•
Quick Ratio 31	0.9	•	•	•	1.8	2.4	1.4	1.6	•	1.4	•	•	•
Net Sales to Working Capital 32	13.3	•	•	4.7	3.5	2.9	5.9	7.4	•	8.5	•	•	•
Coverage Ratio 33	1.7	•	•	•	15.8	365.1	4.3	26.1	•	7.5	•	•	•
Total Asset Turnover 34	0.2	•	•	4.7	1.0	1.3	1.2	1.5	•	1.3	•	•	•
Inventory Turnover 35	11.6	•	•	•	3.2	4.9	7.0	10.1	•	9.6	•	•	•
Receivables Turnover 36	5.5	•	•	11.0	61.2	12.8	•	•	•	6.0	•	•	•
Total Liabilities to Net Worth 37	3.3	•	•	•	1.0	0.9	•	0.6	•	0.8	•	•	•
Current Assets to Working Capital 38	6.7	•	•	1.0	1.6	1.3	1.8	1.9	•	2.1	•	•	•
Current Liabilities to Working Capital 39	5.7	•	•	•	0.6	0.3	0.8	0.9	•	1.1	•	•	•
Working Capital to Net Sales 40	0.1	•	•	0.2	0.3	0.3	0.2	0.1	•	0.1	•	•	•
Inventory to Working Capital 41	0.5	•	•	•	0.4	0.5	0.6	0.4	•	0.4	•	•	•
Total Receipts to Cash Flow 42	6.0	•	•	0.9	3.0	5.0	11.3	5.6	•	5.6	•	•	•
Cost of Goods to Cash Flow 43	2.4	•	•	•	1.1	3.0	7.8	3.2	•	3.1	•	•	•
Cash Flow to Total Debt 44	0.0	•	•	•	0.7	0.6	0.1	0.7	•	0.5	•	•	•

Selected Financial Factors (in Percentages)

Debt Ratio 45	76.9	•	•	•	49.1	48.1	101.6	37.8	•	44.2	•	•	•
Return on Total Assets 46	5.2	•	•	491.3	31.8	18.8	8.2	18.2	•	10.9	•	•	•
Return on Equity Before Income Taxes 47	9.1	•	•	491.3	58.5	36.1	•	28.1	•	16.9	•	•	•
Return on Equity After Income Taxes 48	6.7	•	•	491.3	58.5	35.1	•	27.2	•	16.6	•	•	•
Profit Margin (Before Income Tax) 49	9.3	•	•	104.3	28.9	14.1	5.2	11.4	•	7.5	•	•	•
Profit Margin (After Income Tax) 50	6.8	•	•	104.3	28.9	13.8	3.8	11.1	•	7.4	•	•	•

Table I

Corporations with and without Net Income

WINERIES AND DISTILLERIES

MONEY AMOUNTS AND SIZE OF ASSETS IN THOUSANDS OF DOLLARS

Item Description for Accounting Period 7/11 Through 6/12		Total	Zero Assets	Under 500	500 to 1,000	1,000 to 5,000	5,000 to 10,000	10,000 to 25,000	25,000 to 50,000	50,000 to 100,000	100,000 to 250,000	250,000 to 500,000	500,000 to 2,500,000	2,500,000 and over
Number of Enterprises	1	1448	397	96	253	407	135	64	48	24	9	4	6	5
Revenues ($ in Thousands)														
Net Sales	2	31288789	4967	380478	168517	414921	701928	672679	1151268	1274729	705414	497482	3765045	21551362
Interest	3	101690	0	329	130	708	790	95	746	2678	190	3	4906	91116
Rents	4	10237	0	0	0	367	0	243	99	931	111	10	101	8374
Royalties	5	771630	0	0	0	0	0	0	0	0	0	0	133	771497
Other Portfolio Income	6	516996	0	0	0	119	6338	45	3208	8275	1612	1367	0	496033
Other Receipts	7	543266	45	1334	509	54140	18059	12551	25702	18530	11007	5629	82913	312845
Total Receipts	8	33232608	5012	382141	169156	470255	727115	685613	1181023	1305143	718334	504491	3853098	23231227
Average Total Receipts	9	22951	13	3981	669	1155	5386	10713	24605	54381	79815	126123	642183	4646245
Operating Costs/Operating Income (%)														
Cost of Operations	10	56.4	•	0.0	63.4	41.1	42.4	49.7	49.0	59.5	57.1	53.5	60.1	58.0
Salaries and Wages	11	6.7	•	•	•	8.7	18.6	11.7	10.8	7.6	8.0	9.5	4.8	6.3
Taxes Paid	12	8.9	11.4	0.9	5.7	7.3	4.7	7.4	5.9	8.2	6.6	4.6	10.2	9.4
Interest Paid	13	4.5	•	•	5.9	6.2	5.7	2.8	1.9	2.2	2.1	5.8	1.2	5.5
Depreciation	14	3.2	40.7	2.2	1.4	9.3	5.1	5.6	5.9	6.7	5.5	6.4	4.5	2.2
Amortization and Depletion	15	1.5	•	•	0.4	0.1	0.3	0.2	0.2	0.2	3.4	0.7	0.7	1.9
Pensions and Other Deferred Comp.	16	0.6	•	•	•	0.0	0.2	0.2	0.3	0.3	0.3	0.3	0.4	0.8
Employee Benefits	17	1.5	•	•	1.4	1.9	1.5	0.8	1.6	0.6	1.3	2.5	0.8	1.7
Advertising	18	4.9	1.9	0.0	3.7	1.8	0.9	1.8	2.5	1.2	1.6	3.6	3.2	6.1
Other Expenses	19	10.6	60.8	96.2	5.6	36.1	16.2	17.1	15.7	9.5	5.7	10.2	8.6	8.6
Officers' Compensation	20	1.0	4.8	0.7	23.1	6.1	0.8	2.6	2.5	2.1	2.4	0.4	0.6	0.7
Operating Margin	21	•	•	•	•	•	3.7	0.3	3.6	1.9	6.1	2.3	4.9	•
Operating Margin Before Officers' Comp.	22	1.0	•	0.7	12.4	•	4.5	2.9	6.2	3.9	8.5	2.8	5.5	•

Selected Average Balance Sheet ($ in Thousands)

Net Receivables 23	6306	0	148	24	53	459	1066	3674	6352	11390	21000	138435	1522761
Inventories 24	6417	0	0	228	749	2052	7216	9368	18899	58262	89107	248734	979810
Net Property, Plant and Equipment 25	5548	0	65	346	511	4111	4220	13010	28545	44845	98725	202652	716611
Total Assets 26	45980	0	432	667	1779	7923	15066	35886	73213	135256	283708	861332	10522278
Notes and Loans Payable 27	16947	0	5	664	987	5069	6191	11274	28730	36624	126092	173444	3956668
All Other Liabilities 28	9601	0	32	17	143	634	4772	6745	10976	16057	48747	233053	2224005
Net Worth 29	19432	0	395	-14	649	2220	4103	17867	33507	82575	108868	454835	4341605

Selected Financial Ratios (Times to 1)

Current Ratio 30	1.7	•	11.6	2.8	4.5	3.4	1.6	2.3	1.6	3.3	2.0	2.0	1.6
Quick Ratio 31	0.7	•	11.6	0.5	0.7	0.7	0.2	0.9	0.5	0.8	0.4	0.7	0.8
Net Sales to Working Capital 32	3.1	•	11.8	3.7	1.0	2.3	3.0	2.4	4.4	1.5	2.0	2.7	3.5
Coverage Ratio 33	2.5	•	•	•	0.1	2.3	1.8	4.2	2.9	4.9	1.6	7.2	2.4
Total Asset Turnover 34	0.5	•	9.2	1.0	0.6	0.7	0.7	0.7	0.7	0.6	0.4	0.7	0.4
Inventory Turnover 35	1.9	•	•	1.9	0.6	1.1	0.7	1.3	1.7	0.8	0.7	1.5	2.6
Receivables Turnover 36	5.1	•	•	•	18.0	15.0	9.3	7.9	9.4	6.2	5.9	6.3	4.4
Total Liabilities to Net Worth 37	1.4	•	0.1	•	1.7	2.6	2.7	1.0	1.2	0.6	1.6	0.9	1.4
Current Assets to Working Capital 38	2.3	•	1.1	1.5	1.3	1.4	2.7	1.8	2.8	1.4	2.0	2.0	2.6
Current Liabilities to Working Capital 39	1.3	•	0.1	0.5	0.3	0.4	1.7	0.8	1.8	0.4	1.0	1.0	1.6
Working Capital to Net Sales 40	0.3	•	0.1	0.3	1.0	0.4	0.3	0.4	0.2	0.7	0.5	0.4	0.3
Inventory to Working Capital 41	1.0	•	•	1.3	0.9	1.0	2.2	1.0	1.7	1.0	1.6	1.1	0.9
Total Receipts to Cash Flow 42	7.3	4.9	1.5	•	4.2	5.0	6.2	5.5	9.2	8.7	7.9	8.0	7.9
Cost of Goods to Cash Flow 43	4.1	•	0.0	•	1.7	2.1	3.1	2.7	5.5	5.0	4.2	4.8	4.6
Cash Flow to Total Debt 44	0.1	•	71.8	•	0.2	0.2	0.2	0.2	0.1	0.2	0.1	0.2	0.1

Selected Financial Factors (in Percentages)

Debt Ratio 45	57.7	•	8.5	102.1	63.5	72.0	72.8	50.2	54.2	38.9	61.6	47.2	58.7
Return on Total Assets 46	5.3	•	4.0	•	0.4	8.5	3.5	5.4	4.7	5.8	4.2	6.2	5.3
Return on Equity Before Income Taxes 47	7.5	•	4.4	499.2	•	17.1	5.7	8.2	6.7	7.5	4.3	10.0	7.4
Return on Equity After Income Taxes 48	5.2	•	4.4	499.2	•	16.0	4.2	7.4	6.1	7.2	3.6	8.3	4.8
Profit Margin (Before Income Tax) 49	6.8	•	0.4	•	•	7.3	2.2	6.1	4.2	7.9	3.8	7.3	7.5
Profit Margin (After Income Tax) 50	4.7	•	0.4	•	•	6.8	1.6	5.5	3.8	7.6	3.2	6.0	4.9

Table II

Corporations with Net Income

WINERIES AND DISTILLERIES

MONEY AMOUNTS AND SIZE OF ASSETS IN THOUSANDS OF DOLLARS

Item Description for Accounting Period 7/11 Through 6/12		Total	Zero Assets	Under 500	500 to 1,000	1,000 to 5,000	5,000 to 10,000	10,000 to 25,000	25,000 to 50,000	50,000 to 100,000	100,000 to 250,000	250,000 to 500,000	500,000 to 2,500,000	2,500,000 and over
Number of Enterprises	1	488	0	•	0	178	116	33	32	16	•	0	•	5
Revenues ($ in Thousands)														
Net Sales	2	29451475	0	•	0	238442	674586	488401	809258	1073164	•	0	•	21551362
Interest	3	97260	0	•	0	707	642	90	681	1209	•	0	•	91116
Rents	4	9185	0	•	0	367	0	0	99	244	•	0	•	8374
Royalties	5	771630	0	•	0	0	0	0	0	0	•	0	•	771497
Other Portfolio Income	6	512888	0	•	0	0	6281	31	3046	6689	•	0	•	496033
Other Receipts	7	497487	0	•	0	32414	18826	10837	23734	14927	•	0	•	312845
Total Receipts	8	31339925	0	•	0	271930	700335	499359	836818	1096233	•	0	•	23231227
Average Total Receipts	9	64221	•	•	•	1528	6037	15132	26151	68515	•	•	•	4646245
Operating Costs/Operating Income (%)														
Cost of Operations	10	56.7	•	•	•	36.1	41.8	47.5	41.2	57.3	•	•	•	58.0
Salaries and Wages	11	6.6	•	•	•	7.1	18.2	8.5	11.5	7.7	•	•	•	6.3
Taxes Paid	12	9.0	•	•	•	3.0	4.4	8.6	2.7	9.2	•	•	•	9.4
Interest Paid	13	4.4	•	•	•	2.5	5.4	2.4	2.0	1.2	•	•	•	5.5
Depreciation	14	2.8	•	•	•	4.3	4.4	4.6	6.5	6.1	•	•	•	2.2
Amortization and Depletion	15	1.6	•	•	•	0.1	0.1	0.0	0.2	0.1	•	•	•	1.9
Pensions and Other Deferred Comp.	16	0.7	•	•	•	0.0	0.1	0.1	0.3	0.3	•	•	•	0.8
Employee Benefits	17	1.5	•	•	•	1.8	1.4	0.4	1.3	0.5	•	•	•	1.7
Advertising	18	5.1	•	•	•	0.1	0.9	1.8	2.8	0.9	•	•	•	6.1
Other Expenses	19	9.9	•	•	•	33.4	16.7	15.1	17.6	9.3	•	•	•	8.6
Officers' Compensation	20	0.9	•	•	•	10.1	0.8	2.6	3.4	2.0	•	•	•	0.7
Operating Margin	21	0.9	•	•	•	1.5	5.7	8.3	10.4	5.4	•	•	•	•
Operating Margin Before Officers' Comp.	22	1.8	•	•	•	11.7	6.5	11.0	13.7	7.4	•	•	•	•

	Selected Average Balance Sheet ($ in Thousands)												
Net Receivables **23**	18007	•	•	•	90	509	1472	3032	8055	•	•	•	1522761
Inventories **24**	15391	•	•	•	843	1765	9767	9921	18089	•	•	•	1120833
Net Property, Plant and Equipment **25**	12839	•	•	•	310	4045	3513	12265	24096	•	•	•	716611
Total Assets **26**	127861	•	•	•	1832	7807	15725	37211	71371	•	•	•	10522278
Notes and Loans Payable **27**	45628	•	•	•	722	5222	5606	9632	19189	•	•	•	3956668
All Other Liabilities **28**	27309	•	•	•	61	614	5803	8446	10365	•	•	•	2224005
Net Worth **29**	54924	•	•	•	1049	1971	4315	19133	41817	•	•	•	4341605
	Selected Financial Ratios (Times to 1)												
Current Ratio **30**	1.7	•	•	•	4.5	2.9	1.6	1.9	1.9	•	•	•	1.6
Quick Ratio **31**	0.8	•	•	•	0.8	0.7	0.3	0.8	0.7	•	•	•	0.8
Net Sales to Working Capital **32**	3.2	•	•	•	1.1	2.9	3.6	3.0	4.1	•	•	•	3.5
Coverage Ratio **33**	2.8	•	•	•	7.3	2.8	5.5	7.9	7.3	•	•	•	2.4
Total Asset Turnover **34**	0.5	•	•	•	0.7	0.7	0.9	0.7	0.9	•	•	•	0.4
Inventory Turnover **35**	2.2	•	•	•	0.6	1.4	0.7	1.1	2.1	•	•	•	2.2
Receivables Turnover **36**	5.2	•	•	•	19.6	17.0	8.2	8.0	9.6	•	•	•	•
Total Liabilities to Net Worth **37**	1.3	•	•	•	0.7	3.0	2.6	0.9	0.7	•	•	•	1.4
Current Assets to Working Capital **38**	2.4	•	•	•	1.3	1.5	2.6	2.1	2.2	•	•	•	2.6
Current Liabilities to Working Capital **39**	1.4	•	•	•	0.3	0.5	1.6	1.1	1.2	•	•	•	1.6
Working Capital to Net Sales **40**	0.3	•	•	•	0.9	0.3	0.3	0.3	0.2	•	•	•	0.3
Inventory to Working Capital **41**	1.0	•	•	•	0.8	1.1	2.1	1.2	1.3	•	•	•	0.9
Total Receipts to Cash Flow **42**	7.0	•	•	•	2.5	4.4	4.4	3.7	7.3	•	•	•	7.9
Cost of Goods to Cash Flow **43**	3.9	•	•	•	0.9	1.9	2.1	1.5	4.2	•	•	•	4.6
Cash Flow to Total Debt **44**	0.1	•	•	•	0.7	0.2	0.3	0.4	0.3	•	•	•	0.1
	Selected Financial Factors (in Percentages)												
Debt Ratio **45**	57.0	•	•	•	42.8	74.8	72.6	48.6	41.4	•	•	•	58.7
Return on Total Assets **46**	5.8	•	•	•	13.2	11.1	12.2	10.6	8.2	•	•	•	5.3
Return on Equity Before Income Taxes **47**	8.7	•	•	•	19.9	28.0	36.3	18.0	12.0	•	•	•	7.4
Return on Equity After Income Taxes **48**	6.4	•	•	•	19.8	26.6	33.5	16.8	11.2	•	•	•	4.8
Profit Margin (Before Income Tax) **49**	7.9	•	•	•	15.6	9.5	10.6	13.6	7.5	•	•	•	7.5
Profit Margin (After Income Tax) **50**	5.8	•	•	•	15.5	9.0	9.8	12.7	7.0	•	•	•	4.9

Table I

Corporations with and without Net Income

TOBACCO MANUFACTURING

MONEY AMOUNTS AND SIZE OF ASSETS IN THOUSANDS OF DOLLARS

Item Description for Accounting Period 7/11 Through 6/12		Total	Zero Assets	Under 500	500 to 1,000	1,000 to 5,000	5,000 to 10,000	10,000 to 25,000	25,000 to 50,000	50,000 to 100,000	100,000 to 250,000	250,000 to 500,000	500,000 to 2,500,000	2,500,000 and over
Number of Enterprises	1	31	0	0	0	0	0	13	7	4	3	0	0	4
Revenues ($ in Thousands)														
Net Sales	2	48058458	0	0	0	0	0	890459	392881	576731	1608679	0	0	44589708
Interest	3	68365	0	0	0	0	0	699	0	0	138	0	0	67527
Rents	4	863086	0	0	0	0	0	0	0	0	427	0	0	862658
Royalties	5	35342	0	0	0	0	0	0	0	0	1390	0	0	33952
Other Portfolio Income	6	475646	0	0	0	0	0	1238	129	8	4852	0	0	469418
Other Receipts	7	299823	0	0	0	0	0	84	368	864	796	0	0	297715
Total Receipts	8	49800720	0	0	0	0	0	892480	393378	577603	1616282	0	0	46320978
Average Total Receipts	9	1606475	•	•	•	•	•	68652	56197	144401	538761	•	•	11580244
Operating Costs/Operating Income (%)														
Cost of Operations	10	39.0	•	•	•	•	•	40.1	78.8	51.6	42.6	•	•	38.4
Salaries and Wages	11	2.7	•	•	•	•	•	2.6	4.2	1.4	3.5	•	•	2.6
Taxes Paid	12	27.6	•	•	•	•	•	46.5	0.8	33.8	17.9	•	•	27.8
Interest Paid	13	2.0	•	•	•	•	•	0.2	0.0	1.1	1.1	•	•	2.1
Depreciation	14	1.4	•	•	•	•	•	2.1	1.7	0.4	2.9	•	•	1.4
Amortization and Depletion	15	0.8	•	•	•	•	•	0.0	0.0	0.0	1.4	•	•	0.8
Pensions and Other Deferred Comp.	16	2.0	•	•	•	•	•	0.3	•	0.5	1.1	•	•	2.1
Employee Benefits	17	1.1	•	•	•	•	•	0.4	0.2	0.3	0.4	•	•	1.2
Advertising	18	0.6	•	•	•	•	•	0.9	0.6	0.1	1.0	•	•	0.6
Other Expenses	19	7.6	•	•	•	•	•	5.7	4.5	3.6	13.0	•	•	7.5
Officers' Compensation	20	0.5	•	•	•	•	•	3.8	0.9	0.9	1.8	•	•	0.4
Operating Margin	21	14.6	•	•	•	•	•	•	8.3	6.4	13.3	•	•	15.1
Operating Margin Before Officers' Comp.	22	15.1	•	•	•	•	•	1.3	9.2	7.2	15.1	•	•	15.6

Selected Average Balance Sheet ($ in Thousands)													
Net Receivables 23	17346	•	•	•	•	•	2731	2149	3774	14795	•	•	106922
Inventories 24	118622	•	•	•	•	•	5568	3745	27321	108612	•	•	763926
Net Property, Plant and Equipment 25	129126	•	•	•	•	•	1108	11902	3746	87073	•	•	907244
Total Assets 26	2039615	•	•	•	•	•	14367	29537	70314	898628	•	•	14964348
Notes and Loans Payable 27	741179	•	•	•	•	•	2893	0	42919	111826	•	•	5607948
All Other Liabilities 28	945159	•	•	•	•	•	14937	3952	15782	147030	•	•	7143468
Net Worth 29	353276	•	•	•	•	•	-3463	25585	11613	639771	•	•	2212931

Selected Financial Ratios (Times to 1)													
Current Ratio 30	1.1	•	•	•	•	•	0.9	4.4	1.6	8.1	•	•	1.0
Quick Ratio 31	0.6	•	•	•	•	•	0.3	1.8	0.5	5.6	•	•	0.6
Net Sales to Working Capital 32	39.3	•	•	•	•	•	•	4.2	8.5	1.6	•	•	733.4
Coverage Ratio 33	10.1	•	•	•	•	•	•	33091.0	6.8	13.2	•	•	10.0
Total Asset Turnover 34	0.8	•	•	•	•	•	4.8	1.9	2.1	0.6	•	•	0.7
Inventory Turnover 35	5.1	•	•	•	•	•	4.9	11.8	2.7	2.1	•	•	5.6
Receivables Turnover 36	98.0	•	•	•	•	•	16.4	52.2	25.5	72.5	•	•	125.7
Total Liabilities to Net Worth 37	4.8	•	•	•	•	•	•	0.2	5.1	0.4	•	•	5.8
Current Assets to Working Capital 38	11.6	•	•	•	•	•	•	1.3	2.7	1.1	•	•	206.2
Current Liabilities to Working Capital 39	10.6	•	•	•	•	•	•	0.3	1.7	0.1	•	•	205.2
Working Capital to Net Sales 40	0.0	•	•	•	•	•	•	0.2	0.1	0.6	•	•	0.0
Inventory to Working Capital 41	2.9	•	•	•	•	•	•	0.3	1.4	0.3	•	•	50.1
Total Receipts to Cash Flow 42	4.2	•	•	•	•	•	49.8	8.3	10.9	4.1	•	•	4.1
Cost of Goods to Cash Flow 43	1.6	•	•	•	•	•	20.0	6.5	5.6	1.7	•	•	1.6
Cash Flow to Total Debt 44	0.2	•	•	•	•	•	0.1	1.7	0.2	0.5	•	•	0.2

Selected Financial Factors (in Percentages)													
Debt Ratio 45	82.7	•	•	•	•	•	124.1	13.4	83.5	28.8	•	•	85.2
Return on Total Assets 46	15.6	•	•	•	•	•	•	16.0	15.7	8.7	•	•	16.0
Return on Equity Before Income Taxes 47	81.4	•	•	•	•	•	44.7	18.5	81.0	11.3	•	•	97.6
Return on Equity After Income Taxes 48	53.3	•	•	•	•	•	47.7	18.5	81.0	8.3	•	•	63.6
Profit Margin (Before Income Tax) 49	18.5	•	•	•	•	•	•	8.4	6.5	13.5	•	•	19.4
Profit Margin (After Income Tax) 50	12.1	•	•	•	•	•	•	8.4	6.5	9.9	•	•	12.6

Table II

Corporations with Net Income

TOBACCO MANUFACTURING

MONEY AMOUNTS AND SIZE OF ASSETS IN THOUSANDS OF DOLLARS

Item Description for Accounting Period 7/11 Through 6/12		Total	Zero Assets	Under 500	500 to 1,000	1,000 to 5,000	5,000 to 10,000	10,000 to 25,000	25,000 to 50,000	50,000 to 100,000	100,000 to 250,000	250,000 to 500,000	500,000 to 2,500,000	2,500,000 and over
Number of Enterprises	1	26	0	0	0	0	0	9	7	•	•	0	0	4
Revenues ($ in Thousands)														
Net Sales	2	47749329	0	0	0	0	0	624898	392881	•	•	0	0	44589708
Interest	3	68365	0	0	0	0	0	699	0	•	•	0	0	67527
Rents	4	863086	0	0	0	0	0	0	0	•	•	0	0	862658
Royalties	5	35342	0	0	0	0	0	0	0	•	•	0	0	33952
Other Portfolio Income	6	475646	0	0	0	0	0	1238	129	•	•	0	0	469418
Other Receipts	7	299760	0	0	0	0	0	53	368	•	•	0	0	297715
Total Receipts	8	49491528	0	0	0	0	0	626888	393378	•	•	0	0	46320978
Average Total Receipts	9	1903520	•	•	•	•	•	69654	56197	•	•	•	•	11580244
Operating Costs/Operating Income (%)														
Cost of Operations	10	38.9	•	•	•	•	•	37.3	78.8	•	•	•	•	38.4
Salaries and Wages	11	2.7	•	•	•	•	•	3.5	4.2	•	•	•	•	2.6
Taxes Paid	12	27.5	•	•	•	•	•	42.8	0.8	•	•	•	•	27.8
Interest Paid	13	2.1	•	•	•	•	•	0.1	0.0	•	•	•	•	2.1
Depreciation	14	1.4	•	•	•	•	•	1.9	1.7	•	•	•	•	1.4
Amortization and Depletion	15	0.8	•	•	•	•	•	0.0	0.0	•	•	•	•	0.8
Pensions and Other Deferred Comp.	16	2.0	•	•	•	•	•	0.5	•	•	•	•	•	2.1
Employee Benefits	17	1.1	•	•	•	•	•	0.5	0.2	•	•	•	•	1.2
Advertising	18	0.6	•	•	•	•	•	1.2	0.6	•	•	•	•	0.6
Other Expenses	19	7.6	•	•	•	•	•	5.9	4.5	•	•	•	•	7.5
Officers' Compensation	20	0.5	•	•	•	•	•	5.2	0.9	•	•	•	•	0.4
Operating Margin	21	14.7	•	•	•	•	•	1.1	8.3	•	•	•	•	15.1
Operating Margin Before Officers' Comp.	22	15.3	•	•	•	•	•	6.3	9.2	•	•	•	•	15.6

Selected Average Balance Sheet ($ in Thousands)

Net Receivables 23	20531	•	•	•	•	•	3610	2149	•	•	•	•	106922
Inventories 24	139752	•	•	•	•	•	5062	3745	•	•	•	•	761526
Net Property, Plant and Equipment 25	153927	•	•	•	•	•	1596	11902	•	•	•	•	907244
Total Assets 26	2425878	•	•	•	•	•	13159	29537	•	•	•	•	14964348
Notes and Loans Payable 27	881340	•	•	•	•	•	492	0	•	•	•	•	5607948
All Other Liabilities 28	1120265	•	•	•	•	•	4375	3952	•	•	•	•	7143468
Net Worth 29	424274	•	•	•	•	•	8292	25585	•	•	•	•	2212931

Selected Financial Ratios (Times to 1)

Current Ratio 30	1.1	•	•	•	•	•	2.8	4.4	•	•	•	•	1.0
Quick Ratio 31	0.6	•	•	•	•	•	1.4	1.8	•	•	•	•	0.6
Net Sales to Working Capital 32	36.5	•	•	•	•	•	10.2	4.2	•	•	•	•	733.4
Coverage Ratio 33	10.1	•	•	•	•	•	22.3	33091.0	•	•	•	•	10.0
Total Asset Turnover 34	0.8	•	•	•	•	•	5.3	1.9	•	•	•	•	0.7
Inventory Turnover 35	5.1	•	•	•	•	•	5.1	11.8	•	•	•	•	5.6
Receivables Turnover 36	99.7	•	•	•	•	•	•	52.2	•	•	•	•	•
Total Liabilities to Net Worth 37	4.7	•	•	•	•	•	0.6	0.2	•	•	•	•	5.8
Current Assets to Working Capital 38	10.8	•	•	•	•	•	1.6	1.3	•	•	•	•	206.2
Current Liabilities to Working Capital 39	9.8	•	•	•	•	•	0.6	0.3	•	•	•	•	205.2
Working Capital to Net Sales 40	0.0	•	•	•	•	•	0.1	0.2	•	•	•	•	0.0
Inventory to Working Capital 41	2.7	•	•	•	•	•	0.7	0.3	•	•	•	•	50.1
Total Receipts to Cash Flow 42	4.2	•	•	•	•	•	14.2	8.3	•	•	•	•	4.1
Cost of Goods to Cash Flow 43	1.6	•	•	•	•	•	5.3	6.5	•	•	•	•	1.6
Cash Flow to Total Debt 44	0.2	•	•	•	•	•	1.0	1.7	•	•	•	•	0.2

Selected Financial Factors (in Percentages)

Debt Ratio 45	82.5	•	•	•	•	•	37.0	13.4	•	•	•	•	85.2
Return on Total Assets 46	15.7	•	•	•	•	•	8.1	16.0	•	•	•	•	16.0
Return on Equity Before Income Taxes 47	81.1	•	•	•	•	•	12.3	18.5	•	•	•	•	97.6
Return on Equity After Income Taxes 48	53.2	•	•	•	•	•	10.5	18.5	•	•	•	•	63.6
Profit Margin (Before Income Tax) 49	18.7	•	•	•	•	•	1.5	8.4	•	•	•	•	19.4
Profit Margin (After Income Tax) 50	12.3	•	•	•	•	•	1.2	8.4	•	•	•	•	12.6

Table I

Corporations with and without Net Income

TEXTILE MILLS

MONEY AMOUNTS AND SIZE OF ASSETS IN THOUSANDS OF DOLLARS

Item Description for Accounting Period 7/11 Through 6/12		Total	Zero Assets	Under 500	500 to 1,000	1,000 to 5,000	5,000 to 10,000	10,000 to 25,000	25,000 to 50,000	50,000 to 100,000	100,000 to 250,000	250,000 to 500,000	500,000 to 2,500,000	2,500,000 and over
Number of Enterprises	1	1331	•	•	•	143	40	76	16	17	12	4	5	0
Revenues ($ in Thousands)														
Net Sales	2	13011451	•	•	•	345976	766070	2146904	669616	1748217	2444853	2078969	2036463	0
Interest	3	45455	•	•	•	1567	230	1203	11	2992	361	6438	32651	0
Rents	4	6366	•	•	•	163	0	3640	23	307	54	815	1363	0
Royalties	5	24927	•	•	•	0	0	0	82	93	6735	0	13752	0
Other Portfolio Income	6	88135	•	•	•	8834	6770	2597	170	2670	226	27675	34607	0
Other Receipts	7	113085	•	•	•	212	13225	8862	2248	11599	13566	49412	13336	0
Total Receipts	8	13289419	•	•	•	356752	786295	2163206	672150	1765878	2465795	2163309	2132172	0
Average Total Receipts	9	9985	•	•	•	2495	19657	28463	42009	103875	205483	540827	426434	•
Operating Costs/Operating Income (%)														
Cost of Operations	10	76.2	•	•	•	72.9	80.6	76.7	77.1	80.0	77.4	80.0	69.9	•
Salaries and Wages	11	5.6	•	•	•	2.9	5.7	7.0	6.9	4.7	3.9	4.3	7.5	•
Taxes Paid	12	1.4	•	•	•	2.1	1.0	1.3	0.7	1.2	1.1	1.8	1.8	•
Interest Paid	13	2.1	•	•	•	0.4	1.4	1.0	2.1	0.6	1.4	3.0	5.3	•
Depreciation	14	3.5	•	•	•	3.0	1.8	1.8	4.0	4.0	7.2	2.1	3.0	•
Amortization and Depletion	15	0.4	•	•	•	0.3	0.0	0.0	0.3	0.1	0.5	0.4	1.5	•
Pensions and Other Deferred Comp.	16	0.6	•	•	•	0.5	•	0.3	0.1	0.6	0.4	1.3	0.8	•
Employee Benefits	17	1.4	•	•	•	2.6	0.0	0.9	0.5	1.0	1.4	1.7	2.5	•
Advertising	18	0.3	•	•	•	0.1	0.1	0.3	0.2	0.5	0.1	0.6	0.2	•
Other Expenses	19	8.0	•	•	•	13.1	9.7	7.6	4.5	6.7	6.1	5.5	11.7	•
Officers' Compensation	20	1.4	•	•	•	2.9	0.8	1.2	0.9	1.1	0.9	1.5	1.2	•
Operating Margin	21	•	•	•	•	•	•	1.9	2.7	•	•	•	•	•
Operating Margin Before Officers' Comp.	22	0.4	•	•	•	2.0	•	3.1	3.6	0.7	0.5	•	•	•

Selected Average Balance Sheet ($ in Thousands)

Net Receivables	23	1401	•	•	•	368	2038	3730	8223	12839	28518	82778	73383	•
Inventories	24	1325	•	•	•	426	3484	3875	7579	16659	21068	87706	49725	•
Net Property, Plant and Equipment	25	1663	•	•	•	650	1522	3046	7655	20236	53276	81535	75438	•
Total Assets	26	8188	•	•	•	2628	7677	15522	30137	67141	142112	434940	768584	•
Notes and Loans Payable	27	2974	•	•	•	526	3791	6248	11558	12536	52372	172253	297935	•
All Other Liabilities	28	1866	•	•	•	605	2035	2460	10906	18530	38986	87577	148514	•
Net Worth	29	3349	•	•	•	1496	1851	6814	7674	36075	50755	175110	322135	•

Selected Financial Ratios (Times to 1)

Current Ratio	30	2.1	•	•	•	5.8	2.3	2.9	1.7	2.1	1.9	2.7	1.6	•
Quick Ratio	31	1.1	•	•	•	3.6	1.2	1.4	0.9	1.0	1.0	1.3	1.0	•
Net Sales to Working Capital	32	5.3	•	•	•	1.8	7.2	4.0	5.7	5.2	6.6	4.2	7.1	•
Coverage Ratio	33	1.6	•	•	•	5.9	2.0	3.8	2.5	2.0	1.3	1.7	0.9	•
Total Asset Turnover	34	1.2	•	•	•	0.9	2.5	1.8	1.4	1.5	1.4	1.2	0.5	•
Inventory Turnover	35	5.6	•	•	•	4.1	4.4	5.6	4.3	4.9	7.5	4.7	5.7	•
Receivables Turnover	36	7.0	•	•	•	6.1	7.8	7.9	5.5	8.0	8.3	6.0	5.3	•
Total Liabilities to Net Worth	37	1.4	•	•	•	0.8	3.1	1.3	2.9	0.9	1.8	1.5	1.4	•
Current Assets to Working Capital	38	1.9	•	•	•	1.2	1.8	1.5	2.5	1.9	2.1	1.6	2.6	•
Current Liabilities to Working Capital	39	0.9	•	•	•	0.2	0.8	0.5	1.5	0.9	1.1	0.6	1.6	•
Working Capital to Net Sales	40	0.2	•	•	•	0.5	0.1	0.2	0.2	0.2	0.2	0.2	0.1	•
Inventory to Working Capital	41	0.8	•	•	•	0.3	0.8	0.6	1.1	0.8	0.8	0.8	0.9	•
Total Receipts to Cash Flow	42	14.1	•	•	•	9.7	10.5	12.5	16.1	17.1	22.3	15.2	11.1	•
Cost of Goods to Cash Flow	43	10.7	•	•	•	7.0	8.5	9.6	12.4	13.7	17.3	12.2	7.8	•
Cash Flow to Total Debt	44	0.1	•	•	•	0.2	0.3	0.3	0.1	0.2	0.1	0.1	0.1	•

Selected Financial Factors (in Percentages)

Debt Ratio	45	59.1	•	•	•	43.1	75.9	56.1	74.5	46.3	64.3	59.7	58.1	•
Return on Total Assets	46	4.1	•	•	•	2.4	7.2	6.6	7.2	1.8	2.7	6.1	2.7	•
Return on Equity Before Income Taxes	47	3.7	•	•	•	3.5	14.9	11.2	16.8	1.6	1.9	6.2	•	•
Return on Equity After Income Taxes	48	2.6	•	•	•	2.5	9.8	10.9	16.7	0.9	•	4.9	•	•
Profit Margin (Before Income Tax)	49	1.3	•	•	•	2.2	1.4	2.7	3.1	0.6	0.5	2.1	•	•
Profit Margin (After Income Tax)	50	0.9	•	•	•	1.5	0.9	2.6	3.1	0.3	•	1.7	•	•

Table II

Corporations with Net Income

TEXTILE MILLS

MONEY AMOUNTS AND SIZE OF ASSETS IN THOUSANDS OF DOLLARS

Item Description for Accounting Period 7/11 Through 6/12		Total	Zero Assets	Under 500	500 to 1,000	1,000 to 5,000	5,000 to 10,000	10,000 to 25,000	25,000 to 50,000	50,000 to 100,000	100,000 to 250,000	250,000 to 500,000	500,000 to 2,500,000	2,500,000 and over
Number of Enterprises	1	1090	•	•	0	35	36	50	•	10	7	•	0	0
Revenues ($ in Thousands)														
Net Sales	2	9248908	•	•	0	217425	727893	1661819	•	1109931	2148361	•	0	0
Interest	3	8460	•	•	0	86	230	148	•	503	73	•	0	0
Rents	4	5830	•	•	0	76	0	3465	•	152	0	•	0	0
Royalties	5	11083	•	•	0	0	0	0	•	0	6735	•	0	0
Other Portfolio Income	6	56391	•	•	0	7405	6770	2542	•	543	124	•	0	0
Other Receipts	7	89841	•	•	0	36	13225	3414	•	9082	10199	•	0	0
Total Receipts	8	9420513	•	•	0	225028	748118	1671388	•	1120211	2165492	•	0	0
Average Total Receipts	9	8643	•	•	•	6429	20781	33428	•	112021	309356	•	•	•
Operating Costs/Operating Income (%)														
Cost of Operations	10	73.7	•	•	•	73.9	77.8	75.5	•	77.2	77.5	•	•	•
Salaries and Wages	11	6.3	•	•	•	4.0	6.0	8.0	•	5.1	3.8	•	•	•
Taxes Paid	12	1.4	•	•	•	2.1	1.0	1.1	•	1.2	1.1	•	•	•
Interest Paid	13	1.4	•	•	•	0.4	1.4	0.9	•	0.2	1.2	•	•	•
Depreciation	14	2.6	•	•	•	1.0	1.9	1.0	•	3.5	4.0	•	•	•
Amortization and Depletion	15	0.2	•	•	•	0.5	0.0	0.0	•	0.0	0.2	•	•	•
Pensions and Other Deferred Comp.	16	0.7	•	•	•	0.7	•	0.4	•	0.5	0.4	•	•	•
Employee Benefits	17	1.3	•	•	•	3.2	0.0	0.9	•	1.2	1.2	•	•	•
Advertising	18	0.3	•	•	•	0.1	0.1	0.3	•	0.6	0.1	•	•	•
Other Expenses	19	8.4	•	•	•	11.9	9.8	6.9	•	6.2	6.0	•	•	•
Officers' Compensation	20	1.2	•	•	•	1.3	0.9	1.1	•	0.9	0.8	•	•	•
Operating Margin	21	2.6	•	•	•	0.7	1.1	3.9	•	3.2	3.6	•	•	•
Operating Margin Before Officers' Comp.	22	3.8	•	•	•	2.1	2.0	5.0	•	4.1	4.5	•	•	•

Selected Average Balance Sheet ($ in Thousands)

Net Receivables 23	1202	•	•	•	1098	2187	3101	•	13091	36907	•	•	•
Inventories 24	1076	•	•	•	1182	3008	4073	•	14056	33785	•	•	•
Net Property, Plant and Equipment 25	1121	•	•	•	405	1668	1849	•	22428	48353	•	•	•
Total Assets 26	5434	•	•	•	3688	7973	13202	•	64645	153451	•	•	•
Notes and Loans Payable 27	1797	•	•	•	707	3876	5646	•	8100	58931	•	•	•
All Other Liabilities 28	1225	•	•	•	817	1494	2733	•	15703	41108	•	•	•
Net Worth 29	2412	•	•	•	2164	2603	4823	•	40842	53412	•	•	•

Selected Financial Ratios (Times to 1)

Current Ratio 30	2.1	•	•	•	5.1	2.2	2.3	•	2.5	2.1	•	•	•
Quick Ratio 31	1.1	•	•	•	2.4	1.2	0.9	•	1.3	1.1	•	•	•
Net Sales to Working Capital 32	5.8	•	•	•	3.1	7.3	6.1	•	5.2	7.2	•	•	•
Coverage Ratio 33	4.3	•	•	•	10.6	3.7	6.1	•	20.8	4.7	•	•	•
Total Asset Turnover 34	1.6	•	•	•	1.7	2.5	2.5	•	1.7	2.0	•	•	•
Inventory Turnover 35	5.8	•	•	•	3.9	5.2	6.2	•	6.1	7.0	•	•	•
Receivables Turnover 36	7.3	•	•	•	6.1	9.3	10.8	•	•	•	•	•	•
Total Liabilities to Net Worth 37	1.3	•	•	•	0.7	2.1	1.7	•	0.6	1.9	•	•	•
Current Assets to Working Capital 38	1.9	•	•	•	1.2	1.8	1.8	•	1.6	1.9	•	•	•
Current Liabilities to Working Capital 39	0.9	•	•	•	0.2	0.8	0.8	•	0.6	0.9	•	•	•
Working Capital to Net Sales 40	0.2	•	•	•	0.3	0.1	0.2	•	0.2	0.1	•	•	•
Inventory to Working Capital 41	0.8	•	•	•	0.7	0.9	0.8	•	0.7	0.8	•	•	•
Total Receipts to Cash Flow 42	9.6	•	•	•	10.4	8.3	11.1	•	11.5	12.2	•	•	•
Cost of Goods to Cash Flow 43	7.0	•	•	•	7.7	6.5	8.4	•	8.8	9.5	•	•	•
Cash Flow to Total Debt 44	0.3	•	•	•	0.4	0.5	0.4	•	0.4	0.3	•	•	•

Selected Financial Factors (in Percentages)

Debt Ratio 45	55.6	•	•	•	41.3	67.4	63.5	•	36.8	65.2	•	•	•
Return on Total Assets 46	9.2	•	•	•	7.9	13.5	13.3	•	7.6	11.3	•	•	•
Return on Equity Before Income Taxes 47	15.9	•	•	•	12.2	30.2	30.5	•	11.4	25.5	•	•	•
Return on Equity After Income Taxes 48	14.0	•	•	•	9.2	26.1	29.9	•	10.3	22.0	•	•	•
Profit Margin (Before Income Tax) 49	4.5	•	•	•	4.2	3.9	4.4	•	4.2	4.4	•	•	•
Profit Margin (After Income Tax) 50	4.0	•	•	•	3.2	3.4	4.3	•	3.8	3.8	•	•	•

Table I

Corporations with and without Net Income

TEXTILE PRODUCT MILLS

MONEY AMOUNTS AND SIZE OF ASSETS IN THOUSANDS OF DOLLARS

Item Description for Accounting Period 7/11 Through 6/12		Total	Zero Assets	Under 500	500 to 1,000	1,000 to 5,000	5,000 to 10,000	10,000 to 25,000	25,000 to 50,000	50,000 to 100,000	100,000 to 250,000	250,000 to 500,000	500,000 to 2,500,000	2,500,000 and over
Number of Enterprises	1	2106	•	•	•	562	36	51	37	9	10	8	5	0
Revenues ($ in Thousands)														
Net Sales	2	22726837	•	•	•	3232850	693193	1831820	2486238	961511	2307417	3141238	7115143	0
Interest	3	12547	•	•	•	359	35	22	655	402	2704	2750	5358	0
Rents	4	8011	•	•	•	0	1081	0	1185	0	2154	1297	748	0
Royalties	5	47756	•	•	•	0	0	0	42	20	35	15694	31794	0
Other Portfolio Income	6	86063	•	•	•	6055	3764	979	7659	306	7955	550	58791	0
Other Receipts	7	215108	•	•	•	19941	128	8072	17237	13484	8416	11969	134907	0
Total Receipts	8	23096322	•	•	•	3259205	698201	1840893	2513016	975723	2328681	3173498	7346741	0
Average Total Receipts	9	10967	•	•	•	5799	19394	36096	67919	108414	232868	396687	1469348	•
Operating Costs/Operating Income (%)														
Cost of Operations	10	69.9	•	•	•	59.1	74.8	79.6	78.8	81.1	82.4	72.8	63.7	•
Salaries and Wages	11	9.6	•	•	•	10.9	2.8	4.4	6.2	5.3	5.2	9.6	14.7	•
Taxes Paid	12	1.8	•	•	•	1.9	2.4	2.2	1.3	1.8	1.4	1.5	2.0	•
Interest Paid	13	1.5	•	•	•	0.5	1.9	0.8	1.3	1.1	0.9	2.7	1.9	•
Depreciation	14	3.1	•	•	•	3.4	1.4	1.4	1.8	1.8	2.4	2.3	4.9	•
Amortization and Depletion	15	0.4	•	•	•	0.1	0.0	0.2	0.4	0.4	0.5	0.6	0.7	•
Pensions and Other Deferred Comp.	16	0.5	•	•	•	0.1	0.3	0.1	0.2	0.2	0.3	0.6	1.0	•
Employee Benefits	17	1.1	•	•	•	0.8	0.6	1.0	1.3	1.3	1.1	0.9	1.4	•
Advertising	18	0.6	•	•	•	1.1	0.1	0.5	0.3	0.3	0.4	1.3	0.4	•
Other Expenses	19	10.2	•	•	•	15.8	5.5	7.8	7.2	6.7	7.4	6.8	11.6	•
Officers' Compensation	20	1.9	•	•	•	3.2	4.9	1.7	1.1	0.7	0.6	1.6	0.5	•
Operating Margin	21	•	•	•	•	3.2	5.4	0.4	0.1	•	•	•	•	•
Operating Margin Before Officers' Comp.	22	1.2	•	•	•	6.4	10.3	2.1	1.2	•	•	0.9	•	•

Selected Average Balance Sheet ($ in Thousands)													
Net Receivables 23	1430	•	•	•	678	1133	3257	8097	15974	38184	60227	203415	•
Inventories 24	1734	•	•	•	777	2763	6530	9667	22600	35301	75295	220676	•
Net Property, Plant and Equipment 25	1377	•	•	•	418	1209	2749	5976	12312	35751	46354	276168	•
Total Assets 26	8776	•	•	•	2103	6643	14627	37293	66943	151859	347974	1936776	•
Notes and Loans Payable 27	2825	•	•	•	540	3657	3019	12339	38889	53710	203180	445013	•
All Other Liabilities 28	2561	•	•	•	703	1105	5376	9578	18826	42830	76418	606269	•
Net Worth 29	3390	•	•	•	860	1881	6233	15377	9228	55320	68376	885494	•

Selected Financial Ratios (Times to 1)													
Current Ratio 30	1.6	•	•	•	1.8	2.0	1.5	1.8	2.0	1.4	2.3	1.4	•
Quick Ratio 31	0.8	•	•	•	0.9	0.7	0.7	0.8	1.0	0.7	1.1	0.7	•
Net Sales to Working Capital 32	6.7	•	•	•	8.1	7.8	10.2	6.2	5.4	9.0	3.9	7.5	•
Coverage Ratio 33	1.8	•	•	•	8.4	4.2	2.2	1.9	1.7	•	1.1	1.5	•
Total Asset Turnover 34	1.2	•	•	•	2.7	2.9	2.5	1.8	1.6	1.5	1.1	0.7	•
Inventory Turnover 35	4.4	•	•	•	4.4	5.2	4.4	5.5	3.8	5.4	3.8	4.1	•
Receivables Turnover 36	8.4	•	•	•	9.1	11.9	10.4	9.3	5.6	7.4	5.7	9.7	•
Total Liabilities to Net Worth 37	1.6	•	•	•	1.4	2.5	1.3	1.4	6.3	1.7	4.1	1.2	•
Current Assets to Working Capital 38	2.5	•	•	•	2.3	2.0	2.9	2.2	2.0	3.4	1.8	3.4	•
Current Liabilities to Working Capital 39	1.5	•	•	•	1.3	1.0	1.9	1.2	1.0	2.4	0.8	2.4	•
Working Capital to Net Sales 40	0.1	•	•	•	0.1	0.1	0.1	0.2	0.2	0.1	0.3	0.1	•
Inventory to Working Capital 41	1.1	•	•	•	1.1	1.1	1.6	1.1	1.0	1.6	0.7	1.3	•
Total Receipts to Cash Flow 42	11.7	•	•	•	6.3	9.5	14.1	15.9	18.9	24.3	19.4	10.9	•
Cost of Goods to Cash Flow 43	8.2	•	•	•	3.8	7.1	11.2	12.5	15.3	20.1	14.1	7.0	•
Cash Flow to Total Debt 44	0.2	•	•	•	0.7	0.4	0.3	0.2	0.1	0.1	0.1	0.1	•

Selected Financial Factors (in Percentages)													
Debt Ratio 45	61.4	•	•	•	59.1	71.7	57.4	58.8	86.2	63.6	80.4	54.3	•
Return on Total Assets 46	3.2	•	•	•	12.5	23.4	4.0	4.5	3.1	•	3.5	2.0	•
Return on Equity Before Income Taxes 47	3.6	•	•	•	26.8	62.8	5.1	5.2	9.0	•	1.9	1.4	•
Return on Equity After Income Taxes 48	2.2	•	•	•	24.7	59.4	3.5	3.2	8.0	•	•	0.6	•
Profit Margin (Before Income Tax) 49	1.1	•	•	•	4.0	6.1	0.9	1.2	0.8	•	0.3	0.9	•
Profit Margin (After Income Tax) 50	0.7	•	•	•	3.7	5.8	0.6	0.7	0.7	•	•	0.4	•

Table II

Corporations with Net Income

TEXTILE PRODUCT MILLS

MONEY AMOUNTS AND SIZE OF ASSETS IN THOUSANDS OF DOLLARS

Item Description for Accounting Period 7/11 Through 6/12		Total	Zero Assets	Under 500	500 to 1,000	1,000 to 5,000	5,000 to 10,000	10,000 to 25,000	25,000 to 50,000	50,000 to 100,000	100,000 to 250,000	250,000 to 500,000	500,000 to 2,500,000	2,500,000 and over
Number of Enterprises	1	1519	0	•	139	553	36	34	24	4	3	•	•	0
Revenues ($ in Thousands)														
Net Sales	2	13580847	0	•	126704	3172189	693193	1117716	1605493	450731	725036	•	•	0
Interest	3	3951	0	•	196	359	35	11	638	0	1135	•	•	0
Rents	4	4901	0	•	1273	0	1081	0	906	0	895	•	•	0
Royalties	5	46030	0	•	0	0	0	0	0	0	0	•	•	0
Other Portfolio Income	6	74801	0	•	0	6055	3764	621	4795	102	459	•	•	0
Other Receipts	7	135876	0	•	1	19941	128	1806	13042	12839	2923	•	•	0
Total Receipts	8	13846406	0	•	128174	3198544	698201	1120154	1624874	463672	730448	•	•	0
Average Total Receipts	9	9115	•	•	922	5784	19394	32946	67703	115918	243483	•	•	•
Operating Costs/Operating Income (%)														
Cost of Operations	10	69.7	•	•	66.8	58.2	74.8	77.2	80.4	78.1	83.6	•	•	•
Salaries and Wages	11	7.4	•	•	2.2	11.1	2.8	3.3	5.1	6.4	1.4	•	•	•
Taxes Paid	12	1.6	•	•	1.8	1.8	2.4	2.4	1.0	1.4	1.4	•	•	•
Interest Paid	13	1.2	•	•	0.3	0.6	1.9	0.3	0.6	1.2	0.3	•	•	•
Depreciation	14	2.3	•	•	0.3	3.4	1.4	1.0	1.0	1.1	2.8	•	•	•
Amortization and Depletion	15	0.3	•	•	0.1	0.1	0.0	0.1	0.1	0.3	0.2	•	•	•
Pensions and Other Deferred Comp.	16	0.6	•	•	0.0	0.1	0.3	0.1	0.2	0.2	0.2	•	•	•
Employee Benefits	17	1.3	•	•	•	0.8	0.6	1.3	1.4	0.9	1.4	•	•	•
Advertising	18	0.8	•	•	•	1.1	0.1	0.4	0.3	0.5	0.0	•	•	•
Other Expenses	19	9.9	•	•	7.6	16.0	5.5	8.4	5.6	6.8	5.8	•	•	•
Officers' Compensation	20	2.6	•	•	1.4	3.3	4.9	1.9	1.0	0.8	0.6	•	•	•
Operating Margin	21	2.4	•	•	19.4	3.7	5.4	3.6	3.4	2.1	2.3	•	•	•
Operating Margin Before Officers' Comp.	22	5.0	•	•	20.8	7.0	10.3	5.5	4.4	3.0	2.8	•	•	•

Selected Average Balance Sheet ($ in Thousands)													
Net Receivables	23	1480	•	•	291	685	1133	3424	8564	14566	35382	•	•	•
Inventories	24	1305	•	•	460	782	2558	6421	11307	21966	27362	•	•	•
Net Property, Plant and Equipment	25	887	•	•	83	412	1209	2014	4194	5805	48709	•	•	•
Total Assets	26	6381	•	•	586	2106	6643	13595	37451	65904	154668	•	•	•
Notes and Loans Payable	27	1693	•	•	66	509	3657	2184	6517	10632	16031	•	•	•
All Other Liabilities	28	2135	•	•	184	678	1105	3537	7765	25176	31549	•	•	•
Net Worth	29	2553	•	•	336	919	1881	7874	23170	30097	107088	•	•	•
Selected Financial Ratios (Times to 1)														
Current Ratio	30	1.8	•	•	2.4	1.8	2.0	2.2	2.3	2.4	2.7	•	•	•
Quick Ratio	31	1.1	•	•	1.9	0.9	0.7	1.0	1.1	1.1	1.5	•	•	•
Net Sales to Working Capital	32	5.5	•	•	3.7	7.8	7.8	5.9	4.7	4.4	4.7	•	•	•
Coverage Ratio	33	4.9	•	•	62.2	9.2	4.2	13.9	9.0	5.4	12.1	•	•	•
Total Asset Turnover	34	1.4	•	•	1.6	2.7	2.9	2.4	1.8	1.7	1.6	•	•	•
Inventory Turnover	35	4.8	•	•	1.3	4.3	5.6	4.0	4.8	4.0	7.4	•	•	•
Receivables Turnover	36	6.7	•	•	4.2	9.1	16.0	8.3	8.0	•	•	•	•	•
Total Liabilities to Net Worth	37	1.5	•	•	0.7	1.3	2.5	0.7	0.6	1.2	0.4	•	•	•
Current Assets to Working Capital	38	2.2	•	•	1.7	2.2	2.0	1.8	1.7	1.7	1.6	•	•	•
Current Liabilities to Working Capital	39	1.2	•	•	0.7	1.2	1.0	0.8	0.7	0.7	0.6	•	•	•
Working Capital to Net Sales	40	0.2	•	•	0.3	0.1	0.1	0.2	0.2	0.2	0.2	•	•	•
Inventory to Working Capital	41	0.8	•	•	0.3	1.0	1.1	0.9	0.8	0.9	0.5	•	•	•
Total Receipts to Cash Flow	42	8.5	•	•	4.1	6.1	9.5	9.5	12.3	11.6	11.9	•	•	•
Cost of Goods to Cash Flow	43	5.9	•	•	2.7	3.5	7.1	7.3	9.9	9.1	9.9	•	•	•
Cash Flow to Total Debt	44	0.3	•	•	0.9	0.8	0.4	0.6	0.4	0.3	0.4	•	•	•
Selected Financial Factors (in Percentages)														
Debt Ratio	45	60.0	•	•	42.7	56.4	71.7	42.1	38.1	54.3	30.8	•	•	•
Return on Total Assets	46	8.0	•	•	32.4	13.9	23.4	9.9	9.2	10.8	5.0	•	•	•
Return on Equity Before Income Taxes	47	15.9	•	•	55.7	28.3	62.8	15.9	13.3	19.3	6.7	•	•	•
Return on Equity After Income Taxes	48	13.5	•	•	55.3	26.3	59.4	13.9	11.2	18.5	5.4	•	•	•
Profit Margin (Before Income Tax)	49	4.5	•	•	20.5	4.5	6.1	3.8	4.6	5.2	3.0	•	•	•
Profit Margin (After Income Tax)	50	3.8	•	•	20.4	4.2	5.8	3.3	3.9	5.0	2.4	•	•	•

Table I

Corporations with and without Net Income

APPAREL KNITTING MILLS

MONEY AMOUNTS AND SIZE OF ASSETS IN THOUSANDS OF DOLLARS

Item Description for Accounting Period 7/11 Through 6/12		Total	Zero Assets	Under 500	500 to 1,000	1,000 to 5,000	5,000 to 10,000	10,000 to 25,000	25,000 to 50,000	50,000 to 100,000	100,000 to 250,000	250,000 to 500,000	500,000 to 2,500,000	2,500,000 and over
Number of Enterprises	1	256	0	181	0	35	9	18	4	•	0	•	0	•
Revenues ($ in Thousands)														
Net Sales	2	7531346	0	170205	0	33936	113513	433743	225170	•	0	•	0	•
Interest	3	8195	0	0	0	5296	0	809	216	•	0	•	0	•
Rents	4	150	0	0	0	0	0	11	0	•	0	•	0	•
Royalties	5	50539	0	0	0	0	0	0	0	•	0	•	0	•
Other Portfolio Income	6	26261	0	0	0	1402	0	3109	145	•	0	•	0	•
Other Receipts	7	7935	0	0	0	0	48	5823	347	•	0	•	0	•
Total Receipts	8	7624426	0	170205	0	40634	113561	443495	225878	•	0	•	0	•
Average Total Receipts	9	29783	•	940	•	1161	12618	24639	56470	•	•	•	•	•
Operating Costs/Operating Income (%)														
Cost of Operations	10	74.9	•	56.7	•	89.9	77.2	70.1	77.6	•	•	•	•	•
Salaries and Wages	11	6.5	•	14.0	•	25.4	2.8	7.4	4.8	•	•	•	•	•
Taxes Paid	12	1.2	•	3.5	•	4.8	2.8	1.1	1.8	•	•	•	•	•
Interest Paid	13	2.4	•	0.2	•	0.5	0.8	0.7	0.1	•	•	•	•	•
Depreciation	14	0.9	•	1.2	•	0.2	1.9	2.4	1.3	•	•	•	•	•
Amortization and Depletion	15	0.2	•	•	•	0.0	•	0.0	0.0	•	•	•	•	•
Pensions and Other Deferred Comp.	16	0.8	•	•	•	0.2	•	0.0	0.3	•	•	•	•	•
Employee Benefits	17	1.3	•	0.1	•	1.9	3.1	0.7	0.6	•	•	•	•	•
Advertising	18	3.0	•	1.2	•	0.1	0.1	0.2	1.7	•	•	•	•	•
Other Expenses	19	8.0	•	15.9	•	24.8	8.3	8.3	7.5	•	•	•	•	•
Officers' Compensation	20	0.8	•	2.8	•	4.9	2.1	2.5	1.9	•	•	•	•	•
Operating Margin	21	•	•	4.4	•	•	1.0	6.5	2.4	•	•	•	•	•
Operating Margin Before Officers' Comp.	22	0.7	•	7.2	•	•	3.1	9.0	4.3	•	•	•	•	•

Selected Average Balance Sheet ($ in Thousands)														
Net Receivables	23	3071	•	142	•	74	1920	4015	7472	•	•	•	•	•
Inventories	24	6784	•	111	•	104	3385	2113	8974	•	•	•	•	•
Net Property, Plant and Equipment	25	1486	•	1	•	74	359	1347	2173	•	•	•	•	•
Total Assets	26	29828	•	323	•	2067	6375	15732	28516	•	•	•	•	•
Notes and Loans Payable	27	10521	•	59	•	92	1435	3061	2142	•	•	•	•	•
All Other Liabilities	28	18639	•	71	•	325	873	1461	5933	•	•	•	•	•
Net Worth	29	668	•	193	•	1650	4067	11209	20440	•	•	•	•	•

Selected Financial Ratios (Times to 1)														
Current Ratio	30	2.6	•	4.1	•	0.9	2.7	2.5	3.1	•	•	•	•	•
Quick Ratio	31	0.7	•	2.0	•	0.5	1.0	1.9	1.4	•	•	•	•	•
Net Sales to Working Capital	32	3.9	•	4.2	•	•	3.5	3.8	4.1	•	•	•	•	•
Coverage Ratio	33	1.6	•	23.9	•	•	2.3	13.5	35.3	•	•	•	•	•
Total Asset Turnover	34	1.0	•	2.9	•	0.5	2.0	1.5	2.0	•	•	•	•	•
Inventory Turnover	35	3.2	•	4.8	•	8.4	2.9	8.0	4.9	•	•	•	•	•
Receivables Turnover	36	9.4	•	8.1	•	14.4	5.5	5.9	6.9	•	•	•	•	•
Total Liabilities to Net Worth	37	43.6	•	0.7	•	0.3	0.6	0.4	0.4	•	•	•	•	•
Current Assets to Working Capital	38	1.6	•	1.3	•	•	1.6	1.7	1.5	•	•	•	•	•
Current Liabilities to Working Capital	39	0.6	•	0.3	•	•	0.6	0.7	0.5	•	•	•	•	•
Working Capital to Net Sales	40	0.3	•	0.2	•	•	0.3	0.3	0.2	•	•	•	•	•
Inventory to Working Capital	41	1.0	•	0.6	•	•	1.0	0.3	0.7	•	•	•	•	•
Total Receipts to Cash Flow	42	13.7	•	5.5	•	•	20.3	6.7	11.2	•	•	•	•	•
Cost of Goods to Cash Flow	43	10.3	•	3.1	•	•	15.6	4.7	8.7	•	•	•	•	•
Cash Flow to Total Debt	44	0.1	•	1.3	•	•	0.3	0.8	0.6	•	•	•	•	•

Selected Financial Factors (in Percentages)														
Debt Ratio	45	97.8	•	40.2	•	20.2	36.2	28.7	28.3	•	•	•	•	•
Return on Total Assets	46	3.7	•	13.4	•	•	3.7	14.3	5.5	•	•	•	•	•
Return on Equity Before Income Taxes	47	59.5	•	21.5	•	•	3.2	18.6	7.5	•	•	•	•	•
Return on Equity After Income Taxes	48	35.0	•	18.3	•	•	2.4	18.6	6.4	•	•	•	•	•
Profit Margin (Before Income Tax)	49	1.4	•	4.4	•	•	1.0	8.6	2.7	•	•	•	•	•
Profit Margin (After Income Tax)	50	0.8	•	3.8	•	•	0.8	8.6	2.3	•	•	•	•	•

APPAREL KNITTING MILLS

MONEY AMOUNTS AND SIZE OF ASSETS IN THOUSANDS OF DOLLARS

Item Description for Accounting Period 7/11 Through 6/12		Total	Zero Assets	Under 500	500 to 1,000	1,000 to 5,000	5,000 to 10,000	10,000 to 25,000	25,000 to 50,000	50,000 to 100,000	100,000 to 250,000	250,000 to 500,000	500,000 to 2,500,000	2,500,000 and over
Number of Enterprises	1	218	0	•	0	0	9	18	•	0	•	•	0	•
Revenues ($ in Thousands)														
Net Sales	2	6395589	0	•	0	0	113513	433743	•	0	•	•	0	•
Interest	3	2786	0	•	0	0	0	809	•	0	•	•	0	•
Rents	4	11	0	•	0	0	0	11	•	0	•	•	0	•
Royalties	5	41992	0	•	0	0	0	0	•	0	•	•	0	•
Other Portfolio Income	6	21970	0	•	0	0	0	3109	•	0	•	•	0	•
Other Receipts	7	7178	0	•	0	0	48	5823	•	0	•	•	0	•
Total Receipts	8	6469526	0	•	0	0	113561	443495	•	0	•	•	0	•
Average Total Receipts	9	29677	•	•	•	•	12618	24639	•	•	•	•	•	•
Operating Costs/Operating Income (%)														
Cost of Operations	10	72.9	•	•	•	•	77.2	70.1	•	•	•	•	•	•
Salaries and Wages	11	6.7	•	•	•	•	2.8	7.4	•	•	•	•	•	•
Taxes Paid	12	1.2	•	•	•	•	2.8	1.1	•	•	•	•	•	•
Interest Paid	13	2.7	•	•	•	•	0.8	0.7	•	•	•	•	•	•
Depreciation	14	0.9	•	•	•	•	1.9	2.4	•	•	•	•	•	•
Amortization and Depletion	15	0.2	•	•	•	•	•	0.0	•	•	•	•	•	•
Pensions and Other Deferred Comp.	16	0.6	•	•	•	•	•	0.0	•	•	•	•	•	•
Employee Benefits	17	1.4	•	•	•	•	3.1	0.7	•	•	•	•	•	•
Advertising	18	3.4	•	•	•	•	0.1	0.2	•	•	•	•	•	•
Other Expenses	19	7.5	•	•	•	•	8.3	8.3	•	•	•	•	•	•
Officers' Compensation	20	0.8	•	•	•	•	2.1	2.5	•	•	•	•	•	•
Operating Margin	21	1.7	•	•	•	•	1.0	6.5	•	•	•	•	•	•
Operating Margin Before Officers' Comp.	22	2.5	•	•	•	•	3.1	9.0	•	•	•	•	•	•

	Selected Average Balance Sheet ($ in Thousands)												
Net Receivables **23**	2801	•	•	•	•	1920	4015	•	•	•	•	•	•
Inventories **24**	6543	•	•	•	•	3385	1383	•	•	•	•	•	•
Net Property, Plant and Equipment **25**	1473	•	•	•	•	359	1347	•	•	•	•	•	•
Total Assets **26**	30183	•	•	•	•	6375	15732	•	•	•	•	•	•
Notes and Loans Payable **27**	10536	•	•	•	•	1435	3061	•	•	•	•	•	•
All Other Liabilities **28**	20653	•	•	•	•	873	1461	•	•	•	•	•	•
Net Worth **29**	-1006	•	•	•	•	4067	11209	•	•	•	•	•	•
	Selected Financial Ratios (Times to 1)												
Current Ratio **30**	2.6	•	•	•	•	2.7	2.5	•	•	•	•	•	•
Quick Ratio **31**	0.7	•	•	•	•	1.0	1.9	•	•	•	•	•	•
Net Sales to Working Capital **32**	4.1	•	•	•	•	3.5	3.8	•	•	•	•	•	•
Coverage Ratio **33**	2.2	•	•	•	•	2.3	13.5	•	•	•	•	•	•
Total Asset Turnover **34**	1.0	•	•	•	•	2.0	1.5	•	•	•	•	•	•
Inventory Turnover **35**	3.3	•	•	•	•	2.9	12.2	•	•	•	•	•	•
Receivables Turnover **36**	9.9	•	•	•	•	5.5	7.3	•	•	•	•	•	•
Total Liabilities to Net Worth **37**	•	•	•	•	•	0.6	0.4	•	•	•	•	•	•
Current Assets to Working Capital **38**	1.6	•	•	•	•	1.6	1.7	•	•	•	•	•	•
Current Liabilities to Working Capital **39**	0.6	•	•	•	•	0.6	0.7	•	•	•	•	•	•
Working Capital to Net Sales **40**	0.2	•	•	•	•	0.3	0.3	•	•	•	•	•	•
Inventory to Working Capital **41**	1.0	•	•	•	•	1.0	0.3	•	•	•	•	•	•
Total Receipts to Cash Flow **42**	11.8	•	•	•	•	20.3	6.7	•	•	•	•	•	•
Cost of Goods to Cash Flow **43**	8.6	•	•	•	•	15.6	4.7	•	•	•	•	•	•
Cash Flow to Total Debt **44**	0.1	•	•	•	•	0.3	0.8	•	•	•	•	•	•
	Selected Financial Factors (in Percentages)												
Debt Ratio **45**	103.3	•	•	•	•	36.2	28.7	•	•	•	•	•	•
Return on Total Assets **46**	5.7	•	•	•	•	3.7	14.3	•	•	•	•	•	•
Return on Equity Before Income Taxes **47**	•	•	•	•	•	3.2	18.6	•	•	•	•	•	•
Return on Equity After Income Taxes **48**	•	•	•	•	•	2.4	18.6	•	•	•	•	•	•
Profit Margin (Before Income Tax) **49**	3.2	•	•	•	•	1.0	8.6	•	•	•	•	•	•
Profit Margin (After Income Tax) **50**	2.5	•	•	•	•	0.8	8.6	•	•	•	•	•	•

Table I

Corporations with and without Net Income

CUT AND SEW APPAREL CONTRACTORS AND MFRS.

MONEY AMOUNTS AND SIZE OF ASSETS IN THOUSANDS OF DOLLARS

Item Description for Accounting Period 7/11 Through 6/12		Total	Zero Assets	Under 500	500 to 1,000	1,000 to 5,000	5,000 to 10,000	10,000 to 25,000	25,000 to 50,000	50,000 to 100,000	100,000 to 250,000	250,000 to 500,000	500,000 to 2,500,000	2,500,000 and over
Number of Enterprises	1	6202	1776	3119	291	647	224	76	23	21	•	4	•	•
Revenues ($ in Thousands)														
Net Sales	2	37127379	439442	1475797	741026	3292820	3359088	3100003	2227246	2232571	•	1633103	•	•
Interest	3	22170	101	5	0	2237	549	540	1772	261	•	238	•	•
Rents	4	10361	162	0	0	17	0	0	369	2143	•	0	•	•
Royalties	5	686310	0	0	0	28130	41	68	787	16850	•	0	•	•
Other Portfolio Income	6	87764	24	0	0	7	10	158	4	1941	•	1340	•	•
Other Receipts	7	601537	471	7835	9	24974	99405	20907	9572	12157	•	22763	•	•
Total Receipts	8	38535521	440200	1483637	741035	3348185	3459093	3121676	2239750	2265923	•	1657444	•	•
Average Total Receipts	9	6213	248	476	2547	5175	15442	41075	97380	107901	•	414361	•	•
Operating Costs/Operating Income (%)														
Cost of Operations	10	64.2	54.2	47.3	64.9	71.7	72.2	70.3	73.9	73.6	•	53.5	•	•
Salaries and Wages	11	10.0	10.0	19.7	11.3	9.3	9.1	6.4	5.4	7.3	•	13.0	•	•
Taxes Paid	12	2.0	2.0	2.8	1.5	2.0	2.1	2.0	3.6	1.2	•	3.2	•	•
Interest Paid	13	1.4	4.8	0.3	0.8	1.1	0.6	1.1	0.6	0.8	•	3.8	•	•
Depreciation	14	1.5	1.7	1.3	0.3	0.4	1.2	0.6	0.4	1.0	•	2.5	•	•
Amortization and Depletion	15	0.6	1.1	0.1	0.1	0.1	0.1	0.3	0.2	0.5	•	0.5	•	•
Pensions and Other Deferred Comp.	16	0.7	0.4	•	0.2	0.4	0.2	0.1	0.6	0.4	•	0.8	•	•
Employee Benefits	17	1.0	0.9	1.0	0.7	0.9	1.0	0.5	0.6	1.2	•	1.5	•	•
Advertising	18	2.5	1.4	0.0	0.6	1.7	1.4	1.2	0.9	1.5	•	5.0	•	•
Other Expenses	19	13.4	39.9	26.3	13.7	8.8	7.0	10.8	7.3	8.3	•	16.1	•	•
Officers' Compensation	20	2.2	4.4	3.6	3.5	5.2	4.2	2.3	1.2	1.4	•	1.5	•	•
Operating Margin	21	0.5	•	•	2.3	•	1.0	4.5	5.4	2.7	•	•	•	•
Operating Margin Before Officers' Comp.	22	2.7	•	1.2	5.8	3.5	5.2	6.8	6.6	4.2	•	0.1	•	•

Selected Average Balance Sheet ($ in Thousands)														
Net Receivables	23	705	0	11	121	280	1966	4439	5366	16913	•	54639	•	•
Inventories	24	857	0	9	197	896	1815	6409	15363	23933	•	109298	•	•
Net Property, Plant and Equipment	25	480	0	13	251	200	2242	1318	2601	5286	•	52027	•	•
Total Assets	26	4728	0	82	720	2138	7502	17556	33270	70479	•	357854	•	•
Notes and Loans Payable	27	1789	0	70	333	864	1493	5031	5294	16721	•	105745	•	•
All Other Liabilities	28	1356	0	41	130	660	1924	4608	8526	16136	•	94174	•	•
Net Worth	29	1583	0	-28	258	613	4084	7916	19450	37622	•	157934	•	•
Selected Financial Ratios (Times to 1)														
Current Ratio	30	1.9	•	1.4	1.2	2.0	2.0	2.4	2.4	2.5	•	3.0	•	•
Quick Ratio	31	0.9	•	1.0	0.6	0.8	1.0	0.9	0.7	1.1	•	1.2	•	•
Net Sales to Working Capital	32	5.9	•	28.0	41.5	5.6	6.4	4.7	5.9	3.5	•	3.0	•	•
Coverage Ratio	33	4.3	•	•	4.1	1.0	7.7	5.5	11.6	6.1	•	1.0	•	•
Total Asset Turnover	34	1.3	•	5.8	3.5	2.4	2.0	2.3	2.9	1.5	•	1.1	•	•
Inventory Turnover	35	4.5	•	26.3	8.4	4.1	6.0	4.5	4.7	3.3	•	2.0	•	•
Receivables Turnover	36	8.9	•	41.7	10.3	18.8	10.0	9.2	14.4	•	•	8.0	•	•
Total Liabilities to Net Worth	37	2.0	•	•	1.8	2.5	0.8	1.2	0.7	0.9	•	1.3	•	•
Current Assets to Working Capital	38	2.1	•	3.5	5.7	2.0	2.0	1.7	1.7	1.7	•	1.5	•	•
Current Liabilities to Working Capital	39	1.1	•	2.5	4.7	1.0	1.0	0.7	0.7	0.7	•	0.5	•	•
Working Capital to Net Sales	40	0.2	•	0.0	0.0	0.2	0.2	0.2	0.2	0.3	•	0.3	•	•
Inventory to Working Capital	41	0.9	•	0.8	2.5	0.8	0.9	0.7	1.0	0.8	•	0.9	•	•
Total Receipts to Cash Flow	42	7.2	11.3	6.3	9.5	16.4	11.3	7.1	8.6	9.2	•	9.9	•	•
Cost of Goods to Cash Flow	43	4.6	6.1	3.0	6.2	11.8	8.2	5.0	6.4	6.7	•	5.3	•	•
Cash Flow to Total Debt	44	0.3	•	0.7	0.6	0.2	0.4	0.6	0.8	0.4	•	0.2	•	•
Selected Financial Factors (in Percentages)														
Debt Ratio	45	66.5	•	134.3	64.2	71.3	45.6	54.9	41.5	46.6	•	55.9	•	•
Return on Total Assets	46	7.9	•	•	10.8	2.7	9.1	14.6	18.9	7.5	•	4.4	•	•
Return on Equity Before Income Taxes	47	18.2	•	30.9	22.7	0.1	14.6	26.5	29.5	11.8	•	0.2	•	•
Return on Equity After Income Taxes	48	13.3	•	31.0	22.0	•	14.3	25.0	28.6	11.2	•	•	•	•
Profit Margin (Before Income Tax)	49	4.8	•	•	2.3	0.0	4.0	5.1	5.9	4.2	•	0.1	•	•
Profit Margin (After Income Tax)	50	3.5	•	•	2.2	•	3.9	4.9	5.7	4.0	•	•	•	•

Table II

Corporations with Net Income

CUT AND SEW APPAREL CONTRACTORS AND MFRS.

MONEY AMOUNTS AND SIZE OF ASSETS IN THOUSANDS OF DOLLARS

Item Description for Accounting Period 7/11 Through 6/12		Total	Zero Assets	Under 500	500 to 1,000	1,000 to 5,000	5,000 to 10,000	10,000 to 25,000	25,000 to 50,000	50,000 to 100,000	100,000 to 250,000	250,000 to 500,000	500,000 to 2,500,000	2,500,000 and over
Number of Enterprises	1	3083	•	1522	•	457	136	58	23	16	•	•	8	•
Revenues ($ in Thousands)														
Net Sales	2	32164020	•	823958	•	2415124	2578591	2560453	2227246	1896722	•	•	15880819	•
Interest	3	21148	•	0	•	2231	93	537	1772	231	•	•	15430	•
Rents	4	10188	•	0	•	17	0	0	369	2132	•	•	7405	•
Royalties	5	679848	•	0	•	28130	0	68	787	16546	•	•	634316	•
Other Portfolio Income	6	84428	•	0	•	7	10	61	4	845	•	•	83161	•
Other Receipts	7	521322	•	9	•	17844	59987	20581	9572	12824	•	•	374758	•
Total Receipts	8	33480954	•	823967	•	2463353	2638681	2581700	2239750	1929300	•	•	16995889	•
Average Total Receipts	9	10860	•	541	•	5390	19402	44512	97380	120581	•	•	2124486	•
Operating Costs/Operating Income (%)														
Cost of Operations	10	64.0	•	35.0	•	73.0	71.3	68.1	73.9	72.4	•	•	60.0	•
Salaries and Wages	11	9.2	•	26.8	•	4.8	7.1	6.6	5.4	6.5	•	•	10.6	•
Taxes Paid	12	1.9	•	4.0	•	1.7	1.9	2.0	3.6	1.3	•	•	1.7	•
Interest Paid	13	1.3	•	0.2	•	1.2	0.4	0.9	0.6	0.8	•	•	1.8	•
Depreciation	14	1.5	•	1.6	•	0.4	1.5	0.6	0.4	1.0	•	•	2.0	•
Amortization and Depletion	15	0.6	•	0.0	•	0.0	0.1	0.2	0.2	0.5	•	•	1.0	•
Pensions and Other Deferred Comp.	16	0.7	•	•	•	0.4	0.2	0.1	0.6	0.2	•	•	1.1	•
Employee Benefits	17	1.0	•	1.3	•	0.6	1.3	0.4	0.6	1.3	•	•	1.0	•
Advertising	18	2.5	•	0.1	•	0.5	0.7	1.3	0.9	1.6	•	•	3.8	•
Other Expenses	19	12.8	•	20.9	•	7.2	7.4	10.7	7.3	8.7	•	•	16.2	•
Officers' Compensation	20	2.2	•	5.5	•	5.3	5.3	2.2	1.2	1.5	•	•	1.3	•
Operating Margin	21	2.3	•	4.7	•	5.0	3.0	6.9	5.4	4.2	•	•	•	•
Operating Margin Before Officers' Comp.	22	4.4	•	10.2	•	10.3	8.2	9.1	6.6	5.7	•	•	0.6	•

Selected Average Balance Sheet ($ in Thousands)												
Net Receivables 23	1328	•	21	•	363	2658	5123	5366	19299	•	•	295377	•
Inventories 24	1414	•	7	•	1064	1649	5066	13858	22540	•	•	258855	•
Net Property, Plant and Equipment 25	787	•	14	•	239	1241	1245	2601	6274	•	•	187354	•
Total Assets 26	8667	•	121	•	2255	7509	17914	33270	72753	•	•	2374087	•
Notes and Loans Payable 27	3278	•	112	•	657	1299	4098	5294	17548	•	•	1025005	•
All Other Liabilities 28	2436	•	46	•	765	1311	4486	8526	18358	•	•	711630	•
Net Worth 29	2953	•	-37	•	833	4898	9330	19450	36846	•	•	637452	•

Selected Financial Ratios (Times to 1)													
Current Ratio 30	1.9	•	2.1	•	2.4	2.6	2.5	2.4	2.3	•	•	1.6	•
Quick Ratio 31	1.0	•	1.9	•	1.0	1.5	1.0	0.7	1.1	•	•	0.9	•
Net Sales to Working Capital 32	5.7	•	10.6	•	4.7	5.4	4.8	5.9	3.9	•	•	7.2	•
Coverage Ratio 33	6.3	•	31.2	•	6.9	13.9	10.0	11.6	8.4	•	•	5.2	•
Total Asset Turnover 34	1.2	•	4.5	•	2.3	2.5	2.5	2.9	1.6	•	•	0.8	•
Inventory Turnover 35	4.7	•	28.4	•	3.6	8.2	5.9	5.2	3.8	•	•	4.6	•
Receivables Turnover 36	8.4	•	25.3	•	14.7	10.4	8.6	16.9	7.4	•	•	7.1	•
Total Liabilities to Net Worth 37	1.9	•	•	•	1.7	0.5	0.9	0.7	1.0	•	•	2.7	•
Current Assets to Working Capital 38	2.1	•	1.9	•	1.7	1.6	1.7	1.7	1.8	•	•	2.8	•
Current Liabilities to Working Capital 39	1.1	•	0.9	•	0.7	0.6	0.7	0.7	0.8	•	•	1.8	•
Working Capital to Net Sales 40	0.2	•	0.1	•	0.2	0.2	0.2	0.2	0.3	•	•	0.1	•
Inventory to Working Capital 41	0.8	•	0.2	•	0.6	0.6	0.6	1.0	0.8	•	•	1.0	•
Total Receipts to Cash Flow 42	6.4	•	6.6	•	8.0	9.5	6.0	8.6	7.5	•	•	5.5	•
Cost of Goods to Cash Flow 43	4.1	•	2.3	•	5.8	6.8	4.1	6.4	5.5	•	•	3.3	•
Cash Flow to Total Debt 44	0.3	•	0.5	•	0.5	0.8	0.9	0.8	0.4	•	•	0.2	•

Selected Financial Factors (in Percentages)													
Debt Ratio 45	65.9	•	130.6	•	63.1	34.8	47.9	41.5	49.4	•	•	73.1	•
Return on Total Assets 46	10.0	•	21.7	•	19.1	14.4	21.1	18.9	10.9	•	•	7.8	•
Return on Equity Before Income Taxes 47	24.6	•	•	•	44.2	20.5	36.4	29.5	18.9	•	•	23.6	•
Return on Equity After Income Taxes 48	19.4	•	•	•	43.4	20.0	34.7	28.6	18.1	•	•	15.5	•
Profit Margin (Before Income Tax) 49	7.0	•	4.7	•	7.0	5.3	7.7	5.9	5.9	•	•	7.6	•
Profit Margin (After Income Tax) 50	5.5	•	4.7	•	6.8	5.2	7.3	5.7	5.6	•	•	5.0	•

Table I

Corporations with and without Net Income

APPAREL ACCESSORIES AND OTHER APPAREL

MONEY AMOUNTS AND SIZE OF ASSETS IN THOUSANDS OF DOLLARS

Item Description for Accounting Period 7/11 Through 6/12		Total	Zero Assets	Under 500	500 to 1,000	1,000 to 5,000	5,000 to 10,000	10,000 to 25,000	25,000 to 50,000	50,000 to 100,000	100,000 to 250,000	250,000 to 500,000	500,000 to 2,500,000	2,500,000 and over
Number of Enterprises	1	4135	1269	2499	55	168	77	40	17	•	•	0	•	0
Revenues ($ in Thousands)														
Net Sales	2	7661644	14845	1206084	126191	661073	1121309	1246574	1075562	•	•	0	•	0
Interest	3	1074	0	0	32	29	192	225	95	•	•	0	•	0
Rents	4	184	0	0	0	0	5	0	145	•	•	0	•	0
Royalties	5	2261	0	0	0	0	0	1719	8	•	•	0	•	0
Other Portfolio Income	6	30853	5	27722	0	19	0	1921	91	•	•	0	•	0
Other Receipts	7	54512	0	180	1	5135	11881	4938	2214	•	•	0	•	0
Total Receipts	8	7750528	14850	1233986	126224	666256	1133387	1255377	1078115	•	•	0	•	0
Average Total Receipts	9	1874	12	494	2295	3966	14719	31384	63419	•	•	•	•	•
Operating Costs/Operating Income (%)														
Cost of Operations	10	61.8	189.9	52.7	74.6	51.7	73.8	74.6	62.1	•	•	•	•	•
Salaries and Wages	11	11.7	20.9	21.7	7.8	7.2	10.0	6.0	11.4	•	•	•	•	•
Taxes Paid	12	3.3	1.1	1.7	2.6	2.4	2.8	1.7	2.0	•	•	•	•	•
Interest Paid	13	1.6	•	0.4	1.6	0.1	1.0	2.6	0.7	•	•	•	•	•
Depreciation	14	1.1	•	0.3	1.3	0.7	0.8	0.8	2.2	•	•	•	•	•
Amortization and Depletion	15	0.5	•	0.4	0.1	0.0	0.3	0.3	0.1	•	•	•	•	•
Pensions and Other Deferred Comp.	16	0.4	•	•	•	3.2	0.1	0.2	0.1	•	•	•	•	•
Employee Benefits	17	1.0	1.1	0.3	0.8	1.8	1.2	0.7	1.1	•	•	•	•	•
Advertising	18	1.4	4.1	0.5	0.1	0.6	0.3	1.1	1.7	•	•	•	•	•
Other Expenses	19	12.4	50.9	14.7	8.5	10.7	7.7	7.3	10.8	•	•	•	•	•
Officers' Compensation	20	2.7	0.6	3.0	•	10.6	2.7	2.2	2.5	•	•	•	•	•
Operating Margin	21	2.1	•	4.3	2.7	11.1	•	2.6	5.3	•	•	•	•	•
Operating Margin Before Officers' Comp.	22	4.8	•	7.3	2.7	21.7	2.0	4.8	7.7	•	•	•	•	•

Selected Average Balance Sheet ($ in Thousands)														
Net Receivables	23	240	0	34	263	626	2256	2945	7417	•	•	•	•	•
Inventories	24	329	0	41	566	382	1978	6151	17897	•	•	•	•	•
Net Property, Plant and Equipment	25	77	0	2	89	121	270	1099	4251	•	•	•	•	•
Total Assets	26	981	0	98	893	1782	6601	14300	32197	•	•	•	•	•
Notes and Loans Payable	27	444	0	92	1058	49	1579	9099	12646	•	•	•	•	•
All Other Liabilities	28	423	0	27	280	356	3005	8618	5901	•	•	•	•	•
Net Worth	29	115	0	-22	-445	1376	2017	-3417	13650	•	•	•	•	•

Selected Financial Ratios (Times to 1)														
Current Ratio	30	1.6	•	3.3	3.1	4.7	1.4	1.3	2.0	•	•	•	•	•
Quick Ratio	31	0.7	•	2.1	1.0	3.7	0.8	0.4	0.6	•	•	•	•	•
Net Sales to Working Capital	32	7.1	•	7.7	4.3	3.1	9.4	11.9	4.9	•	•	•	•	•
Coverage Ratio	33	3.0	•	18.5	2.7	157.8	1.4	2.3	8.4	•	•	•	•	•
Total Asset Turnover	34	1.9	•	4.9	2.6	2.2	2.2	2.2	2.0	•	•	•	•	•
Inventory Turnover	35	3.5	•	6.1	3.0	5.3	5.4	3.8	2.2	•	•	•	•	•
Receivables Turnover	36	8.3	•	19.5	9.4	5.9	6.9	9.8	7.9	•	•	•	•	•
Total Liabilities to Net Worth	37	7.6	•	•	•	0.3	2.3	•	1.4	•	•	•	•	•
Current Assets to Working Capital	38	2.7	•	1.4	1.5	1.3	3.5	4.5	2.0	•	•	•	•	•
Current Liabilities to Working Capital	39	1.7	•	0.4	0.5	0.3	2.5	3.5	1.0	•	•	•	•	•
Working Capital to Net Sales	40	0.1	•	0.1	0.2	0.3	0.1	0.1	0.2	•	•	•	•	•
Inventory to Working Capital	41	1.3	•	0.5	1.0	0.2	1.4	2.8	1.3	•	•	•	•	•
Total Receipts to Cash Flow	42	8.2	•	6.0	13.3	5.0	16.8	10.7	6.8	•	•	•	•	•
Cost of Goods to Cash Flow	43	5.1	•	3.2	9.9	2.6	12.4	8.0	4.2	•	•	•	•	•
Cash Flow to Total Debt	44	0.3	•	0.7	0.1	2.0	0.2	0.2	0.5	•	•	•	•	•

Selected Financial Factors (in Percentages)														
Debt Ratio	45	88.3	•	122.2	149.8	22.8	69.5	123.9	57.6	•	•	•	•	•
Return on Total Assets	46	9.1	•	34.4	10.9	26.5	3.1	12.8	12.3	•	•	•	•	•
Return on Equity Before Income Taxes	47	52.0	•	•	•	34.0	2.8	•	25.5	•	•	•	•	•
Return on Equity After Income Taxes	48	49.4	•	•	•	33.4	2.5	•	22.6	•	•	•	•	•
Profit Margin (Before Income Tax)	49	3.2	•	6.6	2.7	11.9	0.4	3.3	5.5	•	•	•	•	•
Profit Margin (After Income Tax)	50	3.1	•	6.6	2.7	11.7	0.3	3.0	4.9	•	•	•	•	•

Table II

Corporations with Net Income

APPAREL ACCESSORIES AND OTHER APPAREL

MONEY AMOUNTS AND SIZE OF ASSETS IN THOUSANDS OF DOLLARS

Item Description for Accounting Period 7/11 Through 6/12		Total	Zero Assets	Under 500	500 to 1,000	1,000 to 5,000	5,000 to 10,000	10,000 to 25,000	25,000 to 50,000	50,000 to 100,000	100,000 to 250,000	250,000 to 500,000	500,000 to 2,500,000	2,500,000 and over
Number of Enterprises	1	2414	•	•	•	134	59	31	17	6	0	0	0	0
Revenues ($ in Thousands)														
Net Sales	2	6084630	•	•	•	610197	1040852	1036770	1075562	992131	0	0	0	0
Interest	3	471	•	•	•	29	0	183	95	163	0	0	0	0
Rents	4	151	•	•	•	0	5	0	145	0	0	0	0	0
Royalties	5	543	•	•	•	0	0	0	8	535	0	0	0	0
Other Portfolio Income	6	29006	•	•	•	14	0	89	91	1084	0	0	0	0
Other Receipts	7	36479	•	•	•	4976	11858	2439	2214	14817	0	0	0	0
Total Receipts	8	6151280	•	•	•	615216	1052715	1039481	1078115	1008730	0	0	0	0
Average Total Receipts	9	2548	•	•	•	4591	17843	33532	63419	168122	•	•	•	•
Operating Costs/Operating Income (%)														
Cost of Operations	10	63.1	•	•	•	49.5	74.5	75.2	62.1	59.0	•	•	•	•
Salaries and Wages	11	10.9	•	•	•	6.4	9.6	4.3	11.4	8.6	•	•	•	•
Taxes Paid	12	2.8	•	•	•	2.4	2.7	1.1	2.0	7.1	•	•	•	•
Interest Paid	13	0.7	•	•	•	0.0	1.0	1.5	0.7	0.4	•	•	•	•
Depreciation	14	0.9	•	•	•	0.7	0.6	0.4	2.2	1.0	•	•	•	•
Amortization and Depletion	15	0.2	•	•	•	•	0.2	0.1	0.1	0.0	•	•	•	•
Pensions and Other Deferred Comp.	16	0.4	•	•	•	3.4	0.1	0.2	0.1	0.1	•	•	•	•
Employee Benefits	17	0.9	•	•	•	1.8	1.1	0.5	1.1	0.9	•	•	•	•
Advertising	18	1.3	•	•	•	0.2	0.1	1.0	1.7	4.4	•	•	•	•
Other Expenses	19	10.1	•	•	•	10.0	6.9	7.5	10.8	9.9	•	•	•	•
Officers' Compensation	20	3.2	•	•	•	10.9	2.3	2.2	2.5	1.6	•	•	•	•
Operating Margin	21	5.6	•	•	•	14.6	0.9	6.1	5.3	7.0	•	•	•	•
Operating Margin Before Officers' Comp.	22	8.8	•	•	•	25.5	3.2	8.3	7.7	8.6	•	•	•	•

Selected Average Balance Sheet ($ in Thousands)

Net Receivables	23	280	•	•	•	403	2792	2722	7417	24737	•	•	•	•
Inventories	24	419	•	•	•	449	2311	6653	16560	28286	•	•	•	•
Net Property, Plant and Equipment	25	76	•	•	•	139	189	962	4251	7072	•	•	•	•
Total Assets	26	1010	•	•	•	1748	6807	13597	32197	90148	•	•	•	•
Notes and Loans Payable	27	357	•	•	•	31	1493	4445	12646	21630	•	•	•	•
All Other Liabilities	28	308	•	•	•	383	3701	4474	5901	25218	•	•	•	•
Net Worth	29	345	•	•	•	1335	1613	4678	13650	43301	•	•	•	•

Selected Financial Ratios (Times to 1)

Current Ratio	30	1.9	•	•	•	4.2	1.2	1.5	2.0	1.9	•	•	•	•
Quick Ratio	31	0.8	•	•	•	3.1	0.6	0.4	0.6	0.8	•	•	•	•
Net Sales to Working Capital	32	6.3	•	•	•	3.7	16.9	8.4	4.9	4.7	•	•	•	•
Coverage Ratio	33	10.2	•	•	•	764.0	3.1	5.1	8.4	23.0	•	•	•	•
Total Asset Turnover	34	2.5	•	•	•	2.6	2.6	2.5	2.0	1.8	•	•	•	•
Inventory Turnover	35	3.8	•	•	•	5.0	5.7	3.8	2.4	3.4	•	•	•	•
Receivables Turnover	36	9.0	•	•	•	10.4	6.7	9.7	•	•	•	•	•	•
Total Liabilities to Net Worth	37	1.9	•	•	•	0.3	3.2	1.9	1.4	1.1	•	•	•	•
Current Assets to Working Capital	38	2.2	•	•	•	1.3	5.3	3.0	2.0	2.1	•	•	•	•
Current Liabilities to Working Capital	39	1.2	•	•	•	0.3	4.3	2.0	1.0	1.1	•	•	•	•
Working Capital to Net Sales	40	0.2	•	•	•	0.3	0.1	0.1	0.2	0.2	•	•	•	•
Inventory to Working Capital	41	1.0	•	•	•	0.3	2.4	2.0	1.3	0.8	•	•	•	•
Total Receipts to Cash Flow	42	7.0	•	•	•	4.4	14.6	8.0	6.8	5.9	•	•	•	•
Cost of Goods to Cash Flow	43	4.4	•	•	•	2.2	10.9	6.0	4.2	3.5	•	•	•	•
Cash Flow to Total Debt	44	0.5	•	•	•	2.5	0.2	0.5	0.5	0.6	•	•	•	•

Selected Financial Factors (in Percentages)

Debt Ratio	45	65.9	•	•	•	23.6	76.3	65.6	57.6	52.0	•	•	•	•
Return on Total Assets	46	18.6	•	•	•	40.1	7.8	19.4	12.3	16.6	•	•	•	•
Return on Equity Before Income Taxes	47	49.3	•	•	•	52.5	22.2	45.4	25.5	33.1	•	•	•	•
Return on Equity After Income Taxes	48	47.8	•	•	•	51.6	21.8	43.0	22.6	32.9	•	•	•	•
Profit Margin (Before Income Tax)	49	6.7	•	•	•	15.4	2.0	6.3	5.5	8.7	•	•	•	•
Profit Margin (After Income Tax)	50	6.5	•	•	•	15.1	2.0	6.0	4.9	8.6	•	•	•	•

Table I

Corporations with and without Net Income

LEATHER AND ALLIED PRODUCT MANUFACTURING

MONEY AMOUNTS AND SIZE OF ASSETS IN THOUSANDS OF DOLLARS

Item Description for Accounting Period 7/11 Through 6/12		Total	Zero Assets	Under 500	500 to 1,000	1,000 to 5,000	5,000 to 10,000	10,000 to 25,000	25,000 to 50,000	50,000 to 100,000	100,000 to 250,000	250,000 to 500,000	500,000 to 2,500,000	2,500,000 and over
Number of Enterprises	1	1469	654	572	0	177	0	27	20	6	7	3	3	0
Revenues ($ in Thousands)														
Net Sales	2	8298687	632539	282346	0	684052	0	552733	1141581	430113	1405172	1158764	2011388	0
Interest	3	5549	512	1	0	598	0	250	244	1642	204	1716	382	0
Rents	4	437	0	0	0	43	0	0	3	0	0	375	17	0
Royalties	5	158821	49470	0	0	0	0	0	0	566	2142	341	106302	0
Other Portfolio Income	6	286016	270359	0	0	1128	0	77	15	51	4	14300	81	0
Other Receipts	7	175914	33872	11	0	1	0	428	7047	31816	17230	3711	81797	0
Total Receipts	8	8925424	986752	282358	0	685822	0	553488	1148890	464188	1424752	1179207	2199967	0
Average Total Receipts	9	6076	1509	494	•	3875	•	20500	57444	77365	203536	393069	733322	•
Operating Costs/Operating Income (%)														
Cost of Operations	10	63.8	57.1	31.2	•	77.7	•	66.5	69.0	58.7	50.5	74.6	66.3	•
Salaries and Wages	11	10.7	9.5	24.3	•	6.3	•	7.9	7.0	13.2	10.6	7.8	14.7	•
Taxes Paid	12	1.8	1.1	5.5	•	2.2	•	1.6	2.0	2.5	1.5	1.2	1.6	•
Interest Paid	13	0.6	0.6	1.9	•	0.1	•	0.4	0.3	2.2	0.5	0.7	0.3	•
Depreciation	14	1.7	1.7	1.0	•	0.3	•	1.2	1.7	1.8	2.0	2.1	1.8	•
Amortization and Depletion	15	0.5	1.9	0.0	•	0.0	•	0.2	0.0	1.0	0.6	0.2	0.8	•
Pensions and Other Deferred Comp.	16	0.8	0.0	0.0	•	0.0	•	0.2	0.1	0.1	0.2	2.3	1.8	•
Employee Benefits	17	2.1	12.9	4.4	•	0.2	•	0.2	0.6	0.7	0.9	1.2	2.1	•
Advertising	18	3.2	3.0	7.4	•	0.4	•	3.2	1.8	3.2	2.5	1.3	6.1	•
Other Expenses	19	10.7	18.7	24.2	•	9.5	•	9.0	9.0	11.5	14.7	8.3	6.6	•
Officers' Compensation	20	3.2	12.9	1.8	•	2.9	•	4.0	1.6	1.7	4.8	1.4	1.5	•
Operating Margin	21	0.9	•	•	•	0.4	•	5.7	6.9	3.5	11.3	•	•	•
Operating Margin Before Officers' Comp.	22	4.2	•	0.1	•	3.3	•	9.6	8.5	5.2	16.1	0.5	•	•

Selected Average Balance Sheet ($ in Thousands)

Net Receivables	23	1249	0	0	•	204	•	2562	7721	7560	25119	65171	386134	•
Inventories	24	974	0	54	•	478	•	5350	9273	23284	39560	57605	159617	•
Net Property, Plant and Equipment	25	389	0	6	•	137	•	1137	3322	6716	10903	35280	74743	•
Total Assets	26	4326	0	182	•	1640	•	13134	30587	71570	125383	343017	885954	•
Notes and Loans Payable	27	736	0	177	•	54	•	1792	6262	26091	21942	62137	100169	•
All Other Liabilities	28	1578	0	0	•	855	•	2625	5583	9014	34905	243665	318416	•
Net Worth	29	2011	0	5	•	731	•	8717	18743	36466	68536	37215	467369	•

Selected Financial Ratios (Times to 1)

Current Ratio	30	1.8	•	7.8	•	1.6	•	3.1	2.6	4.7	1.8	0.9	1.9	•
Quick Ratio	31	0.9	•	1.7	•	0.5	•	1.5	1.3	1.8	0.8	0.3	1.4	•
Net Sales to Working Capital	32	4.5	•	7.7	•	7.1	•	2.8	3.9	2.5	5.0	•	2.4	•
Coverage Ratio	33	17.9	74.8	0.1	•	6.4	•	14.6	26.0	6.2	26.1	3.7	22.7	•
Total Asset Turnover	34	1.3	•	2.7	•	2.4	•	1.6	1.9	1.0	1.6	1.1	0.8	•
Inventory Turnover	35	3.7	•	2.9	•	6.3	•	2.5	4.2	1.8	2.6	5.0	2.8	•
Receivables Turnover	36	3.3	•	2852.0	•	18.6	•	7.2	8.7	5.9	6.8	11.9	1.1	•
Total Liabilities to Net Worth	37	1.2	•	37.1	•	1.2	•	0.5	0.6	1.0	0.8	8.2	0.9	•
Current Assets to Working Capital	38	2.3	•	1.1	•	2.6	•	1.5	1.6	1.3	2.2	•	2.1	•
Current Liabilities to Working Capital	39	1.3	•	0.1	•	1.6	•	0.5	0.6	0.3	1.2	•	1.1	•
Working Capital to Net Sales	40	0.2	•	0.1	•	0.1	•	0.4	0.3	0.4	0.2	•	0.4	•
Inventory to Working Capital	41	0.8	•	0.9	•	1.1	•	0.7	0.8	0.6	1.2	•	0.6	•
Total Receipts to Cash Flow	42	5.9	2.0	5.1	•	14.0	•	7.6	6.5	5.1	4.0	13.7	9.5	•
Cost of Goods to Cash Flow	43	3.8	1.2	1.6	•	10.9	•	5.1	4.5	3.0	2.0	10.2	6.3	•
Cash Flow to Total Debt	44	0.4	•	0.5	•	0.3	•	0.6	0.7	0.4	0.9	0.1	0.2	•

Selected Financial Factors (in Percentages)

Debt Ratio	45	53.5	•	97.4	•	55.4	•	33.6	38.7	49.0	45.3	89.2	47.2	•
Return on Total Assets	46	12.9	•	0.6	•	1.3	•	9.7	14.6	13.7	21.2	2.9	4.8	•
Return on Equity Before Income Taxes	47	26.2	•	•	•	2.5	•	13.6	22.9	22.5	37.3	19.5	8.7	•
Return on Equity After Income Taxes	48	21.6	•	•	•	2.2	•	12.2	22.9	22.1	36.9	11.9	6.5	•
Profit Margin (Before Income Tax)	49	9.3	45.4	•	•	0.5	•	5.8	7.5	11.5	12.7	1.9	6.0	•
Profit Margin (After Income Tax)	50	7.7	30.9	•	•	0.4	•	5.2	7.5	11.3	12.6	1.2	4.5	•

Table II

Corporations with Net Income

LEATHER AND ALLIED PRODUCT MANUFACTURING

MONEY AMOUNTS AND SIZE OF ASSETS IN THOUSANDS OF DOLLARS

Item Description for Accounting Period 7/11 Through 6/12		Total	Zero Assets	Under 500	500 to 1,000	1,000 to 5,000	5,000 to 10,000	10,000 to 25,000	25,000 to 50,000	50,000 to 100,000	100,000 to 250,000	250,000 to 500,000	500,000 to 2,500,000	2,500,000 and over
Number of Enterprises	1	774	401	246	0	76	0	22	16	•	•	0	3	0
Revenues ($ in Thousands)														
Net Sales	2	6403485	583796	28511	0	527168	0	499762	1052255	•	•	0	2011388	0
Interest	3	2205	512	0	0	598	0	250	0	•	•	0	382	0
Rents	4	59	0	0	0	43	0	0	0	•	•	0	17	0
Royalties	5	156504	49470	0	0	0	0	0	0	•	•	0	106302	0
Other Portfolio Income	6	282057	270359	0	0	7	0	76	15	•	•	0	81	0
Other Receipts	7	159532	33872	11	0	2	0	429	6156	•	•	0	81797	0
Total Receipts	8	7003842	938009	28522	0	527818	0	500517	1058426	•	•	0	2199967	0
Average Total Receipts	9	9049	2339	116	•	6945	•	22751	66152	•	•	•	733322	•
Operating Costs/Operating Income (%)														
Cost of Operations	10	62.7	56.9	36.4	•	87.1	•	65.0	68.3	•	•	•	66.3	•
Salaries and Wages	11	10.7	9.2	0.3	•	4.5	•	8.0	6.2	•	•	•	14.7	•
Taxes Paid	12	1.7	1.0	25.1	•	0.9	•	1.5	1.8	•	•	•	1.6	•
Interest Paid	13	0.4	0.7	0.1	•	0.1	•	0.5	0.3	•	•	•	0.3	•
Depreciation	14	1.7	1.9	0.1	•	0.2	•	1.3	1.8	•	•	•	1.8	•
Amortization and Depletion	15	0.5	2.1	0.0	•	0.0	•	0.2	0.0	•	•	•	0.8	•
Pensions and Other Deferred Comp.	16	1.0	0.0	0.0	•	0.0	•	0.2	0.1	•	•	•	1.8	•
Employee Benefits	17	2.3	13.9	1.5	•	0.2	•	0.1	0.6	•	•	•	2.1	•
Advertising	18	3.5	3.2	0.2	•	0.2	•	3.4	1.7	•	•	•	6.1	•
Other Expenses	19	10.3	18.6	27.4	•	5.1	•	9.0	8.8	•	•	•	6.6	•
Officers' Compensation	20	2.6	13.4	0.2	•	1.1	•	4.1	1.7	•	•	•	1.5	•
Operating Margin	21	2.5	•	8.7	•	0.7	•	6.8	8.5	•	•	•	•	•
Operating Margin Before Officers' Comp.	22	5.2	•	8.9	•	1.8	•	10.9	10.2	•	•	•	•	•

Selected Average Balance Sheet ($ in Thousands)													
Net Receivables 23	2074	0	1	•	461	•	2781	9028	•	•	•	386134	•
Inventories 24	1561	0	56	•	981	•	5530	12606	•	•	•	159617	•
Net Property, Plant and Equipment 25	567	0	0	•	137	•	1383	3829	•	•	•	74743	•
Total Assets 26	6372	0	49	•	2187	•	13463	31829	•	•	•	885954	•
Notes and Loans Payable 27	892	0	155	•	125	•	2084	7167	•	•	•	100169	•
All Other Liabilities 28	2590	0	1	•	822	•	2935	6374	•	•	•	318416	•
Net Worth 29	2889	0	-107	•	1239	•	8443	18288	•	•	•	467369	•
Selected Financial Ratios (Times to 1)													
Current Ratio 30	1.7	•	5.5	•	2.3	•	2.8	2.3	•	•	•	1.9	•
Quick Ratio 31	1.0	•	1.1	•	1.0	•	1.3	1.0	•	•	•	1.4	•
Net Sales to Working Capital 32	4.4	•	2.9	•	6.2	•	3.1	4.8	•	•	•	2.4	•
Coverage Ratio 33	36.5	74.9	72.3	•	8.2	•	15.8	32.8	•	•	•	22.7	•
Total Asset Turnover 34	1.3	•	2.4	•	3.2	•	1.7	2.1	•	•	•	0.8	•
Inventory Turnover 35	3.3	•	0.8	•	6.2	•	2.7	3.6	•	•	•	2.8	•
Receivables Turnover 36	2.8	•	298.5	•	14.5	•	7.6	•	•	•	•	1.1	•
Total Liabilities to Net Worth 37	1.2	•	•	•	0.8	•	0.6	0.7	•	•	•	0.9	•
Current Assets to Working Capital 38	2.3	•	1.2	•	1.8	•	1.6	1.8	•	•	•	2.1	•
Current Liabilities to Working Capital 39	1.3	•	0.2	•	0.8	•	0.6	0.8	•	•	•	1.1	•
Working Capital to Net Sales 40	0.2	•	0.3	•	0.2	•	0.3	0.2	•	•	•	0.4	•
Inventory to Working Capital 41	0.8	•	1.0	•	1.0	•	0.7	0.9	•	•	•	0.6	•
Total Receipts to Cash Flow 42	5.1	1.9	2.9	•	23.7	•	7.0	5.9	•	•	•	9.5	•
Cost of Goods to Cash Flow 43	3.2	1.1	1.0	•	20.7	•	4.5	4.0	•	•	•	6.3	•
Cash Flow to Total Debt 44	0.5	•	0.3	•	0.3	•	0.6	0.8	•	•	•	0.2	•
Selected Financial Factors (in Percentages)													
Debt Ratio 45	54.7	•	318.4	•	43.3	•	37.3	42.5	•	•	•	47.2	•
Return on Total Assets 46	17.4	•	21.0	•	2.9	•	12.5	19.3	•	•	•	4.8	•
Return on Equity Before Income Taxes 47	37.3	•	•	•	4.5	•	18.7	32.6	•	•	•	8.7	•
Return on Equity After Income Taxes 48	31.2	•	•	•	4.1	•	17.0	32.6	•	•	•	6.5	•
Profit Margin (Before Income Tax) 49	13.0	49.3	8.8	•	0.8	•	7.0	9.1	•	•	•	6.0	•
Profit Margin (After Income Tax) 50	10.9	33.5	8.8	•	0.7	•	6.3	9.1	•	•	•	4.5	•

Table I

Corporations with and without Net Income

WOOD PRODUCT MANUFACTURING

MONEY AMOUNTS AND SIZE OF ASSETS IN THOUSANDS OF DOLLARS

Item Description for Accounting Period 7/11 Through 6/12		Total	Zero Assets	Under 500	500 to 1,000	1,000 to 5,000	5,000 to 10,000	10,000 to 25,000	25,000 to 50,000	50,000 to 100,000	100,000 to 250,000	250,000 to 500,000	500,000 to 2,500,000	2,500,000 and over
Number of Enterprises	1	10996	416	6572	1424	1628	496	264	87	54	31	9	15	0
Revenues ($ in Thousands)														
Net Sales	2	67881461	239710	3074321	2597522	8572980	8456317	6667891	4216070	4727728	5544116	3874018	19910788	0
Interest	3	129143	1057	1	647	3605	1782	3047	3583	7329	11729	28852	67511	0
Rents	4	30592	14	0	842	5824	254	2729	2874	2229	1871	4147	9809	0
Royalties	5	34883	0	0	0	0	4019	77	1596	1765	335	34	27059	0
Other Portfolio Income	6	748147	50312	4093	29575	23282	10845	8769	8694	38281	54162	42330	477804	0
Other Receipts	7	648762	19677	3774	932	37749	42472	39064	22887	15620	115030	27404	324150	0
Total Receipts	8	69472988	310770	3082189	2629518	8643440	8515689	6721577	4255704	4792952	5727243	3976785	20817121	0
Average Total Receipts	9	6318	747	469	1847	5309	17169	25461	48916	88758	184750	441865	1387808	•
Operating Costs/Operating Income (%)														
Cost of Operations	10	77.0	70.6	58.2	65.7	72.0	80.4	78.3	81.7	81.7	80.0	83.1	77.5	•
Salaries and Wages	11	5.9	6.3	9.5	13.6	6.5	4.6	5.2	4.2	4.6	5.0	4.7	6.2	•
Taxes Paid	12	1.8	2.5	2.2	3.5	2.6	1.7	2.0	1.6	1.6	1.4	1.6	1.2	•
Interest Paid	13	1.8	2.4	1.3	1.6	0.6	0.6	0.8	1.2	1.4	2.2	1.7	3.4	•
Depreciation	14	3.6	3.7	5.1	2.3	2.3	1.4	3.6	3.1	3.8	6.4	3.4	4.4	•
Amortization and Depletion	15	0.5	0.3	0.1	0.1	0.0	0.0	0.1	0.2	0.8	0.4	0.2	1.3	•
Pensions and Other Deferred Comp.	16	0.4	0.0	0.1	0.1	0.2	0.2	0.2	0.3	0.2	0.3	0.1	1.0	•
Employee Benefits	17	1.3	2.7	0.9	1.2	2.0	0.7	1.3	1.0	1.4	1.1	0.5	1.4	•
Advertising	18	0.5	0.1	1.0	0.2	0.3	0.2	0.2	0.3	0.4	0.8	0.9	0.8	•
Other Expenses	19	7.8	48.1	16.2	12.0	8.1	7.2	6.7	5.8	7.8	8.1	7.4	6.5	•
Officers' Compensation	20	1.5	0.3	5.8	3.8	3.8	1.3	1.4	0.9	0.8	1.1	0.3	0.3	•
Operating Margin	21	•	•	•	•	1.6	1.8	0.4	•	•	•	•	•	•
Operating Margin Before Officers' Comp.	22	•	•	5.7	•	5.4	3.0	1.8	0.6	•	•	•	•	•

Selected Average Balance Sheet ($ in Thousands)

Net Receivables 23	617	0	19	162	508	1382	2262	6447	11544	17432	44074	146158	•
Inventories 24	692	0	15	178	529	2311	3606	7740	13035	18961	56556	121935	•
Net Property, Plant and Equipment 25	1651	0	49	177	665	2455	5511	10489	24968	75908	111299	547354	•
Total Assets 26	4723	0	135	718	2357	7250	14709	34084	72409	157367	359455	1581175	•
Notes and Loans Payable 27	1717	0	95	666	740	2579	4478	9702	29460	40423	102505	602092	•
All Other Liabilities 28	1252	0	30	270	406	1370	2397	6880	17627	40558	152034	468777	•
Net Worth 29	1754	0	10	-219	1211	3301	7834	17502	25321	76386	104916	510307	•

Selected Financial Ratios (Times to 1)

Current Ratio 30	1.7	•	1.3	1.0	2.2	2.0	2.2	2.4	1.7	1.7	1.4	1.4	•
Quick Ratio 31	0.8	•	1.0	0.4	1.3	0.9	0.9	1.2	0.8	0.9	0.6	0.7	•
Net Sales to Working Capital 32	8.6	•	31.3	•	6.5	8.0	6.0	4.1	6.5	9.2	11.5	12.5	•
Coverage Ratio 33	1.3	•	1.1	•	5.1	5.1	2.5	1.5	•	•	0.3	1.5	•
Total Asset Turnover 34	1.3	•	3.5	2.5	2.2	2.4	1.7	1.4	1.2	1.1	1.2	0.8	•
Inventory Turnover 35	6.9	•	18.5	6.7	7.2	5.9	5.5	5.1	5.5	7.5	6.3	8.4	•
Receivables Turnover 36	9.9	•	23.7	14.5	9.9	12.6	12.2	8.0	8.4	10.2	11.5	8.0	•
Total Liabilities to Net Worth 37	1.7	•	12.3	•	0.9	1.2	0.9	0.9	1.9	1.1	2.4	2.1	•
Current Assets to Working Capital 38	2.5	•	4.3	•	1.8	2.0	1.8	1.7	2.4	2.5	3.8	3.7	•
Current Liabilities to Working Capital 39	1.5	•	3.3	•	0.8	1.0	0.8	0.7	1.4	1.5	2.8	2.7	•
Working Capital to Net Sales 40	0.1	•	0.0	•	0.2	0.1	0.2	0.2	0.2	0.1	0.1	0.1	•
Inventory to Working Capital 41	1.0	•	0.8	•	0.7	1.0	0.9	0.7	1.0	1.0	1.5	1.2	•
Total Receipts to Cash Flow 42	18.0	11.9	8.2	27.1	13.0	12.4	15.3	20.1	38.4	42.9	27.9	22.2	•
Cost of Goods to Cash Flow 43	13.9	8.4	4.8	17.8	9.3	10.0	12.0	16.4	31.4	34.3	23.1	17.2	•
Cash Flow to Total Debt 44	0.1	•	0.5	0.1	0.4	0.3	0.2	0.1	0.0	0.1	0.1	0.1	•

Selected Financial Factors (in Percentages)

Debt Ratio 45	62.9	•	92.5	130.5	48.6	54.5	46.7	48.6	65.0	51.5	70.8	67.7	•
Return on Total Assets 46	3.1	•	5.0	•	6.6	7.3	3.3	2.5	•	•	0.6	4.3	•
Return on Equity Before Income Taxes 47	2.0	•	6.7	23.6	10.4	12.8	3.8	1.7	•	•	•	4.5	•
Return on Equity After Income Taxes 48	0.8	•	5.8	25.2	9.7	12.3	3.2	1.1	•	•	•	2.7	•
Profit Margin (Before Income Tax) 49	0.6	•	0.1	•	2.4	2.5	1.2	0.6	•	•	•	1.7	•
Profit Margin (After Income Tax) 50	0.2	•	0.1	•	2.2	2.4	1.0	0.4	•	•	•	1.0	•

Table II

Corporations with Net Income

WOOD PRODUCT MANUFACTURING

MONEY AMOUNTS AND SIZE OF ASSETS IN THOUSANDS OF DOLLARS

Item Description for Accounting Period 7/11 Through 6/12		Total	Zero Assets	Under 500	500 to 1,000	1,000 to 5,000	5,000 to 10,000	10,000 to 25,000	25,000 to 50,000	50,000 to 100,000	100,000 to 250,000	250,000 to 500,000	500,000 to 2,500,000	2,500,000 and over
Number of Enterprises	1	5627	401	2707	784	1099	365	172	51	24	13	5	6	0
Revenues ($ in Thousands)														
Net Sales	2	45937171	174101	2207008	1698639	5795615	7911791	4389128	2411023	2272834	2805988	1875841	14395202	0
Interest	3	84072	24	0	282	2254	1043	1731	2062	2378	5291	16861	52145	0
Rents	4	18350	0	0	0	4609	18	2488	2412	675	910	483	6754	0
Royalties	5	30208	0	0	0	0	4019	0	11	0	0	0	26178	0
Other Portfolio Income	6	653754	50312	1492	21424	22585	9854	4110	3632	15366	50237	542	474201	0
Other Receipts	7	461363	16529	322	278	8011	40171	21444	5711	3494	83803	16628	264973	0
Total Receipts	8	47184918	240966	2208822	1720623	5833074	7966896	4418901	2424851	2294747	2946229	1910355	15219453	0
Average Total Receipts	9	8385	601	816	2195	5308	21827	25691	47546	95614	226633	382071	2536576	•
Operating Costs/Operating Income (%)														
Cost of Operations	10	74.8	66.8	58.5	74.8	66.5	80.2	74.4	78.1	77.9	77.6	71.1	76.7	•
Salaries and Wages	11	6.1	4.5	11.6	6.4	6.8	4.6	5.6	4.4	4.5	4.6	7.0	6.8	•
Taxes Paid	12	1.6	3.1	1.8	2.4	2.6	1.7	1.9	1.4	1.6	1.3	1.8	1.0	•
Interest Paid	13	1.7	2.1	0.2	1.0	0.4	0.4	0.5	0.6	1.4	2.2	1.7	3.7	•
Depreciation	14	2.7	3.3	1.7	2.2	2.3	1.2	3.2	3.0	3.4	3.9	2.3	3.3	•
Amortization and Depletion	15	0.4	0.3	0.0	0.1	0.0	0.0	0.0	0.1	0.4	0.2	0.1	0.9	•
Pensions and Other Deferred Comp.	16	0.4	0.0	0.1	•	0.3	0.2	0.2	0.3	0.2	0.2	0.0	0.8	•
Employee Benefits	17	1.0	2.6	0.3	0.4	1.6	0.6	1.1	1.0	1.4	0.8	0.2	1.3	•
Advertising	18	0.5	0.0	1.0	0.1	0.3	0.1	0.2	0.2	0.2	0.5	1.7	0.6	•
Other Expenses	19	7.5	16.8	12.7	5.5	8.7	7.0	7.5	5.1	6.3	9.3	11.1	6.4	•
Officers' Compensation	20	1.6	0.3	4.6	4.3	4.6	1.3	1.5	1.0	0.7	1.1	0.5	0.2	•
Operating Margin	21	1.8	0.1	7.3	3.0	6.0	2.7	3.9	4.6	2.0	•	2.5	•	•
Operating Margin Before Officers' Comp.	22	3.4	0.4	11.9	7.3	10.6	4.0	5.4	5.6	2.7	•	3.0	•	•

Selected Average Balance Sheet ($ in Thousands)													
Net Receivables 23	758	0	33	215	439	1416	2467	6703	11732	17731	31192	262429	•
Inventories 24	834	0	18	90	423	2485	3807	8674	15887	15298	54723	208664	•
Net Property, Plant and Equipment 25	1462	0	55	179	540	2288	4778	10203	24891	64287	63994	568915	•
Total Assets 26	5486	0	189	680	2118	7568	14215	33278	71539	154292	353354	2517718	•
Notes and Loans Payable 27	1867	0	52	589	487	1826	3535	8007	17940	29000	99818	1062818	•
All Other Liabilities 28	1547	0	29	229	309	1389	2295	5732	16759	39322	82906	930515	•
Net Worth 29	2073	0	108	-138	1322	4353	8384	19539	36840	85969	170630	524386	•

Selected Financial Ratios (Times to 1)													
Current Ratio 30	1.8	•	2.9	1.2	3.2	2.5	2.7	2.5	1.7	1.8	3.8	1.2	•
Quick Ratio 31	0.9	•	2.5	0.7	2.2	1.1	1.2	1.2	0.8	1.0	1.3	0.6	•
Net Sales to Working Capital 32	8.2	•	10.7	35.4	5.5	7.3	5.0	3.9	6.9	10.7	3.8	22.8	•
Coverage Ratio 33	4.0	19.1	39.3	5.4	16.1	9.7	9.4	10.0	3.1	2.5	3.6	2.5	•
Total Asset Turnover 34	1.5	•	4.3	3.2	2.5	2.9	1.8	1.4	1.3	1.4	1.1	1.0	•
Inventory Turnover 35	7.3	•	27.2	18.0	8.3	7.0	5.0	4.3	4.6	11.0	4.9	8.8	•
Receivables Turnover 36	10.8	•	24.1	15.0	12.1	17.9	11.0	6.3	9.7	11.0	13.0	8.4	•
Total Liabilities to Net Worth 37	1.6	•	0.8	•	0.6	0.7	0.7	0.7	0.9	0.8	1.1	3.8	•
Current Assets to Working Capital 38	2.3	•	1.5	7.6	1.5	1.7	1.6	1.7	2.4	2.3	1.4	6.5	•
Current Liabilities to Working Capital 39	1.3	•	0.5	6.6	0.5	0.7	0.6	0.7	1.4	1.3	0.4	5.5	•
Working Capital to Net Sales 40	0.1	•	0.1	0.0	0.2	0.1	0.2	0.3	0.1	0.1	0.3	0.0	•
Inventory to Working Capital 41	0.9	•	0.2	2.4	0.4	0.9	0.8	0.7	1.1	0.8	0.6	1.9	•
Total Receipts to Cash Flow 42	10.3	2.0	5.8	14.7	8.1	11.2	9.6	10.9	13.5	9.9	7.5	13.7	•
Cost of Goods to Cash Flow 43	7.7	1.3	3.4	11.0	5.4	9.0	7.1	8.5	10.5	7.6	5.4	10.5	•
Cash Flow to Total Debt 44	0.2	•	1.7	0.2	0.8	0.6	0.5	0.3	0.2	0.3	0.3	0.1	•

Selected Financial Factors (in Percentages)													
Debt Ratio 45	62.2	•	42.9	120.3	37.6	42.5	41.0	41.3	48.5	44.3	51.7	79.2	•
Return on Total Assets 46	10.1	•	32.8	16.6	17.5	10.9	9.2	8.2	5.8	7.6	6.4	8.9	•
Return on Equity Before Income Taxes 47	20.0	•	56.0	•	26.4	17.0	14.0	12.6	7.6	8.2	9.6	25.6	•
Return on Equity After Income Taxes 48	18.1	•	55.8	•	25.5	16.6	13.2	11.6	6.8	7.5	7.8	21.2	•
Profit Margin (Before Income Tax) 49	5.1	38.5	7.4	4.3	6.6	3.4	4.6	5.2	3.0	3.3	4.4	5.6	•
Profit Margin (After Income Tax) 50	4.6	35.6	7.4	4.0	6.4	3.3	4.3	4.8	2.7	3.0	3.5	4.6	•

Table I

Corporations with and without Net Income

PULP, PAPER, AND PAPERBOARD MILLS

Item Description for Accounting Period 7/11 Through 6/12		Total	Zero Assets	Under 500	500 to 1,000	1,000 to 5,000	5,000 to 10,000	10,000 to 25,000	25,000 to 50,000	50,000 to 100,000	100,000 to 250,000	250,000 to 500,000	500,000 to 2,500,000	2,500,000 and over
		MONEY AMOUNTS AND SIZE OF ASSETS IN THOUSANDS OF DOLLARS												
Number of Enterprises	1	382	6	0	164	95	32	13	18	11	15	8	14	6
Revenues ($ in Thousands)														
Net Sales	2	75291438	1210495	0	383176	2749400	414860	387554	1097040	1457671	3032223	3433275	16636662	44489083
Interest	3	500972	1645	0	42	1	439	1	0	964	10598	7951	15156	464176
Rents	4	23229	473	0	0	0	11	0	0	233	3	3585	5742	13183
Royalties	5	128392	0	0	0	0	0	0	0	0	0	186	35739	92467
Other Portfolio Income	6	722390	474173	0	0	0	8657	319	93	1456	12927	6344	95905	122520
Other Receipts	7	912048	19537	0	2627	2	4752	8517	7200	5218	16390	19709	197242	630848
Total Receipts	8	77578469	1706323	0	385845	2749403	428719	396391	1104333	1465542	3072141	3471050	16986446	45812277
Average Total Receipts	9	203085	284387	•	2353	28941	13397	30492	61352	133231	204809	433881	1213318	7635380
Operating Costs/Operating Income (%)														
Cost of Operations	10	78.3	74.7	•	41.7	98.1	81.2	84.8	77.7	80.0	87.3	78.4	78.5	76.7
Salaries and Wages	11	3.5	8.0	•	14.1	0.3	4.4	4.1	6.3	3.6	1.8	4.8	3.7	3.2
Taxes Paid	12	1.1	2.4	•	2.3	0.1	1.9	1.4	1.1	0.8	0.7	1.0	1.0	1.2
Interest Paid	13	3.7	4.9	•	0.9	0.4	1.6	0.7	0.5	0.6	2.1	2.7	2.3	4.9
Depreciation	14	4.7	2.7	•	2.5	0.4	3.7	2.0	3.3	3.0	4.0	6.5	6.1	4.6
Amortization and Depletion	15	0.6	0.2	•	1.8	•	0.1	0.2	0.1	0.1	0.4	0.4	0.6	0.7
Pensions and Other Deferred Comp.	16	1.1	0.1	•	3.3	•	0.0	1.1	0.6	0.6	0.4	1.2	0.9	1.3
Employee Benefits	17	1.5	2.1	•	1.6	•	1.7	0.5	1.6	1.5	2.8	1.9	2.1	1.3
Advertising	18	0.2	0.0	•	0.7	•	0.0	0.4	0.0	0.4	0.2	0.4	0.3	0.2
Other Expenses	19	6.6	12.1	•	15.7	0.8	17.8	5.8	7.6	7.9	3.8	4.1	4.7	7.6
Officers' Compensation	20	0.5	1.5	•	12.5	0.2	0.7	1.7	0.6	0.7	0.6	0.8	0.7	0.2
Operating Margin	21	•	•	•	2.9	•	•	•	0.5	0.7	•	•	•	•
Operating Margin Before Officers' Comp.	22	•	•	•	15.4	•	•	•	1.1	1.4	•	•	•	•

Selected Average Balance Sheet ($ in Thousands)

Net Receivables 23	32273	0	•	207	0	1361	3100	5600	13341	17179	45632	171446	1490022
Inventories 24	18516	0	•	64	103	1943	3319	5853	17146	20412	45910	131027	690959
Net Property, Plant and Equipment 25	76792	0	•	28	388	3879	7776	12389	24687	59770	171042	525095	3159474
Total Assets 26	321837	0	•	853	2298	7097	18868	33525	77442	166178	405570	1181404	16396502
Notes and Loans Payable 27	149398	0	•	436	1238	6768	8915	6804	20044	72845	168527	367262	8103813
All Other Liabilities 28	82102	0	•	270	617	4221	6113	20728	23758	44471	119372	371164	3932132
Net Worth 29	90337	0	•	146	443	-3892	3841	5994	33640	48862	117672	442978	4360558

Selected Financial Ratios (Times to 1)

Current Ratio 30	0.8	•	•	1.2	0.7	0.8	1.5	0.9	1.8	1.6	2.1	2.1	0.6
Quick Ratio 31	0.5	•	•	1.0	0.5	0.3	0.7	0.4	0.8	0.6	1.0	1.1	0.5
Net Sales to Working Capital 32	•	•	•	42.6	•	•	11.1	•	7.8	8.9	6.7	6.1	•
Coverage Ratio 33	1.4	7.5	•	5.2	0.2	•	0.5	3.2	3.0	•	0.6	1.5	1.3
Total Asset Turnover 34	0.6	•	•	2.7	12.6	1.8	1.6	1.8	1.7	1.2	1.1	1.0	0.5
Inventory Turnover 35	8.3	•	•	15.2	275.9	5.4	7.6	8.1	6.2	8.6	7.3	7.1	8.2
Receivables Turnover 36	6.1	•	•	15.6	316.5	11.1	10.5	9.3	8.2	14.5	8.3	7.1	5.0
Total Liabilities to Net Worth 37	2.6	•	•	4.8	4.2	•	3.9	4.6	1.3	2.4	2.4	1.7	2.8
Current Assets to Working Capital 38	•	•	•	6.0	•	•	3.1	•	2.3	2.7	1.9	1.9	•
Current Liabilities to Working Capital 39	•	•	•	5.0	•	•	2.1	•	1.3	1.7	0.9	0.9	•
Working Capital to Net Sales 40	•	•	•	0.0	•	•	0.1	•	0.1	0.1	0.1	0.2	•
Inventory to Working Capital 41	•	•	•	0.9	•	•	1.2	•	0.9	1.0	0.7	0.7	•
Total Receipts to Cash Flow 42	17.8	8.9	•	11.6	250.2	21.5	22.6	13.6	12.7	351.4	48.6	29.8	14.0
Cost of Goods to Cash Flow 43	13.9	6.7	•	4.8	245.4	17.5	19.2	10.6	10.1	306.8	38.1	23.4	10.7
Cash Flow to Total Debt 44	0.0	•	•	0.3	0.1	0.1	0.1	0.2	0.2	0.0	0.0	0.1	0.0

Selected Financial Factors (in Percentages)

Debt Ratio 45	71.9	•	•	82.9	80.7	154.8	79.6	82.1	56.6	70.6	71.0	62.5	73.4
Return on Total Assets 46	3.1	•	•	12.3	1.1	•	0.5	3.0	3.3	•	1.8	3.4	2.8
Return on Equity Before Income Taxes 47	2.9	•	•	57.8	•	32.8	•	11.5	5.1	•	•	3.0	2.1
Return on Equity After Income Taxes 48	1.8	•	•	55.8	•	32.8	•	10.9	3.6	•	•	1.5	1.2
Profit Margin (Before Income Tax) 49	1.3	32.2	•	3.6	•	•	•	1.1	1.3	•	•	1.1	1.2
Profit Margin (After Income Tax) 50	0.8	31.2	•	3.5	•	•	•	1.1	0.9	•	•	0.5	0.7

Table II

Corporations with Net Income

PULP, PAPER, AND PAPERBOARD MILLS

MONEY AMOUNTS AND SIZE OF ASSETS IN THOUSANDS OF DOLLARS

Item Description for Accounting Period 7/11 Through 6/12		Total	Zero Assets	Under 500	500 to 1,000	1,000 to 5,000	5,000 to 10,000	10,000 to 25,000	25,000 to 50,000	50,000 to 100,000	100,000 to 250,000	250,000 to 500,000	500,000 to 2,500,000	2,500,000 and over
Number of Enterprises	1	292	•	0	•	64	9	8	13	7	7	3	10	•
Revenues ($ in Thousands)														
Net Sales	2	57160686	•	0	•	2739113	161739	247254	815068	1000668	945470	1563998	10938855	•
Interest	3	486489	•	0	•	0	3	0	0	498	4910	4215	12396	•
Rents	4	15639	•	0	•	0	0	0	0	233	3	181	1620	•
Royalties	5	127750	•	0	•	0	0	0	0	0	0	0	35283	•
Other Portfolio Income	6	710978	•	0	•	0	10	319	93	121	12401	5740	95620	•
Other Receipts	7	719001	•	0	•	0	0	7743	4553	3987	19926	2479	21945	•
Total Receipts	8	59220543	•	0	•	2739113	161752	255316	819714	1005507	982710	1576613	11105719	•
Average Total Receipts	9	202810	•	•	•	42799	17972	31914	63055	143644	140387	525538	1110572	•
Operating Costs/Operating Income (%)														
Cost of Operations	10	76.4	•	•	•	98.4	58.6	81.6	77.4	83.3	80.1	81.0	76.5	•
Salaries and Wages	11	3.5	•	•	•	0.3	3.9	2.1	4.8	2.3	2.7	5.0	3.6	•
Taxes Paid	12	1.1	•	•	•	0.1	2.9	1.1	1.0	0.7	1.3	1.0	1.1	•
Interest Paid	13	3.4	•	•	•	0.3	2.1	0.5	0.6	0.9	1.1	3.7	1.1	•
Depreciation	14	4.9	•	•	•	0.0	3.8	2.4	3.4	3.3	5.5	4.3	5.3	•
Amortization and Depletion	15	0.7	•	•	•	•	•	0.0	0.1	0.1	0.4	0.0	0.5	•
Pensions and Other Deferred Comp.	16	1.2	•	•	•	•	•	0.1	0.9	0.5	0.6	1.0	1.0	•
Employee Benefits	17	1.1	•	•	•	•	1.5	0.4	1.5	1.9	2.1	1.7	1.5	•
Advertising	18	0.2	•	•	•	•	0.0	0.1	0.0	0.1	0.1	0.4	0.3	•
Other Expenses	19	6.4	•	•	•	0.4	25.0	4.4	8.0	3.8	4.7	•	4.8	•
Officers' Compensation	20	0.5	•	•	•	0.2	1.3	0.9	0.6	0.6	0.7	1.1	0.9	•
Operating Margin	21	0.5	•	•	•	0.2	1.0	6.4	1.7	2.6	0.7	1.5	3.3	•
Operating Margin Before Officers' Comp.	22	1.0	•	•	•	0.4	2.3	7.3	2.3	3.1	1.4	2.7	4.1	•

Selected Average Balance Sheet ($ in Thousands)													
Net Receivables 23	36454	•	•	•	0	1268	3636	5231	11613	11637	53726	184269	•
Inventories 24	16972	•	•	•	38	1330	1271	4700	15668	22591	54152	107103	•
Net Property, Plant and Equipment 25	73618	•	•	•	6	4094	8982	13635	28439	56345	87567	466398	•
Total Assets 26	357922	•	•	•	2663	7044	17981	34721	76949	159559	377745	1092620	•
Notes and Loans Payable 27	176767	•	•	•	1265	7123	4746	5255	20715	57035	281927	215419	•
All Other Liabilities 28	76639	•	•	•	879	1085	2218	9446	16720	37099	110139	357916	•
Net Worth 29	104516	•	•	•	519	-1164	11017	20020	39514	65425	-14321	519284	•

Selected Financial Ratios (Times to 1)													
Current Ratio 30	0.7	•	•	•	0.5	2.7	3.1	1.4	2.3	1.7	2.5	2.2	•
Quick Ratio 31	0.5	•	•	•	0.5	1.5	2.2	0.7	0.8	0.5	1.2	1.3	•
Net Sales to Working Capital 32	•	•	•	•	•	9.6	6.2	16.2	6.6	5.4	5.8	5.6	•
Coverage Ratio 33	2.3	•	•	•	1.7	1.5	20.7	5.1	4.6	5.6	1.6	5.3	•
Total Asset Turnover 34	0.5	•	•	•	16.1	2.6	1.7	1.8	1.9	0.8	1.4	1.0	•
Inventory Turnover 35	8.8	•	•	•	1114.0	7.9	19.8	10.3	7.6	4.8	7.8	7.8	•
Receivables Turnover 36	5.5	•	•	•	346.5	28.4	11.1	•	9.3	9.5	9.5	6.2	•
Total Liabilities to Net Worth 37	2.4	•	•	•	4.1	•	0.6	0.7	0.9	1.4	•	1.1	•
Current Assets to Working Capital 38	•	•	•	•	•	1.6	1.5	3.3	1.8	2.4	1.7	1.8	•
Current Liabilities to Working Capital 39	•	•	•	•	•	0.6	0.5	2.3	0.8	1.4	0.7	0.8	•
Working Capital to Net Sales 40	•	•	•	•	•	0.1	0.2	0.1	0.2	0.2	0.2	0.2	•
Inventory to Working Capital 41	•	•	•	•	•	0.7	0.3	1.2	0.8	0.6	0.6	0.6	•
Total Receipts to Cash Flow 42	11.9	•	•	•	206.6	4.7	7.8	10.8	16.7	12.5	352.7	14.2	•
Cost of Goods to Cash Flow 43	9.1	•	•	•	203.4	2.8	6.4	8.3	13.9	10.0	285.8	10.9	•
Cash Flow to Total Debt 44	0.1	•	•	•	0.1	0.5	0.6	0.4	0.2	0.1	0.0	0.1	•

Selected Financial Factors (in Percentages)													
Debt Ratio 45	70.8	•	•	•	80.5	116.5	38.7	42.3	48.6	59.0	103.8	52.5	•
Return on Total Assets 46	4.2	•	•	•	7.9	7.8	17.5	5.1	7.2	5.2	8.4	5.9	•
Return on Equity Before Income Taxes 47	7.9	•	•	•	16.3	•	27.1	7.1	11.0	10.4	•	10.1	•
Return on Equity After Income Taxes 48	6.7	•	•	•	16.3	•	27.1	6.8	9.0	7.3	•	8.3	•
Profit Margin (Before Income Tax) 49	4.2	•	•	•	0.2	1.0	9.7	2.3	3.0	5.0	2.3	4.8	•
Profit Margin (After Income Tax) 50	3.6	•	•	•	0.2	1.0	9.7	2.2	2.5	3.5	2.0	3.9	•

Table I

Corporations with and without Net Income

CONVERTED PAPER PRODUCT

MONEY AMOUNTS AND SIZE OF ASSETS IN THOUSANDS OF DOLLARS

Item Description for Accounting Period 7/11 Through 6/12		Total	Zero Assets	Under 500	500 to 1,000	1,000 to 5,000	5,000 to 10,000	10,000 to 25,000	25,000 to 50,000	50,000 to 100,000	100,000 to 250,000	250,000 to 500,000	500,000 to 2,500,000	2,500,000 and over
Number of Enterprises	1	2538	582	409	285	797	152	152	72	36	21	11	13	8
Revenues ($ in Thousands)														
Net Sales	2	98659637	704737	502197	649618	5120065	3156261	5401627	4300491	3943319	5000691	5934438	13479466	50466727
Interest	3	534597	1366	994	0	267	109	572	4614	2926	3250	2608	97900	419989
Rents	4	40223	167	2	0	318	378	1083	1576	1434	119	189	29118	5840
Royalties	5	2260432	187	0	0	0	0	1552	146	0	7856	4983	3146	2242563
Other Portfolio Income	6	1016180	31618	0	1	3916	11000	24863	29851	17912	426	72029	285937	538625
Other Receipts	7	1057287	15182	2	224	13527	42078	22528	-15926	12871	4879	8228	52869	900827
Total Receipts	8	103568356	753257	503195	649843	5138093	3209826	5452225	4320752	3978462	5017221	6022475	13948436	54574571
Average Total Receipts	9	40807	1294	1230	2280	6447	21117	35870	60010	110513	238915	547498	1072957	6821821
Operating Costs/Operating Income (%)														
Cost of Operations	10	70.8	76.4	69.4	64.2	66.0	81.5	75.2	76.6	76.1	77.4	77.6	75.4	66.6
Salaries and Wages	11	8.2	15.6	3.1	7.4	11.3	3.6	5.8	5.7	5.7	5.3	5.5	4.7	10.3
Taxes Paid	12	1.2	1.2	2.3	1.5	2.5	2.0	1.6	1.5	1.3	1.1	1.2	1.5	0.9
Interest Paid	13	2.2	0.8	0.2	0.0	0.7	0.8	0.9	1.0	0.8	1.1	1.6	3.5	2.7
Depreciation	14	4.4	2.0	0.0	2.6	1.6	2.4	3.8	5.0	3.7	2.9	2.7	4.1	5.4
Amortization and Depletion	15	0.7	0.5	•	0.0	0.1	0.1	0.1	0.1	0.3	0.3	0.7	0.7	0.9
Pensions and Other Deferred Comp.	16	1.9	1.5	0.2	0.0	0.5	0.3	0.1	0.5	0.4	0.5	1.0	0.8	3.1
Employee Benefits	17	1.9	0.7	0.0	0.7	2.4	0.9	1.2	1.4	1.5	1.0	1.5	2.1	2.1
Advertising	18	0.7	0.2	0.2	0.0	0.2	0.0	0.2	0.1	0.2	0.3	0.6	0.1	1.2
Other Expenses	19	7.8	10.5	14.9	9.7	9.1	5.9	7.5	6.1	6.3	7.9	8.2	6.7	8.2
Officers' Compensation	20	1.0	22.7	5.1	6.6	2.2	1.9	2.6	1.3	1.2	0.7	0.5	0.4	0.4
Operating Margin	21	•	•	4.5	7.2	3.5	0.6	0.9	0.7	2.4	1.4	•	0.1	•
Operating Margin Before Officers' Comp.	22	0.3	•	9.6	13.8	5.6	2.6	3.6	2.0	3.6	2.1	•	0.5	•

Selected Average Balance Sheet ($ in Thousands)													
Net Receivables **23**	5223	0	164	274	703	1745	4075	7661	11665	33892	71825	123955	947641
Inventories **24**	3638	0	34	40	452	1360	3940	7045	14911	26518	55703	97642	569814
Net Property, Plant and Equipment **25**	11055	0	12	37	550	3012	5317	14322	20390	46188	94994	348696	2253089
Total Assets **26**	52875	0	391	871	2246	7475	16069	36405	71099	161369	313506	1117128	12734963
Notes and Loans Payable **27**	17752	0	48	10	827	3416	5779	10919	23696	47409	82822	539374	4052336
All Other Liabilities **28**	12840	0	140	123	455	2455	3993	9833	15391	48129	114860	278456	2999514
Net Worth **29**	22283	0	203	738	964	1604	6296	15652	32012	65831	115824	299299	5683114
Selected Financial Ratios (Times to 1)													
Current Ratio **30**	1.3	•	2.0	6.5	2.5	1.2	1.8	1.5	1.9	1.7	1.6	1.4	1.1
Quick Ratio **31**	0.7	•	1.5	5.5	1.7	0.7	1.0	0.8	0.9	0.9	0.9	0.7	0.6
Net Sales to Working Capital **32**	15.0	•	6.4	3.3	6.5	27.6	8.6	9.5	6.2	8.8	9.5	11.7	37.3
Coverage Ratio **33**	3.5	•	28.2	336.0	6.8	4.0	3.1	2.2	4.9	2.5	1.2	2.1	4.2
Total Asset Turnover **34**	0.7	•	3.1	2.6	2.9	2.8	2.2	1.6	1.5	1.5	1.7	0.9	0.5
Inventory Turnover **35**	7.6	•	24.9	36.3	9.4	12.4	6.8	6.5	5.6	7.0	7.5	8.0	7.4
Receivables Turnover **36**	7.6	•	7.4	8.2	9.2	11.2	8.2	7.4	9.4	6.7	8.0	8.1	7.0
Total Liabilities to Net Worth **37**	1.4	•	0.9	0.2	1.3	3.7	1.6	1.3	1.2	1.5	1.7	2.7	1.2
Current Assets to Working Capital **38**	4.5	•	2.0	1.2	1.7	5.4	2.3	2.9	2.1	2.4	2.7	3.4	11.9
Current Liabilities to Working Capital **39**	3.5	•	1.0	0.2	0.7	4.4	1.3	1.9	1.1	1.4	1.7	2.4	10.9
Working Capital to Net Sales **40**	0.1	•	0.2	0.3	0.2	0.0	0.1	0.1	0.2	0.1	0.1	0.1	0.0
Inventory to Working Capital **41**	1.5	•	0.1	0.0	0.5	1.9	0.9	1.1	0.9	1.0	0.9	1.2	3.6
Total Receipts to Cash Flow **42**	10.4	•	11.8	8.1	12.3	17.6	14.2	19.0	13.1	12.3	15.8	16.3	7.9
Cost of Goods to Cash Flow **43**	7.4	•	8.2	5.2	8.1	14.3	10.7	14.6	10.0	9.5	12.3	12.3	5.3
Cash Flow to Total Debt **44**	0.1	•	0.6	2.1	0.4	0.2	0.3	0.2	0.2	0.2	0.2	0.1	0.1
Selected Financial Factors (in Percentages)													
Debt Ratio **45**	57.9	•	48.0	15.3	57.1	78.5	60.8	57.0	55.0	59.2	63.1	73.2	55.4
Return on Total Assets **46**	5.7	•	15.3	18.9	12.8	8.6	6.2	3.5	6.4	4.3	3.4	6.6	5.7
Return on Equity Before Income Taxes **47**	9.7	•	28.4	22.3	25.4	30.1	10.8	4.4	11.3	6.3	1.4	12.8	9.7
Return on Equity After Income Taxes **48**	6.6	•	28.1	22.3	25.4	27.1	9.1	3.3	9.9	4.8	1.1	8.3	6.4
Profit Margin (Before Income Tax) **49**	5.5	•	4.7	7.2	3.8	2.3	1.9	1.1	3.3	1.7	0.3	3.7	8.7
Profit Margin (After Income Tax) **50**	3.8	•	4.6	7.2	3.8	2.1	1.6	0.9	2.9	1.3	0.2	2.4	5.8

Table II

Corporations with Net Income

CONVERTED PAPER PRODUCT

MONEY AMOUNTS AND SIZE OF ASSETS IN THOUSANDS OF DOLLARS

Item Description for Accounting Period 7/11 Through 6/12		Total	Zero Assets	Under 500	500 to 1,000	1,000 to 5,000	5,000 to 10,000	10,000 to 25,000	25,000 to 50,000	50,000 to 100,000	100,000 to 250,000	250,000 to 500,000	500,000 to 2,500,000	2,500,000 and over
Number of Enterprises	1	1706	•	409	•	598	63	97	44	27	15	5	8	•
Revenues ($ in Thousands)														
Net Sales	2	79154594	•	502197	•	4504149	1365917	2981906	2992264	3154565	3527835	3064620	10177146	•
Interest	3	515042	•	994	•	244	109	447	3131	2741	3069	166	92066	•
Rents	4	18307	•	2	•	318	378	911	1550	1421	86	125	9908	•
Royalties	5	2256841	•	0	•	0	0	1552	0	0	6817	4980	3125	•
Other Portfolio Income	6	967908	•	0	•	2954	10339	22772	25841	17334	426	66858	273745	•
Other Receipts	7	1022262	•	2	•	11477	17015	17052	4596	15387	1536	3925	43299	•
Total Receipts	8	83934954	•	503195	•	4519142	1393758	3024640	3027382	3191448	3539769	3140674	10599289	•
Average Total Receipts	9	49200	•	1230	•	7557	22123	31182	68804	118202	235985	628135	1324911	•
Operating Costs/Operating Income (%)														
Cost of Operations	10	68.4	•	69.4	•	66.6	73.8	73.9	75.6	73.9	75.0	77.7	73.5	•
Salaries and Wages	11	9.1	•	3.1	•	10.7	4.8	5.6	5.6	6.2	5.7	6.0	5.5	•
Taxes Paid	12	1.2	•	2.3	•	2.3	2.0	1.7	1.4	1.4	1.1	1.0	1.5	•
Interest Paid	13	2.3	•	0.2	•	0.6	0.5	0.9	0.7	0.9	1.1	1.4	3.2	•
Depreciation	14	4.4	•	0.0	•	1.2	3.1	3.6	4.7	3.1	3.4	2.0	4.2	•
Amortization and Depletion	15	0.7	•	•	•	0.2	0.2	0.1	0.1	0.3	0.4	0.7	0.5	•
Pensions and Other Deferred Comp.	16	2.2	•	0.2	•	0.5	0.5	0.2	0.5	0.5	0.7	1.0	1.0	•
Employee Benefits	17	2.0	•	0.0	•	2.3	1.5	1.2	1.4	1.4	1.1	1.1	1.8	•
Advertising	18	0.8	•	0.2	•	0.3	0.0	0.2	0.1	0.2	0.4	0.3	0.1	•
Other Expenses	19	7.9	•	14.9	•	7.4	4.9	6.9	5.4	6.5	6.3	7.1	7.0	•
Officers' Compensation	20	0.8	•	5.1	•	2.4	3.3	2.6	1.6	1.2	0.8	0.4	0.4	•
Operating Margin	21	0.3	•	4.5	•	5.6	5.4	3.1	2.9	4.3	4.0	1.3	1.3	•
Operating Margin Before Officers' Comp.	22	1.1	•	9.6	•	8.0	8.6	5.7	4.4	5.5	4.8	1.7	1.7	•

Selected Average Balance Sheet ($ in Thousands)												
Net Receivables 23	6432	•	164	•	666	1652	3685	7788	12372	33794	81234	154457	•
Inventories 24	4428	•	34	•	460	1009	4365	7858	16263	25379	71483	107172	•
Net Property, Plant and Equipment 25	13753	•	12	•	574	2453	5294	15256	18857	44612	81936	472725	•
Total Assets 26	69718	•	391	•	2276	7753	14975	37847	73009	159246	325485	1405910	•
Notes and Loans Payable 27	21961	•	48	•	598	2279	5107	9787	22889	41775	117385	572584	•
All Other Liabilities 28	16254	•	140	•	470	1537	3598	8517	16107	47009	94605	345511	•
Net Worth 29	31504	•	203	•	1207	3937	6269	19543	34013	70463	113495	487816	•
Selected Financial Ratios (Times to 1)												
Current Ratio 30	1.3	•	2.0	•	2.7	2.6	1.9	1.9	2.1	1.7	1.9	1.4	•
Quick Ratio 31	0.7	•	1.5	•	1.8	1.7	1.1	1.1	1.0	0.9	1.1	0.7	•
Net Sales to Working Capital 32	16.3	•	6.4	•	7.4	7.9	7.2	6.9	5.5	9.3	7.1	13.5	•
Coverage Ratio 33	4.4	•	28.2	•	11.5	17.4	6.1	6.7	7.2	5.0	3.8	2.7	•
Total Asset Turnover 34	0.7	•	3.1	•	3.3	2.8	2.1	1.8	1.6	1.5	1.9	0.9	•
Inventory Turnover 35	7.2	•	24.9	•	10.9	15.9	5.2	6.5	5.3	6.9	6.7	8.7	•
Receivables Turnover 36	7.2	•	7.4	•	9.9	12.0	6.4	•	9.4	6.6	7.5	9.2	•
Total Liabilities to Net Worth 37	1.2	•	0.9	•	0.9	1.0	1.4	0.9	1.1	1.3	1.9	1.9	•
Current Assets to Working Capital 38	5.0	•	2.0	•	1.6	1.6	2.1	2.1	1.9	2.5	2.1	3.7	•
Current Liabilities to Working Capital 39	4.0	•	1.0	•	0.6	0.6	1.1	1.1	0.9	1.5	1.1	2.7	•
Working Capital to Net Sales 40	0.1	•	0.2	•	0.1	0.1	0.1	0.1	0.2	0.1	0.1	0.1	•
Inventory to Working Capital 41	1.5	•	0.1	•	0.5	0.4	0.8	0.8	0.8	0.9	0.7	1.2	•
Total Receipts to Cash Flow 42	8.6	•	11.8	•	10.0	9.7	10.6	13.0	10.2	10.8	11.8	13.5	•
Cost of Goods to Cash Flow 43	5.9	•	8.2	•	6.6	7.2	7.8	9.8	7.5	8.1	9.1	9.9	•
Cash Flow to Total Debt 44	0.1	•	0.6	•	0.7	0.6	0.3	0.3	0.3	0.2	0.2	0.1	•
Selected Financial Factors (in Percentages)												
Debt Ratio 45	54.8	•	48.0	•	46.9	49.2	58.1	48.4	53.4	55.8	65.1	65.3	•
Return on Total Assets 46	6.7	•	15.3	•	21.5	21.9	11.4	8.5	10.3	8.0	10.0	8.0	•
Return on Equity Before Income Taxes 47	11.5	•	28.4	•	37.0	40.7	22.7	13.9	18.9	14.5	21.0	14.5	•
Return on Equity After Income Taxes 48	8.3	•	28.1	•	36.9	37.8	20.0	12.5	17.1	12.5	20.3	10.0	•
Profit Margin (Before Income Tax) 49	7.8	•	4.7	•	5.9	7.4	4.6	4.0	5.5	4.3	3.9	5.6	•
Profit Margin (After Income Tax) 50	5.6	•	4.6	•	5.9	6.9	4.1	3.6	5.0	3.7	3.8	3.8	•

Table I

Corporations with and without Net Income

PRINTING AND RELATED SUPPORT ACTIVITIES

MONEY AMOUNTS AND SIZE OF ASSETS IN THOUSANDS OF DOLLARS

Item Description for Accounting Period 7/11 Through 6/12		Total	Zero Assets	Under 500	500 to 1,000	1,000 to 5,000	5,000 to 10,000	10,000 to 25,000	25,000 to 50,000	50,000 to 100,000	100,000 to 250,000	250,000 to 500,000	500,000 to 2,500,000	2,500,000 and over
Number of Enterprises	1	25410	4051	16907	1984	1687	370	239	101	33	14	10	11	3
Revenues ($ in Thousands)														
Net Sales	2	70898796	591961	8156716	5743590	9054906	4656297	6982772	4875727	3201696	2352052	3952867	7518840	13811372
Interest	3	55491	100	84	244	10638	1040	2669	1759	1121	3199	652	15129	18858
Rents	4	19608	0	2048	1774	4677	2	2554	381	111	1425	2061	3304	1273
Royalties	5	151673	1029	0	0	571	2923	8516	201	0	11497	9187	116746	1002
Other Portfolio Income	6	226429	16293	20058	34719	17026	3796	15207	31841	2098	5190	19122	43862	17217
Other Receipts	7	915611	6404	49284	22635	37857	49285	48319	128012	48760	340470	20591	37545	126446
Total Receipts	8	72267608	615787	8228190	5802962	9125675	4713343	7060037	5037921	3253786	2713833	4004480	7735426	13976168
Average Total Receipts	9	2844	152	487	2925	5409	12739	29540	49880	98600	193845	400448	703221	4658723
Operating Costs/Operating Income (%)														
Cost of Operations	10	61.0	51.0	49.7	50.2	63.9	61.1	68.7	71.1	68.8	58.9	64.3	43.8	70.2
Salaries and Wages	11	11.0	8.9	9.9	13.7	11.8	11.3	9.3	9.1	8.2	21.4	10.7	15.8	8.0
Taxes Paid	12	2.2	1.7	2.5	2.5	2.5	2.5	2.0	2.0	2.1	2.5	1.7	2.5	2.0
Interest Paid	13	2.0	2.3	0.7	0.7	1.1	0.5	0.9	1.4	1.4	5.2	2.5	3.9	3.4
Depreciation	14	4.1	2.3	1.9	3.1	2.8	4.2	5.0	5.1	4.5	5.9	4.6	4.5	5.1
Amortization and Depletion	15	0.6	0.6	0.1	0.0	0.2	0.0	0.3	0.6	0.7	1.7	1.7	2.3	0.1
Pensions and Other Deferred Comp.	16	0.4	0.0	0.4	0.1	0.2	0.2	0.3	0.3	0.2	0.3	1.0	0.4	0.8
Employee Benefits	17	1.6	1.4	1.4	0.7	1.6	1.4	1.5	1.6	2.1	2.7	2.9	2.7	1.2
Advertising	18	0.9	0.2	0.5	0.7	0.4	0.6	0.3	0.6	0.4	6.2	0.4	3.3	0.3
Other Expenses	19	13.5	132.6	21.5	15.1	11.1	14.4	8.9	9.1	8.2	10.7	11.5	17.7	8.1
Officers' Compensation	20	2.8	2.0	8.3	6.8	3.7	3.0	2.4	1.7	1.9	1.2	0.7	0.9	0.3
Operating Margin	21	•	•	3.3	6.5	0.8	0.8	0.4	•	1.5	•	•	2.3	0.6
Operating Margin Before Officers' Comp.	22	2.7	•	11.5	13.2	4.5	3.8	2.8	•	3.4	•	•	3.2	0.9

Selected Average Balance Sheet ($ in Thousands)														
Net Receivables	23	373	0	22	208	567	1734	4666	7564	13474	28370	56129	166523	662151
Inventories	24	156	0	8	62	252	1162	2204	3727	9430	14748	37524	32370	232636
Net Property, Plant and Equipment	25	474	0	37	163	674	2076	5107	9553	18893	37342	80203	126872	1217537
Total Assets	26	2098	0	100	704	2291	6720	16475	33768	71987	152753	367744	1039830	5632130
Notes and Loans Payable	27	907	0	77	326	926	1204	5125	13066	22137	89250	137686	425151	2841683
All Other Liabilities	28	603	0	40	164	578	1799	4688	8117	20470	48072	118742	262695	1773759
Net Worth	29	588	0	-17	214	787	3716	6662	12585	29380	15431	111316	351984	1016688

Selected Financial Ratios (Times to 1)														
Current Ratio	30	1.5	•	1.2	2.4	1.5	1.9	1.5	1.7	1.6	0.9	1.7	2.0	1.3
Quick Ratio	31	1.1	•	1.0	2.0	1.0	1.3	1.1	1.2	1.1	0.5	1.1	1.5	0.9
Net Sales to Working Capital	32	10.9	•	48.2	10.5	14.3	6.7	9.6	6.9	7.5	•	8.4	4.9	20.5
Coverage Ratio	33	2.0	•	6.9	12.1	2.5	5.0	2.8	1.5	3.3	0.8	0.9	2.5	1.6
Total Asset Turnover	34	1.3	•	4.8	4.1	2.3	1.9	1.8	1.4	1.3	1.1	1.1	0.7	0.8
Inventory Turnover	35	10.9	•	31.6	23.6	13.6	6.6	9.1	9.2	7.1	6.7	6.8	9.2	13.9
Receivables Turnover	36	7.1	•	21.1	15.0	8.1	6.7	5.8	6.6	7.1	5.8	6.1	4.1	6.6
Total Liabilities to Net Worth	37	2.6	•	•	2.3	1.9	0.8	1.5	1.7	1.5	8.9	2.3	2.0	4.5
Current Assets to Working Capital	38	2.9	•	5.3	1.7	3.2	2.1	2.9	2.4	2.5	•	2.5	2.1	4.9
Current Liabilities to Working Capital	39	1.9	•	4.3	0.7	2.2	1.1	1.9	1.4	1.5	•	1.5	1.1	3.9
Working Capital to Net Sales	40	0.1	•	0.0	0.1	0.1	0.1	0.1	0.1	0.1	•	0.1	0.2	0.0
Inventory to Working Capital	41	0.6	•	0.7	0.2	0.6	0.5	0.6	0.6	0.8	•	0.7	0.3	1.0
Total Receipts to Cash Flow	42	9.5	•	5.3	6.4	11.9	8.8	13.0	15.3	11.7	14.5	13.7	5.0	12.7
Cost of Goods to Cash Flow	43	5.8	•	2.6	3.2	7.6	5.4	9.0	10.9	8.1	8.5	8.8	2.2	8.9
Cash Flow to Total Debt	44	0.2	•	0.8	0.9	0.3	0.5	0.2	0.1	0.2	0.1	0.1	0.2	0.1

Selected Financial Factors (in Percentages)														
Debt Ratio	45	72.0	•	116.7	69.5	65.7	44.7	59.6	62.7	59.2	89.9	69.7	66.1	81.9
Return on Total Assets	46	5.1	•	23.3	33.7	6.3	4.7	4.6	3.1	5.9	4.4	2.3	6.4	4.3
Return on Equity Before Income Taxes	47	8.9	•	•	101.5	11.0	6.8	7.4	2.7	10.0	•	•	11.4	8.6
Return on Equity After Income Taxes	48	6.4	•	•	100.8	10.8	6.0	6.3	1.2	8.3	•	•	7.1	5.3
Profit Margin (Before Income Tax)	49	1.9	•	4.1	7.5	1.6	2.0	1.7	0.7	3.0	•	•	5.9	1.9
Profit Margin (After Income Tax)	50	1.4	•	4.1	7.5	1.6	1.8	1.4	0.3	2.5	•	•	3.7	1.2

Table II

Corporations with Net Income

PRINTING AND RELATED SUPPORT ACTIVITIES

MONEY AMOUNTS AND SIZE OF ASSETS IN THOUSANDS OF DOLLARS

Item Description for Accounting Period 7/11 Through 6/12		Total	Zero Assets	Under 500	500 to 1,000	1,000 to 5,000	5,000 to 10,000	10,000 to 25,000	25,000 to 50,000	50,000 to 100,000	100,000 to 250,000	250,000 to 500,000	500,000 to 2,500,000	2,500,000 and over
Number of Enterprises	1	14325	1907	9073	1758	1021	296	162	60	23	7	•	•	0
Revenues ($ in Thousands)														
Net Sales	2	50826624	266047	5506927	5369615	5592225	3599098	5021176	3164946	2313733	899702	•	•	0
Interest	3	48614	0	10	188	9507	959	2644	537	904	1431	•	•	0
Rents	4	13019	0	2047	44	2763	0	2554	348	63	1409	•	•	0
Royalties	5	136714	0	0	0	0	2923	8516	201	0	0	•	•	0
Other Portfolio Income	6	195689	16273	15578	33988	14836	3523	5387	26971	1904	4248	•	•	0
Other Receipts	7	662940	2250	9131	21329	30243	44100	36825	110727	39786	315216	•	•	0
Total Receipts	8	51883600	284570	5533693	5425164	5649574	3650603	5077102	3303730	2356390	1222006	•	•	0
Average Total Receipts	9	3622	149	610	3086	5533	12333	31340	55062	102452	174572	•	•	•
Operating Costs/Operating Income (%)														
Cost of Operations	10	60.1	38.3	51.0	49.8	63.2	59.4	69.1	72.8	68.0	65.1	•	•	•
Salaries and Wages	11	10.7	0.1	7.4	13.6	11.2	12.0	8.3	8.0	8.0	20.3	•	•	•
Taxes Paid	12	2.2	0.2	2.3	2.4	2.4	2.1	2.0	1.9	2.1	2.4	•	•	•
Interest Paid	13	1.7	0.5	0.5	0.6	0.7	0.4	0.8	1.0	1.1	1.9	•	•	•
Depreciation	14	3.3	1.9	1.5	3.1	1.8	3.9	3.0	3.4	4.5	5.6	•	•	•
Amortization and Depletion	15	0.4	•	0.0	0.0	0.2	0.0	0.2	0.4	0.5	1.7	•	•	•
Pensions and Other Deferred Comp.	16	0.4	•	0.5	0.1	0.2	0.3	0.3	0.2	0.3	0.5	•	•	•
Employee Benefits	17	1.4	0.0	0.9	0.6	1.3	1.2	1.6	1.1	2.1	3.0	•	•	•
Advertising	18	1.1	0.2	0.4	0.7	0.4	0.6	0.3	0.5	0.5	15.3	•	•	•
Other Expenses	19	12.3	36.0	19.4	14.8	11.1	14.0	8.5	7.9	7.3	12.6	•	•	•
Officers' Compensation	20	2.8	1.1	7.6	6.7	3.5	3.0	2.3	1.5	2.1	2.0	•	•	•
Operating Margin	21	3.7	21.8	8.4	7.6	4.0	3.1	3.6	1.3	3.3	•	•	•	•
Operating Margin Before Officers' Comp.	22	6.5	22.9	16.1	14.3	7.5	6.2	6.0	2.8	5.5	•	•	•	•

Selected Average Balance Sheet ($ in Thousands)

Net Receivables	23	483	0	25	216	646	1829	4748	6987	14802	22853	•	•	•
Inventories	24	200	0	11	51	268	1214	2414	4255	9197	20171	•	•	•
Net Property, Plant and Equipment	25	498	0	46	148	707	1776	4504	9128	18960	37503	•	•	•
Total Assets	26	2609	0	115	703	2208	6401	16775	33170	72933	162275	•	•	•
Notes and Loans Payable	27	1040	0	55	312	629	1010	4252	9553	18555	48703	•	•	•
All Other Liabilities	28	740	0	51	158	510	1749	4043	8184	18815	34604	•	•	•
Net Worth	29	829	0	9	233	1069	3642	8479	15432	35563	78968	•	•	•

Selected Financial Ratios (Times to 1)

Current Ratio	30	1.8	•	1.3	2.6	2.0	1.9	1.9	1.7	2.2	1.6	•	•	•
Quick Ratio	31	1.3	•	1.0	2.2	1.5	1.3	1.3	1.1	1.5	1.0	•	•	•
Net Sales to Working Capital	32	8.6	•	43.0	10.1	8.4	6.3	7.0	7.4	4.9	7.2	•	•	•
Coverage Ratio	33	4.5	59.8	20.2	15.4	7.7	12.1	7.2	6.5	5.7	4.0	•	•	•
Total Asset Turnover	34	1.4	•	5.3	4.3	2.5	1.9	1.8	1.6	1.4	0.8	•	•	•
Inventory Turnover	35	10.7	•	28.9	30.0	12.9	5.9	8.9	9.0	7.4	4.1	•	•	•
Receivables Turnover	36	7.0	•	24.1	15.4	7.8	6.8	6.1	7.7	6.6	4.4	•	•	•
Total Liabilities to Net Worth	37	2.1	•	11.8	2.0	1.1	0.8	1.0	1.1	1.1	1.1	•	•	•
Current Assets to Working Capital	38	2.3	•	4.4	1.6	2.0	2.1	2.2	2.4	1.8	2.7	•	•	•
Current Liabilities to Working Capital	39	1.3	•	3.4	0.6	1.0	1.1	1.2	1.4	0.8	1.7	•	•	•
Working Capital to Net Sales	40	0.1	•	0.0	0.1	0.1	0.2	0.1	0.1	0.2	0.1	•	•	•
Inventory to Working Capital	41	0.5	•	0.7	0.2	0.4	0.5	0.5	0.6	0.5	0.8	•	•	•
Total Receipts to Cash Flow	42	7.1	2.0	4.5	6.1	8.2	7.3	9.5	9.9	10.1	6.5	•	•	•
Cost of Goods to Cash Flow	43	4.2	0.8	2.3	3.0	5.2	4.3	6.6	7.2	6.9	4.2	•	•	•
Cash Flow to Total Debt	44	0.3	•	1.3	1.1	0.6	0.6	0.4	0.3	0.3	0.2	•	•	•

Selected Financial Factors (in Percentages)

Debt Ratio	45	68.2	•	92.2	66.8	51.6	43.1	49.5	53.5	51.2	51.3	•	•	•
Return on Total Assets	46	10.2	•	49.7	40.2	14.2	9.5	10.6	10.8	8.6	5.9	•	•	•
Return on Equity Before Income Taxes	47	25.1	•	602.9	113.2	25.6	15.3	18.1	19.6	14.5	9.0	•	•	•
Return on Equity After Income Taxes	48	22.0	•	602.2	112.4	25.4	14.3	17.0	17.6	12.5	6.7	•	•	•
Profit Margin (Before Income Tax)	49	5.9	28.8	8.9	8.6	5.0	4.6	5.0	5.7	5.1	5.5	•	•	•
Profit Margin (After Income Tax)	50	5.1	28.7	8.9	8.6	5.0	4.3	4.6	5.1	4.4	4.1	•	•	•

Table I

Corporations with and without Net Income

PETROLEUM REFINERIES (INCLUDING INTEGRATED)

MONEY AMOUNTS AND SIZE OF ASSETS IN THOUSANDS OF DOLLARS

Item Description for Accounting Period 7/11 Through 6/12		Total	Zero Assets	Under 500	500 to 1,000	1,000 to 5,000	5,000 to 10,000	10,000 to 25,000	25,000 to 50,000	50,000 to 100,000	100,000 to 250,000	250,000 to 500,000	500,000 to 2,500,000	2,500,000 and over
Number of Enterprises	1	202	3	0	0	132	0	15	3	6	12	4	6	21
Revenues ($ in Thousands)														
Net Sales	2	2324182286	10602219	0	0	114417	0	510473	349328	1127863	7309785	2232314	27640649	2274295239
Interest	3	11191822	540	0	0	80	0	286	196	552	1732	3552	54744	11130140
Rents	4	1098743	0	0	0	0	0	1350	46	0	658	1996	26715	1067977
Royalties	5	1268603	0	0	0	0	0	0	0	0	16	0	431	1268155
Other Portfolio Income	6	26784833	128	0	0	49230	0	1524	5	375	106852	338256	13399	26275065
Other Receipts	7	40971137	11639	0	0	59607	0	21245	1509	11579	556192	72064	173822	40063480
Total Receipts	8	2405497424	10614526	0	0	223334	0	534878	351084	1140369	7975235	2648182	27909760	2354100056
Average Total Receipts	9	11908403	3538175	•	•	1692	•	35659	117028	190062	664603	662046	4651627	112100003
Operating Costs/Operating Income (%)														
Cost of Operations	10	90.5	94.2	•	•	96.9	•	85.6	89.2	93.5	88.0	76.7	88.9	90.5
Salaries and Wages	11	1.2	0.2	•	•	9.2	•	3.0	2.1	1.0	1.9	1.2	1.8	1.2
Taxes Paid	12	1.2	0.0	•	•	2.1	•	1.0	0.5	0.3	0.7	0.8	1.2	1.3
Interest Paid	13	1.0	0.2	•	•	5.8	•	0.2	3.4	0.4	2.1	1.7	1.0	1.0
Depreciation	14	1.0	0.3	•	•	3.7	•	0.8	0.7	1.4	1.8	3.4	2.0	1.0
Amortization and Depletion	15	0.4	0.0	•	•	0.4	•	•	0.4	0.0	0.1	0.3	0.6	0.4
Pensions and Other Deferred Comp.	16	0.2	0.0	•	•	0.0	•	0.1	•	0.1	0.1	0.1	0.1	0.2
Employee Benefits	17	0.1	0.1	•	•	0.4	•	0.7	0.0	0.2	0.2	0.1	0.3	0.1
Advertising	18	0.0	0.0	•	•	•	•	0.0	0.0	0.0	0.0	0.0	0.1	0.0
Other Expenses	19	3.4	0.7	•	•	25.1	•	9.4	6.6	2.4	5.0	9.8	2.6	3.4
Officers' Compensation	20	0.0	0.3	•	•	1.5	•	2.1	0.3	0.4	0.2	0.4	0.3	0.0
Operating Margin	21	0.8	4.0	•	•	•	•	•	•	0.3	•	5.6	1.2	0.8
Operating Margin Before Officers' Comp.	22	0.8	4.3	•	•	•	•	•	•	0.7	•	6.0	1.5	0.8

Selected Average Balance Sheet ($ in Thousands)														
Net Receivables	23	4049983	0	•	•	4	•	3778	7150	9958	44903	59834	218593	38850879
Inventories	24	180743	0	•	•	22	•	2614	3254	9400	30131	49240	306163	1624099
Net Property, Plant and Equipment	25	1612567	0	•	•	159	•	572	3324	24723	83348	118286	662695	15242910
Total Assets	26	11619164	0	•	•	2520	•	13616	33222	90243	159554	439990	1679939	111054239
Notes and Loans Payable	27	2534562	0	•	•	357	•	3336	7317	13369	108710	46303	482158	24161877
All Other Liabilities	28	4145627	0	•	•	126	•	6982	14440	22551	97352	99095	554068	39629889
Net Worth	29	4938976	0	•	•	2036	•	3298	11465	54324	-46508	294592	643713	47262473

Selected Financial Ratios (Times to 1)														
Current Ratio	30	1.3	•	•	•	0.9	•	1.7	1.1	1.9	1.8	3.9	1.9	1.3
Quick Ratio	31	1.2	•	•	•	0.2	•	1.0	0.9	1.1	1.2	3.0	0.9	1.2
Net Sales to Working Capital	32	11.7	•	•	•	•	•	8.8	75.9	8.8	10.9	2.7	13.5	11.7
Coverage Ratio	33	6.3	22.1	•	•	9.7	•	11.7	0.2	4.6	5.2	15.6	3.1	6.4
Total Asset Turnover	34	1.0	•	•	•	0.3	•	2.5	3.5	2.1	3.8	1.3	2.7	1.0
Inventory Turnover	35	57.6	•	•	•	38.0	•	11.1	31.9	18.7	17.8	8.7	13.4	60.4
Receivables Turnover	36	2.8	•	•	•	•	•	11.1	20.2	14.4	14.4	18.7	20.4	2.7
Total Liabilities to Net Worth	37	1.4	•	•	•	0.2	•	3.1	1.9	0.7	•	0.5	1.6	1.3
Current Assets to Working Capital	38	4.7	•	•	•	•	•	2.5	14.5	2.1	2.2	1.3	2.1	4.7
Current Liabilities to Working Capital	39	3.7	•	•	•	•	•	1.5	13.5	1.1	1.2	0.3	1.1	3.7
Working Capital to Net Sales	40	0.1	•	•	•	•	•	0.1	0.0	0.1	0.1	0.4	0.1	0.1
Inventory to Working Capital	41	0.2	•	•	•	•	•	1.0	2.3	0.5	0.6	0.2	0.8	0.2
Total Receipts to Cash Flow	42	14.1	23.3	•	•	1.4	•	11.5	38.5	30.3	8.0	3.0	25.8	14.1
Cost of Goods to Cash Flow	43	12.8	22.0	•	•	1.3	•	9.8	34.3	28.3	7.0	2.3	22.9	12.8
Cash Flow to Total Debt	44	0.1	•	•	•	1.3	•	0.3	0.1	0.2	0.4	1.3	0.2	0.1

Selected Financial Factors (in Percentages)														
Debt Ratio	45	57.5	•	•	•	19.2	•	75.8	65.5	39.8	129.1	33.0	61.7	57.4
Return on Total Assets	46	6.3	•	•	•	19.3	•	5.3	2.2	3.8	42.1	32.8	8.8	6.2
Return on Equity Before Income Taxes	47	12.5	•	•	•	21.4	•	20.1	•	4.9	•	45.8	15.6	12.4
Return on Equity After Income Taxes	48	8.1	•	•	•	21.2	•	15.1	•	4.7	•	43.7	9.8	8.0
Profit Margin (Before Income Tax)	49	5.4	4.1	•	•	50.2	•	1.9	•	1.4	8.9	24.2	2.2	5.4
Profit Margin (After Income Tax)	50	3.5	2.7	•	•	49.9	•	1.5	•	1.4	6.9	23.0	1.4	3.5

Table II

Corporations with Net Income

PETROLEUM REFINERIES (INCLUDING INTEGRATED)

MONEY AMOUNTS AND SIZE OF ASSETS IN THOUSANDS OF DOLLARS

Item Description for Accounting Period 7/11 Through 6/12		Total	Zero Assets	Under 500	500 to 1,000	1,000 to 5,000	5,000 to 10,000	10,000 to 25,000	25,000 to 50,000	50,000 to 100,000	100,000 to 250,000	250,000 to 500,000	500,000 to 2,500,000	2,500,000 and over
Number of Enterprises	1	162	•	0	0	111	0	•	0	3	9	4	•	16
Revenues ($ in Thousands)														
Net Sales	2	2242756203	•	0	0	113415	0	•	0	1073134	6408553	2232314	•	2203779331
Interest	3	10987807	•	0	0	0	0	•	0	460	1726	3552	•	10944558
Rents	4	954990	•	0	0	0	0	•	0	0	288	1996	•	932337
Royalties	5	1213839	•	0	0	0	0	•	0	0	5	0	•	1213833
Other Portfolio Income	6	26413564	•	0	0	49230	0	•	0	375	106175	338256	•	25907973
Other Receipts	7	41374050	•	0	0	42990	0	•	0	9467	550088	72064	•	40569405
Total Receipts	8	2323700453	•	0	0	205635	0	•	0	1083436	7066835	2648182	•	2283347437
Average Total Receipts	9	14343830	•	•	•	1853	•	•	•	361145	785204	662046	•	142709215
Operating Costs/Operating Income (%)														
Cost of Operations	10	90.4	•	•	•	96.3	•	•	•	95.5	87.9	76.7	•	90.4
Salaries and Wages	11	1.2	•	•	•	0.6	•	•	•	0.6	2.1	1.2	•	1.2
Taxes Paid	12	1.3	•	•	•	0.9	•	•	•	0.1	0.7	0.8	•	1.3
Interest Paid	13	1.0	•	•	•	4.5	•	•	•	0.1	2.1	1.7	•	1.0
Depreciation	14	0.9	•	•	•	2.2	•	•	•	0.8	1.7	3.4	•	0.9
Amortization and Depletion	15	0.4	•	•	•	0.4	•	•	•	•	0.1	0.3	•	0.4
Pensions and Other Deferred Comp.	16	0.2	•	•	•	0.0	•	•	•	0.1	0.1	0.1	•	0.2
Employee Benefits	17	0.1	•	•	•	0.1	•	•	•	0.1	0.3	0.1	•	0.1
Advertising	18	0.0	•	•	•	•	•	•	•	0.0	0.0	0.0	•	0.0
Other Expenses	19	3.3	•	•	•	4.6	•	•	•	0.6	4.8	9.8	•	3.3
Officers' Compensation	20	0.0	•	•	•	0.0	•	•	•	0.3	0.1	0.4	•	0.0
Operating Margin	21	1.0	•	•	•	•	•	•	•	1.7	0.4	5.6	•	1.0
Operating Margin Before Officers' Comp.	22	1.0	•	•	•	•	•	•	•	2.1	0.5	6.0	•	1.0

Selected Average Balance Sheet ($ in Thousands)												
Net Receivables 23	5020910	•	•	•	3	•	•	•	14025	52001	59834	•	50733856
Inventories 24	183973	•	•	•	0	•	•	•	19513	41984	49240	•	1992431
Net Property, Plant and Equipment 25	1896842	•	•	•	0	•	•	•	29271	81646	118286	•	18991392
Total Assets 26	14190526	•	•	•	2270	•	•	•	91762	159682	439990	•	143044693
Notes and Loans Payable 27	3093258	•	•	•	54	•	•	•	9529	112204	46303	•	31127115
All Other Liabilities 28	5050085	•	•	•	114	•	•	•	23600	106872	99095	•	50908953
Net Worth 29	6047183	•	•	•	2101	•	•	•	58633	-59395	294592	•	61008625

Selected Financial Ratios (Times to 1)												
Current Ratio 30	1.3	•	•	•	0.2	•	•	•	2.6	1.9	3.9	•	1.3
Quick Ratio 31	1.2	•	•	•	0.1	•	•	•	1.7	1.3	3.0	•	1.2
Net Sales to Working Capital 32	11.5	•	•	•	•	•	•	•	9.5	9.9	2.7	•	11.5
Coverage Ratio 33	6.6	•	•	•	17.0	•	•	•	33.8	6.2	15.6	•	6.6
Total Asset Turnover 34	1.0	•	•	•	0.5	•	•	•	3.9	4.5	1.3	•	1.0
Inventory Turnover 35	68.0	•	•	•	•	•	•	•	17.5	14.9	8.7	•	62.5
Receivables Turnover 36	2.7	•	•	•	600.1	•	•	•	•	•	18.7	•	•
Total Liabilities to Net Worth 37	1.3	•	•	•	0.1	•	•	•	0.6	•	0.5	•	1.3
Current Assets to Working Capital 38	4.7	•	•	•	•	•	•	•	1.6	2.1	1.3	•	4.7
Current Liabilities to Working Capital 39	3.7	•	•	•	•	•	•	•	0.6	1.1	0.3	•	3.7
Working Capital to Net Sales 40	0.1	•	•	•	•	•	•	•	0.1	0.1	0.4	•	0.1
Inventory to Working Capital 41	0.2	•	•	•	•	•	•	•	0.5	0.6	0.2	•	0.2
Total Receipts to Cash Flow 42	13.6	•	•	•	1.3	•	•	•	32.9	7.2	3.0	•	13.7
Cost of Goods to Cash Flow 43	12.3	•	•	•	1.3	•	•	•	31.5	6.3	2.3	•	12.4
Cash Flow to Total Debt 44	0.1	•	•	•	4.6	•	•	•	0.3	0.5	1.3	•	0.1

Selected Financial Factors (in Percentages)												
Debt Ratio 45	57.4	•	•	•	7.4	•	•	•	36.1	137.2	33.0	•	57.3
Return on Total Assets 46	6.6	•	•	•	34.3	•	•	•	10.6	56.6	32.8	•	6.5
Return on Equity Before Income Taxes 47	13.1	•	•	•	34.9	•	•	•	16.1	•	45.8	•	12.9
Return on Equity After Income Taxes 48	8.6	•	•	•	34.7	•	•	•	15.8	•	43.7	•	8.4
Profit Margin (Before Income Tax) 49	5.7	•	•	•	71.8	•	•	•	2.6	10.6	24.2	•	5.7
Profit Margin (After Income Tax) 50	3.7	•	•	•	71.4	•	•	•	2.6	8.4	23.0	•	3.7

Table I

Corporations with and without Net Income

ASPHALT PAVING, ROOFING, OTHER PETROLEUM AND COAL PRODUCTS

MONEY AMOUNTS AND SIZE OF ASSETS IN THOUSANDS OF DOLLARS

Item Description for Accounting Period 7/11 Through 6/12		Total	Zero Assets	Under 500	500 to 1,000	1,000 to 5,000	5,000 to 10,000	10,000 to 25,000	25,000 to 50,000	50,000 to 100,000	100,000 to 250,000	250,000 to 500,000	500,000 to 2,500,000	2,500,000 and over
Number of Enterprises	1	779	440	0	58	70	110	51	15	16	13	3	4	0
Revenues ($ in Thousands)														
Net Sales	2	19387210	756571	0	235955	393125	2704647	1535350	917085	2231223	4958863	1093323	4561067	0
Interest	3	19910	148	0	1	91	1	41	526	126	3573	4790	10614	0
Rents	4	1741	18	0	435	0	34	781	0	220	58	196	0	0
Royalties	5	16742	75	0	0	0	0	0	0	153	410	0	16102	0
Other Portfolio Income	6	33605	97	0	0	1112	541	1927	1280	1036	5480	1329	20804	0
Other Receipts	7	216124	15670	0	2	3236	2444	2241	3555	5200	149355	16346	18074	0
Total Receipts	8	19675332	772579	0	236393	397564	2707667	1540340	922446	2237958	5117739	1115984	4626661	0
Average Total Receipts	9	25257	1756	•	4076	5679	24615	30203	61496	139872	393672	371995	1156665	•
Operating Costs/Operating Income (%)														
Cost of Operations	10	74.5	73.1	•	83.3	70.5	82.0	72.0	77.2	80.6	90.4	73.0	50.5	•
Salaries and Wages	11	3.9	1.7	•	1.0	5.5	5.2	5.8	5.2	2.8	2.2	5.0	4.9	•
Taxes Paid	12	0.9	2.0	•	3.3	1.9	0.5	1.3	0.8	0.8	0.4	0.8	1.4	•
Interest Paid	13	2.6	11.1	•	0.3	0.4	0.9	0.6	0.3	0.5	0.5	0.0	7.4	•
Depreciation	14	2.7	2.7	•	0.8	2.4	1.8	4.2	1.6	4.3	1.6	1.3	3.9	•
Amortization and Depletion	15	0.2	0.6	•	0.0	•	0.1	0.0	0.3	0.2	0.1	0.1	0.2	•
Pensions and Other Deferred Comp.	16	0.2	0.1	•	0.0	0.0	0.3	0.2	0.2	0.2	0.3	0.1	0.3	•
Employee Benefits	17	0.8	0.4	•	2.1	0.1	0.8	1.5	0.4	0.4	0.3	1.0	1.3	•
Advertising	18	0.8	0.1	•	1.8	0.6	1.3	0.2	2.5	0.4	0.7	0.3	0.6	•
Other Expenses	19	8.3	10.7	•	3.9	9.3	2.7	7.8	6.6	5.0	3.4	5.9	19.5	•
Officers' Compensation	20	1.1	2.8	•	2.7	6.0	1.4	1.8	1.2	0.9	0.5	1.6	0.4	•
Operating Margin	21	4.0	•	•	0.8	3.2	2.9	4.5	3.7	3.9	•	10.9	9.7	•
Operating Margin Before Officers' Comp.	22	5.1	•	•	3.5	9.3	4.4	6.3	4.9	4.8	0.1	12.5	10.1	•

Selected Average Balance Sheet ($ in Thousands)													
Net Receivables 23	2649	0	•	39	893	3767	3833	6333	14800	38812	36226	110917	•
Inventories 24	1747	0	•	143	592	651	2511	7194	12218	22789	39233	99203	•
Net Property, Plant and Equipment 25	3196	0	•	502	477	2470	6744	7525	20270	25077	35432	235436	•
Total Assets 26	16249	0	•	879	2356	8642	16289	31636	70400	162063	311802	1504362	•
Notes and Loans Payable 27	2881	0	•	247	1025	4424	3517	8328	14116	38934	15527	147228	•
All Other Liabilities 28	6878	0	•	41	538	3134	2694	4053	14960	44377	63877	941861	•
Net Worth 29	6489	0	•	591	792	1085	10079	19255	41324	78752	232398	415273	•

Selected Financial Ratios (Times to 1)													
Current Ratio 30	2.0	•	•	2.0	3.4	1.2	2.2	2.0	2.6	2.4	3.1	1.8	•
Quick Ratio 31	1.2	•	•	1.1	2.1	1.0	1.3	0.9	1.4	1.4	1.0	1.1	•
Net Sales to Working Capital 32	6.3	•	•	24.4	4.3	22.7	6.2	6.1	5.8	7.2	2.7	4.5	•
Coverage Ratio 33	3.1	0.7	•	4.5	11.3	4.2	9.1	15.0	8.8	6.4	428.4	2.5	•
Total Asset Turnover 34	1.5	•	•	4.6	2.4	2.8	1.8	1.9	2.0	2.4	1.2	0.8	•
Inventory Turnover 35	10.6	•	•	23.7	6.7	31.0	8.6	6.6	9.2	15.1	6.8	5.8	•
Receivables Turnover 36	10.4	•	•	27.1	•	•	8.4	11.3	11.4	11.6	8.8	12.3	•
Total Liabilities to Net Worth 37	1.5	•	•	0.5	2.0	7.0	0.6	0.6	0.7	1.1	0.3	2.6	•
Current Assets to Working Capital 38	2.0	•	•	2.0	1.4	5.4	1.8	2.0	1.6	1.7	1.5	2.3	•
Current Liabilities to Working Capital 39	1.0	•	•	1.0	0.4	4.4	0.8	1.0	0.6	0.7	0.5	1.3	•
Working Capital to Net Sales 40	0.2	•	•	0.0	0.2	0.0	0.2	0.2	0.2	0.1	0.4	0.2	•
Inventory to Working Capital 41	0.5	•	•	0.9	0.4	0.6	0.5	1.0	0.6	0.5	0.3	0.5	•
Total Receipts to Cash Flow 42	8.3	16.7	•	34.8	8.4	21.8	8.7	10.1	12.6	17.8	5.7	3.8	•
Cost of Goods to Cash Flow 43	6.2	12.2	•	29.0	5.9	17.9	6.3	7.8	10.1	16.1	4.2	1.9	•
Cash Flow to Total Debt 44	0.3	•	•	0.4	0.4	0.1	0.6	0.5	0.4	0.3	0.8	0.3	•

Selected Financial Factors (in Percentages)													
Debt Ratio 45	60.1	•	•	32.7	66.4	87.4	38.1	39.1	41.3	51.4	25.5	72.4	•
Return on Total Assets 46	12.5	•	•	5.8	11.4	11.3	10.0	8.8	9.4	7.9	15.2	14.1	•
Return on Equity Before Income Taxes 47	21.3	•	•	6.7	30.9	68.7	14.4	13.5	14.1	13.7	20.4	30.7	•
Return on Equity After Income Taxes 48	16.3	•	•	6.7	23.5	64.3	14.2	11.6	11.8	10.3	15.0	23.0	•
Profit Margin (Before Income Tax) 49	5.6	•	•	1.0	4.4	3.0	4.8	4.3	4.2	2.8	13.0	11.2	•
Profit Margin (After Income Tax) 50	4.3	•	•	1.0	3.3	2.8	4.7	3.6	3.5	2.1	9.6	8.4	•

ASPHALT PAVING, ROOFING, OTHER PETROLEUM AND COAL PRODUCTS

MONEY AMOUNTS AND SIZE OF ASSETS IN THOUSANDS OF DOLLARS

Item Description for Accounting Period 7/11 Through 6/12		Total	Zero Assets	Under 500	500 to 1,000	1,000 to 5,000	5,000 to 10,000	10,000 to 25,000	25,000 to 50,000	50,000 to 100,000	100,000 to 250,000	250,000 to 500,000	500,000 to 2,500,000	2,500,000 and over
Number of Enterprises	1	322	•	0	58	70	110	•	15	12	•	3	4	0
Revenues ($ in Thousands)														
Net Sales	2	18033073	•	0	235955	393125	2704647	•	917085	1481077	•	1093323	4561067	0
Interest	3	17558	•	0	1	91	1	•	526	83	•	4790	10614	0
Rents	4	1570	•	0	435	0	34	•	0	220	•	196	0	0
Royalties	5	16513	•	0	0	0	0	•	0	0	•	0	16102	0
Other Portfolio Income	6	33056	•	0	0	1112	541	•	1280	893	•	1329	20804	0
Other Receipts	7	222306	•	0	2	3236	2444	•	3555	4781	•	16346	18074	0
Total Receipts	8	18324076	•	0	236393	397564	2707667	•	922446	1487054	•	1115984	4626661	0
Average Total Receipts	9	56907	•	•	4076	5679	24615	•	61496	123921	•	371995	1156665	•
Operating Costs/Operating Income (%)														
Cost of Operations	10	73.8	•	•	83.3	70.5	82.0	•	77.2	78.2	•	73.0	50.5	•
Salaries and Wages	11	4.0	•	•	1.0	5.5	5.2	•	5.2	2.7	•	5.0	4.9	•
Taxes Paid	12	1.0	•	•	3.3	1.9	0.5	•	0.8	0.8	•	0.8	1.4	•
Interest Paid	13	2.6	•	•	0.3	0.4	0.9	•	0.3	0.4	•	0.0	7.4	•
Depreciation	14	2.5	•	•	0.8	2.4	1.8	•	1.6	3.6	•	1.3	3.9	•
Amortization and Depletion	15	0.1	•	•	0.0	•	0.1	•	0.3	0.1	•	0.1	0.2	•
Pensions and Other Deferred Comp.	16	0.2	•	•	0.0	0.0	0.3	•	0.2	0.2	•	0.1	0.3	•
Employee Benefits	17	0.8	•	•	2.1	0.1	0.8	•	0.4	0.4	•	1.0	1.3	•
Advertising	18	0.8	•	•	1.8	0.6	1.3	•	2.5	0.5	•	0.3	0.6	•
Other Expenses	19	8.4	•	•	3.9	9.3	2.7	•	6.6	5.2	•	5.9	19.5	•
Officers' Compensation	20	1.0	•	•	2.7	6.0	1.4	•	1.2	0.8	•	1.6	0.4	•
Operating Margin	21	4.9	•	•	0.8	3.2	2.9	•	3.7	7.1	•	10.9	9.7	•
Operating Margin Before Officers' Comp.	22	5.9	•	•	3.5	9.3	4.4	•	4.9	7.9	•	12.5	10.1	•

Selected Average Balance Sheet ($ in Thousands)

Net Receivables 23	5800	•	•	39	893	3767	•	6333	13807	•	36226	110917	•
Inventories 24	4003	•	•	153	308	733	•	9766	12521	•	35444	128242	•
Net Property, Plant and Equipment 25	7009	•	•	502	477	2470	•	7525	17692	•	35432	235436	•
Total Assets 26	36836	•	•	879	2356	8642	•	31636	65560	•	311802	1504362	•
Notes and Loans Payable 27	6303	•	•	247	1025	4424	•	8328	9719	•	15527	147228	•
All Other Liabilities 28	16114	•	•	41	538	3134	•	4053	12417	•	63877	941861	•
Net Worth 29	14419	•	•	591	792	1085	•	19255	43424	•	232398	415273	•

Selected Financial Ratios (Times to 1)

Current Ratio 30	2.0	•	•	2.0	3.4	1.2	•	2.0	3.5	•	3.1	1.8	•
Quick Ratio 31	1.2	•	•	1.1	2.1	1.0	•	0.9	1.9	•	1.0	1.1	•
Net Sales to Working Capital 32	6.1	•	•	24.4	4.3	22.7	•	6.1	4.5	•	2.7	4.5	•
Coverage Ratio 33	3.5	•	•	4.5	11.3	4.2	•	15.0	19.8	•	428.4	2.5	•
Total Asset Turnover 34	1.5	•	•	4.6	2.4	2.8	•	1.9	1.9	•	1.2	0.8	•
Inventory Turnover 35	10.3	•	•	22.1	12.9	27.5	•	4.8	7.7	•	7.5	4.5	•
Receivables Turnover 36	11.2	•	•	30.7	5.4	8.0	•	•	•	•	•	•	•
Total Liabilities to Net Worth 37	1.6	•	•	0.5	2.0	7.0	•	0.6	0.5	•	0.3	2.6	•
Current Assets to Working Capital 38	2.0	•	•	2.0	1.4	5.4	•	2.0	1.4	•	1.5	2.3	•
Current Liabilities to Working Capital 39	1.0	•	•	1.0	0.4	4.4	•	1.0	0.4	•	0.5	1.3	•
Working Capital to Net Sales 40	0.2	•	•	0.0	0.2	0.0	•	0.2	0.2	•	0.4	0.2	•
Inventory to Working Capital 41	0.5	•	•	0.9	0.4	0.6	•	1.0	0.5	•	0.3	0.5	•
Total Receipts to Cash Flow 42	7.6	•	•	34.8	8.4	21.8	•	10.1	8.7	•	5.7	3.8	•
Cost of Goods to Cash Flow 43	5.6	•	•	29.0	5.9	17.9	•	7.8	6.8	•	4.2	1.9	•
Cash Flow to Total Debt 44	0.3	•	•	0.4	0.4	0.1	•	0.5	0.6	•	0.8	0.3	•

Selected Financial Factors (in Percentages)

Debt Ratio 45	60.9	•	•	32.7	66.4	87.4	•	39.1	33.8	•	25.5	72.4	•
Return on Total Assets 46	13.9	•	•	5.8	11.4	11.3	•	8.8	14.9	•	15.2	14.1	•
Return on Equity Before Income Taxes 47	25.5	•	•	6.7	30.9	68.7	•	13.5	21.3	•	20.4	30.7	•
Return on Equity After Income Taxes 48	20.1	•	•	6.7	23.5	64.3	•	11.6	18.4	•	15.0	23.0	•
Profit Margin (Before Income Tax) 49	6.6	•	•	1.0	4.4	3.0	•	4.3	7.5	•	13.0	11.2	•
Profit Margin (After Income Tax) 50	5.2	•	•	1.0	3.3	2.8	•	3.6	6.5	•	9.6	8.4	•

Table I

Corporations with and without Net Income

BASIC CHEMICAL

MONEY AMOUNTS AND SIZE OF ASSETS IN THOUSANDS OF DOLLARS

Item Description for Accounting Period 7/11 Through 6/12		Total	Zero Assets	Under 500	500 to 1,000	1,000 to 5,000	5,000 to 10,000	10,000 to 25,000	25,000 to 50,000	50,000 to 100,000	100,000 to 250,000	250,000 to 500,000	500,000 to 2,500,000	2,500,000 and over
Number of Enterprises	1	738	19	117	94	138	51	114	51	36	30	20	40	27
Revenues ($ in Thousands)														
Net Sales	2	239496739	1625992	96969	191808	518502	768427	3070507	2208052	3539309	8941217	6863837	37276773	174395347
Interest	3	1970888	6640	41	28	15	781	726	4854	3971	3438	11024	201699	1737671
Rents	4	229172	464	0	0	0	0	643	267	861	7628	3	19848	199457
Royalties	5	3871790	1648	0	0	0	3878	18	0	1973	19674	6625	167881	3670092
Other Portfolio Income	6	3594095	14573	0	210	4065	388	8989	194	4883	34106	39879	481664	3005145
Other Receipts	7	4593203	1680	5065	4306	8512	4406	26812	17204	-1112	142256	50263	729871	3603940
Total Receipts	8	253755887	1650997	102075	196352	531094	777880	3107695	2230571	3549885	9148319	6971631	38877736	186611652
Average Total Receipts	9	343843	86895	872	2089	3849	15253	27260	43737	98608	304944	348582	971943	6911543
Operating Costs/Operating Income (%)														
Cost of Operations	10	78.3	73.2	69.4	54.8	65.0	75.1	65.8	67.9	76.4	84.7	77.8	75.8	79.1
Salaries and Wages	11	5.0	5.6	13.0	12.6	7.3	3.5	7.8	7.9	4.9	4.1	2.6	5.2	4.9
Taxes Paid	12	0.8	1.0	1.0	2.5	1.3	1.1	1.6	1.5	1.0	0.6	0.6	0.7	0.8
Interest Paid	13	3.9	1.3	8.3	0.8	0.6	0.7	0.5	1.0	1.1	0.7	5.4	5.4	3.9
Depreciation	14	3.6	2.4	2.5	2.2	8.6	2.2	2.7	4.0	3.6	2.9	5.0	3.9	3.5
Amortization and Depletion	15	0.7	1.3	0.9	0.2	0.0	0.0	0.2	0.4	0.7	0.3	1.2	0.7	0.7
Pensions and Other Deferred Comp.	16	1.3	2.1	0.4	•	0.4	0.4	0.3	0.7	0.5	0.3	0.6	1.0	1.5
Employee Benefits	17	1.1	0.4	4.5	3.1	0.9	0.7	1.6	1.7	1.0	0.5	0.6	1.6	1.1
Advertising	18	0.3	0.1	0.1	0.9	0.1	0.1	0.2	0.2	0.2	0.1	0.1	0.1	0.4
Other Expenses	19	6.9	8.2	47.5	24.1	13.4	8.9	10.6	10.9	8.0	4.9	7.7	8.0	6.5
Officers' Compensation	20	0.5	0.3	5.0	20.0	2.9	3.4	2.7	2.6	1.4	0.8	0.5	0.6	0.4
Operating Margin	21	•	4.1	•	•	•	3.8	6.0	1.3	1.2	0.0	•	•	•
Operating Margin Before Officers' Comp.	22	•	4.4	•	•	2.5	7.2	8.8	3.9	2.6	0.9	•	•	•

Selected Average Balance Sheet ($ in Thousands)														
Net Receivables	23	135318	0	69	255	508	1221	3611	6314	13839	26978	59440	146151	3356449
Inventories	24	31476	0	107	238	477	1125	3540	7861	10144	19610	45257	101387	605664
Net Property, Plant and Equipment	25	80153	0	62	127	550	1090	3746	8624	20560	41216	143517	271340	1571674
Total Assets	26	569894	0	353	809	1820	6683	15845	33653	67368	155770	377292	1088651	13265166
Notes and Loans Payable	27	239018	0	15	425	263	1391	12808	7411	19042	50655	194894	439149	5582923
All Other Liabilities	28	150204	0	138	99	451	1242	7869	9808	17586	44779	83032	296844	3473748
Net Worth	29	180673	0	200	284	1106	4049	-4831	16433	30740	60337	99366	352658	4208495
Selected Financial Ratios (Times to 1)														
Current Ratio	30	1.0	•	2.0	1.4	2.8	4.3	1.4	2.0	2.2	1.5	1.8	1.5	1.0
Quick Ratio	31	0.8	•	1.2	0.8	2.2	2.0	0.8	1.2	1.3	0.9	1.0	0.9	0.7
Net Sales to Working Capital	32	48.3	•	6.1	13.0	4.7	3.7	9.1	4.3	5.6	12.2	5.6	7.8	•
Coverage Ratio	33	2.2	5.4	•	•	4.3	7.8	16.9	3.4	2.4	4.4	0.9	1.4	2.4
Total Asset Turnover	34	0.6	•	2.3	2.5	2.1	2.3	1.7	1.3	1.5	1.9	0.9	0.9	0.5
Inventory Turnover	35	8.1	•	5.4	4.7	5.1	10.1	5.0	3.7	7.4	12.9	5.9	7.0	8.4
Receivables Turnover	36	2.7	•	10.3	3.3	6.8	13.3	7.5	5.4	7.2	12.4	4.7	7.1	2.2
Total Liabilities to Net Worth	37	2.2	•	0.8	1.8	0.6	0.7	•	1.0	1.2	1.6	2.8	2.1	2.2
Current Assets to Working Capital	38	30.4	•	2.0	3.8	1.6	1.3	3.6	2.0	1.9	2.9	2.3	3.0	•
Current Liabilities to Working Capital	39	29.4	•	1.0	2.8	0.6	0.3	2.6	1.0	0.9	1.9	1.3	2.0	•
Working Capital to Net Sales	40	0.0	•	0.2	0.1	0.2	0.3	0.1	0.2	0.2	0.1	0.2	0.1	•
Inventory to Working Capital	41	5.0	•	0.7	1.4	0.1	0.3	1.2	0.7	0.6	0.9	0.7	0.9	•
Total Receipts to Cash Flow	42	11.9	7.9	•	53.8	8.2	8.7	6.4	9.3	13.5	16.2	18.3	14.7	11.4
Cost of Goods to Cash Flow	43	9.3	5.8	•	29.5	5.3	6.5	4.2	6.3	10.3	13.8	14.2	11.1	9.0
Cash Flow to Total Debt	44	0.1	•	•	0.1	0.6	0.7	0.2	0.3	0.2	0.2	0.1	0.1	0.1
Selected Financial Factors (in Percentages)														
Debt Ratio	45	68.3	•	43.5	64.8	39.2	39.4	130.5	51.2	54.4	61.3	73.7	67.6	68.3
Return on Total Assets	46	4.8	•	•	•	5.3	13.1	13.1	4.2	3.9	6.0	4.6	6.3	4.6
Return on Equity Before Income Taxes	47	8.2	•	•	•	6.8	18.8	•	6.1	5.0	12.0	•	5.1	8.5
Return on Equity After Income Taxes	48	5.3	•	•	•	4.3	18.3	•	2.4	2.9	7.8	•	0.7	5.9
Profit Margin (Before Income Tax)	49	4.6	5.7	•	•	2.0	5.1	7.3	2.3	1.6	2.4	•	1.9	5.5
Profit Margin (After Income Tax)	50	3.0	5.2	•	•	1.3	4.9	6.4	0.9	0.9	1.6	•	0.3	3.8

Table II

Corporations with Net Income

BASIC CHEMICAL

MONEY AMOUNTS AND SIZE OF ASSETS IN THOUSANDS OF DOLLARS

Item Description for Accounting Period 7/11 Through 6/12		Total	Zero Assets	Under 500	500 to 1,000	1,000 to 5,000	5,000 to 10,000	10,000 to 25,000	25,000 to 50,000	50,000 to 100,000	100,000 to 250,000	250,000 to 500,000	500,000 to 2,500,000	2,500,000 and over
Number of Enterprises	1	478	10	0	58	125	45	96	34	24	19	11	32	24
Revenues ($ in Thousands)														
Net Sales	2	214890910	1625992	0	182726	482075	751583	2879069	1820730	2493245	6383130	3917411	26995184	167359764
Interest	3	1831671	6592	0	0	9	427	481	4692	2330	2870	10198	128386	1675687
Rents	4	204776	464	0	0	0	0	643	0	850	1961	3	19755	181100
Royalties	5	3629342	1648	0	0	0	0	18	0	0	17680	1680	151458	3456858
Other Portfolio Income	6	3510312	14573	0	210	4065	197	8576	109	4809	19216	32281	477124	2949154
Other Receipts	7	4516692	1681	0	4256	1907	4271	20431	14596	1545	130804	42931	693471	3600797
Total Receipts	8	228583703	1650950	0	187192	488056	756478	2909218	1840127	2502779	6555661	4004504	28465378	179223360
Average Total Receipts	9	478209	165095	•	3227	3904	16811	30304	54121	104282	345035	364046	889543	7467640
Operating Costs/Operating Income (%)														
Cost of Operations	10	78.3	73.2	•	55.5	65.0	75.2	66.2	68.6	73.2	86.1	72.6	73.0	79.4
Salaries and Wages	11	4.9	5.2	•	9.7	5.8	2.8	6.8	5.9	5.1	2.5	2.3	5.8	4.8
Taxes Paid	12	0.8	1.0	•	2.0	1.0	1.1	1.5	1.4	1.0	0.6	0.6	0.9	0.8
Interest Paid	13	3.5	1.3	•	0.8	0.1	0.4	0.4	0.2	0.8	0.7	2.7	2.7	3.9
Depreciation	14	3.2	2.2	•	1.3	4.1	1.7	2.3	3.0	3.0	2.1	5.1	3.9	3.1
Amortization and Depletion	15	0.7	1.3	•	•	•	0.0	0.2	0.1	0.7	0.3	1.1	0.8	0.7
Pensions and Other Deferred Comp.	16	1.3	2.1	•	•	0.4	0.4	0.3	0.9	0.7	0.1	0.5	0.9	1.5
Employee Benefits	17	1.1	0.4	•	3.1	0.9	0.7	1.5	1.5	1.2	0.3	0.7	1.9	1.1
Advertising	18	0.3	0.1	•	0.0	0.0	0.1	0.2	0.2	0.2	0.0	0.1	0.1	0.4
Other Expenses	19	6.6	7.7	•	11.2	11.7	6.6	9.1	7.1	6.7	4.5	8.3	8.2	6.3
Officers' Compensation	20	0.5	0.3	•	18.1	2.7	2.8	2.8	2.5	1.4	0.6	0.5	0.7	0.3
Operating Margin	21	•	5.3	•	•	8.2	8.2	8.7	8.5	6.0	2.2	5.5	0.9	•
Operating Margin Before Officers' Comp.	22	•	5.5	•	16.5	11.0	11.0	11.5	11.0	7.5	2.9	5.9	1.6	•

Selected Average Balance Sheet ($ in Thousands)													
Net Receivables 23	203121	0	•	414	534	1382	3909	7322	14728	28050	84661	147065	3741294
Inventories 24	40585	0	•	360	519	977	3760	9602	11675	19209	54002	94001	597023
Net Property, Plant and Equipment 25	99972	0	•	77	320	1040	3054	6457	20776	37406	133343	219473	1561812
Total Assets 26	813385	0	•	858	1611	6654	15568	33108	67586	163741	374345	1021087	14337571
Notes and Loans Payable 27	332918	0	•	564	63	1577	1813	4722	19135	42347	171813	401578	5945187
All Other Liabilities 28	207275	0	•	98	376	1141	3840	7436	15024	38214	84142	262286	3664433
Net Worth 29	273193	0	•	195	1172	3936	9915	20950	33427	83180	118391	357223	4727951

Selected Financial Ratios (Times to 1)													
Current Ratio 30	1.0	•	•	1.4	3.2	4.6	3.2	2.2	2.4	1.8	2.2	1.7	1.0
Quick Ratio 31	0.8	•	•	0.8	2.6	2.0	1.8	1.3	1.4	1.1	1.4	1.0	0.8
Net Sales to Working Capital 32	53.2	•	•	14.1	4.3	3.8	4.0	4.6	5.1	10.5	4.1	6.1	•
Coverage Ratio 33	2.8	6.2	•	2.1	96.6	23.2	24.5	39.4	9.0	8.7	3.9	3.8	2.5
Total Asset Turnover 34	0.6	•	•	3.7	2.4	2.5	1.9	1.6	1.5	2.1	1.0	0.8	0.5
Inventory Turnover 35	8.7	•	•	4.9	4.8	12.8	5.3	3.8	6.5	15.1	4.8	6.6	9.3
Receivables Turnover 36	2.5	•	•	3.1	6.5	15.6	7.8	5.7	6.7	13.0	3.3	6.4	2.2
Total Liabilities to Net Worth 37	2.0	•	•	3.4	0.4	0.7	0.6	0.6	1.0	1.0	2.2	1.9	2.0
Current Assets to Working Capital 38	35.1	•	•	3.4	1.4	1.3	1.5	1.8	1.7	2.2	1.9	2.4	•
Current Liabilities to Working Capital 39	34.1	•	•	2.4	0.4	0.3	0.5	0.8	0.7	1.2	0.9	1.4	•
Working Capital to Net Sales 40	0.0	•	•	0.1	0.2	0.3	0.3	0.2	0.2	0.1	0.2	0.2	•
Inventory to Working Capital 41	5.1	•	•	1.5	0.1	0.4	0.5	0.7	0.6	0.7	0.6	0.7	•
Total Receipts to Cash Flow 42	10.3	7.5	•	10.2	5.4	7.1	5.9	6.7	8.7	11.7	7.3	8.5	11.0
Cost of Goods to Cash Flow 43	8.1	5.5	•	5.7	3.5	5.4	3.9	4.6	6.3	10.0	5.3	6.2	8.8
Cash Flow to Total Debt 44	0.1	•	•	0.5	1.6	0.9	0.9	0.7	0.4	0.4	0.2	0.1	0.1

Selected Financial Factors (in Percentages)													
Debt Ratio 45	66.4	•	•	77.2	27.2	40.8	36.3	36.7	50.5	49.2	68.4	65.0	67.0
Return on Total Assets 46	5.4	•	•	6.0	22.9	23.3	19.6	15.8	11.2	11.7	10.1	8.3	4.8
Return on Equity Before Income Taxes 47	10.3	•	•	13.5	31.1	37.8	29.5	24.4	20.2	20.4	23.8	17.4	8.8
Return on Equity After Income Taxes 48	7.4	•	•	11.5	28.5	37.1	26.8	20.0	17.3	15.6	17.0	11.9	6.2
Profit Margin (Before Income Tax) 49	6.3	6.8	•	0.8	9.5	8.9	9.8	9.5	6.5	5.1	7.9	7.3	6.0
Profit Margin (After Income Tax) 50	4.5	6.3	•	0.7	8.7	8.8	8.9	7.8	5.6	3.9	5.7	5.1	4.2

Table I

Corporations with and without Net Income

RESIN, SYNTHETIC RUBBER AND FIBERS AND FILAMENTS

MONEY AMOUNTS AND SIZE OF ASSETS IN THOUSANDS OF DOLLARS

Item Description for Accounting Period 7/11 Through 6/12		Total	Zero Assets	Under 500	500 to 1,000	1,000 to 5,000	5,000 to 10,000	10,000 to 25,000	25,000 to 50,000	50,000 to 100,000	100,000 to 250,000	250,000 to 500,000	500,000 to 2,500,000	2,500,000 and over
Number of Enterprises	1	568	13	320	0	103	13	53	16	10	14	10	10	6
Revenues ($ in Thousands)														
Net Sales	2	65565597	333662	102976	0	477362	194662	1477039	1061436	1353281	3244857	4964536	15052108	37303677
Interest	3	449187	678	1	0	0	35	87	932	218	2105	14696	26315	404120
Rents	4	26808	0	0	0	0	0	0	100	0	0	1058	7824	17826
Royalties	5	617880	110	0	0	60	0	0	397	0	1779	12286	19730	583519
Other Portfolio Income	6	340884	0	0	0	0	0	21	1	471	2745	89298	37056	211291
Other Receipts	7	2563772	20	14	0	491	37	5166	1194	4441	12318	29305	168030	2342759
Total Receipts	8	69564128	334470	102991	0	477913	194734	1482313	1064060	1358411	3263804	5111179	15311063	40863192
Average Total Receipts	9	122472	25728	322	•	4640	14980	27968	66504	135841	233129	511118	1531106	6810532
Operating Costs/Operating Income (%)														
Cost of Operations	10	72.9	84.1	70.2	•	57.9	63.5	70.7	82.2	83.1	77.9	84.5	83.5	66.2
Salaries and Wages	11	2.7	2.3	1.7	•	4.6	7.2	5.4	2.2	2.9	3.8	3.7	1.9	2.7
Taxes Paid	12	0.5	0.6	2.3	•	1.8	1.8	1.4	1.0	1.5	0.9	0.6	0.4	0.4
Interest Paid	13	2.8	0.5	0.6	•	9.1	0.3	0.7	0.6	0.2	1.2	1.4	2.1	3.6
Depreciation	14	5.6	1.3	2.2	•	2.4	0.6	4.5	2.6	2.4	3.3	3.3	4.9	6.7
Amortization and Depletion	15	0.7	1.1	0.2	•	0.0	0.2	0.1	0.2	0.0	0.4	0.1	0.3	1.1
Pensions and Other Deferred Comp.	16	0.7	0.3	•	•	3.0	•	0.3	0.1	0.8	0.2	0.5	0.2	1.0
Employee Benefits	17	1.5	0.7	4.7	•	1.7	2.0	1.5	0.7	0.5	0.6	1.4	0.7	2.0
Advertising	18	0.2	0.0	0.2	•	0.0	0.6	0.5	0.1	0.1	0.2	0.1	0.0	0.3
Other Expenses	19	15.0	6.7	22.2	•	9.7	19.8	7.8	6.5	3.4	5.2	4.9	3.9	22.8
Officers' Compensation	20	0.4	0.3	6.7	•	5.0	0.5	3.2	0.7	0.5	1.0	0.4	0.5	0.1
Operating Margin	21	•	1.9	•	•	4.8	3.6	4.0	3.0	4.4	5.2	•	1.5	•
Operating Margin Before Officers' Comp.	22	•	2.2	•	•	9.8	4.2	7.2	3.8	4.9	6.2	•	1.9	•

Selected Average Balance Sheet ($ in Thousands)													
Net Receivables **23**	20169	0	44	•	485	3272	4179	8470	18624	29410	102769	172252	1274055
Inventories **24**	14070	0	12	•	588	1339	2595	6117	19417	29576	54648	127507	874078
Net Property, Plant and Equipment **25**	41034	0	33	•	704	249	5100	10209	19448	53164	92296	398373	2823625
Total Assets **26**	183426	0	109	•	3352	7997	16936	37546	74978	171332	387609	1195944	13869920
Notes and Loans Payable **27**	100038	0	48	•	1454	484	4046	7777	9750	45633	99039	458408	8333407
All Other Liabilities **28**	45422	0	18	•	679	1240	5374	13720	22462	40251	160324	307957	3288786
Net Worth **29**	37966	0	42	•	1220	6273	7517	16050	42766	85448	128246	429578	2247727
Selected Financial Ratios (Times to 1)													
Current Ratio **30**	1.5	•	2.2	•	1.9	5.4	2.0	1.9	2.2	2.2	1.3	1.6	1.4
Quick Ratio **31**	0.8	•	1.6	•	0.9	4.2	1.3	1.0	1.1	1.1	0.8	0.8	0.8
Net Sales to Working Capital **32**	8.0	•	8.7	•	7.1	2.9	5.4	6.9	4.9	4.7	10.6	9.6	8.1
Coverage Ratio **33**	2.3	4.9	•	•	1.5	12.4	7.6	6.3	23.2	5.8	2.8	2.5	2.0
Total Asset Turnover **34**	0.6	•	3.0	•	1.4	1.9	1.6	1.8	1.8	1.4	1.3	1.3	0.4
Inventory Turnover **35**	6.0	•	18.4	•	4.6	7.1	7.6	8.9	5.8	6.1	7.7	9.9	4.7
Receivables Turnover **36**	6.3	•	8.2	•	7.8	4.9	7.2	8.8	7.1	7.3	6.0	9.9	5.3
Total Liabilities to Net Worth **37**	3.8	•	1.6	•	1.7	0.3	1.3	1.3	0.8	1.0	2.0	1.8	5.2
Current Assets to Working Capital **38**	3.1	•	1.8	•	2.1	1.2	2.0	2.2	1.8	1.8	4.0	2.8	3.6
Current Liabilities to Working Capital **39**	2.1	•	0.8	•	1.1	0.2	1.0	1.2	0.8	0.8	3.0	1.8	2.6
Working Capital to Net Sales **40**	0.1	•	0.1	•	0.1	0.3	0.2	0.1	0.2	0.2	0.1	0.1	0.1
Inventory to Working Capital **41**	1.1	•	0.4	•	1.0	0.3	0.6	0.7	0.7	0.6	1.3	1.0	1.3
Total Receipts to Cash Flow **42**	6.5	13.0	18.2	•	7.0	4.8	10.4	11.7	14.1	9.9	16.8	17.8	4.6
Cost of Goods to Cash Flow **43**	4.7	10.9	12.8	•	4.1	3.0	7.4	9.7	11.7	7.7	14.2	14.8	3.0
Cash Flow to Total Debt **44**	0.1	•	0.3	•	0.3	1.8	0.3	0.3	0.3	0.3	0.1	0.1	0.1
Selected Financial Factors (in Percentages)													
Debt Ratio **45**	79.3	•	61.3	•	63.6	21.6	55.6	57.3	43.0	50.1	66.9	64.1	83.8
Return on Total Assets **46**	4.1	•	•	•	19.3	7.4	8.2	6.9	9.1	9.5	5.0	6.8	3.3
Return on Equity Before Income Taxes **47**	11.1	•	•	•	18.5	8.7	16.1	13.6	15.2	15.8	9.8	11.5	10.3
Return on Equity After Income Taxes **48**	6.8	•	•	•	18.3	1.2	14.8	6.6	10.2	12.9	5.6	7.2	5.8
Profit Margin (Before Income Tax) **49**	3.6	2.1	•	•	4.9	3.6	4.3	3.3	4.8	5.8	2.5	3.3	3.7
Profit Margin (After Income Tax) **50**	2.2	0.7	•	•	4.8	0.5	4.0	1.6	3.2	4.8	1.4	2.0	2.1

Table II

Corporations with Net Income

RESIN, SYNTHETIC RUBBER AND FIBERS AND FILAMENTS

MONEY AMOUNTS AND SIZE OF ASSETS IN THOUSANDS OF DOLLARS

Item Description for Accounting Period 7/11 Through 6/12		Total	Zero Assets	Under 500	500 to 1,000	1,000 to 5,000	5,000 to 10,000	10,000 to 25,000	25,000 to 50,000	50,000 to 100,000	100,000 to 250,000	250,000 to 500,000	500,000 to 2,500,000	2,500,000 and over
Number of Enterprises	1	300	9	89	0	•	10	43	12	•	10	7	•	3
Revenues ($ in Thousands)														
Net Sales	2	50938412	271258	102093	0	•	193179	1218607	915149	•	2165392	3127445	•	28194776
Interest	3	414954	207	0	0	•	0	86	902	•	1918	5471	•	387408
Rents	4	20428	0	0	0	•	0	0	100	•	0	1058	•	17334
Royalties	5	595118	110	0	0	•	0	0	0	•	1779	4345	•	583519
Other Portfolio Income	6	290445	0	0	0	•	0	21	1	•	2579	75698	•	210965
Other Receipts	7	2538816	20	0	0	•	0	3792	931	•	11672	28759	•	2352373
Total Receipts	8	54798173	271595	102093	0	•	193179	1222506	917083	•	2183340	3242776	•	31746375
Average Total Receipts	9	182661	30177	1147	•	•	19318	28430	76424	•	218334	463254	•	10582125
Operating Costs/Operating Income (%)														
Cost of Operations	10	72.7	82.8	70.4	•	•	61.3	67.2	83.2	•	72.9	80.6	•	64.2
Salaries and Wages	11	2.1	2.3	•	•	•	6.9	6.0	1.1	•	4.4	4.3	•	1.9
Taxes Paid	12	0.5	0.5	2.3	•	•	1.2	1.7	0.8	•	1.0	0.8	•	0.4
Interest Paid	13	2.1	0.2	•	•	•	0.1	0.6	0.4	•	0.6	0.8	•	2.9
Depreciation	14	4.4	1.4	2.0	•	•	0.3	3.6	2.2	•	3.2	2.8	•	6.0
Amortization and Depletion	15	0.4	0.3	0.2	•	•	•	0.0	0.1	•	0.3	0.2	•	0.6
Pensions and Other Deferred Comp.	16	0.7	0.4	•	•	•	•	0.4	0.0	•	0.3	0.5	•	1.0
Employee Benefits	17	1.7	0.9	4.4	•	•	1.9	1.8	0.7	•	0.7	1.7	•	2.5
Advertising	18	0.2	0.0	0.0	•	•	0.6	0.6	0.0	•	0.2	0.1	•	0.4
Other Expenses	19	17.3	5.4	14.0	•	•	18.3	7.4	5.3	•	6.3	6.0	•	27.8
Officers' Compensation	20	0.4	0.4	5.2	•	•	•	3.7	0.6	•	1.3	0.5	•	0.1
Operating Margin	21	•	5.3	1.4	•	•	9.4	7.2	5.5	•	8.8	1.7	•	•
Operating Margin Before Officers' Comp.	22	•	5.8	6.6	•	•	9.4	10.9	6.2	•	10.2	2.2	•	•

Selected Average Balance Sheet ($ in Thousands)

Net Receivables 23	31133	0	157	•	•	3697	4516	7940	•	26582	96899	•	2104934
Inventories 24	20950	0	38	•	•	1718	2529	6696	•	31876	50721	•	1355205
Net Property, Plant and Equipment 25	49762	0	115	•	•	221	4879	11030	•	42334	99109	•	3808739
Total Assets 26	283234	0	369	•	•	8226	17222	37589	•	167687	381854	•	23714362
Notes and Loans Payable 27	157688	0	92	•	•	120	3059	9569	•	44210	73841	•	14656306
All Other Liabilities 28	70808	0	55	•	•	1391	5335	11372	•	33000	152582	•	5671678
Net Worth 29	54737	0	221	•	•	6714	8828	16648	•	90477	155430	•	3386379

Selected Financial Ratios (Times to 1)

Current Ratio 30	1.5	•	4.1	•	•	5.0	2.7	1.9	•	2.2	1.4	•	1.3
Quick Ratio 31	0.8	•	3.2	•	•	3.7	1.8	0.9	•	1.0	0.9	•	0.8
Net Sales to Working Capital 32	8.0	•	6.7	•	•	3.5	4.0	7.6	•	4.5	7.7	•	9.5
Coverage Ratio 33	3.8	24.9	•	•	•	108.8	14.0	16.2	•	17.3	8.5	•	3.1
Total Asset Turnover 34	0.6	•	3.1	•	•	2.3	1.6	2.0	•	1.3	1.2	•	0.4
Inventory Turnover 35	5.9	•	21.4	•	•	6.9	7.5	9.5	•	5.0	7.1	•	4.5
Receivables Turnover 36	5.8	•	8.2	•	•	5.2	7.0	10.0	•	6.9	5.7	•	4.8
Total Liabilities to Net Worth 37	4.2	•	0.7	•	•	0.2	1.0	1.3	•	0.9	1.5	•	6.0
Current Assets to Working Capital 38	3.1	•	1.3	•	•	1.3	1.6	2.1	•	1.9	3.2	•	4.4
Current Liabilities to Working Capital 39	2.1	•	0.3	•	•	0.3	0.6	1.1	•	0.9	2.2	•	3.4
Working Capital to Net Sales 40	0.1	•	0.2	•	•	0.3	0.2	0.1	•	0.2	0.1	•	0.1
Inventory to Working Capital 41	1.1	•	0.2	•	•	0.3	0.4	0.7	•	0.6	1.0	•	1.5
Total Receipts to Cash Flow 42	5.1	10.0	9.7	•	•	4.0	7.8	10.0	•	6.7	9.8	•	3.5
Cost of Goods to Cash Flow 43	3.7	8.3	6.8	•	•	2.4	5.3	8.4	•	4.9	7.9	•	2.3
Cash Flow to Total Debt 44	0.1	•	0.8	•	•	3.2	0.4	0.4	•	0.4	0.2	•	0.1

Selected Financial Factors (in Percentages)

Debt Ratio 45	80.7	•	39.9	•	•	18.4	48.7	55.7	•	46.0	59.3	•	85.7
Return on Total Assets 46	4.8	•	4.5	•	•	22.2	13.3	12.4	•	13.3	7.9	•	3.6
Return on Equity Before Income Taxes 47	18.2	•	7.5	•	•	27.0	24.1	26.3	•	23.2	17.1	•	17.2
Return on Equity After Income Taxes 48	12.5	•	7.5	•	•	17.8	22.7	17.4	•	19.4	12.1	•	11.2
Profit Margin (Before Income Tax) 49	5.9	5.5	1.4	•	•	9.4	7.5	5.8	•	9.7	5.9	•	6.2
Profit Margin (After Income Tax) 50	4.0	3.7	1.4	•	•	6.2	7.1	3.8	•	8.1	4.2	•	4.1

Table I

Corporations with and without Net Income

PHARMACEUTICAL AND MEDICINE

MONEY AMOUNTS AND SIZE OF ASSETS IN THOUSANDS OF DOLLARS

Item Description for Accounting Period 7/11 Through 6/12		Total	Zero Assets	Under 500	500 to 1,000	1,000 to 5,000	5,000 to 10,000	10,000 to 25,000	25,000 to 50,000	50,000 to 100,000	100,000 to 250,000	250,000 to 500,000	500,000 to 2,500,000	2,500,000 and over
Number of Enterprises	1	1412	268	469	40	154	99	130	79	49	46	22	26	30
Revenues ($ in Thousands)														
Net Sales	2	331852894	2195412	66604	69671	873495	787429	2583781	2815265	2884479	4470928	5566758	16850558	292688515
Interest	3	4448948	14141	7	24	292	1672	2061	4467	6568	21583	12923	40204	4345007
Rents	4	179698	15	0	0	0	238	2	111	284	1675	132	6066	171175
Royalties	5	27134831	231820	1636	0	7743	369	27010	42403	71625	85775	120674	765860	25779917
Other Portfolio Income	6	9999074	24764	0	0	27746	15347	797	23160	42038	47026	22418	88604	9707173
Other Receipts	7	32733564	1121732	2606	18228	11274	2528	101407	44885	98249	130236	89054	1648302	29465063
Total Receipts	8	406349009	3587884	70853	87923	920550	807583	2715058	2930291	3103243	4757223	5811959	19399594	362156850
Average Total Receipts	9	287783	13388	151	2198	5978	8157	20885	37092	63331	103418	264180	746138	12071895
Operating Costs/Operating Income (%)														
Cost of Operations	10	54.4	15.3	74.8	10.6	69.3	51.7	62.9	59.0	53.4	48.4	44.4	49.5	55.1
Salaries and Wages	11	13.9	16.2	12.5	8.8	9.2	14.5	10.6	9.7	14.9	15.0	12.5	17.5	13.8
Taxes Paid	12	1.7	3.7	2.7	2.8	1.8	3.1	2.2	2.5	1.8	2.2	1.7	2.1	1.6
Interest Paid	13	5.0	3.6	10.5	0.0	0.6	3.6	2.1	2.4	0.8	2.1	1.7	2.0	5.5
Depreciation	14	3.0	2.7	0.5	1.2	0.9	5.5	3.8	4.3	4.6	6.0	4.0	3.2	2.9
Amortization and Depletion	15	2.0	3.0	0.5	•	1.5	2.0	0.8	3.3	1.5	1.5	2.5	1.6	2.0
Pensions and Other Deferred Comp.	16	1.3	0.6	•	0.2	0.1	0.2	0.2	0.5	0.6	1.0	0.4	0.6	1.4
Employee Benefits	17	2.5	1.7	1.0	•	1.1	1.7	1.6	1.8	1.7	2.4	1.8	2.6	2.5
Advertising	18	3.9	3.7	11.3	0.5	0.5	0.7	1.6	1.2	1.6	2.7	2.5	3.0	4.1
Other Expenses	19	24.6	59.9	110.1	11.4	12.1	23.6	19.9	23.8	24.3	24.4	20.6	25.0	24.5
Officers' Compensation	20	0.6	2.5	20.7	3.3	7.8	6.2	3.4	3.3	1.8	1.8	1.6	1.2	0.4
Operating Margin	21	•	•	•	61.1	•	•	•	•	•	•	6.2	•	•
Operating Margin Before Officers' Comp.	22	•	•	•	64.4	2.9	•	•	•	•	•	7.9	•	•

Selected Average Balance Sheet ($ in Thousands)

Net Receivables 23	69232	0	67	76	557	881	3024	5438	13338	21874	40847	134199	3022610
Inventories 24	32224	0	4	17	421	2063	2483	5279	8003	19858	29580	128022	1306793
Net Property, Plant and Equipment 25	50771	0	1	54	201	1820	3690	7895	13336	27799	49507	130437	2131955
Total Assets 26	740022	0	105	646	2122	7077	15242	33902	70343	155577	311341	1060457	33137461
Notes and Loans Payable 27	287577	0	345	0	1270	2885	5646	12406	18395	47944	52132	281008	13071402
All Other Liabilities 28	227796	0	218	1750	783	1854	5309	8468	23144	38527	104867	287296	10237642
Net Worth 29	224649	0	-458	-1104	69	2338	4287	13028	28803	69106	154342	492154	9828416

Selected Financial Ratios (Times to 1)

Current Ratio 30	0.9	•	0.4	7.6	2.1	1.6	1.4	1.8	1.9	2.4	2.2	1.8	0.9
Quick Ratio 31	0.4	•	0.3	6.6	1.6	0.8	0.9	1.1	1.3	1.5	1.4	1.0	0.4
Net Sales to Working Capital 32	•	•	•	3.4	5.3	5.4	7.3	3.9	3.0	2.3	2.8	3.2	•
Coverage Ratio 33	3.7	15.0	•	3201.4	1.8	•	•	•	1.8	0.6	7.5	4.8	3.6
Total Asset Turnover 34	0.3	•	1.4	2.7	2.7	1.1	1.3	1.1	0.8	0.6	0.8	0.6	0.3
Inventory Turnover 35	4.0	•	28.7	10.7	9.3	2.0	5.0	4.0	3.9	2.4	3.8	2.5	4.1
Receivables Turnover 36	3.7	•	2.2	38.2	11.3	5.4	6.8	7.4	5.2	4.2	7.7	4.8	3.5
Total Liabilities to Net Worth 37	2.3	•	•	•	29.7	2.0	2.6	1.6	1.4	1.3	1.0	1.2	2.4
Current Assets to Working Capital 38	•	•	•	1.2	1.9	2.7	3.5	2.2	2.1	1.7	1.9	2.3	•
Current Liabilities to Working Capital 39	•	•	•	0.2	0.9	1.7	2.5	1.2	1.1	0.7	0.9	1.3	•
Working Capital to Net Sales 40	•	•	•	0.3	0.2	0.2	0.1	0.3	0.3	0.4	0.4	0.3	•
Inventory to Working Capital 41	•	•	•	0.1	0.4	1.0	0.9	0.6	0.4	0.4	0.5	0.5	•
Total Receipts to Cash Flow 42	3.4	1.0	•	1.1	12.4	22.6	7.5	8.1	4.7	5.1	3.5	3.4	3.4
Cost of Goods to Cash Flow 43	1.8	0.1	•	0.1	8.6	11.7	4.7	4.8	2.5	2.5	1.6	1.7	1.8
Cash Flow to Total Debt 44	0.1	•	•	0.9	0.2	0.1	0.2	0.2	0.3	0.2	0.5	0.3	0.1

Selected Financial Factors (in Percentages)

Debt Ratio 45	69.6	•	535.8	270.9	96.7	67.0	71.9	61.6	59.1	55.6	50.4	53.6	70.3
Return on Total Assets 46	5.9	•	•	235.4	2.6	•	•	•	1.2	0.8	10.2	5.7	5.8
Return on Equity Before Income Taxes 47	14.0	•	42.9	•	35.5	•	•	•	1.3	•	17.7	9.8	14.2
Return on Equity After Income Taxes 48	9.1	•	42.9	•	0.8	•	•	•	•	•	11.2	6.3	9.4
Profit Margin (Before Income Tax) 49	13.4	50.5	•	87.3	0.4	•	•	•	0.6	•	10.8	7.5	14.3
Profit Margin (After Income Tax) 50	8.7	31.9	•	80.0	0.0	•	•	•	•	•	6.8	4.8	9.5

Table II

Corporations with Net Income

PHARMACEUTICAL AND MEDICINE

MONEY AMOUNTS AND SIZE OF ASSETS IN THOUSANDS OF DOLLARS

Item Description for Accounting Period 7/11 Through 6/12		Total	Zero Assets	Under 500	500 to 1,000	1,000 to 5,000	5,000 to 10,000	10,000 to 25,000	25,000 to 50,000	50,000 to 100,000	100,000 to 250,000	250,000 to 500,000	500,000 to 2,500,000	2,500,000 and over
Number of Enterprises	1	446	6	0	40	111	43	83	47	29	23	17	20	26
Revenues ($ in Thousands)														
Net Sales	2	318392575	1967437	0	69671	768399	461232	1923761	2218004	2264803	3046113	5049733	14962307	285661116
Interest	3	4341938	14077	0	24	11	1571	1207	2906	3639	11387	3467	23675	4279975
Rents	4	176236	15	0	0	0	238	2	111	284	1287	110	5857	168331
Royalties	5	26260106	229323	0	0	0	0	23988	10905	66841	46035	72487	601946	25208582
Other Portfolio Income	6	9788415	24695	0	0	25233	15300	471	22884	40331	12140	22418	71332	9553609
Other Receipts	7	31976673	1120742	0	18228	5451	968	57664	24384	54994	67475	60131	1147672	29418963
Total Receipts	8	390935943	3356289	0	87923	799094	479309	2007093	2279194	2430892	3184437	5208346	16812789	354290576
Average Total Receipts	9	876538	559382	•	2198	7199	11147	24182	48493	83824	138454	306373	840639	13626561
Operating Costs/Operating Income (%)														
Cost of Operations	10	54.7	12.7	•	10.6	67.9	49.6	63.8	59.2	53.1	44.9	42.3	49.7	55.4
Salaries and Wages	11	13.4	13.7	•	8.8	4.4	10.7	7.7	6.4	12.2	11.5	11.1	15.3	13.5
Taxes Paid	12	1.7	3.9	•	2.8	1.0	2.5	1.8	2.3	1.7	1.9	1.4	2.0	1.6
Interest Paid	13	4.9	3.8	•	0.0	0.1	1.8	0.5	1.0	0.6	1.3	1.4	1.1	5.3
Depreciation	14	2.9	2.6	•	1.2	0.4	2.6	2.6	3.0	4.2	3.9	3.4	2.7	2.9
Amortization and Depletion	15	1.9	3.0	•	•	0.0	0.6	0.3	0.7	0.4	1.3	2.3	1.5	2.0
Pensions and Other Deferred Comp.	16	1.3	0.5	•	0.2	0.1	0.3	0.3	0.5	0.7	0.8	0.3	0.6	1.4
Employee Benefits	17	2.4	1.5	•	•	0.3	0.6	1.3	1.5	1.3	1.6	1.6	2.5	2.5
Advertising	18	4.0	3.5	•	0.5	0.0	0.8	0.8	1.0	1.8	3.3	2.7	3.1	4.2
Other Expenses	19	24.2	61.7	•	11.4	1.9	15.4	11.8	14.3	15.8	17.7	19.2	21.2	24.6
Officers' Compensation	20	0.3	1.7	•	3.3	5.8	5.5	3.0	2.2	1.4	1.6	1.3	1.1	0.2
Operating Margin	21	•	•	•	61.1	18.0	9.6	6.2	8.1	6.8	10.2	12.9	•	•
Operating Margin Before Officers' Comp.	22	•	•	•	64.4	23.8	15.1	9.1	10.3	8.2	11.8	14.2	0.3	•

Selected Average Balance Sheet ($ in Thousands)														
Net Receivables	23	210667	0	•	76	646	903	3303	6465	16842	28558	49598	121823	3416965
Inventories	24	96639	0	•	17	521	2988	2881	6543	9387	26376	31856	154538	1456012
Net Property, Plant and Equipment	25	145752	0	•	54	105	689	3435	7860	16090	26609	43971	122120	2309189
Total Assets	26	2213333	0	•	646	1708	7552	14562	32959	71301	159729	315028	995392	36647842
Notes and Loans Payable	27	834771	0	•	0	272	1718	2676	7954	16176	29742	50280	182218	14075204
All Other Liabilities	28	687207	0	•	1750	327	1186	4082	8061	18762	36203	112204	294463	11401762
Net Worth	29	691356	0	•	-1104	1108	4648	7804	16943	36364	93783	152544	518711	11170876
Selected Financial Ratios (Times to 1)														
Current Ratio	30	0.9	•	•	7.6	5.8	4.0	2.4	2.0	2.0	2.7	2.1	1.6	0.9
Quick Ratio	31	0.4	•	•	6.6	4.5	1.9	1.5	1.1	1.2	1.6	1.3	0.8	0.4
Net Sales to Working Capital	32	•	•	•	3.4	4.4	2.6	4.2	4.7	3.5	3.1	3.2	4.3	•
Coverage Ratio	33	4.1	17.2	•	3201.4	173.1	8.5	22.5	12.3	24.0	12.5	12.4	11.9	3.8
Total Asset Turnover	34	0.3	•	•	2.7	4.1	1.4	1.6	1.4	1.1	0.8	0.9	0.8	0.3
Inventory Turnover	35	4.0	•	•	10.7	9.0	1.8	5.1	4.3	4.4	2.3	3.9	2.4	4.2
Receivables Turnover	36	3.7	•	•	38.2	11.0	4.7	7.0	9.1	5.8	4.7	7.9	5.1	3.5
Total Liabilities to Net Worth	37	2.2	•	•	•	0.5	0.6	0.9	0.9	1.0	0.7	1.1	0.9	2.3
Current Assets to Working Capital	38	•	•	•	1.2	1.2	1.3	1.7	2.0	2.0	1.6	1.9	2.6	•
Current Liabilities to Working Capital	39	•	•	•	0.2	0.2	0.3	0.7	1.0	1.0	0.6	0.9	1.6	•
Working Capital to Net Sales	40	•	•	•	0.3	0.2	0.4	0.2	0.2	0.3	0.3	0.3	0.2	•
Inventory to Working Capital	41	•	•	•	0.1	0.3	0.4	0.5	0.7	0.5	0.4	0.5	0.6	•
Total Receipts to Cash Flow	42	3.3	0.9	•	1.1	4.8	4.7	4.9	4.6	3.9	3.3	3.1	3.3	3.3
Cost of Goods to Cash Flow	43	1.8	0.1	•	0.1	3.3	2.3	3.1	2.7	2.0	1.5	1.3	1.6	1.8
Cash Flow to Total Debt	44	0.1	•	•	0.9	2.4	0.8	0.7	0.6	0.6	0.6	0.6	0.5	0.1
Selected Financial Factors (in Percentages)														
Debt Ratio	45	68.8	•	•	270.9	35.1	38.5	46.4	48.6	49.0	41.3	51.6	47.9	69.5
Return on Total Assets	46	6.4	•	•	235.4	89.8	21.7	17.5	16.9	16.1	13.5	16.7	9.9	6.0
Return on Equity Before Income Taxes	47	15.4	•	•	•	137.6	31.2	31.3	30.2	30.2	21.2	31.7	17.5	14.5
Return on Equity After Income Taxes	48	10.4	•	•	•	134.6	27.5	28.9	25.9	24.8	15.4	23.1	13.2	9.6
Profit Margin (Before Income Tax)	49	14.9	62.0	•	87.3	22.0	13.5	10.5	10.8	14.1	15.0	16.3	12.1	14.7
Profit Margin (After Income Tax)	50	10.0	41.1	•	80.0	21.5	11.9	9.7	9.3	11.6	10.9	11.9	9.1	9.8

Table I

Corporations with and without Net Income

PAINT, COATING, AND ADHESIVE

MONEY AMOUNTS AND SIZE OF ASSETS IN THOUSANDS OF DOLLARS

Item Description for Accounting Period 7/11 Through 6/12		Total	Zero Assets	Under 500	500 to 1,000	1,000 to 5,000	5,000 to 10,000	10,000 to 25,000	25,000 to 50,000	50,000 to 100,000	100,000 to 250,000	250,000 to 500,000	500,000 to 2,500,000	2,500,000 and over
Number of Enterprises	1	1500	11	297	415	535	87	84	27	12	14	7	5	7
Revenues ($ in Thousands)														
Net Sales	2	50306507	83824	250744	1134455	3439633	1228927	2059855	1601361	1148836	2154466	2763207	3526257	30914941
Interest	3	281266	15	0	202	84	158	556	535	1012	1201	13853	33789	229863
Rents	4	24755	0	0	0	0	1833	1732	501	104	357	1329	4336	14562
Royalties	5	438598	0	0	0	0	0	1	1431	1948	1059	3306	53516	377337
Other Portfolio Income	6	534644	0	0	604	17091	0	11127	9861	360	26393	7827	86719	374661
Other Receipts	7	374766	1065	0	7	5755	780	1859	15497	6095	12471	57424	23665	250149
Total Receipts	8	51960536	84904	250744	1135268	3462563	1231698	2075130	1629186	1158355	2195947	2846946	3728282	32161513
Average Total Receipts	9	34640	7719	844	2736	6472	14157	24704	60340	96530	156853	406707	745656	4594502
Operating Costs/Operating Income (%)														
Cost of Operations	10	65.0	62.5	44.4	57.6	65.4	68.6	65.3	72.7	65.4	64.9	66.4	68.9	64.3
Salaries and Wages	11	9.6	22.9	21.4	7.8	6.2	5.8	9.6	9.0	8.5	10.3	9.8	10.6	9.9
Taxes Paid	12	1.6	1.6	2.9	3.1	1.6	4.0	1.6	1.4	2.4	1.8	1.8	1.4	1.4
Interest Paid	13	2.7	0.5	0.3	0.9	0.3	0.5	1.3	0.6	0.7	1.5	2.4	1.5	3.6
Depreciation	14	2.5	0.9	•	0.5	0.9	6.4	1.7	2.1	2.5	3.8	2.5	2.6	2.6
Amortization and Depletion	15	1.0	0.5	•	0.0	0.2	0.1	0.4	0.1	0.2	1.5	1.8	1.2	1.2
Pensions and Other Deferred Comp.	16	1.2	0.2	•	0.8	0.6	0.4	0.6	0.7	1.1	0.6	0.7	2.4	1.3
Employee Benefits	17	1.7	1.3	0.5	2.1	0.6	1.6	1.3	1.0	1.8	1.7	2.0	2.4	1.8
Advertising	18	1.6	0.2	2.8	0.2	1.2	0.8	0.7	0.3	0.7	0.4	0.7	0.5	2.2
Other Expenses	19	11.8	15.1	34.4	11.1	9.7	12.0	10.2	9.7	11.8	10.8	15.4	10.6	11.9
Officers' Compensation	20	1.4	3.0	1.7	6.5	7.1	4.3	3.1	1.1	1.7	0.9	0.8	0.9	0.4
Operating Margin	21	•	•	•	9.4	6.2	•	4.2	1.3	3.1	1.9	•	•	•
Operating Margin Before Officers' Comp.	22	1.4	•	•	15.9	13.3	•	7.4	2.4	4.8	2.8	•	•	•

Selected Average Balance Sheet ($ in Thousands)														
Net Receivables	23	4615	0	92	397	522	1713	3548	8430	16727	26892	53041	75961	635362
Inventories	24	3104	0	5	226	497	1249	3403	7934	12406	20407	40960	48815	388736
Net Property, Plant and Equipment	25	4685	0	0	137	193	1259	2285	6128	18574	35061	49101	119777	677869
Total Assets	26	31581	0	123	813	2165	6642	14794	34876	70922	161777	339456	945840	4693673
Notes and Loans Payable	27	13989	0	574	332	357	2270	4895	7577	9033	60224	126171	183102	2417288
All Other Liabilities	28	13192	0	46	306	384	2076	3261	9282	20816	28238	93248	252112	2311127
Net Worth	29	4400	0	-497	176	1424	2296	6638	18018	41073	73315	120037	510626	-34742
Selected Financial Ratios (Times to 1)														
Current Ratio	30	0.9	•	2.3	1.6	3.9	1.7	2.0	2.0	1.4	1.7	1.5	2.0	0.7
Quick Ratio	31	0.5	•	2.1	1.0	2.5	1.0	1.2	1.1	0.7	1.0	0.8	1.3	0.4
Net Sales to Working Capital	32	•	•	13.3	11.4	5.2	8.1	5.1	5.6	8.9	6.2	10.5	4.9	•
Coverage Ratio	33	2.5	•	•	11.4	25.8	•	4.8	6.8	7.2	3.7	0.5	3.5	2.2
Total Asset Turnover	34	1.1	•	6.9	3.4	3.0	2.1	1.7	1.7	1.3	1.0	1.2	0.7	0.9
Inventory Turnover	35	7.0	•	77.8	7.0	8.5	7.8	4.7	5.4	5.0	4.9	6.4	9.9	7.3
Receivables Turnover	36	7.3	•	11.4	6.8	10.4	10.4	7.4	7.5	6.0	6.1	8.4	9.6	6.8
Total Liabilities to Net Worth	37	6.2	•	•	3.6	0.5	1.9	1.2	0.9	0.7	1.2	1.8	0.9	•
Current Assets to Working Capital	38	•	•	1.8	2.7	1.3	2.4	2.0	2.0	3.5	2.4	3.2	2.0	•
Current Liabilities to Working Capital	39	•	•	0.8	1.7	0.3	1.4	1.0	1.0	2.5	1.4	2.2	1.0	•
Working Capital to Net Sales	40	•	•	0.1	0.1	0.2	0.1	0.2	0.2	0.1	0.2	0.1	0.2	•
Inventory to Working Capital	41	•	•	0.1	0.9	0.4	0.8	0.8	0.8	1.1	0.8	1.2	0.4	•
Total Receipts to Cash Flow	42	8.1	17.1	5.8	6.3	7.3	50.0	7.6	9.1	7.0	8.9	9.9	9.0	7.8
Cost of Goods to Cash Flow	43	5.3	10.7	2.6	3.7	4.8	34.3	4.9	6.6	4.6	5.8	6.6	6.2	5.0
Cash Flow to Total Debt	44	0.2	•	0.2	0.7	1.2	0.1	0.4	0.4	0.5	0.2	0.2	0.2	0.1
Selected Financial Factors (in Percentages)														
Debt Ratio	45	86.1	•	503.2	78.4	34.2	65.4	55.1	48.3	42.1	54.7	64.6	46.0	100.7
Return on Total Assets	46	7.1	•	•	34.8	21.1	•	10.4	6.4	6.5	5.2	1.3	4.0	7.6
Return on Equity Before Income Taxes	47	30.7	•	14.1	146.9	30.9	•	18.3	10.6	9.7	8.4	•	5.3	•
Return on Equity After Income Taxes	48	20.0	•	14.1	146.9	30.0	•	16.2	8.2	8.0	6.9	•	2.8	•
Profit Margin (Before Income Tax)	49	4.0	•	•	9.4	6.8	•	4.9	3.2	4.2	4.0	•	3.8	4.4
Profit Margin (After Income Tax)	50	2.6	•	•	9.4	6.6	•	4.4	2.5	3.4	3.3	•	2.0	2.7

Table II

Corporations with Net Income

PAINT, COATING, AND ADHESIVE

Item Description for Accounting Period 7/11 Through 6/12		MONEY AMOUNTS AND SIZE OF ASSETS IN THOUSANDS OF DOLLARS												
		Total	Zero Assets	Under 500	500 to 1,000	1,000 to 5,000	5,000 to 10,000	10,000 to 25,000	25,000 to 50,000	50,000 to 100,000	100,000 to 250,000	250,000 to 500,000	500,000 to 2,500,000	2,500,000 and over
Number of Enterprises	1	988	•	0	299	535	33	59	18	•	•	4	•	•
Revenues ($ in Thousands)														
Net Sales	2	35332012	•	0	933385	3439633	420751	1330867	1059599	•	•	1733533	•	•
Interest	3	102807	•	0	0	84	98	196	147	•	•	2114	•	•
Rents	4	11790	•	0	0	0	1784	1732	168	•	•	1329	•	•
Royalties	5	427302	•	0	0	0	0	0	69	•	•	54	•	•
Other Portfolio Income	6	506714	•	0	124	17091	0	10879	7453	•	•	7802	•	•
Other Receipts	7	216276	•	0	0	5755	208	1489	5391	•	•	11458	•	•
Total Receipts	8	36596901	•	0	933509	3462563	422841	1345163	1072827	•	•	1756290	•	•
Average Total Receipts	9	37041	•	•	3122	6472	12813	22799	59602	•	•	439072	•	•
Operating Costs/Operating Income (%)														
Cost of Operations	10	63.9	•	•	54.2	65.4	68.5	61.9	70.6	•	•	67.6	•	•
Salaries and Wages	11	9.4	•	•	8.1	6.2	7.0	10.1	8.3	•	•	8.0	•	•
Taxes Paid	12	1.6	•	•	3.3	1.6	1.2	1.8	1.4	•	•	1.8	•	•
Interest Paid	13	2.4	•	•	0.8	0.3	0.3	0.8	0.5	•	•	1.7	•	•
Depreciation	14	2.6	•	•	0.2	0.9	1.5	1.7	2.1	•	•	2.7	•	•
Amortization and Depletion	15	0.7	•	•	0.0	0.2	0.1	0.6	0.1	•	•	1.1	•	•
Pensions and Other Deferred Comp.	16	1.2	•	•	1.0	0.6	1.2	0.6	0.8	•	•	0.2	•	•
Employee Benefits	17	1.7	•	•	2.4	0.6	0.7	1.2	0.9	•	•	1.6	•	•
Advertising	18	1.2	•	•	0.0	1.2	1.4	0.7	0.2	•	•	0.5	•	•
Other Expenses	19	10.9	•	•	11.5	9.7	8.8	8.9	9.0	•	•	11.3	•	•
Officers' Compensation	20	1.6	•	•	6.5	7.1	2.0	3.5	1.4	•	•	1.0	•	•
Operating Margin	21	3.0	•	•	11.8	6.2	7.2	8.1	4.6	•	•	2.5	•	•
Operating Margin Before Officers' Comp.	22	4.6	•	•	18.3	13.3	9.2	11.6	6.0	•	•	3.5	•	•

Selected Average Balance Sheet ($ in Thousands)

Net Receivables 23	4905	•	•	457	522	1235	3635	8854	•	•	60244	•	•
Inventories 24	3239	•	•	219	494	1864	3798	8444	•	•	39784	•	•
Net Property, Plant and Equipment 25	4720	•	•	153	193	429	1886	5277	•	•	60775	•	•
Total Assets 26	34254	•	•	809	2165	6873	14503	34421	•	•	348789	•	•
Notes and Loans Payable 27	14684	•	•	371	357	620	4076	6466	•	•	106478	•	•
All Other Liabilities 28	14973	•	•	329	384	2178	2816	8490	•	•	114013	•	•
Net Worth 29	4597	•	•	108	1424	4075	7611	19465	•	•	128298	•	•

Selected Financial Ratios (Times to 1)

Current Ratio 30	0.8	•	•	1.5	3.9	2.4	2.5	2.3	•	•	1.2	•	•
Quick Ratio 31	0.4	•	•	1.1	2.5	1.1	1.5	1.3	•	•	0.7	•	•
Net Sales to Working Capital 32	•	•	•	14.8	5.2	4.2	4.0	5.6	•	•	25.2	•	•
Coverage Ratio 33	4.2	•	•	15.0	25.8	30.8	12.0	13.2	•	•	3.2	•	•
Total Asset Turnover 34	1.0	•	•	3.9	3.0	1.9	1.6	1.7	•	•	1.2	•	•
Inventory Turnover 35	7.1	•	•	7.7	8.5	4.7	3.7	4.9	•	•	7.4	•	•
Receivables Turnover 36	7.3	•	•	6.7	10.5	9.9	5.6	6.8	•	•	•	•	•
Total Liabilities to Net Worth 37	6.5	•	•	6.5	0.5	0.7	0.9	0.8	•	•	1.7	•	•
Current Assets to Working Capital 38	•	•	•	3.1	1.3	1.7	1.7	1.8	•	•	7.5	•	•
Current Liabilities to Working Capital 39	•	•	•	2.1	0.3	0.7	0.7	0.8	•	•	6.5	•	•
Working Capital to Net Sales 40	•	•	•	0.1	0.2	0.2	0.2	0.2	•	•	0.0	•	•
Inventory to Working Capital 41	•	•	•	0.8	0.4	0.8	0.6	0.7	•	•	2.3	•	•
Total Receipts to Cash Flow 42	6.8	•	•	5.6	7.3	7.1	6.2	7.6	•	•	7.6	•	•
Cost of Goods to Cash Flow 43	4.4	•	•	3.0	4.8	4.9	3.8	5.3	•	•	5.1	•	•
Cash Flow to Total Debt 44	0.2	•	•	0.8	1.2	0.6	0.5	0.5	•	•	0.3	•	•

Selected Financial Factors (in Percentages)

Debt Ratio 45	86.6	•	•	86.6	34.2	40.7	47.5	43.5	•	•	63.2	•	•
Return on Total Assets 46	10.4	•	•	49.0	21.1	14.7	15.6	11.3	•	•	7.0	•	•
Return on Equity Before Income Taxes 47	59.0	•	•	342.6	30.9	24.0	27.2	18.4	•	•	13.2	•	•
Return on Equity After Income Taxes 48	43.5	•	•	342.6	30.0	19.8	24.6	15.0	•	•	8.7	•	•
Profit Margin (Before Income Tax) 49	7.6	•	•	11.9	6.8	7.7	9.2	6.1	•	•	3.9	•	•
Profit Margin (After Income Tax) 50	5.6	•	•	11.9	6.6	6.3	8.3	5.0	•	•	2.6	•	•

Table I

Corporations with and without Net Income

SOAP, CLEANING COMPOUND, AND TOILET PREPARATION

MONEY AMOUNTS AND SIZE OF ASSETS IN THOUSANDS OF DOLLARS

Item Description for Accounting Period 7/11 Through 6/12		Total	Zero Assets	Under 500	500 to 1,000	1,000 to 5,000	5,000 to 10,000	10,000 to 25,000	25,000 to 50,000	50,000 to 100,000	100,000 to 250,000	250,000 to 500,000	500,000 to 2,500,000	2,500,000 and over
Number of Enterprises	1	2166	273	1145	216	346	57	64	16	15	11	6	5	12
Revenues ($ in Thousands)														
Net Sales	2	88988078	92231	422590	670596	2781178	755023	2245956	1176910	1744224	2230457	3021768	5711529	68135617
Interest	3	434044	4	39	33	38	12	318	1642	2566	719	1676	5399	421598
Rents	4	23765	0	0	0	2702	1375	82	48	48	1152	0	2031	16328
Royalties	5	4223343	0	0	0	8357	4	1224	220	430	21	10600	99130	4103358
Other Portfolio Income	6	3394492	0	0	12431	12565	272	67	1123	137	6349	3853	172496	3185197
Other Receipts	7	2094052	0	141	2254	-42267	-27	17848	4353	59727	28261	1226	115911	1906624
Total Receipts	8	99157774	92235	422770	685314	2762573	756659	2265495	1184296	1807132	2266959	3039123	6106496	77768722
Average Total Receipts	9	45779	338	369	3173	7984	13275	35398	74018	120475	206087	506520	1221299	6480727
Operating Costs/Operating Income (%)														
Cost of Operations	10	44.9	72.5	71.3	53.7	64.5	61.9	64.8	68.5	71.7	63.7	58.7	54.7	39.9
Salaries and Wages	11	9.4	1.6	5.6	28.4	13.6	6.0	13.1	8.5	7.9	7.9	9.1	7.7	9.3
Taxes Paid	12	2.0	0.9	3.1	7.1	2.0	1.6	1.8	1.4	1.1	1.0	1.9	1.7	2.1
Interest Paid	13	3.5	2.7	•	0.3	0.3	1.3	0.7	0.8	1.2	1.4	1.4	1.0	4.3
Depreciation	14	2.8	0.7	0.4	1.6	0.3	2.0	2.1	1.7	3.0	2.4	2.7	2.5	3.0
Amortization and Depletion	15	1.6	3.5	0.1	0.1	0.0	0.2	0.2	0.3	1.3	1.5	1.3	0.3	2.0
Pensions and Other Deferred Comp.	16	1.9	•	0.1	0.8	0.7	0.1	0.3	0.2	0.0	0.3	0.9	0.9	2.3
Employee Benefits	17	1.8	0.0	•	1.2	1.2	0.8	1.4	0.9	1.2	0.7	1.4	1.4	2.0
Advertising	18	7.8	1.7	5.8	0.5	0.3	2.0	1.3	2.3	0.7	5.5	3.9	3.2	9.3
Other Expenses	19	19.6	38.6	22.6	14.3	11.1	14.4	9.9	8.4	9.7	12.3	16.2	20.9	21.0
Officers' Compensation	20	1.1	•	11.1	4.6	3.9	2.5	1.6	2.8	2.7	1.1	0.6	1.3	0.8
Operating Margin	21	3.5	•	•	•	2.1	7.2	2.7	4.1	•	2.3	1.9	4.4	4.1
Operating Margin Before Officers' Comp.	22	4.7	•	•	•	5.9	9.7	4.3	6.9	2.2	3.4	2.5	5.7	4.9

Selected Average Balance Sheet ($ in Thousands)														
Net Receivables	23	18036	0	36	200	613	2032	4152	12154	18615	31560	66271	124184	3045705
Inventories	24	3391	0	37	143	645	2521	4604	10542	11585	25080	63855	140946	408571
Net Property, Plant and Equipment	25	8269	0	11	76	266	1345	3396	8848	12595	34376	79258	167217	1289502
Total Assets	26	117919	0	146	756	2399	7089	16522	37418	68310	170115	369415	1082573	20138861
Notes and Loans Payable	27	33294	0	190	415	742	2343	3396	7602	22784	57058	122845	307364	5652885
All Other Liabilities	28	31162	0	7	349	408	2888	6358	11449	19009	59085	104542	365656	5260653
Net Worth	29	53463	0	-50	-8	1249	1857	6768	18367	26517	53972	142028	409553	9225323
Selected Financial Ratios (Times to 1)														
Current Ratio	30	0.9	•	18.8	1.4	2.9	1.4	1.9	2.2	1.7	1.3	1.3	1.4	0.9
Quick Ratio	31	0.7	•	12.4	0.8	1.3	0.7	1.0	1.3	1.0	0.7	0.7	0.9	0.7
Net Sales to Working Capital	32	•	•	3.0	16.8	6.6	9.4	7.0	5.5	7.7	10.7	13.8	9.6	•
Coverage Ratio	33	6.2	•	•	•	5.3	6.9	5.9	7.7	3.6	3.8	2.8	13.0	6.2
Total Asset Turnover	34	0.3	•	2.5	4.1	3.4	1.9	2.1	2.0	1.7	1.2	1.4	1.1	0.3
Inventory Turnover	35	5.4	•	7.1	11.7	8.0	3.3	4.9	4.8	7.2	5.1	4.6	4.4	5.5
Receivables Turnover	36	2.4	•	11.6	15.1	13.0	5.8	8.6	5.4	6.1	7.7	7.6	9.2	2.0
Total Liabilities to Net Worth	37	1.2	•	•	•	0.9	2.8	1.4	1.0	1.6	2.2	1.6	1.6	1.2
Current Assets to Working Capital	38	•	•	1.1	3.4	1.5	3.5	2.1	1.8	2.4	4.0	4.0	3.5	•
Current Liabilities to Working Capital	39	•	•	0.1	2.4	0.5	2.5	1.1	0.8	1.4	3.0	3.0	2.5	•
Working Capital to Net Sales	40	•	•	0.3	0.1	0.2	0.1	0.1	0.2	0.1	0.1	0.1	0.1	•
Inventory to Working Capital	41	•	•	0.3	0.7	0.6	1.6	0.9	0.7	0.8	1.6	1.6	0.8	•
Total Receipts to Cash Flow	42	3.4	6.3	118.1	66.4	11.5	5.3	8.3	8.8	9.1	6.8	5.9	3.4	3.0
Cost of Goods to Cash Flow	43	1.5	4.5	84.2	35.7	7.4	3.3	5.4	6.0	6.5	4.4	3.5	1.9	1.2
Cash Flow to Total Debt	44	0.2	•	0.0	0.1	0.6	0.5	0.4	0.4	0.3	0.3	0.4	0.5	0.2
Selected Financial Factors (in Percentages)														
Debt Ratio	45	54.7	•	134.3	101.1	47.9	73.8	59.0	50.9	61.2	68.3	61.6	62.2	54.2
Return on Total Assets	46	7.5	•	•	•	5.7	16.2	9.2	11.8	7.4	6.4	5.3	14.2	7.4
Return on Equity Before Income Taxes	47	13.9	•	146.7	3976.2	8.9	52.9	18.7	20.9	13.8	15.0	8.8	34.8	13.6
Return on Equity After Income Taxes	48	9.1	•	146.7	4051.8	7.0	50.8	18.7	19.8	9.9	12.1	4.6	22.1	8.9
Profit Margin (Before Income Tax)	49	18.1	•	•	•	1.4	7.4	3.6	5.2	3.1	4.0	2.5	12.5	22.1
Profit Margin (After Income Tax)	50	11.8	•	•	•	1.1	7.1	3.6	5.0	2.3	3.2	1.3	7.9	14.5

Table II

Corporations with Net Income

SOAP, CLEANING COMPOUND, AND TOILET PREPARATION

MONEY AMOUNTS AND SIZE OF ASSETS IN THOUSANDS OF DOLLARS

Item Description for Accounting Period 7/11 Through 6/12		Total	Zero Assets	Under 500	500 to 1,000	1,000 to 5,000	5,000 to 10,000	10,000 to 25,000	25,000 to 50,000	50,000 to 100,000	100,000 to 250,000	250,000 to 500,000	500,000 to 2,500,000	2,500,000 and over
Number of Enterprises	1	625	•	98	115	•	37	49	9	10	11	0	•	•
Revenues ($ in Thousands)														
Net Sales	2	77957400	•	101432	201376	•	408392	1763774	651201	1329244	2511067	0	•	•
Interest	3	432493	•	39	33	•	0	35	1438	2565	2234	0	•	•
Rents	4	21537	•	0	0	•	1375	0	48	48	1152	0	•	•
Royalties	5	4059138	•	0	0	•	0	0	0	108	1809	0	•	•
Other Portfolio Income	6	3374962	•	0	0	•	223	61	809	1	7786	0	•	•
Other Receipts	7	2114426	•	-1	24	•	-862	16433	2934	57474	27468	0	•	•
Total Receipts	8	87959956	•	101470	201433	•	409128	1780303	656430	1389440	2551516	0	•	•
Average Total Receipts	9	140736	•	1035	1752	•	11058	36333	72937	138944	231956	•	•	•
Operating Costs/Operating Income (%)														
Cost of Operations	10	42.1	•	76.7	61.8	•	51.1	64.8	62.9	74.8	55.1	•	•	•
Salaries and Wages	11	9.5	•	5.4	7.4	•	6.9	12.7	8.3	6.0	10.3	•	•	•
Taxes Paid	12	2.0	•	1.0	2.9	•	1.8	1.7	1.3	0.8	1.6	•	•	•
Interest Paid	13	3.5	•	•	0.5	•	0.4	0.4	0.7	1.1	1.1	•	•	•
Depreciation	14	2.7	•	0.3	0.9	•	1.6	1.6	2.2	2.8	2.5	•	•	•
Amortization and Depletion	15	1.6	•	•	0.3	•	0.0	0.1	0.1	0.4	1.4	•	•	•
Pensions and Other Deferred Comp.	16	2.2	•	0.4	1.0	•	0.3	0.3	0.4	0.0	0.8	•	•	•
Employee Benefits	17	1.9	•	•	3.9	•	0.3	1.4	0.8	1.2	0.6	•	•	•
Advertising	18	8.3	•	0.0	0.5	•	3.3	0.9	2.6	0.3	4.8	•	•	•
Other Expenses	19	20.1	•	12.1	9.5	•	14.3	8.8	8.7	9.2	13.6	•	•	•
Officers' Compensation	20	1.1	•	3.9	8.1	•	3.4	1.8	2.9	2.7	1.0	•	•	•
Operating Margin	21	5.0	•	0.1	3.3	•	16.6	5.4	9.1	0.6	7.2	•	•	•
Operating Margin Before Officers' Comp.	22	6.2	•	4.0	11.4	•	20.1	7.2	12.0	3.3	8.2	•	•	•

Selected Average Balance Sheet ($ in Thousands)													
Net Receivables 23	60515	•	44	231	•	1851	4402	10036	20442	34283	•	•	•
Inventories 24	9775	•	102	222	•	2484	5293	12551	13833	28395	•	•	•
Net Property, Plant and Equipment 25	26437	•	13	68	•	1570	3533	10384	15726	47815	•	•	•
Total Assets 26	386965	•	478	867	•	6358	16789	35951	71065	202509	•	•	•
Notes and Loans Payable 27	105160	•	0	172	•	1349	2417	7698	17091	62716	•	•	•
All Other Liabilities 28	100446	•	18	94	•	839	4209	7847	23082	68281	•	•	•
Net Worth 29	181359	•	461	601	•	4170	10162	20407	30892	71512	•	•	•

Selected Financial Ratios (Times to 1)													
Current Ratio 30	0.9	•	26.2	5.0	•	3.2	1.9	2.7	1.9	1.5	•	•	•
Quick Ratio 31	0.7	•	22.5	3.1	•	1.9	1.1	1.5	1.1	0.8	•	•	•
Net Sales to Working Capital 32	•	•	2.3	3.1	•	3.6	6.7	5.1	7.0	9.0	•	•	•
Coverage Ratio 33	7.1	•	•	7.7	•	47.1	17.1	15.4	5.6	8.9	•	•	•
Total Asset Turnover 34	0.3	•	2.2	2.0	•	1.7	2.1	2.0	1.9	1.1	•	•	•
Inventory Turnover 35	5.4	•	7.8	4.9	•	2.3	4.4	3.6	7.2	4.4	•	•	•
Receivables Turnover 36	2.2	•	6.7	5.6	•	4.5	7.9	4.4	5.9	•	•	•	•
Total Liabilities to Net Worth 37	1.1	•	0.0	0.4	•	0.5	0.7	0.8	1.3	1.8	•	•	•
Current Assets to Working Capital 38	•	•	1.0	1.3	•	1.4	2.1	1.6	2.1	3.2	•	•	•
Current Liabilities to Working Capital 39	•	•	0.0	0.3	•	0.4	1.1	0.6	1.1	2.2	•	•	•
Working Capital to Net Sales 40	•	•	0.4	0.3	•	0.3	0.1	0.2	0.1	0.1	•	•	•
Inventory to Working Capital 41	•	•	0.1	0.3	•	0.6	0.9	0.7	0.7	1.1	•	•	•
Total Receipts to Cash Flow 42	3.1	•	14.0	10.2	•	3.6	7.3	5.9	8.0	4.9	•	•	•
Cost of Goods to Cash Flow 43	1.3	•	10.8	6.3	•	1.8	4.7	3.7	6.0	2.7	•	•	•
Cash Flow to Total Debt 44	0.2	•	4.2	0.6	•	1.4	0.7	0.8	0.4	0.4	•	•	•

Selected Financial Factors (in Percentages)													
Debt Ratio 45	53.1	•	3.7	30.6	•	34.4	39.5	43.2	56.5	64.7	•	•	•
Return on Total Assets 46	8.0	•	0.3	7.8	•	29.8	14.5	21.3	11.7	11.2	•	•	•
Return on Equity Before Income Taxes 47	14.7	•	0.4	9.8	•	44.5	22.5	35.2	22.1	28.2	•	•	•
Return on Equity After Income Taxes 48	9.8	•	0.4	7.9	•	43.1	22.5	33.4	17.1	21.5	•	•	•
Profit Margin (Before Income Tax) 49	21.4	•	0.2	3.4	•	16.8	6.3	9.9	5.1	8.8	•	•	•
Profit Margin (After Income Tax) 50	14.3	•	0.2	2.7	•	16.3	6.3	9.4	4.0	6.7	•	•	•

Table I

Corporations with and without Net Income

CHEMICAL PRODUCT AND PREPARATION

MONEY AMOUNTS AND SIZE OF ASSETS IN THOUSANDS OF DOLLARS

Item Description for Accounting Period 7/11 Through 6/12		Total	Zero Assets	Under 500	500 to 1,000	1,000 to 5,000	5,000 to 10,000	10,000 to 25,000	25,000 to 50,000	50,000 to 100,000	100,000 to 250,000	250,000 to 500,000	500,000 to 2,500,000	2,500,000 and over
Number of Enterprises	1	1728	24	772	159	437	56	109	63	43	25	15	16	8
Revenues ($ in Thousands)														
Net Sales	2	76037097	804011	885146	94574	1522133	787052	3072878	3400389	4747576	5699658	4370297	12794283	37859101
Interest	3	307832	772	0	0	838	240	1642	1879	4821	4653	3930	37506	251551
Rents	4	33499	8	0	1473	222	2670	1213	5138	197	392	3386	11649	7150
Royalties	5	616965	0	0	0	0	0	1085	713	7000	18650	17033	37152	535333
Other Portfolio Income	6	873453	169912	1	2685	1325	1519	22052	20572	13958	12217	61244	247894	320076
Other Receipts	7	1495891	53851	7564	186	6203	13401	22352	83437	48032	64062	51697	238866	906236
Total Receipts	8	79364737	1028554	892711	98918	1530721	804882	3121222	3512128	4821584	5799632	4507587	13367350	39879447
Average Total Receipts	9	45929	42856	1156	622	3503	14373	28635	55748	112130	231985	300506	835459	4984931
Operating Costs/Operating Income (%)														
Cost of Operations	10	69.2	66.4	52.8	37.6	56.1	74.4	67.7	74.0	74.4	74.5	68.0	65.9	69.6
Salaries and Wages	11	6.1	11.2	7.5	10.8	7.9	6.0	8.9	6.0	5.4	6.1	6.4	7.6	5.3
Taxes Paid	12	1.2	1.6	3.0	2.5	1.7	1.7	1.9	1.3	1.1	1.1	1.0	1.7	0.9
Interest Paid	13	2.1	2.3	0.2	1.3	0.4	0.6	0.8	1.4	0.7	0.8	2.2	2.2	2.7
Depreciation	14	3.1	4.0	0.2	0.8	1.8	3.2	3.3	2.6	2.1	3.7	4.8	4.0	2.8
Amortization and Depletion	15	0.8	0.1	0.3	•	0.1	0.0	0.2	0.4	0.3	0.6	1.2	1.0	1.0
Pensions and Other Deferred Comp.	16	0.7	0.1	0.0	4.2	3.4	0.3	0.4	0.2	0.5	0.6	0.3	1.3	0.5
Employee Benefits	17	1.1	4.2	1.7	2.6	1.4	1.1	1.1	0.9	0.7	1.1	1.3	2.0	0.6
Advertising	18	0.4	0.3	0.3	1.2	0.3	0.1	0.9	0.5	0.4	0.6	0.3	1.5	0.1
Other Expenses	19	9.9	28.5	13.4	26.6	10.3	10.3	11.2	12.0	7.0	7.3	10.0	10.4	9.6
Officers' Compensation	20	1.1	2.4	11.8	12.5	5.6	3.2	2.3	1.9	2.1	0.6	1.2	0.6	0.5
Operating Margin	21	4.2	•	8.9	•	11.0	•	1.3	•	5.1	3.1	3.3	1.7	6.3
Operating Margin Before Officers' Comp.	22	5.4	•	20.6	12.4	16.6	2.2	3.6	0.7	7.3	3.7	4.5	2.3	6.8

Selected Average Balance Sheet ($ in Thousands)

Net Receivables 23	7126	0	36	105	455	3072	3719	7142	14926	26007	54806	132941	850268
Inventories 24	5611	0	70	236	265	1985	3655	7491	16283	29532	42498	94939	613949
Net Property, Plant and Equipment 25	9395	0	74	108	411	1587	3885	8584	12502	43279	55862	169373	1220034
Total Assets 26	54158	0	280	763	2517	8448	17013	35038	72811	165467	341094	1148710	7106297
Notes and Loans Payable 27	13744	0	29	126	327	7870	4375	9392	15024	33410	105294	366400	1641561
All Other Liabilities 28	16605	0	17	39	335	2323	3427	9807	19324	46036	84336	328553	2362887
Net Worth 29	23809	0	235	598	1855	-1745	9211	15839	38463	86022	151464	453757	3101849

Selected Financial Ratios (Times to 1)

Current Ratio 30	1.3	•	3.4	3.0	3.3	2.3	2.7	1.8	2.3	1.8	1.5	1.7	1.1
Quick Ratio 31	0.8	•	1.6	1.6	2.6	1.5	1.6	1.0	1.2	0.9	0.9	0.9	0.6
Net Sales to Working Capital 32	9.3	•	10.9	2.5	3.6	3.7	4.2	6.1	4.2	6.7	5.8	5.8	32.1
Coverage Ratio 33	5.4	3.8	50.6	4.4	28.2	3.1	4.7	2.5	10.6	7.4	4.0	3.9	5.7
Total Asset Turnover 34	0.8	•	4.1	0.8	1.4	1.7	1.7	1.5	1.5	1.4	0.9	0.7	0.7
Inventory Turnover 35	5.4	•	8.7	0.9	7.4	5.3	5.2	5.3	5.0	5.7	4.7	5.6	5.4
Receivables Turnover 36	6.9	•	37.0	4.0	7.4	5.2	7.3	7.5	7.3	7.8	6.2	6.4	6.8
Total Liabilities to Net Worth 37	1.3	•	0.2	0.3	0.4	•	0.8	1.2	0.9	0.9	1.3	1.5	1.3
Current Assets to Working Capital 38	4.0	•	1.4	1.5	1.4	1.8	1.6	2.2	1.8	2.3	3.0	2.5	14.4
Current Liabilities to Working Capital 39	3.0	•	0.4	0.5	0.4	0.8	0.6	1.2	0.8	1.3	2.0	1.5	13.4
Working Capital to Net Sales 40	0.1	•	0.1	0.4	0.3	0.3	0.2	0.2	0.2	0.1	0.2	0.2	0.0
Inventory to Working Capital 41	1.2	•	0.7	0.6	0.3	0.4	0.5	0.7	0.7	0.8	1.0	0.8	4.2
Total Receipts to Cash Flow 42	6.3	6.7	4.9	3.5	5.3	9.4	8.7	8.4	8.4	9.2	7.1	7.6	5.3
Cost of Goods to Cash Flow 43	4.4	4.4	2.6	1.3	3.0	7.0	5.9	6.2	6.2	6.8	4.8	5.0	3.7
Cash Flow to Total Debt 44	0.2	•	5.1	1.0	1.0	0.1	0.4	0.3	0.4	0.3	0.2	0.2	0.2

Selected Financial Factors (in Percentages)

Debt Ratio 45	56.0	•	16.3	21.6	26.3	120.7	45.9	54.8	47.2	48.0	55.6	60.5	56.4
Return on Total Assets 46	9.3	•	40.5	4.5	16.6	3.0	6.1	5.3	11.8	7.9	7.6	6.1	10.3
Return on Equity Before Income Taxes 47	17.2	•	47.5	4.4	21.8	•	8.9	7.0	20.2	13.1	12.7	11.6	19.5
Return on Equity After Income Taxes 48	11.8	•	47.5	4.1	21.1	•	7.2	5.1	15.1	8.7	11.2	7.7	12.9
Profit Margin (Before Income Tax) 49	9.3	6.6	9.7	4.5	11.6	1.2	2.9	2.1	7.0	4.9	6.6	6.6	12.8
Profit Margin (After Income Tax) 50	6.4	4.6	9.7	4.1	11.3	0.4	2.4	1.5	5.2	3.3	5.8	4.4	8.4

Table II

Corporations with Net Income

CHEMICAL PRODUCT AND PREPARATION

MONEY AMOUNTS AND SIZE OF ASSETS IN THOUSANDS OF DOLLARS

Item Description for Accounting Period 7/11 Through 6/12		Total	Zero Assets	Under 500	500 to 1,000	1,000 to 5,000	5,000 to 10,000	10,000 to 25,000	25,000 to 50,000	50,000 to 100,000	100,000 to 250,000	250,000 to 500,000	500,000 to 2,500,000	2,500,000 and over
Number of Enterprises	1	1382	14	713	159	266	27	85	30	38	•	10	12	•
Revenues ($ in Thousands)														
Net Sales	2	65814566	393713	784640	94574	1312004	674455	2826031	2060114	4527705	•	3232916	9578790	•
Interest	3	284737	100	0	0	402	64	1335	1640	4333	•	3046	23829	•
Rents	4	32145	0	0	1473	153	2670	0	5077	197	•	3386	11649	•
Royalties	5	600264	0	0	0	0	0	1085	181	6693	•	5866	33507	•
Other Portfolio Income	6	810838	152043	1	2685	167	577	10472	18851	13957	•	60560	247681	•
Other Receipts	7	1388768	56302	7556	186	2204	2	21570	74016	46810	•	47705	201877	•
Total Receipts	8	68931318	602158	792197	98918	1314930	677768	2860493	2159879	4599695	•	3353479	10097333	•
Average Total Receipts	9	49878	43011	1111	622	4943	25103	33653	71996	121045	•	335348	841444	•
Operating Costs/Operating Income (%)														
Cost of Operations	10	68.9	65.9	49.9	37.6	52.9	77.2	66.9	79.4	73.9	•	66.8	63.2	•
Salaries and Wages	11	5.8	10.6	7.6	10.8	8.3	4.1	8.0	3.5	5.3	•	5.8	7.7	•
Taxes Paid	12	1.2	1.8	3.1	2.5	1.8	1.3	1.8	1.2	1.1	•	0.9	1.7	•
Interest Paid	13	2.0	1.7	0.2	1.3	0.2	0.3	0.4	0.6	0.7	•	1.2	2.6	•
Depreciation	14	2.7	0.8	•	0.8	1.4	0.6	2.8	2.2	2.1	•	4.7	2.7	•
Amortization and Depletion	15	0.8	0.0	0.3	•	0.1	0.0	0.1	0.2	0.3	•	1.2	1.2	•
Pensions and Other Deferred Comp.	16	0.6	0.2	•	4.2	3.9	0.3	0.5	0.3	0.5	•	0.3	1.3	•
Employee Benefits	17	0.9	0.5	1.8	2.6	1.5	1.0	1.1	0.5	0.7	•	1.5	1.9	•
Advertising	18	0.5	0.4	0.4	1.2	0.3	0.1	0.9	0.3	0.4	•	0.2	1.9	•
Other Expenses	19	9.4	40.2	14.0	26.6	8.9	7.1	9.7	9.0	6.7	•	10.6	11.1	•
Officers' Compensation	20	1.1	4.0	11.9	12.5	5.9	2.9	2.0	1.8	2.1	•	1.1	0.7	•
Operating Margin	21	6.1	•	10.8	•	14.8	5.1	5.8	1.1	6.1	•	5.7	4.0	•
Operating Margin Before Officers' Comp.	22	7.2	•	22.8	12.4	20.7	8.0	7.8	2.9	8.2	•	6.8	4.7	•

Selected Average Balance Sheet ($ in Thousands)													
Net Receivables 23	7858	0	33	105	630	2508	4089	8470	15517	•	63207	135412	•
Inventories 24	6124	0	64	165	253	3212	3797	8656	16688	•	64488	101710	•
Net Property, Plant and Equipment 25	9946	0	74	108	403	1179	3918	9283	13262	•	60474	149057	•
Total Assets 26	58429	0	265	763	2366	8817	16636	34659	74486	•	364569	1125065	•
Notes and Loans Payable 27	12743	0	30	126	202	1405	2804	3777	15390	•	90204	337411	•
All Other Liabilities 28	18318	0	7	39	264	2237	3383	9090	20565	•	93070	336431	•
Net Worth 29	27368	0	228	598	1900	5174	10449	21792	38531	•	181295	451223	•
Selected Financial Ratios (Times to 1)													
Current Ratio 30	1.4	•	3.5	3.0	4.9	2.6	2.7	2.2	2.4	•	1.4	2.0	•
Quick Ratio 31	0.8	•	1.9	1.6	4.1	1.7	1.6	1.3	1.2	•	0.8	1.1	•
Net Sales to Working Capital 32	8.7	•	11.9	2.5	3.5	5.5	4.8	6.4	4.1	•	6.6	4.8	•
Coverage Ratio 33	6.7	17.0	56.8	4.4	61.3	20.2	19.1	11.5	12.1	•	9.1	4.8	•
Total Asset Turnover 34	0.8	•	4.2	0.8	2.1	2.8	2.0	2.0	1.6	•	0.9	0.7	•
Inventory Turnover 35	5.4	•	8.5	1.4	10.3	6.0	5.9	6.3	5.3	•	3.3	5.0	•
Receivables Turnover 36	6.8	•	35.9	4.4	7.5	9.0	8.0	8.0	8.1	•	•	•	•
Total Liabilities to Net Worth 37	1.1	•	0.2	0.3	0.2	0.7	0.6	0.6	0.9	•	1.0	1.5	•
Current Assets to Working Capital 38	3.7	•	1.4	1.5	1.3	1.6	1.6	1.9	1.7	•	3.4	2.0	•
Current Liabilities to Working Capital 39	2.7	•	0.4	0.5	0.3	0.6	0.6	0.9	0.7	•	2.4	1.0	•
Working Capital to Net Sales 40	0.1	•	0.1	0.4	0.3	0.2	0.2	0.2	0.2	•	0.2	0.2	•
Inventory to Working Capital 41	1.1	•	0.6	0.6	0.2	0.5	0.5	0.5	0.7	•	1.3	0.6	•
Total Receipts to Cash Flow 42	5.7	3.0	4.4	3.5	4.6	8.1	6.9	7.7	7.9	•	5.7	6.0	•
Cost of Goods to Cash Flow 43	3.9	2.0	2.2	1.3	2.4	6.3	4.6	6.1	5.8	•	3.8	3.8	•
Cash Flow to Total Debt 44	0.3	•	6.8	1.0	2.3	0.8	0.8	0.7	0.4	•	0.3	0.2	•
Selected Financial Factors (in Percentages)													
Debt Ratio 45	53.2	•	14.0	21.6	19.7	41.3	37.2	37.1	48.3	•	50.3	59.9	•
Return on Total Assets 46	11.1	•	49.8	4.5	31.8	16.8	14.8	12.9	13.9	•	9.7	8.9	•
Return on Equity Before Income Taxes 47	20.1	•	56.9	4.4	39.0	27.2	22.3	18.7	24.7	•	17.3	17.6	•
Return on Equity After Income Taxes 48	14.2	•	56.9	4.1	38.0	22.4	20.4	15.8	19.0	•	15.4	12.4	•
Profit Margin (Before Income Tax) 49	11.6	26.8	11.8	4.5	15.0	5.6	7.0	5.9	8.0	•	9.7	9.9	•
Profit Margin (After Income Tax) 50	8.2	22.5	11.8	4.1	14.6	4.6	6.4	5.0	6.1	•	8.6	7.0	•

Table I

Corporations with and without Net Income

PLASTICS PRODUCT

MONEY AMOUNTS AND SIZE OF ASSETS IN THOUSANDS OF DOLLARS

Item Description for Accounting Period 7/11 Through 6/12		Total	Zero Assets	Under 500	500 to 1,000	1,000 to 5,000	5,000 to 10,000	10,000 to 25,000	25,000 to 50,000	50,000 to 100,000	100,000 to 250,000	250,000 to 500,000	500,000 to 2,500,000	2,500,000 and over
Number of Enterprises	1	9151	1228	2750	1376	2296	563	472	190	118	102	24	28	3
Revenues ($ in Thousands)														
Net Sales	2	123848476	1536653	1260000	2795981	11978229	7867928	13086003	10887168	12665754	21788033	9453810	19782057	10746861
Interest	3	232155	163	370	16	2255	1303	1377	3325	9157	28906	27663	84939	72680
Rents	4	25796	53	3928	0	763	58	2616	2107	1475	4711	8521	1564	0
Royalties	5	234207	876	0	0	1676	0	308	838	8717	24970	43029	69758	84035
Other Portfolio Income	6	768636	16150	358	4368	3202	3689	18323	7713	33630	54739	19674	471828	134967
Other Receipts	7	766141	-14594	5313	5887	42845	20958	72840	68493	53583	244200	35417	260129	-28936
Total Receipts	8	125875411	1539301	1269969	2806252	12028970	7893936	13181467	10969644	12772316	22145559	9588114	20670275	11009607
Average Total Receipts	9	13755	1254	462	2039	5239	14021	27927	57735	108240	217113	399505	738224	3669869
Operating Costs/Operating Income (%)														
Cost of Operations	10	73.1	70.1	54.7	57.1	68.2	72.8	73.9	71.8	74.2	73.9	75.6	76.8	73.2
Salaries and Wages	11	5.4	8.3	10.1	9.4	6.3	5.2	6.2	6.4	5.6	5.5	5.1	3.7	3.4
Taxes Paid	12	1.5	1.8	3.3	2.9	2.5	1.6	1.6	1.7	1.3	1.4	1.3	1.1	0.9
Interest Paid	13	2.0	2.2	0.2	0.3	0.6	0.7	0.9	0.9	1.0	1.6	2.6	3.6	6.1
Depreciation	14	4.1	2.5	4.9	1.0	2.7	3.4	3.9	4.1	4.5	4.8	3.7	4.6	5.0
Amortization and Depletion	15	0.5	1.4	0.0	0.1	0.2	0.0	0.3	0.3	0.4	0.5	1.1	0.8	0.9
Pensions and Other Deferred Comp.	16	0.4	0.4	0.2	0.3	0.4	0.5	0.3	0.3	0.5	0.5	0.5	0.3	0.7
Employee Benefits	17	1.5	1.2	0.4	2.1	1.4	1.1	1.4	1.5	1.6	1.4	1.8	1.1	2.7
Advertising	18	0.4	0.1	0.7	0.4	0.4	0.4	0.3	0.5	0.6	0.3	0.2	0.3	0.1
Other Expenses	19	8.1	13.2	16.1	13.8	10.2	8.4	8.3	7.6	7.0	7.6	6.8	6.9	8.7
Officers' Compensation	20	1.7	2.3	7.2	8.0	5.5	2.4	1.8	1.4	0.9	0.7	0.9	0.8	0.4
Operating Margin	21	1.2	•	2.2	4.6	1.7	3.5	1.0	3.4	2.4	1.7	0.4	•	•
Operating Margin Before Officers' Comp.	22	3.0	•	9.5	12.6	7.1	5.9	2.9	4.8	3.3	2.5	1.4	0.7	•

Selected Average Balance Sheet ($ in Thousands)													
Net Receivables 23	1799	0	39	230	563	1674	3611	7336	15746	27478	49254	114970	546984
Inventories 24	1478	0	22	128	513	1461	3173	7157	13140	24626	41801	79085	383653
Net Property, Plant and Equipment 25	2550	0	20	119	458	1800	4903	10367	20274	49181	80778	173728	851717
Total Assets 26	10926	0	185	721	2177	7043	15223	34099	71398	158438	366609	852814	6198617
Notes and Loans Payable 27	4819	0	65	237	779	2353	5042	9795	22416	51801	160593	383779	4570413
All Other Liabilities 28	2686	0	100	177	488	1440	4931	8312	19356	39380	98682	177510	1527780
Net Worth 29	3421	0	20	307	910	3250	5251	15992	29626	67257	107334	291525	100424
Selected Financial Ratios (Times to 1)													
Current Ratio 30	1.6	•	1.2	1.5	2.3	2.1	1.5	1.9	1.7	1.9	1.3	1.4	1.2
Quick Ratio 31	0.9	•	0.8	1.1	1.4	1.3	0.8	1.0	1.0	1.0	0.7	0.9	0.5
Net Sales to Working Capital 32	8.0	•	24.9	12.1	6.3	6.7	9.7	6.1	6.9	6.3	12.8	8.8	13.6
Coverage Ratio 33	2.5	•	13.1	18.2	4.2	6.2	2.9	5.4	4.3	3.1	1.8	2.4	1.1
Total Asset Turnover 34	1.2	•	2.5	2.8	2.4	2.0	1.8	1.7	1.5	1.3	1.1	0.8	0.6
Inventory Turnover 35	6.7	•	11.4	9.1	6.9	7.0	6.5	5.7	6.1	6.4	7.1	6.9	6.8
Receivables Turnover 36	7.4	•	11.2	10.9	9.0	7.4	8.0	8.2	7.2	8.3	7.7	5.4	6.3
Total Liabilities to Net Worth 37	2.2	•	8.2	1.4	1.4	1.2	1.9	1.1	1.4	1.4	2.4	1.9	60.7
Current Assets to Working Capital 38	2.6	•	6.9	3.2	1.8	1.9	3.0	2.1	2.4	2.1	4.3	3.3	5.9
Current Liabilities to Working Capital 39	1.6	•	5.9	2.2	0.8	0.9	2.0	1.1	1.4	1.1	3.3	2.3	4.9
Working Capital to Net Sales 40	0.1	•	0.0	0.1	0.2	0.1	0.1	0.2	0.1	0.2	0.1	0.1	0.1
Inventory to Working Capital 41	0.9	•	1.2	0.8	0.6	0.7	1.1	0.8	0.9	0.8	1.4	0.9	1.5
Total Receipts to Cash Flow 42	11.5	18.7	7.3	7.2	11.4	10.3	13.1	10.4	11.7	10.7	14.2	11.6	14.4
Cost of Goods to Cash Flow 43	8.4	13.1	4.0	4.1	7.8	7.5	9.7	7.4	8.7	7.9	10.8	8.9	10.5
Cash Flow to Total Debt 44	0.2	•	0.4	0.7	0.4	0.4	0.2	0.3	0.2	0.2	0.1	0.1	0.0
Selected Financial Factors (in Percentages)													
Debt Ratio 45	68.7	•	89.2	57.5	58.2	53.9	65.5	53.1	58.5	57.5	70.7	65.8	98.4
Return on Total Assets 46	6.3	•	8.1	14.8	6.5	9.0	4.9	8.5	6.4	6.8	4.9	7.2	3.9
Return on Equity Before Income Taxes 47	12.1	•	69.3	32.9	11.9	16.4	9.3	14.9	11.8	10.9	7.3	12.1	25.7
Return on Equity After Income Taxes 48	9.6	•	68.9	32.9	10.9	15.9	7.7	13.7	10.0	8.6	5.2	8.9	•
Profit Margin (Before Income Tax) 49	3.0	•	3.0	5.0	2.1	3.8	1.8	4.2	3.3	3.4	2.0	5.0	0.7
Profit Margin (After Income Tax) 50	2.4	•	3.0	5.0	1.9	3.7	1.5	3.8	2.8	2.7	1.4	3.7	•

Table II

Corporations with Net Income

PLASTICS PRODUCT

MONEY AMOUNTS AND SIZE OF ASSETS IN THOUSANDS OF DOLLARS

Item Description for Accounting Period 7/11 Through 6/12		Total	Zero Assets	Under 500	500 to 1,000	1,000 to 5,000	5,000 to 10,000	10,000 to 25,000	25,000 to 50,000	50,000 to 100,000	100,000 to 250,000	250,000 to 500,000	500,000 to 2,500,000	2,500,000 and over
Number of Enterprises	1	5513	343	•	929	1620	392	315	•	76	74	17	20	0
Revenues ($ in Thousands)														
Net Sales	2	84481983	769448	•	2051373	8590222	5935432	9625095	•	8297744	16856462	6454298	16747900	0
Interest	3	122254	120	•	13	1526	1252	845	•	5074	14270	24253	72170	0
Rents	4	18874	16	•	0	0	0	516	•	573	2636	8475	623	0
Royalties	5	211501	822	•	0	1676	0	0	•	8147	22099	33078	144903	0
Other Portfolio Income	6	697562	12663	•	4368	2228	3025	17001	•	17823	35785	18713	580970	0
Other Receipts	7	616101	7985	•	5655	30779	14048	56526	•	33825	184546	29306	203819	0
Total Receipts	8	86148275	791054	•	2061409	8626431	5953757	9699983	•	8363186	17115798	6568123	17750385	0
Average Total Receipts	9	15626	2306	•	2219	5325	15188	30794	•	110042	231295	386360	887519	•
Operating Costs/Operating Income (%)														
Cost of Operations	10	71.3	69.0	•	63.9	65.6	72.7	72.2	•	70.0	73.1	74.1	73.4	•
Salaries and Wages	11	5.3	5.0	•	5.8	5.5	5.0	6.2	•	6.3	5.2	5.4	3.9	•
Taxes Paid	12	1.5	1.5	•	2.3	2.4	1.6	1.6	•	1.3	1.4	1.2	1.1	•
Interest Paid	13	1.4	1.1	•	0.4	0.4	0.7	0.7	•	0.7	1.3	1.6	3.6	•
Depreciation	14	3.7	2.5	•	0.9	2.6	1.9	3.4	•	4.2	4.2	3.3	4.8	•
Amortization and Depletion	15	0.4	0.7	•	0.2	0.1	0.0	0.1	•	0.3	0.4	0.8	0.8	•
Pensions and Other Deferred Comp.	16	0.5	0.1	•	0.4	0.3	0.5	0.4	•	0.5	0.5	0.6	0.5	•
Employee Benefits	17	1.5	1.3	•	1.0	1.5	1.1	1.4	•	1.7	1.3	1.7	1.8	•
Advertising	18	0.3	0.1	•	0.2	0.3	0.5	0.3	•	0.7	0.3	0.3	0.1	•
Other Expenses	19	7.6	8.0	•	11.2	9.4	6.9	7.2	•	6.8	7.3	7.8	7.2	•
Officers' Compensation	20	1.9	2.0	•	5.7	5.9	2.5	2.1	•	1.1	0.8	1.2	0.9	•
Operating Margin	21	4.6	8.6	•	8.1	6.0	6.5	4.6	•	6.3	4.2	2.1	1.8	•
Operating Margin Before Officers' Comp.	22	6.5	10.6	•	13.8	11.8	9.1	6.7	•	7.5	5.0	3.3	2.7	•

Selected Average Balance Sheet ($ in Thousands)

Net Receivables 23	1945	0	•	245	590	1616	3973	•	14888	30048	54450	111178	•
Inventories 24	1644	0	•	120	562	1375	3617	•	14544	24729	41982	85980	•
Net Property, Plant and Equipment 25	2647	0	•	83	341	1803	4549	•	19751	45617	68437	214597	•
Total Assets 26	11743	0	•	701	2038	6963	15614	•	71807	157856	356125	1240603	•
Notes and Loans Payable 27	4153	0	•	124	413	1864	4260	•	16431	43426	129629	600241	•
All Other Liabilities 28	2648	0	•	210	415	1373	3742	•	16465	39894	94261	246114	•
Net Worth 29	4942	0	•	368	1210	3725	7612	•	38910	74536	132235	394249	•

Selected Financial Ratios (Times to 1)

Current Ratio 30	1.8	•	•	1.9	2.7	2.0	1.9	•	2.0	2.2	1.3	1.3	•
Quick Ratio 31	1.0	•	•	1.4	1.8	1.2	1.1	•	1.1	1.2	0.7	0.8	•
Net Sales to Working Capital 32	6.9	•	•	9.1	5.6	7.8	6.7	•	5.8	5.7	11.5	10.5	•
Coverage Ratio 33	5.7	11.2	•	24.5	16.0	10.3	9.3	•	10.9	5.5	3.6	3.4	•
Total Asset Turnover 34	1.3	•	•	3.1	2.6	2.2	2.0	•	1.5	1.4	1.1	0.7	•
Inventory Turnover 35	6.6	•	•	11.8	6.2	8.0	6.1	•	5.3	6.7	6.7	7.2	•
Receivables Turnover 36	7.6	•	•	10.2	7.8	8.5	7.8	•	7.3	8.3	•	6.1	•
Total Liabilities to Net Worth 37	1.4	•	•	0.9	0.7	0.9	1.1	•	0.8	1.1	1.7	2.1	•
Current Assets to Working Capital 38	2.3	•	•	2.2	1.6	2.0	2.1	•	2.0	1.9	4.4	4.0	•
Current Liabilities to Working Capital 39	1.3	•	•	1.2	0.6	1.0	1.1	•	1.0	0.9	3.4	3.0	•
Working Capital to Net Sales 40	0.1	•	•	0.1	0.2	0.1	0.1	•	0.2	0.2	0.1	0.1	•
Inventory to Working Capital 41	0.8	•	•	0.5	0.5	0.7	0.8	•	0.8	0.7	1.3	1.0	•
Total Receipts to Cash Flow 42	8.5	6.2	•	6.7	8.2	8.4	9.7	•	8.0	8.8	10.3	8.2	•
Cost of Goods to Cash Flow 43	6.0	4.3	•	4.3	5.4	6.1	7.0	•	5.6	6.4	7.7	6.0	•
Cash Flow to Total Debt 44	0.3	•	•	1.0	0.8	0.6	0.4	•	0.4	0.3	0.2	0.1	•

Selected Financial Factors (in Percentages)

Debt Ratio 45	57.9	•	•	47.6	40.6	46.5	51.2	•	45.8	52.8	62.9	68.2	•
Return on Total Assets 46	10.7	•	•	28.1	17.8	16.5	11.9	•	12.0	10.3	6.0	8.2	•
Return on Equity Before Income Taxes 47	20.9	•	•	51.5	28.0	27.8	21.8	•	20.2	17.8	11.6	18.3	•
Return on Equity After Income Taxes 48	18.1	•	•	51.4	27.0	27.1	20.2	•	18.1	14.9	9.2	13.8	•
Profit Margin (Before Income Tax) 49	6.7	11.4	•	8.6	6.4	6.8	5.4	•	7.2	5.8	4.1	8.6	•
Profit Margin (After Income Tax) 50	5.9	9.0	•	8.6	6.2	6.7	5.0	•	6.4	4.9	3.2	6.5	•

Table I

Corporations with and without Net Income

RUBBER PRODUCT

MONEY AMOUNTS AND SIZE OF ASSETS IN THOUSANDS OF DOLLARS

Item Description for Accounting Period 7/11 Through 6/12		Total	Zero Assets	Under 500	500 to 1,000	1,000 to 5,000	5,000 to 10,000	10,000 to 25,000	25,000 to 50,000	50,000 to 100,000	100,000 to 250,000	250,000 to 500,000	500,000 to 2,500,000	2,500,000 and over
Number of Enterprises	1	1071	9	440	53	350	92	56	14	26	9	7	9	6
Revenues ($ in Thousands)														
Net Sales	2	63386772	401536	35915	36006	1420446	1906499	1391075	968070	2273489	1591448	2977208	11364836	39020244
Interest	3	348634	8	0	0	653	1164	198	80	641	541	4614	175521	165213
Rents	4	15403	0	0	0	0	0	0	63	1079	181	703	4231	9146
Royalties	5	762402	0	0	0	0	0	0	0	2440	0	18130	72573	669260
Other Portfolio Income	6	719430	0	0	0	1498	843	139	3	7513	1310	689	347847	359588
Other Receipts	7	645171	0	0	54	9351	2958	22401	1375	12818	10570	20313	84046	481284
Total Receipts	8	65877812	401544	35915	36060	1431948	1911464	1413813	969591	2297980	1604050	3021657	12049054	40704735
Average Total Receipts	9	61511	44616	82	680	4091	20777	25247	69256	88384	178228	431665	1338784	6784122
Operating Costs/Operating Income (%)														
Cost of Operations	10	74.3	62.9	51.3	37.4	70.9	66.5	67.0	68.6	75.1	77.5	73.6	80.9	73.4
Salaries and Wages	11	6.0	6.6	1.8	5.2	6.8	9.3	7.8	6.1	5.8	3.3	4.3	3.4	6.8
Taxes Paid	12	1.3	1.4	1.8	2.0	2.0	1.8	1.8	1.6	1.7	1.1	1.2	0.7	1.4
Interest Paid	13	1.7	1.1	0.1	0.1	0.7	0.4	0.4	0.1	1.1	1.0	2.1	4.2	1.2
Depreciation	14	3.5	6.8	0.4	0.4	3.5	0.9	3.3	3.8	3.1	2.5	2.5	3.8	3.6
Amortization and Depletion	15	0.8	0.9	•	•	0.0	0.0	0.1	0.4	0.9	0.6	1.2	0.6	0.9
Pensions and Other Deferred Comp.	16	1.4	0.3	•	0.0	0.3	0.4	0.5	0.2	0.8	0.3	1.4	0.9	1.8
Employee Benefits	17	2.3	1.5	•	0.0	1.0	1.7	1.3	1.1	2.3	1.2	1.5	1.4	2.9
Advertising	18	1.1	0.7	0.0	1.0	0.1	0.2	0.5	3.9	0.3	0.2	0.7	0.8	1.4
Other Expenses	19	8.2	10.5	29.1	27.9	10.1	7.1	7.4	6.6	5.6	9.9	10.0	5.9	8.8
Officers' Compensation	20	0.5	•	16.4	0.6	3.3	3.6	1.8	1.0	1.2	0.4	0.7	0.5	0.1
Operating Margin	21	•	7.3	•	25.4	1.2	8.2	8.2	6.6	2.3	2.1	0.8	•	•
Operating Margin Before Officers' Comp.	22	•	7.3	15.6	26.0	4.5	11.7	10.0	7.6	3.5	2.5	1.5	•	•

Selected Average Balance Sheet ($ in Thousands)

Net Receivables 23	10125	0	56	44	498	2449	3796	6822	13429	28180	92459	155558	1243144
Inventories 24	7515	0	3	17	563	1444	3412	7177	11998	27218	52510	162624	839542
Net Property, Plant and Equipment 25	9788	0	0	22	410	956	3873	13205	14244	23688	51466	257187	1098333
Total Assets 26	51135	0	199	529	1738	6922	14794	36083	66973	146878	327081	1252898	5907096
Notes and Loans Payable 27	14409	0	0	25	531	1124	2288	7079	22237	43835	124839	525163	1390235
All Other Liabilities 28	26293	0	70	90	673	1648	2878	10806	16491	46585	180116	442900	3554974
Net Worth 29	10433	0	129	413	534	4149	9628	18197	28245	56458	22127	284835	961887

Selected Financial Ratios (Times to 1)

Current Ratio 30	1.5	•	1.5	0.7	1.7	3.0	2.8	1.4	1.8	1.3	1.1	1.7	1.4
Quick Ratio 31	0.8	•	1.5	0.6	0.9	1.8	1.8	0.6	1.0	0.6	0.7	0.9	0.8
Net Sales to Working Capital 32	8.7	•	2.5	•	7.4	6.1	3.9	11.8	6.0	10.1	47.5	7.7	9.2
Coverage Ratio 33	3.1	7.5	•	230.7	4.0	19.8	28.7	63.6	4.2	4.0	2.1	2.0	3.4
Total Asset Turnover 34	1.2	•	0.4	1.3	2.3	3.0	1.7	1.9	1.3	1.2	1.3	1.0	1.1
Inventory Turnover 35	5.9	•	16.4	15.3	5.1	9.5	4.9	6.6	5.5	5.0	6.0	6.3	5.7
Receivables Turnover 36	6.6	•	2.5	30.7	8.2	10.0	6.0	13.1	7.3	7.5	3.9	6.2	6.7
Total Liabilities to Net Worth 37	3.9	•	0.5	0.3	2.3	0.7	0.5	1.0	1.4	1.6	13.8	3.4	5.1
Current Assets to Working Capital 38	3.2	•	3.1	•	2.3	1.5	1.6	3.3	2.2	4.2	19.2	2.5	3.6
Current Liabilities to Working Capital 39	2.2	•	2.1	•	1.3	0.5	0.6	2.3	1.2	3.2	18.2	1.5	2.6
Working Capital to Net Sales 40	0.1	•	0.4	•	0.1	0.2	0.3	0.1	0.2	0.1	0.0	0.1	0.1
Inventory to Working Capital 41	1.3	•	0.0	•	1.1	0.5	0.5	1.7	0.9	2.0	6.2	0.9	1.4
Total Receipts to Cash Flow 42	11.5	7.7	4.2	2.5	11.6	7.1	6.4	8.3	13.5	9.0	9.4	13.2	12.3
Cost of Goods to Cash Flow 43	8.6	4.8	2.2	0.9	8.3	4.7	4.3	5.7	10.1	7.0	6.9	10.6	9.0
Cash Flow to Total Debt 44	0.1	•	0.3	2.4	0.3	1.1	0.8	0.5	0.2	0.2	0.1	0.1	0.1

Selected Financial Factors (in Percentages)

Debt Ratio 45	79.6	•	35.2	21.8	69.3	40.1	34.9	49.6	57.8	61.6	93.2	77.3	83.7
Return on Total Assets 46	6.1	•	•	32.9	6.1	26.6	17.1	13.2	5.8	4.7	5.8	8.4	4.5
Return on Equity Before Income Taxes 47	20.0	•	•	41.9	15.0	42.1	25.4	25.8	10.4	9.2	45.5	18.4	19.7
Return on Equity After Income Taxes 48	15.8	•	•	29.7	11.2	39.6	24.4	21.9	8.3	5.1	37.5	10.9	16.3
Profit Margin (Before Income Tax) 49	3.5	7.3	•	25.5	2.0	8.4	9.9	6.8	3.4	2.9	2.4	4.1	2.9
Profit Margin (After Income Tax) 50	2.8	7.2	•	18.0	1.5	7.9	9.5	5.8	2.7	1.6	1.9	2.5	2.4

Table II

Corporations with Net Income

RUBBER PRODUCT

MONEY AMOUNTS AND SIZE OF ASSETS IN THOUSANDS OF DOLLARS

Item Description for Accounting Period 7/11 Through 6/12		Total	Zero Assets	Under 500	500 to 1,000	1,000 to 5,000	5,000 to 10,000	10,000 to 25,000	25,000 to 50,000	50,000 to 100,000	100,000 to 250,000	250,000 to 500,000	500,000 to 2,500,000	2,500,000 and over
Number of Enterprises	1	547	9	•	53	196	92	53	•	17	6	•	6	•
Revenues ($ in Thousands)														
Net Sales	2	56030278	401536	•	36006	1039162	1906499	1364463	•	1708201	1038257	•	8251956	•
Interest	3	301276	8	•	0	228	1164	196	•	443	191	•	152736	•
Rents	4	14274	0	•	0	0	0	0	•	380	1	•	4045	•
Royalties	5	711552	0	•	0	0	0	0	•	2429	0	•	39840	•
Other Portfolio Income	6	712137	0	•	0	1498	843	29	•	6801	239	•	347808	•
Other Receipts	7	572189	0	•	54	2253	2958	20792	•	7954	6147	•	56977	•
Total Receipts	8	58341706	401544	•	36060	1043141	1911464	1385480	•	1726208	1044835	•	8853362	•
Average Total Receipts	9	106658	44616	•	680	5322	20777	26141	•	101542	174139	•	1475560	•
Operating Costs/Operating Income (%)														
Cost of Operations	10	73.4	62.9	•	37.4	70.5	66.5	66.8	•	76.3	72.1	•	80.0	•
Salaries and Wages	11	6.1	6.6	•	5.2	5.7	9.3	7.6	•	5.1	3.8	•	3.4	•
Taxes Paid	12	1.3	1.4	•	2.0	1.9	1.8	1.8	•	1.5	0.8	•	0.9	•
Interest Paid	13	1.6	1.1	•	0.1	0.6	0.4	0.3	•	0.8	1.3	•	5.0	•
Depreciation	14	3.3	6.8	•	0.4	2.3	0.9	3.1	•	2.3	1.9	•	3.0	•
Amortization and Depletion	15	0.8	0.9	•	•	0.0	0.0	0.0	•	0.6	1.0	•	0.2	•
Pensions and Other Deferred Comp.	16	1.5	0.3	•	0.0	0.3	0.4	0.5	•	0.9	0.1	•	1.1	•
Employee Benefits	17	2.4	1.5	•	0.0	1.0	1.7	1.2	•	2.1	0.9	•	1.5	•
Advertising	18	1.2	0.7	•	1.0	0.1	0.2	0.4	•	0.1	0.3	•	0.7	•
Other Expenses	19	8.4	10.5	•	27.9	9.5	7.1	7.0	•	4.7	12.3	•	5.7	•
Officers' Compensation	20	0.5	•	•	0.6	3.9	3.6	1.6	•	1.3	0.4	•	0.6	•
Operating Margin	21	•	7.3	•	25.4	4.1	8.2	9.6	•	4.3	5.2	•	•	•
Operating Margin Before Officers' Comp.	22	•	7.3	•	26.0	8.0	11.7	11.2	•	5.6	5.5	•	•	•

Selected Average Balance Sheet ($ in Thousands)													
Net Receivables 23	13894	0	•	44	629	2449	3965	•	16157	30518	•	176798	•
Inventories 24	11969	0	•	17	731	1444	3479	•	14990	26986	•	407321	•
Net Property, Plant and Equipment 25	15948	0	•	22	337	956	3666	•	9076	19860	•	263611	•
Total Assets 26	78209	0	•	529	2002	6922	14798	•	66501	162881	•	1289263	•
Notes and Loans Payable 27	22662	0	•	25	472	1124	1874	•	17509	53605	•	484177	•
All Other Liabilities 28	41061	0	•	90	795	1648	2923	•	20038	50991	•	541693	•
Net Worth 29	14487	0	•	413	735	4149	10000	•	28954	58286	•	263393	•

Selected Financial Ratios (Times to 1)													
Current Ratio 30	1.7	•	•	0.7	1.9	3.0	2.9	•	1.9	1.3	•	2.1	•
Quick Ratio 31	0.9	•	•	0.6	1.0	1.8	1.9	•	1.0	0.6	•	1.2	•
Net Sales to Working Capital 32	7.6	•	•	•	7.0	6.1	3.8	•	5.9	10.6	•	5.8	•
Coverage Ratio 33	3.7	7.5	•	230.7	8.7	19.8	43.2	•	7.5	5.4	•	2.4	•
Total Asset Turnover 34	1.3	•	•	1.3	2.6	3.0	1.7	•	1.5	1.1	•	1.1	•
Inventory Turnover 35	6.3	•	•	15.3	5.1	9.5	4.9	•	5.1	4.6	•	2.7	•
Receivables Turnover 36	7.8	•	•	30.7	7.7	10.0	6.1	•	6.6	7.4	•	2.6	•
Total Liabilities to Net Worth 37	4.4	•	•	0.3	1.7	0.7	0.5	•	1.3	1.8	•	3.9	•
Current Assets to Working Capital 38	2.5	•	•	•	2.1	1.5	1.5	•	2.1	4.5	•	1.9	•
Current Liabilities to Working Capital 39	1.5	•	•	•	1.1	0.5	0.5	•	1.1	3.5	•	0.9	•
Working Capital to Net Sales 40	0.1	•	•	•	0.1	0.2	0.3	•	0.2	0.1	•	0.2	•
Inventory to Working Capital 41	1.1	•	•	•	0.9	0.5	0.5	•	0.9	2.3	•	0.6	•
Total Receipts to Cash Flow 42	10.3	7.7	•	2.5	9.4	7.1	6.0	•	11.6	6.2	•	10.4	•
Cost of Goods to Cash Flow 43	7.6	4.8	•	0.9	6.6	4.7	4.0	•	8.8	4.5	•	8.3	•
Cash Flow to Total Debt 44	0.2	•	•	2.4	0.4	1.1	0.9	•	0.2	0.3	•	0.1	•

Selected Financial Factors (in Percentages)													
Debt Ratio 45	81.5	•	•	21.8	63.3	40.1	32.4	•	56.5	64.2	•	79.6	•
Return on Total Assets 46	8.0	•	•	32.9	13.4	26.6	19.8	•	9.4	7.7	•	12.6	•
Return on Equity Before Income Taxes 47	31.5	•	•	41.9	32.3	42.1	28.6	•	18.6	17.5	•	35.7	•
Return on Equity After Income Taxes 48	25.6	•	•	29.7	27.3	39.6	27.5	•	15.6	11.6	•	23.6	•
Profit Margin (Before Income Tax) 49	4.5	7.3	•	25.5	4.5	8.4	11.1	•	5.4	5.9	•	6.8	•
Profit Margin (After Income Tax) 50	3.6	7.2	•	18.0	3.8	7.9	10.7	•	4.5	3.9	•	4.5	•

Table I

Corporations with and without Net Income

CLAY, REFRACTORY AND OTHER NONMETALLIC MINERAL PRODUCT

MONEY AMOUNTS AND SIZE OF ASSETS IN THOUSANDS OF DOLLARS

Item Description for Accounting Period 7/11 Through 6/12		Total	Zero Assets	Under 500	500 to 1,000	1,000 to 5,000	5,000 to 10,000	10,000 to 25,000	25,000 to 50,000	50,000 to 100,000	100,000 to 250,000	250,000 to 500,000	500,000 to 2,500,000	2,500,000 and over
Number of Enterprises	1	2688	19	2081	244	186	17	65	33	14	12	8	10	0
Revenues ($ in Thousands)														
Net Sales	2	19874101	625884	1650817	681709	879021	201592	1907432	1013004	912329	1708259	1959260	8334794	0
Interest	3	64087	1813	0	39	3	0	479	398	142	2037	2925	56251	0
Rents	4	30008	0	12	0	409	0	9	5	15	52	496	29010	0
Royalties	5	85510	589	0	0	0	0	1541	31	0	885	366	82099	0
Other Portfolio Income	6	33153	519	0	0	0	0	927	9337	1092	494	3571	17212	0
Other Receipts	7	370803	564	56526	9692	193	11092	3095	24900	20558	15588	-5202	233796	0
Total Receipts	8	20457662	629369	1707355	691440	879626	212684	1913483	1047675	934136	1727315	1961416	8753162	0
Average Total Receipts	9	7611	33125	820	2834	4729	12511	29438	31748	66724	143943	245177	875316	•
Operating Costs/Operating Income (%)														
Cost of Operations	10	68.2	74.2	63.6	51.8	71.9	65.3	71.0	67.5	68.3	61.8	73.4	69.2	•
Salaries and Wages	11	6.4	3.2	5.7	7.2	7.6	7.3	4.7	8.0	8.7	8.7	4.4	6.5	•
Taxes Paid	12	1.7	1.2	2.1	4.3	2.1	1.5	2.2	2.0	1.8	1.7	0.9	1.5	•
Interest Paid	13	1.7	3.5	0.5	0.1	0.6	0.4	0.6	1.2	1.3	0.7	3.1	2.4	•
Depreciation	14	3.9	10.1	1.5	1.0	2.2	0.2	3.4	5.9	5.2	4.7	4.7	3.9	•
Amortization and Depletion	15	0.6	0.1	0.0	0.4	0.0	0.0	0.5	0.4	0.4	0.6	0.7	0.9	•
Pensions and Other Deferred Comp.	16	1.1	0.3	1.2	•	0.1	0.5	0.4	0.3	0.3	1.4	0.5	1.8	•
Employee Benefits	17	1.6	4.7	0.6	•	0.9	1.3	1.3	1.7	1.6	2.4	1.4	1.8	•
Advertising	18	0.7	0.4	0.2	1.0	0.0	0.3	0.6	0.4	0.8	0.3	1.5	0.7	•
Other Expenses	19	11.5	11.3	18.3	17.2	12.6	8.3	6.4	8.7	10.4	11.5	7.6	12.2	•
Officers' Compensation	20	2.0	2.0	7.0	12.7	1.5	2.6	2.6	1.4	1.5	0.9	0.8	0.6	•
Operating Margin	21	0.6	•	•	4.3	0.5	12.4	6.4	2.5	•	5.2	1.0	•	•
Operating Margin Before Officers' Comp.	22	2.6	•	6.3	17.0	2.0	15.0	9.0	4.0	1.1	6.2	1.8	•	•

Selected Average Balance Sheet ($ in Thousands)

Net Receivables	23	897	0	11	252	707	1590	3533	5747	13830	21419	48691	90974	•
Inventories	24	1042	0	36	58	307	1772	3754	5932	15639	35770	49365	114265	•
Net Property, Plant and Equipment	25	2255	0	50	266	680	300	4646	12307	26716	44200	102130	333237	•
Total Assets	26	9928	0	167	883	2526	5767	14669	34415	74329	166964	302842	1799902	•
Notes and Loans Payable	27	3051	0	72	60	1340	1531	3230	14134	22611	17406	113205	565407	•
All Other Liabilities	28	2044	0	13	153	847	1223	4409	8486	20069	43231	64620	336905	•
Net Worth	29	4832	0	82	670	339	3014	7030	11795	31649	106327	125018	897590	•

Selected Financial Ratios (Times to 1)

Current Ratio	30	2.2	•	8.2	2.6	1.9	2.5	2.0	1.7	2.4	3.2	2.5	2.0	•
Quick Ratio	31	0.9	•	5.4	2.3	1.5	1.2	1.0	0.9	1.1	1.5	1.3	0.6	•
Net Sales to Working Capital	32	3.7	•	8.6	9.0	5.8	3.6	6.5	5.1	3.1	2.5	3.3	3.0	•
Coverage Ratio	33	3.1	•	6.1	51.9	2.0	44.9	12.0	6.0	2.5	9.6	1.4	2.6	•
Total Asset Turnover	34	0.7	•	4.8	3.2	1.9	2.1	2.0	0.9	0.9	0.9	0.8	0.5	•
Inventory Turnover	35	4.8	•	14.2	24.9	11.1	4.4	5.6	3.5	2.8	2.5	3.6	5.0	•
Receivables Turnover	36	7.6	•	69.4	10.4	9.2	8.3	10.1	5.0	5.2	5.6	5.9	6.9	•
Total Liabilities to Net Worth	37	1.1	•	1.0	0.3	6.5	0.9	1.1	1.9	1.3	0.6	1.4	1.0	•
Current Assets to Working Capital	38	1.9	•	1.1	1.6	2.2	1.7	2.0	2.4	1.7	1.5	1.7	2.0	•
Current Liabilities to Working Capital	39	0.9	•	0.1	0.6	1.2	0.7	1.0	1.4	0.7	0.5	0.7	1.0	•
Working Capital to Net Sales	40	0.3	•	0.1	0.1	0.2	0.3	0.2	0.2	0.3	0.4	0.3	0.3	•
Inventory to Working Capital	41	0.6	•	0.4	0.2	0.4	0.8	0.9	1.0	0.9	0.6	0.6	0.5	•
Total Receipts to Cash Flow	42	8.4	•	6.9	5.2	8.8	4.4	8.8	7.7	10.4	6.4	14.5	8.1	•
Cost of Goods to Cash Flow	43	5.7	•	4.4	2.7	6.3	2.9	6.3	5.2	7.1	3.9	10.6	5.6	•
Cash Flow to Total Debt	44	0.2	•	1.3	2.5	0.2	1.0	0.4	0.2	0.1	0.4	0.1	0.1	•

Selected Financial Factors (in Percentages)

Debt Ratio	45	51.3	•	51.1	24.1	86.6	47.7	52.1	65.7	57.4	36.3	58.7	50.1	•
Return on Total Assets	46	4.0	•	15.4	18.4	2.2	37.7	14.7	6.4	2.9	6.1	3.5	2.9	•
Return on Equity Before Income Taxes	47	5.5	•	26.3	23.8	8.0	70.5	28.1	15.5	4.1	8.5	2.3	3.5	•
Return on Equity After Income Taxes	48	4.2	•	26.3	23.6	7.7	70.3	26.5	12.9	1.7	7.8	1.1	2.3	•
Profit Margin (Before Income Tax)	49	3.6	•	2.7	5.7	0.6	17.9	6.7	5.9	2.0	6.4	1.2	3.8	•
Profit Margin (After Income Tax)	50	2.8	•	2.7	5.7	0.6	17.9	6.3	5.0	0.8	5.8	0.5	2.4	•

Table II

Corporations with Net Income

CLAY, REFRACTORY AND OTHER NONMETALLIC MINERAL PRODUCT

MONEY AMOUNTS AND SIZE OF ASSETS IN THOUSANDS OF DOLLARS

Item Description for Accounting Period 7/11 Through 6/12		Total	Zero Assets	Under 500	500 to 1,000	1,000 to 5,000	5,000 to 10,000	10,000 to 25,000	25,000 to 50,000	50,000 to 100,000	100,000 to 250,000	250,000 to 500,000	500,000 to 2,500,000	2,500,000 and over
Number of Enterprises	1	1536	16	996	244	157	17	55	23	6	•	•	6	0
Revenues ($ in Thousands)														
Net Sales	2	15318265	0	1280762	681709	782077	201592	1806951	809334	454208	•	•	6724004	0
Interest	3	43497	30	0	39	0	0	422	392	137	•	•	37515	0
Rents	4	29605	0	0	0	409	0	0	0	0	•	•	28649	0
Royalties	5	20482	0	0	0	0	0	1541	31	0	•	•	17660	0
Other Portfolio Income	6	21902	0	0	0	0	0	360	9275	47	•	•	9590	0
Other Receipts	7	316651	398	53510	9692	23	11092	2735	23203	10841	•	•	195864	0
Total Receipts	8	15750402	428	1334272	691440	782509	212684	1812009	842235	465233	•	•	7013282	0
Average Total Receipts	9	10254	27	1340	2834	4984	12511	32946	36619	77539	•	•	1168880	•
Operating Costs/Operating Income (%)														
Cost of Operations	10	66.4	•	65.8	51.8	73.4	65.3	70.9	69.9	68.2	•	•	66.6	•
Salaries and Wages	11	6.3	•	5.0	7.2	7.0	7.3	4.6	6.6	5.5	•	•	6.3	•
Taxes Paid	12	1.7	•	1.7	4.3	2.0	1.5	2.2	1.8	1.4	•	•	1.3	•
Interest Paid	13	1.4	•	0.6	0.1	0.6	0.4	0.6	0.4	1.3	•	•	2.3	•
Depreciation	14	3.5	•	1.7	1.0	2.3	0.2	2.3	4.8	2.8	•	•	3.9	•
Amortization and Depletion	15	0.4	•	•	0.4	0.0	0.0	0.5	0.2	0.6	•	•	0.6	•
Pensions and Other Deferred Comp.	16	1.1	•	0.0	•	0.1	0.5	0.5	0.3	0.4	•	•	1.9	•
Employee Benefits	17	1.4	•	0.8	•	0.4	1.3	1.3	1.2	0.5	•	•	1.6	•
Advertising	18	0.6	•	0.2	1.0	0.0	0.3	0.5	0.3	0.7	•	•	0.8	•
Other Expenses	19	10.7	•	16.7	17.2	12.1	8.3	6.2	8.3	10.3	•	•	10.6	•
Officers' Compensation	20	1.9	•	5.1	12.7	1.3	2.6	2.5	1.5	0.4	•	•	0.6	•
Operating Margin	21	4.7	•	2.6	4.3	0.7	12.4	8.0	4.8	8.0	•	•	3.6	•
Operating Margin Before Officers' Comp.	22	6.6	•	7.7	17.0	2.1	15.0	10.4	6.3	8.3	•	•	4.1	•

Selected Average Balance Sheet ($ in Thousands)

Net Receivables 23	1253	0	23	252	782	1590	3845	7305	20303	•	•	112950	•
Inventories 24	1269	0	40	58	264	2764	3974	5774	10459	•	•	171825	•
Net Property, Plant and Equipment 25	2959	0	94	266	759	300	3469	9647	24186	•	•	430360	•
Total Assets 26	10428	0	261	883	2754	5767	14460	33556	83311	•	•	1556691	•
Notes and Loans Payable 27	2547	0	59	60	1440	1531	3049	13941	8643	•	•	399547	•
All Other Liabilities 28	2713	0	6	153	935	1223	4316	10342	29056	•	•	435103	•
Net Worth 29	5168	0	196	670	379	3014	7096	9273	45612	•	•	722041	•

Selected Financial Ratios (Times to 1)

Current Ratio 30	2.8	•	26.1	2.6	2.0	2.5	2.2	1.8	2.8	•	•	3.0	•
Quick Ratio 31	1.3	•	16.4	2.3	1.6	1.2	1.1	1.0	1.7	•	•	1.1	•
Net Sales to Working Capital 32	3.2	•	9.2	9.0	5.2	3.6	6.1	4.5	3.0	•	•	2.5	•
Coverage Ratio 33	6.5	•	12.2	51.9	2.4	44.9	16.0	25.4	8.8	•	•	4.5	•
Total Asset Turnover 34	1.0	•	4.9	3.2	1.8	2.1	2.3	1.0	0.9	•	•	0.7	•
Inventory Turnover 35	5.2	•	21.0	24.9	13.8	2.8	5.9	4.3	4.9	•	•	4.3	•
Receivables Turnover 36	7.3	•	113.7	10.4	10.0	•	10.5	4.7	4.4	•	•	•	•
Total Liabilities to Net Worth 37	1.0	•	0.3	0.3	6.3	0.9	1.0	2.6	0.8	•	•	1.2	•
Current Assets to Working Capital 38	1.5	•	1.0	1.6	2.0	1.7	1.9	2.2	1.6	•	•	1.5	•
Current Liabilities to Working Capital 39	0.5	•	0.0	0.6	1.0	0.7	0.9	1.2	0.6	•	•	0.5	•
Working Capital to Net Sales 40	0.3	•	0.1	0.1	0.2	0.3	0.2	0.2	0.3	•	•	0.4	•
Inventory to Working Capital 41	0.5	•	0.4	0.2	0.3	0.8	0.8	0.8	0.5	•	•	0.4	•
Total Receipts to Cash Flow 42	6.6	•	5.9	5.2	8.9	4.4	7.9	6.3	5.2	•	•	6.9	•
Cost of Goods to Cash Flow 43	4.4	•	3.9	2.7	6.5	2.9	5.6	4.4	3.5	•	•	4.6	•
Cash Flow to Total Debt 44	0.3	•	3.3	2.5	0.2	1.0	0.6	0.2	0.4	•	•	0.2	•

Selected Financial Factors (in Percentages)

Debt Ratio 45	50.4	•	24.9	24.1	86.3	47.7	50.9	72.4	45.3	•	•	53.6	•
Return on Total Assets 46	8.7	•	36.4	18.4	2.5	37.7	20.0	9.7	10.7	•	•	7.5	•
Return on Equity Before Income Taxes 47	14.8	•	44.4	23.8	10.5	70.5	38.2	33.6	17.3	•	•	12.5	•
Return on Equity After Income Taxes 48	12.7	•	44.4	23.6	10.2	70.3	36.2	29.0	13.4	•	•	9.9	•
Profit Margin (Before Income Tax) 49	7.6	•	6.8	5.7	0.8	17.9	8.2	8.9	10.4	•	•	8.1	•
Profit Margin (After Income Tax) 50	6.6	•	6.8	5.7	0.8	17.9	7.8	7.6	8.1	•	•	6.4	•

Table I

Corporations with and without Net Income

GLASS AND GLASS PRODUCT

Item Description for Accounting Period 7/11 Through 6/12		Total	Zero Assets	Under 500	500 to 1,000	1,000 to 5,000	5,000 to 10,000	10,000 to 25,000	25,000 to 50,000	50,000 to 100,000	100,000 to 250,000	250,000 to 500,000	500,000 to 2,500,000	2,500,000 and over
		Money Amounts and Size of Assets in Thousands of Dollars												
Number of Enterprises	1	2012	0	1348	52	445	109	20	8	10	6	4	6	3
		Revenues ($ in Thousands)												
Net Sales	2	25893007	0	603760	70975	1395450	1686165	708136	253044	464320	827502	1903228	7185172	10795257
Interest	3	41066	0	36	132	340	416	936	118	193	234	7138	5270	26254
Rents	4	9571	0	0	0	28	0	941	0	1115	11	683	188	6606
Royalties	5	1330974	0	0	0	0	0	0	0	375	0	409	15345	1314845
Other Portfolio Income	6	458255	0	0	43	11290	262	167	0	2259	6204	10741	79184	348104
Other Receipts	7	338484	0	18934	704	8516	1415	2689	1001	8589	5977	12411	76461	201784
Total Receipts	8	28071357	0	622730	71854	1415624	1688258	712869	254163	476851	839928	1934610	7361620	12692850
Average Total Receipts	9	13952	•	462	1382	3181	15489	35643	31770	47685	139988	483652	1226937	4230950
		Operating Costs/Operating Income (%)												
Cost of Operations	10	68.3	•	53.8	31.0	57.7	66.4	82.8	70.4	74.1	74.2	77.8	71.8	65.2
Salaries and Wages	11	6.3	•	20.4	33.9	12.2	5.8	3.1	6.2	7.9	5.1	4.4	7.5	4.6
Taxes Paid	12	1.9	•	2.9	4.1	2.7	2.5	2.1	1.1	2.7	2.5	1.4	2.2	1.4
Interest Paid	13	1.9	•	0.1	1.4	1.7	0.5	0.3	2.5	3.0	3.4	5.1	0.5	2.5
Depreciation	14	4.0	•	0.8	2.0	7.8	3.2	3.3	1.6	8.4	5.3	6.0	4.9	2.6
Amortization and Depletion	15	0.5	•	•	•	0.1	0.0	0.4	2.2	1.0	0.8	0.4	0.2	0.9
Pensions and Other Deferred Comp.	16	1.6	•	•	•	0.0	0.1	0.1	0.3	0.6	0.8	2.0	1.5	2.4
Employee Benefits	17	2.1	•	0.2	4.3	1.1	1.6	1.7	0.0	3.9	2.2	2.7	2.7	2.0
Advertising	18	0.3	•	1.7	0.0	0.2	0.0	0.2	0.3	0.2	0.4	0.2	0.1	0.4
Other Expenses	19	15.7	•	22.8	15.7	18.4	10.6	6.0	6.7	11.6	8.2	3.9	9.9	23.4
Officers' Compensation	20	1.4	•	5.1	5.2	4.1	2.4	1.3	4.1	1.2	1.4	0.6	1.2	0.9
Operating Margin	21	•	•	•	2.4	•	6.8	•	4.6	•	•	•	•	•
Operating Margin Before Officers' Comp.	22	•	•	•	7.7	•	9.3	0.0	8.7	•	•	•	•	•

Selected Average Balance Sheet ($ in Thousands)													
Net Receivables 23	1828	•	20	131	348	1657	3268	5213	8297	13624	49454	128472	689464
Inventories 24	1681	•	86	114	309	1860	2488	4663	9771	26913	55905	160592	462213
Net Property, Plant and Equipment 25	5105	•	13	126	859	1897	4847	8451	15637	72566	128565	413609	1968317
Total Assets 26	29830	•	157	553	1983	7534	15996	29183	64941	169415	413337	1249541	15568256
Notes and Loans Payable 27	7288	•	323	177	1206	2364	4284	8472	30612	65899	244116	215890	3432396
All Other Liabilities 28	6434	•	24	164	349	1978	4100	10336	19360	51423	192550	392623	2913849
Net Worth 29	16108	•	-191	212	428	3192	7612	10376	14969	52093	-23329	641028	9222011

Selected Financial Ratios (Times to 1)													
Current Ratio 30	1.4	•	4.5	2.6	2.1	2.0	1.3	1.4	1.2	1.7	1.0	1.7	1.3
Quick Ratio 31	0.8	•	1.5	1.5	1.2	1.0	0.9	1.0	0.5	0.9	0.4	0.8	0.9
Net Sales to Working Capital 32	7.5	•	4.0	5.2	6.0	6.3	16.5	7.8	10.0	4.4	•	7.5	6.9
Coverage Ratio 33	3.8	•	•	3.6	•	16.0	•	3.0	•	0.3	0.5	3.2	6.1
Total Asset Turnover 34	0.4	•	2.9	2.5	1.6	2.1	2.2	1.1	0.7	0.8	1.2	1.0	0.2
Inventory Turnover 35	5.2	•	2.8	3.7	5.9	5.5	11.8	4.8	3.5	3.8	6.6	5.4	5.1
Receivables Turnover 36	6.5	•	23.3	9.5	8.4	12.2	10.6	4.7	8.0	12.3	8.7	6.6	5.2
Total Liabilities to Net Worth 37	0.9	•	•	1.6	3.6	1.4	1.1	1.8	3.3	2.3	•	0.9	0.7
Current Assets to Working Capital 38	3.3	•	1.3	1.6	1.9	2.0	4.1	3.7	6.4	2.4	•	2.5	4.0
Current Liabilities to Working Capital 39	2.3	•	0.3	0.6	0.9	1.0	3.1	2.7	5.4	1.4	•	1.5	3.0
Working Capital to Net Sales 40	0.1	•	0.2	0.2	0.2	0.2	0.1	0.1	0.1	0.2	•	0.1	0.1
Inventory to Working Capital 41	1.0	•	0.9	0.2	0.5	1.0	1.3	0.9	3.5	1.0	•	1.0	0.9
Total Receipts to Cash Flow 42	5.9	•	9.3	6.9	13.2	7.2	28.1	9.8	•	26.6	•	13.8	3.2
Cost of Goods to Cash Flow 43	4.0	•	5.0	2.1	7.6	4.8	23.2	6.9	•	19.7	•	9.9	2.1
Cash Flow to Total Debt 44	0.2	•	0.1	0.6	0.2	0.5	0.2	0.2	•	0.0	•	0.1	0.2

Selected Financial Factors (in Percentages)													
Debt Ratio 45	46.0	•	221.8	61.6	78.4	57.6	52.4	64.4	77.0	69.3	105.6	48.7	40.8
Return on Total Assets 46	3.0	•	•	12.6	•	15.2	•	8.2	•	0.7	2.7	1.5	3.5
Return on Equity Before Income Taxes 47	4.1	•	10.5	23.6	•	33.7	•	15.5	•	•	56.2	2.0	4.9
Return on Equity After Income Taxes 48	3.7	•	10.7	20.1	•	31.8	•	7.7	•	•	57.0	1.0	4.7
Profit Margin (Before Income Tax) 49	5.2	•	•	3.7	•	7.0	•	5.1	•	•	•	1.1	12.5
Profit Margin (After Income Tax) 50	4.7	•	•	3.1	•	6.6	•	2.5	•	•	•	0.5	11.9

Table II

Corporations with Net Income

GLASS AND GLASS PRODUCT

MONEY AMOUNTS AND SIZE OF ASSETS IN THOUSANDS OF DOLLARS

Item Description for Accounting Period 7/11 Through 6/12		Total	Zero Assets	Under 500	500 to 1000	1,000 to 5,000	5,000 to 10,000	10,000 to 25,000	25,000 to 50,000	50,000 to 100,000	100,000 to 250,000	250,000 to 500,000	500,000 to 2,500,000	2,500,000 and over
Number of Enterprises	1	611	0	342	52	77	109	11	4	3	•	0	•	3
Revenues ($ in Thousands)														
Net Sales	2	21931725	0	248559	70975	343438	1686165	476598	214194	162206	•	0	•	10795257
Interest	3	32427	0	36	132	30	416	568	118	101	•	0	•	26254
Rents	4	9008	0	0	0	28	0	941	0	675	•	0	•	6606
Royalties	5	1328343	0	0	0	0	0	0	0	375	•	0	•	1314845
Other Portfolio Income	6	440433	0	0	43	11290	262	12	0	220	•	0	•	348104
Other Receipts	7	279544	0	18799	704	2527	1415	1377	239	4258	•	0	•	201784
Total Receipts	8	24021480	0	267394	71854	357313	1688258	479496	214551	167835	•	0	•	12692850
Average Total Receipts	9	39315	•	782	1382	4640	15489	43591	53638	55945	•	•	•	4230950
Operating Costs/Operating Income (%)														
Cost of Operations	10	67.9	•	70.4	31.0	67.4	66.4	86.7	73.0	71.0	•	•	•	65.2
Salaries and Wages	11	5.7	•	11.1	33.9	6.9	5.8	2.1	4.7	4.7	•	•	•	4.6
Taxes Paid	12	1.8	•	1.5	4.1	2.4	2.5	1.3	0.8	2.0	•	•	•	1.4
Interest Paid	13	1.7	•	0.2	1.4	0.7	0.5	0.0	0.3	0.2	•	•	•	2.5
Depreciation	14	3.5	•	1.2	2.0	1.6	3.2	1.6	1.5	4.2	•	•	•	2.6
Amortization and Depletion	15	0.6	•	•	•	0.0	0.0	0.0	0.1	0.9	•	•	•	0.9
Pensions and Other Deferred Comp.	16	1.7	•	•	•	0.0	0.1	0.1	0.4	0.3	•	•	•	2.4
Employee Benefits	17	2.2	•	0.5	4.3	1.7	1.6	1.1	0.0	4.5	•	•	•	2.0
Advertising	18	0.3	•	0.6	0.0	0.6	0.0	0.3	0.1	0.1	•	•	•	0.4
Other Expenses	19	16.1	•	14.9	15.7	15.6	10.6	2.8	5.6	8.0	•	•	•	23.4
Officers' Compensation	20	1.2	•	3.8	5.2	3.1	2.4	0.5	4.8	1.8	•	•	•	0.9
Operating Margin	21	•	•	•	2.4	•	6.8	3.5	8.7	2.3	•	•	•	•
Operating Margin Before Officers' Comp.	22	•	•	•	7.7	3.1	9.3	4.1	13.5	4.1	•	•	•	•

Selected Average Balance Sheet ($ in Thousands)

Net Receivables **23**	5362	•	50	131	495	1657	4621	9508	11125	•	•	•	689464
Inventories **24**	4337	•	20	52	930	2383	2968	6634	5790	•	•	•	455097
Net Property, Plant and Equipment **25**	14552	•	23	126	868	1897	3413	5366	9981	•	•	•	1968317
Total Assets **26**	91744	•	151	553	2272	7534	18467	33367	58562	•	•	•	15568256
Notes and Loans Payable **27**	19633	•	36	177	779	2364	1734	4968	12639	•	•	•	3432396
All Other Liabilities **28**	18748	•	49	164	206	1978	4824	16236	15193	•	•	•	2913849
Net Worth **29**	53363	•	66	212	1287	3192	11910	12162	30730	•	•	•	9222011

Selected Financial Ratios (Times to 1)

Current Ratio **30**	1.5	•	1.6	2.6	2.3	2.0	2.1	1.3	1.8	•	•	•	1.3
Quick Ratio **31**	0.9	•	1.1	1.5	1.5	1.0	1.4	0.9	1.3	•	•	•	0.9
Net Sales to Working Capital **32**	6.4	•	14.6	5.2	5.9	6.3	6.7	10.2	5.6	•	•	•	6.9
Coverage Ratio **33**	5.7	•	17.7	3.6	6.5	16.0	87.6	27.7	26.3	•	•	•	6.1
Total Asset Turnover **34**	0.4	•	4.8	2.5	2.0	2.1	2.3	1.6	0.9	•	•	•	0.2
Inventory Turnover **35**	5.6	•	25.0	8.1	3.2	4.3	12.7	5.9	6.6	•	•	•	5.2
Receivables Turnover **36**	7.0	•	19.2	11.5	5.6	•	8.5	4.5	•	•	•	•	10.4
Total Liabilities to Net Worth **37**	0.7	•	1.3	1.6	0.8	1.4	0.6	1.7	0.9	•	•	•	0.7
Current Assets to Working Capital **38**	2.9	•	2.6	1.6	1.8	2.0	1.9	4.9	2.2	•	•	•	4.0
Current Liabilities to Working Capital **39**	1.9	•	1.6	0.6	0.8	1.0	0.9	3.9	1.2	•	•	•	3.0
Working Capital to Net Sales **40**	0.2	•	0.1	0.2	0.2	0.2	0.1	0.1	0.2	•	•	•	0.1
Inventory to Working Capital **41**	0.8	•	0.7	0.2	0.5	1.0	0.6	1.1	0.6	•	•	•	0.9
Total Receipts to Cash Flow **42**	5.0	•	6.7	6.9	6.9	7.2	16.6	7.6	8.5	•	•	•	3.2
Cost of Goods to Cash Flow **43**	3.4	•	4.7	2.1	4.6	4.8	14.4	5.5	6.1	•	•	•	2.1
Cash Flow to Total Debt **44**	0.2	•	1.3	0.6	0.7	0.5	0.4	0.3	0.2	•	•	•	0.2

Selected Financial Factors (in Percentages)

Debt Ratio **45**	41.8	•	56.4	61.6	43.3	57.6	35.5	63.5	47.5	•	•	•	40.8
Return on Total Assets **46**	3.8	•	17.2	12.6	9.3	15.2	9.8	14.7	5.6	•	•	•	3.5
Return on Equity Before Income Taxes **47**	5.4	•	37.2	23.6	13.9	33.7	15.0	39.0	10.2	•	•	•	4.9
Return on Equity After Income Taxes **48**	5.0	•	35.5	20.1	10.0	31.8	10.1	25.7	8.6	•	•	•	4.7
Profit Margin (Before Income Tax) **49**	8.0	•	3.4	3.7	4.0	7.0	4.1	8.9	5.8	•	•	•	12.5
Profit Margin (After Income Tax) **50**	7.4	•	3.2	3.1	2.9	6.6	2.8	5.8	4.9	•	•	•	11.9

Table I

Corporations with and without Net Income

CEMENT, CONCRETE, LIME AND GYPSUM PRODUCT

MONEY AMOUNTS AND SIZE OF ASSETS IN THOUSANDS OF DOLLARS

Item Description for Accounting Period 7/11 Through 6/12		Total	Zero Assets	Under 500	500 to 1,000	1,000 to 5,000	5,000 to 10,000	10,000 to 25,000	25,000 to 50,000	50,000 to 100,000	100,000 to 250,000	250,000 to 500,000	500,000 to 2,500,000	2,500,000 and over
Number of Enterprises	1	4376	701	1352	643	1090	336	142	29	30	21	8	18	7
Revenues ($ in Thousands)														
Net Sales	2	53767875	803313	962749	967528	4566715	3787146	2967036	1113825	1891184	3337486	1958345	8903385	22509163
Interest	3	137563	430	138	525	3168	3240	2774	404	689	5173	2743	59196	59083
Rents	4	51360	875	0	0	3287	991	1949	2138	1225	386	9573	8609	22326
Royalties	5	27891	2303	0	0	0	0	0	302	0	1368	4683	11222	8013
Other Portfolio Income	6	791599	11902	26140	921	20225	50724	17754	17838	9812	21970	14111	420432	179770
Other Receipts	7	821788	9130	10692	580	94852	74914	21056	17246	19847	14379	25195	189622	344274
Total Receipts	8	55598076	827953	999719	969554	4688247	3917015	3010569	1151753	1922757	3380762	2014650	9592466	23122629
Average Total Receipts	9	12705	1181	739	1508	4301	11658	21201	39716	64092	160989	251831	532915	3303233
Operating Costs/Operating Income (%)														
Cost of Operations	10	73.0	80.8	46.6	55.8	68.6	69.7	73.0	70.3	75.7	71.5	78.7	72.0	76.0
Salaries and Wages	11	5.9	4.3	16.2	8.1	6.5	4.6	6.6	6.0	5.7	5.4	3.8	4.5	6.3
Taxes Paid	12	2.1	2.0	5.9	3.1	2.6	2.2	2.5	1.9	2.4	2.3	1.6	2.0	1.7
Interest Paid	13	4.2	2.9	1.4	0.5	1.0	1.2	1.0	0.6	1.8	1.4	0.8	4.4	7.1
Depreciation	14	6.0	9.8	4.1	3.8	3.0	5.3	5.0	5.0	7.1	5.4	6.4	9.9	5.5
Amortization and Depletion	15	1.4	2.6	0.1	0.0	0.1	0.1	0.3	0.2	0.6	0.6	1.6	3.1	1.8
Pensions and Other Deferred Comp.	16	0.9	1.4	0.2	0.9	0.4	0.3	0.5	0.4	0.8	0.8	1.3	1.4	1.1
Employee Benefits	17	2.0	3.4	0.3	1.9	1.6	1.0	1.9	1.4	2.0	2.9	1.1	2.6	2.1
Advertising	18	0.4	0.1	0.1	1.1	1.2	0.2	0.6	0.8	0.4	0.4	0.2	0.2	0.3
Other Expenses	19	10.6	14.0	22.9	15.0	10.2	15.0	9.4	8.9	5.8	8.9	5.1	10.6	10.4
Officers' Compensation	20	1.3	4.1	5.9	5.1	3.7	3.3	1.6	2.6	1.2	1.0	0.9	0.6	0.2
Operating Margin	21	•	•	•	4.8	1.1	•	•	2.0	•	•	•	•	•
Operating Margin Before Officers' Comp.	22	•	•	2.2	9.9	4.8	0.5	•	4.5	•	0.3	•	•	•

Selected Average Balance Sheet ($ in Thousands)

Net Receivables	23	1838	0	50	185	527	2074	3207	5484	11431	24542	47011	86383	454473
Inventories	24	1348	0	25	80	273	769	2076	5587	5968	15619	27541	69985	402130
Net Property, Plant and Equipment	25	9519	0	88	263	785	2908	6282	11907	31905	61553	114462	570849	3550846
Total Assets	26	23301	0	216	669	2362	7309	16338	33124	66811	150689	347264	1159005	9160306
Notes and Loans Payable	27	7878	0	151	117	954	2582	5032	5518	23045	37703	35147	333316	3378205
All Other Liabilities	28	5498	0	110	135	572	2450	3215	4268	11634	28010	53574	360030	1992819
Net Worth	29	9925	0	-45	416	836	2277	8090	23337	32131	84976	258542	465659	3789282

Selected Financial Ratios (Times to 1)

Current Ratio	30	1.3	•	0.7	2.5	1.6	1.8	1.7	2.9	1.8	2.3	3.5	1.0	1.2
Quick Ratio	31	0.8	•	0.5	1.8	1.1	1.2	1.2	1.7	1.2	1.5	2.2	0.6	0.6
Net Sales to Working Capital	32	10.4	•	•	6.9	9.1	7.2	5.7	3.3	5.5	4.3	2.6	•	16.9
Coverage Ratio	33	•	•	1.1	11.3	4.6	1.5	0.1	10.4	•	1.4	2.7	0.3	•
Total Asset Turnover	34	0.5	•	3.3	2.3	1.8	1.5	1.3	1.2	0.9	1.1	0.7	0.4	0.4
Inventory Turnover	35	6.7	•	13.5	10.5	10.5	10.2	7.3	4.8	8.0	7.3	7.0	5.1	6.1
Receivables Turnover	36	6.6	•	15.7	9.3	7.9	6.6	6.9	6.2	6.0	7.1	5.5	6.0	6.2
Total Liabilities to Net Worth	37	1.3	•	•	0.6	1.8	2.2	1.0	0.4	1.1	0.8	0.3	1.5	1.4
Current Assets to Working Capital	38	4.1	•	•	1.7	2.6	2.3	2.3	1.5	2.2	1.8	1.4	•	7.1
Current Liabilities to Working Capital	39	3.1	•	•	0.7	1.6	1.3	1.3	0.5	1.2	0.8	0.4	•	6.1
Working Capital to Net Sales	40	0.1	•	•	0.1	0.1	0.1	0.2	0.3	0.2	0.2	0.4	•	0.1
Inventory to Working Capital	41	1.2	•	•	0.4	0.5	0.6	0.6	0.5	0.6	0.5	0.3	•	2.2
Total Receipts to Cash Flow	42	33.9	•	6.0	6.6	9.2	8.7	17.5	9.6	65.2	14.0	22.2	24.1	•
Cost of Goods to Cash Flow	43	24.7	•	2.8	3.7	6.3	6.1	12.8	6.7	49.4	10.0	17.5	17.3	•
Cash Flow to Total Debt	44	0.0	•	0.5	0.9	0.3	0.3	0.1	0.4	0.0	0.2	0.1	0.0	•

Selected Financial Factors (in Percentages)

Debt Ratio	45	57.4	•	120.7	37.8	64.6	68.9	50.5	29.5	51.9	43.6	25.5	59.8	58.6
Return on Total Assets	46	•	•	5.0	12.2	8.4	2.8	0.1	6.9	•	2.1	1.6	0.6	•
Return on Equity Before Income Taxes	47	•	•	•	17.8	18.6	2.9	•	8.8	•	1.1	1.3	•	•
Return on Equity After Income Taxes	48	•	•	•	17.6	17.8	2.8	•	7.1	•	0.3	1.1	•	•
Profit Margin (Before Income Tax)	49	•	•	0.1	4.9	3.7	0.6	•	5.4	•	0.6	1.4	•	•
Profit Margin (After Income Tax)	50	•	•	0.0	4.9	3.6	0.6	•	4.3	•	0.2	1.1	•	•

Table II

Corporations with Net Income

CEMENT, CONCRETE, LIME AND GYPSUM PRODUCT

MONEY AMOUNTS AND SIZE OF ASSETS IN THOUSANDS OF DOLLARS

Item Description for Accounting Period 7/11 Through 6/12		Total	Zero Assets	Under 500	500 to 1,000	1,000 to 5,000	5,000 to 10,000	10,000 to 25,000	25,000 to 50,000	50,000 to 100,000	100,000 to 250,000	250,000 to 500,000	500,000 to 2,500,000	2,500,000 and over
Number of Enterprises	1	1873	0	411	559	583	188	78	21	11	8	•	•	0
Revenues ($ in Thousands)														
Net Sales	2	17314840	0	272028	859123	2757871	2573367	1875893	826504	819520	1188364	•	•	0
Interest	3	33990	0	135	357	2849	2510	2511	190	162	4215	•	•	0
Rents	4	21359	0	0	0	3287	849	1711	2115	504	356	•	•	0
Royalties	5	10774	0	0	0	0	0	0	302	0	1368	•	•	0
Other Portfolio Income	6	470828	0	24475	367	16377	45556	7456	16636	2423	6745	•	•	0
Other Receipts	7	270916	0	2048	579	49399	70400	15256	16195	7923	13836	•	•	0
Total Receipts	8	18122707	0	298686	860426	2829783	2692682	1902827	861942	830532	1214884	•	•	0
Average Total Receipts	9	9676	•	727	1539	4854	14323	24395	41045	75503	151860	•	•	•
Operating Costs/Operating Income (%)														
Cost of Operations	10	65.1	•	31.9	55.2	61.8	65.4	70.2	68.0	68.5	60.9	•	•	•
Salaries and Wages	11	6.1	•	18.9	7.9	6.8	5.3	6.5	6.7	7.2	6.0	•	•	•
Taxes Paid	12	2.4	•	5.6	3.0	2.7	2.3	2.1	2.0	2.9	2.6	•	•	•
Interest Paid	13	1.6	•	1.8	0.3	0.7	1.5	0.7	0.4	1.7	1.4	•	•	•
Depreciation	14	5.7	•	9.0	3.7	3.1	4.4	4.3	4.9	5.2	6.5	•	•	•
Amortization and Depletion	15	1.1	•	0.0	0.0	0.1	0.0	0.2	0.2	0.6	0.7	•	•	•
Pensions and Other Deferred Comp.	16	0.9	•	0.3	1.0	0.6	0.3	0.6	0.3	0.7	1.1	•	•	•
Employee Benefits	17	1.8	•	0.3	2.0	2.1	1.0	1.6	1.5	2.1	3.5	•	•	•
Advertising	18	0.6	•	0.1	1.1	1.8	0.2	0.7	1.1	0.8	0.8	•	•	•
Other Expenses	19	10.2	•	24.3	14.9	8.5	15.8	9.1	8.0	4.6	9.8	•	•	•
Officers' Compensation	20	2.3	•	6.7	5.1	4.3	4.0	1.8	2.7	1.1	0.9	•	•	•
Operating Margin	21	2.3	•	1.3	5.8	7.5	•	2.2	4.1	4.6	5.8	•	•	•
Operating Margin Before Officers' Comp.	22	4.6	•	8.0	10.9	11.8	3.7	4.0	6.8	5.7	6.6	•	•	•

Selected Average Balance Sheet ($ in Thousands)

Net Receivables 23	1373	•	74	192	660	2645	3343	5510	11798	19262	•	•	•
Inventories 24	800	•	28	76	233	711	1987	5581	8239	19181	•	•	•
Net Property, Plant and Equipment 25	3875	•	108	246	651	2279	6111	12482	20295	65077	•	•	•
Total Assets 26	9678	•	303	669	2360	7037	17141	33505	65379	143999	•	•	•
Notes and Loans Payable 27	2305	•	115	81	771	3486	3325	3958	22489	34372	•	•	•
All Other Liabilities 28	2265	•	63	152	662	2004	3079	3862	8807	29310	•	•	•
Net Worth 29	5109	•	126	436	928	1547	10737	25684	34083	80317	•	•	•

Selected Financial Ratios (Times to 1)

Current Ratio 30	2.0	•	1.4	2.5	2.0	1.9	2.2	3.6	3.7	2.6	•	•	•
Quick Ratio 31	1.3	•	1.2	1.9	1.5	1.4	1.5	2.4	2.5	1.7	•	•	•
Net Sales to Working Capital 32	5.2	•	16.7	6.7	6.2	6.4	4.6	3.0	3.1	3.8	•	•	•
Coverage Ratio 33	5.5	•	7.3	18.8	15.3	3.8	6.0	21.2	4.5	6.7	•	•	•
Total Asset Turnover 34	1.0	•	2.2	2.3	2.0	1.9	1.4	1.2	1.1	1.0	•	•	•
Inventory Turnover 35	7.5	•	7.6	11.2	12.6	12.6	8.5	4.8	6.2	4.7	•	•	•
Receivables Turnover 36	7.4	•	10.4	10.0	8.3	8.4	7.8	6.1	•	7.5	•	•	•
Total Liabilities to Net Worth 37	0.9	•	1.4	0.5	1.5	3.5	0.6	0.3	0.9	0.8	•	•	•
Current Assets to Working Capital 38	2.0	•	3.4	1.7	2.0	2.1	1.8	1.4	1.4	1.6	•	•	•
Current Liabilities to Working Capital 39	1.0	•	2.4	0.7	1.0	1.1	0.8	0.4	0.4	0.6	•	•	•
Working Capital to Net Sales 40	0.2	•	0.1	0.1	0.2	0.2	0.2	0.3	0.3	0.3	•	•	•
Inventory to Working Capital 41	0.5	•	0.6	0.4	0.2	0.5	0.5	0.4	0.3	0.5	•	•	•
Total Receipts to Cash Flow 42	7.2	•	3.3	6.4	6.9	6.4	10.5	7.8	12.4	6.3	•	•	•
Cost of Goods to Cash Flow 43	4.7	•	1.1	3.5	4.3	4.2	7.4	5.3	8.5	3.8	•	•	•
Cash Flow to Total Debt 44	0.3	•	1.1	1.0	0.5	0.4	0.4	0.6	0.2	0.4	•	•	•

Selected Financial Factors (in Percentages)

Debt Ratio 45	47.2	•	58.6	34.8	60.7	78.0	37.4	23.3	47.9	44.2	•	•	•
Return on Total Assets 46	8.2	•	28.0	14.3	21.8	11.5	6.2	10.3	8.6	9.7	•	•	•
Return on Equity Before Income Taxes 47	12.8	•	58.4	20.8	51.7	38.5	8.2	12.8	12.9	14.8	•	•	•
Return on Equity After Income Taxes 48	11.7	•	55.9	20.6	50.3	38.2	7.3	10.7	12.2	12.8	•	•	•
Profit Margin (Before Income Tax) 49	7.0	•	11.1	5.9	10.1	4.3	3.7	8.3	5.9	8.0	•	•	•
Profit Margin (After Income Tax) 50	6.4	•	10.6	5.8	9.9	4.3	3.3	7.0	5.6	6.9	•	•	•

Table I

Corporations with and without Net Income

IRON, STEEL MILLS AND STEEL PRODUCT

MONEY AMOUNTS AND SIZE OF ASSETS IN THOUSANDS OF DOLLARS

Item Description for Accounting Period 7/11 Through 6/12		Total	Zero Assets	Under 500	500 to 1,000	1,000 to 5,000	5,000 to 10,000	10,000 to 25,000	25,000 to 50,000	50,000 to 100,000	100,000 to 250,000	250,000 to 500,000	500,000 to 2,500,000	2,500,000 and over
Number of Enterprises	1	3776	1113	1186	491	486	158	149	72	42	33	20	11	14
Revenues ($ in Thousands)														
Net Sales	2	155802858	1261640	1033259	555572	2456491	2992515	4034612	5414212	5157413	8483907	9276023	20118684	95018529
Interest	3	504052	2787	287	240	134	1623	1387	940	11023	4185	44386	71498	365560
Rents	4	53647	38	0	0	0	8	287	17	285	769	9485	3646	39111
Royalties	5	96961	0	0	0	0	0	0	0	0	301	8398	12092	76169
Other Portfolio Income	6	324794	18119	322	9020	696	637	7417	1727	7202	8036	9548	35617	226457
Other Receipts	7	1790772	64541	4323	10500	11043	55514	52575	20261	27706	37743	64635	204257	1237674
Total Receipts	8	158573084	1347125	1038191	575332	2468364	3050297	4096278	5437157	5203629	8534941	9412475	20445794	96963500
Average Total Receipts	9	41995	1210	875	1172	5079	19306	27492	75516	123896	258635	470624	1858709	6925964
Operating Costs/Operating Income (%)														
Cost of Operations	10	84.0	88.5	60.2	67.8	74.9	87.0	74.1	81.5	85.1	84.2	82.4	88.2	84.1
Salaries and Wages	11	2.2	3.8	15.4	6.0	5.9	3.0	4.8	3.8	2.0	3.0	2.8	1.6	1.8
Taxes Paid	12	0.8	1.1	3.6	1.4	1.6	0.8	1.7	1.0	0.9	0.7	0.9	0.6	0.7
Interest Paid	13	1.7	3.3	0.3	0.7	0.6	0.5	0.6	1.2	0.8	1.0	1.4	1.0	2.1
Depreciation	14	3.1	1.0	1.4	3.8	1.7	2.5	3.4	3.1	2.6	2.7	4.1	2.1	3.4
Amortization and Depletion	15	0.7	1.0	0.0	0.0	0.0	0.0	0.2	0.2	0.1	0.1	0.2	0.8	0.9
Pensions and Other Deferred Comp.	16	0.6	0.0	0.3	0.1	0.6	0.1	0.6	0.3	0.6	0.3	0.6	0.1	0.8
Employee Benefits	17	1.1	0.7	0.4	3.8	0.9	0.5	2.0	0.9	0.9	0.9	1.1	0.8	1.2
Advertising	18	0.0	0.0	0.0	0.7	0.1	0.1	0.2	0.1	0.1	0.1	0.1	0.1	0.0
Other Expenses	19	6.4	5.4	10.3	9.6	4.1	2.8	6.1	4.9	3.3	3.9	3.8	2.5	8.2
Officers' Compensation	20	0.5	1.2	8.2	2.0	7.0	1.5	1.8	1.2	1.0	0.6	0.4	0.3	0.2
Operating Margin	21	•	•	•	4.1	2.7	1.1	4.6	1.7	2.7	2.6	2.3	1.8	•
Operating Margin Before Officers' Comp.	22	•	•	8.0	6.1	9.7	2.7	6.4	2.9	3.7	3.2	2.7	2.1	•

Selected Average Balance Sheet ($ in Thousands)													
Net Receivables 23	4596	0	113	78	522	1759	4512	8716	14671	31887	47890	135504	802433
Inventories 24	5140	0	24	92	531	2354	3395	9366	20404	44916	79483	201459	812952
Net Property, Plant and Equipment 25	9621	0	57	171	385	1554	4464	8868	14542	40587	96516	242494	1992225
Total Assets 26	32395	0	228	789	1994	7606	16494	35853	71117	154794	354022	1026668	6284693
Notes and Loans Payable 27	10846	0	279	239	636	1932	3414	13750	17669	42859	103890	196113	2285833
All Other Liabilities 28	10992	0	175	145	494	2692	4081	12688	22717	53323	116673	234014	2244236
Net Worth 29	10556	0	-226	405	864	2983	8999	9415	30731	58612	133459	596541	1754624
Selected Financial Ratios (Times to 1)													
Current Ratio 30	1.8	•	0.9	1.7	2.0	1.5	2.1	1.6	1.7	1.9	2.5	2.4	1.7
Quick Ratio 31	0.8	•	0.7	0.8	1.1	0.7	1.2	0.7	0.8	0.8	1.0	1.0	0.8
Net Sales to Working Capital 32	6.9	•	•	8.9	6.9	10.9	4.9	9.6	6.6	5.6	4.3	7.2	7.2
Coverage Ratio 33	1.3	1.2	2.1	11.4	6.5	7.1	11.9	2.8	5.6	4.1	3.7	4.5	0.4
Total Asset Turnover 34	1.3	•	3.8	1.4	2.5	2.5	1.6	2.1	1.7	1.7	1.3	1.8	1.1
Inventory Turnover 35	6.7	•	22.0	8.3	7.1	7.0	5.9	6.5	5.1	4.8	4.8	8.0	7.0
Receivables Turnover 36	9.8	•	8.6	15.1	11.1	9.2	6.8	9.3	8.7	8.0	10.9	12.6	9.6
Total Liabilities to Net Worth 37	2.1	•	•	0.9	1.3	1.5	0.8	2.8	1.3	1.6	1.7	0.7	2.6
Current Assets to Working Capital 38	2.2	•	•	2.4	2.0	2.8	1.9	2.8	2.4	2.1	1.7	1.7	2.4
Current Liabilities to Working Capital 39	1.2	•	•	1.4	1.0	1.8	0.9	1.8	1.4	1.1	0.7	0.7	1.4
Working Capital to Net Sales 40	0.1	•	•	0.1	0.1	0.1	0.2	0.1	0.2	0.2	0.2	0.1	0.1
Inventory to Working Capital 41	0.9	•	•	1.2	0.8	1.5	0.6	1.3	1.2	1.0	0.8	0.8	1.0
Total Receipts to Cash Flow 42	28.8	18.8	16.6	7.3	17.8	20.4	9.7	17.4	16.6	16.6	15.7	19.6	54.4
Cost of Goods to Cash Flow 43	24.2	16.6	10.0	5.0	13.3	17.8	7.2	14.1	14.1	14.0	12.9	17.3	45.8
Cash Flow to Total Debt 44	0.1	•	0.1	0.4	0.3	0.2	0.4	0.2	0.2	0.2	0.1	0.2	0.0
Selected Financial Factors (in Percentages)													
Debt Ratio 45	67.4	•	199.4	48.7	56.6	60.8	45.4	73.7	56.8	62.1	62.3	41.9	72.1
Return on Total Assets 46	2.9	•	2.0	12.0	9.4	8.9	10.9	6.8	7.6	7.0	6.8	7.9	0.9
Return on Equity Before Income Taxes 47	2.2	•	•	21.3	18.4	19.4	18.3	16.6	14.5	13.9	13.1	10.6	•
Return on Equity After Income Taxes 48	•	•	•	20.7	17.9	19.1	17.1	14.2	11.3	10.2	9.3	6.9	•
Profit Margin (Before Income Tax) 49	0.6	0.8	0.3	7.6	3.1	3.1	6.1	2.1	3.6	3.2	3.8	3.4	•
Profit Margin (After Income Tax) 50	•	0.8	0.3	7.4	3.1	3.0	5.7	1.8	2.8	2.3	2.7	2.2	•

Table II

Corporations with Net Income

IRON, STEEL MILLS AND STEEL PRODUCT

MONEY AMOUNTS AND SIZE OF ASSETS IN THOUSANDS OF DOLLARS

Item Description for Accounting Period 7/11 Through 6/12		Total	Zero Assets	Under 500	500 to 1,000	1,000 to 5,000	5,000 to 10,000	10,000 to 25,000	25,000 to 50,000	50,000 to 100,000	100,000 to 250,000	250,000 to 500,000	500,000 to 2,500,000	2,500,000 and over
Number of Enterprises	1	2539	•	•	402	308	102	104	50	34	27	14	•	10
Revenues ($ in Thousands)														
Net Sales	2	114242568	•	•	356379	1829255	1894742	2836173	4268753	4596779	6914626	7061219	•	64570821
Interest	3	439156	•	•	229	41	1608	1289	911	6626	3771	7069	•	346116
Rents	4	40810	•	•	0	0	8	276	0	285	769	9404	•	26421
Royalties	5	39116	•	•	0	0	0	0	0	0	301	8315	•	18407
Other Portfolio Income	6	305295	•	•	10	681	146	7076	322	6850	8002	7094	•	221534
Other Receipts	7	1090419	•	•	4042	1093	12384	54586	14427	21815	34236	52846	•	641880
Total Receipts	8	116157364	•	•	360660	1831070	1908888	2899400	4284413	4632355	6961705	7145947	•	65825179
Average Total Receipts	9	45749	•	•	897	5945	18715	27879	85688	136246	257841	510425	•	6582518
Operating Costs/Operating Income (%)														
Cost of Operations	10	81.4	•	•	56.8	70.5	82.0	69.9	81.3	84.9	83.3	83.6	•	79.9
Salaries and Wages	11	2.3	•	•	8.1	5.9	3.6	5.0	4.0	2.0	3.1	2.4	•	1.8
Taxes Paid	12	0.9	•	•	1.4	1.7	0.9	1.7	0.9	0.8	0.8	0.8	•	0.9
Interest Paid	13	1.7	•	•	0.2	0.3	0.5	0.4	1.1	0.6	0.7	0.7	•	2.4
Depreciation	14	2.9	•	•	5.2	1.5	2.6	4.0	1.8	2.3	2.6	2.7	•	3.3
Amortization and Depletion	15	0.6	•	•	•	0.0	0.0	0.2	0.2	0.1	0.1	0.2	•	0.7
Pensions and Other Deferred Comp.	16	0.6	•	•	•	0.8	0.2	0.7	0.3	0.3	0.3	0.4	•	0.8
Employee Benefits	17	1.0	•	•	2.9	1.1	0.5	2.1	0.6	0.8	0.8	0.9	•	1.2
Advertising	18	0.1	•	•	0.8	0.1	0.1	0.2	0.1	0.1	0.0	0.1	•	0.0
Other Expenses	19	5.5	•	•	10.0	3.1	3.1	6.4	4.6	3.0	3.6	3.0	•	7.1
Officers' Compensation	20	0.5	•	•	1.0	8.6	1.6	1.7	0.9	1.0	0.5	0.4	•	0.2
Operating Margin	21	2.5	•	•	13.7	6.5	4.9	7.6	4.2	4.1	4.2	4.7	•	1.5
Operating Margin Before Officers' Comp.	22	3.0	•	•	14.6	15.0	6.5	9.4	5.2	5.1	4.8	5.1	•	1.7

Item	No.													
Selected Average Balance Sheet ($ in Thousands)														
Net Receivables	**23**	5324	•	•	59	685	1704	4073	8226	15705	31429	53480	•	861872
Inventories	**24**	4769	•	•	64	276	2791	3774	10825	23225	44713	78941	•	585459
Net Property, Plant and Equipment	**25**	8737	•	•	188	437	1931	4645	7262	13497	36671	87721	•	1569102
Total Assets	**26**	35789	•	•	811	2142	7409	16052	36335	72221	150582	358129	•	6315803
Notes and Loans Payable	**27**	11607	•	•	189	567	1883	2842	13582	14948	40596	81593	•	2308624
All Other Liabilities	**28**	9882	•	•	112	635	2793	3355	12085	23321	50175	121754	•	1722701
Net Worth	**29**	14300	•	•	510	940	2732	9855	10668	33953	59812	154782	•	2284478
Selected Financial Ratios (Times to 1)														
Current Ratio	**30**	2.1	•	•	2.3	2.3	1.5	2.4	1.8	1.8	2.1	2.8	•	2.0
Quick Ratio	**31**	1.0	•	•	1.2	1.5	0.6	1.4	0.7	0.8	0.9	1.1	•	1.0
Net Sales to Working Capital	**32**	5.9	•	•	6.2	6.4	11.4	4.5	8.6	6.2	4.9	3.7	•	5.9
Coverage Ratio	**33**	3.5	•	•	81.5	21.2	13.1	26.6	5.1	9.4	7.6	9.9	•	2.5
Total Asset Turnover	**34**	1.3	•	•	1.1	2.8	2.5	1.7	2.3	1.9	1.7	1.4	•	1.0
Inventory Turnover	**35**	7.7	•	•	7.9	15.2	5.5	5.1	6.4	4.9	4.8	5.3	•	8.8
Receivables Turnover	**36**	10.7	•	•	19.3	13.7	8.2	6.7	10.2	8.6	8.3	12.2	•	10.9
Total Liabilities to Net Worth	**37**	1.5	•	•	0.6	1.3	1.7	0.6	2.4	1.1	1.5	1.3	•	1.8
Current Assets to Working Capital	**38**	1.9	•	•	1.8	1.8	3.0	1.7	2.3	2.3	1.9	1.6	•	2.0
Current Liabilities to Working Capital	**39**	0.9	•	•	0.8	0.8	2.0	0.7	1.3	1.3	0.9	0.6	•	1.0
Working Capital to Net Sales	**40**	0.2	•	•	0.2	0.2	0.1	0.2	0.1	0.2	0.2	0.3	•	0.2
Inventory to Working Capital	**41**	0.8	•	•	0.8	0.5	1.7	0.6	1.2	1.1	0.9	0.8	•	0.7
Total Receipts to Cash Flow	**42**	14.0	•	•	4.7	12.5	13.2	7.0	12.4	14.1	13.5	12.7	•	14.5
Cost of Goods to Cash Flow	**43**	11.4	•	•	2.7	8.8	10.8	4.9	10.0	12.0	11.3	10.7	•	11.6
Cash Flow to Total Debt	**44**	0.1	•	•	0.6	0.4	0.3	0.6	0.3	0.3	0.2	0.2	•	0.1
Selected Financial Factors (in Percentages)														
Debt Ratio	**45**	60.0	•	•	37.1	56.1	63.1	38.6	70.6	53.0	60.3	56.8	•	63.8
Return on Total Assets	**46**	7.5	•	•	16.4	19.1	15.4	17.4	13.5	10.3	9.6	9.2	•	6.1
Return on Equity Before Income Taxes	**47**	13.3	•	•	25.8	41.4	38.5	27.3	36.9	19.6	21.0	19.2	•	10.0
Return on Equity After Income Taxes	**48**	9.6	•	•	25.3	40.8	37.9	25.7	33.8	16.0	16.5	14.6	•	6.2
Profit Margin (Before Income Tax)	**49**	4.2	•	•	14.9	6.6	5.7	9.9	4.6	4.9	4.9	5.9	•	3.5
Profit Margin (After Income Tax)	**50**	3.0	•	•	14.6	6.4	5.6	9.3	4.2	4.0	3.9	4.5	•	2.2

Table I

Corporations with and without Net Income

NONFERROUS METAL PRODUCTION AND PROCESSING

MONEY AMOUNTS AND SIZE OF ASSETS IN THOUSANDS OF DOLLARS

Item Description for Accounting Period 7/11 Through 6/12		Total	Zero Assets	Under 500	500 to 1,000	1,000 to 5,000	5,000 to 10,000	10,000 to 25,000	25,000 to 50,000	50,000 to 100,000	100,000 to 250,000	250,000 to 500,000	500,000 to 2,500,000	2,500,000 and over
Number of Enterprises	1	947	7	•	0	609	•	140	56	39	22	17	29	•
Revenues ($ in Thousands)														
Net Sales	2	113992768	825912	•	0	3762502	•	10968315	8697402	8219682	6469291	9715909	64027271	•
Interest	3	1229413	26	•	0	132	•	420	918	677	3414	18246	1205580	•
Rents	4	64798	0	•	0	3669	•	1653	512	506	10656	742	47060	•
Royalties	5	77787	0	•	0	0	•	2264	164	0	3865	0	71494	•
Other Portfolio Income	6	635437	543	•	0	309	•	48528	18866	5164	13665	22991	525324	•
Other Receipts	7	2206752	17684	•	0	25812	•	38390	14364	12066	66145	95278	1931142	•
Total Receipts	8	118206955	844165	•	0	3792424	•	11059570	8732226	8238095	6567036	9853166	67807871	•
Average Total Receipts	9	124823	120595	•	•	6227	•	78997	155933	211233	298502	579598	2338202	•
Operating Costs/Operating Income (%)														
Cost of Operations	10	87.5	85.5	•	•	74.7	•	90.7	93.5	89.9	88.8	85.6	86.7	•
Salaries and Wages	11	2.3	2.7	•	•	4.2	•	1.9	1.1	1.6	2.0	2.7	2.4	•
Taxes Paid	12	0.5	0.4	•	•	1.1	•	0.6	0.4	0.5	0.7	0.4	0.4	•
Interest Paid	13	2.3	2.0	•	•	1.3	•	0.3	0.2	0.3	1.0	1.4	3.5	•
Depreciation	14	1.7	5.3	•	•	1.7	•	1.4	0.8	1.4	2.1	1.9	1.8	•
Amortization and Depletion	15	0.4	1.9	•	•	0.0	•	0.0	0.1	0.1	0.4	0.4	0.5	•
Pensions and Other Deferred Comp.	16	1.0	0.0	•	•	0.4	•	0.1	0.1	0.2	0.4	0.4	1.5	•
Employee Benefits	17	0.7	0.6	•	•	1.7	•	0.4	0.4	0.4	0.8	1.4	0.7	•
Advertising	18	0.1	0.0	•	•	1.2	•	0.1	0.0	0.0	0.0	0.1	0.1	•
Other Expenses	19	4.9	3.0	•	•	6.6	•	2.7	1.8	2.5	4.5	6.1	5.9	•
Officers' Compensation	20	0.5	2.2	•	•	2.7	•	0.8	0.8	0.7	0.4	0.2	0.3	•
Operating Margin	21	•	•	•	•	4.4	•	1.2	1.0	2.5	•	•	•	•
Operating Margin Before Officers' Comp.	22	•	•	•	•	7.2	•	2.0	1.7	3.1	•	•	•	•

Selected Average Balance Sheet ($ in Thousands)													
Net Receivables **23**	46556	0	•	•	475	•	4508	8637	16907	31847	76619	1377850	•
Inventories **24**	9866	0	•	•	293	•	3913	10590	15545	32323	73267	178991	•
Net Property, Plant and Equipment **25**	16049	0	•	•	433	•	3149	6475	13487	45138	84070	383442	•
Total Assets **26**	162910	0	•	•	2088	•	15906	31957	66561	161839	349803	4712739	•
Notes and Loans Payable **27**	54306	0	•	•	2479	•	4680	10346	16333	57227	120231	1539202	•
All Other Liabilities **28**	51903	0	•	•	1284	•	3903	9624	19176	44442	153100	1476869	•
Net Worth **29**	56700	0	•	•	-1675	•	7323	11987	31051	60170	76472	1696669	•
Selected Financial Ratios (Times to 1)													
Current Ratio **30**	1.3	•	•	•	0.9	•	2.1	1.7	1.9	2.1	1.4	1.2	•
Quick Ratio **31**	1.0	•	•	•	0.5	•	1.2	0.9	1.1	0.9	0.8	1.0	•
Net Sales to Working Capital **32**	8.0	•	•	•	•	•	13.7	17.8	10.0	6.2	12.9	6.2	•
Coverage Ratio **33**	2.0	0.2	•	•	4.9	•	8.9	7.4	10.5	1.3	1.9	1.8	•
Total Asset Turnover **34**	0.7	•	•	•	3.0	•	4.9	4.9	3.2	1.8	1.6	0.5	•
Inventory Turnover **35**	10.7	•	•	•	15.8	•	18.2	13.7	12.2	8.1	6.7	10.7	•
Receivables Turnover **36**	2.4	•	•	•	18.0	•	19.1	15.9	14.5	11.7	6.5	1.5	•
Total Liabilities to Net Worth **37**	1.9	•	•	•	•	•	1.2	1.7	1.1	1.7	3.6	1.8	•
Current Assets to Working Capital **38**	4.5	•	•	•	•	•	1.9	2.5	2.1	1.9	3.8	5.2	•
Current Liabilities to Working Capital **39**	3.5	•	•	•	•	•	0.9	1.5	1.1	0.9	2.8	4.2	•
Working Capital to Net Sales **40**	0.1	•	•	•	•	•	0.1	0.1	0.1	0.2	0.1	0.2	•
Inventory to Working Capital **41**	0.7	•	•	•	•	•	0.7	1.1	0.8	0.8	1.5	0.6	•
Total Receipts to Cash Flow **42**	17.7	146.6	•	•	9.9	•	23.9	40.7	22.2	29.1	18.6	15.0	•
Cost of Goods to Cash Flow **43**	15.5	125.3	•	•	7.4	•	21.7	38.1	20.0	25.9	15.9	13.0	•
Cash Flow to Total Debt **44**	0.1	•	•	•	0.2	•	0.4	0.2	0.3	0.1	0.1	0.0	•
Selected Financial Factors (in Percentages)													
Debt Ratio **45**	65.2	•	•	•	180.2	•	54.0	62.5	53.3	62.8	78.1	64.0	•
Return on Total Assets **46**	3.4	•	•	•	19.4	•	11.1	7.8	9.4	2.4	4.3	2.9	•
Return on Equity Before Income Taxes **47**	4.9	•	•	•	•	•	21.3	17.9	18.2	1.6	9.2	3.6	•
Return on Equity After Income Taxes **48**	3.8	•	•	•	•	•	20.0	16.6	16.3	•	5.0	2.7	•
Profit Margin (Before Income Tax) **49**	2.3	•	•	•	5.2	•	2.0	1.4	2.7	0.3	1.2	2.7	•
Profit Margin (After Income Tax) **50**	1.8	•	•	•	5.2	•	1.9	1.3	2.4	•	0.7	2.1	•

Table II

Corporations with Net Income

NONFERROUS METAL PRODUCTION AND PROCESSING

MONEY AMOUNTS AND SIZE OF ASSETS IN THOUSANDS OF DOLLARS

Item Description for Accounting Period 7/11 Through 6/12		Total	Zero Assets	Under 500	500 to 1,000	1,000 to 5,000	5,000 to 10,000	10,000 to 25,000	25,000 to 50,000	50,000 to 100,000	100,000 to 250,000	250,000 to 500,000	500,000 to 2,500,000	2,500,000 and over
Number of Enterprises	1	723	•	0	0	475	10	115	46	31	•	10	•	•
Revenues ($ in Thousands)														
Net Sales	2	91354473	•	0	0	2949736	1002040	9850833	7627091	7128088	•	7576997	•	•
Interest	3	1159713	•	0	0	65	0	372	737	650	•	17309	•	•
Rents	4	48955	•	0	0	3257	0	135	512	506	•	13	•	•
Royalties	5	76999	•	0	0	0	0	2264	0	0	•	0	•	•
Other Portfolio Income	6	527655	•	0	0	220	0	1327	18642	4988	•	22981	•	•
Other Receipts	7	2030745	•	0	0	25086	46	34095	13327	10721	•	93042	•	•
Total Receipts	8	95198540	•	0	0	2978364	1002086	9889026	7660309	7144953	•	7710342	•	•
Average Total Receipts	9	131672	•	•	•	6270	100209	85992	166528	230482	•	771034	•	•
Operating Costs/Operating Income (%)														
Cost of Operations	10	87.0	•	•	•	73.2	97.6	91.5	93.3	89.9	•	87.7	•	•
Salaries and Wages	11	2.2	•	•	•	4.9	0.4	1.6	1.2	1.6	•	2.1	•	•
Taxes Paid	12	0.5	•	•	•	0.8	0.1	0.5	0.4	0.5	•	0.4	•	•
Interest Paid	13	2.5	•	•	•	0.7	0.1	0.2	0.2	0.2	•	1.5	•	•
Depreciation	14	1.6	•	•	•	2.0	0.1	0.9	0.6	0.9	•	0.9	•	•
Amortization and Depletion	15	0.3	•	•	•	0.0	0.0	0.0	0.0	0.0	•	0.2	•	•
Pensions and Other Deferred Comp.	16	1.0	•	•	•	0.4	0.0	0.2	0.1	0.2	•	0.4	•	•
Employee Benefits	17	0.5	•	•	•	0.4	0.2	0.3	0.4	0.4	•	1.4	•	•
Advertising	18	0.1	•	•	•	0.1	0.0	0.1	0.0	0.0	•	0.1	•	•
Other Expenses	19	4.6	•	•	•	6.7	0.4	1.8	1.7	2.3	•	4.2	•	•
Officers' Compensation	20	0.5	•	•	•	3.1	0.3	0.7	0.8	0.6	•	0.2	•	•
Operating Margin	21	•	•	•	•	7.8	0.7	2.3	1.3	3.3	•	1.0	•	•
Operating Margin Before Officers' Comp.	22	•	•	•	•	10.9	0.9	3.1	2.1	3.9	•	1.2	•	•

Selected Average Balance Sheet ($ in Thousands)

Net Receivables 23	58508	•	•	•	481	1454	4727	8267	17076	•	102795	•	•
Inventories 24	9706	•	•	•	279	18013	4044	10675	14852	•	63144	•	•
Net Property, Plant and Equipment 25	16364	•	•	•	442	782	2595	6193	11674	•	51336	•	•
Total Assets 26	192423	•	•	•	1791	6353	15600	31749	64624	•	369240	•	•
Notes and Loans Payable 27	64032	•	•	•	759	597	4001	10536	11610	•	80008	•	•
All Other Liabilities 28	60157	•	•	•	324	1655	3823	9873	18745	•	201851	•	•
Net Worth 29	68233	•	•	•	708	4102	7776	11339	34269	•	87381	•	•

Selected Financial Ratios (Times to 1)

Current Ratio 30	1.3	•	•	•	2.8	2.5	2.1	1.7	2.1	•	2.0	•	•
Quick Ratio 31	1.0	•	•	•	2.0	0.9	1.2	0.8	1.2	•	1.3	•	•
Net Sales to Working Capital 32	8.0	•	•	•	7.4	30.5	14.1	18.7	10.2	•	7.5	•	•
Coverage Ratio 33	2.5	•	•	•	13.3	6.4	15.7	9.8	17.9	•	3.3	•	•
Total Asset Turnover 34	0.7	•	•	•	3.5	15.8	5.5	5.2	3.6	•	2.1	•	•
Inventory Turnover 35	11.3	•	•	•	16.3	5.4	19.4	14.5	13.9	•	10.5	•	•
Receivables Turnover 36	2.1	•	•	•	16.6	15.7	19.9	19.0	15.1	•	•	•	•
Total Liabilities to Net Worth 37	1.8	•	•	•	1.5	0.5	1.0	1.8	0.9	•	3.2	•	•
Current Assets to Working Capital 38	4.9	•	•	•	1.6	1.7	1.9	2.5	1.9	•	2.0	•	•
Current Liabilities to Working Capital 39	3.9	•	•	•	0.6	0.7	0.9	1.5	0.9	•	1.0	•	•
Working Capital to Net Sales 40	0.1	•	•	•	0.1	0.0	0.1	0.1	0.1	•	0.1	•	•
Inventory to Working Capital 41	0.7	•	•	•	0.3	1.0	0.7	1.1	0.7	•	0.6	•	•
Total Receipts to Cash Flow 42	14.5	•	•	•	7.4	99.3	24.4	37.0	19.3	•	17.7	•	•
Cost of Goods to Cash Flow 43	12.6	•	•	•	5.4	96.9	22.3	34.5	17.3	•	15.5	•	•
Cash Flow to Total Debt 44	0.1	•	•	•	0.8	0.4	0.4	0.2	0.4	•	0.2	•	•

Selected Financial Factors (in Percentages)

Debt Ratio 45	64.5	•	•	•	60.5	35.4	50.2	64.3	47.0	•	76.3	•	•
Return on Total Assets 46	4.1	•	•	•	32.8	12.3	15.9	10.1	13.5	•	10.1	•	•
Return on Equity Before Income Taxes 47	7.0	•	•	•	76.8	16.0	29.8	25.4	24.0	•	29.9	•	•
Return on Equity After Income Taxes 48	5.8	•	•	•	76.2	15.8	28.3	23.8	21.8	•	23.7	•	•
Profit Margin (Before Income Tax) 49	3.8	•	•	•	8.8	0.7	2.7	1.7	3.6	•	3.4	•	•
Profit Margin (After Income Tax) 50	3.1	•	•	•	8.7	0.6	2.6	1.6	3.2	•	2.7	•	•

Table I

Corporations with and without Net Income

FOUNDRIES

Item Description for Accounting Period 7/11 Through 6/12		Total	Zero Assets	Under 500	500 to 1,000	1,000 to 5,000	5,000 to 10,000	10,000 to 25,000	25,000 to 50,000	50,000 to 100,000	100,000 to 250,000	250,000 to 500,000	500,000 to 2,500,000	2,500,000 and over
		MONEY AMOUNTS AND SIZE OF ASSETS IN THOUSANDS OF DOLLARS												
Number of Enterprises	1	1457	3	•	0	200	•	53	14	10	6	4	9	0
Revenues ($ in Thousands)														
Net Sales	2	23896160	234881	•	0	1667586	•	1379073	759102	930870	1163086	1807057	13724133	0
Interest	3	12896	354	•	0	609	•	281	27	248	24	2195	8804	0
Rents	4	3349	0	•	0	314	•	898	274	95	0	1051	716	0
Royalties	5	15982	0	•	0	0	•	0	6	0	1424	0	14552	0
Other Portfolio Income	6	46933	8	•	0	2230	•	147	981	250	2435	370	39503	0
Other Receipts	7	155503	1098	•	0	17974	•	2496	5490	5408	5859	24703	89885	0
Total Receipts	8	24130823	236341	•	0	1688713	•	1382895	765880	936871	1172828	1835376	13877593	0
Average Total Receipts	9	16562	78780	•	•	8444	•	26092	54706	93687	195471	458844	1541955	•
Operating Costs/Operating Income (%)														
Cost of Operations	10	73.3	61.3	•	•	68.0	•	78.0	78.6	76.8	71.4	78.7	72.8	•
Salaries and Wages	11	4.3	4.0	•	•	5.7	•	4.4	2.5	4.9	4.5	3.5	4.3	•
Taxes Paid	12	1.6	3.5	•	•	2.7	•	1.8	1.9	2.0	0.8	1.9	1.4	•
Interest Paid	13	1.1	8.1	•	•	0.4	•	1.0	3.0	0.3	0.5	2.7	0.9	•
Depreciation	14	2.9	3.3	•	•	2.2	•	3.8	4.7	5.0	4.4	3.2	2.6	•
Amortization and Depletion	15	0.8	0.8	•	•	0.0	•	0.1	0.4	0.0	0.2	0.3	1.2	•
Pensions and Other Deferred Comp.	16	0.8	0.4	•	•	0.4	•	0.3	0.1	0.6	0.9	1.0	1.0	•
Employee Benefits	17	1.6	1.9	•	•	2.8	•	2.4	2.1	0.9	3.1	2.4	1.3	•
Advertising	18	0.1	0.1	•	•	0.1	•	0.1	0.0	0.3	0.0	0.1	0.1	•
Other Expenses	19	5.1	11.5	•	•	10.5	•	5.0	5.7	5.6	5.1	6.0	3.7	•
Officers' Compensation	20	1.8	18.0	•	•	5.9	•	2.3	0.8	1.5	0.9	0.7	0.8	•
Operating Margin	21	6.6	•	•	•	1.3	•	0.8	0.3	2.0	7.9	•	9.8	•
Operating Margin Before Officers' Comp.	22	8.4	5.1	•	•	7.1	•	3.1	1.0	3.4	8.8	0.2	10.6	•

Selected Average Balance Sheet ($ in Thousands)

Net Receivables	23	2525	0	•	•	1202	•	3459	8529	10631	27933	73964	253467	•
Inventories	24	2285	0	•	•	747	•	3041	6668	11149	20417	61560	251134	•
Net Property, Plant and Equipment	25	2855	0	•	•	649	•	5089	10267	22373	39547	106966	282482	•
Total Assets	26	16413	0	•	•	3577	•	14282	35634	65491	133813	364954	2028003	•
Notes and Loans Payable	27	2581	0	•	•	707	•	5102	16281	13913	35898	94730	218875	•
All Other Liabilities	28	3843	0	•	•	902	•	3879	8979	9854	32051	170008	430451	•
Net Worth	29	9989	0	•	•	1969	•	5300	10374	41724	65864	100216	1378677	•

Selected Financial Ratios (Times to 1)

Current Ratio	30	2.4	•	•	•	2.8	•	1.4	1.8	2.4	2.9	1.6	2.6	•
Quick Ratio	31	1.3	•	•	•	1.8	•	0.8	1.1	1.4	1.7	0.8	1.4	•
Net Sales to Working Capital	32	4.4	•	•	•	4.9	•	11.3	6.8	4.6	4.1	7.2	3.6	•
Coverage Ratio	33	7.9	•	•	•	6.6	•	2.0	1.4	9.0	17.6	1.4	13.0	•
Total Asset Turnover	34	1.0	•	•	•	2.3	•	1.8	1.5	1.4	1.4	1.2	0.8	•
Inventory Turnover	35	5.3	•	•	•	7.6	•	6.7	6.4	6.4	6.8	5.8	4.4	•
Receivables Turnover	36	7.1	•	•	•	7.1	•	7.4	6.4	7.9	9.0	6.3	6.8	•
Total Liabilities to Net Worth	37	0.6	•	•	•	0.8	•	1.7	2.4	0.6	1.0	2.6	0.5	•
Current Assets to Working Capital	38	1.7	•	•	•	1.6	•	3.3	2.2	1.7	1.5	2.8	1.6	•
Current Liabilities to Working Capital	39	0.7	•	•	•	0.6	•	2.3	1.2	0.7	0.5	1.8	0.6	•
Working Capital to Net Sales	40	0.2	•	•	•	0.2	•	0.1	0.1	0.2	0.2	0.1	0.3	•
Inventory to Working Capital	41	0.7	•	•	•	0.5	•	1.3	0.9	0.6	0.6	1.1	0.7	•
Total Receipts to Cash Flow	42	9.2	•	•	•	11.5	•	20.8	21.7	13.4	7.6	17.3	7.7	•
Cost of Goods to Cash Flow	43	6.8	•	•	•	7.8	•	16.3	17.1	10.3	5.4	13.6	5.6	•
Cash Flow to Total Debt	44	0.3	•	•	•	0.5	•	0.1	0.1	0.3	0.4	0.1	0.3	•

Selected Financial Factors (in Percentages)

Debt Ratio	45	39.1	•	•	•	45.0	•	62.9	70.9	36.3	50.8	72.5	32.0	•
Return on Total Assets	46	8.8	•	•	•	6.6	•	3.7	6.3	4.2	13.2	4.8	9.0	•
Return on Equity Before Income Taxes	47	12.6	•	•	•	10.1	•	5.0	6.0	5.8	25.2	5.2	12.2	•
Return on Equity After Income Taxes	48	9.2	•	•	•	9.9	•	1.7	5.5	4.8	23.2	•	8.7	•
Profit Margin (Before Income Tax)	49	7.6	•	•	•	2.4	•	1.0	1.2	2.6	8.6	1.1	11.0	•
Profit Margin (After Income Tax)	50	5.6	•	•	•	2.3	•	0.3	1.1	2.1	7.9	•	7.8	•

Table II

Corporations with Net Income

FOUNDRIES

MONEY AMOUNTS AND SIZE OF ASSETS IN THOUSANDS OF DOLLARS

Item Description for Accounting Period 7/11 Through 6/12		Total	Zero Assets	Under 500	500 to 1,000	1,000 to 5,000	5,000 to 10,000	10,000 to 25,000	25,000 to 50,000	50,000 to 100,000	100,000 to 250,000	250,000 to 500,000	500,000 to 2,500,000	2,500,000 and over
Number of Enterprises	1	528	0	•	0	88	63	33	8	6	•	0	6	0
Revenues ($ in Thousands)														
Net Sales	2	18139868	0	•	0	1126480	900640	748440	417152	523984	•	0	11416406	0
Interest	3	8331	0	•	0	0	0	250	7	155	•	0	5724	0
Rents	4	2953	0	•	0	314	0	898	274	23	•	0	414	0
Royalties	5	15976	0	•	0	0	0	0	0	0	•	0	14552	0
Other Portfolio Income	6	35493	0	•	0	2230	948	147	369	175	•	0	29070	0
Other Receipts	7	111742	0	•	0	734	513	1143	4968	5026	•	0	73832	0
Total Receipts	8	18314363	0	•	0	1129758	902101	750878	422770	529363	•	0	11539998	0
Average Total Receipts	9	34686	•	•	•	12838	14319	22754	52846	88227	•	•	1923333	•
Operating Costs/Operating Income (%)														
Cost of Operations	10	72.3	•	•	•	71.3	72.0	71.8	78.0	76.1	•	•	71.5	•
Salaries and Wages	11	4.0	•	•	•	3.8	3.6	4.9	3.2	3.0	•	•	4.4	•
Taxes Paid	12	1.5	•	•	•	2.4	1.7	2.1	1.8	1.9	•	•	1.3	•
Interest Paid	13	0.8	•	•	•	0.2	1.5	0.7	1.0	0.3	•	•	0.9	•
Depreciation	14	2.5	•	•	•	1.9	2.0	4.0	4.8	3.1	•	•	2.4	•
Amortization and Depletion	15	0.9	•	•	•	•	0.2	0.2	0.1	0.1	•	•	1.3	•
Pensions and Other Deferred Comp.	16	0.6	•	•	•	0.3	0.6	0.2	0.1	0.7	•	•	0.7	•
Employee Benefits	17	1.3	•	•	•	2.3	2.2	2.3	1.3	1.0	•	•	1.1	•
Advertising	18	0.1	•	•	•	0.1	0.1	0.1	0.0	0.1	•	•	0.1	•
Other Expenses	19	4.3	•	•	•	10.8	4.1	4.9	5.4	3.7	•	•	3.2	•
Officers' Compensation	20	1.4	•	•	•	2.2	1.4	3.4	0.7	1.6	•	•	0.8	•
Operating Margin	21	10.2	•	•	•	4.7	10.5	5.3	3.5	8.3	•	•	12.4	•
Operating Margin Before Officers' Comp.	22	11.6	•	•	•	6.9	12.0	8.7	4.2	9.9	•	•	13.2	•

Selected Average Balance Sheet ($ in Thousands)														
Net Receivables	23	4955	•	•	•	1451	2567	3038	8259	8538	•	•	283012	•
Inventories	24	5028	•	•	•	930	2527	3666	6562	12972	•	•	313984	•
Net Property, Plant and Equipment	25	5732	•	•	•	831	1697	3822	12345	20052	•	•	344257	•
Total Assets	26	37081	•	•	•	4520	7479	13396	33477	63329	•	•	2660764	•
Notes and Loans Payable	27	4130	•	•	•	491	3317	2999	12015	14371	•	•	230622	•
All Other Liabilities	28	7438	•	•	•	1368	1938	2861	9204	8297	•	•	479455	•
Net Worth	29	25514	•	•	•	2660	2224	7536	12258	40661	•	•	1950686	•

Selected Financial Ratios (Times to 1)														
Current Ratio	30	2.6	•	•	•	2.4	2.3	2.8	1.8	4.7	•	•	2.6	•
Quick Ratio	31	1.5	•	•	•	1.8	1.1	1.7	1.1	2.5	•	•	1.4	•
Net Sales to Working Capital	32	4.1	•	•	•	6.2	4.5	4.6	6.0	3.0	•	•	3.7	•
Coverage Ratio	33	15.7	•	•	•	21.9	7.9	8.8	5.7	29.1	•	•	16.6	•
Total Asset Turnover	34	0.9	•	•	•	2.8	1.9	1.7	1.6	1.4	•	•	0.7	•
Inventory Turnover	35	4.9	•	•	•	9.8	4.1	4.4	6.2	5.1	•	•	4.3	•
Receivables Turnover	36	6.9	•	•	•	6.4	4.8	5.5	6.0	7.0	•	•	7.1	•
Total Liabilities to Net Worth	37	0.5	•	•	•	0.7	2.4	0.8	1.7	0.6	•	•	0.4	•
Current Assets to Working Capital	38	1.6	•	•	•	1.7	1.8	1.5	2.2	1.3	•	•	1.6	•
Current Liabilities to Working Capital	39	0.6	•	•	•	0.7	0.8	0.5	1.2	0.3	•	•	0.6	•
Working Capital to Net Sales	40	0.2	•	•	•	0.2	0.2	0.2	0.2	0.3	•	•	0.3	•
Inventory to Working Capital	41	0.7	•	•	•	0.4	0.9	0.6	0.8	0.4	•	•	0.7	•
Total Receipts to Cash Flow	42	7.4	•	•	•	9.4	7.7	11.1	14.4	8.0	•	•	6.7	•
Cost of Goods to Cash Flow	43	5.4	•	•	•	6.7	5.6	8.0	11.3	6.1	•	•	4.8	•
Cash Flow to Total Debt	44	0.4	•	•	•	0.7	0.4	0.3	0.2	0.5	•	•	0.4	•

Selected Financial Factors (in Percentages)														
Debt Ratio	45	31.2	•	•	•	41.1	70.3	43.7	63.4	35.8	•	•	26.7	•
Return on Total Assets	46	11.1	•	•	•	14.2	23.4	10.7	9.1	13.4	•	•	10.3	•
Return on Equity Before Income Taxes	47	15.0	•	•	•	23.1	68.8	16.8	20.4	20.1	•	•	13.3	•
Return on Equity After Income Taxes	48	11.4	•	•	•	22.7	68.4	13.0	19.7	18.3	•	•	9.5	•
Profit Margin (Before Income Tax)	49	11.2	•	•	•	4.8	10.7	5.6	4.8	9.4	•	•	13.6	•
Profit Margin (After Income Tax)	50	8.5	•	•	•	4.7	10.6	4.3	4.6	8.5	•	•	9.7	•

Table I

Corporations with and without Net Income

FORGING AND STAMPING

MONEY AMOUNTS AND SIZE OF ASSETS IN THOUSANDS OF DOLLARS

Item Description for Accounting Period 7/11 Through 6/12		Total	Zero Assets	Under 500	500 to 1,000	1,000 to 5,000	5,000 to 10,000	10,000 to 25,000	25,000 to 50,000	50,000 to 100,000	100,000 to 250,000	250,000 to 500,000	500,000 to 2,500,000	2,500,000 and over
Number of Enterprises	1	1935	•	814	332	497	82	121	•	29	17	•	0	0
Revenues ($ in Thousands)														
Net Sales	2	19249412	•	119581	423309	2766283	1106263	3835579	•	2832993	3338566	•	0	0
Interest	3	33402	•	10	85	102	392	1170	•	897	882	•	0	0
Rents	4	4885	•	249	786	59	625	45	•	245	2668	•	0	0
Royalties	5	169	•	0	0	0	0	0	•	0	0	•	0	0
Other Portfolio Income	6	39706	•	15111	0	6028	1456	2201	•	4785	6164	•	0	0
Other Receipts	7	162135	•	1	205	11665	19748	22621	•	34901	25626	•	0	0
Total Receipts	8	19489709	•	134952	424385	2784137	1128484	3861616	•	2873821	3373906	•	0	0
Average Total Receipts	9	10072	•	166	1278	5602	13762	31914	•	99097	198465	•	•	•
Operating Costs/Operating Income (%)														
Cost of Operations	10	73.9	•	74.8	60.6	69.1	66.5	75.7	•	78.4	74.0	•	•	•
Salaries and Wages	11	4.6	•	11.3	1.0	6.5	3.8	4.1	•	5.1	4.2	•	•	•
Taxes Paid	12	1.7	•	7.0	2.7	2.5	2.0	1.7	•	1.5	1.6	•	•	•
Interest Paid	13	1.1	•	0.7	0.4	0.5	0.5	0.5	•	0.8	1.0	•	•	•
Depreciation	14	4.4	•	1.0	1.1	2.5	3.6	4.2	•	4.9	6.3	•	•	•
Amortization and Depletion	15	0.2	•	0.0	0.1	0.0	0.3	0.0	•	0.3	0.2	•	•	•
Pensions and Other Deferred Comp.	16	0.7	•	0.8	0.2	1.4	0.5	0.5	•	0.7	0.4	•	•	•
Employee Benefits	17	1.9	•	3.1	2.3	2.7	1.9	2.3	•	1.7	2.5	•	•	•
Advertising	18	0.1	•	0.0	0.3	0.2	0.1	0.2	•	0.0	0.1	•	•	•
Other Expenses	19	5.5	•	27.2	16.8	5.3	7.9	4.8	•	4.4	5.1	•	•	•
Officers' Compensation	20	2.1	•	5.9	10.1	3.8	3.3	2.7	•	1.3	1.0	•	•	•
Operating Margin	21	3.7	•	•	4.5	5.5	9.8	3.2	•	0.9	3.6	•	•	•
Operating Margin Before Officers' Comp.	22	5.8	•	•	14.6	9.3	13.1	5.9	•	2.2	4.6	•	•	•

Selected Average Balance Sheet ($ in Thousands)													
Net Receivables 23	1455	•	25	215	727	1726	4212	•	16235	33061	•	•	•
Inventories 24	1087	•	15	140	386	1469	3133	•	12966	20207	•	•	•
Net Property, Plant and Equipment 25	1730	•	6	15	507	1914	4263	•	19465	49258	•	•	•
Total Assets 26	7336	•	55	720	2225	7881	14811	•	68843	149418	•	•	•
Notes and Loans Payable 27	2014	•	167	133	482	1751	3509	•	20112	33665	•	•	•
All Other Liabilities 28	1845	•	11	189	542	1099	4316	•	19201	43088	•	•	•
Net Worth 29	3477	•	-123	397	1201	5032	6986	•	29531	72665	•	•	•

Selected Financial Ratios (Times to 1)													
Current Ratio 30	2.2	•	4.4	3.0	2.7	3.8	2.0	•	2.0	2.0	•	•	•
Quick Ratio 31	1.3	•	3.4	2.3	1.8	2.3	1.3	•	1.2	1.2	•	•	•
Net Sales to Working Capital 32	5.2	•	4.0	2.9	5.5	3.9	6.6	•	5.2	5.1	•	•	•
Coverage Ratio 33	5.6	•	•	12.9	13.1	27.0	9.6	•	4.0	5.8	•	•	•
Total Asset Turnover 34	1.4	•	2.7	1.8	2.5	1.7	2.1	•	1.4	1.3	•	•	•
Inventory Turnover 35	6.8	•	7.5	5.5	10.0	6.1	7.7	•	5.9	7.2	•	•	•
Receivables Turnover 36	7.2	•	6.4	6.3	8.4	7.6	7.7	•	6.1	7.0	•	•	•
Total Liabilities to Net Worth 37	1.1	•	•	0.8	0.9	0.6	1.1	•	1.3	1.1	•	•	•
Current Assets to Working Capital 38	1.9	•	1.3	1.5	1.6	1.4	2.0	•	2.0	2.0	•	•	•
Current Liabilities to Working Capital 39	0.9	•	0.3	0.5	0.6	0.4	1.0	•	1.0	1.0	•	•	•
Working Capital to Net Sales 40	0.2	•	0.2	0.3	0.2	0.3	0.2	•	0.2	0.2	•	•	•
Inventory to Working Capital 41	0.6	•	0.2	0.3	0.5	0.4	0.7	•	0.7	0.6	•	•	•
Total Receipts to Cash Flow 42	11.8	•	3321.7	6.2	12.3	6.0	14.9	•	18.7	11.9	•	•	•
Cost of Goods to Cash Flow 43	8.7	•	2485.2	3.8	8.5	4.0	11.3	•	14.6	8.8	•	•	•
Cash Flow to Total Debt 44	0.2	•	0.0	0.6	0.4	0.8	0.3	•	0.1	0.2	•	•	•

Selected Financial Factors (in Percentages)													
Debt Ratio 45	52.6	•	322.0	44.8	46.0	36.2	52.8	•	57.1	51.4	•	•	•
Return on Total Assets 46	8.2	•	•	9.1	16.6	21.0	9.4	•	4.5	7.4	•	•	•
Return on Equity Before Income Taxes 47	14.2	•	22.7	15.2	28.4	31.7	17.8	•	7.8	12.7	•	•	•
Return on Equity After Income Taxes 48	12.6	•	22.7	13.3	27.8	26.8	15.6	•	6.3	11.2	•	•	•
Profit Margin (Before Income Tax) 49	5.0	•	•	4.7	6.1	11.8	3.9	•	2.3	4.7	•	•	•
Profit Margin (After Income Tax) 50	4.4	•	•	4.2	6.0	10.0	3.4	•	1.9	4.1	•	•	•

Table II

Corporations with Net Income

FORGING AND STAMPING

MONEY AMOUNTS AND SIZE OF ASSETS IN THOUSANDS OF DOLLARS

Item Description for Accounting Period 7/11 Through 6/12		Total	Zero Assets	Under 500	500 to 1,000	1,000 to 5,000	5,000 to 10,000	10,000 to 25,000	25,000 to 50,000	50,000 to 100,000	100,000 to 250,000	250,000 to 500,000	500,000 to 2,500,000	2,500,000 and over
Number of Enterprises	1	1385	•	484	•	347	70	93	23	20	13	•	0	0
Revenues ($ in Thousands)														
Net Sales	2	14547087	•	51469	•	2273241	1020819	3286197	1240221	1833571	2443296	•	0	0
Interest	3	3296	•	0	•	80	360	564	91	796	881	•	0	0
Rents	4	4547	•	249	•	0	625	45	0	88	2668	•	0	0
Royalties	5	169	•	0	•	0	0	0	1	0	0	•	0	0
Other Portfolio Income	6	35611	•	15111	•	6028	1456	424	286	3987	5247	•	0	0
Other Receipts	7	89118	•	0	•	6472	19749	11959	14093	7402	7950	•	0	0
Total Receipts	8	14679828	•	66829	•	2285821	1043009	3299189	1254692	1845844	2460042	•	0	0
Average Total Receipts	9	10599	•	138	•	6587	14900	35475	54552	92292	189234	•	•	•
Operating Costs/Operating Income (%)														
Cost of Operations	10	72.2	•	78.2	•	67.6	65.3	75.9	75.2	73.8	72.4	•	•	•
Salaries and Wages	11	4.2	•	•	•	6.9	3.5	3.5	4.3	5.0	3.7	•	•	•
Taxes Paid	12	1.8	•	11.3	•	2.4	2.1	1.7	1.6	1.5	1.5	•	•	•
Interest Paid	13	0.5	•	1.6	•	0.3	0.4	0.4	0.4	0.5	0.5	•	•	•
Depreciation	14	3.6	•	2.2	•	2.5	3.4	3.2	2.5	5.0	6.2	•	•	•
Amortization and Depletion	15	0.2	•	•	•	0.0	0.3	0.0	0.4	0.2	0.2	•	•	•
Pensions and Other Deferred Comp.	16	0.8	•	•	•	1.5	0.5	0.5	0.5	0.9	0.5	•	•	•
Employee Benefits	17	1.9	•	6.1	•	2.6	2.0	1.8	1.4	1.6	2.5	•	•	•
Advertising	18	0.1	•	0.0	•	0.2	0.1	0.2	0.1	0.1	0.1	•	•	•
Other Expenses	19	5.2	•	18.3	•	5.2	7.3	4.8	4.7	5.0	4.8	•	•	•
Officers' Compensation	20	2.2	•	•	•	3.5	3.5	2.6	1.1	1.3	1.3	•	•	•
Operating Margin	21	7.2	•	•	•	7.3	11.7	5.4	7.8	5.1	6.2	•	•	•
Operating Margin Before Officers' Comp.	22	9.4	•	•	•	10.8	15.2	8.0	8.9	6.4	7.5	•	•	•

Selected Average Balance Sheet ($ in Thousands)

Net Receivables	23	1492	•	31	•	830	1844	4664	7987	15358	32902	•	•	•
Inventories	24	1200	•	1	•	407	1499	3331	6706	13729	23807	•	•	•
Net Property, Plant and Equipment	25	1487	•	8	•	436	1845	3488	7109	17038	49559	•	•	•
Total Assets	26	6672	•	46	•	2360	8186	14075	31387	64688	150233	•	•	•
Notes and Loans Payable	27	1150	•	15	•	327	1682	2899	4615	9340	22646	•	•	•
All Other Liabilities	28	1489	•	7	•	509	1113	4387	6815	17743	41765	•	•	•
Net Worth	29	4034	•	24	•	1523	5391	6789	19956	37605	85823	•	•	•

Selected Financial Ratios (Times to 1)

Current Ratio	30	2.5	•	5.8	•	3.3	3.9	2.0	2.6	1.9	2.3	•	•	•
Quick Ratio	31	1.6	•	5.2	•	2.4	2.4	1.4	1.6	1.2	1.4	•	•	•
Net Sales to Working Capital	32	4.7	•	3.4	•	5.2	3.9	7.2	4.5	5.2	4.0	•	•	•
Coverage Ratio	33	16.3	•	8.5	•	23.9	34.1	17.0	24.9	11.5	16.4	•	•	•
Total Asset Turnover	34	1.6	•	2.3	•	2.8	1.8	2.5	1.7	1.4	1.3	•	•	•
Inventory Turnover	35	6.3	•	120.2	•	10.9	6.4	8.1	6.0	4.9	5.7	•	•	•
Receivables Turnover	36	6.7	•	•	•	8.0	7.8	7.3	5.6	5.5	•	•	•	•
Total Liabilities to Net Worth	37	0.7	•	0.9	•	0.5	0.5	1.1	0.6	0.7	0.8	•	•	•
Current Assets to Working Capital	38	1.7	•	1.2	•	1.4	1.3	2.0	1.6	2.1	1.8	•	•	•
Current Liabilities to Working Capital	39	0.7	•	0.2	•	0.4	0.3	1.0	0.6	1.1	0.8	•	•	•
Working Capital to Net Sales	40	0.2	•	0.3	•	0.2	0.3	0.1	0.2	0.2	0.2	•	•	•
Inventory to Working Capital	41	0.5	•	0.0	•	0.4	0.4	0.6	0.6	0.7	0.5	•	•	•
Total Receipts to Cash Flow	42	8.8	•	3.4	•	10.8	5.4	11.5	8.7	10.6	9.3	•	•	•
Cost of Goods to Cash Flow	43	6.3	•	2.7	•	7.3	3.5	8.8	6.6	7.9	6.7	•	•	•
Cash Flow to Total Debt	44	0.5	•	1.4	•	0.7	1.0	0.4	0.5	0.3	0.3	•	•	•

Selected Financial Factors (in Percentages)

Debt Ratio	45	39.5	•	47.3	•	35.5	34.1	51.8	36.4	41.9	42.9	•	•	•
Return on Total Assets	46	13.7	•	31.5	•	22.7	25.4	15.5	16.0	8.9	9.3	•	•	•
Return on Equity Before Income Taxes	47	21.2	•	52.8	•	33.7	37.5	30.2	24.1	14.0	15.3	•	•	•
Return on Equity After Income Taxes	48	19.3	•	52.8	•	33.0	32.1	27.3	21.9	12.3	13.6	•	•	•
Profit Margin (Before Income Tax)	49	8.1	•	12.1	•	7.8	13.9	5.8	8.9	5.7	7.0	•	•	•
Profit Margin (After Income Tax)	50	7.4	•	12.1	•	7.7	11.9	5.2	8.1	5.0	6.2	•	•	•

Table I

Corporations with and without Net Income

CUTLERY, HARDWARE, SPRING AND WIRE MACHINE SHOPS, NUT, BOLT

MONEY AMOUNTS AND SIZE OF ASSETS IN THOUSANDS OF DOLLARS

Item Description for Accounting Period 7/11 Through 6/12		Total	Zero Assets	Under 500	500 to 1,000	1,000 to 5,000	5,000 to 10,000	10,000 to 25,000	25,000 to 50,000	50,000 to 100,000	100,000 to 250,000	250,000 to 500,000	500,000 to 2,500,000	2,500,000 and over
Number of Enterprises	1	19865	2556	11893	1545	2879	431	392	94	36	21	8	10	0
Revenues ($ in Thousands)														
Net Sales	2	65902495	1100074	4815824	3615623	11601263	5214569	10135739	5144595	3597166	3529789	3716647	13431205	0
Interest	3	211445	169	268	942	5121	1891	1974	11683	3482	2201	1036	182679	0
Rents	4	16686	293	1698	0	1077	544	3576	125	983	5901	1	2488	0
Royalties	5	340846	6	0	0	31	0	2388	109	2964	5780	7511	322057	0
Other Portfolio Income	6	264123	19030	8035	1417	32647	2933	31688	4004	11220	11616	63873	77660	0
Other Receipts	7	645370	9911	10043	7179	75881	16074	67109	30509	26710	26183	170484	205287	0
Total Receipts	8	67380965	1129483	4835868	3625161	11716020	5236011	10242474	5191025	3642525	3581470	3959552	14221376	0
Average Total Receipts	9	3392	442	407	2346	4069	12149	26129	55224	101181	170546	494944	1422138	•
Operating Costs/Operating Income (%)														
Cost of Operations	10	65.7	73.9	52.7	54.8	61.9	66.7	68.6	73.2	75.1	73.7	77.4	62.5	•
Salaries and Wages	11	7.2	3.7	8.9	10.5	7.4	4.6	6.3	5.7	5.0	5.6	7.6	9.1	•
Taxes Paid	12	2.2	1.6	2.8	3.8	3.1	2.7	2.1	1.7	1.4	1.5	1.1	1.5	•
Interest Paid	13	1.5	0.9	0.6	0.7	1.1	0.5	1.1	0.6	0.8	1.4	2.1	3.7	•
Depreciation	14	3.6	2.5	1.8	3.0	4.5	4.6	4.6	3.6	4.0	4.2	2.0	2.7	•
Amortization and Depletion	15	0.5	0.2	0.1	0.0	0.1	0.0	0.2	0.4	0.5	0.8	0.7	1.7	•
Pensions and Other Deferred Comp.	16	0.8	0.4	0.1	0.8	0.4	0.4	0.4	0.5	0.9	0.7	0.8	1.8	•
Employee Benefits	17	1.8	0.6	1.2	1.9	2.2	1.6	1.8	1.6	1.1	1.3	1.1	2.5	•
Advertising	18	0.6	0.2	0.7	0.2	0.2	0.3	0.8	0.3	0.7	0.4	0.8	1.3	•
Other Expenses	19	10.3	15.0	16.5	13.3	8.5	7.4	7.8	6.0	6.7	7.6	8.0	15.4	•
Officers' Compensation	20	3.3	4.3	8.0	7.0	5.8	4.8	2.4	1.9	1.3	1.0	0.5	0.6	•
Operating Margin	21	2.5	•	6.7	4.0	4.7	6.3	3.8	4.4	2.6	1.8	•	•	•
Operating Margin Before Officers' Comp.	22	5.7	1.1	14.6	11.0	10.6	11.1	6.2	6.3	3.9	2.9	•	•	•

Selected Average Balance Sheet ($ in Thousands)													
Net Receivables **23**	464	0	25	242	536	1631	3187	7848	14782	24611	86167	256570	•
Inventories **24**	413	0	21	91	332	1707	4074	9400	14561	27865	66091	140157	•
Net Property, Plant and Equipment **25**	436	0	23	173	613	1432	4358	7759	16606	31793	42107	170297	•
Total Assets **26**	3465	0	149	695	2262	6831	15513	35215	70960	149503	385071	3835912	•
Notes and Loans Payable **27**	821	0	73	256	807	1528	5082	8049	19342	33959	175673	649837	•
All Other Liabilities **28**	652	0	28	216	499	1235	2945	10951	21309	49462	83221	565031	•
Net Worth **29**	1992	0	48	222	956	4068	7487	16215	30309	66082	126177	2621044	•
Selected Financial Ratios (Times to 1)													
Current Ratio **30**	2.0	•	2.8	1.8	2.1	3.2	2.1	2.1	2.0	2.0	2.2	1.6	•
Quick Ratio **31**	1.2	•	1.9	1.3	1.4	1.9	1.0	1.0	1.0	1.0	1.2	0.9	•
Net Sales to Working Capital **32**	5.4	•	5.9	10.7	5.9	3.6	5.2	4.6	5.1	4.7	4.5	6.1	•
Coverage Ratio **33**	4.2	0.5	12.8	7.4	6.2	14.7	5.3	9.7	5.7	3.4	3.1	2.1	•
Total Asset Turnover **34**	1.0	•	2.7	3.4	1.8	1.8	1.7	1.6	1.4	1.1	1.2	0.4	•
Inventory Turnover **35**	5.3	•	10.2	14.1	7.5	4.7	4.4	4.3	5.2	4.4	5.4	6.0	•
Receivables Turnover **36**	7.1	•	16.5	9.8	8.3	7.3	8.6	7.7	7.6	6.5	4.5	8.3	•
Total Liabilities to Net Worth **37**	0.7	•	2.1	2.1	1.4	0.7	1.1	1.2	1.3	1.3	2.1	0.5	•
Current Assets to Working Capital **38**	2.0	•	1.6	2.2	1.9	1.5	1.9	1.9	2.0	2.0	1.8	2.6	•
Current Liabilities to Working Capital **39**	1.0	•	0.6	1.2	0.9	0.5	0.9	0.9	1.0	1.0	0.8	1.6	•
Working Capital to Net Sales **40**	0.2	•	0.2	0.1	0.2	0.3	0.2	0.2	0.2	0.2	0.2	0.2	•
Inventory to Working Capital **41**	0.7	•	0.3	0.5	0.5	0.5	0.9	0.9	0.8	0.9	0.5	0.8	•
Total Receipts to Cash Flow **42**	8.0	9.3	5.5	7.8	9.2	8.7	9.5	10.2	10.8	11.1	9.5	5.9	•
Cost of Goods to Cash Flow **43**	5.3	6.9	2.9	4.2	5.7	5.8	6.5	7.5	8.1	8.2	7.3	3.7	•
Cash Flow to Total Debt **44**	0.3	•	0.7	0.6	0.3	0.5	0.3	0.3	0.2	0.2	0.2	0.2	•
Selected Financial Factors (in Percentages)													
Debt Ratio **45**	42.5	•	68.0	68.0	57.7	40.4	51.7	54.0	57.3	55.8	67.2	31.7	•
Return on Total Assets **46**	6.2	•	21.0	16.7	12.2	12.7	9.9	9.2	6.6	5.2	7.9	2.8	•
Return on Equity Before Income Taxes **47**	8.2	•	60.4	45.1	24.2	19.8	16.6	17.9	12.8	8.4	16.3	2.2	•
Return on Equity After Income Taxes **48**	7.2	•	59.8	42.2	22.6	18.4	15.1	16.2	11.0	6.6	11.7	1.5	•
Profit Margin (Before Income Tax) **49**	4.9	•	7.1	4.3	5.7	6.7	4.8	5.3	3.9	3.3	4.4	4.2	•
Profit Margin (After Income Tax) **50**	4.3	•	7.0	4.0	5.4	6.2	4.4	4.8	3.3	2.6	3.2	3.0	•

Table II

Corporations with Net Income

CUTLERY, HARDWARE, SPRING AND WIRE MACHINE SHOPS, NUT, BOLT

MONEY AMOUNTS AND SIZE OF ASSETS IN THOUSANDS OF DOLLARS

Item Description for Accounting Period 7/11 Through 6/12		Total	Zero Assets	Under 500	500 to 1,000	1,000 to 5,000	5,000 to 10,000	10,000 to 25,000	25,000 to 50,000	50,000 to 100,000	100,000 to 250,000	250,000 to 500,000	500,000 to 2,500,000	2,500,000 and over
Number of Enterprises	1	13959	•	7985	1453	1955	379	313	70	•	15	•	7	0
Revenues ($ in Thousands)														
Net Sales	2	55227992	•	3872135	3124160	9030309	4743982	8221106	4099816	•	2395743	•	12426313	0
Interest	3	193725	•	91	634	3530	1608	1869	10765	•	1961	•	169732	0
Rents	4	14487	•	1698	0	282	544	2797	125	•	5901	•	2488	0
Royalties	5	335487	•	0	0	31	0	2388	109	•	1760	•	321339	0
Other Portfolio Income	6	227543	•	5555	1417	31338	2427	29850	2984	•	3269	•	73796	0
Other Receipts	7	426544	•	8514	7180	67903	15437	48988	26168	•	13920	•	189696	0
Total Receipts	8	56425778	•	3887993	3133391	9133393	4763998	8306998	4139967	•	2422554	•	13183364	0
Average Total Receipts	9	4042	•	487	2156	4672	12570	26540	59142	•	161504	•	1883338	•
Operating Costs/Operating Income (%)														
Cost of Operations	10	64.8	•	54.1	52.0	60.4	65.7	67.7	70.8	•	72.2	•	62.1	•
Salaries and Wages	11	7.1	•	6.7	11.6	8.2	4.6	6.1	6.1	•	5.8	•	9.2	•
Taxes Paid	12	2.1	•	2.6	4.0	3.1	2.8	2.1	1.8	•	1.4	•	1.4	•
Interest Paid	13	1.5	•	0.5	0.8	1.0	0.4	0.8	0.5	•	1.3	•	3.6	•
Depreciation	14	3.0	•	1.1	3.1	3.0	4.6	3.7	3.1	•	3.7	•	2.6	•
Amortization and Depletion	15	0.5	•	0.1	0.0	0.1	0.0	0.1	0.1	•	0.6	•	1.6	•
Pensions and Other Deferred Comp.	16	0.8	•	0.0	0.9	0.4	0.4	0.5	0.5	•	0.5	•	1.9	•
Employee Benefits	17	1.8	•	0.9	2.2	2.2	1.7	1.9	1.8	•	1.0	•	2.5	•
Advertising	18	0.7	•	0.8	0.2	0.2	0.3	0.9	0.3	•	0.5	•	1.3	•
Other Expenses	19	10.1	•	15.7	13.7	7.9	7.6	7.6	5.9	•	6.4	•	15.5	•
Officers' Compensation	20	3.1	•	7.1	6.1	6.2	4.4	2.6	2.1	•	1.0	•	0.6	•
Operating Margin	21	4.5	•	10.5	5.5	7.2	7.6	6.0	6.9	•	5.9	•	•	•
Operating Margin Before Officers' Comp.	22	7.6	•	17.5	11.5	13.5	11.9	8.6	9.0	•	6.9	•	•	•

Selected Average Balance Sheet ($ in Thousands)

Net Receivables **23**	559	•	29	257	589	1688	3209	8854	•	23651	•	338163	•
Inventories **24**	464	•	13	91	392	1845	3929	9990	•	29522	•	221292	•
Net Property, Plant and Equipment **25**	459	•	25	157	583	1462	4007	6432	•	29000	•	208750	•
Total Assets **26**	4263	•	116	704	2328	6861	15246	35224	•	146913	•	5212286	•
Notes and Loans Payable **27**	895	•	73	252	814	1418	3858	7186	•	29347	•	795102	•
All Other Liabilities **28**	734	•	21	226	403	1301	2833	8964	•	45816	•	743266	•
Net Worth **29**	2634	•	22	225	1111	4142	8556	19074	•	71750	•	3673919	•

Selected Financial Ratios (Times to 1)

Current Ratio **30**	2.2	•	2.2	1.8	2.8	3.1	2.5	2.4	•	2.2	•	1.6	•
Quick Ratio **31**	1.3	•	1.6	1.3	1.9	1.8	1.2	1.2	•	1.1	•	1.0	•
Net Sales to Working Capital **32**	5.2	•	10.3	9.5	4.8	3.8	4.6	4.1	•	4.1	•	6.0	•
Coverage Ratio **33**	5.7	•	21.2	8.6	9.2	20.8	9.6	16.4	•	6.3	•	2.4	•
Total Asset Turnover **34**	0.9	•	4.2	3.1	2.0	1.8	1.7	1.7	•	1.1	•	0.3	•
Inventory Turnover **35**	5.5	•	20.4	12.2	7.1	4.5	4.5	4.2	•	3.9	•	5.0	•
Receivables Turnover **36**	7.2	•	19.8	8.8	8.0	7.1	8.7	7.5	•	5.5	•	•	•
Total Liabilities to Net Worth **37**	0.6	•	4.2	2.1	1.1	0.7	0.8	0.8	•	1.0	•	0.4	•
Current Assets to Working Capital **38**	1.9	•	1.8	2.3	1.6	1.5	1.7	1.7	•	1.9	•	2.6	•
Current Liabilities to Working Capital **39**	0.9	•	0.8	1.3	0.6	0.5	0.7	0.7	•	0.9	•	1.6	•
Working Capital to Net Sales **40**	0.2	•	0.1	0.1	0.2	0.3	0.2	0.2	•	0.2	•	0.2	•
Inventory to Working Capital **41**	0.6	•	0.3	0.5	0.4	0.5	0.7	0.8	•	0.8	•	0.7	•
Total Receipts to Cash Flow **42**	7.0	•	4.7	7.0	7.8	7.8	7.8	8.1	•	8.2	•	5.6	•
Cost of Goods to Cash Flow **43**	4.5	•	2.5	3.6	4.7	5.1	5.3	5.8	•	5.9	•	3.5	•
Cash Flow to Total Debt **44**	0.3	•	1.1	0.6	0.5	0.6	0.5	0.4	•	0.3	•	0.2	•

Selected Financial Factors (in Percentages)

Debt Ratio **45**	38.2	•	80.8	68.0	52.3	39.6	43.9	45.8	•	51.2	•	29.5	•
Return on Total Assets **46**	7.8	•	47.6	19.9	18.6	15.2	13.6	14.0	•	9.0	•	3.0	•
Return on Equity Before Income Taxes **47**	10.4	•	235.7	54.8	34.8	24.0	21.7	24.2	•	15.5	•	2.5	•
Return on Equity After Income Taxes **48**	9.3	•	233.9	51.7	32.9	22.4	20.0	22.3	•	13.2	•	1.8	•
Profit Margin (Before Income Tax) **49**	6.9	•	10.9	5.7	8.4	8.0	7.1	7.9	•	7.0	•	5.1	•
Profit Margin (After Income Tax) **50**	6.2	•	10.8	5.4	7.9	7.4	6.5	7.2	•	5.9	•	3.8	•

Table I

Corporations with and without Net Income

ARCHITECTURAL AND STRUCTURAL METALS

Item Description for Accounting Period 7/11 Through 6/12		MONEY AMOUNTS AND SIZE OF ASSETS IN THOUSANDS OF DOLLARS Total	Zero Assets	Under 500	500 to 1,000	1,000 to 5,000	5,000 to 10,000	10,000 to 25,000	25,000 to 50,000	50,000 to 100,000	100,000 to 250,000	250,000 to 500,000	500,000 to 2,500,000	2,500,000 and over
Number of Enterprises	1	8263	1522	3532	995	1629	232	233	71	22	12	10	6	0
Revenues ($ in Thousands)														
Net Sales	2	39918851	915844	2118447	1354079	7074189	3966730	6664389	3356246	2445212	2827472	3344540	5851704	0
Interest	3	66168	232	422	153	1430	2127	2404	2915	2360	6602	10332	37191	0
Rents	4	6657	135	0	0	317	183	877	55	41	646	5	4398	0
Royalties	5	44298	3831	0	0	0	0	0	0	0	454	101	39911	0
Other Portfolio Income	6	511010	147756	7268	803	3890	25282	5627	14499	3423	943	31423	270098	0
Other Receipts	7	246435	6848	3404	22002	15742	8461	28701	26589	20471	27769	27123	59325	0
Total Receipts	8	40793419	1074646	2129541	1377037	7095568	4002783	6701998	3400304	2471507	2863886	3413524	6262627	0
Average Total Receipts	9	4937	706	603	1384	4356	17253	28764	47892	112341	238657	341352	1043771	•
Operating Costs/Operating Income (%)														
Cost of Operations	10	71.9	64.3	62.7	66.5	68.9	76.4	75.4	75.3	74.0	72.1	82.7	64.9	•
Salaries and Wages	11	6.8	10.5	5.4	3.5	7.7	4.4	6.8	7.3	5.7	8.1	5.2	8.2	•
Taxes Paid	12	2.1	2.7	2.9	2.6	2.6	2.1	1.8	1.6	1.6	1.7	1.3	2.1	•
Interest Paid	13	1.7	4.8	0.7	0.5	0.5	0.5	0.7	1.4	0.7	1.6	2.2	5.7	•
Depreciation	14	2.8	2.5	1.6	1.0	2.0	2.7	2.1	2.9	3.3	2.2	3.9	4.7	•
Amortization and Depletion	15	0.3	0.7	0.2	0.0	0.0	0.0	0.3	0.3	0.2	0.6	0.9	0.5	•
Pensions and Other Deferred Comp.	16	0.8	0.3	0.4	0.1	0.4	0.2	0.5	0.4	0.5	3.8	0.3	1.6	•
Employee Benefits	17	2.2	2.9	0.5	2.8	3.0	1.4	2.0	1.4	1.3	1.6	1.6	3.4	•
Advertising	18	0.6	0.4	1.0	1.0	0.4	0.2	0.2	0.5	0.4	0.6	0.1	1.5	•
Other Expenses	19	11.3	86.2	14.9	15.8	10.0	7.9	8.0	6.9	7.4	8.6	5.3	14.0	•
Officers' Compensation	20	2.1	1.9	7.0	7.1	3.2	1.5	1.8	1.1	1.4	0.4	1.0	1.0	•
Operating Margin	21	•	•	2.8	•	1.3	2.5	0.6	0.8	3.4	•	•	•	•
Operating Margin Before Officers' Comp.	22	•	•	9.8	6.1	4.5	4.0	2.3	1.9	4.8	•	•	•	•

Selected Average Balance Sheet ($ in Thousands)													
Net Receivables **23**	757	0	67	183	698	2482	4294	6810	20151	29094	57089	212467	•
Inventories **24**	538	0	13	133	319	1680	3391	6303	14344	26131	33564	192968	•
Net Property, Plant and Equipment **25**	783	0	34	102	404	1625	3455	7220	13989	31169	90129	385832	•
Total Assets **26**	3565	0	182	671	2035	7775	15743	33997	73090	167630	310135	1703554	•
Notes and Loans Payable **27**	1095	0	96	221	577	1882	4391	7516	13849	56483	104482	588784	•
All Other Liabilities **28**	942	0	59	152	600	1997	4701	8553	20412	44130	73541	427641	•
Net Worth **29**	1528	0	28	299	858	3897	6651	17928	38829	67017	132111	687129	•
Selected Financial Ratios (Times to 1)													
Current Ratio **30**	2.0	•	1.1	3.3	2.2	2.6	1.7	1.8	2.4	1.9	2.3	1.7	•
Quick Ratio **31**	1.3	•	0.9	2.1	1.7	1.7	1.0	1.1	1.4	1.1	1.5	1.0	•
Net Sales to Working Capital **32**	5.6	•	53.1	3.6	5.3	5.0	6.6	5.2	3.8	6.3	4.0	5.6	•
Coverage Ratio **33**	1.0	•	6.0	2.6	4.3	7.6	2.7	2.5	6.9	0.9	•	1.1	•
Total Asset Turnover **34**	1.4	•	3.3	2.0	2.1	2.2	1.8	1.4	1.5	1.4	1.1	0.6	•
Inventory Turnover **35**	6.5	•	29.9	6.8	9.4	7.8	6.4	5.6	5.7	6.5	8.2	3.3	•
Receivables Turnover **36**	6.1	•	9.4	7.4	5.9	6.5	7.4	6.8	6.4	7.2	6.4	3.5	•
Total Liabilities to Net Worth **37**	1.3	•	5.5	1.2	1.4	1.0	1.4	0.9	0.9	1.5	1.3	1.5	•
Current Assets to Working Capital **38**	2.0	•	11.8	1.4	1.8	1.6	2.3	2.2	1.7	2.1	1.8	2.5	•
Current Liabilities to Working Capital **39**	1.0	•	10.8	0.4	0.8	0.6	1.3	1.2	0.7	1.1	0.8	1.5	•
Working Capital to Net Sales **40**	0.2	•	0.0	0.3	0.2	0.2	0.2	0.2	0.3	0.2	0.3	0.2	•
Inventory to Working Capital **41**	0.6	•	0.8	0.4	0.4	0.5	0.9	0.6	0.6	0.7	0.4	0.7	•
Total Receipts to Cash Flow **42**	13.4	7.6	8.7	8.1	12.1	12.3	13.8	14.5	9.5	16.0	95.9	16.3	•
Cost of Goods to Cash Flow **43**	9.6	4.9	5.5	5.4	8.3	9.4	10.4	10.9	7.0	11.5	79.4	10.6	•
Cash Flow to Total Debt **44**	0.2	•	0.4	0.5	0.3	0.4	0.2	0.2	0.3	0.1	0.0	0.1	•
Selected Financial Factors (in Percentages)													
Debt Ratio **45**	57.1	•	84.6	55.5	57.8	49.9	57.8	47.3	46.9	60.0	57.4	59.7	•
Return on Total Assets **46**	2.2	•	13.1	2.5	4.4	8.7	3.2	4.8	7.8	2.2	•	3.6	•
Return on Equity Before Income Taxes **47**	•	•	71.1	3.5	8.0	15.0	4.8	5.4	12.6	•	•	0.8	•
Return on Equity After Income Taxes **48**	•	•	69.9	3.4	7.6	13.7	4.4	4.2	11.5	•	•	•	•
Profit Margin (Before Income Tax) **49**	•	•	3.3	0.8	1.6	3.4	1.1	2.0	4.4	•	•	0.5	•
Profit Margin (After Income Tax) **50**	•	•	3.3	0.8	1.5	3.1	1.0	1.6	4.0	•	•	•	•

Table II

Corporations with Net Income

ARCHITECTURAL AND STRUCTURAL METALS

MONEY AMOUNTS AND SIZE OF ASSETS IN THOUSANDS OF DOLLARS

Item Description for Accounting Period 7/11 Through 6/12		Total	Zero Assets	Under 500	500 to 1,000	1,000 to 5,000	5,000 to 10,000	10,000 to 25,000	25,000 to 50,000	50,000 to 100,000	100,000 to 250,000	250,000 to 500,000	500,000 to 2,500,000	2,500,000 and over
Number of Enterprises	1	4511	382	1972	•	1216	192	150	52	18	•	7	0	0
Revenues ($ in Thousands)														
Net Sales	2	27107060	313233	1203530	•	5422285	3726011	4939519	2475363	2210968	•	3558868	0	0
Interest	3	28319	77	110	•	188	591	1452	2139	2056	•	18421	0	0
Rents	4	1865	0	0	•	0	175	303	55	40	•	645	0	0
Royalties	5	17704	0	0	•	0	0	0	0	0	•	17493	0	0
Other Portfolio Income	6	94542	11151	199	•	2072	24955	5612	14154	3191	•	32462	0	0
Other Receipts	7	135770	1134	635	•	12526	6149	17823	20188	18151	•	21056	0	0
Total Receipts	8	27385260	325595	1204474	•	5437071	3757881	4964709	2511899	2234406	•	3648945	0	0
Average Total Receipts	9	6071	852	611	•	4471	19572	33098	48306	124134	•	521278	•	•
Operating Costs/Operating Income (%)														
Cost of Operations	10	71.5	59.7	58.9	•	67.8	75.7	72.4	75.9	74.1	•	72.8	•	•
Salaries and Wages	11	5.9	11.7	0.8	•	6.8	4.3	7.1	5.7	4.8	•	5.9	•	•
Taxes Paid	12	1.9	3.2	2.6	•	2.3	2.1	1.7	1.6	1.7	•	1.4	•	•
Interest Paid	13	0.8	0.8	0.5	•	0.5	0.5	0.5	0.6	0.8	•	2.0	•	•
Depreciation	14	2.4	0.8	2.1	•	2.2	2.7	1.7	3.1	3.0	•	3.7	•	•
Amortization and Depletion	15	0.2	0.2	•	•	0.0	0.0	0.1	0.1	0.2	•	0.6	•	•
Pensions and Other Deferred Comp.	16	0.4	0.7	0.7	•	0.4	0.1	0.3	0.5	0.5	•	0.9	•	•
Employee Benefits	17	1.9	1.6	0.4	•	2.9	1.5	1.9	1.0	1.0	•	2.2	•	•
Advertising	18	0.4	0.5	1.4	•	0.2	0.2	0.2	0.4	0.4	•	0.7	•	•
Other Expenses	19	8.6	10.2	16.3	•	9.2	7.7	8.6	5.6	6.6	•	7.9	•	•
Officers' Compensation	20	2.0	3.0	7.5	•	3.1	1.1	1.7	1.1	1.4	•	0.8	•	•
Operating Margin	21	4.1	7.7	8.8	•	4.7	4.0	3.6	4.5	5.6	•	1.1	•	•
Operating Margin Before Officers' Comp.	22	6.0	10.7	16.3	•	7.8	5.1	5.3	5.6	7.0	•	1.9	•	•

	Selected Average Balance Sheet ($ in Thousands)												
Net Receivables 23	892	0	68	•	729	2668	4350	6683	21233	•	101258	•	•
Inventories 24	592	0	13	•	263	1382	4006	5986	14680	•	30650	•	•
Net Property, Plant and Equipment 25	712	0	38	•	414	1741	3563	7832	14778	•	104057	•	•
Total Assets 26	3833	0	219	•	2049	7733	16071	33853	74652	•	763538	•	•
Notes and Loans Payable 27	1087	0	130	•	423	2104	3668	5241	12144	•	277546	•	•
All Other Liabilities 28	933	0	53	•	638	1798	4263	8691	19961	•	150777	•	•
Net Worth 29	1813	0	37	•	987	3830	8140	19921	42547	•	335215	•	•
	Selected Financial Ratios (Times to 1)												
Current Ratio 30	2.0	•	1.1	•	2.1	2.4	2.0	2.1	2.5	•	1.5	•	•
Quick Ratio 31	1.3	•	0.8	•	1.6	1.6	1.1	1.3	1.4	•	1.0	•	•
Net Sales to Working Capital 32	5.7	•	67.7	•	5.8	5.6	6.0	4.6	4.1	•	6.1	•	•
Coverage Ratio 33	7.6	16.0	19.7	•	12.0	10.1	9.2	11.6	9.4	•	3.2	•	•
Total Asset Turnover 34	1.6	•	2.8	•	2.2	2.5	2.0	1.4	1.6	•	0.7	•	•
Inventory Turnover 35	7.3	•	28.7	•	11.5	10.6	6.0	6.0	6.2	•	12.1	•	•
Receivables Turnover 36	7.2	•	•	•	7.8	10.4	7.9	7.9	7.2	•	7.6	•	•
Total Liabilities to Net Worth 37	1.1	•	5.0	•	1.1	1.0	1.0	0.7	0.8	•	1.3	•	•
Current Assets to Working Capital 38	2.0	•	17.7	•	1.9	1.7	2.0	1.9	1.7	•	2.9	•	•
Current Liabilities to Working Capital 39	1.0	•	16.7	•	0.9	0.7	1.0	0.9	0.7	•	1.9	•	•
Working Capital to Net Sales 40	0.2	•	0.0	•	0.2	0.2	0.2	0.2	0.2	•	0.2	•	•
Inventory to Working Capital 41	0.6	•	1.4	•	0.3	0.5	0.8	0.6	0.6	•	0.6	•	•
Total Receipts to Cash Flow 42	9.0	5.7	5.8	•	9.0	10.8	9.2	10.3	8.3	•	10.2	•	•
Cost of Goods to Cash Flow 43	6.5	3.4	3.4	•	6.1	8.1	6.6	7.8	6.1	•	7.4	•	•
Cash Flow to Total Debt 44	0.3	•	0.6	•	0.5	0.5	0.5	0.3	0.5	•	0.1	•	•
	Selected Financial Factors (in Percentages)												
Debt Ratio 45	52.7	•	83.2	•	51.8	50.5	49.3	41.2	43.0	•	56.1	•	•
Return on Total Assets 46	9.3	•	26.0	•	11.8	13.5	9.5	9.2	12.2	•	4.2	•	•
Return on Equity Before Income Taxes 47	17.1	•	147.4	•	22.5	24.6	16.7	14.3	19.1	•	6.5	•	•
Return on Equity After Income Taxes 48	15.7	•	145.7	•	22.0	23.0	16.1	12.8	17.8	•	4.5	•	•
Profit Margin (Before Income Tax) 49	5.2	11.6	8.9	•	5.0	4.9	4.1	6.0	6.6	•	4.3	•	•
Profit Margin (After Income Tax) 50	4.7	10.7	8.8	•	4.9	4.5	4.0	5.4	6.2	•	3.0	•	•

Table I

Corporations with and without Net Income

BOILER, TANK, AND SHIPPING CONTAINER

Item Description for Accounting Period 7/11 Through 6/12		Money Amounts and Size of Assets in Thousands of Dollars												
		Total	Zero Assets	Under 500	500 to 1,000	1,000 to 5,000	5,000 to 10,000	10,000 to 25,000	25,000 to 50,000	50,000 to 100,000	100,000 to 250,000	250,000 to 500,000	500,000 to 2,500,000	2,500,000 and over
Number of Enterprises	1	511	•	0	202	175	19	60	•	15	8	4	•	•
Revenues ($ in Thousands)														
Net Sales	2	25518881	•	0	337351	871498	240593	1668338	•	1524324	1294591	1440876	•	•
Interest	3	23215	•	0	0	234	3	516	•	908	308	75	•	•
Rents	4	9564	•	0	0	2121	0	657	•	41	123	0	•	•
Royalties	5	131828	•	0	0	0	0	0	•	5067	19	30	•	•
Other Portfolio Income	6	239406	•	0	528	14	1739	4231	•	3142	3541	67	•	•
Other Receipts	7	193268	•	0	2556	161	1209	6840	•	5345	16324	6334	•	•
Total Receipts	8	26116162	•	0	340435	874028	243544	1680582	•	1538827	1314906	1447382	•	•
Average Total Receipts	9	51108	•	•	1685	4994	12818	28010	•	102588	164363	361846	•	•
Operating Costs/Operating Income (%)														
Cost of Operations	10	77.4	•	•	55.2	71.5	81.4	75.6	•	73.4	67.7	82.8	•	•
Salaries and Wages	11	3.3	•	•	8.1	4.7	6.8	5.0	•	5.8	4.8	3.5	•	•
Taxes Paid	12	1.2	•	•	3.2	2.6	0.5	2.1	•	1.8	1.3	2.7	•	•
Interest Paid	13	2.7	•	•	0.7	0.0	1.3	0.5	•	1.1	4.1	3.4	•	•
Depreciation	14	4.2	•	•	2.8	1.1	4.2	2.5	•	3.2	6.2	2.4	•	•
Amortization and Depletion	15	0.8	•	•	•	•	0.3	0.1	•	0.4	0.8	0.4	•	•
Pensions and Other Deferred Comp.	16	1.8	•	•	0.5	1.1	0.1	0.3	•	0.4	0.3	0.1	•	•
Employee Benefits	17	1.5	•	•	1.4	2.2	•	2.1	•	2.4	1.3	1.2	•	•
Advertising	18	0.2	•	•	0.4	0.8	0.2	0.1	•	0.4	0.3	0.1	•	•
Other Expenses	19	5.4	•	•	10.5	6.7	6.0	5.8	•	5.9	7.0	2.4	•	•
Officers' Compensation	20	1.0	•	•	7.9	3.0	0.7	1.7	•	1.5	0.8	1.0	•	•
Operating Margin	21	0.5	•	•	9.3	6.4	•	4.4	•	3.8	5.4	•	•	•
Operating Margin Before Officers' Comp.	22	1.5	•	•	17.2	9.4	•	6.1	•	5.3	6.2	0.8	•	•

Selected Average Balance Sheet ($ in Thousands)													
Net Receivables **23**	5314	•	•	78	709	1462	3858	•	16577	20150	62871	•	•
Inventories **24**	5985	•	•	101	700	1559	2912	•	13789	12023	96724	•	•
Net Property, Plant and Equipment **25**	7843	•	•	380	100	2482	2633	•	15316	33224	43796	•	•
Total Assets **26**	49355	•	•	730	2209	8327	17354	•	70552	176302	373557	•	•
Notes and Loans Payable **27**	23835	•	•	176	64	2969	3286	•	19540	81549	127953	•	•
All Other Liabilities **28**	15261	•	•	45	789	3237	4510	•	21867	36369	195585	•	•
Net Worth **29**	10259	•	•	508	1356	2121	9558	•	29145	58384	50019	•	•
Selected Financial Ratios (Times to 1)													
Current Ratio **30**	1.5	•	•	4.5	2.7	1.8	3.3	•	1.5	1.9	1.2	•	•
Quick Ratio **31**	0.8	•	•	2.9	1.7	0.9	2.1	•	0.8	1.0	0.5	•	•
Net Sales to Working Capital **32**	9.2	•	•	6.1	3.9	5.5	3.6	•	7.1	4.7	14.9	•	•
Coverage Ratio **33**	2.2	•	•	14.7	219.3	0.7	11.9	•	5.3	2.7	1.1	•	•
Total Asset Turnover **34**	1.0	•	•	2.3	2.3	1.5	1.6	•	1.4	0.9	1.0	•	•
Inventory Turnover **35**	6.5	•	•	9.2	5.1	6.6	7.2	•	5.4	9.1	3.1	•	•
Receivables Turnover **36**	10.3	•	•	•	8.2	7.7	8.5	•	6.5	9.6	5.6	•	•
Total Liabilities to Net Worth **37**	3.8	•	•	0.4	0.6	2.9	0.8	•	1.4	2.0	6.5	•	•
Current Assets to Working Capital **38**	2.9	•	•	1.3	1.6	2.3	1.4	•	2.8	2.2	7.1	•	•
Current Liabilities to Working Capital **39**	1.9	•	•	0.3	0.6	1.3	0.4	•	1.8	1.2	6.1	•	•
Working Capital to Net Sales **40**	0.1	•	•	0.2	0.3	0.2	0.3	•	0.1	0.2	0.1	•	•
Inventory to Working Capital **41**	1.1	•	•	0.4	0.6	0.9	0.4	•	1.1	0.4	3.5	•	•
Total Receipts to Cash Flow **42**	15.3	•	•	7.4	9.7	26.6	10.8	•	11.0	7.8	84.9	•	•
Cost of Goods to Cash Flow **43**	11.8	•	•	4.1	7.0	21.6	8.2	•	8.1	5.3	70.3	•	•
Cash Flow to Total Debt **44**	0.1	•	•	1.0	0.6	0.1	0.3	•	0.2	0.2	0.0	•	•
Selected Financial Factors (in Percentages)													
Debt Ratio **45**	79.2	•	•	30.3	38.6	74.5	44.9	•	58.7	66.9	86.6	•	•
Return on Total Assets **46**	5.8	•	•	25.1	15.1	1.3	9.0	•	8.4	10.1	3.7	•	•
Return on Equity Before Income Taxes **47**	15.0	•	•	33.5	24.5	•	14.9	•	16.5	19.4	3.3	•	•
Return on Equity After Income Taxes **48**	11.3	•	•	33.3	19.7	•	13.6	•	14.1	16.1	3.2	•	•
Profit Margin (Before Income Tax) **49**	3.1	•	•	10.2	6.7	•	5.1	•	4.7	7.0	0.5	•	•
Profit Margin (After Income Tax) **50**	2.3	•	•	10.1	5.4	•	4.7	•	4.0	5.8	0.4	•	•

Table II

Corporations with Net Income

BOILER, TANK, AND SHIPPING CONTAINER

MONEY AMOUNTS AND SIZE OF ASSETS IN THOUSANDS OF DOLLARS

Item Description for Accounting Period 7/11 Through 6/12		Total	Zero Assets	Under 500	500 to 1,000	1,000 to 5,000	5,000 to 10,000	10,000 to 25,000	25,000 to 50,000	50,000 to 100,000	100,000 to 250,000	250,000 to 500,000	500,000 to 2,500,000	2,500,000 and over
Number of Enterprises	1	456	0	0	202	147	9	53	18	11	•	•	•	•
Revenues ($ in Thousands)														
Net Sales	2	20521487	0	0	337351	715929	151597	1572914	870605	1190590	•	•	•	•
Interest	3	20385	0	0	0	234	3	482	109	715	•	•	•	•
Rents	4	9142	0	0	0	2121	0	657	0	4	•	•	•	•
Royalties	5	36896	0	0	0	0	0	0	0	1655	•	•	•	•
Other Portfolio Income	6	155075	0	0	528	14	1739	4231	234	1031	•	•	•	•
Other Receipts	7	171916	0	0	2556	161	99	4786	6076	4190	•	•	•	•
Total Receipts	8	20914901	0	0	340435	718459	153438	1583070	877024	1198185	•	•	•	•
Average Total Receipts	9	45866	•	•	1685	4887	17049	29869	48724	108926	•	•	•	•
Operating Costs/Operating Income (%)														
Cost of Operations	10	76.6	•	•	55.2	67.1	80.5	75.2	72.4	72.4	•	•	•	•
Salaries and Wages	11	3.4	•	•	8.1	5.6	6.3	5.0	4.7	5.1	•	•	•	•
Taxes Paid	12	1.1	•	•	3.2	2.6	0.7	2.0	1.7	1.9	•	•	•	•
Interest Paid	13	2.2	•	•	0.7	0.0	1.5	0.5	0.8	1.2	•	•	•	•
Depreciation	14	4.2	•	•	2.8	1.3	5.6	2.5	1.1	3.2	•	•	•	•
Amortization and Depletion	15	0.9	•	•	•	•	0.4	0.1	0.2	0.4	•	•	•	•
Pensions and Other Deferred Comp.	16	0.7	•	•	0.5	1.3	0.2	0.2	0.8	0.5	•	•	•	•
Employee Benefits	17	1.5	•	•	1.4	2.3	•	2.2	1.2	2.1	•	•	•	•
Advertising	18	0.2	•	•	0.4	0.9	0.4	0.1	1.1	0.5	•	•	•	•
Other Expenses	19	5.4	•	•	10.5	7.1	3.1	5.6	6.7	5.4	•	•	•	•
Officers' Compensation	20	1.1	•	•	7.9	3.1	0.8	1.6	2.2	1.4	•	•	•	•
Operating Margin	21	2.7	•	•	9.3	8.6	0.6	5.1	7.1	6.0	•	•	•	•
Operating Margin Before Officers' Comp.	22	3.8	•	•	17.2	11.7	1.4	6.7	9.3	7.4	•	•	•	•

Selected Average Balance Sheet ($ in Thousands)

Net Receivables	23	4660	•	•	78	716	1758	4159	7539	14499	•	•	•	•
Inventories	24	5991	•	•	110	810	985	2954	7582	15676	•	•	•	•
Net Property, Plant and Equipment	25	7319	•	•	380	89	3278	2708	5118	14859	•	•	•	•
Total Assets	26	41077	•	•	730	2414	7269	17888	31650	70628	•	•	•	•
Notes and Loans Payable	27	16391	•	•	176	69	4572	3423	6550	19860	•	•	•	•
All Other Liabilities	28	12774	•	•	45	867	2126	4834	6515	19069	•	•	•	•
Net Worth	29	11912	•	•	508	1478	571	9630	18585	31699	•	•	•	•

Selected Financial Ratios (Times to 1)

Current Ratio	30	1.6	•	•	4.5	2.7	1.1	3.3	2.5	2.1	•	•	•	•
Quick Ratio	31	0.8	•	•	2.9	1.6	0.5	2.1	1.4	1.0	•	•	•	•
Net Sales to Working Capital	32	8.1	•	•	6.1	3.4	39.2	3.7	3.7	5.2	•	•	•	•
Coverage Ratio	33	3.1	•	•	14.7	241.8	2.2	13.8	10.6	6.5	•	•	•	•
Total Asset Turnover	34	1.1	•	•	2.3	2.0	2.3	1.7	1.5	1.5	•	•	•	•
Inventory Turnover	35	5.8	•	•	8.4	4.0	13.8	7.6	4.6	5.0	•	•	•	•
Receivables Turnover	36	9.8	•	•	23.1	7.4	10.9	8.7	7.1	7.0	•	•	•	•
Total Liabilities to Net Worth	37	2.4	•	•	0.4	0.6	11.7	0.9	0.7	1.2	•	•	•	•
Current Assets to Working Capital	38	2.6	•	•	1.3	1.6	8.5	1.4	1.7	1.9	•	•	•	•
Current Liabilities to Working Capital	39	1.6	•	•	0.3	0.6	7.5	0.4	0.7	0.9	•	•	•	•
Working Capital to Net Sales	40	0.1	•	•	0.2	0.3	0.0	0.3	0.3	0.2	•	•	•	•
Inventory to Working Capital	41	1.1	•	•	0.4	0.6	3.5	0.4	0.6	0.9	•	•	•	•
Total Receipts to Cash Flow	42	12.2	•	•	7.4	7.9	24.0	10.4	7.7	9.5	•	•	•	•
Cost of Goods to Cash Flow	43	9.3	•	•	4.1	5.3	19.3	7.8	5.6	6.9	•	•	•	•
Cash Flow to Total Debt	44	0.1	•	•	1.0	0.7	0.1	0.3	0.5	0.3	•	•	•	•

Selected Financial Factors (in Percentages)

Debt Ratio	45	71.0	•	•	30.3	38.8	92.1	46.2	41.3	55.1	•	•	•	•
Return on Total Assets	46	7.6	•	•	25.1	18.1	7.7	10.4	13.3	11.9	•	•	•	•
Return on Equity Before Income Taxes	47	17.8	•	•	33.5	29.5	53.1	17.8	20.5	22.4	•	•	•	•
Return on Equity After Income Taxes	48	14.3	•	•	33.3	24.3	35.3	16.4	19.8	19.4	•	•	•	•
Profit Margin (Before Income Tax)	49	4.7	•	•	10.2	8.9	1.8	5.8	7.9	6.6	•	•	•	•
Profit Margin (After Income Tax)	50	3.8	•	•	10.1	7.4	1.2	5.3	7.6	5.7	•	•	•	•

Table I

Corporations with and without Net Income

COATING, ENGRAVING, HEAT TREATING, AND ALLIED ACTIVITIES

MONEY AMOUNTS AND SIZE OF ASSETS IN THOUSANDS OF DOLLARS

Item Description for Accounting Period 7/11 Through 6/12		Total	Zero Assets	Under 500	500 to 1,000	1,000 to 5,000	5,000 to 10,000	10,000 to 25,000	25,000 to 50,000	50,000 to 100,000	100,000 to 250,000	250,000 to 500,000	500,000 to 2,500,000	2,500,000 and over
Number of Enterprises	1	2701	274	1033	542	667	69	81	•	7	10	0	•	•
Revenues ($ in Thousands)														
Net Sales	2	12428181	69782	911779	634772	3057401	646610	1471754	•	689519	1519354	0	•	•
Interest	3	8511	383	99	80	327	712	599	•	111	5078	0	•	•
Rents	4	10481	0	0	631	2428	571	1085	•	0	2728	0	•	•
Royalties	5	25293	1378	0	0	0	0	0	•	0	14894	0	•	•
Other Portfolio Income	6	90655	17	151	0	37072	11636	738	•	48	10101	0	•	•
Other Receipts	7	111866	3495	2741	1507	33985	7772	7269	•	-3249	15850	0	•	•
Total Receipts	8	12674987	75055	914770	636990	3131213	667301	1481445	•	686429	1568005	0	•	•
Average Total Receipts	9	4693	274	886	1175	4694	9671	18289	•	98061	156800	•	•	•
Operating Costs/Operating Income (%)														
Cost of Operations	10	60.6	63.8	46.6	36.7	52.9	52.7	63.6	•	69.8	58.6	•	•	•
Salaries and Wages	11	7.9	13.8	9.4	9.4	11.5	9.5	6.3	•	7.5	8.9	•	•	•
Taxes Paid	12	2.6	0.9	2.4	3.1	3.7	2.5	2.7	•	1.8	2.2	•	•	•
Interest Paid	13	2.3	6.5	0.2	0.2	0.7	0.8	1.8	•	0.6	3.2	•	•	•
Depreciation	14	3.9	2.1	2.0	4.3	3.1	7.1	4.1	•	2.2	5.6	•	•	•
Amortization and Depletion	15	0.4	0.1	•	•	0.0	0.5	0.2	•	0.2	1.4	•	•	•
Pensions and Other Deferred Comp.	16	0.7	0.1	0.1	0.8	0.9	1.4	0.9	•	0.6	0.5	•	•	•
Employee Benefits	17	2.3	0.9	2.9	1.5	2.7	2.7	1.5	•	1.8	2.1	•	•	•
Advertising	18	0.2	0.1	0.0	0.1	0.2	0.2	0.3	•	0.3	0.2	•	•	•
Other Expenses	19	10.6	32.2	12.0	29.2	13.0	12.6	8.9	•	5.1	11.5	•	•	•
Officers' Compensation	20	4.6	0.2	18.1	4.5	7.8	4.5	3.0	•	1.3	1.4	•	•	•
Operating Margin	21	3.9	•	6.3	10.3	3.6	5.5	6.8	•	8.8	4.6	•	•	•
Operating Margin Before Officers' Comp.	22	8.5	•	24.3	14.8	11.4	10.1	9.8	•	10.1	6.0	•	•	•

Selected Average Balance Sheet ($ in Thousands)

Net Receivables 23	600	0	72	111	582	879	3019	•	10789	22413	•	•	•
Inventories 24	349	0	4	90	148	625	1158	•	10771	13719	•	•	•
Net Property, Plant and Equipment 25	1081	0	115	107	668	2818	5241	•	22201	55892	•	•	•
Total Assets 26	3822	0	267	626	2046	7392	14575	•	63849	185939	•	•	•
Notes and Loans Payable 27	1674	0	56	80	601	1585	6894	•	14854	76276	•	•	•
All Other Liabilities 28	823	0	49	158	392	957	2046	•	13799	50705	•	•	•
Net Worth 29	1325	0	161	389	1053	4851	5635	•	35195	58959	•	•	•

Selected Financial Ratios (Times to 1)

Current Ratio 30	2.0	•	1.7	3.9	2.2	4.0	1.7	•	2.0	1.5	•	•	•
Quick Ratio 31	1.3	•	1.6	2.8	1.7	3.2	1.3	•	1.1	0.9	•	•	•
Net Sales to Working Capital 32	6.7	•	15.6	3.5	7.8	3.6	7.3	•	6.0	7.9	•	•	•
Coverage Ratio 33	3.6	•	34.2	47.0	9.8	12.6	5.1	•	16.1	3.5	•	•	•
Total Asset Turnover 34	1.2	•	3.3	1.9	2.2	1.3	1.2	•	1.5	0.8	•	•	•
Inventory Turnover 35	8.0	•	116.4	4.8	16.4	7.9	10.0	•	6.4	6.5	•	•	•
Receivables Turnover 36	7.2	•	13.0	•	8.0	7.0	6.3	•	8.6	8.7	•	•	•
Total Liabilities to Net Worth 37	1.9	•	0.7	0.6	0.9	0.5	1.6	•	0.8	2.2	•	•	•
Current Assets to Working Capital 38	2.1	•	2.5	1.3	1.8	1.3	2.4	•	2.0	2.8	•	•	•
Current Liabilities to Working Capital 39	1.1	•	1.5	0.3	0.8	0.3	1.4	•	1.0	1.8	•	•	•
Working Capital to Net Sales 40	0.2	•	0.1	0.3	0.1	0.3	0.1	•	0.2	0.1	•	•	•
Inventory to Working Capital 41	0.5	•	0.0	0.3	0.3	0.2	0.4	•	0.7	1.0	•	•	•
Total Receipts to Cash Flow 42	7.6	9.6	6.7	2.8	7.5	5.9	7.4	•	8.1	6.2	•	•	•
Cost of Goods to Cash Flow 43	4.6	6.1	3.1	1.0	4.0	3.1	4.7	•	5.7	3.7	•	•	•
Cash Flow to Total Debt 44	0.2	•	1.2	1.8	0.6	0.6	0.3	•	0.4	0.2	•	•	•

Selected Financial Factors (in Percentages)

Debt Ratio 45	65.3	•	39.6	37.9	48.5	34.4	61.3	•	44.9	68.3	•	•	•
Return on Total Assets 46	9.9	•	22.4	20.4	15.0	12.0	11.5	•	13.8	9.1	•	•	•
Return on Equity Before Income Taxes 47	20.7	•	36.0	32.2	26.1	16.8	23.9	•	23.6	20.6	•	•	•
Return on Equity After Income Taxes 48	18.3	•	36.0	30.2	24.9	16.8	22.7	•	21.8	14.1	•	•	•
Profit Margin (Before Income Tax) 49	6.0	•	6.6	10.7	6.0	8.7	7.4	•	8.4	8.0	•	•	•
Profit Margin (After Income Tax) 50	5.3	•	6.6	10.0	5.7	8.7	7.0	•	7.8	5.5	•	•	•

Table II

Corporations with Net Income

COATING, ENGRAVING, HEAT TREATING, AND ALLIED ACTIVITIES

MONEY AMOUNTS AND SIZE OF ASSETS IN THOUSANDS OF DOLLARS

Item Description for Accounting Period 7/11 Through 6/12		Total	Zero Assets	Under 500	500 to 1,000	1,000 to 5,000	5,000 to 10,000	10,000 to 25,000	25,000 to 50,000	50,000 to 100,000	100,000 to 250,000	250,000 to 500,000	500,000 to 2,500,000	2,500,000 and over
Number of Enterprises	1	1579	•	417	388	635	42	68	11	•	•	3	0	0
Revenues ($ in Thousands)														
Net Sales	2	9536363	•	579200	574235	3023089	540601	1252070	630762	•	•	1188379	0	0
Interest	3	6851	•	1	65	312	5	309	73	•	•	1485	0	0
Rents	4	8443	•	0	0	2428	0	1085	2043	•	•	256	0	0
Royalties	5	16271	•	0	0	0	0	0	0	•	•	0	0	0
Other Portfolio Income	6	57010	•	9	0	36866	8351	738	103	•	•	797	0	0
Other Receipts	7	99354	•	20	1507	29461	7473	18392	887	•	•	31074	0	0
Total Receipts	8	9724292	•	579230	575807	3092156	556430	1272594	633868	•	•	1221991	0	0
Average Total Receipts	9	6159	•	1389	1484	4870	13248	18715	57624	•	•	407330	•	•
Operating Costs/Operating Income (%)														
Cost of Operations	10	55.7	•	29.1	32.5	53.0	51.1	60.7	76.0	•	•	54.9	•	•
Salaries and Wages	11	8.7	•	12.8	8.3	11.2	9.2	6.4	3.3	•	•	7.4	•	•
Taxes Paid	12	2.7	•	2.1	1.7	3.6	2.4	2.8	2.7	•	•	2.6	•	•
Interest Paid	13	1.3	•	0.1	0.3	0.7	0.5	1.7	0.6	•	•	4.1	•	•
Depreciation	14	3.5	•	2.3	4.6	3.0	3.0	4.1	3.3	•	•	4.6	•	•
Amortization and Depletion	15	0.3	•	•	•	0.0	0.6	0.1	0.0	•	•	0.6	•	•
Pensions and Other Deferred Comp.	16	0.8	•	•	0.8	0.9	1.6	1.0	0.5	•	•	1.5	•	•
Employee Benefits	17	2.4	•	3.0	0.9	2.7	3.0	1.5	1.6	•	•	3.6	•	•
Advertising	18	0.2	•	0.0	0.1	0.2	0.1	0.2	0.1	•	•	0.3	•	•
Other Expenses	19	11.0	•	8.5	29.9	12.7	11.2	7.8	2.6	•	•	11.7	•	•
Officers' Compensation	20	5.6	•	27.4	3.5	7.8	4.6	3.2	1.8	•	•	1.7	•	•
Operating Margin	21	7.8	•	14.8	17.4	4.2	12.7	10.3	7.5	•	•	7.1	•	•
Operating Margin Before Officers' Comp.	22	13.4	•	42.2	20.9	11.9	17.3	13.6	9.2	•	•	8.7	•	•

Selected Average Balance Sheet ($ in Thousands)														
Net Receivables	23	793	•	109	129	605	1381	3020	8710	•	•	60583	•	•
Inventories	24	383	•	9	103	138	786	892	1525	•	•	51838	•	•
Net Property, Plant and Equipment	25	1185	•	172	119	664	2278	4680	13156	•	•	122421	•	•
Total Assets	26	4205	•	437	664	2073	7563	14214	32337	•	•	563805	•	•
Notes and Loans Payable	27	1283	•	1	103	613	1364	5773	4312	•	•	262738	•	•
All Other Liabilities	28	980	•	35	215	400	1217	1894	8408	•	•	156474	•	•
Net Worth	29	1942	•	401	347	1061	4981	6547	19617	•	•	144592	•	•
Selected Financial Ratios (Times to 1)														
Current Ratio	30	2.3	•	17.2	3.2	2.2	3.5	2.1	2.2	•	•	2.4	•	•
Quick Ratio	31	1.6	•	16.9	2.2	1.7	2.8	1.7	1.7	•	•	1.5	•	•
Net Sales to Working Capital	32	5.7	•	5.6	4.4	8.1	4.5	5.9	6.6	•	•	3.5	•	•
Coverage Ratio	33	8.6	•	156.6	70.1	10.4	32.4	7.9	14.6	•	•	3.4	•	•
Total Asset Turnover	34	1.4	•	3.2	2.2	2.3	1.7	1.3	1.8	•	•	0.7	•	•
Inventory Turnover	35	8.8	•	46.1	4.7	18.3	8.4	12.5	28.6	•	•	4.2	•	•
Receivables Turnover	36	7.4	•	13.5	11.5	9.7	6.4	6.4	8.5	•	•	13.1	•	•
Total Liabilities to Net Worth	37	1.2	•	0.1	0.9	1.0	0.5	1.2	0.6	•	•	2.9	•	•
Current Assets to Working Capital	38	1.8	•	1.1	1.5	1.8	1.4	1.9	1.8	•	•	1.7	•	•
Current Liabilities to Working Capital	39	0.8	•	0.1	0.5	0.8	0.4	0.9	0.8	•	•	0.7	•	•
Working Capital to Net Sales	40	0.2	•	0.2	0.2	0.1	0.2	0.2	0.2	•	•	0.3	•	•
Inventory to Working Capital	41	0.4	•	0.0	0.4	0.3	0.2	0.3	0.2	•	•	0.5	•	•
Total Receipts to Cash Flow	42	5.7	•	4.6	2.3	7.3	4.3	5.7	10.3	•	•	5.3	•	•
Cost of Goods to Cash Flow	43	3.2	•	1.3	0.7	3.9	2.2	3.5	7.8	•	•	2.9	•	•
Cash Flow to Total Debt	44	0.5	•	8.3	2.1	0.6	1.2	0.4	0.4	•	•	0.2	•	•
Selected Financial Factors (in Percentages)														
Debt Ratio	45	53.8	•	8.3	47.8	48.8	34.1	53.9	39.3	•	•	74.4	•	•
Return on Total Assets	46	16.0	•	47.3	40.0	16.4	27.5	17.7	15.1	•	•	9.9	•	•
Return on Equity Before Income Taxes	47	30.6	•	51.2	75.6	28.9	40.5	33.5	23.3	•	•	27.2	•	•
Return on Equity After Income Taxes	48	27.8	•	51.2	72.5	27.7	40.5	32.3	21.2	•	•	20.1	•	•
Profit Margin (Before Income Tax)	49	9.8	•	14.8	17.7	6.4	15.7	11.9	8.0	•	•	9.9	•	•
Profit Margin (After Income Tax)	50	8.9	•	14.8	17.0	6.2	15.7	11.5	7.2	•	•	7.3	•	•

Table I

Corporations with and without Net Income

OTHER FABRICATED METAL PRODUCT

MONEY AMOUNTS AND SIZE OF ASSETS IN THOUSANDS OF DOLLARS

Item Description for Accounting Period 7/11 Through 6/12		Total	Zero Assets	Under 500	500 to 1,000	1,000 to 5,000	5,000 to 10,000	10,000 to 25,000	25,000 to 50,000	50,000 to 100,000	100,000 to 250,000	250,000 to 500,000	500,000 to 2,500,000	2,500,000 and over
Number of Enterprises	1	14841	2111	7276	1278	2591	921	329	143	90	55	16	23	7
Revenues ($ in Thousands)														
Net Sales	2	125182006	1162858	3655699	2643312	12069597	11721390	9140524	8178832	8540150	10393933	5668329	20905195	31102188
Interest	3	672605	2538	909	657	3270	1356	1760	3830	3187	27735	5117	76944	545303
Rents	4	24493	119	1123	0	384	554	2157	1803	3825	760	457	3129	10183
Royalties	5	1280927	105	0	0	117	0	936	5587	7659	9389	9217	6199	1241718
Other Portfolio Income	6	1315918	12642	29712	1319	15063	20455	20476	5191	22908	59823	24426	91772	1012129
Other Receipts	7	1112719	7437	36430	3950	77291	73934	63090	50352	33039	118109	41401	225877	381809
Total Receipts	8	129588668	1185699	3723873	2649238	12165722	11817689	9228943	8245595	8610768	10609749	5748947	21309116	34293330
Average Total Receipts	9	8732	562	512	2073	4695	12831	28051	57662	95675	192905	359309	926483	4899047
Operating Costs/Operating Income (%)														
Cost of Operations	10	68.1	64.9	63.5	63.8	64.5	66.8	68.6	68.6	70.4	69.6	64.7	71.0	68.4
Salaries and Wages	11	6.8	8.9	5.6	9.4	7.2	7.0	7.3	6.2	6.4	7.1	7.5	5.7	7.0
Taxes Paid	12	1.8	1.5	2.4	2.6	2.5	2.1	2.0	2.0	1.8	1.5	1.9	1.5	1.6
Interest Paid	13	2.1	0.8	0.6	0.8	0.7	0.5	0.5	1.1	1.1	1.3	0.9	3.3	4.4
Depreciation	14	2.9	1.7	1.4	1.8	2.9	3.2	3.9	3.9	3.6	3.5	3.7	3.1	2.0
Amortization and Depletion	15	1.1	0.6	0.2	0.3	0.0	0.0	0.2	0.3	0.5	0.6	0.6	1.1	3.2
Pensions and Other Deferred Comp.	16	1.2	1.8	0.1	0.3	0.5	0.4	0.5	0.6	0.8	0.7	1.6	0.9	2.7
Employee Benefits	17	1.9	1.1	0.8	1.3	1.3	1.7	1.6	1.5	1.8	1.6	2.0	1.6	2.9
Advertising	18	0.5	0.5	0.2	0.2	0.6	0.3	0.5	0.6	0.5	0.5	1.1	0.4	0.7
Other Expenses	19	8.3	12.4	11.9	11.0	10.8	8.7	7.1	8.1	7.1	7.4	8.0	7.9	7.8
Officers' Compensation	20	2.0	4.4	7.2	5.7	5.1	3.4	2.3	1.9	1.4	1.6	1.3	0.5	0.6
Operating Margin	21	3.1	1.4	6.1	2.9	3.9	6.1	5.6	5.2	4.7	4.6	6.8	2.9	•
Operating Margin Before Officers' Comp.	22	5.1	5.8	13.3	8.5	9.0	9.5	7.9	7.1	6.1	6.2	8.2	3.4	•

Selected Average Balance Sheet ($ in Thousands)

Net Receivables 23	1555	0	41	200	606	1765	3951	7383	13677	27624	59590	144614	1420535
Inventories 24	1119	0	22	118	570	1550	4268	10774	14970	26734	62520	147837	461247
Net Property, Plant and Equipment 25	1159	0	38	136	501	1503	3883	8937	15987	31590	61770	155296	539293
Total Assets 26	20219	0	150	737	2220	6886	16094	35538	70843	153504	346768	1230364	32413953
Notes and Loans Payable 27	6546	0	89	244	709	1381	2923	9864	18613	26801	53500	466140	10855626
All Other Liabilities 28	2875	0	33	231	541	1644	3457	8763	17296	55242	80848	353845	3258163
Net Worth 29	10797	0	28	263	971	3862	9714	16911	34934	71461	212421	410379	18300163

Selected Financial Ratios (Times to 1)

Current Ratio 30	1.7	•	2.3	1.5	2.2	2.8	2.8	2.2	2.1	2.0	3.0	2.0	1.1
Quick Ratio 31	1.0	•	1.7	1.0	1.3	1.7	1.4	1.0	1.1	1.0	1.6	1.1	0.8
Net Sales to Working Capital 32	5.5	•	9.4	13.4	5.5	4.0	3.9	4.7	4.6	4.7	2.8	4.1	20.3
Coverage Ratio 33	4.3	5.0	15.3	5.0	7.3	14.5	14.1	6.4	6.1	6.2	10.2	2.5	3.4
Total Asset Turnover 34	0.4	•	3.3	2.8	2.1	1.8	1.7	1.6	1.3	1.2	1.0	0.7	0.1
Inventory Turnover 35	5.1	•	14.2	11.2	5.3	5.5	4.5	3.6	4.5	4.9	3.7	4.4	6.6
Receivables Turnover 36	5.3	•	12.5	10.6	7.7	8.0	7.5	7.5	7.2	7.8	5.9	6.9	2.8
Total Liabilities to Net Worth 37	0.9	•	4.3	1.8	1.3	0.8	0.7	1.1	1.0	1.1	0.6	2.0	0.8
Current Assets to Working Capital 38	2.4	•	1.8	3.1	1.8	1.6	1.6	1.9	1.9	2.0	1.5	2.0	10.8
Current Liabilities to Working Capital 39	1.4	•	0.8	2.1	0.8	0.6	0.6	0.9	0.9	1.0	0.5	1.0	9.8
Working Capital to Net Sales 40	0.2	•	0.1	0.1	0.2	0.3	0.3	0.2	0.2	0.2	0.4	0.2	0.0
Inventory to Working Capital 41	0.7	•	0.4	0.9	0.7	0.5	0.7	0.8	0.7	0.8	0.5	0.7	1.8
Total Receipts to Cash Flow 42	7.8	7.5	6.5	11.7	8.0	7.8	8.8	8.1	8.9	8.4	7.0	8.8	6.8
Cost of Goods to Cash Flow 43	5.3	4.9	4.1	7.5	5.1	5.2	6.0	5.5	6.3	5.8	4.5	6.3	4.6
Cash Flow to Total Debt 44	0.1	•	0.6	0.4	0.5	0.5	0.5	0.4	0.3	0.3	0.4	0.1	0.0

Selected Financial Factors (in Percentages)

Debt Ratio 45	46.6	•	81.1	64.4	56.3	43.9	39.6	52.4	50.7	53.4	38.7	66.6	43.5
Return on Total Assets 46	3.8	•	28.7	10.9	11.4	13.7	12.3	11.5	9.1	10.0	9.4	6.1	2.0
Return on Equity Before Income Taxes 47	5.5	•	142.0	24.4	22.5	22.7	18.9	20.4	15.3	18.0	13.8	11.0	2.5
Return on Equity After Income Taxes 48	4.2	•	140.5	23.6	21.3	21.7	17.3	18.0	12.8	15.4	9.6	6.8	1.6
Profit Margin (Before Income Tax) 49	7.0	3.3	8.0	3.1	4.7	6.9	6.6	6.0	5.6	6.8	8.3	5.0	10.4
Profit Margin (After Income Tax) 50	5.4	2.8	7.9	3.0	4.4	6.6	6.1	5.3	4.7	5.8	5.8	3.0	6.8

Table II

Corporations with Net Income

OTHER FABRICATED METAL PRODUCT

MONEY AMOUNTS AND SIZE OF ASSETS IN THOUSANDS OF DOLLARS

Item Description for Accounting Period 7/11 Through 6/12		Total	Zero Assets	Under 500	500 to 1,000	1,000 to 5,000	5,000 to 10,000	10,000 to 25,000	25,000 to 50,000	50,000 to 100,000	100,000 to 250,000	250,000 to 500,000	500,000 to 2,500,000	2,500,000 and over
Number of Enterprises	1	10737	952	5623	•	2002	758	274	112	70	47	13	17	•
Revenues ($ in Thousands)														
Net Sales	2	103645340	780907	3240697	•	9549973	9953823	8114504	6331936	6874478	9106720	4869642	16330211	•
Interest	3	598893	2392	520	•	3032	1215	1582	2679	2543	18109	4430	53068	•
Rents	4	18808	108	144	•	325	554	50	578	3825	581	455	2996	•
Royalties	5	1262768	105	0	•	117	0	880	5450	746	9389	9217	2546	•
Other Portfolio Income	6	1239983	3479	29211	•	13618	19457	19085	3323	19546	16071	23117	91255	•
Other Receipts	7	948816	6836	29136	•	66436	64936	59923	33985	28397	73780	29716	222668	•
Total Receipts	8	107714608	793827	3299708	•	9633501	10039985	8196024	6377951	6929535	9224650	4936577	16702744	•
Average Total Receipts	9	10032	834	587	•	4812	13245	29912	56946	98993	196269	379737	982514	•
Operating Costs/Operating Income (%)														
Cost of Operations	10	68.4	67.1	64.0	•	63.8	69.1	67.8	67.3	68.2	68.9	63.1	71.6	•
Salaries and Wages	11	6.3	3.7	4.6	•	7.3	5.0	7.2	6.1	6.4	7.3	7.6	5.7	•
Taxes Paid	12	1.8	1.2	2.2	•	2.4	2.1	2.0	1.8	1.9	1.4	1.8	1.3	•
Interest Paid	13	1.8	0.5	0.6	•	0.5	0.5	0.4	1.0	0.8	1.0	0.8	2.4	•
Depreciation	14	2.7	2.0	1.4	•	2.1	3.0	3.4	3.1	3.3	3.5	3.4	2.9	•
Amortization and Depletion	15	1.2	0.3	0.0	•	0.0	0.0	0.2	0.2	0.4	0.4	0.6	1.0	•
Pensions and Other Deferred Comp.	16	1.3	0.6	0.1	•	0.5	0.4	0.5	0.7	0.7	0.8	1.9	0.9	•
Employee Benefits	17	1.8	0.8	0.8	•	1.3	1.6	1.6	1.6	1.8	1.5	2.1	1.5	•
Advertising	18	0.5	0.1	0.3	•	0.6	0.3	0.4	0.4	0.5	0.5	1.0	0.3	•
Other Expenses	19	7.2	7.4	10.3	•	9.5	6.5	7.1	7.7	6.9	6.5	7.4	6.9	•
Officers' Compensation	20	1.9	3.2	7.5	•	4.5	3.7	2.3	2.0	1.6	1.3	1.4	0.5	•
Operating Margin	21	5.0	13.2	8.4	•	7.5	7.9	7.2	8.0	7.6	6.9	8.9	4.9	•
Operating Margin Before Officers' Comp.	22	6.9	16.4	15.8	•	12.0	11.6	9.5	10.0	9.2	8.2	10.3	5.5	•

Selected Average Balance Sheet ($ in Thousands)

Net Receivables 23	1839	0	47	•	636	1713	3992	7071	14006	27940	61843	145536	•
Inventories 24	1235	0	18	•	541	1588	4442	11168	15450	26895	73352	156871	•
Net Property, Plant and Equipment 25	1270	0	45	•	405	1442	3829	7839	15010	29730	63661	160620	•
Total Assets 26	25764	0	160	•	2144	6825	16376	34948	72250	151554	358960	1235527	•
Notes and Loans Payable 27	8047	0	75	•	508	1223	2691	8345	13487	27261	45792	424083	•
All Other Liabilities 28	3414	0	33	•	505	1464	3236	8362	16307	42837	89984	394185	•
Net Worth 29	14303	0	51	•	1132	4138	10449	18242	42456	81456	223183	417259	•

Selected Financial Ratios (Times to 1)

Current Ratio 30	1.7	•	2.4	•	2.8	3.3	3.0	2.4	2.6	2.1	3.2	1.9	•
Quick Ratio 31	1.0	•	1.9	•	1.7	2.0	1.6	1.2	1.4	1.1	1.6	1.1	•
Net Sales to Working Capital 32	5.5	•	9.7	•	4.6	3.7	3.9	4.1	3.9	4.5	2.5	4.5	•
Coverage Ratio 33	6.3	32.5	18.1	•	18.5	19.2	20.3	9.9	11.3	9.7	13.5	4.1	•
Total Asset Turnover 34	0.4	•	3.6	•	2.2	1.9	1.8	1.6	1.4	1.3	1.0	0.8	•
Inventory Turnover 35	5.3	•	20.4	•	5.6	5.7	4.5	3.4	4.3	5.0	3.2	4.4	•
Receivables Turnover 36	5.9	•	13.8	•	8.1	8.2	8.0	7.4	7.2	8.3	•	6.8	•
Total Liabilities to Net Worth 37	0.8	•	2.1	•	0.9	0.6	0.6	0.9	0.7	0.9	0.6	2.0	•
Current Assets to Working Capital 38	2.4	•	1.7	•	1.6	1.4	1.5	1.7	1.6	1.9	1.5	2.1	•
Current Liabilities to Working Capital 39	1.4	•	0.7	•	0.6	0.4	0.5	0.7	0.6	0.9	0.5	1.1	•
Working Capital to Net Sales 40	0.2	•	0.1	•	0.2	0.3	0.3	0.2	0.3	0.2	0.4	0.2	•
Inventory to Working Capital 41	0.8	•	0.3	•	0.6	0.5	0.6	0.8	0.6	0.7	0.5	0.8	•
Total Receipts to Cash Flow 42	7.1	5.1	6.1	•	6.7	7.6	7.8	6.8	7.2	7.7	6.4	7.9	•
Cost of Goods to Cash Flow 43	4.9	3.4	3.9	•	4.3	5.3	5.3	4.6	4.9	5.3	4.0	5.7	•
Cash Flow to Total Debt 44	0.1	•	0.9	•	0.7	0.6	0.6	0.5	0.5	0.4	0.4	0.1	•

Selected Financial Factors (in Percentages)

Debt Ratio 45	44.5	•	68.0	•	47.2	39.4	36.2	47.8	41.2	46.3	37.8	66.2	•
Return on Total Assets 46	4.2	•	38.9	•	19.6	17.7	15.6	15.6	12.7	11.9	11.6	7.6	•
Return on Equity Before Income Taxes 47	6.4	•	114.8	•	35.2	27.7	23.2	26.9	19.7	19.8	17.3	17.0	•
Return on Equity After Income Taxes 48	5.0	•	113.8	•	33.9	26.6	21.5	24.1	17.0	17.1	12.4	11.4	•
Profit Margin (Before Income Tax) 49	9.4	14.9	10.2	•	8.4	8.7	8.2	8.7	8.5	8.3	10.3	7.4	•
Profit Margin (After Income Tax) 50	7.4	14.1	10.1	•	8.0	8.4	7.6	7.8	7.3	7.2	7.4	5.0	•

Table I

Corporations with and without Net Income

AGRICULTURE, CONSTRUCTION, AND MINING MACHINERY

MONEY AMOUNTS AND SIZE OF ASSETS IN THOUSANDS OF DOLLARS

Item Description for Accounting Period 7/11 Through 6/12		Total	Zero Assets	Under 500	500 to 1,000	1,000 to 5,000	5,000 to 10,000	10,000 to 25,000	25,000 to 50,000	50,000 to 100,000	100,000 to 250,000	250,000 to 500,000	500,000 to 2,500,000	2,500,000 and over
Number of Enterprises	1	2688	11	1192	334	689	186	125	50	37	28	11	13	12
Revenues ($ in Thousands)														
Net Sales	2	155657522	2410961	1043177	637491	3579523	2171492	2831579	2841413	2826943	5325186	4090577	11625958	116273223
Interest	3	2703512	21638	110	15	480	1007	2612	1594	2455	5223	14018	29460	2624899
Rents	4	1468862	1129	33	138	7505	56	8325	866	659	3796	2235	134498	1309621
Royalties	5	1447978	51126	0	0	0	0	0	193	260	1562	8124	58336	1328377
Other Portfolio Income	6	2939534	107297	1449	0	151314	867	32806	3748	3175	11807	25618	32158	2569297
Other Receipts	7	2687832	-2719	6768	9068	12776	36841	83663	11624	15845	71200	16511	76765	2349488
Total Receipts	8	166905240	2589432	1051537	646712	3751598	2210263	2958985	2859438	2849337	5418774	4157083	11957175	126454905
Average Total Receipts	9	62093	235403	882	1936	5445	11883	23672	57189	77009	193528	377917	919783	10537909
Operating Costs/Operating Income (%)														
Cost of Operations	10	70.9	70.8	53.4	41.7	71.9	62.7	70.9	70.3	72.6	70.3	66.9	74.1	71.1
Salaries and Wages	11	6.3	11.9	8.5	18.7	6.0	9.6	7.9	5.6	7.3	6.3	7.9	5.5	6.0
Taxes Paid	12	1.0	1.4	1.8	2.1	1.6	2.2	1.8	1.7	1.4	1.1	1.8	1.2	0.8
Interest Paid	13	2.4	3.9	0.3	3.1	0.7	0.7	1.0	0.8	1.4	1.0	1.5	1.9	2.8
Depreciation	14	3.5	1.8	0.8	6.1	5.5	2.8	2.9	2.3	2.5	2.7	3.0	2.8	3.7
Amortization and Depletion	15	0.4	1.3	0.0	•	0.1	0.1	0.2	0.1	0.4	0.4	0.8	0.6	0.4
Pensions and Other Deferred Comp.	16	0.7	0.5	0.7	•	0.7	0.2	0.4	1.0	0.5	0.6	0.6	0.8	0.8
Employee Benefits	17	1.5	1.1	1.2	0.5	0.7	1.0	2.0	1.3	1.5	1.3	1.6	2.6	1.4
Advertising	18	0.3	0.3	0.3	1.0	0.9	1.6	0.7	0.8	0.5	0.6	0.8	0.6	0.2
Other Expenses	19	11.2	8.6	12.3	20.7	6.8	11.9	8.2	7.6	9.5	7.8	10.2	8.1	12.1
Officers' Compensation	20	0.6	3.2	7.3	2.8	4.0	3.9	2.3	1.6	1.1	1.0	0.8	0.4	0.3
Operating Margin	21	1.1	•	13.5	3.5	1.3	3.3	1.8	7.0	1.1	6.8	4.0	1.3	0.5
Operating Margin Before Officers' Comp.	22	1.8	•	20.8	6.3	5.3	7.2	4.1	8.6	2.3	7.8	4.8	1.7	0.8

Selected Average Balance Sheet ($ in Thousands)														
Net Receivables	23	32043	0	42	103	321	1665	3778	7943	11311	31654	75335	217421	6640715
Inventories	24	8785	0	98	120	785	2134	4102	11809	18502	33806	76428	167605	1397019
Net Property, Plant and Equipment	25	9122	0	29	337	412	1013	2240	5824	10433	22367	45253	164858	1639730
Total Assets	26	100002	0	205	851	1868	6437	13828	35804	68643	160546	335134	1129767	19738841
Notes and Loans Payable	27	40157	0	72	949	532	1293	3456	6194	16844	31603	67194	331698	8302727
All Other Liabilities	28	35457	0	70	77	547	2422	3659	9068	24627	46508	99230	377692	7103882
Net Worth	29	24388	0	63	-175	790	2722	6712	20542	27172	82435	168710	420378	4332233

Selected Financial Ratios (Times to 1)														
Current Ratio	30	1.4	•	2.2	4.9	2.7	1.8	2.2	2.5	1.6	2.2	1.9	1.5	1.3
Quick Ratio	31	1.0	•	0.9	3.4	1.4	0.8	1.1	1.1	0.8	1.3	1.0	0.8	1.0
Net Sales to Working Capital	32	4.2	•	8.9	5.8	5.9	5.5	4.0	3.6	4.6	3.5	4.1	5.8	3.9
Coverage Ratio	33	5.1	1.7	43.4	2.6	9.9	8.1	7.3	10.7	2.5	9.5	5.1	4.1	5.1
Total Asset Turnover	34	0.6	•	4.3	2.2	2.8	1.8	1.6	1.6	1.1	1.2	1.1	0.8	0.5
Inventory Turnover	35	4.7	•	4.7	6.6	4.8	3.4	3.9	3.4	3.0	4.0	3.3	4.0	4.9
Receivables Turnover	36	2.0	•	30.6	17.9	12.9	7.9	6.2	7.2	6.5	6.7	4.8	4.9	1.6
Total Liabilities to Net Worth	37	3.1	•	2.3	•	1.4	1.4	1.1	0.7	1.5	0.9	1.0	1.7	3.6
Current Assets to Working Capital	38	3.5	•	1.8	1.3	1.6	2.3	1.8	1.6	2.6	1.8	2.1	3.2	3.9
Current Liabilities to Working Capital	39	2.5	•	0.8	0.3	0.6	1.3	0.8	0.6	1.6	0.8	1.1	2.2	2.9
Working Capital to Net Sales	40	0.2	•	0.1	0.2	0.2	0.2	0.2	0.3	0.2	0.3	0.2	0.2	0.3
Inventory to Working Capital	41	0.7	•	1.0	0.3	0.7	1.1	0.8	0.9	1.2	0.6	0.8	1.1	0.6
Total Receipts to Cash Flow	42	5.6	10.0	4.5	4.4	9.1	7.0	7.9	7.4	9.8	6.6	7.5	9.8	5.1
Cost of Goods to Cash Flow	43	4.0	7.0	2.4	1.8	6.5	4.4	5.6	5.2	7.2	4.6	5.0	7.3	3.6
Cash Flow to Total Debt	44	0.1	•	1.4	0.4	0.5	0.5	0.4	0.5	0.2	0.4	0.3	0.1	0.1

Selected Financial Factors (in Percentages)														
Debt Ratio	45	75.6	•	69.3	120.5	57.7	57.7	51.5	42.6	60.4	48.7	49.7	62.8	78.1
Return on Total Assets	46	7.2	•	62.6	18.0	18.9	10.5	12.0	13.3	3.9	11.4	8.1	6.1	6.9
Return on Equity Before Income Taxes	47	23.6	•	199.2	•	40.1	21.8	21.3	21.1	5.9	19.8	13.0	12.3	25.1
Return on Equity After Income Taxes	48	15.9	•	195.5	•	38.7	18.7	17.8	17.9	3.1	16.8	8.7	7.9	16.4
Profit Margin (Before Income Tax)	49	9.9	2.6	14.3	4.9	6.1	5.1	6.3	7.6	2.1	8.6	5.9	5.8	11.2
Profit Margin (After Income Tax)	50	6.7	2.3	14.0	4.9	5.9	4.4	5.3	6.5	1.1	7.3	3.9	3.7	7.3

Table II

Corporations with Net Income

AGRICULTURE, CONSTRUCTION, AND MINING MACHINERY

MONEY AMOUNTS AND SIZE OF ASSETS IN THOUSANDS OF DOLLARS

Item Description for Accounting Period 7/11 Through 6/12		Total	Zero Assets	Under 500	500 to 1,000	1,000 to 5,000	5,000 to 10,000	10,000 to 25,000	25,000 to 50,000	50,000 to 100,000	100,000 to 250,000	250,000 to 500,000	500,000 to 2,500,000	2,500,000 and over
Number of Enterprises	1	1951	•	752	212	563	186	108	43	23	23	•	10	•
Revenues ($ in Thousands)														
Net Sales	2	148339500	•	945724	345936	3422416	2171492	2584782	2668766	1954800	4692347	•	10408279	•
Interest	3	2677272	•	110	15	473	1007	2523	1583	1181	2511	•	29096	•
Rents	4	1429154	•	33	0	6883	56	8194	866	500	991	•	99705	•
Royalties	5	1385626	•	0	0	0	0	0	193	260	530	•	56244	•
Other Portfolio Income	6	2909382	•	1449	0	151306	867	13779	3748	2703	11679	•	22424	•
Other Receipts	7	2609258	•	6769	2074	12775	36841	36805	11117	13288	62789	•	72978	•
Total Receipts	8	159350192	•	954085	348025	3593853	2210263	2646083	2686273	1972732	4770847	•	10688726	•
Average Total Receipts	9	81676	•	1269	1642	6383	11883	24501	62471	85771	207428	•	1068873	•
Operating Costs/Operating Income (%)														
Cost of Operations	10	70.7	•	53.6	26.9	71.7	62.7	70.4	70.2	70.3	69.6	•	74.6	•
Salaries and Wages	11	6.0	•	7.0	16.9	5.6	9.6	7.1	5.2	6.5	6.1	•	5.1	•
Taxes Paid	12	0.9	•	1.6	2.4	1.3	2.2	1.7	1.6	1.4	1.2	•	1.1	•
Interest Paid	13	2.3	•	0.4	5.1	0.3	0.7	0.9	0.6	0.5	0.8	•	1.0	•
Depreciation	14	3.5	•	0.9	10.4	5.6	2.8	2.2	2.1	1.9	2.7	•	2.2	•
Amortization and Depletion	15	0.4	•	0.0	•	0.1	0.1	0.2	0.1	0.1	0.3	•	0.5	•
Pensions and Other Deferred Comp.	16	0.8	•	0.8	•	0.7	0.2	0.4	1.0	0.7	0.6	•	0.9	•
Employee Benefits	17	1.5	•	1.1	0.3	0.6	1.0	1.6	1.1	1.4	1.1	•	2.8	•
Advertising	18	0.3	•	0.4	0.6	0.8	1.6	0.7	0.8	0.6	0.6	•	0.7	•
Other Expenses	19	11.3	•	11.3	18.8	6.6	11.9	7.6	7.1	7.2	7.2	•	7.8	•
Officers' Compensation	20	0.6	•	5.7	3.6	3.9	3.9	2.2	1.4	1.2	1.0	•	0.4	•
Operating Margin	21	1.8	•	17.4	15.0	2.8	3.3	5.0	8.7	8.1	8.7	•	2.8	•
Operating Margin Before Officers' Comp.	22	2.4	•	23.1	18.6	6.7	7.2	7.2	10.2	9.3	9.7	•	3.1	•

Selected Average Balance Sheet ($ in Thousands)

Net Receivables 23	43386	•	38	26	363	1665	3691	8859	11191	32496	•	252933	•
Inventories 24	11210	•	56	133	696	1935	3732	11548	17884	35365	•	201486	•
Net Property, Plant and Equipment 25	11776	•	45	433	488	1013	2086	5478	9100	23118	•	123234	•
Total Assets 26	132827	•	193	925	1953	6437	13652	36773	65023	167005	•	1158932	•
Notes and Loans Payable 27	53546	•	46	1413	348	1293	3011	5456	9080	34104	•	293350	•
All Other Liabilities 28	46950	•	49	39	348	2422	3762	9425	14956	42886	•	398998	•
Net Worth 29	32331	•	98	-527	1256	2722	6878	21893	40987	90015	•	466584	•

Selected Financial Ratios (Times to 1)

Current Ratio 30	1.4	•	2.4	7.1	3.8	1.8	2.3	2.6	2.7	2.4	•	1.4	•
Quick Ratio 31	1.0	•	1.2	5.6	2.1	0.8	1.1	1.1	1.4	1.4	•	0.8	•
Net Sales to Working Capital 32	4.0	•	14.4	4.8	5.5	5.5	4.2	3.7	3.2	3.4	•	6.3	•
Coverage Ratio 33	5.7	•	50.2	4.1	27.2	8.1	9.0	15.6	20.1	13.7	•	8.1	•
Total Asset Turnover 34	0.6	•	6.5	1.8	3.1	1.8	1.8	1.7	1.3	1.2	•	0.9	•
Inventory Turnover 35	4.8	•	11.9	3.3	6.3	3.8	4.5	3.8	3.3	4.0	•	3.9	•
Receivables Turnover 36	2.0	•	56.0	16.3	13.6	8.6	7.2	7.8	•	7.2	•	4.8	•
Total Liabilities to Net Worth 37	3.1	•	1.0	•	0.6	1.4	1.0	0.7	0.6	0.9	•	1.5	•
Current Assets to Working Capital 38	3.5	•	1.7	1.2	1.4	2.3	1.8	1.6	1.6	1.7	•	3.5	•
Current Liabilities to Working Capital 39	2.5	•	0.7	0.2	0.4	1.3	0.8	0.6	0.6	0.7	•	2.5	•
Working Capital to Net Sales 40	0.2	•	0.1	0.2	0.2	0.2	0.2	0.3	0.3	0.3	•	0.2	•
Inventory to Working Capital 41	0.7	•	0.8	0.2	0.6	1.1	0.8	0.8	0.7	0.6	•	1.3	•
Total Receipts to Cash Flow 42	5.4	•	3.9	3.3	7.8	7.0	7.5	6.8	6.6	6.1	•	8.9	•
Cost of Goods to Cash Flow 43	3.8	•	2.1	0.9	5.6	4.4	5.3	4.8	4.6	4.2	•	6.7	•
Cash Flow to Total Debt 44	0.1	•	3.4	0.3	1.1	0.5	0.5	0.6	0.5	0.4	•	0.2	•

Selected Financial Factors (in Percentages)

Debt Ratio 45	75.7	•	49.1	157.0	35.7	57.7	49.6	40.5	37.0	46.1	•	59.7	•
Return on Total Assets 46	7.6	•	121.9	36.4	25.3	10.5	14.5	16.9	12.4	13.7	•	7.5	•
Return on Equity Before Income Taxes 47	25.6	•	234.9	•	37.9	21.8	25.6	26.6	18.8	23.6	•	16.3	•
Return on Equity After Income Taxes 48	17.5	•	231.2	•	36.8	18.7	21.6	23.1	15.8	20.2	•	11.1	•
Profit Margin (Before Income Tax) 49	10.9	•	18.3	15.6	7.8	5.1	7.4	9.4	9.0	10.4	•	7.3	•
Profit Margin (After Income Tax) 50	7.5	•	18.0	15.6	7.6	4.4	6.2	8.2	7.6	8.9	•	5.0	•

Table I

Corporations with and without Net Income

INDUSTRIAL MACHINERY

MONEY AMOUNTS AND SIZE OF ASSETS IN THOUSANDS OF DOLLARS

Item Description for Accounting Period 7/11 Through 6/12		Total	Zero Assets	Under 500	500 to 1,000	1,000 to 5,000	5,000 to 10,000	10,000 to 25,000	25,000 to 50,000	50,000 to 100,000	100,000 to 250,000	250,000 to 500,000	500,000 to 2,500,000	2,500,000 and over
Number of Enterprises	1	2901	95	999	466	666	343	179	59	34	37	8	12	3
Revenues ($ in Thousands)														
Net Sales	2	50995132	233326	463391	825228	4034034	3342096	3899934	2887560	2753480	4975275	3116542	9663597	14800668
Interest	3	141459	714	1	1810	1835	1095	4319	1714	4168	23425	8402	29122	64854
Rents	4	92910	3785	0	0	3125	1072	370	5946	2381	15206	274	59689	1062
Royalties	5	382714	2797	0	0	0	2422	388	2099	125	11405	9948	61814	291717
Other Portfolio Income	6	440763	1827	0	403	4680	2699	31368	6222	13432	43896	22066	138712	175456
Other Receipts	7	678720	116044	192	714	46512	16002	27498	14772	20750	33690	27872	243756	130919
Total Receipts	8	52731698	358493	463584	828155	4090186	3365386	3963877	2918313	2794336	5102897	3185104	10196690	15464676
Average Total Receipts	9	18177	3774	464	1777	6141	9812	22145	49463	82186	137916	398138	849724	5154892
Operating Costs/Operating Income (%)														
Cost of Operations	10	65.0	100.5	61.5	63.9	64.0	62.9	69.1	67.3	70.6	69.0	71.6	62.4	61.8
Salaries and Wages	11	10.0	71.3	6.0	3.9	9.8	11.1	9.1	8.0	8.3	8.2	8.0	10.2	11.2
Taxes Paid	12	1.6	2.0	2.9	3.1	2.4	2.3	1.9	1.9	1.8	1.4	1.1	1.4	1.3
Interest Paid	13	1.4	9.6	0.9	1.0	1.4	0.8	0.5	0.6	1.4	1.2	1.2	1.5	1.7
Depreciation	14	2.8	3.2	0.4	2.8	2.4	2.6	1.8	3.1	2.8	2.9	1.7	3.7	2.7
Amortization and Depletion	15	0.7	0.5	0.1	0.0	0.3	0.1	0.2	0.2	0.8	1.1	1.0	0.9	1.0
Pensions and Other Deferred Comp.	16	0.8	0.7	•	0.0	0.2	0.9	0.3	1.0	0.9	0.7	0.9	1.1	0.8
Employee Benefits	17	2.0	9.0	6.1	4.9	2.3	2.7	1.8	1.6	1.8	1.7	2.2	1.6	1.8
Advertising	18	0.5	0.2	0.8	0.9	0.4	0.7	0.5	0.6	0.3	0.3	0.3	0.3	0.6
Other Expenses	19	9.9	6.0	16.4	7.5	10.5	8.2	7.4	10.6	6.6	10.8	7.6	10.5	10.9
Officers' Compensation	20	1.7	8.5	6.2	6.8	3.1	2.8	5.2	1.4	1.5	1.3	1.1	1.0	0.4
Operating Margin	21	3.7	•	•	5.2	3.2	4.8	2.1	3.7	3.1	1.5	3.3	5.6	5.7
Operating Margin Before Officers' Comp.	22	5.4	•	5.1	11.9	6.3	7.6	7.3	5.2	4.6	2.8	4.4	6.6	6.1

Selected Average Balance Sheet ($ in Thousands)														
Net Receivables	23	4355	0	45	190	872	1447	2885	8675	14977	29132	91905	166522	2025327
Inventories	24	2372	0	38	207	841	1786	3238	7770	13191	19009	70774	168488	530693
Net Property, Plant and Equipment	25	2036	0	31	129	472	1588	1839	7438	10201	16191	32065	98804	599849
Total Assets	26	23988	0	125	801	3202	7535	14478	36908	70026	153957	357676	1174425	11524353
Notes and Loans Payable	27	5172	0	11	519	1122	2307	3058	6115	16616	31385	94274	245820	2291886
All Other Liabilities	28	6906	0	74	80	1077	2131	5273	11593	24817	55733	146488	366209	2791266
Net Worth	29	11910	0	40	202	1003	3097	6147	19201	28593	66839	116914	562396	6441202
Selected Financial Ratios (Times to 1)														
Current Ratio	30	1.9	•	1.1	6.0	1.8	2.4	1.8	2.4	1.5	1.9	1.4	1.8	2.0
Quick Ratio	31	1.3	•	0.8	4.4	1.0	1.4	1.0	1.3	0.9	1.2	0.7	1.1	1.7
Net Sales to Working Capital	32	3.1	•	77.0	3.6	6.0	3.2	4.7	3.4	5.7	3.3	5.9	3.6	2.0
Coverage Ratio	33	6.8	•	•	6.5	4.3	8.0	7.9	9.4	4.3	4.7	5.8	8.9	8.0
Total Asset Turnover	34	0.7	•	3.7	2.2	1.9	1.3	1.5	1.3	1.2	0.9	1.1	0.7	0.4
Inventory Turnover	35	4.8	•	7.5	5.5	4.6	3.4	4.6	4.2	4.3	4.9	3.9	3.0	5.7
Receivables Turnover	36	4.0	•	11.7	10.9	6.2	7.7	8.2	6.7	5.2	5.3	4.2	1.8	4.9
Total Liabilities to Net Worth	37	1.0	•	2.1	3.0	2.2	1.4	1.4	0.9	1.4	1.3	2.1	1.1	0.8
Current Assets to Working Capital	38	2.1	•	14.8	1.2	2.2	1.7	2.3	1.7	2.9	2.1	3.7	2.2	2.0
Current Liabilities to Working Capital	39	1.1	•	13.8	0.2	1.2	0.7	1.3	0.7	1.9	1.1	2.7	1.2	1.0
Working Capital to Net Sales	40	0.3	•	0.0	0.3	0.2	0.3	0.2	0.3	0.2	0.3	0.2	0.3	0.5
Inventory to Working Capital	41	0.4	•	4.0	0.3	0.8	0.6	0.8	0.6	0.9	0.5	1.1	0.5	0.2
Total Receipts to Cash Flow	42	6.9	•	11.0	9.6	8.2	8.4	11.7	7.3	10.4	8.0	8.3	5.4	5.5
Cost of Goods to Cash Flow	43	4.5	•	6.8	6.2	5.3	5.3	8.1	4.9	7.3	5.5	6.0	3.4	3.4
Cash Flow to Total Debt	44	0.2	•	0.5	0.3	0.3	0.3	0.2	0.4	0.2	0.2	0.2	0.2	0.2
Selected Financial Factors (in Percentages)														
Debt Ratio	45	50.4	•	67.7	74.8	68.7	58.9	57.5	48.0	59.2	56.6	67.3	52.1	44.1
Return on Total Assets	46	6.8	•	•	14.5	11.3	8.1	6.4	7.1	7.0	4.9	7.6	9.3	5.9
Return on Equity Before Income Taxes	47	11.7	•	•	48.4	27.6	17.3	13.1	12.2	13.1	8.8	19.2	17.2	9.3
Return on Equity After Income Taxes	48	8.3	•	•	44.1	26.1	15.7	12.1	10.8	11.3	6.4	14.3	12.1	6.0
Profit Margin (Before Income Tax)	49	7.9	•	•	5.5	4.6	5.5	3.7	4.8	4.6	4.4	5.7	12.0	12.1
Profit Margin (After Income Tax)	50	5.6	•	•	5.0	4.3	5.0	3.4	4.2	4.0	3.2	4.3	8.4	7.9

Table II

Corporations with Net Income

INDUSTRIAL MACHINERY

MONEY AMOUNTS AND SIZE OF ASSETS IN THOUSANDS OF DOLLARS

Item Description for Accounting Period 7/11 Through 6/12		Total	Zero Assets	Under 500	500 to 1,000	1,000 to 5,000	5,000 to 10,000	10,000 to 25,000	25,000 to 50,000	50,000 to 100,000	100,000 to 250,000	250,000 to 500,000	500,000 to 2,500,000	2,500,000 and over
Number of Enterprises	1	1880	•	452	376	536	250	137	45	•	25	8	•	3
Revenues ($ in Thousands)														
Net Sales	2	45100352	•	55000	796467	3494970	2791167	2788135	2390436	•	3901415	3116542	•	14800668
Interest	3	120951	•	1	2	584	658	3033	1354	•	16902	8402	•	64854
Rents	4	72482	•	0	0	2542	1072	64	4023	•	1707	274	•	1062
Royalties	5	368977	•	0	0	0	1074	388	1899	•	2012	9948	•	291717
Other Portfolio Income	6	417361	•	0	0	4614	1916	29963	3129	•	32814	22066	•	175456
Other Receipts	7	494079	•	0	87	7176	12656	19215	12340	•	19937	27872	•	130919
Total Receipts	8	46574202	•	55001	796556	3509886	2808543	2840798	2413181	•	3974787	3185104	•	15464676
Average Total Receipts	9	24774	•	122	2118	6548	11234	20736	53626	•	158991	398138	•	5154892
Operating Costs/Operating Income (%)														
Cost of Operations	10	64.4	•	40.4	64.0	63.5	61.8	68.2	68.5	•	68.8	71.6	•	61.8
Salaries and Wages	11	9.8	•	0.0	3.9	10.3	10.9	8.5	7.2	•	8.0	8.0	•	11.2
Taxes Paid	12	1.5	•	0.2	3.0	2.2	2.1	1.9	1.7	•	1.2	1.1	•	1.3
Interest Paid	13	1.3	•	0.0	0.8	1.1	0.6	0.5	0.6	•	1.0	1.2	•	1.7
Depreciation	14	2.3	•	0.1	2.5	2.2	2.4	1.7	2.2	•	2.4	1.7	•	2.7
Amortization and Depletion	15	0.7	•	•	0.0	0.3	0.1	0.2	0.2	•	0.9	1.0	•	1.0
Pensions and Other Deferred Comp.	16	0.8	•	•	0.0	0.2	1.0	0.4	1.1	•	0.8	0.9	•	0.8
Employee Benefits	17	1.9	•	7.7	5.0	2.0	2.7	1.6	1.4	•	1.6	2.2	•	1.8
Advertising	18	0.5	•	•	1.0	0.2	0.7	0.5	0.7	•	0.2	0.3	•	0.6
Other Expenses	19	9.5	•	12.5	7.1	7.3	7.1	7.6	9.7	•	8.6	7.6	•	10.9
Officers' Compensation	20	1.4	•	14.5	6.8	3.1	3.0	3.6	1.3	•	1.1	1.1	•	0.4
Operating Margin	21	5.9	•	24.5	6.0	7.6	7.5	5.3	5.6	•	5.4	3.3	•	5.7
Operating Margin Before Officers' Comp.	22	7.3	•	39.0	12.8	10.7	10.5	8.9	6.9	•	6.6	4.4	•	6.1

Selected Average Balance Sheet ($ in Thousands)													
Net Receivables **23**	6192	•	0	223	906	1597	2757	9099	•	31076	91905	•	2025327
Inventories **24**	3119	•	0	256	764	1424	3062	7639	•	22132	70803	•	530693
Net Property, Plant and Equipment **25**	2608	•	0	129	396	1626	1422	5359	•	16491	32065	•	599849
Total Assets **26**	33877	•	31	840	3152	7699	13583	37134	•	158145	357676	•	11524353
Notes and Loans Payable **27**	6629	•	1	328	852	1363	1796	5009	•	26223	94274	•	2291886
All Other Liabilities **28**	9718	•	0	98	955	2064	5314	13308	•	59542	146488	•	2791266
Net Worth **29**	17530	•	30	413	1345	4273	6474	18817	•	72380	116914	•	6441202
Selected Financial Ratios (Times to 1)													
Current Ratio **30**	2.0	•	45.1	6.0	2.2	2.8	1.8	2.3	•	2.0	1.4	•	2.0
Quick Ratio **31**	1.4	•	44.4	4.4	1.3	1.8	1.0	1.3	•	1.2	0.7	•	1.7
Net Sales to Working Capital **32**	2.9	•	4.0	3.6	5.2	3.3	4.1	3.6	•	3.2	5.9	•	2.0
Coverage Ratio **33**	8.8	•	675.8	8.6	8.3	14.9	15.6	12.5	•	8.5	5.8	•	8.0
Total Asset Turnover **34**	0.7	•	3.9	2.5	2.1	1.5	1.5	1.4	•	1.0	1.1	•	0.4
Inventory Turnover **35**	5.0	•	•	5.3	5.4	4.8	4.5	4.8	•	4.9	3.9	•	5.7
Receivables Turnover **36**	3.8	•	•	10.9	6.7	8.3	8.4	7.3	•	5.9	•	•	4.9
Total Liabilities to Net Worth **37**	0.9	•	0.0	1.0	1.3	0.8	1.1	1.0	•	1.2	2.1	•	0.8
Current Assets to Working Capital **38**	2.0	•	1.0	1.2	1.8	1.6	2.2	1.7	•	2.0	3.7	•	2.0
Current Liabilities to Working Capital **39**	1.0	•	0.0	0.2	0.8	0.6	1.2	0.7	•	1.0	2.7	•	1.0
Working Capital to Net Sales **40**	0.3	•	0.3	0.3	0.2	0.3	0.2	0.3	•	0.3	0.2	•	0.5
Inventory to Working Capital **41**	0.4	•	•	0.3	0.7	0.5	0.7	0.6	•	0.5	1.1	•	0.2
Total Receipts to Cash Flow **42**	6.2	•	2.8	9.7	7.8	7.3	8.3	6.7	•	7.3	8.3	•	5.5
Cost of Goods to Cash Flow **43**	4.0	•	1.1	6.2	5.0	4.5	5.7	4.6	•	5.0	6.0	•	3.4
Cash Flow to Total Debt **44**	0.2	•	39.6	0.5	0.5	0.4	0.3	0.4	•	0.2	0.2	•	0.2
Selected Financial Factors (in Percentages)													
Debt Ratio **45**	48.3	•	3.5	50.8	57.3	44.5	52.3	49.3	•	54.2	67.3	•	44.1
Return on Total Assets **46**	8.0	•	95.4	17.0	19.0	12.6	11.4	10.1	•	8.4	7.6	•	5.9
Return on Equity Before Income Taxes **47**	13.7	•	98.7	30.6	39.1	21.2	22.5	18.4	•	16.3	19.2	•	9.3
Return on Equity After Income Taxes **48**	10.2	•	98.7	28.0	37.7	19.5	21.2	16.5	•	12.9	14.3	•	6.0
Profit Margin (Before Income Tax) **49**	10.0	•	24.5	6.0	8.1	8.1	7.1	6.5	•	7.5	5.7	•	12.1
Profit Margin (After Income Tax) **50**	7.5	•	24.5	5.5	7.8	7.5	6.7	5.8	•	6.0	4.3	•	7.9

Table I

Corporations with and without Net Income

COMMERCIAL AND SERVICE INDUSTRY MACHINERY

Item Description for Accounting Period 7/11 Through 6/12		MONEY AMOUNTS AND SIZE OF ASSETS IN THOUSANDS OF DOLLARS												
		Total	Zero Assets	Under 500	500 to 1,000	1,000 to 5,000	5,000 to 10,000	10,000 to 25,000	25,000 to 50,000	50,000 to 100,000	100,000 to 250,000	250,000 to 500,000	500,000 to 2,500,000	2,500,000 and over
Number of Enterprises	1	1544	33	893	11	354	97	75	31	17	14	8	8	4
Revenues ($ in Thousands)														
Net Sales	2	45469748	165371	845478	9571	1512878	1279265	1647758	1520645	1632912	2154340	2657852	6092216	25951462
Interest	3	535536	24	0	2	276	847	1860	1435	1369	6952	4278	66759	451733
Rents	4	140422	0	0	0	0	0	289	1962	324	4369	1040	37720	94718
Royalties	5	739218	23	0	0	0	365	140	86	251	2464	28109	57988	649792
Other Portfolio Income	6	427761	0	0	0	1662	238	1564	4576	5850	22413	4848	81487	305123
Other Receipts	7	1923885	-561	16472	1606	5000	16439	14012	14425	18044	32384	16367	85819	1703878
Total Receipts	8	49236570	164857	861950	11179	1519816	1297154	1665623	1543129	1658750	2222922	2712494	6421989	29156706
Average Total Receipts	9	31889	4996	965	1016	4293	13373	22208	49778	97574	158780	339062	802749	7289176
Operating Costs/Operating Income (%)														
Cost of Operations	10	51.3	43.1	73.6	111.2	53.9	64.3	63.9	62.9	63.1	63.1	67.4	51.5	44.9
Salaries and Wages	11	18.2	14.3	0.7	89.1	12.3	10.4	7.2	9.3	10.5	12.6	9.0	15.9	23.1
Taxes Paid	12	2.6	37.2	0.9	6.9	2.3	1.8	1.8	1.9	1.6	2.3	1.8	1.9	3.0
Interest Paid	13	2.7	1.2	•	14.3	1.1	0.1	1.5	0.8	1.2	0.7	2.7	2.6	3.6
Depreciation	14	5.8	3.6	0.6	3.0	1.7	1.2	10.0	2.6	2.9	1.7	2.1	2.8	8.0
Amortization and Depletion	15	3.1	0.1	•	•	0.6	0.1	0.4	0.3	0.9	0.9	1.7	1.6	4.7
Pensions and Other Deferred Comp.	16	1.9	0.2	0.4	0.1	0.6	0.5	0.3	0.3	1.0	0.7	0.9	0.6	2.9
Employee Benefits	17	2.3	1.0	2.8	2.8	2.3	3.4	1.3	1.5	2.5	2.9	2.2	1.4	2.6
Advertising	18	0.8	1.3	0.7	0.9	2.5	0.4	0.5	1.3	1.0	0.5	0.7	0.8	0.7
Other Expenses	19	16.4	10.8	3.2	43.4	12.5	8.2	7.5	12.0	9.6	12.7	10.7	17.5	19.3
Officers' Compensation	20	1.0	•	7.5	12.7	4.1	2.0	1.8	1.5	1.5	1.4	1.0	1.2	0.4
Operating Margin	21	•	•	9.5	•	6.2	7.6	3.9	5.5	4.1	0.4	•	2.3	•
Operating Margin Before Officers' Comp.	22	•	•	17.0	•	10.3	9.6	5.6	7.0	5.6	1.8	0.8	3.4	•

Selected Average Balance Sheet ($ in Thousands)														
Net Receivables	23	7113	0	138	302	658	1512	3390	8080	14853	44023	89520	88383	1919816
Inventories	24	2630	0	21	514	678	1588	3814	9494	14789	25185	46616	73414	374280
Net Property, Plant and Equipment	25	3170	0	35	27	334	487	2190	4123	9076	17360	36924	108062	712066
Total Assets	26	42665	0	294	662	2272	6162	14776	34173	71575	153215	426864	994928	11824884
Notes and Loans Payable	27	17119	0	21	1606	590	671	4397	5549	10162	17973	259692	381415	5016537
All Other Liabilities	28	14346	0	191	2463	738	2768	5046	13554	28809	65269	138157	216352	4096287
Net Worth	29	11200	0	82	-3407	944	2723	5333	15069	32603	69973	29016	397161	2712061
Selected Financial Ratios (Times to 1)														
Current Ratio	30	1.3	•	1.2	0.2	2.0	2.4	1.8	1.6	2.0	1.5	0.7	0.9	1.3
Quick Ratio	31	0.7	•	1.1	0.1	0.9	1.6	0.9	0.8	1.1	1.0	0.5	0.5	0.8
Net Sales to Working Capital	32	9.8	•	22.6	•	4.9	4.7	4.9	5.4	4.0	4.5	•	•	7.8
Coverage Ratio	33	2.0	•	•	•	7.3	89.9	4.4	9.7	5.7	6.6	1.8	4.3	1.0
Total Asset Turnover	34	0.7	•	3.2	1.3	1.9	2.1	1.5	1.4	1.3	1.0	0.8	0.8	0.5
Inventory Turnover	35	5.7	•	33.5	1.9	3.4	5.3	3.7	3.3	4.1	3.9	4.8	5.3	7.8
Receivables Turnover	36	3.1	•	9.3	0.5	9.1	7.7	6.7	6.0	7.2	3.5	4.7	9.9	2.3
Total Liabilities to Net Worth	37	2.8	•	2.6	•	1.4	1.3	1.8	1.3	1.2	1.2	13.7	1.5	3.4
Current Assets to Working Capital	38	4.9	•	5.6	•	2.0	1.7	2.3	2.7	2.0	2.9	•	•	4.2
Current Liabilities to Working Capital	39	3.9	•	4.6	•	1.0	0.7	1.3	1.7	1.0	1.9	•	•	3.2
Working Capital to Net Sales	40	0.1	•	0.0	•	0.2	0.2	0.2	0.2	0.2	0.2	•	•	0.1
Inventory to Working Capital	41	0.9	•	0.5	•	0.9	0.5	0.9	1.2	0.6	0.7	•	•	0.5
Total Receipts to Cash Flow	42	6.7	•	7.0	•	6.2	6.8	8.9	5.8	7.5	7.0	9.0	4.5	7.2
Cost of Goods to Cash Flow	43	3.5	•	5.2	•	3.3	4.4	5.7	3.7	4.7	4.4	6.1	2.3	3.2
Cash Flow to Total Debt	44	0.1	•	0.6	•	0.5	0.6	0.3	0.4	0.3	0.3	0.1	0.3	0.1
Selected Financial Factors (in Percentages)														
Debt Ratio	45	73.7	•	72.2	614.9	58.4	55.8	63.9	55.9	54.4	54.3	93.2	60.1	77.1
Return on Total Assets	46	3.8	•	36.7	•	14.5	19.6	9.5	11.4	9.3	4.9	3.8	8.4	2.0
Return on Equity Before Income Taxes	47	7.1	•	131.9	42.8	30.2	43.8	20.3	23.2	16.8	9.2	24.8	16.1	0.1
Return on Equity After Income Taxes	48	4.2	•	131.9	42.8	28.7	42.3	16.1	21.6	13.7	7.4	12.1	11.6	•
Profit Margin (Before Income Tax)	49	2.7	•	11.4	•	6.7	9.0	4.9	7.1	5.7	4.2	2.2	8.4	0.0
Profit Margin (After Income Tax)	50	1.6	•	11.4	•	6.3	8.7	3.9	6.6	4.6	3.3	1.1	6.1	•

Table II

Corporations with Net Income

COMMERCIAL AND SERVICE INDUSTRY MACHINERY

MONEY AMOUNTS AND SIZE OF ASSETS IN THOUSANDS OF DOLLARS

Item Description for Accounting Period 7/11 Through 6/12		Total	Zero Assets	Under 500	500 to 1,000	1,000 to 5,000	5,000 to 10,000	10,000 to 25,000	25,000 to 50,000	50,000 to 100,000	100,000 to 250,000	250,000 to 500,000	500,000 to 2,500,000	2,500,000 and over
Number of Enterprises	1	1380	16	•	0	276	74	56	26	14	10	5	•	0
Revenues ($ in Thousands)														
Net Sales	2	34146518	142283	•	0	868756	1037511	1300681	1310061	1323584	1409078	1982323	•	0
Interest	3	459592	0	•	0	233	155	1339	1387	913	4895	2017	•	0
Rents	4	42960	0	•	0	0	0	289	1962	198	2041	750	•	0
Royalties	5	570759	23	•	0	0	365	0	86	251	2424	28064	•	0
Other Portfolio Income	6	194755	0	•	0	1196	238	354	3425	5719	21442	3778	•	0
Other Receipts	7	1760365	-110	•	0	2451	9176	11671	6914	16815	12877	10714	•	0
Total Receipts	8	37174949	142196	•	0	872636	1047445	1314334	1323835	1347480	1452757	2027646	•	0
Average Total Receipts	9	26938	8887	•	•	3162	14155	23470	50917	96249	145276	405529	•	•
Operating Costs/Operating Income (%)														
Cost of Operations	10	44.3	42.6	•	•	54.1	63.6	60.1	59.8	60.6	58.7	65.8	•	•
Salaries and Wages	11	18.8	1.9	•	•	4.7	10.2	7.6	10.4	10.3	14.3	8.7	•	•
Taxes Paid	12	2.8	43.1	•	•	1.6	1.8	1.8	1.9	1.7	2.7	1.8	•	•
Interest Paid	13	2.8	0.6	•	•	1.2	0.0	0.8	0.6	1.2	0.8	0.7	•	•
Depreciation	14	5.7	4.0	•	•	0.8	1.3	10.1	2.4	3.3	1.7	2.5	•	•
Amortization and Depletion	15	3.9	•	•	•	0.4	0.0	0.4	0.4	0.7	0.6	1.5	•	•
Pensions and Other Deferred Comp.	16	2.2	0.2	•	•	0.8	0.6	0.2	0.3	0.8	0.5	1.1	•	•
Employee Benefits	17	1.6	1.1	•	•	1.7	2.1	1.3	1.7	2.6	2.1	2.0	•	•
Advertising	18	0.7	0.9	•	•	0.5	0.3	0.4	1.5	1.2	0.5	0.5	•	•
Other Expenses	19	18.8	5.0	•	•	13.2	4.4	7.2	12.0	9.1	11.8	11.5	•	•
Officers' Compensation	20	1.1	•	•	•	5.0	2.1	1.7	1.5	1.5	1.6	1.0	•	•
Operating Margin	21	•	0.6	•	•	16.1	13.5	8.3	7.5	6.8	4.8	2.9	•	•
Operating Margin Before Officers' Comp.	22	•	0.6	•	•	21.1	15.6	10.0	9.0	8.3	6.4	3.9	•	•

Selected Average Balance Sheet ($ in Thousands)													
Net Receivables 23	6747	0	•	•	553	1313	3674	8073	13674	38955	72603	•	•
Inventories 24	1902	0	•	•	588	1552	3867	9937	15382	21837	58814	•	•
Net Property, Plant and Equipment 25	2649	0	•	•	64	529	1297	3833	9284	13626	51352	•	•
Total Assets 26	37724	0	•	•	1728	5990	14871	34166	70859	150420	417762	•	•
Notes and Loans Payable 27	13058	0	•	•	395	64	3239	5858	9143	18372	117491	•	•
All Other Liabilities 28	11770	0	•	•	490	1432	5115	14086	30096	52764	81790	•	•
Net Worth 29	12896	0	•	•	842	4494	6517	14223	31620	79284	218481	•	•
Selected Financial Ratios (Times to 1)													
Current Ratio 30	1.5	•	•	•	2.5	3.8	1.9	1.6	1.9	1.7	2.6	•	•
Quick Ratio 31	1.0	•	•	•	1.2	2.6	1.0	0.7	1.0	1.1	1.5	•	•
Net Sales to Working Capital 32	6.6	•	•	•	3.7	4.0	4.6	5.1	4.3	3.8	3.9	•	•
Coverage Ratio 33	3.3	1.9	•	•	14.5	531.5	12.2	16.0	7.9	11.8	9.2	•	•
Total Asset Turnover 34	0.7	•	•	•	1.8	2.3	1.6	1.5	1.3	0.9	0.9	•	•
Inventory Turnover 35	5.8	•	•	•	2.9	5.7	3.6	3.0	3.7	3.8	4.4	•	•
Receivables Turnover 36	2.7	•	•	•	7.4	8.7	6.4	7.2	•	3.4	•	•	•
Total Liabilities to Net Worth 37	1.9	•	•	•	1.1	0.3	1.3	1.4	1.2	0.9	0.9	•	•
Current Assets to Working Capital 38	3.1	•	•	•	1.7	1.4	2.2	2.7	2.1	2.5	1.6	•	•
Current Liabilities to Working Capital 39	2.1	•	•	•	0.7	0.4	1.2	1.7	1.1	1.5	0.6	•	•
Working Capital to Net Sales 40	0.2	•	•	•	0.3	0.2	0.2	0.2	0.2	0.3	0.3	•	•
Inventory to Working Capital 41	0.6	•	•	•	0.8	0.4	0.9	1.2	0.7	0.6	0.6	•	•
Total Receipts to Cash Flow 42	4.7	27.8	•	•	3.8	5.9	6.4	5.5	6.3	5.8	6.5	•	•
Cost of Goods to Cash Flow 43	2.1	11.8	•	•	2.1	3.8	3.9	3.3	3.8	3.4	4.3	•	•
Cash Flow to Total Debt 44	0.2	•	•	•	0.9	1.6	0.4	0.5	0.4	0.3	0.3	•	•
Selected Financial Factors (in Percentages)													
Debt Ratio 45	65.8	•	•	•	51.3	25.0	56.2	58.4	55.4	47.3	47.7	•	•
Return on Total Assets 46	6.2	•	•	•	32.5	33.9	15.9	13.7	13.1	8.7	5.9	•	•
Return on Equity Before Income Taxes 47	12.5	•	•	•	62.0	45.1	33.4	30.8	25.7	15.2	10.0	•	•
Return on Equity After Income Taxes 48	9.7	•	•	•	60.0	44.0	28.8	28.8	21.8	12.9	7.3	•	•
Profit Margin (Before Income Tax) 49	6.5	0.5	•	•	16.6	14.5	9.4	8.7	8.6	8.5	5.5	•	•
Profit Margin (After Income Tax) 50	5.1	0.4	•	•	16.0	14.1	8.1	8.1	7.3	7.3	4.0	•	•

Table I

Corporations with and without Net Income

VENTILATION, HEATING, A.C. & COMMERCIAL REFRIGERATION EQUIP.

MONEY AMOUNTS AND SIZE OF ASSETS IN THOUSANDS OF DOLLARS

Item Description for Accounting Period 7/11 Through 6/12		Total	Zero Assets	Under 500	500 to 1,000	1,000 to 5,000	5,000 to 10,000	10,000 to 25,000	25,000 to 50,000	50,000 to 100,000	100,000 to 250,000	250,000 to 500,000	500,000 to 2,500,000	2,500,000 and over
Number of Enterprises	1	829	3	288	126	152	93	64	39	27	20	4	11	0
Revenues ($ in Thousands)														
Net Sales	2	34260255	248263	11260	287598	890761	1777399	1574596	2620031	2767152	3860414	1086830	19135952	0
Interest	3	74542	157	0	2	590	51	503	1653	1835	3392	4699	61660	0
Rents	4	9609	0	0	0	0	361	267	5293	406	1771	194	1317	0
Royalties	5	172293	0	0	0	0	0	0	2403	6741	2662	2187	158300	0
Other Portfolio Income	6	537794	10257	0	61	57	910	2134	7025	3313	28246	47072	438718	0
Other Receipts	7	449719	1566	154	437	826	3952	16508	19473	12301	39222	11302	343977	0
Total Receipts	8	35504212	260243	11414	288098	892234	1782673	1594008	2655878	2791748	3935707	1152284	20139924	0
Average Total Receipts	9	42828	86748	40	2286	5870	19169	24906	68099	103398	196785	288071	1830902	•
Operating Costs/Operating Income (%)														
Cost of Operations	10	71.7	62.0	78.9	69.9	69.9	82.6	68.7	72.3	70.0	70.4	74.3	71.5	•
Salaries and Wages	11	8.0	16.5	2.4	9.8	10.4	4.6	9.7	6.7	8.4	6.5	7.4	8.3	•
Taxes Paid	12	1.3	10.3	3.8	2.9	3.1	0.9	1.5	1.5	1.6	1.5	1.2	1.0	•
Interest Paid	13	3.4	19.2	0.2	0.2	1.3	0.5	0.5	0.5	0.8	1.7	4.1	4.9	•
Depreciation	14	2.1	1.4	9.7	0.5	1.3	1.2	2.1	1.8	2.7	3.6	1.7	1.9	•
Amortization and Depletion	15	1.1	1.2	0.5	0.0	0.1	0.0	0.4	0.3	0.4	0.4	1.9	1.6	•
Pensions and Other Deferred Comp.	16	0.6	0.1	•	0.2	0.7	0.4	0.9	0.4	0.5	0.9	0.2	0.7	•
Employee Benefits	17	2.8	0.8	0.2	1.6	0.8	0.5	1.1	1.8	2.1	2.3	1.9	3.7	•
Advertising	18	0.7	0.7	7.2	1.4	0.5	0.2	0.9	0.9	0.5	0.7	0.4	0.8	•
Other Expenses	19	8.4	18.4	56.9	7.5	11.5	6.2	7.8	10.6	8.5	7.3	11.4	8.2	•
Officers' Compensation	20	1.0	9.7	3.3	7.9	5.2	1.4	2.2	0.8	1.2	0.7	0.5	0.6	•
Operating Margin	21	•	•	•	•	•	1.6	4.2	2.4	3.3	4.0	•	•	•
Operating Margin Before Officers' Comp.	22	•	•	•	6.0	0.5	3.0	6.4	3.2	4.5	4.7	•	•	•

Selected Average Balance Sheet ($ in Thousands)

Net Receivables 23	5771	0	1	257	924	1934	4406	9417	15024	30921	103044	213257	•
Inventories 24	4506	0	9	178	597	2019	3653	6485	10092	28929	42589	134315	•
Net Property, Plant and Equipment 25	4672	0	43	31	278	1583	2167	6816	14178	30958	30839	194327	•
Total Assets 26	45671	0	55	769	2842	6878	15688	35835	69169	152294	432107	2512162	•
Notes and Loans Payable 27	20441	0	95	136	984	2194	3521	5437	16677	53971	169646	1263782	•
All Other Liabilities 28	11947	0	4	247	1161	1655	3841	11927	20773	55110	112020	610856	•
Net Worth 29	13283	0	-44	386	696	3029	8326	18471	31719	43212	150441	637524	•

Selected Financial Ratios (Times to 1)

Current Ratio 30	1.6	•	2.3	1.7	1.9	3.5	2.6	2.3	1.7	1.3	2.6	1.5	•
Quick Ratio 31	0.9	•	0.4	1.2	1.4	2.2	1.4	1.6	1.0	0.6	1.9	0.8	•
Net Sales to Working Capital 32	7.7	•	7.5	8.8	4.9	5.5	3.5	5.7	6.5	11.2	2.7	10.3	•
Coverage Ratio 33	1.9	•	•	•	•	5.1	10.9	8.7	6.1	4.7	1.3	1.6	•
Total Asset Turnover 34	0.9	•	0.7	3.0	2.1	2.8	1.6	1.9	1.5	1.3	0.6	0.7	•
Inventory Turnover 35	6.6	•	3.5	9.0	6.9	7.8	4.6	7.5	7.1	4.7	4.7	9.3	•
Receivables Turnover 36	7.0	•	2.5	•	•	9.0	7.0	6.8	7.4	6.2	2.5	10.3	•
Total Liabilities to Net Worth 37	2.4	•	•	1.0	3.1	1.3	0.9	0.9	1.2	2.5	1.9	2.9	•
Current Assets to Working Capital 38	2.6	•	1.8	2.4	2.1	1.4	1.6	1.8	2.5	4.9	1.6	3.1	•
Current Liabilities to Working Capital 39	1.6	•	0.8	1.4	1.1	0.4	0.6	0.8	1.5	3.9	0.6	2.1	•
Working Capital to Net Sales 40	0.1	•	0.1	0.1	0.2	0.2	0.3	0.2	0.2	0.1	0.4	0.1	•
Inventory to Working Capital 41	0.8	•	1.5	0.7	0.5	0.5	0.7	0.5	0.7	1.8	0.4	1.0	•
Total Receipts to Cash Flow 42	11.5	•	•	23.5	23.8	14.0	8.3	7.8	8.8	8.7	9.1	13.2	•
Cost of Goods to Cash Flow 43	8.3	•	•	16.4	16.6	11.5	5.7	5.6	6.2	6.2	6.7	9.4	•
Cash Flow to Total Debt 44	0.1	•	•	0.3	0.1	0.4	0.4	0.5	0.3	0.2	0.1	0.1	•

Selected Financial Factors (in Percentages)

Debt Ratio 45	70.9	•	180.5	49.8	75.5	56.0	46.9	48.5	54.1	71.6	65.2	74.6	•
Return on Total Assets 46	5.7	•	•	•	•	6.7	9.2	8.1	7.4	9.9	3.2	5.4	•
Return on Equity Before Income Taxes 47	9.1	•	54.7	•	•	12.2	15.8	13.9	13.5	27.6	1.9	8.0	•
Return on Equity After Income Taxes 48	6.1	•	54.7	•	•	10.5	13.6	9.6	10.7	21.7	1.8	5.1	•
Profit Margin (Before Income Tax) 49	2.9	•	•	•	•	1.9	5.4	3.8	4.2	6.2	1.0	2.9	•
Profit Margin (After Income Tax) 50	2.0	•	•	•	•	1.7	4.6	2.6	3.3	4.8	1.0	1.9	•

Table II

Corporations with Net Income

VENTILATION, HEATING, A.C. & COMMERCIAL REFRIGERATION EQUIP.

MONEY AMOUNTS AND SIZE OF ASSETS IN THOUSANDS OF DOLLARS

Item Description for Accounting Period 7/11 Through 6/12		Total	Zero Assets	Under 500	500 to 1,000	1,000 to 5,000	5,000 to 10,000	10,000 to 25,000	25,000 to 50,000	50,000 to 100,000	100,000 to 250,000	250,000 to 500,000	500,000 to 2,500,000	2,500,000 and over
Number of Enterprises	1	406	0	•	116	79	86	46	33	20	•	0	6	0
Revenues ($ in Thousands)														
Net Sales	2	27000803	0	•	281984	666717	1725379	1105789	1983661	1817624	•	0	15582179	0
Interest	3	70160	0	•	2	232	14	250	1367	1756	•	0	60299	0
Rents	4	9156	0	•	0	0	350	267	5293	47	•	0	1233	0
Royalties	5	152595	0	•	0	0	0	0	2403	3071	•	0	142878	0
Other Portfolio Income	6	514874	0	•	5	9	887	269	6912	3090	•	0	430917	0
Other Receipts	7	424336	0	•	437	518	3473	15668	18326	8481	•	0	335674	0
Total Receipts	8	28171924	0	•	282428	667476	1730103	1122243	2017962	1834069	•	0	16553180	0
Average Total Receipts	9	69389	•	•	2435	8449	20117	24397	61150	91703	•	•	2758863	•
Operating Costs/Operating Income (%)														
Cost of Operations	10	70.8	•	•	70.1	68.6	82.6	65.0	66.8	67.0	•	•	71.2	•
Salaries and Wages	11	7.9	•	•	6.6	10.9	4.0	8.8	7.8	8.5	•	•	8.3	•
Taxes Paid	12	1.2	•	•	2.6	2.9	0.8	1.7	1.5	1.8	•	•	1.0	•
Interest Paid	13	3.3	•	•	0.1	0.2	0.2	0.4	0.4	0.6	•	•	5.2	•
Depreciation	14	2.0	•	•	0.4	1.2	0.9	1.4	2.0	3.1	•	•	2.0	•
Amortization and Depletion	15	1.1	•	•	0.0	0.1	0.0	0.6	0.2	0.5	•	•	1.7	•
Pensions and Other Deferred Comp.	16	0.7	•	•	0.2	0.4	0.4	0.6	0.6	0.6	•	•	0.7	•
Employee Benefits	17	3.2	•	•	1.1	0.5	0.4	1.0	2.0	2.0	•	•	4.2	•
Advertising	18	0.7	•	•	1.4	0.5	0.1	0.5	1.1	0.6	•	•	0.8	•
Other Expenses	19	7.8	•	•	6.0	8.3	5.2	8.7	11.8	7.6	•	•	7.5	•
Officers' Compensation	20	1.1	•	•	8.0	4.8	1.2	2.1	0.9	1.4	•	•	0.7	•
Operating Margin	21	0.2	•	•	3.6	1.7	4.1	9.3	5.0	6.3	•	•	•	•
Operating Margin Before Officers' Comp.	22	1.3	•	•	11.6	6.5	5.3	11.4	5.9	7.7	•	•	•	•

Selected Average Balance Sheet ($ in Thousands)														
Net Receivables	23	8722	•	•	260	1123	2022	4196	9511	12633	•	•	299088	•
Inventories	24	6484	•	•	148	770	1827	3549	5994	11043	•	•	234645	•
Net Property, Plant and Equipment	25	7260	•	•	19	417	1472	2163	6827	14926	•	•	277036	•
Total Assets	26	76099	•	•	772	3015	6677	15190	36020	68005	•	•	3906233	•
Notes and Loans Payable	27	33378	•	•	23	591	1365	2700	4203	15965	•	•	1963699	•
All Other Liabilities	28	19101	•	•	189	714	1424	3647	10484	15707	•	•	915958	•
Net Worth	29	23620	•	•	560	1710	3888	8843	21332	36333	•	•	1026575	•

Selected Financial Ratios (Times to 1)														
Current Ratio	30	1.8	•	•	3.3	3.0	5.3	3.0	2.7	2.1	•	•	1.6	•
Quick Ratio	31	1.0	•	•	2.3	2.0	3.4	1.6	1.8	1.3	•	•	0.9	•
Net Sales to Working Capital	32	7.0	•	•	5.6	4.9	5.1	3.2	4.7	4.6	•	•	8.9	•
Coverage Ratio	33	2.6	•	•	43.6	10.6	20.9	26.0	19.2	13.4	•	•	1.8	•
Total Asset Turnover	34	0.9	•	•	3.1	2.8	3.0	1.6	1.7	1.3	•	•	0.7	•
Inventory Turnover	35	7.3	•	•	11.5	7.5	9.1	4.4	6.7	5.5	•	•	7.9	•
Receivables Turnover	36	8.4	•	•	15.0	8.5	9.1	6.7	6.5	6.7	•	•	•	•
Total Liabilities to Net Worth	37	2.2	•	•	0.4	0.8	0.7	0.7	0.7	0.9	•	•	2.8	•
Current Assets to Working Capital	38	2.3	•	•	1.4	1.5	1.2	1.5	1.6	1.9	•	•	2.6	•
Current Liabilities to Working Capital	39	1.3	•	•	0.4	0.5	0.2	0.5	0.6	0.9	•	•	1.6	•
Working Capital to Net Sales	40	0.1	•	•	0.2	0.2	0.2	0.3	0.2	0.2	•	•	0.1	•
Inventory to Working Capital	41	0.7	•	•	0.4	0.5	0.4	0.6	0.4	0.5	•	•	0.8	•
Total Receipts to Cash Flow	42	10.0	•	•	11.8	14.2	11.5	5.4	5.8	7.5	•	•	13.3	•
Cost of Goods to Cash Flow	43	7.1	•	•	8.2	9.7	9.5	3.5	3.9	5.0	•	•	9.5	•
Cash Flow to Total Debt	44	0.1	•	•	1.0	0.5	0.6	0.7	0.7	0.4	•	•	0.1	•

Selected Financial Factors (in Percentages)														
Debt Ratio	45	69.0	•	•	27.4	43.3	41.8	41.8	40.8	46.6	•	•	73.7	•
Return on Total Assets	46	7.4	•	•	12.0	5.5	13.6	17.8	12.0	10.4	•	•	6.2	•
Return on Equity Before Income Taxes	47	14.7	•	•	16.2	8.8	22.3	29.4	19.2	18.0	•	•	10.3	•
Return on Equity After Income Taxes	48	11.2	•	•	12.0	6.2	20.9	26.5	14.7	14.7	•	•	7.0	•
Profit Margin (Before Income Tax)	49	5.2	•	•	3.7	1.8	4.3	10.8	6.8	7.2	•	•	4.1	•
Profit Margin (After Income Tax)	50	4.0	•	•	2.8	1.3	4.0	9.8	5.2	5.9	•	•	2.8	•

Table I

Corporations with and without Net Income

METALWORKING MACHINERY

Item Description for Accounting Period 7/11 Through 6/12		Total	Zero Assets	Under 500	500 to 1,000	1,000 to 5,000	5,000 to 10,000	10,000 to 25,000	25,000 to 50,000	50,000 to 100,000	100,000 to 250,000	250,000 to 500,000	500,000 to 2,500,000	2,500,000 and over
		MONEY AMOUNTS AND SIZE OF ASSETS IN THOUSANDS OF DOLLARS												
Number of Enterprises	1	6509	645	3670	957	884	141	128	33	28	12	5	5	0
Revenues ($ in Thousands)														
Net Sales	2	25433666	55412	1691492	1282011	4363148	1501907	2613471	1308920	2106368	2205308	1246825	7058804	0
Interest	3	61585	1	164	113	4134	237	872	564	2178	2659	1255	49409	0
Rents	4	12365	0	1246	0	1436	3427	211	680	168	3414	1334	449	0
Royalties	5	6968	62	0	0	0	892	0	0	347	2500	55	3113	0
Other Portfolio Income	6	48144	33	0	35	4481	3951	3684	2780	4620	2793	4040	21727	0
Other Receipts	7	163499	-42	7035	9813	41259	4266	33425	6360	11995	29156	13582	6647	0
Total Receipts	8	25726227	55466	1699937	1291972	4414458	1514680	2651663	1319304	2125676	2245830	1267091	7140149	0
Average Total Receipts	9	3952	86	463	1350	4994	10742	20716	39979	75917	187152	253418	1428030	•
Operating Costs/Operating Income (%)														
Cost of Operations	10	66.5	64.3	45.3	53.6	70.0	67.3	68.3	72.9	69.3	68.5	61.1	69.4	•
Salaries and Wages	11	7.0	15.0	6.9	9.6	5.6	5.4	5.8	5.0	5.7	9.9	10.5	7.5	•
Taxes Paid	12	2.0	0.7	3.5	4.0	2.7	2.8	2.5	1.6	1.9	1.5	2.1	0.8	•
Interest Paid	13	1.7	2.9	1.5	1.5	0.5	1.2	0.6	1.1	1.1	1.6	3.3	3.1	•
Depreciation	14	3.5	1.4	1.9	4.3	4.1	4.2	5.0	4.9	4.2	2.6	3.9	2.5	•
Amortization and Depletion	15	0.5	5.8	0.0	0.0	0.0	0.0	0.0	0.2	0.6	0.3	0.7	1.3	•
Pensions and Other Deferred Comp.	16	0.4	0.1	0.0	•	0.4	0.5	0.4	0.8	0.4	0.7	0.7	0.2	•
Employee Benefits	17	2.7	2.1	2.1	2.9	1.4	1.3	3.2	1.4	2.0	2.7	2.0	4.3	•
Advertising	18	0.3	0.3	0.2	0.1	0.2	0.2	0.3	0.2	0.3	0.4	0.4	0.5	•
Other Expenses	19	9.4	22.7	27.9	9.7	7.2	8.0	8.0	6.7	7.1	7.6	11.7	8.5	•
Officers' Compensation	20	2.6	7.5	7.1	6.0	5.4	3.8	2.2	1.4	1.5	0.9	0.7	0.4	•
Operating Margin	21	3.2	•	3.6	8.2	2.5	5.3	3.7	3.9	5.8	3.1	3.0	1.5	•
Operating Margin Before Officers' Comp.	22	5.8	•	10.7	14.2	7.9	9.1	5.9	5.2	7.3	4.1	3.7	1.9	•

Selected Average Balance Sheet ($ in Thousands)

Net Receivables 23	606	0	31	179	585	1266	3839	7874	13175	29578	38326	259262	•
Inventories 24	556	0	10	102	595	1344	3325	9964	15242	30438	50464	194007	•
Net Property, Plant and Equipment 25	590	0	27	278	597	1784	3810	8267	13253	21674	39603	220798	•
Total Assets 26	3754	0	125	691	2634	6774	15107	34276	65309	157882	289210	2358953	•
Notes and Loans Payable 27	1240	0	133	379	549	2168	2984	7649	15864	40343	93466	880015	•
All Other Liabilities 28	1109	0	62	94	690	2205	3894	9482	18759	46577	66832	750306	•
Net Worth 29	1405	0	-70	218	1396	2401	8230	17146	30686	70962	128912	728631	•

Selected Financial Ratios (Times to 1)

Current Ratio 30	1.5	•	1.0	2.2	2.2	1.9	2.1	1.7	1.8	1.7	2.0	1.0	•
Quick Ratio 31	0.8	•	0.7	1.5	1.3	1.1	1.2	0.9	0.9	0.8	1.1	0.5	•
Net Sales to Working Capital 32	7.6	•	•	6.3	4.9	5.2	4.2	4.7	4.3	5.6	4.3	•	•
Coverage Ratio 33	3.8	•	3.7	6.8	8.1	6.2	9.8	5.1	6.9	4.2	2.8	2.2	•
Total Asset Turnover 34	1.0	•	3.7	1.9	1.9	1.6	1.4	1.2	1.2	1.2	0.9	0.6	•
Inventory Turnover 35	4.7	•	21.5	7.1	5.8	5.3	4.2	2.9	3.4	4.1	3.0	5.0	•
Receivables Turnover 36	7.0	•	11.9	7.1	8.8	8.3	5.9	4.5	6.6	7.2	7.4	6.4	•
Total Liabilities to Net Worth 37	1.7	•	•	2.2	0.9	1.8	0.8	1.0	1.1	1.2	1.2	2.2	•
Current Assets to Working Capital 38	3.2	•	•	1.8	1.8	2.2	1.9	2.4	2.3	2.5	2.0	•	•
Current Liabilities to Working Capital 39	2.2	•	•	0.8	0.8	1.2	0.9	1.4	1.3	1.5	1.0	•	•
Working Capital to Net Sales 40	0.1	•	•	0.2	0.2	0.2	0.2	0.2	0.2	0.2	0.2	•	•
Inventory to Working Capital 41	1.2	•	•	0.4	0.6	0.8	0.8	1.1	1.0	1.2	0.7	•	•
Total Receipts to Cash Flow 42	8.6	•	4.0	6.4	12.5	8.0	9.9	10.0	8.2	8.9	6.7	9.8	•
Cost of Goods to Cash Flow 43	5.7	•	1.8	3.4	8.8	5.4	6.7	7.3	5.7	6.1	4.1	6.8	•
Cash Flow to Total Debt 44	0.2	•	0.6	0.4	0.3	0.3	0.3	0.2	0.3	0.2	0.2	0.1	•

Selected Financial Factors (in Percentages)

Debt Ratio 45	62.6	•	156.2	68.4	47.0	64.6	45.5	50.0	53.0	55.1	55.4	69.1	•
Return on Total Assets 46	6.8	•	20.8	20.4	7.9	11.4	7.7	6.7	9.1	8.1	8.1	4.1	•
Return on Equity Before Income Taxes 47	13.3	•	•	55.1	13.0	27.1	12.8	10.8	16.5	13.7	11.8	7.2	•
Return on Equity After Income Taxes 48	11.0	•	•	54.8	11.6	23.9	11.6	8.5	13.9	9.7	8.6	5.0	•
Profit Margin (Before Income Tax) 49	4.8	•	4.1	9.0	3.7	6.1	5.1	4.7	6.7	5.3	6.1	3.7	•
Profit Margin (After Income Tax) 50	3.9	•	3.9	8.9	3.3	5.4	4.7	3.7	5.7	3.8	4.4	2.6	•

Table II

Corporations with Net Income

METALWORKING MACHINERY

MONEY AMOUNTS AND SIZE OF ASSETS IN THOUSANDS OF DOLLARS

Item Description for Accounting Period 7/11 Through 6/12		Total	Zero Assets	Under 500	500 to 1,000	1,000 to 5,000	5,000 to 10,000	10,000 to 25,000	25,000 to 50,000	50,000 to 100,000	100,000 to 250,000	250,000 to 500,000	500,000 to 2,500,000	2,500,000 and over
Number of Enterprises	1	5399	382	3415	617	692	124	105	22	23	•	•	5	0
Revenues ($ in Thousands)														
Net Sales	2	22849937	10591	1481415	962641	3450957	1363734	2377852	1078632	1847658	•	•	7058804	0
Interest	3	59430	0	136	113	2968	230	441	391	1912	•	•	49409	0
Rents	4	10979	0	1246	0	1436	3427	124	204	168	•	•	449	0
Royalties	5	6906	0	0	0	0	892	0	0	347	•	•	3113	0
Other Portfolio Income	6	43091	0	0	0	4481	3951	3436	1392	2837	•	•	21727	0
Other Receipts	7	111859	0	6281	9806	12903	3949	14480	4227	10991	•	•	6647	0
Total Receipts	8	23082202	10591	1489078	972560	3472745	1376183	2396333	1084846	1863913	•	•	7140149	0
Average Total Receipts	9	4275	28	436	1576	5018	11098	22822	49311	81040	•	•	1428030	•
Operating Costs/Operating Income (%)														
Cost of Operations	10	65.8	7.3	44.7	48.2	66.7	65.9	67.7	74.2	68.6	•	•	69.4	•
Salaries and Wages	11	6.8	•	4.2	10.4	5.8	5.1	5.4	4.4	5.9	•	•	7.5	•
Taxes Paid	12	1.9	•	3.4	3.9	2.8	2.9	2.4	1.5	1.7	•	•	0.8	•
Interest Paid	13	1.7	•	1.6	1.7	0.4	1.1	0.6	0.8	0.9	•	•	3.1	•
Depreciation	14	3.2	•	1.8	3.9	3.8	4.3	4.7	4.4	3.5	•	•	2.5	•
Amortization and Depletion	15	0.5	•	0.0	0.0	0.0	0.0	0.0	0.2	0.7	•	•	1.3	•
Pensions and Other Deferred Comp.	16	0.3	•	0.0	•	0.3	0.6	0.4	0.9	0.4	•	•	0.2	•
Employee Benefits	17	2.7	9.8	1.9	2.8	1.3	1.4	3.2	1.1	1.7	•	•	4.3	•
Advertising	18	0.4	•	0.2	0.1	0.3	0.3	0.3	0.2	0.3	•	•	0.5	•
Other Expenses	19	9.4	6.5	28.5	10.3	7.0	8.5	7.5	5.7	7.5	•	•	8.5	•
Officers' Compensation	20	2.5	•	6.8	6.8	5.9	3.9	2.1	1.2	1.6	•	•	0.4	•
Operating Margin	21	4.7	76.4	6.8	12.0	5.5	6.1	5.7	5.5	7.3	•	•	1.5	•
Operating Margin Before Officers' Comp.	22	7.2	76.4	13.6	18.8	11.4	10.0	7.8	6.8	8.9	•	•	1.9	•

Selected Average Balance Sheet ($ in Thousands)													
Net Receivables 23	648	0	32	175	580	1373	4205	8816	13013	•	•	259262	•
Inventories 24	554	0	8	116	634	1235	3468	12407	14005	•	•	234844	•
Net Property, Plant and Equipment 25	621	0	22	347	572	1872	4151	7804	13020	•	•	220798	•
Total Assets 26	3997	0	115	705	2541	6829	15249	34844	64677	•	•	2358953	•
Notes and Loans Payable 27	1305	0	100	412	449	2229	2766	5860	14502	•	•	880015	•
All Other Liabilities 28	1187	0	34	106	674	1988	3785	11306	17023	•	•	750306	•
Net Worth 29	1505	0	-19	187	1418	2612	8698	17678	33152	•	•	728631	•

Selected Financial Ratios (Times to 1)													
Current Ratio 30	1.5	•	1.8	1.8	2.3	2.1	2.3	1.7	2.1	•	•	1.0	•
Quick Ratio 31	0.8	•	1.4	1.3	1.4	1.2	1.3	0.8	1.0	•	•	0.5	•
Net Sales to Working Capital 32	7.5	•	11.0	10.9	4.8	4.6	4.1	5.1	3.8	•	•	•	•
Coverage Ratio 33	4.6	•	5.6	8.9	15.3	7.2	12.2	8.3	10.0	•	•	2.2	•
Total Asset Turnover 34	1.1	•	3.8	2.2	2.0	1.6	1.5	1.4	1.2	•	•	0.6	•
Inventory Turnover 35	5.0	•	24.9	6.5	5.2	5.9	4.4	2.9	3.9	•	•	4.2	•
Receivables Turnover 36	7.7	•	13.6	7.2	8.2	9.5	6.0	4.8	7.3	•	•	•	•
Total Liabilities to Net Worth 37	1.7	•	•	2.8	0.8	1.6	0.8	1.0	1.0	•	•	2.2	•
Current Assets to Working Capital 38	3.1	•	2.3	2.3	1.8	1.9	1.8	2.4	1.9	•	•	•	•
Current Liabilities to Working Capital 39	2.1	•	1.3	1.3	0.8	0.9	0.8	1.4	0.9	•	•	•	•
Working Capital to Net Sales 40	0.1	•	0.1	0.1	0.2	0.2	0.2	0.2	0.3	•	•	•	•
Inventory to Working Capital 41	1.2	•	0.4	0.6	0.6	0.7	0.7	1.2	0.8	•	•	•	•
Total Receipts to Cash Flow 42	7.7	1.2	3.4	5.0	9.9	7.2	9.0	9.5	7.1	•	•	9.8	•
Cost of Goods to Cash Flow 43	5.1	0.1	1.5	2.4	6.6	4.7	6.1	7.0	4.9	•	•	6.8	•
Cash Flow to Total Debt 44	0.2	•	0.9	0.6	0.4	0.4	0.4	0.3	0.4	•	•	0.1	•

Selected Financial Factors (in Percentages)													
Debt Ratio 45	62.4	•	116.2	73.5	44.2	61.7	43.0	49.3	48.7	•	•	69.1	•
Return on Total Assets 46	8.2	•	33.5	32.5	12.8	13.2	10.6	9.8	11.3	•	•	4.1	•
Return on Equity Before Income Taxes 47	17.1	•	•	108.7	21.4	29.6	17.0	17.0	19.7	•	•	7.2	•
Return on Equity After Income Taxes 48	14.4	•	•	108.1	19.7	26.3	15.6	13.6	16.8	•	•	5.0	•
Profit Margin (Before Income Tax) 49	6.1	76.4	7.3	13.0	6.1	7.0	6.5	6.1	8.1	•	•	3.7	•
Profit Margin (After Income Tax) 50	5.1	76.4	7.0	13.0	5.6	6.2	6.0	4.9	6.9	•	•	2.6	•

Table I

Corporations with and without Net Income

ENGINE, TURBINE AND POWER TRANSMISSION EQUIPMENT

MONEY AMOUNTS AND SIZE OF ASSETS IN THOUSANDS OF DOLLARS

Item Description for Accounting Period 7/11 Through 6/12		Total	Zero Assets	Under 500	500 to 1,000	1,000 to 5,000	5,000 to 10,000	10,000 to 25,000	25,000 to 50,000	50,000 to 100,000	100,000 to 250,000	250,000 to 500,000	500,000 to 2,500,000	2,500,000 and over
Number of Enterprises	1	341	8	52	33	131	23	36	21	9	8	7	5	8
Revenues ($ in Thousands)														
Net Sales	2	62486706	0	43075	162543	710293	147551	588741	926827	753155	1751577	1742188	8095537	47565218
Interest	3	757196	0	0	0	4	37	63	482	465	7461	11345	9887	727452
Rents	4	729273	0	0	0	0	0	0	0	0	118	9	467	728679
Royalties	5	785440	0	0	0	0	0	0	0	0	274	2389	27595	755182
Other Portfolio Income	6	678802	0	0	0	0	43	9491	908	322	8317	2526	14822	642373
Other Receipts	7	1000378	0	0	0	10882	248	779	7827	6941	5755	-5825	49510	924262
Total Receipts	8	66437795	0	43075	162543	721179	147879	599074	936044	760883	1773502	1752632	8197818	51343166
Average Total Receipts	9	194832	0	828	4926	5505	6430	16641	44574	84543	221688	250376	1639564	6417896
Operating Costs/Operating Income (%)														
Cost of Operations	10	73.1	•	83.9	58.5	74.0	58.6	59.9	76.1	70.5	77.8	71.3	73.9	73.1
Salaries and Wages	11	13.3	•	8.0	22.8	5.3	8.0	11.8	6.3	9.3	4.2	10.7	5.8	15.3
Taxes Paid	12	1.2	•	6.9	0.0	1.8	3.5	2.0	2.1	0.9	1.0	2.2	1.4	1.1
Interest Paid	13	1.8	•	6.6	•	0.9	1.0	2.1	0.4	1.0	0.8	1.7	2.2	1.9
Depreciation	14	3.2	•	0.1	3.1	0.5	4.0	5.3	5.5	3.2	4.1	2.9	2.9	3.3
Amortization and Depletion	15	0.4	•	•	•	0.0	2.3	0.2	0.3	0.3	0.9	0.2	1.0	0.3
Pensions and Other Deferred Comp.	16	1.8	•	•	•	0.2	0.3	0.2	0.4	0.4	0.9	0.8	1.8	2.0
Employee Benefits	17	2.9	•	•	•	1.6	1.2	1.3	2.8	1.0	1.0	2.1	3.5	2.9
Advertising	18	0.4	•	0.0	0.4	0.9	0.3	0.5	0.2	0.2	0.4	0.2	1.2	0.3
Other Expenses	19	2.1	•	17.4	3.1	7.5	20.9	18.4	11.3	10.8	7.7	5.2	5.4	0.5
Officers' Compensation	20	0.6	•	8.9	•	3.7	3.4	3.2	1.6	1.7	0.7	1.0	0.4	0.5
Operating Margin	21	•	•	•	12.0	3.6	•	•	•	0.7	0.5	1.6	0.7	•
Operating Margin Before Officers' Comp.	22	•	•	•	12.0	7.3	•	•	•	2.3	1.2	2.6	1.1	•

Selected Average Balance Sheet ($ in Thousands)

Net Receivables 23	27453	0	30	0	429	1125	2147	7020	16388	35736	86253	186566	885376
Inventories 24	19705	0	236	0	1233	2170	3233	7152	14162	41870	37551	275926	524769
Net Property, Plant and Equipment 25	26715	0	3	284	467	2811	4349	10158	8262	43139	52930	223877	836890
Total Assets 26	226850	0	283	909	2348	8365	14930	33200	72672	190598	369400	1233625	8080460
Notes and Loans Payable 27	35991	0	778	1	881	4406	6079	7023	10846	33764	113901	284692	1132580
All Other Liabilities 28	117965	0	591	270	395	1062	4220	14128	28980	87291	239141	632789	4233065
Net Worth 29	72894	0	-1086	638	1072	2897	4630	12049	32846	69542	16358	316144	2714815

Selected Financial Ratios (Times to 1)

Current Ratio 30	1.3	•	0.2	2.3	3.4	3.5	1.8	1.3	1.8	1.6	1.1	1.8	1.2
Quick Ratio 31	0.6	•	0.0	2.3	1.1	2.3	0.9	0.6	1.2	0.8	0.6	0.9	0.5
Net Sales to Working Capital 32	9.9	•	•	13.8	4.1	3.1	4.5	8.4	3.5	5.4	8.2	5.8	12.6
Coverage Ratio 33	4.5	•	•	•	6.7	•	•	•	2.8	3.6	2.3	1.9	5.3
Total Asset Turnover 34	0.8	•	2.9	5.4	2.3	0.8	1.1	1.3	1.2	1.1	0.7	1.3	0.7
Inventory Turnover 35	6.8	•	2.9	•	3.3	1.7	3.0	4.7	4.2	4.1	4.7	4.3	8.3
Receivables Turnover 36	8.6	•	55.4	•	•	3.7	7.2	9.3	5.5	6.2	3.1	5.2	10.7
Total Liabilities to Net Worth 37	2.1	•	•	0.4	1.2	1.9	2.2	1.8	1.2	1.7	21.6	2.9	2.0
Current Assets to Working Capital 38	4.3	•	•	1.8	1.4	1.4	2.3	3.9	2.3	2.6	7.9	2.2	5.3
Current Liabilities to Working Capital 39	3.3	•	•	0.8	0.4	0.4	1.3	2.9	1.3	1.6	6.9	1.2	4.3
Working Capital to Net Sales 40	0.1	•	•	0.1	0.2	0.3	0.2	0.1	0.3	0.2	0.1	0.2	0.1
Inventory to Working Capital 41	1.4	•	•	•	0.9	0.5	0.9	1.8	0.7	1.0	1.2	0.9	1.7
Total Receipts to Cash Flow 42	20.2	•	•	6.8	9.5	8.0	16.2	29.3	10.1	12.3	18.7	16.2	22.6
Cost of Goods to Cash Flow 43	14.8	•	•	4.0	7.0	4.7	9.7	22.3	7.1	9.5	13.3	12.0	16.5
Cash Flow to Total Debt 44	0.1	•	•	2.7	0.4	0.1	0.1	0.1	0.2	0.1	0.0	0.1	0.0

Selected Financial Factors (in Percentages)

Debt Ratio 45	67.9	•	483.8	29.9	54.4	65.4	69.0	63.7	54.8	63.5	95.6	74.4	66.4
Return on Total Assets 46	6.7	•	•	65.2	14.0	•	•	•	3.0	3.4	2.6	5.6	7.3
Return on Equity Before Income Taxes 47	16.3	•	24.2	93.0	26.1	•	•	•	4.3	6.7	33.2	10.6	17.6
Return on Equity After Income Taxes 48	10.4	•	24.2	62.6	26.1	•	•	•	1.5	2.2	9.9	6.2	11.7
Profit Margin (Before Income Tax) 49	6.5	•	•	12.0	5.2	•	•	•	1.7	2.1	2.2	2.1	8.0
Profit Margin (After Income Tax) 50	4.2	•	•	8.1	5.2	•	•	•	0.6	0.7	0.7	1.2	5.3

Table II

Corporations with Net Income

ENGINE, TURBINE AND POWER TRANSMISSION EQUIPMENT

MONEY AMOUNTS AND SIZE OF ASSETS IN THOUSANDS OF DOLLARS

Item Description for Accounting Period 7/11 Through 6/12		Total	Zero Assets	Under 500	500 to 1,000	1,000 to 5,000	5,000 to 10,000	10,000 to 25,000	25,000 to 50,000	50,000 to 100,000	100,000 to 250,000	250,000 to 500,000	500,000 to 2,500,000	2,500,000 and over
Number of Enterprises	1	205	0	0	33	102	13	22	11	•	5	3	•	•
Revenues ($ in Thousands)														
Net Sales	2	52888737	0	0	162543	619036	124220	436205	687761	•	1425601	1402401	•	•
Interest	3	735526	0	0	0	0	29	37	0	•	2322	1730	•	•
Rents	4	728689	0	0	0	0	0	0	0	•	0	9	•	•
Royalties	5	769334	0	0	0	0	0	0	0	•	274	2389	•	•
Other Portfolio Income	6	653887	0	0	0	0	23	2044	0	•	5369	2100	•	•
Other Receipts	7	965197	0	0	0	10715	177	1922	1678	•	4232	-13819	•	•
Total Receipts	8	56741370	0	0	162543	629751	124449	440208	689439	•	1437798	1394810	•	•
Average Total Receipts	9	276787	•	•	4926	6174	9573	20009	62676	•	287560	464937	•	•
Operating Costs/Operating Income (%)														
Cost of Operations	10	72.4	•	•	58.5	77.2	52.6	67.7	76.6	•	77.4	71.2	•	•
Salaries and Wages	11	14.5	•	•	22.8	2.1	5.2	6.9	2.8	•	3.6	9.6	•	•
Taxes Paid	12	1.2	•	•	0.0	1.4	3.3	1.8	1.7	•	0.6	2.6	•	•
Interest Paid	13	1.8	•	•	•	0.2	1.1	0.7	0.3	•	0.2	0.2	•	•
Depreciation	14	3.1	•	•	3.1	0.3	3.4	2.9	4.6	•	4.0	2.4	•	•
Amortization and Depletion	15	0.3	•	•	•	0.0	2.8	0.3	0.0	•	0.1	0.1	•	•
Pensions and Other Deferred Comp.	16	1.9	•	•	•	0.2	0.3	0.1	0.4	•	1.0	0.5	•	•
Employee Benefits	17	2.8	•	•	•	1.8	1.4	0.6	2.0	•	0.9	2.6	•	•
Advertising	18	0.4	•	•	0.4	0.9	0.1	0.5	0.1	•	0.4	0.2	•	•
Other Expenses	19	1.2	•	•	3.1	4.5	6.3	9.0	7.3	•	6.8	3.8	•	•
Officers' Compensation	20	0.6	•	•	•	4.0	2.8	3.3	1.1	•	0.7	0.8	•	•
Operating Margin	21	•	•	•	12.0	7.5	20.8	6.1	3.1	•	4.3	6.1	•	•
Operating Margin Before Officers' Comp.	22	0.4	•	•	12.0	11.5	23.6	9.5	4.2	•	5.0	6.9	•	•

Selected Average Balance Sheet ($ in Thousands)														
Net Receivables	23	39667	•	•	0	521	1257	2739	9547	•	46492	96528	•	•
Inventories	24	27024	•	•	0	816	3361	3457	10218	•	53957	63340	•	•
Net Property, Plant and Equipment	25	34016	•	•	284	240	3124	2130	8495	•	49190	43334	•	•
Total Assets	26	328449	•	•	909	2400	7745	13377	34129	•	213291	354882	•	•
Notes and Loans Payable	27	43748	•	•	1	311	2234	2873	5538	•	33839	10115	•	•
All Other Liabilities	28	173772	•	•	270	400	921	3511	17571	•	100222	138860	•	•
Net Worth	29	110929	•	•	638	1689	4590	6993	11020	•	79230	205908	•	•
Selected Financial Ratios (Times to 1)														
Current Ratio	30	1.3	•	•	2.3	3.7	4.7	1.6	1.2	•	1.7	2.1	•	•
Quick Ratio	31	0.6	•	•	2.3	1.3	3.4	0.7	0.5	•	0.9	1.3	•	•
Net Sales to Working Capital	32	9.1	•	•	13.8	3.9	3.3	6.9	12.7	•	5.0	3.6	•	•
Coverage Ratio	33	5.7	•	•	•	48.2	20.8	12.4	12.4	•	23.7	35.6	•	•
Total Asset Turnover	34	0.8	•	•	5.4	2.5	1.2	1.5	1.8	•	1.3	1.3	•	•
Inventory Turnover	35	6.9	•	•	•	5.7	1.5	3.9	4.7	•	4.1	5.3	•	•
Receivables Turnover	36	8.6	•	•	•	19.1	3.5	7.1	9.6	•	6.2	5.8	•	•
Total Liabilities to Net Worth	37	2.0	•	•	0.4	0.4	0.7	0.9	2.1	•	1.7	0.7	•	•
Current Assets to Working Capital	38	3.9	•	•	1.8	1.4	1.3	2.8	5.2	•	2.5	1.9	•	•
Current Liabilities to Working Capital	39	2.9	•	•	0.8	0.4	0.3	1.8	4.2	•	1.5	0.9	•	•
Working Capital to Net Sales	40	0.1	•	•	0.1	0.3	0.3	0.1	0.1	•	0.2	0.3	•	•
Inventory to Working Capital	41	1.3	•	•	•	0.9	0.4	1.4	2.8	•	1.0	0.4	•	•
Total Receipts to Cash Flow	42	17.6	•	•	6.8	8.2	4.0	7.0	11.0	•	9.2	14.2	•	•
Cost of Goods to Cash Flow	43	12.7	•	•	4.0	6.3	2.1	4.7	8.4	•	7.1	10.1	•	•
Cash Flow to Total Debt	44	0.1	•	•	2.7	1.0	0.8	0.4	0.2	•	0.2	0.2	•	•
Selected Financial Factors (in Percentages)														
Debt Ratio	45	66.2	•	•	29.9	29.6	40.7	47.7	67.7	•	62.9	42.0	•	•
Return on Total Assets	46	7.9	•	•	65.2	23.7	27.2	12.0	6.7	•	7.6	7.5	•	•
Return on Equity Before Income Taxes	47	19.4	•	•	93.0	33.0	43.7	21.1	19.1	•	19.6	12.5	•	•
Return on Equity After Income Taxes	48	13.0	•	•	62.6	33.0	28.8	16.7	17.5	•	13.3	8.2	•	•
Profit Margin (Before Income Tax)	49	8.3	•	•	12.0	9.2	21.0	7.4	3.4	•	5.4	5.5	•	•
Profit Margin (After Income Tax)	50	5.6	•	•	8.1	9.2	13.8	5.9	3.1	•	3.7	3.6	•	•

Table I

Corporations with and without Net Income

OTHER GENERAL PURPOSE MACHINERY

MONEY AMOUNTS AND SIZE OF ASSETS IN THOUSANDS OF DOLLARS

Item Description for Accounting Period 7/11 Through 6/12		Total	Zero Assets	Under 500	500 to 1,000	1,000 to 5,000	5,000 to 10,000	10,000 to 25,000	25,000 to 50,000	50,000 to 100,000	100,000 to 250,000	250,000 to 500,000	500,000 to 2,500,000	2,500,000 and over
Number of Enterprises	1	5346	294	3024	571	742	316	217	76	47	18	15	19	7
Revenues ($ in Thousands)														
Net Sales	2	75564960	1298621	1304558	2033451	3552726	3482518	5375573	3639889	4161289	3236987	6138407	17833832	23507110
Interest	3	542488	4863	263	1348	460	650	2586	1883	4924	4952	8348	241433	270777
Rents	4	21136	208	0	829	62	518	2691	8470	387	605	1329	5327	709
Royalties	5	318781	774	0	0	0	0	1288	7913	2940	8570	7066	191303	98926
Other Portfolio Income	6	759232	9881	986	732	9636	3071	31626	1593	14174	9508	36112	207048	434861
Other Receipts	7	1027016	-18112	39704	976	12046	16185	56204	38868	43662	26466	21423	115794	673806
Total Receipts	8	78233613	1296235	1345511	2037336	3574930	3502942	5469968	3698616	4227376	3287088	6212685	18594737	24986189
Average Total Receipts	9	14634	4409	445	3568	4818	11085	25207	48666	89944	182616	414179	978670	3569456
Operating Costs/Operating Income (%)														
Cost of Operations	10	67.7	60.0	47.6	53.9	66.0	61.2	67.4	73.3	69.3	66.6	68.0	66.7	71.4
Salaries and Wages	11	9.4	16.8	13.2	8.9	6.9	9.8	8.9	7.7	8.5	10.8	6.8	9.9	9.8
Taxes Paid	12	1.6	2.2	2.6	3.4	2.1	2.7	2.0	1.4	1.6	1.4	1.3	1.9	0.9
Interest Paid	13	2.6	1.6	0.5	0.6	0.4	0.5	0.5	1.0	1.2	4.9	0.4	2.9	4.6
Depreciation	14	3.5	1.7	1.0	1.5	1.7	2.0	2.5	2.8	2.9	1.7	2.4	2.5	6.3
Amortization and Depletion	15	0.8	1.0	0.1	0.0	0.3	0.0	0.2	0.1	0.5	0.9	0.4	1.1	1.1
Pensions and Other Deferred Comp.	16	0.9	0.8	0.8	1.6	0.5	0.6	0.6	0.4	0.7	0.6	0.9	0.7	1.4
Employee Benefits	17	2.1	2.6	1.0	1.0	2.1	2.0	1.9	1.0	1.7	2.1	1.9	2.7	2.0
Advertising	18	0.5	0.7	0.3	1.1	0.4	0.6	0.5	0.3	0.5	0.3	0.5	0.4	0.7
Other Expenses	19	9.7	8.4	23.9	14.5	9.3	9.9	8.0	5.3	7.7	8.6	9.5	9.7	10.1
Officers' Compensation	20	1.7	2.2	7.5	11.6	5.1	3.1	2.6	1.9	1.4	1.2	1.7	0.6	0.5
Operating Margin	21	•	2.0	1.4	2.0	5.3	7.5	4.8	4.7	4.2	0.8	6.1	0.9	•
Operating Margin Before Officers' Comp.	22	1.2	4.2	8.9	13.6	10.4	10.5	7.5	6.6	5.6	2.0	7.8	1.5	•

Selected Average Balance Sheet ($ in Thousands)													
Net Receivables 23	2574	0	27	145	435	1463	3797	8291	16793	41727	72698	152154	833366
Inventories 24	1863	0	12	218	557	2223	3577	8200	14702	26828	52780	116257	444437
Net Property, Plant and Equipment 25	1896	0	27	67	376	826	2449	4989	11434	15072	43583	102626	736109
Total Assets 26	19008	0	103	704	2120	7380	14545	34626	71122	161099	333192	901804	8976232
Notes and Loans Payable 27	5470	0	74	556	379	1084	2752	7491	17483	47016	40131	280674	2758231
All Other Liabilities 28	5440	0	33	84	650	2253	4272	11908	22528	28378	105728	356088	2283790
Net Worth 29	8098	0	-4	65	1091	4043	7521	15227	31111	85704	187333	265042	3934212
Selected Financial Ratios (Times to 1)													
Current Ratio 30	1.2	•	1.8	2.7	2.3	2.5	2.2	1.8	1.8	1.8	2.0	1.5	0.9
Quick Ratio 31	0.6	•	1.3	1.8	1.4	1.4	1.2	1.0	0.9	1.1	1.1	0.7	0.4
Net Sales to Working Capital 32	10.5	•	16.8	11.8	5.6	3.4	4.4	4.5	4.5	4.1	4.5	7.5	•
Coverage Ratio 33	2.5	2.6	9.8	4.8	16.7	17.9	13.7	7.1	5.9	1.5	18.0	3.4	0.7
Total Asset Turnover 34	0.7	•	4.2	5.1	2.3	1.5	1.7	1.4	1.2	1.1	1.2	1.0	0.4
Inventory Turnover 35	5.1	•	16.7	8.8	5.7	3.0	4.7	4.3	4.2	4.5	5.3	5.4	5.4
Receivables Turnover 36	5.5	•	19.8	22.4	10.6	7.6	7.1	5.9	6.4	4.4	6.5	6.5	3.7
Total Liabilities to Net Worth 37	1.3	•	•	9.8	0.9	0.8	0.9	1.3	1.3	0.9	0.8	2.4	1.3
Current Assets to Working Capital 38	5.1	•	2.3	1.6	1.8	1.7	1.9	2.2	2.2	2.2	2.1	3.2	•
Current Liabilities to Working Capital 39	4.1	•	1.3	0.6	0.8	0.7	0.9	1.2	1.2	1.2	1.1	2.2	•
Working Capital to Net Sales 40	0.1	•	0.1	0.1	0.2	0.3	0.2	0.2	0.2	0.2	0.2	0.1	•
Inventory to Working Capital 41	1.5	•	0.5	0.5	0.7	0.7	0.7	0.9	0.8	0.6	0.7	1.0	•
Total Receipts to Cash Flow 42	9.5	12.5	4.9	6.6	7.7	6.6	7.9	9.7	8.4	10.8	6.7	7.9	17.9
Cost of Goods to Cash Flow 43	6.4	7.5	2.3	3.6	5.1	4.0	5.3	7.1	5.9	7.2	4.6	5.3	12.8
Cash Flow to Total Debt 44	0.1	•	0.8	0.8	0.6	0.5	0.4	0.3	0.3	0.2	0.4	0.2	0.0
Selected Financial Factors (in Percentages)													
Debt Ratio 45	57.4	•	104.1	90.8	48.5	45.2	48.3	56.0	56.3	46.8	43.8	70.6	56.2
Return on Total Assets 46	4.8	•	21.2	14.0	14.1	12.8	12.1	10.1	8.8	8.2	9.9	10.3	1.2
Return on Equity Before Income Taxes 47	6.7	•	•	119.9	25.8	22.0	21.7	19.7	16.7	5.1	16.6	24.8	•
Return on Equity After Income Taxes 48	4.2	•	•	118.4	24.2	18.8	19.2	17.1	12.9	2.7	11.2	15.9	•
Profit Margin (Before Income Tax) 49	3.8	2.5	4.5	2.2	5.9	8.1	6.6	6.3	5.9	2.4	7.6	7.0	•
Profit Margin (After Income Tax) 50	2.4	0.8	4.4	2.2	5.5	6.9	5.8	5.4	4.5	1.3	5.1	4.5	•

Table II

Corporations with Net Income

OTHER GENERAL PURPOSE MACHINERY

MONEY AMOUNTS AND SIZE OF ASSETS IN THOUSANDS OF DOLLARS

Item Description for Accounting Period 7/11 Through 6/12		Total	Zero Assets	Under 500	500 to 1,000	1,000 to 5,000	5,000 to 10,000	10,000 to 25,000	25,000 to 50,000	50,000 to 100,000	100,000 to 250,000	250,000 to 500,000	500,000 to 2,500,000	2,500,000 and over
Number of Enterprises	1	4038	11	2277	466	663	302	175	60	34	14	•	16	•
Revenues ($ in Thousands)														
Net Sales	2	57417430	830664	1243203	1999536	3268637	3443301	4322775	2850517	3052990	2564564	•	15569305	•
Interest	3	92339	4388	0	9	434	585	2358	1316	4673	4296	•	21453	•
Rents	4	16102	208	0	0	0	518	1649	8350	29	605	•	3040	•
Royalties	5	297100	114	0	0	0	0	1288	7879	2940	111	•	180058	•
Other Portfolio Income	6	736247	3686	7	42	9496	3071	29669	1593	13118	7662	•	205014	•
Other Receipts	7	741874	-18287	196	962	6008	16212	51987	35115	40385	23754	•	85946	•
Total Receipts	8	59301092	820773	1243406	2000549	3284575	3463687	4409726	2904770	3114135	2600992	•	16064816	•
Average Total Receipts	9	14686	74616	546	4293	4954	11469	25198	48413	91592	185785	•	1004051	•
Operating Costs/Operating Income (%)														
Cost of Operations	10	64.6	63.2	43.1	54.2	66.2	61.0	65.2	72.1	66.5	70.5	•	66.3	•
Salaries and Wages	11	9.7	8.9	13.5	8.6	6.8	9.6	8.0	7.7	8.7	11.0	•	10.1	•
Taxes Paid	12	1.6	1.7	2.5	3.3	1.8	2.7	2.1	1.5	1.7	1.3	•	1.9	•
Interest Paid	13	1.8	1.5	0.5	0.6	0.3	0.5	0.5	0.5	0.9	0.6	•	1.1	•
Depreciation	14	2.5	1.7	1.0	1.4	1.7	2.0	2.2	3.0	2.7	1.4	•	2.4	•
Amortization and Depletion	15	0.7	0.9	0.1	0.0	0.3	0.0	0.2	0.1	0.5	0.2	•	1.1	•
Pensions and Other Deferred Comp.	16	0.9	1.1	0.8	1.7	0.5	0.6	0.6	0.5	0.8	0.6	•	0.7	•
Employee Benefits	17	2.2	2.6	1.0	1.0	2.0	2.0	2.1	1.1	2.0	2.3	•	2.6	•
Advertising	18	0.5	0.6	0.3	1.1	0.4	0.6	0.5	0.3	0.4	0.3	•	0.4	•
Other Expenses	19	9.8	6.2	23.3	14.5	8.1	9.9	8.2	4.2	7.3	6.5	•	9.5	•
Officers' Compensation	20	2.0	1.1	7.9	11.4	5.0	3.1	2.8	2.3	1.5	1.2	•	0.7	•
Operating Margin	21	3.7	10.5	6.0	2.3	6.8	8.0	7.4	6.8	7.0	4.0	•	3.3	•
Operating Margin Before Officers' Comp.	22	5.7	11.5	13.9	13.7	11.8	11.1	10.2	9.1	8.6	5.2	•	4.0	•

Selected Average Balance Sheet ($ in Thousands)

Net Receivables 23	2245	0	35	163	397	1493	3755	8668	16322	48870	•	158159	•
Inventories 24	1877	0	16	211	511	1978	3444	7172	14847	29082	•	125149	•
Net Property, Plant and Equipment 25	1442	0	35	62	396	858	2357	4485	9982	14453	•	99852	•
Total Assets 26	19172	0	123	695	2053	7295	14432	33983	69369	162072	•	895253	•
Notes and Loans Payable 27	5081	0	97	639	371	1128	2396	5384	12886	25854	•	264177	•
All Other Liabilities 28	4658	0	43	99	568	2315	3856	11704	22389	61132	•	314703	•
Net Worth 29	9434	0	-17	-44	1114	3853	8180	16894	34095	75085	•	316372	•

Selected Financial Ratios (Times to 1)

Current Ratio 30	1.6	•	1.6	2.3	2.4	2.5	2.5	2.1	1.9	2.0	•	1.5	•
Quick Ratio 31	0.9	•	1.3	1.7	1.5	1.4	1.5	1.2	1.0	1.3	•	0.7	•
Net Sales to Working Capital 32	5.9	•	18.9	15.1	5.6	3.4	3.9	3.7	4.4	3.2	•	7.5	•
Coverage Ratio 33	5.4	7.6	13.3	5.1	22.8	19.1	20.6	19.8	11.5	10.7	•	8.9	•
Total Asset Turnover 34	0.7	•	4.4	6.2	2.4	1.6	1.7	1.4	1.3	1.1	•	1.1	•
Inventory Turnover 35	4.9	•	14.7	11.0	6.4	3.5	4.7	4.8	4.0	4.4	•	5.2	•
Receivables Turnover 36	6.7	•	20.6	23.0	12.1	8.7	7.5	5.7	6.5	4.2	•	6.5	•
Total Liabilities to Net Worth 37	1.0	•	•	•	0.8	0.9	0.8	1.0	1.0	1.2	•	1.8	•
Current Assets to Working Capital 38	2.6	•	2.6	1.7	1.7	1.7	1.7	1.9	2.1	2.0	•	3.2	•
Current Liabilities to Working Capital 39	1.6	•	1.6	0.7	0.7	0.7	0.7	0.9	1.1	1.0	•	2.2	•
Working Capital to Net Sales 40	0.2	•	0.1	0.1	0.2	0.3	0.3	0.3	0.2	0.3	•	0.1	•
Inventory to Working Capital 41	0.9	•	0.5	0.5	0.6	0.7	0.6	0.7	0.8	0.5	•	1.1	•
Total Receipts to Cash Flow 42	6.9	7.4	4.6	6.5	7.3	6.4	6.4	8.7	6.7	9.8	•	7.2	•
Cost of Goods to Cash Flow 43	4.4	4.7	2.0	3.5	4.8	3.9	4.2	6.3	4.5	6.9	•	4.8	•
Cash Flow to Total Debt 44	0.2	•	0.9	0.9	0.7	0.5	0.6	0.3	0.4	0.2	•	0.2	•

Selected Financial Factors (in Percentages)

Debt Ratio 45	50.8	•	114.2	106.3	45.7	47.2	43.3	50.3	50.9	53.7	•	64.7	•
Return on Total Assets 46	7.3	•	29.0	17.7	18.3	14.2	16.9	12.8	13.1	6.8	•	10.6	•
Return on Equity Before Income Taxes 47	12.1	•	•	•	32.3	25.4	28.4	24.5	24.3	13.3	•	26.6	•
Return on Equity After Income Taxes 48	9.2	•	•	•	30.4	21.9	25.6	21.4	19.5	9.8	•	17.7	•
Profit Margin (Before Income Tax) 49	8.0	10.1	6.0	2.3	7.3	8.6	9.4	8.7	9.2	5.5	•	8.6	•
Profit Margin (After Income Tax) 50	6.1	7.4	5.9	2.3	6.9	7.4	8.5	7.6	7.4	4.0	•	5.8	•

Table I

Corporations with and without Net Income

COMPUTER AND PERIPHERAL EQUIPMENT

MONEY AMOUNTS AND SIZE OF ASSETS IN THOUSANDS OF DOLLARS

Item Description for Accounting Period 7/11 Through 6/12		Total	Zero Assets	Under 500	500 to 1,000	1,000 to 5,000	5,000 to 10,000	10,000 to 25,000	25,000 to 50,000	50,000 to 100,000	100,000 to 250,000	250,000 to 500,000	500,000 to 2,500,000	2,500,000 and over
Number of Enterprises	1	2505	468	1162	108	462	89	85	60	24	10	9	15	12
Revenues ($ in Thousands)														
Net Sales	2	224435743	327535	114532	200465	1563121	601359	2089233	3128309	2125831	2783822	3036008	12071201	196394326
Interest	3	1587652	6608	0	26	3584	522	2697	4058	4251	2727	2456	23427	1537296
Rents	4	2168872	0	18	0	0	0	0	96	244	0	0	17056	2151459
Royalties	5	27003284	0	0	2034	0	0	0	3847	28005	7020	69392	189392	26703594
Other Portfolio Income	6	2706030	4482	0	0	41756	82	2021	3291	7296	406	872	139762	2506061
Other Receipts	7	5035139	18889	408	55	2955	364	4153	7030	21370	79	83907	690081	4205849
Total Receipts	8	262936720	357514	114958	202580	1611416	602327	2098104	3146631	2186997	2794054	3192635	13130919	233498585
Average Total Receipts	9	104965	764	99	1876	3488	6768	24684	52444	91125	279405	354737	875395	19458215
Operating Costs/Operating Income (%)														
Cost of Operations	10	61.2	72.6	76.3	58.8	66.4	45.6	60.5	58.4	60.6	77.0	60.1	69.4	60.6
Salaries and Wages	11	16.2	18.5	21.6	12.8	18.9	27.0	16.5	17.0	15.4	11.5	13.1	17.9	16.2
Taxes Paid	12	1.9	1.3	1.3	3.6	2.4	2.0	2.1	1.9	2.1	1.0	1.3	1.4	1.9
Interest Paid	13	1.2	7.5	1.6	3.1	2.1	1.3	0.5	0.7	1.4	0.2	1.0	0.8	1.2
Depreciation	14	4.4	1.6	0.4	0.6	1.2	3.3	1.1	2.0	1.7	2.0	2.2	3.2	4.7
Amortization and Depletion	15	0.6	0.4	0.0	1.9	0.5	0.7	0.8	1.1	1.0	0.4	0.9	0.9	0.5
Pensions and Other Deferred Comp.	16	0.5	0.0	•	0.5	0.5	0.0	0.2	0.1	0.3	0.2	0.2	0.2	0.6
Employee Benefits	17	1.4	1.2	0.2	0.7	1.3	3.1	1.5	1.7	1.5	0.9	1.1	1.3	1.4
Advertising	18	1.4	0.2	0.1	0.4	1.9	1.3	2.0	0.8	0.9	0.6	1.5	0.7	1.5
Other Expenses	19	21.4	28.2	42.8	18.1	16.2	23.8	11.7	14.4	16.3	4.2	21.9	11.9	22.5
Officers' Compensation	20	0.7	3.7	3.9	10.4	4.6	4.8	2.5	2.2	1.6	1.0	1.6	1.3	0.6
Operating Margin	21	•	•	•	•	•	•	0.5	•	•	1.1	•	•	•
Operating Margin Before Officers' Comp.	22	•	•	•	•	•	•	3.0	1.9	•	2.1	•	•	•

Selected Average Balance Sheet ($ in Thousands)													
Net Receivables 23	21545	0	4	272	381	1211	4944	10649	14506	44669	61169	132724	4104750
Inventories 24	3601	0	10	115	257	995	3588	6159	11025	24084	46287	53321	532752
Net Property, Plant and Equipment 25	11407	0	0	36	133	1560	729	2613	4551	14081	14997	73155	2222474
Total Assets 26	160382	0	9	713	1906	6988	15851	35417	72616	160522	335795	857892	31454570
Notes and Loans Payable 27	44885	0	3	409	1228	1687	2147	5401	13905	16210	53516	162457	8979178
All Other Liabilities 28	52962	0	49	296	1053	1967	5331	14102	31896	60052	155378	252031	10339646
Net Worth 29	62534	0	-43	9	-376	3333	8373	15914	26815	84260	126901	443405	12135746
Selected Financial Ratios (Times to 1)													
Current Ratio 30	1.0	•	1.5	1.6	1.7	1.9	2.5	1.9	1.7	1.9	1.7	2.1	0.9
Quick Ratio 31	0.6	•	1.4	1.2	1.1	1.0	1.7	1.2	1.0	1.4	1.1	1.3	0.5
Net Sales to Working Capital 32	692.8	•	33.0	7.1	5.6	3.5	3.1	4.3	4.9	6.1	4.5	3.6	•
Coverage Ratio 33	8.3	•	•	•	•	•	3.0	1.6	1.1	8.0	2.0	2.4	9.1
Total Asset Turnover 34	0.6	•	10.5	2.6	1.8	1.0	1.6	1.5	1.2	1.7	1.0	0.9	0.5
Inventory Turnover 35	15.2	•	7.6	9.5	8.7	3.1	4.1	4.9	4.9	8.9	4.4	10.5	18.6
Receivables Turnover 36	4.2	•	16.6	8.0	9.3	5.9	4.4	5.9	5.4	5.5	4.3	7.0	4.1
Total Liabilities to Net Worth 37	1.6	•	•	79.8	•	1.1	0.9	1.2	1.7	0.9	1.6	0.9	1.6
Current Assets to Working Capital 38	405.3	•	3.0	2.6	2.4	2.1	1.7	2.1	2.5	2.2	2.5	1.9	•
Current Liabilities to Working Capital 39	404.3	•	2.0	1.6	1.4	1.1	0.7	1.1	1.5	1.2	1.5	0.9	•
Working Capital to Net Sales 40	0.0	•	0.0	0.1	0.2	0.3	0.3	0.2	0.2	0.2	0.2	0.3	•
Inventory to Working Capital 41	29.2	•	•	0.5	0.4	0.6	0.4	0.5	0.6	0.4	0.4	0.4	•
Total Receipts to Cash Flow 42	3.9	•	•	45.9	•	16.6	9.4	7.5	6.9	21.5	4.9	11.0	3.6
Cost of Goods to Cash Flow 43	2.4	•	•	27.0	•	7.6	5.7	4.4	4.2	16.5	2.9	7.7	2.2
Cash Flow to Total Debt 44	0.2	•	•	0.1	•	0.1	0.4	0.4	0.3	0.2	0.3	0.2	0.2
Selected Financial Factors (in Percentages)													
Debt Ratio 45	61.0	•	563.3	98.8	119.7	52.3	47.2	55.1	63.1	47.5	62.2	48.3	61.4
Return on Total Assets 46	5.6	•	•	•	•	•	2.4	1.7	1.9	2.9	1.9	1.8	5.9
Return on Equity Before Income Taxes 47	12.6	•	108.7	•	116.6	•	3.0	1.4	0.6	4.9	2.5	2.0	13.7
Return on Equity After Income Taxes 48	8.1	•	108.7	•	117.1	•	0.2	•	•	3.1	•	•	9.1
Profit Margin (Before Income Tax) 49	8.8	•	•	•	•	•	1.0	0.4	0.2	1.5	0.9	1.1	10.1
Profit Margin (After Income Tax) 50	5.7	•	•	•	•	•	0.1	•	•	0.9	•	•	6.7

Table II

Corporations with Net Income

COMPUTER AND PERIPHERAL EQUIPMENT

MONEY AMOUNTS AND SIZE OF ASSETS IN THOUSANDS OF DOLLARS

Item Description for Accounting Period 7/11 Through 6/12		Total	Zero Assets	Under 500	500 to 1,000	1,000 to 5,000	5,000 to 10,000	10,000 to 25,000	25,000 to 50,000	50,000 to 100,000	100,000 to 250,000	250,000 to 500,000	500,000 to 2,500,000	2,500,000 and over
Number of Enterprises	1	808	3	416	60	155	35	61	31	•	7	6	10	•
Revenues ($ in Thousands)														
Net Sales	2	176470880	129256	107440	159759	915269	258592	1732711	1778513	•	2107397	1572421	7914973	•
Interest	3	1338342	10	0	0	565	471	2381	1871	•	1630	2184	16357	•
Rents	4	754816	0	0	0	0	0	0	96	•	0	0	17056	•
Royalties	5	21760095	0	0	0	0	0	0	108	•	980	11392	176444	•
Other Portfolio Income	6	2252438	4482	0	0	41756	78	1950	2468	•	395	55	138808	•
Other Receipts	7	2433150	7467	407	0	1802	102	2817	4160	•	-7	13260	533051	•
Total Receipts	8	205009721	141215	107847	159759	959392	259243	1739859	1787216	•	2110395	1599312	8796689	•
Average Total Receipts	9	253725	47072	259	2663	6190	7407	28522	57652	•	301485	266552	879669	•
Operating Costs/Operating Income (%)														
Cost of Operations	10	55.0	88.8	80.0	62.7	60.9	44.1	61.6	58.2	•	80.8	49.3	63.6	•
Salaries and Wages	11	15.6	3.4	8.7	7.8	14.1	21.5	12.6	13.6	•	11.3	14.7	19.3	•
Taxes Paid	12	1.9	0.3	0.0	3.6	2.2	2.1	1.9	1.8	•	0.7	1.0	1.9	•
Interest Paid	13	1.1	8.2	1.6	0.6	1.8	1.1	0.4	1.0	•	0.2	0.9	1.0	•
Depreciation	14	4.4	0.7	•	0.5	1.2	4.1	0.7	2.1	•	1.3	2.2	4.0	•
Amortization and Depletion	15	0.6	0.3	•	0.0	0.4	0.0	0.3	0.6	•	0.2	0.4	0.8	•
Pensions and Other Deferred Comp.	16	0.5	0.0	•	0.5	0.9	0.0	0.2	0.2	•	0.1	0.1	0.3	•
Employee Benefits	17	1.4	0.1	•	0.1	1.2	2.1	0.8	1.5	•	0.8	1.6	1.3	•
Advertising	18	1.1	0.0	•	0.0	0.5	2.0	1.7	0.6	•	0.2	2.6	0.9	•
Other Expenses	19	23.7	3.3	8.6	13.3	10.5	16.9	9.7	9.9	•	1.7	17.9	11.8	•
Officers' Compensation	20	0.7	1.0	•	7.9	3.4	4.1	1.6	2.1	•	0.6	2.0	0.9	•
Operating Margin	21	•	•	1.1	2.9	2.9	2.1	8.5	8.3	•	2.1	7.3	•	•
Operating Margin Before Officers' Comp.	22	•	•	1.1	10.8	6.3	6.2	10.1	10.4	•	2.7	9.2	•	•

Selected Average Balance Sheet ($ in Thousands)													
Net Receivables **23**	52146	0	12	413	437	1793	5530	9129	•	47698	51724	152402	•
Inventories **24**	8479	0	27	249	419	1264	4189	6554	•	24681	41375	70754	•
Net Property, Plant and Equipment **25**	28440	0	0	58	248	885	705	3581	•	11407	12904	96101	•
Total Assets **26**	421211	0	14	751	2316	6505	15846	33352	•	148434	318215	953320	•
Notes and Loans Payable **27**	85272	0	0	212	333	2393	2219	6302	•	20512	58811	102732	•
All Other Liabilities **28**	135294	0	14	331	559	761	3494	11320	•	63340	101954	275945	•
Net Worth **29**	200644	0	1	208	1425	3351	10133	15730	•	64582	157450	574643	•
Selected Financial Ratios (Times to 1)													
Current Ratio **30**	1.2	•	1.1	1.3	2.8	5.7	3.9	2.0	•	1.6	2.1	2.1	•
Quick Ratio **31**	0.6	•	0.9	0.8	1.9	4.0	2.6	1.4	•	1.1	1.4	1.4	•
Net Sales to Working Capital **32**	12.3	•	294.4	15.7	5.4	1.9	2.8	4.9	•	8.5	2.9	3.3	•
Coverage Ratio **33**	11.8	1.4	1.9	5.6	5.4	3.2	22.5	10.3	•	13.9	12.4	7.7	•
Total Asset Turnover **34**	0.5	•	17.8	3.5	2.5	1.1	1.8	1.7	•	2.0	0.8	0.8	•
Inventory Turnover **35**	14.2	•	7.7	6.7	8.6	2.6	4.2	5.1	•	9.9	3.1	7.1	•
Receivables Turnover **36**	3.8	•	16.1	•	14.8	•	5.1	6.6	•	5.5	3.3	•	•
Total Liabilities to Net Worth **37**	1.1	•	15.6	2.6	0.6	0.9	0.6	1.1	•	1.3	1.0	0.7	•
Current Assets to Working Capital **38**	7.5	•	16.5	4.1	1.6	1.2	1.3	2.0	•	2.7	1.9	1.9	•
Current Liabilities to Working Capital **39**	6.5	•	15.5	3.1	0.6	0.2	0.3	1.0	•	1.7	0.9	0.9	•
Working Capital to Net Sales **40**	0.1	•	0.0	0.1	0.2	0.5	0.4	0.2	•	0.1	0.3	0.3	•
Inventory to Working Capital **41**	0.4	•	•	1.5	0.4	0.3	0.4	0.5	•	0.6	0.2	0.3	•
Total Receipts to Cash Flow **42**	3.2	44.0	14.9	9.5	9.3	7.1	5.9	5.7	•	33.0	4.0	7.4	•
Cost of Goods to Cash Flow **43**	1.8	39.1	11.9	6.0	5.7	3.1	3.6	3.3	•	26.6	2.0	4.7	•
Cash Flow to Total Debt **44**	0.3	•	1.3	0.5	0.7	0.3	0.8	0.6	•	0.1	0.4	0.3	•
Selected Financial Factors (in Percentages)													
Debt Ratio **45**	52.4	•	94.0	72.3	38.5	48.5	36.1	52.8	•	56.5	50.5	39.7	•
Return on Total Assets **46**	6.9	•	54.8	12.6	24.2	3.9	16.8	17.1	•	5.0	8.7	6.7	•
Return on Equity Before Income Taxes **47**	13.2	•	433.0	37.4	32.1	5.2	25.2	32.7	•	10.7	16.2	9.7	•
Return on Equity After Income Taxes **48**	8.9	•	433.0	30.4	31.7	4.8	21.9	26.8	•	7.3	12.6	6.8	•
Profit Margin (Before Income Tax) **49**	12.2	3.1	1.5	2.9	7.7	2.4	9.0	9.0	•	2.3	9.7	7.0	•
Profit Margin (After Income Tax) **50**	8.2	2.3	1.5	2.4	7.6	2.2	7.8	7.3	•	1.6	7.6	5.0	•

COMMUNICATIONS EQUIPMENT

MONEY AMOUNTS AND SIZE OF ASSETS IN THOUSANDS OF DOLLARS

Item Description for Accounting Period 7/11 Through 6/12		Total	Zero Assets	Under 500	500 to 1,000	1,000 to 5,000	5,000 to 10,000	10,000 to 25,000	25,000 to 50,000	50,000 to 100,000	100,000 to 250,000	250,000 to 500,000	500,000 to 2,500,000	2,500,000 and over
Number of Enterprises	1	1029	16	395	113	301	40	68	37	17	12	6	14	9
Revenues ($ in Thousands)														
Net Sales	2	77942807	306400	51206	276876	1607733	472429	1914557	1564084	1634995	1621620	1873893	10944542	55674471
Interest	3	298446	1203	203	215	103	212	204	2796	2319	4391	21854	99762	165185
Rents	4	37997	62	0	0	131	0	218	711	0	303	12232	2851	21490
Royalties	5	1078604	13	0	0	0	0	22684	0	3555	1318	56	40448	1010530
Other Portfolio Income	6	1979850	80726	0	0	0	142	51	12965	6580	66916	1821	216813	1593838
Other Receipts	7	308147	10404	6234	0	6895	8326	26125	-11364	12846	2240	18745	127752	99941
Total Receipts	8	81645851	398808	57643	277091	1614862	481109	1963839	1569192	1660295	1696788	1928601	11432168	58565455
Average Total Receipts	9	79345	24926	146	2452	5365	12028	28880	42411	97664	141399	321434	816583	6507273
Operating Costs/Operating Income (%)														
Cost of Operations	10	60.3	56.8	76.5	36.5	41.4	50.2	65.9	59.1	55.4	59.5	68.3	67.5	59.4
Salaries and Wages	11	11.4	28.4	42.0	34.1	25.9	16.0	12.0	14.4	12.8	14.0	15.6	9.3	10.8
Taxes Paid	12	2.0	2.3	1.9	3.8	5.2	1.7	3.1	1.9	1.7	1.4	1.1	1.7	2.0
Interest Paid	13	2.6	1.5	•	0.3	0.2	0.8	1.6	1.1	2.0	0.4	0.4	3.8	2.7
Depreciation	14	2.6	2.8	•	0.5	0.8	0.9	1.1	4.2	2.3	2.5	2.8	5.6	2.1
Amortization and Depletion	15	3.0	0.4	2.0	0.1	0.9	0.1	0.5	3.3	1.1	1.8	0.9	2.4	3.5
Pensions and Other Deferred Comp.	16	1.6	0.4	•	0.8	0.0	0.6	0.2	0.2	0.4	0.2	0.5	1.1	1.9
Employee Benefits	17	2.0	2.2	•	3.9	1.1	1.3	1.7	2.6	2.0	3.1	1.5	2.3	1.9
Advertising	18	1.0	0.5	0.2	0.0	1.7	1.3	0.9	0.3	0.6	0.5	0.3	0.4	1.1
Other Expenses	19	14.1	34.2	22.8	15.8	17.0	12.8	9.5	12.7	12.7	11.3	14.2	11.6	14.7
Officers' Compensation	20	0.8	8.2	6.3	15.9	6.8	5.6	2.6	1.8	1.8	1.7	1.0	0.7	0.3
Operating Margin	21	•	•	•	•	•	8.7	0.9	•	7.4	3.5	•	•	•
Operating Margin Before Officers' Comp.	22	•	•	•	4.3	5.7	14.2	3.4	0.1	9.1	5.3	•	•	0.1

Selected Average Balance Sheet ($ in Thousands)

Net Receivables 23	19458	0	25	269	826	2708	3922	6188	15819	36088	128856	167811	1700471
Inventories 24	6355	0	48	94	618	1439	2426	6091	10889	27716	29056	80545	450695
Net Property, Plant and Equipment 25	6958	0	15	16	389	409	1264	4536	6283	11693	19802	139588	493871
Total Assets 26	98629	0	163	751	2834	6852	16086	37470	71159	169389	384785	1208307	8362753
Notes and Loans Payable 27	28499	0	15	255	985	3409	5767	3876	23645	20113	53124	280919	2603002
All Other Liabilities 28	41781	0	7	186	1734	2412	5882	13931	17398	37328	118471	714637	3330663
Net Worth 29	28349	0	141	310	115	1031	4437	19663	30116	111948	213190	212751	2429088

Selected Financial Ratios (Times to 1)

Current Ratio 30	1.6	•	6.8	2.8	1.3	2.2	1.8	1.6	2.1	3.1	2.0	0.9	1.9
Quick Ratio 31	1.1	•	4.7	2.2	0.8	1.5	1.1	1.0	1.4	2.1	1.6	0.6	1.3
Net Sales to Working Capital 32	4.6	•	1.0	6.2	9.0	4.2	6.0	5.3	4.6	2.0	2.3	•	3.6
Coverage Ratio 33	2.7	•	•	•	•	13.4	3.2	•	5.6	23.8	•	0.6	3.3
Total Asset Turnover 34	0.8	•	0.8	3.3	1.9	1.7	1.8	1.1	1.4	0.8	0.8	0.6	0.7
Inventory Turnover 35	7.2	•	2.1	9.5	3.6	4.1	7.6	4.1	4.9	2.9	7.3	6.5	8.1
Receivables Turnover 36	4.0	•	6.6	12.6	6.9	5.2	7.6	5.7	6.0	2.9	3.5	4.6	3.7
Total Liabilities to Net Worth 37	2.5	•	0.2	1.4	23.5	5.6	2.6	0.9	1.4	0.5	0.8	4.7	2.4
Current Assets to Working Capital 38	2.6	•	1.2	1.5	3.9	1.9	2.3	2.7	1.9	1.5	2.0	•	2.1
Current Liabilities to Working Capital 39	1.6	•	0.2	0.5	2.9	0.9	1.3	1.7	0.9	0.5	1.0	•	1.1
Working Capital to Net Sales 40	0.2	•	1.0	0.2	0.1	0.2	0.2	0.2	0.2	0.5	0.4	•	0.3
Inventory to Working Capital 41	0.4	•	0.3	0.3	1.1	0.4	0.6	0.7	0.5	0.4	0.3	•	0.3
Total Receipts to Cash Flow 42	6.7	•	•	•	8.3	4.6	8.9	11.8	5.2	7.6	14.6	19.7	5.7
Cost of Goods to Cash Flow 43	4.1	•	•	•	3.4	2.3	5.9	7.0	2.9	4.5	10.0	13.3	3.4
Cash Flow to Total Debt 44	0.2	•	•	•	0.2	0.4	0.3	0.2	0.5	0.3	0.1	0.0	0.2

Selected Financial Factors (in Percentages)

Debt Ratio 45	71.3	•	13.7	58.7	95.9	85.0	72.4	47.5	57.7	33.9	44.6	82.4	71.0
Return on Total Assets 46	5.4	•	•	•	•	19.5	8.8	•	15.0	7.1	•	1.5	6.5
Return on Equity Before Income Taxes 47	12.0	•	•	•	•	120.2	21.9	•	29.1	10.3	•	•	15.7
Return on Equity After Income Taxes 48	6.8	•	•	•	•	107.8	16.1	•	20.8	8.9	•	•	9.7
Profit Margin (Before Income Tax) 49	4.5	•	•	•	•	10.5	3.5	•	9.1	8.5	•	•	6.1
Profit Margin (After Income Tax) 50	2.5	•	•	•	•	9.4	2.5	•	6.5	7.3	•	•	3.8

Table II

Corporations with Net Income

COMMUNICATIONS EQUIPMENT

MONEY AMOUNTS AND SIZE OF ASSETS IN THOUSANDS OF DOLLARS

Item Description for Accounting Period 7/11 Through 6/12		Total	Zero Assets	Under 500	500 to 1,000	1,000 to 5,000	5,000 to 10,000	10,000 to 25,000	25,000 to 50,000	50,000 to 100,000	100,000 to 250,000	250,000 to 500,000	500,000 to 2,500,000	2,500,000 and over
Number of Enterprises	1	578	3	273	0	164	35	41	23	•	9	0	•	6
Revenues ($ in Thousands)														
Net Sales	2	57198707	120798	29463	0	774572	417980	1478292	941938	•	1419851	0	•	41194106
Interest	3	243080	54	0	0	63	209	99	2384	•	3764	0	•	146589
Rents	4	22112	62	0	0	131	0	0	711	•	303	0	•	18975
Royalties	5	662634	13	0	0	0	0	0	0	•	1158	0	•	630004
Other Portfolio Income	6	1915714	80508	0	0	0	142	7	12836	•	66564	0	•	1532325
Other Receipts	7	291647	23	0	0	1411	8327	25896	-13307	•	2151	0	•	146560
Total Receipts	8	60333894	201458	29463	0	776177	426658	1504294	944562	•	1493791	0	•	43668559
Average Total Receipts	9	104384	67153	108	•	4733	12190	36690	41068	•	165977	•	•	7278093
Operating Costs/Operating Income (%)														
Cost of Operations	10	57.5	26.3	75.3	•	49.6	48.2	67.4	58.1	•	59.8	•	•	54.7
Salaries and Wages	11	10.3	15.2	•	•	15.6	13.3	6.9	13.7	•	12.4	•	•	10.8
Taxes Paid	12	2.1	2.5	0.6	•	1.9	1.6	2.9	2.1	•	1.4	•	•	2.3
Interest Paid	13	2.4	2.5	•	•	0.1	0.6	0.6	0.7	•	0.3	•	•	2.4
Depreciation	14	2.2	1.3	•	•	1.0	0.8	0.9	3.1	•	2.3	•	•	2.3
Amortization and Depletion	15	2.7	0.0	•	•	0.1	0.1	0.1	1.3	•	0.9	•	•	3.2
Pensions and Other Deferred Comp.	16	1.9	•	•	•	0.1	0.6	0.2	0.1	•	0.2	•	•	2.3
Employee Benefits	17	2.0	2.3	•	•	1.3	1.1	1.3	2.5	•	2.5	•	•	2.0
Advertising	18	0.6	0.1	•	•	2.0	0.4	1.0	0.5	•	0.4	•	•	0.7
Other Expenses	19	13.3	52.1	2.6	•	12.1	11.7	4.4	11.0	•	10.9	•	•	14.7
Officers' Compensation	20	0.7	3.2	•	•	8.0	5.9	2.5	1.6	•	1.7	•	•	0.3
Operating Margin	21	4.1	•	21.5	•	8.2	15.6	12.0	5.3	•	7.1	•	•	4.3
Operating Margin Before Officers' Comp.	22	4.8	•	21.5	•	16.3	21.5	14.5	6.9	•	8.8	•	•	4.6

Selected Average Balance Sheet ($ in Thousands)														
Net Receivables	**23**	27373	0	0	•	705	2673	4443	4641	•	26640	•	•	2196696
Inventories	**24**	8617	0	0	•	864	1126	2681	5034	•	30956	•	•	580817
Net Property, Plant and Equipment	**25**	8674	0	0	•	620	376	1125	4655	•	14072	•	•	592526
Total Assets	**26**	125698	0	74	•	3082	6818	15384	33580	•	169664	•	•	9492137
Notes and Loans Payable	**27**	35414	0	22	•	54	3319	4917	4013	•	15478	•	•	2878225
All Other Liabilities	**28**	46880	0	1	•	1539	2143	4663	7717	•	25278	•	•	3803994
Net Worth	**29**	43403	0	51	•	1489	1357	5804	21849	•	128908	•	•	2809918
Selected Financial Ratios (Times to 1)														
Current Ratio	**30**	2.1	•	3.3	•	1.7	2.4	2.5	1.9	•	3.6	•	•	2.1
Quick Ratio	**31**	1.4	•	3.3	•	1.2	1.7	1.6	1.3	•	2.3	•	•	1.4
Net Sales to Working Capital	**32**	3.4	•	2.1	•	4.6	4.0	5.0	4.7	•	2.2	•	•	3.3
Coverage Ratio	**33**	5.4	25.2	•	•	86.3	28.8	24.5	9.1	•	37.6	•	•	5.8
Total Asset Turnover	**34**	0.8	•	1.5	•	1.5	1.8	2.3	1.2	•	0.9	•	•	0.7
Inventory Turnover	**35**	6.6	•	•	•	2.7	5.1	9.1	4.7	•	3.0	•	•	6.5
Receivables Turnover	**36**	4.6	•	•	•	5.0	•	7.5	7.2	•	4.5	•	•	•
Total Liabilities to Net Worth	**37**	1.9	•	0.4	•	1.1	4.0	1.7	0.5	•	0.3	•	•	2.4
Current Assets to Working Capital	**38**	1.9	•	1.4	•	2.3	1.7	1.7	2.1	•	1.4	•	•	1.9
Current Liabilities to Working Capital	**39**	0.9	•	0.4	•	1.3	0.7	0.7	1.1	•	0.4	•	•	0.9
Working Capital to Net Sales	**40**	0.3	•	0.5	•	0.2	0.2	0.2	0.2	•	0.5	•	•	0.3
Inventory to Working Capital	**41**	0.3	•	•	•	0.7	0.4	0.4	0.5	•	0.4	•	•	0.3
Total Receipts to Cash Flow	**42**	5.0	2.3	4.1	•	5.7	3.6	5.9	7.4	•	6.0	•	•	4.5
Cost of Goods to Cash Flow	**43**	2.9	0.6	3.1	•	2.8	1.7	3.9	4.3	•	3.6	•	•	2.4
Cash Flow to Total Debt	**44**	0.2	•	1.1	•	0.5	0.6	0.6	0.5	•	0.6	•	•	0.2
Selected Financial Factors (in Percentages)														
Debt Ratio	**45**	65.5	•	30.7	•	51.7	80.1	62.3	34.9	•	24.0	•	•	70.4
Return on Total Assets	**46**	10.3	•	31.4	•	13.0	32.0	33.5	7.6	•	12.1	•	•	10.2
Return on Equity Before Income Taxes	**47**	24.3	•	45.4	•	26.7	155.3	85.2	10.5	•	15.5	•	•	28.6
Return on Equity After Income Taxes	**48**	18.3	•	38.7	•	23.9	144.6	77.9	9.2	•	13.8	•	•	20.9
Profit Margin (Before Income Tax)	**49**	10.7	61.3	21.5	•	8.4	17.6	13.7	5.6	•	12.6	•	•	11.7
Profit Margin (After Income Tax)	**50**	8.0	58.5	18.3	•	7.5	16.4	12.5	4.9	•	11.3	•	•	8.6

Table I

Corporations with and without Net Income

AUDIO AND VIDEO EQUIP., REPRODUCING MAGNETIC & OPTICAL MEDIA

MONEY AMOUNTS AND SIZE OF ASSETS IN THOUSANDS OF DOLLARS

Item Description for Accounting Period 7/11 Through 6/12		Total	Zero Assets	Under 500	500 to 1,000	1,000 to 5,000	5,000 to 10,000	10,000 to 25,000	25,000 to 50,000	50,000 to 100,000	100,000 to 250,000	250,000 to 500,000	500,000 to 2,500,000	2,500,000 and over
Number of Enterprises	1	1143	18	750	112	136	31	43	21	11	8	7	6	0
Revenues ($ in Thousands)														
Net Sales	2	27775531	6279	183827	144146	624949	354960	1176874	1015425	1159298	1628315	2003162	19478295	0
Interest	3	24735	146	6	0	469	658	372	427	149	1008	14708	6792	0
Rents	4	11466	0	0	0	0	0	0	78	0	0	1122	10266	0
Royalties	5	79138	0	0	0	0	0	46	0	0	972	3596	74525	0
Other Portfolio Income	6	184527	0	0	0	306	61	10078	4	365	73	7948	165694	0
Other Receipts	7	384899	843	8197	3061	1769	687	10234	18196	60429	6406	55435	219640	0
Total Receipts	8	28460296	7268	192030	147207	627493	356366	1197604	1034130	1220241	1636774	2085971	19955212	0
Average Total Receipts	9	24900	404	256	1314	4614	11496	27851	49244	110931	204597	297996	3325869	•
Operating Costs/Operating Income (%)														
Cost of Operations	10	62.2	8.0	27.9	74.5	55.8	59.2	66.1	68.3	70.0	65.7	55.2	62.1	•
Salaries and Wages	11	10.9	136.9	19.8	18.7	11.9	12.7	12.0	10.5	8.3	12.4	14.0	10.3	•
Taxes Paid	12	1.0	13.0	3.3	3.2	2.2	2.4	1.3	1.6	1.8	2.2	2.0	0.6	•
Interest Paid	13	2.2	13.0	0.8	0.2	0.8	0.3	2.4	2.0	2.4	0.5	4.5	2.2	•
Depreciation	14	2.2	19.9	0.0	0.3	0.6	6.5	1.3	2.3	1.0	2.9	6.1	1.9	•
Amortization and Depletion	15	0.9	9.0	0.0	0.3	0.0	0.3	0.6	1.1	0.4	0.8	2.3	0.9	•
Pensions and Other Deferred Comp.	16	1.8	•	0.8	0.1	1.0	0.1	0.4	0.1	0.0	0.2	0.8	2.4	•
Employee Benefits	17	1.8	15.5	1.6	2.6	0.7	0.5	2.4	0.8	0.9	0.8	1.8	2.0	•
Advertising	18	2.0	•	1.4	4.4	1.2	1.5	0.9	0.4	1.6	2.5	1.6	2.2	•
Other Expenses	19	14.1	159.0	17.9	36.8	14.5	22.5	11.3	12.9	12.6	13.1	15.1	14.0	•
Officers' Compensation	20	1.0	15.4	12.3	4.8	9.0	6.3	2.0	1.9	0.6	1.0	1.3	0.4	•
Operating Margin	21	•	•	14.2	•	2.2	•	•	•	0.4	•	•	1.1	•
Operating Margin Before Officers' Comp.	22	0.9	•	26.5	•	11.2	•	1.2	0.0	1.1	•	•	1.5	•

Selected Average Balance Sheet ($ in Thousands)													
Net Receivables 23	5096	0	7	139	529	1862	6014	9742	17367	28924	51312	738194	•
Inventories 24	3346	0	16	418	809	807	3683	5002	19839	26170	29290	459660	•
Net Property, Plant and Equipment 25	2149	0	0	62	98	1213	1453	2625	7173	12908	55092	285590	•
Total Assets 26	42286	0	112	693	2983	6592	17264	34006	72751	142998	356119	6944513	•
Notes and Loans Payable 27	17636	0	2	251	347	1657	6989	14434	24105	57204	113180	2985281	•
All Other Liabilities 28	9063	0	16	194	902	4000	9441	12742	25916	71965	110397	1295147	•
Net Worth 29	15587	0	94	248	1734	935	834	6830	22731	13829	132542	2664084	•

Selected Financial Ratios (Times to 1)													
Current Ratio 30	1.3	•	6.3	3.1	2.4	1.1	1.6	1.8	1.9	1.6	1.5	1.2	•
Quick Ratio 31	0.5	•	5.4	1.0	1.9	0.8	1.2	1.2	0.8	0.8	0.8	0.4	•
Net Sales to Working Capital 32	5.6	•	2.8	3.2	3.6	48.0	5.7	5.4	4.0	5.8	6.1	5.8	•
Coverage Ratio 33	2.2	•	24.2	•	4.1	•	1.5	1.0	3.4	•	1.0	2.7	•
Total Asset Turnover 34	0.6	•	2.2	1.9	1.5	1.7	1.6	1.4	1.4	1.4	0.8	0.5	•
Inventory Turnover 35	4.5	•	4.4	2.3	3.2	8.4	4.9	6.6	3.7	5.1	5.4	4.4	•
Receivables Turnover 36	5.8	•	27.1	18.5	8.6	7.0	5.1	7.4	5.5	8.1	7.4	5.4	•
Total Liabilities to Net Worth 37	1.7	•	0.2	1.8	0.7	6.0	19.7	4.0	2.2	9.3	1.7	1.6	•
Current Assets to Working Capital 38	4.3	•	1.2	1.5	1.7	19.1	2.7	2.2	2.1	2.8	3.2	5.1	•
Current Liabilities to Working Capital 39	3.3	•	0.2	0.5	0.7	18.1	1.7	1.2	1.1	1.8	2.2	4.1	•
Working Capital to Net Sales 40	0.2	•	0.4	0.3	0.3	0.0	0.2	0.2	0.2	0.2	0.2	0.2	•
Inventory to Working Capital 41	0.8	•	0.2	1.0	0.3	4.7	0.6	0.6	0.8	0.7	0.7	0.8	•
Total Receipts to Cash Flow 42	6.9	•	2.9	•	7.9	12.7	9.8	8.9	5.8	10.8	8.1	6.3	•
Cost of Goods to Cash Flow 43	4.3	•	0.8	•	4.4	7.5	6.5	6.1	4.0	7.1	4.5	3.9	•
Cash Flow to Total Debt 44	0.1	•	4.7	•	0.5	0.2	0.2	0.2	0.4	0.1	0.2	0.1	•

Selected Financial Factors (in Percentages)													
Debt Ratio 45	63.1	•	16.1	64.1	41.9	85.8	95.2	79.9	68.8	90.3	62.8	61.6	•
Return on Total Assets 46	2.7	•	42.6	•	5.3	•	6.0	2.9	11.7	•	3.5	2.8	•
Return on Equity Before Income Taxes 47	4.0	•	48.6	•	6.9	•	43.9	0.1	26.6	•	•	4.5	•
Return on Equity After Income Taxes 48	2.8	•	47.0	•	4.7	•	19.5	•	24.0	•	•	3.6	•
Profit Margin (Before Income Tax) 49	2.5	•	18.7	•	2.6	•	1.3	0.0	5.7	•	•	3.7	•
Profit Margin (After Income Tax) 50	1.8	•	18.1	•	1.8	•	0.6	•	5.2	•	•	3.0	•

Table II

Corporations with Net Income

AUDIO AND VIDEO EQUIP., REPRODUCING MAGNETIC & OPTICAL MEDIA

MONEY AMOUNTS AND SIZE OF ASSETS IN THOUSANDS OF DOLLARS

Item Description for Accounting Period 7/11 Through 6/12		Total	Zero Assets	Under 500	500 to 1,000	1,000 to 5,000	5,000 to 10,000	10,000 to 25,000	25,000 to 50,000	50,000 to 100,000	100,000 to 250,000	250,000 to 500,000	500,000 to 2,500,000	2,500,000 and over
Number of Enterprises	1	645	8	•	0	114	10	27	9	8	4	3	•	0
Revenues ($ in Thousands)														
Net Sales	2	21490555	0	•	0	488785	166059	893771	425110	826059	594897	914829	•	0
Interest	3	10570	145	•	0	440	0	172	391	9	547	2784	•	0
Rents	4	10370	0	•	0	0	0	0	78	0	0	26	•	0
Royalties	5	79041	0	•	0	0	0	0	0	0	972	3544	•	0
Other Portfolio Income	6	175868	0	•	0	306	61	10070	0	355	67	4053	•	0
Other Receipts	7	315176	844	•	0	93	-1	8810	17083	59782	81	3577	•	0
Total Receipts	8	22081580	989	•	0	489624	166119	912823	442662	886205	596564	928813	•	0
Average Total Receipts	9	34235	124	•	•	4295	16612	33808	49185	110776	149141	309604	•	•
Operating Costs/Operating Income (%)														
Cost of Operations	10	58.2	•	•	•	47.4	46.9	66.6	65.6	68.5	50.9	47.2	•	•
Salaries and Wages	11	11.3	•	•	•	13.2	11.3	8.3	6.8	7.6	13.3	19.9	•	•
Taxes Paid	12	0.9	•	•	•	1.8	3.7	1.0	1.2	1.8	2.1	2.1	•	•
Interest Paid	13	2.2	•	•	•	1.0	0.1	0.4	0.4	1.1	0.7	3.3	•	•
Depreciation	14	1.9	•	•	•	0.7	2.0	0.9	1.0	0.9	2.7	2.7	•	•
Amortization and Depletion	15	0.9	•	•	•	•	•	0.4	0.0	0.4	0.3	0.6	•	•
Pensions and Other Deferred Comp.	16	2.3	•	•	•	1.3	•	0.6	0.3	0.0	0.7	1.6	•	•
Employee Benefits	17	2.0	•	•	•	0.4	•	2.4	0.0	1.1	1.6	2.1	•	•
Advertising	18	2.2	•	•	•	1.5	2.7	0.3	0.7	1.0	5.6	2.1	•	•
Other Expenses	19	14.5	•	•	•	13.6	24.5	8.1	12.3	13.1	9.3	14.2	•	•
Officers' Compensation	20	0.9	•	•	•	10.7	4.5	1.6	2.5	0.6	1.1	0.9	•	•
Operating Margin	21	2.7	•	•	•	8.4	4.5	9.4	9.2	3.8	11.7	3.2	•	•
Operating Margin Before Officers' Comp.	22	3.6	•	•	•	19.1	8.9	11.0	11.7	4.4	12.7	4.1	•	•

Selected Average Balance Sheet ($ in Thousands)

Net Receivables 23	6823	0	•	•	317	1676	8032	7602	15190	24896	50290	•	•
Inventories 24	4481	0	•	•	883	1550	2716	7643	17800	16275	32870	•	•
Net Property, Plant and Equipment 25	2931	0	•	•	83	622	1821	2336	8126	7900	43150	•	•
Total Assets 26	66806	0	•	•	2954	5420	19824	31419	68782	133192	372779	•	•
Notes and Loans Payable 27	28586	0	•	•	100	97	2523	5541	14258	2385	103882	•	•
All Other Liabilities 28	12351	0	•	•	863	1668	6811	4511	21846	35299	104725	•	•
Net Worth 29	25869	0	•	•	1991	3654	10490	21367	32678	95508	164172	•	•

Selected Financial Ratios (Times to 1)

Current Ratio 30	1.3	•	•	•	2.2	2.8	1.8	3.2	2.4	2.1	1.4	•	•
Quick Ratio 31	0.5	•	•	•	1.8	1.5	1.5	1.7	1.0	1.5	0.8	•	•
Net Sales to Working Capital 32	5.5	•	•	•	4.0	5.4	4.9	3.5	3.8	3.9	6.5	•	•
Coverage Ratio 33	3.5	•	•	•	9.3	86.2	30.6	35.5	10.7	17.7	2.7	•	•
Total Asset Turnover 34	0.5	•	•	•	1.5	3.1	1.7	1.5	1.5	1.1	0.8	•	•
Inventory Turnover 35	4.3	•	•	•	2.3	5.0	8.1	4.1	4.0	4.6	4.4	•	•
Receivables Turnover 36	6.0	•	•	•	9.6	5.8	5.7	8.3	6.3	•	12.1	•	•
Total Liabilities to Net Worth 37	1.6	•	•	•	0.5	0.5	0.9	0.5	1.1	0.4	1.3	•	•
Current Assets to Working Capital 38	4.6	•	•	•	1.8	1.6	2.2	1.5	1.7	1.9	3.4	•	•
Current Liabilities to Working Capital 39	3.6	•	•	•	0.8	0.6	1.2	0.5	0.7	0.9	2.4	•	•
Working Capital to Net Sales 40	0.2	•	•	•	0.2	0.2	0.2	0.3	0.3	0.3	0.2	•	•
Inventory to Working Capital 41	0.7	•	•	•	0.3	0.7	0.3	0.5	0.7	0.4	0.7	•	•
Total Receipts to Cash Flow 42	5.5	•	•	•	5.6	3.7	5.5	4.2	4.3	4.9	5.8	•	•
Cost of Goods to Cash Flow 43	3.2	•	•	•	2.6	1.7	3.7	2.7	2.9	2.5	2.7	•	•
Cash Flow to Total Debt 44	0.1	•	•	•	0.8	2.6	0.6	1.1	0.7	0.8	0.3	•	•

Selected Financial Factors (in Percentages)

Debt Ratio 45	61.3	•	•	•	32.6	32.6	47.1	32.0	52.5	28.3	56.0	•	•
Return on Total Assets 46	3.9	•	•	•	14.0	14.0	20.8	20.6	18.4	14.1	7.4	•	•
Return on Equity Before Income Taxes 47	7.3	•	•	•	18.6	20.5	38.0	29.4	35.1	18.6	10.6	•	•
Return on Equity After Income Taxes 48	6.1	•	•	•	16.3	13.5	34.9	27.3	32.6	15.1	7.4	•	•
Profit Margin (Before Income Tax) 49	5.7	•	•	•	8.6	4.5	12.0	13.3	11.1	12.0	5.7	•	•
Profit Margin (After Income Tax) 50	4.7	•	•	•	7.6	3.0	11.1	12.3	10.3	9.7	4.0	•	•

Table I

Corporations with and without Net Income

SEMICONDUCTOR AND OTHER ELECTRONIC COMPONENT

MONEY AMOUNTS AND SIZE OF ASSETS IN THOUSANDS OF DOLLARS

Item Description for Accounting Period 7/11 Through 6/12		Total	Zero Assets	Under 500	500 to 1,000	1,000 to 5,000	5,000 to 10,000	10,000 to 25,000	25,000 to 50,000	50,000 to 100,000	100,000 to 250,000	250,000 to 500,000	500,000 to 2,500,000	2,500,000 and over
Number of Enterprises	1	4925	1055	1423	329	1122	473	221	82	47	63	34	52	23
Revenues ($ in Thousands)														
Net Sales	2	215412802	1314557	1224731	532227	5317281	5795761	4938655	3780918	3806770	11891654	9277530	37195912	130336805
Interest	3	581922	1490	890	128	687	3379	3890	6757	7703	21030	24082	137379	374507
Rents	4	54525	23	0	0	150	3010	1624	1693	845	2868	7398	9019	27897
Royalties	5	8767603	19994	0	0	95021	1063	1246	6092	12671	75249	95995	1103846	7356425
Other Portfolio Income	6	1691838	25642	0	84	2896	16343	36082	3783	28439	167851	23858	641068	745789
Other Receipts	7	3340185	107818	97	227	9872	52792	43064	61093	79734	403159	261274	988605	1332453
Total Receipts	8	229848875	1469524	1225718	532666	5425907	5872348	5024561	3860336	3936162	12561811	9690137	40075829	140173876
Average Total Receipts	9	46670	1393	861	1619	4836	12415	22736	47077	83748	199394	285004	770689	6094516
Operating Costs/Operating Income (%)														
Cost of Operations	10	62.6	56.1	47.4	58.6	62.0	64.1	70.8	66.7	74.4	77.8	64.2	67.3	59.2
Salaries and Wages	11	12.4	20.8	11.6	10.7	13.6	8.6	12.3	9.0	10.1	10.1	14.7	14.2	12.1
Taxes Paid	12	1.4	1.5	2.1	2.8	2.8	2.0	1.9	2.1	1.5	1.1	1.3	1.4	1.3
Interest Paid	13	1.4	2.0	0.7	0.8	0.8	0.5	1.1	1.7	1.4	0.9	1.7	1.7	1.4
Depreciation	14	7.1	3.5	2.9	1.5	3.3	1.8	2.8	4.8	3.2	3.2	3.7	4.7	9.3
Amortization and Depletion	15	1.2	3.5	0.0	0.1	0.2	0.2	0.4	0.4	0.9	1.0	1.8	1.6	1.2
Pensions and Other Deferred Comp.	16	0.5	0.7	•	0.0	0.6	1.0	0.6	0.6	0.2	0.2	0.5	0.6	0.4
Employee Benefits	17	1.9	1.7	1.6	1.6	1.7	2.0	1.5	1.7	1.2	1.3	1.7	2.2	1.9
Advertising	18	1.3	0.2	0.8	0.4	0.3	0.9	0.3	0.3	0.2	0.4	0.5	0.3	1.9
Other Expenses	19	9.1	28.3	21.9	15.2	12.7	9.2	8.3	17.2	10.8	9.7	12.4	10.4	7.7
Officers' Compensation	20	1.1	9.3	7.4	6.7	6.5	3.9	2.7	2.4	2.0	1.2	1.5	1.6	0.2
Operating Margin	21	0.0	•	3.5	1.7	•	5.8	•	•	•	•	•	•	3.3
Operating Margin Before Officers' Comp.	22	1.1	•	10.9	8.4	2.1	9.7	0.1	•	•	•	•	•	3.6

Selected Average Balance Sheet ($ in Thousands)													
Net Receivables **23**	8057	0	38	202	507	1648	2813	7095	21531	33598	54750	147486	1058593
Inventories **24**	3520	0	34	183	643	1329	3805	6500	10687	22571	35602	67622	341384
Net Property, Plant and Equipment **25**	9494	0	26	54	618	939	2128	6041	10109	23551	40327	143776	1469367
Total Assets **26**	63283	0	234	705	2435	7125	15598	36211	75407	163205	353012	1111739	9345461
Notes and Loans Payable **27**	11470	0	32	228	829	1490	4802	10118	16400	38145	41894	240905	1553017
All Other Liabilities **28**	17505	0	90	129	571	1504	4355	12287	24995	54409	69356	249228	2730527
Net Worth **29**	34307	0	112	348	1035	4131	6441	13806	34013	70651	241762	621607	5061917

Selected Financial Ratios (Times to 1)													
Current Ratio **30**	1.8	•	1.9	3.5	2.0	2.8	2.3	2.0	1.7	1.6	2.7	2.4	1.6
Quick Ratio **31**	1.1	•	1.3	2.5	1.1	1.7	1.3	1.2	1.1	1.0	1.8	1.6	0.9
Net Sales to Working Capital **32**	4.3	•	10.1	4.0	6.2	3.5	3.8	4.1	4.3	5.2	2.6	2.7	5.4
Coverage Ratio **33**	6.6	•	6.0	3.1	•	15.1	0.2	•	•	•	1.6	2.8	9.6
Total Asset Turnover **34**	0.7	•	3.7	2.3	1.9	1.7	1.4	1.3	1.1	1.2	0.8	0.6	0.6
Inventory Turnover **35**	7.8	•	11.9	5.2	4.6	5.9	4.2	4.7	5.6	6.5	4.9	7.1	9.8
Receivables Turnover **36**	4.1	•	24.3	7.4	8.5	9.3	7.4	7.2	4.4	5.7	4.4	4.4	3.6
Total Liabilities to Net Worth **37**	0.8	•	1.1	1.0	1.4	0.7	1.4	1.6	1.2	1.3	0.5	0.8	0.8
Current Assets to Working Capital **38**	2.2	•	2.1	1.4	2.0	1.5	1.8	2.0	2.4	2.5	1.6	1.7	2.7
Current Liabilities to Working Capital **39**	1.2	•	1.1	0.4	1.0	0.5	0.8	1.0	1.4	1.5	0.6	0.7	1.7
Working Capital to Net Sales **40**	0.2	•	0.1	0.3	0.2	0.3	0.3	0.2	0.2	0.2	0.4	0.4	0.2
Inventory to Working Capital **41**	0.4	•	0.6	0.4	0.8	0.5	0.7	0.6	0.6	0.7	0.3	0.2	0.3
Total Receipts to Cash Flow **42**	7.6	17.5	5.7	8.9	14.5	7.6	20.8	11.7	17.9	18.6	10.4	10.0	6.2
Cost of Goods to Cash Flow **43**	4.7	9.8	2.7	5.2	9.0	4.9	14.7	7.8	13.4	14.5	6.7	6.7	3.7
Cash Flow to Total Debt **44**	0.2	•	1.2	0.5	0.2	0.5	0.1	0.2	0.1	0.1	0.2	0.1	0.2

Selected Financial Factors (in Percentages)													
Debt Ratio **45**	45.8	•	52.0	50.6	57.5	42.0	58.7	61.9	54.9	56.7	31.5	44.1	45.8
Return on Total Assets **46**	6.4	•	15.7	6.0	•	13.2	0.4	•	•	•	2.1	3.1	8.3
Return on Equity Before Income Taxes **47**	10.1	•	27.2	8.3	•	21.3	•	•	•	•	1.2	3.6	13.8
Return on Equity After Income Taxes **48**	6.1	•	26.5	8.0	•	19.5	•	•	•	•	•	1.7	8.9
Profit Margin (Before Income Tax) **49**	7.9	•	3.6	1.8	•	7.2	•	•	•	•	1.0	3.2	12.3
Profit Margin (After Income Tax) **50**	4.8	•	3.5	1.7	•	6.6	•	•	•	•	•	1.5	8.0

Table II

Corporations with Net Income

SEMICONDUCTOR AND OTHER ELECTRONIC COMPONENT

MONEY AMOUNTS AND SIZE OF ASSETS IN THOUSANDS OF DOLLARS

Item Description for Accounting Period 7/11 Through 6/12		Total	Zero Assets	Under 500	500 to 1,000	1,000 to 5,000	5,000 to 10,000	10,000 to 25,000	25,000 to 50,000	50,000 to 100,000	100,000 to 250,000	250,000 to 500,000	500,000 to 2,500,000	2,500,000 and over
Number of Enterprises	1	3247	753	897	241	712	333	153	45	24	30	19	29	12
Revenues ($ in Thousands)														
Net Sales	2	139304891	470759	639891	395292	3788716	4330273	3875328	2611487	2357163	6347193	5248151	19221416	90019222
Interest	3	365597	103	567	100	404	3001	2484	2221	3506	6133	14198	86802	246079
Rents	4	42370	0	0	0	150	3010	1624	78	112	171	6245	8767	22214
Royalties	5	8203333	0	0	0	0	51	1154	1700	526	53421	86580	906987	7152914
Other Portfolio Income	6	1027100	497	0	0	1696	15840	20585	1108	4900	121778	20310	271033	569353
Other Receipts	7	1479580	55568	104	227	3904	4510	33490	9174	71239	174216	140409	266794	719944
Total Receipts	8	150422871	526927	640562	395619	3794870	4356685	3934665	2625768	2437446	6702912	5515893	20761799	98729726
Average Total Receipts	9	46327	700	714	1642	5330	13083	25717	58350	101560	223430	290310	715924	8227477
Operating Costs/Operating Income (%)														
Cost of Operations	10	53.6	69.2	44.9	52.6	56.9	61.3	67.9	63.0	72.4	75.5	57.7	57.2	49.1
Salaries and Wages	11	12.6	6.0	6.3	10.0	12.8	6.7	9.9	7.4	7.0	8.1	13.8	16.2	12.9
Taxes Paid	12	1.5	1.5	2.3	2.6	2.8	2.0	1.7	2.0	1.2	1.0	1.3	1.7	1.5
Interest Paid	13	0.9	1.5	0.1	0.6	0.7	0.4	0.7	0.7	0.8	0.9	0.8	1.9	0.8
Depreciation	14	8.9	1.1	0.5	1.6	2.2	1.5	2.3	3.3	2.3	2.4	3.1	4.5	12.1
Amortization and Depletion	15	1.0	1.5	•	•	0.2	0.1	0.2	0.1	0.6	0.5	1.5	1.8	1.1
Pensions and Other Deferred Comp.	16	0.6	0.5	•	0.0	0.5	1.1	0.7	0.3	0.2	0.2	0.6	0.8	0.6
Employee Benefits	17	2.2	0.7	1.3	2.1	1.5	2.1	1.1	1.4	1.2	1.0	1.7	2.7	2.4
Advertising	18	1.6	0.1	0.0	0.4	0.3	1.0	0.4	0.2	0.2	0.2	0.6	0.4	2.3
Other Expenses	19	9.1	12.8	18.1	17.4	10.4	6.6	6.0	7.1	7.9	6.7	10.0	10.2	9.1
Officers' Compensation	20	0.9	1.1	8.8	7.0	7.8	4.1	2.8	2.1	1.2	0.8	1.4	1.2	0.2
Operating Margin	21	6.9	4.0	17.6	5.5	4.0	13.1	6.4	12.3	5.2	2.5	7.5	1.4	8.0
Operating Margin Before Officers' Comp.	22	7.8	5.1	26.4	12.4	11.7	17.2	9.2	14.4	6.3	3.4	9.0	2.6	8.2

Selected Average Balance Sheet ($ in Thousands)

Net Receivables 23	6726	0	46	231	568	1620	3135	8715	21634	33425	50618	135539	1125878
Inventories 24	3783	0	14	203	712	1452	4391	8827	13180	28109	44090	72131	509691
Net Property, Plant and Equipment 25	10374	0	14	39	568	826	2086	6212	9502	19903	37566	127147	2263269
Total Assets 26	61020	0	245	662	2134	7056	15638	36853	77905	156139	355417	1197541	11816499
Notes and Loans Payable 27	9315	0	4	180	722	1166	3098	7183	14275	31946	22902	228317	1678403
All Other Liabilities 28	16489	0	31	92	428	1422	4151	8583	21380	47796	62298	236458	3475217
Net Worth 29	35217	0	210	390	984	4468	8390	21087	42250	76398	270217	732766	6662879

Selected Financial Ratios (Times to 1)

Current Ratio 30	2.0	•	5.7	5.9	2.3	3.4	2.6	2.7	2.3	2.2	2.7	2.8	1.7
Quick Ratio 31	1.0	•	5.2	3.5	1.4	1.9	1.4	1.6	1.5	1.3	1.7	1.7	0.8
Net Sales to Working Capital 32	4.2	•	4.7	3.7	6.7	3.3	3.8	3.8	3.8	4.4	2.7	2.3	5.4
Coverage Ratio 33	18.3	12.0	197.2	9.6	6.9	36.4	12.0	20.0	12.3	10.6	18.7	6.8	25.0
Total Asset Turnover 34	0.7	•	2.9	2.5	2.5	1.8	1.6	1.6	1.3	1.4	0.8	0.6	0.6
Inventory Turnover 35	6.1	•	23.5	4.2	4.2	5.5	3.9	4.1	5.4	5.7	3.6	5.3	7.2
Receivables Turnover 36	3.7	•	17.6	•	7.6	9.0	6.9	6.9	5.0	•	4.9	3.7	3.3
Total Liabilities to Net Worth 37	0.7	•	0.2	0.7	1.2	0.6	0.9	0.7	0.8	1.0	0.3	0.6	0.8
Current Assets to Working Capital 38	2.0	•	1.2	1.2	1.8	1.4	1.6	1.6	1.8	1.9	1.6	1.6	2.5
Current Liabilities to Working Capital 39	1.0	•	0.2	0.2	0.8	0.4	0.6	0.6	0.8	0.9	0.6	0.6	1.5
Working Capital to Net Sales 40	0.2	•	0.2	0.3	0.1	0.3	0.3	0.3	0.3	0.2	0.4	0.4	0.2
Inventory to Working Capital 41	0.3	•	0.1	0.5	0.7	0.5	0.6	0.5	0.5	0.6	0.4	0.2	0.3
Total Receipts to Cash Flow 42	4.7	3.8	3.3	6.3	9.3	5.8	8.6	5.7	6.6	8.4	4.8	5.8	4.2
Cost of Goods to Cash Flow 43	2.5	2.7	1.5	3.3	5.3	3.5	5.8	3.6	4.8	6.4	2.8	3.3	2.1
Cash Flow to Total Debt 44	0.4	•	6.2	1.0	0.5	0.9	0.4	0.6	0.4	0.3	0.7	0.2	0.3

Selected Financial Factors (in Percentages)

Debt Ratio 45	42.3	•	14.3	41.0	53.9	36.7	46.3	42.8	45.8	51.1	24.0	38.8	43.6
Return on Total Assets 46	12.1	•	51.7	15.3	12.1	25.9	14.1	21.3	11.8	12.8	11.2	7.2	12.9
Return on Equity Before Income Taxes 47	19.9	•	60.1	23.3	22.4	39.8	24.1	35.3	20.0	23.6	13.9	10.0	21.9
Return on Equity After Income Taxes 48	14.1	•	59.5	22.9	22.1	37.4	20.1	31.5	14.8	20.3	11.2	7.1	14.9
Profit Margin (Before Income Tax) 49	16.3	16.0	17.7	5.5	4.1	13.7	8.0	12.8	8.6	8.5	13.6	11.1	19.5
Profit Margin (After Income Tax) 50	11.6	14.7	17.5	5.5	4.1	12.9	6.7	11.5	6.4	7.3	10.9	7.9	13.3

Table I

Corporations with and without Net Income

NAVIGATIONAL, MEASURING, ELECTROMEDICAL, AND CONTROL

MONEY AMOUNTS AND SIZE OF ASSETS IN THOUSANDS OF DOLLARS

Item Description for Accounting Period 7/11 Through 6/12		Total	Zero Assets	Under 500	500 to 1,000	1,000 to 5,000	5,000 to 10,000	10,000 to 25,000	25,000 to 50,000	50,000 to 100,000	100,000 to 250,000	250,000 to 500,000	500,000 to 2,500,000	2,500,000 and over
Number of Enterprises	1	3921	90	2205	433	458	357	175	71	35	31	23	26	18
Revenues ($ in Thousands)														
Net Sales	2	113718927	3159252	1169895	605174	2391738	4650159	4232802	3169895	2920864	5305355	5672525	17456487	62984779
Interest	3	2317024	35151	7	114	457	624	2796	2504	4927	10478	31292	54769	2173906
Rents	4	82261	6780	0	950	588	2610	329	2585	880	2403	825	49195	15116
Royalties	5	1083072	50728	0	0	0	0	2028	2221	6736	44758	15141	224611	736850
Other Portfolio Income	6	2499125	117787	0	0	907	1722	32596	2281	12811	3996	98171	56735	2172119
Other Receipts	7	1881734	41978	1	11347	4077	31220	34197	44297	54431	70427	73384	262118	1254258
Total Receipts	8	121582143	3411676	1169903	617585	2397767	4686335	4304748	3223783	3000649	5437417	5891338	18103915	69337028
Average Total Receipts	9	31008	37908	531	1426	5235	13127	24599	45405	85733	175401	256145	696304	3852057
Operating Costs/Operating Income (%)														
Cost of Operations	10	57.0	55.8	42.1	35.4	58.7	61.0	57.2	57.6	59.8	60.8	50.8	57.6	57.0
Salaries and Wages	11	14.3	26.1	14.3	21.1	13.8	13.2	15.0	15.5	14.6	11.4	17.2	14.2	13.7
Taxes Paid	12	2.1	6.0	2.5	3.7	2.5	2.5	2.3	2.1	1.7	1.7	2.0	1.8	1.9
Interest Paid	13	3.9	7.0	0.3	0.3	0.5	0.5	0.6	1.5	0.6	0.6	2.7	2.0	5.5
Depreciation	14	2.7	7.6	0.7	1.8	1.4	1.2	1.6	2.2	2.2	2.8	3.5	2.7	2.6
Amortization and Depletion	15	1.5	0.8	0.0	0.0	0.3	0.4	0.3	1.0	0.7	0.6	2.0	1.8	1.7
Pensions and Other Deferred Comp.	16	1.3	0.2	0.6	0.6	0.3	0.4	0.6	0.9	0.7	0.7	0.5	0.9	1.9
Employee Benefits	17	2.1	0.9	1.3	2.2	1.5	2.3	2.1	2.0	2.5	2.5	2.6	1.9	2.2
Advertising	18	0.7	0.7	1.1	0.2	1.3	0.9	0.8	0.7	1.4	0.7	1.8	0.6	0.5
Other Expenses	19	13.9	10.3	15.8	25.3	12.7	11.9	11.1	13.2	13.0	11.6	15.7	12.0	15.0
Officers' Compensation	20	1.5	3.7	11.6	6.4	4.5	3.5	4.3	3.0	1.5	2.1	1.6	1.4	0.6
Operating Margin	21	•	•	9.7	3.0	2.5	2.3	4.0	0.1	1.0	4.6	•	3.1	•
Operating Margin Before Officers' Comp.	22	0.6	•	21.4	9.4	7.0	5.8	8.4	3.1	2.6	6.7	1.4	4.5	•

Selected Average Balance Sheet ($ in Thousands)

Net Receivables 23	5496	0	33	214	731	2337	3291	7633	15336	30581	82709	151490	653962
Inventories 24	2906	0	39	84	579	1285	3307	6645	11351	26392	31928	90699	288365
Net Property, Plant and Equipment 25	2906	0	3	54	184	640	1794	5666	7293	21131	30984	75192	375458
Total Assets 26	72333	0	197	643	2232	7049	15394	36355	71794	159182	352027	1223886	12595925
Notes and Loans Payable 27	18334	0	36	371	551	914	2677	9630	15450	23044	72815	331330	3242835
All Other Liabilities 28	25968	0	20	137	995	1991	4288	9408	21318	47192	106381	302374	4811913
Net Worth 29	28031	0	141	135	685	4144	8429	17317	35026	88946	172831	590182	4541176

Selected Financial Ratios (Times to 1)

Current Ratio 30	1.2	•	7.7	3.2	1.9	2.5	2.1	2.3	1.5	2.2	1.7	1.3	0.9
Quick Ratio 31	0.7	•	5.7	2.6	1.1	1.8	1.2	1.2	0.9	1.2	1.2	0.8	0.6
Net Sales to Working Capital 32	14.9	•	3.6	3.9	5.7	3.9	4.3	3.5	6.0	3.4	3.5	7.3	•
Coverage Ratio 33	2.8	•	38.8	16.5	6.1	6.8	10.4	2.2	7.4	12.5	2.6	4.6	2.6
Total Asset Turnover 34	0.4	•	2.7	2.2	2.3	1.8	1.6	1.2	1.2	1.1	0.7	0.5	0.3
Inventory Turnover 35	5.7	•	5.7	5.9	5.3	6.2	4.2	3.9	4.4	3.9	3.9	4.3	6.9
Receivables Turnover 36	5.6	•	20.9	6.9	7.5	5.6	7.6	6.2	5.7	5.0	3.5	4.8	5.7
Total Liabilities to Net Worth 37	1.6	•	0.4	3.8	2.3	0.7	0.8	1.1	1.0	0.8	1.0	1.1	1.8
Current Assets to Working Capital 38	6.7	•	1.1	1.5	2.1	1.6	1.9	1.8	3.1	1.8	2.4	4.5	•
Current Liabilities to Working Capital 39	5.7	•	0.1	0.5	1.1	0.6	0.9	0.8	2.1	0.8	1.4	3.5	•
Working Capital to Net Sales 40	0.1	•	0.3	0.3	0.2	0.3	0.2	0.3	0.2	0.3	0.3	0.1	•
Inventory to Working Capital 41	1.5	•	0.3	0.2	0.7	0.4	0.6	0.6	0.8	0.5	0.5	1.0	•
Total Receipts to Cash Flow 42	5.9	•	4.6	3.8	8.1	7.9	7.1	7.5	6.7	5.8	5.7	5.9	5.3
Cost of Goods to Cash Flow 43	3.4	•	1.9	1.4	4.7	4.8	4.1	4.3	4.0	3.5	2.9	3.4	3.0
Cash Flow to Total Debt 44	0.1	•	2.1	0.7	0.4	0.6	0.5	0.3	0.3	0.4	0.2	0.2	0.1

Selected Financial Factors (in Percentages)

Debt Ratio 45	61.2	•	28.4	79.0	69.3	41.2	45.2	52.4	51.2	44.1	50.9	51.8	63.9
Return on Total Assets 46	4.3	•	26.9	11.7	7.6	6.6	10.0	4.1	5.5	8.4	4.8	5.1	4.0
Return on Equity Before Income Taxes 47	7.2	•	36.6	52.5	20.9	9.6	16.5	4.8	9.8	13.8	6.0	8.4	6.8
Return on Equity After Income Taxes 48	4.8	•	35.2	50.1	16.2	8.2	13.7	2.5	6.7	10.9	3.8	6.0	4.4
Profit Margin (Before Income Tax) 49	7.0	•	9.7	5.1	2.7	3.0	5.8	1.8	4.1	7.2	4.2	7.4	8.8
Profit Margin (After Income Tax) 50	4.7	•	9.4	4.8	2.1	2.6	4.8	1.0	2.8	5.7	2.7	5.3	5.7

Table II

Corporations with Net Income

NAVIGATIONAL, MEASURING, ELECTROMEDICAL, AND CONTROL

MONEY AMOUNTS AND SIZE OF ASSETS IN THOUSANDS OF DOLLARS

Item Description for Accounting Period 7/11 Through 6/12		Total	Zero Assets	Under 500	500 to 1,000	1,000 to 5,000	5,000 to 10,000	10,000 to 25,000	25,000 to 50,000	50,000 to 100,000	100,000 to 250,000	250,000 to 500,000	500,000 to 2,500,000	2,500,000 and over
Number of Enterprises	1	3176	62	•	351	408	272	133	50	27	25	16	23	•
Revenues ($ in Thousands)														
Net Sales	2	97188856	411449	•	536944	2338145	4097368	3414712	2659777	2328076	4784709	4455856	16078049	•
Interest	3	2266518	140	•	13	92	489	1988	2128	4524	9206	29452	51009	•
Rents	4	78919	3601	•	950	501	2596	329	2585	880	2382	810	49195	•
Royalties	5	986865	0	•	0	0	0	2028	1213	6723	44497	11276	195289	•
Other Portfolio Income	6	2367322	76153	•	0	907	963	21829	2272	12166	3077	78087	51384	•
Other Receipts	7	1738069	492	•	11284	2857	24916	35102	43714	53092	63227	74229	194557	•
Total Receipts	8	104626549	491835	•	549191	2342502	4126332	3475988	2711689	2405461	4907098	4649710	16619483	•
Average Total Receipts	9	32943	7933	•	1565	5741	15170	26135	54234	89091	196284	290607	722586	•
Operating Costs/Operating Income (%)														
Cost of Operations	10	55.2	51.8	•	36.3	58.3	61.5	53.5	56.1	62.2	61.1	51.8	56.5	•
Salaries and Wages	11	14.5	6.5	•	23.6	12.5	11.8	14.4	14.6	12.0	10.9	16.4	14.5	•
Taxes Paid	12	2.0	1.6	•	4.2	2.4	2.3	2.3	2.0	1.8	1.6	2.0	1.9	•
Interest Paid	13	3.9	0.9	•	0.3	0.4	0.1	0.5	1.2	0.8	0.4	1.7	1.6	•
Depreciation	14	2.5	2.5	•	1.8	1.2	1.1	1.4	2.2	2.0	2.5	3.7	2.8	•
Amortization and Depletion	15	1.3	1.3	•	0.0	0.0	0.4	0.1	0.2	0.7	0.5	0.9	1.3	•
Pensions and Other Deferred Comp.	16	1.3	0.2	•	0.7	0.3	0.4	0.7	1.0	0.8	0.7	0.3	0.9	•
Employee Benefits	17	2.1	1.4	•	2.4	1.3	1.7	2.0	2.0	2.0	2.6	2.6	2.0	•
Advertising	18	0.7	1.0	•	0.1	1.0	0.6	0.6	0.8	1.7	0.6	2.2	0.6	•
Other Expenses	19	13.9	19.4	•	18.2	10.3	9.4	10.4	10.3	9.5	11.7	14.3	12.0	•
Officers' Compensation	20	1.5	0.5	•	7.2	4.3	3.0	4.8	3.0	1.4	1.9	1.6	1.5	•
Operating Margin	21	1.2	12.9	•	5.1	8.1	7.7	9.3	6.5	5.2	5.6	2.5	4.5	•
Operating Margin Before Officers' Comp.	22	2.6	13.5	•	12.3	12.4	10.7	14.1	9.5	6.5	7.5	4.2	5.9	•

Selected Average Balance Sheet ($ in Thousands)

Net Receivables 23	5899	0	•	173	730	2786	3428	8953	15224	32555	88442	149097	•
Inventories 24	3152	0	•	78	571	1371	3500	8236	12221	27903	43619	89892	•
Net Property, Plant and Equipment 25	3158	0	•	62	180	722	1733	7122	6843	20540	32731	78731	•
Total Assets 26	83281	0	•	581	2256	7055	15132	37256	69881	159377	361352	1239076	•
Notes and Loans Payable 27	20998	0	•	112	423	580	2366	10692	19841	17727	41427	264345	•
All Other Liabilities 28	28872	0	•	132	704	2253	3819	8713	19331	52293	99206	327293	•
Net Worth 29	33410	0	•	338	1129	4221	8947	17850	30709	89357	220718	647438	•

Selected Financial Ratios (Times to 1)

Current Ratio 30	1.2	•	•	3.1	2.3	2.5	2.6	2.3	1.3	2.2	2.3	1.3	•
Quick Ratio 31	0.7	•	•	2.5	1.3	1.9	1.5	1.2	0.8	1.2	1.5	0.8	•
Net Sales to Working Capital 32	12.7	•	•	4.5	5.1	4.2	3.7	3.8	8.4	3.6	2.7	6.6	•
Coverage Ratio 33	3.5	37.8	•	29.9	22.2	60.1	23.3	7.8	12.6	21.3	5.5	6.3	•
Total Asset Turnover 34	0.4	•	•	2.6	2.5	2.1	1.7	1.4	1.2	1.2	0.8	0.6	•
Inventory Turnover 35	5.4	•	•	7.1	5.9	6.8	3.9	3.6	4.4	4.2	3.3	4.4	•
Receivables Turnover 36	5.6	•	•	8.7	9.5	5.3	7.4	6.2	5.7	5.6	•	5.2	•
Total Liabilities to Net Worth 37	1.5	•	•	0.7	1.0	0.7	0.7	1.1	1.3	0.8	0.6	0.9	•
Current Assets to Working Capital 38	5.9	•	•	1.5	1.8	1.7	1.6	1.8	4.2	1.8	1.8	4.2	•
Current Liabilities to Working Capital 39	4.9	•	•	0.5	0.8	0.7	0.6	0.8	3.2	0.8	0.8	3.2	•
Working Capital to Net Sales 40	0.1	•	•	0.2	0.2	0.2	0.3	0.3	0.1	0.3	0.4	0.2	•
Inventory to Working Capital 41	1.4	•	•	0.3	0.6	0.4	0.5	0.7	1.2	0.5	0.4	1.0	•
Total Receipts to Cash Flow 42	5.1	2.2	•	4.7	6.4	6.3	5.3	5.9	6.2	5.5	5.1	5.6	•
Cost of Goods to Cash Flow 43	2.8	1.1	•	1.7	3.7	3.9	2.8	3.3	3.8	3.3	2.6	3.2	•
Cash Flow to Total Debt 44	0.1	•	•	1.3	0.8	0.8	0.8	0.5	0.4	0.5	0.4	0.2	•

Selected Financial Factors (in Percentages)

Debt Ratio 45	59.9	•	•	41.9	49.9	40.2	40.9	52.1	56.1	43.9	38.9	47.7	•
Return on Total Assets 46	5.1	•	•	20.1	22.0	18.3	19.7	13.8	11.9	10.4	7.1	5.7	•
Return on Equity Before Income Taxes 47	9.1	•	•	33.5	42.1	30.0	31.9	25.1	25.0	17.7	9.5	9.1	•
Return on Equity After Income Taxes 48	6.6	•	•	32.3	38.9	28.2	28.4	22.1	20.5	14.1	7.0	6.7	•
Profit Margin (Before Income Tax) 49	9.9	32.5	•	7.4	8.3	8.4	11.1	8.4	8.9	8.3	7.5	8.4	•
Profit Margin (After Income Tax) 50	7.2	29.1	•	7.1	7.7	7.9	9.9	7.4	7.3	6.6	5.6	6.2	•

Table I

Corporations with and without Net Income

ELECTRICAL LIGHTING EQUIPMENT AND HOUSEHOLD APPLIANCE

Item Description for Accounting Period 7/11 Through 6/12		MONEY AMOUNTS AND SIZE OF ASSETS IN THOUSANDS OF DOLLARS												
		Total	Zero Assets	Under 500	500 to 1,000	1,000 to 5,000	5,000 to 10,000	10,000 to 25,000	25,000 to 50,000	50,000 to 100,000	100,000 to 250,000	250,000 to 500,000	500,000 to 2,500,000	2,500,000 and over
Number of Enterprises	1	1552	275	•	0	296	•	101	18	15	17	7	6	6
Revenues ($ in Thousands)														
Net Sales	2	125616425	778075	•	0	1665549	•	2497655	862578	1415800	3707646	2159454	9791841	101982749
Interest	3	45601240	95	•	0	119	•	319	383	755	3260	7551	20599	45568033
Rents	4	9226379	0	•	0	0	•	4541	0	1071	950	0	613	9219203
Royalties	5	2857362	0	•	0	0	•	0	0	133	145	2643	24218	2830223
Other Portfolio Income	6	10360332	3405	•	0	604	•	1668	41	3431	14239	1523	525881	9809539
Other Receipts	7	23931954	2510	•	0	262	•	15454	-21933	3728	13636	31071	42078	23844702
Total Receipts	8	217593692	784085	•	0	1666534	•	2519637	841069	1424918	3739876	2202242	10405230	193254449
Average Total Receipts	9	140202	2851	•	•	5630	•	24947	46726	94995	219993	314606	1734205	32209075
Operating Costs/Operating Income (%)														
Cost of Operations	10	68.6	91.2	•	•	58.5	•	64.0	70.8	67.5	66.7	66.6	71.2	68.7
Salaries and Wages	11	11.8	14.7	•	•	18.6	•	12.4	7.5	7.4	9.1	5.6	6.4	12.5
Taxes Paid	12	1.0	0.4	•	•	2.5	•	1.8	2.4	1.5	1.4	1.3	1.1	0.9
Interest Paid	13	36.0	0.1	•	•	0.3	•	0.7	1.0	1.4	1.0	4.1	0.8	44.1
Depreciation	14	8.3	2.8	•	•	0.3	•	2.9	2.4	2.1	2.8	2.4	1.8	9.7
Amortization and Depletion	15	1.4	6.0	•	•	0.3	•	0.1	0.2	1.3	0.5	0.6	0.5	1.5
Pensions and Other Deferred Comp.	16	0.7	0.8	•	•	0.5	•	0.3	0.2	0.8	0.7	0.2	2.4	0.5
Employee Benefits	17	2.8	0.0	•	•	0.8	•	2.0	1.2	1.0	2.1	1.3	2.2	3.0
Advertising	18	1.3	0.2	•	•	2.4	•	0.9	1.7	0.8	1.4	5.6	2.4	1.1
Other Expenses	19	35.0	17.0	•	•	13.3	•	10.6	10.9	9.4	11.2	9.6	11.6	40.3
Officers' Compensation	20	0.5	2.5	•	•	4.2	•	2.8	2.0	1.3	1.1	1.4	0.6	0.3
Operating Margin	21	•	•	•	•	•	•	1.3	•	5.6	1.9	1.1	•	•
Operating Margin Before Officers' Comp.	22	•	•	•	•	2.4	•	4.1	1.5	6.9	2.9	2.6	•	•

Selected Average Balance Sheet ($ in Thousands)													
Net Receivables 23	104676	0	•	•	819	•	3171	8581	11837	37978	53960	293868	26448261
Inventories 24	8143	0	•	•	728	•	4420	8519	15579	35026	48644	164715	1584445
Net Property, Plant and Equipment 25	24323	0	•	•	120	•	2624	6780	10182	28995	42736	195733	5863141
Total Assets 26	550631	0	•	•	1900	•	14284	33973	72169	160493	300941	1536398	139409556
Notes and Loans Payable 27	317806	0	•	•	345	•	4003	11634	17555	42498	137299	180639	81550862
All Other Liabilities 28	89784	0	•	•	1393	•	4369	7650	21498	50011	82719	555212	22181632
Net Worth 29	143040	0	•	•	162	•	5912	14690	33115	67984	80924	800547	35677062

Selected Financial Ratios (Times to 1)													
Current Ratio 30	0.7	•	•	•	1.6	•	2.3	2.1	2.0	2.3	1.7	1.7	0.7
Quick Ratio 31	0.6	•	•	•	0.9	•	1.2	1.0	1.0	1.3	0.8	1.1	0.6
Net Sales to Working Capital 32	•	•	•	•	9.5	•	4.5	3.9	4.5	4.3	5.9	7.3	•
Coverage Ratio 33	1.4	•	•	•	•	•	4.1	•	5.4	4.0	1.8	8.9	1.3
Total Asset Turnover 34	0.1	•	•	•	3.0	•	1.7	1.4	1.3	1.4	1.0	1.1	0.1
Inventory Turnover 35	6.8	•	•	•	4.5	•	3.6	4.0	4.1	4.2	4.2	7.1	7.4
Receivables Turnover 36	0.7	•	•	•	7.9	•	7.9	7.4	8.2	6.0	5.4	5.8	0.6
Total Liabilities to Net Worth 37	2.8	•	•	•	10.7	•	1.4	1.3	1.2	1.4	2.7	0.9	2.9
Current Assets to Working Capital 38	•	•	•	•	2.7	•	1.8	1.9	2.1	1.7	2.5	2.5	•
Current Liabilities to Working Capital 39	•	•	•	•	1.7	•	0.8	0.9	1.1	0.7	1.5	1.5	•
Working Capital to Net Sales 40	•	•	•	•	0.1	•	0.2	0.3	0.2	0.2	0.2	0.1	•
Inventory to Working Capital 41	•	•	•	•	1.0	•	0.8	0.9	0.8	0.7	0.8	0.7	•
Total Receipts to Cash Flow 42	2.8	•	•	•	11.4	•	10.2	16.2	7.1	8.3	9.0	8.1	2.5
Cost of Goods to Cash Flow 43	2.0	•	•	•	6.7	•	6.5	11.5	4.8	5.6	6.0	5.7	1.7
Cash Flow to Total Debt 44	0.1	•	•	•	0.3	•	0.3	0.2	0.3	0.3	0.2	0.3	0.1

Selected Financial Factors (in Percentages)													
Debt Ratio 45	74.0	•	•	•	91.5	•	58.6	56.8	54.1	57.6	73.1	47.9	74.4
Return on Total Assets 46	7.2	•	•	•	•	•	5.0	•	10.0	5.5	7.6	8.0	7.2
Return on Equity Before Income Taxes 47	7.3	•	•	•	•	•	9.1	•	17.8	9.8	12.6	13.6	7.2
Return on Equity After Income Taxes 48	4.7	•	•	•	•	•	7.4	•	15.1	7.2	9.7	9.5	4.7
Profit Margin (Before Income Tax) 49	12.8	•	•	•	•	•	2.2	•	6.2	3.0	3.3	6.7	15.2
Profit Margin (After Income Tax) 50	8.4	•	•	•	•	•	1.8	•	5.3	2.2	2.5	4.7	10.0

Table II

Corporations with Net Income

ELECTRICAL LIGHTING EQUIPMENT AND HOUSEHOLD APPLIANCE

MONEY AMOUNTS AND SIZE OF ASSETS IN THOUSANDS OF DOLLARS

Item Description for Accounting Period 7/11 Through 6/12		Total	Zero Assets	Under 500	500 to 1,000	1,000 to 5,000	5,000 to 10,000	10,000 to 25,000	25,000 to 50,000	50,000 to 100,000	100,000 to 250,000	250,000 to 500,000	500,000 to 2,500,000	2,500,000 and over
Number of Enterprises	1	648	0	384	0	140	20	59	9	11	•	•	6	•
Revenues ($ in Thousands)														
Net Sales	2	109677574	0	6345	0	968699	318720	1631155	505566	1257343	•	•	9791841	•
Interest	3	45557750	0	0	0	0	0	222	324	211	•	•	20599	•
Rents	4	9216346	0	0	0	0	0	1242	0	1071	•	•	613	•
Royalties	5	2291259	0	0	0	0	0	0	0	69	•	•	24218	•
Other Portfolio Income	6	10329902	0	0	0	0	0	479	41	3431	•	•	525881	•
Other Receipts	7	23841912	0	7	0	253	1329	11929	1467	3141	•	•	42078	•
Total Receipts	8	200914743	0	6352	0	968952	320049	1645027	507398	1265266	•	•	10405230	•
Average Total Receipts	9	310054	•	17	•	6921	16002	27882	56378	115024	•	•	1734205	•
Operating Costs/Operating Income (%)														
Cost of Operations	10	67.9	•	56.7	•	56.7	50.0	65.0	62.3	68.2	•	•	71.2	•
Salaries and Wages	11	12.6	•	3.1	•	21.5	11.7	10.6	7.7	7.0	•	•	6.4	•
Taxes Paid	12	1.0	•	2.1	•	3.8	2.3	1.4	1.6	1.4	•	•	1.1	•
Interest Paid	13	40.9	•	0.2	•	0.1	0.3	0.5	1.4	1.0	•	•	0.8	•
Depreciation	14	9.1	•	0.4	•	0.0	1.4	1.8	1.7	2.0	•	•	1.8	•
Amortization and Depletion	15	1.4	•	•	•	0.4	•	0.0	0.3	0.8	•	•	0.5	•
Pensions and Other Deferred Comp.	16	0.5	•	0.2	•	0.8	1.1	0.5	0.2	0.8	•	•	2.4	•
Employee Benefits	17	2.8	•	•	•	•	0.5	1.3	0.9	1.0	•	•	2.2	•
Advertising	18	1.2	•	1.0	•	0.5	0.7	1.2	2.3	0.7	•	•	2.4	•
Other Expenses	19	37.7	•	30.6	•	11.1	11.2	6.9	12.2	9.0	•	•	11.6	•
Officers' Compensation	20	0.5	•	3.5	•	1.6	0.6	3.3	2.1	1.3	•	•	0.6	•
Operating Margin	21	•	•	2.3	•	3.4	20.2	7.5	7.3	6.8	•	•	•	•
Operating Margin Before Officers' Comp.	22	•	•	5.8	•	5.0	20.8	10.8	9.3	8.1	•	•	•	•

Selected Average Balance Sheet ($ in Thousands)													
Net Receivables 23	227745	•	1	•	708	1993	3539	10011	14655	•	•	293868	•
Inventories 24	16446	•	1	•	966	5118	5370	10458	19192	•	•	165895	•
Net Property, Plant and Equipment 25	55302	•	0	•	8	369	2398	6628	11035	•	•	195733	•
Total Assets 26	1259305	•	4	•	1481	7894	15020	38451	74583	•	•	1536398	•
Notes and Loans Payable 27	748350	•	11	•	116	1230	2963	14101	18374	•	•	180639	•
All Other Liabilities 28	189603	•	2	•	833	2211	3601	7221	20907	•	•	555212	•
Net Worth 29	321352	•	-9	•	532	4453	8456	17129	35302	•	•	800547	•

Selected Financial Ratios (Times to 1)													
Current Ratio 30	0.7	•	2.2	•	2.6	2.6	2.7	2.6	2.2	•	•	1.7	•
Quick Ratio 31	0.6	•	1.3	•	1.5	1.1	1.3	1.2	1.1	•	•	1.1	•
Net Sales to Working Capital 32	•	•	6.9	•	8.0	3.5	3.8	3.6	4.5	•	•	7.3	•
Coverage Ratio 33	1.4	•	16.1	•	56.1	74.0	16.9	6.3	8.5	•	•	8.9	•
Total Asset Turnover 34	0.1	•	3.7	•	4.7	2.0	1.8	1.5	1.5	•	•	1.1	•
Inventory Turnover 35	7.0	•	6.7	•	4.1	1.6	3.3	3.3	4.1	•	•	7.0	•
Receivables Turnover 36	0.7	•	48.1	•	9.3	4.9	7.8	6.5	8.0	•	•	•	•
Total Liabilities to Net Worth 37	2.9	•	•	•	1.8	0.8	0.8	1.2	1.1	•	•	0.9	•
Current Assets to Working Capital 38	•	•	1.8	•	1.6	1.6	1.6	1.6	1.9	•	•	2.5	•
Current Liabilities to Working Capital 39	•	•	0.8	•	0.6	0.6	0.6	0.6	0.9	•	•	1.5	•
Working Capital to Net Sales 40	•	•	0.1	•	0.1	0.3	0.3	0.3	0.2	•	•	0.1	•
Inventory to Working Capital 41	•	•	0.6	•	0.7	0.8	0.7	0.8	0.8	•	•	0.7	•
Total Receipts to Cash Flow 42	2.6	•	6.5	•	8.1	3.5	7.8	5.6	6.7	•	•	8.1	•
Cost of Goods to Cash Flow 43	1.7	•	3.7	•	4.6	1.8	5.1	3.5	4.6	•	•	5.7	•
Cash Flow to Total Debt 44	0.1	•	0.2	•	0.9	1.3	0.5	0.5	0.4	•	•	0.3	•

Selected Financial Factors (in Percentages)													
Debt Ratio 45	74.5	•	290.5	•	64.1	43.6	43.7	55.5	52.7	•	•	47.9	•
Return on Total Assets 46	7.6	•	9.3	•	16.4	42.2	16.4	13.2	12.8	•	•	8.0	•
Return on Equity Before Income Taxes 47	8.2	•	•	•	44.8	73.8	27.4	25.0	23.9	•	•	13.6	•
Return on Equity After Income Taxes 48	5.5	•	•	•	44.8	67.5	25.4	20.3	20.4	•	•	9.5	•
Profit Margin (Before Income Tax) 49	15.6	•	2.4	•	3.4	20.6	8.4	7.6	7.4	•	•	6.7	•
Profit Margin (After Income Tax) 50	10.5	•	2.3	•	3.4	18.9	7.8	6.2	6.3	•	•	4.7	•

Table I

Corporations with and without Net Income

ELECTRICAL EQUIPMENT

MONEY AMOUNTS AND SIZE OF ASSETS IN THOUSANDS OF DOLLARS

Item Description for Accounting Period 7/11 Through 6/12		Total	Zero Assets	Under 500	500 to 1,000	1,000 to 5,000	5,000 to 10,000	10,000 to 25,000	25,000 to 50,000	50,000 to 100,000	100,000 to 250,000	250,000 to 500,000	500,000 to 2,500,000	2,500,000 and over
Number of Enterprises	1	733	10	•	153	316	•	73	25	17	7	10	3	4
Revenues ($ in Thousands)														
Net Sales	2	45935945	13405	•	490535	1717948	•	1619105	882507	1673508	841554	3905256	1867716	30991600
Interest	3	231554	0	•	0	289	•	75	839	2102	1122	2107	1461	223472
Rents	4	53603	0	•	0	3006	•	42	404	575	172	0	0	49404
Royalties	5	464138	0	•	0	0	•	0	2067	40	3527	17913	2840	437752
Other Portfolio Income	6	574207	9	•	0	1	•	93	5336	1584	16978	25802	5486	518805
Other Receipts	7	435253	33	•	2378	4860	•	2241	10188	2311	4907	20247	5087	374873
Total Receipts	8	47694700	13447	•	492913	1726104	•	1621556	901341	1680120	868260	3971325	1882590	32595906
Average Total Receipts	9	65068	1345	•	3222	5462	•	22213	36054	98831	124037	397132	627530	8148976
Operating Costs/Operating Income (%)														
Cost of Operations	10	67.4	59.9	•	77.4	64.9	•	63.4	66.2	74.9	67.3	65.7	62.0	67.9
Salaries and Wages	11	7.9	6.2	•	4.0	7.5	•	7.7	8.8	6.4	11.7	11.3	7.2	7.7
Taxes Paid	12	1.9	3.5	•	1.9	3.0	•	1.5	1.7	1.3	2.0	2.0	0.5	2.0
Interest Paid	13	2.0	0.5	•	0.2	1.1	•	0.5	1.2	0.7	3.4	0.4	4.5	2.3
Depreciation	14	1.9	1.2	•	0.4	1.7	•	2.0	2.2	2.1	3.6	3.2	2.8	1.6
Amortization and Depletion	15	1.1	1.2	•	•	0.0	•	0.2	1.3	0.4	1.1	0.6	9.2	0.8
Pensions and Other Deferred Comp.	16	1.9	1.1	•	•	0.4	•	0.9	0.2	0.4	0.5	2.5	0.4	2.4
Employee Benefits	17	1.8	3.4	•	0.7	1.3	•	2.1	1.8	1.5	1.9	1.8	1.1	1.9
Advertising	18	0.4	0.1	•	0.3	0.4	•	0.3	0.4	0.6	0.4	0.4	0.8	0.5
Other Expenses	19	9.0	59.6	•	10.3	12.4	•	10.5	12.6	6.0	5.0	11.5	8.5	8.6
Officers' Compensation	20	1.7	•	•	4.1	6.4	•	2.5	1.6	1.2	1.1	1.3	0.9	1.2
Operating Margin	21	2.8	•	•	0.7	1.0	•	8.6	1.9	4.4	2.0	•	2.0	3.1
Operating Margin Before Officers' Comp.	22	4.5	•	•	4.8	7.4	•	11.1	3.5	5.7	3.1	0.6	2.9	4.2

Selected Average Balance Sheet ($ in Thousands)													
Net Receivables 23	15885	0	•	391	494	•	3683	6615	19026	20079	70339	91893	2328443
Inventories 24	5977	0	•	172	838	•	3183	6995	13797	32512	44377	136224	541968
Net Property, Plant and Equipment 25	7771	0	•	63	481	•	2121	5209	11257	42726	77631	62613	901385
Total Assets 26	106545	0	•	741	2290	•	15075	33534	69244	162023	332447	983395	16433606
Notes and Loans Payable 27	29283	0	•	165	972	•	3050	9326	10727	34118	58622	439644	4535468
All Other Liabilities 28	26282	0	•	348	483	•	3843	9793	22339	40950	89812	131718	4099098
Net Worth 29	50980	0	•	228	836	•	8181	14415	36178	86955	184013	412033	7799039
Selected Financial Ratios (Times to 1)													
Current Ratio 30	1.2	•	•	1.7	2.8	•	2.2	1.6	2.3	1.5	1.7	2.3	1.0
Quick Ratio 31	0.8	•	•	1.2	1.4	•	1.2	0.9	1.3	1.1	0.9	1.3	0.7
Net Sales to Working Capital 32	14.0	•	•	11.5	4.8	•	3.7	6.0	3.8	5.0	5.3	4.2	363.1
Coverage Ratio 33	4.8	•	•	6.2	2.4	•	20.0	4.5	8.4	2.6	4.3	1.6	5.0
Total Asset Turnover 34	0.6	•	•	4.3	2.4	•	1.5	1.1	1.4	0.7	1.2	0.6	0.5
Inventory Turnover 35	7.1	•	•	14.4	4.2	•	4.4	3.3	5.3	2.5	5.8	2.8	9.7
Receivables Turnover 36	4.1	•	•	8.3	10.6	•	7.6	4.2	6.7	3.4	6.7	5.2	3.5
Total Liabilities to Net Worth 37	1.1	•	•	2.3	1.7	•	0.8	1.3	0.9	0.9	0.8	1.4	1.1
Current Assets to Working Capital 38	6.0	•	•	2.4	1.6	•	1.8	2.7	1.8	2.9	2.5	1.8	157.7
Current Liabilities to Working Capital 39	5.0	•	•	1.4	0.6	•	0.8	1.7	0.8	1.9	1.5	0.8	156.7
Working Capital to Net Sales 40	0.1	•	•	0.1	0.2	•	0.3	0.2	0.3	0.2	0.2	0.2	0.0
Inventory to Working Capital 41	1.4	•	•	0.7	0.7	•	0.6	0.9	0.6	0.8	0.7	0.7	28.4
Total Receipts to Cash Flow 42	7.4	4.3	•	12.6	8.7	•	5.8	6.6	10.3	11.7	9.0	10.0	6.9
Cost of Goods to Cash Flow 43	5.0	2.6	•	9.7	5.6	•	3.7	4.4	7.7	7.9	5.9	6.2	4.7
Cash Flow to Total Debt 44	0.2	•	•	0.5	0.4	•	0.6	0.3	0.3	0.1	0.3	0.1	0.1
Selected Financial Factors (in Percentages)													
Debt Ratio 45	52.2	•	•	69.3	63.5	•	45.7	57.0	47.8	46.3	44.6	58.1	52.5
Return on Total Assets 46	5.6	•	•	5.9	6.1	•	13.5	5.8	8.5	6.4	2.0	4.7	5.5
Return on Equity Before Income Taxes 47	9.2	•	•	16.2	9.8	•	23.6	10.4	14.3	7.2	2.8	4.3	9.3
Return on Equity After Income Taxes 48	6.7	•	•	13.4	6.5	•	21.8	5.8	11.4	4.6	1.6	3.8	6.7
Profit Margin (Before Income Tax) 49	7.5	•	•	1.1	1.5	•	8.7	4.2	5.2	5.2	1.3	2.8	9.4
Profit Margin (After Income Tax) 50	5.5	•	•	1.0	1.0	•	8.1	2.4	4.2	3.3	0.7	2.5	6.7

Table II

Corporations with Net Income

ELECTRICAL EQUIPMENT

MONEY AMOUNTS AND SIZE OF ASSETS IN THOUSANDS OF DOLLARS

Item Description for Accounting Period 7/11 Through 6/12		Total	Zero Assets	Under 500	500 to 1,000	1,000 to 5,000	5,000 to 10,000	10,000 to 25,000	25,000 to 50,000	50,000 to 100,000	100,000 to 250,000	250,000 to 500,000	500,000 to 2,500,000	2,500,000 and over
Number of Enterprises	1	562	0	0	121	263	64	67	14	14	•	•	3	•
Revenues ($ in Thousands)														
Net Sales	2	42920032	0	0	407389	1526458	862269	1537267	527451	1306184	•	•	1867716	•
Interest	3	230853	0	0	0	195	2	65	835	2092	•	•	1461	•
Rents	4	53603	0	0	0	3006	0	42	404	575	•	•	0	•
Royalties	5	464009	0	0	0	0	0	0	2067	40	•	•	2840	•
Other Portfolio Income	6	546579	0	0	0	1	101	93	2950	1584	•	•	5486	•
Other Receipts	7	425685	0	0	2379	4476	1117	2251	9665	5249	•	•	5087	•
Total Receipts	8	44640761	0	0	409768	1534136	863489	1539718	543372	1315724	•	•	1882590	•
Average Total Receipts	9	79432	•	•	3387	5833	13492	22981	38812	93980	•	•	627530	•
Operating Costs/Operating Income (%)														
Cost of Operations	10	66.6	•	•	80.5	65.3	50.9	62.9	60.8	70.9	•	•	62.0	•
Salaries and Wages	11	7.9	•	•	3.1	6.1	3.7	7.3	11.6	7.3	•	•	7.2	•
Taxes Paid	12	1.9	•	•	1.8	2.8	2.6	1.5	2.0	1.3	•	•	0.5	•
Interest Paid	13	2.0	•	•	0.2	1.1	0.6	0.4	0.8	0.8	•	•	4.5	•
Depreciation	14	1.8	•	•	0.4	1.3	1.4	2.0	2.1	2.0	•	•	2.8	•
Amortization and Depletion	15	1.1	•	•	•	0.0	0.0	0.1	1.3	0.4	•	•	9.2	•
Pensions and Other Deferred Comp.	16	2.1	•	•	•	0.3	0.5	0.9	0.3	0.4	•	•	0.4	•
Employee Benefits	17	1.8	•	•	0.6	1.2	0.3	2.2	1.9	0.9	•	•	1.1	•
Advertising	18	0.5	•	•	0.1	0.2	0.4	0.3	0.4	0.7	•	•	0.8	•
Other Expenses	19	8.9	•	•	8.8	11.8	11.1	9.4	11.0	6.7	•	•	8.5	•
Officers' Compensation	20	1.7	•	•	3.7	6.7	15.2	2.5	1.5	1.4	•	•	0.9	•
Operating Margin	21	3.7	•	•	1.0	3.2	13.4	10.6	6.1	7.1	•	•	2.0	•
Operating Margin Before Officers' Comp.	22	5.4	•	•	4.6	9.9	28.6	13.1	7.6	8.5	•	•	2.9	•

Selected Average Balance Sheet ($ in Thousands)

Net Receivables	23	19906	•	•	409	533	1577	3573	7016	18897	•	•	91893	•
Inventories	24	6441	•	•	189	948	2229	3183	8825	15891	•	•	103808	•
Net Property, Plant and Equipment	25	8907	•	•	2	511	822	2002	6196	9466	•	•	62613	•
Total Assets	26	134763	•	•	673	2361	8561	14775	33742	67375	•	•	983395	•
Notes and Loans Payable	27	36951	•	•	155	997	1739	2876	6586	10748	•	•	439644	•
All Other Liabilities	28	33092	•	•	403	504	1283	3832	7565	22156	•	•	131718	•
Net Worth	29	64720	•	•	115	859	5540	8067	19591	34470	•	•	412033	•

Selected Financial Ratios (Times to 1)

Current Ratio	30	1.2	•	•	1.4	2.8	2.9	2.2	2.1	2.4	•	•	2.3	•
Quick Ratio	31	0.8	•	•	1.0	1.3	2.0	1.2	1.2	1.4	•	•	1.3	•
Net Sales to Working Capital	32	14.7	•	•	16.5	5.0	3.1	3.9	4.0	3.7	•	•	4.2	•
Coverage Ratio	33	5.3	•	•	9.6	4.5	24.5	25.6	12.2	11.4	•	•	1.6	•
Total Asset Turnover	34	0.6	•	•	5.0	2.5	1.6	1.6	1.1	1.4	•	•	0.6	•
Inventory Turnover	35	7.9	•	•	14.3	4.0	3.1	4.5	2.6	4.2	•	•	3.7	•
Receivables Turnover	36	4.3	•	•	7.6	10.0	6.0	8.3	3.5	•	•	•	•	•
Total Liabilities to Net Worth	37	1.1	•	•	4.9	1.7	0.5	0.8	0.7	1.0	•	•	1.4	•
Current Assets to Working Capital	38	6.4	•	•	3.2	1.6	1.5	1.8	1.9	1.7	•	•	1.8	•
Current Liabilities to Working Capital	39	5.4	•	•	2.2	0.6	0.5	0.8	0.9	0.7	•	•	0.8	•
Working Capital to Net Sales	40	0.1	•	•	0.1	0.2	0.3	0.3	0.3	0.3	•	•	0.2	•
Inventory to Working Capital	41	1.4	•	•	0.9	0.8	0.4	0.6	0.7	0.6	•	•	0.7	•
Total Receipts to Cash Flow	42	6.9	•	•	15.0	7.5	4.7	5.5	5.6	7.6	•	•	10.0	•
Cost of Goods to Cash Flow	43	4.6	•	•	12.1	4.9	2.4	3.4	3.4	5.4	•	•	6.2	•
Cash Flow to Total Debt	44	0.2	•	•	0.4	0.5	1.0	0.6	0.5	0.4	•	•	0.1	•

Selected Financial Factors (in Percentages)

Debt Ratio	45	52.0	•	•	82.9	63.6	35.3	45.4	41.9	48.8	•	•	58.1	•
Return on Total Assets	46	6.0	•	•	8.6	11.8	22.2	17.3	11.4	12.7	•	•	4.7	•
Return on Equity Before Income Taxes	47	10.2	•	•	45.3	25.2	32.9	30.5	18.0	22.6	•	•	4.3	•
Return on Equity After Income Taxes	48	7.6	•	•	38.3	21.5	32.9	28.6	11.9	19.0	•	•	3.8	•
Profit Margin (Before Income Tax)	49	8.6	•	•	1.5	3.7	13.5	10.7	9.3	8.3	•	•	2.8	•
Profit Margin (After Income Tax)	50	6.4	•	•	1.3	3.2	13.5	10.0	6.2	7.0	•	•	2.5	•

Table I

Corporations with and without Net Income

OTHER ELECTRICAL EQUIPMENT AND COMPONENT

Item Description for Accounting Period 7/11 Through 6/12		Total	Zero Assets	Under 500	500 to 1,000	1,000 to 5,000	5,000 to 10,000	10,000 to 25,000	25,000 to 50,000	50,000 to 100,000	100,000 to 250,000	250,000 to 500,000	500,000 to 2,500,000	2,500,000 and over
		Money Amounts and Size of Assets in Thousands of Dollars												
Number of Enterprises	1	3284	995	490	265	818	299	194	96	53	34	19	18	4
		Revenues ($ in Thousands)												
Net Sales	2	65314962	1075930	404912	524326	3669788	3532824	5259160	4676441	4605606	5663867	5660812	12704552	17536744
Interest	3	285989	1764	2	24	641	816	1577	2147	8729	7826	20990	61966	179508
Rents	4	16603	0	0	0	863	514	3809	115	1586	116	310	1581	7709
Royalties	5	197834	1092	0	0	0	0	1544	4121	6318	7297	41371	55179	80912
Other Portfolio Income	6	274555	17289	0	0	3640	1594	1129	18290	8360	34163	10243	71686	108163
Other Receipts	7	392132	18919	1855	172	6160	14672	42897	44220	14723	9717	16708	107223	114863
Total Receipts	8	66482075	1114994	406769	524522	3681092	3550420	5310116	4745334	4645322	5722986	5750434	13002187	18027899
Average Total Receipts	9	20244	1121	830	1979	4500	11874	27372	49431	87648	168323	302654	722344	4506975
		Operating Costs/Operating Income (%)												
Cost of Operations	10	69.4	67.1	62.5	80.8	57.5	71.8	67.6	65.6	70.5	73.1	66.4	68.7	73.1
Salaries and Wages	11	8.6	15.0	10.7	5.9	12.2	8.3	7.8	10.0	8.1	9.1	10.0	8.4	7.0
Taxes Paid	12	1.6	1.4	2.5	2.6	2.3	2.1	2.2	1.7	2.0	1.5	1.3	1.5	1.3
Interest Paid	13	2.4	2.7	6.7	1.5	0.5	1.0	0.7	0.8	1.3	2.2	2.3	2.6	4.3
Depreciation	14	2.5	2.3	1.0	0.3	2.5	2.4	2.2	2.5	3.0	3.4	3.1	3.9	1.2
Amortization and Depletion	15	1.4	2.2	0.0	1.6	0.4	0.6	0.3	0.6	1.3	0.5	2.8	1.4	2.1
Pensions and Other Deferred Comp.	16	0.6	0.3	0.1	•	0.6	0.3	0.5	0.4	0.4	0.8	0.5	1.0	0.4
Employee Benefits	17	1.7	2.1	0.4	1.8	2.2	1.6	1.7	1.8	1.9	1.9	1.6	1.8	1.4
Advertising	18	1.2	0.9	0.0	0.1	0.9	0.3	0.5	1.0	0.5	0.6	1.0	0.7	2.5
Other Expenses	19	9.4	15.0	28.9	3.7	12.3	7.9	9.4	10.1	8.7	8.8	9.3	10.6	7.7
Officers' Compensation	20	1.7	6.7	5.5	5.4	5.7	2.9	3.6	1.8	1.5	1.1	1.7	1.1	0.3
Operating Margin	21	•	•	•	•	2.9	0.8	3.5	3.6	0.8	•	0.1	•	•
Operating Margin Before Officers' Comp.	22	1.2	•	•	1.7	8.5	3.7	7.1	5.4	2.3	•	1.8	•	•

Selected Average Balance Sheet ($ in Thousands)														
Net Receivables	23	4267	0	84	218	667	1482	4276	7816	15409	26125	62409	110162	1617564
Inventories	24	2572	0	40	413	555	1902	4428	7448	12754	29813	38375	90236	419201
Net Property, Plant and Equipment	25	2628	0	15	27	541	1294	2013	5463	10130	36246	40260	168301	326713
Total Assets	26	31393	0	269	635	2509	7082	15977	34232	69475	154444	304026	1070041	14567002
Notes and Loans Payable	27	5466	0	689	307	596	2591	3173	7524	18314	52415	97051	328351	1106316
All Other Liabilities	28	9981	0	117	275	763	1664	4299	9305	21382	53710	69557	293089	5060487
Net Worth	29	15946	0	-537	53	1150	2827	8506	17402	29779	48318	137418	448601	8400199
Selected Financial Ratios (Times to 1)														
Current Ratio	30	1.6	•	0.9	1.7	2.4	1.8	2.3	2.2	1.9	1.7	1.8	2.2	1.1
Quick Ratio	31	1.0	•	0.7	1.0	1.5	0.8	1.3	1.3	1.0	0.9	1.0	1.2	0.8
Net Sales to Working Capital	32	5.8	•	•	8.1	4.5	6.3	4.0	4.1	4.6	5.6	4.6	4.3	15.6
Coverage Ratio	33	1.7	•	•	•	7.3	2.3	7.8	7.4	2.4	0.1	2.3	1.3	1.6
Total Asset Turnover	34	0.6	•	3.1	3.1	1.8	1.7	1.7	1.4	1.3	1.1	1.0	0.7	0.3
Inventory Turnover	35	5.4	•	12.8	3.9	4.7	4.5	4.1	4.3	4.8	4.1	5.2	5.4	7.6
Receivables Turnover	36	4.8	•	11.1	5.5	6.9	7.8	5.8	6.7	6.1	5.0	5.2	7.4	2.8
Total Liabilities to Net Worth	37	1.0	•	•	10.9	1.2	1.5	0.9	1.0	1.3	2.2	1.2	1.4	0.7
Current Assets to Working Capital	38	2.6	•	•	2.5	1.7	2.3	1.8	1.8	2.2	2.4	2.2	1.8	7.9
Current Liabilities to Working Capital	39	1.6	•	•	1.5	0.7	1.3	0.8	0.8	1.2	1.4	1.2	0.8	6.9
Working Capital to Net Sales	40	0.2	•	•	0.1	0.2	0.2	0.3	0.2	0.2	0.2	0.2	0.2	0.1
Inventory to Working Capital	41	0.8	•	•	1.0	0.6	1.1	0.7	0.7	0.7	0.9	0.6	0.6	1.3
Total Receipts to Cash Flow	42	11.5	68.0	32.9	•	8.1	16.2	8.1	7.4	11.2	21.9	10.6	11.1	12.9
Cost of Goods to Cash Flow	43	8.0	45.6	20.6	•	4.6	11.6	5.5	4.8	7.9	16.0	7.0	7.7	9.4
Cash Flow to Total Debt	44	0.1	•	0.0	•	0.4	0.2	0.4	0.4	0.2	0.1	0.2	0.1	0.1
Selected Financial Factors (in Percentages)														
Debt Ratio	45	49.2	•	299.2	91.6	54.2	60.1	46.8	49.2	57.1	68.7	54.8	58.1	42.3
Return on Total Assets	46	2.6	•	•	•	6.6	3.9	8.7	8.8	3.7	0.3	5.0	2.3	2.1
Return on Equity Before Income Taxes	47	2.2	•	27.4	•	12.5	5.5	14.2	15.0	5.0	•	6.2	1.4	1.4
Return on Equity After Income Taxes	48	0.9	•	27.4	•	10.3	2.9	12.5	11.5	3.0	•	3.7	•	0.8
Profit Margin (Before Income Tax)	49	1.7	•	•	•	3.2	1.3	4.5	5.4	1.7	•	2.8	0.9	2.6
Profit Margin (After Income Tax)	50	0.8	•	•	•	2.6	0.7	3.9	4.1	1.0	•	1.7	•	1.5

Table II

Corporations with Net Income

OTHER ELECTRICAL EQUIPMENT AND COMPONENT

MONEY AMOUNTS AND SIZE OF ASSETS IN THOUSANDS OF DOLLARS

Item Description for Accounting Period 7/11 Through 6/12		Total	Zero Assets	Under 500	500 to 1000	1,000 to 5,000	5,000 to 10,000	10,000 to 25,000	25,000 to 50,000	50,000 to 100,000	100,000 to 250,000	250,000 to 500,000	500,000 to 2,500,000	2,500,000 and over
Number of Enterprises	1	1899	528	308	61	543	165	146	75	33	17	12	11	0
Revenues ($ in Thousands)														
Net Sales	2	46562652	107946	265632	113749	3245876	2287172	4044521	3960729	3429775	3179559	3758778	22168916	0
Interest	3	229381	1639	0	0	326	302	860	1811	5131	1999	12319	204993	0
Rents	4	15352	0	0	0	684	0	3623	102	1322	116	296	9210	0
Royalties	5	149424	0	0	0	0	0	1544	4121	6109	2125	7139	128386	0
Other Portfolio Income	6	205211	17093	0	0	1635	74	678	17015	3496	13001	4228	147991	0
Other Receipts	7	324809	12572	1157	91	5490	7688	38266	41583	11164	21002	5980	179815	0
Total Receipts	8	47486829	139250	266789	113840	3254011	2295236	4089492	4025361	3456997	3217802	3788740	22839311	0
Average Total Receipts	9	25006	264	866	1866	5993	13911	28010	53671	104757	189282	315728	2076301	•
Operating Costs/Operating Income (%)														
Cost of Operations	10	68.3	76.9	48.5	63.3	61.0	68.7	64.6	64.6	68.3	70.5	67.4	70.8	•
Salaries and Wages	11	7.8	7.7	2.6	7.7	9.2	7.4	7.5	9.9	7.9	6.8	8.3	7.3	•
Taxes Paid	12	1.6	2.7	1.8	3.4	2.3	2.0	2.3	1.7	2.0	1.5	1.2	1.4	•
Interest Paid	13	2.1	1.0	6.9	2.0	0.4	0.6	0.7	0.7	0.8	1.9	1.9	3.1	•
Depreciation	14	2.0	0.6	0.1	1.3	2.3	0.6	1.4	2.3	2.1	2.3	3.2	2.0	•
Amortization and Depletion	15	1.1	0.7	•	0.1	0.4	0.6	0.2	0.4	0.7	0.4	0.7	1.7	•
Pensions and Other Deferred Comp.	16	0.5	0.0	•	•	0.7	0.3	0.5	0.4	0.6	0.9	0.5	0.5	•
Employee Benefits	17	1.6	0.8	0.0	3.6	1.9	1.7	1.8	1.9	1.7	1.3	1.3	1.6	•
Advertising	18	1.3	0.0	0.0	0.7	0.8	0.3	0.3	1.0	0.6	0.6	1.1	2.0	•
Other Expenses	19	7.8	10.3	30.6	10.6	7.2	5.0	9.7	9.3	8.3	4.2	7.1	7.8	•
Officers' Compensation	20	1.6	0.2	4.9	5.5	5.1	3.3	3.4	1.6	1.2	1.2	1.9	0.5	•
Operating Margin	21	4.3	•	4.6	1.8	8.7	9.6	7.5	6.3	6.0	8.4	5.4	1.3	•
Operating Margin Before Officers' Comp.	22	5.9	•	9.4	7.3	13.8	12.9	10.9	7.9	7.1	9.5	7.3	1.8	•

Selected Average Balance Sheet ($ in Thousands)														
Net Receivables	**23**	5833	0	101	187	765	1757	4653	8259	16437	28854	71832	648613	•
Inventories	**24**	3230	0	6	1016	692	2295	4715	8253	16959	28813	38267	148374	•
Net Property, Plant and Equipment	**25**	2613	0	15	115	333	892	1820	5441	8469	22733	42024	252518	•
Total Assets	**26**	38553	0	317	839	2569	7143	15721	34078	70607	144461	302681	5201901	•
Notes and Loans Payable	**27**	4859	0	141	579	449	1545	2898	6272	13000	55998	83719	488260	•
All Other Liabilities	**28**	13276	0	160	205	707	1209	4613	9091	24079	40673	67003	1901873	•
Net Worth	**29**	20418	0	16	56	1412	4389	8210	18716	33529	47790	151959	2811768	•
Selected Financial Ratios (Times to 1)														
Current Ratio	**30**	1.6	•	0.5	1.2	2.6	2.8	2.4	2.3	2.0	2.2	2.0	1.2	•
Quick Ratio	**31**	1.0	•	0.5	0.5	1.5	1.6	1.4	1.3	1.1	1.1	1.2	0.9	•
Net Sales to Working Capital	**32**	6.0	•	•	13.1	4.8	4.9	3.7	4.0	4.4	4.4	3.9	10.5	•
Coverage Ratio	**33**	4.3	30.7	1.7	2.0	22.1	18.6	13.2	12.5	9.9	6.0	5.1	2.6	•
Total Asset Turnover	**34**	0.6	•	2.7	2.2	2.3	1.9	1.8	1.5	1.5	1.3	1.0	0.4	•
Inventory Turnover	**35**	5.2	•	73.5	1.2	5.3	4.1	3.8	4.1	4.2	4.6	5.5	9.6	•
Receivables Turnover	**36**	4.1	•	•	2.0	8.1	6.5	5.3	6.6	•	•	5.2	5.3	•
Total Liabilities to Net Worth	**37**	0.9	•	18.8	14.0	0.8	0.6	0.9	0.8	1.1	2.0	1.0	0.9	•
Current Assets to Working Capital	**38**	2.7	•	•	5.0	1.6	1.6	1.7	1.8	2.0	1.8	2.0	5.0	•
Current Liabilities to Working Capital	**39**	1.7	•	•	4.0	0.6	0.6	0.7	0.8	1.0	0.8	1.0	4.0	•
Working Capital to Net Sales	**40**	0.2	•	•	0.1	0.2	0.2	0.3	0.3	0.2	0.2	0.3	0.1	•
Inventory to Working Capital	**41**	0.8	•	•	3.2	0.7	0.6	0.6	0.7	0.7	0.7	0.6	1.0	•
Total Receipts to Cash Flow	**42**	8.0	2.8	3.9	8.2	7.3	7.3	6.0	6.4	7.2	8.2	8.4	9.6	•
Cost of Goods to Cash Flow	**43**	5.5	2.1	1.9	5.2	4.5	5.0	3.9	4.1	4.9	5.8	5.7	6.8	•
Cash Flow to Total Debt	**44**	0.2	•	0.7	0.3	0.7	0.7	0.6	0.5	0.4	0.2	0.2	0.1	•
Selected Financial Factors (in Percentages)														
Debt Ratio	**45**	47.0	•	94.9	93.3	45.0	38.6	47.8	45.1	52.5	66.9	49.8	45.9	•
Return on Total Assets	**46**	5.7	•	32.4	8.7	21.8	20.4	16.4	13.8	11.2	15.1	10.1	3.2	•
Return on Equity Before Income Taxes	**47**	8.3	•	269.2	64.3	37.9	31.4	29.0	23.1	21.1	38.0	16.1	3.7	•
Return on Equity After Income Taxes	**48**	6.6	•	269.2	64.0	35.2	28.4	26.7	19.0	18.2	30.8	12.6	2.5	•
Profit Margin (Before Income Tax)	**49**	6.9	28.2	5.0	1.9	8.9	9.9	8.6	8.2	6.8	9.7	7.8	5.2	•
Profit Margin (After Income Tax)	**50**	5.5	26.4	5.0	1.9	8.3	9.0	7.9	6.7	5.9	7.9	6.1	3.5	•

Table I

Corporations with and without Net Income

MOTOR VEHICLES AND PARTS

MONEY AMOUNTS AND SIZE OF ASSETS IN THOUSANDS OF DOLLARS

Item Description for Accounting Period 7/11 Through 6/12		Total	Zero Assets	Under 500	500 to 1,000	1,000 to 5,000	5,000 to 10,000	10,000 to 25,000	25,000 to 50,000	50,000 to 100,000	100,000 to 250,000	250,000 to 500,000	500,000 to 2,500,000	2,500,000 and over
Number of Enterprises	1	5654	438	2540	842	786	299	221	179	108	103	56	56	26
Revenues ($ in Thousands)														
Net Sales	2	594083475	2487987	884638	1424500	4775273	2997390	6547009	11737838	13155282	26544572	28405382	70827777	424295827
Interest	3	9648904	3936	82	11	868	426	1953	1500	4955	13382	77515	459609	9084667
Rents	4	8997146	1481	0	0	1829	86	1370	3142	3515	5646	35896	74415	8869766
Royalties	5	6006370	115	0	0	0	0	0	785	5779	3452	34306	364133	5597800
Other Portfolio Income	6	9825583	21197	6	4591	11708	2964	14091	39356	18512	45389	86532	611176	8970059
Other Receipts	7	12541176	1664718	5688	10360	25099	51730	64954	94121	79381	227987	300174	550983	9465983
Total Receipts	8	641102654	4179434	890414	1439462	4814777	3052596	6629377	11876742	13267424	26840428	28939805	72888093	466284102
Average Total Receipts	9	113389	9542	351	1710	6126	10209	29997	66351	122847	260587	516782	1301573	17934004
Operating Costs/Operating Income (%)														
Cost of Operations	10	81.7	81.1	62.1	71.3	74.3	85.6	78.0	79.9	83.0	84.0	84.7	82.8	81.4
Salaries and Wages	11	3.5	4.8	13.6	7.7	6.1	5.0	4.4	4.5	3.4	3.3	3.3	4.1	3.2
Taxes Paid	12	0.8	1.2	2.9	3.1	2.1	1.8	1.6	1.5	1.2	1.0	1.0	1.0	0.6
Interest Paid	13	1.9	3.0	0.9	0.6	1.0	2.2	0.7	0.6	0.9	0.8	1.3	1.7	2.2
Depreciation	14	6.4	3.3	4.2	0.7	1.5	4.2	3.0	3.5	4.4	3.6	3.8	3.4	7.5
Amortization and Depletion	15	0.9	2.1	1.1	0.9	0.1	0.1	0.1	0.1	0.4	0.3	0.4	0.5	1.2
Pensions and Other Deferred Comp.	16	0.9	0.2	0.0	0.1	0.1	0.3	0.2	0.2	0.2	0.2	0.4	0.8	1.0
Employee Benefits	17	1.3	0.9	1.0	1.2	0.5	1.4	1.1	1.8	1.6	1.4	1.3	1.3	1.3
Advertising	18	1.7	0.8	1.2	0.6	1.1	0.2	0.4	0.3	0.2	0.3	0.1	0.5	2.2
Other Expenses	19	7.1	125.3	20.0	12.8	8.9	5.2	7.4	6.5	4.6	4.7	5.2	5.4	7.0
Officers' Compensation	20	0.3	0.8	2.3	2.3	3.6	1.2	1.4	0.9	0.5	0.4	0.5	0.4	0.1
Operating Margin	21	•	•	•	•	0.7	•	1.8	0.0	•	0.1	•	•	•
Operating Margin Before Officers' Comp.	22	•	•	•	1.0	4.3	•	3.1	1.0	0.1	0.5	•	•	•

Selected Average Balance Sheet ($ in Thousands)														
Net Receivables	23	40345	0	13	322	360	1063	3571	8739	16913	33305	71008	205688	7850064
Inventories	24	7175	0	62	149	1041	3361	4643	7787	12395	27996	56102	109141	867818
Net Property, Plant and Equipment	25	22568	0	12	99	343	1872	3776	9746	22034	44577	87092	202632	3879987
Total Assets	26	146329	0	114	705	2322	7120	16387	35460	71211	159277	339253	954877	27537390
Notes and Loans Payable	27	44490	0	93	276	1199	6233	5715	10376	22418	43081	105269	289008	8315756
All Other Liabilities	28	58823	0	60	243	872	2326	4969	13214	25569	55376	136681	386026	11140306
Net Worth	29	43017	0	-39	186	250	-1439	5702	11869	23223	60819	97302	279843	8081328

Selected Financial Ratios (Times to 1)														
Current Ratio	30	1.5	•	1.1	1.5	2.1	1.9	1.6	1.5	1.3	1.4	1.3	1.4	1.5
Quick Ratio	31	1.1	•	0.3	1.0	0.7	0.6	0.7	0.8	0.7	0.7	0.7	0.9	1.1
Net Sales to Working Capital	32	4.4	•	86.1	9.2	6.8	4.2	7.2	9.2	14.1	11.0	13.8	9.9	3.6
Coverage Ratio	33	2.0	•	•	0.7	2.6	•	5.5	3.0	1.5	2.7	0.9	1.9	2.2
Total Asset Turnover	34	0.7	•	3.1	2.4	2.6	1.4	1.8	1.8	1.7	1.6	1.5	1.3	0.6
Inventory Turnover	35	12.0	•	3.5	8.1	4.3	2.6	5.0	6.7	8.2	7.7	7.7	9.6	15.3
Receivables Turnover	36	2.6	•	22.7	8.6	13.9	9.5	8.9	8.0	8.0	7.8	7.6	6.5	2.1
Total Liabilities to Net Worth	37	2.4	•	•	2.8	8.3	•	1.9	2.0	2.1	1.6	2.5	2.4	2.4
Current Assets to Working Capital	38	2.9	•	20.5	2.9	1.9	2.1	2.7	3.0	4.6	3.5	4.7	3.6	2.8
Current Liabilities to Working Capital	39	1.9	•	19.5	1.9	0.9	1.1	1.7	2.0	3.6	2.5	3.7	2.6	1.8
Working Capital to Net Sales	40	0.2	•	0.0	0.1	0.1	0.2	0.1	0.1	0.1	0.1	0.1	0.1	0.3
Inventory to Working Capital	41	0.3	•	13.9	0.8	1.2	1.4	1.2	1.1	1.6	1.2	1.7	1.0	0.2
Total Receipts to Cash Flow	42	13.1	2.5	32.3	10.8	13.8	•	11.0	16.7	24.5	20.5	26.9	18.5	11.8
Cost of Goods to Cash Flow	43	10.7	2.0	20.1	7.7	10.2	•	8.6	13.3	20.4	17.2	22.8	15.3	9.6
Cash Flow to Total Debt	44	0.1	•	0.1	0.3	0.2	•	0.3	0.2	0.1	0.1	0.1	0.1	0.1

Selected Financial Factors (in Percentages)														
Debt Ratio	45	70.6	•	134.3	73.6	89.2	120.2	65.2	66.5	67.4	61.8	71.3	70.7	70.7
Return on Total Assets	46	2.8	•	•	1.0	6.5	•	6.7	3.6	2.4	3.3	1.8	4.3	2.9
Return on Equity Before Income Taxes	47	4.8	•	77.7	•	36.7	36.7	15.8	7.1	2.6	5.3	•	6.9	5.4
Return on Equity After Income Taxes	48	4.2	•	77.9	•	35.1	38.5	13.9	4.0	0.2	3.0	•	3.8	5.1
Profit Margin (Before Income Tax)	49	2.0	•	•	•	1.5	•	3.0	1.3	0.5	1.3	•	1.5	2.7
Profit Margin (After Income Tax)	50	1.7	•	•	•	1.4	•	2.7	0.7	0.0	0.7	•	0.8	2.5

Table II

Corporations with Net Income

MOTOR VEHICLES AND PARTS

MONEY AMOUNTS AND SIZE OF ASSETS IN THOUSANDS OF DOLLARS

Item Description for Accounting Period 7/11 Through 6/12		Total	Zero Assets	Under 500	500 to 1,000	1,000 to 5,000	5,000 to 10,000	10,000 to 25,000	25,000 to 50,000	50,000 to 100,000	100,000 to 250,000	250,000 to 500,000	500,000 to 2,500,000	2,500,000 and over
Number of Enterprises	1	2321	401	207	523	646	55	178	109	60	67	27	32	16
Revenues ($ in Thousands)														
Net Sales	2	431757477	2084548	251808	1073154	4319322	610516	5101910	7992614	8062328	17432325	13957241	46838553	324033158
Interest	3	7161929	542	82	11	751	406	1479	566	1753	9938	35095	352968	6758339
Rents	4	3485749	112	0	0	1353	86	1369	1350	940	5223	32352	3904	3439059
Royalties	5	5832407	115	0	0	0	0	0	785	5394	3429	12692	334008	5475983
Other Portfolio Income	6	7267101	21189	0	4591	11513	6	14066	29228	13409	32467	60164	524544	6555920
Other Receipts	7	8729973	11232	29	353	18937	1119	50995	55243	45361	129293	214101	257615	7945698
Total Receipts	8	464234636	2117738	251919	1078109	4351876	612133	5169819	8079786	8129185	17612675	14311645	48311592	354208157
Average Total Receipts	9	200015	5281	1217	2061	6737	11130	29044	74126	135486	262876	530061	1509737	22138010
Operating Costs/Operating Income (%)														
Cost of Operations	10	80.8	80.3	54.3	69.1	73.9	74.7	75.6	77.2	81.0	82.7	83.5	81.2	80.8
Salaries and Wages	11	3.4	4.3	18.3	7.1	6.2	7.2	4.1	4.6	3.1	3.3	3.4	4.2	3.2
Taxes Paid	12	0.7	1.1	2.9	3.3	2.0	1.6	1.6	1.6	1.3	0.9	1.1	1.0	0.6
Interest Paid	13	1.8	0.6	1.0	0.6	0.8	1.4	0.6	0.5	0.6	0.7	1.3	1.9	1.9
Depreciation	14	4.5	2.2	0.3	0.5	1.2	3.1	2.8	2.7	3.2	2.9	2.2	3.0	5.1
Amortization and Depletion	15	1.0	0.2	•	0.8	0.0	0.0	0.1	0.1	0.2	0.3	0.3	0.3	1.3
Pensions and Other Deferred Comp.	16	0.9	0.2	•	0.1	0.1	0.1	0.2	0.3	0.3	0.2	0.3	0.9	1.0
Employee Benefits	17	1.4	0.8	0.2	1.2	0.4	1.7	1.2	1.8	1.5	1.1	1.3	1.2	1.4
Advertising	18	1.9	0.9	0.5	0.0	1.1	0.1	0.5	0.4	0.2	0.3	0.2	0.4	2.4
Other Expenses	19	6.4	7.1	13.1	12.5	7.9	4.6	7.5	6.0	4.7	4.4	4.6	4.1	6.9
Officers' Compensation	20	0.3	0.7	4.4	2.4	3.7	1.1	1.6	1.1	0.6	0.4	0.5	0.4	0.1
Operating Margin	21	•	1.4	5.1	2.2	2.7	4.4	4.3	3.8	3.4	2.7	1.3	1.4	•
Operating Margin Before Officers' Comp.	22	•	2.2	9.5	4.6	6.4	5.5	5.9	4.9	3.9	3.1	1.8	1.8	•

Selected Average Balance Sheet ($ in Thousands)

Net Receivables 23	71304	0	62	333	340	1201	3372	9641	17560	33720	69549	200611	9485130
Inventories 24	10757	0	73	196	851	3832	4554	8381	14478	30581	65988	113334	872578
Net Property, Plant and Equipment 25	33962	0	11	51	236	1955	3127	8346	18857	39920	63977	196664	4077709
Total Assets 26	232830	0	325	747	2290	6675	15356	35165	70322	157762	328619	1030013	29681618
Notes and Loans Payable 27	77134	0	52	231	1037	2298	4236	8537	18156	39887	84418	300869	10046639
All Other Liabilities 28	90315	0	404	264	822	1564	4441	10308	26414	52786	131288	391002	11605605
Net Worth 29	65381	0	-131	252	431	2813	6679	16319	25752	65089	112912	338143	8029374

Selected Financial Ratios (Times to 1)

Current Ratio 30	1.7	•	0.5	2.0	2.7	2.3	1.9	1.8	1.5	1.5	1.3	1.6	1.7
Quick Ratio 31	1.3	•	0.3	1.3	0.8	1.3	0.9	1.0	0.8	0.8	0.7	1.0	1.4
Net Sales to Working Capital 32	3.8	•	•	6.8	6.0	4.2	5.3	7.1	9.5	8.6	13.1	8.2	3.2
Coverage Ratio 33	3.8	6.1	6.3	5.3	5.5	4.3	10.2	10.4	8.1	6.3	4.0	3.7	3.6
Total Asset Turnover 34	0.8	•	3.7	2.7	2.9	1.7	1.9	2.1	1.9	1.6	1.6	1.4	0.7
Inventory Turnover 35	14.0	•	9.1	7.2	5.8	2.2	4.8	6.8	7.5	7.0	6.5	10.5	18.8
Receivables Turnover 36	3.7	•	•	•	15.6	4.3	9.2	8.0	7.5	7.2	7.3	7.4	3.2
Total Liabilities to Net Worth 37	2.6	•	•	2.0	4.3	1.4	1.3	1.2	1.7	1.4	1.9	2.0	2.7
Current Assets to Working Capital 38	2.4	•	•	2.0	1.6	1.7	2.1	2.2	3.0	2.9	4.5	2.7	2.3
Current Liabilities to Working Capital 39	1.4	•	•	1.0	0.6	0.7	1.1	1.2	2.0	1.9	3.5	1.7	1.3
Working Capital to Net Sales 40	0.3	•	•	0.1	0.2	0.2	0.2	0.1	0.1	0.1	0.1	0.1	0.3
Inventory to Working Capital 41	0.2	•	•	0.7	1.1	0.7	1.0	0.9	1.0	1.0	1.6	0.7	0.2
Total Receipts to Cash Flow 42	10.0	12.3	7.8	8.2	12.0	13.5	8.6	10.6	12.6	14.0	14.2	13.0	9.3
Cost of Goods to Cash Flow 43	8.1	9.9	4.2	5.7	8.9	10.1	6.5	8.2	10.2	11.6	11.8	10.6	7.5
Cash Flow to Total Debt 44	0.1	•	0.3	0.5	0.3	0.2	0.4	0.4	0.2	0.2	0.2	0.2	0.1

Selected Financial Factors (in Percentages)

Debt Ratio 45	71.9	•	140.5	66.3	81.2	57.9	56.5	53.6	63.4	58.7	65.6	67.2	72.9
Return on Total Assets 46	5.3	•	22.7	9.2	12.3	10.1	11.7	11.5	9.3	7.4	8.1	9.9	4.7
Return on Equity Before Income Taxes 47	13.9	•	•	22.1	53.5	18.4	24.3	22.4	22.2	15.0	17.7	22.0	12.7
Return on Equity After Income Taxes 48	12.9	•	•	21.7	52.4	13.4	22.4	18.7	18.5	11.7	14.9	17.5	12.2
Profit Margin (Before Income Tax) 49	4.9	3.0	5.1	2.7	3.4	4.7	5.7	5.0	4.3	3.8	3.9	5.1	5.0
Profit Margin (After Income Tax) 50	4.5	2.5	5.0	2.7	3.4	3.4	5.2	4.2	3.5	2.9	3.3	4.0	4.8

Table I

Corporations with and without Net Income

AEROSPACE PRODUCT AND PARTS

MONEY AMOUNTS AND SIZE OF ASSETS IN THOUSANDS OF DOLLARS

Item Description for Accounting Period 7/11 Through 6/12		Total	Zero Assets	Under 500	500 to 1,000	1,000 to 5,000	5,000 to 10,000	10,000 to 25,000	25,000 to 50,000	50,000 to 100,000	100,000 to 250,000	250,000 to 500,000	500,000 to 2,500,000	2,500,000 and over
Number of Enterprises	1	1437	21	572	121	379	110	108	44	21	23	7	9	21
Revenues ($ in Thousands)														
Net Sales	2	296667752	179884	590835	83022	1614467	1243379	2862670	1747004	1415378	3186568	1730675	12538286	269475583
Interest	3	676658	0	21	0	470	681	2009	582	830	2152	161	19446	650307
Rents	4	659583	19	121	0	0	0	302	674	417	597	527	8512	648413
Royalties	5	1876493	0	0	0	0	268	0	0	298	2047	1170	7003	1865707
Other Portfolio Income	6	1697555	0	39050	0	7096	735	29098	6822	12878	2829	6706	8875	1583465
Other Receipts	7	3920203	269	2177	1	107	1932	11715	14464	5563	19921	5582	94201	3764274
Total Receipts	8	305498244	180172	632204	83023	1622140	1246995	2905794	1769546	1435364	3214114	1744821	12676323	277987749
Average Total Receipts	9	212594	8580	1105	686	4280	11336	26906	40217	68351	139744	249260	1408480	13237512
Operating Costs/Operating Income (%)														
Cost of Operations	10	70.4	40.6	58.9	37.0	55.7	63.1	66.4	68.2	64.3	63.2	57.7	70.6	70.8
Salaries and Wages	11	4.7	25.9	1.9	7.9	11.8	7.5	6.4	6.3	9.9	7.6	11.0	8.0	4.3
Taxes Paid	12	1.5	1.9	1.0	3.4	3.3	2.5	2.5	2.2	1.9	1.6	3.2	1.6	1.4
Interest Paid	13	1.5	3.4	0.9	0.1	0.4	1.1	1.0	1.8	1.8	3.1	3.7	1.0	1.5
Depreciation	14	2.8	2.3	1.5	8.1	0.6	2.0	2.4	3.8	2.5	4.3	7.7	3.7	2.7
Amortization and Depletion	15	0.7	0.1	•	3.3	0.7	0.0	0.4	0.3	0.5	0.4	1.9	0.8	0.7
Pensions and Other Deferred Comp.	16	3.2	3.5	•	•	0.4	0.2	0.5	0.6	0.6	0.6	0.2	0.9	3.5
Employee Benefits	17	2.3	1.9	0.3	1.7	1.4	2.1	2.8	2.6	1.7	2.1	1.4	3.8	2.2
Advertising	18	0.3	0.1	0.1	0.4	0.1	0.1	0.2	0.2	0.5	0.2	0.4	0.2	0.3
Other Expenses	19	10.6	25.1	16.0	24.5	5.9	7.7	9.2	7.8	11.1	11.6	14.6	6.2	10.8
Officers' Compensation	20	0.3	2.5	7.9	11.3	4.3	2.7	2.9	2.6	3.2	0.9	1.3	0.7	0.2
Operating Margin	21	1.7	•	11.5	2.4	15.4	11.0	5.3	3.6	2.0	4.5	•	2.6	1.4
Operating Margin Before Officers' Comp.	22	2.0	•	19.4	13.6	19.8	13.7	8.2	6.2	5.2	5.3	•	3.3	1.6

Selected Average Balance Sheet ($ in Thousands)														
Net Receivables	23	27259	0	0	107	570	1246	3972	6661	10525	23684	34328	259274	1654418
Inventories	24	42385	0	0	163	453	3077	4965	8713	16163	29615	93061	249744	2644700
Net Property, Plant and Equipment	25	28581	0	7	180	329	791	2739	7314	12272	30705	78763	245599	1737610
Total Assets	26	267639	0	146	520	2182	6840	16938	35141	70117	156991	340605	1582019	17037653
Notes and Loans Payable	27	53425	0	117	295	563	2663	4696	10160	19475	53457	136795	297709	3330124
All Other Liabilities	28	145414	0	3	131	323	3211	3464	8760	17662	62244	130732	707682	9458107
Net Worth	29	68801	0	27	94	1295	966	8778	16221	32981	41291	73078	576627	4249422
Selected Financial Ratios (Times to 1)														
Current Ratio	30	1.3	•	5.4	1.3	4.2	3.0	2.4	2.2	2.9	1.5	2.0	1.7	1.3
Quick Ratio	31	0.6	•	3.9	0.9	3.0	1.1	1.2	1.0	1.3	0.7	0.8	0.9	0.6
Net Sales to Working Capital	32	8.3	•	78.3	15.5	3.3	3.2	4.0	3.4	2.4	5.6	3.1	4.6	9.2
Coverage Ratio	33	4.3	•	21.6	36.3	38.6	10.9	7.9	3.7	2.9	2.7	0.4	4.7	4.2
Total Asset Turnover	34	0.8	•	7.1	1.3	2.0	1.7	1.6	1.1	1.0	0.9	0.7	0.9	0.8
Inventory Turnover	35	3.4	•	•	1.6	5.2	2.3	3.5	3.1	2.7	3.0	1.5	3.9	3.4
Receivables Turnover	36	7.7	•	6457.2	8.2	8.5	10.4	7.3	6.6	6.2	6.9	6.1	4.5	8.0
Total Liabilities to Net Worth	37	2.9	•	4.5	4.5	0.7	6.1	0.9	1.2	1.1	2.8	3.7	1.7	3.0
Current Assets to Working Capital	38	4.0	•	1.2	4.5	1.3	1.5	1.7	1.8	1.5	3.2	2.0	2.5	4.4
Current Liabilities to Working Capital	39	3.0	•	0.2	3.5	0.3	0.5	0.7	0.8	0.5	2.2	1.0	1.5	3.4
Working Capital to Net Sales	40	0.1	•	0.0	0.1	0.3	0.3	0.2	0.3	0.4	0.2	0.3	0.2	0.1
Inventory to Working Capital	41	1.8	•	•	1.5	0.3	0.8	0.8	0.9	0.6	1.3	1.1	0.8	2.1
Total Receipts to Cash Flow	42	7.5	6.2	4.3	4.8	5.2	6.3	7.9	9.6	8.6	6.7	10.0	12.5	7.4
Cost of Goods to Cash Flow	43	5.3	2.5	2.5	1.8	2.9	4.0	5.2	6.6	5.6	4.3	5.7	8.8	5.2
Cash Flow to Total Debt	44	0.1	•	2.0	0.3	0.9	0.3	0.4	0.2	0.2	0.2	0.1	0.1	0.1
Selected Financial Factors (in Percentages)														
Debt Ratio	45	74.3	•	81.8	81.9	40.6	85.9	48.2	53.8	53.0	73.7	78.5	63.6	75.1
Return on Total Assets	46	5.0	•	136.9	3.2	31.9	20.5	12.1	7.6	5.0	7.5	1.0	4.2	4.9
Return on Equity Before Income Taxes	47	14.9	•	718.4	17.4	52.3	131.8	20.4	12.0	7.0	17.9	•	9.0	15.0
Return on Equity After Income Taxes	48	9.7	•	718.4	17.4	49.0	129.4	19.1	10.8	2.6	15.4	•	5.9	9.5
Profit Margin (Before Income Tax)	49	5.0	•	18.5	2.4	15.9	11.3	6.8	4.9	3.4	5.3	•	3.7	5.0
Profit Margin (After Income Tax)	50	3.2	•	18.5	2.4	14.9	11.1	6.3	4.4	1.3	4.6	•	2.5	3.1

Table II

Corporations with Net Income

AEROSPACE PRODUCT AND PARTS

MONEY AMOUNTS AND SIZE OF ASSETS IN THOUSANDS OF DOLLARS

Item Description for Accounting Period 7/11 Through 6/12		Total	Zero Assets	Under 500	500 to 1,000	1,000 to 5,000	5,000 to 10,000	10,000 to 25,000	25,000 to 50,000	50,000 to 100,000	100,000 to 250,000	250,000 to 500,000	500,000 to 2,500,000	2,500,000 and over
Number of Enterprises	1	1266	5	572	60	379	81	81	33	14	•	0	•	17
Revenues ($ in Thousands)														
Net Sales	2	208211107	95624	590835	50385	1614467	1107819	2257510	1397624	922224	•	0	•	187210961
Interest	3	356003	0	21	0	470	506	1130	582	367	•	0	•	332876
Rents	4	46829	19	121	0	0	0	302	674	14	•	0	•	36810
Royalties	5	1609744	0	0	0	0	263	0	0	298	•	0	•	1600356
Other Portfolio Income	6	1361406	0	39050	0	7096	460	20538	6441	11489	•	0	•	1266726
Other Receipts	7	3040781	269	2177	0	107	1228	7089	14015	5022	•	0	•	2897186
Total Receipts	8	214625870	95912	632204	50385	1622140	1110276	2286569	1419336	939414	•	0	•	193344915
Average Total Receipts	9	169531	19182	1105	840	4280	13707	28229	43010	67101	•	•	•	11373230
Operating Costs/Operating Income (%)														
Cost of Operations	10	69.3	69.1	58.9	40.2	55.7	62.5	65.1	65.5	64.3	•	•	•	69.7
Salaries and Wages	11	5.4	7.0	1.9	5.7	11.8	6.9	5.3	6.6	5.6	•	•	•	5.1
Taxes Paid	12	1.5	3.3	1.0	3.6	3.3	2.5	2.7	2.2	1.8	•	•	•	1.5
Interest Paid	13	1.5	1.5	0.9	0.1	0.4	0.9	1.0	1.5	1.7	•	•	•	1.6
Depreciation	14	2.5	2.7	1.5	1.7	0.6	1.4	2.3	3.7	2.4	•	•	•	2.5
Amortization and Depletion	15	0.7	•	•	5.5	0.7	•	0.2	0.4	0.3	•	•	•	0.7
Pensions and Other Deferred Comp.	16	3.5	•	•	•	0.4	0.2	0.6	0.4	0.5	•	•	•	3.8
Employee Benefits	17	2.7	0.1	0.3	2.8	1.4	2.2	3.1	2.4	1.4	•	•	•	2.6
Advertising	18	0.4	0.2	0.1	0.6	0.1	0.1	0.2	0.2	0.2	•	•	•	0.4
Other Expenses	19	8.0	13.0	16.0	17.3	5.9	7.0	7.8	7.1	7.1	•	•	•	8.0
Officers' Compensation	20	0.4	•	7.9	18.6	4.3	1.9	3.4	2.6	4.2	•	•	•	0.2
Operating Margin	21	4.2	3.2	11.5	3.9	15.4	14.6	8.3	7.3	10.5	•	•	•	3.8
Operating Margin Before Officers' Comp.	22	4.5	3.2	19.4	22.5	19.8	16.5	11.7	10.0	14.7	•	•	•	4.0

Selected Average Balance Sheet ($ in Thousands)

Net Receivables 23	22591	0	0	97	570	1458	4021	6465	10767	•	•	•	1477584
Inventories 24	29531	0	0	136	453	2540	5124	7996	14554	•	•	•	1434482
Net Property, Plant and Equipment 25	20265	0	7	17	329	785	3112	7850	10107	•	•	•	1336675
Total Assets 26	218957	0	146	530	2182	6733	16581	35068	68694	•	•	•	15157146
Notes and Loans Payable 27	40416	0	117	595	563	3050	4967	9228	18705	•	•	•	2774347
All Other Liabilities 28	107445	0	3	150	323	3583	3057	5486	14374	•	•	•	7532072
Net Worth 29	71096	0	27	-215	1295	100	8558	20354	35615	•	•	•	4850727

Selected Financial Ratios (Times to 1)

Current Ratio 30	1.4	•	5.4	1.2	4.2	3.4	2.7	2.7	3.9	•	•	•	1.3
Quick Ratio 31	0.8	•	3.9	0.5	3.0	1.5	1.3	1.3	1.6	•	•	•	0.7
Net Sales to Working Capital 32	9.6	•	78.3	25.7	3.3	3.9	3.9	3.1	1.9	•	•	•	11.2
Coverage Ratio 33	6.1	3.4	21.6	36.3	38.6	16.9	10.3	7.0	8.2	•	•	•	5.9
Total Asset Turnover 34	0.8	•	7.1	1.6	2.0	2.0	1.7	1.2	1.0	•	•	•	0.7
Inventory Turnover 35	3.9	•	•	2.5	5.2	3.4	3.5	3.5	2.9	•	•	•	5.4
Receivables Turnover 36	7.4	•	6457.2	•	8.5	10.9	7.7	7.2	6.7	•	•	•	•
Total Liabilities to Net Worth 37	2.1	•	4.5	•	0.7	66.1	0.9	0.7	0.9	•	•	•	2.1
Current Assets to Working Capital 38	3.7	•	1.2	7.2	1.3	1.4	1.6	1.6	1.3	•	•	•	4.2
Current Liabilities to Working Capital 39	2.7	•	0.2	6.2	0.3	0.4	0.6	0.6	0.3	•	•	•	3.2
Working Capital to Net Sales 40	0.1	•	0.0	0.0	0.3	0.3	0.3	0.3	0.5	•	•	•	0.1
Inventory to Working Capital 41	1.3	•	•	4.2	0.3	0.7	0.8	0.7	0.5	•	•	•	1.5
Total Receipts to Cash Flow 42	7.8	6.4	4.3	5.9	5.2	5.3	7.3	7.3	6.2	•	•	•	7.9
Cost of Goods to Cash Flow 43	5.4	4.4	2.5	2.4	2.9	3.3	4.7	4.8	4.0	•	•	•	5.5
Cash Flow to Total Debt 44	0.1	•	2.0	0.2	0.9	0.4	0.5	0.4	0.3	•	•	•	0.1

Selected Financial Factors (in Percentages)

Debt Ratio 45	67.5	•	81.8	140.5	40.6	98.5	48.4	42.0	48.2	•	•	•	68.0
Return on Total Assets 46	6.9	•	136.9	6.4	31.9	32.0	17.8	12.5	13.5	•	•	•	6.7
Return on Equity Before Income Taxes 47	17.8	•	718.4	•	52.3	2019.7	31.1	18.5	22.9	•	•	•	17.3
Return on Equity After Income Taxes 48	12.1	•	718.4	•	49.0	1988.3	29.3	17.2	16.7	•	•	•	11.4
Profit Margin (Before Income Tax) 49	7.7	3.5	18.5	3.9	15.9	14.8	9.6	8.9	12.4	•	•	•	7.6
Profit Margin (After Income Tax) 50	5.2	2.3	18.5	3.9	14.9	14.6	9.0	8.3	9.0	•	•	•	5.0

Table I

Corporations with and without Net Income

SHIP AND BOAT BUILDING

MONEY AMOUNTS AND SIZE OF ASSETS IN THOUSANDS OF DOLLARS

Item Description for Accounting Period 7/11 Through 6/12		Total	Zero Assets	Under 500	500 to 1,000	1,000 to 5,000	5,000 to 10,000	10,000 to 25,000	25,000 to 50,000	50,000 to 100,000	100,000 to 250,000	250,000 to 500,000	500,000 to 2,500,000	2,500,000 and over
Number of Enterprises	1	822	19	468	0	130	71	81	25	10	11	3	5	0
Revenues ($ in Thousands)														
Net Sales	2	46009015	475097	242229	0	412503	1252070	1972014	1023844	788854	1661297	783700	37397407	0
Interest	3	19226	0	0	0	739	450	586	646	111	577	1568	14547	0
Rents	4	11793	0	0	0	210	0	116	639	530	254	1539	8505	0
Royalties	5	497	0	0	0	0	0	0	0	0	0	0	497	0
Other Portfolio Income	6	125765	33476	0	0	3788	0	1641	2096	738	4108	392	79525	0
Other Receipts	7	301584	3005	18	0	11280	5532	47579	20464	12713	14124	26311	160561	0
Total Receipts	8	46467880	511578	242247	0	428520	1258052	2021936	1047689	802946	1680360	813510	37661042	0
Average Total Receipts	9	56530	26925	518	•	3296	17719	24962	41908	80295	152760	271170	7532208	•
Operating Costs/Operating Income (%)														
Cost of Operations	10	76.2	95.8	35.2	•	65.8	60.4	81.2	67.2	80.8	82.9	69.9	76.6	•
Salaries and Wages	11	4.5	1.1	31.7	•	7.0	8.6	3.3	6.7	3.8	2.8	5.3	4.3	•
Taxes Paid	12	1.6	0.3	5.4	•	4.3	2.1	1.5	2.0	1.9	1.7	1.6	1.5	•
Interest Paid	13	0.8	0.0	0.4	•	3.4	0.4	1.2	0.8	2.6	0.5	1.5	0.7	•
Depreciation	14	2.3	0.3	2.1	•	2.5	3.7	3.2	4.1	3.0	3.5	4.1	2.1	•
Amortization and Depletion	15	0.7	0.0	•	•	0.0	0.0	0.2	0.2	0.7	0.0	0.0	0.8	•
Pensions and Other Deferred Comp.	16	1.1	0.1	•	•	0.0	0.2	0.2	0.1	0.3	0.8	1.3	1.3	•
Employee Benefits	17	1.5	0.4	10.5	•	2.2	2.4	1.0	1.7	1.1	1.7	5.4	1.4	•
Advertising	18	0.2	0.0	0.2	•	0.2	0.3	0.7	0.2	1.0	0.4	0.1	0.2	•
Other Expenses	19	4.4	0.7	17.6	•	19.5	11.8	4.6	12.7	7.8	3.6	5.5	3.7	•
Officers' Compensation	20	0.8	0.4	14.9	•	4.1	3.2	2.4	1.6	1.7	1.1	1.1	0.4	•
Operating Margin	21	5.8	0.7	•	•	•	6.9	0.7	2.8	•	1.1	4.2	6.9	•
Operating Margin Before Officers' Comp.	22	6.6	1.1	•	•	•	10.1	3.0	4.4	•	2.1	5.3	7.4	•

Selected Average Balance Sheet ($ in Thousands)

Item	No.	1	2	3	4	5	6	7	8	9	10	11	12	13
Net Receivables	23	3620	0	149	•	217	1830	3056	4324	7506	18398	26175	407262	•
Inventories	24	5772	0	30	•	684	3044	2295	3444	9877	19568	2620	829611	•
Net Property, Plant and Equipment	25	8976	0	90	•	1257	2314	5319	8601	23696	38065	76451	1095483	•
Total Assets	26	54763	0	263	•	2642	8729	16101	35296	67904	129737	337096	7724935	•
Notes and Loans Payable	27	10946	0	68	•	2447	1401	6271	10680	33393	41629	67945	1355501	•
All Other Liabilities	28	23629	0	50	•	492	2773	5846	10543	16203	30428	158144	3486114	•
Net Worth	29	20187	0	144	•	-298	4554	3985	14073	18308	57680	111007	2883320	•

Selected Financial Ratios (Times to 1)

Item	No.	1	2	3	4	5	6	7	8	9	10	11	12	13
Current Ratio	30	1.3	•	2.0	•	0.9	2.2	1.4	2.1	1.1	1.6	0.8	1.3	•
Quick Ratio	31	0.5	•	1.8	•	0.2	1.1	0.7	1.1	0.5	0.8	0.5	0.5	•
Net Sales to Working Capital	32	12.2	•	6.0	•	•	5.2	8.5	4.4	27.4	5.9	•	13.4	•
Coverage Ratio	33	9.7	179.6	•	•	•	19.7	3.7	7.6	•	5.4	6.5	11.6	•
Total Asset Turnover	34	1.0	•	2.0	•	1.2	2.0	1.5	1.2	1.2	1.2	0.8	1.0	•
Inventory Turnover	35	7.4	•	6.1	•	3.0	3.5	8.6	8.0	6.5	6.4	69.7	6.9	•
Receivables Turnover	36	15.1	•	3.8	•	16.4	8.7	9.7	8.6	7.5	9.9	•	•	•
Total Liabilities to Net Worth	37	1.7	•	0.8	•	•	0.9	3.0	1.5	2.7	1.2	2.0	1.7	•
Current Assets to Working Capital	38	4.1	•	2.0	•	•	1.8	3.3	1.9	8.2	2.7	•	4.4	•
Current Liabilities to Working Capital	39	3.1	•	1.0	•	•	0.8	2.3	0.9	7.2	1.7	•	3.4	•
Working Capital to Net Sales	40	0.1	•	0.2	•	•	0.2	0.1	0.2	0.0	0.2	•	0.1	•
Inventory to Working Capital	41	1.3	•	0.1	•	•	0.9	1.0	0.4	2.4	0.8	•	1.5	•
Total Receipts to Cash Flow	42	11.0	11.0	•	•	10.9	6.3	15.3	7.1	29.1	23.3	9.1	10.8	•
Cost of Goods to Cash Flow	43	8.4	10.6	•	•	7.2	3.8	12.4	4.8	23.5	19.3	6.4	8.3	•
Cash Flow to Total Debt	44	0.1	•	•	•	0.1	0.7	0.1	0.3	0.1	0.1	0.1	0.1	•

Selected Financial Factors (in Percentages)

Item	No.	1	2	3	4	5	6	7	8	9	10	11	12	13
Debt Ratio	45	63.1	•	45.1	•	111.3	47.8	75.3	60.1	73.0	55.5	67.1	62.7	•
Return on Total Assets	46	7.8	•	•	•	•	15.8	6.6	6.9	•	2.9	7.3	8.2	•
Return on Equity Before Income Taxes	47	19.1	•	•	•	54.2	28.7	19.5	14.9	•	5.3	18.8	20.1	•
Return on Equity After Income Taxes	48	12.8	•	•	•	54.9	28.7	17.5	13.5	•	3.8	12.4	13.3	•
Profit Margin (Before Income Tax)	49	6.9	8.3	•	•	•	7.4	3.2	5.1	•	2.0	8.0	7.8	•
Profit Margin (After Income Tax)	50	4.6	8.3	•	•	•	7.4	2.9	4.6	•	1.4	5.3	5.1	•

Table II

Corporations with Net Income

SHIP AND BOAT BUILDING

Item Description for Accounting Period 7/11 Through 6/12		MONEY AMOUNTS AND SIZE OF ASSETS IN THOUSANDS OF DOLLARS												
		Total	Zero Assets	Under 500	500 to 1,000	1,000 to 5,000	5,000 to 10,000	10,000 to 25,000	25,000 to 50,000	50,000 to 100,000	100,000 to 250,000	250,000 to 500,000	500,000 to 2,500,000	2,500,000 and over
Number of Enterprises	1	158	•	0	0	29	50	45	19	0	7	•	•	0
Revenues ($ in Thousands)														
Net Sales	2	42693595	•	0	0	254570	972569	1477134	1095511	0	1193314	•	•	0
Interest	3	17882	•	0	0	341	0	528	353	0	564	•	•	0
Rents	4	10063	•	0	0	0	0	0	18	0	0	•	•	0
Royalties	5	497	•	0	0	0	0	0	0	0	0	•	•	0
Other Portfolio Income	6	118065	•	0	0	44	0	754	1032	0	2842	•	•	0
Other Receipts	7	261786	•	0	0	4734	5053	34549	21379	0	12507	•	•	0
Total Receipts	8	43101888	•	0	0	259689	977622	1512965	1118293	0	1209227	•	•	0
Average Total Receipts	9	272797	•	•	•	8955	19552	33621	58858	•	172747	•	•	•
Operating Costs/Operating Income (%)														
Cost of Operations	10	76.0	•	•	•	72.7	57.9	79.5	69.4	•	80.5	•	•	•
Salaries and Wages	11	4.4	•	•	•	1.1	10.4	3.0	5.6	•	2.8	•	•	•
Taxes Paid	12	1.5	•	•	•	4.5	2.1	1.4	1.9	•	1.6	•	•	•
Interest Paid	13	0.7	•	•	•	3.4	0.3	0.8	0.9	•	0.3	•	•	•
Depreciation	14	2.1	•	•	•	1.2	0.9	1.8	3.5	•	3.4	•	•	•
Amortization and Depletion	15	0.7	•	•	•	•	•	0.1	0.4	•	0.0	•	•	•
Pensions and Other Deferred Comp.	16	1.2	•	•	•	•	0.2	0.2	0.1	•	1.1	•	•	•
Employee Benefits	17	1.5	•	•	•	1.1	2.6	1.1	1.3	•	1.6	•	•	•
Advertising	18	0.2	•	•	•	0.1	0.3	0.6	0.1	•	0.1	•	•	•
Other Expenses	19	4.0	•	•	•	8.9	12.2	4.5	10.9	•	2.0	•	•	•
Officers' Compensation	20	0.6	•	•	•	5.2	1.7	1.6	1.5	•	1.2	•	•	•
Operating Margin	21	7.0	•	•	•	1.7	11.4	5.4	4.3	•	5.1	•	•	•
Operating Margin Before Officers' Comp.	22	7.6	•	•	•	6.9	13.2	7.0	5.8	•	6.4	•	•	•

Selected Average Balance Sheet ($ in Thousands)														
Net Receivables	23	16421	•	•	•	499	1512	4227	5588	•	25274	•	•	•
Inventories	24	26865	•	•	•	816	4055	1293	2683	•	14615	•	•	•
Net Property, Plant and Equipment	25	39206	•	•	•	2956	1388	3480	11609	•	36162	•	•	•
Total Assets	26	265734	•	•	•	4237	8711	15171	39053	•	137944	•	•	•
Notes and Loans Payable	27	46351	•	•	•	2730	736	3217	9547	•	20782	•	•	•
All Other Liabilities	28	116917	•	•	•	872	3303	5440	11585	•	35587	•	•	•
Net Worth	29	102466	•	•	•	636	4672	6515	17920	•	81575	•	•	•
Selected Financial Ratios (Times to 1)														
Current Ratio	30	1.4	•	•	•	1.1	2.2	2.5	2.4	•	2.1	•	•	•
Quick Ratio	31	0.6	•	•	•	0.5	1.0	1.3	1.4	•	1.2	•	•	•
Net Sales to Working Capital	32	11.5	•	•	•	78.2	4.9	5.2	4.8	•	4.1	•	•	•
Coverage Ratio	33	11.7	•	•	•	2.1	45.6	10.6	8.0	•	20.2	•	•	•
Total Asset Turnover	34	1.0	•	•	•	2.1	2.2	2.2	1.5	•	1.2	•	•	•
Inventory Turnover	35	7.6	•	•	•	7.8	2.8	20.2	14.9	•	9.4	•	•	•
Receivables Turnover	36	15.8	•	•	•	17.3	9.8	10.3	10.0	•	•	•	•	•
Total Liabilities to Net Worth	37	1.6	•	•	•	5.7	0.9	1.3	1.2	•	0.7	•	•	•
Current Assets to Working Capital	38	3.8	•	•	•	10.1	1.8	1.7	1.7	•	1.9	•	•	•
Current Liabilities to Working Capital	39	2.8	•	•	•	9.1	0.8	0.7	0.7	•	0.9	•	•	•
Working Capital to Net Sales	40	0.1	•	•	•	0.0	0.2	0.2	0.2	•	0.2	•	•	•
Inventory to Working Capital	41	1.2	•	•	•	0.6	1.0	0.3	0.4	•	0.4	•	•	•
Total Receipts to Cash Flow	42	10.2	•	•	•	9.3	4.7	9.1	7.3	•	13.2	•	•	•
Cost of Goods to Cash Flow	43	7.7	•	•	•	6.7	2.7	7.2	5.1	•	10.6	•	•	•
Cash Flow to Total Debt	44	0.2	•	•	•	0.3	1.0	0.4	0.4	•	0.2	•	•	•
Selected Financial Factors (in Percentages)														
Debt Ratio	45	61.4	•	•	•	85.0	46.4	57.1	54.1	•	40.9	•	•	•
Return on Total Assets	46	8.9	•	•	•	14.8	27.2	18.7	10.8	•	8.1	•	•	•
Return on Equity Before Income Taxes	47	21.1	•	•	•	51.1	49.7	39.5	20.5	•	13.1	•	•	•
Return on Equity After Income Taxes	48	14.7	•	•	•	49.6	49.7	37.2	18.3	•	11.3	•	•	•
Profit Margin (Before Income Tax)	49	8.0	•	•	•	3.7	11.9	7.8	6.4	•	6.3	•	•	•
Profit Margin (After Income Tax)	50	5.6	•	•	•	3.6	11.9	7.4	5.7	•	5.4	•	•	•

Table I

Corporations with and without Net Income

OTHER TRANSPORTATION EQUIPMENT AND RAILROAD ROLLING STOCK

Item Description for Accounting Period 7/11 Through 6/12		MONEY AMOUNTS AND SIZE OF ASSETS IN THOUSANDS OF DOLLARS												
		Total	Zero Assets	Under 500	500 to 1,000	1,000 to 5,000	5,000 to 10,000	10,000 to 25,000	25,000 to 50,000	50,000 to 100,000	100,000 to 250,000	250,000 to 500,000	500,000 to 2,500,000	2,500,000 and over
Number of Enterprises	1	1695	4	1142	185	185	77	42	22	12	11	6	9	0
Revenues ($ in Thousands)														
Net Sales	2	26520730	685660	191523	249161	601242	1026249	1145524	1365851	1396746	1960231	2985979	14912564	0
Interest	3	597906	143	0	376	0	61	155	632	1603	678	1295	592963	0
Rents	4	52082	0	0	0	0	0	0	6	1417	256	570	49832	0
Royalties	5	81943	0	0	0	0	0	0	0	151	0	12742	69050	0
Other Portfolio Income	6	122918	35903	0	2203	0	3748	9	1109	1343	1755	6894	69955	0
Other Receipts	7	228800	41215	146	3	7586	12988	7683	16173	30142	22079	22218	68567	0
Total Receipts	8	27604379	762921	191669	251743	608828	1043046	1153371	1383771	1431402	1984999	3029698	15762931	0
Average Total Receipts	9	16286	190730	168	1361	3291	13546	27461	62899	119284	180454	504950	1751437	•
Operating Costs/Operating Income (%)														
Cost of Operations	10	69.4	80.0	63.4	88.5	67.8	70.9	72.3	73.8	73.9	75.3	84.9	63.7	•
Salaries and Wages	11	6.2	3.7	6.3	2.6	4.6	8.0	6.1	6.8	4.8	3.8	3.0	7.3	•
Taxes Paid	12	1.3	0.4	7.8	0.7	2.3	1.7	1.2	1.5	1.7	1.0	0.8	1.3	•
Interest Paid	13	2.7	0.1	2.2	0.8	1.0	6.0	0.3	0.3	0.7	1.8	0.4	3.9	•
Depreciation	14	5.1	2.5	3.1	6.5	1.2	5.8	1.5	2.1	1.5	3.1	1.6	7.2	•
Amortization and Depletion	15	0.7	0.0	0.8	0.6	0.5	0.4	0.0	0.5	0.4	0.7	0.4	0.9	•
Pensions and Other Deferred Comp.	16	1.4	0.0	•	•	•	0.2	0.1	0.1	0.7	0.4	0.2	2.4	•
Employee Benefits	17	1.7	0.3	0.6	0.2	0.8	1.1	0.8	0.8	1.6	2.3	1.0	2.0	•
Advertising	18	1.1	0.2	1.5	0.5	1.4	0.3	0.5	0.7	0.2	0.1	2.7	1.1	•
Other Expenses	19	9.3	10.6	19.0	7.7	11.8	23.2	7.5	7.0	6.0	3.3	5.3	10.4	•
Officers' Compensation	20	1.1	1.4	1.8	1.9	4.9	5.1	2.0	1.0	1.5	0.6	0.3	0.8	•
Operating Margin	21	•	0.7	•	•	3.7	•	7.8	5.2	6.9	7.6	•	•	•
Operating Margin Before Officers' Comp.	22	1.1	2.1	•	•	8.7	•	9.8	6.3	8.4	8.2	•	•	•

Selected Average Balance Sheet ($ in Thousands)

Net Receivables 23	5085	0	20	7	339	2529	3494	8569	22872	17933	62163	795261	•
Inventories 24	2134	0	56	114	867	1229	3691	6490	13617	20989	52046	224507	•
Net Property, Plant and Equipment 25	3529	0	20	252	362	1045	1675	4746	10650	22657	42268	551141	•
Total Assets 26	16384	0	99	730	1809	7005	13915	32995	75191	152876	322598	2313291	•
Notes and Loans Payable 27	7170	0	123	1016	700	5495	2597	3928	23997	47752	57603	1102064	•
All Other Liabilities 28	4172	0	15	49	436	2860	3865	8165	19510	40116	181818	515117	•
Net Worth 29	5042	0	-40	-334	674	-1349	7453	20901	31684	65008	83177	696111	•

Selected Financial Ratios (Times to 1)

Current Ratio 30	1.5	•	0.8	6.9	1.4	1.4	2.3	2.9	1.9	2.1	1.0	1.5	•
Quick Ratio 31	1.0	•	0.2	3.7	0.6	0.8	1.3	1.6	1.2	1.2	0.5	1.0	•
Net Sales to Working Capital 32	4.8	•	•	4.7	9.4	8.2	5.4	4.1	4.8	4.2	238.2	3.7	•
Coverage Ratio 33	2.5	81.6	•	•	5.9	•	32.8	23.5	14.3	6.0	3.0	2.2	•
Total Asset Turnover 34	1.0	•	1.7	1.8	1.8	1.9	2.0	1.9	1.5	1.2	1.5	0.7	•
Inventory Turnover 35	5.1	•	1.9	10.4	2.5	7.7	5.3	7.1	6.3	6.4	8.1	4.7	•
Receivables Turnover 36	2.9	•	12.1	388.1	5.2	9.9	7.8	8.3	6.9	10.9	•	•	•
Total Liabilities to Net Worth 37	2.2	•	•	•	1.7	•	0.9	0.6	1.4	1.4	2.9	2.3	•
Current Assets to Working Capital 38	3.1	•	•	1.2	3.7	3.5	1.8	1.5	2.1	1.9	91.7	3.2	•
Current Liabilities to Working Capital 39	2.1	•	•	0.2	2.7	2.5	0.8	0.5	1.1	0.9	90.7	2.2	•
Working Capital to Net Sales 40	0.2	•	•	0.2	0.1	0.1	0.2	0.2	0.2	0.2	0.0	0.3	•
Inventory to Working Capital 41	0.6	•	•	0.4	2.0	1.3	0.7	0.5	0.6	0.6	24.9	0.5	•
Total Receipts to Cash Flow 42	9.3	4.6	11.1	•	7.5	•	6.8	8.5	7.4	9.1	18.1	8.0	•
Cost of Goods to Cash Flow 43	6.5	3.7	7.0	•	5.1	•	4.9	6.3	5.5	6.8	15.4	5.1	•
Cash Flow to Total Debt 44	0.1	•	0.1	•	0.4	•	0.6	0.6	0.4	0.2	0.1	0.1	•

Selected Financial Factors (in Percentages)

Debt Ratio 45	69.2	•	140.1	145.8	62.8	119.3	46.4	36.7	57.9	57.5	74.2	69.9	•
Return on Total Assets 46	6.6	•	•	•	10.8	•	17.1	12.8	16.1	12.3	1.9	6.3	•
Return on Equity Before Income Taxes 47	12.9	•	26.8	37.2	24.1	207.6	30.9	19.4	35.4	24.2	5.0	11.5	•
Return on Equity After Income Taxes 48	8.5	•	26.8	37.2	23.5	211.7	30.8	18.6	30.4	20.1	4.0	6.5	•
Profit Margin (Before Income Tax) 49	4.2	11.9	•	•	5.0	•	8.4	6.5	9.6	8.8	0.8	4.8	•
Profit Margin (After Income Tax) 50	2.7	11.9	•	•	4.9	•	8.4	6.3	8.3	7.3	0.7	2.7	•

OTHER TRANSPORTATION EQUIPMENT AND RAILROAD ROLLING STOCK

Item Description for Accounting Period 7/11 Through 6/12		Total	Zero Assets	Under 500	500 to 1,000	1,000 to 5,000	5,000 to 10,000	10,000 to 25,000	25,000 to 50,000	50,000 to 100,000	100,000 to 250,000	250,000 to 500,000	500,000 to 2,500,000	2,500,000 and over
		MONEY AMOUNTS AND SIZE OF ASSETS IN THOUSANDS OF DOLLARS												
Number of Enterprises	1	754	•	388	32	181	67	36	18	12	•	•	5	0
		Revenues ($ in Thousands)												
Net Sales	2	19707800	•	94287	18861	593087	961360	1026116	1327023	1396746	•	•	10005790	0
Interest	3	577829	•	0	0	0	32	155	323	1603	•	•	573990	0
Rents	4	2754	•	0	0	0	0	0	0	1417	•	•	1059	0
Royalties	5	80073	•	0	0	0	0	0	0	151	•	•	67181	0
Other Portfolio Income	6	53014	•	0	0	0	3503	9	259	1343	•	•	3353	0
Other Receipts	7	168862	•	0	0	7162	122	5498	7894	30142	•	•	38992	0
Total Receipts	8	20590332	•	94287	18861	600249	965017	1031778	1335499	1431402	•	•	10690365	0
Average Total Receipts	9	27308	•	243	589	3316	14403	28660	74194	119284	•	•	2138073	•
		Operating Costs/Operating Income (%)												
Cost of Operations	10	70.2	•	57.3	67.6	67.6	71.9	73.4	74.0	73.9	•	•	65.0	•
Salaries and Wages	11	5.8	•	•	1.3	4.2	6.0	5.3	6.5	4.8	•	•	7.1	•
Taxes Paid	12	1.3	•	8.5	3.0	2.3	1.3	1.2	1.4	1.7	•	•	1.2	•
Interest Paid	13	1.9	•	2.3	8.3	0.7	0.2	0.3	0.3	0.7	•	•	3.0	•
Depreciation	14	2.8	•	3.9	3.4	1.2	1.8	1.6	1.2	1.5	•	•	3.6	•
Amortization and Depletion	15	0.6	•	•	8.3	0.5	0.1	0.0	0.5	0.4	•	•	0.8	•
Pensions and Other Deferred Comp.	16	1.8	•	•	•	•	0.2	0.1	0.1	0.7	•	•	3.2	•
Employee Benefits	17	1.7	•	1.1	•	0.8	0.8	0.7	0.8	1.6	•	•	2.2	•
Advertising	18	1.3	•	0.3	1.0	1.4	0.3	0.4	0.7	0.2	•	•	1.5	•
Other Expenses	19	7.3	•	18.8	6.2	9.7	5.7	5.3	6.1	6.0	•	•	8.9	•
Officers' Compensation	20	1.3	•	3.7	0.2	4.7	4.9	2.1	1.0	1.5	•	•	0.9	•
Operating Margin	21	4.2	•	4.2	0.7	6.9	6.8	9.5	7.3	6.9	•	•	2.5	•
Operating Margin Before Officers' Comp.	22	5.4	•	7.9	0.9	11.6	11.7	11.6	8.4	8.4	•	•	3.4	•

Selected Average Balance Sheet ($ in Thousands)													
Net Receivables 23	10052	•	18	0	329	2775	3122	9166	22872	•	•	1275382	•
Inventories 24	3207	•	49	300	775	1237	3892	7597	13980	•	•	246169	•
Net Property, Plant and Equipment 25	2919	•	28	398	369	1044	1931	3329	10650	•	•	266234	•
Total Assets 26	24391	•	96	1000	1784	7007	13463	33960	75191	•	•	2579552	•
Notes and Loans Payable 27	10654	•	82	1000	653	1930	2795	2584	23997	•	•	1329187	•
All Other Liabilities 28	5721	•	30	24	352	1688	3043	7266	19510	•	•	529669	•
Net Worth 29	8016	•	-15	-24	779	3389	7625	24109	31684	•	•	720696	•
Selected Financial Ratios (Times to 1)													
Current Ratio 30	1.4	•	0.9	1.6	1.4	1.8	2.9	3.7	1.9	•	•	1.3	•
Quick Ratio 31	1.0	•	0.2	1.2	0.6	1.1	1.5	2.0	1.2	•	•	1.0	•
Net Sales to Working Capital 32	4.9	•	•	43.8	8.5	5.6	4.7	3.9	4.8	•	•	4.0	•
Coverage Ratio 33	5.6	•	2.8	1.1	12.1	33.4	35.1	31.3	14.3	•	•	4.1	•
Total Asset Turnover 34	1.1	•	2.5	0.6	1.8	2.0	2.1	2.2	1.5	•	•	0.8	•
Inventory Turnover 35	5.7	•	2.9	1.3	2.9	8.3	5.4	7.2	6.2	•	•	5.3	•
Receivables Turnover 36	2.4	•	•	•	5.3	9.7	8.6	9.0	•	•	•	1.4	•
Total Liabilities to Net Worth 37	2.0	•	•	•	1.3	1.1	0.8	0.4	1.4	•	•	2.6	•
Current Assets to Working Capital 38	3.4	•	•	2.8	3.3	2.2	1.5	1.4	2.1	•	•	4.0	•
Current Liabilities to Working Capital 39	2.4	•	•	1.8	2.3	1.2	0.5	0.4	1.1	•	•	3.0	•
Working Capital to Net Sales 40	0.2	•	•	0.0	0.1	0.2	0.2	0.3	0.2	•	•	0.2	•
Inventory to Working Capital 41	0.6	•	•	0.5	1.7	0.9	0.6	0.5	0.6	•	•	0.4	•
Total Receipts to Cash Flow 42	7.0	•	5.8	15.2	6.9	8.8	7.1	8.1	7.4	•	•	6.1	•
Cost of Goods to Cash Flow 43	4.9	•	3.3	10.3	4.7	6.3	5.2	6.0	5.5	•	•	4.0	•
Cash Flow to Total Debt 44	0.2	•	0.4	0.0	0.5	0.4	0.7	0.9	0.4	•	•	0.2	•
Selected Financial Factors (in Percentages)													
Debt Ratio 45	67.1	•	115.7	102.4	56.3	51.6	43.4	29.0	57.9	•	•	72.1	•
Return on Total Assets 46	11.4	•	16.2	5.3	16.3	15.1	22.0	17.9	16.1	•	•	9.8	•
Return on Equity Before Income Taxes 47	28.6	•	•	•	34.2	30.3	37.7	24.3	35.4	•	•	26.5	•
Return on Equity After Income Taxes 48	22.4	•	•	•	33.7	28.4	37.7	23.5	30.4	•	•	17.8	•
Profit Margin (Before Income Tax) 49	8.8	•	4.2	0.7	8.1	7.1	10.1	8.0	9.6	•	•	9.5	•
Profit Margin (After Income Tax) 50	6.9	•	4.2	0.7	8.0	6.7	10.1	7.7	8.3	•	•	6.4	•

Table I

Corporations with and without Net Income

FURNITURE AND RELATED PRODUCT MANUFACTURING

MONEY AMOUNTS AND SIZE OF ASSETS IN THOUSANDS OF DOLLARS

Item Description for Accounting Period 7/11 Through 6/12		Total	Zero Assets	Under 500	500 to 1,000	1,000 to 5,000	5,000 to 10,000	10,000 to 25,000	25,000 to 50,000	50,000 to 100,000	100,000 to 250,000	250,000 to 500,000	500,000 to 2,500,000	2,500,000 and over
Number of Enterprises	1	12778	3245	7874	355	875	142	162	60	27	20	6	13	0
Revenues ($ in Thousands)														
Net Sales	2	53997467	1160068	4692007	710241	4766912	2581716	4518389	4033978	2968320	4443250	3716496	20406090	0
Interest	3	82961	33406	71	377	2350	209	1959	2137	2316	3824	11992	24319	0
Rents	4	34218	437	0	0	874	0	1905	2187	203	7833	2711	18068	0
Royalties	5	74787	6194	0	0	0	0	0	882	699	128	4	66879	0
Other Portfolio Income	6	196518	42398	13914	1579	1573	6052	10362	4525	4921	82883	250	28061	0
Other Receipts	7	639687	9285	74113	662	13247	17572	19575	18340	40348	18292	4267	423987	0
Total Receipts	8	55025638	1251788	4780105	712859	4784956	2605549	4552190	4062049	3016807	4556210	3735720	20967404	0
Average Total Receipts	9	4306	386	607	2008	5469	18349	28100	67701	111734	227810	622620	1612877	•
Operating Costs/Operating Income (%)														
Cost of Operations	10	66.8	64.6	59.9	57.3	69.7	72.6	69.3	74.0	74.2	71.1	64.3	63.9	•
Salaries and Wages	11	8.5	7.9	10.0	8.0	9.3	8.3	8.2	7.5	7.0	7.3	10.4	8.5	•
Taxes Paid	12	2.1	2.1	3.0	3.3	2.9	1.7	1.9	1.9	1.7	1.9	1.9	1.9	•
Interest Paid	13	1.1	3.5	0.8	1.1	0.8	0.5	0.8	0.8	1.1	0.9	0.4	1.6	•
Depreciation	14	1.9	1.8	1.3	1.5	1.1	1.9	1.9	1.6	2.2	2.3	2.5	2.1	•
Amortization and Depletion	15	0.4	0.3	0.4	0.2	0.0	0.0	0.1	0.3	0.4	0.4	0.2	0.8	•
Pensions and Other Deferred Comp.	16	0.6	1.8	0.6	0.0	0.1	0.2	0.2	0.3	0.5	0.8	0.6	0.8	•
Employee Benefits	17	1.8	2.4	1.3	4.2	1.2	2.0	1.6	1.4	2.4	1.9	1.3	2.1	•
Advertising	18	2.4	2.2	0.6	0.3	0.8	1.3	2.0	1.4	0.5	1.2	3.9	4.0	•
Other Expenses	19	12.2	17.6	16.2	16.8	10.5	9.2	10.8	9.9	10.6	8.7	11.6	13.4	•
Officers' Compensation	20	1.8	0.9	7.2	9.4	2.4	2.2	2.0	1.4	1.0	1.1	0.7	0.6	•
Operating Margin	21	0.3	•	•	•	1.3	0.0	1.2	•	•	2.5	2.1	0.3	•
Operating Margin Before Officers' Comp.	22	2.1	•	5.8	7.2	3.7	2.2	3.2	1.0	•	3.6	2.9	0.9	•

Selected Average Balance Sheet ($ in Thousands)													
Net Receivables 23	433	0	33	317	535	1697	3044	8427	17359	25892	65140	159901	•
Inventories 24	397	0	24	146	606	1503	3665	7494	18258	27628	43004	133460	•
Net Property, Plant and Equipment 25	480	0	32	188	544	1792	3558	8526	13492	32820	78974	193040	•
Total Assets 26	2497	0	137	761	2231	6398	14234	34662	70128	142218	305752	1287162	•
Notes and Loans Payable 27	783	0	82	363	829	2461	3389	9999	22902	36346	22259	425052	•
All Other Liabilities 28	763	0	71	236	656	1822	3744	7453	22124	37164	99687	406559	•
Net Worth 29	950	0	-16	162	746	2114	7101	17209	25102	68708	183806	455551	•
Selected Financial Ratios (Times to 1)													
Current Ratio 30	1.7	•	1.1	1.3	1.8	1.8	2.0	2.0	1.9	2.7	2.2	1.4	•
Quick Ratio 31	0.9	•	0.6	1.1	1.0	1.1	1.0	1.1	1.0	1.4	1.5	0.7	•
Net Sales to Working Capital 32	8.5	•	87.4	15.3	7.8	9.0	6.2	6.4	5.1	4.9	6.5	10.6	•
Coverage Ratio 33	3.0	1.8	1.7	•	3.2	2.8	3.5	1.3	1.1	6.6	7.9	3.0	•
Total Asset Turnover 34	1.7	•	4.3	2.6	2.4	2.8	2.0	1.9	1.6	1.6	2.0	1.2	•
Inventory Turnover 35	7.1	•	14.8	7.8	6.3	8.8	5.3	6.6	4.5	5.7	9.3	7.5	•
Receivables Turnover 36	9.7	•	18.8	4.5	9.1	10.8	9.3	8.7	6.9	9.3	11.7	9.1	•
Total Liabilities to Net Worth 37	1.6	•	•	3.7	2.0	2.0	1.0	1.0	1.8	1.1	0.7	1.8	•
Current Assets to Working Capital 38	2.5	•	12.9	4.0	2.2	2.2	2.0	2.0	2.2	1.6	1.8	3.3	•
Current Liabilities to Working Capital 39	1.5	•	11.9	3.0	1.2	1.2	1.0	1.0	1.2	0.6	0.8	2.3	•
Working Capital to Net Sales 40	0.1	•	0.0	0.1	0.1	0.1	0.2	0.2	0.2	0.2	0.2	0.1	•
Inventory to Working Capital 41	0.8	•	4.2	0.7	0.9	0.7	0.8	0.7	0.8	0.7	0.5	0.9	•
Total Receipts to Cash Flow 42	8.8	6.9	8.4	15.6	11.6	14.3	9.8	12.5	11.7	10.5	8.5	7.1	•
Cost of Goods to Cash Flow 43	5.9	4.4	5.0	8.9	8.1	10.4	6.8	9.2	8.7	7.4	5.5	4.5	•
Cash Flow to Total Debt 44	0.3	•	0.5	0.2	0.3	0.3	0.4	0.3	0.2	0.3	0.6	0.3	•
Selected Financial Factors (in Percentages)													
Debt Ratio 45	61.9	•	111.7	78.7	66.6	67.0	50.1	50.4	64.2	51.7	39.9	64.6	•
Return on Total Assets 46	5.8	•	5.9	•	5.9	4.2	5.5	2.1	1.9	9.3	6.2	5.8	•
Return on Equity Before Income Taxes 47	10.1	•	•	•	12.2	8.2	7.8	1.1	0.5	16.3	9.0	10.9	•
Return on Equity After Income Taxes 48	8.0	•	•	•	11.3	8.0	7.4	0.7	0.1	12.9	6.9	8.3	•
Profit Margin (Before Income Tax) 49	2.3	2.9	0.5	•	1.7	1.0	2.0	0.3	0.1	5.0	2.7	3.2	•
Profit Margin (After Income Tax) 50	1.8	2.7	0.5	•	1.5	0.9	1.9	0.2	0.0	4.0	2.0	2.4	•

Table II

Corporations with Net Income

FURNITURE AND RELATED PRODUCT MANUFACTURING

MONEY AMOUNTS AND SIZE OF ASSETS IN THOUSANDS OF DOLLARS

Item Description for Accounting Period 7/11 Through 6/12		Total	Zero Assets	Under 500	500 to 1,000	1,000 to 5,000	5,000 to 10,000	10,000 to 25,000	25,000 to 50,000	50,000 to 100,000	100,000 to 250,000	250,000 to 500,000	500,000 to 2,500,000	2,500,000 and over
Number of Enterprises	1	6933	1300	4627	280	500	69	83	34	13	17	0	9	0
Revenues ($ in Thousands)														
Net Sales	2	33513238	1019585	1807606	641821	2920065	1396812	2538313	2145721	1556949	5259756	0	14226607	0
Interest	3	54261	33406	1	3	946	72	392	1572	388	817	0	16664	0
Rents	4	26497	437	0	0	14	0	1154	1226	163	7475	0	16027	0
Royalties	5	38874	6194	0	0	0	0	0	0	0	128	0	32551	0
Other Portfolio Income	6	166782	42396	4872	88	613	2508	8514	2303	1227	80902	0	23358	0
Other Receipts	7	504400	9286	70099	520	4241	9342	7478	10386	10061	17139	0	365853	0
Total Receipts	8	34304052	1111304	1882578	642432	2925879	1408734	2555851	2161208	1568788	5366217	0	14681060	0
Average Total Receipts	9	4948	855	407	2294	5852	20416	30793	63565	120676	315660	•	1631229	•
Operating Costs/Operating Income (%)														
Cost of Operations	10	64.2	64.7	50.3	58.6	66.5	70.6	69.0	71.5	70.9	63.4	•	62.7	•
Salaries and Wages	11	8.6	6.8	10.7	7.4	8.6	8.1	7.3	7.7	7.2	9.7	•	8.6	•
Taxes Paid	12	2.1	2.1	3.0	3.3	2.4	0.9	1.8	2.4	1.6	2.0	•	2.0	•
Interest Paid	13	1.0	3.9	1.4	0.4	0.9	0.2	0.4	0.8	0.7	0.7	•	1.1	•
Depreciation	14	1.7	2.0	1.4	1.0	1.0	1.3	1.3	1.6	1.5	2.0	•	2.0	•
Amortization and Depletion	15	0.4	0.3	0.2	0.2	0.0	0.0	0.1	0.1	0.2	0.3	•	0.8	•
Pensions and Other Deferred Comp.	16	0.7	2.1	0.9	0.0	0.2	0.1	0.2	0.3	0.4	0.9	•	0.9	•
Employee Benefits	17	1.9	2.6	0.5	4.2	1.0	1.2	1.3	2.0	2.1	1.9	•	2.3	•
Advertising	18	2.3	2.3	0.3	0.3	1.0	1.1	2.4	1.1	0.5	2.6	•	3.2	•
Other Expenses	19	11.9	15.7	16.9	12.8	9.9	6.7	8.1	7.9	7.9	10.4	•	14.1	•
Officers' Compensation	20	1.7	1.0	9.7	9.1	2.5	2.1	2.1	1.2	1.0	1.0	•	0.5	•
Operating Margin	21	3.6	•	4.6	2.6	5.8	7.7	6.1	3.5	5.9	5.1	•	1.9	•
Operating Margin Before Officers' Comp.	22	5.2	•	14.3	11.8	8.4	9.8	8.2	4.7	6.9	6.1	•	2.3	•

Selected Average Balance Sheet ($ in Thousands)

Net Receivables 23	494	0	22	398	577	2440	3124	7677	17185	31515	•	163690	•
Inventories 24	447	0	24	131	613	1844	3898	7533	17584	26947	•	125586	•
Net Property, Plant and Equipment 25	509	0	25	122	692	1336	2993	7989	10784	35325	•	186139	•
Total Assets 26	2872	0	126	739	2479	6934	14209	32668	67075	157450	•	1285010	•
Notes and Loans Payable 27	794	0	77	241	966	1022	1859	10466	12605	39810	•	352997	•
All Other Liabilities 28	799	0	24	192	572	2548	3493	6663	11887	53037	•	371399	•
Net Worth 29	1279	0	25	306	941	3364	8857	15539	42582	64603	•	560614	•

Selected Financial Ratios (Times to 1)

Current Ratio 30	2.0	•	2.6	1.5	2.3	2.0	2.8	2.4	2.7	2.2	•	1.7	•
Quick Ratio 31	1.1	•	0.9	1.2	1.3	1.3	1.6	1.3	1.5	1.2	•	0.9	•
Net Sales to Working Capital 32	6.7	•	7.4	12.4	6.1	7.5	4.7	5.7	4.1	6.2	•	7.6	•
Coverage Ratio 33	7.1	2.4	7.5	7.5	7.4	54.6	20.2	6.4	9.9	11.4	•	5.7	•
Total Asset Turnover 34	1.7	•	3.1	3.1	2.4	2.9	2.2	1.9	1.8	2.0	•	1.2	•
Inventory Turnover 35	6.9	•	8.1	10.3	6.3	7.7	5.4	6.0	4.8	7.3	•	7.9	•
Receivables Turnover 36	9.0	•	15.7	6.3	9.1	8.0	8.6	7.2	•	12.1	•	8.6	•
Total Liabilities to Net Worth 37	1.2	•	4.1	1.4	1.6	1.1	0.6	1.1	0.6	1.4	•	1.3	•
Current Assets to Working Capital 38	2.0	•	1.6	3.2	1.8	2.0	1.5	1.7	1.6	1.8	•	2.5	•
Current Liabilities to Working Capital 39	1.0	•	0.6	2.2	0.8	1.0	0.5	0.7	0.6	0.8	•	1.5	•
Working Capital to Net Sales 40	0.1	•	0.1	0.1	0.2	0.1	0.2	0.2	0.2	0.2	•	0.1	•
Inventory to Working Capital 41	0.6	•	0.7	0.6	0.7	0.6	0.5	0.6	0.6	0.7	•	0.5	•
Total Receipts to Cash Flow 42	6.7	6.4	4.7	10.8	7.9	8.1	7.7	10.1	7.4	7.7	•	5.9	•
Cost of Goods to Cash Flow 43	4.3	4.1	2.4	6.3	5.3	5.7	5.3	7.3	5.2	4.9	•	3.7	•
Cash Flow to Total Debt 44	0.5	•	0.8	0.5	0.5	0.7	0.7	0.4	0.7	0.4	•	0.4	•

Selected Financial Factors (in Percentages)

Debt Ratio 45	55.5	•	80.2	58.6	62.0	51.5	37.7	52.4	36.5	59.0	•	56.4	•
Return on Total Assets 46	11.8	•	31.3	9.8	16.4	25.5	15.4	9.5	13.3	15.3	•	7.9	•
Return on Equity Before Income Taxes 47	22.8	•	137.1	20.5	37.5	51.7	23.5	16.9	18.8	34.0	•	14.9	•
Return on Equity After Income Taxes 48	19.9	•	137.1	16.9	36.2	51.5	22.9	16.3	18.4	27.7	•	11.7	•
Profit Margin (Before Income Tax) 49	6.0	5.5	8.8	2.7	6.0	8.6	6.8	4.2	6.7	7.1	•	5.3	•
Profit Margin (After Income Tax) 50	5.3	5.3	8.8	2.3	5.8	8.6	6.6	4.0	6.5	5.8	•	4.2	•

Table I

Corporations with and without Net Income

MEDICAL EQUIPMENT AND SUPPLIES

MONEY AMOUNTS AND SIZE OF ASSETS IN THOUSANDS OF DOLLARS

Item Description for Accounting Period 7/11 Through 6/12		Total	Zero Assets	Under 500	500 to 1,000	1,000 to 5,000	5,000 to 10,000	10,000 to 25,000	25,000 to 50,000	50,000 to 100,000	100,000 to 250,000	250,000 to 500,000	500,000 to 2,500,000	2,500,000 and over
Number of Enterprises	1	9499	533	7074	369	909	174	161	84	63	47	27	39	19
Revenues ($ in Thousands)														
Net Sales	2	130380294	2039441	2782913	722458	5211185	2202110	3004659	3524589	4015895	5988104	6972140	31256068	62660732
Interest	3	784087	4120	62	1036	458	1486	2645	2734	10256	10517	15306	282530	452937
Rents	4	57610	53	0	0	148	533	198	114	1681	1472	2438	42763	8212
Royalties	5	3202908	53520	0	0	66	5000	2227	1843	27120	1280	89385	132539	2889927
Other Portfolio Income	6	2203259	4289	4	8	513	13004	16162	62388	8039	20192	77508	340516	1660636
Other Receipts	7	3189531	213338	3	0	51515	26965	24329	64960	45046	60712	41653	552218	2108790
Total Receipts	8	139817689	2314761	2782982	723502	5263885	2249098	3050220	3656628	4108037	6082277	7198430	32606634	69781234
Average Total Receipts	9	14719	4343	393	1961	5791	12926	18945	43531	65207	129410	266609	836068	3672697
Operating Costs/Operating Income (%)														
Cost of Operations	10	52.4	38.9	34.5	51.9	59.9	59.3	49.8	55.3	53.3	55.2	50.7	54.9	51.3
Salaries and Wages	11	15.0	21.3	14.8	6.3	11.3	10.9	18.1	14.8	16.6	12.6	17.2	14.2	15.5
Taxes Paid	12	1.7	2.6	3.4	3.8	2.7	2.5	2.8	2.3	2.2	1.4	1.7	1.4	1.5
Interest Paid	13	3.8	3.1	1.2	0.7	0.5	1.4	1.0	1.8	1.6	2.7	1.8	3.8	5.0
Depreciation	14	3.7	2.7	2.9	3.3	1.7	2.6	3.0	3.3	3.8	3.6	3.8	3.7	4.1
Amortization and Depletion	15	1.6	2.7	3.9	0.0	0.3	0.6	0.7	1.0	1.1	2.0	1.6	1.6	1.8
Pensions and Other Deferred Comp.	16	0.8	1.0	0.2	0.7	0.4	0.1	0.4	0.4	0.5	0.4	0.3	0.6	1.1
Employee Benefits	17	2.6	3.3	1.2	4.9	1.4	1.6	2.0	2.6	2.0	1.9	2.3	1.9	3.3
Advertising	18	0.9	2.2	0.6	0.3	1.2	0.9	1.3	1.1	2.0	1.3	1.3	0.6	0.8
Other Expenses	19	16.4	28.5	21.7	23.1	15.1	14.3	22.1	17.7	17.4	14.3	16.1	15.1	16.3
Officers' Compensation	20	1.7	3.7	13.4	5.7	5.6	7.6	6.6	2.7	2.5	1.6	1.9	1.1	0.5
Operating Margin	21	•	•	2.2	•	•	•	•	•	•	2.8	1.3	1.0	•
Operating Margin Before Officers' Comp.	22	1.2	•	15.6	5.0	5.5	5.7	•	•	•	4.4	3.2	2.1	•

Selected Average Balance Sheet ($ in Thousands)

Net Receivables	23	2740	0	16	395	704	1372	3381	6996	11324	24007	50106	147350	779719
Inventories	24	2073	0	10	83	511	1417	3435	6504	9664	16996	33280	111465	585409
Net Property, Plant and Equipment	25	2089	0	22	104	233	1180	1970	5392	9152	18594	40432	139848	550727
Total Assets	26	23311	0	101	792	2002	6911	15831	37211	68758	155317	347929	1091091	7797566
Notes and Loans Payable	27	7595	0	83	118	641	2597	3276	10087	16134	43985	60054	321460	2729836
All Other Liabilities	28	7100	0	36	327	971	1750	3608	9111	15819	32947	79846	299845	2533443
Net Worth	29	8616	0	-18	347	391	2564	8947	18014	36805	78385	208029	469787	2534287

Selected Financial Ratios (Times to 1)

Current Ratio	30	1.9	•	1.1	1.7	1.5	2.2	3.3	2.2	2.4	2.2	2.6	2.0	1.8
Quick Ratio	31	1.1	•	0.7	1.4	0.9	1.4	2.3	1.3	1.5	1.3	1.8	1.1	0.9
Net Sales to Working Capital	32	3.8	•	66.3	7.6	12.0	5.0	2.2	3.7	3.0	3.5	3.0	3.8	3.5
Coverage Ratio	33	3.2	2.2	2.8	0.1	2.6	1.2	•	1.4	0.6	2.6	3.8	2.7	3.6
Total Asset Turnover	34	0.6	•	3.9	2.5	2.9	1.8	1.2	1.1	0.9	0.8	0.7	0.7	0.4
Inventory Turnover	35	3.5	•	13.8	12.3	6.7	5.3	2.7	3.6	3.5	4.1	3.9	3.9	2.9
Receivables Turnover	36	4.8	•	31.7	5.4	7.3	9.6	5.3	5.9	5.6	4.9	5.6	5.1	4.0
Total Liabilities to Net Worth	37	1.7	•	•	1.3	4.1	1.7	0.8	1.1	0.9	1.0	0.7	1.3	2.1
Current Assets to Working Capital	38	2.1	•	8.1	2.5	3.2	1.8	1.4	1.8	1.7	1.8	1.6	2.0	2.2
Current Liabilities to Working Capital	39	1.1	•	7.1	1.5	2.2	0.8	0.4	0.8	0.7	0.8	0.6	1.0	1.2
Working Capital to Net Sales	40	0.3	•	0.0	0.1	0.1	0.2	0.5	0.3	0.3	0.3	0.3	0.3	0.3
Inventory to Working Capital	41	0.5	•	2.0	0.3	0.9	0.6	0.4	0.6	0.5	0.5	0.4	0.5	0.6
Total Receipts to Cash Flow	42	4.9	3.4	5.4	5.4	8.4	8.7	8.1	6.7	7.3	5.9	5.4	5.4	4.2
Cost of Goods to Cash Flow	43	2.6	1.3	1.9	2.8	5.0	5.1	4.0	3.7	3.9	3.2	2.7	3.0	2.2
Cash Flow to Total Debt	44	0.2	•	0.6	0.8	0.4	0.3	0.3	0.3	0.3	0.3	0.3	0.2	0.1

Selected Financial Factors (in Percentages)

Debt Ratio	45	63.0	•	118.2	56.2	80.5	62.9	43.5	51.6	46.5	49.5	40.2	56.9	67.5
Return on Total Assets	46	7.1	•	13.3	0.2	4.0	2.9	•	2.9	1.0	5.9	5.0	7.7	7.6
Return on Equity Before Income Taxes	47	13.2	•	•	•	12.8	1.2	•	1.9	•	7.1	6.2	11.3	16.8
Return on Equity After Income Taxes	48	8.9	•	•	•	6.2	•	•	•	•	5.2	3.7	8.6	11.5
Profit Margin (Before Income Tax)	49	8.3	3.7	2.2	•	0.9	0.2	•	0.8	•	4.4	5.0	6.6	12.9
Profit Margin (After Income Tax)	50	5.6	0.1	2.2	•	0.4	•	•	•	•	3.2	3.0	5.0	8.8

Table II

Corporations with Net Income

MEDICAL EQUIPMENT AND SUPPLIES

MONEY AMOUNTS AND SIZE OF ASSETS IN THOUSANDS OF DOLLARS

Item Description for Accounting Period 7/11 Through 6/12		Total	Zero Assets	Under 500	500 to 1,000	1,000 to 5,000	5,000 to 10,000	10,000 to 25,000	25,000 to 50,000	50,000 to 100,000	100,000 to 250,000	250,000 to 500,000	500,000 to 2,500,000	2,500,000 and over
Number of Enterprises	1	7607	9	6293	279	640	126	81	49	33	32	18	30	16
Revenues ($ in Thousands)														
Net Sales	2	114978300	1347982	2556509	712512	4267286	1870884	2188725	2464419	2710296	4906143	5065700	27617412	59270430
Interest	3	567292	3757	59	1012	267	792	942	2154	7258	7243	12909	85444	445454
Rents	4	47109	53	0	0	148	491	198	1	1668	1472	2438	32520	8120
Royalties	5	3023476	10785	0	0	0	539	0	193	15917	1268	89385	46752	2858638
Other Portfolio Income	6	1943827	1085	0	8	263	10209	11290	14785	1056	9012	69462	267929	1558728
Other Receipts	7	2826418	205002	1	1	23056	20593	18497	52045	19693	46125	33421	359589	2048397
Total Receipts	8	123386422	1568664	2556569	713533	4291020	1903508	2219652	2533597	2755888	4971263	5273315	28409646	66189767
Average Total Receipts	9	16220	174296	406	2557	6705	15107	27403	51706	83512	155352	292962	946988	4136860
Operating Costs/Operating Income (%)														
Cost of Operations	10	52.4	40.6	30.9	52.0	58.7	60.3	46.3	58.4	51.7	57.4	46.4	55.6	51.5
Salaries and Wages	11	14.3	15.5	15.3	6.0	9.5	6.4	13.0	10.9	12.0	11.2	17.3	13.4	15.7
Taxes Paid	12	1.6	2.3	3.5	3.7	2.7	2.3	2.3	2.1	1.8	1.4	1.8	1.5	1.5
Interest Paid	13	3.2	1.3	0.4	0.7	0.4	0.7	0.6	0.9	0.8	1.7	1.6	2.2	4.6
Depreciation	14	3.6	2.4	3.0	3.3	1.4	2.6	2.3	2.4	2.7	3.5	3.9	3.4	4.1
Amortization and Depletion	15	1.3	1.8	0.7	0.0	0.0	0.1	0.2	0.8	0.8	1.2	0.8	1.2	1.6
Pensions and Other Deferred Comp.	16	0.8	1.2	0.3	0.7	0.5	0.1	0.5	0.6	0.6	0.4	0.4	0.6	1.1
Employee Benefits	17	2.6	2.9	0.9	5.0	1.4	1.1	1.7	1.5	1.4	1.9	2.4	1.7	3.4
Advertising	18	0.8	2.5	0.6	0.2	1.0	0.6	0.9	0.5	2.1	1.4	1.7	0.5	0.7
Other Expenses	19	15.3	28.4	21.1	19.9	12.0	6.7	15.3	12.2	14.2	12.6	15.9	14.7	15.9
Officers' Compensation	20	1.5	1.0	14.2	5.5	5.3	7.2	5.7	2.3	2.1	1.4	2.0	1.0	0.5
Operating Margin	21	2.6	0.1	9.1	2.9	7.0	11.9	11.1	7.4	9.7	5.9	5.8	4.2	•
Operating Margin Before Officers' Comp.	22	4.1	1.1	23.2	8.4	12.3	19.0	16.8	9.7	11.8	7.3	7.8	5.2	0.1

Selected Average Balance Sheet ($ in Thousands)													
Net Receivables **23**	2970	0	15	515	791	1498	4801	7791	14198	25517	48305	169121	853494
Inventories **24**	2249	0	7	28	647	1481	3813	6498	14303	19623	32730	128137	591798
Net Property, Plant and Equipment **25**	2270	0	22	137	200	1408	2433	5134	9093	23437	45523	151885	619217
Total Assets **26**	24925	0	94	801	2069	6951	16243	37821	66736	153920	349082	1115461	8534042
Notes and Loans Payable **27**	7557	0	40	152	603	1707	2012	8581	12165	37302	43976	261105	2861884
All Other Liabilities **28**	7770	0	14	364	676	1411	3900	8901	15488	33454	80757	317237	2812433
Net Worth **29**	9598	0	40	285	789	3833	10332	20339	39084	83164	224349	537119	2859725
Selected Financial Ratios (Times to 1)													
Current Ratio **30**	2.0	•	1.7	1.4	2.2	2.9	2.9	2.6	2.8	2.4	3.0	2.2	1.9
Quick Ratio **31**	1.1	•	1.2	1.4	1.4	1.6	1.9	1.5	1.6	1.3	2.1	1.2	0.9
Net Sales to Working Capital **32**	3.7	•	24.6	12.5	6.9	5.0	3.2	3.9	3.3	3.8	2.8	3.6	3.4
Coverage Ratio **33**	4.7	13.6	24.2	5.7	18.9	19.4	23.6	12.1	15.2	5.3	7.5	4.8	4.0
Total Asset Turnover **34**	0.6	•	4.3	3.2	3.2	2.1	1.7	1.3	1.2	1.0	0.8	0.8	0.4
Inventory Turnover **35**	3.5	•	19.0	47.6	6.1	6.0	3.3	4.5	3.0	4.5	4.0	4.0	3.2
Receivables Turnover **36**	4.9	•	35.1	•	7.4	10.3	5.6	6.1	5.1	5.5	6.0	5.0	•
Total Liabilities to Net Worth **37**	1.6	•	1.4	1.8	1.6	0.8	0.6	0.9	0.7	0.9	0.6	1.1	2.0
Current Assets to Working Capital **38**	2.0	•	2.5	3.2	1.8	1.5	1.5	1.6	1.6	1.7	1.5	1.8	2.2
Current Liabilities to Working Capital **39**	1.0	•	1.5	2.2	0.8	0.5	0.5	0.6	0.6	0.7	0.5	0.8	1.2
Working Capital to Net Sales **40**	0.3	•	0.0	0.1	0.1	0.2	0.3	0.3	0.3	0.3	0.4	0.3	0.3
Inventory to Working Capital **41**	0.5	•	0.6	0.1	0.6	0.6	0.4	0.5	0.5	0.5	0.3	0.5	0.5
Total Receipts to Cash Flow **42**	4.5	2.4	3.9	5.2	6.2	5.6	4.0	5.0	4.3	5.5	4.2	5.1	4.2
Cost of Goods to Cash Flow **43**	2.3	1.0	1.2	2.7	3.6	3.4	1.9	2.9	2.3	3.1	2.0	2.8	2.1
Cash Flow to Total Debt **44**	0.2	•	1.9	1.0	0.8	0.8	1.1	0.6	0.7	0.4	0.5	0.3	0.2
Selected Financial Factors (in Percentages)													
Debt Ratio **45**	61.5	•	57.7	64.4	61.9	44.9	36.4	46.2	41.4	46.0	35.7	51.8	66.5
Return on Total Assets **46**	8.9	•	40.8	11.8	25.9	30.7	21.8	14.9	15.0	8.9	9.7	8.6	8.1
Return on Equity Before Income Taxes **47**	18.2	•	92.4	27.3	64.2	52.7	32.8	25.4	23.9	13.4	13.1	14.2	18.0
Return on Equity After Income Taxes **48**	13.4	•	92.3	24.1	59.5	49.8	30.3	20.9	19.4	10.8	9.6	11.1	12.4
Profit Margin (Before Income Tax) **49**	11.6	16.6	9.1	3.0	7.6	13.6	12.5	10.3	11.4	7.3	10.5	8.3	13.9
Profit Margin (After Income Tax) **50**	8.5	11.1	9.1	2.7	7.0	12.9	11.6	8.4	9.3	5.9	7.7	6.5	9.5

Table I

Corporations with and without Net Income

OTHER MISCELLANEOUS MANUFACTURING

Item Description for Accounting Period 7/11 Through 6/12		MONEY AMOUNTS AND SIZE OF ASSETS IN THOUSANDS OF DOLLARS Total	Zero Assets	Under 500	500 to 1,000	1,000 to 5,000	5,000 to 10,000	10,000 to 25,000	25,000 to 50,000	50,000 to 100,000	100,000 to 250,000	250,000 to 500,000	500,000 to 2,500,000	2,500,000 and over
Number of Enterprises	1	19758	1087	15101	1013	1524	485	302	107	54	43	22	16	4
Revenues ($ in Thousands)														
Net Sales	2	74550143	217114	5260849	1602958	7064575	6421492	7283667	5513930	5286957	7113251	6886400	11855688	10043260
Interest	3	511254	267	283	501	2842	1409	1884	4937	10766	9429	27448	39094	412393
Rents	4	20800	0	0	0	1451	12	1554	455	264	11027	3402	2157	479
Royalties	5	1192625	154	0	0	0	210	9079	1295	10837	28920	28056	112430	1001644
Other Portfolio Income	6	273537	3418	33597	522	659	35841	20267	1565	13856	10055	13189	43553	97014
Other Receipts	7	1445704	17697	72508	3535	46686	24928	108065	161443	20983	31089	176837	53740	728198
Total Receipts	8	77994063	238650	5367237	1607516	7116213	6483892	7424516	5683625	5343663	7203771	7135332	12106662	12282988
Average Total Receipts	9	3947	220	355	1587	4669	13369	24584	53118	98957	167530	324333	756666	3070747
Operating Costs/Operating Income (%)														
Cost of Operations	10	60.2	67.5	48.0	58.7	64.0	68.4	68.8	66.5	63.1	64.9	58.6	55.1	51.5
Salaries and Wages	11	10.6	9.7	11.9	9.9	9.4	9.7	7.8	8.9	10.0	8.4	12.9	11.5	13.9
Taxes Paid	12	2.1	2.1	3.0	2.1	2.4	1.6	2.0	1.9	1.8	2.0	1.9	2.0	2.2
Interest Paid	13	2.6	1.4	1.3	0.8	0.5	1.0	1.2	1.1	1.4	1.8	4.3	3.4	7.2
Depreciation	14	3.1	2.3	1.2	1.2	2.1	2.7	2.9	3.1	2.6	3.3	3.6	3.9	4.5
Amortization and Depletion	15	0.9	2.0	0.4	0.0	0.3	0.5	0.5	0.3	0.9	1.2	1.0	1.3	2.2
Pensions and Other Deferred Comp.	16	0.7	0.1	0.1	0.8	0.6	0.4	0.3	0.4	0.5	0.9	0.9	0.8	1.2
Employee Benefits	17	1.8	0.7	1.3	0.6	1.0	1.8	1.5	1.4	1.8	2.1	1.8	2.5	2.0
Advertising	18	1.9	2.5	1.5	1.6	0.9	0.9	1.0	1.7	2.6	1.8	2.5	1.7	3.8
Other Expenses	19	13.9	33.6	20.3	16.3	11.0	8.9	10.0	11.4	10.6	10.1	14.1	14.8	22.3
Officers' Compensation	20	2.4	4.5	8.3	5.8	5.7	3.1	2.4	1.7	1.8	0.9	1.0	0.9	0.6
Operating Margin	21	•	•	2.9	2.3	2.2	1.1	1.6	1.5	3.0	2.6	•	2.0	•
Operating Margin Before Officers' Comp.	22	2.2	•	11.1	8.1	7.9	4.2	4.0	3.3	4.7	3.5	•	3.0	•

Selected Average Balance Sheet ($ in Thousands)													
Net Receivables 23	573	0	17	94	611	1505	3917	6848	12349	26740	49125	126938	616857
Inventories 24	604	0	22	199	698	2121	4065	9102	15102	26601	62674	97461	554854
Net Property, Plant and Equipment 25	481	0	24	45	319	1243	2507	6200	12238	29205	53023	112461	426061
Total Assets 26	3562	0	98	637	2187	6796	15994	35173	70633	163849	352631	1094675	4227762
Notes and Loans Payable 27	1228	0	72	116	799	3306	5009	8289	24678	48806	115897	361064	1520126
All Other Liabilities 28	1148	0	57	194	628	1145	4063	14505	18621	45734	114049	382254	1436825
Net Worth 29	1186	0	-31	326	760	2346	6922	12380	27334	69310	122685	351358	1270810
Selected Financial Ratios (Times to 1)													
Current Ratio 30	1.8	•	1.0	1.6	1.8	1.6	1.9	2.0	1.9	1.7	2.4	1.8	1.6
Quick Ratio 31	0.9	•	0.6	0.7	1.1	0.7	1.0	0.9	0.9	0.9	1.1	0.9	0.8
Net Sales to Working Capital 32	5.3	•	686.0	9.1	6.4	8.0	4.8	4.4	5.3	5.1	3.6	5.1	3.8
Coverage Ratio 33	2.8	•	4.9	4.5	6.4	3.1	4.1	5.0	3.8	3.2	1.7	2.3	2.6
Total Asset Turnover 34	1.1	•	3.6	2.5	2.1	1.9	1.5	1.5	1.4	1.0	0.9	0.7	0.6
Inventory Turnover 35	3.8	•	7.7	4.7	4.2	4.3	4.1	3.8	4.1	4.0	2.9	4.2	2.3
Receivables Turnover 36	6.6	•	17.3	15.9	7.0	9.2	6.4	7.4	6.8	6.3	5.7	5.9	4.6
Total Liabilities to Net Worth 37	2.0	•	•	1.0	1.9	1.9	1.3	1.8	1.6	1.4	1.9	2.1	2.3
Current Assets to Working Capital 38	2.3	•	116.9	2.6	2.2	2.7	2.1	2.0	2.1	2.4	1.7	2.3	2.6
Current Liabilities to Working Capital 39	1.3	•	115.9	1.6	1.2	1.7	1.1	1.0	1.1	1.4	0.7	1.3	1.6
Working Capital to Net Sales 40	0.2	•	0.0	0.1	0.2	0.1	0.2	0.2	0.2	0.2	0.3	0.2	0.3
Inventory to Working Capital 41	0.8	•	35.1	1.4	0.7	1.4	0.8	0.8	0.8	0.8	0.7	0.7	0.9
Total Receipts to Cash Flow 42	6.7	10.9	5.1	6.5	9.3	12.7	9.4	7.2	7.9	8.2	8.4	6.1	3.6
Cost of Goods to Cash Flow 43	4.0	7.4	2.4	3.8	6.0	8.7	6.5	4.8	5.0	5.3	4.9	3.3	1.9
Cash Flow to Total Debt 44	0.2	•	0.5	0.8	0.3	0.2	0.3	0.3	0.3	0.2	0.2	0.2	0.2
Selected Financial Factors (in Percentages)													
Debt Ratio 45	66.7	•	131.6	48.8	65.3	65.5	56.7	64.8	61.3	57.7	65.2	67.9	69.9
Return on Total Assets 46	7.8	•	21.9	8.4	7.3	6.0	7.5	8.5	7.6	5.8	6.2	5.3	11.2
Return on Equity Before Income Taxes 47	15.0	•	•	12.7	17.8	11.8	13.0	19.2	14.5	9.5	7.1	9.3	23.1
Return on Equity After Income Taxes 48	11.3	•	•	11.9	15.8	11.3	11.6	15.3	11.1	8.0	5.3	5.3	15.5
Profit Margin (Before Income Tax) 49	4.7	•	4.9	2.6	2.9	2.1	3.7	4.6	4.1	4.0	2.8	4.4	11.7
Profit Margin (After Income Tax) 50	3.5	•	4.8	2.5	2.6	2.0	3.3	3.7	3.1	3.4	2.1	2.5	7.8

Table II

Corporations with Net Income

OTHER MISCELLANEOUS MANUFACTURING

MONEY AMOUNTS AND SIZE OF ASSETS IN THOUSANDS OF DOLLARS

Item Description for Accounting Period 7/11 Through 6/12		Total	Zero Assets	Under 500	500 to 1,000	1,000 to 5,000	5,000 to 10,000	10,000 to 25,000	25,000 to 50,000	50,000 to 100,000	100,000 to 250,000	250,000 to 500,000	500,000 to 2,500,000	2,500,000 and over
Number of Enterprises	1	10340	25	7547	943	1146	288	219	68	42	29	16	11	4
Revenues ($ in Thousands)														
Net Sales	2	58230521	117149	3525218	1441999	6359212	4221628	5076921	4122557	4340554	4492761	5532901	8956361	10043260
Interest	3	467249	2	40	497	1390	129	1609	1121	10629	4051	8219	27170	412393
Rents	4	11867	0	0	0	1451	12	1468	79	264	4928	1030	2157	479
Royalties	5	1125131	154	0	0	0	210	8152	450	3678	7443	19528	83872	1001644
Other Portfolio Income	6	259293	2493	30657	522	659	34874	19289	1224	13832	7016	13182	38532	97014
Other Receipts	7	1309062	22444	51774	374	44746	16094	93706	148366	20552	19255	113723	49828	728198
Total Receipts	8	61403123	142242	3607689	1443392	6407458	4272947	5201145	4273797	4389509	4535454	5688583	9157920	12282988
Average Total Receipts	9	5938	5690	478	1531	5591	14837	23750	62850	104512	156395	355536	832538	3070747
Operating Costs/Operating Income (%)														
Cost of Operations	10	58.8	67.7	47.1	56.3	64.4	69.0	68.4	64.7	62.3	60.7	58.6	52.7	51.5
Salaries and Wages	11	10.7	5.5	12.2	10.0	8.2	7.6	7.3	9.2	9.5	9.0	12.8	12.5	13.9
Taxes Paid	12	2.0	2.0	2.4	2.1	2.4	1.4	2.0	2.0	1.9	1.6	1.9	2.2	2.2
Interest Paid	13	2.3	0.5	1.0	0.7	0.4	0.6	1.0	0.9	1.1	1.6	2.1	2.3	7.2
Depreciation	14	2.8	0.8	1.2	1.0	1.3	1.5	2.2	2.1	2.8	3.1	3.3	3.8	4.5
Amortization and Depletion	15	0.9	2.8	0.3	0.0	0.2	0.1	0.3	0.2	0.5	0.8	0.8	1.4	2.2
Pensions and Other Deferred Comp.	16	0.7	0.1	0.1	0.9	0.6	0.4	0.3	0.5	0.5	1.0	1.1	0.8	1.2
Employee Benefits	17	1.7	0.4	1.1	0.3	0.9	1.9	1.4	1.6	1.7	2.3	1.4	2.2	2.0
Advertising	18	1.9	2.1	1.1	1.6	0.8	0.7	0.7	1.4	2.1	1.4	2.7	1.8	3.8
Other Expenses	19	13.2	14.8	15.9	14.7	9.6	7.3	8.9	10.6	10.0	10.0	13.2	13.7	22.3
Officers' Compensation	20	2.4	1.0	8.1	5.8	5.8	3.2	2.2	1.9	1.8	1.0	1.1	0.9	0.6
Operating Margin	21	2.6	2.3	9.4	6.7	5.4	6.4	5.3	5.0	5.5	7.7	1.0	5.8	•
Operating Margin Before Officers' Comp.	22	5.0	3.3	17.5	12.5	11.1	9.5	7.5	6.8	7.3	8.7	2.2	6.6	•

Selected Average Balance Sheet ($ in Thousands)														
Net Receivables	23	865	0	17	95	743	1655	3747	7978	12300	20652	51394	148502	616857
Inventories	24	861	0	23	240	727	2088	4197	10371	15148	25977	63152	101747	594133
Net Property, Plant and Equipment	25	698	0	38	40	281	1366	2199	5540	13036	29177	54678	122957	426061
Total Assets	26	5207	0	112	622	2291	6709	15562	36356	71675	157482	349466	1081172	4227762
Notes and Loans Payable	27	1618	0	44	74	749	2565	4250	7897	21425	42173	103121	310296	1520126
All Other Liabilities	28	1495	0	33	178	677	988	2953	9826	18737	34466	112024	303481	1436825
Net Worth	29	2094	0	35	370	865	3156	8359	18633	31513	80843	134321	467395	1270810

Selected Financial Ratios (Times to 1)														
Current Ratio	30	1.9	•	1.7	1.9	2.0	2.1	2.2	2.4	2.1	2.2	2.2	2.0	1.6
Quick Ratio	31	1.0	•	1.3	0.8	1.3	0.9	1.1	1.1	1.0	1.2	1.0	1.0	0.8
Net Sales to Working Capital	32	4.7	•	16.8	7.4	6.1	5.8	4.0	4.0	5.1	4.5	4.0	4.3	3.8
Coverage Ratio	33	4.7	46.4	12.9	11.4	15.6	14.1	9.2	10.6	7.0	6.5	3.9	4.7	2.6
Total Asset Turnover	34	1.1	•	4.2	2.5	2.4	2.2	1.5	1.7	1.4	1.0	1.0	0.8	0.6
Inventory Turnover	35	3.8	•	9.8	3.6	4.9	4.8	3.8	3.8	4.3	3.6	3.2	4.2	2.2
Receivables Turnover	36	6.8	•	16.8	•	7.0	8.6	6.8	8.0	7.7	6.9	5.4	6.0	•
Total Liabilities to Net Worth	37	1.5	•	2.2	0.7	1.6	1.1	0.9	1.0	1.3	0.9	1.6	1.3	2.3
Current Assets to Working Capital	38	2.1	•	2.3	2.1	2.0	1.9	1.8	1.7	1.9	1.9	1.8	2.0	2.6
Current Liabilities to Working Capital	39	1.1	•	1.3	1.1	1.0	0.9	0.8	0.7	0.9	0.9	0.8	1.0	1.6
Working Capital to Net Sales	40	0.2	•	0.1	0.1	0.2	0.2	0.3	0.2	0.2	0.2	0.2	0.2	0.3
Inventory to Working Capital	41	0.7	•	0.6	1.2	0.6	1.0	0.7	0.7	0.7	0.7	0.7	0.6	0.9
Total Receipts to Cash Flow	42	5.6	2.9	4.3	5.5	7.8	8.8	7.2	5.8	6.8	6.0	7.3	5.2	3.6
Cost of Goods to Cash Flow	43	3.3	2.0	2.0	3.1	5.0	6.1	4.9	3.8	4.2	3.6	4.3	2.8	1.9
Cash Flow to Total Debt	44	0.3	•	1.4	1.1	0.5	0.5	0.4	0.6	0.4	0.3	0.2	0.3	0.2

Selected Financial Factors (in Percentages)														
Debt Ratio	45	59.8	•	68.8	40.5	62.2	53.0	46.3	48.7	56.0	48.7	61.6	56.8	69.9
Return on Total Assets	46	11.7	•	53.1	18.3	15.9	17.8	13.4	15.9	11.2	10.2	8.0	8.0	11.2
Return on Equity Before Income Taxes	47	22.9	•	157.0	28.1	39.5	35.2	22.3	28.2	21.9	16.7	15.4	14.6	23.1
Return on Equity After Income Taxes	48	18.9	•	155.2	27.3	37.2	34.6	20.7	24.1	18.1	15.0	13.3	10.2	15.5
Profit Margin (Before Income Tax)	49	8.5	23.7	11.7	6.8	6.2	7.6	8.0	8.7	6.7	8.7	6.0	8.4	11.7
Profit Margin (After Income Tax)	50	7.0	23.1	11.6	6.6	5.8	7.5	7.5	7.4	5.5	7.8	5.2	5.9	7.8

Table I

Corporations with and without Net Income

MOTOR VEHICLE AND MOTOR VEHICLE PARTS AND SUPPLIES

MONEY AMOUNTS AND SIZE OF ASSETS IN THOUSANDS OF DOLLARS

Item Description for Accounting Period 7/11 Through 6/12		Total	Zero Assets	Under 500	500 to 1,000	1,000 to 5,000	5,000 to 10,000	10,000 to 25,000	25,000 to 50,000	50,000 to 100,000	100,000 to 250,000	250,000 to 500,000	500,000 to 2,500,000	2,500,000 and over
Number of Enterprises	1	19934	1976	11596	2707	2590	471	328	136	44	44	16	19	6
Revenues ($ in Thousands)														
Net Sales	2	234104103	787234	10020073	5759121	16914924	7311884	12526877	11301448	6259918	11527881	14022946	58120924	79550873
Interest	3	2731313	1163	2370	731	5866	3761	7313	2059	777	12622	6630	134360	2553662
Rents	4	875351	0	0	2012	1398	526	2474	1963	6256	8967	1112	63861	786782
Royalties	5	52394	0	0	2919	2845	0	0	0	0	136	129	10055	36309
Other Portfolio Income	6	972237	9191	3625	3897	13638	7183	42895	8660	12526	31912	60094	328198	450417
Other Receipts	7	1693162	17485	-15056	14219	105753	64118	99862	149182	37610	129222	84628	277746	728395
Total Receipts	8	240428560	815073	10011012	5782899	17044424	7387472	12679421	11463312	6317087	11710740	14175539	58935144	84106438
Average Total Receipts	9	12061	412	863	2136	6581	15685	38657	84289	143570	266153	885971	3101850	14017740
Operating Costs/Operating Income (%)														
Cost of Operations	10	81.9	69.8	86.2	79.2	79.0	75.9	80.3	78.3	79.2	79.6	86.1	87.8	79.2
Salaries and Wages	11	4.3	10.0	4.5	7.3	5.4	8.3	6.6	7.6	7.0	5.6	3.4	2.9	3.5
Taxes Paid	12	0.8	1.0	0.9	1.5	1.2	1.4	1.2	1.5	1.3	1.1	0.6	0.7	0.5
Interest Paid	13	1.1	0.4	0.4	0.5	0.5	0.8	0.5	0.5	0.6	0.9	0.7	0.5	2.2
Depreciation	14	5.5	0.3	0.2	0.5	0.7	0.8	1.6	1.3	1.6	2.0	0.6	1.5	13.7
Amortization and Depletion	15	0.1	0.5	0.0	0.1	0.0	0.1	0.0	0.2	0.1	0.3	0.2	0.1	0.2
Pensions and Other Deferred Comp.	16	0.2	0.1	0.0	0.1	0.2	0.3	0.2	0.2	0.1	0.2	0.1	0.1	0.3
Employee Benefits	17	0.5	0.4	0.2	0.6	0.5	0.5	0.7	0.9	0.8	0.7	0.4	0.4	0.5
Advertising	18	1.5	0.5	0.2	0.5	0.3	0.4	0.4	0.3	0.3	0.8	1.4	2.5	1.9
Other Expenses	19	5.7	16.9	6.8	8.3	7.4	8.4	6.0	6.7	6.1	6.2	3.9	4.2	5.7
Officers' Compensation	20	0.7	0.8	1.8	2.6	2.6	1.7	1.3	1.2	1.2	0.6	0.4	0.2	0.1
Operating Margin	21	•	•	•	•	2.2	1.5	1.4	1.3	1.6	2.1	2.1	•	•
Operating Margin Before Officers' Comp.	22	•	0.0	0.6	1.4	4.8	3.2	2.7	2.5	2.9	2.7	2.5	•	•

Selected Average Balance Sheet ($ in Thousands)

Net Receivables 23	2918	0	27	122	511	1790	4098	8282	14967	24022	66746	276797	7473955
Inventories 24	1367	0	40	259	838	2403	7099	14971	25199	43551	123391	379733	1035441
Net Property, Plant and Equipment 25	1899	0	7	63	194	907	1658	3853	11893	18670	37364	133182	5187869
Total Assets 26	8201	0	103	712	2102	7043	15602	35031	68925	148485	349913	1292010	16999535
Notes and Loans Payable 27	2934	0	52	214	475	2243	4719	11324	25099	54528	74236	417998	6548713
All Other Liabilities 28	3575	0	32	247	716	2245	5527	13247	20765	47448	179151	593996	7756914
Net Worth 29	1692	0	18	251	911	2555	5357	10460	23061	46509	96526	280017	2693908

Selected Financial Ratios (Times to 1)

Current Ratio 30	1.6	•	2.6	1.9	2.1	1.9	1.7	1.5	1.5	1.5	1.5	1.2	1.6
Quick Ratio 31	1.0	•	1.2	0.9	1.0	0.9	0.7	0.6	0.6	0.6	0.6	0.5	1.3
Net Sales to Working Capital 32	6.3	•	15.4	7.3	7.0	5.6	7.0	8.7	9.3	8.7	11.6	17.2	3.6
Coverage Ratio 33	1.3	7.5	•	•	7.4	4.3	6.1	6.3	5.5	5.2	5.5	1.7	0.1
Total Asset Turnover 34	1.4	•	8.4	3.0	3.1	2.2	2.4	2.4	2.1	1.8	2.5	2.4	0.8
Inventory Turnover 35	7.0	•	18.7	6.5	6.2	4.9	4.3	4.3	4.5	4.8	6.1	7.1	10.1
Receivables Turnover 36	4.2	•	27.2	21.0	12.4	10.3	9.0	10.3	9.9	11.5	12.7	11.8	1.8
Total Liabilities to Net Worth 37	3.8	•	4.6	1.8	1.3	1.8	1.9	2.3	2.0	2.2	2.6	3.6	5.3
Current Assets to Working Capital 38	2.8	•	1.6	2.1	1.9	2.1	2.4	2.9	3.2	3.1	3.2	5.0	2.7
Current Liabilities to Working Capital 39	1.8	•	0.6	1.1	0.9	1.1	1.4	1.9	2.2	2.1	2.2	4.0	1.7
Working Capital to Net Sales 40	0.2	•	0.1	0.1	0.1	0.2	0.1	0.1	0.1	0.1	0.1	0.1	0.3
Inventory to Working Capital 41	0.8	•	0.8	1.1	1.0	1.0	1.3	1.5	1.7	1.6	1.7	2.4	0.3
Total Receipts to Cash Flow 42	20.6	6.4	26.5	19.6	11.7	11.4	14.4	12.8	14.6	11.8	17.2	26.8	33.7
Cost of Goods to Cash Flow 43	16.9	4.5	22.8	15.5	9.3	8.6	11.5	10.0	11.6	9.4	14.8	23.5	26.7
Cash Flow to Total Debt 44	0.1	•	0.4	0.2	0.5	0.3	0.3	0.3	0.2	0.2	0.2	0.1	0.0

Selected Financial Factors (in Percentages)

Debt Ratio 45	79.4	•	82.0	64.7	56.7	63.7	65.7	70.1	66.5	68.7	72.4	78.3	84.2
Return on Total Assets 46	2.1	•	•	•	10.8	7.3	7.6	7.7	6.4	8.1	9.7	2.1	0.2
Return on Equity Before Income Taxes 47	2.6	•	•	•	21.6	15.4	18.6	21.7	15.6	21.0	28.7	4.2	•
Return on Equity After Income Taxes 48	•	•	•	•	19.8	12.9	15.4	20.6	14.6	15.9	22.7	0.1	•
Profit Margin (Before Income Tax) 49	0.4	2.8	•	•	3.0	2.5	2.6	2.7	2.5	3.7	3.2	0.4	•
Profit Margin (After Income Tax) 50	•	2.7	•	•	2.8	2.1	2.2	2.6	2.4	2.8	2.5	0.0	•

Table II

Corporations with Net Income

MOTOR VEHICLE AND MOTOR VEHICLE PARTS AND SUPPLIES

MONEY AMOUNTS AND SIZE OF ASSETS IN THOUSANDS OF DOLLARS

Item Description for Accounting Period 7/11 Through 6/12		Total	Zero Assets	Under 500	500 to 1,000	1,000 to 5,000	5,000 to 10,000	10,000 to 25,000	25,000 to 50,000	50,000 to 100,000	100,000 to 250,000	250,000 to 500,000	500,000 to 2,500,000	2,500,000 and over
Number of Enterprises	1	10421	574	5367	1651	2006	325	283	113	36	38	11	13	3
Revenues ($ in Thousands)														
Net Sales	2	145983880	362114	7683246	3878742	14282818	5581537	11191544	9838146	5331496	10584238	11256113	44050573	21943313
Interest	3	455376	1162	1312	551	5276	3374	4223	1197	641	12547	4132	49962	370999
Rents	4	395119	0	0	0	1332	526	2080	1963	277	8967	715	58366	320894
Royalties	5	50705	0	0	2919	2845	0	0	0	0	136	27	9593	35186
Other Portfolio Income	6	570021	7712	3220	1290	12488	5435	33338	3780	12085	27621	60033	317109	85913
Other Receipts	7	981328	1842	8893	6611	87669	46333	65740	124074	33685	107406	70513	135444	293113
Total Receipts	8	148436429	372830	7696671	3890113	14392428	5637205	11296925	9969160	5378184	10740915	11391533	44621047	23049418
Average Total Receipts	9	14244	650	1434	2356	7175	17345	39918	88223	149394	282656	1035594	3432388	7683139
Operating Costs/Operating Income (%)														
Cost of Operations	10	81.6	49.9	89.8	75.1	78.4	76.0	80.0	78.1	79.0	80.3	86.2	86.8	74.5
Salaries and Wages	11	5.0	12.6	3.2	6.6	5.1	7.6	6.5	7.6	6.8	5.4	3.1	2.8	7.6
Taxes Paid	12	1.0	1.1	0.7	1.5	1.1	1.3	1.2	1.2	1.3	1.1	0.6	0.7	1.1
Interest Paid	13	0.6	0.5	0.1	0.4	0.5	0.5	0.5	0.4	0.5	0.8	0.2	0.5	1.3
Depreciation	14	1.4	0.5	0.1	0.5	0.6	0.6	1.1	1.1	1.4	1.8	0.5	1.5	2.7
Amortization and Depletion	15	0.1	1.0	0.0	0.1	0.0	0.0	0.0	0.1	0.1	0.2	0.1	0.0	0.3
Pensions and Other Deferred Comp.	16	0.2	0.1	0.0	0.2	0.3	0.3	0.2	0.2	0.1	0.2	0.1	0.1	0.7
Employee Benefits	17	0.6	0.5	0.2	0.5	0.4	0.5	0.6	0.9	0.7	0.7	0.3	0.4	1.2
Advertising	18	1.1	0.6	0.1	0.6	0.3	0.3	0.3	0.3	0.3	0.6	1.2	2.4	0.6
Other Expenses	19	5.9	20.5	3.4	9.1	7.1	7.7	5.6	6.6	5.9	5.5	3.7	3.5	10.6
Officers' Compensation	20	0.9	1.4	1.2	3.2	2.7	1.9	1.2	1.3	1.3	0.6	0.4	0.2	0.4
Operating Margin	21	1.7	11.3	1.1	2.2	3.5	3.2	2.7	2.3	2.5	2.9	3.4	0.9	•
Operating Margin Before Officers' Comp.	22	2.6	12.7	2.3	5.3	6.2	5.1	3.9	3.6	3.8	3.4	3.9	1.2	•

Selected Average Balance Sheet ($ in Thousands)														
Net Receivables	23	1583	0	24	134	561	1832	4250	8816	14503	25498	76925	296903	2011655
Inventories	24	1877	0	29	284	851	3028	6655	14585	24868	45543	137932	450048	677741
Net Property, Plant and Equipment	25	739	0	5	73	227	399	1519	3375	9891	17558	30577	133366	1021389
Total Assets	26	6385	0	80	759	2209	7157	15529	35365	68653	148256	350530	1390171	6557914
Notes and Loans Payable	27	1787	0	18	170	452	1141	4528	10145	23674	53464	59992	365732	2080015
All Other Liabilities	28	2473	0	19	236	667	2669	5363	13752	19447	46438	141948	663543	2451931
Net Worth	29	2125	0	43	353	1090	3347	5638	11468	25533	48354	148591	360896	2025968
Selected Financial Ratios (Times to 1)														
Current Ratio	30	1.4	•	3.3	2.0	2.2	2.1	1.8	1.5	1.5	1.6	1.8	1.2	1.0
Quick Ratio	31	0.7	•	2.0	1.0	1.1	1.0	0.7	0.6	0.6	0.6	0.8	0.5	0.8
Net Sales to Working Capital	32	11.8	•	30.6	7.2	7.0	5.2	6.8	8.5	8.4	7.8	9.1	19.7	105.3
Coverage Ratio	33	6.8	32.3	14.1	7.3	9.9	10.4	8.9	9.2	7.7	6.8	25.3	5.8	4.1
Total Asset Turnover	34	2.2	•	17.8	3.1	3.2	2.4	2.5	2.5	2.2	1.9	2.9	2.4	1.1
Inventory Turnover	35	6.1	•	44.5	6.2	6.6	4.3	4.8	4.7	4.7	4.9	6.4	6.5	8.0
Receivables Turnover	36	5.7	•	36.0	20.3	12.1	9.7	9.6	10.2	10.3	11.7	12.9	•	•
Total Liabilities to Net Worth	37	2.0	•	0.9	1.2	1.0	1.1	1.8	2.1	1.7	2.1	1.4	2.9	2.2
Current Assets to Working Capital	38	3.6	•	1.4	2.0	1.8	1.9	2.3	2.8	2.8	2.8	2.3	5.5	46.9
Current Liabilities to Working Capital	39	2.6	•	0.4	1.0	0.8	0.9	1.3	1.8	1.8	1.8	1.3	4.5	45.9
Working Capital to Net Sales	40	0.1	•	0.0	0.1	0.1	0.2	0.1	0.1	0.1	0.1	0.1	0.1	0.0
Inventory to Working Capital	41	1.6	•	0.5	0.9	0.9	0.9	1.2	1.5	1.5	1.4	1.2	2.6	9.8
Total Receipts to Cash Flow	42	12.7	3.1	27.2	11.1	10.5	10.2	13.1	11.7	13.6	11.8	14.1	20.6	7.6
Cost of Goods to Cash Flow	43	10.4	1.5	24.4	8.4	8.2	7.8	10.5	9.1	10.7	9.5	12.2	17.9	5.7
Cash Flow to Total Debt	44	0.3	•	1.4	0.5	0.6	0.4	0.3	0.3	0.3	0.2	0.4	0.2	0.2
Selected Financial Factors (in Percentages)														
Debt Ratio	45	66.7	•	46.0	53.5	50.6	53.2	63.7	67.6	62.8	67.4	57.6	74.0	69.1
Return on Total Assets	46	8.6	•	23.8	8.9	15.3	11.2	10.4	9.9	8.2	9.6	14.0	6.6	6.1
Return on Equity Before Income Taxes	47	22.1	•	40.9	16.5	27.9	21.7	25.4	27.3	19.3	25.2	31.8	20.9	14.9
Return on Equity After Income Taxes	48	18.1	•	37.7	15.8	26.0	19.0	21.9	26.1	18.1	19.6	26.1	16.3	9.9
Profit Margin (Before Income Tax)	49	3.4	14.2	1.2	2.5	4.3	4.2	3.6	3.6	3.3	4.4	4.6	2.2	4.1
Profit Margin (After Income Tax)	50	2.7	14.1	1.1	2.4	4.0	3.7	3.1	3.4	3.1	3.4	3.8	1.7	2.7

Table I

Corporations with and without Net Income

LUMBER AND OTHER CONSTRUCTION MATERIALS

Item Description for Accounting Period 7/11 Through 6/12		Total	Zero Assets	Under 500	500 to 1,000	1,000 to 5,000	5,000 to 10,000	10,000 to 25,000	25,000 to 50,000	50,000 to 100,000	100,000 to 250,000	250,000 to 500,000	500,000 to 2,500,000	2,500,000 and over
		MONEY AMOUNTS AND SIZE OF ASSETS IN THOUSANDS OF DOLLARS												
Number of Enterprises	1	15111	2567	6041	1317	3871	777	378	84	48	16	7	4	0
		Revenues ($ in Thousands)												
Net Sales	2	96587926	1140152	5361473	2251331	25287149	14710552	14357248	7226493	7284984	4792313	5115730	9060501	0
Interest	3	58697	2353	740	916	14187	4783	6630	4434	1045	4693	11756	7161	0
Rents	4	29304	73	11	841	10348	2206	6243	2089	818	2381	3497	796	0
Royalties	5	3201	0	0	0	0	37	0	40	0	20	3104	0	0
Other Portfolio Income	6	183456	43371	2	35258	34163	14897	11484	3167	4938	7275	28387	514	0
Other Receipts	7	663196	107459	17513	15904	163686	85805	95695	30578	52798	24105	52037	17617	0
Total Receipts	8	97525780	1293408	5379739	2304250	25509533	14818280	14477300	7266801	7344583	4830787	5214511	9086589	0
Average Total Receipts	9	6454	504	891	1750	6590	19071	38300	86510	153012	301924	744930	2271647	•
		Operating Costs/Operating Income (%)												
Cost of Operations	10	78.6	82.5	66.1	63.8	78.2	79.1	80.9	81.8	80.7	82.9	82.1	77.5	•
Salaries and Wages	11	7.2	4.7	6.6	10.8	6.9	7.1	7.2	7.0	7.5	5.8	9.2	7.1	•
Taxes Paid	12	1.3	2.0	1.8	3.5	1.5	1.1	1.2	1.0	1.1	0.9	1.3	0.9	•
Interest Paid	13	0.7	1.1	0.4	0.7	0.6	0.6	0.4	0.7	0.5	0.7	1.4	1.3	•
Depreciation	14	1.1	0.4	0.4	1.6	0.7	1.2	1.2	0.9	1.3	1.3	1.7	1.2	•
Amortization and Depletion	15	0.1	0.6	0.0	0.0	0.0	0.1	0.0	0.1	0.1	0.3	0.6	0.5	•
Pensions and Other Deferred Comp.	16	0.2	0.1	0.5	0.2	0.2	0.1	0.2	0.1	0.2	0.2	0.2	0.2	•
Employee Benefits	17	0.6	0.3	0.3	0.6	0.5	0.7	0.9	0.7	0.8	0.7	0.6	0.5	•
Advertising	18	0.3	0.1	1.4	0.9	0.3	0.1	0.2	0.2	0.2	0.2	0.3	0.2	•
Other Expenses	19	7.9	18.4	16.6	15.5	7.4	7.7	6.1	6.8	7.0	7.2	6.6	6.5	•
Officers' Compensation	20	1.6	1.5	3.4	5.3	2.5	1.4	1.3	0.9	0.7	0.5	0.8	0.3	•
Operating Margin	21	0.4	•	2.6	•	1.2	0.6	0.3	•	•	•	•	3.7	•
Operating Margin Before Officers' Comp.	22	2.0	•	6.0	2.3	3.6	2.0	1.6	0.7	0.7	•	•	3.9	•

Selected Average Balance Sheet ($ in Thousands)													
Net Receivables 23	676	0	37	151	735	2257	4540	9020	16100	36309	67809	222310	•
Inventories 24	724	0	50	274	715	2572	4451	12522	18855	31494	59575	238614	•
Net Property, Plant and Equipment 25	407	0	13	132	321	853	2307	5059	10005	27733	109790	251601	•
Total Assets 26	2486	0	143	801	2301	6984	15158	34182	63499	153047	386813	1125216	•
Notes and Loans Payable 27	752	0	51	353	700	1884	3812	15693	17095	50046	132752	275381	•
All Other Liabilities 28	749	0	88	213	658	2482	3306	8816	14704	50632	109195	438704	•
Net Worth 29	985	0	4	234	943	2618	8040	9673	31700	52368	144865	411130	•
Selected Financial Ratios (Times to 1)													
Current Ratio 30	1.9	•	1.3	1.9	2.0	1.7	2.3	1.7	2.2	1.6	2.0	2.0	•
Quick Ratio 31	1.0	•	0.7	0.8	1.1	0.8	1.2	0.7	1.0	0.7	0.9	1.0	•
Net Sales to Working Capital 32	7.8	•	36.9	5.9	7.2	8.1	5.7	8.7	6.3	9.5	9.2	8.6	•
Coverage Ratio 33	3.1	2.8	8.0	0.2	4.7	3.2	3.6	1.5	2.5	1.2	•	4.0	•
Total Asset Turnover 34	2.6	•	6.2	2.1	2.8	2.7	2.5	2.5	2.4	2.0	1.9	2.0	•
Inventory Turnover 35	6.9	•	11.8	4.0	7.1	5.8	6.9	5.6	6.5	7.9	10.1	7.4	•
Receivables Turnover 36	9.7	•	26.5	9.5	8.8	9.3	8.7	9.4	10.4	9.7	9.9	10.0	•
Total Liabilities to Net Worth 37	1.5	•	31.8	2.4	1.4	1.7	0.9	2.5	1.0	1.9	1.7	1.7	•
Current Assets to Working Capital 38	2.1	•	4.9	2.1	2.0	2.4	1.8	2.5	1.9	2.7	2.0	2.0	•
Current Liabilities to Working Capital 39	1.1	•	3.9	1.1	1.0	1.4	0.8	1.5	0.9	1.7	1.0	1.0	•
Working Capital to Net Sales 40	0.1	•	0.0	0.2	0.1	0.1	0.2	0.1	0.2	0.1	0.1	0.1	•
Inventory to Working Capital 41	0.9	•	1.9	0.9	0.8	1.0	0.7	1.2	0.8	1.2	0.9	0.9	•
Total Receipts to Cash Flow 42	14.5	7.6	6.3	11.3	13.8	14.5	19.5	20.4	18.3	19.3	79.8	11.5	•
Cost of Goods to Cash Flow 43	11.4	6.3	4.1	7.2	10.8	11.4	15.8	16.7	14.8	16.0	65.6	8.9	•
Cash Flow to Total Debt 44	0.3	•	1.0	0.3	0.3	0.3	0.3	0.2	0.3	0.2	0.0	0.3	•
Selected Financial Factors (in Percentages)													
Debt Ratio 45	60.4	•	96.9	70.8	59.0	62.5	47.0	71.7	50.1	65.8	62.5	63.5	•
Return on Total Assets 46	5.4	•	20.8	0.3	7.4	5.4	3.9	2.7	2.9	1.6	•	10.8	•
Return on Equity Before Income Taxes 47	9.1	•	596.7	•	14.2	9.9	5.4	3.3	3.5	0.8	•	22.1	•
Return on Equity After Income Taxes 48	7.7	•	595.2	•	13.8	9.0	4.9	2.5	3.1	0.2	•	13.9	•
Profit Margin (Before Income Tax) 49	1.4	1.9	2.9	•	2.1	1.4	1.1	0.4	0.7	0.1	•	4.0	•
Profit Margin (After Income Tax) 50	1.2	1.8	2.9	•	2.0	1.2	1.0	0.3	0.6	0.0	•	2.5	•

Table II

Corporations with Net Income

LUMBER AND OTHER CONSTRUCTION MATERIALS

MONEY AMOUNTS AND SIZE OF ASSETS IN THOUSANDS OF DOLLARS

Item Description for Accounting Period 7/11 Through 6/12		Total	Zero Assets	Under 500	500 to 1,000	1,000 to 5,000	5,000 to 10,000	10,000 to 25,000	25,000 to 50,000	50,000 to 100,000	100,000 to 250,000	250,000 to 500,000	500,000 to 2,500,000	2,500,000 and over
Number of Enterprises	1	10563	2009	4498	•	2552	521	254	53	30	6	•	0	0
Revenues ($ in Thousands)														
Net Sales	2	66930306	355921	4602788	•	18371496	11301191	10394065	5528600	5072083	2090090	•	0	0
Interest	3	24175	1580	4	•	9265	2065	3611	1364	288	404	•	0	0
Rents	4	13961	73	11	•	3149	1993	5957	577	782	0	•	0	0
Royalties	5	7	0	0	•	0	7	0	0	0	0	•	0	0
Other Portfolio Income	6	120835	43371	2	•	20000	11166	6584	2463	3492	222	•	0	0
Other Receipts	7	447586	59740	13550	•	123678	42171	95331	16379	39542	2172	•	0	0
Total Receipts	8	67536870	460685	4616355	•	18527588	11358593	10505548	5549383	5116187	2092888	•	0	0
Average Total Receipts	9	6394	229	1026	•	7260	21802	41360	104705	170540	348815	•	•	•
Operating Costs/Operating Income (%)														
Cost of Operations	10	78.0	49.9	65.7	•	77.5	80.7	81.5	82.6	81.0	80.2	•	•	•
Salaries and Wages	11	6.9	10.0	6.5	•	6.7	6.8	6.5	6.2	6.9	5.8	•	•	•
Taxes Paid	12	1.2	1.9	1.8	•	1.3	0.9	1.0	0.9	1.0	0.9	•	•	•
Interest Paid	13	0.5	2.6	0.3	•	0.4	0.6	0.3	0.5	0.4	0.3	•	•	•
Depreciation	14	0.7	0.7	0.4	•	0.5	0.7	0.9	0.7	1.0	0.8	•	•	•
Amortization and Depletion	15	0.1	1.8	0.0	•	0.0	0.1	0.0	0.1	0.1	0.4	•	•	•
Pensions and Other Deferred Comp.	16	0.2	0.2	0.3	•	0.2	0.1	0.2	0.1	0.2	0.3	•	•	•
Employee Benefits	17	0.5	0.6	0.2	•	0.4	0.5	0.8	0.6	0.8	0.6	•	•	•
Advertising	18	0.3	0.2	1.4	•	0.3	0.1	0.2	0.2	0.1	0.2	•	•	•
Other Expenses	19	7.1	20.0	16.4	•	6.7	5.7	5.7	5.8	6.1	6.8	•	•	•
Officers' Compensation	20	1.6	4.6	2.5	•	2.4	1.5	1.3	1.0	0.8	0.6	•	•	•
Operating Margin	21	2.8	7.7	4.3	•	3.5	2.3	1.5	1.5	1.5	3.0	•	•	•
Operating Margin Before Officers' Comp.	22	4.4	12.3	6.9	•	5.9	3.8	2.8	2.4	2.3	3.6	•	•	•

Selected Average Balance Sheet ($ in Thousands)

Net Receivables 23	664	0	38	•	785	2496	4716	10392	16753	43852	•	•	•
Inventories 24	668	0	43	•	661	2589	4688	14167	21766	44671	•	•	•
Net Property, Plant and Equipment 25	245	0	15	•	221	595	1843	4069	8127	9556	•	•	•
Total Assets 26	2182	0	147	•	2310	7059	14932	35043	63003	140128	•	•	•
Notes and Loans Payable 27	591	0	52	•	565	2109	3157	14659	17371	20554	•	•	•
All Other Liabilities 28	629	0	96	•	671	1944	3354	9927	14682	54840	•	•	•
Net Worth 29	963	0	-1	•	1074	3006	8422	10456	30950	64734	•	•	•

Selected Financial Ratios (Times to 1)

Current Ratio 30	2.0	•	1.3	•	2.2	2.0	2.4	1.7	2.1	1.7	•	•	•
Quick Ratio 31	1.1	•	0.7	•	1.2	1.0	1.3	0.7	1.0	0.8	•	•	•
Net Sales to Working Capital 32	7.4	•	33.9	•	6.9	7.3	5.8	9.7	6.8	8.1	•	•	•
Coverage Ratio 33	8.2	15.2	15.7	•	12.1	5.8	8.2	4.6	6.3	10.3	•	•	•
Total Asset Turnover 34	2.9	•	7.0	•	3.1	3.1	2.7	3.0	2.7	2.5	•	•	•
Inventory Turnover 35	7.4	•	15.5	•	8.4	6.8	7.1	6.1	6.3	6.3	•	•	•
Receivables Turnover 36	10.3	•	36.1	•	9.8	9.8	9.2	10.4	•	7.9	•	•	•
Total Liabilities to Net Worth 37	1.3	•	•	•	1.2	1.3	0.8	2.4	1.0	1.2	•	•	•
Current Assets to Working Capital 38	2.0	•	4.2	•	1.8	2.0	1.7	2.5	1.9	2.4	•	•	•
Current Liabilities to Working Capital 39	1.0	•	3.2	•	0.8	1.0	0.7	1.5	0.9	1.4	•	•	•
Working Capital to Net Sales 40	0.1	•	0.0	•	0.1	0.1	0.2	0.1	0.1	0.1	•	•	•
Inventory to Working Capital 41	0.8	•	1.7	•	0.7	0.8	0.6	1.3	0.9	1.1	•	•	•
Total Receipts to Cash Flow 42	11.3	1.9	5.7	•	10.9	14.3	15.3	17.8	15.6	12.9	•	•	•
Cost of Goods to Cash Flow 43	8.8	0.9	3.7	•	8.4	11.6	12.5	14.7	12.7	10.4	•	•	•
Cash Flow to Total Debt 44	0.5	•	1.2	•	0.5	0.4	0.4	0.2	0.3	0.4	•	•	•

Selected Financial Factors (in Percentages)

Debt Ratio 45	55.9	•	100.6	•	53.5	57.4	43.6	70.2	50.9	53.8	•	•	•
Return on Total Assets 46	12.3	•	34.4	•	14.8	10.4	7.9	7.1	7.5	8.6	•	•	•
Return on Equity Before Income Taxes 47	24.5	•	•	•	29.2	20.2	12.3	18.6	12.8	16.9	•	•	•
Return on Equity After Income Taxes 48	22.4	•	•	•	28.7	19.0	11.6	17.4	12.1	15.6	•	•	•
Profit Margin (Before Income Tax) 49	3.7	37.2	4.6	•	4.4	2.8	2.5	1.9	2.3	3.1	•	•	•
Profit Margin (After Income Tax) 50	3.4	36.7	4.6	•	4.3	2.6	2.4	1.7	2.2	2.9	•	•	•

PROFESSIONAL AND COMMERCIAL EQUIPMENT AND SUPPLIES

MONEY AMOUNTS AND SIZE OF ASSETS IN THOUSANDS OF DOLLARS

Item Description for Accounting Period 7/11 Through 6/12		Total	Zero Assets	Under 500	500 to 1,000	1,000 to 5,000	5,000 to 10,000	10,000 to 25,000	25,000 to 50,000	50,000 to 100,000	100,000 to 250,000	250,000 to 500,000	500,000 to 2,500,000	2,500,000 and over
Number of Enterprises	1	35514	3724	22857	3603	3921	635	420	143	83	60	30	28	10
Revenues ($ in Thousands)														
Net Sales	2	269972795	15191141	11175559	8045699	27183099	11719343	16546958	11370381	10472246	19294800	13644366	46463972	78865232
Interest	3	501050	239	1283	1354	4571	5294	2910	7568	5923	19473	23521	73550	355364
Rents	4	339929	0	0	0	7790	940	881	608	14656	3407	40205	39713	231729
Royalties	5	399507	371	37	0	399	7083	169829	238	3846	10058	101974	53895	51778
Other Portfolio Income	6	703478	7874	5817	20664	32877	34849	26005	16299	105558	31639	48182	63036	310678
Other Receipts	7	2047306	8077	108137	91678	119435	167236	64223	98404	74444	88527	290750	689942	246450
Total Receipts	8	273964065	15207702	11290833	8159395	27348171	11934745	16810806	11493498	10676673	19447904	14148998	47384108	80061231
Average Total Receipts	9	7714	4084	494	2265	6975	18795	40026	80374	128635	324132	471633	1692290	8006123
Operating Costs/Operating Income (%)														
Cost of Operations	10	73.4	92.8	57.0	58.8	67.2	69.5	73.6	73.6	73.5	78.4	70.8	80.0	71.5
Salaries and Wages	11	11.0	3.1	10.1	11.5	11.0	10.6	9.2	10.5	10.1	6.9	11.7	7.9	16.0
Taxes Paid	12	1.1	0.5	1.9	2.2	1.6	1.3	1.2	1.2	1.1	1.0	1.2	0.8	0.9
Interest Paid	13	0.8	0.3	0.3	0.3	0.5	0.5	0.4	0.5	0.6	0.9	0.7	0.9	1.2
Depreciation	14	1.9	0.3	0.7	0.9	0.9	0.8	1.0	1.0	2.3	1.3	1.5	1.3	3.7
Amortization and Depletion	15	0.4	0.0	0.0	0.1	0.1	0.2	0.1	0.3	0.5	0.5	0.7	0.8	0.4
Pensions and Other Deferred Comp.	16	0.2	0.0	0.4	0.8	0.3	0.3	0.3	0.3	0.2	0.2	0.3	0.2	0.2
Employee Benefits	17	0.8	0.3	0.6	1.0	1.3	0.9	0.7	0.9	1.0	0.9	1.3	1.0	0.4
Advertising	18	0.9	0.2	0.8	1.6	0.7	1.0	0.7	0.9	0.6	0.8	1.5	1.1	0.9
Other Expenses	19	6.4	3.2	15.6	16.0	9.9	11.3	9.4	8.3	9.4	7.9	10.6	5.9	0.6
Officers' Compensation	20	1.5	0.3	9.1	4.9	3.6	3.6	1.9	1.1	1.0	0.7	0.8	0.3	0.2
Operating Margin	21	1.7	•	3.2	1.9	2.9	0.0	1.4	1.4	•	0.7	•	•	3.9
Operating Margin Before Officers' Comp.	22	3.2	•	12.3	6.9	6.6	3.6	3.3	2.5	0.7	1.3	•	0.2	4.2

Selected Average Balance Sheet ($ in Thousands)													
Net Receivables 23	1047	0	21	235	679	2264	5323	12732	17957	49422	94367	232862	1389824
Inventories 24	585	0	30	147	592	1429	4199	7251	15272	30091	52184	140775	493586
Net Property, Plant and Equipment 25	355	0	11	62	279	456	1329	2740	6167	12150	27518	64051	594175
Total Assets 26	4762	0	99	710	2258	6932	15712	35670	68430	159904	359200	1109134	8224744
Notes and Loans Payable 27	1325	0	71	249	929	1985	3693	7132	15855	37110	59229	287504	2368471
All Other Liabilities 28	1769	0	41	382	959	3137	6997	15897	23598	68413	118080	370688	2957434
Net Worth 29	1668	0	-13	79	370	1811	5022	12641	28977	54381	181891	450942	2898839

Selected Financial Ratios (Times to 1)													
Current Ratio 30	1.4	•	1.6	1.4	1.7	1.6	1.6	1.7	1.6	1.6	1.6	1.7	1.2
Quick Ratio 31	0.9	•	0.9	0.9	1.0	1.0	1.0	1.1	0.9	0.9	1.0	0.9	0.8
Net Sales to Working Capital 32	9.8	•	17.1	13.8	9.1	9.5	8.2	7.2	8.0	8.5	5.6	6.5	14.6
Coverage Ratio 33	5.9	•	14.7	11.6	7.8	4.9	8.6	6.4	4.0	2.7	4.9	3.1	7.3
Total Asset Turnover 34	1.6	•	4.9	3.1	3.1	2.7	2.5	2.2	1.8	2.0	1.3	1.5	1.0
Inventory Turnover 35	9.5	•	9.2	8.9	7.9	9.0	6.9	8.1	6.1	8.4	6.2	9.4	11.4
Receivables Turnover 36	7.3	•	19.8	11.0	10.4	8.7	7.5	6.7	6.3	6.6	5.2	8.0	5.3
Total Liabilities to Net Worth 37	1.9	•	•	8.0	5.1	2.8	2.1	1.8	1.4	1.9	1.0	1.5	1.8
Current Assets to Working Capital 38	3.2	•	2.6	3.6	2.3	2.8	2.5	2.5	2.7	2.8	2.6	2.4	6.1
Current Liabilities to Working Capital 39	2.2	•	1.6	2.6	1.3	1.8	1.5	1.5	1.7	1.8	1.6	1.4	5.1
Working Capital to Net Sales 40	0.1	•	0.1	0.1	0.1	0.1	0.1	0.1	0.1	0.1	0.2	0.2	0.1
Inventory to Working Capital 41	0.8	•	1.1	1.0	0.8	0.8	0.9	0.7	0.9	0.8	0.7	0.6	0.9
Total Receipts to Cash Flow 42	12.7	52.2	5.9	6.4	9.0	8.9	9.3	10.7	11.1	13.1	8.8	15.4	21.9
Cost of Goods to Cash Flow 43	9.3	48.5	3.4	3.7	6.1	6.2	6.8	7.9	8.1	10.3	6.2	12.3	15.6
Cash Flow to Total Debt 44	0.2	•	0.7	0.6	0.4	0.4	0.4	0.3	0.3	0.2	0.3	0.2	0.1

Selected Financial Factors (in Percentages)													
Debt Ratio 45	65.0	•	112.7	88.9	83.6	73.9	68.0	64.6	57.7	66.0	49.4	59.3	64.8
Return on Total Assets 46	7.3	•	22.5	11.6	12.5	6.3	8.5	6.6	4.2	4.7	4.2	4.1	8.4
Return on Equity Before Income Taxes 47	17.2	•	•	94.8	66.6	19.1	23.5	15.7	7.4	8.8	6.6	6.8	20.4
Return on Equity After Income Taxes 48	12.2	•	•	86.5	62.8	15.4	20.4	12.6	5.4	4.8	4.1	4.0	13.5
Profit Margin (Before Income Tax) 49	3.8	•	4.3	3.4	3.6	1.9	3.0	2.5	1.7	1.5	2.7	1.9	7.5
Profit Margin (After Income Tax) 50	2.7	•	4.2	3.1	3.4	1.5	2.6	2.0	1.2	0.8	1.6	1.1	5.0

PROFESSIONAL AND COMMERCIAL EQUIPMENT AND SUPPLIES

MONEY AMOUNTS AND SIZE OF ASSETS IN THOUSANDS OF DOLLARS

Item Description for Accounting Period 7/11 Through 6/12		Total	Zero Assets	Under 500	500 to 1,000	1,000 to 5,000	5,000 to 10,000	10,000 to 25,000	25,000 to 50,000	50,000 to 100,000	100,000 to 250,000	250,000 to 500,000	500,000 to 2,500,000	2,500,000 and over
Number of Enterprises	1	22988	1697	15156	2162	2934	455	332	99	63	40	21	21	7
Revenues ($ in Thousands)														
Net Sales	2	208336381	13969467	9872300	4649352	23417485	8310513	14188033	8391409	9142269	14182012	11194012	39126132	51893397
Interest	3	442084	126	1007	895	3598	4596	1772	5460	4602	14571	15425	66471	323559
Rents	4	230005	0	0	0	5540	940	0	163	14523	3246	39949	4480	161164
Royalties	5	365026	371	23	0	399	7083	169774	0	3846	10058	92995	34829	45649
Other Portfolio Income	6	529421	7786	5712	20528	23661	114	25872	15967	84717	17033	24986	31852	271191
Other Receipts	7	1612884	9867	101783	35044	79466	151603	55489	42710	52462	53974	254333	656237	119920
Total Receipts	8	211515801	13987617	9980825	4705819	23530149	8474849	14440940	8455709	9302419	14280894	11621700	39920001	52814880
Average Total Receipts	9	9201	8243	659	2177	8020	18626	43497	85411	147657	357022	553414	1900952	7544983
Operating Costs/Operating Income (%)														
Cost of Operations	10	73.0	95.0	55.6	52.7	67.8	67.9	72.8	75.8	77.1	78.0	71.1	82.3	66.2
Salaries and Wages	11	11.6	1.8	9.5	10.8	10.2	10.5	9.0	8.2	8.6	6.7	11.4	6.8	22.2
Taxes Paid	12	1.1	0.2	1.9	2.1	1.4	1.4	1.2	1.0	1.0	1.0	1.4	0.7	1.1
Interest Paid	13	0.7	0.1	0.2	0.1	0.4	0.4	0.4	0.4	0.5	0.6	0.5	0.6	1.3
Depreciation	14	1.5	0.1	0.7	0.6	0.9	0.8	0.9	0.8	1.0	1.3	1.5	0.7	3.8
Amortization and Depletion	15	0.3	0.0	0.0	0.1	0.0	0.2	0.1	0.2	0.3	0.4	0.6	0.4	0.4
Pensions and Other Deferred Comp.	16	0.2	0.0	0.5	0.2	0.3	0.4	0.3	0.2	0.2	0.2	0.3	0.2	0.2
Employee Benefits	17	0.7	0.2	0.6	0.8	1.2	0.9	0.7	0.6	0.8	0.9	1.0	0.5	0.5
Advertising	18	0.9	0.2	0.6	2.3	0.4	0.7	0.7	0.8	0.6	1.0	1.6	1.2	0.9
Other Expenses	19	4.8	1.6	14.1	17.5	8.8	9.2	9.2	6.7	7.5	6.3	9.4	5.6	•
Officers' Compensation	20	1.5	0.1	9.5	4.8	3.4	4.1	1.9	1.2	1.0	0.6	0.6	0.3	0.3
Operating Margin	21	3.7	0.8	6.7	8.0	5.0	3.6	2.7	4.0	1.5	3.2	0.5	0.7	6.7
Operating Margin Before Officers' Comp.	22	5.3	0.8	16.2	12.7	8.5	7.7	4.6	5.2	2.4	3.7	1.1	1.0	7.0

Selected Average Balance Sheet ($ in Thousands)													
Net Receivables 23	1225	0	26	214	760	2684	5520	12240	20542	51766	108589	247713	1425162
Inventories 24	674	0	33	184	567	1298	4352	7853	15507	33406	60021	157546	463026
Net Property, Plant and Equipment 25	401	0	14	34	297	484	1312	2535	4856	13148	24724	44145	694955
Total Assets 26	5561	0	124	736	2362	7212	15819	36141	68364	159649	362455	1037315	9321836
Notes and Loans Payable 27	1408	0	54	112	521	1649	3778	6309	14360	34787	57367	236234	2669821
All Other Liabilities 28	2113	0	35	299	915	2749	6282	15479	24365	68648	120385	408484	3496145
Net Worth 29	2040	0	35	325	926	2814	5759	14352	29638	56214	184703	392597	3155870
Selected Financial Ratios (Times to 1)													
Current Ratio 30	1.5	•	2.3	2.2	2.0	1.7	1.8	1.7	1.6	1.6	1.7	1.6	1.2
Quick Ratio 31	0.9	•	1.4	1.4	1.2	1.1	1.1	1.1	1.0	0.9	1.0	0.9	0.8
Net Sales to Working Capital 32	9.6	•	11.9	6.2	8.5	8.3	7.4	7.5	7.8	8.7	5.6	8.1	14.2
Coverage Ratio 33	10.2	8.9	33.3	67.6	15.1	13.7	12.6	14.3	7.7	7.8	10.0	5.7	9.7
Total Asset Turnover 34	1.6	•	5.3	2.9	3.4	2.5	2.7	2.3	2.1	2.2	1.5	1.8	0.8
Inventory Turnover 35	9.8	•	11.1	6.2	9.5	9.5	7.1	8.2	7.2	8.3	6.3	9.7	10.6
Receivables Turnover 36	7.1	•	26.7	10.8	11.7	7.4	8.0	6.8	7.1	6.7	5.2	8.2	4.4
Total Liabilities to Net Worth 37	1.7	•	2.6	1.3	1.6	1.6	1.7	1.5	1.3	1.8	1.0	1.6	2.0
Current Assets to Working Capital 38	3.1	•	1.8	1.8	2.0	2.5	2.2	2.4	2.6	2.7	2.4	2.6	6.9
Current Liabilities to Working Capital 39	2.1	•	0.8	0.8	1.0	1.5	1.2	1.4	1.6	1.7	1.4	1.6	5.9
Working Capital to Net Sales 40	0.1	•	0.1	0.2	0.1	0.1	0.1	0.1	0.1	0.1	0.2	0.1	0.1
Inventory to Working Capital 41	0.7	•	0.7	0.6	0.7	0.6	0.8	0.7	0.8	0.8	0.6	0.7	0.9
Total Receipts to Cash Flow 42	11.8	46.1	5.2	4.6	8.2	7.6	8.3	9.7	11.5	10.9	8.4	13.3	32.5
Cost of Goods to Cash Flow 43	8.6	43.7	2.9	2.4	5.5	5.2	6.0	7.4	8.9	8.5	5.9	10.9	21.5
Cash Flow to Total Debt 44	0.2	•	1.4	1.1	0.7	0.5	0.5	0.4	0.3	0.3	0.4	0.2	0.0
Selected Financial Factors (in Percentages)													
Debt Ratio 45	63.3	•	71.9	55.9	60.8	61.0	63.6	60.3	56.6	64.8	49.0	62.2	66.1
Return on Total Assets 46	10.9	•	42.3	27.2	20.0	15.2	13.1	12.1	7.9	9.9	7.2	6.1	10.3
Return on Equity Before Income Taxes 47	26.9	•	146.0	60.7	47.7	36.2	33.2	28.4	15.9	24.6	12.7	13.3	27.3
Return on Equity After Income Taxes 48	20.5	•	144.6	57.4	45.7	32.8	29.8	24.5	13.3	18.7	9.1	9.1	18.2
Profit Margin (Before Income Tax) 49	6.0	0.9	7.8	9.2	5.5	5.6	4.5	4.8	3.2	3.9	4.4	2.8	11.6
Profit Margin (After Income Tax) 50	4.6	0.7	7.7	8.7	5.3	5.1	4.0	4.2	2.7	3.0	3.2	1.9	7.7

Table I

Corporations with and without Net Income

METAL AND MINERAL (EXCEPT PETROLEUM)

MONEY AMOUNTS AND SIZE OF ASSETS IN THOUSANDS OF DOLLARS

Item Description for Accounting Period 7/11 Through 6/12		Total	Zero Assets	Under 500	500 to 1,000	1,000 to 5,000	5,000 to 10,000	10,000 to 25,000	25,000 to 50,000	50,000 to 100,000	100,000 to 250,000	250,000 to 500,000	500,000 to 2,500,000	2,500,000 and over
Number of Enterprises	1	4956	64	2351	660	812	503	300	110	62	58	20	17	0
Revenues ($ in Thousands)														
Net Sales	2	131068460	1284565	2025866	2459409	5322292	11870900	13269852	10113626	12080182	17623116	16620383	38398270	0
Interest	3	152543	1766	5	668	2243	3277	3083	3721	2618	16636	21184	97343	0
Rents	4	38467	2734	0	2047	9	856	749	1661	256	2573	10441	17141	0
Royalties	5	85	0	0	0	0	0	85	0	0	0	0	0	0
Other Portfolio Income	6	187702	16538	0	41	10802	600	3221	5439	2532	93558	9118	45855	0
Other Receipts	7	1182443	29051	447	2765	9078	51454	26630	17901	33600	503586	117025	390903	0
Total Receipts	8	132629700	1334654	2026318	2464930	5344424	11927087	13303620	10142348	12119188	18239469	16778151	38949512	0
Average Total Receipts	9	26761	20854	862	3735	6582	23712	44345	92203	195471	314474	838908	2291148	•
Operating Costs/Operating Income (%)														
Cost of Operations	10	88.0	91.7	72.2	81.6	80.2	92.1	88.2	88.0	88.9	88.6	92.5	86.5	•
Salaries and Wages	11	3.1	3.5	4.4	2.5	6.2	1.3	3.1	2.8	2.5	2.8	1.6	4.1	•
Taxes Paid	12	0.6	0.5	1.4	0.8	0.9	0.4	0.6	0.8	0.5	0.6	0.4	0.6	•
Interest Paid	13	0.8	0.2	0.2	0.1	0.3	0.2	0.3	0.4	0.3	0.4	1.0	1.6	•
Depreciation	14	0.7	0.4	0.2	0.6	0.6	0.2	0.6	0.9	0.6	0.6	0.4	1.2	•
Amortization and Depletion	15	0.2	0.1	0.0	0.0	0.0	0.0	0.0	0.0	0.1	0.1	0.2	0.5	•
Pensions and Other Deferred Comp.	16	0.2	0.1	0.2	0.1	0.4	0.1	0.1	0.2	0.1	0.2	0.1	0.3	•
Employee Benefits	17	0.5	0.2	0.2	0.4	0.8	0.2	0.3	0.4	0.3	0.4	0.3	0.9	•
Advertising	18	0.0	0.0	0.1	0.1	0.1	0.0	0.1	0.0	0.0	0.1	0.0	0.0	•
Other Expenses	19	3.4	4.8	3.9	4.8	7.0	2.2	3.3	2.8	2.7	4.1	3.1	3.4	•
Officers' Compensation	20	0.9	0.3	14.3	3.6	3.2	1.1	1.0	1.0	0.6	0.4	0.4	0.3	•
Operating Margin	21	1.5	•	3.0	5.3	0.4	2.3	2.2	2.7	3.3	1.6	0.1	0.7	•
Operating Margin Before Officers' Comp.	22	2.5	•	17.3	8.9	3.6	3.3	3.2	3.7	3.9	2.0	0.4	1.0	•

Selected Average Balance Sheet ($ in Thousands)													
Net Receivables 23	2790	0	45	251	610	1614	4800	9905	23355	36162	88742	258853	•
Inventories 24	3429	0	25	143	732	2059	5420	13517	29789	55492	94118	302958	•
Net Property, Plant and Equipment 25	1365	0	35	92	128	214	1283	4128	5198	12282	30122	231263	•
Total Assets 26	11399	0	168	715	2492	6851	15790	35469	70210	152645	352438	1250654	•
Notes and Loans Payable 27	3493	0	39	93	326	961	4312	10053	19226	38816	117455	483529	•
All Other Liabilities 28	3926	0	15	219	1099	2910	4636	10714	26644	49449	136953	417080	•
Net Worth 29	3980	0	115	403	1067	2980	6842	14702	24340	64380	98030	350046	•

Selected Financial Ratios (Times to 1)													
Current Ratio 30	1.8	•	2.9	2.6	1.9	1.8	1.8	2.0	1.8	1.9	1.6	1.7	•
Quick Ratio 31	0.8	•	2.2	2.0	1.1	0.9	0.9	0.8	0.8	0.7	0.8	0.8	•
Net Sales to Working Capital 32	7.4	•	11.9	10.1	6.2	9.9	7.6	6.5	7.2	5.4	8.7	7.6	•
Coverage Ratio 33	4.5	12.2	14.1	48.1	3.6	16.2	8.7	8.5	11.3	14.6	2.1	2.4	•
Total Asset Turnover 34	2.3	•	5.1	5.2	2.6	3.4	2.8	2.6	2.8	2.0	2.4	1.8	•
Inventory Turnover 35	6.8	•	24.7	21.3	7.2	10.6	7.2	6.0	5.8	4.9	8.2	6.4	•
Receivables Turnover 36	10.4	•	15.1	16.4	9.0	18.8	10.3	9.5	8.7	8.6	11.3	9.9	•
Total Liabilities to Net Worth 37	1.9	•	0.5	0.8	1.3	1.3	1.3	1.4	1.9	1.4	2.6	2.6	•
Current Assets to Working Capital 38	2.2	•	1.5	1.6	2.1	2.3	2.2	2.0	2.2	2.1	2.6	2.3	•
Current Liabilities to Working Capital 39	1.2	•	0.5	0.6	1.1	1.3	1.2	1.0	1.2	1.1	1.6	1.3	•
Working Capital to Net Sales 40	0.1	•	0.1	0.1	0.2	0.1	0.1	0.2	0.1	0.2	0.1	0.1	•
Inventory to Working Capital 41	1.1	•	0.3	0.4	0.7	1.1	1.0	1.1	1.1	1.1	1.2	1.2	•
Total Receipts to Cash Flow 42	19.3	19.1	15.5	10.8	17.8	22.6	20.2	20.4	17.8	11.9	30.0	22.7	•
Cost of Goods to Cash Flow 43	17.0	17.6	11.2	8.8	14.3	20.9	17.8	18.0	15.8	10.5	27.8	19.7	•
Cash Flow to Total Debt 44	0.2	•	1.0	1.1	0.3	0.3	0.2	0.2	0.2	0.3	0.1	0.1	•

Selected Financial Factors (in Percentages)													
Debt Ratio 45	65.1	•	31.9	43.7	57.2	56.5	56.7	58.5	65.3	57.8	72.2	72.0	•
Return on Total Assets 46	8.1	•	16.8	29.5	2.8	10.0	7.9	8.8	10.9	11.0	4.7	6.8	•
Return on Equity Before Income Taxes 47	18.1	•	22.9	51.2	4.8	21.6	16.1	18.8	28.8	24.2	8.7	14.0	•
Return on Equity After Income Taxes 48	14.6	•	22.5	50.6	4.0	20.4	14.3	16.8	23.5	19.5	5.4	9.4	•
Profit Margin (Before Income Tax) 49	2.7	2.2	3.0	5.5	0.8	2.7	2.5	3.0	3.6	5.1	1.0	2.2	•
Profit Margin (After Income Tax) 50	2.2	1.8	3.0	5.5	0.6	2.6	2.2	2.7	2.9	4.1	0.6	1.5	•

Table II

Corporations with Net Income

METAL AND MINERAL (EXCEPT PETROLEUM)

MONEY AMOUNTS AND SIZE OF ASSETS IN THOUSANDS OF DOLLARS

Item Description for Accounting Period 7/11 Through 6/12		Total	Zero Assets	Under 500	500 to 1,000	1,000 to 5,000	5,000 to 10,000	10,000 to 25,000	25,000 to 50,000	50,000 to 100,000	100,000 to 250,000	250,000 to 500,000	500,000 to 2,500,000	2,500,000 and over
Number of Enterprises	1	4248	7	1974	•	645	494	241	94	54	53	15	•	0
Revenues ($ in Thousands)														
Net Sales	2	112515649	1219747	1330107	•	4531892	11783070	11639234	8856494	10226911	16567624	15107901	•	0
Interest	3	51362	1765	0	•	1565	3277	2587	2287	1583	16636	4678	•	0
Rents	4	35397	2734	0	•	9	856	678	1382	256	2573	10403	•	0
Royalties	5	0	0	0	•	0	0	0	0	0	0	0	•	0
Other Portfolio Income	6	170676	3639	0	•	8048	600	2363	5412	2357	93452	8913	•	0
Other Receipts	7	1121572	29051	447	•	8499	51399	23436	16354	32178	506765	106990	•	0
Total Receipts	8	113894656	1256936	1330554	•	4550013	11839202	11668298	8881929	10263285	17187050	15238885	•	0
Average Total Receipts	9	26811	179562	674	•	7054	23966	48416	94489	190061	324284	1015926	•	•
Operating Costs/Operating Income (%)														
Cost of Operations	10	87.2	93.4	58.8	•	79.8	92.2	87.5	87.3	88.2	88.0	92.5	•	•
Salaries and Wages	11	3.1	2.8	6.6	•	5.3	1.3	3.2	3.0	2.4	3.0	1.6	•	•
Taxes Paid	12	0.6	0.4	2.0	•	1.0	0.4	0.6	0.6	0.5	0.6	0.4	•	•
Interest Paid	13	0.5	0.2	0.4	•	0.3	0.2	0.3	0.4	0.3	0.4	0.3	•	•
Depreciation	14	0.7	0.4	0.3	•	0.4	0.1	0.4	0.9	0.6	0.7	0.4	•	•
Amortization and Depletion	15	0.2	0.0	0.0	•	0.0	0.0	0.0	0.0	0.0	0.1	0.1	•	•
Pensions and Other Deferred Comp.	16	0.2	0.1	0.3	•	0.5	0.1	0.1	0.2	0.2	0.2	0.2	•	•
Employee Benefits	17	0.5	0.2	0.2	•	1.0	0.2	0.3	0.5	0.3	0.4	0.3	•	•
Advertising	18	0.1	0.1	0.1	•	0.1	0.0	0.1	0.0	0.0	0.1	0.0	•	•
Other Expenses	19	3.7	1.7	4.8	•	6.3	2.2	3.2	2.8	2.7	4.3	2.8	•	•
Officers' Compensation	20	1.0	0.3	21.6	•	3.7	1.1	0.9	1.0	0.7	0.5	0.4	•	•
Operating Margin	21	2.3	0.5	4.9	•	1.6	2.3	3.3	3.3	4.1	1.8	1.0	•	•
Operating Margin Before Officers' Comp.	22	3.4	0.8	26.5	•	5.3	3.3	4.2	4.4	4.8	2.2	1.4	•	•

Selected Average Balance Sheet ($ in Thousands)													
Net Receivables **23**	2764	0	50	•	623	1629	5089	10317	22762	35240	87131	•	•
Inventories **24**	3089	0	21	•	748	2055	5383	13577	29826	50164	81990	•	•
Net Property, Plant and Equipment **25**	1143	0	38	•	105	217	1025	4153	5476	13309	39449	•	•
Total Assets **26**	10835	0	173	•	2627	6869	15815	35991	71261	153663	349745	•	•
Notes and Loans Payable **27**	2706	0	46	•	398	944	3545	8526	17004	35693	75866	•	•
All Other Liabilities **28**	3527	0	15	•	1021	2953	4759	10723	25653	47007	150517	•	•
Net Worth **29**	4602	0	112	•	1208	2972	7511	16741	28604	70963	123362	•	•
Selected Financial Ratios (Times to 1)													
Current Ratio **30**	1.9	•	2.8	•	2.0	1.7	1.9	2.2	1.9	2.0	1.6	•	•
Quick Ratio **31**	0.9	•	2.2	•	1.2	0.9	1.0	0.9	0.8	0.8	0.7	•	•
Net Sales to Working Capital **32**	7.0	•	8.5	•	6.0	10.2	7.6	5.8	6.6	5.5	11.2	•	•
Coverage Ratio **33**	8.2	24.8	14.9	•	7.2	16.7	13.6	10.3	16.0	15.1	6.5	•	•
Total Asset Turnover **34**	2.4	•	3.9	•	2.7	3.5	3.1	2.6	2.7	2.0	2.9	•	•
Inventory Turnover **35**	7.5	•	19.2	•	7.5	10.7	7.8	6.1	5.6	5.5	11.4	•	•
Receivables Turnover **36**	11.1	•	13.1	•	9.7	18.8	10.8	9.7	8.7	9.5	16.1	•	•
Total Liabilities to Net Worth **37**	1.4	•	0.5	•	1.2	1.3	1.1	1.1	1.5	1.2	1.8	•	•
Current Assets to Working Capital **38**	2.1	•	1.5	•	2.0	2.3	2.1	1.8	2.1	2.0	2.8	•	•
Current Liabilities to Working Capital **39**	1.1	•	0.5	•	1.0	1.3	1.1	0.8	1.1	1.0	1.8	•	•
Working Capital to Net Sales **40**	0.1	•	0.1	•	0.2	0.1	0.1	0.2	0.2	0.2	0.1	•	•
Inventory to Working Capital **41**	1.0	•	0.3	•	0.6	1.2	0.9	1.0	1.1	1.1	1.3	•	•
Total Receipts to Cash Flow **42**	15.9	21.2	10.9	•	15.2	22.6	16.9	18.1	15.5	11.1	25.9	•	•
Cost of Goods to Cash Flow **43**	13.8	19.8	6.4	•	12.1	20.8	14.8	15.8	13.6	9.8	23.9	•	•
Cash Flow to Total Debt **44**	0.3	•	1.0	•	0.3	0.3	0.3	0.3	0.3	0.3	0.2	•	•
Selected Financial Factors (in Percentages)													
Debt Ratio **45**	57.5	•	35.1	•	54.0	56.7	52.5	53.5	59.9	53.8	64.7	•	•
Return on Total Assets **46**	9.9	•	20.5	•	6.3	10.2	11.8	10.5	12.6	12.1	6.4	•	•
Return on Equity Before Income Taxes **47**	20.5	•	29.5	•	11.7	22.1	23.0	20.4	29.3	24.4	15.4	•	•
Return on Equity After Income Taxes **48**	17.0	•	29.0	•	10.9	20.9	21.0	18.4	24.2	19.8	11.9	•	•
Profit Margin (Before Income Tax) **49**	3.6	3.6	4.9	•	2.0	2.8	3.6	3.6	4.4	5.5	1.9	•	•
Profit Margin (After Income Tax) **50**	2.9	3.2	4.8	•	1.9	2.6	3.3	3.3	3.7	4.5	1.5	•	•

Table I

Corporations with and without Net Income

ELECTRICAL GOODS

MONEY AMOUNTS AND SIZE OF ASSETS IN THOUSANDS OF DOLLARS

Item Description for Accounting Period 7/11 Through 6/12		Total	Zero Assets	Under 500	500 to 1,000	1,000 to 5,000	5,000 to 10,000	10,000 to 25,000	25,000 to 50,000	50,000 to 100,000	100,000 to 250,000	250,000 to 500,000	500,000 to 2,500,000	2,500,000 and over
Number of Enterprises	1	28758	4298	15289	3129	4332	789	422	207	127	86	26	40	12
Revenues ($ in Thousands)														
Net Sales	2	387510992	3119748	10287698	6805397	25138350	18746870	15078348	16455293	20833647	31564006	13852869	98644309	126984458
Interest	3	607527	302	2382	697	3087	2384	4252	10338	13185	29577	6036	132803	402485
Rents	4	135194	120	0	559	665	152	2912	3796	1776	3351	5649	34542	81670
Royalties	5	2285063	0	0	1	0	0	0	2368	22621	145263	5470	78700	2030640
Other Portfolio Income	6	374069	9293	2569	3679	44635	5399	1190	12980	10219	7267	13627	102276	160933
Other Receipts	7	4965994	45768	71534	84482	106764	431850	92757	162781	82806	176718	81768	1082337	2546430
Total Receipts	8	395878839	3175231	10364183	6894815	25293501	19186655	15179459	16647556	20964254	31926182	13965419	100074967	132206616
Average Total Receipts	9	13766	739	678	2204	5839	24318	35970	80423	165073	371235	537132	2501874	11017218
Operating Costs/Operating Income (%)														
Cost of Operations	10	82.8	86.3	64.5	67.2	73.7	79.6	79.4	79.5	80.4	84.5	79.3	88.9	83.8
Salaries and Wages	11	5.9	4.4	9.5	8.8	8.3	7.7	7.1	7.7	7.1	5.6	7.7	4.2	5.5
Taxes Paid	12	0.7	0.5	2.0	1.7	1.4	1.2	1.0	0.9	0.9	0.6	0.8	0.5	0.5
Interest Paid	13	0.5	0.3	1.0	0.5	0.3	0.3	0.4	0.4	0.4	0.4	0.5	0.4	0.6
Depreciation	14	1.1	0.3	0.5	0.7	0.4	1.0	0.6	0.6	1.0	0.6	2.2	0.6	2.0
Amortization and Depletion	15	0.8	0.2	0.1	0.1	0.0	0.1	0.1	0.2	0.2	0.1	0.2	0.2	2.2
Pensions and Other Deferred Comp.	16	0.2	0.1	0.2	0.4	0.3	0.2	0.1	0.3	0.3	0.2	0.2	0.2	0.2
Employee Benefits	17	0.7	0.5	0.9	0.7	0.7	0.5	0.6	0.7	0.7	0.7	0.9	0.6	0.7
Advertising	18	0.7	0.1	0.7	1.1	0.4	1.1	0.4	0.4	0.7	0.7	0.3	0.5	1.1
Other Expenses	19	5.6	6.6	13.4	10.1	8.2	7.2	6.4	6.4	5.8	4.6	6.4	3.6	5.4
Officers' Compensation	20	0.9	1.2	6.1	6.3	3.7	1.6	1.5	1.1	0.7	0.7	0.8	0.3	0.1
Operating Margin	21	•	•	1.0	2.4	2.6	•	2.4	1.7	1.9	1.2	0.8	•	•
Operating Margin Before Officers' Comp.	22	0.8	0.6	7.1	8.8	6.3	1.2	3.9	2.8	2.6	1.9	1.6	0.3	•

Selected Average Balance Sheet ($ in Thousands)													
Net Receivables 23	1930	0	29	192	755	2691	5110	12724	23034	60216	102926	339973	1658398
Inventories 24	1114	0	26	222	659	2053	4848	9780	18248	35400	49837	189964	678238
Net Property, Plant and Equipment 25	634	0	8	130	112	545	991	1918	5744	10083	24504	60223	945510
Total Assets 26	7197	0	120	699	2178	7228	15012	34656	69881	159044	349425	1156642	8033079
Notes and Loans Payable 27	1716	0	167	290	513	2031	3334	5560	12615	24573	52584	115155	2483930
All Other Liabilities 28	2931	0	51	249	894	3356	6593	15607	30445	68349	152569	488208	3078865
Net Worth 29	2550	0	-98	160	771	1841	5085	13489	26821	66121	144272	553278	2470283

Selected Financial Ratios (Times to 1)													
Current Ratio 30	1.4	•	1.7	1.6	1.9	1.6	1.6	1.7	1.7	1.7	1.6	1.5	1.1
Quick Ratio 31	0.8	•	1.2	0.9	1.1	0.9	0.9	0.9	0.9	1.1	1.0	0.9	0.6
Net Sales to Working Capital 32	11.7	•	16.8	12.5	6.6	10.1	7.9	7.2	7.5	7.2	6.8	9.5	52.2
Coverage Ratio 33	5.6	4.7	2.7	8.4	10.4	8.7	8.8	8.9	6.7	7.9	4.5	5.1	4.4
Total Asset Turnover 34	1.9	•	5.6	3.1	2.7	3.3	2.4	2.3	2.3	2.3	1.5	2.1	1.3
Inventory Turnover 35	10.0	•	16.8	6.6	6.5	9.2	5.8	6.5	7.2	8.8	8.5	11.5	13.1
Receivables Turnover 36	7.0	•	23.0	11.3	8.0	9.9	6.5	6.8	7.3	6.7	5.8	7.0	6.2
Total Liabilities to Net Worth 37	1.8	•	•	3.4	1.8	2.9	2.0	1.6	1.6	1.4	1.4	1.1	2.3
Current Assets to Working Capital 38	3.8	•	2.4	2.8	2.1	2.6	2.7	2.5	2.5	2.4	2.7	2.9	18.1
Current Liabilities to Working Capital 39	2.8	•	1.4	1.8	1.1	1.6	1.7	1.5	1.5	1.4	1.7	1.9	17.1
Working Capital to Net Sales 40	0.1	•	0.1	0.1	0.2	0.1	0.1	0.1	0.1	0.1	0.1	0.1	0.0
Inventory to Working Capital 41	1.0	•	0.7	1.0	0.8	1.0	1.1	0.9	0.9	0.7	0.7	0.7	3.6
Total Receipts to Cash Flow 42	15.4	15.7	9.0	8.9	11.0	12.4	12.0	12.7	13.8	15.9	14.6	22.5	16.0
Cost of Goods to Cash Flow 43	12.7	13.6	5.8	6.0	8.1	9.9	9.6	10.1	11.1	13.4	11.6	20.0	13.5
Cash Flow to Total Debt 44	0.2	•	0.3	0.5	0.4	0.4	0.3	0.3	0.3	0.2	0.2	0.2	0.1

Selected Financial Factors (in Percentages)													
Debt Ratio 45	64.6	•	181.9	77.1	64.6	74.5	66.1	61.1	61.6	58.4	58.7	52.2	69.2
Return on Total Assets 46	4.7	•	15.3	13.2	9.3	7.2	8.4	7.3	7.0	6.4	3.1	4.2	3.3
Return on Equity Before Income Taxes 47	11.0	•	•	50.9	23.8	24.9	21.9	16.7	15.6	13.4	5.9	7.0	8.2
Return on Equity After Income Taxes 48	8.5	•	•	47.8	21.8	21.7	19.1	14.4	12.2	10.7	4.1	5.0	5.5
Profit Margin (Before Income Tax) 49	2.1	1.1	1.7	3.7	3.2	1.9	3.1	2.8	2.6	2.4	1.6	1.6	1.9
Profit Margin (After Income Tax) 50	1.6	0.9	1.6	3.5	2.9	1.7	2.7	2.4	2.0	1.9	1.1	1.1	1.3

Table II

Corporations with Net Income

Electrical Goods

Money Amounts and Size of Assets in Thousands of Dollars

Item Description for Accounting Period 7/11 Through 6/12		Total	Zero Assets	Under 500	500 to 1,000	1,000 to 5,000	5,000 to 10,000	10,000 to 25,000	25,000 to 50,000	50,000 to 100,000	100,000 to 250,000	250,000 to 500,000	500,000 to 2,500,000	2,500,000 and over
Number of Enterprises	1	18454	2223	9035	•	3342	668	332	178	103	72	17	31	•
Revenues ($ in Thousands)														
Net Sales	2	357748237	2517560	9071575	•	22650728	17084457	13285958	14615456	18525547	26848134	9489369	94696132	•
Interest	3	330946	211	464	•	2470	1839	2104	9868	8601	21188	5329	129271	•
Rents	4	117958	0	0	•	438	52	1468	3796	1365	1746	4123	27723	•
Royalties	5	1912927	0	0	•	0	0	0	0	16613	145263	5463	43723	•
Other Portfolio Income	6	298380	70	206	•	42083	5366	961	9378	9870	7231	11122	54185	•
Other Receipts	7	3870338	43926	73417	•	64077	427316	71969	77827	79250	154513	73088	954982	•
Total Receipts	8	364278786	2561767	9145662	•	22759796	17519030	13362460	14716325	18641246	27178075	9588494	95906016	•
Average Total Receipts	9	19740	1152	1012	•	6810	26226	40248	82676	180983	377473	564029	3093742	•
Operating Costs/Operating Income (%)														
Cost of Operations	10	83.2	89.3	66.3	•	74.2	79.0	79.2	79.0	81.0	83.6	78.3	89.3	•
Salaries and Wages	11	5.5	2.9	8.1	•	7.6	7.7	6.7	7.4	6.7	5.7	8.5	4.0	•
Taxes Paid	12	0.7	0.4	1.7	•	1.3	1.2	0.9	0.9	0.8	0.7	0.8	0.5	•
Interest Paid	13	0.3	0.1	0.1	•	0.3	0.3	0.4	0.3	0.3	0.3	0.5	0.3	•
Depreciation	14	1.0	0.2	0.4	•	0.4	1.1	0.6	0.5	0.8	0.5	0.9	0.5	•
Amortization and Depletion	15	0.9	0.0	0.0	•	0.0	0.1	0.1	0.2	0.1	0.1	0.2	0.1	•
Pensions and Other Deferred Comp.	16	0.2	0.1	0.2	•	0.3	0.2	0.1	0.4	0.3	0.3	0.3	0.2	•
Employee Benefits	17	0.7	0.4	0.8	•	0.6	0.5	0.5	0.7	0.7	0.7	0.9	0.5	•
Advertising	18	0.7	0.0	0.6	•	0.3	1.1	0.4	0.4	0.4	0.8	0.2	0.5	•
Other Expenses	19	5.0	3.5	10.4	•	7.0	7.1	5.9	5.9	5.1	4.6	5.9	3.0	•
Officers' Compensation	20	0.9	0.8	6.4	•	3.7	1.6	1.5	1.1	0.7	0.7	0.5	0.2	•
Operating Margin	21	1.0	2.3	5.0	•	4.4	0.1	3.7	3.2	3.1	2.1	2.9	0.8	•
Operating Margin Before Officers' Comp.	22	1.9	3.1	11.4	•	8.0	1.7	5.2	4.3	3.8	2.8	3.4	1.0	•

Selected Average Balance Sheet ($ in Thousands)													
Net Receivables **23**	2675	0	39	•	857	2639	5309	13106	24647	58943	106462	407479	•
Inventories **24**	1494	0	25	•	685	1963	5189	10093	19196	36475	61396	229869	•
Net Property, Plant and Equipment **25**	769	0	8	•	115	615	998	1864	5418	10036	20486	67523	•
Total Assets **26**	9195	0	152	•	2200	7321	14782	34821	70564	157658	366242	1209296	•
Notes and Loans Payable **27**	2022	0	18	•	397	1534	2946	5628	11169	25061	60730	109608	•
All Other Liabilities **28**	3946	0	57	•	888	3304	6398	14709	29156	66431	158373	529197	•
Net Worth **29**	3228	0	77	•	916	2482	5438	14484	30238	66167	147139	570491	•
Selected Financial Ratios (Times to 1)													
Current Ratio **30**	1.4	•	2.3	•	2.0	1.7	1.7	1.8	1.8	1.7	1.6	1.6	•
Quick Ratio **31**	0.8	•	1.6	•	1.2	1.0	0.9	1.0	1.0	1.1	1.0	1.0	•
Net Sales to Working Capital **32**	12.3	•	13.2	•	7.1	9.6	8.1	6.5	7.0	7.2	6.2	10.0	•
Coverage Ratio **33**	9.2	35.2	72.9	•	17.6	11.5	11.7	12.9	13.9	11.8	9.0	8.3	•
Total Asset Turnover **34**	2.1	•	6.6	•	3.1	3.5	2.7	2.4	2.5	2.4	1.5	2.5	•
Inventory Turnover **35**	10.8	•	26.2	•	7.3	10.3	6.1	6.4	7.6	8.5	7.1	11.9	•
Receivables Turnover **36**	7.9	•	30.8	•	8.4	10.9	6.8	6.8	7.8	6.8	5.2	7.2	•
Total Liabilities to Net Worth **37**	1.8	•	1.0	•	1.4	1.9	1.7	1.4	1.3	1.4	1.5	1.1	•
Current Assets to Working Capital **38**	3.8	•	1.8	•	2.0	2.3	2.5	2.3	2.2	2.4	2.6	2.7	•
Current Liabilities to Working Capital **39**	2.8	•	0.8	•	1.0	1.3	1.5	1.3	1.2	1.4	1.6	1.7	•
Working Capital to Net Sales **40**	0.1	•	0.1	•	0.1	0.1	0.1	0.2	0.1	0.1	0.2	0.1	•
Inventory to Working Capital **41**	1.0	•	0.4	•	0.7	0.9	1.0	0.8	0.8	0.8	0.6	0.7	•
Total Receipts to Cash Flow **42**	14.8	15.0	7.9	•	10.2	11.4	11.2	11.8	12.7	13.8	11.3	21.8	•
Cost of Goods to Cash Flow **43**	12.3	13.4	5.3	•	7.6	9.0	8.8	9.3	10.3	11.5	8.8	19.4	•
Cash Flow to Total Debt **44**	0.2	•	1.7	•	0.5	0.5	0.4	0.3	0.4	0.3	0.2	0.2	•
Selected Financial Factors (in Percentages)													
Debt Ratio **45**	64.9	•	49.6	•	58.4	66.1	63.2	58.4	57.1	58.0	59.8	52.8	•
Return on Total Assets **46**	6.7	•	39.3	•	15.7	10.2	12.6	9.9	10.3	8.8	6.9	6.1	•
Return on Equity Before Income Taxes **47**	17.1	•	76.8	•	35.7	27.6	31.4	22.1	22.4	19.1	15.2	11.4	•
Return on Equity After Income Taxes **48**	14.0	•	75.6	•	33.6	24.8	28.0	19.6	18.6	15.9	12.6	9.0	•
Profit Margin (Before Income Tax) **49**	2.8	4.1	5.9	•	4.8	2.7	4.3	3.9	3.8	3.4	4.0	2.1	•
Profit Margin (After Income Tax) **50**	2.3	3.8	5.8	•	4.5	2.4	3.8	3.5	3.1	2.8	3.3	1.7	•

Table I

Corporations with and without Net Income

HARDWARE, PLUMBING, HEATING EQUIPMENT, AND SUPPLIES

MONEY AMOUNTS AND SIZE OF ASSETS IN THOUSANDS OF DOLLARS

Item Description for Accounting Period 7/11 Through 6/12		Total	Zero Assets	Under 500	500 to 1,000	1,000 to 5,000	5,000 to 10,000	10,000 to 25,000	25,000 to 50,000	50,000 to 100,000	100,000 to 250,000	250,000 to 500,000	500,000 to 2,500,000	2,500,000 and over
Number of Enterprises	1	12912	1877	5772	1227	2860	633	342	112	48	25	6	9	0
Revenues ($ in Thousands)														
Net Sales	2	89682195	484466	4203065	2205944	16060706	10619723	11708508	8872602	6677110	6219857	3617438	19012777	0
Interest	3	47805	202	22	1926	7140	4069	3407	4169	3842	629	1309	21089	0
Rents	4	11973	49	0	0	3656	394	1230	1210	279	1341	0	3814	0
Royalties	5	4527	0	0	0	0	0	0	0	0	0	0	4527	0
Other Portfolio Income	6	89996	4642	0	1828	12832	2560	10343	9308	2094	2220	105	44064	0
Other Receipts	7	931359	-393	16101	38398	295319	122048	79772	78117	70162	26242	59779	145813	0
Total Receipts	8	90767855	488966	4219188	2248096	16379653	10748794	11803260	8965406	6753487	6250289	3678631	19232084	0
Average Total Receipts	9	7030	261	731	1832	5727	16981	34512	80048	140698	250012	613105	2136898	•
Operating Costs/Operating Income (%)														
Cost of Operations	10	72.0	62.0	66.5	66.8	72.6	69.4	74.3	74.7	74.8	74.3	83.4	68.3	•
Salaries and Wages	11	10.0	8.5	9.9	9.3	9.6	10.6	9.8	9.9	9.7	8.8	6.7	11.3	•
Taxes Paid	12	1.5	4.5	2.0	1.7	1.7	1.5	1.3	1.3	1.3	1.3	1.0	1.6	•
Interest Paid	13	0.7	1.4	0.6	0.4	0.4	0.6	0.4	0.5	0.4	0.7	0.4	1.4	•
Depreciation	14	1.1	0.7	1.2	0.5	0.4	1.5	0.7	0.9	1.4	1.2	0.9	1.7	•
Amortization and Depletion	15	0.2	0.9	0.2	0.0	0.1	0.0	0.0	0.1	0.2	0.2	0.1	0.4	•
Pensions and Other Deferred Comp.	16	0.4	0.2	0.2	0.8	0.3	0.4	0.4	0.4	0.4	0.2	0.1	0.7	•
Employee Benefits	17	0.9	0.3	0.6	0.4	0.9	1.2	0.9	1.0	1.0	0.8	0.7	1.1	•
Advertising	18	0.5	0.4	1.1	0.2	0.4	0.8	0.5	0.5	0.7	0.7	0.1	0.3	•
Other Expenses	19	8.4	16.8	13.2	11.6	8.7	8.7	7.1	6.7	8.0	8.8	4.8	8.5	•
Officers' Compensation	20	2.1	5.7	4.7	6.8	3.8	2.9	2.4	1.2	0.8	0.9	0.4	0.3	•
Operating Margin	21	2.3	•	•	1.5	1.1	2.4	2.3	2.8	1.3	2.2	1.5	4.3	•
Operating Margin Before Officers' Comp.	22	4.4	4.4	4.6	8.3	4.9	5.3	4.6	4.0	2.1	3.1	1.9	4.5	•

Selected Average Balance Sheet ($ in Thousands)

Net Receivables 23	919	0	58	193	736	2226	4268	9584	18523	44019	86138	304157	•
Inventories 24	1038	0	28	225	806	2983	6212	12127	24387	51175	107779	243504	•
Net Property, Plant and Equipment 25	376	0	11	31	157	677	1285	3737	9835	21066	22197	209173	•
Total Assets 26	3401	0	134	694	2283	7137	15783	33697	70459	155396	323988	1429414	•
Notes and Loans Payable 27	931	0	129	114	463	2021	3636	8438	14004	34340	87794	475508	•
All Other Liabilities 28	1004	0	80	107	805	1995	4066	8842	19079	52404	128553	380812	•
Net Worth 29	1467	0	-76	473	1016	3122	8081	16416	37376	68652	107642	573095	•

Selected Financial Ratios (Times to 1)

Current Ratio 30	2.1	•	0.9	4.5	2.2	2.1	2.1	2.2	2.3	2.0	1.7	2.4	•
Quick Ratio 31	1.1	•	0.7	2.6	1.2	0.9	1.0	1.0	1.1	0.9	0.7	1.3	•
Net Sales to Working Capital 32	5.3	•	•	4.1	5.4	5.1	5.2	5.3	4.7	4.5	6.8	4.7	•
Coverage Ratio 33	6.1	0.7	1.3	9.3	8.3	6.8	8.7	8.6	6.9	5.0	8.2	4.9	•
Total Asset Turnover 34	2.0	•	5.4	2.6	2.5	2.4	2.2	2.4	2.0	1.6	1.9	1.5	•
Inventory Turnover 35	4.8	•	17.4	5.3	5.1	3.9	4.1	4.9	4.3	3.6	4.7	5.9	•
Receivables Turnover 36	7.9	•	16.3	9.2	7.6	8.5	7.6	9.2	7.9	5.5	8.0	7.5	•
Total Liabilities to Net Worth 37	1.3	•	•	0.5	1.2	1.3	1.0	1.1	0.9	1.3	2.0	1.5	•
Current Assets to Working Capital 38	1.9	•	•	1.3	1.8	1.9	1.9	1.8	1.8	2.0	2.5	1.7	•
Current Liabilities to Working Capital 39	0.9	•	•	0.3	0.8	0.9	0.9	0.8	0.8	1.0	1.5	0.7	•
Working Capital to Net Sales 40	0.2	•	•	0.2	0.2	0.2	0.2	0.2	0.2	0.2	0.1	0.2	•
Inventory to Working Capital 41	0.8	•	•	0.5	0.8	1.0	1.0	0.9	0.8	1.0	1.3	0.7	•
Total Receipts to Cash Flow 42	10.6	6.9	9.0	8.2	10.6	9.9	13.1	12.3	11.9	10.7	16.2	9.0	•
Cost of Goods to Cash Flow 43	7.6	4.3	6.0	5.5	7.7	6.9	9.7	9.2	8.9	8.0	13.5	6.2	•
Cash Flow to Total Debt 44	0.3	•	0.4	1.0	0.4	0.4	0.3	0.4	0.4	0.3	0.2	0.3	•

Selected Financial Factors (in Percentages)

Debt Ratio 45	56.9	•	156.4	31.8	55.5	56.3	48.8	51.3	47.0	55.8	66.8	59.9	•
Return on Total Assets 46	8.6	•	4.7	9.8	8.5	9.9	7.5	10.3	5.7	5.4	6.7	10.3	•
Return on Equity Before Income Taxes 47	16.6	•	•	12.8	16.7	19.4	13.0	18.7	9.2	9.8	17.6	20.4	•
Return on Equity After Income Taxes 48	14.1	•	•	11.2	14.4	18.1	11.8	16.5	8.1	8.5	15.0	15.9	•
Profit Margin (Before Income Tax) 49	3.5	•	0.2	3.4	3.0	3.6	3.1	3.9	2.5	2.7	3.2	5.5	•
Profit Margin (After Income Tax) 50	3.0	•	0.2	2.9	2.6	3.4	2.8	3.4	2.2	2.3	2.7	4.3	•

Table II

Corporations with Net Income

HARDWARE, PLUMBING, HEATING EQUIPMENT, AND SUPPLIES

MONEY AMOUNTS AND SIZE OF ASSETS IN THOUSANDS OF DOLLARS

Item Description for Accounting Period 7/11 Through 6/12		Total	Zero Assets	Under 500	500 to 1,000	1,000 to 5,000	5,000 to 10,000	10,000 to 25,000	25,000 to 50,000	50,000 to 100,000	100,000 to 250,000	250,000 to 500,000	500,000 to 2,500,000	2,500,000 and over
Number of Enterprises	1	9443	1069	4067	1027	2222	583	309	98	38	19	•	•	0
Revenues ($ in Thousands)														
Net Sales	2	78725826	191315	2970540	1855775	13844331	9826505	10759363	7862662	5909173	4896354	•	•	0
Interest	3	38304	12	4	1294	6901	3545	3369	3381	798	254	•	•	0
Rents	4	10452	49	0	0	2680	378	1230	1210	270	1000	•	•	0
Royalties	5	4527	0	0	0	0	0	0	0	0	0	•	•	0
Other Portfolio Income	6	62816	2	0	450	7170	2546	9222	9088	1655	2152	•	•	0
Other Receipts	7	884194	853	5956	37266	286822	108197	67553	76529	78223	25156	•	•	0
Total Receipts	8	79726119	192231	2976500	1894785	14147904	9941171	10840737	7952870	5990119	4924916	•	•	0
Average Total Receipts	9	8443	180	732	1845	6367	17052	35083	81152	157635	259206	•	•	•
Operating Costs/Operating Income (%)														
Cost of Operations	10	71.6	35.0	66.0	65.5	72.8	68.4	73.6	74.6	75.0	74.8	•	•	•
Salaries and Wages	11	10.0	17.3	8.0	9.6	9.8	10.8	9.8	9.9	9.6	8.8	•	•	•
Taxes Paid	12	1.5	6.1	1.8	1.5	1.6	1.6	1.3	1.3	1.3	1.3	•	•	•
Interest Paid	13	0.7	2.7	0.4	0.2	0.4	0.6	0.3	0.5	0.3	0.5	•	•	•
Depreciation	14	0.9	1.1	1.3	0.4	0.4	1.5	0.6	0.7	0.9	1.3	•	•	•
Amortization and Depletion	15	0.1	2.1	0.0	0.0	0.0	0.0	0.0	0.1	0.1	0.1	•	•	•
Pensions and Other Deferred Comp.	16	0.5	0.2	0.2	0.9	0.4	0.4	0.4	0.4	0.4	0.2	•	•	•
Employee Benefits	17	0.9	0.3	0.7	0.3	0.9	1.1	0.8	1.0	1.0	0.6	•	•	•
Advertising	18	0.5	0.2	1.4	0.2	0.4	0.8	0.5	0.5	0.7	0.8	•	•	•
Other Expenses	19	7.9	16.8	11.6	11.0	7.7	8.8	6.8	6.1	7.4	7.4	•	•	•
Officers' Compensation	20	2.0	3.2	4.1	6.6	3.5	3.0	2.5	1.2	0.8	0.7	•	•	•
Operating Margin	21	3.4	14.9	4.4	3.7	2.0	2.9	3.4	3.6	2.6	3.4	•	•	•
Operating Margin Before Officers' Comp.	22	5.4	18.1	8.5	10.3	5.6	5.9	5.8	4.9	3.4	4.1	•	•	•

Selected Average Balance Sheet ($ in Thousands)													
Net Receivables 23	1089	0	57	209	790	2183	4250	9418	20143	45470	•	•	•
Inventories 24	1189	0	16	214	819	2874	5971	12647	26266	48124	•	•	•
Net Property, Plant and Equipment 25	377	0	11	12	143	690	1127	3400	9286	21831	•	•	•
Total Assets 26	3917	0	115	706	2358	7045	15493	33840	71315	152725	•	•	•
Notes and Loans Payable 27	1011	0	53	39	460	1905	2980	8568	12305	28338	•	•	•
All Other Liabilities 28	1047	0	62	115	726	1938	3889	8374	18001	47982	•	•	•
Net Worth 29	1859	0	1	552	1172	3202	8625	16898	41008	76405	•	•	•

Selected Financial Ratios (Times to 1)													
Current Ratio 30	2.3	•	1.2	4.6	2.3	2.1	2.2	2.4	2.6	2.1	•	•	•
Quick Ratio 31	1.2	•	1.0	2.7	1.2	0.9	1.0	1.1	1.2	1.0	•	•	•
Net Sales to Working Capital 32	5.1	•	50.7	3.9	5.4	5.1	5.0	5.0	4.4	4.4	•	•	•
Coverage Ratio 33	8.0	6.7	11.7	29.3	11.3	7.4	13.7	9.9	14.1	8.6	•	•	•
Total Asset Turnover 34	2.1	•	6.4	2.6	2.6	2.4	2.2	2.4	2.2	1.7	•	•	•
Inventory Turnover 35	5.0	•	29.4	5.5	5.5	4.0	4.3	4.7	4.4	4.0	•	•	•
Receivables Turnover 36	8.1	•	16.9	8.7	8.1	9.2	8.2	9.0	8.2	5.4	•	•	•
Total Liabilities to Net Worth 37	1.1	•	189.2	0.3	1.0	1.2	0.8	1.0	0.7	1.0	•	•	•
Current Assets to Working Capital 38	1.8	•	6.6	1.3	1.8	1.9	1.8	1.7	1.6	1.9	•	•	•
Current Liabilities to Working Capital 39	0.8	•	5.6	0.3	0.8	0.9	0.8	0.7	0.6	0.9	•	•	•
Working Capital to Net Sales 40	0.2	•	0.0	0.3	0.2	0.2	0.2	0.2	0.2	0.2	•	•	•
Inventory to Working Capital 41	0.8	•	1.0	0.5	0.7	1.0	0.9	0.9	0.8	0.9	•	•	•
Total Receipts to Cash Flow 42	9.8	3.2	7.1	7.2	10.1	9.4	11.8	11.6	10.8	10.9	•	•	•
Cost of Goods to Cash Flow 43	7.0	1.1	4.7	4.7	7.3	6.4	8.7	8.6	8.1	8.1	•	•	•
Cash Flow to Total Debt 44	0.4	•	0.9	1.6	0.5	0.5	0.4	0.4	0.5	0.3	•	•	•

Selected Financial Factors (in Percentages)													
Debt Ratio 45	52.5	•	99.5	21.8	50.3	54.6	44.3	50.1	42.5	50.0	•	•	•
Return on Total Assets 46	11.5	•	31.9	15.3	12.2	11.3	10.0	12.6	9.2	7.6	•	•	•
Return on Equity Before Income Taxes 47	21.2	•	5545.1	18.9	22.3	21.5	16.6	22.7	14.8	13.5	•	•	•
Return on Equity After Income Taxes 48	18.6	•	5480.2	17.3	19.8	20.2	15.3	20.3	13.6	11.9	•	•	•
Profit Margin (Before Income Tax) 49	4.7	15.4	4.6	5.8	4.2	4.1	4.1	4.8	3.9	4.0	•	•	•
Profit Margin (After Income Tax) 50	4.1	14.8	4.5	5.3	3.7	3.8	3.8	4.3	3.6	3.5	•	•	•

Table I

Corporations with and without Net Income

MACHINERY, EQUIPMENT, AND SUPPLIES

Item Description for Accounting Period 7/11 Through 6/12		MONEY AMOUNTS AND SIZE OF ASSETS IN THOUSANDS OF DOLLARS												
		Total	Zero Assets	Under 500	500 to 1,000	1,000 to 5,000	5,000 to 10,000	10,000 to 25,000	25,000 to 50,000	50,000 to 100,000	100,000 to 250,000	250,000 to 500,000	500,000 to 2,500,000	2,500,000 and over
Number of Enterprises	1	48092	5883	25776	4350	8700	1529	1115	398	165	106	38	26	5
Revenues ($ in Thousands)														
Net Sales	2	290328564	9411147	14529644	8140982	50171758	24958493	37037211	27480589	19128915	23027769	16270499	28108564	32062993
Interest	3	321345	12382	1240	3117	19325	10787	12889	12634	22652	14549	25151	38963	147656
Rents	4	134828	174	1681	10358	11146	10462	32842	11989	8954	4794	32881	5670	3876
Royalties	5	55477	186	0	0	7419	4495	30190	29	7308	491	450	2416	2494
Other Portfolio Income	6	1298730	80218	1311	23395	155022	60956	114999	159515	144617	203100	97367	238713	19517
Other Receipts	7	2249701	63811	122640	42252	330746	250147	306232	258249	227902	231381	143139	204763	68440
Total Receipts	8	294388645	9567918	14656516	8220104	50695416	25295340	37534363	27923005	19540348	23482084	16569487	28599089	32304976
Average Total Receipts	9	6121	1626	569	1890	5827	16544	33663	70158	118426	221529	436039	1099965	6460995
Operating Costs/Operating Income (%)														
Cost of Operations	10	76.3	91.6	66.3	73.4	73.0	75.3	76.8	80.2	77.6	74.5	73.9	70.4	85.8
Salaries and Wages	11	6.8	2.3	6.3	5.3	8.0	6.7	7.5	6.1	7.0	7.7	7.9	7.9	4.5
Taxes Paid	12	1.2	0.6	1.5	1.5	1.5	1.4	1.1	1.0	1.1	1.1	1.1	1.2	0.8
Interest Paid	13	0.7	0.3	0.3	0.6	0.5	0.5	0.5	0.5	0.8	0.9	1.0	1.4	0.7
Depreciation	14	2.2	0.4	0.7	1.1	0.9	1.8	1.8	2.3	3.2	3.7	5.0	5.1	0.8
Amortization and Depletion	15	0.2	0.1	0.0	0.0	0.1	0.1	0.1	0.1	0.2	0.1	0.2	1.1	0.1
Pensions and Other Deferred Comp.	16	0.4	0.1	1.2	0.2	0.3	0.3	0.3	0.3	0.3	0.4	0.4	0.6	0.6
Employee Benefits	17	0.9	0.3	0.7	0.7	0.8	0.8	0.7	0.8	0.8	1.2	1.7	1.7	0.7
Advertising	18	0.3	0.2	0.3	0.4	0.3	0.4	0.4	0.3	0.3	0.3	0.3	0.4	0.5
Other Expenses	19	6.7	3.8	11.2	9.7	8.4	7.6	6.2	5.3	6.4	7.6	6.9	6.1	2.8
Officers' Compensation	20	2.0	0.9	8.3	4.1	3.6	2.5	1.8	1.1	1.0	0.8	0.6	0.6	0.3
Operating Margin	21	2.3	•	3.0	3.0	2.6	2.7	2.8	2.1	1.2	1.8	0.9	3.5	2.5
Operating Margin Before Officers' Comp.	22	4.3	0.3	11.4	7.1	6.2	5.2	4.6	3.2	2.3	2.6	1.5	4.1	2.8

Selected Average Balance Sheet ($ in Thousands)

Net Receivables 23	770	0	35	186	592	1778	3790	7558	14721	35776	84840	174560	1248896
Inventories 24	958	0	39	240	748	3287	5812	13711	23195	45341	92607	229533	482878
Net Property, Plant and Equipment 25	429	0	13	91	199	856	1865	4940	10572	26368	55972	183494	280542
Total Assets 26	3137	0	140	685	2144	7165	14869	34038	67418	156794	360720	943542	3710928
Notes and Loans Payable 27	882	0	56	295	541	2112	3646	8807	16554	45947	89797	292605	1111248
All Other Liabilities 28	1079	0	41	186	762	2461	5334	12475	24230	55789	133010	275499	1314662
Net Worth 29	1176	0	43	204	841	2593	5889	12755	26634	55057	137913	375438	1285018

Selected Financial Ratios (Times to 1)

Current Ratio 30	1.8	•	2.7	2.6	1.9	1.9	1.7	1.6	1.7	1.5	1.6	1.8	1.9
Quick Ratio 31	0.8	•	1.7	1.3	1.0	0.8	0.8	0.7	0.7	0.7	0.7	0.8	1.1
Net Sales to Working Capital 32	6.2	•	8.1	5.4	6.7	5.9	6.7	6.7	5.7	5.9	5.1	4.8	5.5
Coverage Ratio 33	6.7	4.7	13.8	7.9	9.0	9.5	9.8	8.3	5.5	5.1	3.9	4.8	5.8
Total Asset Turnover 34	1.9	•	4.0	2.7	2.7	2.3	2.2	2.0	1.7	1.4	1.2	1.1	1.7
Inventory Turnover 35	4.8	•	9.5	5.7	5.6	3.7	4.4	4.0	3.9	3.6	3.4	3.3	11.4
Receivables Turnover 36	8.4	•	16.2	10.2	10.2	9.0	9.1	10.3	8.0	6.8	5.9	6.7	5.5
Total Liabilities to Net Worth 37	1.7	•	2.3	2.4	1.5	1.8	1.5	1.7	1.5	1.8	1.6	1.5	1.9
Current Assets to Working Capital 38	2.3	•	1.6	1.6	2.1	2.1	2.4	2.6	2.4	2.9	2.7	2.3	2.1
Current Liabilities to Working Capital 39	1.3	•	0.6	0.6	1.1	1.1	1.4	1.6	1.4	1.9	1.7	1.3	1.1
Working Capital to Net Sales 40	0.2	•	0.1	0.2	0.1	0.2	0.1	0.2	0.2	0.2	0.2	0.2	0.2
Inventory to Working Capital 41	1.0	•	0.6	0.7	0.9	1.2	1.2	1.4	1.2	1.3	1.3	1.2	0.4
Total Receipts to Cash Flow 42	11.4	27.2	7.8	9.0	10.0	9.8	11.3	12.9	11.7	10.5	12.3	10.7	19.1
Cost of Goods to Cash Flow 43	8.7	24.9	5.2	6.6	7.3	7.4	8.7	10.3	9.1	7.8	9.1	7.5	16.4
Cash Flow to Total Debt 44	0.3	•	0.7	0.4	0.4	0.4	0.3	0.3	0.2	0.2	0.2	0.2	0.1

Selected Financial Factors (in Percentages)

Debt Ratio 45	62.5	•	69.3	70.2	60.8	63.8	60.4	62.5	60.5	64.9	61.8	60.2	65.4
Return on Total Assets 46	8.5	•	16.9	12.4	11.1	10.2	10.4	8.7	7.2	6.5	4.5	7.5	6.9
Return on Equity Before Income Taxes 47	19.3	•	51.0	36.4	25.1	25.2	23.5	20.3	14.8	14.8	8.6	15.0	16.5
Return on Equity After Income Taxes 48	15.7	•	49.7	35.4	23.1	22.8	20.5	17.7	12.4	11.1	6.7	8.9	10.8
Profit Margin (Before Income Tax) 49	3.8	1.1	3.9	4.0	3.7	4.0	4.2	3.8	3.4	3.7	2.8	5.2	3.3
Profit Margin (After Income Tax) 50	3.1	0.7	3.8	3.9	3.4	3.6	3.6	3.3	2.8	2.8	2.1	3.1	2.2

Table II

Corporations with Net Income

MACHINERY, EQUIPMENT, AND SUPPLIES

MONEY AMOUNTS AND SIZE OF ASSETS IN THOUSANDS OF DOLLARS

Item Description for Accounting Period 7/11 Through 6/12		Total	Zero Assets	Under 500	500 to 1,000	1,000 to 5,000	5,000 to 10,000	10,000 to 25,000	25,000 to 50,000	50,000 to 100,000	100,000 to 250,000	250,000 to 500,000	500,000 to 2,500,000	2,500,000 and over
Number of Enterprises	1	32522	3642	16159	3025	6847	1318	934	344	124	77	29	19	5
Revenues ($ in Thousands)														
Net Sales	2	250348257	9057925	12178992	6242137	41717707	23068544	32336024	24942930	15897624	18457198	13216752	21169430	32062993
Interest	3	286887	10249	1031	2304	15634	6801	10225	10973	16855	10114	20376	34669	147656
Rents	4	94309	174	0	10066	10486	7871	25734	11067	4715	3095	12432	4791	3876
Royalties	5	19605	186	0	0	7419	4495	1494	29	215	491	366	2416	2494
Other Portfolio Income	6	878035	73089	1146	20753	144801	50156	68449	113429	49759	99251	65438	172246	19517
Other Receipts	7	1914406	45681	116747	30516	279770	219228	245890	217269	183586	246803	101002	159479	68440
Total Receipts	8	253541499	9187304	12297916	6305776	42175817	23357095	32687816	25295697	16152754	18816952	13416366	21543031	32304976
Average Total Receipts	9	7796	2523	761	2085	6160	17722	34998	73534	130264	244376	462633	1133844	6460995
Operating Costs/Operating Income (%)														
Cost of Operations	10	76.4	92.1	66.2	71.2	72.2	75.3	76.7	80.2	78.3	75.3	74.3	67.9	85.8
Salaries and Wages	11	6.6	1.7	5.4	5.4	7.9	6.6	7.5	6.0	6.7	7.6	7.7	8.4	4.5
Taxes Paid	12	1.2	0.5	1.5	1.5	1.5	1.4	1.1	1.0	1.0	1.1	1.1	1.3	0.8
Interest Paid	13	0.6	0.3	0.1	0.5	0.4	0.4	0.4	0.4	0.6	0.7	0.9	1.2	0.7
Depreciation	14	1.5	0.3	0.7	1.0	0.8	1.6	1.3	1.7	1.6	1.9	3.8	3.5	0.8
Amortization and Depletion	15	0.1	0.1	0.0	0.0	0.0	0.0	0.1	0.1	0.1	0.1	0.2	0.8	0.1
Pensions and Other Deferred Comp.	16	0.4	0.1	1.4	0.2	0.4	0.3	0.3	0.3	0.3	0.3	0.5	0.7	0.6
Employee Benefits	17	0.9	0.2	0.7	0.7	0.8	0.8	0.7	0.8	0.8	1.0	1.7	1.7	0.7
Advertising	18	0.3	0.1	0.2	0.3	0.3	0.3	0.4	0.4	0.3	0.3	0.3	0.4	0.5
Other Expenses	19	6.1	2.8	9.2	8.4	7.9	7.2	5.8	4.9	5.4	7.0	6.5	6.6	2.8
Officers' Compensation	20	2.0	0.7	8.1	4.5	3.7	2.6	1.7	1.0	1.0	0.7	0.5	0.7	0.3
Operating Margin	21	3.9	1.2	6.4	6.3	4.2	3.5	4.1	3.2	3.7	3.9	2.4	6.8	2.5
Operating Margin Before Officers' Comp.	22	5.9	1.9	14.5	10.8	7.9	6.2	5.8	4.3	4.7	4.6	2.9	7.5	2.8

Selected Average Balance Sheet ($ in Thousands)

Net Receivables	23	956	0	45	209	591	1867	3820	7669	15027	38716	92243	171339	1248896
Inventories	24	1144	0	39	189	775	3337	6099	13667	26524	48989	91354	229913	514138
Net Property, Plant and Equipment	25	441	0	12	106	176	782	1493	4549	8012	19835	48916	172732	280542
Total Assets	26	3723	0	157	697	2122	7187	14872	34229	66757	158275	362404	907034	3710928
Notes and Loans Payable	27	968	0	51	218	499	2138	3228	8214	13875	37611	83189	280234	1111248
All Other Liabilities	28	1256	0	42	169	657	2179	5290	12598	24817	60342	145274	235961	1314662
Net Worth	29	1500	0	64	309	965	2870	6354	13417	28065	60323	133940	390839	1285018

Selected Financial Ratios (Times to 1)

Current Ratio	30	1.9	•	2.6	2.9	2.2	2.0	1.8	1.7	1.7	1.7	1.5	2.0	1.9
Quick Ratio	31	0.9	•	1.7	1.6	1.2	0.8	0.8	0.7	0.7	0.8	0.8	0.9	1.1
Net Sales to Working Capital	32	6.0	•	9.4	5.6	6.1	5.8	6.4	6.5	5.8	5.2	5.4	4.3	5.5
Coverage Ratio	33	10.4	11.1	57.4	16.3	13.3	12.9	14.1	11.7	10.5	8.8	5.2	8.4	5.8
Total Asset Turnover	34	2.1	•	4.8	3.0	2.9	2.4	2.3	2.1	1.9	1.5	1.3	1.2	1.7
Inventory Turnover	35	5.1	•	12.7	7.8	5.7	4.0	4.4	4.3	3.8	3.7	3.7	3.3	10.7
Receivables Turnover	36	8.8	•	19.7	10.2	10.2	9.4	9.4	10.9	•	6.8	5.8	7.7	•
Total Liabilities to Net Worth	37	1.5	•	1.5	1.3	1.2	1.5	1.3	1.6	1.4	1.6	1.7	1.3	1.9
Current Assets to Working Capital	38	2.1	•	1.6	1.5	1.8	2.0	2.3	2.5	2.3	2.4	2.9	2.0	2.1
Current Liabilities to Working Capital	39	1.1	•	0.6	0.5	0.8	1.0	1.3	1.5	1.3	1.4	1.9	1.0	1.1
Working Capital to Net Sales	40	0.2	•	0.1	0.2	0.2	0.2	0.2	0.2	0.2	0.2	0.2	0.2	0.2
Inventory to Working Capital	41	1.0	•	0.5	0.5	0.8	1.1	1.1	1.4	1.2	1.1	1.3	1.0	0.4
Total Receipts to Cash Flow	42	10.2	22.0	6.8	7.5	8.8	9.5	10.5	12.0	10.4	8.8	11.1	7.7	19.1
Cost of Goods to Cash Flow	43	7.8	20.2	4.5	5.4	6.4	7.1	8.1	9.6	8.2	6.6	8.2	5.2	16.4
Cash Flow to Total Debt	44	0.3	•	1.2	0.7	0.6	0.4	0.4	0.3	0.3	0.3	0.2	0.3	0.1

Selected Financial Factors (in Percentages)

Debt Ratio	45	59.7	•	59.3	55.6	54.5	60.1	57.3	60.8	58.0	61.9	63.0	56.9	65.4
Return on Total Assets	46	12.0	•	35.9	23.0	16.5	12.7	13.1	10.8	11.4	10.0	6.1	12.0	6.9
Return on Equity Before Income Taxes	47	26.8	•	86.6	48.7	33.5	29.3	28.4	25.1	24.5	23.2	13.4	24.5	16.5
Return on Equity After Income Taxes	48	22.7	•	85.3	47.7	31.3	26.7	25.1	22.2	21.4	18.6	10.7	16.4	10.8
Profit Margin (Before Income Tax)	49	5.2	2.6	7.4	7.3	5.3	4.8	5.2	4.6	5.4	5.8	3.9	8.6	3.3
Profit Margin (After Income Tax)	50	4.4	2.2	7.2	7.2	5.0	4.4	4.6	4.1	4.7	4.7	3.2	5.8	2.2

Table I

Corporations with and without Net Income

FURNITURE, SPORTS, TOYS, JEWELRY, OTHER DURABLE GOODS

MONEY AMOUNTS AND SIZE OF ASSETS IN THOUSANDS OF DOLLARS

Item Description for Accounting Period 7/11 Through 6/12		Total	Zero Assets	Under 500	500 to 1,000	1,000 to 5,000	5,000 to 10,000	10,000 to 25,000	25,000 to 50,000	50,000 to 100,000	100,000 to 250,000	250,000 to 500,000	500,000 to 2,500,000	2,500,000 and over
Number of Enterprises	1	68410	9470	42560	6332	7267	1407	874	243	150	66	26	10	4
Revenues ($ in Thousands)														
Net Sales	2	271561413	2931552	17687156	13846694	50369084	25106668	37387078	22707680	21681347	20615016	21236012	10413961	27579166
Interest	3	279097	10715	1777	1921	12440	4650	15059	16754	16227	9714	21322	22532	145987
Rents	4	80703	98	4731	2221	3732	1894	2912	4094	8322	5666	1618	33599	11818
Royalties	5	389457	5643	0	0	4584	3086	20953	7246	85178	72078	108768	422	81498
Other Portfolio Income	6	272309	3170	5595	9001	47548	6900	35750	39135	6487	52292	12710	16364	37359
Other Receipts	7	1493358	80408	170005	32543	281622	140248	211409	99645	97979	84880	148500	33423	112689
Total Receipts	8	274076337	3031586	17869264	13892380	50719010	25263446	37673161	22874554	21895540	20839646	21528930	10520301	27968517
Average Total Receipts	9	4006	320	420	2194	6979	17956	43104	94134	145970	315752	828036	1052030	6992129
Operating Costs/Operating Income (%)														
Cost of Operations	10	81.1	87.4	68.6	72.5	78.6	81.8	80.5	85.5	80.9	82.0	86.5	80.2	89.9
Salaries and Wages	11	5.1	2.9	5.4	7.4	6.2	5.3	5.4	3.7	4.9	4.6	3.8	6.4	3.8
Taxes Paid	12	0.9	0.6	1.2	1.4	1.0	0.9	0.9	1.0	0.8	0.8	0.6	1.0	0.4
Interest Paid	13	0.5	0.8	0.4	0.4	0.4	0.4	0.5	0.5	0.6	0.8	0.6	1.7	0.4
Depreciation	14	0.7	0.2	0.6	0.7	0.6	0.6	0.8	0.6	1.0	0.8	1.0	1.4	0.6
Amortization and Depletion	15	0.2	0.1	0.1	0.2	0.0	0.1	0.1	0.1	0.3	0.3	0.2	0.9	0.7
Pensions and Other Deferred Comp.	16	0.2	0.2	0.3	0.1	0.2	0.1	0.2	0.1	0.2	0.2	0.1	0.3	0.3
Employee Benefits	17	0.4	0.7	0.4	0.5	0.4	0.4	0.4	0.3	0.5	0.5	0.7	0.8	0.1
Advertising	18	1.1	0.2	1.0	1.0	0.4	0.7	1.0	0.9	1.5	2.3	1.1	1.0	2.2
Other Expenses	19	6.8	11.9	14.7	10.7	7.9	6.9	7.0	4.6	6.2	6.3	4.0	5.8	2.0
Officers' Compensation	20	1.7	0.9	5.8	2.7	2.6	2.1	1.5	0.9	0.9	0.5	0.3	0.7	0.4
Operating Margin	21	1.2	•	1.2	2.5	1.8	0.9	1.6	1.7	2.1	1.0	1.1	•	•
Operating Margin Before Officers' Comp.	22	2.9	•	7.1	5.2	4.4	3.0	3.2	2.6	3.0	1.5	1.5	0.6	•

Selected Average Balance Sheet ($ in Thousands)													
Net Receivables 23	389	0	12	175	596	1763	4471	9819	19422	36119	104572	125437	650959
Inventories 24	495	0	42	238	882	2977	5614	11848	20826	36591	67890	168600	796112
Net Property, Plant and Equipment 25	131	0	11	84	146	414	1398	3551	6818	11488	30786	81732	200269
Total Assets 26	1648	0	100	718	2191	7145	15354	34661	68448	143959	320378	979309	4552335
Notes and Loans Payable 27	482	0	68	230	657	1877	4094	9741	19529	38767	90933	261752	1206535
All Other Liabilities 28	782	0	27	336	2511	3113	6005	12190	23874	51560	122704	227640	1723852
Net Worth 29	384	0	5	153	-977	2155	5254	12731	25045	53632	106741	489917	1621948
Selected Financial Ratios (Times to 1)													
Current Ratio 30	1.6	•	2.3	1.5	1.7	1.6	1.6	1.7	1.6	1.6	1.7	2.2	1.5
Quick Ratio 31	0.7	•	1.1	0.7	0.8	0.7	0.7	0.8	0.8	0.8	1.0	0.8	0.5
Net Sales to Working Capital 32	8.8	•	9.3	12.3	9.2	8.5	9.5	8.9	7.5	8.5	9.7	4.9	8.6
Coverage Ratio 33	5.1	•	6.2	8.1	8.0	5.1	5.9	5.8	6.0	3.9	6.2	1.6	2.7
Total Asset Turnover 34	2.4	•	4.1	3.0	3.2	2.5	2.8	2.7	2.1	2.2	2.5	1.1	1.5
Inventory Turnover 35	6.5	•	6.8	6.7	6.2	4.9	6.1	6.7	5.6	7.0	10.4	5.0	7.8
Receivables Turnover 36	10.1	•	37.2	14.0	11.2	9.0	9.5	9.8	7.8	8.6	8.3	8.9	9.5
Total Liabilities to Net Worth 37	3.3	•	18.2	3.7	•	2.3	1.9	1.7	1.7	1.7	2.0	1.0	1.8
Current Assets to Working Capital 38	2.6	•	1.8	3.1	2.4	2.8	2.8	2.5	2.6	2.7	2.5	1.9	3.1
Current Liabilities to Working Capital 39	1.6	•	0.8	2.1	1.4	1.8	1.8	1.5	1.6	1.7	1.5	0.9	2.1
Working Capital to Net Sales 40	0.1	•	0.1	0.1	0.1	0.1	0.1	0.1	0.1	0.1	0.1	0.2	0.1
Inventory to Working Capital 41	1.1	•	0.9	1.4	1.1	1.5	1.3	1.1	1.1	1.1	0.9	0.8	1.0
Total Receipts to Cash Flow 42	14.1	12.1	7.7	9.3	12.3	14.8	13.3	17.0	12.6	14.1	19.2	20.8	54.8
Cost of Goods to Cash Flow 43	11.4	10.6	5.3	6.8	9.6	12.1	10.7	14.5	10.2	11.5	16.6	16.7	49.3
Cash Flow to Total Debt 44	0.2	•	0.6	0.4	0.2	0.2	0.3	0.3	0.3	0.2	0.2	0.1	0.0
Selected Financial Factors (in Percentages)													
Debt Ratio 45	76.7	•	94.8	78.7	144.6	69.8	65.8	63.3	63.4	62.7	66.7	50.0	64.4
Return on Total Assets 46	6.4	•	11.2	9.7	9.1	4.6	8.0	8.0	7.7	6.3	8.8	2.9	1.6
Return on Equity Before Income Taxes 47	22.1	•	179.5	39.9	•	12.3	19.4	18.0	17.6	12.5	22.2	2.1	2.8
Return on Equity After Income Taxes 48	18.9	•	169.1	38.9	•	10.8	18.1	15.8	15.3	9.0	17.0	0.6	0.8
Profit Margin (Before Income Tax) 49	2.1	•	2.3	2.8	2.5	1.5	2.4	2.4	3.0	2.2	2.9	1.0	0.7
Profit Margin (After Income Tax) 50	1.8	•	2.1	2.7	2.4	1.3	2.2	2.1	2.6	1.5	2.2	0.3	0.2

Table II

Corporations with Net Income

FURNITURE, SPORTS, TOYS, JEWELRY, OTHER DURABLE GOODS

MONEY AMOUNTS AND SIZE OF ASSETS IN THOUSANDS OF DOLLARS

Item Description for Accounting Period 7/11 Through 6/12		Total	Zero Assets	Under 500	500 to 1,000	1,000 to 5,000	5,000 to 10,000	10,000 to 25,000	25,000 to 50,000	50,000 to 100,000	100,000 to 250,000	250,000 to 500,000	500,000 to 2,500,000	2,500,000 and over
Number of Enterprises	1	41320	2389	26514	•	5562	1065	704	202	121	51	22	4	•
Revenues ($ in Thousands)														
Net Sales	2	231609770	903031	13856108	•	42332780	22320342	32452206	21077912	18445495	17636368	19896346	7516589	•
Interest	3	237232	10616	380	•	9359	3446	6138	14470	7714	7321	20924	15234	•
Rents	4	69334	0	4731	•	1003	924	2022	3148	7806	3852	1618	33555	•
Royalties	5	313239	97	0	•	282	110	20778	6401	84551	28229	108768	0	•
Other Portfolio Income	6	233243	628	3982	•	38988	3124	32238	35188	5553	51951	12710	9008	•
Other Receipts	7	1164400	30250	120791	•	224270	108057	179091	76433	104008	60898	139996	18541	•
Total Receipts	8	233627218	944622	13985992	•	42606682	22436003	32692473	21213552	18655127	17788619	20180362	7592927	•
Average Total Receipts	9	5654	395	527	•	7660	21067	46438	105018	154175	348796	917289	1898232	•
Operating Costs/Operating Income (%)														
Cost of Operations	10	81.8	68.2	66.4	•	79.8	82.6	81.6	86.0	81.0	83.1	87.2	80.9	•
Salaries and Wages	11	4.6	2.5	4.6	•	5.1	4.6	4.9	3.5	4.7	4.1	3.7	6.9	•
Taxes Paid	12	0.8	0.9	1.1	•	0.9	0.8	0.9	1.0	0.8	0.6	0.5	1.2	•
Interest Paid	13	0.4	0.0	0.3	•	0.3	0.2	0.4	0.4	0.5	0.5	0.5	0.6	•
Depreciation	14	0.6	0.2	0.5	•	0.6	0.4	0.7	0.5	1.0	0.7	0.9	0.8	•
Amortization and Depletion	15	0.2	0.0	0.1	•	0.0	0.1	0.1	0.0	0.2	0.2	0.2	0.3	•
Pensions and Other Deferred Comp.	16	0.2	0.4	0.4	•	0.2	0.1	0.2	0.1	0.2	0.1	0.1	0.3	•
Employee Benefits	17	0.4	0.3	0.4	•	0.3	0.3	0.4	0.3	0.5	0.4	0.6	0.8	•
Advertising	18	0.9	0.2	1.1	•	0.3	0.4	0.8	0.8	1.5	1.8	1.1	0.8	•
Other Expenses	19	5.8	15.8	13.5	•	6.3	5.7	6.2	4.2	5.9	5.6	3.7	5.0	•
Officers' Compensation	20	1.6	1.9	6.3	•	2.4	2.2	1.5	0.9	0.9	0.5	0.2	0.5	•
Operating Margin	21	2.6	9.7	5.3	•	3.7	2.6	2.6	2.3	2.9	2.4	1.3	1.9	•
Operating Margin Before Officers' Comp.	22	4.3	11.5	11.6	•	6.1	4.8	4.0	3.2	3.8	2.9	1.6	2.4	•

Selected Average Balance Sheet ($ in Thousands)														
Net Receivables	23	544	0	12	•	610	1949	4828	10729	20711	38893	112930	235981	•
Inventories	24	649	0	37	•	811	3184	5786	11944	22540	38255	67446	322574	•
Net Property, Plant and Equipment	25	157	0	14	•	163	323	1267	2919	6507	9625	32795	131208	•
Total Assets	26	2107	0	112	•	2219	7334	15603	34587	67934	140459	320781	1160488	•
Notes and Loans Payable	27	550	0	49	•	523	1425	3694	9191	17469	29917	92529	248996	•
All Other Liabilities	28	769	0	27	•	729	3161	6094	12589	22783	46387	121408	319344	•
Net Worth	29	788	0	36	•	967	2749	5815	12807	27682	64155	106844	592148	•
Selected Financial Ratios (Times to 1)														
Current Ratio	30	1.7	•	2.5	•	2.1	1.7	1.7	1.7	1.7	2.0	1.6	2.1	•
Quick Ratio	31	0.8	•	1.1	•	1.1	0.7	0.8	0.8	0.9	1.0	1.0	0.9	•
Net Sales to Working Capital	32	8.7	•	10.5	•	7.8	8.0	9.0	9.4	6.9	6.6	10.5	5.9	•
Coverage Ratio	33	10.2	896.6	20.4	•	14.6	15.5	10.2	7.9	9.4	7.9	7.1	5.8	•
Total Asset Turnover	34	2.7	•	4.7	•	3.4	2.9	3.0	3.0	2.2	2.5	2.8	1.6	•
Inventory Turnover	35	7.1	•	9.4	•	7.5	5.4	6.5	7.5	5.5	7.5	11.7	4.7	•
Receivables Turnover	36	10.3	•	48.2	•	12.3	9.5	9.5	10.3	•	9.4	9.6	•	•
Total Liabilities to Net Worth	37	1.7	•	2.1	•	1.3	1.7	1.7	1.7	1.5	1.2	2.0	1.0	•
Current Assets to Working Capital	38	2.4	•	1.7	•	1.9	2.4	2.5	2.5	2.4	2.0	2.6	1.9	•
Current Liabilities to Working Capital	39	1.4	•	0.7	•	0.9	1.4	1.5	1.5	1.4	1.0	1.6	0.9	•
Working Capital to Net Sales	40	0.1	•	0.1	•	0.1	0.1	0.1	0.1	0.1	0.2	0.1	0.2	•
Inventory to Working Capital	41	1.0	•	0.9	•	0.8	1.3	1.1	1.1	1.0	0.8	0.9	1.0	•
Total Receipts to Cash Flow	42	12.8	3.4	6.1	•	11.3	13.5	12.7	16.5	11.4	12.9	18.9	17.1	•
Cost of Goods to Cash Flow	43	10.5	2.3	4.1	•	9.0	11.1	10.3	14.2	9.3	10.7	16.5	13.8	•
Cash Flow to Total Debt	44	0.3	•	1.1	•	0.5	0.3	0.4	0.3	0.3	0.4	0.2	0.2	•
Selected Financial Factors (in Percentages)														
Debt Ratio	45	62.6	•	67.5	•	56.4	62.5	62.7	63.0	59.3	54.3	66.7	49.0	•
Return on Total Assets	46	10.5	•	30.6	•	15.9	9.4	10.9	10.3	10.1	9.3	10.4	5.7	•
Return on Equity Before Income Taxes	47	25.3	•	89.7	•	34.0	23.6	26.5	24.3	22.2	17.8	26.9	9.3	•
Return on Equity After Income Taxes	48	22.7	•	87.3	•	32.6	22.0	25.0	21.6	19.6	13.9	20.8	6.2	•
Profit Margin (Before Income Tax)	49	3.6	14.3	6.2	•	4.3	3.1	3.3	3.0	4.0	3.3	3.2	2.9	•
Profit Margin (After Income Tax)	50	3.2	13.5	6.1	•	4.1	2.9	3.2	2.7	3.6	2.6	2.5	1.9	•

Table I

Corporations with and without Net Income

PAPER AND PAPER PRODUCT

MONEY AMOUNTS AND SIZE OF ASSETS IN THOUSANDS OF DOLLARS

Item Description for Accounting Period 7/11 Through 6/12		Total	Zero Assets	Under 500	500 to 1,000	1,000 to 5,000	5,000 to 10,000	10,000 to 25,000	25,000 to 50,000	50,000 to 100,000	100,000 to 250,000	250,000 to 500,000	500,000 to 2,500,000	2,500,000 and over
Number of Enterprises	1	9704	1988	5636	800	857	201	122	55	22	14	4	6	0
Revenues ($ in Thousands)														
Net Sales	2	55811501	121639	1974674	2224136	5056841	5092624	5664174	5999544	5114095	6793414	5191756	12578604	0
Interest	3	20042	211	79	66	1692	1125	3222	819	290	3855	1647	7034	0
Rents	4	9373	0	0	0	167	2891	141	1234	1171	25	498	3247	0
Royalties	5	31587	0	16844	0	0	0	0	0	0	20	0	14724	0
Other Portfolio Income	6	70417	6009	12309	10	22766	1720	608	1658	1929	536	0	22870	0
Other Receipts	7	252128	5086	24622	2450	41239	18871	36526	42735	26633	25915	62409	-34356	0
Total Receipts	8	56195048	132945	2028528	2226662	5122705	5117231	5704671	6045990	5144118	6823765	5256310	12592123	0
Average Total Receipts	9	5791	67	360	2783	5977	25459	46760	109927	233824	487412	1314078	2098687	•
Operating Costs/Operating Income (%)														
Cost of Operations	10	82.9	86.2	65.5	64.9	72.8	81.8	81.0	83.8	86.0	88.6	92.7	85.2	•
Salaries and Wages	11	5.8	2.4	7.1	9.6	9.2	7.2	6.7	6.2	5.3	3.5	2.5	5.1	•
Taxes Paid	12	0.8	1.3	1.6	1.4	1.3	0.9	1.0	0.8	0.7	0.5	0.3	0.7	•
Interest Paid	13	0.6	2.7	0.3	0.2	0.3	0.3	0.3	0.4	0.5	0.3	0.7	1.4	•
Depreciation	14	0.8	1.1	1.0	1.1	0.6	0.6	0.7	1.3	1.3	0.6	0.4	0.7	•
Amortization and Depletion	15	0.2	0.2	0.2	0.0	0.1	0.0	0.1	0.2	0.1	0.1	0.1	0.5	•
Pensions and Other Deferred Comp.	16	0.3	2.0	0.6	0.5	0.4	0.0	0.3	0.3	0.2	0.1	0.0	0.4	•
Employee Benefits	17	0.5	0.6	0.2	0.8	0.9	0.4	0.4	0.6	0.4	0.3	0.4	0.6	•
Advertising	18	0.2	0.7	0.7	0.3	0.2	0.1	0.5	0.2	0.1	0.0	0.0	0.1	•
Other Expenses	19	5.9	38.0	18.5	11.0	8.5	5.3	6.2	5.0	5.0	5.3	3.2	3.9	•
Officers' Compensation	20	1.2	4.9	6.9	3.6	2.4	1.1	1.4	1.0	0.7	0.4	0.3	0.3	•
Operating Margin	21	1.0	•	•	6.7	3.3	2.3	1.5	0.2	•	0.3	•	1.2	•
Operating Margin Before Officers' Comp.	22	2.2	•	4.3	10.3	5.7	3.4	2.8	1.3	0.6	0.7	•	1.4	•

Selected Average Balance Sheet ($ in Thousands)													
Net Receivables 23	676	0	23	204	696	2216	4981	14175	22877	72268	216751	243308	•
Inventories 24	419	0	31	115	544	1402	4248	9934	21298	34415	63459	130004	•
Net Property, Plant and Equipment 25	182	0	10	90	229	905	1334	4041	9429	14055	21027	63933	•
Total Assets 26	1883	0	108	755	2240	6408	15429	36182	70639	157337	316914	826058	•
Notes and Loans Payable 27	567	0	92	95	591	2218	3228	11280	28312	38826	109750	223118	•
All Other Liabilities 28	774	0	29	263	561	1730	5631	13511	23065	81607	180440	418390	•
Net Worth 29	541	0	-13	396	1087	2460	6570	11392	19262	36905	26724	184549	•

Selected Financial Ratios (Times to 1)													
Current Ratio 30	1.5	•	2.5	2.0	1.7	2.1	1.7	1.6	1.6	1.5	1.7	1.0	•
Quick Ratio 31	0.9	•	1.6	1.5	1.1	1.1	1.0	0.9	0.7	0.9	1.3	0.6	•
Net Sales to Working Capital 32	13.4	•	7.4	9.0	9.1	9.5	9.0	11.0	11.2	12.0	10.9	•	•
Coverage Ratio 33	3.7	•	1.6	31.6	17.3	10.5	7.8	3.4	1.9	3.7	2.1	1.9	•
Total Asset Turnover 34	3.1	•	3.2	3.7	2.6	4.0	3.0	3.0	3.3	3.1	4.1	2.5	•
Inventory Turnover 35	11.4	•	7.4	15.6	7.9	14.8	8.9	9.2	9.4	12.5	19.0	13.7	•
Receivables Turnover 36	8.5	•	11.3	13.7	8.2	14.2	8.4	7.8	11.1	6.5	5.6	9.2	•
Total Liabilities to Net Worth 37	2.5	•	•	0.9	1.1	1.6	1.3	2.2	2.7	3.3	10.9	3.5	•
Current Assets to Working Capital 38	3.1	•	1.7	2.0	2.3	1.9	2.4	2.8	2.7	3.2	2.5	•	•
Current Liabilities to Working Capital 39	2.1	•	0.7	1.0	1.3	0.9	1.4	1.8	1.7	2.2	1.5	•	•
Working Capital to Net Sales 40	0.1	•	0.1	0.1	0.1	0.1	0.1	0.1	0.1	0.1	0.1	•	•
Inventory to Working Capital 41	1.0	•	0.5	0.4	0.7	0.8	0.9	1.0	1.1	0.9	0.5	•	•
Total Receipts to Cash Flow 42	17.1	•	7.5	6.5	10.6	15.3	14.7	21.0	26.6	20.5	31.0	24.9	•
Cost of Goods to Cash Flow 43	14.1	•	4.9	4.2	7.7	12.5	11.9	17.6	22.8	18.2	28.7	21.2	•
Cash Flow to Total Debt 44	0.3	•	0.4	1.2	0.5	0.4	0.4	0.2	0.2	0.2	0.1	0.1	•

Selected Financial Factors (in Percentages)													
Debt Ratio 45	71.2	•	111.9	47.5	51.5	61.6	57.4	68.5	72.7	76.5	91.6	77.7	•
Return on Total Assets 46	7.2	•	1.8	25.8	13.0	12.3	7.5	4.6	3.2	3.2	5.9	6.9	•
Return on Equity Before Income Taxes 47	18.3	•	•	47.6	25.3	28.9	15.4	10.3	5.5	10.0	36.7	14.6	•
Return on Equity After Income Taxes 48	15.7	•	•	47.3	24.1	27.6	13.6	7.4	3.5	9.0	35.4	8.9	•
Profit Margin (Before Income Tax) 49	1.7	•	0.2	6.8	4.7	2.8	2.2	1.1	0.5	0.8	0.8	1.3	•
Profit Margin (After Income Tax) 50	1.5	•	0.0	6.7	4.4	2.7	1.9	0.8	0.3	0.7	0.7	0.8	•

Table II

Corporations with Net Income

PAPER AND PAPER PRODUCT

MONEY AMOUNTS AND SIZE OF ASSETS IN THOUSANDS OF DOLLARS

Item Description for Accounting Period 7/11 Through 6/12		Total	Zero Assets	Under 500	500 to 1,000	1,000 to 5,000	5,000 to 10,000	10,000 to 25,000	25,000 to 50,000	50,000 to 100,000	100,000 to 250,000	250,000 to 500,000	500,000 to 2,500,000	2,500,000 and over
Number of Enterprises	1	5248	401	3109	670	750	140	98	44	19	•	4	•	0
Revenues ($ in Thousands)														
Net Sales	2	43850161	2921	789730	1919396	4298829	4552127	4532144	4898598	4042328	•	5191756	•	0
Interest	3	10019	0	24	26	1680	1112	3166	662	175	•	1647	•	0
Rents	4	4991	0	0	0	0	2891	141	266	1171	•	498	•	0
Royalties	5	16970	0	16844	0	0	0	0	0	0	•	0	•	0
Other Portfolio Income	6	29535	0	0	0	22289	1720	517	257	1498	•	0	•	0
Other Receipts	7	210625	0	24148	1250	40284	18870	28770	36132	26170	•	62409	•	0
Total Receipts	8	44122301	2921	830746	1920672	4363082	4576720	4564738	4935915	4071342	•	5256310	•	0
Average Total Receipts	9	8407	7	267	2867	5817	32691	46579	112180	214281	•	1314078	•	•
Operating Costs/Operating Income (%)														
Cost of Operations	10	82.9	•	51.9	63.8	72.3	83.0	81.8	84.9	85.1	•	92.7	•	•
Salaries and Wages	11	5.3	•	7.7	7.7	8.3	7.1	5.8	5.5	5.4	•	2.5	•	•
Taxes Paid	12	0.8	•	1.3	1.0	1.3	0.9	1.0	0.7	0.8	•	0.3	•	•
Interest Paid	13	0.4	•	0.3	0.0	0.2	0.2	0.2	0.4	0.3	•	0.7	•	•
Depreciation	14	0.5	•	0.5	1.1	0.5	0.3	0.5	0.6	0.7	•	0.4	•	•
Amortization and Depletion	15	0.1	•	0.2	•	0.1	0.0	0.1	0.2	0.1	•	0.1	•	•
Pensions and Other Deferred Comp.	16	0.2	•	0.0	0.6	0.4	0.0	0.3	0.1	0.1	•	0.0	•	•
Employee Benefits	17	0.5	•	•	0.6	1.0	0.4	0.5	0.4	0.3	•	0.4	•	•
Advertising	18	0.2	•	0.9	0.3	0.2	0.1	0.6	0.2	0.1	•	0.0	•	•
Other Expenses	19	5.4	75.8	26.5	9.9	8.8	3.8	5.9	4.5	4.9	•	3.2	•	•
Officers' Compensation	20	1.1	•	7.8	3.3	2.5	1.1	1.1	1.1	0.9	•	0.3	•	•
Operating Margin	21	2.5	24.2	2.6	11.6	4.5	3.2	2.4	1.4	1.4	•	•	•	•
Operating Margin Before Officers' Comp.	22	3.6	24.2	10.5	14.8	6.9	4.2	3.5	2.5	2.3	•	•	•	•

Selected Average Balance Sheet ($ in Thousands)

Net Receivables	23	968	0	22	224	668	2679	4993	14458	23824	•	216751	•	•
Inventories	24	602	0	22	95	511	1281	4345	11682	22587	•	62207	•	•
Net Property, Plant and Equipment	25	226	0	4	92	217	835	1198	2214	6603	•	21027	•	•
Total Assets	26	2592	0	90	768	2226	6681	15306	35322	66906	•	316914	•	•
Notes and Loans Payable	27	627	0	104	4	523	1946	2976	8528	18762	•	109750	•	•
All Other Liabilities	28	1072	0	20	192	593	1998	5194	13935	22405	•	180440	•	•
Net Worth	29	893	0	-34	572	1110	2736	7136	12858	25740	•	26724	•	•

Selected Financial Ratios (Times to 1)

Current Ratio	30	1.5	•	3.3	3.2	1.7	2.0	1.9	1.7	1.7	•	1.7	•	•
Quick Ratio	31	0.9	•	2.4	2.7	1.0	1.2	1.1	1.0	0.8	•	1.3	•	•
Net Sales to Working Capital	32	13.5	•	6.7	6.7	9.7	12.6	7.9	9.5	8.9	•	10.9	•	•
Coverage Ratio	33	8.5	•	23.4	476.5	26.9	17.7	14.1	7.2	7.7	•	2.1	•	•
Total Asset Turnover	34	3.2	•	2.8	3.7	2.6	4.9	3.0	3.2	3.2	•	4.1	•	•
Inventory Turnover	35	11.5	•	6.1	19.1	8.1	21.1	8.7	8.1	8.0	•	19.3	•	•
Receivables Turnover	36	8.7	•	8.7	12.4	8.6	16.4	8.0	7.3	9.3	•	•	•	•
Total Liabilities to Net Worth	37	1.9	•	•	0.3	1.0	1.4	1.1	1.7	1.6	•	10.9	•	•
Current Assets to Working Capital	38	3.0	•	1.4	1.5	2.5	2.0	2.1	2.5	2.3	•	2.5	•	•
Current Liabilities to Working Capital	39	2.0	•	0.4	0.5	1.5	1.0	1.1	1.5	1.3	•	1.5	•	•
Working Capital to Net Sales	40	0.1	•	0.2	0.2	0.1	0.1	0.1	0.1	0.1	•	0.1	•	•
Inventory to Working Capital	41	1.0	•	0.2	0.2	0.8	0.7	0.8	0.9	1.0	•	0.5	•	•
Total Receipts to Cash Flow	42	14.3	1.0	3.2	5.1	9.3	15.6	13.4	18.0	18.8	•	31.0	•	•
Cost of Goods to Cash Flow	43	11.9	•	1.7	3.2	6.7	13.0	11.0	15.3	16.0	•	28.7	•	•
Cash Flow to Total Debt	44	0.3	•	0.6	2.9	0.6	0.5	0.4	0.3	0.3	•	0.1	•	•

Selected Financial Factors (in Percentages)

Debt Ratio	45	65.6	•	138.1	25.5	50.1	59.0	53.4	63.6	61.5	•	91.6	•	•
Return on Total Assets	46	11.4	•	23.1	43.4	16.0	19.1	10.0	8.0	7.6	•	5.9	•	•
Return on Equity Before Income Taxes	47	29.1	•	•	58.2	30.8	43.9	20.0	19.0	17.3	•	36.7	•	•
Return on Equity After Income Taxes	48	26.3	•	•	58.0	29.5	42.3	17.9	15.7	15.5	•	35.4	•	•
Profit Margin (Before Income Tax)	49	3.1	24.2	7.8	11.6	6.0	3.7	3.1	2.2	2.1	•	0.8	•	•
Profit Margin (After Income Tax)	50	2.8	24.2	7.4	11.6	5.7	3.6	2.8	1.8	1.9	•	0.7	•	•

Table I

Corporations with and without Net Income

DRUGS AND DRUGGISTS' SUNDRIES

MONEY AMOUNTS AND SIZE OF ASSETS IN THOUSANDS OF DOLLARS

Item Description for Accounting Period 7/11 Through 6/12		Total	Zero Assets	Under 500	500 to 1,000	1,000 to 5,000	5,000 to 10,000	10,000 to 25,000	25,000 to 50,000	50,000 to 100,000	100,000 to 250,000	250,000 to 500,000	500,000 to 2,500,000	2,500,000 and over
Number of Enterprises	1	6251	741	3536	602	800	209	161	73	40	29	18	22	20
Revenues ($ in Thousands)														
Net Sales	2	479881135	2442413	2097620	1054997	5980509	2871749	5376639	6222210	5420289	6047438	5544530	28717183	408105560
Interest	3	298857	1678	3	7	1195	594	317	3689	6025	2333	13510	121489	148018
Rents	4	45284	215	0	968	13410	0	0	505	90	1119	1400	1339	26237
Royalties	5	4019449	139982	0	0	35	19363	260	44158	27399	70754	64258	58157	3595083
Other Portfolio Income	6	993127	10019	0	0	15794	231	16674	13122	68905	18402	12083	85460	752435
Other Receipts	7	4547554	133089	6076	9023	11989	22268	220832	51651	38388	59836	112588	1316192	2565622
Total Receipts	8	489785406	2727396	2103699	1064995	6022932	2914205	5614722	6335335	5561096	6199882	5748369	30299820	415192955
Average Total Receipts	9	78353	3681	595	1769	7529	13944	34874	86785	139027	213789	319354	1377265	20759648
Operating Costs/Operating Income (%)														
Cost of Operations	10	81.2	52.0	61.6	62.8	58.4	67.2	70.7	74.8	72.7	60.2	65.9	65.8	84.0
Salaries and Wages	11	3.7	19.5	8.1	5.9	10.8	7.0	9.3	7.4	8.0	12.1	8.6	8.7	2.7
Taxes Paid	12	0.5	2.0	1.6	1.3	1.7	0.9	1.3	0.7	1.0	1.1	1.0	1.0	0.4
Interest Paid	13	0.6	1.8	0.1	0.3	0.4	0.6	0.4	0.3	1.4	0.7	3.7	0.9	0.5
Depreciation	14	0.6	2.6	0.1	1.2	0.5	0.3	0.8	0.8	0.9	1.5	0.9	0.8	0.5
Amortization and Depletion	15	0.5	1.0	0.1	0.1	0.1	0.3	0.1	0.5	2.0	1.1	1.1	1.1	0.4
Pensions and Other Deferred Comp.	16	0.1	1.3	•	0.1	0.2	0.2	0.2	0.1	0.1	0.2	0.4	0.3	0.1
Employee Benefits	17	0.5	2.1	0.4	0.3	0.4	0.4	0.6	0.7	0.8	1.1	1.0	1.6	0.4
Advertising	18	0.9	2.7	1.1	0.7	1.6	0.8	1.3	2.2	3.5	2.6	4.1	2.0	0.7
Other Expenses	19	9.5	21.4	17.2	21.0	18.4	15.2	14.0	9.8	16.2	13.2	15.6	15.4	8.5
Officers' Compensation	20	0.4	3.3	3.1	1.8	4.7	2.1	2.6	1.6	1.8	0.9	1.6	0.5	0.2
Operating Margin	21	1.5	•	6.6	4.4	2.7	5.0	•	1.0	•	5.3	•	1.8	1.7
Operating Margin Before Officers' Comp.	22	1.9	•	9.6	6.2	7.4	7.1	1.2	2.6	•	6.2	•	2.3	1.8

Selected Average Balance Sheet ($ in Thousands)

Net Receivables 23	6708	0	4	120	575	1944	4017	11896	14090	23949	72831	180528	1646133
Inventories 24	5606	0	19	197	785	2418	4964	6611	15354	37049	53461	120426	1357151
Net Property, Plant and Equipment 25	2148	0	1	95	440	154	1205	1825	4621	18494	19412	54145	519702
Total Assets 26	40237	0	62	835	2900	6132	16716	35326	71149	151837	333490	1131959	10188494
Notes and Loans Payable 27	10018	0	50	92	623	1370	3730	3603	22266	39266	114649	271180	2534360
All Other Liabilities 28	17326	0	55	95	1470	2893	6465	16625	27293	49799	202873	360486	4494922
Net Worth 29	12892	0	-42	647	807	1869	6520	15099	21590	62771	15967	500294	3159212

Selected Financial Ratios (Times to 1)

Current Ratio 30	0.9	•	3.9	4.3	1.4	1.5	1.7	1.7	1.1	1.4	1.2	1.5	0.8
Quick Ratio 31	0.5	•	1.1	2.0	0.8	0.9	0.8	1.1	0.6	0.7	0.6	0.8	0.5
Net Sales to Working Capital 32	•	•	18.3	4.8	12.9	7.8	6.3	7.7	23.0	8.1	10.1	7.1	•
Coverage Ratio 33	7.5	2.1	82.7	16.4	8.9	11.3	8.1	10.0	•	12.3	1.0	9.0	8.2
Total Asset Turnover 34	1.9	•	9.5	2.1	2.6	2.2	2.0	2.4	1.9	1.4	0.9	1.2	2.0
Inventory Turnover 35	11.1	•	18.9	5.6	5.6	3.8	4.8	9.6	6.4	3.4	3.8	7.1	12.6
Receivables Turnover 36	12.2	•	214.6	14.5	11.2	5.9	7.9	7.4	9.7	7.4	4.6	8.3	13.3
Total Liabilities to Net Worth 37	2.1	•	•	0.3	2.6	2.3	1.6	1.3	2.3	1.4	19.9	1.3	2.2
Current Assets to Working Capital 38	•	•	1.3	1.3	3.6	2.9	2.5	2.5	7.8	3.4	6.8	2.8	•
Current Liabilities to Working Capital 39	•	•	0.3	0.3	2.6	1.9	1.5	1.5	6.8	2.4	5.8	1.8	•
Working Capital to Net Sales 40	•	•	0.1	0.2	0.1	0.1	0.2	0.1	0.0	0.1	0.1	0.1	•
Inventory to Working Capital 41	•	•	0.8	0.7	1.5	1.1	1.0	0.6	2.4	1.5	2.3	0.8	•
Total Receipts to Cash Flow 42	8.2	4.6	5.4	4.3	5.2	4.9	6.6	8.9	28.1	5.1	7.8	4.6	8.8
Cost of Goods to Cash Flow 43	6.6	2.4	3.3	2.7	3.1	3.3	4.6	6.7	20.4	3.1	5.1	3.1	7.4
Cash Flow to Total Debt 44	0.3	•	1.1	2.2	0.7	0.7	0.5	0.5	0.1	0.5	0.1	0.4	0.3

Selected Financial Factors (in Percentages)

Debt Ratio 45	68.0	•	168.3	22.5	72.2	69.5	61.0	57.3	69.7	58.7	95.2	55.8	69.0
Return on Total Assets 46	8.3	•	66.2	11.9	9.8	16.0	6.7	7.6	•	12.0	3.4	9.8	8.2
Return on Equity Before Income Taxes 47	22.4	•	•	14.4	31.4	47.8	15.1	16.0	•	26.6	•	19.7	23.3
Return on Equity After Income Taxes 48	14.9	•	•	14.3	26.6	41.2	13.3	14.1	•	21.0	•	12.3	15.6
Profit Margin (Before Income Tax) 49	3.8	2.1	6.9	5.3	3.4	6.5	2.9	2.8	•	8.0	•	7.5	3.6
Profit Margin (After Income Tax) 50	2.5	•	6.9	5.3	2.9	5.6	2.6	2.5	•	6.3	•	4.7	2.4

Table II

Corporations with Net Income

DRUGS AND DRUGGISTS' SUNDRIES

MONEY AMOUNTS AND SIZE OF ASSETS IN THOUSANDS OF DOLLARS

Item Description for Accounting Period 7/11 Through 6/12		Total	Zero Assets	Under 500	500 to 1,000	1,000 to 5,000	5,000 to 10,000	10,000 to 25,000	25,000 to 50,000	50,000 to 100,000	100,000 to 250,000	250,000 to 500,000	500,000 to 2,500,000	2,500,000 and over
Number of Enterprises	1	3727	6	2448	300	519	182	110	61	25	24	14	17	20
Revenues ($ in Thousands)														
Net Sales	2	467906113	2338173	1796083	460122	5547240	2536701	4432496	5744786	4497144	4762803	4605829	23079175	408105560
Interest	3	271744	1555	0	7	934	260	153	3304	2880	2199	4031	108404	148018
Rents	4	31977	215	0	968	590	0	0	505	90	1119	1400	853	26237
Royalties	5	3931226	139982	0	0	35	19363	0	25132	8426	70708	63118	9378	3595083
Other Portfolio Income	6	930585	0	0	0	15712	222	13188	9637	60829	18402	8577	51582	752435
Other Receipts	7	4142403	130347	6083	476	10944	31782	81177	41801	22480	55725	99384	1096585	2565622
Total Receipts	8	477214048	2610272	1802166	461573	5575455	2588328	4527014	5825165	4591849	4910956	4782339	24345977	415192955
Average Total Receipts	9	128042	435045	736	1539	10743	14222	41155	95495	183674	204623	341596	1432116	20759648
Operating Costs/Operating Income (%)														
Cost of Operations	10	81.5	50.4	58.5	54.3	59.7	66.6	71.9	76.7	77.5	53.8	67.8	61.6	84.0
Salaries and Wages	11	3.6	18.5	8.8	10.3	10.4	5.4	6.3	6.7	6.0	14.1	8.0	9.3	2.7
Taxes Paid	12	0.5	1.9	1.3	1.9	1.6	0.8	1.1	0.6	0.7	1.2	0.9	1.1	0.4
Interest Paid	13	0.5	1.9	0.1	0.5	0.2	0.6	0.3	0.2	0.5	0.7	2.4	0.7	0.5
Depreciation	14	0.6	2.7	0.1	1.2	0.5	0.3	0.7	0.6	0.6	1.6	0.8	0.8	0.5
Amortization and Depletion	15	0.4	0.9	0.1	0.0	0.0	0.1	0.0	0.2	0.5	0.9	0.9	0.9	0.4
Pensions and Other Deferred Comp.	16	0.1	1.4	•	0.2	0.2	0.2	0.2	0.1	0.1	0.3	0.4	0.4	0.1
Employee Benefits	17	0.5	2.0	0.5	0.5	0.4	0.3	0.4	0.7	0.6	1.3	1.1	1.8	0.4
Advertising	18	0.8	2.5	1.0	1.4	1.6	0.7	1.0	1.7	3.3	2.7	1.9	1.9	0.7
Other Expenses	19	9.2	18.6	16.0	14.3	15.6	14.7	10.4	7.0	6.9	14.9	12.0	16.0	8.5
Officers' Compensation	20	0.3	2.5	2.0	2.4	4.4	2.1	2.6	1.6	1.0	1.0	1.9	0.5	0.2
Operating Margin	21	2.1	•	11.6	13.0	5.5	8.2	4.9	3.8	2.4	7.4	2.0	5.0	1.7
Operating Margin Before Officers' Comp.	22	2.4	•	13.7	15.4	9.9	10.4	7.5	5.4	3.4	8.4	3.9	5.5	1.8

Selected Average Balance Sheet ($ in Thousands)													
Net Receivables 23	10882	0	5	66	790	1936	4919	13670	16694	25312	86995	189482	1646133
Inventories 24	8974	0	11	191	1032	2633	6147	7575	18969	35292	49198	127666	1402449
Net Property, Plant and Equipment 25	3361	0	1	116	222	150	1266	1493	2923	17964	19996	55234	519702
Total Assets 26	64700	0	53	754	3392	5994	16778	35694	70765	146226	339718	1182618	10188494
Notes and Loans Payable 27	15739	0	26	119	385	1421	3822	2735	11988	33760	94890	258181	2534360
All Other Liabilities 28	28039	0	13	59	1731	2655	6703	17011	26653	51988	214313	381400	4494922
Net Worth 29	20922	0	13	576	1275	1918	6253	15948	32123	60477	30515	543038	3159212

Selected Financial Ratios (Times to 1)													
Current Ratio 30	0.9	•	2.5	3.8	1.6	1.7	1.7	1.8	1.8	1.5	1.1	1.6	0.8
Quick Ratio 31	0.5	•	1.1	1.9	0.9	1.0	0.9	1.2	1.0	0.7	0.7	0.8	0.5
Net Sales to Working Capital 32	•	•	35.9	6.8	10.7	6.4	6.8	7.2	7.9	7.4	19.2	6.6	•
Coverage Ratio 33	9.0	5.4	127.3	27.5	30.9	19.0	21.2	22.0	9.8	16.5	3.5	15.3	8.2
Total Asset Turnover 34	1.9	•	14.0	2.0	3.2	2.3	2.4	2.6	2.5	1.4	1.0	1.1	2.0
Inventory Turnover 35	11.4	•	38.7	4.3	6.2	3.5	4.7	9.5	7.3	3.0	4.5	6.5	12.2
Receivables Turnover 36	12.4	•	270.3	12.4	12.7	5.8	7.5	•	10.3	6.7	4.4	8.3	•
Total Liabilities to Net Worth 37	2.1	•	2.9	0.3	1.7	2.1	1.7	1.2	1.2	1.4	10.1	1.2	2.2
Current Assets to Working Capital 38	•	•	1.7	1.4	2.8	2.4	2.4	2.3	2.3	3.2	13.0	2.8	•
Current Liabilities to Working Capital 39	•	•	0.7	0.4	1.8	1.4	1.4	1.3	1.3	2.2	12.0	1.8	•
Working Capital to Net Sales 40	•	•	0.0	0.1	0.1	0.2	0.1	0.1	0.1	0.1	0.1	0.2	•
Inventory to Working Capital 41	•	•	0.9	0.6	1.2	0.9	1.0	0.6	0.8	1.2	3.7	0.8	•
Total Receipts to Cash Flow 42	8.0	3.9	4.6	3.9	5.1	4.2	6.3	9.1	10.6	4.2	6.0	3.9	8.8
Cost of Goods to Cash Flow 43	6.5	2.0	2.7	2.1	3.1	2.8	4.5	6.9	8.2	2.3	4.1	2.4	7.4
Cash Flow to Total Debt 44	0.4	•	4.1	2.2	1.0	0.8	0.6	0.5	0.4	0.6	0.2	0.5	0.3

Selected Financial Factors (in Percentages)													
Debt Ratio 45	67.7	•	74.5	23.5	62.4	68.0	62.7	55.3	54.6	58.6	91.0	54.1	69.0
Return on Total Assets 46	9.3	•	168.5	28.2	19.6	25.2	17.8	14.4	13.1	15.5	8.3	13.1	8.2
Return on Equity Before Income Taxes 47	25.5	•	655.3	35.5	50.4	74.7	45.4	30.7	25.9	35.3	66.2	26.7	23.3
Return on Equity After Income Taxes 48	17.7	•	654.9	35.2	45.7	67.4	42.7	28.5	18.8	28.4	53.0	17.9	15.6
Profit Margin (Before Income Tax) 49	4.2	8.3	12.0	13.3	6.0	10.3	7.0	5.2	4.6	10.8	6.1	10.7	3.6
Profit Margin (After Income Tax) 50	3.0	6.1	12.0	13.2	5.4	9.3	6.6	4.8	3.4	8.6	4.9	7.2	2.4

Table I

Corporations with and without Net Income

APPAREL, PIECE GOODS, AND NOTIONS

MONEY AMOUNTS AND SIZE OF ASSETS IN THOUSANDS OF DOLLARS

Item Description for Accounting Period 7/11 Through 6/12		Total	Zero Assets	Under 500	500 to 1,000	1,000 to 5,000	5,000 to 10,000	10,000 to 25,000	25,000 to 50,000	50,000 to 100,000	100,000 to 250,000	250,000 to 500,000	500,000 to 2,500,000	2,500,000 and over
Number of Enterprises	1	19593	988	14803	498	2493	348	241	108	43	33	16	•	6
Revenues ($ in Thousands)														
Net Sales	2	113934975	2124175	9887376	1443855	13876069	6210704	9304364	7657493	5817439	7303763	7189849	•	28419218
Interest	3	155199	75	1152	32	1999	612	1397	1436	2252	7112	6490	•	27657
Rents	4	46969	1087	0	0	382	2668	26	233	5119	6310	18405	•	4805
Royalties	5	1828278	60375	0	0	12603	0	2529	15335	7763	37677	73924	•	1316016
Other Portfolio Income	6	1057988	0	0	0	3571	17	399	112	13258	20429	49704	•	794491
Other Receipts	7	1096389	7691	48057	32813	33125	-2061	78618	100350	35154	57568	98748	•	438797
Total Receipts	8	118119798	2193403	9936585	1476700	13927749	6211940	9387333	7774959	5880985	7432859	7437120	•	31000984
Average Total Receipts	9	6029	2220	671	2965	5587	17850	38952	71990	136767	225238	464820	•	5166831
Operating Costs/Operating Income (%)														
Cost of Operations	10	67.1	69.9	71.9	67.8	74.0	83.9	74.7	71.5	73.2	65.7	62.4	•	58.7
Salaries and Wages	11	9.3	6.2	4.3	5.5	5.8	3.9	7.1	7.2	7.5	8.7	10.5	•	14.4
Taxes Paid	12	2.1	2.9	1.1	2.0	2.1	1.4	3.1	1.5	1.7	2.2	2.1	•	2.1
Interest Paid	13	0.9	0.2	0.3	0.2	0.7	0.6	0.6	0.5	0.5	1.2	2.1	•	0.8
Depreciation	14	1.6	2.2	0.3	0.2	0.4	0.2	0.4	0.8	0.9	1.8	2.3	•	2.4
Amortization and Depletion	15	0.4	0.5	0.1	0.0	0.0	0.0	0.2	0.2	0.1	0.6	0.8	•	0.6
Pensions and Other Deferred Comp.	16	0.3	0.0	0.6	0.8	0.2	0.6	0.1	0.1	0.1	0.4	0.4	•	0.4
Employee Benefits	17	0.6	0.3	0.2	0.4	0.6	0.2	0.4	0.4	0.8	0.7	1.1	•	0.7
Advertising	18	2.4	0.9	0.7	0.2	0.8	0.5	1.0	1.1	1.3	3.1	2.3	•	4.8
Other Expenses	19	13.3	13.2	13.5	10.6	12.3	6.0	7.7	10.2	10.0	12.3	15.3	•	17.0
Officers' Compensation	20	1.8	0.9	5.1	5.2	2.4	1.1	2.8	2.0	1.6	1.5	0.6	•	0.8
Operating Margin	21	0.3	2.7	1.9	7.0	0.7	1.6	1.9	4.4	2.3	1.8	0.1	•	•
Operating Margin Before Officers' Comp.	22	2.1	3.6	7.1	12.2	3.2	2.7	4.7	6.4	3.9	3.4	0.8	•	•

Selected Average Balance Sheet ($ in Thousands)

Net Receivables **23**	794	0	16	405	528	2908	4921	9775	17691	35458	48943	•	920501
Inventories **24**	817	0	28	410	640	2706	5671	13896	24947	49638	93244	•	562886
Net Property, Plant and Equipment **25**	358	0	8	46	108	718	662	3136	4906	15193	40984	•	516986
Total Assets **26**	5609	0	100	793	2008	7397	15188	35623	69853	161967	373471	•	10830720
Notes and Loans Payable **27**	923	0	81	217	562	2451	4945	7888	16467	51786	138971	•	954553
All Other Liabilities **28**	1289	0	52	361	944	3536	5487	12478	23306	47451	142022	•	1643039
Net Worth **29**	3396	0	-33	215	502	1409	4756	15257	30080	62729	92478	•	8233128

Selected Financial Ratios (Times to 1)

Current Ratio **30**	1.6	•	1.6	1.5	1.6	1.5	1.7	1.8	1.6	2.2	1.6	•	1.3
Quick Ratio **31**	0.8	•	1.0	1.1	0.7	0.8	0.8	0.7	0.7	0.9	0.6	•	0.7
Net Sales to Working Capital **32**	6.9	•	20.3	12.1	8.6	9.0	7.4	5.5	6.6	3.8	6.0	•	8.7
Coverage Ratio **33**	6.5	27.4	10.3	56.0	2.6	3.6	5.5	13.0	8.1	3.9	2.7	•	13.9
Total Asset Turnover **34**	1.0	•	6.7	3.7	2.8	2.4	2.5	2.0	1.9	1.4	1.2	•	0.4
Inventory Turnover **35**	4.8	•	16.9	4.8	6.4	5.5	5.1	3.7	4.0	2.9	3.0	•	4.9
Receivables Turnover **36**	8.3	•	38.4	7.5	10.8	6.9	8.4	7.3	8.0	6.5	8.2	•	6.8
Total Liabilities to Net Worth **37**	0.7	•	•	2.7	3.0	4.2	2.2	1.3	1.3	1.6	3.0	•	0.3
Current Assets to Working Capital **38**	2.6	•	2.6	2.8	2.7	3.1	2.5	2.3	2.6	1.8	2.6	•	4.1
Current Liabilities to Working Capital **39**	1.6	•	1.6	1.8	1.7	2.1	1.5	1.3	1.6	0.8	1.6	•	3.1
Working Capital to Net Sales **40**	0.1	•	0.0	0.1	0.1	0.1	0.1	0.2	0.2	0.3	0.2	•	0.1
Inventory to Working Capital **41**	1.0	•	0.9	0.8	1.1	1.2	1.1	1.1	1.2	0.9	1.2	•	1.1
Total Receipts to Cash Flow **42**	7.5	6.1	9.0	6.2	9.2	15.6	11.6	7.3	9.2	8.1	7.6	•	5.4
Cost of Goods to Cash Flow **43**	5.0	4.3	6.5	4.2	6.8	13.1	8.7	5.2	6.7	5.3	4.7	•	3.1
Cash Flow to Total Debt **44**	0.4	•	0.6	0.8	0.4	0.2	0.3	0.5	0.4	0.3	0.2	•	0.3

Selected Financial Factors (in Percentages)

Debt Ratio **45**	39.4	•	133.3	72.9	75.0	80.9	68.7	57.2	56.9	61.3	75.2	•	24.0
Return on Total Assets **46**	5.9	•	18.0	34.5	4.9	5.3	8.6	12.8	7.4	6.6	6.9	•	4.7
Return on Equity Before Income Taxes **47**	8.2	•	•	124.9	12.1	20.2	22.6	27.5	15.1	12.8	17.4	•	5.7
Return on Equity After Income Taxes **48**	5.9	•	•	120.8	11.1	15.5	21.0	25.3	13.8	7.8	10.7	•	3.8
Profit Margin (Before Income Tax) **49**	4.8	5.9	2.4	9.3	1.1	1.6	2.8	5.9	3.3	3.6	3.6	•	9.9
Profit Margin (After Income Tax) **50**	3.4	3.7	2.4	9.0	1.0	1.2	2.6	5.4	3.1	2.2	2.2	•	6.6

Table II

Corporations with Net Income

APPAREL, PIECE GOODS, AND NOTIONS

MONEY AMOUNTS AND SIZE OF ASSETS IN THOUSANDS OF DOLLARS

Item Description for Accounting Period 7/11 Through 6/12		Total	Zero Assets	Under 500	500 to 1,000	1,000 to 5,000	5,000 to 10,000	10,000 to 25,000	25,000 to 50,000	50,000 to 100,000	100,000 to 250,000	250,000 to 500,000	500,000 to 2,500,000	2,500,000 and over
Number of Enterprises	1	10917	315	7791	412	1721	323	180	93	31	22	12	11	6
Revenues ($ in Thousands)														
Net Sales	2	94456566	1815601	6390804	1387645	10637621	5860837	7939122	6678503	4386279	5005898	4964188	10970849	28419218
Interest	3	53107	74	122	32	990	596	739	579	1029	2031	5032	14226	27657
Rents	4	40694	0	0	0	382	2657	26	233	618	5967	18073	7934	4805
Royalties	5	1593263	60375	0	0	0	0	0	4867	1324	22886	36518	151277	1316016
Other Portfolio Income	6	910311	0	0	0	3483	12	365	74	758	18030	47167	45931	794491
Other Receipts	7	908616	6292	11227	32756	29455	-3849	60966	94018	27908	43241	47067	120739	438797
Total Receipts	8	97962557	1882342	6402153	1420433	10671931	5860253	8001218	6778274	4417916	5098053	5118045	11310956	31000984
Average Total Receipts	9	8973	5976	822	3448	6201	18143	44451	72885	142513	231730	426504	1028269	5166831
Operating Costs/Operating Income (%)														
Cost of Operations	10	66.2	69.2	70.1	67.9	72.1	83.8	74.8	70.4	72.7	62.6	61.9	60.1	58.7
Salaries and Wages	11	9.3	6.3	3.5	5.1	5.6	3.7	6.6	7.1	7.2	8.9	9.7	10.8	14.4
Taxes Paid	12	2.1	3.3	1.0	2.0	2.0	1.4	3.3	1.5	1.9	2.5	2.3	2.7	2.1
Interest Paid	13	0.7	0.2	0.2	0.1	0.6	0.4	0.5	0.5	0.4	1.1	1.7	0.6	0.8
Depreciation	14	1.4	2.2	0.3	0.2	0.4	0.2	0.3	0.6	0.6	1.4	2.5	2.1	2.4
Amortization and Depletion	15	0.3	0.3	0.1	•	0.0	0.0	0.1	0.2	0.1	0.5	0.7	0.5	0.6
Pensions and Other Deferred Comp.	16	0.3	0.0	0.9	0.9	0.2	0.7	0.1	0.1	0.1	0.4	0.1	0.3	0.4
Employee Benefits	17	0.5	0.4	0.1	0.4	0.4	0.1	0.3	0.4	0.6	0.7	1.0	0.6	0.7
Advertising	18	2.4	1.0	0.8	0.2	0.7	0.4	0.6	1.1	1.1	3.1	2.2	2.8	4.8
Other Expenses	19	12.4	10.9	11.5	10.0	11.7	5.1	6.7	9.8	8.7	12.2	13.7	12.8	17.0
Officers' Compensation	20	1.8	1.1	5.0	5.4	2.6	1.1	3.1	2.2	1.9	1.3	0.6	1.3	0.8
Operating Margin	21	2.5	5.0	6.5	7.7	3.6	3.1	3.6	5.9	4.8	5.1	3.6	5.3	•
Operating Margin Before Officers' Comp.	22	4.3	6.1	11.5	13.1	6.2	4.2	6.7	8.1	6.7	6.4	4.2	6.6	•

Selected Average Balance Sheet ($ in Thousands)

Net Receivables	23	1176	0	18	421	531	2958	5301	9812	18860	37759	43672	120249	920501
Inventories	24	1185	0	28	428	641	2361	6323	15257	26349	56913	93234	196237	598291
Net Property, Plant and Equipment	25	517	0	6	54	111	751	655	2885	3151	14153	35566	74876	516986
Total Assets	26	8859	0	109	812	1881	7300	15532	35344	70061	165867	357564	796102	10830720
Notes and Loans Payable	27	1180	0	27	99	494	1972	4537	8080	14670	48444	97755	104761	954553
All Other Liabilities	28	1872	0	38	392	714	3499	5414	11611	22966	52254	118623	220210	1643039
Net Worth	29	5807	0	44	321	672	1828	5580	15653	32425	65168	141187	471131	8233128

Selected Financial Ratios (Times to 1)

Current Ratio	30	1.7	•	2.2	1.6	1.8	1.5	1.8	1.8	1.8	2.4	1.8	2.4	1.3
Quick Ratio	31	0.8	•	1.5	1.2	0.9	0.9	0.9	0.7	0.7	1.0	0.6	1.1	0.7
Net Sales to Working Capital	32	6.7	•	16.5	12.2	8.4	8.5	7.4	5.2	5.2	3.6	5.1	3.8	8.7
Coverage Ratio	33	11.9	37.6	39.8	103.7	7.2	8.9	9.9	15.1	14.9	7.2	4.9	14.5	13.9
Total Asset Turnover	34	1.0	•	7.5	4.1	3.3	2.5	2.8	2.0	2.0	1.4	1.2	1.3	0.4
Inventory Turnover	35	4.8	•	20.4	5.3	7.0	6.4	5.2	3.3	3.9	2.5	2.7	3.1	4.6
Receivables Turnover	36	8.4	•	40.1	8.5	12.3	6.9	8.7	6.9	8.0	5.7	7.4	•	•
Total Liabilities to Net Worth	37	0.5	•	1.5	1.5	1.8	3.0	1.8	1.3	1.2	1.5	1.5	0.7	0.3
Current Assets to Working Capital	38	2.5	•	1.8	2.6	2.2	2.9	2.3	2.2	2.2	1.7	2.3	1.7	4.1
Current Liabilities to Working Capital	39	1.5	•	0.8	1.6	1.2	1.9	1.3	1.2	1.2	0.7	1.3	0.7	3.1
Working Capital to Net Sales	40	0.1	•	0.1	0.1	0.1	0.1	0.1	0.2	0.2	0.3	0.2	0.3	0.1
Inventory to Working Capital	41	1.0	•	0.5	0.7	1.0	1.1	1.0	1.1	1.0	0.9	1.1	0.8	1.1
Total Receipts to Cash Flow	42	6.6	5.8	7.0	6.0	7.4	13.7	10.6	6.6	7.9	6.2	6.8	5.7	5.4
Cost of Goods to Cash Flow	43	4.4	4.0	4.9	4.1	5.4	11.5	7.9	4.7	5.7	3.9	4.2	3.5	3.1
Cash Flow to Total Debt	44	0.4	•	1.8	1.1	0.7	0.2	0.4	0.6	0.5	0.4	0.3	0.5	0.3

Selected Financial Factors (in Percentages)

Debt Ratio	45	34.4	•	59.5	60.5	64.2	75.0	64.1	55.7	53.7	60.7	60.5	40.8	24.0
Return on Total Assets	46	7.7	•	51.2	42.2	14.9	8.6	14.0	16.1	11.9	11.0	9.7	11.7	4.7
Return on Equity Before Income Taxes	47	10.8	•	123.3	105.9	35.9	30.6	35.0	34.0	23.9	24.2	19.6	18.4	5.7
Return on Equity After Income Taxes	48	8.4	•	122.4	102.5	34.8	26.8	33.1	31.5	22.3	17.0	13.7	13.7	3.8
Profit Margin (Before Income Tax)	49	7.2	8.7	6.7	10.1	3.9	3.1	4.4	7.4	5.5	6.9	6.7	8.7	9.9
Profit Margin (After Income Tax)	50	5.6	6.0	6.6	9.8	3.8	2.7	4.2	6.9	5.1	4.9	4.7	6.5	6.6

Table I

Corporations with and without Net Income

GROCERY AND RELATED PRODUCT

MONEY AMOUNTS AND SIZE OF ASSETS IN THOUSANDS OF DOLLARS

Item Description for Accounting Period 7/11 Through 6/12		Total	Zero Assets	Under 500	500 to 1,000	1,000 to 5,000	5,000 to 10,000	10,000 to 25,000	25,000 to 50,000	50,000 to 100,000	100,000 to 250,000	250,000 to 500,000	500,000 to 2,500,000	2,500,000 and over
Number of Enterprises	1	37917	5916	21434	3692	5063	681	635	247	139	67	17	18	8
Revenues ($ in Thousands)														
Net Sales	2	609202392	4916444	17513069	16407860	67079150	19508251	46892052	32210111	33565936	34469703	18927221	55640966	262071629
Interest	3	4395709	904	3399	567	15931	12142	7303	8057	17694	12488	14617	41495	4261113
Rents	4	1729058	793	1953	7456	4138	6250	13212	3381	7319	7451	10363	41120	1625623
Royalties	5	537196	0	151	0	0	388	296	0	197	522	7322	21600	506720
Other Portfolio Income	6	7025281	67907	12994	34805	24896	12598	17336	2161	13535	13715	38833	31671	6754830
Other Receipts	7	6844259	61996	71574	41943	162411	80957	180980	160861	180284	303859	232260	435995	4931138
Total Receipts	8	629733895	5048044	17603140	16492631	67286526	19620586	47111179	32384571	33784965	34807738	19230616	56212847	280151053
Average Total Receipts	9	16608	853	821	4467	13290	28811	74191	131112	243057	519518	1131213	3122936	35018882
Operating Costs/Operating Income (%)														
Cost of Operations	10	81.1	88.4	76.6	82.7	86.1	87.9	87.8	88.0	85.2	88.3	89.6	83.6	74.8
Salaries and Wages	11	5.9	2.4	4.3	4.5	3.7	3.4	3.9	3.9	4.7	3.8	3.4	5.1	8.3
Taxes Paid	12	1.1	0.5	1.1	0.9	0.8	0.6	0.7	0.6	1.3	0.5	0.5	0.8	1.5
Interest Paid	13	1.0	0.1	0.2	0.4	0.2	0.3	0.3	0.2	0.4	0.5	0.5	0.5	1.8
Depreciation	14	2.3	0.5	0.9	0.6	0.5	0.5	0.4	0.7	0.9	0.8	1.1	1.3	4.3
Amortization and Depletion	15	0.3	0.1	0.0	0.1	0.0	0.1	0.0	0.0	0.1	0.1	0.1	0.2	0.5
Pensions and Other Deferred Comp.	16	0.4	0.0	0.2	0.1	0.2	0.1	0.1	0.1	0.2	0.1	0.2	0.2	0.7
Employee Benefits	17	0.8	0.1	0.4	0.4	0.4	0.4	0.4	0.4	0.5	0.5	0.5	0.6	1.3
Advertising	18	0.6	0.3	0.4	0.3	0.1	0.2	0.4	0.3	0.7	0.6	0.3	0.8	0.9
Other Expenses	19	6.1	6.9	9.9	7.4	5.1	4.6	3.7	3.8	4.5	3.5	3.7	5.0	7.8
Officers' Compensation	20	0.7	1.2	4.5	1.6	1.5	1.0	1.1	0.8	0.6	0.6	0.2	0.2	0.2
Operating Margin	21	•	•	1.5	0.8	1.4	1.1	1.2	1.1	0.7	0.6	•	1.5	•
Operating Margin Before Officers' Comp.	22	0.4	0.5	6.0	2.5	2.9	2.1	2.2	2.0	1.4	1.2	0.2	1.8	•

Selected Average Balance Sheet ($ in Thousands)													
Net Receivables 23	1116	0	20	228	810	2379	5475	10498	18797	36855	69391	173258	2482653
Inventories 24	917	0	15	122	482	1859	4111	9031	19813	43774	87540	202501	1831068
Net Property, Plant and Equipment 25	3126	0	19	184	232	592	1808	4472	10010	20890	71274	216181	13213639
Total Assets 26	20112	0	111	740	2204	7047	15721	33935	68267	147892	372558	948837	85044542
Notes and Loans Payable 27	2724	0	57	373	574	1698	4123	8322	19386	49448	98192	234385	10004259
All Other Liabilities 28	5580	0	30	322	809	2266	5693	12170	24656	47137	108529	336896	22873024
Net Worth 29	11809	0	24	45	821	3083	5905	13442	24225	51307	165837	377557	52167260
Selected Financial Ratios (Times to 1)													
Current Ratio 30	1.1	•	2.3	1.4	1.9	1.8	1.6	1.7	1.6	1.6	1.7	1.8	0.9
Quick Ratio 31	0.6	•	1.5	0.9	1.3	1.0	1.0	0.9	0.8	0.8	0.7	0.8	0.5
Net Sales to Working Capital 32	73.0	•	21.9	34.1	16.2	11.2	16.0	12.1	13.8	13.1	13.4	14.4	•
Coverage Ratio 33	4.4	17.2	10.8	4.1	11.1	7.6	7.1	7.9	4.3	4.2	4.4	6.3	3.9
Total Asset Turnover 34	0.8	•	7.4	6.0	6.0	4.1	4.7	3.8	3.5	3.5	3.0	3.3	0.4
Inventory Turnover 35	14.2	•	41.8	30.2	23.7	13.5	15.8	12.7	10.4	10.4	11.4	12.8	13.4
Receivables Turnover 36	13.9	•	48.5	20.9	17.0	10.9	13.3	13.4	13.3	16.0	16.6	18.8	11.8
Total Liabilities to Net Worth 37	0.7	•	3.7	15.5	1.7	1.3	1.7	1.5	1.8	1.9	1.2	1.5	0.6
Current Assets to Working Capital 38	18.7	•	1.8	3.5	2.2	2.2	2.6	2.5	2.7	2.6	2.5	2.3	•
Current Liabilities to Working Capital 39	17.7	•	0.8	2.5	1.2	1.2	1.6	1.5	1.7	1.6	1.5	1.3	•
Working Capital to Net Sales 40	0.0	•	0.0	0.0	0.1	0.1	0.1	0.1	0.1	0.1	0.1	0.1	•
Inventory to Working Capital 41	4.4	•	0.4	1.0	0.6	0.7	0.9	0.9	1.2	1.2	1.2	0.9	•
Total Receipts to Cash Flow 42	13.8	15.1	10.4	13.4	18.2	19.2	22.7	22.8	19.8	23.5	23.8	16.9	10.3
Cost of Goods to Cash Flow 43	11.2	13.3	8.0	11.0	15.7	16.8	19.9	20.1	16.9	20.8	21.3	14.2	7.7
Cash Flow to Total Debt 44	0.1	•	0.9	0.5	0.5	0.4	0.3	0.3	0.3	0.2	0.2	0.3	0.1
Selected Financial Factors (in Percentages)													
Debt Ratio 45	41.3	•	78.5	94.0	62.8	56.3	62.4	60.4	64.5	65.3	55.5	60.2	38.7
Return on Total Assets 46	3.3	•	16.7	10.8	11.3	7.8	8.9	7.4	6.4	7.1	6.0	10.0	2.7
Return on Equity Before Income Taxes 47	4.4	•	70.8	135.4	27.7	15.4	20.3	16.4	13.8	15.6	10.5	21.1	3.2
Return on Equity After Income Taxes 48	3.3	•	69.7	134.9	26.6	13.7	18.7	15.2	12.0	13.3	9.2	14.4	2.2
Profit Margin (Before Income Tax) 49	3.2	2.0	2.1	1.4	1.7	1.7	1.6	1.7	1.4	1.6	1.6	2.6	5.1
Profit Margin (After Income Tax) 50	2.4	1.5	2.0	1.4	1.6	1.5	1.5	1.6	1.2	1.3	1.4	1.8	3.6

Table II

Corporations with Net Income

GROCERY AND RELATED PRODUCT

MONEY AMOUNTS AND SIZE OF ASSETS IN THOUSANDS OF DOLLARS

Item Description for Accounting Period 7/11 Through 6/12		Total	Zero Assets	Under 500	500 to 1,000	1,000 to 5,000	5,000 to 10,000	10,000 to 25,000	25,000 to 50,000	50,000 to 100,000	100,000 to 250,000	250,000 to 500,000	500,000 to 2,500,000	2,500,000 and over
Number of Enterprises	1	26025	2755	14966	2620	4123	603	559	199	109	54	13	•	•
Revenues ($ in Thousands)														
Net Sales	2	527451252	2216903	12788661	13341928	59127701	17988910	44051219	26439833	26732128	31103707	15795910	•	•
Interest	3	4380084	595	2989	477	15133	7281	5967	7605	13267	10850	14124	•	•
Rents	4	1716816	793	437	5862	3152	6163	13170	3262	3503	4118	10363	•	•
Royalties	5	537041	0	0	0	0	388	296	0	193	522	7322	•	•
Other Portfolio Income	6	6965309	40610	9770	32684	23550	10044	17161	1938	12104	10219	38825	•	•
Other Receipts	7	6160233	54604	2070	29086	129263	61141	165292	151128	137670	311262	237078	•	•
Total Receipts	8	547210735	2313505	12803927	13410037	59298799	18073927	44253105	26603766	26898865	31440678	16103622	•	•
Average Total Receipts	9	21026	840	856	5118	14382	29973	79165	133687	246779	582235	1238740	•	•
Operating Costs/Operating Income (%)														
Cost of Operations	10	80.3	87.3	74.4	86.1	86.5	87.9	87.8	87.7	84.1	89.3	90.0	•	•
Salaries and Wages	11	6.0	1.0	3.5	2.9	3.5	3.3	3.9	3.5	5.0	3.4	3.3	•	•
Taxes Paid	12	1.2	0.4	1.0	0.7	0.7	0.6	0.7	0.6	1.5	0.5	0.5	•	•
Interest Paid	13	1.0	0.1	0.2	0.3	0.2	0.2	0.2	0.2	0.4	0.4	0.3	•	•
Depreciation	14	2.5	0.5	0.5	0.5	0.5	0.4	0.4	0.6	0.8	0.7	0.9	•	•
Amortization and Depletion	15	0.3	0.0	0.0	0.1	0.0	0.1	0.0	0.0	0.1	0.1	0.1	•	•
Pensions and Other Deferred Comp.	16	0.4	0.0	0.2	0.1	0.2	0.1	0.1	0.1	0.2	0.1	0.1	•	•
Employee Benefits	17	0.8	0.2	0.4	0.3	0.4	0.3	0.4	0.4	0.5	0.4	0.5	•	•
Advertising	18	0.7	0.6	0.2	0.2	0.1	0.2	0.3	0.2	0.7	0.6	0.3	•	•
Other Expenses	19	6.1	5.6	9.6	5.5	4.4	4.3	3.5	3.8	4.4	3.1	3.6	•	•
Officers' Compensation	20	0.7	0.6	5.2	1.3	1.5	1.0	1.1	0.9	0.7	0.6	0.2	•	•
Operating Margin	21	0.1	3.7	4.7	2.0	2.1	1.7	1.5	2.0	1.5	0.9	0.2	•	•
Operating Margin Before Officers' Comp.	22	0.8	4.4	9.8	3.4	3.6	2.7	2.6	2.9	2.2	1.5	0.4	•	•

Selected Average Balance Sheet ($ in Thousands)

Net Receivables	23	1442	0	19	216	832	2442	5720	10497	19554	40418	73411	•	•
Inventories	24	1169	0	9	115	450	2001	4245	9796	21464	47499	92275	•	•
Net Property, Plant and Equipment	25	4374	0	12	136	236	407	1892	4176	9457	19288	66786	•	•
Total Assets	26	28367	0	103	710	2245	6968	15768	33633	69414	147348	378660	•	•
Notes and Loans Payable	27	3584	0	48	292	538	1516	3841	7525	20549	48371	83779	•	•
All Other Liabilities	28	7791	0	23	316	801	2231	5777	12039	22720	47717	110516	•	•
Net Worth	29	16991	0	31	102	906	3221	6150	14070	26145	51261	184366	•	•

Selected Financial Ratios (Times to 1)

Current Ratio	30	1.0	•	3.1	1.5	1.9	1.9	1.6	1.7	1.6	1.7	1.8	•	•
Quick Ratio	31	0.6	•	2.5	1.0	1.3	1.1	1.0	0.9	0.8	0.8	0.9	•	•
Net Sales to Working Capital	32	106.3	•	22.4	32.0	16.4	10.4	16.5	11.4	12.6	12.5	12.8	•	•
Coverage Ratio	33	5.0	115.9	27.3	9.6	16.9	11.1	9.1	12.5	6.1	5.8	7.5	•	•
Total Asset Turnover	34	0.7	•	8.3	7.2	6.4	4.3	5.0	4.0	3.5	3.9	3.2	•	•
Inventory Turnover	35	13.9	•	74.7	38.0	27.6	13.1	16.3	11.9	9.6	10.8	11.8	•	•
Receivables Turnover	36	13.5	•	56.8	26.7	18.6	10.7	13.7	13.3	12.8	17.0	•	•	•
Total Liabilities to Net Worth	37	0.7	•	2.3	6.0	1.5	1.2	1.6	1.4	1.7	1.9	1.1	•	•
Current Assets to Working Capital	38	28.9	•	1.5	2.9	2.1	2.1	2.6	2.4	2.6	2.4	2.2	•	•
Current Liabilities to Working Capital	39	27.9	•	0.5	1.9	1.1	1.1	1.6	1.4	1.6	1.4	1.2	•	•
Working Capital to Net Sales	40	0.0	•	0.0	0.0	0.1	0.1	0.1	0.1	0.1	0.1	0.1	•	•
Inventory to Working Capital	41	6.4	•	0.1	0.9	0.5	0.6	0.9	0.9	1.1	1.1	1.0	•	•
Total Receipts to Cash Flow	42	12.8	9.1	8.3	14.6	17.8	18.1	22.1	18.8	17.5	23.1	21.9	•	•
Cost of Goods to Cash Flow	43	10.3	8.0	6.2	12.6	15.4	16.0	19.4	16.5	14.7	20.6	19.7	•	•
Cash Flow to Total Debt	44	0.1	•	1.4	0.6	0.6	0.4	0.4	0.4	0.3	0.3	0.3	•	•

Selected Financial Factors (in Percentages)

Debt Ratio	45	40.1	•	69.7	85.6	59.7	53.8	61.0	58.2	62.3	65.2	51.3	•	•
Return on Total Assets	46	3.6	•	41.6	20.5	16.4	10.2	10.8	11.3	9.2	9.3	8.0	•	•
Return on Equity Before Income Taxes	47	4.8	•	132.1	127.9	38.3	20.0	24.7	24.8	20.3	22.1	14.2	•	•
Return on Equity After Income Taxes	48	3.6	•	130.9	127.6	37.1	18.1	23.0	23.3	18.2	19.2	12.7	•	•
Profit Margin (Before Income Tax)	49	4.0	8.1	4.8	2.6	2.4	2.2	1.9	2.6	2.2	2.0	2.2	•	•
Profit Margin (After Income Tax)	50	3.0	7.0	4.8	2.6	2.3	2.0	1.8	2.5	1.9	1.7	1.9	•	•

Table I

Corporations with and without Net Income

FARM PRODUCT RAW MATERIAL

MONEY AMOUNTS AND SIZE OF ASSETS IN THOUSANDS OF DOLLARS

Item Description for Accounting Period 7/11 Through 6/12		Total	Zero Assets	Under 500	500 to 1,000	1,000 to 5,000	5,000 to 10,000	10,000 to 25,000	25,000 to 50,000	50,000 to 100,000	100,000 to 250,000	250,000 to 500,000	500,000 to 2,500,000	2,500,000 and over
Number of Enterprises	1	4249	426	1581	•	1046	289	186	49	•	23	0	9	4
Revenues ($ in Thousands)														
Net Sales	2	190680917	2283	1337293	•	9422965	6234627	12048797	7605039	•	16032095	0	33341391	93531762
Interest	3	393570	288	893	•	5341	5402	3244	3013	•	9024	0	15969	347233
Rents	4	137167	0	13	•	11370	826	1653	2117	•	5282	0	95636	19532
Royalties	5	132927	0	0	•	0	301	0	0	•	3633	0	1896	127098
Other Portfolio Income	6	383330	1679	20462	•	4355	38828	20213	3621	•	21717	0	48223	221779
Other Receipts	7	2157489	1621	47453	•	111610	20033	149042	35245	•	73530	0	190001	1407121
Total Receipts	8	193885400	5871	1406114	•	9555641	6300017	12222949	7649035	•	16145281	0	33693116	95654525
Average Total Receipts	9	45631	14	889	•	9135	21799	65715	156103	•	701969	•	3743680	23913631
Operating Costs/Operating Income (%)														
Cost of Operations	10	94.1	87.5	80.5	•	88.6	88.8	92.7	92.5	•	95.3	•	96.0	94.9
Salaries and Wages	11	1.7	2.3	3.5	•	2.2	2.4	2.3	2.9	•	1.2	•	1.0	1.7
Taxes Paid	12	0.3	11.6	1.2	•	0.7	0.5	0.3	0.3	•	0.3	•	0.2	0.3
Interest Paid	13	0.8	22.5	1.4	•	0.3	0.4	0.4	0.4	•	0.4	•	0.5	1.1
Depreciation	14	1.0	5.4	2.4	•	0.6	1.6	1.0	0.7	•	0.7	•	0.7	1.1
Amortization and Depletion	15	0.0	•	0.0	•	0.0	0.0	0.0	0.0	•	0.0	•	0.1	0.1
Pensions and Other Deferred Comp.	16	0.2	0.1	0.0	•	0.2	0.0	0.1	0.1	•	0.1	•	0.1	0.3
Employee Benefits	17	0.4	0.9	0.3	•	0.2	0.2	0.2	0.3	•	0.1	•	0.1	0.6
Advertising	18	0.1	•	0.3	•	0.1	0.1	0.0	0.0	•	0.0	•	0.1	0.1
Other Expenses	19	2.2	172.3	13.0	•	5.4	3.6	2.4	1.6	•	1.6	•	1.1	2.1
Officers' Compensation	20	0.5	0.4	3.0	•	1.8	0.9	0.6	0.5	•	0.3	•	0.2	0.4
Operating Margin	21	•	•	•	•	•	1.5	•	0.6	•	0.1	•	•	•
Operating Margin Before Officers' Comp.	22	•	•	•	•	1.7	2.4	0.5	1.2	•	0.3	•	0.1	•

Selected Average Balance Sheet ($ in Thousands)

Net Receivables 23	4389	0	40	•	653	1599	3923	11432	•	55615	•	210469	3063238
Inventories 24	4329	0	4	•	529	1284	4321	12534	•	54133	•	437364	2505138
Net Property, Plant and Equipment 25	2364	0	36	•	249	1532	2586	5547	•	20948	•	191295	1492538
Total Assets 26	21961	0	192	•	2419	7064	14841	38535	•	184665	•	1186744	16624057
Notes and Loans Payable 27	8115	0	267	•	653	1800	5303	12400	•	68772	•	495251	6155251
All Other Liabilities 28	5710	0	18	•	1081	3226	5076	17209	•	52297	•	422135	3639313
Net Worth 29	8137	0	-92	•	686	2039	4462	8926	•	63596	•	269358	6829493

Selected Financial Ratios (Times to 1)

Current Ratio 30	1.6	•	5.3	•	1.5	1.3	1.6	1.4	•	1.4	•	1.1	1.9
Quick Ratio 31	0.8	•	4.8	•	0.9	0.9	0.7	0.7	•	0.6	•	0.3	1.0
Net Sales to Working Capital 32	10.1	•	9.1	•	13.4	19.8	16.7	18.0	•	18.3	•	70.2	6.5
Coverage Ratio 33	2.0	•	0.6	•	5.0	7.0	4.2	3.8	•	2.9	•	2.9	1.3
Total Asset Turnover 34	2.0	•	4.4	•	3.7	3.1	4.4	4.0	•	3.8	•	3.1	1.4
Inventory Turnover 35	9.8	•	186.3	•	15.1	14.9	13.9	11.5	•	12.3	•	8.1	8.9
Receivables Turnover 36	7.8	•	23.0	•	15.2	17.5	18.6	13.1	•	16.2	•	12.1	5.3
Total Liabilities to Net Worth 37	1.7	•	•	•	2.5	2.5	2.3	3.3	•	1.9	•	3.4	1.4
Current Assets to Working Capital 38	2.6	•	1.2	•	3.0	4.8	2.7	3.6	•	3.6	•	14.4	2.1
Current Liabilities to Working Capital 39	1.6	•	0.2	•	2.0	3.8	1.7	2.6	•	2.6	•	13.4	1.1
Working Capital to Net Sales 40	0.1	•	0.1	•	0.1	0.1	0.1	0.1	•	0.1	•	0.0	0.2
Inventory to Working Capital 41	0.9	•	0.1	•	0.7	1.3	1.1	1.5	•	1.6	•	8.4	0.6
Total Receipts to Cash Flow 42	53.1	•	10.6	•	19.8	21.0	31.9	46.7	•	52.0	•	66.9	107.0
Cost of Goods to Cash Flow 43	50.0	•	8.5	•	17.6	18.7	29.5	43.2	•	49.5	•	64.2	101.5
Cash Flow to Total Debt 44	0.1	•	0.3	•	0.3	0.2	0.2	0.1	•	0.1	•	0.1	0.0

Selected Financial Factors (in Percentages)

Debt Ratio 45	63.0	•	148.1	•	71.6	71.1	69.9	76.8	•	65.6	•	77.3	58.9
Return on Total Assets 46	3.1	•	3.5	•	5.9	9.1	7.6	6.7	•	4.5	•	4.4	2.1
Return on Equity Before Income Taxes 47	4.2	•	5.4	•	16.8	27.0	19.2	21.3	•	8.6	•	12.8	1.1
Return on Equity After Income Taxes 48	3.2	•	10.5	•	15.3	26.0	16.8	19.8	•	6.0	•	8.2	0.7
Profit Margin (Before Income Tax) 49	0.8	•	•	•	1.3	2.6	1.3	1.2	•	0.8	•	0.9	0.3
Profit Margin (After Income Tax) 50	0.6	•	•	•	1.2	2.5	1.2	1.1	•	0.5	•	0.6	0.2

Table II

Corporations with Net Income

FARM PRODUCT RAW MATERIAL

MONEY AMOUNTS AND SIZE OF ASSETS IN THOUSANDS OF DOLLARS

Item Description for Accounting Period 7/11 Through 6/12		Total	Zero Assets	Under 500	500 to 1,000	1,000 to 5,000	5,000 to 10,000	10,000 to 25,000	25,000 to 50,000	50,000 to 100,000	100,000 to 250,000	250,000 to 500,000	500,000 to 2,500,000	2,500,000 and over
Number of Enterprises	1	2573	16	847	551	675	263	138	40	17	16	0	•	•
Revenues ($ in Thousands)														
Net Sales	2	112266095	0	1206979	4723267	5093197	5254800	8253970	6025322	4474329	13562543	0	•	•
Interest	3	250558	288	82	866	5301	4890	1661	2349	1879	7592	0	•	•
Rents	4	110989	0	13	216	5561	705	1468	2020	191	5212	0	•	•
Royalties	5	5881	0	0	0	0	301	0	0	0	3633	0	•	•
Other Portfolio Income	6	252464	0	20462	710	4355	38798	16986	3592	1456	19943	0	•	•
Other Receipts	7	792620	1620	47404	85442	38977	18279	120297	29334	28505	59393	0	•	•
Total Receipts	8	113678607	1908	1274940	4810501	5147391	5317773	8394382	6062617	4506360	13658316	0	•	•
Average Total Receipts	9	44181	119	1505	8730	7626	20220	60829	151565	265080	853645	•	•	•
Operating Costs/Operating Income (%)														
Cost of Operations	10	93.7	•	82.1	89.9	83.8	88.2	91.6	92.7	93.3	95.5	•	•	•
Salaries and Wages	11	1.5	•	2.7	2.1	3.3	2.5	2.6	2.2	1.6	1.1	•	•	•
Taxes Paid	12	0.3	•	0.9	0.5	0.7	0.6	0.4	0.3	0.3	0.3	•	•	•
Interest Paid	13	0.6	•	0.8	0.1	0.3	0.5	0.4	0.4	0.3	0.3	•	•	•
Depreciation	14	0.7	•	1.5	0.6	0.7	1.6	0.6	0.6	0.6	0.5	•	•	•
Amortization and Depletion	15	0.0	•	•	•	0.0	0.0	0.0	0.0	0.0	0.0	•	•	•
Pensions and Other Deferred Comp.	16	0.1	•	0.0	0.1	0.2	0.0	0.2	0.1	0.0	0.1	•	•	•
Employee Benefits	17	0.2	•	0.2	0.0	0.2	0.2	0.2	0.2	0.1	0.1	•	•	•
Advertising	18	0.1	•	0.3	0.1	0.2	0.1	0.0	0.0	0.1	0.0	•	•	•
Other Expenses	19	2.1	•	10.0	3.5	6.0	3.4	2.5	1.9	2.6	1.3	•	•	•
Officers' Compensation	20	0.5	•	2.9	1.7	2.5	1.0	0.7	0.6	0.3	0.3	•	•	•
Operating Margin	21	0.2	•	•	1.4	2.2	1.9	0.8	1.0	0.9	0.4	•	•	•
Operating Margin Before Officers' Comp.	22	0.7	•	1.5	3.0	4.6	2.9	1.5	1.5	1.1	0.7	•	•	•

Selected Average Balance Sheet ($ in Thousands)													
Net Receivables 23	3014	0	49	125	696	1539	4006	10448	29230	72508	•	•	•
Inventories 24	5381	0	1	121	664	1143	4485	11207	24017	47188	•	•	•
Net Property, Plant and Equipment 25	1760	0	51	134	227	1531	2391	5867	8276	18599	•	•	•
Total Assets 26	15670	0	247	775	2535	7017	14765	37408	73048	200419	•	•	•
Notes and Loans Payable 27	7280	0	207	155	519	1840	4528	10564	18279	72458	•	•	•
All Other Liabilities 28	4931	0	13	96	974	3082	5147	16510	30892	60437	•	•	•
Net Worth 29	3459	0	27	525	1042	2095	5090	10334	23876	67524	•	•	•

Selected Financial Ratios (Times to 1)													
Current Ratio 30	1.4	•	4.5	3.6	1.8	1.3	1.7	1.5	1.5	1.4	•	•	•
Quick Ratio 31	0.5	•	4.3	2.1	0.8	0.9	0.8	0.7	0.8	0.7	•	•	•
Net Sales to Working Capital 32	14.5	•	11.8	20.4	7.9	19.4	14.2	16.3	13.4	20.9	•	•	•
Coverage Ratio 33	3.7	5.6	6.1	25.4	10.5	7.7	7.2	5.1	6.1	4.4	•	•	•
Total Asset Turnover 34	2.8	•	5.8	11.1	3.0	2.8	4.1	4.0	3.6	4.2	•	•	•
Inventory Turnover 35	7.6	•	2321.4	63.8	9.5	15.4	12.2	12.5	10.2	17.2	•	•	•
Receivables Turnover 36	6.1	•	•	78.4	10.6	16.9	16.5	15.3	9.2	17.5	•	•	•
Total Liabilities to Net Worth 37	3.5	•	8.1	0.5	1.4	2.3	1.9	2.6	2.1	2.0	•	•	•
Current Assets to Working Capital 38	3.5	•	1.3	1.4	2.3	4.9	2.5	3.2	3.0	3.8	•	•	•
Current Liabilities to Working Capital 39	2.5	•	0.3	0.4	1.3	3.9	1.5	2.2	2.0	2.8	•	•	•
Working Capital to Net Sales 40	0.1	•	0.1	0.0	0.1	0.1	0.1	0.1	0.1	0.0	•	•	•
Inventory to Working Capital 41	1.3	•	0.0	0.5	0.6	1.1	0.9	1.4	1.1	1.5	•	•	•
Total Receipts to Cash Flow 42	35.0	•	8.6	16.3	13.5	20.0	22.9	33.9	26.1	47.8	•	•	•
Cost of Goods to Cash Flow 43	32.8	•	7.1	14.6	11.3	17.6	21.0	31.5	24.4	45.6	•	•	•
Cash Flow to Total Debt 44	0.1	•	0.8	2.1	0.4	0.2	0.3	0.2	0.2	0.1	•	•	•

Selected Financial Factors (in Percentages)													
Debt Ratio 45	77.9	•	89.0	32.3	58.9	70.1	65.5	72.4	67.3	66.3	•	•	•
Return on Total Assets 46	6.0	•	29.0	36.8	10.7	10.1	11.9	8.0	6.8	6.4	•	•	•
Return on Equity Before Income Taxes 47	19.6	•	220.7	52.3	23.5	29.4	29.7	23.4	17.3	14.7	•	•	•
Return on Equity After Income Taxes 48	15.9	•	188.2	52.0	22.0	28.3	26.8	21.7	14.3	11.2	•	•	•
Profit Margin (Before Income Tax) 49	1.6	•	4.2	3.2	3.2	3.1	2.5	1.6	1.6	1.2	•	•	•
Profit Margin (After Income Tax) 50	1.3	•	3.6	3.2	3.0	3.0	2.3	1.5	1.3	0.9	•	•	•

Table I

Corporations with and without Net Income

CHEMICAL AND ALLIED PRODUCTS

MONEY AMOUNTS AND SIZE OF ASSETS IN THOUSANDS OF DOLLARS

Item Description for Accounting Period 7/11 Through 6/12		Total	Zero Assets	Under 500	500 to 1,000	1,000 to 5,000	5,000 to 10,000	10,000 to 25,000	25,000 to 50,000	50,000 to 100,000	100,000 to 250,000	250,000 to 500,000	500,000 to 2,500,000	2,500,000 and over
Number of Enterprises	1	8227	1256	4412	337	1534	274	260	72	40	27	•	•	3
Revenues ($ in Thousands)														
Net Sales	2	91957662	1583157	2868158	954345	12087987	5267594	10985747	7012434	5931375	10818306	•	•	17221529
Interest	3	76041	977	148	963	826	948	3092	2740	3665	4528	•	•	37711
Rents	4	14016	607	0	0	0	658	480	188	2416	95	•	•	2466
Royalties	5	1200	0	0	0	0	0	0	0	63	732	•	•	0
Other Portfolio Income	6	281255	17025	23039	433	24706	2550	26049	3351	1862	10028	•	•	92376
Other Receipts	7	1100295	11798	17104	8333	44958	19481	51251	57414	24068	41031	•	•	644929
Total Receipts	8	93430469	1613564	2908449	964074	12158477	5291231	11066619	7076127	5963449	10874720	•	•	17999011
Average Total Receipts	9	11357	1285	659	2861	7926	19311	42564	98280	149086	402767	•	•	5999670
Operating Costs/Operating Income (%)														
Cost of Operations	10	80.3	81.5	65.5	69.7	72.1	71.8	81.1	83.8	84.6	88.0	•	•	76.9
Salaries and Wages	11	5.5	5.5	5.8	5.5	8.4	9.1	5.4	5.3	4.3	2.6	•	•	7.0
Taxes Paid	12	0.9	0.9	1.0	1.3	1.1	1.1	1.0	1.0	0.8	0.5	•	•	0.8
Interest Paid	13	0.9	1.0	0.2	0.2	0.5	0.2	0.3	0.3	0.5	0.4	•	•	2.4
Depreciation	14	1.4	0.8	0.4	0.7	1.1	0.8	0.7	1.2	1.1	0.9	•	•	3.4
Amortization and Depletion	15	0.5	0.2	0.0	•	0.1	0.0	0.0	0.2	0.2	0.2	•	•	1.7
Pensions and Other Deferred Comp.	16	0.3	0.5	•	0.5	0.3	0.5	0.3	0.3	0.4	0.2	•	•	0.6
Employee Benefits	17	0.9	0.7	0.2	0.8	0.5	0.5	0.4	0.4	0.6	0.5	•	•	2.4
Advertising	18	0.1	0.1	0.3	0.3	0.2	0.2	0.2	0.3	0.2	0.1	•	•	0.0
Other Expenses	19	5.9	6.1	21.0	12.8	9.0	8.2	5.2	4.7	4.1	3.2	•	•	5.1
Officers' Compensation	20	1.2	0.4	1.9	7.7	2.7	3.6	1.5	1.1	1.0	0.5	•	•	0.3
Operating Margin	21	2.1	2.4	3.7	0.5	4.0	4.1	3.8	1.3	2.4	3.0	•	•	•
Operating Margin Before Officers' Comp.	22	3.3	2.8	5.5	8.2	6.7	7.6	5.4	2.4	3.4	3.5	•	•	•

Selected Average Balance Sheet ($ in Thousands)													
Net Receivables	23	1435	0	43	316	833	2225	5500	12060	21432	47256	•	• 1148929
Inventories	24	932	0	30	154	424	2216	4701	9626	16686	35338	•	• 430606
Net Property, Plant and Equipment	25	1012	0	3	69	222	585	2286	5552	8190	19318	•	• 1547028
Total Assets	26	6272	0	152	711	2226	6985	16029	34094	66435	159849	•	• 7159618
Notes and Loans Payable	27	1723	0	58	80	521	1411	3069	9173	17039	28673	•	• 2091527
All Other Liabilities	28	2149	0	40	233	1064	2795	5283	12614	20961	62871	•	• 2483024
Net Worth	29	2400	0	53	399	641	2779	7676	12307	28435	68305	•	• 2585068
Selected Financial Ratios (Times to 1)													
Current Ratio	30	1.5	•	1.9	2.0	1.5	1.4	1.9	1.5	1.6	1.6	•	• 1.3
Quick Ratio	31	0.8	•	1.5	1.6	1.0	0.8	1.1	0.8	0.9	0.8	•	• 0.5
Net Sales to Working Capital	32	10.3	•	9.8	9.6	15.1	12.6	7.1	11.5	8.3	10.0	•	• 8.8
Coverage Ratio	33	5.3	5.3	29.0	10.6	10.6	19.9	18.8	7.8	6.9	10.9	•	• 2.7
Total Asset Turnover	34	1.8	•	4.3	4.0	3.5	2.8	2.6	2.9	2.2	2.5	•	• 0.8
Inventory Turnover	35	9.6	•	14.1	12.9	13.4	6.2	7.3	8.5	7.5	10.0	•	• 10.2
Receivables Turnover	36	8.3	•	15.5	8.4	11.2	7.3	7.6	8.5	7.1	9.2	•	• 5.7
Total Liabilities to Net Worth	37	1.6	•	1.8	0.8	2.5	1.5	1.1	1.8	1.3	1.3	•	• 1.8
Current Assets to Working Capital	38	3.1	•	2.1	2.0	3.1	3.6	2.1	3.0	2.7	2.7	•	• 4.4
Current Liabilities to Working Capital	39	2.1	•	1.1	1.0	2.1	2.6	1.1	2.0	1.7	1.7	•	• 3.4
Working Capital to Net Sales	40	0.1	•	0.1	0.1	0.1	0.1	0.1	0.1	0.1	0.1	•	• 0.1
Inventory to Working Capital	41	0.9	•	0.5	0.4	0.9	1.3	0.8	1.2	1.0	1.0	•	• 0.7
Total Receipts to Cash Flow	42	12.5	11.3	4.2	8.7	8.8	8.9	11.3	16.8	16.6	16.8	•	• 16.9
Cost of Goods to Cash Flow	43	10.0	9.2	2.8	6.0	6.3	6.4	9.2	14.1	14.0	14.8	•	• 13.0
Cash Flow to Total Debt	44	0.2	•	1.6	1.0	0.6	0.5	0.4	0.3	0.2	0.3	•	• 0.1
Selected Financial Factors (in Percentages)													
Debt Ratio	45	61.7	•	64.9	43.9	71.2	60.2	52.1	63.9	57.2	57.3	•	• 63.9
Return on Total Assets	46	8.2	•	22.5	6.9	17.8	13.1	12.8	7.4	7.7	9.8	•	• 5.1
Return on Equity Before Income Taxes	47	17.4	•	61.8	11.1	56.0	31.3	25.2	17.8	15.3	20.8	•	• 8.8
Return on Equity After Income Taxes	48	14.2	•	60.0	9.5	54.5	27.6	22.9	14.4	13.7	16.7	•	• 5.7
Profit Margin (Before Income Tax)	49	3.7	4.3	5.1	1.6	4.6	4.5	4.6	2.3	2.9	3.5	•	• 4.0
Profit Margin (After Income Tax)	50	3.1	2.9	4.9	1.3	4.4	4.0	4.2	1.8	2.6	2.8	•	• 2.5

Table II

Corporations with Net Income

CHEMICAL AND ALLIED PRODUCTS

MONEY AMOUNTS AND SIZE OF ASSETS IN THOUSANDS OF DOLLARS

Item Description for Accounting Period 7/11 Through 6/12		Total	Zero Assets	Under 500	500 to 1,000	1,000 to 5,000	5,000 to 10,000	10,000 to 25,000	25,000 to 50,000	50,000 to 100,000	100,000 to 250,000	250,000 to 500,000	500,000 to 2,500,000	2,500,000 and over
Number of Enterprises	1	4691	827	1855	278	1113	239	247	58	36	•	•	•	0
Revenues ($ in Thousands)														
Net Sales	2	80051449	1162277	2410431	891257	10029720	4818481	10631144	6557810	5713984	•	•	•	0
Interest	3	57615	928	0	569	528	948	847	1792	3664	•	•	•	0
Rents	4	11340	607	0	0	0	658	480	102	2416	•	•	•	0
Royalties	5	1019	0	0	0	0	0	0	0	63	•	•	•	0
Other Portfolio Income	6	278897	17025	23039	433	23935	2550	26049	3257	1855	•	•	•	0
Other Receipts	7	1012661	13798	670	1496	39957	17480	43573	54761	14523	•	•	•	0
Total Receipts	8	81412981	1194635	2434140	893755	10094140	4840117	10702093	6617722	5736505	•	•	•	0
Average Total Receipts	9	17355	1445	1312	3215	9069	20252	43328	114099	159347	•	•	•	•
Operating Costs/Operating Income (%)														
Cost of Operations	10	80.5	77.0	67.3	67.9	73.0	70.1	80.9	85.1	84.4	•	•	•	•
Salaries and Wages	11	5.5	7.1	6.8	5.7	7.9	9.7	5.4	4.7	4.2	•	•	•	•
Taxes Paid	12	0.8	1.0	1.0	1.3	1.0	1.2	1.0	0.9	0.8	•	•	•	•
Interest Paid	13	0.5	1.1	0.2	0.1	0.4	0.2	0.2	0.3	0.5	•	•	•	•
Depreciation	14	1.4	0.9	0.4	0.7	0.9	0.8	0.7	0.8	1.1	•	•	•	•
Amortization and Depletion	15	0.5	0.3	0.0	•	0.1	0.0	0.0	0.1	0.2	•	•	•	•
Pensions and Other Deferred Comp.	16	0.3	0.4	•	0.6	0.3	0.6	0.3	0.3	0.4	•	•	•	•
Employee Benefits	17	0.9	0.8	0.2	0.8	0.5	0.5	0.4	0.4	0.6	•	•	•	•
Advertising	18	0.1	0.1	0.3	0.3	0.2	0.2	0.2	0.2	0.2	•	•	•	•
Other Expenses	19	5.4	6.8	14.5	13.1	7.9	8.3	5.2	3.9	3.8	•	•	•	•
Officers' Compensation	20	1.2	0.4	1.9	7.8	2.2	3.8	1.5	1.1	1.0	•	•	•	•
Operating Margin	21	2.9	4.2	7.4	1.6	5.6	4.7	4.2	2.3	2.9	•	•	•	•
Operating Margin Before Officers' Comp.	22	4.1	4.6	9.4	9.4	7.8	8.4	5.7	3.4	3.9	•	•	•	•

Selected Average Balance Sheet ($ in Thousands)													
Net Receivables **23**	2173	0	75	307	897	2190	5556	13619	21810	•	•	•	•
Inventories **24**	1446	0	55	174	431	2135	4663	11368	16892	•	•	•	•
Net Property, Plant and Equipment **25**	1570	0	5	84	241	634	2321	4326	8812	•	•	•	•
Total Assets **26**	8883	0	207	655	2172	7037	15958	34863	66715	•	•	•	•
Notes and Loans Payable **27**	2636	0	16	80	431	1277	3006	9417	15634	•	•	•	•
All Other Liabilities **28**	2534	0	56	231	1096	2765	5153	12590	22044	•	•	•	•
Net Worth **29**	3713	0	136	344	645	2996	7799	12856	29037	•	•	•	•
Selected Financial Ratios (Times to 1)													
Current Ratio **30**	1.5	•	3.5	1.7	1.6	1.4	1.9	1.5	1.7	•	•	•	•
Quick Ratio **31**	0.8	•	2.3	1.3	1.1	0.8	1.1	0.8	1.0	•	•	•	•
Net Sales to Working Capital **32**	10.1	•	10.0	14.7	13.4	12.4	7.2	11.7	8.2	•	•	•	•
Coverage Ratio **33**	10.4	7.3	49.0	14.3	17.6	28.0	20.6	13.3	8.0	•	•	•	•
Total Asset Turnover **34**	1.9	•	6.3	4.9	4.1	2.9	2.7	3.2	2.4	•	•	•	•
Inventory Turnover **35**	9.5	•	16.0	12.5	15.3	6.6	7.5	8.5	7.9	•	•	•	•
Receivables Turnover **36**	8.1	•	17.2	8.6	11.5	7.5	7.9	•	7.3	•	•	•	•
Total Liabilities to Net Worth **37**	1.4	•	0.5	0.9	2.4	1.3	1.0	1.7	1.3	•	•	•	•
Current Assets to Working Capital **38**	3.1	•	1.4	2.3	2.6	3.4	2.1	2.9	2.5	•	•	•	•
Current Liabilities to Working Capital **39**	2.1	•	0.4	1.3	1.6	2.4	1.1	1.9	1.5	•	•	•	•
Working Capital to Net Sales **40**	0.1	•	0.1	0.1	0.1	0.1	0.1	0.1	0.1	•	•	•	•
Inventory to Working Capital **41**	0.9	•	0.5	0.6	0.7	1.2	0.8	1.2	0.9	•	•	•	•
Total Receipts to Cash Flow **42**	11.8	8.5	4.9	8.2	8.1	8.4	11.1	16.1	16.2	•	•	•	•
Cost of Goods to Cash Flow **43**	9.5	6.5	3.3	5.6	5.9	5.9	9.0	13.7	13.7	•	•	•	•
Cash Flow to Total Debt **44**	0.3	•	3.7	1.3	0.7	0.6	0.5	0.3	0.3	•	•	•	•
Selected Financial Factors (in Percentages)													
Debt Ratio **45**	58.2	•	34.5	47.5	70.3	57.4	51.1	63.1	56.5	•	•	•	•
Return on Total Assets **46**	9.9	•	53.9	10.0	27.4	15.2	13.7	11.3	8.9	•	•	•	•
Return on Equity Before Income Taxes **47**	21.3	•	80.5	17.8	86.9	34.5	26.6	28.4	17.9	•	•	•	•
Return on Equity After Income Taxes **48**	17.7	•	78.8	15.4	84.8	30.6	24.2	24.3	16.1	•	•	•	•
Profit Margin (Before Income Tax) **49**	4.6	6.9	8.4	1.9	6.2	5.1	4.8	3.2	3.3	•	•	•	•
Profit Margin (After Income Tax) **50**	3.9	4.9	8.3	1.7	6.1	4.5	4.4	2.8	2.9	•	•	•	•

Table I

Corporations with and without Net Income

PETROLEUM AND PETROLEUM PRODUCTS

MONEY AMOUNTS AND SIZE OF ASSETS IN THOUSANDS OF DOLLARS

Item Description for Accounting Period 7/11 Through 6/12		Total	Zero Assets	Under 500	500 to 1,000	1,000 to 5,000	5,000 to 10,000	10,000 to 25,000	25,000 to 50,000	50,000 to 100,000	100,000 to 250,000	250,000 to 500,000	500,000 to 2,500,000	2,500,000 and over
Number of Enterprises	1	7168	1237	1787	605	2084	762	390	146	79	26	17	27	8
Revenues ($ in Thousands)														
Net Sales	2	668206498	51002644	1675353	3802984	49016142	55224195	58961286	41375892	46127706	32086303	46294339	151477670	131161987
Interest	3	274907	6612	551	3958	3967	5053	9973	6406	3840	6847	2489	31415	193797
Rents	4	283017	7	17488	320	11884	12680	42633	17816	13793	29751	25133	34852	76660
Royalties	5	45146	0	0	0	0	59	19	212	6	369	126	3538	40817
Other Portfolio Income	6	1874218	11332	16940	0	73728	81754	36066	32269	25737	4792	19023	42764	1529813
Other Receipts	7	2486885	102908	8973	4873	367060	113480	108891	106931	143114	61087	73024	143677	1252865
Total Receipts	8	673170671	51123503	1719305	3812135	49472781	55437221	59158868	41539526	46314196	32189149	46414134	151733916	134255939
Average Total Receipts	9	93913	41329	962	6301	23739	72752	151689	284517	586256	1238044	2730243	5619775	16781992
Operating Costs/Operating Income (%)														
Cost of Operations	10	95.0	99.0	88.7	90.7	93.8	95.7	95.0	95.3	95.7	96.6	98.0	97.9	88.4
Salaries and Wages	11	1.0	0.3	3.5	1.0	1.8	1.4	1.5	1.5	1.1	0.9	0.4	0.6	1.2
Taxes Paid	12	0.3	0.0	1.3	2.5	0.4	0.3	0.5	0.2	0.2	0.2	0.3	0.1	0.6
Interest Paid	13	0.4	0.2	0.7	0.1	0.1	0.2	0.1	0.2	0.1	0.2	0.1	0.2	1.4
Depreciation	14	0.8	0.0	1.4	0.4	0.4	0.4	0.5	0.6	0.5	0.4	0.2	0.3	2.8
Amortization and Depletion	15	0.2	0.0	0.3	0.0	0.0	0.0	0.0	0.0	0.1	0.1	0.0	0.0	1.1
Pensions and Other Deferred Comp.	16	0.1	0.0	•	0.1	0.0	0.1	0.0	0.0	0.0	0.0	0.0	0.0	0.2
Employee Benefits	17	0.1	0.0	0.2	0.3	0.1	0.1	0.1	0.1	0.1	0.1	0.1	0.1	0.1
Advertising	18	0.0	0.0	0.1	0.0	0.1	0.0	0.0	0.0	0.0	0.0	0.0	0.0	0.0
Other Expenses	19	3.0	3.4	5.5	2.6	3.0	1.5	1.9	1.8	1.6	1.6	1.0	0.9	8.4
Officers' Compensation	20	0.2	0.0	3.2	1.8	0.5	0.3	0.2	0.2	0.2	0.2	0.1	0.1	0.1
Operating Margin	21	•	•	•	0.6	•	•	0.0	0.0	0.2	•	•	•	•
Operating Margin Before Officers' Comp.	22	•	•	•	2.4	0.2	0.3	0.2	0.2	0.4	0.0	•	•	•

Selected Average Balance Sheet ($ in Thousands)

Net Receivables	23	4207	0	31	378	695	2707	5042	10665	25061	51442	127180	254073	1312148
Inventories	24	2263	0	11	123	421	743	2376	4450	8340	32990	73272	189564	653496
Net Property, Plant and Equipment	25	9339	0	24	44	490	1678	4344	11077	14593	35666	33574	91414	7017916
Total Assets	26	24236	0	174	758	2321	7135	16177	34924	69200	150465	310315	978213	13776276
Notes and Loans Payable	27	8950	0	166	154	630	2054	4215	11268	17523	41131	75411	290336	5752650
All Other Liabilities	28	8321	0	58	168	814	2904	6052	13117	30904	72439	186559	415830	4066582
Net Worth	29	6966	0	-50	436	877	2177	5911	10539	20773	36896	48346	272047	3957044

Selected Financial Ratios (Times to 1)

Current Ratio	30	1.3	•	0.9	2.6	1.6	1.4	1.3	1.2	1.3	1.4	1.2	1.3	1.4
Quick Ratio	31	0.8	•	0.7	2.2	1.1	1.1	0.9	0.8	0.9	0.8	0.7	0.7	0.9
Net Sales to Working Capital	32	42.6	•	•	15.0	39.5	54.4	61.8	82.7	53.0	46.7	65.8	44.7	21.5
Coverage Ratio	33	•	•	•	9.0	6.7	3.3	3.7	3.2	5.3	1.7	1.8	0.4	•
Total Asset Turnover	34	3.8	•	5.4	8.3	10.1	10.2	9.3	8.1	8.4	8.2	8.8	5.7	1.2
Inventory Turnover	35	39.1	•	77.4	46.5	52.4	93.4	60.5	60.7	67.0	36.1	36.4	29.0	22.2
Receivables Turnover	36	23.5	•	29.4	15.2	28.9	29.9	30.3	26.4	23.9	22.9	20.2	24.8	14.1
Total Liabilities to Net Worth	37	2.5	•	•	0.7	1.6	2.3	1.7	2.3	2.3	3.1	5.4	2.6	2.5
Current Assets to Working Capital	38	4.0	•	•	1.6	2.6	3.6	4.0	5.8	4.1	3.5	5.8	4.7	3.8
Current Liabilities to Working Capital	39	3.0	•	•	0.6	1.6	2.6	3.0	4.8	3.1	2.5	4.8	3.7	2.8
Working Capital to Net Sales	40	0.0	•	•	0.1	0.0	0.0	0.0	0.0	0.0	0.0	0.0	0.0	0.0
Inventory to Working Capital	41	1.1	•	•	0.2	0.7	0.6	0.9	1.5	0.8	0.9	2.0	1.6	0.9
Total Receipts to Cash Flow	42	47.2	218.6	49.0	36.2	34.1	73.7	55.5	57.6	56.3	82.4	142.6	225.8	17.3
Cost of Goods to Cash Flow	43	44.9	216.5	43.5	32.8	32.0	70.5	52.8	54.9	53.9	79.6	139.7	221.1	15.3
Cash Flow to Total Debt	44	0.1	•	0.1	0.5	0.5	0.2	0.3	0.2	0.2	0.1	0.1	0.0	0.1

Selected Financial Factors (in Percentages)

Debt Ratio	45	71.3	•	128.9	42.5	62.2	69.5	63.5	69.8	70.0	75.5	84.4	72.2	71.3
Return on Total Assets	46	•	•	•	7.6	7.1	5.3	4.6	4.7	6.6	2.3	1.5	0.6	•
Return on Equity Before Income Taxes	47	•	•	44.1	11.7	16.0	12.0	9.2	10.8	17.8	4.0	4.3	•	•
Return on Equity After Income Taxes	48	•	•	45.0	11.2	15.7	11.3	8.2	10.0	15.6	3.0	1.9	•	•
Profit Margin (Before Income Tax)	49	•	•	•	0.8	0.6	0.4	0.4	0.4	0.6	0.1	0.1	•	•
Profit Margin (After Income Tax)	50	•	•	•	0.8	0.6	0.3	0.3	0.4	0.6	0.1	0.0	•	•

Table II

Corporations with Net Income

PETROLEUM AND PETROLEUM PRODUCTS

MONEY AMOUNTS AND SIZE OF ASSETS IN THOUSANDS OF DOLLARS

Item Description for Accounting Period 7/11 Through 6/12		Total	Zero Assets	Under 500	500 to 1,000	1,000 to 5,000	5,000 to 10,000	10,000 to 25,000	25,000 to 50,000	50,000 to 100,000	100,000 to 250,000	250,000 to 500,000	500,000 to 2,500,000	2,500,000 and over
Number of Enterprises	1	4483	804	•	437	1545	516	313	100	59	16	•	15	5
Revenues ($ in Thousands)														
Net Sales	2	460744470	4978109	•	2053052	42055971	35531703	46705169	31015961	37136604	16063053	•	106813107	101925657
Interest	3	151205	2613	•	2774	3119	4610	8339	3751	3219	4717	•	16962	98346
Rents	4	190232	0	•	320	9390	12141	30775	11471	12740	344	•	5845	64863
Royalties	5	3754	0	•	0	0	59	19	0	6	159	•	3385	0
Other Portfolio Income	6	1531650	4224	•	0	64449	78738	28658	25332	24400	2540	•	37083	1237202
Other Receipts	7	1185832	18371	•	2388	343711	84755	75423	89174	148777	61382	•	91106	212525
Total Receipts	8	463807143	5003317	•	2058534	42476640	35712006	46848383	31145689	37325746	16132195	•	106967488	103538593
Average Total Receipts	9	103459	6223	•	4711	27493	69209	149675	311457	632640	1008262	•	7131166	20707719
Operating Costs/Operating Income (%)														
Cost of Operations	10	96.0	97.6	•	87.8	94.2	95.6	94.9	95.4	95.6	96.0	•	98.2	95.1
Salaries and Wages	11	0.8	0.3	•	0.9	1.5	1.4	1.4	1.4	1.1	1.0	•	0.4	0.5
Taxes Paid	12	0.2	0.1	•	4.3	0.4	0.3	0.5	0.2	0.2	0.2	•	0.1	0.1
Interest Paid	13	0.2	0.2	•	0.2	0.1	0.1	0.1	0.1	0.1	0.2	•	0.2	0.4
Depreciation	14	0.5	0.1	•	0.6	0.4	0.3	0.5	0.5	0.5	0.4	•	0.2	1.0
Amortization and Depletion	15	0.2	0.0	•	0.0	0.0	0.0	0.0	0.0	0.0	0.1	•	0.0	0.6
Pensions and Other Deferred Comp.	16	0.0	0.0	•	0.2	0.0	0.1	0.0	0.0	0.0	0.0	•	0.0	0.0
Employee Benefits	17	0.1	0.0	•	0.1	0.1	0.1	0.1	0.1	0.1	0.1	•	0.0	0.1
Advertising	18	0.0	0.0	•	0.0	0.1	0.0	0.0	0.0	0.0	0.0	•	0.0	0.0
Other Expenses	19	1.8	0.6	•	2.4	2.9	1.4	1.8	1.7	1.6	1.4	•	0.5	3.0
Officers' Compensation	20	0.2	0.0	•	1.8	0.5	0.4	0.2	0.2	0.2	0.1	•	0.1	0.0
Operating Margin	21	•	1.0	•	1.6	•	0.3	0.3	0.2	0.4	0.4	•	0.2	•
Operating Margin Before Officers' Comp.	22	0.2	1.1	•	3.5	0.3	0.7	0.6	0.5	0.6	0.6	•	0.4	•

Selected Average Balance Sheet ($ in Thousands)													
Net Receivables 23	4305	0	•	409	787	2949	5439	12412	25589	56244	•	315332	861509
Inventories 24	2569	0	•	122	459	855	2353	4846	8028	40670	•	224467	757259
Net Property, Plant and Equipment 25	3226	0	•	33	484	1105	3810	8266	14201	29405	•	65098	1651686
Total Assets 26	15206	0	•	761	2353	6717	15842	34436	69739	148511	•	967369	5335750
Notes and Loans Payable 27	5324	0	•	157	577	1731	3799	8673	16976	35172	•	338984	2461195
All Other Liabilities 28	5963	0	•	145	956	2760	6016	15017	29894	69536	•	378598	1832878
Net Worth 29	3918	0	•	458	820	2226	6027	10746	22869	43803	•	249786	1041677
Selected Financial Ratios (Times to 1)													
Current Ratio 30	1.4	•	•	3.1	1.5	1.4	1.4	1.3	1.3	1.6	•	1.3	1.5
Quick Ratio 31	0.8	•	•	2.6	1.1	1.1	1.0	0.9	1.0	0.9	•	0.7	0.8
Net Sales to Working Capital 32	41.0	•	•	9.5	46.6	49.1	51.9	64.8	54.9	26.9	•	46.9	27.9
Coverage Ratio 33	4.3	8.4	•	13.3	10.0	6.3	6.4	6.4	9.4	5.3	•	3.3	2.7
Total Asset Turnover 34	6.8	•	•	6.2	11.6	10.3	9.4	9.0	9.0	6.8	•	7.4	3.8
Inventory Turnover 35	38.4	•	•	33.8	55.9	76.9	60.2	61.1	74.9	23.7	•	31.2	25.6
Receivables Turnover 36	25.2	•	•	10.9	30.0	23.4	30.5	24.6	26.7	16.1	•	29.0	23.0
Total Liabilities to Net Worth 37	2.9	•	•	0.7	1.9	2.0	1.6	2.2	2.0	2.4	•	2.9	4.1
Current Assets to Working Capital 38	3.5	•	•	1.5	2.8	3.6	3.5	4.8	3.9	2.7	•	4.3	3.0
Current Liabilities to Working Capital 39	2.5	•	•	0.5	1.8	2.6	2.5	3.8	2.9	1.7	•	3.3	2.0
Working Capital to Net Sales 40	0.0	•	•	0.1	0.0	0.0	0.0	0.0	0.0	0.0	•	0.0	0.0
Inventory to Working Capital 41	1.1	•	•	0.2	0.7	0.7	0.8	1.3	0.7	0.7	•	1.7	1.0
Total Receipts to Cash Flow 42	51.5	51.9	•	25.9	31.9	61.0	49.3	52.6	48.5	53.4	•	147.6	32.9
Cost of Goods to Cash Flow 43	49.4	50.7	•	22.7	30.1	58.3	46.8	50.2	46.3	51.2	•	144.9	31.3
Cash Flow to Total Debt 44	0.2	•	•	0.6	0.6	0.3	0.3	0.2	0.3	0.2	•	0.1	0.1
Selected Financial Factors (in Percentages)													
Debt Ratio 45	74.2	•	•	39.7	65.1	66.9	62.0	68.8	67.2	70.5	•	74.2	80.5
Return on Total Assets 46	5.8	•	•	12.6	10.8	9.4	7.1	7.1	9.5	7.0	•	4.3	4.2
Return on Equity Before Income Taxes 47	17.2	•	•	19.4	27.9	23.8	15.8	19.1	25.9	19.2	•	11.6	13.5
Return on Equity After Income Taxes 48	15.0	•	•	18.7	27.4	22.8	14.5	18.0	23.2	17.9	•	9.8	10.0
Profit Margin (Before Income Tax) 49	0.7	1.6	•	1.9	0.8	0.8	0.6	0.7	0.9	0.8	•	0.4	0.7
Profit Margin (After Income Tax) 50	0.6	1.3	•	1.8	0.8	0.7	0.6	0.6	0.8	0.8	•	0.3	0.5

Table I

Corporations with and without Net Income

BEER, WINE, AND DISTILLED ALCOHOLIC BEVERAGE

MONEY AMOUNTS AND SIZE OF ASSETS IN THOUSANDS OF DOLLARS

Item Description for Accounting Period 7/11 Through 6/12		Total	Zero Assets	Under 500	500 to 1,000	1,000 to 5,000	5,000 to 10,000	10,000 to 25,000	25,000 to 50,000	50,000 to 100,000	100,000 to 250,000	250,000 to 500,000	500,000 to 2,500,000	2,500,000 and over
Number of Enterprises	1	4007	1363	916	140	733	428	229	76	61	39	11	8	3
Revenues ($ in Thousands)														
Net Sales	2	79118551	263550	289927	388490	6000622	8902124	9336298	6417181	8587258	10500487	6016172	10117364	12299077
Interest	3	46371	14	0	0	1583	1225	386	631	5298	1209	9977	10357	15690
Rents	4	42844	907	0	0	15	975	0	1022	128	416	11535	27091	754
Royalties	5	87686	0	0	0	0	0	0	3330	0	36144	65	6999	41148
Other Portfolio Income	6	162277	3298	4676	0	30019	18237	38356	4735	20961	12313	5587	21588	2506
Other Receipts	7	1034129	9340	2855	12000	69306	85725	109322	39106	127494	186323	90903	165198	136562
Total Receipts	8	80491858	277109	297458	400490	6101545	9008286	9484362	6466005	8741139	10736892	6134239	10348597	12495737
Average Total Receipts	9	20088	203	325	2861	8324	21047	41416	85079	143297	275305	557658	1293575	4165246
Operating Costs/Operating Income (%)														
Cost of Operations	10	75.3	60.6	37.9	68.6	75.5	75.0	73.6	75.5	77.9	75.2	78.4	74.1	75.8
Salaries and Wages	11	8.2	9.1	2.5	9.0	8.1	8.5	8.5	8.6	7.3	8.2	6.8	8.0	9.1
Taxes Paid	12	2.7	2.7	4.8	1.1	2.4	2.6	3.5	1.7	1.7	2.6	2.5	5.6	1.2
Interest Paid	13	0.9	0.0	0.4	0.4	0.2	0.5	0.6	0.4	0.6	0.6	0.6	1.0	2.4
Depreciation	14	0.7	0.5	0.4	0.9	0.7	0.7	0.6	0.7	1.0	0.7	0.6	1.2	0.4
Amortization and Depletion	15	1.5	0.3	0.9	0.2	0.1	0.3	0.7	0.7	0.9	0.7	1.0	1.7	5.4
Pensions and Other Deferred Comp.	16	0.4	0.2	•	•	0.2	0.6	0.3	0.2	0.3	0.3	0.4	0.4	0.5
Employee Benefits	17	0.9	0.5	0.0	0.1	0.5	1.0	1.0	1.0	1.0	0.9	0.6	0.5	1.1
Advertising	18	1.8	0.1	0.4	1.9	0.5	0.7	0.7	1.5	1.3	3.0	2.1	1.9	3.1
Other Expenses	19	5.7	25.2	20.5	16.2	7.6	5.0	5.7	6.5	5.5	5.5	5.0	6.0	3.9
Officers' Compensation	20	1.0	2.4	19.8	•	2.4	1.7	1.3	1.0	0.7	1.2	0.4	0.3	0.2
Operating Margin	21	1.0	•	12.5	1.6	1.7	3.3	3.4	2.4	1.9	1.1	1.8	•	•
Operating Margin Before Officers' Comp.	22	2.1	0.8	32.3	1.6	4.1	5.1	4.7	3.4	2.6	2.3	2.2	•	•

Selected Average Balance Sheet ($ in Thousands)													
Net Receivables 23	1854	0	15	225	441	884	2088	4738	10327	29886	48980	170835	714667
Inventories 24	2171	0	22	326	808	1793	3150	7445	10038	31020	46500	168298	768406
Net Property, Plant and Equipment 25	1008	0	26	43	245	1306	1774	3669	8489	12232	36296	73747	200640
Total Assets 26	13156	0	142	792	2112	7481	15721	33388	71030	145288	335270	977110	6695136
Notes and Loans Payable 27	4239	0	51	399	339	1540	5444	9823	22645	37418	108366	275888	2581092
All Other Liabilities 28	3365	0	51	351	853	2110	2851	7356	15406	43690	90163	288206	1568631
Net Worth 29	5552	0	40	41	919	3831	7427	16209	32980	64180	136741	413016	2545413
Selected Financial Ratios (Times to 1)													
Current Ratio 30	1.4	•	1.3	2.0	1.9	2.4	2.1	1.8	1.6	1.7	1.9	1.7	0.8
Quick Ratio 31	0.6	•	0.5	1.2	0.9	1.2	1.1	0.8	0.8	0.8	1.0	0.9	0.3
Net Sales to Working Capital 32	13.0	•	17.3	9.1	10.8	8.5	10.5	11.2	13.2	8.4	8.2	6.9	•
Coverage Ratio 33	4.2	99.4	35.5	13.2	18.4	10.1	9.6	9.1	6.9	6.7	7.5	2.4	0.3
Total Asset Turnover 34	1.5	•	2.2	3.5	3.9	2.8	2.6	2.5	2.0	1.9	1.6	1.3	0.6
Inventory Turnover 35	6.9	•	5.5	5.8	7.7	8.7	9.5	8.6	10.9	6.5	9.2	5.6	4.0
Receivables Turnover 36	11.1	•	42.6	15.5	19.2	23.7	20.8	19.2	14.8	9.2	10.1	8.5	5.9
Total Liabilities to Net Worth 37	1.4	•	2.6	18.1	1.3	1.0	1.1	1.1	1.2	1.3	1.5	1.4	1.6
Current Assets to Working Capital 38	3.6	•	4.0	2.0	2.2	1.7	1.9	2.3	2.8	2.5	2.1	2.3	•
Current Liabilities to Working Capital 39	2.6	•	3.0	1.0	1.2	0.7	0.9	1.3	1.8	1.5	1.1	1.3	•
Working Capital to Net Sales 40	0.1	•	0.1	0.1	0.1	0.1	0.1	0.1	0.1	0.1	0.1	0.1	•
Inventory to Working Capital 41	1.5	•	2.4	0.6	1.1	0.8	0.8	1.0	0.9	1.0	0.8	1.0	•
Total Receipts to Cash Flow 42	14.1	5.7	3.5	5.4	10.4	11.9	11.0	12.1	13.1	12.9	12.9	16.1	90.9
Cost of Goods to Cash Flow 43	10.6	3.5	1.3	3.7	7.9	8.9	8.1	9.2	10.2	9.7	10.1	11.9	68.9
Cash Flow to Total Debt 44	0.2	•	0.9	0.7	0.7	0.5	0.4	0.4	0.3	0.3	0.2	0.1	0.0
Selected Financial Factors (in Percentages)													
Debt Ratio 45	57.8	•	71.8	94.8	56.5	48.8	52.8	51.5	53.6	55.8	59.2	57.7	62.0
Return on Total Assets 46	5.4	•	34.5	17.8	14.0	13.9	14.4	8.9	8.5	7.1	7.1	3.2	0.5
Return on Equity Before Income Taxes 47	9.8	•	119.2	315.3	30.5	24.5	27.4	16.3	15.6	13.7	15.0	4.5	•
Return on Equity After Income Taxes 48	9.1	•	119.2	296.0	27.4	23.7	26.5	15.1	15.2	12.8	12.5	3.7	•
Profit Margin (Before Income Tax) 49	2.8	3.5	15.1	4.7	3.4	4.5	5.0	3.1	3.6	3.3	3.8	1.5	•
Profit Margin (After Income Tax) 50	2.6	3.1	15.1	4.4	3.1	4.4	4.8	2.9	3.6	3.1	3.1	1.2	•

Table II

Corporations with Net Income

BEER, WINE, AND DISTILLED ALCOHOLIC BEVERAGE

MONEY AMOUNTS AND SIZE OF ASSETS IN THOUSANDS OF DOLLARS

Item Description for Accounting Period 7/11 Through 6/12		Total	Zero Assets	Under 500	500 to 1,000	1,000 to 5,000	5,000 to 10,000	10,000 to 25,000	25,000 to 50,000	50,000 to 100,000	100,000 to 250,000	250,000 to 500,000	500,000 to 2,500,000	2,500,000 and over
Number of Enterprises	1	2451	669	•	140	658	416	211	60	•	34	8	•	0
Revenues ($ in Thousands)														
Net Sales	2	68990009	231919	•	388490	5227878	8647983	8789930	5508252	•	8977241	5557540	•	0
Interest	3	23025	14	•	0	1496	1221	386	433	•	1135	7312	•	0
Rents	4	16172	907	•	0	15	975	0	106	•	416	11535	•	0
Royalties	5	40098	0	•	0	0	0	0	3330	•	35611	0	•	0
Other Portfolio Income	6	139576	3155	•	0	30019	18237	38337	4660	•	11525	5418	•	0
Other Receipts	7	736970	7519	•	12000	12881	84762	106608	38718	•	155971	89640	•	0
Total Receipts	8	69945850	243514	•	400490	5272289	8753178	8935261	5555499	•	9181899	5671445	•	0
Average Total Receipts	9	28538	364	•	2861	8013	21041	42347	92592	•	270056	708931	•	•
Operating Costs/Operating Income (%)														
Cost of Operations	10	76.3	66.0	•	68.6	72.5	74.7	73.6	75.6	•	75.2	78.7	•	•
Salaries and Wages	11	8.0	9.5	•	9.0	8.5	8.6	8.4	8.2	•	7.8	6.6	•	•
Taxes Paid	12	2.8	2.5	•	1.1	2.7	2.6	3.6	1.8	•	2.8	2.5	•	•
Interest Paid	13	0.5	0.0	•	0.4	0.1	0.5	0.5	0.3	•	0.5	0.6	•	•
Depreciation	14	0.6	0.5	•	0.9	0.8	0.6	0.6	0.7	•	0.7	0.6	•	•
Amortization and Depletion	15	0.6	0.3	•	0.2	0.1	0.3	0.6	0.5	•	0.7	0.7	•	•
Pensions and Other Deferred Comp.	16	0.3	0.3	•	•	0.2	0.6	0.4	0.2	•	0.3	0.3	•	•
Employee Benefits	17	0.8	0.5	•	0.1	0.6	1.0	0.9	0.9	•	0.9	0.6	•	•
Advertising	18	1.1	0.1	•	1.9	0.4	0.7	0.7	1.5	•	2.4	2.1	•	•
Other Expenses	19	5.2	17.5	•	16.2	7.8	5.0	5.6	5.9	•	5.4	4.7	•	•
Officers' Compensation	20	1.1	1.8	•	•	2.6	1.8	1.4	1.1	•	1.2	0.5	•	•
Operating Margin	21	2.7	0.9	•	1.6	3.8	3.5	3.7	3.3	•	2.0	2.2	•	•
Operating Margin Before Officers' Comp.	22	3.8	2.7	•	1.6	6.4	5.3	5.1	4.4	•	3.2	2.7	•	•

Selected Average Balance Sheet ($ in Thousands)													
Net Receivables **23**	2375	0	•	225	376	897	2054	5025	•	27420	56711	•	•
Inventories **24**	3112	0	•	175	774	1743	2963	7978	•	28717	67438	•	•
Net Property, Plant and Equipment **25**	1370	0	•	43	258	1243	1857	3969	•	12222	47036	•	•
Total Assets **26**	13063	0	•	792	2099	7403	15755	32549	•	140440	348661	•	•
Notes and Loans Payable **27**	3924	0	•	399	287	1452	4877	7597	•	33955	117230	•	•
All Other Liabilities **28**	3605	0	•	351	705	2037	2873	7084	•	40614	103618	•	•
Net Worth **29**	5533	0	•	41	1107	3914	8005	17867	•	65871	127813	•	•
Selected Financial Ratios (Times to 1)													
Current Ratio **30**	1.9	•	•	2.0	2.2	2.5	2.1	2.1	•	1.9	1.8	•	•
Quick Ratio **31**	0.9	•	•	1.2	1.0	1.3	1.2	1.0	•	1.0	0.9	•	•
Net Sales to Working Capital **32**	8.4	•	•	9.1	9.2	8.5	10.5	9.7	•	7.9	9.9	•	•
Coverage Ratio **33**	8.9	152.4	•	13.2	32.1	11.1	11.4	14.4	•	9.1	8.7	•	•
Total Asset Turnover **34**	2.2	•	•	3.5	3.8	2.8	2.6	2.8	•	1.9	2.0	•	•
Inventory Turnover **35**	6.9	•	•	10.9	7.4	8.9	10.3	8.7	•	6.9	8.1	•	•
Receivables Turnover **36**	12.2	•	•	18.8	22.6	24.3	21.9	21.6	•	9.5	•	•	•
Total Liabilities to Net Worth **37**	1.4	•	•	18.1	0.9	0.9	1.0	0.8	•	1.1	1.7	•	•
Current Assets to Working Capital **38**	2.1	•	•	2.0	1.8	1.7	1.9	1.9	•	2.2	2.2	•	•
Current Liabilities to Working Capital **39**	1.1	•	•	1.0	0.8	0.7	0.9	0.9	•	1.2	1.2	•	•
Working Capital to Net Sales **40**	0.1	•	•	0.1	0.1	0.1	0.1	0.1	•	0.1	0.1	•	•
Inventory to Working Capital **41**	1.0	•	•	0.6	0.9	0.8	0.8	0.9	•	0.9	1.0	•	•
Total Receipts to Cash Flow **42**	12.5	5.9	•	5.4	9.2	11.6	10.7	11.3	•	11.7	12.6	•	•
Cost of Goods to Cash Flow **43**	9.6	3.9	•	3.7	6.7	8.6	7.8	8.6	•	8.8	9.9	•	•
Cash Flow to Total Debt **44**	0.3	•	•	0.7	0.9	0.5	0.5	0.6	•	0.3	0.3	•	•
Selected Financial Factors (in Percentages)													
Debt Ratio **45**	57.6	•	•	94.8	47.2	47.1	49.2	45.1	•	53.1	63.3	•	•
Return on Total Assets **46**	9.8	•	•	17.8	18.2	14.5	15.6	12.7	•	8.9	9.6	•	•
Return on Equity Before Income Taxes **47**	20.5	•	•	315.3	33.5	25.0	28.0	21.5	•	16.8	23.2	•	•
Return on Equity After Income Taxes **48**	19.4	•	•	296.0	30.6	24.2	27.1	20.2	•	15.8	19.5	•	•
Profit Margin (Before Income Tax) **49**	4.0	5.9	•	4.7	4.7	4.7	5.4	4.2	•	4.2	4.3	•	•
Profit Margin (After Income Tax) **50**	3.8	5.5	•	4.4	4.3	4.6	5.2	3.9	•	3.9	3.6	•	•

Table I

Corporations with and without Net Income

MISCELLANEOUS NONDURABLE GOODS

MONEY AMOUNTS AND SIZE OF ASSETS IN THOUSANDS OF DOLLARS

Item Description for Accounting Period 7/11 Through 6/12		Total	Zero Assets	Under 500	500 to 1,000	1,000 to 5,000	5,000 to 10,000	10,000 to 25,000	25,000 to 50,000	50,000 to 100,000	100,000 to 250,000	250,000 to 500,000	500,000 to 2,500,000	2,500,000 and over
Number of Enterprises	1	30136	5214	17529	2534	3838	307	420	142	72	46	13	15	5
Revenues ($ in Thousands)														
Net Sales	2	185090687	1331237	7918958	6372484	31930765	8366290	20900839	13239328	13751337	16271300	6369109	29526341	29112699
Interest	3	148626	4033	1803	804	6928	6692	8649	4708	3546	14057	1740	18522	77143
Rents	4	36630	844	0	169	2992	533	1574	1748	1196	106	2131	6530	18808
Royalties	5	963348	38	0	0	1088	0	277	2474	1507	3481	22302	5216	926965
Other Portfolio Income	6	1066862	18009	8716	34901	3076	4747	4066	4030	4713	15902	4820	70939	892943
Other Receipts	7	2639544	38825	26920	21477	201762	65763	261787	136900	114135	140600	109334	137606	1384435
Total Receipts	8	189945697	1392986	7956397	6429835	32146611	8444025	21177192	13389188	13876434	16445446	6509436	29765154	32412993
Average Total Receipts	9	6303	267	454	2537	8376	27505	50422	94290	192728	357510	500726	1984344	6482599
Operating Costs/Operating Income (%)														
Cost of Operations	10	79.8	66.5	67.6	80.7	84.5	86.7	80.9	81.5	86.3	82.0	79.6	78.8	71.7
Salaries and Wages	11	4.9	5.7	5.0	5.6	3.8	3.8	5.8	5.0	4.4	5.0	6.1	4.8	5.7
Taxes Paid	12	1.6	3.2	1.5	1.2	0.7	0.6	3.0	1.7	0.9	0.6	0.9	2.7	1.4
Interest Paid	13	0.7	1.0	0.5	0.5	0.2	0.3	0.3	0.4	0.5	0.9	0.3	1.2	1.3
Depreciation	14	1.0	0.7	0.6	0.5	0.5	0.5	0.7	1.0	0.8	0.9	1.8	1.6	1.6
Amortization and Depletion	15	0.3	2.1	0.1	0.0	0.0	0.0	0.1	0.1	0.2	0.3	0.3	0.4	1.1
Pensions and Other Deferred Comp.	16	0.3	0.5	0.1	0.0	0.3	0.1	0.2	0.2	0.2	0.2	0.2	0.4	0.4
Employee Benefits	17	0.7	0.7	0.3	0.3	0.3	0.2	0.5	0.5	0.3	0.4	0.5	0.7	2.4
Advertising	18	1.0	0.5	1.1	0.4	0.3	0.6	0.4	1.2	0.9	1.5	0.3	1.2	1.8
Other Expenses	19	7.0	16.1	15.3	7.7	6.0	5.1	6.0	5.9	4.5	5.8	5.5	6.8	9.3
Officers' Compensation	20	1.1	7.4	3.7	2.2	1.9	1.5	1.1	1.0	0.6	0.5	0.8	0.3	0.4
Operating Margin	21	1.7	•	4.0	1.0	1.5	0.7	1.0	1.6	0.4	1.9	3.7	1.2	2.9
Operating Margin Before Officers' Comp.	22	2.8	3.1	7.8	3.2	3.4	2.2	2.1	2.6	1.0	2.3	4.4	1.4	3.3

Selected Average Balance Sheet ($ in Thousands)													
Net Receivables 23	496	0	15	177	602	1559	4837	8971	19048	34041	74831	149538	397178
Inventories 24	588	0	29	257	542	2451	4540	9913	19924	41261	74017	177736	788394
Net Property, Plant and Equipment 25	396	0	17	61	263	479	1581	4289	9046	18344	48622	155626	917964
Total Assets 26	3297	0	106	663	2193	7157	15473	33557	67608	153846	356728	862918	8883354
Notes and Loans Payable 27	983	0	49	189	532	1982	4515	8995	21307	67190	51845	284944	2575918
All Other Liabilities 28	1179	0	32	261	872	2157	5219	12721	24735	65254	124444	345799	2940624
Net Worth 29	1135	0	24	213	789	3018	5739	11842	21567	21402	180440	232174	3366812
Selected Financial Ratios (Times to 1)													
Current Ratio 30	1.4	•	1.9	1.7	1.7	2.1	1.7	1.5	1.5	1.3	1.5	1.4	1.1
Quick Ratio 31	0.6	•	1.0	1.0	1.0	1.1	0.9	0.8	0.8	0.6	0.8	0.7	0.3
Net Sales to Working Capital 32	12.7	•	13.9	11.1	11.9	9.0	10.3	11.2	11.1	15.7	7.1	15.3	20.0
Coverage Ratio 33	7.2	1.4	9.2	4.8	9.6	7.0	8.1	7.6	3.7	4.4	19.3	2.7	11.9
Total Asset Turnover 34	1.9	•	4.3	3.8	3.8	3.8	3.2	2.8	2.8	2.3	1.4	2.3	0.7
Inventory Turnover 35	8.3	•	10.5	7.9	13.0	9.6	8.9	7.7	8.3	7.0	5.3	8.7	5.3
Receivables Turnover 36	12.4	•	32.4	12.0	15.1	13.3	10.2	10.8	•	10.6	•	•	13.5
Total Liabilities to Net Worth 37	1.9	•	3.3	2.1	1.8	1.4	1.7	1.8	2.1	6.2	1.0	2.7	1.6
Current Assets to Working Capital 38	3.8	•	2.1	2.4	2.4	1.9	2.5	2.9	2.9	4.4	2.9	3.5	12.4
Current Liabilities to Working Capital 39	2.8	•	1.1	1.4	1.4	0.9	1.5	1.9	1.9	3.4	1.9	2.5	11.4
Working Capital to Net Sales 40	0.1	•	0.1	0.1	0.1	0.1	0.1	0.1	0.1	0.1	0.1	0.1	0.1
Inventory to Working Capital 41	1.3	•	0.9	1.0	0.8	0.8	1.0	1.2	1.2	2.1	1.1	1.4	2.8
Total Receipts to Cash Flow 42	10.3	7.9	6.0	14.3	14.6	18.6	14.1	13.1	20.1	12.8	9.5	13.8	4.7
Cost of Goods to Cash Flow 43	8.2	5.3	4.0	11.6	12.3	16.1	11.4	10.7	17.3	10.5	7.6	10.9	3.4
Cash Flow to Total Debt 44	0.3	•	0.9	0.4	0.4	0.4	0.4	0.3	0.2	0.2	0.3	0.2	0.2
Selected Financial Factors (in Percentages)													
Debt Ratio 45	65.6	•	77.0	67.9	64.0	57.8	62.9	64.7	68.1	86.1	49.4	73.1	62.1
Return on Total Assets 46	9.3	•	21.6	9.5	9.0	7.2	8.6	8.9	5.4	8.8	8.5	7.3	10.3
Return on Equity Before Income Taxes 47	23.4	•	83.5	23.6	22.5	14.6	20.4	21.8	12.3	48.8	16.0	17.0	24.9
Return on Equity After Income Taxes 48	18.4	•	81.9	20.2	21.1	13.3	18.6	19.0	11.2	39.9	13.2	13.7	17.6
Profit Margin (Before Income Tax) 49	4.3	0.4	4.5	2.0	2.1	1.6	2.4	2.8	1.4	3.0	5.9	2.0	14.4
Profit Margin (After Income Tax) 50	3.4	•	4.4	1.7	2.0	1.5	2.1	2.4	1.3	2.4	4.9	1.6	10.2

Table II

Corporations with Net Income

MISCELLANEOUS NONDURABLE GOODS

MONEY AMOUNTS AND SIZE OF ASSETS IN THOUSANDS OF DOLLARS

Item Description for Accounting Period 7/11 Through 6/12		Total	Zero Assets	Under 500	500 to 1,000	1,000 to 5,000	5,000 to 10,000	10,000 to 25,000	25,000 to 50,000	50,000 to 100,000	100,000 to 250,000	250,000 to 500,000	500,000 to 2,500,000	2,500,000 and over
Number of Enterprises	1	17535	2270	9932	1577	2918	255	336	129	53	36	13	10	5
Revenues ($ in Thousands)														
Net Sales	2	162332337	793522	6356015	5179263	26227196	7814075	18538556	12373760	11200182	13559783	6369109	24808176	29112699
Interest	3	127916	544	1476	373	5741	4212	5403	4667	2782	12002	1740	11835	77143
Rents	4	28888	57	0	169	1887	404	945	1748	1188	104	2131	1446	18808
Royalties	5	957108	38	0	0	13	0	0	1561	1371	1607	22302	3250	926965
Other Portfolio Income	6	1044713	5683	8653	32275	3047	3695	3389	3915	3451	12913	4820	69927	892943
Other Receipts	7	2388630	28864	20953	4307	159011	92829	157257	116900	81669	138681	109334	94394	1384435
Total Receipts	8	166879592	828708	6387097	5216387	26396895	7915215	18705550	12502551	11290643	13725090	6509436	24989028	32412993
Average Total Receipts	9	9517	365	643	3308	9046	31040	55671	96919	213031	381252	500726	2498903	6482599
Operating Costs/Operating Income (%)														
Cost of Operations	10	79.8	60.8	68.1	82.0	83.5	87.2	80.5	82.6	87.0	82.3	79.6	79.4	71.7
Salaries and Wages	11	4.7	4.4	4.2	4.9	3.5	3.3	5.4	4.8	4.1	4.6	6.1	4.4	5.7
Taxes Paid	12	1.5	3.4	1.5	0.8	0.6	0.5	3.3	0.8	1.0	0.6	0.9	3.0	1.4
Interest Paid	13	0.6	1.5	0.5	0.4	0.2	0.2	0.3	0.4	0.5	0.7	0.3	0.7	1.3
Depreciation	14	0.9	0.5	0.4	0.3	0.4	0.4	0.6	0.8	0.7	0.9	1.8	1.3	1.6
Amortization and Depletion	15	0.3	2.5	0.1	0.0	0.0	0.0	0.1	0.1	0.1	0.1	0.3	0.2	1.1
Pensions and Other Deferred Comp.	16	0.3	0.1	0.1	0.0	0.3	0.1	0.2	0.2	0.2	0.2	0.2	0.4	0.4
Employee Benefits	17	0.7	0.5	0.2	0.1	0.2	0.1	0.5	0.4	0.3	0.4	0.5	0.6	2.4
Advertising	18	0.9	0.3	0.8	0.3	0.3	0.6	0.4	1.1	0.4	1.7	0.3	1.2	1.8
Other Expenses	19	6.5	12.7	13.8	6.0	5.8	4.4	5.3	5.6	3.5	5.1	5.5	6.5	9.3
Officers' Compensation	20	1.1	7.9	3.5	1.7	2.0	1.5	1.1	1.0	0.6	0.5	0.8	0.3	0.4
Operating Margin	21	2.7	5.4	6.9	3.4	3.2	1.8	2.4	2.1	1.5	2.9	3.7	1.9	2.9
Operating Margin Before Officers' Comp.	22	3.8	13.3	10.3	5.1	5.2	3.4	3.5	3.1	2.1	3.4	4.4	2.2	3.3

Selected Average Balance Sheet ($ in Thousands)

Net Receivables 23	712	0	20	135	632	1669	5197	9319	19759	35261	74831	158346	397178
Inventories 24	861	0	39	268	593	2560	4615	9723	19915	42528	74017	175828	788394
Net Property, Plant and Equipment 25	563	0	13	31	190	514	1542	4090	8714	16078	48622	170794	917964
Total Assets 26	4949	0	121	652	2222	7206	15501	33604	68052	149382	356728	864919	8883354
Notes and Loans Payable 27	1369	0	55	151	435	1814	3767	8742	18999	58291	51845	244809	2575918
All Other Liabilities 28	1759	0	26	279	892	2028	5126	12484	23460	62999	124444	385726	2940624
Net Worth 29	1821	0	41	222	895	3365	6607	12379	25593	28092	180440	234385	3366812

Selected Financial Ratios (Times to 1)

Current Ratio 30	1.4	•	2.5	1.7	1.8	2.5	1.8	1.5	1.7	1.5	1.5	1.3	1.1
Quick Ratio 31	0.6	•	1.4	1.0	1.0	1.3	1.0	0.8	0.8	0.6	0.8	0.6	0.3
Net Sales to Working Capital 32	12.5	•	11.8	14.7	11.1	8.4	9.8	11.1	9.7	11.3	7.1	23.7	20.0
Coverage Ratio 33	10.3	7.5	16.6	11.6	18.0	16.5	11.8	8.8	5.9	6.7	19.3	4.8	11.9
Total Asset Turnover 34	1.9	•	5.3	5.0	4.0	4.3	3.6	2.9	3.1	2.5	1.4	2.9	0.7
Inventory Turnover 35	8.6	•	11.1	10.0	12.7	10.4	9.6	8.1	9.2	7.3	5.3	11.2	5.3
Receivables Turnover 36	13.0	•	35.8	15.5	15.1	13.9	11.1	11.1	10.6	10.8	•	•	13.5
Total Liabilities to Net Worth 37	1.7	•	2.0	1.9	1.5	1.1	1.3	1.7	1.7	4.3	1.0	2.7	1.6
Current Assets to Working Capital 38	3.7	•	1.7	2.4	2.3	1.7	2.2	2.9	2.4	3.1	2.9	4.3	12.4
Current Liabilities to Working Capital 39	2.7	•	0.7	1.4	1.3	0.7	1.2	1.9	1.4	2.1	1.9	3.3	11.4
Working Capital to Net Sales 40	0.1	•	0.1	0.1	0.1	0.1	0.1	0.1	0.1	0.1	0.1	0.0	0.1
Inventory to Working Capital 41	1.2	•	0.7	1.0	0.7	0.7	0.9	1.2	1.0	1.4	1.1	1.7	2.8
Total Receipts to Cash Flow 42	9.4	5.2	5.4	12.3	11.8	15.6	13.6	12.7	19.6	12.0	9.5	13.3	4.7
Cost of Goods to Cash Flow 43	7.5	3.2	3.7	10.1	9.8	13.6	11.0	10.5	17.0	9.9	7.6	10.6	3.4
Cash Flow to Total Debt 44	0.3	•	1.5	0.6	0.6	0.5	0.5	0.4	0.3	0.3	0.3	0.3	0.2

Selected Financial Factors (in Percentages)

Debt Ratio 45	63.2	•	66.4	65.9	59.7	53.3	57.4	63.2	62.4	81.2	49.4	72.9	62.1
Return on Total Assets 46	11.6	•	41.3	23.5	16.5	14.2	12.7	10.2	8.9	12.2	8.5	9.7	10.3
Return on Equity Before Income Taxes 47	28.5	•	115.7	63.0	38.8	28.5	27.2	24.7	19.6	55.4	16.0	28.4	24.9
Return on Equity After Income Taxes 48	23.1	•	114.0	57.9	37.1	27.1	25.3	21.7	18.4	46.7	13.2	23.4	17.6
Profit Margin (Before Income Tax) 49	5.6	9.8	7.4	4.3	3.9	3.1	3.3	3.2	2.4	4.1	5.9	2.7	14.4
Profit Margin (After Income Tax) 50	4.5	8.7	7.3	3.9	3.7	3.0	3.0	2.8	2.2	3.5	4.9	2.2	10.2

Table I

Corporations with and without Net Income

WHOLESALE ELECTRONIC MARKETS AND AGENTS AND BROKERS

MONEY AMOUNTS AND SIZE OF ASSETS IN THOUSANDS OF DOLLARS

Item Description for Accounting Period 7/11 Through 6/12		Total	Zero Assets	Under 500	500 to 1,000	1,000 to 5,000	5,000 to 10,000	10,000 to 25,000	25,000 to 50,000	50,000 to 100,000	100,000 to 250,000	250,000 to 500,000	500,000 to 2,500,000	2,500,000 and over
Number of Enterprises	1	14533	3856	10243	•	174	5	11	8	•	0	•	•	0
Revenues ($ in Thousands)														
Net Sales	2	6620344	362219	2652790	•	300181	3656	391035	101159	•	0	•	•	0
Interest	3	4082	5	1458	•	1578	0	183	168	•	0	•	•	0
Rents	4	5519	0	0	•	0	0	1143	153	•	0	•	•	0
Royalties	5	10391	0	0	•	0	0	0	0	•	0	•	•	0
Other Portfolio Income	6	27092	0	0	•	438	0	13826	11223	•	0	•	•	0
Other Receipts	7	337014	1403	61321	•	2500	16399	8949	14575	•	0	•	•	0
Total Receipts	8	7004442	363627	2715569	•	304697	20055	415136	127278	•	0	•	•	0
Average Total Receipts	9	482	94	265	•	1751	4011	37740	15910	•	•	•	•	•
Operating Costs/Operating Income (%)														
Cost of Operations	10	4.9	•	•	•	•	•	78.0	•	•	•	•	•	•
Salaries and Wages	11	24.4	8.6	15.8	•	25.1	•	9.4	47.5	•	•	•	•	•
Taxes Paid	12	4.0	2.8	3.2	•	4.0	•	1.2	4.9	•	•	•	•	•
Interest Paid	13	0.7	0.9	0.5	•	1.8	1.3	0.2	3.2	•	•	•	•	•
Depreciation	14	2.7	19.9	1.2	•	3.4	•	1.4	3.9	•	•	•	•	•
Amortization and Depletion	15	0.3	•	0.1	•	•	•	0.2	2.1	•	•	•	•	•
Pensions and Other Deferred Comp.	16	0.9	2.0	1.6	•	•	•	1.2	0.3	•	•	•	•	•
Employee Benefits	17	2.0	0.0	2.8	•	1.1	•	0.7	0.5	•	•	•	•	•
Advertising	18	0.5	0.0	0.6	•	2.2	•	0.1	0.1	•	•	•	•	•
Other Expenses	19	28.9	16.8	37.9	•	47.5	5.0	8.6	26.5	•	•	•	•	•
Officers' Compensation	20	22.9	22.6	22.7	•	9.9	•	4.4	15.9	•	•	•	•	•
Operating Margin	21	7.7	26.3	13.7	•	5.0	93.7	•	•	•	•	•	•	•
Operating Margin Before Officers' Comp.	22	30.6	48.9	36.4	•	14.9	93.7	•	11.0	•	•	•	•	•

Selected Average Balance Sheet ($ in Thousands)													
Net Receivables 23	59	0	3	•	377	0	2940	486	•	•	•	•	•
Inventories 24	4	0	2	•	282	0	1281	0	•	•	•	•	•
Net Property, Plant and Equipment 25	48	0	7	•	80	0	862	586	•	•	•	•	•
Total Assets 26	271	0	72	•	1971	6545	14060	32032	•	•	•	•	•
Notes and Loans Payable 27	97	0	28	•	1172	359	4827	5118	•	•	•	•	•
All Other Liabilities 28	45	0	9	•	726	43	6252	10208	•	•	•	•	•
Net Worth 29	129	0	35	•	74	6143	2982	16706	•	•	•	•	•
Selected Financial Ratios (Times to 1)													
Current Ratio 30	2.5	•	3.0	•	3.3	•	1.0	2.2	•	•	•	•	•
Quick Ratio 31	1.7	•	2.3	•	1.1	•	0.7	0.2	•	•	•	•	•
Net Sales to Working Capital 32	5.3	•	8.5	•	1.8	•	206.7	1.1	•	•	•	•	•
Coverage Ratio 33	20.7	30.8	31.9	•	4.7	414.0	6.5	7.6	•	•	•	•	•
Total Asset Turnover 34	1.7	•	3.6	•	0.9	0.1	2.5	0.4	•	•	•	•	•
Inventory Turnover 35	5.0	•	•	•	•	•	21.6	•	•	•	•	•	•
Receivables Turnover 36	11.6	•	93.8	•	5.0	•	24.2	52.1	•	•	•	•	•
Total Liabilities to Net Worth 37	1.1	•	1.1	•	25.7	0.1	3.7	0.9	•	•	•	•	•
Current Assets to Working Capital 38	1.7	•	1.5	•	1.4	•	37.0	1.9	•	•	•	•	•
Current Liabilities to Working Capital 39	0.7	•	0.5	•	0.4	•	36.0	0.9	•	•	•	•	•
Working Capital to Net Sales 40	0.2	•	0.1	•	0.6	•	0.0	0.9	•	•	•	•	•
Inventory to Working Capital 41	0.1	•	0.0	•	0.2	•	7.4	•	•	•	•	•	•
Total Receipts to Cash Flow 42	2.6	2.4	2.0	•	2.4	0.2	23.7	2.4	•	•	•	•	•
Cost of Goods to Cash Flow 43	0.1	•	•	•	•	•	18.5	•	•	•	•	•	•
Cash Flow to Total Debt 44	1.2	•	3.5	•	0.4	10.0	0.1	0.3	•	•	•	•	•
Selected Financial Factors (in Percentages)													
Debt Ratio 45	52.5	•	51.6	•	96.3	6.1	78.8	47.8	•	•	•	•	•
Return on Total Assets 46	23.9	•	60.0	•	7.3	60.7	2.6	9.5	•	•	•	•	•
Return on Equity Before Income Taxes 47	47.9	•	120.1	•	152.2	64.5	10.2	15.8	•	•	•	•	•
Return on Equity After Income Taxes 48	41.4	•	115.7	•	122.9	64.5	1.0	15.2	•	•	•	•	•
Profit Margin (Before Income Tax) 49	13.5	26.7	16.1	•	6.5	542.2	0.9	20.8	•	•	•	•	•
Profit Margin (After Income Tax) 50	11.7	26.7	15.5	•	5.3	542.2	0.1	20.1	•	•	•	•	•

Table II

Corporations with Net Income

WHOLESALE ELECTRONIC MARKETS AND AGENTS AND BROKERS

MONEY AMOUNTS AND SIZE OF ASSETS IN THOUSANDS OF DOLLARS

Item Description for Accounting Period 7/11 Through 6/12		Total	Zero Assets	Under 500	500 to 1000	1,000 to 5,000	5,000 to 10,000	10,000 to 25,000	25,000 to 50,000	50,000 to 100,000	100,000 to 250,000	250,000 to 500,000	500,000 to 2,500,000	2,500,000 and over
Number of Enterprises	1	9730	1674	7744	187	100	5	7	8	•	0	•	•	0
Revenues ($ in Thousands)														
Net Sales	2	6108621	360121	2500316	1517685	274642	3656	67251	101159	•	0	•	•	0
Interest	3	2594	0	1343	0	215	0	183	168	•	0	•	•	0
Rents	4	5519	0	0	0	0	0	1143	153	•	0	•	•	0
Royalties	5	10391	0	0	0	0	0	0	0	•	0	•	•	0
Other Portfolio Income	6	26575	0	0	0	0	0	13747	11223	•	0	•	•	0
Other Receipts	7	331659	537	61322	218199	1792	16399	8412	14575	•	0	•	•	0
Total Receipts	8	6485359	360658	2562981	1735884	276649	20055	90736	127278	•	0	•	•	0
Average Total Receipts	9	667	215	331	9283	2766	4011	12962	15910	•	•	•	•	•
Operating Costs/Operating Income (%)														
Cost of Operations	10	0.4	•	•	•	•	•	•	•	•	•	•	•	•
Salaries and Wages	11	25.0	8.7	14.2	34.5	25.1	•	47.0	47.5	•	•	•	•	•
Taxes Paid	12	4.2	2.8	3.2	4.2	4.0	•	5.7	4.9	•	•	•	•	•
Interest Paid	13	0.7	0.2	0.5	0.0	1.9	1.3	0.7	3.2	•	•	•	•	•
Depreciation	14	2.8	20.0	1.2	0.5	3.6	•	5.9	3.9	•	•	•	•	•
Amortization and Depletion	15	0.3	•	0.1	•	•	•	0.8	2.1	•	•	•	•	•
Pensions and Other Deferred Comp.	16	1.0	2.0	1.7	0.0	•	•	7.0	0.3	•	•	•	•	•
Employee Benefits	17	2.0	0.0	2.5	1.1	0.4	•	3.5	0.5	•	•	•	•	•
Advertising	18	0.5	0.0	0.6	0.0	2.4	•	0.1	0.1	•	•	•	•	•
Other Expenses	19	29.2	15.5	36.8	19.6	48.9	5.0	32.1	26.5	•	•	•	•	•
Officers' Compensation	20	24.4	22.7	23.9	50.0	5.0	•	18.5	15.9	•	•	•	•	•
Operating Margin	21	9.8	28.1	15.4	•	8.6	93.7	•	•	•	•	•	•	•
Operating Margin Before Officers' Comp.	22	34.1	50.8	39.2	40.1	13.6	93.7	•	11.0	•	•	•	•	•

Selected Average Balance Sheet ($ in Thousands)													
Net Receivables 23	84	0	2	0	578	0	2037	486	•	•	•	•	•
Inventories 24	6	0	2	0	491	0	0	0	•	•	•	•	•
Net Property, Plant and Equipment 25	69	0	9	83	137	0	856	586	•	•	•	•	•
Total Assets 26	360	0	77	814	2137	6545	13343	32032	•	•	•	•	•
Notes and Loans Payable 27	114	0	32	605	651	359	748	5118	•	•	•	•	•
All Other Liabilities 28	51	0	12	3	612	43	2510	10208	•	•	•	•	•
Net Worth 29	195	0	33	206	874	6143	10085	16706	•	•	•	•	•

Selected Financial Ratios (Times to 1)													
Current Ratio 30	2.7	•	2.7	1.1	3.3	•	2.4	2.2	•	•	•	•	•
Quick Ratio 31	1.8	•	2.0	1.1	1.0	•	1.9	0.2	•	•	•	•	•
Net Sales to Working Capital 32	5.0	•	9.5	107.2	2.0	•	3.8	1.1	•	•	•	•	•
Coverage Ratio 33	25.4	141.8	35.1	91.7	5.8	414.0	19.6	7.6	•	•	•	•	•
Total Asset Turnover 34	1.7	•	4.2	10.0	1.3	0.1	0.7	0.4	•	•	•	•	•
Inventory Turnover 35	0.4	•	•	•	•	•	•	•	•	•	•	•	•
Receivables Turnover 36	11.3	•	167.4	•	5.2	•	9.4	52.1	•	•	•	•	•
Total Liabilities to Net Worth 37	0.9	•	1.3	3.0	1.4	0.1	0.3	0.9	•	•	•	•	•
Current Assets to Working Capital 38	1.6	•	1.6	9.0	1.4	•	1.7	1.9	•	•	•	•	•
Current Liabilities to Working Capital 39	0.6	•	0.6	8.0	0.4	•	0.7	0.9	•	•	•	•	•
Working Capital to Net Sales 40	0.2	•	0.1	0.0	0.5	•	0.3	0.9	•	•	•	•	•
Inventory to Working Capital 41	0.0	•	0.1	•	0.3	•	•	•	•	•	•	•	•
Total Receipts to Cash Flow 42	2.5	2.3	2.0	5.1	2.2	0.2	5.6	2.4	•	•	•	•	•
Cost of Goods to Cash Flow 43	0.0	•	•	•	•	•	•	•	•	•	•	•	•
Cash Flow to Total Debt 44	1.5	•	3.7	2.6	1.0	10.0	0.5	0.3	•	•	•	•	•

Selected Financial Factors (in Percentages)													
Debt Ratio 45	46.0	•	57.3	74.7	59.1	6.1	24.4	47.8	•	•	•	•	•
Return on Total Assets 46	28.9	•	76.8	45.0	14.5	60.7	10.3	9.5	•	•	•	•	•
Return on Equity Before Income Taxes 47	51.4	•	174.9	176.3	29.2	64.5	13.0	15.8	•	•	•	•	•
Return on Equity After Income Taxes 48	45.0	•	168.7	176.3	24.9	64.5	8.7	15.2	•	•	•	•	•
Profit Margin (Before Income Tax) 49	16.0	28.2	17.9	4.5	9.3	542.2	13.6	20.8	•	•	•	•	•
Profit Margin (After Income Tax) 50	14.0	28.2	17.3	4.5	7.9	542.2	9.1	20.1	•	•	•	•	•

Table I

Corporations with and without Net Income

NEW AND USED CAR DEALERS

MONEY AMOUNTS AND SIZE OF ASSETS IN THOUSANDS OF DOLLARS

Item Description for Accounting Period 7/11 Through 6/12		Total	Zero Assets	Under 500	500 to 1,000	1,000 to 5,000	5,000 to 10,000	10,000 to 25,000	25,000 to 50,000	50,000 to 100,000	100,000 to 250,000	250,000 to 500,000	500,000 to 2,500,000	2,500,000 and over
Number of Enterprises	1	45559	4129	21118	3391	8575	4193	3266	669	140	56	11	6	4
Revenues ($ in Thousands)														
Net Sales	2	604851503	777208	17751762	10530697	84287503	114037254	184893769	79672928	30611602	21924356	7495031	16168717	36700676
Interest	3	722499	54	9357	6382	121853	88221	147254	48920	28276	56036	8081	85234	122831
Rents	4	299130	0	4661	757	10291	4150	24418	28097	16626	26276	30085	18748	135021
Royalties	5	8061	0	0	0	55	7444	0	34	0	0	0	527	0
Other Portfolio Income	6	625630	0	40905	18432	29280	57583	198823	115837	32939	37259	11376	75947	7251
Other Receipts	7	12714860	13836	93715	160499	1262710	2600052	4381674	1714011	710324	475692	194939	403749	703658
Total Receipts	8	619221683	791098	17900400	10716767	85711692	116794704	189645938	81579827	31399767	22519619	7739512	16752922	37669437
Average Total Receipts	9	13592	192	848	3160	9996	27855	58067	121943	224284	402136	703592	2792154	9417359
Operating Costs/Operating Income (%)														
Cost of Operations	10	87.4	81.9	81.5	85.5	87.5	87.7	88.0	88.0	88.0	86.8	86.2	83.7	86.2
Salaries and Wages	11	5.2	4.0	3.5	2.8	5.0	5.1	5.3	5.0	5.3	5.4	6.0	6.8	6.3
Taxes Paid	12	0.9	2.6	1.9	1.3	1.0	0.9	0.8	0.8	0.8	0.8	0.9	0.9	1.2
Interest Paid	13	0.4	0.9	0.6	0.3	0.4	0.4	0.3	0.4	0.4	0.4	0.7	1.2	0.8
Depreciation	14	0.6	0.6	0.3	0.4	0.3	0.3	0.6	0.8	0.8	1.2	1.1	1.2	0.6
Amortization and Depletion	15	0.1	0.0	0.0	0.0	0.0	0.1	0.1	0.1	0.1	0.1	0.1	0.9	0.5
Pensions and Other Deferred Comp.	16	0.0	0.0	0.0	0.1	0.0	0.0	0.0	0.0	0.0	0.1	0.1	0.0	0.1
Employee Benefits	17	0.4	0.2	0.2	0.1	0.4	0.5	0.4	0.4	0.4	0.5	0.6	0.7	0.4
Advertising	18	1.0	1.2	0.6	0.7	1.0	1.1	1.1	0.9	1.0	0.9	0.9	1.0	0.6
Other Expenses	19	4.2	17.0	9.0	6.0	4.3	4.2	3.9	3.8	3.7	4.5	5.0	6.1	2.9
Officers' Compensation	20	0.8	0.9	2.4	2.1	0.9	0.9	0.7	0.6	0.6	0.5	0.5	0.1	0.2
Operating Margin	21	•	•	•	0.7	•	•	•	•	•	•	•	•	0.1
Operating Margin Before Officers' Comp.	22	•	•	2.4	2.8	0.1	•	•	•	•	•	•	•	0.3

Selected Average Balance Sheet ($ in Thousands)

Net Receivables 23	462	0	16	127	350	800	1778	4021	9200	18473	51870	228362	293780
Inventories 24	1835	0	95	307	1494	4230	7867	14849	30240	47391	85003	422130	1006777
Net Property, Plant and Equipment 25	490	0	24	32	161	422	1563	5207	10726	28835	74412	316661	1035639
Total Assets 26	3864	0	175	713	2563	7167	15076	33814	68326	142818	291908	1478206	4102595
Notes and Loans Payable 27	2399	0	133	322	1613	4926	10165	21433	40826	80531	161882	607952	1932377
All Other Liabilities 28	502	0	24	85	377	830	1644	3571	9232	19677	42163	451701	506987
Net Worth 29	964	0	19	306	573	1410	3267	8811	18268	42611	87863	418552	1663230

Selected Financial Ratios (Times to 1)

Current Ratio 30	1.4	•	3.1	4.7	1.6	1.4	1.3	1.3	1.2	1.3	1.4	1.2	1.3
Quick Ratio 31	0.4	•	0.9	2.1	0.5	0.4	0.4	0.4	0.4	0.5	0.6	0.5	0.3
Net Sales to Working Capital 32	16.4	•	8.9	6.4	11.5	14.8	20.2	19.2	24.5	21.1	14.8	22.0	28.4
Coverage Ratio 33	4.1	•	2.4	9.1	3.0	3.9	5.1	4.8	4.9	4.5	2.6	1.9	4.6
Total Asset Turnover 34	3.4	•	4.8	4.4	3.8	3.8	3.8	3.5	3.2	2.7	2.3	1.8	2.2
Inventory Turnover 35	6.3	•	7.2	8.6	5.8	5.6	6.3	7.1	6.4	7.2	6.9	5.3	7.9
Receivables Turnover 36	30.0	•	45.9	24.5	29.5	29.9	34.2	33.2	24.7	20.3	13.3	16.0	37.0
Total Liabilities to Net Worth 37	3.0	•	8.4	1.3	3.5	4.1	3.6	2.8	2.7	2.4	2.3	2.5	1.5
Current Assets to Working Capital 38	3.6	•	1.5	1.3	2.6	3.4	4.4	4.0	5.5	4.9	3.7	5.5	4.9
Current Liabilities to Working Capital 39	2.6	•	0.5	0.3	1.6	2.4	3.4	3.0	4.5	3.9	2.7	4.5	3.9
Working Capital to Net Sales 40	0.1	•	0.1	0.2	0.1	0.1	0.0	0.1	0.0	0.0	0.1	0.0	0.0
Inventory to Working Capital 41	2.4	•	1.0	0.7	1.8	2.4	3.0	2.5	3.4	2.8	1.9	3.1	3.4
Total Receipts to Cash Flow 42	24.1	61.0	13.2	16.5	25.7	25.5	25.5	24.2	24.8	23.0	21.6	22.9	24.0
Cost of Goods to Cash Flow 43	21.1	49.9	10.7	14.1	22.5	22.3	22.5	21.3	21.9	20.0	18.6	19.2	20.7
Cash Flow to Total Debt 44	0.2	•	0.4	0.5	0.2	0.2	0.2	0.2	0.2	0.2	0.2	0.1	0.2

Selected Financial Factors (in Percentages)

Debt Ratio 45	75.1	•	89.4	57.1	77.6	80.3	78.3	73.9	73.3	70.2	69.9	71.7	59.5
Return on Total Assets 46	6.1	•	6.4	12.2	5.2	6.1	6.3	6.4	5.8	5.5	4.2	4.1	8.0
Return on Equity Before Income Taxes 47	18.6	•	35.0	25.4	15.7	23.0	23.2	19.6	17.2	14.2	8.5	6.7	15.4
Return on Equity After Income Taxes 48	17.0	•	33.3	24.9	15.0	22.3	22.5	19.0	16.1	13.0	6.9	4.2	10.2
Profit Margin (Before Income Tax) 49	1.3	•	0.8	2.5	0.9	1.2	1.3	1.4	1.4	1.6	1.1	1.0	2.8
Profit Margin (After Income Tax) 50	1.2	•	0.7	2.5	0.9	1.2	1.3	1.4	1.3	1.4	0.9	0.7	1.9

Table II

Corporations with Net Income

NEW AND USED CAR DEALERS

MONEY AMOUNTS AND SIZE OF ASSETS IN THOUSANDS OF DOLLARS

Item Description for Accounting Period 7/11 Through 6/12		Total	Zero Assets	Under 500	500 to 1,000	1,000 to 5,000	5,000 to 10,000	10,000 to 25,000	25,000 to 50,000	50,000 to 100,000	100,000 to 250,000	250,000 to 500,000	500,000 to 2,500,000	2,500,000 and over
Number of Enterprises	1	28149	697	11695	3050	5994	3258	2718	554	118	46	•	•	4
Revenues ($ in Thousands)														
Net Sales	2	503831051	213881	10893266	9502684	63272505	91097054	159583470	64868268	27203005	18493436	•	•	36700676
Interest	3	658308	17	1347	6353	95952	77155	141765	42765	24927	51881	•	•	122831
Rents	4	277293	0	0	757	8137	2827	21639	24549	9770	25760	•	•	135021
Royalties	5	8061	0	0	0	55	7444	0	34	0	0	•	•	0
Other Portfolio Income	6	430932	0	17494	17601	20989	51378	110472	67847	17231	33634	•	•	7251
Other Receipts	7	10815970	8323	47871	118740	965026	2076893	3783440	1481217	667721	403464	•	•	703658
Total Receipts	8	516021615	222221	10959978	9646135	64362664	93312751	163640786	66484680	27922654	19008175	•	•	37669437
Average Total Receipts	9	18332	319	937	3163	10738	28641	60206	120008	236633	413221	•	•	9417359
Operating Costs/Operating Income (%)														
Cost of Operations	10	87.2	76.1	76.8	85.7	87.1	87.7	88.0	87.5	88.1	86.7	•	•	86.2
Salaries and Wages	11	5.2	3.9	3.4	2.6	4.9	5.0	5.2	5.2	5.3	5.4	•	•	6.3
Taxes Paid	12	0.9	1.5	2.3	1.3	0.9	0.9	0.8	0.8	0.8	0.8	•	•	1.2
Interest Paid	13	0.4	0.4	0.4	0.3	0.4	0.4	0.3	0.4	0.3	0.4	•	•	0.8
Depreciation	14	0.5	0.8	0.3	0.4	0.3	0.3	0.4	0.7	0.6	0.9	•	•	0.6
Amortization and Depletion	15	0.1	0.0	0.0	0.0	0.0	0.1	0.1	0.1	0.1	0.1	•	•	0.5
Pensions and Other Deferred Comp.	16	0.1	0.0	0.0	0.1	0.0	0.0	0.0	0.0	0.0	0.1	•	•	0.1
Employee Benefits	17	0.4	0.4	0.2	0.1	0.4	0.5	0.4	0.4	0.4	0.5	•	•	0.4
Advertising	18	1.0	0.3	0.5	0.6	0.9	1.1	1.0	1.0	1.0	0.9	•	•	0.6
Other Expenses	19	4.0	11.0	10.0	5.2	4.1	3.9	3.8	3.7	3.5	4.5	•	•	2.9
Officers' Compensation	20	0.7	3.0	2.6	1.7	0.9	0.9	0.7	0.6	0.6	0.5	•	•	0.2
Operating Margin	21	•	2.7	3.5	1.9	0.0	•	•	•	•	•	•	•	0.1
Operating Margin Before Officers' Comp.	22	0.2	5.7	6.1	3.6	0.9	0.3	•	0.1	•	•	•	•	0.3

Selected Average Balance Sheet ($ in Thousands)

Net Receivables 23	598	0	17	132	361	799	1848	4142	9701	16828	•	•	293780
Inventories 24	2404	0	102	266	1599	4119	7864	15087	31544	50124	•	•	1094292
Net Property, Plant and Equipment 25	662	0	26	31	147	443	1473	5218	10111	28683	•	•	1035639
Total Assets 26	5165	0	197	701	2725	7141	15101	34105	68619	142303	•	•	4102595
Notes and Loans Payable 27	3063	0	87	314	1660	4644	9844	21298	40998	81985	•	•	1932377
All Other Liabilities 28	666	0	21	77	350	853	1697	3391	9536	15213	•	•	506987
Net Worth 29	1437	0	89	310	716	1644	3560	9416	18085	45106	•	•	1663230

Selected Financial Ratios (Times to 1)

Current Ratio 30	1.4	•	4.5	5.9	1.6	1.4	1.3	1.3	1.2	1.3	•	•	1.3
Quick Ratio 31	0.4	•	1.4	2.8	0.4	0.4	0.4	0.5	0.4	0.5	•	•	0.3
Net Sales to Working Capital 32	16.3	•	7.8	6.1	11.6	14.8	19.0	18.0	25.0	20.6	•	•	28.4
Coverage Ratio 33	5.6	19.0	10.5	13.1	5.1	5.6	6.7	6.3	6.2	5.5	•	•	4.6
Total Asset Turnover 34	3.5	•	4.7	4.4	3.9	3.9	3.9	3.4	3.4	2.8	•	•	2.2
Inventory Turnover 35	6.5	•	7.0	10.0	5.7	6.0	6.6	6.8	6.4	7.0	•	•	7.2
Receivables Turnover 36	31.0	•	42.9	26.4	31.3	30.1	35.0	31.5	25.1	•	•	•	62.5
Total Liabilities to Net Worth 37	2.6	•	1.2	1.3	2.8	3.3	3.2	2.6	2.8	2.2	•	•	1.5
Current Assets to Working Capital 38	3.5	•	1.3	1.2	2.6	3.3	4.0	3.9	5.5	4.5	•	•	4.9
Current Liabilities to Working Capital 39	2.5	•	0.3	0.2	1.6	2.3	3.0	2.9	4.5	3.5	•	•	3.9
Working Capital to Net Sales 40	0.1	•	0.1	0.2	0.1	0.1	0.1	0.1	0.0	0.0	•	•	0.0
Inventory to Working Capital 41	2.3	•	0.8	0.6	1.8	2.3	2.7	2.4	3.5	2.6	•	•	3.4
Total Receipts to Cash Flow 42	21.9	7.8	8.6	15.1	21.8	23.2	23.7	22.1	23.9	21.1	•	•	24.0
Cost of Goods to Cash Flow 43	19.1	6.0	6.6	12.9	19.0	20.4	20.8	19.4	21.1	18.3	•	•	20.7
Cash Flow to Total Debt 44	0.2	•	1.0	0.5	0.2	0.2	0.2	0.2	0.2	0.2	•	•	0.2

Selected Financial Factors (in Percentages)

Debt Ratio 45	72.2	•	54.8	55.8	73.7	77.0	76.4	72.4	73.6	68.3	•	•	59.5
Return on Total Assets 46	8.1	•	21.4	16.4	8.5	8.5	7.8	8.1	7.2	7.0	•	•	8.0
Return on Equity Before Income Taxes 47	24.0	•	42.9	34.4	25.9	30.4	28.3	24.7	22.9	18.1	•	•	15.4
Return on Equity After Income Taxes 48	22.3	•	42.2	33.9	25.1	29.7	27.5	24.0	21.6	16.7	•	•	10.2
Profit Margin (Before Income Tax) 49	1.9	6.6	4.1	3.4	1.8	1.8	1.7	2.0	1.8	2.0	•	•	2.8
Profit Margin (After Income Tax) 50	1.8	6.0	4.0	3.4	1.7	1.7	1.7	1.9	1.7	1.9	•	•	1.9

Table I

Corporations with and without Net Income

OTHER MOTOR VEHICLE AND PARTS DEALERS

MONEY AMOUNTS AND SIZE OF ASSETS IN THOUSANDS OF DOLLARS

Item Description for Accounting Period 7/11 Through 6/12		Total	Zero Assets	Under 500	500 to 1,000	1,000 to 5,000	5,000 to 10,000	10,000 to 25,000	25,000 to 50,000	50,000 to 100,000	100,000 to 250,000	250,000 to 500,000	500,000 to 2,500,000	2,500,000 and over
Number of Enterprises	1	40500	3829	24478	4481	6330	925	279	96	44	23	7	4	4
Revenues ($ in Thousands)														
Net Sales	2	135088733	822980	13197613	8500765	32917503	16420835	9435671	7624459	7602165	6511092	3070603	6311512	22673533
Interest	3	73042	21	4657	4128	11812	4630	9718	7707	7290	2992	7893	2313	9881
Rents	4	79811	0	134	7474	21959	6639	2976	227	9535	24553	0	4746	1569
Royalties	5	14345	0	0	0	1810	2073	774	0	748	0	0	0	8940
Other Portfolio Income	6	304917	20529	29386	3795	49416	37297	34012	48616	36510	26866	17983	177	332
Other Receipts	7	1837602	7653	50619	76584	845809	139824	121057	53149	81125	50975	56778	279046	74983
Total Receipts	8	137398450	851183	13282409	8592746	33848309	16611298	9604208	7734158	7737373	6616478	3153257	6597794	22769238
Average Total Receipts	9	3393	222	543	1918	5347	17958	34424	80564	175849	287673	450465	1649448	5692310
Operating Costs/Operating Income (%)														
Cost of Operations	10	69.5	69.0	67.5	67.4	74.3	78.8	79.3	81.3	76.2	72.3	68.3	59.6	49.4
Salaries and Wages	11	10.2	4.2	8.9	8.4	8.9	6.9	7.6	6.5	8.7	9.8	10.4	16.7	17.2
Taxes Paid	12	2.0	4.0	2.2	2.1	1.8	1.4	1.2	1.0	1.5	1.7	1.7	2.5	3.1
Interest Paid	13	0.9	0.7	0.6	0.9	1.0	0.8	0.9	0.7	0.8	0.6	0.5	1.9	1.1
Depreciation	14	1.7	1.0	1.1	0.9	0.9	0.6	1.4	1.8	1.9	3.5	6.8	2.3	2.9
Amortization and Depletion	15	0.1	0.5	0.0	0.1	0.1	0.0	0.1	0.1	0.1	0.1	0.4	0.4	0.2
Pensions and Other Deferred Comp.	16	0.2	0.0	0.0	0.1	0.1	0.1	0.1	0.2	0.3	0.3	0.3	0.3	0.3
Employee Benefits	17	0.8	0.4	0.4	0.7	0.6	0.5	0.7	0.7	0.9	1.2	1.7	1.0	1.4
Advertising	18	1.1	1.2	0.9	1.4	1.1	1.2	0.9	0.7	1.1	0.5	0.9	2.1	1.1
Other Expenses	19	10.3	16.1	13.0	12.2	9.6	8.0	6.9	5.5	7.4	8.2	10.2	16.5	13.3
Officers' Compensation	20	1.6	5.9	3.9	4.0	2.2	1.1	0.9	0.6	1.1	0.7	0.4	0.3	0.2
Operating Margin	21	1.7	•	1.3	1.8	•	0.6	0.1	1.0	0.0	1.1	•	•	9.7
Operating Margin Before Officers' Comp.	22	3.3	2.8	5.3	5.9	1.5	1.7	1.0	1.6	1.1	1.8	•	•	9.9

Selected Average Balance Sheet ($ in Thousands)													
Net Receivables 23	167	0	13	71	183	542	1689	3525	11538	29173	31880	266807	293829
Inventories 24	712	0	62	396	1272	3414	6809	15724	29831	46376	108955	319370	1630792
Net Property, Plant and Equipment 25	303	0	22	89	292	873	2393	6204	11523	30847	93755	214839	1177298
Total Assets 26	1574	0	131	693	2195	6472	14497	32335	68855	147188	312329	1058351	4397944
Notes and Loans Payable 27	622	0	61	351	913	3101	7675	14654	29467	49448	121667	310427	1350346
All Other Liabilities 28	529	0	21	187	656	1948	2988	6018	21482	44757	53628	489896	2098736
Net Worth 29	423	0	49	155	627	1424	3835	11663	17906	52983	137035	258028	948863

Selected Financial Ratios (Times to 1)													
Current Ratio 30	1.5	•	3.4	1.8	1.8	1.5	1.5	1.5	1.4	1.6	1.6	1.8	1.2
Quick Ratio 31	0.4	•	1.2	0.5	0.4	0.4	0.4	0.4	0.4	0.6	0.4	0.9	0.2
Net Sales to Working Capital 32	9.0	•	8.0	8.2	6.9	10.6	9.4	9.8	13.2	7.8	6.5	5.7	19.5
Coverage Ratio 33	4.7	1.4	4.3	4.2	3.1	3.1	3.2	4.6	3.3	5.6	3.1	1.5	10.1
Total Asset Turnover 34	2.1	•	4.1	2.7	2.4	2.7	2.3	2.5	2.5	1.9	1.4	1.5	1.3
Inventory Turnover 35	3.3	•	5.9	3.2	3.0	4.1	3.9	4.1	4.4	4.4	2.7	2.9	1.7
Receivables Turnover 36	21.0	•	40.7	25.1	28.5	33.9	19.9	18.7	16.4	11.7	15.3	5.5	25.6
Total Liabilities to Net Worth 37	2.7	•	1.7	3.5	2.5	3.5	2.8	1.8	2.8	1.8	1.3	3.1	3.6
Current Assets to Working Capital 38	2.9	•	1.4	2.3	2.3	3.1	2.9	2.9	3.8	2.8	2.8	2.3	7.6
Current Liabilities to Working Capital 39	1.9	•	0.4	1.3	1.3	2.1	1.9	1.9	2.8	1.8	1.8	1.3	6.6
Working Capital to Net Sales 40	0.1	•	0.1	0.1	0.1	0.1	0.1	0.1	0.1	0.1	0.2	0.2	0.1
Inventory to Working Capital 41	2.0	•	0.9	1.6	1.7	2.2	1.9	1.9	2.5	1.5	1.8	1.0	6.0
Total Receipts to Cash Flow 42	9.6	8.8	8.9	8.8	10.9	12.8	15.2	16.6	15.3	12.1	12.7	8.2	5.5
Cost of Goods to Cash Flow 43	6.7	6.1	6.0	5.9	8.1	10.1	12.1	13.5	11.7	8.7	8.7	4.9	2.7
Cash Flow to Total Debt 44	0.3	•	0.7	0.4	0.3	0.3	0.2	0.2	0.2	0.2	0.2	0.2	0.3

Selected Financial Factors (in Percentages)													
Debt Ratio 45	73.1	•	62.9	77.7	71.4	78.0	73.5	63.9	74.0	64.0	56.1	75.6	78.4
Return on Total Assets 46	9.2	•	10.6	10.5	7.5	7.2	6.5	7.7	6.6	6.3	2.1	4.4	14.5
Return on Equity Before Income Taxes 47	26.8	•	21.8	35.8	17.9	22.2	16.9	16.9	17.6	14.4	3.2	6.4	60.7
Return on Equity After Income Taxes 48	21.3	•	21.0	34.4	17.2	20.9	14.8	16.0	16.3	13.1	2.8	6.0	39.6
Profit Margin (Before Income Tax) 49	3.4	0.3	2.0	2.9	2.2	1.8	1.9	2.5	1.8	2.7	1.0	1.0	10.2
Profit Margin (After Income Tax) 50	2.7	•	1.9	2.8	2.1	1.7	1.7	2.4	1.7	2.5	0.9	1.0	6.6

Table II

Corporations with Net Income

OTHER MOTOR VEHICLE AND PARTS DEALERS

MONEY AMOUNTS AND SIZE OF ASSETS IN THOUSANDS OF DOLLARS

Item Description for Accounting Period 7/11 Through 6/12		Total	Zero Assets	Under 500	500 to 1,000	1,000 to 5,000	5,000 to 10,000	10,000 to 25,000	25,000 to 50,000	50,000 to 100,000	100,000 to 250,000	250,000 to 500,000	500,000 to 2,500,000	2,500,000 and over
Number of Enterprises	1	26268	2258	15397	3076	4445	756	195	73	38	18	7	0	4
Revenues ($ in Thousands)														
Net Sales	2	110790173	583092	10073925	6662129	24680567	14208683	7719328	6295754	6448529	5323034	6121599	0	22673533
Interest	3	54115	21	2485	3150	10327	2279	9545	6975	6841	2575	34	0	9881
Rents	4	64917	0	132	5949	18213	4541	2532	227	9508	22247	0	0	1569
Royalties	5	13658	0	0	0	1810	2073	87	0	748	0	0	0	8940
Other Portfolio Income	6	239285	19517	26535	2409	33202	37179	19945	37483	33198	26445	3041	0	332
Other Receipts	7	1348776	1667	46563	8349	624760	82674	64388	29967	66533	38461	310432	0	74983
Total Receipts	8	112510924	604297	10149640	6681986	25368879	14337429	7815825	6370406	6565357	5412762	6435106	0	22769238
Average Total Receipts	9	4283	268	659	2172	5707	18965	40081	87266	172773	300709	919301	•	5692310
Operating Costs/Operating Income (%)														
Cost of Operations	10	68.9	61.5	67.3	66.7	73.9	78.7	80.0	81.1	77.2	71.2	66.2	•	49.4
Salaries and Wages	11	10.0	2.4	8.0	8.3	8.5	6.4	7.4	6.4	8.3	10.1	12.5	•	17.2
Taxes Paid	12	1.9	2.8	2.0	2.0	1.9	1.4	1.1	0.9	1.4	1.8	1.8	•	3.1
Interest Paid	13	0.8	0.5	0.5	0.8	0.8	0.8	0.8	0.6	0.8	0.5	1.1	•	1.1
Depreciation	14	1.5	1.2	0.8	0.8	0.7	0.6	0.9	1.2	1.6	3.3	2.6	•	2.9
Amortization and Depletion	15	0.1	0.0	0.1	0.1	0.1	0.0	0.1	0.1	0.1	0.1	0.3	•	0.2
Pensions and Other Deferred Comp.	16	0.2	0.0	0.0	0.1	0.2	0.1	0.1	0.1	0.3	0.3	0.4	•	0.3
Employee Benefits	17	0.8	0.2	0.3	0.5	0.6	0.5	0.6	0.7	0.9	1.3	0.9	•	1.4
Advertising	18	1.0	1.5	0.9	1.3	0.9	1.0	0.9	0.8	1.1	0.4	1.2	•	1.1
Other Expenses	19	10.0	17.4	11.7	10.9	9.6	7.9	5.7	5.3	7.0	8.2	15.1	•	13.3
Officers' Compensation	20	1.4	7.5	3.7	3.7	2.1	1.1	0.8	0.7	0.8	0.7	0.3	•	0.2
Operating Margin	21	3.3	4.9	4.7	4.7	0.7	1.6	1.6	2.2	0.6	2.1	•	•	9.7
Operating Margin Before Officers' Comp.	22	4.8	12.4	8.4	8.4	2.8	2.7	2.4	2.8	1.4	2.8	•	•	9.9

Selected Average Balance Sheet ($ in Thousands)													
Net Receivables **23**	209	0	15	83	220	517	1753	3632	12434	27493	124627	•	293829
Inventories **24**	849	0	58	351	1252	3223	7860	15903	26641	61436	139071	•	1630792
Net Property, Plant and Equipment **25**	352	0	19	88	229	845	1868	5861	10647	26787	91759	•	1177298
Total Assets **26**	1925	0	137	720	2207	6505	14504	32153	69697	152561	478467	•	4397944
Notes and Loans Payable **27**	701	0	42	344	876	2636	7030	13653	28856	52075	145110	•	1350346
All Other Liabilities **28**	649	0	15	198	558	2112	2992	6230	21425	46329	150444	•	2098736
Net Worth **29**	575	0	80	177	772	1757	4481	12269	19416	54158	182913	•	948863
Selected Financial Ratios (Times to 1)													
Current Ratio **30**	1.6	•	4.5	1.9	1.9	1.5	1.5	1.6	1.4	1.7	2.5	•	1.2
Quick Ratio **31**	0.4	•	1.6	0.6	0.5	0.4	0.4	0.5	0.4	0.6	1.3	•	0.2
Net Sales to Working Capital **32**	8.7	•	7.8	7.8	6.3	10.0	10.4	9.4	12.0	6.7	4.8	•	19.5
Coverage Ratio **33**	6.9	18.4	10.9	7.0	5.3	4.3	4.7	6.4	4.0	8.2	3.5	•	10.1
Total Asset Turnover **34**	2.2	•	4.8	3.0	2.5	2.9	2.7	2.7	2.4	1.9	1.8	•	1.3
Inventory Turnover **35**	3.4	•	7.6	4.1	3.3	4.6	4.0	4.4	4.9	3.4	4.2	•	1.7
Receivables Turnover **36**	21.3	•	46.3	26.5	25.0	36.9	20.3	20.1	16.4	•	•	•	25.6
Total Liabilities to Net Worth **37**	2.4	•	0.7	3.1	1.9	2.7	2.2	1.6	2.6	1.8	1.6	•	3.6
Current Assets to Working Capital **38**	2.7	•	1.3	2.2	2.1	2.8	2.9	2.6	3.7	2.4	1.7	•	7.6
Current Liabilities to Working Capital **39**	1.7	•	0.3	1.2	1.1	1.8	1.9	1.6	2.7	1.4	0.7	•	6.6
Working Capital to Net Sales **40**	0.1	•	0.1	0.1	0.2	0.1	0.1	0.1	0.1	0.1	0.2	•	0.1
Inventory to Working Capital **41**	1.9	•	0.8	1.4	1.5	2.0	2.0	1.7	2.4	1.4	0.8	•	6.0
Total Receipts to Cash Flow **42**	8.5	4.9	7.2	7.6	9.4	11.8	14.8	15.0	14.4	10.8	7.6	•	5.5
Cost of Goods to Cash Flow **43**	5.9	3.0	4.9	5.1	7.0	9.3	11.9	12.1	11.1	7.7	5.0	•	2.7
Cash Flow to Total Debt **44**	0.4	•	1.6	0.5	0.4	0.3	0.3	0.3	0.2	0.3	0.4	•	0.3
Selected Financial Factors (in Percentages)													
Debt Ratio **45**	70.2	•	41.8	75.4	65.0	73.0	69.1	61.8	72.1	64.5	61.8	•	78.4
Return on Total Assets **46**	12.5	•	28.5	17.7	10.9	9.4	9.9	10.6	7.9	8.3	7.1	•	14.5
Return on Equity Before Income Taxes **47**	35.9	•	44.5	61.4	25.3	26.9	25.2	23.4	21.3	20.5	13.3	•	60.7
Return on Equity After Income Taxes **48**	29.6	•	43.6	59.7	24.4	25.6	22.6	22.4	19.8	18.9	12.6	•	39.6
Profit Margin (Before Income Tax) **49**	4.9	8.6	5.4	5.0	3.5	2.5	2.9	3.3	2.4	3.8	2.8	•	10.2
Profit Margin (After Income Tax) **50**	4.0	7.4	5.3	4.9	3.4	2.4	2.6	3.2	2.3	3.5	2.6	•	6.6

Table I

Corporations with and without Net Income

FURNITURE AND HOME FURNISHINGS STORES

MONEY AMOUNTS AND SIZE OF ASSETS IN THOUSANDS OF DOLLARS

Item Description for Accounting Period 7/11 Through 6/12		Total	Zero Assets	Under 500	500 to 1,000	1,000 to 5,000	5,000 to 10,000	10,000 to 25,000	25,000 to 50,000	50,000 to 100,000	100,000 to 250,000	250,000 to 500,000	500,000 to 2,500,000	2,500,000 and over
Number of Enterprises	1	33172	3142	23047	3828	2704	212	154	35	21	10	8	10	0
Revenues ($ in Thousands)														
Net Sales	2	75407336	1026167	9982560	6541128	13441153	3045905	5973903	2676462	2704905	3073394	3927314	23014446	0
Interest	3	188395	340	2550	13346	20169	5861	4141	2	71	6458	129485	5972	0
Rents	4	26094	0	4869	6	6975	1548	1728	472	2577	1688	1765	4467	0
Royalties	5	9518	0	0	0	0	0	0	0	668	0	0	8850	0
Other Portfolio Income	6	98095	17	28783	54006	6922	73	921	30	5317	134	255	1637	0
Other Receipts	7	773020	11027	49688	41901	129128	69714	76215	33458	72603	42397	75593	171294	0
Total Receipts	8	76502458	1037551	10068450	6650387	13604347	3123101	6056908	2710424	2786141	3124071	4134412	23206666	0
Average Total Receipts	9	2306	330	437	1737	5031	14732	39331	77441	132673	312407	516802	2320667	•
Operating Costs/Operating Income (%)														
Cost of Operations	10	57.9	63.6	60.4	65.4	59.9	64.8	57.7	62.3	53.1	54.0	54.9	53.6	•
Salaries and Wages	11	11.8	8.6	8.4	8.0	12.5	8.9	13.7	15.6	15.4	14.1	16.9	12.0	•
Taxes Paid	12	2.4	3.0	2.6	2.2	2.4	1.6	2.1	1.9	2.5	2.5	2.4	2.7	•
Interest Paid	13	0.6	1.8	0.6	0.6	0.6	1.0	0.5	0.6	0.5	0.5	0.8	0.6	•
Depreciation	14	1.6	1.0	0.7	0.8	0.8	1.8	0.8	1.3	1.9	2.5	2.2	2.7	•
Amortization and Depletion	15	0.2	•	0.1	0.0	0.2	0.0	0.1	0.1	0.5	0.2	0.1	0.2	•
Pensions and Other Deferred Comp.	16	0.1	0.1	0.1	0.1	0.1	0.0	0.1	0.3	0.2	0.1	0.4	0.1	•
Employee Benefits	17	0.9	0.5	0.8	0.6	0.4	0.6	0.9	1.5	0.8	1.2	0.6	1.3	•
Advertising	18	3.9	2.3	2.4	3.0	2.9	3.8	6.3	2.3	4.0	4.7	5.3	4.6	•
Other Expenses	19	16.0	15.9	17.6	14.6	15.8	15.1	15.4	13.2	22.1	19.7	20.0	14.5	•
Officers' Compensation	20	2.5	1.6	7.1	4.3	3.5	4.0	1.0	0.8	1.0	0.5	0.8	0.6	•
Operating Margin	21	2.0	1.6	•	0.5	1.1	•	1.3	•	•	0.0	•	7.1	•
Operating Margin Before Officers' Comp.	22	4.5	3.2	6.2	4.7	4.5	2.3	2.4	0.8	•	0.5	•	7.7	•

Selected Average Balance Sheet ($ in Thousands)													
Net Receivables 23	195	0	17	98	318	1050	1742	8870	7690	15172	113644	282242	•
Inventories 24	359	0	48	222	852	3672	5858	9517	23143	44342	118493	376911	•
Net Property, Plant and Equipment 25	293	0	21	164	357	1868	2509	6640	17111	58553	76656	507134	•
Total Assets 26	1184	0	112	665	2074	7551	15013	31839	71255	149688	329349	1786916	•
Notes and Loans Payable 27	313	0	74	199	698	2736	3335	9106	20287	30624	101390	306538	•
All Other Liabilities 28	444	0	46	169	819	1661	6202	10426	23207	70498	82191	729671	•
Net Worth 29	427	0	-7	297	557	3154	5475	12307	27760	48566	145768	750707	•

Selected Financial Ratios (Times to 1)													
Current Ratio 30	1.6	•	1.7	2.3	1.7	1.9	1.6	1.5	1.9	1.2	1.9	1.4	•
Quick Ratio 31	0.7	•	0.8	1.1	0.6	0.6	0.5	0.7	0.8	0.4	1.0	0.6	•
Net Sales to Working Capital 32	8.2	•	12.5	7.3	8.4	5.9	9.4	10.3	6.6	28.1	4.7	7.3	•
Coverage Ratio 33	6.7	2.5	0.9	4.5	4.9	1.8	6.8	3.0	3.2	4.2	2.2	14.5	•
Total Asset Turnover 34	1.9	•	3.9	2.6	2.4	1.9	2.6	2.4	1.8	2.1	1.5	1.3	•
Inventory Turnover 35	3.7	•	5.4	5.0	3.5	2.5	3.8	5.0	3.0	3.7	2.3	3.3	•
Receivables Turnover 36	10.8	•	21.6	16.8	14.3	13.3	17.1	9.5	19.2	15.8	4.4	7.4	•
Total Liabilities to Net Worth 37	1.8	•	•	1.2	2.7	1.4	1.7	1.6	1.6	2.1	1.3	1.4	•
Current Assets to Working Capital 38	2.7	•	2.4	1.8	2.5	2.1	2.6	2.9	2.2	7.0	2.2	3.3	•
Current Liabilities to Working Capital 39	1.7	•	1.4	0.8	1.5	1.1	1.6	1.9	1.2	6.0	1.2	2.3	•
Working Capital to Net Sales 40	0.1	•	0.1	0.1	0.1	0.2	0.1	0.1	0.2	0.0	0.2	0.1	•
Inventory to Working Capital 41	1.3	•	1.3	0.9	1.4	1.3	1.5	1.4	1.1	4.2	0.9	1.3	•
Total Receipts to Cash Flow 42	7.7	7.0	8.8	8.4	8.4	11.3	9.1	10.5	6.7	7.0	7.3	6.4	•
Cost of Goods to Cash Flow 43	4.5	4.4	5.3	5.5	5.0	7.3	5.3	6.5	3.6	3.8	4.0	3.5	•
Cash Flow to Total Debt 44	0.4	•	0.4	0.6	0.4	0.3	0.4	0.4	0.4	0.4	0.4	0.3	•

Selected Financial Factors (in Percentages)													
Debt Ratio 45	63.9	•	106.0	55.4	73.2	58.2	63.5	61.3	61.0	67.6	55.7	58.0	•
Return on Total Assets 46	7.9	•	1.9	7.0	6.8	3.4	8.1	4.5	2.8	4.5	2.6	11.0	•
Return on Equity Before Income Taxes 47	18.5	•	4.0	12.3	20.2	3.6	19.0	7.7	4.9	10.7	3.2	24.3	•
Return on Equity After Income Taxes 48	13.5	•	5.5	11.6	19.3	3.2	18.3	7.7	4.2	8.6	2.0	15.7	•
Profit Margin (Before Income Tax) 49	3.5	2.7	•	2.1	2.3	0.8	2.7	1.2	1.1	1.7	0.9	7.9	•
Profit Margin (After Income Tax) 50	2.5	2.1	•	2.0	2.2	0.7	2.6	1.2	0.9	1.4	0.6	5.1	•

Table II

Corporations with Net Income

FURNITURE AND HOME FURNISHINGS STORES

MONEY AMOUNTS AND SIZE OF ASSETS IN THOUSANDS OF DOLLARS

Item Description for Accounting Period 7/11 Through 6/12		Total	Zero Assets	Under 500	500 to 1,000	1,000 to 5,000	5,000 to 10,000	10,000 to 25,000	25,000 to 50,000	50,000 to 100,000	100,000 to 250,000	250,000 to 500,000	500,000 to 2,500,000	2,500,000 and over
Number of Enterprises	1	19430	1933	12942	2246	1966	•	135	26	14	6	5	•	0
Revenues ($ in Thousands)														
Net Sales	2	59805253	875959	6273599	4400563	9566469	•	5626699	2061421	2053833	1582629	2824475	•	0
Interest	3	137422	325	713	1951	16780	•	4052	1	13	6410	101114	•	0
Rents	4	13857	0	671	4	1508	•	95	200	2148	1688	1765	•	0
Royalties	5	8850	0	0	0	0	•	0	0	0	0	0	•	0
Other Portfolio Income	6	80393	0	21180	53438	1770	•	919	30	1038	87	223	•	0
Other Receipts	7	628463	9696	23612	27132	96718	•	76709	31116	63897	13790	74416	•	0
Total Receipts	8	60674238	885980	6319775	4483088	9683245	•	5708474	2092768	2120929	1604604	3001993	•	0
Average Total Receipts	9	3123	458	488	1996	4925	•	42285	80491	151495	267434	600399	•	•
Operating Costs/Operating Income (%)														
Cost of Operations	10	57.7	61.9	59.5	67.9	58.7	•	57.2	65.7	52.7	53.5	56.4	•	•
Salaries and Wages	11	11.4	8.9	7.2	8.0	11.9	•	13.3	14.7	14.5	14.2	16.4	•	•
Taxes Paid	12	2.3	3.3	2.2	2.0	2.3	•	2.1	1.6	2.4	2.5	2.2	•	•
Interest Paid	13	0.5	2.0	0.4	0.3	0.5	•	0.4	0.7	0.4	0.5	0.8	•	•
Depreciation	14	1.6	1.0	0.4	0.7	0.8	•	0.9	1.0	2.0	2.1	1.6	•	•
Amortization and Depletion	15	0.2	•	0.1	0.1	0.1	•	0.1	0.0	0.0	0.3	0.1	•	•
Pensions and Other Deferred Comp.	16	0.1	0.1	0.1	0.0	0.1	•	0.1	0.3	0.3	0.1	0.2	•	•
Employee Benefits	17	0.9	0.2	0.9	0.5	0.4	•	0.8	1.4	1.0	1.1	0.3	•	•
Advertising	18	3.8	2.1	2.0	2.7	2.5	•	6.5	1.9	3.9	3.9	5.4	•	•
Other Expenses	19	14.9	13.1	15.3	11.3	16.0	•	15.4	10.9	19.3	18.5	18.9	•	•
Officers' Compensation	20	2.3	1.7	7.3	4.2	3.5	•	1.0	0.9	0.9	0.5	0.7	•	•
Operating Margin	21	4.4	5.8	4.5	2.5	3.1	•	2.2	1.1	2.6	2.7	•	•	•
Operating Margin Before Officers' Comp.	22	6.6	7.5	11.7	6.7	6.6	•	3.3	1.9	3.5	3.2	•	•	•

Selected Average Balance Sheet ($ in Thousands)

Net Receivables 23	278	0	12	104	342	•	1672	10266	8534	23490	138396	•	•
Inventories 24	468	0	50	220	829	•	5600	9003	24478	35968	113494	•	•
Net Property, Plant and Equipment 25	400	0	19	98	358	•	2680	6841	19485	46392	72227	•	•
Total Assets 26	1602	0	121	677	2011	•	15007	32238	69831	145197	345460	•	•
Notes and Loans Payable 27	347	0	57	142	573	•	2270	11119	19504	24537	107950	•	•
All Other Liabilities 28	615	0	51	177	704	•	6440	9373	23852	51900	91465	•	•
Net Worth 29	641	0	13	358	734	•	6298	11746	26474	68761	146045	•	•

Selected Financial Ratios (Times to 1)

Current Ratio 30	1.6	•	1.6	2.3	2.1	•	1.6	1.6	1.8	1.6	2.3	•	•
Quick Ratio 31	0.7	•	0.7	1.1	0.8	•	0.5	0.8	0.7	0.8	1.2	•	•
Net Sales to Working Capital 32	7.6	•	14.3	7.5	6.2	•	9.9	9.3	7.6	8.7	3.9	•	•
Coverage Ratio 33	11.9	4.4	12.8	17.0	9.5	•	10.1	4.7	17.0	9.1	5.4	•	•
Total Asset Turnover 34	1.9	•	4.0	2.9	2.4	•	2.8	2.5	2.1	1.8	1.6	•	•
Inventory Turnover 35	3.8	•	5.7	6.0	3.4	•	4.3	5.8	3.2	3.9	2.8	•	•
Receivables Turnover 36	10.5	•	25.8	18.5	14.7	•	20.7	10.2	18.6	10.6	•	•	•
Total Liabilities to Net Worth 37	1.5	•	8.0	0.9	1.7	•	1.4	1.7	1.6	1.1	1.4	•	•
Current Assets to Working Capital 38	2.6	•	2.6	1.8	1.9	•	2.6	2.6	2.2	2.5	1.8	•	•
Current Liabilities to Working Capital 39	1.6	•	1.6	0.8	0.9	•	1.6	1.6	1.2	1.5	0.8	•	•
Working Capital to Net Sales 40	0.1	•	0.1	0.1	0.2	•	0.1	0.1	0.1	0.1	0.3	•	•
Inventory to Working Capital 41	1.2	•	1.5	0.9	1.1	•	1.5	1.2	1.3	1.0	0.8	•	•
Total Receipts to Cash Flow 42	6.9	6.1	6.6	9.3	6.8	•	8.4	10.2	5.5	6.3	6.4	•	•
Cost of Goods to Cash Flow 43	4.0	3.8	4.0	6.3	4.0	•	4.8	6.7	2.9	3.4	3.6	•	•
Cash Flow to Total Debt 44	0.5	•	0.7	0.7	0.6	•	0.6	0.4	0.6	0.5	0.4	•	•

Selected Financial Factors (in Percentages)

Debt Ratio 45	60.0	•	88.8	47.1	63.5	•	58.0	63.6	62.1	52.6	57.7	•	•
Return on Total Assets 46	12.2	•	22.7	13.4	11.7	•	11.3	8.0	13.1	8.4	6.9	•	•
Return on Equity Before Income Taxes 47	27.9	•	187.9	23.8	28.7	•	24.3	17.4	32.5	15.8	13.3	•	•
Return on Equity After Income Taxes 48	22.2	•	186.6	22.8	27.8	•	23.5	17.4	31.5	13.4	11.4	•	•
Profit Margin (Before Income Tax) 49	5.8	6.9	5.2	4.3	4.3	•	3.7	2.6	5.9	4.1	3.4	•	•
Profit Margin (After Income Tax) 50	4.6	6.2	5.2	4.2	4.2	•	3.5	2.6	5.7	3.5	3.0	•	•

Table I

Corporations with and without Net Income

ELECTRONICS AND APPLIANCE STORES

MONEY AMOUNTS AND SIZE OF ASSETS IN THOUSANDS OF DOLLARS

Item Description for Accounting Period 7/11 Through 6/12		Total	Zero Assets	Under 500	500 to 1,000	1,000 to 5,000	5,000 to 10,000	10,000 to 25,000	25,000 to 50,000	50,000 to 100,000	100,000 to 250,000	250,000 to 500,000	500,000 to 2,500,000	2,500,000 and over
Number of Enterprises	1	27260	4355	19657	1602	1375	110	101	18	16	12	3	10	0
Revenues ($ in Thousands)														
Net Sales	2	101924632	1059108	8312057	3935512	7595770	1316456	4672933	1354902	3641543	4622684	1347281	64066386	0
Interest	3	161328	175	1506	663	3044	203	300	96	1093	67	6	154174	0
Rents	4	29525	0	3533	676	168	33	66	0	347	0	0	24703	0
Royalties	5	49635	1465	0	0	0	0	0	0	0	0	0	48171	0
Other Portfolio Income	6	64273	24296	3456	2039	4595	13277	1496	0	480	831	6	13796	0
Other Receipts	7	1979595	15385	493749	13075	47551	28154	20553	3705	27502	56844	-2390	1275468	0
Total Receipts	8	104208988	1100429	8814301	3951965	7651128	1358123	4695348	1358703	3670965	4680426	1344903	65582698	0
Average Total Receipts	9	3823	253	448	2467	5564	12347	46489	75484	229435	390036	448301	6558270	•
Operating Costs/Operating Income (%)														
Cost of Operations	10	71.4	49.4	55.4	55.4	64.7	62.4	73.3	66.2	69.5	77.1	75.6	75.3	•
Salaries and Wages	11	9.9	10.4	14.9	18.7	14.3	16.0	12.3	13.5	11.7	8.9	10.6	7.8	•
Taxes Paid	12	1.7	1.8	2.7	2.6	2.0	1.8	1.0	1.7	1.3	0.9	1.4	1.6	•
Interest Paid	13	0.6	3.2	0.8	0.5	0.5	1.2	0.3	0.6	0.2	0.1	4.4	0.5	•
Depreciation	14	1.1	1.2	1.0	0.8	0.6	2.2	1.8	0.9	1.8	1.6	0.5	1.1	•
Amortization and Depletion	15	0.2	0.9	0.1	0.1	0.3	0.0	0.1	0.4	0.0	0.1	0.9	0.2	•
Pensions and Other Deferred Comp.	16	0.2	1.5	0.2	0.8	0.3	0.2	0.1	0.3	0.1	0.1	0.0	0.1	•
Employee Benefits	17	0.7	0.7	0.6	1.5	1.4	1.0	0.6	0.4	0.7	0.4	0.8	0.7	•
Advertising	18	1.9	1.9	1.9	0.8	1.4	2.3	0.8	1.7	1.4	0.5	0.2	2.2	•
Other Expenses	19	10.3	20.9	19.5	15.5	8.6	10.6	7.8	11.3	7.6	9.4	4.6	9.4	•
Officers' Compensation	20	1.5	2.9	7.2	5.4	3.1	3.0	1.3	1.0	5.3	0.8	0.2	0.1	•
Operating Margin	21	0.5	5.3	•	•	2.9	•	0.6	2.2	0.3	0.1	0.8	0.9	•
Operating Margin Before Officers' Comp.	22	1.9	8.2	2.8	3.4	6.0	2.3	1.9	3.2	5.7	0.9	1.0	1.0	•

Selected Average Balance Sheet ($ in Thousands)													
Net Receivables 23	251	0	14	94	501	1482	5917	9834	19208	41050	59149	381633	•
Inventories 24	367	0	31	198	672	1941	2803	6654	18018	30898	14292	684406	•
Net Property, Plant and Equipment 25	207	0	18	129	232	1624	1039	6979	7563	20453	7090	395731	•
Total Assets 26	1445	0	105	703	1997	6711	15410	35286	74043	168538	279423	2648327	•
Notes and Loans Payable 27	259	0	65	215	466	2789	3711	6300	15169	7249	204638	305974	•
All Other Liabilities 28	692	0	72	264	783	2203	7956	15212	31047	71965	149872	1282650	•
Net Worth 29	494	0	-32	225	748	1719	3743	13774	27827	89324	-75086	1059703	•

Selected Financial Ratios (Times to 1)													
Current Ratio 30	1.2	•	0.9	2.0	1.7	1.1	1.4	2.1	1.4	1.4	1.0	1.2	•
Quick Ratio 31	0.6	•	0.5	1.0	0.9	0.6	0.9	1.3	0.8	0.8	0.4	0.5	•
Net Sales to Working Capital 32	22.8	•	•	11.2	9.3	29.5	14.9	6.8	14.1	14.0	•	26.4	•
Coverage Ratio 33	5.9	3.9	2.9	•	8.9	3.1	4.6	5.0	6.1	18.5	1.1	7.9	•
Total Asset Turnover 34	2.6	•	4.0	3.5	2.8	1.8	3.0	2.1	3.1	2.3	1.6	2.4	•
Inventory Turnover 35	7.3	•	7.5	6.9	5.3	3.8	12.1	7.5	8.8	9.6	23.7	7.1	•
Receivables Turnover 36	11.6	•	35.7	31.5	9.6	7.3	9.0	7.7	11.3	11.7	5.9	11.1	•
Total Liabilities to Net Worth 37	1.9	•	•	2.1	1.7	2.9	3.1	1.6	1.7	0.9	•	1.5	•
Current Assets to Working Capital 38	5.1	•	•	2.0	2.4	9.6	3.7	1.9	3.3	3.6	•	5.8	•
Current Liabilities to Working Capital 39	4.1	•	•	1.0	1.4	8.6	2.7	0.9	2.3	2.6	•	4.8	•
Working Capital to Net Sales 40	0.0	•	•	0.1	0.1	0.0	0.1	0.1	0.1	0.1	•	0.0	•
Inventory to Working Capital 41	2.2	•	•	0.9	1.0	4.1	0.9	0.5	1.2	1.0	•	2.8	•
Total Receipts to Cash Flow 42	10.1	3.8	6.3	10.5	9.9	10.8	14.2	8.2	14.1	11.2	33.8	10.6	•
Cost of Goods to Cash Flow 43	7.2	1.9	3.5	5.8	6.4	6.8	10.4	5.4	9.8	8.6	25.6	8.0	•
Cash Flow to Total Debt 44	0.4	•	0.5	0.5	0.4	0.2	0.3	0.4	0.3	0.4	0.0	0.4	•

Selected Financial Factors (in Percentages)													
Debt Ratio 45	65.8	•	130.8	68.1	62.5	74.4	75.7	61.0	62.4	47.0	126.9	60.0	•
Return on Total Assets 46	9.0	•	10.1	•	11.1	6.5	4.3	6.5	4.3	3.1	8.1	9.8	•
Return on Equity Before Income Taxes 47	21.9	•	•	•	26.4	17.2	13.7	13.4	9.5	5.6	•	21.4	•
Return on Equity After Income Taxes 48	15.1	•	•	•	24.7	12.6	13.6	10.9	6.2	5.5	•	13.4	•
Profit Margin (Before Income Tax) 49	2.9	9.4	1.6	•	3.6	2.5	1.1	2.4	1.2	1.3	0.7	3.5	•
Profit Margin (After Income Tax) 50	2.0	9.3	1.6	•	3.3	1.8	1.1	2.0	0.8	1.3	0.5	2.2	•

Table II

Corporations with Net Income

Electronics and Appliance Stores

Money Amounts and Size of Assets in Thousands of Dollars

Item Description for Accounting Period 7/11 Through 6/12		Total	Zero Assets	Under 500	500 to 1,000	1,000 to 5,000	5,000 to 10,000	10,000 to 25,000	25,000 to 50,000	50,000 to 100,000	100,000 to 250,000	250,000 to 500,000	500,000 to 2,500,000	2,500,000 and over
Number of Enterprises	1	14584	2178	10440	814	994	•	65	12	12	9	0	•	0
Revenues ($ in Thousands)														
Net Sales	2	86066083	717536	5592952	2164202	5963235	•	3801602	954851	2718909	4112708	0	•	0
Interest	3	34902	120	218	431	2132	•	112	94	1051	40	0	•	0
Rents	4	25345	0	0	676	0	•	0	0	347	0	0	•	0
Royalties	5	46874	0	0	0	0	•	0	0	0	0	0	•	0
Other Portfolio Income	6	45701	14706	334	657	2459	•	1253	0	12	755	0	•	0
Other Receipts	7	1652245	11036	252274	11436	23690	•	18611	680	24006	48189	0	•	0
Total Receipts	8	87871150	743398	5845778	2177402	5991516	•	3821578	955625	2744325	4161692	0	•	0
Average Total Receipts	9	6025	341	560	2675	6028	•	58794	79635	228694	462410	•	•	•
Operating Costs/Operating Income (%)														
Cost of Operations	10	72.6	49.7	51.5	43.2	63.2	•	75.3	62.9	70.1	76.3	•	•	•
Salaries and Wages	11	9.2	6.5	14.3	25.3	14.3	•	11.0	15.9	12.6	11.6	•	•	•
Taxes Paid	12	1.6	0.9	2.5	3.2	2.0	•	1.0	1.7	1.1	1.3	•	•	•
Interest Paid	13	0.5	0.0	0.5	0.2	0.3	•	0.3	0.7	0.2	1.5	•	•	•
Depreciation	14	0.9	0.9	0.6	0.8	0.5	•	0.9	0.8	0.4	0.6	•	•	•
Amortization and Depletion	15	0.2	0.3	0.0	0.1	0.3	•	0.0	0.6	0.0	0.3	•	•	•
Pensions and Other Deferred Comp.	16	0.2	2.0	0.2	1.0	0.4	•	0.1	0.3	0.1	0.1	•	•	•
Employee Benefits	17	0.8	1.0	0.6	1.7	1.5	•	0.4	0.5	0.6	0.7	•	•	•
Advertising	18	1.7	2.7	1.9	0.6	1.3	•	0.3	0.2	1.0	0.4	•	•	•
Other Expenses	19	9.0	19.7	17.4	16.8	7.8	•	6.8	10.5	5.3	5.3	•	•	•
Officers' Compensation	20	1.3	3.0	8.1	6.1	3.5	•	1.1	1.1	6.6	0.6	•	•	•
Operating Margin	21	2.1	13.2	2.3	1.1	4.9	•	2.9	4.7	2.0	1.5	•	•	•
Operating Margin Before Officers' Comp.	22	3.5	16.3	10.4	7.2	8.3	•	4.0	5.7	8.7	2.1	•	•	•

Selected Average Balance Sheet ($ in Thousands)													
Net Receivables 23	347	0	15	93	563	•	7014	12910	22934	51071	•	•	•
Inventories 24	570	0	31	199	655	•	3148	2780	14739	31230	•	•	•
Net Property, Plant and Equipment 25	302	0	14	73	255	•	780	2356	5074	12195	•	•	•
Total Assets 26	2175	0	112	640	2072	•	15553	34649	71601	203008	•	•	•
Notes and Loans Payable 27	279	0	44	97	349	•	3018	8601	10169	71641	•	•	•
All Other Liabilities 28	1053	0	54	224	762	•	8576	16580	31531	74667	•	•	•
Net Worth 29	844	0	14	319	961	•	3959	9467	29901	56700	•	•	•

Selected Financial Ratios (Times to 1)													
Current Ratio 30	1.2	•	1.3	2.9	1.9	•	1.3	2.5	1.7	1.5	•	•	•
Quick Ratio 31	0.6	•	0.8	1.8	1.1	•	0.9	1.9	1.2	0.9	•	•	•
Net Sales to Working Capital 32	30.6	•	28.7	10.4	8.7	•	19.8	6.0	10.5	11.9	•	•	•
Coverage Ratio 33	10.7	568.2	13.6	10.6	17.1	•	14.4	7.4	18.1	2.8	•	•	•
Total Asset Turnover 34	2.7	•	4.8	4.2	2.9	•	3.8	2.3	3.2	2.3	•	•	•
Inventory Turnover 35	7.5	•	8.9	5.8	5.8	•	14.0	18.0	10.8	11.2	•	•	•
Receivables Turnover 36	11.5	•	42.9	26.4	9.4	•	9.5	•	9.8	11.8	•	•	•
Total Liabilities to Net Worth 37	1.6	•	7.2	1.0	1.2	•	2.9	2.7	1.4	2.6	•	•	•
Current Assets to Working Capital 38	6.2	•	4.5	1.5	2.1	•	4.4	1.7	2.5	3.1	•	•	•
Current Liabilities to Working Capital 39	5.2	•	3.5	0.5	1.1	•	3.4	0.7	1.5	2.1	•	•	•
Working Capital to Net Sales 40	0.0	•	0.0	0.1	0.1	•	0.1	0.2	0.1	0.1	•	•	•
Inventory to Working Capital 41	2.8	•	1.5	0.4	0.8	•	1.1	0.2	0.6	0.9	•	•	•
Total Receipts to Cash Flow 42	9.6	3.0	5.0	7.1	8.9	•	11.6	7.2	14.4	16.0	•	•	•
Cost of Goods to Cash Flow 43	7.0	1.5	2.6	3.1	5.6	•	8.8	4.5	10.1	12.2	•	•	•
Cash Flow to Total Debt 44	0.5	•	1.1	1.2	0.6	•	0.4	0.4	0.4	0.2	•	•	•

Selected Financial Factors (in Percentages)													
Debt Ratio 45	61.2	•	87.8	50.1	53.6	•	74.5	72.7	58.2	72.1	•	•	•
Return on Total Assets 46	13.2	•	35.3	7.8	16.3	•	13.9	12.6	10.0	9.3	•	•	•
Return on Equity Before Income Taxes 47	30.9	•	268.3	14.1	33.1	•	51.0	39.8	22.5	21.4	•	•	•
Return on Equity After Income Taxes 48	23.6	•	266.8	13.4	31.3	•	50.7	34.5	18.5	20.7	•	•	•
Profit Margin (Before Income Tax) 49	4.4	16.8	6.8	1.7	5.3	•	3.4	4.7	3.0	2.7	•	•	•
Profit Margin (After Income Tax) 50	3.4	16.8	6.8	1.6	5.0	•	3.4	4.1	2.4	2.6	•	•	•

Table I

Corporations with and without Net Income

HOMES CENTERS; PAINT AND WALLPAPER STORES

MONEY AMOUNTS AND SIZE OF ASSETS IN THOUSANDS OF DOLLARS

Item Description for Accounting Period 7/11 Through 6/12		Total	Zero Assets	Under 500	500 to 1,000	1,000 to 5,000	5,000 to 10,000	10,000 to 25,000	25,000 to 50,000	50,000 to 100,000	100,000 to 250,000	250,000 to 500,000	500,000 to 2,500,000	2,500,000 and over
Number of Enterprises	1	2761	16	1733	445	485	35	33	6	5	0	0	0	3
Revenues ($ in Thousands)														
Net Sales	2	130679835	8710	915845	899290	2761015	681223	1040196	508535	799734	0	0	0	123065285
Interest	3	38820	0	450	726	3035	1219	626	327	375	0	0	0	32061
Rents	4	377012	0	0	158	589	3032	1009	0	0	0	0	0	372224
Royalties	5	256258	0	0	0	0	0	0	0	0	0	0	0	256258
Other Portfolio Income	6	64765	0	1115	0	26783	194	572	386	345	0	0	0	35368
Other Receipts	7	1865561	0	91	6042	11667	3809	9084	1928	7447	0	0	0	1825498
Total Receipts	8	133282251	8710	917501	906216	2803089	689477	1051487	511176	807901	0	0	0	125586694
Average Total Receipts	9	48273	544	529	2036	5780	19699	31863	85196	161580	•	•	•	41862231
Operating Costs/Operating Income (%)														
Cost of Operations	10	66.3	42.5	59.3	68.3	70.0	70.1	72.5	71.1	72.5	•	•	•	66.1
Salaries and Wages	11	13.1	•	7.1	11.5	13.0	14.4	10.5	12.4	9.9	•	•	•	13.2
Taxes Paid	12	2.3	3.6	2.5	7.3	2.4	2.3	1.7	1.9	1.8	•	•	•	2.3
Interest Paid	13	0.9	•	0.4	1.1	0.3	0.5	0.5	0.7	0.8	•	•	•	0.9
Depreciation	14	2.8	•	0.2	0.7	0.6	3.0	1.0	2.4	1.8	•	•	•	2.9
Amortization and Depletion	15	0.0	•	0.0	•	0.1	0.2	0.0	0.1	0.0	•	•	•	0.0
Pensions and Other Deferred Comp.	16	0.2	•	0.0	0.0	0.4	0.1	0.3	0.0	0.9	•	•	•	0.2
Employee Benefits	17	1.4	0.8	0.4	0.2	0.9	0.6	0.9	0.9	1.5	•	•	•	1.5
Advertising	18	1.5	•	1.1	0.4	0.6	1.3	1.1	0.7	1.3	•	•	•	1.5
Other Expenses	19	7.1	11.2	19.7	9.3	9.0	9.9	9.3	8.4	8.4	•	•	•	6.9
Officers' Compensation	20	0.2	•	8.8	2.2	2.8	1.5	1.1	2.1	0.9	•	•	•	0.1
Operating Margin	21	4.1	41.9	0.5	•	•	•	1.2	•	0.2	•	•	•	4.4
Operating Margin Before Officers' Comp.	22	4.4	41.9	9.2	1.3	2.7	•	2.3	1.4	1.1	•	•	•	4.5

Selected Average Balance Sheet ($ in Thousands)													
Net Receivables **23**	1534	0	28	142	515	727	3603	7266	10653	•	•	•	1210749
Inventories **24**	7236	0	83	158	811	3822	4907	11138	35318	•	•	•	6281564
Net Property, Plant and Equipment **25**	14238	0	10	252	210	2427	3760	10324	28102	•	•	•	12889668
Total Assets **26**	46175	0	112	652	2273	7797	16194	33352	88609	•	•	•	41483803
Notes and Loans Payable **27**	15729	0	26	362	273	1933	5503	9436	21259	•	•	•	14225827
All Other Liabilities **28**	16936	0	40	218	427	1808	3524	8883	18602	•	•	•	15353946
Net Worth **29**	13509	0	46	71	1573	4056	7167	15033	48748	•	•	•	11904031
Selected Financial Ratios (Times to 1)													
Current Ratio **30**	1.2	•	2.4	0.9	4.1	1.6	1.7	2.4	4.1	•	•	•	1.1
Quick Ratio **31**	0.2	•	1.0	0.4	2.1	0.4	0.8	1.0	1.1	•	•	•	0.1
Net Sales to Working Capital **32**	17.3	•	8.8	•	4.1	9.7	7.3	7.4	4.1	•	•	•	19.5
Coverage Ratio **33**	8.0	•	2.7	0.9	5.9	•	5.7	0.6	2.6	•	•	•	8.2
Total Asset Turnover **34**	1.0	•	4.7	3.1	2.5	2.5	1.9	2.5	1.8	•	•	•	1.0
Inventory Turnover **35**	4.3	•	3.8	8.7	4.9	3.6	4.7	5.4	3.3	•	•	•	4.3
Receivables Turnover **36**	35.1	•	12.3	23.0	11.3	•	9.4	10.5	•	•	•	•	39.3
Total Liabilities to Net Worth **37**	2.4	•	1.4	8.2	0.4	0.9	1.3	1.2	0.8	•	•	•	2.5
Current Assets to Working Capital **38**	6.8	•	1.7	•	1.3	2.6	2.5	1.7	1.3	•	•	•	7.8
Current Liabilities to Working Capital **39**	5.8	•	0.7	•	0.3	1.6	1.5	0.7	0.3	•	•	•	6.8
Working Capital to Net Sales **40**	0.1	•	0.1	•	0.2	0.1	0.1	0.1	0.2	•	•	•	0.1
Inventory to Working Capital **41**	2.6	•	1.0	•	0.6	1.9	1.2	1.0	0.9	•	•	•	3.0
Total Receipts to Cash Flow **42**	9.4	1.9	6.4	18.5	13.9	35.1	11.9	18.5	15.6	•	•	•	9.2
Cost of Goods to Cash Flow **43**	6.2	0.8	3.8	12.6	9.8	24.6	8.7	13.1	11.3	•	•	•	6.1
Cash Flow to Total Debt **44**	0.2	•	1.3	0.2	0.6	0.1	0.3	0.3	0.3	•	•	•	0.2
Selected Financial Factors (in Percentages)													
Debt Ratio **45**	70.7	•	58.8	89.1	30.8	48.0	55.7	54.9	45.0	•	•	•	71.3
Return on Total Assets **46**	7.2	•	4.7	3.0	4.2	•	5.3	1.1	3.6	•	•	•	7.3
Return on Equity Before Income Taxes **47**	21.4	•	7.3	•	5.1	•	9.9	•	4.1	•	•	•	22.2
Return on Equity After Income Taxes **48**	14.6	•	7.3	•	4.8	•	8.6	•	3.6	•	•	•	15.1
Profit Margin (Before Income Tax) **49**	6.1	41.9	0.6	•	1.4	•	2.3	•	1.2	•	•	•	6.4
Profit Margin (After Income Tax) **50**	4.2	41.9	0.6	•	1.3	•	2.0	•	1.1	•	•	•	4.4

Table II

Corporations with Net Income

Homes Centers; Paint and Wallpaper Stores

Money Amounts and Size of Assets in Thousands of Dollars

Item Description for Accounting Period 7/11 Through 6/12		Total	Zero Assets	Under 500	500 to 1,000	1,000 to 5,000	5,000 to 10,000	10,000 to 25,000	25,000 to 50,000	50,000 to 100,000	100,000 to 250,000	250,000 to 500,000	500,000 to 2,500,000	2,500,000 and over
Number of Enterprises	1	1193	16	743	104	276	23	•	0	•	0	0	0	3
Revenues ($ in Thousands)														
Net Sales	2	126746539	8710	497955	92943	1465733	312464	•	0	•	0	0	0	123065285
Interest	3	34284	0	0	726	208	750	•	0	•	0	0	0	32061
Rents	4	375425	0	0	158	11	3032	•	0	•	0	0	0	372224
Royalties	5	256258	0	0	0	0	0	•	0	•	0	0	0	256258
Other Portfolio Income	6	38101	0	0	0	1876	194	•	0	•	0	0	0	35368
Other Receipts	7	1846227	0	0	1465	6320	1910	•	0	•	0	0	0	1825498
Total Receipts	8	129296834	8710	497955	95292	1474148	318350	•	0	•	0	0	0	125586694
Average Total Receipts	9	108380	544	670	916	5341	13841	•	•	•	•	•	•	41862231
Operating Costs/Operating Income (%)														
Cost of Operations	10	66.2	42.5	55.7	66.6	70.9	73.8	•	•	•	•	•	•	66.1
Salaries and Wages	11	13.2	•	6.4	5.8	10.5	11.1	•	•	•	•	•	•	13.2
Taxes Paid	12	2.3	3.6	1.8	2.4	2.3	2.1	•	•	•	•	•	•	2.3
Interest Paid	13	0.9	•	•	3.1	0.3	0.4	•	•	•	•	•	•	0.9
Depreciation	14	2.8	•	0.1	2.3	0.4	1.5	•	•	•	•	•	•	2.9
Amortization and Depletion	15	0.0	•	•	•	0.0	0.0	•	•	•	•	•	•	0.0
Pensions and Other Deferred Comp.	16	0.2	•	•	0.2	0.4	0.1	•	•	•	•	•	•	0.2
Employee Benefits	17	1.4	0.8	•	1.5	0.8	1.3	•	•	•	•	•	•	1.5
Advertising	18	1.5	•	1.7	2.1	0.4	1.1	•	•	•	•	•	•	1.5
Other Expenses	19	7.0	11.2	22.6	8.4	6.4	7.9	•	•	•	•	•	•	6.9
Officers' Compensation	20	0.2	•	8.8	8.8	3.9	1.3	•	•	•	•	•	•	0.1
Operating Margin	21	4.3	41.9	2.8	•	3.7	•	•	•	•	•	•	•	4.4
Operating Margin Before Officers' Comp.	22	4.5	41.9	11.6	7.7	7.7	0.6	•	•	•	•	•	•	4.5

Selected Average Balance Sheet ($ in Thousands)														
Net Receivables	23	3353	0	57	142	602	576	•	•	•	•	•	•	1210749
Inventories	24	16262	0	33	303	749	2883	•	•	•	•	•	•	6281564
Net Property, Plant and Equipment	25	32666	0	11	198	124	2380	•	•	•	•	•	•	12889668
Total Assets	26	105601	0	116	749	1924	7106	•	•	•	•	•	•	41483803
Notes and Loans Payable	27	36031	0	0	473	216	1815	•	•	•	•	•	•	14225827
All Other Liabilities	28	38860	0	50	51	419	870	•	•	•	•	•	•	15353946
Net Worth	29	30710	0	66	225	1290	4421	•	•	•	•	•	•	11904031
Selected Financial Ratios (Times to 1)														
Current Ratio	30	1.2	•	2.1	2.7	4.0	1.9	•	•	•	•	•	•	1.1
Quick Ratio	31	0.2	•	1.4	1.2	2.1	0.5	•	•	•	•	•	•	0.1
Net Sales to Working Capital	32	18.0	•	12.2	3.0	4.2	6.6	•	•	•	•	•	•	19.5
Coverage Ratio	33	8.2	•	•	1.5	16.5	4.0	•	•	•	•	•	•	8.2
Total Asset Turnover	34	1.0	•	5.8	1.2	2.8	1.9	•	•	•	•	•	•	1.0
Inventory Turnover	35	4.3	•	11.4	2.0	5.0	3.5	•	•	•	•	•	•	4.3
Receivables Turnover	36	36.5	•	•	8.1	9.5	20.5	•	•	•	•	•	•	39.3
Total Liabilities to Net Worth	37	2.4	•	0.8	2.3	0.5	0.6	•	•	•	•	•	•	2.5
Current Assets to Working Capital	38	7.1	•	1.9	1.6	1.3	2.1	•	•	•	•	•	•	7.8
Current Liabilities to Working Capital	39	6.1	•	0.9	0.6	0.3	1.1	•	•	•	•	•	•	6.8
Working Capital to Net Sales	40	0.1	•	0.1	0.3	0.2	0.2	•	•	•	•	•	•	0.1
Inventory to Working Capital	41	2.8	•	0.6	0.9	0.6	1.5	•	•	•	•	•	•	3.0
Total Receipts to Cash Flow	42	9.2	1.9	4.5	11.9	10.9	13.4	•	•	•	•	•	•	9.2
Cost of Goods to Cash Flow	43	6.1	0.8	2.5	7.9	7.7	9.9	•	•	•	•	•	•	6.1
Cash Flow to Total Debt	44	0.2	•	3.0	0.1	0.8	0.4	•	•	•	•	•	•	0.2
Selected Financial Factors (in Percentages)														
Debt Ratio	45	70.9	•	43.1	70.0	33.0	37.8	•	•	•	•	•	•	71.3
Return on Total Assets	46	7.3	•	16.4	5.5	12.6	3.1	•	•	•	•	•	•	7.3
Return on Equity Before Income Taxes	47	22.0	•	28.9	6.0	17.7	3.7	•	•	•	•	•	•	22.2
Return on Equity After Income Taxes	48	15.1	•	28.9	6.0	17.0	2.6	•	•	•	•	•	•	15.1
Profit Margin (Before Income Tax)	49	6.4	41.9	2.8	1.5	4.3	1.2	•	•	•	•	•	•	6.4
Profit Margin (After Income Tax)	50	4.4	41.9	2.8	1.5	4.1	0.8	•	•	•	•	•	•	4.4

Table I

Corporations with and without Net Income

HARDWARE STORES

MONEY AMOUNTS AND SIZE OF ASSETS IN THOUSANDS OF DOLLARS

Item Description for Accounting Period 7/11 Through 6/12		Total	Zero Assets	Under 500	500 to 1,000	1,000 to 5,000	5,000 to 10,000	10,000 to 25,000	25,000 to 50,000	50,000 to 100,000	100,000 to 250,000	250,000 to 500,000	500,000 to 2,500,000	2,500,000 and over
Number of Enterprises	1	7162	•	2623	2560	1870	•	•	12	0	3	0	0	0
Revenues ($ in Thousands)														
Net Sales	2	18138987	•	1543062	4108273	6832626	•	•	1040552	0	2855640	0	0	0
Interest	3	8096	•	2063	223	4915	•	•	600	0	2	0	0	0
Rents	4	12149	•	0	8543	1342	•	•	1363	0	868	0	0	0
Royalties	5	14	•	0	14	0	•	•	0	0	0	0	0	0
Other Portfolio Income	6	33591	•	1125	1742	5117	•	•	762	0	24033	0	0	0
Other Receipts	7	173667	•	21083	58174	58717	•	•	3407	0	9451	0	0	0
Total Receipts	8	18366504	•	1567333	4176969	6902717	•	•	1046684	0	2889994	0	0	0
Average Total Receipts	9	2564	•	598	1632	3691	•	•	87224	•	963331	•	•	•
Operating Costs/Operating Income (%)														
Cost of Operations	10	64.0	•	59.7	63.5	64.0	•	•	63.4	•	63.5	•	•	•
Salaries and Wages	11	12.3	•	12.0	11.9	12.6	•	•	13.0	•	12.4	•	•	•
Taxes Paid	12	2.4	•	2.6	2.6	2.7	•	•	2.8	•	1.7	•	•	•
Interest Paid	13	1.0	•	0.7	0.9	0.7	•	•	0.9	•	2.4	•	•	•
Depreciation	14	1.6	•	0.9	1.6	1.2	•	•	2.0	•	2.6	•	•	•
Amortization and Depletion	15	0.1	•	0.0	0.1	0.0	•	•	0.4	•	0.1	•	•	•
Pensions and Other Deferred Comp.	16	0.2	•	0.1	0.2	0.2	•	•	0.3	•	0.0	•	•	•
Employee Benefits	17	1.1	•	1.3	0.8	1.1	•	•	1.2	•	1.1	•	•	•
Advertising	18	2.0	•	1.0	2.1	1.6	•	•	1.3	•	4.4	•	•	•
Other Expenses	19	10.9	•	14.4	13.6	11.6	•	•	10.8	•	4.4	•	•	•
Officers' Compensation	20	3.3	•	7.8	4.6	3.2	•	•	1.1	•	0.7	•	•	•
Operating Margin	21	1.3	•	•	•	1.2	•	•	2.8	•	6.7	•	•	•
Operating Margin Before Officers' Comp.	22	4.6	•	7.2	2.9	4.4	•	•	3.9	•	7.4	•	•	•

Selected Average Balance Sheet ($ in Thousands)

Net Receivables 23	94	•	21	51	175	•	•	2901	•	11034	•	•	•
Inventories 24	591	•	126	459	857	•	•	18078	•	215210	•	•	•
Net Property, Plant and Equipment 25	227	•	37	69	272	•	•	11436	•	130415	•	•	•
Total Assets 26	1185	•	265	703	1775	•	•	40925	•	448890	•	•	•
Notes and Loans Payable 27	488	•	163	367	465	•	•	15836	•	317224	•	•	•
All Other Liabilities 28	240	•	86	101	291	•	•	9260	•	150544	•	•	•
Net Worth 29	458	•	16	234	1019	•	•	15829	•	-18878	•	•	•

Selected Financial Ratios (Times to 1)

Current Ratio 30	3.0	•	1.8	4.3	3.5	•	•	2.0	•	2.2	•	•	•
Quick Ratio 31	0.8	•	0.3	0.8	1.1	•	•	0.4	•	0.4	•	•	•
Net Sales to Working Capital 32	4.7	•	8.2	3.9	4.0	•	•	7.0	•	6.1	•	•	•
Coverage Ratio 33	3.6	•	2.4	0.9	4.1	•	•	4.7	•	4.3	•	•	•
Total Asset Turnover 34	2.1	•	2.2	2.3	2.1	•	•	2.1	•	2.1	•	•	•
Inventory Turnover 35	2.7	•	2.8	2.2	2.7	•	•	3.0	•	2.8	•	•	•
Receivables Turnover 36	26.0	•	30.0	25.0	21.0	•	•	31.2	•	105.3	•	•	•
Total Liabilities to Net Worth 37	1.6	•	16.0	2.0	0.7	•	•	1.6	•	•	•	•	•
Current Assets to Working Capital 38	1.5	•	2.3	1.3	1.4	•	•	2.0	•	1.8	•	•	•
Current Liabilities to Working Capital 39	0.5	•	1.3	0.3	0.4	•	•	1.0	•	0.8	•	•	•
Working Capital to Net Sales 40	0.2	•	0.1	0.3	0.3	•	•	0.1	•	0.2	•	•	•
Inventory to Working Capital 41	1.1	•	1.8	1.0	0.9	•	•	1.5	•	1.4	•	•	•
Total Receipts to Cash Flow 42	11.9	•	10.7	14.0	10.7	•	•	10.3	•	14.3	•	•	•
Cost of Goods to Cash Flow 43	7.6	•	6.4	8.9	6.8	•	•	6.5	•	9.1	•	•	•
Cash Flow to Total Debt 44	0.3	•	0.2	0.2	0.5	•	•	0.3	•	0.1	•	•	•

Selected Financial Factors (in Percentages)

Debt Ratio 45	61.4	•	94.1	66.6	42.6	•	•	61.3	•	104.2	•	•	•
Return on Total Assets 46	7.5	•	3.8	1.8	6.0	•	•	9.2	•	21.9	•	•	•
Return on Equity Before Income Taxes 47	13.9	•	37.2	•	7.9	•	•	18.7	•	•	•	•	•
Return on Equity After Income Taxes 48	12.8	•	32.1	•	7.5	•	•	13.1	•	•	•	•	•
Profit Margin (Before Income Tax) 49	2.5	•	1.0	•	2.2	•	•	3.4	•	7.9	•	•	•
Profit Margin (After Income Tax) 50	2.3	•	0.8	•	2.1	•	•	2.4	•	7.6	•	•	•

HARDWARE STORES

MONEY AMOUNTS AND SIZE OF ASSETS IN THOUSANDS OF DOLLARS

Item Description for Accounting Period 7/11 Through 6/12		Total	Zero Assets	Under 500	500 to 1,000	1,000 to 5,000	5,000 to 10,000	10,000 to 25,000	25,000 to 50,000	50,000 to 100,000	100,000 to 250,000	250,000 to 500,000	500,000 to 2,500,000	2,500,000 and over
Number of Enterprises	1	4012	0	1210	1147	1569	56	18	9	0	3	0	0	0
Revenues ($ in Thousands)														
Net Sales	2	14192734	0	1097222	2311311	5715722	494642	802676	915522	0	2855640	0	0	0
Interest	3	5312	0	201	186	4270	170	4	480	0	2	0	0	0
Rents	4	9160	0	0	6335	942	0	0	1014	0	868	0	0	0
Royalties	5	14	0	0	14	0	0	0	0	0	0	0	0	0
Other Portfolio Income	6	31141	0	136	549	4872	499	292	762	0	24033	0	0	0
Other Receipts	7	114560	0	18285	27590	49377	2901	3691	3262	0	9451	0	0	0
Total Receipts	8	14352921	0	1115844	2345985	5775183	498212	806663	921040	0	2889994	0	0	0
Average Total Receipts	9	3577	•	922	2045	3681	8897	44815	102338	•	963331	•	•	•
Operating Costs/Operating Income (%)														
Cost of Operations	10	63.6	•	59.2	63.3	63.9	62.2	69.5	63.9	•	63.5	•	•	•
Salaries and Wages	11	12.1	•	11.5	11.1	12.2	11.6	12.9	12.9	•	12.4	•	•	•
Taxes Paid	12	2.3	•	2.2	2.2	2.7	2.4	1.8	2.8	•	1.7	•	•	•
Interest Paid	13	0.9	•	0.5	0.5	0.7	0.1	0.3	0.6	•	2.4	•	•	•
Depreciation	14	1.5	•	0.7	1.0	1.2	3.3	1.0	1.9	•	2.6	•	•	•
Amortization and Depletion	15	0.0	•	0.0	0.0	0.0	0.2	0.0	0.0	•	0.1	•	•	•
Pensions and Other Deferred Comp.	16	0.2	•	•	0.3	0.2	0.5	0.1	0.3	•	0.0	•	•	•
Employee Benefits	17	1.1	•	0.7	1.2	1.1	1.7	1.3	1.1	•	1.1	•	•	•
Advertising	18	2.0	•	1.1	1.5	1.6	0.7	0.8	1.4	•	4.4	•	•	•
Other Expenses	19	10.0	•	13.9	12.9	11.2	7.7	8.7	10.5	•	4.4	•	•	•
Officers' Compensation	20	3.2	•	8.2	4.4	3.3	5.4	1.8	1.0	•	0.7	•	•	•
Operating Margin	21	3.0	•	2.1	1.6	2.0	4.3	1.7	3.4	•	6.7	•	•	•
Operating Margin Before Officers' Comp.	22	6.2	•	10.3	5.9	5.3	9.8	3.4	4.5	•	7.4	•	•	•

Selected Average Balance Sheet ($ in Thousands)													
Net Receivables 23	126	•	24	63	170	550	2583	2831	•	11034	•	•	•
Inventories 24	771	•	139	561	792	1250	8143	21931	•	218893	•	•	•
Net Property, Plant and Equipment 25	314	•	12	44	277	3334	4987	10036	•	130415	•	•	•
Total Assets 26	1588	•	338	680	1767	6934	16894	41340	•	448890	•	•	•
Notes and Loans Payable 27	544	•	91	209	432	475	2855	13955	•	317224	•	•	•
All Other Liabilities 28	340	•	159	94	266	289	4934	10168	•	150544	•	•	•
Net Worth 29	704	•	87	376	1069	6170	9105	17217	•	-18878	•	•	•

Selected Financial Ratios (Times to 1)													
Current Ratio 30	2.9	•	1.3	5.1	3.9	8.6	1.8	2.1	•	2.2	•	•	•
Quick Ratio 31	0.8	•	0.2	1.1	1.3	4.1	0.7	0.4	•	0.4	•	•	•
Net Sales to Working Capital 32	5.0	•	17.4	4.9	3.8	3.4	9.9	7.0	•	6.1	•	•	•
Coverage Ratio 33	5.4	•	9.0	6.8	5.4	70.9	7.5	7.3	•	4.3	•	•	•
Total Asset Turnover 34	2.2	•	2.7	3.0	2.1	1.3	2.6	2.5	•	2.1	•	•	•
Inventory Turnover 35	2.9	•	3.9	2.3	2.9	4.4	3.8	3.0	•	2.8	•	•	•
Receivables Turnover 36	29.7	•	47.0	24.2	25.1	18.5	14.1	•	•	•	•	•	•
Total Liabilities to Net Worth 37	1.3	•	2.9	0.8	0.7	0.1	0.9	1.4	•	•	•	•	•
Current Assets to Working Capital 38	1.5	•	4.1	1.2	1.3	1.1	2.3	2.0	•	1.8	•	•	•
Current Liabilities to Working Capital 39	0.5	•	3.1	0.2	0.3	0.1	1.3	1.0	•	0.8	•	•	•
Working Capital to Net Sales 40	0.2	•	0.1	0.2	0.3	0.3	0.1	0.1	•	0.2	•	•	•
Inventory to Working Capital 41	1.0	•	3.1	0.9	0.9	0.6	1.4	1.5	•	1.4	•	•	•
Total Receipts to Cash Flow 42	10.5	•	8.8	9.8	9.9	9.5	12.6	10.0	•	14.3	•	•	•
Cost of Goods to Cash Flow 43	6.7	•	5.2	6.2	6.3	5.9	8.8	6.4	•	9.1	•	•	•
Cash Flow to Total Debt 44	0.4	•	0.4	0.7	0.5	1.2	0.5	0.4	•	0.1	•	•	•

Selected Financial Factors (in Percentages)													
Debt Ratio 45	55.7	•	74.2	44.6	39.5	11.0	46.1	58.4	•	104.2	•	•	•
Return on Total Assets 46	11.3	•	11.6	10.7	7.5	6.6	6.5	11.4	•	21.9	•	•	•
Return on Equity Before Income Taxes 47	20.9	•	40.0	16.5	10.2	7.3	10.5	23.7	•	•	•	•	•
Return on Equity After Income Taxes 48	19.6	•	38.0	16.0	9.7	5.7	10.5	16.9	•	•	•	•	•
Profit Margin (Before Income Tax) 49	4.2	•	3.8	3.1	3.0	5.1	2.1	4.0	•	7.9	•	•	•
Profit Margin (After Income Tax) 50	3.9	•	3.6	3.0	2.8	4.0	2.1	2.9	•	7.6	•	•	•

Table I

Corporations with and without Net Income

OTHER BUILDING MATERIAL DEALERS

MONEY AMOUNTS AND SIZE OF ASSETS IN THOUSANDS OF DOLLARS

Item Description for Accounting Period 7/11 Through 6/12		Total	Zero Assets	Under 500	500 to 1,000	1,000 to 5,000	5,000 to 10,000	10,000 to 25,000	25,000 to 50,000	50,000 to 100,000	100,000 to 250,000	250,000 to 500,000	500,000 to 2,500,000	2,500,000 and over
Number of Enterprises	1	18626	2319	10600	2227	2871	391	150	39	•	5	•	3	0
Revenues ($ in Thousands)														
Net Sales	2	45120312	760794	5615386	4671437	13915795	6026966	3782943	2477271	•	1384328	•	870575	0
Interest	3	355209	3897	88	4147	12049	1055	2104	1382	•	633	•	322082	0
Rents	4	18076	3894	2776	295	3753	28	3052	981	•	0	•	0	0
Royalties	5	38747	0	3825	0	0	0	0	92	•	0	•	33421	0
Other Portfolio Income	6	64512	4685	1980	24826	14353	1408	3454	6119	•	739	•	15	0
Other Receipts	7	385575	9293	5291	61254	58790	18022	33646	25600	•	2751	•	141741	0
Total Receipts	8	45982431	782563	5629346	4761959	14004740	6047479	3825199	2511445	•	1388451	•	1367834	0
Average Total Receipts	9	2469	337	531	2138	4878	15467	25501	64396	•	277690	•	455945	•
Operating Costs/Operating Income (%)														
Cost of Operations	10	71.9	80.3	62.5	72.5	71.2	75.9	73.3	74.6	•	79.4	•	60.6	•
Salaries and Wages	11	9.5	5.1	8.6	6.9	8.9	10.4	11.0	11.4	•	7.5	•	20.4	•
Taxes Paid	12	2.0	1.9	2.2	2.9	1.9	1.9	1.9	1.8	•	1.3	•	2.7	•
Interest Paid	13	1.5	2.0	0.6	0.2	0.6	0.6	0.7	0.8	•	0.3	•	44.0	•
Depreciation	14	1.1	1.0	1.1	1.2	0.7	0.4	1.4	1.2	•	1.3	•	3.9	•
Amortization and Depletion	15	0.2	0.9	0.0	0.0	0.0	0.0	0.1	0.1	•	0.1	•	6.5	•
Pensions and Other Deferred Comp.	16	0.2	0.0	0.1	0.4	0.2	0.2	0.3	0.3	•	0.1	•	0.4	•
Employee Benefits	17	0.9	0.7	0.8	0.8	0.8	0.6	1.0	1.3	•	0.3	•	1.1	•
Advertising	18	0.9	0.2	1.6	1.7	0.7	0.4	0.8	0.4	•	0.3	•	0.7	•
Other Expenses	19	10.6	12.7	17.8	12.1	9.8	8.6	9.6	8.5	•	5.8	•	20.9	•
Officers' Compensation	20	2.4	1.0	3.9	4.3	2.8	1.8	1.3	1.0	•	0.4	•	1.7	•
Operating Margin	21	•	•	0.6	•	2.4	•	•	•	•	3.3	•	•	•
Operating Margin Before Officers' Comp.	22	1.2	•	4.6	1.3	5.2	1.1	•	•	•	3.8	•	•	•

Selected Average Balance Sheet ($ in Thousands)														
Net Receivables	23	253	0	21	159	405	1596	2927	9629	•	22330	•	281278	•
Inventories	24	380	0	55	285	830	2884	4150	8180	•	42460	•	146895	•
Net Property, Plant and Equipment	25	240	0	40	108	261	903	2736	7846	•	40357	•	297924	•
Total Assets	26	1549	0	151	734	2048	6889	13932	34930	•	157488	•	3027388	•
Notes and Loans Payable	27	780	0	124	324	657	1980	4031	9357	•	22145	•	2563315	•
All Other Liabilities	28	354	0	85	154	434	954	3227	7572	•	64532	•	676981	•
Net Worth	29	415	0	-58	257	956	3954	6674	18001	•	70811	•	-212909	•
Selected Financial Ratios (Times to 1)														
Current Ratio	30	2.0	•	0.9	3.6	2.9	2.4	2.1	2.1	•	3.6	•	1.0	•
Quick Ratio	31	1.0	•	0.3	2.0	1.3	1.1	0.9	1.1	•	2.3	•	0.6	•
Net Sales to Working Capital	32	5.7	•	•	4.8	4.6	4.7	4.9	5.5	•	3.9	•	•	•
Coverage Ratio	33	1.5	•	2.4	•	6.3	0.3	0.6	1.1	•	12.7	•	0.9	•
Total Asset Turnover	34	1.6	•	3.5	2.9	2.4	2.2	1.8	1.8	•	1.8	•	0.1	•
Inventory Turnover	35	4.6	•	6.0	5.3	4.2	4.1	4.5	5.8	•	5.2	•	1.2	•
Receivables Turnover	36	10.0	•	22.8	13.6	12.2	8.6	8.5	6.8	•	16.2	•	1.4	•
Total Liabilities to Net Worth	37	2.7	•	•	1.9	1.1	0.7	1.1	0.9	•	1.2	•	•	•
Current Assets to Working Capital	38	2.0	•	•	1.4	1.5	1.7	1.9	1.9	•	1.4	•	•	•
Current Liabilities to Working Capital	39	1.0	•	•	0.4	0.5	0.7	0.9	0.9	•	0.4	•	•	•
Working Capital to Net Sales	40	0.2	•	•	0.2	0.2	0.2	0.2	0.2	•	0.3	•	•	•
Inventory to Working Capital	41	0.9	•	•	0.6	0.8	0.8	0.8	0.7	•	0.5	•	•	•
Total Receipts to Cash Flow	42	12.2	17.9	7.6	12.4	10.1	17.8	16.7	15.5	•	12.5	•	12.1	•
Cost of Goods to Cash Flow	43	8.8	14.4	4.7	9.0	7.2	13.5	12.3	11.5	•	9.9	•	7.3	•
Cash Flow to Total Debt	44	0.2	•	0.3	0.4	0.4	0.3	0.2	0.2	•	0.3	•	0.0	•
Selected Financial Factors (in Percentages)														
Debt Ratio	45	73.2	•	138.4	65.0	53.3	42.6	52.1	48.5	•	55.0	•	107.0	•
Return on Total Assets	46	3.5	•	5.3	•	8.5	0.4	0.7	1.5	•	7.0	•	3.7	•
Return on Equity Before Income Taxes	47	4.4	•	•	•	15.3	•	•	0.1	•	14.3	•	8.1	•
Return on Equity After Income Taxes	48	3.9	•	•	•	14.9	•	•	•	•	13.6	•	8.1	•
Profit Margin (Before Income Tax)	49	0.8	•	0.9	•	3.0	•	•	0.0	•	3.6	•	•	•
Profit Margin (After Income Tax)	50	0.7	•	0.8	•	2.9	•	•	•	•	3.5	•	•	•

Table II

Corporations with Net Income

OTHER BUILDING MATERIAL DEALERS

MONEY AMOUNTS AND SIZE OF ASSETS IN THOUSANDS OF DOLLARS

Item Description for Accounting Period 7/11 Through 6/12		Total	Zero Assets	Under 500	500 to 1,000	1,000 to 5,000	5,000 to 10,000	10,000 to 25,000	25,000 to 50,000	50,000 to 100,000	100,000 to 250,000	250,000 to 500,000	500,000 to 2,500,000	2,500,000 and over
Number of Enterprises	1	10573	443	6585	1195	1991	226	90	23	12	•	•	0	0
Revenues ($ in Thousands)														
Net Sales	2	30920328	100179	3489764	3156012	11156936	4347608	2311788	1375291	1426474	•	•	0	0
Interest	3	21194	0	9	2560	8726	665	1194	959	961	•	•	0	0
Rents	4	7667	0	2776	212	256	28	791	835	3	•	•	0	0
Royalties	5	5327	0	3825	0	0	0	0	92	0	•	•	0	0
Other Portfolio Income	6	23098	0	1967	1801	5139	796	1752	5164	1271	•	•	0	0
Other Receipts	7	202860	0	2571	44380	34034	6147	21327	5595	15947	•	•	0	0
Total Receipts	8	31180474	100179	3500912	3204965	11205091	4355244	2336852	1387936	1444656	•	•	0	0
Average Total Receipts	9	2949	226	532	2682	5628	19271	25965	60345	120388	•	•	•	•
Operating Costs/Operating Income (%)														
Cost of Operations	10	71.4	34.6	62.1	71.3	70.6	77.5	72.5	74.9	72.4	•	•	•	•
Salaries and Wages	11	8.2	16.5	7.3	4.5	8.0	9.2	10.0	9.7	11.6	•	•	•	•
Taxes Paid	12	1.8	1.6	1.8	2.9	1.8	1.4	2.0	1.6	1.7	•	•	•	•
Interest Paid	13	0.5	•	0.4	0.2	0.4	0.6	0.5	0.3	0.7	•	•	•	•
Depreciation	14	1.0	•	1.3	0.8	0.7	0.3	1.2	1.3	1.8	•	•	•	•
Amortization and Depletion	15	0.0	•	0.0	0.0	0.0	0.0	0.1	0.1	0.1	•	•	•	•
Pensions and Other Deferred Comp.	16	0.2	•	0.2	0.3	0.2	0.1	0.3	0.2	0.4	•	•	•	•
Employee Benefits	17	0.8	4.7	1.0	0.8	0.8	0.5	1.0	1.4	1.4	•	•	•	•
Advertising	18	1.0	1.1	1.8	2.1	0.5	0.2	0.9	0.5	0.6	•	•	•	•
Other Expenses	19	9.6	35.3	15.2	10.0	9.7	7.9	9.2	6.7	6.6	•	•	•	•
Officers' Compensation	20	2.3	•	4.1	3.7	2.7	1.5	1.4	0.9	0.7	•	•	•	•
Operating Margin	21	3.2	6.2	4.8	3.3	4.6	0.9	1.0	2.3	1.8	•	•	•	•
Operating Margin Before Officers' Comp.	22	5.5	6.2	8.9	7.1	7.3	2.4	2.4	3.3	2.5	•	•	•	•

Selected Average Balance Sheet ($ in Thousands)

Net Receivables	23	260	0	13	191	414	1925	2840	7214	14151	•	•	•	•
Inventories	24	414	0	46	303	835	2692	4428	7879	15928	•	•	•	•
Net Property, Plant and Equipment	25	249	0	43	99	253	479	2384	6677	21534	•	•	•	•
Total Assets	26	1409	0	126	728	2185	7188	13844	32914	74527	•	•	•	•
Notes and Loans Payable	27	474	0	78	208	639	2709	3420	1866	17529	•	•	•	•
All Other Liabilities	28	283	0	39	167	469	968	3025	7356	11982	•	•	•	•
Net Worth	29	652	0	9	353	1078	3511	7399	23692	45017	•	•	•	•

Selected Financial Ratios (Times to 1)

Current Ratio	30	2.4	•	1.7	3.7	2.8	2.2	2.3	3.0	2.3	•	•	•	•
Quick Ratio	31	1.1	•	0.7	1.9	1.2	1.1	1.0	1.4	1.2	•	•	•	•
Net Sales to Working Capital	32	5.3	•	15.3	6.0	4.9	5.3	4.5	4.2	5.2	•	•	•	•
Coverage Ratio	33	9.3	•	13.5	33.3	12.6	2.7	5.6	13.1	5.3	•	•	•	•
Total Asset Turnover	34	2.1	•	4.2	3.6	2.6	2.7	1.9	1.8	1.6	•	•	•	•
Inventory Turnover	35	5.0	•	7.2	6.2	4.7	5.5	4.2	5.7	5.4	•	•	•	•
Receivables Turnover	36	12.7	•	30.2	13.6	14.7	11.0	8.4	9.9	9.6	•	•	•	•
Total Liabilities to Net Worth	37	1.2	•	12.9	1.1	1.0	1.0	0.9	0.4	0.7	•	•	•	•
Current Assets to Working Capital	38	1.7	•	2.3	1.4	1.5	1.8	1.8	1.5	1.7	•	•	•	•
Current Liabilities to Working Capital	39	0.7	•	1.3	0.4	0.5	0.8	0.8	0.5	0.7	•	•	•	•
Working Capital to Net Sales	40	0.2	•	0.1	0.2	0.2	0.2	0.2	0.2	0.2	•	•	•	•
Inventory to Working Capital	41	0.8	•	1.2	0.6	0.8	0.9	0.7	0.6	0.8	•	•	•	•
Total Receipts to Cash Flow	42	9.4	2.8	6.6	8.5	8.4	15.6	12.8	12.5	14.4	•	•	•	•
Cost of Goods to Cash Flow	43	6.7	1.0	4.1	6.0	5.9	12.1	9.3	9.4	10.4	•	•	•	•
Cash Flow to Total Debt	44	0.4	•	0.7	0.8	0.6	0.3	0.3	0.5	0.3	•	•	•	•

Selected Financial Factors (in Percentages)

Debt Ratio	45	53.7	•	92.8	51.4	50.7	51.2	46.6	28.0	39.6	•	•	•	•
Return on Total Assets	46	9.3	•	23.2	18.2	13.9	4.4	4.7	6.4	6.0	•	•	•	•
Return on Equity Before Income Taxes	47	18.0	•	298.3	36.4	26.0	5.7	7.2	8.2	8.1	•	•	•	•
Return on Equity After Income Taxes	48	17.4	•	293.9	35.7	25.4	5.6	6.8	7.8	7.8	•	•	•	•
Profit Margin (Before Income Tax)	49	4.0	6.2	5.1	4.9	5.0	1.0	2.1	3.3	3.1	•	•	•	•
Profit Margin (After Income Tax)	50	3.9	6.2	5.0	4.8	4.9	1.0	2.0	3.1	2.9	•	•	•	•

Table I

Corporations with and without Net Income

LAWN AND GARDEN EQUIPMENT AND SUPPLIES STORES

MONEY AMOUNTS AND SIZE OF ASSETS IN THOUSANDS OF DOLLARS

Item Description for Accounting Period 7/11 Through 6/12		Total	Zero Assets	Under 500	500 to 1,000	1,000 to 5,000	5,000 to 10,000	10,000 to 25,000	25,000 to 50,000	50,000 to 100,000	100,000 to 250,000	250,000 to 500,000	500,000 to 2,500,000	2,500,000 and over
Number of Enterprises	1	8148	•	5140	1622	918	•	•	12	•	0	•	0	0
Revenues ($ in Thousands)														
Net Sales	2	14419950	•	2582878	3598319	4835652	•	•	1021213	•	0	•	0	0
Interest	3	12798	•	132	363	10463	•	•	834	•	0	•	0	0
Rents	4	3432	•	0	0	3384	•	•	48	•	0	•	0	0
Royalties	5	0	•	0	0	0	•	•	0	•	0	•	0	0
Other Portfolio Income	6	15285	•	12	10927	3222	•	•	100	•	0	•	0	0
Other Receipts	7	79842	•	6692	5828	32466	•	•	1987	•	0	•	0	0
Total Receipts	8	14531307	•	2589714	3615437	4885187	•	•	1024182	•	0	•	0	0
Average Total Receipts	9	1783	•	504	2229	5322	•	•	85348	•	•	•	•	•
Operating Costs/Operating Income (%)														
Cost of Operations	10	71.5	•	66.1	72.1	72.6	•	•	70.2	•	•	•	•	•
Salaries and Wages	11	9.2	•	9.7	10.3	9.2	•	•	10.2	•	•	•	•	•
Taxes Paid	12	2.1	•	2.9	2.6	1.8	•	•	1.9	•	•	•	•	•
Interest Paid	13	0.8	•	0.9	0.7	0.8	•	•	0.8	•	•	•	•	•
Depreciation	14	1.5	•	1.6	1.5	1.5	•	•	2.4	•	•	•	•	•
Amortization and Depletion	15	0.0	•	0.0	0.0	0.0	•	•	0.1	•	•	•	•	•
Pensions and Other Deferred Comp.	16	0.2	•	0.0	0.1	0.2	•	•	0.0	•	•	•	•	•
Employee Benefits	17	0.7	•	0.7	0.7	0.7	•	•	0.5	•	•	•	•	•
Advertising	18	1.1	•	1.4	0.8	1.1	•	•	0.8	•	•	•	•	•
Other Expenses	19	10.0	•	12.6	9.0	9.3	•	•	8.5	•	•	•	•	•
Officers' Compensation	20	2.8	•	5.0	3.0	2.4	•	•	1.2	•	•	•	•	•
Operating Margin	21	0.2	•	•	•	0.5	•	•	3.3	•	•	•	•	•
Operating Margin Before Officers' Comp.	22	3.0	•	4.1	2.1	2.9	•	•	4.6	•	•	•	•	•

Selected Average Balance Sheet ($ in Thousands)													
Net Receivables 23	69	•	10	86	230	•	•	4732	•	•	•	•	•
Inventories 24	344	•	77	308	1183	•	•	17232	•	•	•	•	•
Net Property, Plant and Equipment 25	178	•	56	172	617	•	•	5698	•	•	•	•	•
Total Assets 26	752	•	173	791	2400	•	•	35397	•	•	•	•	•
Notes and Loans Payable 27	368	•	116	323	1066	•	•	13560	•	•	•	•	•
All Other Liabilities 28	201	•	73	211	460	•	•	7469	•	•	•	•	•
Net Worth 29	182	•	-15	257	873	•	•	14368	•	•	•	•	•
Selected Financial Ratios (Times to 1)													
Current Ratio 30	1.5	•	1.4	2.3	1.5	•	•	1.9	•	•	•	•	•
Quick Ratio 31	0.4	•	0.3	1.0	0.4	•	•	0.5	•	•	•	•	•
Net Sales to Working Capital 32	10.7	•	15.9	6.6	10.1	•	•	7.9	•	•	•	•	•
Coverage Ratio 33	2.2	•	0.2	0.4	3.0	•	•	5.7	•	•	•	•	•
Total Asset Turnover 34	2.4	•	2.9	2.8	2.2	•	•	2.4	•	•	•	•	•
Inventory Turnover 35	3.7	•	4.3	5.2	3.2	•	•	3.5	•	•	•	•	•
Receivables Turnover 36	25.0	•	43.6	29.0	20.8	•	•	17.4	•	•	•	•	•
Total Liabilities to Net Worth 37	3.1	•	•	2.1	1.7	•	•	1.5	•	•	•	•	•
Current Assets to Working Capital 38	3.0	•	3.5	1.8	3.1	•	•	2.1	•	•	•	•	•
Current Liabilities to Working Capital 39	2.0	•	2.5	0.8	2.1	•	•	1.1	•	•	•	•	•
Working Capital to Net Sales 40	0.1	•	0.1	0.2	0.1	•	•	0.1	•	•	•	•	•
Inventory to Working Capital 41	2.0	•	2.7	1.0	2.2	•	•	1.5	•	•	•	•	•
Total Receipts to Cash Flow 42	12.2	•	11.5	17.0	12.5	•	•	11.1	•	•	•	•	•
Cost of Goods to Cash Flow 43	8.7	•	7.6	12.3	9.1	•	•	7.8	•	•	•	•	•
Cash Flow to Total Debt 44	0.3	•	0.2	0.2	0.3	•	•	0.4	•	•	•	•	•
Selected Financial Factors (in Percentages)													
Debt Ratio 45	75.8	•	108.6	67.5	63.6	•	•	59.4	•	•	•	•	•
Return on Total Assets 46	4.0	•	0.6	0.9	5.0	•	•	10.6	•	•	•	•	•
Return on Equity Before Income Taxes 47	9.2	•	21.5	•	9.0	•	•	21.5	•	•	•	•	•
Return on Equity After Income Taxes 48	7.9	•	22.0	•	7.4	•	•	20.6	•	•	•	•	•
Profit Margin (Before Income Tax) 49	0.9	•	•	•	1.5	•	•	3.6	•	•	•	•	•
Profit Margin (After Income Tax) 50	0.8	•	•	•	1.2	•	•	3.5	•	•	•	•	•

Table II

Corporations with Net Income

LAWN AND GARDEN EQUIPMENT AND SUPPLIES STORES

MONEY AMOUNTS AND SIZE OF ASSETS IN THOUSANDS OF DOLLARS

Item Description for Accounting Period 7/11 Through 6/12		Total	Zero Assets	Under 500	500 to 1,000	1,000 to 5,000	5,000 to 10,000	10,000 to 25,000	25,000 to 50,000	50,000 to 100,000	100,000 to 250,000	250,000 to 500,000	500,000 to 2,500,000	2,500,000 and over
Number of Enterprises	1	3742	352	1932	871	523	23	•	12	•	0	0	0	0
Revenues ($ in Thousands)														
Net Sales	2	8905179	14299	915485	2497694	2529959	510982	•	1021213	•	0	0	0	0
Interest	3	11271	0	131	284	9024	997	•	834	•	0	0	0	0
Rents	4	1272	0	0	0	1224	0	•	48	•	0	0	0	0
Royalties	5	0	0	0	0	0	0	•	0	•	0	0	0	0
Other Portfolio Income	6	8582	0	0	4974	2617	0	•	100	•	0	0	0	0
Other Receipts	7	58774	0	4958	3511	19650	5352	•	1987	•	0	0	0	0
Total Receipts	8	8985078	14299	920574	2506463	2562474	517331	•	1024182	•	0	0	0	0
Average Total Receipts	9	2401	41	476	2878	4900	22493	•	85348	•	•	•	•	•
Operating Costs/Operating Income (%)														
Cost of Operations	10	71.3	•	57.1	72.5	73.2	73.2	•	70.2	•	•	•	•	•
Salaries and Wages	11	8.5	•	9.9	9.5	7.8	8.7	•	10.2	•	•	•	•	•
Taxes Paid	12	1.9	•	2.8	2.2	2.0	1.3	•	1.9	•	•	•	•	•
Interest Paid	13	0.5	6.3	0.4	0.4	0.6	0.7	•	0.8	•	•	•	•	•
Depreciation	14	1.5	28.5	2.1	1.0	1.6	0.6	•	2.4	•	•	•	•	•
Amortization and Depletion	15	0.0	•	•	•	0.0	•	•	0.1	•	•	•	•	•
Pensions and Other Deferred Comp.	16	0.2	•	•	0.2	0.3	0.4	•	0.0	•	•	•	•	•
Employee Benefits	17	0.5	•	0.4	0.4	0.5	0.4	•	0.5	•	•	•	•	•
Advertising	18	1.0	•	2.0	0.5	0.9	0.2	•	0.8	•	•	•	•	•
Other Expenses	19	9.3	60.6	16.2	8.1	7.2	11.6	•	8.5	•	•	•	•	•
Officers' Compensation	20	2.3	•	3.8	2.7	2.9	2.2	•	1.2	•	•	•	•	•
Operating Margin	21	2.9	4.6	5.4	2.5	3.0	0.6	•	3.3	•	•	•	•	•
Operating Margin Before Officers' Comp.	22	5.2	4.6	9.1	5.2	5.9	2.8	•	4.6	•	•	•	•	•

Selected Average Balance Sheet ($ in Thousands)													
Net Receivables 23	97	0	6	124	246	801	•	4732	•	•	•	•	•
Inventories 24	406	0	98	223	1150	2641	•	16154	•	•	•	•	•
Net Property, Plant and Equipment 25	192	0	57	132	664	1270	•	5698	•	•	•	•	•
Total Assets 26	896	0	181	839	2213	7614	•	35397	•	•	•	•	•
Notes and Loans Payable 27	296	0	112	214	571	3815	•	13560	•	•	•	•	•
All Other Liabilities 28	243	0	67	229	513	1758	•	7469	•	•	•	•	•
Net Worth 29	357	0	2	396	1129	2042	•	14368	•	•	•	•	•
Selected Financial Ratios (Times to 1)													
Current Ratio 30	1.9	•	1.7	2.4	2.1	2.0	•	1.9	•	•	•	•	•
Quick Ratio 31	0.6	•	0.3	1.4	0.7	0.3	•	0.5	•	•	•	•	•
Net Sales to Working Capital 32	7.7	•	9.7	7.2	6.4	8.0	•	7.9	•	•	•	•	•
Coverage Ratio 33	8.1	1.7	15.5	7.4	8.6	3.5	•	5.7	•	•	•	•	•
Total Asset Turnover 34	2.7	•	2.6	3.4	2.2	2.9	•	2.4	•	•	•	•	•
Inventory Turnover 35	4.2	•	2.7	9.3	3.1	6.2	•	3.7	•	•	•	•	•
Receivables Turnover 36	25.3	•	•	27.9	17.6	45.4	•	•	•	•	•	•	•
Total Liabilities to Net Worth 37	1.5	•	87.5	1.1	1.0	2.7	•	1.5	•	•	•	•	•
Current Assets to Working Capital 38	2.1	•	2.5	1.7	1.9	2.0	•	2.1	•	•	•	•	•
Current Liabilities to Working Capital 39	1.1	•	1.5	0.7	0.9	1.0	•	1.1	•	•	•	•	•
Working Capital to Net Sales 40	0.1	•	0.1	0.1	0.2	0.1	•	0.1	•	•	•	•	•
Inventory to Working Capital 41	1.3	•	2.0	0.7	1.2	1.3	•	1.5	•	•	•	•	•
Total Receipts to Cash Flow 42	9.5	2.7	5.7	11.8	10.8	9.1	•	11.1	•	•	•	•	•
Cost of Goods to Cash Flow 43	6.8	•	3.2	8.5	7.9	6.7	•	7.8	•	•	•	•	•
Cash Flow to Total Debt 44	0.5	•	0.5	0.6	0.4	0.4	•	0.4	•	•	•	•	•
Selected Financial Factors (in Percentages)													
Debt Ratio 45	60.2	•	98.9	52.8	49.0	73.2	•	59.4	•	•	•	•	•
Return on Total Assets 46	11.4	•	16.6	11.2	10.5	7.5	•	10.6	•	•	•	•	•
Return on Equity Before Income Taxes 47	25.1	•	1375.1	20.6	18.3	20.0	•	21.5	•	•	•	•	•
Return on Equity After Income Taxes 48	23.7	•	1365.7	19.7	16.0	18.6	•	20.6	•	•	•	•	•
Profit Margin (Before Income Tax) 49	3.8	4.6	5.9	2.8	4.3	1.8	•	3.6	•	•	•	•	•
Profit Margin (After Income Tax) 50	3.6	4.6	5.9	2.7	3.7	1.7	•	3.5	•	•	•	•	•

Table I

Corporations with and without Net Income

FOOD AND BEVERAGE STORES

MONEY AMOUNTS AND SIZE OF ASSETS IN THOUSANDS OF DOLLARS

Item Description for Accounting Period 7/11 Through 6/12		Total	Zero Assets	Under 500	500 to 1,000	1,000 to 5,000	5,000 to 10,000	10,000 to 25,000	25,000 to 50,000	50,000 to 100,000	100,000 to 250,000	250,000 to 500,000	500,000 to 2,500,000	2,500,000 and over
Number of Enterprises	1	75845	6938	59640	3878	4375	588	218	63	51	42	14	26	11
Revenues ($ in Thousands)														
Net Sales	2	530720317	6798244	44628295	14209935	34526475	16120913	17442431	8215635	12411489	22244451	16103966	92539534	245478949
Interest	3	492380	93	2491	2263	3992	6107	1017	2567	1988	1958	1591	58244	410069
Rents	4	509277	0	511	5153	7633	19404	10675	9167	3691	21718	16066	116639	298620
Royalties	5	1826102	0	0	82	0	103	2310	9414	11306	12834	0	71562	1718492
Other Portfolio Income	6	1866459	5079	8436	10197	17626	2562	9913	21418	3255	5804	3309	349870	1428993
Other Receipts	7	5034253	123629	648608	-103305	326084	155739	140412	78900	159949	181239	87823	1671538	1563632
Total Receipts	8	540448788	6927045	45288341	14124325	34881810	16304828	17606758	8337101	12591678	22468004	16212755	94807387	250898755
Average Total Receipts	9	7126	998	759	3642	7973	27729	80765	132335	246896	534952	1158054	3646438	22808978
Operating Costs/Operating Income (%)														
Cost of Operations	10	74.8	68.0	74.5	75.7	74.5	75.0	78.0	81.0	74.7	72.5	74.6	76.3	74.2
Salaries and Wages	11	9.3	12.8	7.0	8.5	9.2	10.1	8.4	7.1	10.1	11.3	10.5	9.5	9.4
Taxes Paid	12	1.5	1.7	2.0	1.3	1.5	1.5	1.2	1.4	1.6	1.7	1.6	1.4	1.5
Interest Paid	13	0.5	0.3	0.2	0.3	0.3	0.4	0.3	0.3	0.5	0.4	0.4	0.9	0.6
Depreciation	14	2.1	1.6	0.8	0.5	1.3	1.3	1.2	1.3	2.3	2.1	2.6	2.4	2.6
Amortization and Depletion	15	0.1	0.2	0.3	0.3	0.1	0.2	0.1	0.0	0.1	0.1	0.2	0.3	0.1
Pensions and Other Deferred Comp.	16	0.4	0.1	0.0	0.0	0.1	0.1	0.1	0.2	0.4	0.3	0.2	0.6	0.6
Employee Benefits	17	1.2	0.1	0.2	0.3	0.7	0.7	0.8	1.3	1.6	1.5	1.2	1.5	1.4
Advertising	18	0.7	1.0	0.4	0.4	1.2	0.9	0.8	0.7	0.8	0.8	0.7	0.7	0.5
Other Expenses	19	8.9	16.4	12.4	9.0	10.5	8.1	8.8	6.7	8.5	9.1	7.7	7.6	8.5
Officers' Compensation	20	0.5	1.1	2.5	1.6	1.1	0.8	0.5	0.6	0.4	0.3	0.2	0.1	0.1
Operating Margin	21	0.0	•	•	2.2	•	0.9	•	•	•	•	0.1	•	0.6
Operating Margin Before Officers' Comp.	22	0.5	•	2.3	3.8	0.7	1.7	0.3	•	•	0.2	0.3	•	0.7

Selected Average Balance Sheet ($ in Thousands)

Net Receivables	23	183	0	2	71	265	292	745	2698	4885	7069	18931	45509	892712
Inventories	24	346	0	37	204	370	1461	3317	6645	11700	25952	50183	179340	1145289
Net Property, Plant and Equipment	25	1013	0	28	142	643	2286	4834	11702	23974	70603	177322	585547	4251829
Total Assets	26	2435	0	120	755	1878	6822	15539	34903	68453	148552	325367	1220718	10064997
Notes and Loans Payable	27	647	0	67	319	726	2420	4149	10896	22052	44798	92702	329289	2252683
All Other Liabilities	28	1045	0	21	145	543	1659	4838	12675	22926	48066	112907	501199	4947796
Net Worth	29	743	0	33	291	609	2743	6552	11333	23475	55688	119757	390230	2864518

Selected Financial Ratios (Times to 1)

Current Ratio	30	1.0	•	2.8	2.7	1.7	1.6	1.4	1.4	1.2	1.2	1.0	1.1	0.8
Quick Ratio	31	0.5	•	1.0	1.4	0.9	0.6	0.6	0.6	0.6	0.4	0.4	0.4	0.4
Net Sales to Working Capital	32	648.7	•	17.8	13.7	20.0	25.4	38.9	27.0	44.6	76.9	259.9	95.9	•
Coverage Ratio	33	4.6	•	7.7	6.3	2.9	6.2	3.5	4.2	1.9	3.4	2.6	2.3	6.3
Total Asset Turnover	34	2.9	•	6.2	4.9	4.2	4.0	5.1	3.7	3.6	3.6	3.5	2.9	2.2
Inventory Turnover	35	15.1	•	15.1	13.6	15.9	14.1	18.8	15.9	15.5	14.8	17.1	15.2	14.5
Receivables Turnover	36	40.3	•	365.2	55.9	33.1	64.9	77.2	39.7	51.3	74.1	62.5	77.0	27.1
Total Liabilities to Net Worth	37	2.3	•	2.7	1.6	2.1	1.5	1.4	2.1	1.9	1.7	1.7	2.1	2.5
Current Assets to Working Capital	38	79.3	•	1.6	1.6	2.4	2.8	3.7	3.4	5.4	7.6	21.5	9.4	•
Current Liabilities to Working Capital	39	78.3	•	0.6	0.6	1.4	1.8	2.7	2.4	4.4	6.6	20.5	8.4	•
Working Capital to Net Sales	40	0.0	•	0.1	0.1	0.0	0.0	0.0	0.0	0.0	0.0	0.0	0.0	•
Inventory to Working Capital	41	32.4	•	0.9	0.6	1.1	1.3	1.6	1.3	2.1	4.0	12.1	4.8	•
Total Receipts to Cash Flow	42	13.1	14.1	12.4	13.5	13.5	13.3	15.5	20.1	18.0	15.0	17.6	16.5	11.5
Cost of Goods to Cash Flow	43	9.8	9.6	9.2	10.2	10.1	10.0	12.1	16.3	13.4	10.9	13.1	12.6	8.5
Cash Flow to Total Debt	44	0.3	•	0.7	0.6	0.5	0.5	0.6	0.3	0.3	0.4	0.3	0.3	0.3

Selected Financial Factors (in Percentages)

Debt Ratio	45	69.5	•	73.0	61.5	67.6	59.8	57.8	67.5	65.7	62.5	63.2	68.0	71.5
Return on Total Assets	46	7.1	•	9.1	9.1	3.8	9.7	5.3	4.5	3.0	4.3	4.2	5.9	8.0
Return on Equity Before Income Taxes	47	18.3	•	29.5	19.8	7.6	20.2	8.9	10.5	4.1	8.0	7.1	10.4	23.6
Return on Equity After Income Taxes	48	12.8	•	28.5	19.5	6.6	19.1	8.4	9.5	2.9	6.8	5.3	6.9	15.5
Profit Margin (Before Income Tax)	49	1.9	•	1.3	1.6	0.6	2.0	0.7	0.9	0.4	0.8	0.7	1.1	3.0
Profit Margin (After Income Tax)	50	1.4	•	1.2	1.5	0.5	1.9	0.7	0.8	0.3	0.7	0.6	0.8	2.0

Table II

Corporations with Net Income

FOOD AND BEVERAGE STORES

MONEY AMOUNTS AND SIZE OF ASSETS IN THOUSANDS OF DOLLARS

Item Description for Accounting Period 7/11 Through 6/12		Total	Zero Assets	Under 500	500 to 1,000	1,000 to 5,000	5,000 to 10,000	10,000 to 25,000	25,000 to 50,000	50,000 to 100,000	100,000 to 250,000	250,000 to 500,000	500,000 to 2,500,000	2,500,000 and over
Number of Enterprises	1	45603	3050	36662	2646	2495	462	146	39	33	28	10	20	11
Revenues ($ in Thousands)														
Net Sales	2	464597682	5381554	34907672	12219922	23973601	12556186	10890957	5802344	9132486	14977628	12048686	77227698	245478949
Interest	3	488619	44	1690	969	3661	5925	852	2336	1909	1646	1591	57928	410069
Rents	4	447945	0	500	4483	4296	16674	2236	4313	2299	14688	16066	83772	298620
Royalties	5	1813262	0	0	0	0	83	444	9414	433	12834	0	71562	1718492
Other Portfolio Income	6	1822891	0	6208	9472	12978	2339	8062	20771	1843	4096	2529	325603	1428993
Other Receipts	7	4235155	99730	463918	-117791	193098	133021	105453	54120	110420	123905	74711	1430929	1563632
Total Receipts	8	473405554	5481328	35379988	12117055	24187634	12714228	11008004	5893298	9249390	15134797	12143583	79197492	250898755
Average Total Receipts	9	10381	1797	965	4579	9694	27520	75397	151110	280285	540528	1214358	3959875	22808978
Operating Costs/Operating Income (%)														
Cost of Operations	10	75.0	68.0	75.7	76.3	76.1	74.8	76.6	82.3	74.8	72.5	74.2	76.9	74.2
Salaries and Wages	11	9.1	13.9	6.3	7.7	7.6	9.7	9.1	6.3	10.0	11.1	10.9	9.1	9.4
Taxes Paid	12	1.5	1.4	1.8	1.2	1.4	1.4	1.3	1.2	1.5	1.7	1.7	1.3	1.5
Interest Paid	13	0.5	0.1	0.1	0.3	0.2	0.3	0.2	0.2	0.3	0.3	0.3	0.7	0.6
Depreciation	14	2.1	1.4	0.5	0.5	0.8	1.1	1.0	1.1	1.9	2.0	2.6	2.4	2.6
Amortization and Depletion	15	0.1	0.2	0.2	0.1	0.1	0.2	0.1	0.0	0.1	0.1	0.1	0.2	0.1
Pensions and Other Deferred Comp.	16	0.4	0.1	0.0	0.0	0.1	0.1	0.2	0.2	0.4	0.3	0.3	0.6	0.6
Employee Benefits	17	1.2	0.0	0.1	0.3	0.6	0.7	0.7	0.8	1.3	1.5	1.2	1.5	1.4
Advertising	18	0.6	1.1	0.4	0.3	0.9	1.1	0.9	0.7	0.6	0.9	0.7	0.6	0.5
Other Expenses	19	8.4	14.2	11.0	8.0	9.2	8.0	8.4	5.8	8.3	8.8	7.3	6.9	8.5
Officers' Compensation	20	0.4	0.9	2.1	1.6	1.2	0.9	0.5	0.6	0.5	0.3	0.2	0.2	0.1
Operating Margin	21	0.7	•	1.6	3.5	1.9	1.8	0.9	0.9	0.4	0.7	0.4	•	0.6
Operating Margin Before Officers' Comp.	22	1.1	•	3.7	5.1	3.1	2.7	1.5	1.5	0.9	1.0	0.7	•	0.7

Selected Average Balance Sheet ($ in Thousands)													
Net Receivables 23	276	0	3	95	273	279	693	3361	3915	7061	12336	47168	892712
Inventories 24	468	0	42	196	416	1481	3667	7669	13230	28070	59823	168308	1045625
Net Property, Plant and Equipment 25	1492	0	27	136	539	1839	4136	10530	24378	65894	191322	606128	4251829
Total Assets 26	3601	0	144	749	1836	6659	14982	34288	67580	147840	313125	1276659	10064997
Notes and Loans Payable 27	844	0	54	247	477	2241	2868	7034	16191	38428	78316	289063	2252683
All Other Liabilities 28	1546	0	24	138	455	1516	4362	9506	21313	45486	115366	443698	4947796
Net Worth 29	1210	0	66	364	905	2902	7752	17748	30076	63925	119444	543898	2864518

Selected Financial Ratios (Times to 1)													
Current Ratio 30	1.0	•	3.1	2.9	1.9	2.0	1.7	1.8	1.4	1.4	1.0	1.1	0.8
Quick Ratio 31	0.5	•	1.3	1.6	1.0	0.8	0.8	0.9	0.6	0.5	0.3	0.4	0.4
Net Sales to Working Capital 32	•	•	16.7	14.7	20.8	17.2	21.4	22.1	36.8	35.5	534.9	122.0	•
Coverage Ratio 33	6.6	4.9	23.7	10.6	13.0	9.8	11.7	12.1	7.8	7.8	4.7	4.3	6.3
Total Asset Turnover 34	2.8	•	6.6	6.2	5.2	4.1	5.0	4.3	4.1	3.6	3.8	3.0	2.2
Inventory Turnover 35	16.3	•	17.1	17.9	17.6	13.7	15.6	16.0	15.7	13.8	15.0	17.7	15.8
Receivables Turnover 36	40.3	•	420.9	57.1	43.4	63.7	64.8	47.9	60.8	•	•	84.3	28.0
Total Liabilities to Net Worth 37	2.0	•	1.2	1.1	1.0	1.3	0.9	0.9	1.2	1.3	1.6	1.3	2.5
Current Assets to Working Capital 38	•	•	1.5	1.5	2.2	2.0	2.4	2.3	3.8	3.7	41.5	11.8	•
Current Liabilities to Working Capital 39	•	•	0.5	0.5	1.2	1.0	1.4	1.3	2.8	2.7	40.5	10.8	•
Working Capital to Net Sales 40	•	•	0.1	0.1	0.0	0.1	0.0	0.0	0.0	0.0	0.0	0.0	•
Inventory to Working Capital 41	•	•	0.8	0.6	0.9	0.9	1.1	0.9	1.7	1.9	26.6	5.8	•
Total Receipts to Cash Flow 42	12.3	11.7	11.3	12.4	11.3	12.1	13.0	16.8	14.6	14.0	16.9	14.6	11.5
Cost of Goods to Cash Flow 43	9.2	7.9	8.6	9.5	8.6	9.1	9.9	13.8	10.9	10.1	12.5	11.2	8.5
Cash Flow to Total Debt 44	0.3	•	1.1	1.0	0.9	0.6	0.8	0.5	0.5	0.5	0.4	0.4	0.3

Selected Financial Factors (in Percentages)													
Debt Ratio 45	66.4	•	54.1	51.4	50.7	56.4	48.3	48.2	55.5	56.8	61.9	57.4	71.5
Return on Total Assets 46	9.0	•	20.7	18.3	16.0	13.7	10.9	11.6	8.1	7.3	6.0	8.6	8.0
Return on Equity Before Income Taxes 47	22.7	•	43.2	34.1	30.0	28.3	19.3	20.5	15.8	14.7	12.3	15.4	23.6
Return on Equity After Income Taxes 48	17.1	•	42.4	33.8	28.9	27.0	18.6	19.5	14.3	13.0	9.8	12.1	15.5
Profit Margin (Before Income Tax) 49	2.7	0.5	3.0	2.7	2.8	3.0	2.0	2.4	1.7	1.8	1.2	2.2	3.0
Profit Margin (After Income Tax) 50	2.0	0.5	2.9	2.7	2.7	2.9	1.9	2.3	1.6	1.6	1.0	1.7	2.0

Table I

Corporations with and without Net Income

BEER, WINE, AND LIQUOR STORES

Item Description for Accounting Period 7/11 Through 6/12		Total	Zero Assets	Under 500	500 to 1,000	1,000 to 5,000	5,000 to 10,000	10,000 to 25,000	25,000 to 50,000	50,000 to 100,000	100,000 to 250,000	250,000 to 500,000	500,000 to 2,500,000	2,500,000 and over
		MONEY AMOUNTS AND SIZE OF ASSETS IN THOUSANDS OF DOLLARS												
Number of Enterprises	1	19793	408	15282	3087	891	87	23	8	0	5	0	0	0
Revenues ($ in Thousands)														
Net Sales	2	27969636	102287	11825729	5479998	4840279	1807694	1090741	502478	0	2320432	0	0	0
Interest	3	6102	0	638	80	2388	1714	857	0	0	426	0	0	0
Rents	4	2886	0	1254	110	567	0	0	0	0	956	0	0	0
Royalties	5	0	0	0	0	0	0	0	0	0	0	0	0	0
Other Portfolio Income	6	60313	5901	48710	0	4160	0	3	0	0	1538	0	0	0
Other Receipts	7	396059	2	268692	74206	9894	12797	16172	4822	0	9471	0	0	0
Total Receipts	8	28434996	108190	12145023	5554394	4857288	1822205	1107773	507300	0	2332823	0	0	0
Average Total Receipts	9	1437	265	795	1799	5452	20945	48164	63412	•	466565	•	•	•
Operating Costs/Operating Income (%)														
Cost of Operations	10	77.8	106.4	76.3	79.2	78.3	82.8	77.8	78.5	•	76.0	•	•	•
Salaries and Wages	11	5.4	0.4	5.3	4.8	5.3	5.0	6.4	6.3	•	8.0	•	•	•
Taxes Paid	12	2.1	0.3	3.3	1.4	1.6	0.6	0.9	1.1	•	1.1	•	•	•
Interest Paid	13	0.6	0.1	0.6	0.5	0.5	0.1	0.2	1.6	•	1.0	•	•	•
Depreciation	14	0.7	1.5	0.6	0.5	0.4	0.3	0.3	1.1	•	2.0	•	•	•
Amortization and Depletion	15	0.4	0.3	0.5	0.5	0.1	0.1	0.1	0.7	•	0.2	•	•	•
Pensions and Other Deferred Comp.	16	0.1	•	0.1	0.0	0.1	0.0	0.0	0.0	•	0.1	•	•	•
Employee Benefits	17	0.2	0.0	0.1	0.2	0.3	•	0.4	0.2	•	0.7	•	•	•
Advertising	18	0.6	2.0	0.3	0.7	0.7	0.6	0.9	0.7	•	1.3	•	•	•
Other Expenses	19	9.7	22.0	10.3	10.2	9.0	6.9	11.1	10.0	•	7.7	•	•	•
Officers' Compensation	20	2.6	0.2	4.1	1.8	1.9	0.6	1.1	1.6	•	0.7	•	•	•
Operating Margin	21	•	•	•	0.3	1.9	3.2	0.8	•	•	1.3	•	•	•
Operating Margin Before Officers' Comp.	22	2.5	•	2.6	2.2	3.9	3.7	1.8	•	•	1.9	•	•	•

Selected Average Balance Sheet ($ in Thousands)													
Net Receivables **23**	13	0	1	11	76	691	150	4926	•	5884	•	•	•
Inventories **24**	219	0	92	364	977	3624	5089	23420	•	62248	•	•	•
Net Property, Plant and Equipment **25**	83	0	33	120	400	624	1382	7177	•	52831	•	•	•
Total Assets **26**	487	0	218	758	2046	6728	12089	44798	•	187169	•	•	•
Notes and Loans Payable **27**	237	0	130	378	956	754	2321	20174	•	79837	•	•	•
All Other Liabilities **28**	102	0	36	121	490	1429	5487	13162	•	57973	•	•	•
Net Worth **29**	149	0	51	259	600	4544	4281	11462	•	49359	•	•	•
Selected Financial Ratios (Times to 1)													
Current Ratio **30**	2.8	•	3.1	4.0	2.5	2.7	1.3	2.4	•	1.6	•	•	•
Quick Ratio **31**	0.7	•	0.8	1.1	0.5	1.2	0.3	0.5	•	0.2	•	•	•
Net Sales to Working Capital **32**	6.8	•	8.2	4.8	6.0	5.5	25.5	3.3	•	12.1	•	•	•
Coverage Ratio **33**	3.8	•	2.8	4.5	5.6	54.7	14.8	0.5	•	2.8	•	•	•
Total Asset Turnover **34**	2.9	•	3.6	2.3	2.7	3.1	3.9	1.4	•	2.5	•	•	•
Inventory Turnover **35**	5.0	•	6.4	3.9	4.4	4.7	7.2	2.1	•	5.7	•	•	•
Receivables Turnover **36**	93.4	•	770.2	222.3	81.6	14.0	462.1	11.8	•	90.7	•	•	•
Total Liabilities to Net Worth **37**	2.3	•	3.3	1.9	2.4	0.5	1.8	2.9	•	2.8	•	•	•
Current Assets to Working Capital **38**	1.6	•	1.5	1.3	1.7	1.6	4.3	1.7	•	2.6	•	•	•
Current Liabilities to Working Capital **39**	0.6	•	0.5	0.3	0.7	0.6	3.3	0.7	•	1.6	•	•	•
Working Capital to Net Sales **40**	0.1	•	0.1	0.2	0.2	0.2	0.0	0.3	•	0.1	•	•	•
Inventory to Working Capital **41**	1.1	•	1.1	1.0	1.3	0.9	3.2	0.9	•	1.8	•	•	•
Total Receipts to Cash Flow **42**	14.0	•	14.3	13.0	13.4	12.1	8.7	17.7	•	19.6	•	•	•
Cost of Goods to Cash Flow **43**	10.9	•	10.9	10.3	10.5	10.1	6.8	13.9	•	14.9	•	•	•
Cash Flow to Total Debt **44**	0.3	•	0.3	0.3	0.3	0.8	0.7	0.1	•	0.2	•	•	•
Selected Financial Factors (in Percentages)													
Debt Ratio **45**	69.4	•	76.5	65.8	70.7	32.5	64.6	74.4	•	73.6	•	•	•
Return on Total Assets **46**	6.3	•	6.4	5.0	7.3	12.5	9.8	1.0	•	6.9	•	•	•
Return on Equity Before Income Taxes **47**	15.1	•	17.6	11.5	20.5	18.2	25.7	•	•	16.8	•	•	•
Return on Equity After Income Taxes **48**	14.2	•	17.1	11.3	17.8	17.9	25.7	•	•	14.2	•	•	•
Profit Margin (Before Income Tax) **49**	1.6	•	1.2	1.7	2.3	4.0	2.3	•	•	1.8	•	•	•
Profit Margin (After Income Tax) **50**	1.5	•	1.1	1.6	2.0	3.9	2.3	•	•	1.5	•	•	•

BEER, WINE, AND LIQUOR STORES

MONEY AMOUNTS AND SIZE OF ASSETS IN THOUSANDS OF DOLLARS

Item Description for Accounting Period 7/11 Through 6/12		Total	Zero Assets	Under 500	500 to 1,000	1,000 to 5,000	5,000 to 10,000	10,000 to 25,000	25,000 to 50,000	50,000 to 100,000	100,000 to 250,000	250,000 to 500,000	500,000 to 2,500,000	2,500,000 and over
Number of Enterprises	1	12200	81	9535	1721	746	87	20	4	0	5	0	0	0
Revenues ($ in Thousands)														
Net Sales	2	21394615	12882	8261893	3697488	4097094	1807694	900763	296370	0	2320432	0	0	0
Interest	3	4811	0	238	61	2372	1714	0	0	0	426	0	0	0
Rents	4	2843	0	1254	66	567	0	0	0	0	956	0	0	0
Royalties	5	0	0	0	0	0	0	0	0	0	0	0	0	0
Other Portfolio Income	6	46197	5901	38680	0	74	0	3	0	0	1538	0	0	0
Other Receipts	7	266814	2	184310	43201	9485	12797	4424	3124	0	9471	0	0	0
Total Receipts	8	21715280	18785	8486375	3740816	4109592	1822205	905190	299494	0	2332823	0	0	0
Average Total Receipts	9	1780	232	890	2174	5509	20945	45260	74874	•	466565	•	•	•
Operating Costs/Operating Income (%)														
Cost of Operations	10	77.9	80.6	76.6	78.8	78.6	82.8	76.7	79.7	•	76.0	•	•	•
Salaries and Wages	11	5.1	3.1	4.3	4.8	5.1	5.0	6.4	5.3	•	8.0	•	•	•
Taxes Paid	12	1.7	1.3	2.4	1.2	1.6	0.6	0.9	1.1	•	1.1	•	•	•
Interest Paid	13	0.4	0.7	0.2	0.4	0.4	0.1	0.2	1.1	•	1.0	•	•	•
Depreciation	14	0.5	0.1	0.4	0.3	0.4	0.3	0.2	0.7	•	2.0	•	•	•
Amortization and Depletion	15	0.2	2.4	0.3	0.1	0.1	0.1	0.1	0.4	•	0.2	•	•	•
Pensions and Other Deferred Comp.	16	0.1	•	0.1	0.0	0.1	0.0	0.0	0.0	•	0.1	•	•	•
Employee Benefits	17	0.2	0.2	0.1	0.2	0.3	•	0.5	0.3	•	0.7	•	•	•
Advertising	18	0.6	0.4	0.3	1.0	0.5	0.6	0.8	0.7	•	1.3	•	•	•
Other Expenses	19	8.6	28.2	9.5	8.4	7.7	6.9	10.4	8.0	•	7.7	•	•	•
Officers' Compensation	20	2.6	1.3	4.4	2.1	1.8	0.6	1.2	2.8	•	0.7	•	•	•
Operating Margin	21	2.1	•	1.4	2.5	3.4	3.2	2.5	0.1	•	1.3	•	•	•
Operating Margin Before Officers' Comp.	22	4.7	•	5.8	4.7	5.2	3.7	3.7	2.9	•	1.9	•	•	•

Selected Average Balance Sheet ($ in Thousands)													
Net Receivables 23	14	0	1	11	54	691	27	2247	•	5884	•	•	•
Inventories 24	258	0	102	361	969	3624	4203	23392	•	70187	•	•	•
Net Property, Plant and Equipment 25	85	0	21	81	454	624	1500	2746	•	52831	•	•	•
Total Assets 26	575	0	228	756	2136	6728	11307	50401	•	187169	•	•	•
Notes and Loans Payable 27	206	0	64	345	954	754	2670	19608	•	79837	•	•	•
All Other Liabilities 28	136	0	44	161	496	1429	5000	21232	•	57973	•	•	•
Net Worth 29	232	0	120	250	686	4544	3637	9561	•	49359	•	•	•
Selected Financial Ratios (Times to 1)													
Current Ratio 30	2.7	•	3.9	3.4	2.5	2.7	1.4	2.1	•	1.6	•	•	•
Quick Ratio 31	0.7	•	1.1	1.1	0.5	1.2	0.3	0.2	•	0.2	•	•	•
Net Sales to Working Capital 32	6.6	•	7.0	5.3	5.8	5.5	20.9	3.1	•	12.1	•	•	•
Coverage Ratio 33	11.0	39.6	20.0	11.6	9.7	54.7	15.9	2.0	•	2.8	•	•	•
Total Asset Turnover 34	3.0	•	3.8	2.8	2.6	3.1	4.0	1.5	•	2.5	•	•	•
Inventory Turnover 35	5.3	•	6.5	4.7	4.5	4.7	8.2	2.5	•	5.0	•	•	•
Receivables Turnover 36	92.1	•	1287.1	281.7	92.0	14.0	1279.5	•	•	•	•	•	•
Total Liabilities to Net Worth 37	1.5	•	0.9	2.0	2.1	0.5	2.1	4.3	•	2.8	•	•	•
Current Assets to Working Capital 38	1.6	•	1.3	1.4	1.7	1.6	3.7	1.9	•	2.6	•	•	•
Current Liabilities to Working Capital 39	0.6	•	0.3	0.4	0.7	0.6	2.7	0.9	•	1.6	•	•	•
Working Capital to Net Sales 40	0.2	•	0.1	0.2	0.2	0.2	0.0	0.3	•	0.1	•	•	•
Inventory to Working Capital 41	1.1	•	0.9	0.9	1.3	0.9	2.8	1.0	•	1.8	•	•	•
Total Receipts to Cash Flow 42	11.8	•	10.9	11.7	11.8	12.1	8.8	16.3	•	19.6	•	•	•
Cost of Goods to Cash Flow 43	9.2	•	8.3	9.2	9.2	10.1	6.8	13.0	•	14.9	•	•	•
Cash Flow to Total Debt 44	0.4	•	0.7	0.4	0.3	0.8	0.7	0.1	•	0.2	•	•	•
Selected Financial Factors (in Percentages)													
Debt Ratio 45	59.6	•	47.5	66.9	67.9	32.5	67.8	81.0	•	73.6	•	•	•
Return on Total Assets 46	12.2	•	16.5	11.5	10.5	12.5	12.9	3.3	•	6.9	•	•	•
Return on Equity Before Income Taxes 47	27.4	•	29.9	31.9	29.4	18.2	37.5	8.8	•	16.8	•	•	•
Return on Equity After Income Taxes 48	26.4	•	29.6	31.5	26.5	17.9	37.5	8.8	•	14.2	•	•	•
Profit Margin (Before Income Tax) 49	3.6	27.6	4.1	3.7	3.7	4.0	3.0	1.1	•	1.8	•	•	•
Profit Margin (After Income Tax) 50	3.5	27.3	4.1	3.7	3.3	3.9	3.0	1.1	•	1.5	•	•	•

Table I

Corporations with and without Net Income

HEALTH AND PERSONAL CARE STORES

MONEY AMOUNTS AND SIZE OF ASSETS IN THOUSANDS OF DOLLARS

Item Description for Accounting Period 7/11 Through 6/12		Total	Zero Assets	Under 500	500 to 1,000	1,000 to 5,000	5,000 to 10,000	10,000 to 25,000	25,000 to 50,000	50,000 to 100,000	100,000 to 250,000	250,000 to 500,000	500,000 to 2,500,000	2,500,000 and over
Number of Enterprises	1	43603	4282	31044	3939	4028	146	96	25	12	16	3	6	5
Revenues ($ in Thousands)														
Net Sales	2	310795563	1115682	26847099	12782382	25405866	4029839	4337419	2122720	2440415	6351853	2228254	10739044	212394991
Interest	3	77347	70	1165	1326	3318	1133	5524	829	22	12688	46	4281	46945
Rents	4	168742	0	8	2265	187	737	45	0	0	7140	4428	973	152960
Royalties	5	115360	0	0	0	0	0	0	0	0	10918	0	53860	50582
Other Portfolio Income	6	1088232	14091	3204	2325	15954	430	4976	6814	1148	7092	65	28261	1003870
Other Receipts	7	4511346	48407	47852	30288	192414	42505	33826	36376	17431	73766	16039	43294	3929149
Total Receipts	8	316756590	1178250	26899328	12818586	25617739	4074644	4381790	2166739	2459016	6463457	2248832	10869713	217578497
Average Total Receipts	9	7265	275	866	3254	6360	27909	45644	86670	204918	403966	749611	1811619	43515699
Operating Costs/Operating Income (%)														
Cost of Operations	10	72.0	66.4	68.9	75.0	69.7	78.9	67.6	56.4	74.2	72.9	51.1	60.7	73.4
Salaries and Wages	11	9.9	14.7	7.3	8.4	11.4	7.8	13.6	20.3	12.5	10.3	18.6	12.9	9.7
Taxes Paid	12	1.2	1.8	1.9	1.5	1.3	0.8	1.3	3.3	1.1	1.2	2.7	2.2	1.1
Interest Paid	13	0.7	0.2	0.2	0.2	0.5	0.2	0.6	1.1	1.0	1.0	1.8	1.9	0.7
Depreciation	14	1.3	0.4	0.6	0.3	0.9	1.2	2.3	1.7	1.2	1.6	3.8	2.1	1.4
Amortization and Depletion	15	0.3	0.1	0.1	0.1	0.3	0.1	0.4	0.3	0.5	0.4	0.6	1.0	0.3
Pensions and Other Deferred Comp.	16	0.3	0.3	0.2	0.4	0.3	0.2	0.2	0.3	0.2	0.2	0.1	0.2	0.3
Employee Benefits	17	0.9	0.3	0.3	0.6	0.5	0.9	0.8	0.5	1.1	1.3	1.4	0.7	1.0
Advertising	18	0.8	1.0	0.6	0.6	0.8	0.6	1.8	1.0	0.7	2.0	2.3	1.2	0.7
Other Expenses	19	9.7	20.2	11.2	6.3	9.7	6.4	9.1	15.2	8.2	9.9	15.0	11.9	9.5
Officers' Compensation	20	1.1	2.7	6.6	4.8	2.5	1.0	0.9	1.1	0.5	0.4	0.9	0.9	0.0
Operating Margin	21	1.9	•	2.3	1.9	2.1	2.0	1.3	•	•	•	1.7	4.3	2.0
Operating Margin Before Officers' Comp.	22	3.0	•	8.9	6.6	4.7	3.0	2.2	•	•	•	2.7	5.2	2.0

Selected Average Balance Sheet ($ in Thousands)													
Net Receivables 23	662	0	14	83	269	2339	4636	9261	18804	32750	19911	103673	4915682
Inventories 24	671	0	60	284	428	1181	2570	7265	12582	26470	125873	181592	4378769
Net Property, Plant and Equipment 25	522	0	18	43	222	1365	2194	5044	7124	18207	100522	152810	3795787
Total Assets 26	3539	0	139	713	1673	6918	15337	33331	75013	162969	369670	1165903	25102173
Notes and Loans Payable 27	864	0	57	128	556	1437	4779	13906	28746	55536	95574	487116	5545946
All Other Liabilities 28	1076	0	37	175	446	3428	14161	21123	28385	59811	151859	289697	7485403
Net Worth 29	1598	0	46	409	671	2053	-3603	-1698	17882	47622	122237	389090	12070824

Selected Financial Ratios (Times to 1)													
Current Ratio 30	1.5	•	2.9	3.0	2.2	1.2	0.6	1.1	1.3	1.5	0.9	2.3	1.4
Quick Ratio 31	0.8	•	1.3	1.3	1.2	0.9	0.4	0.6	0.8	0.8	0.2	0.9	0.8
Net Sales to Working Capital 32	12.6	•	12.1	8.9	9.9	31.2	•	84.5	28.1	14.6	•	6.9	12.7
Coverage Ratio 33	6.9	•	14.8	13.5	7.5	20.8	4.7	2.0	0.4	1.5	2.5	3.8	7.4
Total Asset Turnover 34	2.0	•	6.2	4.6	3.8	4.0	2.9	2.5	2.7	2.4	2.0	1.5	1.7
Inventory Turnover 35	7.7	•	9.9	8.6	10.3	18.4	11.9	6.6	12.0	10.9	3.0	6.0	7.1
Receivables Turnover 36	11.6	•	69.2	37.2	23.2	12.9	10.6	11.9	9.6	19.0	15.3	18.2	9.3
Total Liabilities to Net Worth 37	1.2	•	2.0	0.7	1.5	2.4	•	•	3.2	2.4	2.0	2.0	1.1
Current Assets to Working Capital 38	2.9	•	1.5	1.5	1.8	5.7	•	20.9	4.8	3.1	•	1.7	3.2
Current Liabilities to Working Capital 39	1.9	•	0.5	0.5	0.8	4.7	•	19.9	3.8	2.1	•	0.7	2.2
Working Capital to Net Sales 40	0.1	•	0.1	0.1	0.1	0.0	•	0.0	0.0	0.1	•	0.1	0.1
Inventory to Working Capital 41	1.2	•	0.8	0.8	0.7	1.3	•	7.7	1.5	1.1	•	0.9	1.3
Total Receipts to Cash Flow 42	10.2	11.3	11.6	15.9	9.5	12.1	10.7	8.7	18.1	13.9	10.3	8.4	9.9
Cost of Goods to Cash Flow 43	7.3	7.5	8.0	12.0	6.6	9.5	7.3	4.9	13.4	10.1	5.3	5.1	7.2
Cash Flow to Total Debt 44	0.4	•	0.8	0.7	0.7	0.5	0.2	0.3	0.2	0.2	0.3	0.3	0.3

Selected Financial Factors (in Percentages)													
Debt Ratio 45	54.8	•	67.0	42.5	59.9	70.3	123.5	105.1	76.2	70.8	66.9	66.6	51.9
Return on Total Assets 46	9.2	•	16.6	10.6	12.9	12.9	8.6	5.5	1.1	3.6	8.9	11.3	8.8
Return on Equity Before Income Taxes 47	17.4	•	46.8	17.1	27.9	41.4	•	•	•	4.3	16.1	25.0	15.8
Return on Equity After Income Taxes 48	12.2	•	45.9	16.5	27.0	36.6	•	•	•	2.7	10.8	17.4	10.3
Profit Margin (Before Income Tax) 49	3.9	•	2.5	2.2	3.0	3.1	2.3	1.1	•	0.5	2.7	5.4	4.5
Profit Margin (After Income Tax) 50	2.7	•	2.4	2.1	2.9	2.7	2.2	0.7	•	0.3	1.8	3.8	2.9

Table II

Corporations with Net Income

HEALTH AND PERSONAL CARE STORES

MONEY AMOUNTS AND SIZE OF ASSETS IN THOUSANDS OF DOLLARS

Item Description for Accounting Period 7/11 Through 6/12		Total	Zero Assets	Under 500	500 to 1,000	1,000 to 5,000	5,000 to 10,000	10,000 to 25,000	25,000 to 50,000	50,000 to 100,000	100,000 to 250,000	250,000 to 500,000	500,000 to 2,500,000	2,500,000 and over
Number of Enterprises	1	29064	951	21491	3084	3309	114	68	19	•	12	0	6	•
Revenues ($ in Thousands)														
Net Sales	2	266802595	719035	21560422	9130779	21364255	3855192	3370036	1742871	•	6643262	0	10739044	•
Interest	3	62591	21	793	939	2913	450	3807	816	•	1645	0	4281	•
Rents	4	123209	0	8	2146	68	737	0	0	•	10944	0	973	•
Royalties	5	104442	0	0	0	0	0	0	0	•	0	0	53860	•
Other Portfolio Income	6	1075738	13778	3203	1645	7379	262	4860	6814	•	4563	0	28261	•
Other Receipts	7	3700900	41951	40253	20635	176247	13161	27292	35434	•	59958	0	43294	•
Total Receipts	8	271869475	774785	21604679	9156144	21550862	3869802	3405995	1785935	•	6720372	0	10869713	•
Average Total Receipts	9	9354	815	1005	2969	6513	33946	50088	93997	•	560031	•	1811619	•
Operating Costs/Operating Income (%)														
Cost of Operations	10	71.5	64.3	66.9	72.8	68.8	79.7	70.4	53.2	•	71.2	•	60.7	•
Salaries and Wages	11	9.6	10.9	6.9	8.7	11.7	7.2	11.8	22.9	•	11.2	•	12.9	•
Taxes Paid	12	1.2	1.6	1.8	1.5	1.3	0.7	1.2	2.9	•	1.5	•	2.2	•
Interest Paid	13	0.5	0.1	0.2	0.2	0.4	0.1	0.3	0.8	•	0.8	•	1.9	•
Depreciation	14	1.3	0.4	0.4	0.3	0.7	0.8	1.9	1.7	•	1.6	•	2.1	•
Amortization and Depletion	15	0.3	•	0.1	0.2	0.2	0.1	0.3	0.3	•	0.2	•	1.0	•
Pensions and Other Deferred Comp.	16	0.4	0.5	0.2	0.5	0.3	0.2	0.3	0.3	•	0.2	•	0.2	•
Employee Benefits	17	0.8	0.2	0.3	0.6	0.4	0.8	0.8	0.6	•	1.3	•	0.7	•
Advertising	18	0.7	0.2	0.5	0.6	0.8	0.5	0.7	1.1	•	1.0	•	1.2	•
Other Expenses	19	9.8	15.2	10.9	7.0	9.3	5.4	7.8	14.7	•	9.2	•	11.9	•
Officers' Compensation	20	1.0	3.6	6.7	4.5	2.5	0.7	1.0	1.2	•	0.4	•	0.9	•
Operating Margin	21	3.0	2.9	5.1	3.2	3.3	3.6	3.6	0.0	•	1.4	•	4.3	•
Operating Margin Before Officers' Comp.	22	4.0	6.5	11.8	7.7	5.9	4.3	4.6	1.3	•	1.9	•	5.2	•

Selected Average Balance Sheet ($ in Thousands)												
Net Receivables 23	924	0	13	83	281	2544	5328	11245	•	28190	•	103673	•
Inventories 24	841	0	70	260	410	1117	2350	6295	•	47402	•	1682367	•
Net Property, Plant and Equipment 25	687	0	18	47	212	1042	1660	5568	•	31173	•	152810	•
Total Assets 26	4867	0	154	693	1674	6859	14884	35220	•	200720	•	1165903	•
Notes and Loans Payable 27	988	0	46	98	490	1528	3307	12356	•	55594	•	487116	•
All Other Liabilities 28	1384	0	33	148	416	3550	5317	22628	•	72326	•	289697	•
Net Worth 29	2495	0	75	447	768	1782	6259	236	•	72800	•	389090	•
Selected Financial Ratios (Times to 1)												
Current Ratio 30	1.5	•	3.3	3.3	2.5	1.1	1.7	0.9	•	1.4	•	2.3	•
Quick Ratio 31	0.8	•	1.4	1.5	1.4	0.8	1.2	0.6	•	0.6	•	0.9	•
Net Sales to Working Capital 32	11.9	•	11.7	8.4	9.0	91.4	11.7	•	•	22.0	•	6.9	•
Coverage Ratio 33	10.4	87.8	33.2	16.7	11.0	28.7	19.7	4.5	•	4.1	•	3.8	•
Total Asset Turnover 34	1.9	•	6.5	4.3	3.9	4.9	3.3	2.6	•	2.8	•	1.5	•
Inventory Turnover 35	7.8	•	9.6	8.3	10.8	24.1	14.8	7.8	•	8.3	•	0.6	•
Receivables Turnover 36	11.1	•	79.0	33.3	24.7	20.9	10.5	10.7	•	•	•	1.1	•
Total Liabilities to Net Worth 37	1.0	•	1.0	0.5	1.2	2.8	1.4	148.2	•	1.8	•	2.0	•
Current Assets to Working Capital 38	2.8	•	1.4	1.4	1.7	14.2	2.4	•	•	3.8	•	1.7	•
Current Liabilities to Working Capital 39	1.8	•	0.4	0.4	0.7	13.2	1.4	•	•	2.8	•	0.7	•
Working Capital to Net Sales 40	0.1	•	0.1	0.1	0.1	0.0	0.1	•	•	0.0	•	0.1	•
Inventory to Working Capital 41	1.1	•	0.8	0.7	0.6	3.4	0.7	•	•	1.9	•	0.9	•
Total Receipts to Cash Flow 42	9.1	5.5	8.9	12.6	8.8	12.0	9.1	7.7	•	13.4	•	8.4	•
Cost of Goods to Cash Flow 43	6.5	3.5	6.0	9.2	6.1	9.6	6.4	4.1	•	9.5	•	5.1	•
Cash Flow to Total Debt 44	0.4	•	1.4	1.0	0.8	0.6	0.6	0.3	•	0.3	•	0.3	•
Selected Financial Factors (in Percentages)												
Debt Ratio 45	48.7	•	50.9	35.5	54.1	74.0	57.9	99.3	•	63.7	•	66.6	•
Return on Total Assets 46	10.3	•	35.6	15.7	17.8	20.3	16.5	9.9	•	9.5	•	11.3	•
Return on Equity Before Income Taxes 47	18.2	•	70.3	22.8	35.2	75.3	37.2	1147.4	•	19.8	•	25.0	•
Return on Equity After Income Taxes 48	13.2	•	69.5	22.1	34.2	68.2	36.5	961.4	•	16.2	•	17.4	•
Profit Margin (Before Income Tax) 49	4.9	10.7	5.3	3.4	4.2	4.0	4.7	3.0	•	2.6	•	5.4	•
Profit Margin (After Income Tax) 50	3.6	10.6	5.2	3.3	4.1	3.6	4.6	2.5	•	2.1	•	3.8	•

Table I

Corporations with and without Net Income

GASOLINE STATIONS

MONEY AMOUNTS AND SIZE OF ASSETS IN THOUSANDS OF DOLLARS

Item Description for Accounting Period 7/11 Through 6/12		Total	Zero Assets	Under 500	500 to 1,000	1,000 to 5,000	5,000 to 10,000	10,000 to 25,000	25,000 to 50,000	50,000 to 100,000	100,000 to 250,000	250,000 to 500,000	500,000 to 2,500,000	2,500,000 and over
Number of Enterprises	1	42898	3639	28486	5817	4343	267	203	67	39	22	0	14	0
Revenues ($ in Thousands)														
Net Sales	2	343811669	4567242	58270040	31585125	54046290	6952050	21446883	19820407	15864057	27446407	0	103813168	0
Interest	3	53026	0	378	924	2430	564	1069	2878	3426	370	0	40987	0
Rents	4	155971	0	5642	6413	7933	8865	10280	7344	8448	7581	0	93465	0
Royalties	5	50328	0	0	0	399	0	0	1	0	0	0	49928	0
Other Portfolio Income	6	261643	43335	37374	3561	67277	9114	16561	4125	8883	9770	0	61643	0
Other Receipts	7	1983882	8402	429083	99777	203917	29707	194303	93976	78942	138157	0	707618	0
Total Receipts	8	346316519	4618979	58742517	31695800	54328246	7000300	21669096	19928731	15963756	27602285	0	104766809	0
Average Total Receipts	9	8073	1269	2062	5449	12509	26218	106744	297444	409327	1254649	•	7483344	•
Operating Costs/Operating Income (%)														
Cost of Operations	10	90.8	91.3	89.3	91.0	90.7	89.9	90.3	92.5	92.6	91.8	•	90.9	•
Salaries and Wages	11	2.6	1.3	2.4	2.0	2.8	2.6	3.7	2.6	2.3	2.8	•	2.6	•
Taxes Paid	12	0.8	0.5	0.9	0.9	0.8	0.7	0.7	0.5	0.5	0.5	•	1.0	•
Interest Paid	13	0.3	0.1	0.1	0.3	0.5	0.8	0.2	0.2	0.3	0.2	•	0.3	•
Depreciation	14	1.0	0.0	0.3	0.6	0.6	0.9	1.1	0.8	1.1	1.2	•	1.5	•
Amortization and Depletion	15	0.1	0.0	0.1	0.1	0.1	0.1	0.0	0.0	0.0	0.1	•	0.1	•
Pensions and Other Deferred Comp.	16	0.0	0.1	0.0	0.0	0.0	0.0	0.0	0.0	0.0	0.0	•	0.1	•
Employee Benefits	17	0.1	0.0	0.1	0.0	0.1	0.1	0.1	0.1	0.1	0.2	•	0.2	•
Advertising	18	0.1	0.0	0.1	0.0	0.1	0.1	0.1	0.1	0.1	0.1	•	0.1	•
Other Expenses	19	4.0	4.4	6.1	4.3	4.1	4.0	4.2	3.2	3.1	2.9	•	3.3	•
Officers' Compensation	20	0.4	1.6	0.9	0.7	0.5	0.4	0.3	0.2	0.2	0.1	•	0.1	•
Operating Margin	21	•	0.7	•	0.1	•	0.4	•	•	•	0.2	•	•	•
Operating Margin Before Officers' Comp.	22	0.2	2.3	0.6	0.8	0.2	0.8	•	•	•	0.3	•	•	•

Selected Average Balance Sheet ($ in Thousands)

Item	No.													
Net Receivables	23	93	0	6	27	135	209	1960	4434	6289	14768	•	125165	•
Inventories	24	140	0	48	109	192	771	1829	4169	6028	19117	•	113559	•
Net Property, Plant and Equipment	25	599	0	56	374	1044	3190	7064	16892	34788	109016	•	730873	•
Total Assets	26	1214	0	181	704	1852	6388	15794	35541	65461	198112	•	1470109	•
Notes and Loans Payable	27	468	0	100	436	1459	3908	5515	10283	23329	52701	•	245149	•
All Other Liabilities	28	349	0	34	99	375	945	5187	13125	17808	67089	•	530689	•
Net Worth	29	397	0	47	168	18	1535	5092	12133	24323	78322	•	694271	•

Selected Financial Ratios (Times to 1)

Item	No.													
Current Ratio	30	1.4	•	2.7	2.1	1.6	1.7	1.1	1.2	1.2	1.0	•	1.2	•
Quick Ratio	31	0.7	•	1.2	0.8	0.9	0.8	0.7	0.6	0.7	0.5	•	0.7	•
Net Sales to Working Capital	32	70.0	•	34.7	45.8	56.7	35.5	157.6	138.2	133.1	•	•	100.4	•
Coverage Ratio	33	3.0	36.5	4.5	2.5	1.4	2.4	2.3	2.9	2.0	4.4	•	3.9	•
Total Asset Turnover	34	6.6	•	11.3	7.7	6.7	4.1	6.7	8.3	6.2	6.3	•	5.0	•
Inventory Turnover	35	52.0	•	38.3	45.4	58.7	30.3	52.2	65.7	62.5	59.9	•	59.4	•
Receivables Turnover	36	90.4	•	242.1	202.3	105.9	58.0	58.7	67.0	69.7	105.2	•	67.3	•
Total Liabilities to Net Worth	37	2.1	•	2.9	3.2	101.9	3.2	2.1	1.9	1.7	1.5	•	1.1	•
Current Assets to Working Capital	38	3.5	•	1.6	1.9	2.6	2.5	8.5	6.8	7.6	•	•	5.7	•
Current Liabilities to Working Capital	39	2.5	•	0.6	0.9	1.6	1.5	7.5	5.8	6.6	•	•	4.7	•
Working Capital to Net Sales	40	0.0	•	0.0	0.0	0.0	0.0	0.0	0.0	0.0	•	•	0.0	•
Inventory to Working Capital	41	1.2	•	0.8	1.0	0.9	0.9	2.7	2.0	2.0	•	•	1.6	•
Total Receipts to Cash Flow	42	31.6	22.0	25.6	29.2	32.6	24.0	32.9	38.8	39.8	36.1	•	34.1	•
Cost of Goods to Cash Flow	43	28.7	20.1	22.8	26.5	29.6	21.5	29.7	35.9	36.8	33.1	•	31.0	•
Cash Flow to Total Debt	44	0.3	•	0.6	0.3	0.2	0.2	0.3	0.3	0.2	0.3	•	0.3	•

Selected Financial Factors (in Percentages)

Item	No.													
Debt Ratio	45	67.3	•	74.0	76.1	99.0	76.0	67.8	65.9	62.8	60.5	•	52.8	•
Return on Total Assets	46	5.5	•	7.4	5.7	4.8	7.7	3.4	4.0	3.3	6.1	•	5.4	•
Return on Equity Before Income Taxes	47	11.3	•	22.3	14.3	151.0	18.7	5.9	7.6	4.4	11.9	•	8.6	•
Return on Equity After Income Taxes	48	10.1	•	21.7	14.2	146.4	16.8	5.2	7.1	3.8	11.4	•	7.1	•
Profit Margin (Before Income Tax)	49	0.6	1.8	0.5	0.4	0.2	1.1	0.3	0.3	0.3	0.7	•	0.8	•
Profit Margin (After Income Tax)	50	0.5	1.8	0.5	0.4	0.2	1.0	0.2	0.3	0.2	0.7	•	0.7	•

Table II

Corporations with Net Income

GASOLINE STATIONS

MONEY AMOUNTS AND SIZE OF ASSETS IN THOUSANDS OF DOLLARS

Item Description for Accounting Period 7/11 Through 6/12		Total	Zero Assets	Under 500	500 to 1,000	1,000 to 5,000	5,000 to 10,000	10,000 to 25,000	25,000 to 50,000	50,000 to 100,000	100,000 to 250,000	250,000 to 500,000	500,000 to 2,500,000	2,500,000 and over
Number of Enterprises	1	27144	1538	17871	4053	3229	226	128	45	28	17	0	10	0
Revenues ($ in Thousands)														
Net Sales	2	258772933	4087626	41521431	25429910	37902897	5967391	15092951	12563072	12123911	25438998	0	78644746	0
Interest	3	48228	0	318	19	1931	564	664	1502	2137	322	0	40772	0
Rents	4	91805	0	5642	6393	7284	8865	6345	2012	7196	6619	0	41450	0
Royalties	5	49929	0	0	0	0	0	0	1	0	0	0	49928	0
Other Portfolio Income	6	178015	43335	18263	2640	27596	8722	12219	2086	3220	6977	0	52956	0
Other Receipts	7	1715107	7315	345604	77367	174215	23008	159597	65306	60657	132510	0	669526	0
Total Receipts	8	260856017	4138276	41891258	25516329	38113923	6008550	15271776	12633979	12197121	25585426	0	79499378	0
Average Total Receipts	9	9610	2691	2344	6296	11804	26587	119311	280755	435611	1505025	•	7949938	•
Operating Costs/Operating Income (%)														
Cost of Operations	10	90.8	91.5	88.8	91.1	90.8	89.4	90.0	93.2	93.1	91.9	•	90.9	•
Salaries and Wages	11	2.4	1.1	2.1	2.0	2.6	2.7	3.9	2.3	2.1	2.7	•	2.4	•
Taxes Paid	12	0.8	0.4	0.9	0.9	0.7	0.8	0.6	0.5	0.5	0.5	•	1.1	•
Interest Paid	13	0.3	0.1	0.1	0.3	0.5	0.6	0.2	0.2	0.2	0.2	•	0.3	•
Depreciation	14	0.9	0.0	0.3	0.5	0.6	0.9	0.8	0.6	1.0	1.2	•	1.4	•
Amortization and Depletion	15	0.1	0.0	0.1	0.1	0.1	0.1	0.0	0.0	0.0	0.1	•	0.0	•
Pensions and Other Deferred Comp.	16	0.0	0.1	0.0	0.0	0.0	0.0	0.0	0.0	0.0	0.0	•	0.1	•
Employee Benefits	17	0.1	0.0	0.0	0.0	0.1	0.1	0.1	0.1	0.1	0.1	•	0.2	•
Advertising	18	0.1	0.0	0.1	0.0	0.1	0.1	0.1	0.1	0.1	0.1	•	0.1	•
Other Expenses	19	3.8	3.7	6.1	3.9	3.4	4.1	4.2	2.8	2.9	2.8	•	3.3	•
Officers' Compensation	20	0.4	1.5	1.0	0.7	0.5	0.4	0.2	0.2	0.1	0.1	•	0.0	•
Operating Margin	21	0.3	1.6	0.6	0.4	0.5	0.7	•	0.1	•	0.3	•	0.1	•
Operating Margin Before Officers' Comp.	22	0.7	3.1	1.5	1.2	1.1	1.1	•	0.3	0.1	0.4	•	0.1	•

Selected Average Balance Sheet ($ in Thousands)

Net Receivables 23	111	0	7	29	96	230	2389	5000	6195	16545	•	143343	•
Inventories 24	150	0	48	110	155	752	1975	4299	5954	22580	•	102517	•
Net Property, Plant and Equipment 25	662	0	45	358	970	3017	5771	15548	33398	123463	•	742146	•
Total Assets 26	1394	0	181	713	1698	6431	15861	35700	65035	214256	•	1569095	•
Notes and Loans Payable 27	386	0	74	393	950	3392	5331	9422	18956	57808	•	109083	•
All Other Liabilities 28	415	0	32	112	256	1033	5332	12297	17316	75522	•	617591	•
Net Worth 29	593	0	74	207	492	2007	5197	13980	28762	80925	•	842421	•

Selected Financial Ratios (Times to 1)

Current Ratio 30	1.4	•	3.2	2.1	2.3	1.5	1.2	1.3	1.3	0.9	•	1.2	•
Quick Ratio 31	0.7	•	1.5	0.8	1.3	0.7	0.8	0.7	0.8	0.5	•	0.6	•
Net Sales to Working Capital 32	67.9	•	32.9	49.9	40.2	39.3	108.7	78.4	82.0	•	•	133.4	•
Coverage Ratio 33	5.3	50.7	16.5	3.7	3.2	3.2	6.3	5.0	4.6	5.2	•	5.6	•
Total Asset Turnover 34	6.8	•	12.8	8.8	6.9	4.1	7.4	7.8	6.7	7.0	•	5.0	•
Inventory Turnover 35	57.8	•	42.9	51.8	68.9	31.4	53.7	60.5	67.7	60.9	•	69.7	•
Receivables Turnover 36	97.2	•	258.2	205.0	135.3	118.0	56.3	54.0	•	111.9	•	72.5	•
Total Liabilities to Net Worth 37	1.3	•	1.4	2.4	2.5	2.2	2.1	1.6	1.3	1.6	•	0.9	•
Current Assets to Working Capital 38	3.3	•	1.5	1.9	1.8	2.9	6.1	4.2	4.6	•	•	7.6	•
Current Liabilities to Working Capital 39	2.3	•	0.5	0.9	0.8	1.9	5.1	3.2	3.6	•	•	6.6	•
Working Capital to Net Sales 40	0.0	•	0.0	0.0	0.0	0.0	0.0	0.0	0.0	•	•	0.0	•
Inventory to Working Capital 41	1.2	•	0.7	1.0	0.6	1.1	1.7	1.0	1.1	•	•	2.1	•
Total Receipts to Cash Flow 42	28.3	20.6	21.4	29.0	29.2	22.4	27.5	36.7	38.3	35.2	•	29.8	•
Cost of Goods to Cash Flow 43	25.7	18.9	19.0	26.4	26.5	20.1	24.7	34.2	35.7	32.4	•	27.0	•
Cash Flow to Total Debt 44	0.4	•	1.0	0.4	0.3	0.3	0.4	0.4	0.3	0.3	•	0.4	•

Selected Financial Factors (in Percentages)

Debt Ratio 45	57.4	•	58.9	70.9	71.0	68.8	67.2	60.8	55.8	62.2	•	46.3	•
Return on Total Assets 46	9.2	•	19.9	9.5	11.0	8.0	8.1	6.6	4.9	7.3	•	7.1	•
Return on Equity Before Income Taxes 47	17.6	•	45.5	23.6	26.2	17.8	20.7	13.4	8.7	15.5	•	10.9	•
Return on Equity After Income Taxes 48	16.4	•	44.9	23.5	26.0	16.1	19.5	12.8	7.9	14.9	•	9.1	•
Profit Margin (Before Income Tax) 49	1.1	2.8	1.5	0.8	1.1	1.4	0.9	0.7	0.6	0.8	•	1.2	•
Profit Margin (After Income Tax) 50	1.0	2.8	1.4	0.8	1.1	1.2	0.9	0.6	0.5	0.8	•	1.0	•

CLOTHING AND CLOTHING ACCESSORIES STORES

MONEY AMOUNTS AND SIZE OF ASSETS IN THOUSANDS OF DOLLARS

Item Description for Accounting Period 7/11 Through 6/12		Total	Zero Assets	Under 500	500 to 1,000	1,000 to 5,000	5,000 to 10,000	10,000 to 25,000	25,000 to 50,000	50,000 to 100,000	100,000 to 250,000	250,000 to 500,000	500,000 to 2,500,000	2,500,000 and over
Number of Enterprises	1	51829	11043	33831	3697	2705	250	143	36	38	23	21	32	10
Revenues ($ in Thousands)														
Net Sales	2	192820345	2519174	12571175	5131970	10414935	2707375	3472126	2753304	4613164	7570627	13988237	56791955	70286302
Interest	3	531453	3285	682	2117	5060	854	18536	1588	696	1194	13079	87908	396454
Rents	4	108847	149	1539	0	3210	0	1062	357	1025	9820	1123	34712	55850
Royalties	5	555745	21	0	0	0	0	1894	5096	1601	48862	37536	194844	265890
Other Portfolio Income	6	473681	28	31911	3666	5950	579	8586	48128	6479	403	5913	14584	347457
Other Receipts	7	2459095	24264	42612	31752	101981	21121	66840	30032	50042	130532	141984	511237	1306696
Total Receipts	8	196949166	2546921	12647919	5169505	10531136	2729929	3569044	2838505	4673007	7761438	14187872	57635240	72658649
Average Total Receipts	9	3800	231	374	1398	3893	10920	24958	78847	122974	337454	675613	1801101	7265865
Operating Costs/Operating Income (%)														
Cost of Operations	10	52.8	44.8	53.6	59.5	59.8	67.3	57.3	57.3	56.1	51.6	54.1	50.2	52.1
Salaries and Wages	11	14.0	13.6	9.6	12.8	11.6	9.7	13.9	14.6	14.9	15.2	15.4	14.7	14.3
Taxes Paid	12	2.4	2.3	2.7	2.6	2.2	1.4	2.5	4.1	2.7	2.7	2.0	2.5	2.2
Interest Paid	13	1.0	0.9	0.5	0.4	0.6	0.4	0.5	0.4	0.8	0.4	0.8	0.9	1.4
Depreciation	14	3.2	1.9	0.8	1.0	1.4	2.1	2.0	2.1	3.4	4.1	3.4	3.8	3.6
Amortization and Depletion	15	0.2	0.2	0.1	0.0	0.1	0.0	0.2	0.2	0.3	0.2	0.2	0.3	0.3
Pensions and Other Deferred Comp.	16	0.2	0.1	0.2	0.1	0.2	0.5	0.2	0.1	0.1	0.1	0.0	0.2	0.4
Employee Benefits	17	1.1	0.6	0.4	0.8	0.5	0.3	0.7	0.8	1.0	1.0	1.5	0.9	1.4
Advertising	18	2.3	2.2	1.9	3.3	2.2	3.3	3.4	3.6	2.6	1.7	2.2	2.7	2.0
Other Expenses	19	18.8	35.2	22.2	14.9	17.2	13.0	19.4	19.5	18.3	23.8	20.9	20.8	15.8
Officers' Compensation	20	1.4	1.6	5.9	4.8	4.2	1.4	2.2	1.1	1.0	0.7	0.6	0.6	0.8
Operating Margin	21	2.7	•	2.0	•	•	0.6	•	•	•	•	•	2.4	5.8
Operating Margin Before Officers' Comp.	22	4.1	•	7.9	4.6	4.1	2.0	•	•	•	•	•	3.0	6.6

Selected Average Balance Sheet ($ in Thousands)

Net Receivables 23	141	0	4	42	76	245	1460	3516	4074	11768	10522	51193	413294
Inventories 24	603	0	73	468	1037	3606	7375	16623	24687	47697	102193	282137	847218
Net Property, Plant and Equipment 25	509	0	10	59	273	539	3127	6204	14937	44365	92739	311597	1076033
Total Assets 26	2196	0	133	708	1962	6658	15920	34702	68133	170566	354641	1090139	4735898
Notes and Loans Payable 27	609	0	63	270	547	2339	3852	8598	16226	26043	57012	210427	1636393
All Other Liabilities 28	751	0	40	140	712	2132	5791	15293	32442	81289	122726	376995	1546187
Net Worth 29	836	0	30	297	703	2187	6277	10811	19465	63234	174903	502716	1553317

Selected Financial Ratios (Times to 1)

Current Ratio 30	1.7	•	2.5	3.3	2.0	2.1	1.8	1.6	1.5	1.5	2.3	1.8	1.4
Quick Ratio 31	0.6	•	0.8	0.8	0.4	0.3	0.5	0.5	0.4	0.5	0.8	0.6	0.7
Net Sales to Working Capital 32	7.7	•	5.5	3.4	5.2	3.6	4.9	8.2	8.4	10.1	5.7	7.5	11.3
Coverage Ratio 33	6.2	•	5.8	2.1	2.6	4.2	1.7	•	1.3	3.8	1.8	5.5	8.0
Total Asset Turnover 34	1.7	•	2.8	2.0	2.0	1.6	1.5	2.2	1.8	1.9	1.9	1.6	1.5
Inventory Turnover 35	3.3	•	2.7	1.8	2.2	2.0	1.9	2.6	2.8	3.6	3.5	3.2	4.3
Receivables Turnover 36	24.8	•	112.8	30.8	49.9	17.0	16.6	22.0	33.6	26.8	60.1	35.1	15.5
Total Liabilities to Net Worth 37	1.6	•	3.4	1.4	1.8	2.0	1.5	2.2	2.5	1.7	1.0	1.2	2.0
Current Assets to Working Capital 38	2.4	•	1.7	1.4	2.0	1.9	2.3	2.7	3.1	2.8	1.8	2.3	3.3
Current Liabilities to Working Capital 39	1.4	•	0.7	0.4	1.0	0.9	1.3	1.7	2.1	1.8	0.8	1.3	2.3
Working Capital to Net Sales 40	0.1	•	0.2	0.3	0.2	0.3	0.2	0.1	0.1	0.1	0.2	0.1	0.1
Inventory to Working Capital 41	1.3	•	1.1	1.0	1.4	1.1	1.4	1.7	1.8	1.6	0.9	1.2	1.4
Total Receipts to Cash Flow 42	7.0	5.1	6.6	10.9	10.2	10.7	9.6	12.6	11.8	7.7	10.1	7.5	5.6
Cost of Goods to Cash Flow 43	3.7	2.3	3.5	6.5	6.1	7.2	5.5	7.2	6.6	4.0	5.5	3.7	2.9
Cash Flow to Total Debt 44	0.4	•	0.5	0.3	0.3	0.2	0.3	0.3	0.2	0.4	0.4	0.4	0.4

Selected Financial Factors (in Percentages)

Debt Ratio 45	61.9	•	77.3	58.0	64.2	67.2	60.6	68.8	71.4	62.9	50.7	53.9	67.2
Return on Total Assets 46	10.1	•	8.7	1.7	3.3	3.0	1.2	•	1.9	2.8	2.6	7.9	16.3
Return on Equity Before Income Taxes 47	22.2	•	31.7	2.2	5.7	6.9	1.3	•	1.5	5.5	2.3	14.0	43.5
Return on Equity After Income Taxes 48	14.1	•	31.1	1.5	4.2	5.0	0.2	•	•	•	•	8.3	28.6
Profit Margin (Before Income Tax) 49	5.0	•	2.6	0.5	1.0	1.4	0.3	•	0.2	1.1	0.6	4.0	9.6
Profit Margin (After Income Tax) 50	3.2	•	2.5	0.3	0.8	1.0	0.1	•	•	•	•	2.4	6.3

CLOTHING AND CLOTHING ACCESSORIES STORES

MONEY AMOUNTS AND SIZE OF ASSETS IN THOUSANDS OF DOLLARS

Item Description for Accounting Period 7/11 Through 6/12		Total	Zero Assets	Under 500	500 to 1,000	1,000 to 5,000	5,000 to 10,000	10,000 to 25,000	25,000 to 50,000	50,000 to 100,000	100,000 to 250,000	250,000 to 500,000	500,000 to 2,500,000	2,500,000 and over
Number of Enterprises	1	30369	5217	20010	2567	2215	175	88	20	21	•	11	22	•
Revenues ($ in Thousands)														
Net Sales	2	153446014	781551	8448427	3940505	8563980	2124230	2481670	1319997	3116389	•	6649359	41482783	•
Interest	3	446694	0	480	1635	2843	480	18483	1178	102	•	2002	28174	•
Rents	4	85367	0	1539	0	3166	0	764	289	920	•	295	21884	•
Royalties	5	440501	0	0	0	0	0	0	5096	1098	•	19700	148717	•
Other Portfolio Income	6	441715	28	28109	3274	2609	468	460	46653	6477	•	4647	8172	•
Other Receipts	7	2030536	0	4783	20670	99713	20711	60100	19561	33943	•	9151	356315	•
Total Receipts	8	156890827	781579	8483338	3966084	8672311	2145889	2561477	1392774	3158929	•	6685154	42046045	•
Average Total Receipts	9	5166	150	424	1545	3915	12262	29108	69639	150425	•	607741	1911184	•
Operating Costs/Operating Income (%)														
Cost of Operations	10	52.0	29.3	51.1	60.3	61.3	65.9	58.9	51.2	56.8	•	50.9	48.1	•
Salaries and Wages	11	13.7	7.1	10.1	10.8	10.1	10.0	13.1	15.8	13.6	•	14.1	14.7	•
Taxes Paid	12	2.3	3.0	2.4	2.6	1.9	1.5	2.5	4.8	2.3	•	2.3	2.4	•
Interest Paid	13	0.7	0.0	0.5	0.4	0.7	0.3	0.4	0.5	0.7	•	0.1	0.2	•
Depreciation	14	3.2	0.3	0.7	0.6	1.2	0.4	1.5	1.7	2.6	•	4.0	4.1	•
Amortization and Depletion	15	0.2	•	0.1	0.0	0.1	0.0	0.2	0.1	0.2	•	0.2	0.2	•
Pensions and Other Deferred Comp.	16	0.3	•	0.3	0.0	0.2	0.6	0.2	0.1	0.1	•	0.0	0.2	•
Employee Benefits	17	1.1	0.0	0.4	0.8	0.5	0.3	0.6	0.8	0.9	•	1.0	0.9	•
Advertising	18	2.2	0.1	1.8	2.8	1.9	3.2	3.3	4.2	2.7	•	2.0	2.3	•
Other Expenses	19	17.8	47.4	20.7	14.0	15.0	12.6	16.2	19.4	16.3	•	19.6	20.8	•
Officers' Compensation	20	1.3	2.4	5.1	4.9	3.9	1.3	1.5	1.3	1.3	•	0.8	0.7	•
Operating Margin	21	5.3	10.4	6.9	2.6	3.1	3.9	1.7	0.3	2.5	•	5.1	5.3	•
Operating Margin Before Officers' Comp.	22	6.6	12.8	12.0	7.6	7.0	5.3	3.1	1.6	3.8	•	5.9	6.0	•

Selected Average Balance Sheet ($ in Thousands)

Net Receivables 23	199	0	3	56	61	138	2197	3913	3873	•	11529	40202	•
Inventories 24	797	0	75	485	1001	4098	7500	21908	30500	•	125801	293192	•
Net Property, Plant and Equipment 25	680	0	8	50	260	485	2528	4717	11251	•	84013	321965	•
Total Assets 26	2915	0	147	712	1969	6441	15696	35456	65893	•	364962	1072545	•
Notes and Loans Payable 27	647	0	67	211	524	1735	2318	6383	8214	•	29362	52038	•
All Other Liabilities 28	977	0	45	127	618	1650	6868	14090	29615	•	91831	362220	•
Net Worth 29	1292	0	36	374	827	3056	6511	14984	28064	•	243769	658286	•

Selected Financial Ratios (Times to 1)

Current Ratio 30	1.7	•	2.8	3.5	2.2	2.2	1.8	1.7	2.0	•	3.3	1.8	•
Quick Ratio 31	0.7	•	0.9	1.0	0.5	0.2	0.6	0.5	0.5	•	1.3	0.6	•
Net Sales to Working Capital 32	7.5	•	5.1	3.5	4.8	4.0	5.2	5.5	6.3	•	3.6	7.3	•
Coverage Ratio 33	11.9	249.4	15.9	8.7	7.1	17.4	13.4	12.8	6.6	•	77.1	27.8	•
Total Asset Turnover 34	1.7	•	2.9	2.2	2.0	1.9	1.8	1.9	2.3	•	1.7	1.8	•
Inventory Turnover 35	3.3	•	2.9	1.9	2.4	2.0	2.2	1.5	2.8	•	2.4	3.1	•
Receivables Turnover 36	23.8	•	140.3	25.7	57.0	17.3	14.6	14.2	47.4	•	43.6	38.6	•
Total Liabilities to Net Worth 37	1.3	•	3.1	0.9	1.4	1.1	1.4	1.4	1.3	•	0.5	0.6	•
Current Assets to Working Capital 38	2.4	•	1.5	1.4	1.8	1.8	2.3	2.4	2.0	•	1.4	2.2	•
Current Liabilities to Working Capital 39	1.4	•	0.5	0.4	0.8	0.8	1.3	1.4	1.0	•	0.4	1.2	•
Working Capital to Net Sales 40	0.1	•	0.2	0.3	0.2	0.2	0.2	0.2	0.2	•	0.3	0.1	•
Inventory to Working Capital 41	1.2	•	1.0	1.0	1.3	1.2	1.4	1.6	1.3	•	0.6	1.1	•
Total Receipts to Cash Flow 42	6.0	2.5	5.3	9.1	8.3	7.7	7.2	7.4	8.4	•	6.7	6.3	•
Cost of Goods to Cash Flow 43	3.1	0.7	2.7	5.5	5.1	5.1	4.2	3.8	4.8	•	3.4	3.0	•
Cash Flow to Total Debt 44	0.5	•	0.7	0.5	0.4	0.5	0.4	0.4	0.5	•	0.7	0.7	•

Selected Financial Factors (in Percentages)

Debt Ratio 45	55.7	•	75.8	47.5	58.0	52.6	58.5	57.7	57.4	•	33.2	38.6	•
Return on Total Assets 46	14.7	•	22.4	8.0	10.0	9.9	9.4	11.7	10.8	•	9.9	12.2	•
Return on Equity Before Income Taxes 47	30.5	•	86.8	13.5	20.5	19.7	21.1	25.5	21.6	•	14.6	19.2	•
Return on Equity After Income Taxes 48	21.5	•	85.9	12.8	18.9	17.8	19.5	19.2	17.8	•	10.9	12.8	•
Profit Margin (Before Income Tax) 49	7.8	10.4	7.3	3.3	4.4	5.0	4.9	5.8	4.1	•	5.9	6.7	•
Profit Margin (After Income Tax) 50	5.5	10.4	7.2	3.1	4.0	4.5	4.5	4.4	3.4	•	4.4	4.5	•

Table I

Corporations with and without Net Income

SPORTING GOODS, HOBBY, BOOK, AND MUSIC STORES

MONEY AMOUNTS AND SIZE OF ASSETS IN THOUSANDS OF DOLLARS

Item Description for Accounting Period 7/11 Through 6/12		Total	Zero Assets	Under 500	500 to 1,000	1,000 to 5,000	5,000 to 10,000	10,000 to 25,000	25,000 to 50,000	50,000 to 100,000	100,000 to 250,000	250,000 to 500,000	500,000 to 2,500,000	2,500,000 and over
Number of Enterprises	1	27028	4496	18795	1546	1854	216	61	17	7	14	8	11	4
Revenues ($ in Thousands)														
Net Sales	2	80127489	2272697	6081810	2480966	6453357	3166972	1355497	902786	1111315	4941246	4559524	22027639	24773680
Interest	3	594519	11464	1101	1365	3983	2528	2549	212	4	9518	401	3725	557669
Rents	4	46660	1024	451	0	3220	360	0	3368	0	3138	148	11848	23103
Royalties	5	142422	752	0	36	0	0	0	0	0	13721	28936	7516	91460
Other Portfolio Income	6	396161	69264	2244	52	1635	369	8800	18	124	14	13	224802	88825
Other Receipts	7	1186129	-6482	40594	12999	126452	47749	14570	9631	13671	64679	18697	238395	605176
Total Receipts	8	82493380	2348719	6126200	2495418	6588647	3217978	1381416	916015	1125114	5032316	4607719	22513925	26139913
Average Total Receipts	9	3052	522	326	1614	3554	14898	22646	53883	160731	359451	575965	2046720	6534978
Operating Costs/Operating Income (%)														
Cost of Operations	10	60.8	85.4	60.1	60.4	58.6	72.0	60.6	66.1	57.0	59.0	63.1	54.6	63.3
Salaries and Wages	11	12.5	9.7	8.4	12.6	14.1	9.3	14.1	8.8	15.6	14.2	12.8	14.0	11.9
Taxes Paid	12	2.3	1.5	2.7	2.3	2.7	2.3	2.1	1.4	2.7	2.0	2.0	2.5	2.2
Interest Paid	13	2.0	3.9	0.7	0.7	0.8	0.7	0.2	0.8	2.2	0.8	1.5	3.2	2.3
Depreciation	14	2.7	0.9	1.1	0.8	2.0	0.3	5.8	3.4	1.5	2.6	2.9	2.9	3.6
Amortization and Depletion	15	0.2	0.1	0.0	0.1	0.1	0.1	0.2	0.6	0.4	0.4	0.5	0.3	0.2
Pensions and Other Deferred Comp.	16	0.2	0.0	0.0	0.1	0.2	0.0	0.7	0.0	0.1	0.2	0.1	0.1	0.2
Employee Benefits	17	0.7	0.6	0.7	0.9	0.8	0.3	1.0	0.8	1.5	1.0	0.4	0.5	0.9
Advertising	18	2.7	0.5	1.7	1.4	1.8	1.8	2.4	5.6	1.9	3.3	2.2	3.2	3.2
Other Expenses	19	16.5	35.9	18.7	16.7	14.7	11.9	12.8	12.7	17.5	17.7	14.5	16.2	15.8
Officers' Compensation	20	1.3	0.6	5.3	4.9	4.4	1.0	1.3	1.2	0.5	0.8	0.6	0.3	0.5
Operating Margin	21	•	•	0.6	•	•	0.3	•	•	•	•	•	2.3	•
Operating Margin Before Officers' Comp.	22	•	•	5.9	4.1	4.2	1.3	0.0	•	•	•	•	2.5	•

Selected Average Balance Sheet ($ in Thousands)

Net Receivables	23	182	0	5	37	112	699	1126	1925	15322	4092	23175	32253	905023
Inventories	24	631	0	73	464	823	3690	3876	11397	41448	80200	145468	431849	1218449
Net Property, Plant and Equipment	25	389	0	14	111	294	333	2350	6436	10046	33304	59130	268502	1312983
Total Assets	26	1827	0	119	737	1927	7131	14863	32137	73785	160569	342573	1294158	4924560
Notes and Loans Payable	27	763	0	80	499	488	2044	1614	9223	46899	45554	69949	723566	1810406
All Other Liabilities	28	704	0	25	163	447	2751	5577	10120	31037	73169	178562	470511	2129218
Net Worth	29	360	0	13	74	992	2336	7671	12794	-4151	41846	94062	100081	984936

Selected Financial Ratios (Times to 1)

Current Ratio	30	1.7	•	2.8	2.6	2.3	1.9	1.7	1.8	1.6	1.7	1.8	1.5	1.5
Quick Ratio	31	0.6	•	0.7	0.5	0.8	0.4	0.6	0.5	0.5	0.2	0.6	0.3	0.7
Net Sales to Working Capital	32	7.2	•	5.2	4.7	4.7	6.0	7.2	5.9	7.1	7.9	6.0	10.6	6.8
Coverage Ratio	33	1.5	•	2.9	0.7	3.4	3.9	3.8	1.1	1.1	0.9	1.3	2.4	1.7
Total Asset Turnover	34	1.6	•	2.7	2.2	1.8	2.1	1.5	1.7	2.2	2.2	1.7	1.5	1.3
Inventory Turnover	35	2.9	•	2.6	2.1	2.5	2.9	3.5	3.1	2.2	2.6	2.5	2.5	3.2
Receivables Turnover	36	17.8	•	73.0	34.2	37.8	22.9	24.1	34.4	9.6	84.0	27.3	59.6	7.6
Total Liabilities to Net Worth	37	4.1	•	8.1	8.9	0.9	2.1	0.9	1.5	•	2.8	2.6	11.9	4.0
Current Assets to Working Capital	38	2.5	•	1.6	1.6	1.7	2.2	2.5	2.3	2.6	2.4	2.2	3.0	2.9
Current Liabilities to Working Capital	39	1.5	•	0.6	0.6	0.7	1.2	1.5	1.3	1.6	1.4	1.2	2.0	1.9
Working Capital to Net Sales	40	0.1	•	0.2	0.2	0.2	0.2	0.1	0.2	0.1	0.1	0.2	0.1	0.1
Inventory to Working Capital	41	1.5	•	1.2	1.3	1.1	1.6	1.5	1.5	1.7	1.9	1.5	2.0	1.4
Total Receipts to Cash Flow	42	9.9	•	8.1	11.5	9.0	13.3	10.9	10.4	11.9	12.9	12.7	7.6	9.6
Cost of Goods to Cash Flow	43	6.0	•	4.9	6.9	5.3	9.5	6.6	6.9	6.8	7.6	8.0	4.1	6.1
Cash Flow to Total Debt	44	0.2	•	0.4	0.2	0.4	0.2	0.3	0.3	0.2	0.2	0.2	0.2	0.2

Selected Financial Factors (in Percentages)

Debt Ratio	45	80.3	•	89.0	89.9	48.5	67.2	48.4	60.2	105.6	73.9	72.5	92.3	80.0
Return on Total Assets	46	5.1	•	5.5	1.1	4.9	5.3	1.3	1.5	5.4	1.6	3.3	11.8	5.0
Return on Equity Before Income Taxes	47	9.0	•	32.6	•	6.8	11.9	1.8	0.4	•	•	2.9	89.5	10.6
Return on Equity After Income Taxes	48	5.0	•	32.1	•	6.2	11.0	1.4	•	•	•	•	76.4	6.6
Profit Margin (Before Income Tax)	49	1.1	•	1.3	•	1.9	1.9	0.6	0.1	0.3	•	0.5	4.5	1.7
Profit Margin (After Income Tax)	50	0.6	•	1.3	•	1.8	1.8	0.5	•	0.3	•	•	3.8	1.0

Table II

Corporations with Net Income

SPORTING GOODS, HOBBY, BOOK, AND MUSIC STORES

MONEY AMOUNTS AND SIZE OF ASSETS IN THOUSANDS OF DOLLARS

Item Description for Accounting Period 7/11 Through 6/12		Total	Zero Assets	Under 500	500 to 1,000	1,000 to 5,000	5,000 to 10,000	10,000 to 25,000	25,000 to 50,000	50,000 to 100,000	100,000 to 250,000	250,000 to 500,000	500,000 to 2,500,000	2,500,000 and over
Number of Enterprises	1	15206	2109	10675	976	1176	192	42	11	•	5	4	8	•
Revenues ($ in Thousands)														
Net Sales	2	57378831	808712	4215795	1849266	4799623	2822837	945331	596244	•	1731723	2645724	18456571	•
Interest	3	568674	3	787	1365	2787	1894	2540	212	•	254	53	1223	•
Rents	4	27240	706	0	0	2625	360	0	3368	•	0	3	1664	•
Royalties	5	132715	0	0	36	0	0	0	0	•	5441	28936	7516	•
Other Portfolio Income	6	384574	69264	2244	22	574	369	520	18	•	0	13	222601	•
Other Receipts	7	596885	-12032	38758	5065	108952	41412	6568	8196	•	7128	-23313	194850	•
Total Receipts	8	59088919	866653	4257584	1855754	4914561	2866872	954959	608038	•	1744546	2651416	18884425	•
Average Total Receipts	9	3886	411	399	1901	4179	14932	22737	55276	•	348909	662854	2360553	•
Operating Costs/Operating Income (%)														
Cost of Operations	10	59.0	73.1	57.6	59.6	58.8	72.0	61.5	66.5	•	57.9	59.6	53.0	•
Salaries and Wages	11	12.4	7.8	7.3	13.1	13.7	9.3	13.0	8.6	•	13.3	13.9	14.4	•
Taxes Paid	12	2.4	1.1	2.7	2.0	2.4	2.4	1.6	1.4	•	2.3	2.0	2.7	•
Interest Paid	13	2.0	1.3	0.7	0.6	0.6	0.6	0.2	0.8	•	0.4	0.5	2.8	•
Depreciation	14	2.7	0.6	1.3	0.7	1.7	0.3	1.1	3.1	•	2.6	2.6	2.8	•
Amortization and Depletion	15	0.1	0.2	0.0	0.1	0.2	0.1	0.3	0.8	•	0.1	0.1	0.2	•
Pensions and Other Deferred Comp.	16	0.2	0.0	0.0	0.1	0.2	0.0	1.0	0.1	•	0.0	0.1	0.1	•
Employee Benefits	17	0.6	0.2	0.4	1.1	0.7	0.2	1.1	0.5	•	0.9	0.4	0.5	•
Advertising	18	2.9	0.5	1.5	1.5	1.8	1.8	2.6	1.9	•	2.9	2.8	3.3	•
Other Expenses	19	14.9	10.1	17.4	13.3	13.6	10.5	12.7	13.7	•	14.6	11.8	16.4	•
Officers' Compensation	20	1.3	1.5	5.2	4.8	4.4	0.9	1.2	1.1	•	1.3	0.6	0.3	•
Operating Margin	21	1.4	3.6	5.7	3.0	1.9	1.9	3.8	1.6	•	3.6	5.7	3.5	•
Operating Margin Before Officers' Comp.	22	2.8	5.0	10.9	7.8	6.3	2.9	5.0	2.6	•	4.9	6.4	3.8	•

Selected Average Balance Sheet ($ in Thousands)													
Net Receivables 23	281	0	6	53	147	613	923	2569	•	3541	16516	35092	•
Inventories 24	740	0	73	429	892	3557	4606	11416	•	100355	180489	433898	•
Net Property, Plant and Equipment 25	550	0	19	91	177	226	727	7184	•	33697	86707	318914	•
Total Assets 26	2352	0	137	737	1811	7297	14110	35353	•	170004	336642	1397165	•
Notes and Loans Payable 27	1060	0	78	265	381	1965	612	12082	•	34351	59083	811657	•
All Other Liabilities 28	770	0	23	164	439	1724	6232	10621	•	64088	118882	473946	•
Net Worth 29	521	0	36	307	991	3607	7266	12650	•	71565	158678	111563	•
Selected Financial Ratios (Times to 1)													
Current Ratio 30	1.9	•	2.9	2.4	2.6	1.9	1.6	1.7	•	1.7	2.0	1.5	•
Quick Ratio 31	0.7	•	0.8	0.7	1.0	0.4	0.4	0.4	•	0.3	0.4	0.3	•
Net Sales to Working Capital 32	6.2	•	5.6	5.5	4.8	5.6	7.4	6.0	•	6.6	6.5	11.8	•
Coverage Ratio 33	3.2	9.1	10.4	6.7	8.3	6.7	21.9	5.3	•	13.1	13.7	3.1	•
Total Asset Turnover 34	1.6	•	2.9	2.6	2.3	2.0	1.6	1.5	•	2.0	2.0	1.7	•
Inventory Turnover 35	3.0	•	3.1	2.6	2.7	3.0	3.0	3.2	•	2.0	2.2	2.8	•
Receivables Turnover 36	14.9	•	104.8	37.8	33.9	27.4	28.3	30.0	•	67.9	32.0	70.7	•
Total Liabilities to Net Worth 37	3.5	•	2.8	1.4	0.8	1.0	0.9	1.8	•	1.4	1.1	11.5	•
Current Assets to Working Capital 38	2.2	•	1.5	1.7	1.6	2.1	2.6	2.4	•	2.4	2.0	3.2	•
Current Liabilities to Working Capital 39	1.2	•	0.5	0.7	0.6	1.1	1.6	1.4	•	1.4	1.0	2.2	•
Working Capital to Net Sales 40	0.2	•	0.2	0.2	0.2	0.2	0.1	0.2	•	0.2	0.2	0.1	•
Inventory to Working Capital 41	1.2	•	1.1	1.2	1.0	1.6	1.8	1.7	•	1.7	1.5	2.1	•
Total Receipts to Cash Flow 42	7.8	11.2	5.9	8.8	7.4	11.6	7.8	7.2	•	9.8	8.5	6.8	•
Cost of Goods to Cash Flow 43	4.6	8.2	3.4	5.2	4.4	8.4	4.8	4.8	•	5.7	5.1	3.6	•
Cash Flow to Total Debt 44	0.3	•	0.7	0.5	0.7	0.3	0.4	0.3	•	0.4	0.4	0.3	•
Selected Financial Factors (in Percentages)													
Debt Ratio 45	77.8	•	73.8	58.3	45.3	50.6	48.5	64.2	•	57.9	52.9	92.0	•
Return on Total Assets 46	10.5	•	21.5	10.1	11.1	8.3	8.1	6.7	•	10.2	12.6	14.2	•
Return on Equity Before Income Taxes 47	32.6	•	74.0	20.7	17.8	14.3	14.9	15.2	•	22.4	24.9	120.8	•
Return on Equity After Income Taxes 48	27.7	•	73.7	18.7	16.9	13.6	14.2	13.4	•	20.4	16.2	104.7	•
Profit Margin (Before Income Tax) 49	4.5	10.7	6.7	3.4	4.3	3.5	4.8	3.5	•	4.6	6.0	5.8	•
Profit Margin (After Income Tax) 50	3.8	10.1	6.7	3.0	4.1	3.3	4.6	3.1	•	4.2	3.9	5.1	•

Table I

Corporations with and without Net Income

GENERAL MERCHANDISE STORES

Item Description for Accounting Period 7/11 Through 6/12		Total	Zero Assets	Under 500	500 to 1,000	1,000 to 5,000	5,000 to 10,000	10,000 to 25,000	25,000 to 50,000	50,000 to 100,000	100,000 to 250,000	250,000 to 500,000	500,000 to 2,500,000	2,500,000 and over
		MONEY AMOUNTS AND SIZE OF ASSETS IN THOUSANDS OF DOLLARS												
Number of Enterprises	1	10736	1970	7250	1106	302	15	34	14	8	10	6	8	14
		Revenues ($ in Thousands)												
Net Sales	2	651183732	7887354	2379098	2959463	3050526	758730	800196	1179161	862764	3897046	4057196	26727790	596624406
Interest	3	843183	20	1647	816	3477	5	306	11	10164	1232	4437	6977	814091
Rents	4	949611	3080	0	0	369	0	0	9	7948	3934	1297	13084	919890
Royalties	5	1397041	0	0	0	48	0	0	0	0	0	16297	52671	1328025
Other Portfolio Income	6	209584	0	16	148	883	80	1354	160	30	2586	3087	3413	197826
Other Receipts	7	14494283	290151	52138	70159	15137	774	11885	2596	12139	44939	21399	225236	13747733
Total Receipts	8	669077434	8180605	2432899	3030586	3070440	759589	813741	1181937	893045	3949737	4103713	27029171	613631971
Average Total Receipts	9	62321	4153	336	2740	10167	50639	23934	84424	111631	394974	683952	3378646	43830855
		Operating Costs/Operating Income (%)												
Cost of Operations	10	73.5	86.5	61.6	77.0	60.0	86.5	60.0	71.3	64.9	66.0	68.7	64.1	73.9
Salaries and Wages	11	11.0	5.2	8.3	6.2	14.3	4.8	16.2	10.5	15.0	11.6	11.8	12.7	11.0
Taxes Paid	12	1.9	1.2	2.5	1.2	1.6	0.6	2.5	1.4	2.3	1.8	1.5	2.8	1.8
Interest Paid	13	0.8	0.0	0.6	0.2	0.3	0.1	0.2	0.4	0.4	0.5	0.5	0.6	0.9
Depreciation	14	2.5	1.5	0.7	0.4	0.4	0.4	1.3	0.8	1.7	1.8	2.7	2.8	2.5
Amortization and Depletion	15	0.0	0.0	0.1	0.1	0.0	•	•	0.1	0.1	0.0	0.1	0.1	0.0
Pensions and Other Deferred Comp.	16	0.4	0.1	0.0	0.7	0.5	0.1	0.4	0.1	0.3	0.2	0.1	0.2	0.4
Employee Benefits	17	0.9	0.8	0.1	0.1	1.2	0.7	0.6	0.9	1.3	1.1	1.6	1.1	0.9
Advertising	18	1.3	0.2	0.3	3.0	2.1	0.7	1.5	1.7	1.4	1.9	0.9	1.3	1.3
Other Expenses	19	6.6	6.6	21.8	6.6	17.5	6.5	14.0	8.9	13.1	12.7	10.6	9.6	6.2
Officers' Compensation	20	0.2	0.4	3.8	2.9	1.7	0.4	1.4	0.4	0.3	1.7	0.6	0.6	0.1
Operating Margin	21	0.9	•	0.2	1.5	0.5	•	1.8	3.5	•	0.7	0.9	4.1	0.8
Operating Margin Before Officers' Comp.	22	1.1	•	4.0	4.4	2.2	•	3.2	3.9	•	2.4	1.5	4.7	0.9

Selected Average Balance Sheet ($ in Thousands)													
Net Receivables 23	535	0	3	10	304	1008	1660	444	13763	10286	31223	23335	354091
Inventories 24	6821	0	57	169	992	8262	2443	20729	21952	71355	114881	635006	4655435
Net Property, Plant and Equipment 25	14006	0	8	90	243	1248	1920	4684	9399	45000	73350	486838	10366029
Total Assets 26	35112	0	96	605	2514	7985	13210	35178	68120	187714	344033	1433696	25558876
Notes and Loans Payable 27	9984	0	66	275	375	14	1666	10578	8830	51330	48708	232963	7381770
All Other Liabilities 28	12139	0	22	99	549	6002	84733	5705	20198	57750	108228	476291	8688965
Net Worth 29	12990	0	9	230	1589	1969	-73189	18895	39091	78634	187097	724442	9488141
Selected Financial Ratios (Times to 1)													
Current Ratio 30	0.9	•	2.1	2.6	4.0	1.1	0.1	3.8	2.6	1.4	1.9	2.2	0.9
Quick Ratio 31	0.2	•	0.7	1.4	1.6	0.3	0.1	0.7	1.0	0.3	0.5	0.4	0.2
Net Sales to Working Capital 32	•	•	9.3	10.4	6.6	64.6	•	4.3	3.4	13.1	8.1	7.5	•
Coverage Ratio 33	5.8	28.4	5.3	17.5	5.2	•	21.8	11.3	7.8	5.2	5.1	9.6	5.7
Total Asset Turnover 34	1.7	•	3.4	4.4	4.0	6.3	1.8	2.4	1.6	2.1	2.0	2.3	1.7
Inventory Turnover 35	6.5	•	3.5	12.2	6.1	5.3	5.8	2.9	3.2	3.6	4.0	3.4	6.8
Receivables Turnover 36	67.0	•	136.6	275.9	41.5	24.0	15.8	190.2	8.1	35.1	21.8	100.9	67.4
Total Liabilities to Net Worth 37	1.7	•	9.7	1.6	0.6	3.1	•	0.9	0.7	1.4	0.8	1.0	1.7
Current Assets to Working Capital 38	•	•	1.9	1.6	1.3	8.6	•	1.4	1.6	3.2	2.1	1.9	•
Current Liabilities to Working Capital 39	•	•	0.9	0.6	0.3	7.6	•	0.4	0.6	2.2	1.1	0.9	•
Working Capital to Net Sales 40	•	•	0.1	0.1	0.2	0.0	•	0.2	0.3	0.1	0.1	0.1	•
Inventory to Working Capital 41	•	•	1.2	0.7	0.8	6.0	•	1.0	0.8	2.3	1.5	1.3	•
Total Receipts to Cash Flow 42	12.0	21.6	7.0	12.6	7.4	27.9	10.0	11.3	10.6	9.9	13.6	9.6	12.2
Cost of Goods to Cash Flow 43	8.8	18.7	4.3	9.7	4.4	24.2	6.0	8.1	6.9	6.5	9.3	6.1	9.0
Cash Flow to Total Debt 44	0.2	•	0.5	0.6	1.5	0.3	0.0	0.5	0.3	0.4	0.3	0.5	0.2
Selected Financial Factors (in Percentages)													
Debt Ratio 45	63.0	•	90.6	61.9	36.8	75.3	654.1	46.3	42.6	58.1	45.6	49.5	62.9
Return on Total Assets 46	8.3	•	10.4	18.4	5.6	•	6.3	9.8	5.0	5.2	5.0	13.7	8.1
Return on Equity Before Income Taxes 47	18.5	•	90.0	45.6	7.2	•	•	16.7	7.5	10.0	7.4	24.3	17.9
Return on Equity After Income Taxes 48	11.8	•	89.9	44.7	6.0	•	•	16.6	6.8	8.2	5.8	16.1	11.3
Profit Margin (Before Income Tax) 49	4.0	1.2	2.5	3.9	1.1	•	3.4	3.7	2.7	2.0	2.1	5.3	4.0
Profit Margin (After Income Tax) 50	2.5	0.7	2.5	3.9	0.9	•	3.4	3.7	2.5	1.6	1.6	3.5	2.5

Table II

Corporations with Net Income

GENERAL MERCHANDISE STORES

MONEY AMOUNTS AND SIZE OF ASSETS IN THOUSANDS OF DOLLARS

Item Description for Accounting Period 7/11 Through 6/12		Total	Zero Assets	Under 500	500 to 1,000	1,000 to 5,000	5,000 to 10,000	10,000 to 25,000	25,000 to 50,000	50,000 to 100,000	100,000 to 250,000	250,000 to 500,000	500,000 to 2,500,000	2,500,000 and over
Number of Enterprises	1	6475	816	4608	749	220	•	19	11	•	•	•	•	•
Revenues ($ in Thousands)														
Net Sales	2	604350369	7789449	2057215	2779031	1546458	•	654986	1155398	•	•	•	•	•
Interest	3	835055	20	1646	512	3397	•	0	9	•	•	•	•	•
Rents	4	901216	3080	0	0	369	•	0	9	•	•	•	•	•
Royalties	5	1312590	0	0	0	48	•	0	0	•	•	•	•	•
Other Portfolio Income	6	193867	0	0	6	883	•	164	160	•	•	•	•	•
Other Receipts	7	13676839	290150	34044	60011	15018	•	1775	2593	•	•	•	•	•
Total Receipts	8	621269936	8082699	2092905	2839560	1566173	•	656925	1158169	•	•	•	•	•
Average Total Receipts	9	95949	9905	454	3791	7119	•	34575	105288	•	•	•	•	•
Operating Costs/Operating Income (%)														
Cost of Operations	10	73.9	86.8	60.5	78.3	63.7	•	58.6	71.1	•	•	•	•	•
Salaries and Wages	11	10.7	5.1	6.9	5.3	9.8	•	17.9	10.1	•	•	•	•	•
Taxes Paid	12	1.8	1.1	2.4	1.1	1.5	•	2.7	1.4	•	•	•	•	•
Interest Paid	13	0.8	0.0	0.7	0.1	0.5	•	0.1	0.4	•	•	•	•	•
Depreciation	14	2.5	1.5	0.7	0.2	0.5	•	0.7	0.8	•	•	•	•	•
Amortization and Depletion	15	0.0	0.0	0.1	•	0.0	•	•	0.1	•	•	•	•	•
Pensions and Other Deferred Comp.	16	0.4	0.1	•	0.7	0.9	•	0.1	0.1	•	•	•	•	•
Employee Benefits	17	0.9	0.8	•	0.0	0.7	•	0.5	0.9	•	•	•	•	•
Advertising	18	1.1	0.2	0.3	3.1	1.6	•	1.4	1.1	•	•	•	•	•
Other Expenses	19	6.2	6.3	19.6	5.5	16.5	•	10.2	8.2	•	•	•	•	•
Officers' Compensation	20	0.2	0.3	3.6	2.7	2.4	•	1.4	0.3	•	•	•	•	•
Operating Margin	21	1.4	•	5.2	2.9	1.9	•	6.4	5.5	•	•	•	•	•
Operating Margin Before Officers' Comp.	22	1.6	•	8.8	5.6	4.3	•	7.8	5.9	•	•	•	•	•

Selected Average Balance Sheet ($ in Thousands)													
Net Receivables **23**	780	0	4	4	256	•	2884	548	•	•	•	•	•
Inventories **24**	10485	0	53	171	907	•	4100	25791	•	•	•	•	•
Net Property, Plant and Equipment **25**	22141	0	11	106	145	•	837	4595	•	•	•	•	•
Total Assets **26**	53724	0	130	593	2180	•	12330	36748	•	•	•	•	•
Notes and Loans Payable **27**	14619	0	50	216	468	•	537	10271	•	•	•	•	•
All Other Liabilities **28**	17740	0	27	115	519	•	1961	6348	•	•	•	•	•
Net Worth **29**	21365	0	53	262	1194	•	9832	20130	•	•	•	•	•
Selected Financial Ratios (Times to 1)													
Current Ratio **30**	1.0	•	2.1	3.5	3.6	•	5.5	3.7	•	•	•	•	•
Quick Ratio **31**	0.2	•	0.6	2.0	1.6	•	2.9	0.3	•	•	•	•	•
Net Sales to Working Capital **32**	642.2	•	9.7	11.0	5.5	•	3.7	4.9	•	•	•	•	•
Coverage Ratio **33**	6.4	34.1	11.6	90.9	7.2	•	68.6	16.6	•	•	•	•	•
Total Asset Turnover **34**	1.7	•	3.4	6.3	3.2	•	2.8	2.9	•	•	•	•	•
Inventory Turnover **35**	6.6	•	5.1	17.0	4.9	•	4.9	2.9	•	•	•	•	•
Receivables Turnover **36**	64.8	•	174.4	1912.6	31.0	•	13.2	•	•	•	•	•	•
Total Liabilities to Net Worth **37**	1.5	•	1.4	1.3	0.8	•	0.3	0.8	•	•	•	•	•
Current Assets to Working Capital **38**	98.2	•	1.9	1.4	1.4	•	1.2	1.4	•	•	•	•	•
Current Liabilities to Working Capital **39**	97.2	•	0.9	0.4	0.4	•	0.2	0.4	•	•	•	•	•
Working Capital to Net Sales **40**	0.0	•	0.1	0.1	0.2	•	0.3	0.2	•	•	•	•	•
Inventory to Working Capital **41**	69.8	•	1.3	0.6	0.7	•	0.6	1.2	•	•	•	•	•
Total Receipts to Cash Flow **42**	11.7	20.7	5.9	11.8	6.6	•	8.5	9.5	•	•	•	•	•
Cost of Goods to Cash Flow **43**	8.6	17.9	3.6	9.2	4.2	•	5.0	6.8	•	•	•	•	•
Cash Flow to Total Debt **44**	0.2	•	1.0	0.9	1.1	•	1.6	0.7	•	•	•	•	•
Selected Financial Factors (in Percentages)													
Debt Ratio **45**	60.2	•	59.0	55.9	45.3	•	20.3	45.2	•	•	•	•	•
Return on Total Assets **46**	9.3	•	26.1	32.0	12.0	•	18.9	17.6	•	•	•	•	•
Return on Equity Before Income Taxes **47**	19.8	•	58.1	71.8	18.9	•	23.3	30.2	•	•	•	•	•
Return on Equity After Income Taxes **48**	13.0	•	58.1	70.7	16.7	•	23.3	30.0	•	•	•	•	•
Profit Margin (Before Income Tax) **49**	4.5	1.5	7.0	5.1	3.2	•	6.7	5.8	•	•	•	•	•
Profit Margin (After Income Tax) **50**	3.0	1.0	7.0	5.0	2.8	•	6.7	5.8	•	•	•	•	•

Table I

Corporations with and without Net Income

MISCELLANEOUS STORE RETAILERS

MONEY AMOUNTS AND SIZE OF ASSETS IN THOUSANDS OF DOLLARS

Item Description for Accounting Period 7/11 Through 6/12		Total	Zero Assets	Under 500	500 to 1,000	1,000 to 5,000	5,000 to 10,000	10,000 to 25,000	25,000 to 50,000	50,000 to 100,000	100,000 to 250,000	250,000 to 500,000	500,000 to 2,500,000	2,500,000 and over
Number of Enterprises	1	73293	11986	55418	2085	3142	395	176	38	19	15	6	9	3
Revenues ($ in Thousands)														
Net Sales	2	103064870	1026189	24322748	3910783	11518213	3649209	5353321	1977273	1835235	2663785	4056720	12387470	30363924
Interest	3	195448	398	1180	1275	9225	1824	754	761	826	2687	1904	20969	153645
Rents	4	43179	0	1844	3734	2289	3991	11520	1549	0	1754	3023	2410	11065
Royalties	5	233969	0	10625	0	1078	35587	4888	7268	30840	2330	3345	55329	82679
Other Portfolio Income	6	395654	14767	17686	1257	11553	908	4001	23363	6012	115	4422	36248	275322
Other Receipts	7	1687881	69498	142300	39362	212972	25490	94887	38344	11647	11747	51564	813452	176618
Total Receipts	8	105621001	1110852	24496383	3956411	11755330	3717009	5469371	2048558	1884560	2682418	4120978	13315878	31063253
Average Total Receipts	9	1441	93	442	1898	3741	9410	31076	53909	99187	178828	686830	1479542	10354418
Operating Costs/Operating Income (%)														
Cost of Operations	10	62.0	51.0	55.2	64.8	67.8	71.0	72.4	66.6	73.0	52.9	62.5	50.7	66.7
Salaries and Wages	11	12.1	8.5	11.5	11.9	11.1	8.9	9.8	10.3	8.6	12.8	13.4	17.4	11.9
Taxes Paid	12	2.2	2.7	2.6	2.5	2.7	1.3	1.5	2.1	1.4	2.5	2.0	3.4	1.4
Interest Paid	13	1.2	1.3	0.7	0.6	0.7	1.3	0.6	0.7	1.0	3.0	1.7	2.8	1.0
Depreciation	14	1.7	1.9	1.3	1.4	1.0	1.1	1.2	2.3	4.0	2.9	2.0	3.1	1.7
Amortization and Depletion	15	0.2	0.1	0.2	0.0	0.1	0.1	0.0	0.4	0.2	0.3	1.0	0.2	0.2
Pensions and Other Deferred Comp.	16	0.1	0.0	0.2	0.1	0.3	0.2	0.2	0.2	0.2	0.1	0.0	0.1	0.1
Employee Benefits	17	1.0	0.5	0.6	0.6	0.6	0.4	0.5	0.9	1.0	0.8	1.5	1.7	1.2
Advertising	18	1.8	3.3	1.3	1.1	0.9	1.4	0.7	0.5	1.6	2.2	2.7	2.2	2.8
Other Expenses	19	15.5	39.6	20.5	14.5	12.5	13.2	10.1	12.8	9.8	18.1	12.6	18.9	12.4
Officers' Compensation	20	2.2	3.8	5.1	3.1	3.5	2.1	1.9	1.6	1.4	1.0	0.5	0.9	0.0
Operating Margin	21	0.1	•	0.9	•	•	•	1.0	1.6	•	3.3	0.1	•	0.7
Operating Margin Before Officers' Comp.	22	2.2	•	6.0	2.5	2.4	1.1	2.9	3.2	•	4.3	0.6	•	0.7

Selected Average Balance Sheet ($ in Thousands)													
Net Receivables 23	131	0	9	122	252	1637	2006	6302	7278	22509	51266	88503	1759344
Inventories 24	204	0	43	360	785	2508	6515	12154	21022	55045	82166	226722	999136
Net Property, Plant and Equipment 25	126	0	19	130	310	510	2412	4978	12480	31464	44780	293524	823518
Total Assets 26	804	0	108	728	1996	6625	15001	36445	66624	168961	344278	1371116	6779819
Notes and Loans Payable 27	292	0	67	315	575	2529	4728	7749	17693	103728	141379	548114	1802468
All Other Liabilities 28	268	0	23	260	371	2191	4577	9151	22100	51709	113724	482608	2801328
Net Worth 29	245	0	18	153	1050	1905	5696	19546	26830	13525	89174	340394	2176023
Selected Financial Ratios (Times to 1)													
Current Ratio 30	2.1	•	2.2	1.8	2.6	1.9	2.2	2.6	1.3	2.1	1.5	1.4	2.5
Quick Ratio 31	1.0	•	0.9	0.8	1.0	0.7	0.8	0.9	0.5	0.9	0.6	0.6	1.7
Net Sales to Working Capital 32	5.8	•	11.2	7.7	4.5	3.3	4.9	3.2	11.8	3.1	10.8	8.6	4.4
Coverage Ratio 33	3.5	•	3.2	1.9	2.3	1.7	6.5	8.4	1.4	2.3	2.0	3.6	4.8
Total Asset Turnover 34	1.7	•	4.1	2.6	1.8	1.4	2.0	1.4	1.4	1.1	2.0	1.0	1.5
Inventory Turnover 35	4.3	•	5.7	3.4	3.2	2.6	3.4	2.9	3.4	1.7	5.1	3.1	6.8
Receivables Turnover 36	11.0	•	49.2	14.9	12.9	7.6	15.5	7.7	8.8	5.9	20.0	13.8	6.2
Total Liabilities to Net Worth 37	2.3	•	5.1	3.8	0.9	2.5	1.6	0.9	1.5	11.5	2.9	3.0	2.1
Current Assets to Working Capital 38	1.9	•	1.9	2.3	1.6	2.1	1.8	1.6	4.2	1.9	2.9	3.3	1.7
Current Liabilities to Working Capital 39	0.9	•	0.9	1.3	0.6	1.1	0.8	0.6	3.2	0.9	1.9	2.3	0.7
Working Capital to Net Sales 40	0.2	•	0.1	0.1	0.2	0.3	0.2	0.3	0.1	0.3	0.1	0.1	0.2
Inventory to Working Capital 41	0.9	•	1.0	1.3	0.9	1.2	1.0	0.8	2.4	1.0	1.5	1.5	0.4
Total Receipts to Cash Flow 42	8.3	5.1	7.0	10.6	10.4	9.5	11.7	9.3	16.6	6.8	12.7	6.3	8.9
Cost of Goods to Cash Flow 43	5.1	2.6	3.9	6.9	7.0	6.7	8.5	6.2	12.1	3.6	8.0	3.2	5.9
Cash Flow to Total Debt 44	0.3	•	0.7	0.3	0.4	0.2	0.3	0.3	0.1	0.2	0.2	0.2	0.2
Selected Financial Factors (in Percentages)													
Debt Ratio 45	69.6	•	83.5	79.0	47.4	71.3	62.0	46.4	59.7	92.0	74.1	75.2	67.9
Return on Total Assets 46	7.0	•	9.4	3.1	3.0	3.1	7.6	8.4	2.1	7.4	6.8	9.9	6.8
Return on Equity Before Income Taxes 47	16.3	•	39.2	7.0	3.2	4.5	17.0	13.8	1.6	52.8	13.0	28.6	16.7
Return on Equity After Income Taxes 48	11.7	•	37.8	5.1	2.8	4.2	16.2	12.4	0.1	30.7	9.3	19.4	10.4
Profit Margin (Before Income Tax) 49	2.8	•	1.6	0.6	0.9	0.9	3.2	5.2	0.4	4.0	1.7	7.1	3.6
Profit Margin (After Income Tax) 50	2.0	•	1.5	0.4	0.8	0.9	3.0	4.6	0.0	2.3	1.2	4.8	2.2

Table II

Corporations with Net Income

MISCELLANEOUS STORE RETAILERS

Item Description for Accounting Period 7/11 Through 6/12		MONEY AMOUNTS AND SIZE OF ASSETS IN THOUSANDS OF DOLLARS Total	Zero Assets	Under 500	500 to 1,000	1,000 to 5,000	5,000 to 10,000	10,000 to 25,000	25,000 to 50,000	50,000 to 100,000	100,000 to 250,000	250,000 to 500,000	500,000 to 2,500,000	2,500,000 and over
Number of Enterprises	1	35538	3619	28082	1282	2080	288	126	25	11	10	•	•	0
Revenues ($ in Thousands)														
Net Sales	2	71963726	436779	15770150	2408427	8826161	2744323	4581003	1515880	789146	2326663	•	•	0
Interest	3	40777	359	614	1015	8586	859	754	524	795	2676	•	•	0
Rents	4	33396	0	26	1500	2150	2992	11267	1549	0	1754	•	•	0
Royalties	5	173024	0	0	0	0	0	298	0	30418	2330	•	•	0
Other Portfolio Income	6	369605	10080	7368	861	6429	650	3656	20048	5509	115	•	•	0
Other Receipts	7	1510315	55363	65715	30737	160343	12961	93969	38573	8869	4241	•	•	0
Total Receipts	8	74090843	502581	15843873	2442540	9003669	2761785	4690947	1576574	834737	2337779	•	•	0
Average Total Receipts	9	2085	139	564	1905	4329	9590	37230	63063	75885	233778	•	•	•
Operating Costs/Operating Income (%)														
Cost of Operations	10	60.1	54.1	51.5	64.2	69.4	72.0	74.3	69.2	60.5	49.8	•	•	•
Salaries and Wages	11	12.1	7.2	11.6	12.2	9.9	6.2	8.5	8.8	11.9	13.8	•	•	•
Taxes Paid	12	2.2	1.9	2.6	2.0	2.5	0.9	1.2	1.8	2.1	2.6	•	•	•
Interest Paid	13	1.2	0.5	0.5	0.5	0.6	1.4	0.4	0.3	0.9	3.4	•	•	•
Depreciation	14	1.7	0.8	1.0	0.8	0.6	0.6	1.2	1.4	6.5	2.9	•	•	•
Amortization and Depletion	15	0.2	0.1	0.1	0.0	0.1	0.0	0.0	0.0	0.2	0.3	•	•	•
Pensions and Other Deferred Comp.	16	0.1	0.0	0.2	0.0	0.3	0.2	0.2	0.1	0.5	0.1	•	•	•
Employee Benefits	17	1.0	0.2	0.7	0.5	0.4	0.2	0.3	0.6	1.5	0.9	•	•	•
Advertising	18	1.5	2.1	1.2	0.5	0.7	1.0	0.4	0.3	1.4	2.4	•	•	•
Other Expenses	19	15.0	31.6	19.5	12.3	10.7	12.8	8.4	11.0	13.2	17.4	•	•	•
Officers' Compensation	20	2.2	1.2	5.5	3.4	3.1	1.7	1.9	1.9	2.0	1.1	•	•	•
Operating Margin	21	2.7	0.2	5.7	3.5	1.5	3.1	3.1	4.7	•	5.3	•	•	•
Operating Margin Before Officers' Comp.	22	4.9	1.4	11.2	6.9	4.6	4.8	4.9	6.5	1.3	6.4	•	•	•

Selected Average Balance Sheet ($ in Thousands)													
Net Receivables **23**	145	0	12	162	333	1725	2357	6613	5645	20059	•	•	•
Inventories **24**	271	0	43	265	745	2525	5907	12897	19779	64889	•	•	•
Net Property, Plant and Equipment **25**	182	0	22	95	266	322	2628	6332	10772	29699	•	•	•
Total Assets **26**	1064	0	118	738	2006	6649	15566	37260	64937	179669	•	•	•
Notes and Loans Payable **27**	363	0	52	135	544	2148	3528	5970	14585	116002	•	•	•
All Other Liabilities **28**	286	0	29	287	366	2377	4956	8507	24039	37191	•	•	•
Net Worth **29**	415	0	37	316	1096	2123	7082	22783	26314	26476	•	•	•
Selected Financial Ratios (Times to 1)													
Current Ratio **30**	2.1	•	2.3	1.9	2.7	2.0	2.5	3.2	1.2	2.6	•	•	•
Quick Ratio **31**	0.9	•	1.1	1.0	1.2	0.7	1.1	1.1	0.5	1.0	•	•	•
Net Sales to Working Capital **32**	6.4	•	12.7	6.8	4.6	3.0	5.4	3.0	15.5	3.3	•	•	•
Coverage Ratio **33**	6.2	33.9	14.5	11.0	6.6	3.8	16.1	26.8	6.3	2.7	•	•	•
Total Asset Turnover **34**	1.9	•	4.8	2.5	2.1	1.4	2.3	1.6	1.1	1.3	•	•	•
Inventory Turnover **35**	4.5	•	6.8	4.6	4.0	2.7	4.6	3.3	2.2	1.8	•	•	•
Receivables Turnover **36**	14.1	•	45.1	12.0	11.9	8.7	15.8	8.1	6.3	9.7	•	•	•
Total Liabilities to Net Worth **37**	1.6	•	2.2	1.3	0.8	2.1	1.2	0.6	1.5	5.8	•	•	•
Current Assets to Working Capital **38**	1.9	•	1.8	2.1	1.6	2.0	1.7	1.4	7.0	1.6	•	•	•
Current Liabilities to Working Capital **39**	0.9	•	0.8	1.1	0.6	1.0	0.7	0.4	6.0	0.6	•	•	•
Working Capital to Net Sales **40**	0.2	•	0.1	0.1	0.2	0.3	0.2	0.3	0.1	0.3	•	•	•
Inventory to Working Capital **41**	0.9	•	0.9	1.0	0.8	1.2	0.9	0.6	3.3	0.9	•	•	•
Total Receipts to Cash Flow **42**	6.8	3.3	5.4	7.8	9.2	7.6	9.7	7.8	7.5	6.5	•	•	•
Cost of Goods to Cash Flow **43**	4.1	1.8	2.8	5.0	6.4	5.5	7.2	5.4	4.5	3.2	•	•	•
Cash Flow to Total Debt **44**	0.5	•	1.3	0.6	0.5	0.3	0.4	0.5	0.2	0.2	•	•	•
Selected Financial Factors (in Percentages)													
Debt Ratio **45**	61.0	•	68.4	57.2	45.4	68.1	54.5	38.9	59.5	85.3	•	•	•
Return on Total Assets **46**	13.7	•	31.8	13.6	8.8	7.3	13.6	14.6	6.6	11.9	•	•	•
Return on Equity Before Income Taxes **47**	29.6	•	93.9	29.0	13.7	16.8	28.1	23.0	13.8	50.9	•	•	•
Return on Equity After Income Taxes **48**	24.0	•	92.6	27.5	13.0	16.4	27.2	21.1	11.1	33.9	•	•	•
Profit Margin (Before Income Tax) **49**	6.1	15.3	6.2	4.9	3.5	3.8	5.5	8.7	5.1	5.8	•	•	•
Profit Margin (After Income Tax) **50**	4.9	14.9	6.1	4.6	3.3	3.7	5.3	7.9	4.1	3.9	•	•	•

Table I

Corporations with and without Net Income

NONSTORE RETAILERS

MONEY AMOUNTS AND SIZE OF ASSETS IN THOUSANDS OF DOLLARS

Item Description for Accounting Period 7/11 Through 6/12		Total	Zero Assets	Under 500	500 to 1,000	1,000 to 5,000	5,000 to 10,000	10,000 to 25,000	25,000 to 50,000	50,000 to 100,000	100,000 to 250,000	250,000 to 500,000	500,000 to 2,500,000	2,500,000 and over
Number of Enterprises	1	56063	15574	35616	1922	2263	338	152	70	57	33	15	14	10
Revenues ($ in Thousands)														
Net Sales	2	192504688	2196665	18215688	5670640	21837755	6724685	9028067	5352216	9420704	11652503	11599048	23860972	66945746
Interest	3	585378	1567	3096	2376	4582	4433	3926	1219	10395	40352	18112	232347	262974
Rents	4	90775	370	1889	8276	306	6823	2335	1938	8373	3690	254	3239	53283
Royalties	5	843553	0	0	0	913	585	0	72	3094	233	118	215659	622879
Other Portfolio Income	6	1059421	23629	45661	2293	50012	16865	22662	3250	17430	2369	21970	42124	811156
Other Receipts	7	2263844	192140	67763	6201	155818	77791	63869	47169	107156	83427	170171	388538	903797
Total Receipts	8	197347659	2414371	18334097	5689786	22049386	6831182	9120859	5405864	9567152	11782574	11809673	24742879	69599835
Average Total Receipts	9	3520	155	515	2960	9743	20211	60006	77227	167845	357048	787312	1767348	6959984
Operating Costs/Operating Income (%)														
Cost of Operations	10	69.9	45.9	65.9	76.6	76.4	78.0	77.3	61.0	70.8	64.6	75.8	79.6	64.3
Salaries and Wages	11	8.1	15.6	6.5	6.9	6.1	6.5	6.6	9.5	8.1	9.7	6.9	5.5	10.2
Taxes Paid	12	1.1	2.6	1.4	1.5	1.1	1.4	0.8	1.4	1.2	1.1	0.9	0.7	1.0
Interest Paid	13	1.2	1.5	0.4	0.3	0.4	0.5	0.3	0.4	0.8	0.6	1.1	0.8	2.3
Depreciation	14	2.2	4.1	0.8	0.6	0.8	1.2	1.3	1.7	1.8	1.4	1.0	1.0	4.2
Amortization and Depletion	15	0.4	0.8	0.0	0.0	0.2	0.2	0.1	0.3	0.4	0.4	0.3	0.3	0.6
Pensions and Other Deferred Comp.	16	0.3	0.1	0.2	0.4	0.1	0.1	0.2	0.1	0.1	0.2	0.1	0.9	0.2
Employee Benefits	17	0.7	0.9	0.4	0.7	0.5	0.6	0.5	1.0	0.9	0.7	0.8	0.6	0.8
Advertising	18	2.4	4.3	2.1	0.9	2.3	0.9	2.9	4.2	2.8	3.3	2.3	3.1	2.1
Other Expenses	19	13.2	36.3	15.6	8.1	9.7	8.3	8.5	18.8	12.2	15.2	10.7	8.3	16.0
Officers' Compensation	20	1.4	9.7	5.2	3.0	1.7	2.0	1.0	1.5	0.7	0.8	0.4	0.6	0.5
Operating Margin	21	•	•	1.5	0.9	0.8	0.4	0.4	0.1	0.1	2.0	•	•	•
Operating Margin Before Officers' Comp.	22	0.6	•	6.6	3.9	2.4	2.3	1.4	1.5	0.8	2.8	0.0	•	•

Selected Average Balance Sheet ($ in Thousands)														
Net Receivables	23	386	0	11	133	627	1656	2872	5898	16153	33584	73178	261333	1134745
Inventories	24	226	0	19	129	501	1210	3720	5815	11946	31539	78760	109256	482857
Net Property, Plant and Equipment	25	221	0	10	118	314	885	2736	4138	10909	13647	26087	59638	778506
Total Assets	26	2242	0	74	670	2270	6266	15921	33346	72868	162543	376638	1044149	7994703
Notes and Loans Payable	27	512	0	35	165	513	2078	3839	4426	17526	29624	82583	192538	1847428
All Other Liabilities	28	883	0	27	163	910	1836	6445	13353	26104	59056	109797	446373	3233929
Net Worth	29	847	0	13	342	847	2351	5637	15567	29238	73863	184258	405238	2913346

Selected Financial Ratios (Times to 1)														
Current Ratio	30	1.5	•	2.0	2.1	1.7	1.8	1.6	1.6	1.4	1.5	1.9	1.6	1.4
Quick Ratio	31	0.9	•	1.3	1.4	1.1	1.1	0.9	1.0	0.9	0.9	1.1	0.9	0.8
Net Sales to Working Capital	32	9.9	•	17.3	14.4	13.1	10.5	15.8	9.7	12.6	9.3	8.3	7.7	8.3
Coverage Ratio	33	3.2	•	6.6	4.9	5.3	5.0	5.6	3.9	3.3	6.5	2.3	4.4	2.8
Total Asset Turnover	34	1.5	•	6.9	4.4	4.3	3.2	3.7	2.3	2.3	2.2	2.1	1.6	0.8
Inventory Turnover	35	10.6	•	18.2	17.4	14.7	12.8	12.3	8.0	9.8	7.2	7.4	12.4	8.9
Receivables Turnover	36	8.4	•	48.6	18.4	14.8	13.7	19.5	11.4	10.9	10.5	9.8	6.8	5.3
Total Liabilities to Net Worth	37	1.6	•	4.6	1.0	1.7	1.7	1.8	1.1	1.5	1.2	1.0	1.6	1.7
Current Assets to Working Capital	38	3.0	•	2.0	1.9	2.4	2.2	2.8	2.7	3.2	2.8	2.1	2.7	3.6
Current Liabilities to Working Capital	39	2.0	•	1.0	0.9	1.4	1.2	1.8	1.7	2.2	1.8	1.1	1.7	2.6
Working Capital to Net Sales	40	0.1	•	0.1	0.1	0.1	0.1	0.1	0.1	0.1	0.1	0.1	0.1	0.1
Inventory to Working Capital	41	0.7	•	0.7	0.6	0.8	0.6	1.0	0.8	0.9	0.9	0.8	0.6	0.7
Total Receipts to Cash Flow	42	7.4	5.0	6.8	12.7	9.5	11.1	11.2	5.5	8.0	6.0	9.0	10.5	6.1
Cost of Goods to Cash Flow	43	5.2	2.3	4.5	9.7	7.3	8.7	8.7	3.3	5.6	3.9	6.8	8.4	3.9
Cash Flow to Total Debt	44	0.3	•	1.2	0.7	0.7	0.5	0.5	0.8	0.5	0.7	0.4	0.3	0.2

Selected Financial Factors (in Percentages)														
Debt Ratio	45	62.2	•	82.2	49.0	62.7	62.5	64.6	53.3	59.9	54.6	51.1	61.2	63.6
Return on Total Assets	46	5.8	•	17.2	6.8	9.1	7.8	6.4	3.3	5.8	8.0	5.1	5.6	5.5
Return on Equity Before Income Taxes	47	10.6	•	81.9	10.7	19.7	16.7	14.8	5.3	10.0	14.9	5.9	11.1	9.7
Return on Equity After Income Taxes	48	7.5	•	80.9	10.0	18.9	14.5	13.0	2.4	6.6	12.8	3.9	8.1	6.2
Profit Margin (Before Income Tax)	49	2.6	•	2.1	1.2	1.7	2.0	1.4	1.1	1.8	3.1	1.4	2.6	4.2
Profit Margin (After Income Tax)	50	1.9	•	2.1	1.2	1.7	1.7	1.2	0.5	1.2	2.7	0.9	1.9	2.7

Table II

Corporations with Net Income

NONSTORE RETAILERS

MONEY AMOUNTS AND SIZE OF ASSETS IN THOUSANDS OF DOLLARS

Item Description for Accounting Period 7/11 Through 6/12		Total	Zero Assets	Under 500	500 to 1,000	1,000 to 5,000	5,000 to 10,000	10,000 to 25,000	25,000 to 50,000	50,000 to 100,000	100,000 to 250,000	250,000 to 500,000	500,000 to 2,500,000	2,500,000 and over
Number of Enterprises	1	27824	4640	19285	1633	1785	258	103	39	29	25	8	11	7
Revenues ($ in Thousands)														
Net Sales	2	126800920	998227	12809840	4947577	19431775	5755296	6581636	3321976	5549401	8708877	7873758	19136861	31685696
Interest	3	520511	355	2628	200	3523	2732	1763	402	5315	39356	766	232211	231262
Rents	4	65623	370	0	1346	306	1993	148	59	1311	3568	0	3239	53283
Royalties	5	753444	0	0	0	913	25	0	72	3094	233	118	215659	533329
Other Portfolio Income	6	990535	23611	28002	699	47003	5084	22588	2795	10668	1866	1	41317	806901
Other Receipts	7	1920273	26610	50999	2525	147578	42433	53553	45656	93952	36169	55689	385517	979591
Total Receipts	8	131051306	1049173	12891469	4952347	19631098	5807563	6659688	3370960	5663741	8790069	7930332	20014804	34290062
Average Total Receipts	9	4710	226	668	3033	10998	22510	64657	86435	195301	351603	991292	1819528	4898580
Operating Costs/Operating Income (%)														
Cost of Operations	10	67.5	36.1	62.6	76.4	77.8	79.2	74.4	55.5	71.1	64.2	80.7	76.4	52.1
Salaries and Wages	11	7.9	6.9	6.1	6.8	5.2	5.4	7.2	8.7	7.2	7.9	5.2	6.2	12.9
Taxes Paid	12	1.1	2.1	1.5	1.5	0.9	1.0	0.9	1.5	1.2	0.9	0.6	0.8	1.3
Interest Paid	13	1.5	0.6	0.4	0.3	0.3	0.4	0.2	0.3	0.5	0.7	0.7	0.9	4.4
Depreciation	14	1.5	0.5	0.6	0.5	0.7	1.0	1.1	1.8	1.1	1.3	0.7	1.1	3.4
Amortization and Depletion	15	0.5	0.9	0.1	0.0	0.1	0.2	0.1	0.2	0.2	0.4	0.5	0.4	1.2
Pensions and Other Deferred Comp.	16	0.4	0.2	0.2	0.5	0.1	0.1	0.3	0.2	0.1	0.2	0.0	1.2	0.4
Employee Benefits	17	0.7	0.3	0.4	0.7	0.5	0.6	0.6	0.9	0.7	0.6	0.5	0.7	1.2
Advertising	18	2.7	7.3	1.9	0.7	2.2	0.6	3.2	2.3	2.6	3.9	1.9	3.7	3.0
Other Expenses	19	13.4	29.4	15.1	6.8	8.5	6.2	7.4	21.1	11.7	15.0	6.1	9.5	21.8
Officers' Compensation	20	1.5	5.4	5.8	2.7	1.5	1.7	1.2	1.5	0.7	0.8	0.3	0.3	0.8
Operating Margin	21	1.4	10.4	5.3	3.0	2.2	3.8	3.5	6.0	3.0	4.1	2.7	•	•
Operating Margin Before Officers' Comp.	22	2.9	15.7	11.1	5.7	3.7	5.4	4.7	7.5	3.7	4.9	3.0	•	•

Selected Average Balance Sheet ($ in Thousands)

Net Receivables 23	638	0	15	126	691	2063	2907	6540	19637	35232	64026	312647	1363669
Inventories 24	329	0	24	125	511	1449	4157	6777	17131	30032	112380	146119	281380
Net Property, Plant and Equipment 25	264	0	14	126	314	1002	2141	4630	6257	12599	22562	65725	608248
Total Assets 26	3119	0	98	664	2354	6358	16598	33487	72977	156257	423144	1147134	7560184
Notes and Loans Payable 27	810	0	38	180	468	2147	3497	4224	12742	35953	64853	204285	2224682
All Other Liabilities 28	1178	0	27	153	924	1924	6541	11667	27518	55393	128407	504811	2853461
Net Worth 29	1131	0	34	331	963	2288	6560	17596	32718	64911	229884	438039	2482041

Selected Financial Ratios (Times to 1)

Current Ratio 30	1.6	•	2.6	2.1	1.8	1.9	1.6	1.8	1.6	1.4	2.0	1.5	1.5
Quick Ratio 31	1.1	•	1.6	1.3	1.1	1.3	0.8	1.1	0.9	0.9	1.0	0.9	1.1
Net Sales to Working Capital 32	9.2	•	13.7	16.6	12.9	10.3	14.7	8.4	10.3	11.5	8.8	7.7	6.4
Coverage Ratio 33	5.0	25.8	15.8	10.1	10.2	12.2	21.9	28.2	12.2	8.4	6.2	5.3	3.4
Total Asset Turnover 34	1.5	•	6.8	4.6	4.6	3.5	3.8	2.5	2.6	2.2	2.3	1.5	0.6
Inventory Turnover 35	9.3	•	17.5	18.5	16.6	12.2	11.4	7.0	7.9	7.4	7.1	9.1	8.4
Receivables Turnover 36	6.5	•	48.1	21.8	15.3	12.6	19.3	12.5	9.8	9.9	9.9	•	•
Total Liabilities to Net Worth 37	1.8	•	1.9	1.0	1.4	1.8	1.5	0.9	1.2	1.4	0.8	1.6	2.0
Current Assets to Working Capital 38	2.7	•	1.6	1.9	2.2	2.1	2.6	2.2	2.6	3.2	2.0	3.0	3.2
Current Liabilities to Working Capital 39	1.7	•	0.6	0.9	1.2	1.1	1.6	1.2	1.6	2.2	1.0	2.0	2.2
Working Capital to Net Sales 40	0.1	•	0.1	0.1	0.1	0.1	0.1	0.1	0.1	0.1	0.1	0.1	0.2
Inventory to Working Capital 41	0.6	•	0.6	0.7	0.7	0.6	1.0	0.6	0.8	1.0	0.9	0.6	0.4
Total Receipts to Cash Flow 42	6.0	2.5	5.5	11.5	9.2	10.1	9.0	3.7	6.3	5.4	11.0	8.7	3.9
Cost of Goods to Cash Flow 43	4.1	0.9	3.4	8.8	7.2	8.0	6.7	2.1	4.5	3.4	8.9	6.6	2.0
Cash Flow to Total Debt 44	0.4	•	1.9	0.8	0.9	0.5	0.7	1.4	0.8	0.7	0.5	0.3	0.2

Selected Financial Factors (in Percentages)

Debt Ratio 45	63.7	•	65.8	50.2	59.1	64.0	60.5	47.5	55.2	58.5	45.7	61.8	67.2
Return on Total Assets 46	11.0	•	42.9	15.6	16.3	17.8	18.8	19.8	15.0	12.8	9.5	7.0	9.1
Return on Equity Before Income Taxes 47	24.2	•	117.5	28.2	36.0	45.5	45.3	36.4	30.7	27.1	14.7	14.9	19.5
Return on Equity After Income Taxes 48	19.6	•	116.8	27.3	35.2	42.6	43.0	31.8	24.8	24.0	11.7	11.3	13.6
Profit Margin (Before Income Tax) 49	6.0	15.5	5.9	3.1	3.2	4.7	4.7	7.5	5.3	5.0	3.4	3.7	10.7
Profit Margin (After Income Tax) 50	4.9	14.5	5.9	3.0	3.1	4.4	4.4	6.6	4.2	4.5	2.7	2.8	7.4

Table I

Corporations with and without Net Income

AIR TRANSPORTATION

Item Description for Accounting Period 7/11 Through 6/12		MONEY AMOUNTS AND SIZE OF ASSETS IN THOUSANDS OF DOLLARS												
		Total	Zero Assets	Under 500	500 to 1,000	1,000 to 5,000	5,000 to 10,000	10,000 to 25,000	25,000 to 50,000	50,000 to 100,000	100,000 to 250,000	250,000 to 500,000	500,000 to 2,500,000	2,500,000 and over
Number of Enterprises	1	7124	2121	3568	593	533	122	92	32	23	11	4	15	9
Revenues ($ in Thousands)														
Net Sales	2	164796315	1100446	1195785	252970	1469924	1123624	3185700	950918	2380544	1662798	873267	13622932	136977409
Interest	3	225340	730	14	9	420	277	1172	3588	256	748	33	28661	189433
Rents	4	429519	0	0	1760	1002	0	37	3889	45	83	0	48558	374146
Royalties	5	959	0	0	0	0	0	21	0	0	0	0	938	1
Other Portfolio Income	6	825568	34968	56574	15468	5845	693	15794	40564	8305	10816	164	132820	503559
Other Receipts	7	5142068	7183	4158	996	37197	39341	49435	11155	25935	19711	2366	87382	4857201
Total Receipts	8	171419769	1143327	1256531	271203	1514388	1163935	3252159	1010114	2415085	1694156	875830	13921291	142901749
Average Total Receipts	9	24062	539	352	457	2841	9540	35350	31566	105004	154014	218958	928086	15877972
Operating Costs/Operating Income (%)														
Cost of Operations	10	28.9	3.2	92.0	5.0	60.5	60.9	65.5	62.8	21.2	30.1	26.0	34.7	26.5
Salaries and Wages	11	16.2	10.8	0.6	19.8	9.4	8.7	8.8	7.5	14.5	16.1	14.6	12.7	17.1
Taxes Paid	12	1.9	0.6	1.1	3.5	1.4	2.8	1.1	2.3	1.6	1.8	1.8	1.9	1.9
Interest Paid	13	2.4	0.5	0.3	2.0	1.4	1.3	1.1	2.1	0.8	2.2	3.9	3.2	2.4
Depreciation	14	5.6	14.8	2.3	33.5	9.5	7.8	3.8	7.1	3.2	6.3	13.3	12.0	4.8
Amortization and Depletion	15	0.3	0.0	•	0.5	0.1	0.0	0.1	0.0	0.2	1.8	0.1	0.4	0.3
Pensions and Other Deferred Comp.	16	2.1	0.0	•	•	0.1	0.0	0.1	0.1	0.2	0.1	0.2	0.4	2.5
Employee Benefits	17	2.8	0.1	0.1	2.9	0.6	1.1	0.4	2.2	1.6	2.1	1.3	1.6	3.1
Advertising	18	0.7	0.9	0.4	0.1	0.3	0.1	0.2	0.3	0.1	0.3	0.3	0.9	0.7
Other Expenses	19	43.5	89.9	14.8	80.6	30.6	22.2	16.7	17.3	56.6	43.0	47.2	41.1	44.5
Officers' Compensation	20	0.4	1.5	4.5	9.1	1.3	1.1	2.3	1.8	1.2	0.9	0.7	0.7	0.2
Operating Margin	21	•	•	•	•	•	•	•	•	•	•	•	•	•
Operating Margin Before Officers' Comp.	22	•	•	•	•	•	•	2.1	•	0.0	•	•	•	•

Selected Average Balance Sheet ($ in Thousands)													
Net Receivables 23	1088	0	5	81	155	1594	3877	2705	12741	31667	112159	58562	555328
Inventories 24	390	0	26	49	72	34	293	930	2048	11065	13630	23388	220416
Net Property, Plant and Equipment 25	12999	0	23	528	1535	2131	7505	15419	28692	52273	220981	521341	8889712
Total Assets 26	24980	0	81	695	2092	7109	16921	32727	72181	168404	424263	1017439	16910885
Notes and Loans Payable 27	9328	0	244	1413	1096	4181	7781	18257	28517	74428	317025	397945	5959424
All Other Liabilities 28	14300	0	40	1153	307	1764	4441	7842	26046	68434	35115	335925	10386665
Net Worth 29	1352	0	-203	-1872	689	1164	4698	6627	17618	25541	72123	283568	564795
Selected Financial Ratios (Times to 1)													
Current Ratio 30	0.9	•	1.9	0.1	1.3	1.7	1.3	1.2	1.0	1.9	5.0	1.3	0.9
Quick Ratio 31	0.6	•	0.8	0.1	0.8	1.2	1.1	0.8	0.7	1.3	3.9	0.8	0.6
Net Sales to Working Capital 32	•	•	11.9	•	31.7	7.4	23.3	14.6	•	4.5	1.4	14.0	•
Coverage Ratio 33	0.7	•	•	•	•	•	2.7	2.3	1.3	•	•	•	1.1
Total Asset Turnover 34	0.9	•	4.1	0.6	1.3	1.3	2.0	0.9	1.4	0.9	0.5	0.9	0.9
Inventory Turnover 35	17.2	•	11.7	0.4	23.1	165.3	77.3	20.1	10.7	4.1	4.2	13.5	18.3
Receivables Turnover 36	20.6	•	35.9	4.5	18.6	7.6	8.5	7.7	9.9	5.0	3.2	14.0	25.6
Total Liabilities to Net Worth 37	17.5	•	•	•	2.0	5.1	2.6	3.9	3.1	5.6	4.9	2.6	28.9
Current Assets to Working Capital 38	•	•	2.1	•	4.7	2.4	4.1	5.3	•	2.1	1.3	4.7	•
Current Liabilities to Working Capital 39	•	•	1.1	•	3.7	1.4	3.1	4.3	•	1.1	0.3	3.7	•
Working Capital to Net Sales 40	•	•	0.1	•	0.0	0.1	0.0	0.1	•	0.2	0.7	0.1	•
Inventory to Working Capital 41	•	•	1.1	•	0.7	0.0	0.2	0.4	•	0.2	0.2	0.3	•
Total Receipts to Cash Flow 42	3.4	1.8	•	5.7	12.5	8.2	9.3	7.2	2.5	3.6	5.3	6.7	3.1
Cost of Goods to Cash Flow 43	1.0	0.1	•	0.3	7.6	5.0	6.1	4.5	0.5	1.1	1.4	2.3	0.8
Cash Flow to Total Debt 44	0.3	•	•	0.0	0.2	0.2	0.3	0.2	0.8	0.3	0.1	0.2	0.3
Selected Financial Factors (in Percentages)													
Debt Ratio 45	94.6	•	350.0	369.3	67.1	83.6	72.2	79.8	75.6	84.8	83.0	72.1	96.7
Return on Total Assets 46	1.5	•	•	•	•	•	6.0	4.4	1.6	•	•	•	2.4
Return on Equity Before Income Taxes 47	•	•	18.2	11.4	•	•	13.7	12.3	1.7	•	•	•	9.1
Return on Equity After Income Taxes 48	•	•	18.2	11.4	•	•	11.5	11.1	0.2	•	•	•	9.1
Profit Margin (Before Income Tax) 49	•	•	•	•	•	•	1.9	2.7	0.3	•	•	•	0.3
Profit Margin (After Income Tax) 50	•	•	•	•	•	•	1.6	2.5	0.0	•	•	•	0.3

Table II

Corporations with Net Income

AIR TRANSPORTATION

MONEY AMOUNTS AND SIZE OF ASSETS IN THOUSANDS OF DOLLARS

Item Description for Accounting Period 7/11 Through 6/12		Total	Zero Assets	Under 500	500 to 1,000	1,000 to 5,000	5,000 to 10,000	10,000 to 25,000	25,000 to 50,000	50,000 to 100,000	100,000 to 250,000	250,000 to 500,000	500,000 to 2,500,000	2,500,000 and over
Number of Enterprises	1	1799	20	1232	56	330	73	45	20	11	6	0	3	3
Revenues ($ in Thousands)														
Net Sales	2	63973103	13316	978535	2739	698919	959201	2431045	584448	936511	970641	0	2329627	54068120
Interest	3	76873	704	0	0	106	275	103	1409	14	46	0	7152	67063
Rents	4	19789	0	0	0	0	0	36	3889	45	83	0	0	15736
Royalties	5	0	0	0	0	0	0	0	0	0	0	0	0	0
Other Portfolio Income	6	209811	30840	34332	15468	0	685	13728	38679	4867	162	0	54703	16349
Other Receipts	7	3407211	0	4158	914	34748	3137	39627	7091	16151	9196	0	11408	3280782
Total Receipts	8	67686787	44860	1017025	19121	733773	963298	2484539	635516	957588	980128	0	2402890	57448050
Average Total Receipts	9	37625	2243	826	341	2224	13196	55212	31776	87053	163355	•	800963	19149350
Operating Costs/Operating Income (%)														
Cost of Operations	10	16.7	•	88.0	•	50.3	68.2	67.9	53.9	29.9	45.9	•	16.2	10.6
Salaries and Wages	11	16.2	44.2	0.0	4.6	10.1	9.2	6.8	9.4	18.1	13.5	•	14.5	17.2
Taxes Paid	12	1.6	19.5	0.6	0.8	1.9	2.6	1.0	2.3	1.9	1.2	•	2.3	1.5
Interest Paid	13	2.3	12.1	0.3	3.0	0.9	0.4	0.5	1.5	0.8	0.3	•	3.2	2.5
Depreciation	14	4.3	30.2	1.8	5.2	6.9	2.3	1.4	8.0	2.3	2.2	•	7.6	4.4
Amortization and Depletion	15	0.3	•	•	•	0.1	•	0.0	0.0	0.1	0.1	•	0.0	0.3
Pensions and Other Deferred Comp.	16	2.0	0.1	•	•	0.3	0.1	0.1	0.1	0.3	0.4	•	0.2	2.3
Employee Benefits	17	3.2	4.2	0.1	0.8	0.7	1.2	0.3	2.3	2.7	1.0	•	1.3	3.5
Advertising	18	0.7	0.0	0.4	•	0.2	0.1	0.2	0.3	0.1	0.1	•	0.4	0.8
Other Expenses	19	55.3	41.0	2.9	48.9	25.0	11.8	15.7	21.0	35.6	29.1	•	50.2	60.6
Officers' Compensation	20	0.5	•	5.0	•	2.8	1.2	2.7	3.0	2.0	1.1	•	0.6	0.2
Operating Margin	21	•	•	0.9	36.7	1.0	2.9	3.3	•	6.2	5.3	•	3.3	•
Operating Margin Before Officers' Comp.	22	•	•	5.9	36.7	3.8	4.1	6.0	1.0	8.2	6.4	•	3.9	•

Selected Average Balance Sheet ($ in Thousands)														
Net Receivables	23	1776	0	3	0	174	1406	5229	3706	13486	116605	•	45403	579087
Inventories	24	629	0	0	0	88	32	449	1154	3756	17396	•	30897	150304
Net Property, Plant and Equipment	25	19982	0	49	675	1291	706	5234	16726	16347	37773	•	330196	11134940
Total Assets	26	39601	0	93	707	1905	6167	16810	32793	69634	213642	•	1130798	21052005
Notes and Loans Payable	27	13298	0	79	0	771	864	4279	11367	20133	99374	•	312105	7111342
All Other Liabilities	28	18536	0	27	19	171	1829	5694	8269	29659	53332	•	222885	10461716
Net Worth	29	7767	0	-12	688	963	3474	6836	13157	19842	60934	•	595808	3478947
Selected Financial Ratios (Times to 1)														
Current Ratio	30	1.1	•	1.4	1.5	2.5	2.0	1.3	1.1	1.2	5.2	•	2.6	1.0
Quick Ratio	31	0.8	•	1.2	1.2	1.7	1.6	1.1	0.9	0.9	4.6	•	1.5	0.7
Net Sales to Working Capital	32	44.0	•	61.9	4.6	9.3	9.3	26.8	22.7	17.3	1.2	•	2.9	•
Coverage Ratio	33	2.3	16.3	18.4	213.0	8.0	9.2	11.3	5.5	12.2	20.9	•	3.4	1.9
Total Asset Turnover	34	0.9	•	8.5	0.1	1.1	2.1	3.2	0.9	1.2	0.8	•	0.7	0.9
Inventory Turnover	35	9.4	•	•	•	12.1	277.4	81.7	13.6	6.8	4.3	•	4.1	12.7
Receivables Turnover	36	13.6	•	114.6	•	14.2	13.8	9.5	11.1	6.6	•	•	5.1	•
Total Liabilities to Net Worth	37	4.1	•	•	0.0	1.0	0.8	1.5	1.5	2.5	2.5	•	0.9	5.1
Current Assets to Working Capital	38	14.1	•	3.4	2.8	1.7	2.0	4.1	8.7	7.4	1.2	•	1.6	•
Current Liabilities to Working Capital	39	13.1	•	2.4	1.8	0.7	1.0	3.1	7.7	6.4	0.2	•	0.6	•
Working Capital to Net Sales	40	0.0	•	0.0	0.2	0.1	0.1	0.0	0.0	0.1	0.8	•	0.3	•
Inventory to Working Capital	41	0.5	•	•	•	0.4	0.0	0.1	0.8	1.2	0.1	•	0.1	•
Total Receipts to Cash Flow	42	2.2	0.5	20.1	0.1	4.3	11.1	7.8	5.3	2.9	4.4	•	2.6	2.0
Cost of Goods to Cash Flow	43	0.4	•	17.7	•	2.2	7.6	5.3	2.9	0.9	2.0	•	0.4	0.2
Cash Flow to Total Debt	44	0.5	•	0.4	17.1	0.5	0.4	0.7	0.3	0.6	0.2	•	0.6	0.5
Selected Financial Factors (in Percentages)														
Debt Ratio	45	80.4	•	113.3	2.8	49.5	43.7	59.3	59.9	71.5	71.5	•	47.3	83.5
Return on Total Assets	46	4.7	•	43.7	44.1	7.6	7.8	19.5	7.4	11.2	5.0	•	7.5	4.0
Return on Equity Before Income Taxes	47	13.4	•	•	45.2	13.1	12.4	43.8	15.0	36.2	16.7	•	10.1	11.6
Return on Equity After Income Taxes	48	13.0	•	•	44.5	12.4	12.0	40.7	14.1	33.4	14.6	•	8.7	11.6
Profit Margin (Before Income Tax)	49	2.9	185.5	4.8	634.8	5.9	3.3	5.5	6.8	8.4	6.3	•	7.7	2.2
Profit Margin (After Income Tax)	50	2.8	185.0	4.8	625.5	5.6	3.2	5.2	6.3	7.8	5.5	•	6.7	2.2

Table I

Corporations with and without Net Income

RAIL TRANSPORTATION

MONEY AMOUNTS AND SIZE OF ASSETS IN THOUSANDS OF DOLLARS

Item Description for Accounting Period 7/11 Through 6/12		Total	Zero Assets	Under 500	500 to 1,000	1,000 to 5,000	5,000 to 10,000	10,000 to 25,000	25,000 to 50,000	50,000 to 100,000	100,000 to 250,000	250,000 to 500,000	500,000 to 2,500,000	2,500,000 and over
Number of Enterprises	1	213	17	94	9	21	9	18	12	10	9	3	4	7
Revenues ($ in Thousands)														
Net Sales	2	53623978	35021	0	40	46744	174665	204015	293493	239714	474820	581432	1321646	50252387
Interest	3	155180	0	343	0	6	68	1352	269	986	1224	542	32194	118195
Rents	4	440971	0	38	0	1689	0	1775	4925	2430	4826	2826	16435	406027
Royalties	5	60832	0	0	0	5	253	0	0	0	14590	0	0	45983
Other Portfolio Income	6	554556	206	0	0	2366	413	11961	5181	17192	76105	4305	24042	412786
Other Receipts	7	1009682	-6393	0	436	6982	5863	5279	3207	6805	14160	4365	149575	819404
Total Receipts	8	55845199	28834	381	476	57792	181262	224382	307075	267127	585725	593470	1543892	52054782
Average Total Receipts	9	262184	1696	4	53	2752	20140	12466	25590	26713	65081	197823	385973	7436397
Operating Costs/Operating Income (%)														
Cost of Operations	10	16.8	•	•	•	11.9	•	21.9	21.0	11.3	28.6	36.0	4.0	16.8
Salaries and Wages	11	17.8	11.9	•	•	13.4	•	17.0	10.0	17.6	17.3	7.7	22.7	17.9
Taxes Paid	12	5.3	5.1	•	70.0	7.4	0.0	4.6	5.0	4.8	4.4	2.6	5.2	5.3
Interest Paid	13	5.0	1.2	•	1547.5	0.3	0.7	1.4	1.7	3.7	2.8	0.4	11.1	5.0
Depreciation	14	16.8	4.8	•	72.5	14.2	7.2	4.9	10.9	18.6	14.8	11.2	15.5	17.0
Amortization and Depletion	15	0.1	0.1	•	1295.0	•	0.0	0.3	0.1	0.0	0.2	0.1	0.8	0.1
Pensions and Other Deferred Comp.	16	1.5	•	•	•	•	•	•	0.2	1.0	1.3	0.1	0.2	1.5
Employee Benefits	17	5.7	1.3	•	•	0.9	•	3.8	1.2	3.9	2.7	0.1	7.2	5.8
Advertising	18	0.2	0.0	•	245.0	0.3	•	0.1	0.1	0.1	0.3	0.0	0.0	0.2
Other Expenses	19	27.5	52.6	•	35415.0	49.1	96.1	27.2	26.1	29.3	31.9	19.4	40.5	27.0
Officers' Compensation	20	0.5	•	•	•	1.2	0.1	0.6	2.6	1.8	1.9	0.5	2.7	0.4
Operating Margin	21	2.8	23.1	•	•	1.3	•	18.0	21.0	7.8	•	21.8	•	2.9
Operating Margin Before Officers' Comp.	22	3.3	23.1	•	•	2.5	•	18.7	23.5	9.6	•	22.4	•	3.3

Selected Average Balance Sheet ($ in Thousands)

Net Receivables 23	27055	0	1	0	96	2141	4157	3134	3225	9079	30571	179758	672025
Inventories 24	5800	0	0	6	0	4	181	552	835	401	6087	839	170269
Net Property, Plant and Equipment 25	568278	0	101	3	1532	2203	4688	19115	38246	106705	256411	761949	16501161
Total Assets 26	704809	0	301	970	2933	8305	14812	38220	66362	146343	430499	1707657	19874687
Notes and Loans Payable 27	147434	0	0	1098	120	3385	4366	5375	18191	36951	94488	435639	4096709
All Other Liabilities 28	297694	0	0	1535	68	2343	3722	5881	17150	48557	144734	438408	8634087
Net Worth 29	259681	0	301	-1662	2745	2577	6724	26964	31021	60836	191277	833610	7143891

Selected Financial Ratios (Times to 1)

Current Ratio 30	0.7	•	990.3	0.1	10.9	1.4	1.8	2.8	2.0	1.3	0.7	1.4	0.7
Quick Ratio 31	0.6	•	990.3	0.0	9.7	1.3	1.6	2.3	1.6	1.0	0.5	1.3	0.5
Net Sales to Working Capital 32	•	•	•	•	4.4	20.6	3.3	3.8	2.6	10.9	•	4.4	•
Coverage Ratio 33	2.4	5.5	•	•	72.6	0.5	20.7	15.7	6.2	7.2	69.2	1.6	2.3
Total Asset Turnover 34	0.4	•	•	0.0	0.8	2.3	0.8	0.6	0.4	0.4	0.5	0.2	0.4
Inventory Turnover 35	7.3	•	•	•	1858.3	•	13.7	9.3	3.3	37.6	11.5	15.6	7.1
Receivables Turnover 36	10.2	•	•	•	22.7	10.2	3.7	6.8	8.9	6.3	7.4	1.9	11.8
Total Liabilities to Net Worth 37	1.7	•	0.0	•	0.1	2.2	1.2	0.4	1.1	1.4	1.3	1.0	1.8
Current Assets to Working Capital 38	•	•	1.0	•	1.1	3.9	2.2	1.6	2.0	4.9	•	3.3	•
Current Liabilities to Working Capital 39	•	•	0.0	•	0.1	2.9	1.2	0.6	1.0	3.9	•	2.3	•
Working Capital to Net Sales 40	•	•	•	•	0.2	0.0	0.3	0.3	0.4	0.1	•	0.2	•
Inventory to Working Capital 41	•	•	•	•	0.0	•	0.1	0.1	0.2	0.1	•	0.0	•
Total Receipts to Cash Flow 42	3.9	2.1	•	•	1.5	2.0	2.5	2.2	2.4	2.9	2.7	2.7	4.1
Cost of Goods to Cash Flow 43	0.7	•	•	•	0.2	•	0.5	0.5	0.3	0.8	1.0	0.1	0.7
Cash Flow to Total Debt 44	0.1	•	17.3	•	7.9	1.7	0.6	1.0	0.3	0.2	0.3	0.1	0.1

Selected Financial Factors (in Percentages)

Debt Ratio 45	63.2	•	0.1	271.3	6.4	69.0	54.6	29.5	53.3	58.4	55.6	51.2	64.1
Return on Total Assets 46	4.3	•	•	•	19.2	0.8	22.5	17.5	8.3	7.2	10.9	3.5	4.2
Return on Equity Before Income Taxes 47	6.8	•	•	100.2	20.2	•	47.2	23.2	14.8	15.0	24.2	2.7	6.6
Return on Equity After Income Taxes 48	4.2	•	•	100.2	13.7	•	39.2	19.4	9.8	12.7	20.6	1.3	4.0
Profit Margin (Before Income Tax) 49	7.0	5.5	•	•	25.0	•	28.0	25.6	19.2	17.3	23.9	6.8	6.5
Profit Margin (After Income Tax) 50	4.4	•	•	•	16.9	•	23.3	21.3	12.7	14.6	20.3	3.3	3.9

Table II

Corporations with Net Income

RAIL TRANSPORTATION

MONEY AMOUNTS AND SIZE OF ASSETS IN THOUSANDS OF DOLLARS

Item Description for Accounting Period 7/11 Through 6/12		Total	Zero Assets	Under 500	500 to 1,000	1,000 to 5,000	5,000 to 10,000	10,000 to 25,000	25,000 to 50,000	50,000 to 100,000	100,000 to 250,000	250,000 to 500,000	500,000 to 2,500,000	2,500,000 and over
Number of Enterprises	1	79	9	0	0	21	0	14	•	•	9	0	•	•
Revenues ($ in Thousands)														
Net Sales	2	47144872	35021	0	0	46744	0	174101	•	•	740837	0	•	•
Interest	3	147058	0	0	0	6	0	1351	•	•	1715	0	•	•
Rents	4	355385	0	0	0	1689	0	1775	•	•	3734	0	•	•
Royalties	5	60206	0	0	0	5	0	0	•	•	14576	0	•	•
Other Portfolio Income	6	522143	206	0	0	2366	0	11961	•	•	76475	0	•	•
Other Receipts	7	264406	0	0	0	6982	0	462	•	•	11796	0	•	•
Total Receipts	8	48494070	35227	0	0	57792	0	189650	•	•	849133	0	•	•
Average Total Receipts	9	613849	3914	•	•	2752	•	13546	•	•	94348	•	•	•
Operating Costs/Operating Income (%)														
Cost of Operations	10	18.1	•	•	•	11.9	•	8.8	•	•	25.1	•	•	•
Salaries and Wages	11	16.2	11.9	•	•	13.4	•	19.6	•	•	11.4	•	•	•
Taxes Paid	12	5.0	5.1	•	•	7.4	•	5.2	•	•	3.3	•	•	•
Interest Paid	13	5.0	1.2	•	•	0.3	•	1.7	•	•	0.9	•	•	•
Depreciation	14	17.4	4.8	•	•	14.2	•	3.2	•	•	13.9	•	•	•
Amortization and Depletion	15	0.1	0.1	•	•	•	•	0.0	•	•	0.0	•	•	•
Pensions and Other Deferred Comp.	16	1.5	•	•	•	•	•	•	•	•	0.8	•	•	•
Employee Benefits	17	5.8	1.3	•	•	0.9	•	4.4	•	•	1.5	•	•	•
Advertising	18	0.0	0.0	•	•	0.3	•	0.1	•	•	0.2	•	•	•
Other Expenses	19	24.0	52.6	•	•	49.1	•	30.6	•	•	24.2	•	•	•
Officers' Compensation	20	0.5	•	•	•	1.2	•	0.7	•	•	1.2	•	•	•
Operating Margin	21	6.3	23.1	•	•	1.3	•	25.7	•	•	17.3	•	•	•
Operating Margin Before Officers' Comp.	22	6.8	23.1	•	•	2.5	•	26.4	•	•	18.5	•	•	•

Selected Average Balance Sheet ($ in Thousands)														
Net Receivables	23	66196	0	•	•	96	•	4174	•	•	12342	•	•	•
Inventories	24	13254	0	•	•	0	•	226	•	•	754	•	•	•
Net Property, Plant and Equipment	25	1304459	0	•	•	1532	•	5402	•	•	132311	•	•	•
Total Assets	26	1614448	0	•	•	2933	•	15556	•	•	205083	•	•	•
Notes and Loans Payable	27	353057	0	•	•	120	•	4626	•	•	51720	•	•	•
All Other Liabilities	28	699258	0	•	•	68	•	3981	•	•	63869	•	•	•
Net Worth	29	562133	0	•	•	2745	•	6948	•	•	89494	•	•	•

Selected Financial Ratios (Times to 1)														
Current Ratio	30	0.8	•	•	•	10.9	•	2.1	•	•	0.9	•	•	•
Quick Ratio	31	0.6	•	•	•	9.7	•	2.0	•	•	0.7	•	•	•
Net Sales to Working Capital	32	•	•	•	•	4.4	•	3.1	•	•	•	•	•	•
Coverage Ratio	33	2.8	20.6	•	•	72.6	•	21.7	•	•	35.4	•	•	•
Total Asset Turnover	34	0.4	•	•	•	0.8	•	0.8	•	•	0.4	•	•	•
Inventory Turnover	35	8.2	•	•	•	1858.3	•	4.9	•	•	27.4	•	•	•
Receivables Turnover	36	9.7	•	•	•	22.7	•	3.7	•	•	•	•	•	•
Total Liabilities to Net Worth	37	1.9	•	•	•	0.1	•	1.2	•	•	1.3	•	•	•
Current Assets to Working Capital	38	•	•	•	•	1.1	•	1.9	•	•	•	•	•	•
Current Liabilities to Working Capital	39	•	•	•	•	0.1	•	0.9	•	•	•	•	•	•
Working Capital to Net Sales	40	•	•	•	•	0.2	•	0.3	•	•	•	•	•	•
Inventory to Working Capital	41	•	•	•	•	0.0	•	0.1	•	•	•	•	•	•
Total Receipts to Cash Flow	42	4.1	1.5	•	•	1.5	•	2.1	•	•	2.3	•	•	•
Cost of Goods to Cash Flow	43	0.7	•	•	•	0.2	•	0.2	•	•	0.6	•	•	•
Cash Flow to Total Debt	44	0.1	•	•	•	7.9	•	0.7	•	•	0.3	•	•	•

Selected Financial Factors (in Percentages)														
Debt Ratio	45	65.2	•	•	•	6.4	•	55.3	•	•	56.4	•	•	•
Return on Total Assets	46	5.2	•	•	•	19.2	•	29.0	•	•	13.2	•	•	•
Return on Equity Before Income Taxes	47	9.7	•	•	•	20.2	•	61.9	•	•	29.4	•	•	•
Return on Equity After Income Taxes	48	6.5	•	•	•	13.7	•	52.0	•	•	25.2	•	•	•
Profit Margin (Before Income Tax)	49	9.2	23.7	•	•	25.0	•	34.6	•	•	31.9	•	•	•
Profit Margin (After Income Tax)	50	6.1	15.5	•	•	16.9	•	29.0	•	•	27.4	•	•	•

Table I

Corporations with and without Net Income

WATER TRANSPORTATION

MONEY AMOUNTS AND SIZE OF ASSETS IN THOUSANDS OF DOLLARS

Item Description for Accounting Period 7/11 Through 6/12		Total	Zero Assets	Under 500	500 to 1,000	1,000 to 5,000	5,000 to 10,000	10,000 to 25,000	25,000 to 50,000	50,000 to 100,000	100,000 to 250,000	250,000 to 500,000	500,000 to 2,500,000	2,500,000 and over
Number of Enterprises	1	4160	417	2383	157	858	175	76	19	24	25	12	14	0
Revenues ($ in Thousands)														
Net Sales	2	28074682	1060044	671024	442159	2865338	589936	1683378	477480	1218689	2066840	1392089	15607704	0
Interest	3	32783	189	1	100	172	0	937	499	487	3226	2295	24878	0
Rents	4	113442	36	0	0	0	359	108	397	18	460	2060	110004	0
Royalties	5	538	530	0	0	0	0	0	0	0	0	8	1	0
Other Portfolio Income	6	335005	35178	0	25	14479	0	16907	6956	23953	29229	64317	143961	0
Other Receipts	7	781038	312337	153177	524	15612	1	26957	10379	-37447	19588	15161	264747	0
Total Receipts	8	29337488	1408314	824202	442808	2895601	590296	1728287	495711	1205700	2119343	1475930	16151295	0
Average Total Receipts	9	7052	3377	346	2820	3375	3373	22741	26090	50238	84774	122994	1153664	•
Operating Costs/Operating Income (%)														
Cost of Operations	10	41.9	25.7	13.8	36.6	22.0	58.5	51.1	43.3	49.6	40.0	40.9	46.1	•
Salaries and Wages	11	9.8	8.9	14.2	16.7	14.7	20.4	7.7	10.5	7.5	10.0	10.3	8.5	•
Taxes Paid	12	1.8	1.0	2.0	4.2	2.6	2.4	1.7	3.7	1.9	2.3	1.9	1.4	•
Interest Paid	13	2.3	1.6	0.3	0.4	1.4	2.1	1.3	3.4	2.5	3.6	3.7	2.4	•
Depreciation	14	10.4	1.7	5.3	2.9	12.3	20.5	5.5	9.6	11.3	19.4	19.8	9.2	•
Amortization and Depletion	15	0.4	0.4	•	0.0	0.0	0.0	0.0	0.0	0.5	0.3	0.4	0.5	•
Pensions and Other Deferred Comp.	16	0.7	0.6	1.6	•	0.1	0.1	0.3	0.6	0.3	0.6	0.6	0.9	•
Employee Benefits	17	2.2	1.5	0.3	0.9	1.2	1.7	1.4	2.9	1.0	3.4	2.5	2.5	•
Advertising	18	0.2	2.1	0.2	0.5	0.2	0.0	0.1	0.6	0.6	0.1	0.4	0.1	•
Other Expenses	19	37.0	91.2	67.0	26.2	41.1	5.3	32.8	18.7	24.5	26.8	61.7	33.9	•
Officers' Compensation	20	1.5	0.3	9.0	15.0	2.2	4.3	1.5	2.4	0.6	1.1	0.8	0.8	•
Operating Margin	21	•	•	•	•	2.2	•	•	4.2	•	•	•	•	•
Operating Margin Before Officers' Comp.	22	•	•	•	11.7	4.4	•	•	6.7	0.3	•	•	•	•

Selected Average Balance Sheet ($ in Thousands)														
Net Receivables	23	1122	0	5	161	151	1244	3896	2471	7594	12571	13793	234181	•
Inventories	24	103	0	7	0	6	66	156	523	369	723	2628	22826	•
Net Property, Plant and Equipment	25	4989	0	36	324	1189	4011	7656	15623	42114	114431	183798	852864	•
Total Assets	26	9153	0	130	713	2065	7521	15872	37761	74126	162080	356904	1609043	•
Notes and Loans Payable	27	3465	0	82	1342	986	3155	7834	14658	23408	76824	75106	596561	•
All Other Liabilities	28	2146	0	34	178	280	811	4216	10128	20227	18425	113313	401126	•
Net Worth	29	3542	0	14	-807	798	3555	3822	12975	30490	66832	168486	611356	•
Selected Financial Ratios (Times to 1)														
Current Ratio	30	1.2	•	1.9	1.5	1.8	1.6	1.2	1.5	1.1	1.0	0.6	1.3	•
Quick Ratio	31	0.9	•	0.7	1.5	1.4	0.9	0.9	1.1	0.7	0.8	0.5	1.0	•
Net Sales to Working Capital	32	18.7	•	9.2	30.6	15.1	3.2	23.1	8.2	20.2	•	•	12.8	•
Coverage Ratio	33	•	•	27.6	•	3.4	•	0.5	3.4	0.6	•	•	•	•
Total Asset Turnover	34	0.7	•	2.2	3.9	1.6	0.4	1.4	0.7	0.7	0.5	0.3	0.7	•
Inventory Turnover	35	27.5	•	5.3	•	115.7	29.9	72.7	20.8	68.2	45.7	18.0	22.5	•
Receivables Turnover	36	6.1	•	48.9	32.7	16.9	2.3	5.9	8.0	6.2	8.1	3.0	5.4	•
Total Liabilities to Net Worth	37	1.6	•	8.4	•	1.6	1.1	3.2	1.9	1.4	1.4	1.1	1.6	•
Current Assets to Working Capital	38	5.9	•	2.1	2.9	2.3	2.7	6.2	2.8	8.9	•	•	4.5	•
Current Liabilities to Working Capital	39	4.9	•	1.1	1.9	1.3	1.7	5.2	1.8	7.9	•	•	3.5	•
Working Capital to Net Sales	40	0.1	•	0.1	0.0	0.1	0.3	0.0	0.1	0.0	•	•	0.1	•
Inventory to Working Capital	41	0.3	•	0.0	•	0.0	0.1	0.1	0.1	0.2	•	•	0.3	•
Total Receipts to Cash Flow	42	4.0	1.2	1.4	9.1	3.1	•	7.2	5.4	5.7	7.0	4.9	4.3	•
Cost of Goods to Cash Flow	43	1.7	0.3	0.2	3.3	0.7	•	3.7	2.3	2.8	2.8	2.0	2.0	•
Cash Flow to Total Debt	44	0.3	•	1.7	0.2	0.8	•	0.3	0.2	0.2	0.1	0.1	0.3	•
Selected Financial Factors (in Percentages)														
Debt Ratio	45	61.3	•	89.4	213.1	61.3	52.7	75.9	65.6	58.9	58.8	52.8	62.0	•
Return on Total Assets	46	•	•	20.6	•	7.4	•	0.9	7.6	1.0	•	•	•	•
Return on Equity Before Income Taxes	47	•	•	186.5	10.9	13.5	•	•	15.6	•	•	•	•	•
Return on Equity After Income Taxes	48	•	•	186.5	11.0	13.1	•	•	12.6	•	•	•	•	•
Profit Margin (Before Income Tax)	49	•	•	9.2	•	3.2	•	•	8.0	•	•	•	•	•
Profit Margin (After Income Tax)	50	•	•	9.2	•	3.1	•	•	6.5	•	•	•	•	•

Table II

Corporations with Net Income

WATER TRANSPORTATION

MONEY AMOUNTS AND SIZE OF ASSETS IN THOUSANDS OF DOLLARS

Item Description for Accounting Period 7/11 Through 6/12		Total	Zero Assets	Under 500	500 to 1,000	1,000 to 5,000	5,000 to 10,000	10,000 to 25,000	25,000 to 50,000	50,000 to 100,000	100,000 to 250,000	250,000 to 500,000	500,000 to 2,500,000	2,500,000 and over
Number of Enterprises	1	2744	14	1945	140	549	10	40	•	•	9	3	•	0
Revenues ($ in Thousands)														
Net Sales	2	19954025	800678	623163	356983	2541673	51579	1042013	•	•	1015567	492000	•	0
Interest	3	9988	113	1	0	36	0	935	•	•	41	1102	•	0
Rents	4	113424	36	0	0	0	359	108	•	•	460	2060	•	0
Royalties	5	530	530	0	0	0	0	0	•	•	0	0	•	0
Other Portfolio Income	6	219709	35178	0	0	14081	0	16619	•	•	21994	36929	•	0
Other Receipts	7	398635	3183	135321	324	15428	0	22656	•	•	7394	9555	•	0
Total Receipts	8	20696311	839718	758485	357307	2571218	51938	1082331	•	•	1045456	541646	•	0
Average Total Receipts	9	7542	59980	390	2552	4683	5194	27058	•	•	116162	180549	•	•
Operating Costs/Operating Income (%)														
Cost of Operations	10	41.8	17.0	14.8	45.3	19.6	68.2	58.9	•	•	43.8	10.8	•	•
Salaries and Wages	11	7.8	5.8	10.2	12.9	13.1	2.5	5.1	•	•	9.7	15.2	•	•
Taxes Paid	12	1.8	0.6	1.8	4.3	2.6	1.5	1.3	•	•	2.8	3.2	•	•
Interest Paid	13	1.0	0.4	0.2	0.2	1.2	1.9	0.7	•	•	1.4	1.5	•	•
Depreciation	14	6.2	1.0	1.9	2.7	12.5	8.7	3.2	•	•	5.9	13.0	•	•
Amortization and Depletion	15	0.2	0.0	•	0.0	0.0	•	0.0	•	•	0.2	0.0	•	•
Pensions and Other Deferred Comp.	16	0.8	0.2	1.7	•	0.1	•	0.3	•	•	0.6	0.8	•	•
Employee Benefits	17	1.8	1.0	0.3	•	1.0	•	1.2	•	•	5.0	3.6	•	•
Advertising	18	0.3	2.8	0.2	0.5	0.2	0.0	0.1	•	•	0.1	1.0	•	•
Other Expenses	19	36.9	70.5	65.4	13.3	43.3	11.5	24.5	•	•	26.2	50.1	•	•
Officers' Compensation	20	1.4	0.2	9.7	18.5	1.5	3.0	1.5	•	•	0.8	0.7	•	•
Operating Margin	21	0.2	0.7	•	2.2	4.9	2.6	3.2	•	•	3.4	•	•	•
Operating Margin Before Officers' Comp.	22	1.5	0.9	3.4	20.8	6.4	5.6	4.7	•	•	4.2	0.6	•	•

Selected Average Balance Sheet ($ in Thousands)														
Net Receivables	23	1199	0	7	181	157	808	5234	•	•	15784	13862	•	•
Inventories	24	90	0	9	0	2	0	294	•	•	1328	2317	•	•
Net Property, Plant and Equipment	25	3621	0	44	359	1280	4895	6773	•	•	103917	263703	•	•
Total Assets	26	6552	0	157	700	2039	5893	16752	•	•	149499	348148	•	•
Notes and Loans Payable	27	1926	0	91	154	1152	4841	4250	•	•	67371	17139	•	•
All Other Liabilities	28	1748	0	42	195	312	842	4382	•	•	19011	94639	•	•
Net Worth	29	2878	0	25	351	575	210	8119	•	•	63117	236369	•	•
Selected Financial Ratios (Times to 1)														
Current Ratio	30	1.3	•	1.9	1.1	1.6	0.2	2.0	•	•	1.1	0.5	•	•
Quick Ratio	31	1.0	•	0.6	1.1	1.1	0.2	1.6	•	•	0.8	0.3	•	•
Net Sales to Working Capital	32	14.5	•	8.7	238.1	21.9	•	6.1	•	•	37.2	•	•	•
Coverage Ratio	33	5.1	15.5	72.9	14.1	6.0	2.7	11.0	•	•	5.5	7.5	•	•
Total Asset Turnover	34	1.1	•	2.0	3.6	2.3	0.9	1.6	•	•	0.8	0.5	•	•
Inventory Turnover	35	33.6	•	5.3	•	425.4	•	52.2	•	•	37.2	7.6	•	•
Receivables Turnover	36	6.4	•	96.8	28.2	31.5	1.6	5.2	•	•	8.3	1.9	•	•
Total Liabilities to Net Worth	37	1.3	•	5.2	1.0	2.5	27.0	1.1	•	•	1.4	0.5	•	•
Current Assets to Working Capital	38	4.0	•	2.1	19.2	2.7	•	2.0	•	•	10.4	•	•	•
Current Liabilities to Working Capital	39	3.0	•	1.1	18.2	1.7	•	1.0	•	•	9.4	•	•	•
Working Capital to Net Sales	40	0.1	•	0.1	0.0	0.0	•	0.2	•	•	0.0	•	•	•
Inventory to Working Capital	41	0.2	•	0.0	•	0.0	•	0.1	•	•	0.4	•	•	•
Total Receipts to Cash Flow	42	3.1	1.4	1.3	8.6	2.8	7.2	8.5	•	•	3.6	1.8	•	•
Cost of Goods to Cash Flow	43	1.3	0.2	0.2	3.9	0.5	4.9	5.0	•	•	1.6	0.2	•	•
Cash Flow to Total Debt	44	0.6	•	1.9	0.8	1.1	0.1	0.4	•	•	0.4	0.8	•	•
Selected Financial Factors (in Percentages)														
Debt Ratio	45	56.1	•	83.9	49.8	71.8	96.4	51.5	•	•	57.8	32.1	•	•
Return on Total Assets	46	5.4	•	31.9	9.1	16.6	4.6	12.1	•	•	5.8	5.5	•	•
Return on Equity Before Income Taxes	47	9.9	•	195.8	16.9	49.0	81.6	22.8	•	•	11.3	7.0	•	•
Return on Equity After Income Taxes	48	8.5	•	195.8	16.4	48.2	65.3	21.5	•	•	10.1	6.5	•	•
Profit Margin (Before Income Tax)	49	3.9	5.6	15.5	2.3	6.1	3.3	7.1	•	•	6.3	10.1	•	•
Profit Margin (After Income Tax)	50	3.4	3.8	15.5	2.3	6.0	2.7	6.7	•	•	5.6	9.4	•	•

TRUCK TRANSPORTATION

Item Description for Accounting Period 7/11 Through 6/12		Total	Zero Assets	Under 500	500 to 1,000	1,000 to 5,000	5,000 to 10,000	10,000 to 25,000	25,000 to 50,000	50,000 to 100,000	100,000 to 250,000	250,000 to 500,000	500,000 to 2,500,000	2,500,000 and over
		MONEY AMOUNTS AND SIZE OF ASSETS IN THOUSANDS OF DOLLARS												
Number of Enterprises	1	115589	32389	71172	5100	5350	863	387	168	63	52	18	27	0
		Revenues ($ in Thousands)												
Net Sales	2	239902522	6712403	45853326	12734426	44330770	17983635	15988444	12888204	8542826	14457322	10040477	50370688	0
Interest	3	702272	169	4168	2474	10808	5497	3693	1693	5187	7310	40757	620516	0
Rents	4	369709	0	521	466	32116	7222	21986	17035	14800	46999	74648	153917	0
Royalties	5	9184	0	0	45	0	0	5	166	0	1602	1304	6061	0
Other Portfolio Income	6	2272170	78980	325013	250665	459842	115588	145371	75252	81239	113582	123746	502886	0
Other Receipts	7	3846064	435141	661113	187102	844475	206764	82021	86176	70500	138698	695714	438366	0
Total Receipts	8	247101921	7226693	46844141	13175178	45678011	18318706	16241520	13068526	8714552	14765513	10976646	52092434	0
Average Total Receipts	9	2138	223	658	2583	8538	21227	41968	77789	138326	283952	609814	1929349	•
		Operating Costs/Operating Income (%)												
Cost of Operations	10	31.7	18.7	23.9	32.1	36.8	44.3	46.6	41.1	30.6	27.5	47.9	22.2	•
Salaries and Wages	11	15.7	13.2	11.7	12.6	12.4	15.8	12.9	13.8	19.7	20.0	16.9	22.6	•
Taxes Paid	12	3.3	2.8	2.8	3.4	3.3	2.6	3.0	3.1	4.0	3.5	3.3	4.1	•
Interest Paid	13	1.1	0.9	0.5	0.8	0.7	0.6	0.9	0.6	1.2	2.1	1.5	2.0	•
Depreciation	14	5.3	4.2	3.0	4.4	4.4	3.6	5.2	6.4	8.5	7.7	6.8	7.5	•
Amortization and Depletion	15	0.1	0.0	0.0	0.3	0.1	0.1	0.1	0.1	0.2	0.4	0.4	0.1	•
Pensions and Other Deferred Comp.	16	0.4	0.1	0.1	0.1	0.3	0.2	0.1	0.4	0.1	0.5	0.2	1.2	•
Employee Benefits	17	2.1	1.1	1.0	1.0	1.6	2.0	1.8	1.5	2.8	2.8	2.1	4.1	•
Advertising	18	0.2	0.1	0.4	0.1	0.2	0.2	0.2	0.2	0.2	0.2	0.2	0.2	•
Other Expenses	19	38.0	58.0	43.3	43.0	38.9	29.0	28.8	33.2	34.4	38.2	29.7	37.9	•
Officers' Compensation	20	3.4	4.2	12.5	2.8	2.1	1.2	1.4	1.1	0.8	0.5	0.4	0.3	•
Operating Margin	21	•	•	1.0	•	•	0.4	•	•	•	•	•	•	•
Operating Margin Before Officers' Comp.	22	2.1	0.9	13.4	2.3	1.4	1.6	0.4	•	•	•	•	•	•

Selected Average Balance Sheet ($ in Thousands)														
Net Receivables	23	182	0	11	98	668	2261	4312	8594	15894	32299	74893	261561	•
Inventories	24	10	0	1	19	28	175	234	638	1109	1415	8004	8787	•
Net Property, Plant and Equipment	25	336	0	31	273	797	2362	5963	15359	32566	78400	169588	550342	•
Total Assets	26	923	0	71	679	2246	6992	15292	34225	68232	165200	377511	1807995	•
Notes and Loans Payable	27	338	0	48	323	1148	2704	6311	12567	28914	85307	107635	471471	•
All Other Liabilities	28	330	0	17	135	575	2020	4077	6231	16847	43104	135225	852583	•
Net Worth	29	256	0	5	221	523	2267	4903	15427	22471	36790	134652	483940	•
Selected Financial Ratios (Times to 1)														
Current Ratio	30	1.1	•	1.3	1.1	1.4	1.4	1.3	1.7	1.3	1.0	1.2	0.9	•
Quick Ratio	31	0.8	•	1.1	0.8	1.2	1.2	1.1	1.4	1.1	0.7	0.9	0.5	•
Net Sales to Working Capital	32	47.9	•	103.6	85.7	23.9	17.9	22.7	13.2	21.0	318.8	21.2	•	•
Coverage Ratio	33	2.5	5.7	7.5	5.0	4.5	4.8	1.7	0.8	0.7	0.4	0.9	1.5	•
Total Asset Turnover	34	2.2	•	9.1	3.7	3.7	3.0	2.7	2.2	2.0	1.7	1.5	1.0	•
Inventory Turnover	35	64.7	•	220.8	41.2	108.5	52.7	82.2	49.4	37.4	54.1	33.4	47.2	•
Receivables Turnover	36	12.0	•	60.2	25.0	13.2	8.9	9.7	9.7	8.9	10.0	6.5	8.0	•
Total Liabilities to Net Worth	37	2.6	•	12.1	2.1	3.3	2.1	2.1	1.2	2.0	3.5	1.8	2.7	•
Current Assets to Working Capital	38	8.7	•	4.7	8.2	3.5	3.4	3.9	2.4	4.4	62.1	5.2	•	•
Current Liabilities to Working Capital	39	7.7	•	3.7	7.2	2.5	2.4	2.9	1.4	3.4	61.1	4.2	•	•
Working Capital to Net Sales	40	0.0	•	0.0	0.0	0.0	0.1	0.0	0.1	0.0	0.0	0.0	•	•
Inventory to Working Capital	41	0.2	•	0.1	0.6	0.1	0.1	0.1	0.1	0.1	2.0	0.3	•	•
Total Receipts to Cash Flow	42	3.1	2.1	2.6	2.5	3.0	4.1	4.8	4.5	3.7	3.5	4.6	3.0	•
Cost of Goods to Cash Flow	43	1.0	0.4	0.6	0.8	1.1	1.8	2.3	1.8	1.1	1.0	2.2	0.7	•
Cash Flow to Total Debt	44	1.0	•	3.8	2.1	1.6	1.1	0.8	0.9	0.8	0.6	0.5	0.5	•
Selected Financial Factors (in Percentages)														
Debt Ratio	45	72.3	•	92.4	67.4	76.7	67.6	67.9	54.9	67.1	77.7	64.3	73.2	•
Return on Total Assets	46	6.1	•	32.5	13.9	11.2	8.6	3.9	1.2	1.6	1.3	2.0	3.2	•
Return on Equity Before Income Taxes	47	13.4	•	369.9	34.1	37.5	20.8	4.9	•	•	•	•	4.2	•
Return on Equity After Income Taxes	48	12.0	•	366.4	33.3	35.4	19.8	3.4	•	•	•	•	2.7	•
Profit Margin (Before Income Tax)	49	1.7	4.4	3.1	3.0	2.4	2.3	0.6	•	•	•	•	1.1	•
Profit Margin (After Income Tax)	50	1.5	4.3	3.1	2.9	2.2	2.2	0.4	•	•	•	•	0.7	•

Table II

Corporations with Net Income

TRUCK TRANSPORTATION

MONEY AMOUNTS AND SIZE OF ASSETS IN THOUSANDS OF DOLLARS

Item Description for Accounting Period 7/11 Through 6/12		Total	Zero Assets	Under 500	500 to 1,000	1,000 to 5,000	5,000 to 10,000	10,000 to 25,000	25,000 to 50,000	50,000 to 100,000	100,000 to 250,000	250,000 to 500,000	500,000 to 2,500,000	2,500,000 and over
Number of Enterprises	1	74122	18120	48223	3137	3566	689	218	93	22	24	10	20	0
Revenues ($ in Thousands)														
Net Sales	2	161260990	3456425	35740516	8665416	33076584	13686889	10566569	7619032	3599787	6501505	5725643	32622623	0
Interest	3	71332	127	3839	2187	8562	2799	3054	1050	2058	1320	33294	13041	0
Rents	4	278675	0	110	466	22146	3348	8352	13465	7960	22238	66416	134175	0
Royalties	5	15	0	0	0	0	0	0	0	0	15	0	0	0
Other Portfolio Income	6	1624546	7243	292251	240083	345870	68902	50044	42533	20902	59124	100696	396898	0
Other Receipts	7	3404634	428040	642804	179231	812460	178757	60908	113642	16248	52868	666909	252767	0
Total Receipts	8	166640192	3891835	36679520	9087383	34265622	13940695	10688927	7789722	3646955	6637070	6592958	33419504	0
Average Total Receipts	9	2248	215	761	2897	9609	20233	49032	83760	165771	276545	659296	1670975	•
Operating Costs/Operating Income (%)														
Cost of Operations	10	33.1	9.1	21.3	26.4	37.5	39.7	51.9	43.2	36.7	21.7	46.9	34.3	•
Salaries and Wages	11	13.8	8.0	9.9	13.7	12.3	18.2	11.5	13.1	15.3	19.6	15.9	17.5	•
Taxes Paid	12	3.0	2.7	2.6	3.9	3.2	2.7	2.6	2.7	2.9	3.3	3.1	3.5	•
Interest Paid	13	0.6	1.0	0.5	0.7	0.6	0.5	0.5	0.5	0.6	1.3	1.2	0.7	•
Depreciation	14	4.5	2.3	2.8	3.6	3.2	3.7	3.0	4.5	4.3	5.9	7.2	8.4	•
Amortization and Depletion	15	0.1	0.0	0.0	0.4	0.1	0.1	0.1	0.1	0.1	0.2	0.1	0.2	•
Pensions and Other Deferred Comp.	16	0.2	0.0	0.1	0.1	0.2	0.3	0.1	0.3	0.1	0.5	0.3	0.2	•
Employee Benefits	17	1.6	1.0	0.8	1.0	1.6	2.3	1.9	1.6	2.1	2.1	1.9	2.1	•
Advertising	18	0.2	0.1	0.3	0.1	0.1	0.1	0.2	0.3	0.1	0.1	0.2	0.1	•
Other Expenses	19	37.4	71.1	44.3	46.1	38.1	29.4	24.5	31.6	34.0	42.6	35.2	31.8	•
Officers' Compensation	20	4.3	3.8	14.9	2.6	2.1	1.1	1.6	1.1	0.8	0.6	0.3	0.3	•
Operating Margin	21	1.1	0.9	2.7	1.4	0.9	1.9	2.2	1.0	3.0	2.0	•	0.9	•
Operating Margin Before Officers' Comp.	22	5.4	4.7	17.6	4.1	3.0	3.0	3.8	2.1	3.8	2.6	•	1.2	•

Selected Average Balance Sheet ($ in Thousands)													
Net Receivables 23	174	0	12	91	729	2020	5283	8619	22687	32132	94295	194990	•
Inventories 24	10	0	0	17	25	164	288	901	2029	2171	7870	7306	•
Net Property, Plant and Equipment 25	312	0	34	275	719	2400	4872	13545	24190	77551	163410	504753	•
Total Assets 26	733	0	76	733	2340	6894	15219	33242	65787	168062	377277	980223	•
Notes and Loans Payable 27	242	0	47	317	993	2291	4744	9029	19031	61216	91228	242180	•
All Other Liabilities 28	205	0	16	117	602	1862	4224	6436	20314	40295	137040	314453	•
Net Worth 29	287	0	13	299	744	2741	6251	17777	26442	66551	149009	423590	•
Selected Financial Ratios (Times to 1)													
Current Ratio 30	1.6	•	1.5	1.1	1.6	1.5	1.6	2.0	1.6	1.2	1.5	1.7	•
Quick Ratio 31	1.3	•	1.3	0.8	1.4	1.3	1.4	1.5	1.4	0.8	1.2	1.4	•
Net Sales to Working Capital 32	19.4	•	73.9	133.2	18.0	15.7	14.7	10.3	11.8	27.3	11.0	12.8	•
Coverage Ratio 33	8.0	14.8	12.5	9.8	9.2	7.9	7.3	7.6	8.3	4.2	3.2	5.7	•
Total Asset Turnover 34	3.0	•	9.8	3.8	4.0	2.9	3.2	2.5	2.5	1.6	1.5	1.7	•
Inventory Turnover 35	71.7	•	353.1	44.1	136.5	48.0	87.4	39.3	29.6	27.0	34.1	76.7	•
Receivables Turnover 36	12.9	•	65.7	38.7	12.6	10.3	10.7	9.1	7.1	8.8	6.9	8.5	•
Total Liabilities to Net Worth 37	1.6	•	5.0	1.5	2.1	1.5	1.4	0.9	1.5	1.5	1.5	1.3	•
Current Assets to Working Capital 38	2.8	•	3.1	11.2	2.7	3.0	2.6	2.0	2.6	5.8	3.1	2.4	•
Current Liabilities to Working Capital 39	1.8	•	2.1	10.2	1.7	2.0	1.6	1.0	1.6	4.8	2.1	1.4	•
Working Capital to Net Sales 40	0.1	•	0.0	0.0	0.1	0.1	0.1	0.1	0.1	0.0	0.1	0.1	•
Inventory to Working Capital 41	0.1	•	0.0	1.0	0.0	0.1	0.1	0.2	0.1	0.3	0.1	0.1	•
Total Receipts to Cash Flow 42	3.0	1.6	2.4	2.2	2.9	3.9	5.2	4.6	3.1	2.7	3.8	3.4	•
Cost of Goods to Cash Flow 43	1.0	0.1	0.5	0.6	1.1	1.5	2.7	2.0	1.2	0.6	1.8	1.2	•
Cash Flow to Total Debt 44	1.6	•	4.9	2.9	2.0	1.2	1.0	1.2	1.3	1.0	0.7	0.9	•
Selected Financial Factors (in Percentages)													
Debt Ratio 45	60.9	•	83.3	59.3	68.2	60.2	58.9	46.5	59.8	60.4	60.5	56.8	•
Return on Total Assets 46	15.1	•	56.5	26.5	20.1	12.4	12.3	9.1	12.3	8.9	6.0	6.8	•
Return on Equity Before Income Taxes 47	33.8	•	311.4	58.4	56.2	27.2	25.9	14.8	26.9	17.0	10.3	12.9	•
Return on Equity After Income Taxes 48	31.9	•	309.3	57.5	54.1	26.1	23.8	13.9	24.4	16.5	7.7	10.6	•
Profit Margin (Before Income Tax) 49	4.5	13.5	5.3	6.3	4.5	3.7	3.3	3.2	4.3	4.2	2.7	3.3	•
Profit Margin (After Income Tax) 50	4.2	13.3	5.3	6.2	4.3	3.6	3.1	3.0	3.9	4.1	2.0	2.8	•

Table I

Corporations with and without Net Income

TRANSIT AND GROUND PASSENGER TRANSPORTATION

MONEY AMOUNTS AND SIZE OF ASSETS IN THOUSANDS OF DOLLARS

Item Description for Accounting Period 7/11 Through 6/12		Total	Zero Assets	Under 500	500 to 1,000	1,000 to 5,000	5,000 to 10,000	10,000 to 25,000	25,000 to 50,000	50,000 to 100,000	100,000 to 250,000	250,000 to 500,000	500,000 to 2,500,000	2,500,000 and over
Number of Enterprises	1	32090	7900	19247	2447	2300	53	108	11	10	8	4	3	0
Revenues ($ in Thousands)														
Net Sales	2	26482340	560570	4802758	897197	6314838	647491	2486710	608044	698855	2480278	1368581	5617018	0
Interest	3	99165	33	50	218	2039	127	204	204	280	2125	4311	89574	0
Rents	4	18048	0	51	0	1080	38	492	0	218	4666	0	11504	0
Royalties	5	11731	0	0	0	0	0	0	0	0	0	0	11731	0
Other Portfolio Income	6	204201	34	9940	31	22766	11103	69075	3833	1870	8599	18440	58508	0
Other Receipts	7	399742	7916	167380	11210	58273	7378	57173	1856	5845	1916	25157	55639	0
Total Receipts	8	27215227	568553	4980179	908656	6398996	666137	2613654	613937	707068	2497584	1416489	5843974	0
Average Total Receipts	9	848	72	259	371	2782	12569	24200	55812	70707	312198	354122	1947991	•
Operating Costs/Operating Income (%)														
Cost of Operations	10	25.0	32.8	7.6	17.6	32.4	43.8	47.6	53.7	54.8	24.9	23.5	13.4	•
Salaries and Wages	11	27.0	2.4	31.5	21.9	17.6	17.2	11.6	15.3	12.6	36.6	24.5	44.5	•
Taxes Paid	12	4.7	2.0	5.3	3.5	3.9	4.8	3.3	4.6	4.0	5.2	5.3	5.9	•
Interest Paid	13	2.5	1.4	1.2	7.8	1.9	0.4	1.0	1.4	2.3	2.6	4.4	4.3	•
Depreciation	14	6.2	3.8	5.4	7.9	6.3	9.1	11.2	7.1	11.7	4.0	8.1	3.9	•
Amortization and Depletion	15	0.7	0.1	0.2	3.2	0.4	0.1	0.1	0.1	0.2	0.3	0.8	1.7	•
Pensions and Other Deferred Comp.	16	0.4	•	0.1	•	0.3	0.5	0.7	0.6	0.2	0.4	0.1	0.9	•
Employee Benefits	17	2.1	0.0	0.3	0.8	1.1	2.8	2.5	1.8	2.7	5.6	4.1	3.0	•
Advertising	18	0.5	1.1	0.7	0.8	0.7	1.1	0.5	0.2	0.3	0.1	1.2	0.2	•
Other Expenses	19	28.9	44.1	41.0	30.4	30.7	21.3	21.7	14.9	13.6	20.4	34.3	24.5	•
Officers' Compensation	20	2.7	10.6	5.9	2.6	4.2	1.6	1.2	0.8	1.1	0.4	0.2	0.3	•
Operating Margin	21	•	1.7	0.8	3.5	0.6	•	•	•	•	•	•	•	•
Operating Margin Before Officers' Comp.	22	1.9	12.3	6.7	6.1	4.8	•	•	0.1	•	•	•	•	•

Selected Average Balance Sheet ($ in Thousands)													
Net Receivables 23	71	0	5	0	263	1081	2343	5048	11257	68027	23273	159991	•
Inventories 24	4	0	0	0	4	97	70	366	1864	2134	943	19109	•
Net Property, Plant and Equipment 25	202	0	25	122	564	2263	7681	12366	29083	46683	156334	681252	•
Total Assets 26	631	0	88	730	1750	7628	14922	31000	68608	180987	374902	2253588	•
Notes and Loans Payable 27	354	0	55	612	1123	1450	5069	13531	33679	69730	230402	1207898	•
All Other Liabilities 28	134	0	13	23	282	3249	2745	5106	12286	70628	76909	601131	•
Net Worth 29	144	0	19	95	345	2929	7109	12363	22642	40628	67592	444559	•

Selected Financial Ratios (Times to 1)													
Current Ratio 30	1.1	•	1.0	1.8	1.3	1.1	1.2	2.3	1.2	1.4	1.0	0.7	•
Quick Ratio 31	0.8	•	0.6	0.3	1.1	0.8	0.9	1.9	0.9	1.1	0.7	0.5	•
Net Sales to Working Capital 32	49.6	•	•	9.4	21.2	31.1	24.7	6.1	21.1	12.1	•	•	•
Coverage Ratio 33	1.8	3.3	4.7	1.6	2.0	1.4	4.9	1.2	•	1.1	0.3	1.3	•
Total Asset Turnover 34	1.3	•	2.9	0.5	1.6	1.6	1.5	1.8	1.0	1.7	0.9	0.8	•
Inventory Turnover 35	54.3	•	233.3	280.1	249.9	55.4	156.9	81.1	20.6	36.2	85.1	13.1	•
Receivables Turnover 36	12.9	•	84.1	221.8	10.4	11.1	12.6	10.0	6.0	5.6	29.4	12.3	•
Total Liabilities to Net Worth 37	3.4	•	3.5	6.7	4.1	1.6	1.1	1.5	2.0	3.5	4.5	4.1	•
Current Assets to Working Capital 38	8.9	•	•	2.2	3.9	9.3	5.5	1.8	6.4	3.5	•	•	•
Current Liabilities to Working Capital 39	7.9	•	•	1.2	2.9	8.3	4.5	0.8	5.4	2.5	•	•	•
Working Capital to Net Sales 40	0.0	•	•	0.1	0.0	0.0	0.0	0.2	0.0	0.1	•	•	•
Inventory to Working Capital 41	0.2	•	•	0.0	0.0	0.0	0.1	0.0	0.4	0.1	•	•	•
Total Receipts to Cash Flow 42	4.3	2.6	2.5	3.9	5.1	6.7	4.9	8.9	16.3	5.9	5.6	5.0	•
Cost of Goods to Cash Flow 43	1.1	0.9	0.2	0.7	1.7	2.9	2.3	4.8	8.9	1.5	1.3	0.7	•
Cash Flow to Total Debt 44	0.4	•	1.5	0.1	0.4	0.4	0.6	0.3	0.1	0.4	0.2	0.2	•

Selected Financial Factors (in Percentages)													
Debt Ratio 45	77.2	•	77.8	86.9	80.3	61.6	52.4	60.1	67.0	77.6	82.0	80.3	•
Return on Total Assets 46	5.9	•	16.3	6.3	5.9	0.8	7.2	3.0	•	4.7	1.3	4.8	•
Return on Equity Before Income Taxes 47	11.3	•	58.0	18.5	14.9	0.6	12.1	1.3	•	1.1	•	6.2	•
Return on Equity After Income Taxes 48	10.2	•	57.4	18.1	14.7	•	10.9	1.2	•	•	•	6.2	•
Profit Margin (Before Income Tax) 49	2.0	3.1	4.5	4.8	1.9	0.1	3.7	0.3	•	0.1	•	1.5	•
Profit Margin (After Income Tax) 50	1.8	3.1	4.5	4.7	1.9	•	3.4	0.3	•	•	•	1.5	•

Table II

Corporations with Net Income

TRANSIT AND GROUND PASSENGER TRANSPORTATION

MONEY AMOUNTS AND SIZE OF ASSETS IN THOUSANDS OF DOLLARS

Item Description for Accounting Period 7/11 Through 6/12		Total	Zero Assets	Under 500	500 to 1,000	1,000 to 5,000	5,000 to 10,000	10,000 to 25,000	25,000 to 50,000	50,000 to 100,000	100,000 to 250,000	250,000 to 500,000	500,000 to 2,500,000	2,500,000 and over
Number of Enterprises	1	18495	•	12600	1300	1659	24	80	•	4	•	0	3	0
Revenues ($ in Thousands)														
Net Sales	2	20769879	•	3271526	762425	5471528	382532	2043052	•	178599	•	0	5617018	0
Interest	3	97766	•	12	0	1902	27	55	•	67	•	0	89574	0
Rents	4	16549	•	51	0	1080	38	76	•	0	•	0	11504	0
Royalties	5	11731	•	0	0	0	0	0	•	0	•	0	11731	0
Other Portfolio Income	6	144954	•	9933	31	19847	484	26759	•	653	•	0	58508	0
Other Receipts	7	354832	•	162126	11073	35001	6180	53572	•	2697	•	0	55639	0
Total Receipts	8	21395711	•	3443648	773529	5529358	389261	2123514	•	182016	•	0	5843974	0
Average Total Receipts	9	1157	•	273	595	3333	16219	26544	•	45504	•	•	1947991	•
Operating Costs/Operating Income (%)														
Cost of Operations	10	22.9	•	10.3	20.7	34.3	24.2	45.2	•	41.9	•	•	13.4	•
Salaries and Wages	11	27.5	•	21.3	21.5	15.9	23.6	12.8	•	17.2	•	•	44.5	•
Taxes Paid	12	4.6	•	3.9	3.3	3.9	7.4	2.9	•	3.4	•	•	5.9	•
Interest Paid	13	2.1	•	0.8	3.1	1.6	0.1	0.8	•	1.3	•	•	4.3	•
Depreciation	14	5.1	•	5.4	8.5	5.6	4.1	7.6	•	9.4	•	•	3.9	•
Amortization and Depletion	15	0.6	•	0.0	0.3	0.3	•	0.1	•	0.0	•	•	1.7	•
Pensions and Other Deferred Comp.	16	0.5	•	0.1	•	0.4	0.6	0.8	•	0.2	•	•	0.9	•
Employee Benefits	17	2.2	•	0.3	0.9	1.1	4.3	3.0	•	2.8	•	•	3.0	•
Advertising	18	0.5	•	0.8	0.9	0.7	0.0	0.6	•	0.3	•	•	0.2	•
Other Expenses	19	29.2	•	46.1	30.4	28.8	26.7	22.6	•	15.1	•	•	24.5	•
Officers' Compensation	20	2.9	•	7.2	2.4	4.7	1.2	1.2	•	1.7	•	•	0.3	•
Operating Margin	21	1.9	•	3.7	8.2	2.8	7.8	2.5	•	6.7	•	•	•	•
Operating Margin Before Officers' Comp.	22	4.7	•	10.9	10.5	7.5	9.0	3.7	•	8.4	•	•	•	•

Selected Average Balance Sheet ($ in Thousands)

Item	No.													
Net Receivables	23	92	•	6	0	332	1287	2890	•	5975	•	•	159991	•
Inventories	24	5	•	0	0	2	30	72	•	2788	•	•	17938	•
Net Property, Plant and Equipment	25	266	•	30	192	594	1760	7016	•	22832	•	•	681252	•
Total Assets	26	833	•	88	674	1892	6550	15175	•	64939	•	•	2253588	•
Notes and Loans Payable	27	418	•	38	452	1098	639	4422	•	26443	•	•	1207898	•
All Other Liabilities	28	183	•	13	20	247	2011	3175	•	15285	•	•	601131	•
Net Worth	29	232	•	37	202	548	3900	7578	•	23211	•	•	444559	•

Selected Financial Ratios (Times to 1)

Item	No.													
Current Ratio	30	1.2	•	1.2	1.2	1.9	2.0	1.3	•	0.6	•	•	0.7	•
Quick Ratio	31	0.9	•	1.1	0.4	1.5	1.8	1.0	•	0.5	•	•	0.5	•
Net Sales to Working Capital	32	40.3	•	73.5	67.1	10.9	8.0	20.1	•	•	•	•	•	•
Coverage Ratio	33	3.3	•	11.9	4.1	3.4	157.9	9.1	•	7.5	•	•	1.3	•
Total Asset Turnover	34	1.3	•	3.0	0.9	1.7	2.4	1.7	•	0.7	•	•	0.8	•
Inventory Turnover	35	51.2	•	256.4	•	653.6	129.6	160.1	•	6.7	•	•	14.0	•
Receivables Turnover	36	13.7	•	67.9	38121.2	9.4	11.2	12.3	•	3.3	•	•	•	•
Total Liabilities to Net Worth	37	2.6	•	1.4	2.3	2.5	0.7	1.0	•	1.8	•	•	4.1	•
Current Assets to Working Capital	38	6.6	•	5.3	5.2	2.1	2.0	4.7	•	•	•	•	•	•
Current Liabilities to Working Capital	39	5.6	•	4.3	4.2	1.1	1.0	3.7	•	•	•	•	•	•
Working Capital to Net Sales	40	0.0	•	0.0	0.0	0.1	0.1	0.0	•	•	•	•	•	•
Inventory to Working Capital	41	0.2	•	0.0	•	0.0	0.0	0.1	•	•	•	•	•	•
Total Receipts to Cash Flow	42	3.8	•	2.1	3.3	4.9	3.8	4.2	•	5.0	•	•	5.0	•
Cost of Goods to Cash Flow	43	0.9	•	0.2	0.7	1.7	0.9	1.9	•	2.1	•	•	0.7	•
Cash Flow to Total Debt	44	0.5	•	2.5	0.4	0.5	1.6	0.8	•	0.2	•	•	0.2	•

Selected Financial Factors (in Percentages)

Item	No.													
Debt Ratio	45	72.1	•	57.6	70.0	71.0	40.5	50.1	•	64.3	•	•	80.3	•
Return on Total Assets	46	9.4	•	29.0	11.0	9.3	23.3	12.2	•	6.8	•	•	4.8	•
Return on Equity Before Income Taxes	47	23.7	•	62.7	27.8	22.8	38.9	21.8	•	16.5	•	•	6.2	•
Return on Equity After Income Taxes	48	22.5	•	62.2	27.5	22.7	37.6	20.3	•	16.4	•	•	6.2	•
Profit Margin (Before Income Tax)	49	4.9	•	9.0	9.6	3.8	9.5	6.5	•	8.6	•	•	1.5	•
Profit Margin (After Income Tax)	50	4.7	•	8.9	9.5	3.8	9.2	6.0	•	8.5	•	•	1.5	•

Table I

Corporations with and without Net Income

PIPELINE TRANSPORTATION

MONEY AMOUNTS AND SIZE OF ASSETS IN THOUSANDS OF DOLLARS

Item Description for Accounting Period 7/11 Through 6/12		Total	Zero Assets	Under 500	500 to 1,000	1,000 to 5,000	5,000 to 10,000	10,000 to 25,000	25,000 to 50,000	50,000 to 100,000	100,000 to 250,000	250,000 to 500,000	500,000 to 2,500,000	2,500,000 and over
Number of Enterprises	1	264	3	0	0	155	46	28	11	5	5	0	7	4
Revenues ($ in Thousands)														
Net Sales	2	11814531	1414734	0	0	691855	127088	410603	313763	325163	610829	0	3170617	4749878
Interest	3	105865	21234	0	0	170	0	39	99	111	95	0	1651	82464
Rents	4	39177	52	0	0	0	0	298	3745	164	0	0	17586	17332
Royalties	5	3778	180	0	0	245	0	0	0	0	0	0	2897	456
Other Portfolio Income	6	6528304	4862582	0	0	0	0	206	423	124	65	0	144802	1520100
Other Receipts	7	1330447	252472	0	0	28804	-11092	46872	424	450	90485	0	225880	696157
Total Receipts	8	19822102	6551254	0	0	721074	115996	458018	318454	326012	701474	0	3563433	7066387
Average Total Receipts	9	75084	2183751	•	•	4652	2522	16358	28950	65202	140295	•	509062	1766597
Operating Costs/Operating Income (%)														
Cost of Operations	10	22.6	11.1	•	•	43.7	13.0	68.9	21.7	9.1	25.2	•	39.4	8.6
Salaries and Wages	11	10.8	11.8	•	•	21.4	0.2	2.9	2.0	25.9	2.5	•	5.7	13.9
Taxes Paid	12	5.3	9.6	•	•	3.2	0.7	1.6	6.5	6.5	3.0	•	4.0	5.6
Interest Paid	13	14.2	18.7	•	•	0.3	0.0	0.3	0.5	0.5	2.8	•	7.9	23.9
Depreciation	14	37.2	14.8	•	•	0.1	9.5	3.3	6.6	7.7	9.6	•	12.1	77.2
Amortization and Depletion	15	2.8	5.1	•	•	0.2	•	0.0	•	0.0	0.3	•	1.1	4.7
Pensions and Other Deferred Comp.	16	0.7	1.0	•	•	•	0.1	•	•	1.3	0.3	•	0.7	0.9
Employee Benefits	17	1.5	•	•	•	•	1.1	0.8	0.5	6.4	1.2	•	0.8	2.4
Advertising	18	0.0	0.0	•	•	0.7	•	0.0	•	0.0	•	•	0.0	0.0
Other Expenses	19	65.2	108.9	•	•	19.2	52.5	8.4	21.5	26.1	51.4	•	26.4	97.5
Officers' Compensation	20	1.2	4.2	•	•	1.7	0.7	0.0	•	0.2	0.1	•	0.4	1.2
Operating Margin	21	•	•	•	•	9.5	22.2	13.8	40.7	16.4	3.5	•	1.4	•
Operating Margin Before Officers' Comp.	22	•	•	•	•	11.2	22.9	13.8	40.7	16.6	3.6	•	1.8	•

Selected Average Balance Sheet ($ in Thousands)													
Net Receivables **23**	10804	0	•	•	443	1268	1464	2824	7243	16815	•	69648	511342
Inventories **24**	1880	0	•	•	159	246	404	369	1092	356	•	12951	86569
Net Property, Plant and Equipment **25**	97993	0	•	•	39	437	4377	22114	39531	143119	•	606143	5080477
Total Assets **26**	164175	0	•	•	2443	7875	13558	37803	73769	191791	•	925115	8500545
Notes and Loans Payable **27**	88879	0	•	•	282	4181	306	29434	6336	55218	•	382797	4977106
All Other Liabilities **28**	38106	0	•	•	332	172	3434	10356	27404	51040	•	277950	1863178
Net Worth **29**	37190	0	•	•	1830	3522	9818	-1987	40028	85533	•	264368	1660262
Selected Financial Ratios (Times to 1)													
Current Ratio **30**	1.1	•	•	•	2.9	10.7	2.0	1.4	2.6	1.4	•	1.1	1.0
Quick Ratio **31**	0.6	•	•	•	2.5	10.5	1.7	1.2	2.4	1.1	•	0.9	0.5
Net Sales to Working Capital **32**	37.3	•	•	•	4.9	1.6	5.7	13.6	4.1	10.6	•	64.6	•
Coverage Ratio **33**	1.4	15.8	•	•	44.4	4274.2	101.2	86.3	36.9	7.5	•	2.7	•
Total Asset Turnover **34**	0.3	•	•	•	1.8	0.4	1.1	0.8	0.9	0.6	•	0.5	0.1
Inventory Turnover **35**	5.4	•	•	•	12.2	1.5	25.0	16.8	5.4	86.4	•	13.8	1.2
Receivables Turnover **36**	4.6	•	•	•	13.3	2.0	14.7	12.3	9.7	8.8	•	7.0	2.6
Total Liabilities to Net Worth **37**	3.4	•	•	•	0.3	1.2	0.4	•	0.8	1.2	•	2.5	4.1
Current Assets to Working Capital **38**	19.5	•	•	•	1.5	1.1	2.0	3.6	1.6	3.6	•	19.4	•
Current Liabilities to Working Capital **39**	18.5	•	•	•	0.5	0.1	1.0	2.6	0.6	2.6	•	18.4	•
Working Capital to Net Sales **40**	0.0	•	•	•	0.2	0.6	0.2	0.1	0.2	0.1	•	0.0	•
Inventory to Working Capital **41**	1.0	•	•	•	0.2	0.0	0.3	0.2	0.1	0.0	•	0.9	•
Total Receipts to Cash Flow **42**	1.5	0.3	•	•	3.5	1.5	3.2	1.7	2.9	1.5	•	2.7	20.2
Cost of Goods to Cash Flow **43**	0.3	0.0	•	•	1.5	0.2	2.2	0.4	0.3	0.4	•	1.1	1.7
Cash Flow to Total Debt **44**	0.2	•	•	•	2.1	0.4	1.2	0.4	0.7	0.7	•	0.3	0.0
Selected Financial Factors (in Percentages)													
Debt Ratio **45**	77.3	•	•	•	25.1	55.3	27.6	105.3	45.7	55.4	•	71.4	80.5
Return on Total Assets **46**	5.6	•	•	•	25.7	4.7	27.7	32.2	15.1	13.5	•	10.6	•
Return on Equity Before Income Taxes **47**	7.5	•	•	•	33.6	10.6	37.9	•	27.0	26.2	•	23.7	•
Return on Equity After Income Taxes **48**	4.2	•	•	•	30.9	10.6	28.3	•	18.9	17.0	•	13.3	•
Profit Margin (Before Income Tax) **49**	6.3	277.7	•	•	13.8	13.4	25.4	42.2	16.6	18.3	•	13.8	•
Profit Margin (After Income Tax) **50**	3.5	277.7	•	•	12.7	13.4	18.9	27.5	11.6	11.9	•	7.8	•

Table II

Corporations with Net Income

PIPELINE TRANSPORTATION

MONEY AMOUNTS AND SIZE OF ASSETS IN THOUSANDS OF DOLLARS

Item Description for Accounting Period 7/11 Through 6/12		Total	Zero Assets	Under 500	500 to 1,000	1,000 to 5,000	5,000 to 10,000	10,000 to 25,000	25,000 to 50,000	50,000 to 100,000	100,000 to 250,000	250,000 to 500,000	500,000 to 2,500,000	2,500,000 and over
Number of Enterprises	1	208	•	0	0	155	4	24	•	5	•	0	•	0
Revenues ($ in Thousands)														
Net Sales	2	5075450	•	0	0	691855	42844	400504	•	325163	•	0	•	0
Interest	3	21975	•	0	0	170	0	25	•	111	•	0	•	0
Rents	4	9970	•	0	0	0	0	298	•	164	•	0	•	0
Royalties	5	425	•	0	0	245	0	0	•	0	•	0	•	0
Other Portfolio Income	6	4985856	•	0	0	0	0	206	•	124	•	0	•	0
Other Receipts	7	590744	•	0	0	28804	0	46873	•	450	•	0	•	0
Total Receipts	8	10684420	•	0	0	721074	42844	447906	•	326012	•	0	•	0
Average Total Receipts	9	51367	•	•	•	4652	10711	18663	•	65202	•	•	•	•
Operating Costs/Operating Income (%)														
Cost of Operations	10	19.0	•	•	•	43.7	38.6	68.4	•	9.1	•	•	•	•
Salaries and Wages	11	10.1	•	•	•	21.4	0.7	3.0	•	25.9	•	•	•	•
Taxes Paid	12	6.6	•	•	•	3.2	1.6	1.7	•	6.5	•	•	•	•
Interest Paid	13	9.4	•	•	•	0.3	0.0	0.3	•	0.5	•	•	•	•
Depreciation	14	11.4	•	•	•	0.1	3.2	2.3	•	7.7	•	•	•	•
Amortization and Depletion	15	1.8	•	•	•	0.2	•	0.0	•	0.0	•	•	•	•
Pensions and Other Deferred Comp.	16	0.8	•	•	•	•	0.2	•	•	1.3	•	•	•	•
Employee Benefits	17	0.9	•	•	•	•	3.2	0.8	•	6.4	•	•	•	•
Advertising	18	0.1	•	•	•	0.7	•	0.0	•	0.0	•	•	•	•
Other Expenses	19	48.7	•	•	•	19.2	2.1	8.3	•	26.1	•	•	•	•
Officers' Compensation	20	1.6	•	•	•	1.7	2.1	0.0	•	0.2	•	•	•	•
Operating Margin	21	•	•	•	•	9.5	48.2	15.2	•	16.4	•	•	•	•
Operating Margin Before Officers' Comp.	22	•	•	•	•	11.2	50.3	15.2	•	16.6	•	•	•	•

Selected Average Balance Sheet ($ in Thousands)													
Net Receivables **23**	2194	•	•	•	443	1275	1708	•	7243	•	•	•	•
Inventories **24**	997	•	•	•	146	214	470	•	1092	•	•	•	•
Net Property, Plant and Equipment **25**	21273	•	•	•	39	984	3897	•	39531	•	•	•	•
Total Assets **26**	32835	•	•	•	2443	7945	13717	•	73769	•	•	•	•
Notes and Loans Payable **27**	14207	•	•	•	282	0	357	•	6336	•	•	•	•
All Other Liabilities **28**	9340	•	•	•	332	1983	3502	•	27404	•	•	•	•
Net Worth **29**	9288	•	•	•	1830	5962	9858	•	40028	•	•	•	•
Selected Financial Ratios (Times to 1)													
Current Ratio **30**	1.3	•	•	•	2.9	3.5	1.9	•	2.6	•	•	•	•
Quick Ratio **31**	1.1	•	•	•	2.5	3.3	1.6	•	2.4	•	•	•	•
Net Sales to Working Capital **32**	19.7	•	•	•	4.9	2.2	6.4	•	4.1	•	•	•	•
Coverage Ratio **33**	11.7	•	•	•	44.4	5165.0	105.1	•	36.9	•	•	•	•
Total Asset Turnover **34**	0.7	•	•	•	1.8	1.3	1.2	•	0.9	•	•	•	•
Inventory Turnover **35**	4.6	•	•	•	13.4	19.3	24.3	•	5.4	•	•	•	•
Receivables Turnover **36**	4.3	•	•	•	20.1	9.0	14.7	•	9.7	•	•	•	•
Total Liabilities to Net Worth **37**	2.5	•	•	•	0.3	0.3	0.4	•	0.8	•	•	•	•
Current Assets to Working Capital **38**	4.6	•	•	•	1.5	1.4	2.1	•	1.6	•	•	•	•
Current Liabilities to Working Capital **39**	3.6	•	•	•	0.5	0.4	1.1	•	0.6	•	•	•	•
Working Capital to Net Sales **40**	0.1	•	•	•	0.2	0.5	0.2	•	0.2	•	•	•	•
Inventory to Working Capital **41**	0.3	•	•	•	0.2	0.1	0.3	•	0.1	•	•	•	•
Total Receipts to Cash Flow **42**	0.7	•	•	•	3.5	2.0	3.0	•	2.9	•	•	•	•
Cost of Goods to Cash Flow **43**	0.1	•	•	•	1.5	0.8	2.1	•	0.3	•	•	•	•
Cash Flow to Total Debt **44**	1.5	•	•	•	2.1	2.7	1.4	•	0.7	•	•	•	•
Selected Financial Factors (in Percentages)													
Debt Ratio **45**	71.7	•	•	•	25.1	25.0	28.1	•	45.7	•	•	•	•
Return on Total Assets **46**	81.4	•	•	•	25.7	65.0	33.2	•	15.1	•	•	•	•
Return on Equity Before Income Taxes **47**	263.0	•	•	•	33.6	86.6	45.7	•	27.0	•	•	•	•
Return on Equity After Income Taxes **48**	246.1	•	•	•	30.9	86.6	34.6	•	18.9	•	•	•	•
Profit Margin (Before Income Tax) **49**	100.1	•	•	•	13.8	48.2	27.0	•	16.6	•	•	•	•
Profit Margin (After Income Tax) **50**	93.7	•	•	•	12.7	48.2	20.4	•	11.6	•	•	•	•

Table I

Corporations with and without Net Income

OTHER TRANSPORTATION AND SUPPORT ACTIVITIES

MONEY AMOUNTS AND SIZE OF ASSETS IN THOUSANDS OF DOLLARS

Item Description for Accounting Period 7/11 Through 6/12		Total	Zero Assets	Under 500	500 to 1,000	1,000 to 5,000	5,000 to 10,000	10,000 to 25,000	25,000 to 50,000	50,000 to 100,000	100,000 to 250,000	250,000 to 500,000	500,000 to 2,500,000	2,500,000 and over
Number of Enterprises	1	44514	7459	29879	3391	2859	355	297	112	60	49	25	22	5
Revenues ($ in Thousands)														
Net Sales	2	240677597	1682172	24270041	11275447	19325759	6282876	12904716	7413660	9154722	10159788	8982126	14095304	115130987
Interest	3	376259	2029	187	1123	6571	2678	3192	2488	9040	6358	22065	115124	205403
Rents	4	263581	521	14	0	12139	7006	741	0	9917	32814	22007	77002	101419
Royalties	5	1915729	648	0	7	0	0	0	0	1908	447	9	0	1912710
Other Portfolio Income	6	1128549	18742	7125	71629	35977	17124	15196	21635	75791	25935	54749	382581	402065
Other Receipts	7	3408537	43564	150415	21164	172811	49410	51463	206286	197725	51413	242958	229696	1991632
Total Receipts	8	247770252	1747676	24427782	11369370	19553257	6359094	12975308	7644069	9449103	10276755	9323914	14899707	119744216
Average Total Receipts	9	5566	234	818	3353	6839	17913	43688	68251	157485	209730	372957	677259	23948843
Operating Costs/Operating Income (%)														
Cost of Operations	10	40.7	57.7	50.0	63.2	64.2	67.2	65.1	62.4	66.5	57.8	40.1	47.1	22.6
Salaries and Wages	11	16.2	10.5	6.5	9.7	17.0	9.1	11.6	10.6	11.9	10.0	16.2	16.3	21.1
Taxes Paid	12	2.4	1.5	1.4	2.3	2.4	3.8	1.7	2.1	2.1	1.7	1.9	2.7	2.8
Interest Paid	13	0.9	1.1	0.4	1.0	0.5	0.7	0.4	0.9	0.7	1.1	2.0	4.5	0.7
Depreciation	14	3.9	1.8	1.1	2.2	2.2	1.9	1.5	2.6	1.7	3.0	3.2	4.2	5.7
Amortization and Depletion	15	0.3	0.4	0.0	0.1	0.1	0.0	0.1	0.4	0.3	1.1	0.7	2.5	0.2
Pensions and Other Deferred Comp.	16	1.6	1.0	0.4	0.5	0.2	0.2	0.5	0.2	0.2	0.4	0.5	0.5	3.0
Employee Benefits	17	3.4	0.6	0.3	0.6	1.1	1.3	1.4	1.1	1.5	2.1	2.7	5.3	5.4
Advertising	18	0.3	0.5	0.2	0.3	0.2	0.2	0.1	0.1	0.1	0.2	0.2	0.2	0.5
Other Expenses	19	28.4	29.0	33.1	14.4	8.4	11.9	14.2	17.8	13.6	22.6	33.6	20.2	37.5
Officers' Compensation	20	1.2	2.3	3.6	4.7	2.4	2.3	1.2	1.8	0.9	0.7	1.0	0.4	0.3
Operating Margin	21	0.4	•	2.9	0.9	1.4	1.3	2.3	•	0.4	•	•	•	0.3
Operating Margin Before Officers' Comp.	22	1.6	•	6.4	5.6	3.8	3.6	3.5	1.8	1.3	•	•	•	0.6

Selected Average Balance Sheet ($ in Thousands)

Net Receivables 23	726	0	9	150	783	2287	6068	10647	23527	36799	76017	200396	3189720
Inventories 24	45	0	1	17	48	58	223	351	3226	4945	13424	15072	105786
Net Property, Plant and Equipment 25	1026	0	23	180	529	1208	4009	9003	16818	34247	67711	175220	6400112
Total Assets 26	3495	0	89	690	2194	6919	15047	33067	71123	144921	341557	1140304	17732211
Notes and Loans Payable 27	1016	0	46	478	887	2104	4959	10413	21308	38767	124530	406283	4217403
All Other Liabilities 28	1538	0	39	277	740	3092	5362	14280	26013	53046	124751	422973	8669622
Net Worth 29	941	0	4	-65	567	1724	4725	8374	23801	53109	92276	311048	4845187

Selected Financial Ratios (Times to 1)

Current Ratio 30	1.2	•	1.4	1.2	1.5	1.3	1.3	1.1	1.4	1.3	1.2	1.4	1.0
Quick Ratio 31	1.0	•	1.2	1.0	1.3	1.1	1.1	0.9	1.1	1.0	0.9	1.1	0.9
Net Sales to Working Capital 32	31.5	•	64.9	49.4	14.7	19.1	20.1	33.1	14.7	13.5	19.3	6.7	193.5
Coverage Ratio 33	4.6	•	10.7	2.7	6.7	4.8	7.9	4.4	6.5	1.3	2.0	1.4	7.4
Total Asset Turnover 34	1.5	•	9.1	4.8	3.1	2.6	2.9	2.0	2.1	1.4	1.1	0.6	1.3
Inventory Turnover 35	49.3	•	328.1	125.8	89.8	206.2	127.0	117.5	31.5	24.3	10.7	20.0	49.1
Receivables Turnover 36	7.2	•	77.8	27.0	9.2	7.3	7.5	7.7	6.6	6.1	5.5	3.8	6.2
Total Liabilities to Net Worth 37	2.7	•	22.5	•	2.9	3.0	2.2	2.9	2.0	1.7	2.7	2.7	2.7
Current Assets to Working Capital 38	7.3	•	3.5	5.9	3.0	4.4	4.2	8.6	3.7	4.2	7.3	3.8	44.0
Current Liabilities to Working Capital 39	6.3	•	2.5	4.9	2.0	3.4	3.2	7.6	2.7	3.2	6.3	2.8	43.0
Working Capital to Net Sales 40	0.0	•	0.0	0.0	0.1	0.1	0.0	0.0	0.1	0.1	0.1	0.1	0.0
Inventory to Working Capital 41	0.3	•	0.1	0.3	0.1	0.1	0.1	0.2	0.3	0.3	1.0	0.2	0.9
Total Receipts to Cash Flow 42	3.9	5.1	3.2	7.1	13.6	9.2	7.4	5.4	6.9	5.8	3.3	6.1	2.9
Cost of Goods to Cash Flow 43	1.6	3.0	1.6	4.5	8.7	6.2	4.8	3.4	4.6	3.3	1.3	2.9	0.7
Cash Flow to Total Debt 44	0.5	•	3.0	0.6	0.3	0.4	0.6	0.5	0.5	0.4	0.4	0.1	0.6

Selected Financial Factors (in Percentages)

Debt Ratio 45	73.1	•	95.7	109.4	74.1	75.1	68.6	74.7	66.5	63.4	73.0	72.7	72.7
Return on Total Assets 46	6.7	•	35.2	13.3	9.4	8.1	9.3	8.0	9.1	2.1	4.1	3.6	6.7
Return on Equity Before Income Taxes 47	19.6	•	751.0	•	30.8	25.8	26.0	24.4	23.1	1.5	7.6	4.0	21.1
Return on Equity After Income Taxes 48	13.8	•	734.5	•	29.1	21.0	23.3	19.9	18.9	•	2.5	0.2	13.8
Profit Margin (Before Income Tax) 49	3.4	•	3.5	1.8	2.6	2.5	2.8	3.1	3.6	0.4	1.9	2.0	4.4
Profit Margin (After Income Tax) 50	2.4	•	3.4	1.7	2.4	2.0	2.5	2.5	2.9	•	0.7	0.1	2.9

Table II

Corporations with Net Income

OTHER TRANSPORTATION AND SUPPORT ACTIVITIES

MONEY AMOUNTS AND SIZE OF ASSETS IN THOUSANDS OF DOLLARS

Item Description for Accounting Period 7/11 Through 6/12		Total	Zero Assets	Under 500	500 to 1,000	1,000 to 5,000	5,000 to 10,000	10,000 to 25,000	25,000 to 50,000	50,000 to 100,000	100,000 to 250,000	250,000 to 500,000	500,000 to 2,500,000	2,500,000 and over
Number of Enterprises	1	28558	2376	21315	2180	2015	269	221	•	41	26	14	13	•
Revenues ($ in Thousands)														
Net Sales	2	203274353	442576	19861796	8791058	14987014	5002911	10152378	•	6376750	4566438	4616222	9684634	•
Interest	3	285140	2010	120	685	6238	1653	2991	•	7253	4552	5005	67603	•
Rents	4	210452	0	0	0	4013	6646	141	•	9171	23077	16658	49328	•
Royalties	5	1915081	0	0	7	0	0	0	•	1908	447	9	0	•
Other Portfolio Income	6	802378	18699	5040	71617	18147	17090	14397	•	64252	15355	51496	109365	•
Other Receipts	7	3004707	7828	146556	19036	106680	44870	47134	•	199459	47580	204688	99388	•
Total Receipts	8	209492111	471113	20013512	8882403	15122092	5073170	10217041	•	6658793	4657449	4894078	10010318	•
Average Total Receipts	9	7336	198	939	4074	7505	18859	46231	•	162410	179133	349577	770024	•
Operating Costs/Operating Income (%)														
Cost of Operations	10	38.3	24.3	55.3	70.6	61.5	66.3	63.4	•	62.2	54.6	54.2	41.7	•
Salaries and Wages	11	17.3	6.8	7.3	8.7	19.6	9.4	12.0	•	12.5	11.7	12.0	18.5	•
Taxes Paid	12	2.6	1.2	1.6	2.3	2.5	4.3	1.8	•	2.4	2.0	2.1	2.3	•
Interest Paid	13	0.7	0.9	0.3	0.4	0.4	0.2	0.3	•	0.5	1.2	1.3	2.5	•
Depreciation	14	4.2	0.5	1.0	2.0	1.9	1.1	1.3	•	1.7	3.4	4.4	4.7	•
Amortization and Depletion	15	0.2	0.3	0.0	0.1	0.1	0.0	0.0	•	0.3	0.6	0.2	0.9	•
Pensions and Other Deferred Comp.	16	1.9	•	0.5	0.4	0.2	0.2	0.6	•	0.2	0.5	0.3	0.6	•
Employee Benefits	17	3.6	0.5	0.3	0.6	1.2	1.1	1.5	•	1.5	2.2	2.7	3.7	•
Advertising	18	0.4	1.6	0.3	0.3	0.2	0.2	0.1	•	0.2	0.3	0.1	0.1	•
Other Expenses	19	27.9	53.5	24.9	7.0	6.1	10.6	13.8	•	15.8	19.6	20.0	18.9	•
Officers' Compensation	20	1.2	5.9	4.0	4.6	2.6	2.7	1.3	•	0.9	0.9	1.2	0.3	•
Operating Margin	21	1.8	4.6	4.5	3.0	3.5	3.7	3.8	•	1.8	3.0	1.5	5.8	•
Operating Margin Before Officers' Comp.	22	3.1	10.5	8.5	7.7	6.1	6.4	5.1	•	2.7	3.9	2.7	6.1	•

Selected Average Balance Sheet ($ in Thousands)

Net Receivables 23	974	0	10	163	839	2414	6968	•	25594	34036	69154	295941	•
Inventories 24	49	0	0	15	48	52	216	•	2819	5465	23444	26282	•
Net Property, Plant and Equipment 25	1444	0	22	148	405	1116	3296	•	15449	41981	88534	235671	•
Total Assets 26	4471	0	97	725	2263	6924	15358	•	71192	145081	321381	1184128	•
Notes and Loans Payable 27	1109	0	33	274	632	829	3902	•	15853	26915	80733	271043	•
All Other Liabilities 28	1996	0	44	160	776	3168	5910	•	28028	45865	110577	482440	•
Net Worth 29	1366	0	20	291	854	2927	5547	•	27311	72301	130071	430645	•

Selected Financial Ratios (Times to 1)

Current Ratio 30	1.2	•	1.3	2.4	1.7	1.5	1.5	•	1.4	1.7	1.6	1.3	•
Quick Ratio 31	1.0	•	1.1	2.2	1.4	1.3	1.3	•	1.1	1.4	1.0	1.0	•
Net Sales to Working Capital 32	29.6	•	98.2	16.3	12.0	13.0	13.6	•	14.4	6.3	6.3	7.5	•
Coverage Ratio 33	8.3	13.8	17.7	11.7	11.8	22.7	13.8	•	14.0	5.3	7.1	4.7	•
Total Asset Turnover 34	1.6	•	9.6	5.6	3.3	2.7	3.0	•	2.2	1.2	1.0	0.6	•
Inventory Turnover 35	55.1	•	2336.7	184.8	94.9	235.5	135.2	•	34.3	17.5	7.6	11.8	•
Receivables Turnover 36	7.1	•	90.8	28.5	9.8	6.9	7.5	•	6.2	5.2	4.9	0.7	•
Total Liabilities to Net Worth 37	2.3	•	3.8	1.5	1.6	1.4	1.8	•	1.6	1.0	1.5	1.7	•
Current Assets to Working Capital 38	6.8	•	4.7	1.7	2.5	3.0	3.0	•	3.8	2.4	2.8	4.7	•
Current Liabilities to Working Capital 39	5.8	•	3.7	0.7	1.5	2.0	2.0	•	2.8	1.4	1.8	3.7	•
Working Capital to Net Sales 40	0.0	•	0.0	0.1	0.1	0.1	0.1	•	0.1	0.2	0.2	0.1	•
Inventory to Working Capital 41	0.2	•	0.0	0.1	0.1	0.1	0.1	•	0.2	0.2	0.6	0.1	•
Total Receipts to Cash Flow 42	3.7	1.9	4.2	11.3	13.6	7.6	6.4	•	5.1	5.5	4.5	4.2	•
Cost of Goods to Cash Flow 43	1.4	0.5	2.3	8.0	8.4	5.0	4.0	•	3.2	3.0	2.4	1.7	•
Cash Flow to Total Debt 44	0.6	•	2.9	0.8	0.4	0.6	0.7	•	0.7	0.4	0.4	0.2	•

Selected Financial Factors (in Percentages)

Debt Ratio 45	69.5	•	79.0	59.9	62.2	57.7	63.9	•	61.6	50.2	59.5	63.6	•
Return on Total Assets 46	9.0	•	53.4	24.6	15.9	14.3	14.3	•	14.7	7.7	9.3	7.4	•
Return on Equity Before Income Taxes 47	26.0	•	240.1	56.1	38.4	32.2	36.8	•	35.5	12.5	19.7	16.1	•
Return on Equity After Income Taxes 48	19.8	•	235.8	55.2	36.9	28.5	33.7	•	30.1	10.3	13.4	11.4	•
Profit Margin (Before Income Tax) 49	5.0	11.0	5.2	4.1	4.4	5.1	4.4	•	6.2	5.1	7.8	9.3	•
Profit Margin (After Income Tax) 50	3.8	10.5	5.1	4.0	4.2	4.5	4.1	•	5.3	4.2	5.3	6.6	•

Table I

Corporations with and without Net Income

WAREHOUSING AND STORAGE

MONEY AMOUNTS AND SIZE OF ASSETS IN THOUSANDS OF DOLLARS

Item Description for Accounting Period 7/11 Through 6/12		Total	Zero Assets	Under 500	500 to 1,000	1,000 to 5,000	5,000 to 10,000	10,000 to 25,000	25,000 to 50,000	50,000 to 100,000	100,000 to 250,000	250,000 to 500,000	500,000 to 2,500,000	2,500,000 and over
Number of Enterprises	1	4537	553	1931	664	918	161	208	57	18	15	3	10	0
Revenues ($ in Thousands)														
Net Sales	2	25336987	271180	819294	879304	3332795	2254870	4173201	2169204	1666465	1226469	471207	8072998	0
Interest	3	76229	288	2076	425	1239	1365	5819	408	1450	2164	9552	51443	0
Rents	4	17412	284	0	2188	794	7172	544	1561	2279	1372	0	1218	0
Royalties	5	14899	0	0	0	0	1289	0	0	0	0	5	13605	0
Other Portfolio Income	6	180270	181	16110	796	6414	12947	6743	4984	7350	2813	12410	109521	0
Other Receipts	7	426472	28579	891	2520	47431	17493	95615	27745	2302	69477	35052	99367	0
Total Receipts	8	26052269	300512	838371	885233	3388673	2295136	4281922	2203902	1679846	1302295	528226	8348152	0
Average Total Receipts	9	5742	543	434	1333	3691	14256	20586	38665	93325	86820	176075	834815	•
Operating Costs/Operating Income (%)														
Cost of Operations	10	41.5	72.7	22.2	12.5	65.1	60.2	42.8	63.4	50.1	24.1	1.0	27.3	•
Salaries and Wages	11	17.4	14.4	35.2	25.1	9.5	9.0	19.1	8.3	14.1	23.0	20.7	21.7	•
Taxes Paid	12	3.0	1.0	0.9	4.4	2.3	2.3	3.6	2.0	2.2	3.8	5.6	3.6	•
Interest Paid	13	2.5	0.9	0.4	0.8	1.2	0.9	1.1	1.5	1.1	2.2	4.0	5.1	•
Depreciation	14	5.2	1.3	0.9	4.5	2.7	2.8	5.6	4.6	4.0	13.0	24.0	5.5	•
Amortization and Depletion	15	0.6	0.1	•	0.0	0.1	0.0	0.0	0.2	0.5	0.5	0.0	1.7	•
Pensions and Other Deferred Comp.	16	0.4	0.0	•	0.8	0.2	0.7	0.3	0.2	0.4	0.7	2.4	0.3	•
Employee Benefits	17	2.2	0.8	0.2	2.8	1.4	1.4	1.0	1.1	3.8	3.2	5.4	3.1	•
Advertising	18	0.2	0.1	0.2	1.4	0.1	0.1	0.1	0.1	0.1	0.1	0.1	0.3	•
Other Expenses	19	25.5	35.7	39.2	39.8	16.3	19.7	23.9	15.2	20.3	34.8	42.4	29.9	•
Officers' Compensation	20	1.3	0.1	0.0	6.0	2.3	1.7	2.3	0.7	1.3	1.2	0.5	0.2	•
Operating Margin	21	0.1	•	0.9	1.9	•	1.1	•	2.8	2.1	•	•	1.2	•
Operating Margin Before Officers' Comp.	22	1.4	•	0.9	7.9	1.1	2.9	2.3	3.5	3.3	•	•	1.5	•

Selected Average Balance Sheet ($ in Thousands)													
Net Receivables 23	1189	0	46	114	408	1553	2114	4601	12178	16543	15200	339068	•
Inventories 24	211	0	0	34	242	625	596	2269	5239	10716	64	10404	•
Net Property, Plant and Equipment 25	2197	0	98	319	1255	2127	6649	19070	26860	54113	267602	350433	•
Total Assets 26	7328	0	223	650	2547	7358	14945	35533	68307	131715	470750	1911038	•
Notes and Loans Payable 27	3152	0	141	574	1207	1891	5219	14798	18393	26584	132812	917444	•
All Other Liabilities 28	1457	0	9	316	828	1748	2563	5962	12211	29478	137723	339266	•
Net Worth 29	2719	0	72	-241	511	3718	7162	14772	37703	75652	200215	654328	•

Selected Financial Ratios (Times to 1)													
Current Ratio 30	1.3	•	3.1	0.9	0.9	2.2	1.8	1.6	1.5	1.8	1.1	1.2	•
Quick Ratio 31	1.0	•	3.0	0.6	0.6	1.4	1.2	1.1	0.9	1.2	0.6	1.1	•
Net Sales to Working Capital 32	11.1	•	5.7	•	•	6.4	7.7	9.5	10.0	4.6	36.9	12.6	•
Coverage Ratio 33	2.2	•	9.4	4.1	1.4	4.3	3.2	3.9	3.5	0.8	2.6	1.9	•
Total Asset Turnover 34	0.8	•	1.9	2.0	1.4	1.9	1.3	1.1	1.4	0.6	0.3	0.4	•
Inventory Turnover 35	11.0	•	•	4.9	9.8	13.5	14.4	10.6	8.9	1.8	24.5	21.2	•
Receivables Turnover 36	6.0	•	12.3	7.9	9.1	8.7	9.2	10.0	7.8	4.5	9.3	3.6	•
Total Liabilities to Net Worth 37	1.7	•	2.1	•	4.0	1.0	1.1	1.4	0.8	0.7	1.4	1.9	•
Current Assets to Working Capital 38	3.9	•	1.5	•	•	1.9	2.2	2.7	2.8	2.3	8.4	6.3	•
Current Liabilities to Working Capital 39	2.9	•	0.5	•	•	0.9	1.2	1.7	1.8	1.3	7.4	5.3	•
Working Capital to Net Sales 40	0.1	•	0.2	•	•	0.2	0.1	0.1	0.1	0.2	0.0	0.1	•
Inventory to Working Capital 41	0.4	•	•	•	•	0.3	0.2	0.6	0.6	0.6	0.0	0.2	•
Total Receipts to Cash Flow 42	5.1	8.4	5.5	3.7	9.3	7.5	5.5	7.3	5.9	4.1	2.5	4.0	•
Cost of Goods to Cash Flow 43	2.1	6.1	1.2	0.5	6.0	4.5	2.3	4.6	3.0	1.0	0.0	1.1	•
Cash Flow to Total Debt 44	0.2	•	0.5	0.4	0.2	0.5	0.5	0.3	0.5	0.4	0.2	0.2	•

Selected Financial Factors (in Percentages)													
Debt Ratio 45	62.9	•	67.4	137.1	79.9	49.5	52.1	58.4	44.8	42.6	57.5	65.8	•
Return on Total Assets 46	4.1	•	6.9	6.9	2.5	7.2	4.8	6.4	5.4	1.1	3.4	4.1	•
Return on Equity Before Income Taxes 47	6.0	•	18.9	•	3.4	11.0	6.9	11.4	7.0	•	4.9	5.8	•
Return on Equity After Income Taxes 48	4.2	•	17.4	•	•	10.5	6.0	10.3	5.1	•	2.0	3.7	•
Profit Margin (Before Income Tax) 49	2.9	•	3.2	2.6	0.5	2.9	2.5	4.4	2.8	•	6.2	4.7	•
Profit Margin (After Income Tax) 50	2.0	•	3.0	2.5	•	2.8	2.2	4.0	2.1	•	2.5	3.0	•

Table II

Corporations with Net Income

WAREHOUSING AND STORAGE

MONEY AMOUNTS AND SIZE OF ASSETS IN THOUSANDS OF DOLLARS

Item Description for Accounting Period 7/11 Through 6/12		Total	Zero Assets	Under 500	500 to 1000	1,000 to 5,000	5,000 to 10,000	10,000 to 25,000	25,000 to 50,000	50,000 to 100,000	100,000 to 250,000	250,000 to 500,000	500,000 to 2,500,000	2,500,000 and over
Number of Enterprises	1	2015	23	710	561	430	100	130	•	13	•	0	6	0
Revenues ($ in Thousands)														
Net Sales	2	16634706	69473	368125	662756	1487551	1812444	2994139	•	1413634	•	0	4960014	0
Interest	3	22431	7	2075	20	1155	1310	1898	•	1334	•	0	2545	0
Rents	4	14635	0	0	2188	761	5976	544	•	1914	•	0	1209	0
Royalties	5	14856	0	0	0	0	1289	0	•	0	•	0	13562	0
Other Portfolio Income	6	160384	143	16110	0	6025	9728	5564	•	4657	•	0	102348	0
Other Receipts	7	241505	237	892	2519	40511	17421	23815	•	1670	•	0	26236	0
Total Receipts	8	17088517	69860	387202	667483	1536003	1848168	3025960	•	1423209	•	0	5105914	0
Average Total Receipts	9	8481	3037	545	1190	3572	18482	23277	•	109478	•	•	850986	•
Operating Costs/Operating Income (%)														
Cost of Operations	10	36.3	32.4	49.3	16.6	52.9	63.6	44.0	•	50.9	•	•	10.4	•
Salaries and Wages	11	19.3	36.5	12.0	24.6	11.6	7.8	19.6	•	13.8	•	•	28.7	•
Taxes Paid	12	3.3	0.6	1.1	4.7	3.1	1.6	3.6	•	1.9	•	•	4.4	•
Interest Paid	13	2.3	0.1	0.9	1.1	1.4	0.6	1.1	•	0.7	•	•	4.9	•
Depreciation	14	4.4	3.6	0.1	5.8	3.3	2.9	3.5	•	3.1	•	•	5.3	•
Amortization and Depletion	15	0.6	•	•	0.0	0.0	0.0	0.0	•	0.2	•	•	1.7	•
Pensions and Other Deferred Comp.	16	0.5	•	•	0.9	0.4	0.6	0.4	•	0.5	•	•	0.4	•
Employee Benefits	17	2.7	1.7	•	3.4	2.4	0.9	0.8	•	4.2	•	•	4.4	•
Advertising	18	0.2	0.2	0.4	0.3	0.1	0.0	0.1	•	0.1	•	•	0.4	•
Other Expenses	19	24.6	24.2	27.9	32.5	18.8	16.5	19.5	•	19.7	•	•	32.8	•
Officers' Compensation	20	1.3	•	•	6.6	2.6	1.6	1.9	•	1.3	•	•	0.2	•
Operating Margin	21	4.5	0.7	8.3	3.6	3.4	3.9	5.5	•	3.5	•	•	6.3	•
Operating Margin Before Officers' Comp.	22	5.9	0.7	8.3	10.2	6.1	5.5	7.4	•	4.8	•	•	6.4	•

Selected Average Balance Sheet ($ in Thousands)													
Net Receivables **23**	2121	0	61	66	331	1299	2401	•	13864	•	•	502815	•
Inventories **24**	301	0	0	19	94	759	679	•	5083	•	•	13758	•
Net Property, Plant and Equipment **25**	2982	0	3	355	1057	2541	7002	•	31232	•	•	379223	•
Total Assets **26**	9742	0	138	645	2039	7624	14602	•	69893	•	•	1867651	•
Notes and Loans Payable **27**	4504	0	113	674	861	1965	5250	•	9675	•	•	1066334	•
All Other Liabilities **28**	1929	0	11	354	347	1155	2365	•	14200	•	•	362440	•
Net Worth **29**	3308	0	14	-383	831	4504	6987	•	46018	•	•	438878	•
Selected Financial Ratios (Times to 1)													
Current Ratio **30**	1.4	•	4.6	0.7	2.0	2.9	2.0	•	1.9	•	•	1.2	•
Quick Ratio **31**	1.2	•	4.6	0.4	1.5	1.8	1.6	•	1.2	•	•	1.1	•
Net Sales to Working Capital **32**	8.3	•	7.1	•	8.7	6.2	8.3	•	8.3	•	•	7.7	•
Coverage Ratio **33**	4.2	24.5	16.9	4.9	5.6	10.9	7.1	•	7.2	•	•	2.9	•
Total Asset Turnover **34**	0.8	•	3.8	1.8	1.7	2.4	1.6	•	1.6	•	•	0.4	•
Inventory Turnover **35**	10.0	•	•	10.3	19.6	15.2	14.9	•	10.9	•	•	6.3	•
Receivables Turnover **36**	5.2	•	17.1	12.7	10.0	11.9	8.9	•	7.6	•	•	2.6	•
Total Liabilities to Net Worth **37**	1.9	•	9.0	•	1.5	0.7	1.1	•	0.5	•	•	3.3	•
Current Assets to Working Capital **38**	3.3	•	1.3	•	2.0	1.5	2.0	•	2.1	•	•	5.5	•
Current Liabilities to Working Capital **39**	2.3	•	0.3	•	1.0	0.5	1.0	•	1.1	•	•	4.5	•
Working Capital to Net Sales **40**	0.1	•	0.1	•	0.1	0.2	0.1	•	0.1	•	•	0.1	•
Inventory to Working Capital **41**	0.3	•	•	•	0.3	0.3	0.2	•	0.3	•	•	0.1	•
Total Receipts to Cash Flow **42**	4.3	5.7	3.9	4.3	5.6	7.5	4.8	•	5.6	•	•	3.3	•
Cost of Goods to Cash Flow **43**	1.6	1.9	1.9	0.7	3.0	4.7	2.1	•	2.8	•	•	0.3	•
Cash Flow to Total Debt **44**	0.3	•	1.1	0.3	0.5	0.8	0.6	•	0.8	•	•	0.2	•
Selected Financial Factors (in Percentages)													
Debt Ratio **45**	66.0	•	90.0	159.4	59.3	40.9	52.1	•	34.2	•	•	76.5	•
Return on Total Assets **46**	8.1	•	54.1	9.9	13.8	15.5	11.9	•	7.5	•	•	6.3	•
Return on Equity Before Income Taxes **47**	18.2	•	507.0	•	27.8	23.8	21.4	•	9.8	•	•	17.6	•
Return on Equity After Income Taxes **48**	14.9	•	486.6	•	23.2	23.0	19.9	•	7.7	•	•	12.2	•
Profit Margin (Before Income Tax) **49**	7.3	1.3	13.5	4.3	6.7	5.9	6.5	•	4.2	•	•	9.3	•
Profit Margin (After Income Tax) **50**	6.0	1.1	13.0	4.2	5.6	5.7	6.0	•	3.3	•	•	6.5	•

Table I

Corporations with and without Net Income

NEWSPAPER PUBLISHERS

MONEY AMOUNTS AND SIZE OF ASSETS IN THOUSANDS OF DOLLARS

Item Description for Accounting Period 7/11 Through 6/12		Total	Zero Assets	Under 500	500 to 1,000	1,000 to 5,000	5,000 to 10,000	10,000 to 25,000	25,000 to 50,000	50,000 to 100,000	100,000 to 250,000	250,000 to 500,000	500,000 to 2,500,000	2,500,000 and over
Number of Enterprises	1	4393	549	2909	265	433	68	87	29	21	10	9	7	5
Revenues ($ in Thousands)														
Net Sales	2	25600754	188595	1100687	98638	2921702	751582	1333966	1011028	1176979	1418199	2145111	3256719	10197550
Interest	3	48508	40	257	2	17546	1018	6968	2713	1056	1205	5562	1875	10266
Rents	4	59851	48	0	0	0	77	1817	6355	369	8352	9175	8554	25105
Royalties	5	20367	113	0	0	0	0	79	0	13	619	127	254	19162
Other Portfolio Income	6	504833	10569	0	0	10950	971	15977	1670	8585	80556	57964	24424	293168
Other Receipts	7	1143060	8978	140	196	44293	-15186	42031	18468	22413	30358	29983	53246	908137
Total Receipts	8	27377373	208343	1101084	98836	2994491	738462	1400838	1040234	1209415	1539289	2247922	3345072	11453388
Average Total Receipts	9	6232	379	379	373	6916	10860	16102	35870	57591	153929	249769	477867	2290678
Operating Costs/Operating Income (%)														
Cost of Operations	10	30.7	12.5	38.4	40.9	62.7	32.0	32.3	26.9	28.9	17.2	26.9	17.9	27.9
Salaries and Wages	11	24.7	40.6	20.1	19.7	12.3	24.7	27.2	25.0	28.5	32.2	24.3	28.5	25.4
Taxes Paid	12	3.6	4.7	4.0	4.2	2.3	2.5	4.5	3.8	3.8	4.5	3.8	3.4	3.6
Interest Paid	13	6.3	0.6	0.3	0.0	2.0	0.8	1.0	2.0	2.3	2.3	3.1	8.5	10.8
Depreciation	14	3.7	2.1	2.1	0.6	0.7	1.7	3.0	2.7	5.9	5.9	5.4	3.9	4.2
Amortization and Depletion	15	4.7	1.8	0.1	9.8	0.3	1.0	0.5	2.0	2.2	2.8	6.1	10.3	6.1
Pensions and Other Deferred Comp.	16	3.1	1.7	0.1	0.1	0.2	0.9	0.9	1.2	1.7	1.4	5.0	1.2	5.4
Employee Benefits	17	3.4	8.0	0.9	1.9	2.1	2.0	4.1	4.3	4.4	4.5	3.5	3.8	3.4
Advertising	18	1.8	2.1	2.7	4.0	0.5	7.1	0.8	1.6	1.6	1.7	2.0	1.1	2.1
Other Expenses	19	22.7	55.7	26.3	56.2	14.3	12.7	25.3	31.1	24.1	29.6	26.5	31.0	18.9
Officers' Compensation	20	1.6	0.9	7.4	6.8	2.1	2.7	2.3	2.3	2.7	1.6	1.1	1.1	0.7
Operating Margin	21	•	•	•	•	0.5	11.8	•	•	•	•	•	•	•
Operating Margin Before Officers' Comp.	22	•	•	5.0	•	2.6	14.5	0.3	•	•	•	•	•	•

Selected Average Balance Sheet ($ in Thousands)													
Net Receivables **23**	851	0	27	185	918	1114	1795	4260	6623	17544	41606	58977	350965
Inventories **24**	95	0	1	7	225	126	275	563	866	3092	4069	7766	25868
Net Property, Plant and Equipment **25**	1953	0	21	36	554	816	4039	12189	25944	51126	90736	177788	877890
Total Assets **26**	9793	0	77	553	2837	7613	14790	35302	67253	178477	331523	774711	5397227
Notes and Loans Payable **27**	2803	0	61	1640	1122	1476	2698	10971	30670	38882	107440	611136	856386
All Other Liabilities **28**	6247	0	26	147	2852	4602	2931	8296	18070	54399	111445	220116	4363898
Net Worth **29**	743	0	-10	-1233	-1137	1536	9161	16036	18513	85196	112638	-56542	176944
Selected Financial Ratios (Times to 1)													
Current Ratio **30**	1.2	•	1.4	0.1	1.1	4.9	2.3	1.0	1.4	2.3	1.6	0.4	1.5
Quick Ratio **31**	0.9	•	1.4	0.1	0.8	3.3	1.8	0.9	0.9	2.1	1.1	0.3	1.2
Net Sales to Working Capital **32**	15.0	•	29.2	•	97.5	2.8	5.0	79.2	9.1	4.2	6.8	•	6.3
Coverage Ratio **33**	1.1	•	•	•	2.5	13.1	3.9	0.9	•	3.1	0.1	0.0	1.4
Total Asset Turnover **34**	0.6	•	4.9	0.7	2.4	1.5	1.0	1.0	0.8	0.8	0.7	0.6	0.4
Inventory Turnover **35**	18.7	•	227.9	22.0	18.8	28.0	18.0	16.7	18.7	7.9	15.8	10.7	22.0
Receivables Turnover **36**	6.8	•	11.4	1.4	8.3	11.9	9.0	6.5	8.6	7.6	5.7	7.6	5.8
Total Liabilities to Net Worth **37**	12.2	•	•	•	•	4.0	0.6	1.2	2.6	1.1	1.9	•	29.5
Current Assets to Working Capital **38**	5.3	•	3.4	•	19.7	1.3	1.8	22.6	3.3	1.8	2.6	•	2.9
Current Liabilities to Working Capital **39**	4.3	•	2.4	•	18.7	0.3	0.8	21.6	2.3	0.8	1.6	•	1.9
Working Capital to Net Sales **40**	0.1	•	0.0	•	0.0	0.4	0.2	0.0	0.1	0.2	0.1	•	0.2
Inventory to Working Capital **41**	0.2	•	0.0	•	3.7	0.1	0.1	1.2	0.1	0.1	0.1	•	0.1
Total Receipts to Cash Flow **42**	5.3	4.7	5.3	15.1	6.6	4.6	4.2	3.6	5.7	3.5	5.4	5.2	6.0
Cost of Goods to Cash Flow **43**	1.6	0.6	2.0	6.2	4.2	1.5	1.3	1.0	1.6	0.6	1.5	0.9	1.7
Cash Flow to Total Debt **44**	0.1	•	0.8	0.0	0.3	0.4	0.7	0.5	0.2	0.4	0.2	0.1	0.1
Selected Financial Factors (in Percentages)													
Debt Ratio **45**	92.4	•	112.8	322.8	140.1	79.8	38.1	54.6	72.5	52.3	66.0	107.3	96.7
Return on Total Assets **46**	4.2	•	•	•	11.8	15.8	4.0	1.8	•	5.5	0.1	0.2	5.5
Return on Equity Before Income Taxes **47**	5.6	•	88.2	13.3	•	72.2	4.8	•	•	7.8	•	67.3	44.1
Return on Equity After Income Taxes **48**	•	•	92.0	13.3	•	70.6	3.0	•	•	6.9	•	70.0	31.2
Profit Margin (Before Income Tax) **49**	0.7	•	•	•	3.0	10.0	2.9	•	•	4.7	•	•	3.8
Profit Margin (After Income Tax) **50**	•	•	•	•	2.8	9.8	1.8	•	•	4.1	•	•	2.7

Table II

Corporations with Net Income

NEWSPAPER PUBLISHERS

MONEY AMOUNTS AND SIZE OF ASSETS IN THOUSANDS OF DOLLARS

Item Description for Accounting Period 7/11 Through 6/12		Total	Zero Assets	Under 500	500 to 1,000	1,000 to 5,000	5,000 to 10,000	10,000 to 25,000	25,000 to 50,000	50,000 to 100,000	100,000 to 250,000	250,000 to 500,000	500,000 to 2,500,000	2,500,000 and over
Number of Enterprises	1	1438	20	872	59	339	62	46	12	12	7	•	0	•
Revenues ($ in Thousands)														
Net Sales	2	13753829	58465	314865	46716	2627794	700205	788473	381160	615700	1049521	•	0	•
Interest	3	21875	28	256	1	12	977	4146	375	804	1067	•	0	•
Rents	4	33493	36	0	0	0	59	687	3249	349	8296	•	0	•
Royalties	5	226	0	0	0	0	0	77	0	0	1	•	0	•
Other Portfolio Income	6	423805	10180	0	0	10944	120	11177	740	2803	76126	•	0	•
Other Receipts	7	697329	5339	137	21	43924	-15026	41617	6490	18871	4891	•	0	•
Total Receipts	8	14930557	74048	315258	46738	2682674	686335	846177	392014	638527	1139902	•	0	•
Average Total Receipts	9	10383	3702	362	792	7913	11070	18395	32668	53211	162843	•	•	•
Operating Costs/Operating Income (%)														
Cost of Operations	10	33.8	15.5	20.1	37.8	65.5	33.0	36.3	33.2	27.6	15.5	•	•	•
Salaries and Wages	11	24.2	39.1	27.5	29.4	11.8	23.7	23.0	19.5	25.7	29.6	•	•	•
Taxes Paid	12	3.6	5.4	3.4	2.3	2.3	2.3	4.3	2.9	3.7	4.5	•	•	•
Interest Paid	13	3.7	1.1	0.0	0.0	0.6	0.5	1.0	2.6	1.5	1.7	•	•	•
Depreciation	14	2.9	0.4	0.4	0.2	0.3	1.7	2.3	2.6	4.1	5.9	•	•	•
Amortization and Depletion	15	3.3	0.9	•	5.6	0.3	0.6	0.4	2.7	2.6	2.8	•	•	•
Pensions and Other Deferred Comp.	16	3.1	0.5	0.5	•	0.2	0.4	0.6	1.1	1.4	1.2	•	•	•
Employee Benefits	17	3.3	2.4	2.8	0.3	2.1	1.9	2.6	2.8	3.9	3.9	•	•	•
Advertising	18	1.7	0.9	0.7	0.4	0.5	7.2	0.7	0.4	0.6	0.9	•	•	•
Other Expenses	19	18.8	31.0	36.5	17.5	11.9	12.0	23.5	28.4	21.6	31.5	•	•	•
Officers' Compensation	20	1.6	•	6.3	0.4	2.2	1.2	2.3	2.8	3.0	1.7	•	•	•
Operating Margin	21	•	3.0	1.7	6.1	2.4	15.5	3.1	1.1	4.3	0.9	•	•	•
Operating Margin Before Officers' Comp.	22	1.5	3.0	8.0	6.5	4.6	16.8	5.4	3.9	7.3	2.6	•	•	•

Selected Average Balance Sheet ($ in Thousands)													
Net Receivables 23	1476	0	46	133	1102	1132	1741	3879	5901	17038	•	•	•
Inventories 24	192	0	0	31	278	129	238	579	744	2905	•	•	•
Net Property, Plant and Equipment 25	2866	0	2	27	230	706	3899	9331	19502	53075	•	•	•
Total Assets 26	18703	0	80	596	2853	7443	14709	32751	69955	197309	•	•	•
Notes and Loans Payable 27	4418	0	0	265	652	1071	2991	11366	16221	30383	•	•	•
All Other Liabilities 28	5772	0	58	27	1291	4312	2601	7403	11552	59192	•	•	•
Net Worth 29	8513	0	22	304	909	2060	9118	13982	42182	107734	•	•	•
Selected Financial Ratios (Times to 1)													
Current Ratio 30	1.0	•	1.1	10.7	1.2	5.5	2.6	1.2	1.6	2.3	•	•	•
Quick Ratio 31	0.8	•	1.1	10.7	0.9	3.7	2.0	1.1	0.9	2.2	•	•	•
Net Sales to Working Capital 32	330.8	•	70.3	3.0	26.0	2.7	4.2	16.2	5.2	4.0	•	•	•
Coverage Ratio 33	3.3	27.5	173.8	261.6	8.6	26.7	11.6	2.5	6.2	6.6	•	•	•
Total Asset Turnover 34	0.5	•	4.5	1.3	2.7	1.5	1.2	1.0	0.7	0.8	•	•	•
Inventory Turnover 35	16.8	•	2306.7	9.6	18.3	28.9	26.1	18.2	19.0	8.0	•	•	•
Receivables Turnover 36	6.2	•	6.2	1.7	8.7	12.7	10.0	6.1	7.8	8.4	•	•	•
Total Liabilities to Net Worth 37	1.2	•	2.7	1.0	2.1	2.6	0.6	1.3	0.7	0.8	•	•	•
Current Assets to Working Capital 38	99.0	•	10.7	1.1	5.3	1.2	1.6	5.6	2.6	1.8	•	•	•
Current Liabilities to Working Capital 39	98.0	•	9.7	0.1	4.3	0.2	0.6	4.6	1.6	0.8	•	•	•
Working Capital to Net Sales 40	0.0	•	0.0	0.3	0.0	0.4	0.2	0.1	0.2	0.3	•	•	•
Inventory to Working Capital 41	6.5	•	0.0	0.0	1.1	0.1	0.1	0.3	0.1	0.1	•	•	•
Total Receipts to Cash Flow 42	4.6	1.7	2.9	4.9	7.1	4.0	3.3	3.3	3.7	2.9	•	•	•
Cost of Goods to Cash Flow 43	1.5	0.3	0.6	1.9	4.6	1.3	1.2	1.1	1.0	0.5	•	•	•
Cash Flow to Total Debt 44	0.2	•	2.1	0.6	0.6	0.5	0.9	0.5	0.5	0.6	•	•	•
Selected Financial Factors (in Percentages)													
Debt Ratio 45	54.5	•	72.8	48.9	68.1	72.3	38.0	57.3	39.7	45.4	•	•	•
Return on Total Assets 46	6.2	•	8.5	8.2	13.8	21.4	13.1	6.3	7.0	8.5	•	•	•
Return on Equity Before Income Taxes 47	9.5	•	30.9	16.0	38.3	74.4	19.3	8.8	9.7	13.3	•	•	•
Return on Equity After Income Taxes 48	8.0	•	25.2	15.9	37.0	73.0	15.7	7.2	8.5	12.2	•	•	•
Profit Margin (Before Income Tax) 49	8.4	29.6	1.9	6.1	4.5	13.6	10.3	3.9	8.0	9.5	•	•	•
Profit Margin (After Income Tax) 50	7.1	22.7	1.5	6.1	4.3	13.3	8.4	3.2	7.0	8.8	•	•	•

PERIODICAL PUBLISHERS

MONEY AMOUNTS AND SIZE OF ASSETS IN THOUSANDS OF DOLLARS

Item Description for Accounting Period 7/11 Through 6/12		Total	Zero Assets	Under 500	500 to 1,000	1,000 to 5,000	5,000 to 10,000	10,000 to 25,000	25,000 to 50,000	50,000 to 100,000	100,000 to 250,000	250,000 to 500,000	500,000 to 2,500,000	2,500,000 and over
Number of Enterprises	1	7130	1882	4282	302	501	24	65	24	15	15	7	9	3
Revenues ($ in Thousands)														
Net Sales	2	24751062	104226	1024256	391520	2384905	348906	1541205	1023541	1002227	1793017	1051275	4576417	9509567
Interest	3	85775	40	0	210	498	23	544	403	978	3440	3348	24335	51958
Rents	4	127675	88	0	0	0	0	1761	41	327	3107	3191	7209	111951
Royalties	5	363826	0	0	0	0	1767	0	0	18201	47236	85725	23978	186918
Other Portfolio Income	6	730606	0	708	61	1693	2	1240	2434	15372	7452	758	74029	626857
Other Receipts	7	1296763	2572	2832	1763	26876	36087	55792	22569	34273	103699	55371	3705	951223
Total Receipts	8	27355707	106926	1027796	393554	2413972	386785	1600542	1048988	1071378	1957951	1199668	4709673	11438474
Average Total Receipts	9	3837	57	240	1303	4818	16116	24624	43708	71425	130530	171381	523297	3812825
Operating Costs/Operating Income (%)														
Cost of Operations	10	32.7	14.1	14.2	44.6	59.9	18.4	52.1	47.4	25.5	39.1	30.3	30.7	24.1
Salaries and Wages	11	21.6	1.6	16.7	8.8	7.6	40.8	14.5	19.0	23.2	18.3	28.5	19.2	27.9
Taxes Paid	12	2.7	1.2	2.6	2.3	3.4	2.2	2.0	2.5	2.7	2.2	3.0	2.2	3.1
Interest Paid	13	5.5	1.0	0.3	0.2	1.9	0.4	1.5	2.6	2.9	3.6	7.4	6.2	8.5
Depreciation	14	2.6	0.2	2.5	2.8	1.3	0.9	2.4	1.6	2.1	2.0	5.3	2.0	3.2
Amortization and Depletion	15	2.8	1.4	2.3	2.7	0.6	3.7	0.8	1.4	4.4	4.7	9.2	0.1	4.0
Pensions and Other Deferred Comp.	16	1.2	•	0.0	1.1	1.4	0.4	0.4	0.3	0.6	0.4	0.3	0.7	2.1
Employee Benefits	17	2.9	0.1	2.0	1.0	1.3	4.2	2.0	2.6	4.3	2.1	3.3	1.8	4.1
Advertising	18	2.0	0.0	2.6	0.2	4.0	4.6	1.3	5.0	2.0	4.1	1.9	1.1	1.1
Other Expenses	19	29.7	90.7	46.5	23.9	13.7	39.0	24.6	21.8	26.2	27.0	27.3	34.5	31.7
Officers' Compensation	20	3.0	2.0	18.8	6.4	3.3	2.3	1.8	2.7	2.0	2.3	3.5	1.6	2.1
Operating Margin	21	•	•	•	5.9	1.5	•	•	•	4.0	•	•	•	•
Operating Margin Before Officers' Comp.	22	•	•	10.2	12.4	4.8	•	•	•	6.0	•	•	1.4	•

Selected Average Balance Sheet ($ in Thousands)

Net Receivables 23	552	0	19	141	559	2512	3009	4880	10810	20231	37162	67577	608107
Inventories 24	75	0	7	7	40	149	1362	1305	1486	4943	2748	7720	57741
Net Property, Plant and Equipment 25	430	0	17	33	214	411	3652	5109	5778	13281	17279	49351	550372
Total Assets 26	7619	0	78	727	2130	6832	15498	33223	73723	156149	393675	1007198	11822233
Notes and Loans Payable 27	2521	0	155	0	476	2555	5457	15831	28425	54182	252733	444038	3090679
All Other Liabilities 28	2965	0	52	124	2030	7495	8979	15339	32111	62283	96598	306560	4627809
Net Worth 29	2133	0	-129	603	-376	-3218	1063	2054	13188	39684	44344	256600	4103745

Selected Financial Ratios (Times to 1)

Current Ratio 30	1.0	•	0.8	2.7	1.2	0.6	1.4	1.4	1.0	1.0	1.7	0.8	1.0
Quick Ratio 31	0.8	•	0.6	2.7	0.9	0.5	0.8	1.0	0.6	0.8	1.4	0.6	0.8
Net Sales to Working Capital 32	73.2	•	•	7.8	17.1	•	11.4	8.9	411.1	350.8	3.9	•	5400.1
Coverage Ratio 33	1.7	•	•	27.6	2.5	•	1.2	•	5.0	2.0	0.2	1.5	2.0
Total Asset Turnover 34	0.5	•	3.1	1.8	2.2	2.1	1.5	1.3	0.9	0.8	0.4	0.5	0.3
Inventory Turnover 35	15.1	•	4.9	86.7	71.0	17.9	9.1	15.5	11.4	9.5	16.6	20.2	13.2
Receivables Turnover 36	3.6	•	12.8	9.8	7.0	7.4	7.5	7.0	6.1	5.1	5.0	7.4	2.0
Total Liabilities to Net Worth 37	2.6	•	•	0.2	•	•	13.6	15.2	4.6	2.9	7.9	2.9	1.9
Current Assets to Working Capital 38	28.6	•	•	1.6	5.3	•	3.8	3.3	168.3	150.4	2.5	•	2578.2
Current Liabilities to Working Capital 39	27.6	•	•	0.6	4.3	•	2.8	2.3	167.3	149.4	1.5	•	2577.2
Working Capital to Net Sales 40	0.0	•	•	0.1	0.1	•	0.1	0.1	0.0	0.0	0.3	•	0.0
Inventory to Working Capital 41	1.5	•	•	•	0.1	•	0.7	0.3	8.0	14.8	0.1	•	91.3
Total Receipts to Cash Flow 42	3.5	2.4	2.9	3.7	8.0	3.7	4.5	7.2	3.0	3.9	6.3	3.0	2.9
Cost of Goods to Cash Flow 43	1.1	0.3	0.4	1.7	4.8	0.7	2.3	3.4	0.8	1.5	1.9	0.9	0.7
Cash Flow to Total Debt 44	0.2	•	0.4	2.8	0.2	0.4	0.4	0.2	0.4	0.3	0.1	0.2	0.1

Selected Financial Factors (in Percentages)

Debt Ratio 45	72.0	•	264.6	17.0	117.7	147.1	93.1	93.8	82.1	74.6	88.7	74.5	65.3
Return on Total Assets 46	4.4	•	•	12.0	10.4	•	2.9	•	13.3	5.5	0.5	4.6	4.6
Return on Equity Before Income Taxes 47	6.7	•	15.3	13.9	•	27.5	8.4	•	59.8	10.7	•	5.6	6.8
Return on Equity After Income Taxes 48	4.8	•	15.3	10.7	•	27.5	5.6	•	45.4	8.8	•	1.7	5.6
Profit Margin (Before Income Tax) 49	4.1	•	•	6.5	2.8	•	0.4	•	11.8	3.6	•	2.8	8.8
Profit Margin (After Income Tax) 50	3.0	•	•	5.0	2.7	•	0.3	•	9.0	2.9	•	0.8	7.3

Table II

Corporations with Net Income

PERIODICAL PUBLISHERS

MONEY AMOUNTS AND SIZE OF ASSETS IN THOUSANDS OF DOLLARS

Item Description for Accounting Period 7/11 Through 6/12		Total	Zero Assets	Under 500	500 to 1,000	1,000 to 5,000	5,000 to 10,000	10,000 to 25,000	25,000 to 50,000	50,000 to 100,000	100,000 to 250,000	250,000 to 500,000	500,000 to 2,500,000	2,500,000 and over
Number of Enterprises	1	3512	421	2382	302	325	9	35	•	10	7	3	•	0
Revenues ($ in Thousands)														
Net Sales	2	14526845	74306	739977	391520	2155816	180067	748102	•	745017	1065767	288594	•	0
Interest	3	63242	40	0	210	447	21	465	•	930	2537	2613	•	0
Rents	4	93373	39	0	0	0	0	51	•	327	3107	220	•	0
Royalties	5	137064	0	0	0	0	3	0	•	15247	733	0	•	0
Other Portfolio Income	6	657741	0	708	61	1693	0	27	•	15372	1007	758	•	0
Other Receipts	7	1117699	2367	894	1763	26535	191	1570	•	27205	94666	1727	•	0
Total Receipts	8	16595964	76752	741579	393554	2184491	180282	750215	•	804098	1167817	293912	•	0
Average Total Receipts	9	4726	182	311	1303	6722	20031	21435	•	80410	166831	97971	•	•
Operating Costs/Operating Income (%)														
Cost of Operations	10	34.4	14.3	16.3	44.6	60.4	35.7	56.6	•	22.1	33.7	18.6	•	•
Salaries and Wages	11	19.8	•	10.3	8.8	7.7	30.0	11.1	•	22.8	19.6	23.2	•	•
Taxes Paid	12	3.1	1.3	2.4	2.3	3.4	2.5	1.5	•	2.7	2.1	3.5	•	•
Interest Paid	13	1.8	0.0	0.0	0.2	2.1	0.7	1.0	•	1.4	0.8	4.6	•	•
Depreciation	14	2.3	0.0	3.0	2.8	1.5	0.2	2.1	•	2.2	2.0	2.8	•	•
Amortization and Depletion	15	3.4	•	3.2	2.7	0.6	5.2	1.1	•	2.4	1.9	10.5	•	•
Pensions and Other Deferred Comp.	16	1.4	•	0.0	1.1	0.2	0.2	0.6	•	0.8	0.7	0.4	•	•
Employee Benefits	17	2.9	0.0	1.4	1.0	1.0	2.5	2.6	•	4.9	1.8	1.1	•	•
Advertising	18	1.9	•	0.0	0.2	4.2	7.8	0.7	•	2.6	5.4	1.8	•	•
Other Expenses	19	26.9	59.8	24.0	23.9	12.4	13.1	9.8	•	26.1	26.4	24.8	•	•
Officers' Compensation	20	4.2	2.7	25.8	6.4	3.2	1.1	2.8	•	2.1	3.1	5.4	•	•
Operating Margin	21	•	21.7	13.6	5.9	3.4	0.9	10.2	•	9.8	2.6	3.5	•	•
Operating Margin Before Officers' Comp.	22	2.2	24.4	39.4	12.4	6.5	2.0	13.0	•	11.9	5.7	8.8	•	•

Selected Average Balance Sheet ($ in Thousands)													
Net Receivables 23	634	0	23	141	770	1960	3120	•	10782	19491	50193	•	•
Inventories 24	80	0	12	7	11	388	1740	•	1804	7314	456	•	•
Net Property, Plant and Equipment 25	637	0	24	33	326	55	3555	•	7001	19064	11412	•	•
Total Assets 26	10463	0	98	727	2620	7570	15054	•	73659	160624	349085	•	•
Notes and Loans Payable 27	1226	0	52	0	488	2963	3626	•	13035	12687	164728	•	•
All Other Liabilities 28	4258	0	74	124	2624	5568	6907	•	39570	77733	74261	•	•
Net Worth 29	4979	0	-28	603	-492	-961	4522	•	21054	70204	110097	•	•

Selected Financial Ratios (Times to 1)													
Current Ratio 30	1.7	•	0.7	2.7	1.2	0.8	1.6	•	1.0	1.0	2.9	•	•
Quick Ratio 31	1.3	•	0.6	2.7	0.9	0.4	1.1	•	0.5	0.8	2.8	•	•
Net Sales to Working Capital 32	5.7	•	•	7.8	22.9	•	7.2	•	•	72.7	1.1	•	•
Coverage Ratio 33	7.9	563.8	430.6	27.6	3.2	2.4	11.9	•	14.6	16.2	2.1	•	•
Total Asset Turnover 34	0.4	•	3.2	1.8	2.5	2.6	1.4	•	1.0	0.9	0.3	•	•
Inventory Turnover 35	17.8	•	4.3	86.7	349.1	18.4	6.9	•	9.1	7.0	39.2	•	•
Receivables Turnover 36	6.1	•	18.0	9.8	10.7	13.1	5.0	•	6.7	5.8	3.8	•	•
Total Liabilities to Net Worth 37	1.1	•	•	0.2	•	•	2.3	•	2.5	1.3	2.2	•	•
Current Assets to Working Capital 38	2.5	•	•	1.6	5.6	•	2.6	•	•	27.7	1.5	•	•
Current Liabilities to Working Capital 39	1.5	•	•	0.6	4.6	•	1.6	•	•	26.7	0.5	•	•
Working Capital to Net Sales 40	0.2	•	•	0.1	0.0	•	0.1	•	•	0.0	0.9	•	•
Inventory to Working Capital 41	0.1	•	•	•	0.0	•	0.5	•	•	3.3	0.0	•	•
Total Receipts to Cash Flow 42	2.9	1.2	2.9	3.7	7.7	9.4	5.3	•	2.4	2.8	4.0	•	•
Cost of Goods to Cash Flow 43	1.0	0.2	0.5	1.7	4.6	3.4	3.0	•	0.5	1.0	0.7	•	•
Cash Flow to Total Debt 44	0.3	•	0.9	2.8	0.3	0.2	0.4	•	0.6	0.6	0.1	•	•

Selected Financial Factors (in Percentages)													
Debt Ratio 45	52.4	•	128.1	17.0	118.8	112.7	70.0	•	71.4	56.3	68.5	•	•
Return on Total Assets 46	5.7	•	43.8	12.0	17.1	4.5	16.2	•	20.5	12.6	2.7	•	•
Return on Equity Before Income Taxes 47	10.5	•	•	13.9	•	•	49.5	•	66.9	27.1	4.5	•	•
Return on Equity After Income Taxes 48	8.8	•	•	10.7	•	•	48.3	•	53.5	24.7	4.5	•	•
Profit Margin (Before Income Tax) 49	12.6	25.0	13.8	6.5	4.7	1.0	10.5	•	18.9	12.5	5.2	•	•
Profit Margin (After Income Tax) 50	10.6	24.1	13.8	5.0	4.6	1.0	10.2	•	15.1	11.4	5.2	•	•

Table I

Corporations with and without Net Income

BOOK PUBLISHERS

MONEY AMOUNTS AND SIZE OF ASSETS IN THOUSANDS OF DOLLARS

Item Description for Accounting Period 7/11 Through 6/12		Total	Zero Assets	Under 500	500 to 1,000	1,000 to 5,000	5,000 to 10,000	10,000 to 25,000	25,000 to 50,000	50,000 to 100,000	100,000 to 250,000	250,000 to 500,000	500,000 to 2,500,000	2,500,000 and over
Number of Enterprises	1	4979	867	3404	408	155	52	40	19	12	7	4	4	6
Revenues ($ in Thousands)														
Net Sales	2	28494545	33286	617143	573704	555177	437429	906431	660719	913465	945321	706372	3610955	18534543
Interest	3	175892	0	635	1763	1482	0	25	1912	1127	1138	20211	6744	140854
Rents	4	26575	0	0	0	0	212	0	1624	891	0	0	5844	18004
Royalties	5	238422	9	0	0	2360	0	1944	5478	7764	9170	5799	36716	169182
Other Portfolio Income	6	540788	0	0	0	253	80	392	21	835	1025	339	299326	238515
Other Receipts	7	781157	28	1604	3	722	2895	4011	28217	58611	68614	69075	202779	344600
Total Receipts	8	30257379	33323	619382	575470	559994	440616	912803	697971	982693	1025268	801796	4162364	19445698
Average Total Receipts	9	6077	38	182	1410	3613	8473	22820	36735	81891	146467	200449	1040591	3240950
Operating Costs/Operating Income (%)														
Cost of Operations	10	33.0	17.4	37.9	40.2	30.0	41.3	42.9	56.6	40.0	38.2	37.0	44.7	28.1
Salaries and Wages	11	21.8	30.3	19.3	6.3	12.8	15.9	19.5	14.7	18.4	17.3	9.4	23.5	23.7
Taxes Paid	12	2.5	3.8	2.2	1.2	1.5	1.9	2.6	1.8	1.9	2.6	1.2	2.8	2.6
Interest Paid	13	5.5	2.9	0.0	0.5	0.2	1.0	0.5	4.3	1.4	4.0	11.3	1.9	7.2
Depreciation	14	3.4	0.2	0.3	0.6	0.4	0.4	2.6	1.1	2.9	1.1	1.5	3.2	4.2
Amortization and Depletion	15	4.7	0.5	0.2	0.0	0.0	0.0	0.5	1.6	2.6	5.8	3.7	3.3	6.0
Pensions and Other Deferred Comp.	16	1.1	0.4	1.1	4.2	1.1	0.2	0.5	0.5	0.6	1.2	1.0	0.6	1.2
Employee Benefits	17	2.6	6.8	2.0	0.7	1.3	1.7	2.6	2.1	1.8	1.5	2.4	3.4	2.7
Advertising	18	1.4	0.2	1.5	0.2	1.3	1.7	1.9	2.7	4.8	2.0	2.3	2.7	0.9
Other Expenses	19	20.5	70.9	17.4	20.4	32.0	25.0	18.6	12.6	27.7	35.3	37.3	17.4	19.3
Officers' Compensation	20	1.4	17.9	5.4	9.6	10.5	2.8	4.3	2.8	2.2	2.9	1.6	0.7	0.5
Operating Margin	21	2.1	•	12.8	16.1	8.9	8.1	3.4	•	•	•	•	•	3.8
Operating Margin Before Officers' Comp.	22	3.5	•	18.2	25.7	19.4	10.9	7.6	1.9	•	•	•	•	4.2

Selected Average Balance Sheet ($ in Thousands)

Net Receivables 23	1114	0	10	75	385	1516	3932	4754	14699	33727	68937	231101	580472
Inventories 24	564	0	7	244	896	1559	2137	7321	7385	28590	15493	90838	259971
Net Property, Plant and Equipment 25	411	0	9	131	116	459	1694	1823	6462	7141	14480	111059	197630
Total Assets 26	10198	0	81	611	2935	6933	14590	34383	69141	170286	338339	1566554	6426348
Notes and Loans Payable 27	4070	0	53	1397	96	2115	3239	9094	13010	107664	249012	392950	2601793
All Other Liabilities 28	4092	0	17	277	423	2365	4700	29364	33521	49156	133234	563954	2622740
Net Worth 29	2035	0	11	-1062	2416	2454	6651	-4074	22610	13467	-43907	609651	1201816

Selected Financial Ratios (Times to 1)

Current Ratio 30	0.9	•	1.9	1.2	5.8	2.0	1.8	2.3	1.4	1.1	1.1	1.4	0.8
Quick Ratio 31	0.5	•	1.5	0.4	3.6	1.1	1.1	0.7	0.8	0.6	0.7	0.9	0.4
Net Sales to Working Capital 32	•	•	7.3	23.7	1.7	3.7	5.1	2.8	6.7	18.7	24.4	7.0	•
Coverage Ratio 33	2.6	•	281.0	33.9	52.2	10.0	8.8	2.1	3.4	0.1	1.4	7.8	2.3
Total Asset Turnover 34	0.6	•	2.2	2.3	1.2	1.2	1.6	1.0	1.1	0.8	0.5	0.6	0.5
Inventory Turnover 35	3.3	•	10.2	2.3	1.2	2.2	4.6	2.7	4.1	1.8	4.2	4.4	3.3
Receivables Turnover 36	4.7	•	22.2	16.7	8.8	6.3	6.8	8.9	5.8	3.3	5.1	2.5	5.1
Total Liabilities to Net Worth 37	4.0	•	6.4	•	0.2	1.8	1.2	•	2.1	11.6	•	1.6	4.3
Current Assets to Working Capital 38	•	•	2.1	5.8	1.2	2.0	2.2	1.8	3.6	11.0	18.0	3.8	•
Current Liabilities to Working Capital 39	•	•	1.1	4.8	0.2	1.0	1.2	0.8	2.6	10.0	17.0	2.8	•
Working Capital to Net Sales 40	•	•	0.1	0.0	0.6	0.3	0.2	0.4	0.1	0.1	0.0	0.1	•
Inventory to Working Capital 41	•	•	0.4	4.0	0.4	0.7	0.6	0.5	0.7	3.3	2.1	0.7	•
Total Receipts to Cash Flow 42	4.2	5.8	3.5	3.2	2.7	3.1	4.9	6.7	3.6	3.5	2.8	5.7	4.3
Cost of Goods to Cash Flow 43	1.4	1.0	1.3	1.3	0.8	1.3	2.1	3.8	1.4	1.3	1.0	2.5	1.2
Cash Flow to Total Debt 44	0.2	•	0.7	0.3	2.5	0.6	0.6	0.1	0.5	0.2	0.2	0.2	0.1

Selected Financial Factors (in Percentages)

Debt Ratio 45	80.0	•	86.4	273.7	17.7	64.6	54.4	111.8	67.3	92.1	113.0	61.1	81.3
Return on Total Assets 46	8.0	•	29.4	38.8	12.1	11.8	7.1	9.2	5.1	0.4	8.3	8.7	7.8
Return on Equity Before Income Taxes 47	24.6	•	215.7	•	14.4	30.1	13.8	•	11.0	•	•	19.4	23.2
Return on Equity After Income Taxes 48	17.5	•	209.9	•	13.8	29.7	11.3	•	9.4	•	•	13.4	15.9
Profit Margin (Before Income Tax) 49	8.8	•	13.1	16.4	9.7	8.8	4.1	4.8	3.3	•	4.6	13.1	9.0
Profit Margin (After Income Tax) 50	6.2	•	12.8	16.4	9.3	8.7	3.3	3.5	2.8	•	2.8	9.1	6.2

Table II

Corporations with Net Income

BOOK PUBLISHERS

MONEY AMOUNTS AND SIZE OF ASSETS IN THOUSANDS OF DOLLARS

Item Description for Accounting Period 7/11 Through 6/12		Total	Zero Assets	Under 500	500 to 1,000	1,000 to 5,000	5,000 to 10,000	10,000 to 25,000	25,000 to 50,000	50,000 to 100,000	100,000 to 250,000	250,000 to 500,000	500,000 to 2,500,000	2,500,000 and over
Number of Enterprises	1	2347	608	1318	219	109	33	23	15	8	3	•	•	•
Revenues ($ in Thousands)														
Net Sales	2	24630605	23641	564226	568095	506832	361281	685043	586191	519395	357541	•	•	•
Interest	3	152493	0	600	1763	650	0	23	1912	315	852	•	•	•
Rents	4	26260	0	0	0	0	212	0	1624	891	0	•	•	•
Royalties	5	217721	9	0	0	665	0	1462	5478	3220	8829	•	•	•
Other Portfolio Income	6	530487	0	0	0	177	10	124	21	675	327	•	•	•
Other Receipts	7	603432	27	1575	3	555	1194	1051	25904	52652	13062	•	•	•
Total Receipts	8	26160998	23677	566401	569861	508879	362697	687703	621130	577148	380611	•	•	•
Average Total Receipts	9	11147	39	430	2602	4669	10991	29900	41409	72144	126870	•	•	•
Operating Costs/Operating Income (%)														
Cost of Operations	10	31.8	•	36.2	39.7	26.8	42.9	37.6	55.2	41.5	55.5	•	•	•
Salaries and Wages	11	22.2	26.3	17.5	6.4	13.1	13.7	22.6	14.5	14.5	13.9	•	•	•
Taxes Paid	12	2.6	4.0	1.7	1.2	1.4	1.6	2.5	1.9	1.7	2.3	•	•	•
Interest Paid	13	5.3	•	0.0	0.3	0.0	0.5	0.2	4.2	0.6	0.1	•	•	•
Depreciation	14	3.6	0.3	0.1	0.6	0.3	0.2	0.6	1.2	1.7	0.5	•	•	•
Amortization and Depletion	15	3.9	0.3	•	0.0	0.0	0.0	0.0	1.8	2.1	1.5	•	•	•
Pensions and Other Deferred Comp.	16	1.2	0.5	1.2	4.2	1.3	0.2	0.6	0.6	0.4	1.5	•	•	•
Employee Benefits	17	2.6	9.2	2.0	0.7	1.4	0.8	2.5	1.9	1.6	1.1	•	•	•
Advertising	18	1.2	•	1.4	0.0	1.3	1.1	1.7	2.2	7.0	4.7	•	•	•
Other Expenses	19	19.1	49.7	15.1	19.5	32.5	17.4	16.3	12.5	29.1	9.7	•	•	•
Officers' Compensation	20	1.4	1.0	4.8	9.7	10.6	2.8	5.0	3.1	2.0	5.3	•	•	•
Operating Margin	21	5.1	8.8	19.9	17.6	11.2	18.8	10.5	0.8	•	3.9	•	•	•
Operating Margin Before Officers' Comp.	22	6.4	9.7	24.8	27.3	21.8	21.6	15.4	3.9	•	9.2	•	•	•

Selected Average Balance Sheet ($ in Thousands)

Net Receivables 23	1924	0	21	125	487	2057	4975	6005	10929	34085	•	•	•
Inventories 24	862	0	1	1	1123	1810	2165	6944	6630	24638	•	•	•
Net Property, Plant and Equipment 25	734	0	0	245	156	231	779	2279	5266	2379	•	•	•
Total Assets 26	18461	0	90	589	3419	6041	15698	34382	66392	126976	•	•	•
Notes and Loans Payable 27	6383	0	43	244	4	1464	1428	11519	6966	10686	•	•	•
All Other Liabilities 28	7450	0	9	131	535	2493	6198	31832	26400	40495	•	•	•
Net Worth 29	4629	0	38	214	2880	2083	8072	-8969	33026	75795	•	•	•

Selected Financial Ratios (Times to 1)

Current Ratio 30	0.9	•	7.7	1.3	5.4	1.9	1.9	2.2	1.5	1.9	•	•	•
Quick Ratio 31	0.4	•	7.6	1.2	3.4	1.1	1.3	0.7	0.9	1.0	•	•	•
Net Sales to Working Capital 32	•	•	6.9	71.1	2.0	4.0	5.5	2.8	4.7	3.0	•	•	•
Coverage Ratio 33	3.2	•	452.5	59.6	590.2	36.9	65.6	2.6	16.2	98.6	•	•	•
Total Asset Turnover 34	0.6	•	4.7	4.4	1.4	1.8	1.9	1.1	1.0	0.9	•	•	•
Inventory Turnover 35	3.9	•	120.2	719.5	1.1	2.6	5.2	3.1	4.1	2.7	•	•	•
Receivables Turnover 36	5.5	•	39.2	18.5	8.9	6.5	7.2	8.8	•	2.4	•	•	•
Total Liabilities to Net Worth 37	3.0	•	1.4	1.8	0.2	1.9	0.9	•	1.0	0.7	•	•	•
Current Assets to Working Capital 38	•	•	1.1	4.9	1.2	2.1	2.2	1.8	2.8	2.1	•	•	•
Current Liabilities to Working Capital 39	•	•	0.1	3.9	0.2	1.1	1.2	0.8	1.8	1.1	•	•	•
Working Capital to Net Sales 40	•	•	0.1	0.0	0.5	0.3	0.2	0.4	0.2	0.3	•	•	•
Inventory to Working Capital 41	•	•	0.0	0.0	0.4	0.7	0.5	0.5	0.5	0.5	•	•	•
Total Receipts to Cash Flow 42	3.9	1.8	3.0	3.1	2.6	2.9	4.0	6.0	2.8	6.0	•	•	•
Cost of Goods to Cash Flow 43	1.3	•	1.1	1.2	0.7	1.2	1.5	3.3	1.2	3.3	•	•	•
Cash Flow to Total Debt 44	0.2	•	2.8	2.2	3.4	1.0	1.0	0.2	0.7	0.4	•	•	•

Selected Financial Factors (in Percentages)

Debt Ratio 45	74.9	•	57.6	63.7	15.8	65.5	48.6	126.1	50.3	40.3	•	•	•
Return on Total Assets 46	9.7	•	96.5	80.2	15.8	35.8	20.9	12.5	9.5	9.7	•	•	•
Return on Equity Before Income Taxes 47	26.9	•	227.4	217.0	18.8	100.9	40.0	•	18.0	16.1	•	•	•
Return on Equity After Income Taxes 48	20.2	•	223.1	216.7	18.1	100.2	36.4	•	16.3	12.0	•	•	•
Profit Margin (Before Income Tax) 49	11.8	8.9	20.3	17.9	11.6	19.2	10.8	6.7	9.1	10.3	•	•	•
Profit Margin (After Income Tax) 50	8.9	7.2	19.9	17.9	11.2	19.1	9.9	5.3	8.3	7.6	•	•	•

Table I

Corporations with and without Net Income

DATABASE, DIRECTORY, AND OTHER PUBLISHERS

MONEY AMOUNTS AND SIZE OF ASSETS IN THOUSANDS OF DOLLARS

Item Description for Accounting Period 7/11 Through 6/12		Total	Zero Assets	Under 500	500 to 1,000	1,000 to 5,000	5,000 to 10,000	10,000 to 25,000	25,000 to 50,000	50,000 to 100,000	100,000 to 250,000	250,000 to 500,000	500,000 to 2,500,000	2,500,000 and over
Number of Enterprises	1	3859	823	2618	174	150	25	39	6	8	7	0	6	3
Revenues ($ in Thousands)														
Net Sales	2	16390876	31358	343973	283326	1328113	177530	748746	352877	742155	919039	0	4565859	6897900
Interest	3	21132	58	39	513	95	172	70	592	4321	534	0	9991	4747
Rents	4	75976	0	0	0	0	79	0	63	957	0	0	1229	73648
Royalties	5	64891	0	0	0	1597	989	0	0	0	322	0	29758	32225
Other Portfolio Income	6	54886	0	238	0	0	9	57	151	10275	763	0	23349	20044
Other Receipts	7	106651	3812	59	803	1221	11636	4098	389	81485	-85810	0	32732	56225
Total Receipts	8	16714412	35228	344309	284642	1331026	190415	752971	354072	839193	834848	0	4662918	7084789
Average Total Receipts	9	4331	43	132	1636	8874	7617	19307	59012	104899	119264	•	777153	2361596
Operating Costs/Operating Income (%)														
Cost of Operations	10	30.6	37.2	50.9	45.7	39.8	53.4	52.9	23.0	27.5	30.6	•	21.6	30.8
Salaries and Wages	11	19.5	1.3	31.1	19.6	25.3	29.0	12.6	25.7	20.8	19.9	•	24.3	14.7
Taxes Paid	12	3.2	0.2	3.9	4.5	2.4	2.8	1.9	2.7	2.4	1.5	•	3.3	3.7
Interest Paid	13	6.3	50.3	2.9	0.2	0.1	1.7	2.4	1.2	3.8	9.9	•	8.1	7.1
Depreciation	14	2.7	0.9	6.3	0.1	1.4	2.2	2.5	3.8	2.1	2.1	•	3.6	2.4
Amortization and Depletion	15	4.8	35.4	0.4	0.0	0.1	1.8	1.9	2.0	2.5	14.9	•	4.7	5.5
Pensions and Other Deferred Comp.	16	0.9	•	•	1.7	0.4	•	0.3	0.4	0.8	0.3	•	0.9	1.3
Employee Benefits	17	2.0	0.3	1.4	2.8	0.3	0.9	1.2	2.7	3.6	3.8	•	3.4	1.2
Advertising	18	3.5	0.2	13.4	0.0	0.9	0.5	2.4	0.8	6.1	7.5	•	3.5	3.2
Other Expenses	19	25.2	42.4	28.8	12.5	7.9	21.1	13.3	25.4	38.7	16.2	•	26.2	29.3
Officers' Compensation	20	2.6	0.8	•	16.4	16.6	2.3	2.5	1.7	1.8	1.2	•	0.8	0.9
Operating Margin	21	•	•	•	•	4.8	•	6.1	10.7	•	•	•	•	•
Operating Margin Before Officers' Comp.	22	1.1	•	•	12.9	21.4	•	8.7	12.3	•	•	•	0.3	0.7

Selected Average Balance Sheet ($ in Thousands)													
Net Receivables 23	666	0	5	203	1423	925	1995	4330	20779	10593	•	105712	435113
Inventories 24	222	0	15	0	3	153	242	930	65	721	•	29920	203691
Net Property, Plant and Equipment 25	415	0	22	16	235	716	1498	7220	10970	3947	•	83827	256172
Total Assets 26	5345	0	60	716	2601	6582	15993	36482	72947	204039	•	1058346	3528227
Notes and Loans Payable 27	2670	0	32	5	298	1516	3252	12215	58074	198174	•	681714	1330940
All Other Liabilities 28	2169	0	62	426	888	4304	4714	12098	45606	26623	•	341200	1678349
Net Worth 29	507	0	-34	285	1415	762	8027	12170	-30732	-20758	•	35432	518939

Selected Financial Ratios (Times to 1)													
Current Ratio 30	0.8	•	0.9	1.1	2.6	0.5	2.0	2.0	0.7	0.3	•	1.1	0.7
Quick Ratio 31	0.5	•	0.3	0.8	2.3	0.4	1.6	1.8	0.7	0.3	•	0.6	0.5
Net Sales to Working Capital 32	•	•	•	54.2	6.1	•	4.9	5.9	•	•	•	26.1	•
Coverage Ratio 33	1.2	•	•	•	43.1	•	3.8	10.3	5.5	•	•	1.2	1.4
Total Asset Turnover 34	0.8	•	2.2	2.3	3.4	1.1	1.2	1.6	1.3	0.6	•	0.7	0.7
Inventory Turnover 35	5.9	•	4.3	•	1399.8	24.7	42.0	14.6	394.6	55.7	•	5.5	3.5
Receivables Turnover 36	5.5	•	5.3	13.1	6.6	10.7	9.6	8.7	5.6	8.7	•	5.7	4.6
Total Liabilities to Net Worth 37	9.5	•	•	1.5	0.8	7.6	1.0	2.0	•	•	•	28.9	5.8
Current Assets to Working Capital 38	•	•	•	15.4	1.6	•	2.1	2.0	•	•	•	8.9	•
Current Liabilities to Working Capital 39	•	•	•	14.4	0.6	•	1.1	1.0	•	•	•	7.9	•
Working Capital to Net Sales 40	•	•	•	0.0	0.2	•	0.2	0.2	•	•	•	0.0	•
Inventory to Working Capital 41	•	•	•	•	•	•	0.1	0.1	•	•	•	1.1	•
Total Receipts to Cash Flow 42	5.5	•	•	18.8	8.7	11.9	6.0	3.0	2.6	•	•	4.9	4.7
Cost of Goods to Cash Flow 43	1.7	•	•	8.6	3.5	6.4	3.2	0.7	0.7	•	•	1.1	1.5
Cash Flow to Total Debt 44	0.2	•	•	0.2	0.9	0.1	0.4	0.8	0.3	•	•	0.2	0.2

Selected Financial Factors (in Percentages)													
Debt Ratio 45	90.5	•	156.1	60.3	45.6	88.4	49.8	66.6	142.1	110.2	•	96.7	85.3
Return on Total Assets 46	6.2	•	•	•	17.5	•	10.9	19.6	26.9	•	•	7.2	6.6
Return on Equity Before Income Taxes 47	12.1	•	151.7	•	31.4	•	16.0	53.1	•	108.2	•	39.7	13.0
Return on Equity After Income Taxes 48	6.6	•	151.7	•	28.4	•	13.3	43.3	•	108.2	•	10.4	13.0
Profit Margin (Before Income Tax) 49	1.4	•	•	•	5.0	•	6.7	11.0	17.3	•	•	1.9	2.9
Profit Margin (After Income Tax) 50	0.8	•	•	•	4.5	•	5.6	9.0	14.4	•	•	0.5	2.9

Table II

Corporations with Net Income

DATABASE, DIRECTORY, AND OTHER PUBLISHERS

MONEY AMOUNTS AND SIZE OF ASSETS IN THOUSANDS OF DOLLARS

Item Description for Accounting Period 7/11 Through 6/12		Total	Zero Assets	Under 500	500 to 1,000	1,000 to 5,000	5,000 to 10,000	10,000 to 25,000	25,000 to 50,000	50,000 to 100,000	100,000 to 250,000	250,000 to 500,000	500,000 to 2,500,000	2,500,000 and over
Number of Enterprises	1	972	406	251	113	146	10	28	•	•	0	0	•	0
Revenues ($ in Thousands)														
Net Sales	2	8504030	5850	0	227357	1308032	51816	617086	•	•	0	0	•	0
Interest	3	13238	0	22	471	95	112	66	•	•	0	0	•	0
Rents	4	2328	0	0	0	0	79	0	•	•	0	0	•	0
Royalties	5	31355	0	0	0	1597	0	0	•	•	0	0	•	0
Other Portfolio Income	6	35446	0	238	0	0	9	28	•	•	0	0	•	0
Other Receipts	7	119104	419	-1	767	1047	581	4075	•	•	0	0	•	0
Total Receipts	8	8705501	6269	259	228595	1310771	52597	621255	•	•	0	0	•	0
Average Total Receipts	9	8956	15	1	2023	8978	5260	22188	•	•	•	•	•	•
Operating Costs/Operating Income (%)														
Cost of Operations	10	25.3	•	•	51.2	39.3	44.9	59.1	•	•	•	•	•	•
Salaries and Wages	11	21.3	•	•	17.0	25.2	21.3	8.5	•	•	•	•	•	•
Taxes Paid	12	2.9	•	•	3.9	2.4	2.2	1.4	•	•	•	•	•	•
Interest Paid	13	6.5	•	•	0.2	0.0	4.9	1.3	•	•	•	•	•	•
Depreciation	14	2.4	•	•	0.0	1.4	1.2	2.6	•	•	•	•	•	•
Amortization and Depletion	15	3.1	•	•	0.1	•	5.9	0.7	•	•	•	•	•	•
Pensions and Other Deferred Comp.	16	0.9	•	•	1.0	0.4	•	0.2	•	•	•	•	•	•
Employee Benefits	17	2.4	•	•	2.0	0.3	0.5	0.6	•	•	•	•	•	•
Advertising	18	2.7	•	•	•	0.9	0.1	2.6	•	•	•	•	•	•
Other Expenses	19	23.3	•	•	10.0	7.5	11.8	10.9	•	•	•	•	•	•
Officers' Compensation	20	3.9	•	•	12.1	16.9	2.6	1.7	•	•	•	•	•	•
Operating Margin	21	5.5	100.0	•	2.4	5.8	4.6	10.4	•	•	•	•	•	•
Operating Margin Before Officers' Comp.	22	9.4	100.0	•	14.5	22.6	7.2	12.1	•	•	•	•	•	•

Selected Average Balance Sheet ($ in Thousands)													
Net Receivables 23	1648	0	0	297	1423	1075	2112	•	•	•	•	•	•
Inventories 24	450	0	0	0	1	34	337	•	•	•	•	•	•
Net Property, Plant and Equipment 25	783	0	0	20	239	126	1888	•	•	•	•	•	•
Total Assets 26	9808	0	34	739	2601	6042	15452	•	•	•	•	•	•
Notes and Loans Payable 27	5529	0	0	0	277	3006	3090	•	•	•	•	•	•
All Other Liabilities 28	3329	0	0	355	903	2115	4218	•	•	•	•	•	•
Net Worth 29	950	0	34	384	1421	921	8144	•	•	•	•	•	•
Selected Financial Ratios (Times to 1)													
Current Ratio 30	1.2	•	•	1.0	2.6	0.6	2.1	•	•	•	•	•	•
Quick Ratio 31	0.9	•	•	1.0	2.2	0.5	1.5	•	•	•	•	•	•
Net Sales to Working Capital 32	15.6	•	•	1263.1	6.1	•	5.7	•	•	•	•	•	•
Coverage Ratio 33	2.4	•	•	13.8	162.6	2.2	9.3	•	•	•	•	•	•
Total Asset Turnover 34	0.9	•	•	2.7	3.4	0.9	1.4	•	•	•	•	•	•
Inventory Turnover 35	4.9	•	•	•	3445.7	68.8	38.6	•	•	•	•	•	•
Receivables Turnover 36	5.2	•	•	10.9	9.8	9.6	9.9	•	•	•	•	•	•
Total Liabilities to Net Worth 37	9.3	•	•	0.9	0.8	5.6	0.9	•	•	•	•	•	•
Current Assets to Working Capital 38	6.4	•	1.0	224.0	1.6	•	2.0	•	•	•	•	•	•
Current Liabilities to Working Capital 39	5.4	•	•	223.0	0.6	•	1.0	•	•	•	•	•	•
Working Capital to Net Sales 40	0.1	•	•	0.0	0.2	•	0.2	•	•	•	•	•	•
Inventory to Working Capital 41	0.4	•	•	•	•	•	0.1	•	•	•	•	•	•
Total Receipts to Cash Flow 42	3.8	0.9	•	10.2	8.3	8.5	5.4	•	•	•	•	•	•
Cost of Goods to Cash Flow 43	1.0	•	•	5.2	3.2	3.8	3.2	•	•	•	•	•	•
Cash Flow to Total Debt 44	0.3	•	•	0.6	0.9	0.1	0.6	•	•	•	•	•	•
Selected Financial Factors (in Percentages)													
Debt Ratio 45	90.3	•	•	48.1	45.4	84.8	47.3	•	•	•	•	•	•
Return on Total Assets 46	14.0	•	1.3	8.8	20.7	9.5	17.6	•	•	•	•	•	•
Return on Equity Before Income Taxes 47	84.9	•	1.3	15.7	37.6	34.5	29.9	•	•	•	•	•	•
Return on Equity After Income Taxes 48	73.5	•	1.3	12.7	34.5	30.1	27.2	•	•	•	•	•	•
Profit Margin (Before Income Tax) 49	9.2	107.2	•	3.0	6.0	6.1	11.0	•	•	•	•	•	•
Profit Margin (After Income Tax) 50	8.0	107.2	•	2.4	5.5	5.3	10.1	•	•	•	•	•	•

Table I

Corporations with and without Net Income

SOFTWARE PUBLISHERS

MONEY AMOUNTS AND SIZE OF ASSETS IN THOUSANDS OF DOLLARS

Item Description for Accounting Period 7/11 Through 6/12		Total	Zero Assets	Under 500	500 to 1,000	1,000 to 5,000	5,000 to 10,000	10,000 to 25,000	25,000 to 50,000	50,000 to 100,000	100,000 to 250,000	250,000 to 500,000	500,000 to 2,500,000	2,500,000 and over
Number of Enterprises	1	8126	1102	5206	642	574	143	198	82	47	46	26	42	18
Revenues ($ in Thousands)														
Net Sales	2	114679115	3132938	1788356	1011085	1950230	2392003	3404943	3146427	2160089	4601993	4726883	20580600	65783570
Interest	3	452799	9664	527	44696	1295	1405	4298	11629	4667	13553	12414	92492	256160
Rents	4	165361	0	0	0	3390	114	0	21	582	548	4711	24087	131908
Royalties	5	9999398	16876	38084	0	199	219	396	1429	60081	322437	118929	1870829	7569919
Other Portfolio Income	6	2066728	61115	68546	29725	17439	4811	45336	881	55199	44476	38649	483990	1216560
Other Receipts	7	42503621	319064	967	28399	34076	50382	27367	38397	91558	224313	55633	224286	41409178
Total Receipts	8	169867022	3539657	1896480	1113905	2006629	2448934	3482340	3198784	2372176	5207320	4957219	23276284	116367295
Average Total Receipts	9	20904	3212	364	1735	3496	17125	17588	39010	50472	113203	190662	554197	6464850
Operating Costs/Operating Income (%)														
Cost of Operations	10	33.7	36.9	28.6	6.0	22.8	61.0	16.9	19.6	31.7	20.5	21.0	15.4	42.6
Salaries and Wages	11	38.3	23.2	21.2	50.2	39.9	19.6	37.4	36.4	29.4	33.9	31.3	39.3	40.8
Taxes Paid	12	3.7	3.5	3.6	4.5	4.7	2.1	3.7	2.9	3.4	3.8	3.8	2.8	4.0
Interest Paid	13	2.8	3.9	1.0	6.0	2.6	0.4	1.1	1.3	1.4	2.1	2.5	3.2	3.1
Depreciation	14	4.0	0.9	1.0	1.6	1.5	1.3	2.8	2.3	3.6	3.5	3.8	3.3	4.8
Amortization and Depletion	15	2.2	2.5	0.8	0.3	3.3	0.1	1.2	1.1	2.6	3.4	3.1	3.1	2.0
Pensions and Other Deferred Comp.	16	0.5	1.5	0.1	0.2	1.2	0.6	0.6	0.3	0.9	0.6	0.4	0.8	0.4
Employee Benefits	17	3.9	2.5	2.8	2.3	4.3	1.6	3.1	2.8	3.4	3.0	3.1	3.9	4.3
Advertising	18	4.4	1.2	2.5	1.1	3.2	1.6	2.7	1.9	3.2	4.7	2.7	2.2	5.8
Other Expenses	19	35.0	36.7	31.0	36.4	31.5	12.8	31.4	32.4	24.8	39.2	23.2	27.8	39.4
Officers' Compensation	20	2.1	2.9	13.6	7.9	9.1	3.1	3.9	2.9	3.4	3.1	2.9	2.4	1.1
Operating Margin	21	•	•	•	•	•	•	•	•	•	•	2.1	•	•
Operating Margin Before Officers' Comp.	22	•	•	7.5	•	•	•	•	•	•	•	5.0	•	•

Selected Average Balance Sheet ($ in Thousands)														
Net Receivables	23	4105	0	5	167	542	2650	3157	9057	9829	21953	55816	145664	1229336
Inventories	24	237	0	0	0	51	82	198	289	445	623	3690	2991	86181
Net Property, Plant and Equipment	25	2016	0	3	153	126	553	1043	2389	2758	7527	14920	58974	687496
Total Assets	26	39133	0	43	793	2467	6869	15845	33414	70038	162647	361478	1147848	13366891
Notes and Loans Payable	27	5313	0	63	248	1254	997	2380	7141	13397	22333	68935	173507	1668220
All Other Liabilities	28	18254	0	50	596	2000	4749	10573	18300	36061	72774	138352	399508	6491341
Net Worth	29	15567	0	-71	-51	-786	1124	2893	7973	20580	67540	154191	574833	5207330

Selected Financial Ratios (Times to 1)														
Current Ratio	30	0.6	•	0.7	1.3	0.8	1.5	1.1	1.3	1.1	1.4	1.6	1.2	0.5
Quick Ratio	31	0.5	•	0.7	1.2	0.7	1.3	0.9	1.1	0.9	1.1	1.3	1.1	0.4
Net Sales to Working Capital	32	•	•	•	12.3	•	10.4	14.8	7.5	11.6	5.3	3.2	7.2	•
Coverage Ratio	33	8.1	0.3	0.9	•	•	•	•	•	2.8	•	3.9	4.0	11.7
Total Asset Turnover	34	0.4	•	8.0	2.0	1.4	2.4	1.1	1.1	0.7	0.6	0.5	0.4	0.3
Inventory Turnover	35	20.0	•	1616.5	233.0	15.2	123.9	14.6	26.0	32.7	32.9	10.4	25.2	18.1
Receivables Turnover	36	3.5	•	35.6	9.5	7.0	8.3	6.3	4.7	5.3	5.1	3.5	3.3	3.0
Total Liabilities to Net Worth	37	1.5	•	•	•	•	5.1	4.5	3.2	2.4	1.4	1.3	1.0	1.6
Current Assets to Working Capital	38	•	•	•	4.6	•	3.1	7.9	4.6	8.1	3.7	2.7	5.0	•
Current Liabilities to Working Capital	39	•	•	•	3.6	•	2.1	6.9	3.6	7.1	2.7	1.7	4.0	•
Working Capital to Net Sales	40	•	•	•	0.1	•	0.1	0.1	0.1	0.1	0.2	0.3	0.1	•
Inventory to Working Capital	41	•	•	•	0.0	•	0.1	0.2	0.1	0.1	0.0	0.1	0.0	•
Total Receipts to Cash Flow	42	2.1	3.7	4.2	4.4	19.3	10.9	4.1	3.7	4.6	3.2	3.8	3.0	1.6
Cost of Goods to Cash Flow	43	0.7	1.4	1.2	0.3	4.4	6.7	0.7	0.7	1.5	0.7	0.8	0.5	0.7
Cash Flow to Total Debt	44	0.3	•	0.7	0.4	0.1	0.3	0.3	0.4	0.2	0.3	0.2	0.3	0.3

Selected Financial Factors (in Percentages)														
Debt Ratio	45	60.2	•	265.5	106.4	131.9	83.6	81.7	76.1	70.6	58.5	57.3	49.9	61.0
Return on Total Assets	46	8.2	•	6.9	•	•	•	•	•	2.6	•	4.9	5.5	9.8
Return on Equity Before Income Taxes	47	18.1	•	0.5	201.9	92.0	•	•	•	5.7	•	8.4	8.2	22.9
Return on Equity After Income Taxes	48	11.7	•	1.4	219.8	96.6	•	•	•	1.7	•	4.8	5.8	15.3
Profit Margin (Before Income Tax)	49	20.0	•	•	•	•	•	•	•	2.6	•	7.2	9.6	32.7
Profit Margin (After Income Tax)	50	12.9	•	•	•	•	•	•	•	0.8	•	4.0	6.8	21.8

Table II

Corporations with Net Income

SOFTWARE PUBLISHERS

Item Description for Accounting Period 7/11 Through 6/12		Total	Zero Assets	Under 500	500 to 1,000	1,000 to 5,000	5,000 to 10,000	10,000 to 25,000	25,000 to 50,000	50,000 to 100,000	100,000 to 250,000	250,000 to 500,000	500,000 to 2,500,000	2,500,000 and over
		MONEY AMOUNTS AND SIZE OF ASSETS IN THOUSANDS OF DOLLARS												
Number of Enterprises	1	2814	26	1995	270	180	97	93	44	•	25	15	28	•
		Revenues ($ in Thousands)												
Net Sales	2	97261574	2589871	765953	577584	763286	2133202	1936330	1734137	•	2668557	2662873	15167227	•
Interest	3	390242	4967	2	44685	632	874	1837	3342	•	3498	5415	75833	•
Rents	4	153251	0	0	0	3390	114	0	0	•	0	4283	13038	•
Royalties	5	9513537	0	7331	0	0	0	0	0	•	76265	20840	1780623	•
Other Portfolio Income	6	1868037	27123	19927	29725	16787	535	44701	881	•	19812	27907	409223	•
Other Receipts	7	42095863	149289	515	28168	23983	3392	23550	11112	•	150610	31820	213205	•
Total Receipts	8	151282504	2771250	793728	680162	808078	2138117	2006418	1749472	•	2918742	2753138	17659149	•
Average Total Receipts	9	53761	106587	398	2519	4489	22042	21574	39761	•	116750	183543	630684	•
		Operating Costs/Operating Income (%)												
Cost of Operations	10	35.1	40.5	8.9	6.2	12.2	64.6	14.4	15.8	•	18.2	19.6	11.9	•
Salaries and Wages	11	38.1	14.0	19.7	37.4	33.7	11.6	35.1	28.3	•	30.0	27.1	41.2	•
Taxes Paid	12	3.7	3.1	3.1	3.5	4.5	1.4	3.7	2.8	•	3.6	4.5	3.1	•
Interest Paid	13	2.7	3.6	0.5	10.2	1.2	0.2	0.5	0.5	•	1.5	2.4	2.8	•
Depreciation	14	4.1	0.5	1.3	1.0	0.8	1.1	2.5	1.7	•	3.3	3.0	3.3	•
Amortization and Depletion	15	2.0	0.8	0.1	0.5	1.1	0.0	1.1	0.7	•	2.2	2.7	2.8	•
Pensions and Other Deferred Comp.	16	0.5	1.7	•	0.1	0.4	0.4	0.8	0.5	•	0.6	0.5	0.9	•
Employee Benefits	17	3.9	2.1	1.2	0.6	2.7	1.0	2.6	2.5	•	3.2	3.3	3.8	•
Advertising	18	4.4	1.0	0.7	0.2	1.3	1.1	2.4	2.0	•	2.5	1.2	1.7	•
Other Expenses	19	34.8	27.2	21.7	32.8	24.0	8.7	23.9	27.6	•	28.8	18.0	27.8	•
Officers' Compensation	20	1.6	0.8	11.8	9.1	8.1	2.7	3.9	3.3	•	3.3	2.3	1.7	•
Operating Margin	21	•	4.5	31.0	•	10.2	7.2	9.1	14.5	•	2.9	15.4	•	•
Operating Margin Before Officers' Comp.	22	•	5.4	42.7	7.7	18.3	9.9	13.1	17.8	•	6.2	17.7	0.8	•

Selected Average Balance Sheet ($ in Thousands)													
Net Receivables 23	10211	0	2	155	640	3301	3562	10219	•	17959	63335	162493	•
Inventories 24	605	0	0	1	134	94	107	225	•	460	699	2673	•
Net Property, Plant and Equipment 25	5311	0	4	12	178	703	1022	2516	•	7627	10986	70894	•
Total Assets 26	100851	0	68	779	2653	6914	16596	34087	•	157543	365270	1230266	•
Notes and Loans Payable 27	13135	0	37	24	146	570	1110	3072	•	21556	80535	165793	•
All Other Liabilities 28	47055	0	35	934	1809	3972	9726	16752	•	56503	122689	460208	•
Net Worth 29	40661	0	-4	-180	698	2372	5760	14263	•	79483	162046	604265	•
Selected Financial Ratios (Times to 1)													
Current Ratio 30	0.5	•	1.4	2.1	1.4	1.7	1.4	1.4	•	1.3	1.5	1.1	•
Quick Ratio 31	0.5	•	1.3	1.8	1.2	1.6	1.1	1.1	•	1.0	1.2	1.0	•
Net Sales to Working Capital 32	•	•	28.3	5.8	7.4	10.9	8.2	6.2	•	8.8	3.6	11.8	•
Coverage Ratio 33	11.2	4.2	73.8	2.6	14.4	40.9	25.7	32.2	•	9.6	8.7	6.9	•
Total Asset Turnover 34	0.3	•	5.7	2.7	1.6	3.2	1.3	1.2	•	0.7	0.5	0.4	•
Inventory Turnover 35	20.1	•	270.1	135.5	3.8	151.0	28.0	27.7	•	42.4	49.9	24.2	•
Receivables Turnover 36	3.5	•	67.4	12.8	8.3	9.8	7.5	4.0	•	5.4	•	3.5	•
Total Liabilities to Net Worth 37	1.5	•	•	•	2.8	1.9	1.9	1.4	•	1.0	1.3	1.0	•
Current Assets to Working Capital 38	•	•	3.6	1.9	3.5	2.5	3.8	3.6	•	4.7	3.0	7.7	•
Current Liabilities to Working Capital 39	•	•	2.6	0.9	2.5	1.5	2.8	2.6	•	3.7	2.0	6.7	•
Working Capital to Net Sales 40	•	•	0.0	0.2	0.1	0.1	0.1	0.2	•	0.1	0.3	0.1	•
Inventory to Working Capital 41	•	•	0.0	0.0	0.3	0.1	0.1	0.0	•	0.0	0.0	0.1	•
Total Receipts to Cash Flow 42	1.8	2.7	1.9	2.5	2.8	6.7	3.1	2.5	•	2.6	3.0	2.6	•
Cost of Goods to Cash Flow 43	0.6	1.1	0.2	0.2	0.3	4.3	0.5	0.4	•	0.5	0.6	0.3	•
Cash Flow to Total Debt 44	0.3	•	2.9	0.9	0.8	0.7	0.6	0.8	•	0.5	0.3	0.3	•
Selected Financial Factors (in Percentages)													
Debt Ratio 45	59.7	•	105.7	123.1	73.7	65.7	65.3	58.2	•	49.5	55.6	50.9	•
Return on Total Assets 46	10.3	•	198.6	72.7	27.6	24.3	16.7	18.4	•	9.8	10.3	8.3	•
Return on Equity Before Income Taxes 47	23.2	•	•	•	97.6	69.2	46.2	42.5	•	17.5	20.5	14.5	•
Return on Equity After Income Taxes 48	16.1	•	•	•	81.3	60.7	40.4	36.3	•	14.8	14.4	11.0	•
Profit Margin (Before Income Tax) 49	27.3	11.5	34.6	16.3	16.1	7.5	12.8	15.4	•	13.0	18.7	16.2	•
Profit Margin (After Income Tax) 50	18.9	8.6	34.2	15.3	13.4	6.5	11.2	13.1	•	11.0	13.2	12.3	•

Table I

Corporations with and without Net Income

MOTION PICTURE AND VIDEO INDUSTRIES (EXCEPT VIDEO RENTAL)

MONEY AMOUNTS AND SIZE OF ASSETS IN THOUSANDS OF DOLLARS

Item Description for Accounting Period 7/11 Through 6/12		Total	Zero Assets	Under 500	500 to 1,000	1,000 to 5,000	5,000 to 10,000	10,000 to 25,000	25,000 to 50,000	50,000 to 100,000	100,000 to 250,000	250,000 to 500,000	500,000 to 2,500,000	2,500,000 and over
Number of Enterprises	1	27355	5676	19548	958	707	226	124	53	16	22	8	7	10
Revenues ($ in Thousands)														
Net Sales	2	99481967	961784	4811829	1553081	2077521	1640525	3108085	909507	750327	2698134	1319160	5476481	74175534
Interest	3	564827	1500	430	57	2049	123	990	1267	5789	10944	9247	33280	499149
Rents	4	369040	404	0	0	1212	273	0	731	2487	2603	6330	10878	344121
Royalties	5	1897418	229968	1142	0	0	0	0	0	2	7285	3513	9342	1646167
Other Portfolio Income	6	1064605	5810	182	3006	14357	17919	1553	123	8731	1023	3	77731	934169
Other Receipts	7	4510770	187542	84097	8728	443354	57355	74287	73656	16314	32736	50820	437442	3044437
Total Receipts	8	107888627	1387008	4897680	1564872	2538493	1716195	3184915	985284	783650	2752725	1389073	6045154	80643577
Average Total Receipts	9	3944	244	251	1633	3591	7594	25685	18590	48978	125124	173634	863593	8064358
Operating Costs/Operating Income (%)														
Cost of Operations	10	21.9	42.8	26.2	24.4	27.8	33.5	53.3	41.7	40.1	45.7	52.2	14.9	18.3
Salaries and Wages	11	10.4	3.4	3.2	27.3	20.0	16.3	7.8	13.4	10.8	5.1	9.6	11.6	10.4
Taxes Paid	12	2.9	1.9	1.9	3.8	4.9	2.5	2.2	3.0	3.2	0.9	2.4	3.7	3.0
Interest Paid	13	4.3	7.6	0.2	1.1	0.6	1.5	1.1	2.1	3.9	3.5	4.6	4.1	4.9
Depreciation	14	6.6	18.6	1.5	3.9	2.5	7.8	8.0	10.3	7.1	7.1	6.6	6.1	6.8
Amortization and Depletion	15	15.5	0.2	0.0	1.2	1.8	0.3	4.1	1.9	6.4	5.1	2.1	5.8	19.8
Pensions and Other Deferred Comp.	16	0.6	0.7	2.5	0.9	1.0	0.1	0.0	0.2	0.1	0.1	0.1	0.5	0.5
Employee Benefits	17	1.5	0.3	1.7	1.8	0.7	0.5	0.8	0.6	2.9	0.3	2.0	1.9	1.6
Advertising	18	5.3	1.1	0.2	2.0	0.4	0.6	0.6	1.1	1.3	1.0	0.2	2.5	6.8
Other Expenses	19	27.9	84.7	27.5	36.0	44.5	36.6	16.0	37.2	28.4	32.4	20.9	43.4	25.5
Officers' Compensation	20	2.9	10.2	23.8	7.2	15.6	3.6	5.6	1.7	5.9	2.8	1.0	1.8	1.0
Operating Margin	21	0.1	•	11.1	•	•	•	0.4	•	•	•	•	3.8	1.4
Operating Margin Before Officers' Comp.	22	3.1	•	35.0	•	•	0.2	6.0	•	•	•	•	5.6	2.4

Selected Average Balance Sheet ($ in Thousands)

Net Receivables 23	1141	0	2	23	108	565	2626	3868	7221	20582	125489	109713	2806860
Inventories 24	402	0	1	19	3	134	575	861	1552	5731	8061	14229	1049343
Net Property, Plant and Equipment 25	626	0	8	379	500	1990	3151	8433	19571	12882	78801	498558	1024521
Total Assets 26	8107	0	65	754	1872	6804	16188	38653	68205	150693	365290	1474032	19522340
Notes and Loans Payable 27	2303	0	161	696	1281	3224	7382	12025	22254	65703	157399	574721	4889755
All Other Liabilities 28	2575	0	29	260	337	867	7639	14185	25517	86335	177535	463388	6051650
Net Worth 29	3230	0	-126	-201	254	2713	1167	12443	20434	-1345	30356	435923	8580935

Selected Financial Ratios (Times to 1)

Current Ratio 30	1.4	•	1.4	0.6	3.2	2.5	1.0	1.2	1.3	0.7	1.1	1.1	1.5
Quick Ratio 31	1.0	•	1.2	0.5	2.7	1.8	0.8	0.7	0.9	0.5	0.7	0.8	1.1
Net Sales to Working Capital 32	5.4	•	22.9	•	5.0	3.4	148.9	7.1	6.7	•	8.4	36.6	4.2
Coverage Ratio 33	3.1	•	65.7	•	4.8	1.8	3.6	•	•	0.4	1.8	4.4	3.2
Total Asset Turnover 34	0.4	•	3.8	2.1	1.6	1.1	1.5	0.4	0.7	0.8	0.5	0.5	0.4
Inventory Turnover 35	2.0	•	69.6	21.2	259.6	18.1	23.2	8.3	12.1	9.8	10.7	8.2	1.3
Receivables Turnover 36	3.4	•	99.0	64.0	16.0	10.6	8.2	4.2	5.6	7.6	1.3	5.9	2.9
Total Liabilities to Net Worth 37	1.5	•	•	•	6.4	1.5	12.9	2.1	2.3	•	11.0	2.4	1.3
Current Assets to Working Capital 38	3.5	•	3.6	•	1.5	1.7	42.4	5.3	3.9	•	12.4	11.6	3.2
Current Liabilities to Working Capital 39	2.5	•	2.6	•	0.5	0.7	41.4	4.3	2.9	•	11.4	10.6	2.2
Working Capital to Net Sales 40	0.2	•	0.0	•	0.2	0.3	0.0	0.1	0.1	•	0.1	0.0	0.2
Inventory to Working Capital 41	0.6	•	0.1	•	0.0	0.0	3.2	0.5	0.3	•	0.5	0.2	0.6
Total Receipts to Cash Flow 42	3.5	2.2	2.8	6.0	2.6	5.8	9.2	4.7	7.4	3.9	6.8	4.1	3.3
Cost of Goods to Cash Flow 43	0.8	0.9	0.7	1.5	0.7	2.0	4.9	2.0	3.0	1.8	3.5	0.6	0.6
Cash Flow to Total Debt 44	0.2	•	0.5	0.3	0.7	0.3	0.2	0.1	0.1	0.2	0.1	0.2	0.2

Selected Financial Factors (in Percentages)

Debt Ratio 45	60.2	•	294.2	126.6	86.4	60.1	92.8	67.8	70.0	100.9	91.7	70.4	56.0
Return on Total Assets 46	6.0	•	49.8	•	4.6	2.9	6.0	•	•	1.3	3.7	9.7	5.9
Return on Equity Before Income Taxes 47	10.2	•	•	71.5	27.0	3.2	60.8	•	•	176.5	19.6	25.5	9.3
Return on Equity After Income Taxes 48	6.5	•	•	71.8	26.3	2.4	54.8	•	•	252.5	7.2	18.8	5.8
Profit Margin (Before Income Tax) 49	9.1	•	12.9	•	2.3	1.2	2.8	•	•	•	3.6	14.2	10.7
Profit Margin (After Income Tax) 50	5.7	•	12.7	•	2.3	0.9	2.5	•	•	•	1.3	10.4	6.7

Table II

Corporations with Net Income

MOTION PICTURE AND VIDEO INDUSTRIES (EXCEPT VIDEO RENTAL)

MONEY AMOUNTS AND SIZE OF ASSETS IN THOUSANDS OF DOLLARS

Item Description for Accounting Period 7/11 Through 6/12		Total	Zero Assets	Under 500	500 to 1,000	1,000 to 5,000	5,000 to 10,000	10,000 to 25,000	25,000 to 50,000	50,000 to 100,000	100,000 to 250,000	250,000 to 500,000	500,000 to 2,500,000	2,500,000 and over
Number of Enterprises	1	15718	2549	12586	96	297	•	62	•	6	•	3	•	•
Revenues ($ in Thousands)														
Net Sales	2	82074247	614969	3454690	222244	1240907	•	2490245	•	452293	•	1013264	•	•
Interest	3	314755	98	288	5	877	•	856	•	772	•	1013	•	•
Rents	4	333799	34	0	0	0	•	0	•	2428	•	917	•	•
Royalties	5	1615260	0	1142	0	0	•	0	•	0	•	0	•	•
Other Portfolio Income	6	809700	5810	36	1049	14357	•	1139	•	107	•	0	•	•
Other Receipts	7	3857801	10841	60776	3100	424964	•	50365	•	4898	•	43394	•	•
Total Receipts	8	89005562	631752	3516932	226398	1681105	•	2542605	•	460498	•	1058588	•	•
Average Total Receipts	9	5663	248	279	2358	5660	•	41010	•	76750	•	352863	•	•
Operating Costs/Operating Income (%)														
Cost of Operations	10	20.2	40.2	27.6	66.1	7.2	•	53.1	•	38.8	•	58.1	•	•
Salaries and Wages	11	10.1	4.7	3.7	7.0	26.4	•	5.2	•	9.2	•	9.2	•	•
Taxes Paid	12	2.9	1.2	1.8	0.8	6.2	•	1.6	•	2.2	•	2.3	•	•
Interest Paid	13	3.8	0.0	0.2	0.7	0.3	•	0.3	•	0.6	•	1.4	•	•
Depreciation	14	6.5	0.1	1.2	5.0	1.3	•	8.0	•	1.7	•	4.0	•	•
Amortization and Depletion	15	17.6	0.0	0.1	•	0.1	•	4.9	•	0.0	•	0.1	•	•
Pensions and Other Deferred Comp.	16	0.5	•	0.5	0.4	0.9	•	0.0	•	0.1	•	0.1	•	•
Employee Benefits	17	1.5	0.0	1.0	0.8	1.0	•	0.6	•	3.4	•	2.1	•	•
Advertising	18	6.2	0.0	0.2	2.3	0.2	•	0.6	•	1.8	•	•	•	•
Other Expenses	19	23.3	20.7	25.5	10.7	50.1	•	12.8	•	24.3	•	17.8	•	•
Officers' Compensation	20	2.4	9.7	17.0	5.7	21.2	•	6.5	•	8.0	•	0.9	•	•
Operating Margin	21	4.9	23.3	21.2	0.5	•	•	6.3	•	10.0	•	4.0	•	•
Operating Margin Before Officers' Comp.	22	7.3	33.0	38.2	6.1	6.4	•	12.8	•	18.0	•	4.9	•	•

Selected Average Balance Sheet ($ in Thousands)														
Net Receivables	23	1800	0	1	90	42	•	4158	•	12503	•	124438	•	•
Inventories	24	672	0	0	0	1	•	162	•	1623	•	19574	•	•
Net Property, Plant and Equipment	25	586	0	7	282	353	•	2946	•	17817	•	120895	•	•
Total Assets	26	11948	0	67	636	1820	•	15404	•	70104	•	406166	•	•
Notes and Loans Payable	27	2922	0	70	303	255	•	3501	•	11071	•	157413	•	•
All Other Liabilities	28	3590	0	6	207	120	•	8610	•	31766	•	213220	•	•
Net Worth	29	5435	0	-9	126	1445	•	3294	•	27266	•	35534	•	•
Selected Financial Ratios (Times to 1)														
Current Ratio	30	1.5	•	6.9	1.1	8.8	•	1.0	•	1.4	•	1.0	•	•
Quick Ratio	31	1.1	•	6.1	1.1	7.7	•	0.9	•	0.9	•	0.5	•	•
Net Sales to Working Capital	32	4.5	•	7.7	71.4	3.8	•	1312.0	•	5.6	•	33.5	•	•
Coverage Ratio	33	4.6	1253.7	122.4	4.3	65.1	•	26.4	•	20.1	•	7.2	•	•
Total Asset Turnover	34	0.4	•	4.1	3.6	2.3	•	2.6	•	1.1	•	0.8	•	•
Inventory Turnover	35	1.6	•	160.5	•	230.7	•	131.6	•	18.0	•	10.0	•	•
Receivables Turnover	36	3.1	•	100.4	24.4	23.1	•	9.3	•	7.0	•	2.4	•	•
Total Liabilities to Net Worth	37	1.2	•	•	4.1	0.3	•	3.7	•	1.6	•	10.4	•	•
Current Assets to Working Capital	38	3.0	•	1.2	9.7	1.1	•	299.1	•	3.3	•	27.3	•	•
Current Liabilities to Working Capital	39	2.0	•	0.2	8.7	0.1	•	298.1	•	2.3	•	26.3	•	•
Working Capital to Net Sales	40	0.2	•	0.1	0.0	0.3	•	0.0	•	0.2	•	0.0	•	•
Inventory to Working Capital	41	0.6	•	0.0	•	0.0	•	2.7	•	0.2	•	2.3	•	•
Total Receipts to Cash Flow	42	3.1	2.4	2.3	9.7	1.6	•	7.3	•	2.9	•	6.0	•	•
Cost of Goods to Cash Flow	43	0.6	1.0	0.6	6.4	0.1	•	3.9	•	1.1	•	3.5	•	•
Cash Flow to Total Debt	44	0.3	•	1.6	0.5	7.1	•	0.5	•	0.6	•	0.2	•	•
Selected Financial Factors (in Percentages)														
Debt Ratio	45	54.5	•	113.6	80.2	20.6	•	78.6	•	61.1	•	91.3	•	•
Return on Total Assets	46	7.7	•	95.2	11.0	48.2	•	22.7	•	13.5	•	8.2	•	•
Return on Equity Before Income Taxes	47	13.3	•	•	42.6	59.8	•	102.1	•	32.9	•	80.5	•	•
Return on Equity After Income Taxes	48	9.4	•	•	37.9	59.5	•	97.8	•	30.4	•	52.3	•	•
Profit Margin (Before Income Tax)	49	13.9	26.1	23.0	2.3	20.7	•	8.4	•	11.9	•	8.5	•	•
Profit Margin (After Income Tax)	50	9.8	24.8	22.7	2.1	20.6	•	8.0	•	11.0	•	5.5	•	•

Table I

Corporations with and without Net Income

SOUND RECORDING INDUSTRIES

MONEY AMOUNTS AND SIZE OF ASSETS IN THOUSANDS OF DOLLARS

Item Description for Accounting Period 7/11 Through 6/12		Total	Zero Assets	Under 500	500 to 1,000	1,000 to 5,000	5,000 to 10,000	10,000 to 25,000	25,000 to 50,000	50,000 to 100,000	100,000 to 250,000	250,000 to 500,000	500,000 to 2,500,000	2,500,000 and over
Number of Enterprises	1	5278	1544	3613	0	34	47	14	10	10	0	0	5	0
Revenues ($ in Thousands)														
Net Sales	2	6132279	107769	552361	0	23581	80399	152691	98304	539171	0	0	4578002	0
Interest	3	36388	105	0	0	0	0	258	1046	2760	0	0	32219	0
Rents	4	9598	0	0	0	0	0	0	294	17	0	0	9287	0
Royalties	5	2052643	53260	0	0	17924	0	0	80063	33330	0	0	1868066	0
Other Portfolio Income	6	526992	0	0	0	0	0	0	1619	1	0	0	525370	0
Other Receipts	7	901835	7429	19	0	1	0	109	5942	27545	0	0	860794	0
Total Receipts	8	9659735	168563	552380	0	41506	80399	153058	187268	602824	0	0	7873738	0
Average Total Receipts	9	1830	109	153	•	1221	1711	10933	18727	60282	•	•	1574748	•
Operating Costs/Operating Income (%)														
Cost of Operations	10	39.0	42.1	25.1	•	•	27.9	2.5	27.6	50.6	•	•	41.1	•
Salaries and Wages	11	13.6	7.4	6.2	•	•	13.5	16.3	28.5	11.8	•	•	14.5	•
Taxes Paid	12	3.6	3.6	1.7	•	0.4	4.6	2.2	4.8	2.0	•	•	4.0	•
Interest Paid	13	8.0	5.0	0.3	•	•	0.3	0.5	2.3	3.4	•	•	10.1	•
Depreciation	14	5.3	0.3	0.9	•	•	1.1	2.1	3.1	2.2	•	•	6.5	•
Amortization and Depletion	15	6.2	19.0	0.0	•	•	•	3.3	21.4	5.3	•	•	6.6	•
Pensions and Other Deferred Comp.	16	1.0	•	1.5	•	•	•	•	1.2	0.5	•	•	1.1	•
Employee Benefits	17	1.4	0.6	5.2	•	•	•	0.5	4.3	1.0	•	•	1.0	•
Advertising	18	2.3	2.0	0.5	•	•	0.1	8.3	0.8	3.4	•	•	2.3	•
Other Expenses	19	67.7	65.1	36.1	•	79.9	34.0	77.7	69.0	25.4	•	•	76.7	•
Officers' Compensation	20	2.7	4.7	15.9	•	•	•	5.2	16.8	2.8	•	•	0.7	•
Operating Margin	21	•	•	6.7	•	19.7	18.6	•	•	•	•	•	•	•
Operating Margin Before Officers' Comp.	22	•	•	22.6	•	19.7	18.6	•	•	•	•	•	•	•

Selected Average Balance Sheet ($ in Thousands)													
Net Receivables 23	130	0	3	•	0	704	503	594	7200	•	•	111265	•
Inventories 24	54	0	0	•	0	764	19	88	4624	•	•	41022	•
Net Property, Plant and Equipment 25	95	0	15	•	0	1904	276	4598	2327	•	•	57170	•
Total Assets 26	5167	0	46	•	1901	6262	18041	38449	84426	•	•	5053408	•
Notes and Loans Payable 27	1164	0	296	•	0	946	1464	14667	29715	•	•	913190	•
All Other Liabilities 28	1401	0	4	•	104	1173	8212	8296	42646	•	•	1339164	•
Net Worth 29	2602	0	-254	•	1797	4143	8365	15486	12064	•	•	2801055	•

Selected Financial Ratios (Times to 1)													
Current Ratio 30	0.6	•	5.0	•	2.0	3.3	1.6	1.2	1.1	•	•	0.5	•
Quick Ratio 31	0.2	•	4.8	•	1.2	1.4	1.1	0.8	0.7	•	•	0.1	•
Net Sales to Working Capital 32	•	•	8.3	•	6.4	0.6	2.3	3.3	13.3	•	•	•	•
Coverage Ratio 33	2.2	2.3	24.9	•	•	56.7	•	6.5	2.0	•	•	2.0	•
Total Asset Turnover 34	0.2	•	3.3	•	0.4	0.3	0.6	0.3	0.6	•	•	0.2	•
Inventory Turnover 35	8.3	•	•	•	•	0.6	14.4	30.8	5.9	•	•	9.2	•
Receivables Turnover 36	2.4	•	46.3	•	•	2.2	25.3	22.1	12.9	•	•	1.9	•
Total Liabilities to Net Worth 37	1.0	•	•	•	0.1	0.5	1.2	1.5	6.0	•	•	0.8	•
Current Assets to Working Capital 38	•	•	1.2	•	2.0	1.4	2.8	5.9	9.6	•	•	•	•
Current Liabilities to Working Capital 39	•	•	0.2	•	1.0	0.4	1.8	4.9	8.6	•	•	•	•
Working Capital to Net Sales 40	•	•	0.1	•	0.2	1.6	0.4	0.3	0.1	•	•	•	•
Inventory to Working Capital 41	•	•	•	•	•	0.3	0.0	0.0	1.1	•	•	•	•
Total Receipts to Cash Flow 42	1.5	1.6	3.5	•	0.6	2.1	1.7	1.3	3.8	•	•	1.3	•
Cost of Goods to Cash Flow 43	0.6	0.7	0.9	•	•	0.6	0.0	0.4	1.9	•	•	0.5	•
Cash Flow to Total Debt 44	0.3	•	0.1	•	11.7	0.4	0.7	0.3	0.2	•	•	0.3	•

Selected Financial Factors (in Percentages)													
Debt Ratio 45	49.6	•	657.0	•	5.5	33.8	53.6	59.7	85.7	•	•	44.6	•
Return on Total Assets 46	3.9	•	23.5	•	34.9	5.2	•	3.9	4.5	•	•	3.7	•
Return on Equity Before Income Taxes 47	4.1	•	•	•	36.9	7.7	•	8.1	16.0	•	•	3.4	•
Return on Equity After Income Taxes 48	4.0	•	•	•	36.6	7.7	•	5.9	6.0	•	•	3.4	•
Profit Margin (Before Income Tax) 49	9.3	6.7	6.7	•	95.7	18.6	•	12.8	3.6	•	•	10.5	•
Profit Margin (After Income Tax) 50	9.0	6.3	6.3	•	94.9	18.6	•	9.3	1.3	•	•	10.5	•

Table II

Corporations with Net Income

SOUND RECORDING INDUSTRIES

MONEY AMOUNTS AND SIZE OF ASSETS IN THOUSANDS OF DOLLARS

Item Description for Accounting Period 7/11 Through 6/12		Total	Zero Assets	Under 500	500 to 1,000	1,000 to 5,000	5,000 to 10,000	10,000 to 25,000	25,000 to 50,000	50,000 to 100,000	100,000 to 250,000	250,000 to 500,000	500,000 to 2,500,000	2,500,000 and over
Number of Enterprises	1	2689	475	2117	0	34	•	0	•	3	•	0	•	•
Revenues ($ in Thousands)														
Net Sales	2	4156578	103986	476259	0	23581	•	0	•	168281	•	0	•	•
Interest	3	12448	0	0	0	0	•	0	•	462	•	0	•	•
Rents	4	9545	0	0	0	0	•	0	•	12	•	0	•	•
Royalties	5	1579643	0	0	0	17924	•	0	•	0	•	0	•	•
Other Portfolio Income	6	472241	0	0	0	0	•	0	•	0	•	0	•	•
Other Receipts	7	608696	6575	19	0	1	•	0	•	140	•	0	•	•
Total Receipts	8	6839151	110561	476278	0	41506	•	0	•	168895	•	0	•	•
Average Total Receipts	9	2543	233	225	•	1221	•	•	•	56298	•	•	•	•
Operating Costs/Operating Income (%)														
Cost of Operations	10	37.4	42.8	28.2	•	•	•	•	•	44.6	•	•	•	•
Salaries and Wages	11	10.7	1.7	3.5	•	•	•	•	•	6.3	•	•	•	•
Taxes Paid	12	2.5	2.1	1.6	•	0.4	•	•	•	2.9	•	•	•	•
Interest Paid	13	5.1	0.0	0.0	•	•	•	•	•	4.3	•	•	•	•
Depreciation	14	1.9	0.1	0.5	•	•	•	•	•	2.2	•	•	•	•
Amortization and Depletion	15	3.9	0.2	•	•	•	•	•	•	2.1	•	•	•	•
Pensions and Other Deferred Comp.	16	1.4	•	1.7	•	•	•	•	•	0.2	•	•	•	•
Employee Benefits	17	1.5	0.2	2.9	•	•	•	•	•	0.6	•	•	•	•
Advertising	18	2.9	1.9	0.4	•	•	•	•	•	0.3	•	•	•	•
Other Expenses	19	76.8	25.9	19.4	•	79.9	•	•	•	15.3	•	•	•	•
Officers' Compensation	20	3.0	4.8	18.5	•	•	•	•	•	1.6	•	•	•	•
Operating Margin	21	•	20.2	23.4	•	19.7	•	•	•	19.6	•	•	•	•
Operating Margin Before Officers' Comp.	22	•	25.0	41.8	•	19.7	•	•	•	21.2	•	•	•	•

Selected Average Balance Sheet ($ in Thousands)													
Net Receivables 23	166	0	5	•	0	•	•	•	4096	•	•	•	•
Inventories 24	62	0	0	•	0	•	•	•	0	•	•	•	•
Net Property, Plant and Equipment 25	118	0	8	•	0	•	•	•	789	•	•	•	•
Total Assets 26	7740	0	41	•	1901	•	•	•	79310	•	•	•	•
Notes and Loans Payable 27	701	0	6	•	0	•	•	•	44846	•	•	•	•
All Other Liabilities 28	2131	0	4	•	104	•	•	•	20418	•	•	•	•
Net Worth 29	4908	0	30	•	1797	•	•	•	14045	•	•	•	•
Selected Financial Ratios (Times to 1)													
Current Ratio 30	0.5	•	7.4	•	2.0	•	•	•	2.2	•	•	•	•
Quick Ratio 31	0.1	•	7.3	•	1.2	•	•	•	1.2	•	•	•	•
Net Sales to Working Capital 32	•	•	7.9	•	6.4	•	•	•	2.1	•	•	•	•
Coverage Ratio 33	5.0	1623.6	1392.4	•	•	•	•	•	5.8	•	•	•	•
Total Asset Turnover 34	0.2	•	5.6	•	0.4	•	•	•	0.7	•	•	•	•
Inventory Turnover 35	9.3	•	•	•	•	•	•	•	•	•	•	•	•
Receivables Turnover 36	1.9	•	40.0	•	•	•	•	•	27.4	•	•	•	•
Total Liabilities to Net Worth 37	0.6	•	0.3	•	0.1	•	•	•	4.6	•	•	•	•
Current Assets to Working Capital 38	•	•	1.2	•	2.0	•	•	•	1.9	•	•	•	•
Current Liabilities to Working Capital 39	•	•	0.2	•	1.0	•	•	•	0.9	•	•	•	•
Working Capital to Net Sales 40	•	•	0.1	•	0.2	•	•	•	0.5	•	•	•	•
Inventory to Working Capital 41	•	•	•	•	•	•	•	•	•	•	•	•	•
Total Receipts to Cash Flow 42	1.2	2.2	2.8	•	0.6	•	•	•	3.0	•	•	•	•
Cost of Goods to Cash Flow 43	0.4	0.9	0.8	•	•	•	•	•	1.3	•	•	•	•
Cash Flow to Total Debt 44	0.5	•	7.9	•	11.7	•	•	•	0.3	•	•	•	•
Selected Financial Factors (in Percentages)													
Debt Ratio 45	36.6	•	25.0	•	5.5	•	•	•	82.3	•	•	•	•
Return on Total Assets 46	5.1	•	129.9	•	34.9	•	•	•	17.7	•	•	•	•
Return on Equity Before Income Taxes 47	6.4	•	173.0	•	36.9	•	•	•	82.8	•	•	•	•
Return on Equity After Income Taxes 48	6.3	•	169.3	•	36.6	•	•	•	54.1	•	•	•	•
Profit Margin (Before Income Tax) 49	20.5	26.5	23.4	•	95.7	•	•	•	20.7	•	•	•	•
Profit Margin (After Income Tax) 50	20.0	26.1	22.9	•	94.9	•	•	•	13.6	•	•	•	•

Table I

Corporations with and without Net Income

BROADCASTING (EXCEPT INTERNET)

MONEY AMOUNTS AND SIZE OF ASSETS IN THOUSANDS OF DOLLARS

Item Description for Accounting Period 7/11 Through 6/12		Total	Zero Assets	Under 500	500 to 1,000	1,000 to 5,000	5,000 to 10,000	10,000 to 25,000	25,000 to 50,000	50,000 to 100,000	100,000 to 250,000	250,000 to 500,000	500,000 to 2,500,000	2,500,000 and over
Number of Enterprises	1	7141	576	4936	619	642	102	116	45	32	18	21	22	12
Revenues ($ in Thousands)														
Net Sales	2	98546378	494627	1009127	877568	1178945	862146	1456053	1036854	1035195	1705236	6141883	6597562	76151183
Interest	3	1922892	1210	31	256	3763	716	4168	428	1775	9844	23944	213242	1663517
Rents	4	293351	505	0	0	4408	619	1034	3884	907	5916	14965	19342	241770
Royalties	5	5106198	0	0	0	0	8484	0	1233	3423	154	44684	6936	5041285
Other Portfolio Income	6	836719	53633	160	0	2141	11653	12515	6841	7546	2174	183150	316625	240278
Other Receipts	7	4312456	-18823	675	4751	34265	27603	42558	4593	38231	28821	67448	359532	3722801
Total Receipts	8	111017994	531152	1009993	882575	1223522	911221	1516328	1053833	1087077	1752145	6476074	7513239	87060834
Average Total Receipts	9	15547	922	205	1426	1906	8934	13072	23419	33971	97341	308384	341511	7255070
Operating Costs/Operating Income (%)														
Cost of Operations	10	12.0	•	0.2	16.4	15.8	19.5	36.4	16.6	4.4	25.5	52.0	4.1	8.8
Salaries and Wages	11	15.5	29.0	12.1	33.2	36.3	15.5	17.6	22.0	20.9	19.2	11.7	23.8	14.2
Taxes Paid	12	2.1	3.3	2.3	6.0	6.6	3.6	3.6	3.1	3.2	3.4	1.9	3.1	1.8
Interest Paid	13	7.5	7.1	0.1	1.7	1.7	1.9	4.8	6.2	11.8	10.1	5.0	13.3	7.5
Depreciation	14	5.5	2.2	3.7	3.4	6.2	3.9	5.2	7.9	6.3	6.3	6.4	7.3	5.3
Amortization and Depletion	15	9.1	14.0	0.4	0.3	2.0	2.8	2.0	10.3	11.1	9.2	4.5	13.1	9.5
Pensions and Other Deferred Comp.	16	0.7	•	0.8	•	0.6	0.6	0.3	0.4	0.5	0.2	0.8	0.7	0.8
Employee Benefits	17	3.7	1.9	1.2	2.8	2.5	1.6	1.1	1.2	1.5	1.6	1.7	1.8	4.2
Advertising	18	3.3	0.9	0.4	0.7	1.4	6.6	1.5	1.6	2.9	2.3	1.1	1.7	3.8
Other Expenses	19	45.5	52.8	63.1	23.5	33.7	50.3	21.0	34.5	50.0	25.3	19.1	45.1	48.7
Officers' Compensation	20	1.7	1.5	14.4	8.4	6.0	1.5	2.4	1.7	2.6	2.0	1.2	1.7	1.4
Operating Margin	21	•	•	1.1	3.8	•	•	3.9	•	•	•	•	•	•
Operating Margin Before Officers' Comp.	22	•	•	15.5	12.2	•	•	6.4	•	•	•	•	•	•

Selected Average Balance Sheet ($ in Thousands)

Net Receivables 23	2390	0	2	143	205	1009	2023	4415	5872	20331	40378	77609	1098882
Inventories 24	161	0	0	15	12	11	11	150	291	2964	2195	573	83262
Net Property, Plant and Equipment 25	4385	0	32	120	625	1571	2138	7271	9256	31458	70682	99339	2117445
Total Assets 26	36075	0	53	665	2493	7538	14576	35601	70621	152997	354233	1129094	17832282
Notes and Loans Payable 27	12689	0	82	680	3483	2231	7899	28177	51764	105600	185939	630608	5316959
All Other Liabilities 28	12371	0	14	422	-3009	1410	3631	9572	23495	27825	69311	361350	6523838
Net Worth 29	11015	0	-44	-437	2019	3896	3047	-2149	-4638	19572	98984	137135	5991486

Selected Financial Ratios (Times to 1)

Current Ratio 30	0.8	•	2.4	0.4	1.1	1.7	1.2	1.0	1.1	1.2	1.8	1.1	0.7
Quick Ratio 31	0.5	•	1.7	0.3	0.6	1.3	0.9	0.8	0.8	0.9	1.4	1.0	0.4
Net Sales to Working Capital 32	•	•	23.1	•	19.9	7.7	13.8	•	20.2	15.7	5.9	19.1	•
Coverage Ratio 33	1.8	0.6	12.8	3.6	•	•	2.7	0.3	0.1	0.7	1.0	0.9	2.1
Total Asset Turnover 34	0.4	•	3.9	2.1	0.7	1.1	0.9	0.6	0.5	0.6	0.8	0.3	0.4
Inventory Turnover 35	10.3	•	•	15.1	24.0	150.5	418.1	25.5	4.9	8.2	69.3	21.3	6.7
Receivables Turnover 36	6.0	•	59.4	12.8	5.6	8.2	6.0	5.8	5.0	4.5	6.7	3.6	6.2
Total Liabilities to Net Worth 37	2.3	•	•	•	0.2	0.9	3.8	•	•	6.8	2.6	7.2	2.0
Current Assets to Working Capital 38	•	•	1.7	•	12.4	2.5	7.0	•	9.4	6.8	2.3	10.6	•
Current Liabilities to Working Capital 39	•	•	0.7	•	11.4	1.5	6.0	•	8.4	5.8	1.3	9.6	•
Working Capital to Net Sales 40	•	•	0.0	•	0.1	0.1	0.1	•	0.0	0.1	0.2	0.1	•
Inventory to Working Capital 41	•	•	•	•	0.1	0.0	0.0	•	0.2	0.0	0.0	0.0	•
Total Receipts to Cash Flow 42	2.1	2.4	1.7	4.9	6.2	2.2	3.8	4.1	2.8	5.3	7.1	2.7	1.9
Cost of Goods to Cash Flow 43	0.3	•	0.0	0.8	1.0	0.4	1.4	0.7	0.1	1.4	3.7	0.1	0.2
Cash Flow to Total Debt 44	0.3	•	1.3	0.3	0.6	1.1	0.3	0.2	0.2	0.1	0.2	0.1	0.3

Selected Financial Factors (in Percentages)

Debt Ratio 45	69.5	•	183.9	165.8	19.0	48.3	79.1	106.0	106.6	87.2	72.1	87.9	66.4
Return on Total Assets 46	5.3	•	5.1	13.0	•	•	11.1	1.4	0.8	4.7	4.1	3.2	5.7
Return on Equity Before Income Taxes 47	7.9	•	•	•	•	•	33.1	43.1	70.6	•	•	•	9.0
Return on Equity After Income Taxes 48	4.1	•	•	•	•	•	26.8	46.5	81.2	•	•	•	5.2
Profit Margin (Before Income Tax) 49	6.3	•	1.2	4.4	•	•	8.0	•	•	•	•	•	8.5
Profit Margin (After Income Tax) 50	3.2	•	1.2	4.3	•	•	6.5	•	•	•	•	•	4.9

Table II

Corporations with Net Income

BROADCASTING (EXCEPT INTERNET)

MONEY AMOUNTS AND SIZE OF ASSETS IN THOUSANDS OF DOLLARS

Item Description for Accounting Period 7/11 Through 6/12		Total	Zero Assets	Under 500	500 to 1,000	1,000 to 5,000	5,000 to 10,000	10,000 to 25,000	25,000 to 50,000	50,000 to 100,000	100,000 to 250,000	250,000 to 500,000	500,000 to 2,500,000	2,500,000 and over
Number of Enterprises	1	2757	555	1276	401	297	63	85	27	14	11	11	10	7
Revenues ($ in Thousands)														
Net Sales	2	74301789	25269	630690	717694	742576	694713	931449	766335	527086	1268463	2286446	2793674	62917394
Interest	3	1458546	289	0	255	4	715	3248	139	1478	8807	2062	92162	1349386
Rents	4	224627	0	0	0	0	205	823	794	532	2749	2355	7775	209394
Royalties	5	5104001	0	0	0	0	8484	0	1233	3423	154	42635	6930	5041142
Other Portfolio Income	6	537217	53633	0	0	261	11653	12515	6182	5008	2006	176534	153002	116421
Other Receipts	7	3454288	5142	688	4717	8446	27210	41363	1475	25172	19802	55192	209807	3055279
Total Receipts	8	85080468	84333	631378	722666	751287	742980	989398	776158	562699	1301981	2565224	3263350	72689016
Average Total Receipts	9	30860	152	495	1802	2530	11793	11640	28747	40193	118362	233202	326335	10384145
Operating Costs/Operating Income (%)														
Cost of Operations	10	11.0	•	•	20.0	20.5	22.0	13.4	22.4	3.5	27.4	26.4	8.9	9.8
Salaries and Wages	11	13.6	25.4	6.6	28.6	33.3	10.7	24.5	19.8	23.1	19.9	19.2	17.9	12.5
Taxes Paid	12	1.6	1.7	1.0	5.3	5.6	3.6	5.2	2.9	3.0	3.3	2.5	3.1	1.3
Interest Paid	13	4.6	•	•	1.7	1.5	0.6	5.6	2.9	3.5	5.6	5.2	13.6	4.3
Depreciation	14	4.1	5.9	4.5	3.8	5.5	3.1	4.1	5.6	3.5	4.1	8.4	6.3	3.8
Amortization and Depletion	15	9.2	0.6	•	•	2.1	0.3	2.6	9.3	4.7	9.3	4.3	9.8	9.9
Pensions and Other Deferred Comp.	16	0.8	•	•	•	0.9	0.1	0.4	0.2	1.0	0.2	0.7	0.7	0.8
Employee Benefits	17	4.2	0.2	•	3.0	2.6	1.3	1.2	0.9	1.7	1.7	2.4	1.6	4.7
Advertising	18	3.9	1.9	0.4	0.3	0.9	7.6	2.3	1.6	3.9	2.7	1.9	1.7	4.2
Other Expenses	19	46.9	96.8	78.7	19.2	14.5	44.5	24.1	27.4	39.6	21.3	29.3	29.1	49.9
Officers' Compensation	20	1.8	28.6	1.1	10.1	6.3	1.3	3.1	1.6	3.1	2.0	1.6	1.7	1.7
Operating Margin	21	•	•	7.6	8.0	6.4	4.9	13.5	5.5	9.3	2.5	•	5.5	•
Operating Margin Before Officers' Comp.	22	0.2	•	8.7	18.1	12.7	6.3	16.6	7.1	12.5	4.5	•	7.2	•

Selected Average Balance Sheet ($ in Thousands)

Net Receivables 23	5040	0	0	200	327	1252	2473	5326	6302	28341	31740	101127	1646470
Inventories 24	397	0	0	30	12	6	11	192	344	4831	3787	1179	131996
Net Property, Plant and Equipment 25	7945	0	100	141	774	1541	1930	5201	6934	23174	71703	74832	2742907
Total Assets 26	70940	0	122	731	2874	7589	14008	33422	74012	154514	352130	1247038	24661056
Notes and Loans Payable 27	14153	0	27	592	2078	897	8163	15494	20586	95438	139047	521069	4126204
All Other Liabilities 28	20958	0	0	400	198	1431	2820	8554	25540	33840	49927	522001	7214668
Net Worth 29	35828	0	94	-260	598	5261	3025	9375	27886	25236	163156	203967	13320184

Selected Financial Ratios (Times to 1)

Current Ratio 30	1.1	•	71.8	0.7	0.8	1.7	1.2	1.3	1.6	1.3	2.3	1.0	1.0
Quick Ratio 31	0.7	•	44.3	0.6	0.5	1.3	0.9	1.1	1.2	1.1	1.8	0.9	0.6
Net Sales to Working Capital 32	32.3	•	23.8	•	•	8.0	10.2	9.5	5.9	9.0	2.8	31.0	63.4
Coverage Ratio 33	3.9	•	•	6.1	5.9	21.1	4.5	3.4	5.6	1.9	2.9	2.7	4.0
Total Asset Turnover 34	0.4	•	4.1	2.4	0.9	1.5	0.8	0.8	0.5	0.7	0.6	0.2	0.4
Inventory Turnover 35	7.4	•	•	11.8	41.9	402.7	130.8	33.1	3.8	6.5	14.5	21.2	6.7
Receivables Turnover 36	5.6	•	113.0	•	4.5	9.3	4.5	5.7	4.7	5.0	4.6	2.5	•
Total Liabilities to Net Worth 37	1.0	•	0.3	•	3.8	0.4	3.6	2.6	1.7	5.1	1.2	5.1	0.9
Current Assets to Working Capital 38	15.2	•	1.0	•	•	2.5	6.1	4.2	2.8	3.9	1.8	24.8	29.3
Current Liabilities to Working Capital 39	14.2	•	0.0	•	•	1.5	5.1	3.2	1.8	2.9	0.8	23.8	28.3
Working Capital to Net Sales 40	0.0	•	0.0	•	•	0.1	0.1	0.1	0.2	0.1	0.4	0.0	0.0
Inventory to Working Capital 41	0.4	•	•	•	•	0.0	0.0	0.1	0.0	0.0	0.1	0.1	0.9
Total Receipts to Cash Flow 42	1.8	0.4	1.2	4.1	5.3	1.8	2.5	3.6	1.9	4.4	3.4	2.1	1.7
Cost of Goods to Cash Flow 43	0.2	•	•	0.8	1.1	0.4	0.3	0.8	0.1	1.2	0.9	0.2	0.2
Cash Flow to Total Debt 44	0.4	•	15.0	0.4	0.2	2.6	0.4	0.3	0.4	0.2	0.3	0.1	0.5

Selected Financial Factors (in Percentages)

Debt Ratio 45	49.5	•	22.6	135.6	79.2	30.7	78.4	72.0	62.3	83.7	53.7	83.6	46.0
Return on Total Assets 46	6.7	•	31.2	25.5	7.8	18.1	19.7	8.2	10.0	8.0	8.9	8.3	6.3
Return on Equity Before Income Taxes 47	9.9	•	40.3	•	31.3	24.9	71.1	20.5	21.7	23.4	12.5	32.4	8.8
Return on Equity After Income Taxes 48	6.8	•	40.3	•	31.3	21.0	62.4	19.2	17.7	17.8	9.5	24.7	5.9
Profit Margin (Before Income Tax) 49	13.2	222.3	7.7	8.7	7.5	11.9	19.6	6.8	16.1	5.1	9.8	23.7	13.1
Profit Margin (After Income Tax) 50	9.1	170.4	7.7	8.6	7.5	10.0	17.2	6.3	13.1	3.9	7.5	18.0	8.7

TELECOMMUNICATIONS (WIRED, WIRELESS, SATELLITE, INTERNET PROVIDERS)

MONEY AMOUNTS AND SIZE OF ASSETS IN THOUSANDS OF DOLLARS

Item Description for Accounting Period 7/11 Through 6/12		Total	Zero Assets	Under 500	500 to 1,000	1,000 to 5,000	5,000 to 10,000	10,000 to 25,000	25,000 to 50,000	50,000 to 100,000	100,000 to 250,000	250,000 to 500,000	500,000 to 2,500,000	2,500,000 and over
Number of Enterprises	1	18246	2751	11846	938	1321	493	397	173	123	91	36	47	28
Revenues ($ in Thousands)														
Net Sales	2	421740756	4815230	8316321	2468580	8791793	7275600	5718315	4124840	5052060	8893188	9554646	24804008	331926175
Interest	3	9810687	2657	721	92	8970	5075	22333	9444	19636	33642	15740	391811	9300567
Rents	4	7362034	148	0	0	1287	19936	11882	5272	12329	18427	5828	59815	7227110
Royalties	5	4799887	0	3	0	0	12063	4500	15	1086	4	891	15290	4766035
Other Portfolio Income	6	5117363	35306	1112	14282	17427	43179	107018	64161	47367	49986	141074	882627	3713824
Other Receipts	7	17438319	61049	31090	1468	55447	51665	150959	297473	224643	318824	258689	1524938	14462072
Total Receipts	8	466269046	4914390	8349247	2484422	8874924	7407518	6015007	4501205	5357121	9314071	9976868	27678489	371395783
Average Total Receipts	9	25555	1786	705	2649	6718	15025	15151	26019	43554	102352	277135	588904	13264135
Operating Costs/Operating Income (%)														
Cost of Operations	10	24.8	49.7	63.8	68.9	52.8	67.7	47.1	39.3	34.6	44.9	51.4	43.9	18.0
Salaries and Wages	11	13.6	18.4	7.8	12.8	15.9	11.0	12.0	12.3	9.0	11.0	14.5	18.0	13.5
Taxes Paid	12	2.6	1.9	1.3	1.2	2.5	1.5	2.4	2.3	2.1	2.1	2.0	2.4	2.8
Interest Paid	13	6.8	4.5	1.3	1.5	0.7	1.1	1.7	2.8	2.8	2.5	4.6	7.8	7.6
Depreciation	14	14.1	9.2	0.9	1.3	1.8	4.6	9.4	11.6	13.3	11.8	7.6	13.3	15.6
Amortization and Depletion	15	1.7	1.8	0.2	0.0	0.2	0.2	0.8	1.6	1.1	1.1	1.5	2.2	1.8
Pensions and Other Deferred Comp.	16	1.5	0.2	0.5	0.1	0.2	0.2	0.3	0.2	0.2	0.3	0.2	0.8	1.8
Employee Benefits	17	2.2	1.8	0.5	0.5	1.3	0.7	1.3	1.8	1.1	1.2	1.6	1.8	2.5
Advertising	18	1.8	0.7	0.4	0.4	0.4	0.8	0.6	3.6	2.3	0.9	0.9	2.1	1.9
Other Expenses	19	40.4	19.3	15.6	8.4	20.5	15.6	29.2	31.7	36.0	25.9	19.8	22.4	45.4
Officers' Compensation	20	0.6	4.8	6.4	2.1	3.3	1.3	1.7	1.6	1.7	1.5	0.9	1.1	0.2
Operating Margin	21	•	•	1.4	2.7	0.5	•	•	•	•	•	•	•	•
Operating Margin Before Officers' Comp.	22	•	•	7.8	4.8	3.8	•	•	•	•	•	•	•	•

Selected Average Balance Sheet ($ in Thousands)														
Net Receivables	23	9134	0	6	98	591	1448	2220	3562	5141	22144	47275	194068	5358452
Inventories	24	270	0	6	26	96	183	327	772	864	3282	7433	10054	114520
Net Property, Plant and Equipment	25	15427	0	11	74	389	2250	6299	12804	28911	54411	81025	260931	8972977
Total Assets	26	70046	0	79	669	2302	7225	16351	35387	69472	158368	350510	1050542	41868746
Notes and Loans Payable	27	24420	0	67	1275	725	2421	4743	10198	17898	38713	124312	372690	14645022
All Other Liabilities	28	23373	0	102	596	1179	2797	3793	9492	14532	44873	110715	363832	13988032
Net Worth	29	22252	0	-90	-1201	399	2007	7815	15697	37043	74782	115483	314020	13235692

Selected Financial Ratios (Times to 1)														
Current Ratio	30	1.0	•	0.5	0.7	1.1	1.3	1.5	1.5	1.7	1.5	1.4	2.1	0.9
Quick Ratio	31	0.9	•	0.4	0.5	0.8	0.9	1.2	1.0	1.4	1.1	1.1	1.7	0.8
Net Sales to Working Capital	32	152.0	•	•	•	66.3	17.6	6.9	6.9	5.4	5.7	7.1	3.0	•
Coverage Ratio	33	1.1	•	2.4	3.2	3.1	•	0.3	1.1	1.7	1.7	0.9	0.5	1.1
Total Asset Turnover	34	0.3	•	8.9	3.9	2.9	2.0	0.9	0.7	0.6	0.6	0.8	0.5	0.3
Inventory Turnover	35	21.3	•	80.0	69.7	36.7	54.6	20.7	12.1	16.4	13.4	18.3	23.1	18.7
Receivables Turnover	36	2.8	•	69.3	18.2	12.2	12.1	7.3	6.8	6.7	5.1	5.5	3.7	2.4
Total Liabilities to Net Worth	37	2.1	•	•	•	4.8	2.6	1.1	1.3	0.9	1.1	2.0	2.3	2.2
Current Assets to Working Capital	38	84.0	•	•	•	14.4	4.8	3.0	3.2	2.5	3.0	3.4	1.9	•
Current Liabilities to Working Capital	39	83.0	•	•	•	13.4	3.8	2.0	2.2	1.5	2.0	2.4	0.9	•
Working Capital to Net Sales	40	0.0	•	•	•	0.0	0.1	0.1	0.1	0.2	0.2	0.1	0.3	•
Inventory to Working Capital	41	1.7	•	•	•	1.0	0.2	0.2	0.2	0.1	0.2	0.2	0.1	•
Total Receipts to Cash Flow	42	2.9	34.7	6.8	10.0	5.3	10.2	4.4	3.7	3.4	4.3	6.4	8.4	2.5
Cost of Goods to Cash Flow	43	0.7	17.3	4.3	6.9	2.8	6.9	2.1	1.5	1.2	1.9	3.3	3.7	0.4
Cash Flow to Total Debt	44	0.2	•	0.6	0.1	0.7	0.3	0.4	0.3	0.4	0.3	0.2	0.1	0.2

Selected Financial Factors (in Percentages)														
Debt Ratio	45	68.2	•	214.5	279.4	82.7	72.2	52.2	55.6	46.7	52.8	67.1	70.1	68.4
Return on Total Assets	46	2.4	•	27.2	19.2	6.2	•	0.5	2.1	2.9	2.6	3.2	1.8	2.4
Return on Equity Before Income Taxes	47	0.4	•	•	•	24.0	•	•	0.6	2.3	2.2	•	•	0.8
Return on Equity After Income Taxes	48	•	•	•	•	18.8	•	•	•	1.1	0.6	•	•	•
Profit Margin (Before Income Tax)	49	0.4	•	1.8	3.4	1.4	•	•	0.4	2.1	1.7	•	•	0.9
Profit Margin (After Income Tax)	50	•	•	1.7	3.3	1.1	•	•	•	1.0	0.5	•	•	•

Table II

Corporations with Net Income

TELECOMMUNICATIONS (WIRED, WIRELESS, SATELLITE, INTERNET PROVIDERS)

MONEY AMOUNTS AND SIZE OF ASSETS IN THOUSANDS OF DOLLARS

Item Description for Accounting Period 7/11 Through 6/12		Total	Zero Assets	Under 500	500 to 1,000	1,000 to 5,000	5,000 to 10,000	10,000 to 25,000	25,000 to 50,000	50,000 to 100,000	100,000 to 250,000	250,000 to 500,000	500,000 to 2,500,000	2,500,000 and over
Number of Enterprises	1	10796	2132	6585	435	865	258	233	107	72	53	19	21	16
Revenues ($ in Thousands)														
Net Sales	2	201580919	939347	3328279	854484	6719262	5950245	3681821	2571510	3019641	6105558	5813275	14147889	148449610
Interest	3	1483565	1459	663	90	6988	2440	7825	6251	10981	21315	12878	155206	1257469
Rents	4	772152	0	0	0	745	18690	10812	3020	7518	16163	4015	13064	698123
Royalties	5	7703	0	3	0	0	0	840	0	170	0	2	1065	5624
Other Portfolio Income	6	2434123	27927	0	14282	12328	40647	97104	60078	36364	42583	74368	70896	1957545
Other Receipts	7	8023793	31949	20635	530	25789	46353	123979	245646	166113	249068	245562	1331286	5536883
Total Receipts	8	214302255	1000682	3349580	869386	6765112	6058375	3922381	2886505	3240787	6434687	6150100	15719406	157905254
Average Total Receipts	9	19850	469	509	1999	7821	23482	16834	26977	45011	121409	323689	748543	9869078
Operating Costs/Operating Income (%)														
Cost of Operations	10	36.7	43.7	24.1	60.4	51.7	72.8	58.2	36.1	34.2	50.9	55.9	47.8	31.9
Salaries and Wages	11	10.8	18.5	15.1	11.6	14.5	9.2	6.5	8.5	8.5	9.1	9.8	20.3	10.0
Taxes Paid	12	2.1	1.4	2.3	0.9	2.4	1.1	2.1	2.3	2.0	1.9	1.9	2.5	2.1
Interest Paid	13	5.7	1.2	0.3	0.1	0.3	0.8	0.9	2.1	2.4	1.7	2.1	3.3	7.1
Depreciation	14	11.7	3.1	1.3	0.6	1.4	2.1	6.9	10.1	11.3	8.4	5.5	7.3	13.9
Amortization and Depletion	15	2.2	0.5	0.2	•	0.1	0.1	0.4	0.4	0.6	0.7	1.1	1.3	2.8
Pensions and Other Deferred Comp.	16	0.9	1.2	0.6	0.3	0.1	0.1	0.4	0.3	0.2	0.2	0.2	0.9	1.1
Employee Benefits	17	1.6	2.0	0.9	0.7	1.2	0.4	0.7	1.5	1.2	1.1	1.3	1.5	1.7
Advertising	18	1.6	0.5	0.7	0.6	0.4	0.7	0.3	3.8	2.0	0.6	0.9	2.9	1.7
Other Expenses	19	24.4	21.4	26.5	6.4	19.2	10.9	20.9	30.9	32.9	21.5	19.6	14.5	26.3
Officers' Compensation	20	0.7	1.7	12.6	2.5	2.7	1.1	1.2	1.5	1.9	0.8	0.9	0.6	0.3
Operating Margin	21	1.4	4.9	15.3	15.9	6.0	0.8	1.4	2.6	2.8	3.1	0.8	•	1.1
Operating Margin Before Officers' Comp.	22	2.1	6.5	27.9	18.4	8.7	1.8	2.6	4.1	4.8	3.9	1.7	•	1.4

Selected Average Balance Sheet ($ in Thousands)

Net Receivables	23	3121	0	7	96	634	1482	2384	3347	5970	24115	56291	254209	1477899
Inventories	24	285	0	1	43	83	88	322	869	940	4484	9769	9835	130768
Net Property, Plant and Equipment	25	9605	0	11	10	413	2075	5398	13525	26603	50107	56661	171117	5673650
Total Assets	26	50369	0	88	646	2344	7116	16264	34416	68277	158428	336894	1040838	30625862
Notes and Loans Payable	27	18012	0	39	36	324	2342	2801	8054	15704	34538	62510	278960	11361317
All Other Liabilities	28	15927	0	105	296	920	3601	3688	7591	14909	49511	119988	338255	9666008
Net Worth	29	16429	0	-56	314	1100	1173	9775	18770	37664	74380	154396	423623	9598536

Selected Financial Ratios (Times to 1)

Current Ratio	30	1.0	•	0.5	1.1	1.7	1.1	2.4	2.5	1.9	1.5	1.8	1.9	0.8
Quick Ratio	31	0.8	•	0.5	0.8	1.3	0.8	1.8	1.9	1.5	1.1	1.5	1.6	0.6
Net Sales to Working Capital	32	•	•	•	47.0	13.8	59.9	3.8	3.7	4.3	6.3	4.5	3.2	•
Coverage Ratio	33	2.4	10.8	50.1	145.7	22.7	4.1	10.2	8.2	5.3	6.1	4.2	3.6	2.1
Total Asset Turnover	34	0.4	•	5.7	3.0	3.3	3.2	1.0	0.7	0.6	0.7	0.9	0.6	0.3
Inventory Turnover	35	24.0	•	90.7	27.4	48.3	191.0	28.6	10.0	15.3	13.1	17.5	32.7	22.6
Receivables Turnover	36	2.8	•	44.7	10.5	15.7	21.1	7.7	6.4	6.5	5.0	5.2	3.5	2.4
Total Liabilities to Net Worth	37	2.1	•	•	1.1	1.1	5.1	0.7	0.8	0.8	1.1	1.2	1.5	2.2
Current Assets to Working Capital	38	•	•	•	8.8	2.5	10.6	1.7	1.7	2.1	3.0	2.2	2.1	•
Current Liabilities to Working Capital	39	•	•	•	7.8	1.5	9.6	0.7	0.7	1.1	2.0	1.2	1.1	•
Working Capital to Net Sales	40	•	•	•	0.0	0.1	0.0	0.3	0.3	0.2	0.2	0.2	0.3	•
Inventory to Working Capital	41	•	•	•	0.9	0.2	0.1	0.1	0.1	0.1	0.3	0.1	0.1	•
Total Receipts to Cash Flow	42	3.7	3.9	2.7	4.7	4.3	9.3	4.3	2.5	3.1	3.8	4.5	5.1	3.6
Cost of Goods to Cash Flow	43	1.4	1.7	0.6	2.8	2.2	6.7	2.5	0.9	1.0	1.9	2.5	2.5	1.1
Cash Flow to Total Debt	44	0.1	•	1.3	1.3	1.4	0.4	0.6	0.6	0.4	0.4	0.4	0.2	0.1

Selected Financial Factors (in Percentages)

Debt Ratio	45	67.4	•	163.9	51.4	53.1	83.5	39.9	45.5	44.8	53.1	54.2	59.3	68.7
Return on Total Assets	46	5.0	•	93.6	53.9	23.3	11.1	8.9	11.7	8.0	7.4	7.9	7.6	4.5
Return on Equity Before Income Taxes	47	8.9	•	•	110.2	47.4	50.9	13.3	18.9	11.7	13.2	13.1	13.4	7.4
Return on Equity After Income Taxes	48	6.8	•	•	109.0	44.5	46.1	10.4	14.9	9.7	10.4	10.4	11.7	5.3
Profit Margin (Before Income Tax)	49	7.9	11.4	16.0	17.6	6.7	2.6	8.2	14.8	10.5	8.5	6.6	8.4	7.7
Profit Margin (After Income Tax)	50	5.9	10.0	15.7	17.4	6.3	2.3	6.5	11.6	8.7	6.7	5.2	7.3	5.5

Table I

Corporations with and without Net Income

DATA PROCESSING, HOSTING AND RELATED SERVICES

MONEY AMOUNTS AND SIZE OF ASSETS IN THOUSANDS OF DOLLARS

Item Description for Accounting Period 7/11 Through 6/12		Total	Zero Assets	Under 500	500 to 1,000	1,000 to 5,000	5,000 to 10,000	10,000 to 25,000	25,000 to 50,000	50,000 to 100,000	100,000 to 250,000	250,000 to 500,000	500,000 to 2,500,000	2,500,000 and over
Number of Enterprises	1	9844	1791	6892	106	792	81	76	27	25	23	10	14	6
Revenues ($ in Thousands)														
Net Sales	2	36481983	192912	2543346	58184	2642717	1445338	1699528	949664	1359461	1857192	1877688	7422530	14433425
Interest	3	178917	58	1576	385	592	395	1151	568	1825	12805	1516	10167	147879
Rents	4	34727	664	0	0	0	0	0	0	347	0	0	21540	12176
Royalties	5	853505	0	0	0	0	0	0	0	336	3650	8605	19161	821753
Other Portfolio Income	6	641508	10136	10798	1304	604	362	335	11589	7887	4168	46	452025	142255
Other Receipts	7	531732	8443	5218	5306	15554	4485	25918	3664	9101	9639	126909	61351	256142
Total Receipts	8	38722372	212213	2560938	65179	2659467	1450580	1726932	965485	1378957	1887454	2014764	7986774	15813630
Average Total Receipts	9	3934	118	372	615	3358	17908	22723	35759	55158	82063	201476	570484	2635605
Operating Costs/Operating Income (%)														
Cost of Operations	10	23.7	3.7	32.6	22.8	28.1	42.3	47.4	31.1	39.2	19.1	11.4	24.5	16.8
Salaries and Wages	11	28.5	46.3	14.4	30.6	23.2	16.0	23.5	26.3	26.6	30.0	33.2	27.2	33.6
Taxes Paid	12	2.9	5.9	2.8	4.6	2.6	1.9	2.8	3.8	2.8	3.3	3.2	4.0	2.4
Interest Paid	13	5.0	3.2	1.4	0.1	1.0	1.4	0.6	2.3	2.3	5.6	1.4	4.4	8.3
Depreciation	14	8.9	1.6	0.8	0.6	3.3	3.3	4.0	10.4	3.6	10.4	5.8	10.6	12.4
Amortization and Depletion	15	2.3	0.7	0.6	0.0	1.5	0.5	0.7	1.2	1.7	3.0	4.0	4.1	2.1
Pensions and Other Deferred Comp.	16	0.4	0.5	0.2	•	1.1	0.4	0.7	0.8	0.2	0.5	0.1	0.5	0.3
Employee Benefits	17	2.1	4.1	1.5	4.3	2.0	1.2	2.1	2.9	2.4	2.0	2.8	2.6	1.8
Advertising	18	1.9	0.7	0.6	0.8	0.9	2.0	2.2	3.0	1.4	1.1	7.1	3.7	0.9
Other Expenses	19	26.7	58.3	36.8	77.5	31.5	29.3	18.9	22.2	27.5	28.6	36.3	16.2	28.3
Officers' Compensation	20	3.0	26.2	8.1	28.9	11.3	4.6	2.9	3.1	2.1	1.6	3.1	2.4	0.4
Operating Margin	21	•	•	0.4	•	•	•	•	•	•	•	•	•	•
Operating Margin Before Officers' Comp.	22	•	•	8.5	•	4.7	1.8	•	•	•	•	•	2.2	•

Selected Average Balance Sheet ($ in Thousands)													
Net Receivables 23	608	0	17	23	296	1350	3043	3831	11783	16139	30262	43623	601170
Inventories 24	10	0	0	14	27	76	117	131	322	565	136	2237	0
Net Property, Plant and Equipment 25	1356	0	10	4	281	832	1923	9153	6471	25896	25267	117808	1654984
Total Assets 26	7683	0	96	761	2089	6986	15474	34421	66900	146451	374269	1126328	7668448
Notes and Loans Payable 27	2722	0	128	4	692	2013	2104	7573	13256	48043	44227	411280	2867339
All Other Liabilities 28	1798	0	102	491	1163	2506	6332	12775	19251	47958	126698	249050	1442549
Net Worth 29	3163	0	-134	267	234	2468	7038	14073	34393	50450	203344	465998	3358560

Selected Financial Ratios (Times to 1)													
Current Ratio 30	1.3	•	0.7	2.1	1.5	1.7	1.8	1.7	1.5	1.2	1.2	0.9	1.4
Quick Ratio 31	1.0	•	0.6	2.0	1.4	1.6	1.6	1.4	1.3	0.9	0.8	0.7	1.0
Net Sales to Working Capital 32	10.0	•	•	8.3	6.7	10.2	5.7	4.8	5.4	12.6	13.1	•	5.7
Coverage Ratio 33	1.2	•	1.8	•	•	•	•	•	•	0.4	0.4	2.7	1.3
Total Asset Turnover 34	0.5	•	3.8	0.7	1.6	2.6	1.4	1.0	0.8	0.6	0.5	0.5	0.3
Inventory Turnover 35	92.0	•	383.6	8.7	35.3	98.7	90.6	83.3	66.2	27.2	156.4	58.0	•
Receivables Turnover 36	7.1	•	21.6	3.2	15.2	16.4	8.6	9.1	4.2	5.4	6.0	11.5	5.1
Total Liabilities to Net Worth 37	1.4	•	•	1.9	7.9	1.8	1.2	1.4	0.9	1.9	0.8	1.4	1.3
Current Assets to Working Capital 38	4.6	•	•	1.9	2.9	2.4	2.2	2.4	3.0	6.7	6.4	•	3.6
Current Liabilities to Working Capital 39	3.6	•	•	0.9	1.9	1.4	1.2	1.4	2.0	5.7	5.4	•	2.6
Working Capital to Net Sales 40	0.1	•	•	0.1	0.1	0.1	0.2	0.2	0.2	0.1	0.1	•	0.2
Inventory to Working Capital 41	0.0	•	•	•	0.0	0.0	0.0	0.0	0.0	0.1	0.0	•	•
Total Receipts to Cash Flow 42	4.7	13.6	3.0	6.1	4.8	4.0	8.3	7.9	6.6	5.4	3.1	5.0	4.9
Cost of Goods to Cash Flow 43	1.1	0.5	1.0	1.4	1.4	1.7	3.9	2.5	2.6	1.0	0.4	1.2	0.8
Cash Flow to Total Debt 44	0.2	•	0.5	0.2	0.4	1.0	0.3	0.2	0.3	0.2	0.4	0.2	0.1

Selected Financial Factors (in Percentages)													
Debt Ratio 45	58.8	•	238.7	64.9	88.8	64.7	54.5	59.1	48.6	65.6	45.7	58.6	56.2
Return on Total Assets 46	2.8	•	9.4	•	•	•	•	•	•	1.2	0.2	5.6	3.3
Return on Equity Before Income Taxes 47	0.9	•	•	•	•	•	•	•	•	•	•	8.5	1.6
Return on Equity After Income Taxes 48	•	•	•	•	•	•	•	•	•	•	•	5.1	•
Profit Margin (Before Income Tax) 49	0.8	•	1.1	•	•	•	•	•	•	•	•	7.4	2.3
Profit Margin (After Income Tax) 50	•	•	1.1	•	•	•	•	•	•	•	•	4.5	•

Table II

Corporations with Net Income

DATA PROCESSING, HOSTING AND RELATED SERVICES

MONEY AMOUNTS AND SIZE OF ASSETS IN THOUSANDS OF DOLLARS

Item Description for Accounting Period 7/11 Through 6/12		Total	Zero Assets	Under 500	500 to 1,000	1,000 to 5,000	5,000 to 10,000	10,000 to 25,000	25,000 to 50,000	50,000 to 100,000	100,000 to 250,000	250,000 to 500,000	500,000 to 2,500,000	2,500,000 and over
Number of Enterprises	1	5514	834	4065	57	439	30	42	9	10	11	6	8	3
Revenues ($ in Thousands)														
Net Sales	2	22663072	65008	2010966	39360	1609808	672860	1202592	362803	726125	1169955	1355628	5462129	7985838
Interest	3	26840	2	1569	0	195	44	733	244	15	6991	1087	8541	7418
Rents	4	32326	664	0	0	0	0	0	0	0	0	0	21259	10403
Royalties	5	792432	0	0	0	0	0	0	0	0	3650	1412	16819	770552
Other Portfolio Income	6	419939	10136	959	1304	73	292	103	703	7347	3563	19	376779	18661
Other Receipts	7	414955	7349	2735	5306	760	2580	19565	606	1410	9761	13384	46548	304950
Total Receipts	8	24349564	83159	2016229	45970	1610836	675776	1222993	364356	734897	1193920	1371530	5932075	9097822
Average Total Receipts	9	4416	100	496	806	3669	22526	29119	40484	73490	108538	228588	741509	3032607
Operating Costs/Operating Income (%)														
Cost of Operations	10	21.9	•	35.4	4.7	31.4	40.6	50.5	20.0	36.9	14.6	12.3	25.0	10.1
Salaries and Wages	11	28.2	40.9	11.2	7.3	15.2	15.1	15.5	31.2	21.4	33.1	22.9	30.7	37.1
Taxes Paid	12	2.2	4.2	2.1	0.9	1.8	2.1	2.2	2.5	3.3	3.5	2.4	2.7	1.5
Interest Paid	13	3.1	0.1	0.4	•	0.3	0.1	0.6	0.1	2.7	3.2	0.5	3.8	5.1
Depreciation	14	6.0	1.8	0.3	0.1	2.3	4.1	2.8	2.5	4.4	5.8	3.8	5.9	9.8
Amortization and Depletion	15	2.0	•	0.0	•	1.0	0.0	0.4	0.1	1.7	2.2	2.3	4.4	1.4
Pensions and Other Deferred Comp.	16	0.5	1.1	0.2	•	1.8	0.6	0.5	1.7	0.3	0.6	0.1	0.7	0.2
Employee Benefits	17	1.9	3.0	1.2	0.3	2.0	0.8	1.7	3.1	2.0	1.2	1.3	2.7	1.7
Advertising	18	2.2	0.1	0.6	1.1	0.6	0.8	1.6	0.5	0.4	0.8	9.1	4.1	1.1
Other Expenses	19	23.6	21.5	34.1	34.0	15.0	17.0	14.9	23.4	19.9	27.0	37.4	11.9	30.1
Officers' Compensation	20	3.0	34.5	7.1	4.7	13.0	5.1	2.6	4.9	1.3	1.6	3.2	2.3	0.3
Operating Margin	21	5.5	•	7.3	46.7	15.6	13.5	6.7	9.9	5.7	6.4	4.5	5.8	1.6
Operating Margin Before Officers' Comp.	22	8.5	27.3	14.3	51.4	28.7	18.7	9.3	14.9	7.0	7.9	7.7	8.1	1.9

Selected Average Balance Sheet ($ in Thousands)														
Net Receivables	23	681	0	16	0	213	2392	3698	3211	14520	16142	19729	51169	829791
Inventories	24	12	0	0	5	47	0	84	384	222	192	122	3864	0
Net Property, Plant and Equipment	25	904	0	4	1	156	1066	1873	2869	9596	13776	19408	85793	1237593
Total Assets	26	7660	0	111	801	1961	7091	14927	36025	64433	158528	396274	1243676	8333362
Notes and Loans Payable	27	2393	0	74	0	368	386	2791	321	26786	31446	38840	452787	2709865
All Other Liabilities	28	1470	0	57	771	724	2002	5073	22205	20517	54548	120578	297908	1042963
Net Worth	29	3797	0	-20	31	869	4702	7063	13499	17130	72534	236856	492980	4580533
Selected Financial Ratios (Times to 1)														
Current Ratio	30	1.4	•	1.2	•	2.7	2.7	1.8	1.8	0.9	1.1	1.1	0.8	1.6
Quick Ratio	31	1.1	•	0.9	•	2.3	2.6	1.6	1.4	0.8	0.9	0.9	0.7	1.3
Net Sales to Working Capital	32	9.2	•	33.6	24.4	3.7	7.9	8.5	3.0	•	25.8	41.5	•	4.5
Coverage Ratio	33	5.2	277.2	18.6	•	50.9	175.9	15.9	192.3	3.7	3.6	11.6	4.8	4.1
Total Asset Turnover	34	0.5	•	4.5	0.9	1.9	3.2	1.9	1.1	1.1	0.7	0.6	0.5	0.3
Inventory Turnover	35	76.9	•	849.8	7.2	24.4	•	172.3	21.0	120.8	80.6	227.2	44.2	•
Receivables Turnover	36	7.3	•	31.4	5.4	19.8	10.5	9.1	11.4	6.4	8.9	7.4	5.1	6.4
Total Liabilities to Net Worth	37	1.0	•	•	25.0	1.3	0.5	1.1	1.7	2.8	1.2	0.7	1.5	0.8
Current Assets to Working Capital	38	3.7	•	5.9	1.0	1.6	1.6	2.3	2.2	•	11.4	12.1	•	2.8
Current Liabilities to Working Capital	39	2.7	•	4.9	•	0.6	0.6	1.3	1.2	•	10.4	11.1	•	1.8
Working Capital to Net Sales	40	0.1	•	0.0	0.0	0.3	0.1	0.1	0.3	•	0.0	0.0	•	0.2
Inventory to Working Capital	41	0.0	•	0.0	•	0.0	•	0.0	0.0	•	0.1	0.0	•	•
Total Receipts to Cash Flow	42	3.2	4.0	2.6	1.0	3.5	3.5	4.8	3.2	4.5	3.2	2.5	4.1	2.8
Cost of Goods to Cash Flow	43	0.7	•	0.9	0.0	1.1	1.4	2.4	0.6	1.7	0.5	0.3	1.0	0.3
Cash Flow to Total Debt	44	0.3	•	1.4	0.9	1.0	2.7	0.8	0.6	0.3	0.4	0.6	0.2	0.3
Selected Financial Factors (in Percentages)														
Debt Ratio	45	50.4	•	118.3	96.2	55.7	33.7	52.7	62.5	73.4	54.2	40.2	60.4	45.0
Return on Total Assets	46	8.6	•	35.4	54.7	29.9	44.5	17.1	11.4	11.2	7.8	3.6	10.0	6.6
Return on Equity Before Income Taxes	47	14.0	•	•	1424.7	66.2	66.7	33.8	30.4	30.6	12.3	5.4	20.0	9.0
Return on Equity After Income Taxes	48	10.6	•	•	1424.7	64.0	59.3	29.3	20.9	29.1	10.2	4.4	14.4	6.0
Profit Margin (Before Income Tax)	49	12.9	21.2	7.5	63.5	15.7	14.0	8.3	10.2	7.2	8.4	5.7	14.4	15.6
Profit Margin (After Income Tax)	50	9.8	17.7	7.5	63.5	15.2	12.4	7.2	7.0	6.9	7.0	4.6	10.4	10.4

Table I

Corporations with and without Net Income

OTHER INFORMATION SERVICES, INTERNET PUBLISHING, WEB PORTALS

MONEY AMOUNTS AND SIZE OF ASSETS IN THOUSANDS OF DOLLARS

Item Description for Accounting Period 7/11 Through 6/12		Total	Zero Assets	Under 500	500 to 1,000	1,000 to 5,000	5,000 to 10,000	10,000 to 25,000	25,000 to 50,000	50,000 to 100,000	100,000 to 250,000	250,000 to 500,000	500,000 to 2,500,000	2,500,000 and over
Number of Enterprises	1	24450	6462	15953	772	641	336	119	81	32	25	8	13	8
Revenues ($ in Thousands)														
Net Sales	2	71215202	1802323	4520542	1311541	2580776	4205150	1829267	2507206	1229911	2551785	1888207	8415168	38373326
Interest	3	956682	347	276	185	2072	2581	1177	1787	3704	6223	5252	72295	860781
Rents	4	147613	0	178	0	0	0	36	0	163	20	2984	5581	138650
Royalties	5	1294575	26	46	0	46	0	0	809	3179	152	604032	31906	654377
Other Portfolio Income	6	944556	3	255	141	48577	11044	23776	1620	56565	312	3935	197322	601009
Other Receipts	7	4074249	70906	154256	7666	5158	18466	10463	25299	79673	20274	19050	195441	3467599
Total Receipts	8	78632877	1873605	4675553	1319533	2636629	4237241	1864719	2536721	1373195	2578766	2523460	8917713	44095742
Average Total Receipts	9	3216	290	293	1709	4113	12611	15670	31318	42912	103151	315432	685978	5511968
Operating Costs/Operating Income (%)														
Cost of Operations	10	23.0	17.1	52.5	17.9	29.8	51.3	25.6	39.7	24.2	21.7	10.8	26.6	15.1
Salaries and Wages	11	26.9	31.8	7.8	27.6	37.8	20.5	30.7	46.2	33.0	25.4	36.3	28.7	26.4
Taxes Paid	12	3.2	2.7	1.3	1.4	2.8	3.1	3.2	5.2	4.4	2.6	4.3	2.3	3.5
Interest Paid	13	3.4	1.8	0.9	0.5	0.8	0.6	2.3	1.5	1.5	0.7	4.6	3.9	4.6
Depreciation	14	5.9	1.2	0.6	0.5	2.3	2.2	3.5	3.3	3.5	5.3	4.7	5.6	8.1
Amortization and Depletion	15	2.0	4.0	0.2	1.4	2.2	0.4	2.8	0.7	3.1	1.7	2.6	3.7	1.9
Pensions and Other Deferred Comp.	16	0.8	0.1	0.3	0.0	0.1	0.8	0.1	0.1	0.1	0.7	5.2	0.5	0.8
Employee Benefits	17	2.0	1.0	0.7	5.0	1.5	2.6	2.3	2.6	2.6	2.9	3.4	2.6	1.7
Advertising	18	3.2	2.7	4.0	1.8	4.3	4.8	5.4	2.9	4.3	6.1	9.2	3.7	2.2
Other Expenses	19	33.5	40.5	29.7	34.0	28.6	16.3	40.5	27.4	43.9	29.2	41.2	25.9	37.2
Officers' Compensation	20	2.4	3.4	6.7	8.8	8.5	3.4	4.1	2.9	2.5	4.8	2.9	2.0	0.8
Operating Margin	21	•	•	•	1.1	•	•	•	•	•	•	•	•	•
Operating Margin Before Officers' Comp.	22	•	•	2.2	9.9	•	•	•	•	•	3.8	•	•	•

Selected Average Balance Sheet ($ in Thousands)														
Net Receivables	23	504	0	2	55	491	1533	3094	7311	8047	20694	41090	97090	1012047
Inventories	24	22	0	0	13	24	34	110	52	957	261	60	29412	7068
Net Property, Plant and Equipment	25	557	0	6	12	139	678	1501	2253	3111	12820	33897	98065	1357195
Total Assets	26	6309	0	45	649	2144	6754	14621	33594	68348	159040	366810	1157397	15099562
Notes and Loans Payable	27	895	0	87	163	710	1460	4262	5818	19923	11459	68027	351492	1551500
All Other Liabilities	28	1892	0	35	306	1401	4700	7946	12300	22985	47552	115310	352768	4201686
Net Worth	29	3522	0	-77	180	32	594	2413	15476	25440	100029	183472	453136	9346377

Selected Financial Ratios (Times to 1)														
Current Ratio	30	2.2	•	0.6	3.4	1.0	1.8	1.3	1.9	1.6	1.6	1.7	1.7	2.7
Quick Ratio	31	1.1	•	0.4	3.2	0.9	1.5	1.1	1.7	1.1	1.5	1.5	1.1	1.0
Net Sales to Working Capital	32	2.3	•	•	4.6	159.8	6.4	6.0	3.1	3.4	3.4	5.9	2.8	1.6
Coverage Ratio	33	2.6	•	•	4.6	•	•	•	•	•	1.2	3.1	1.1	4.1
Total Asset Turnover	34	0.5	•	6.3	2.6	1.9	1.9	1.1	0.9	0.6	0.6	0.6	0.6	0.3
Inventory Turnover	35	30.8	•	858.2	22.9	50.3	191.8	35.9	234.5	9.7	84.9	424.6	5.9	102.6
Receivables Turnover	36	5.5	•	44.0	26.5	10.9	8.2	5.1	6.8	4.3	6.1	5.4	6.3	4.2
Total Liabilities to Net Worth	37	0.8	•	•	2.6	65.3	10.4	5.1	1.2	1.7	0.6	1.0	1.6	0.6
Current Assets to Working Capital	38	1.8	•	•	1.4	56.3	2.2	4.0	2.2	2.8	2.5	2.4	2.4	1.6
Current Liabilities to Working Capital	39	0.8	•	•	0.4	55.3	1.2	3.0	1.2	1.8	1.5	1.4	1.4	0.6
Working Capital to Net Sales	40	0.4	•	•	0.2	0.0	0.2	0.2	0.3	0.3	0.3	0.2	0.4	0.6
Inventory to Working Capital	41	0.0	•	•	0.0	0.8	0.0	0.0	0.0	0.1	0.0	0.0	0.1	0.0
Total Receipts to Cash Flow	42	2.9	2.8	3.8	3.0	14.5	12.4	5.7	•	3.9	3.8	2.3	4.3	2.2
Cost of Goods to Cash Flow	43	0.7	0.5	2.0	0.5	4.3	6.4	1.5	•	0.9	0.8	0.3	1.1	0.3
Cash Flow to Total Debt	44	0.4	•	0.6	1.2	0.1	0.2	0.2	•	0.2	0.5	0.6	0.2	0.4

Selected Financial Factors (in Percentages)														
Debt Ratio	45	44.2	•	271.7	72.2	98.5	91.2	83.5	53.9	62.8	37.1	50.0	60.8	38.1
Return on Total Assets	46	4.0	•	•	5.7	•	•	•	•	•	0.5	9.2	2.5	6.0
Return on Equity Before Income Taxes	47	4.4	•	4.2	16.1	•	•	•	•	•	0.1	12.5	0.8	7.4
Return on Equity After Income Taxes	48	1.8	•	4.7	10.0	•	•	•	•	•	•	5.7	•	4.8
Profit Margin (Before Income Tax)	49	5.3	•	•	1.7	•	•	•	•	•	0.1	9.7	0.6	14.4
Profit Margin (After Income Tax)	50	2.1	•	•	1.1	•	•	•	•	•	•	4.5	•	9.4

Table II

Corporations with Net Income

OTHER INFORMATION SERVICES, INTERNET PUBLISHING, WEB PORTALS

MONEY AMOUNTS AND SIZE OF ASSETS IN THOUSANDS OF DOLLARS

Item Description for Accounting Period 7/11 Through 6/12		Total	Zero Assets	Under 500	500 to 1,000	1,000 to 5,000	5,000 to 10,000	10,000 to 25,000	25,000 to 50,000	50,000 to 100,000	100,000 to 250,000	250,000 to 500,000	500,000 to 2,500,000	2,500,000 and over
Number of Enterprises	1	12728	3911	7719	547	267	182	42	19	11	13	5	7	5
Revenues ($ in Thousands)														
Net Sales	2	55431426	772126	3409949	1123665	1810885	3203902	781460	919092	647151	1431899	1522394	4877861	34931041
Interest	3	884911	233	19	117	1156	345	589	699	915	4864	4795	69112	802069
Rents	4	134560	0	178	0	0	0	36	0	65	0	46	4208	130026
Royalties	5	677243	26	46	0	0	0	0	809	0	152	1083	25070	650056
Other Portfolio Income	6	843731	3	255	0	48550	8351	23308	1617	56502	249	3783	109444	591673
Other Receipts	7	3766667	80132	150319	757	376	-3256	11564	8824	34702	10369	821	95859	3376197
Total Receipts	8	61738538	852520	3560766	1124539	1860967	3209342	816957	931041	739335	1447533	1532922	5181554	40481062
Average Total Receipts	9	4851	218	461	2056	6970	17634	19451	49002	67212	111349	306584	740222	8096212
Operating Costs/Operating Income (%)														
Cost of Operations	10	23.1	8.9	61.4	12.7	30.6	54.3	19.4	46.8	18.9	20.1	6.3	28.9	16.3
Salaries and Wages	11	23.8	27.4	4.7	24.6	32.6	15.4	19.5	17.0	30.6	26.7	23.7	23.3	26.0
Taxes Paid	12	2.9	1.8	1.0	0.7	0.8	3.1	1.8	2.6	3.7	2.8	2.8	2.2	3.5
Interest Paid	13	3.2	3.7	0.4	0.1	0.3	0.2	1.4	0.5	1.1	0.4	0.6	2.7	4.4
Depreciation	14	5.9	2.2	0.3	0.2	0.3	1.5	1.5	1.4	3.6	3.4	3.3	2.8	8.3
Amortization and Depletion	15	1.6	6.6	0.1	0.0	0.2	•	1.0	0.7	1.6	1.5	2.6	2.3	1.9
Pensions and Other Deferred Comp.	16	0.7	0.2	0.3	0.0	0.0	1.0	0.2	0.1	0.0	0.9	3.8	0.5	0.7
Employee Benefits	17	1.7	1.2	0.5	5.3	0.6	2.5	1.6	0.9	2.6	2.5	2.2	2.3	1.6
Advertising	18	3.1	2.1	2.3	1.7	3.3	4.3	4.4	6.1	2.3	9.8	9.4	5.5	2.2
Other Expenses	19	30.2	35.7	13.8	28.4	13.6	9.8	38.5	14.3	36.4	18.6	26.9	24.1	36.1
Officers' Compensation	20	1.8	3.7	6.1	9.7	8.5	2.5	1.6	1.4	1.8	2.1	2.0	1.4	0.7
Operating Margin	21	1.9	6.5	9.1	16.5	9.1	5.5	9.1	8.3	•	11.3	16.3	3.9	•
Operating Margin Before Officers' Comp.	22	3.6	10.2	15.2	26.2	17.5	8.0	10.7	9.7	•	13.4	18.3	5.3	•

Selected Average Balance Sheet ($ in Thousands)														
Net Receivables	23	619	0	3	45	858	1738	4626	4794	12958	20804	51615	118170	1099800
Inventories	24	26	0	0	0	31	1	2	130	1320	282	0	34071	12618
Net Property, Plant and Equipment	25	881	0	5	0	91	853	759	2864	3713	11311	19938	55644	2046670
Total Assets	26	9199	0	50	626	2129	6386	14284	36812	67769	169255	349824	1232084	20002340
Notes and Loans Payable	27	1071	0	32	75	375	1468	2840	5461	12568	11764	13393	402172	1915297
All Other Liabilities	28	2782	0	16	134	1139	1820	8343	14558	37553	45050	46414	452935	5908944
Net Worth	29	5347	0	1	417	615	3097	3101	16794	17649	112440	290017	376977	12178099

Selected Financial Ratios (Times to 1)														
Current Ratio	30	2.8	•	1.6	4.4	1.4	2.3	1.4	1.7	1.0	2.2	2.5	1.6	3.3
Quick Ratio	31	1.1	•	1.0	4.3	1.3	1.7	0.9	1.5	0.7	2.0	2.2	1.0	1.0
Net Sales to Working Capital	32	2.0	•	31.6	4.5	14.8	7.5	6.5	5.7	356.0	2.0	4.3	3.2	1.4
Coverage Ratio	33	5.5	5.6	39.0	260.9	38.3	26.5	10.8	22.9	12.1	30.9	33.4	4.8	4.6
Total Asset Turnover	34	0.5	•	8.9	3.3	3.2	2.8	1.3	1.3	0.9	0.7	0.9	0.6	0.3
Inventory Turnover	35	39.3	•	1240.2	•	66.0	8209.8	2155.2	173.8	8.4	78.4	•	5.9	90.1
Receivables Turnover	36	6.6	•	44.0	•	12.4	11.6	4.8	11.3	4.0	5.5	5.7	5.2	•
Total Liabilities to Net Worth	37	0.7	•	35.8	0.5	2.5	1.1	3.6	1.2	2.8	0.5	0.2	2.3	0.6
Current Assets to Working Capital	38	1.6	•	2.5	1.3	3.4	1.8	3.8	2.5	197.2	1.9	1.7	2.6	1.4
Current Liabilities to Working Capital	39	0.6	•	1.5	0.3	2.4	0.8	2.8	1.5	196.2	0.9	0.7	1.6	0.4
Working Capital to Net Sales	40	0.5	•	0.0	0.2	0.1	0.1	0.2	0.2	0.0	0.5	0.2	0.3	0.7
Inventory to Working Capital	41	0.0	•	0.0	•	0.1	0.0	•	0.0	5.6	0.0	•	0.2	0.0
Total Receipts to Cash Flow	42	2.5	2.0	3.8	2.3	4.7	8.0	2.1	4.5	2.6	3.5	2.5	3.2	2.2
Cost of Goods to Cash Flow	43	0.6	0.2	2.4	0.3	1.4	4.3	0.4	2.1	0.5	0.7	0.2	0.9	0.4
Cash Flow to Total Debt	44	0.4	•	2.4	4.3	1.0	0.7	0.8	0.5	0.4	0.5	2.0	0.3	0.4

Selected Financial Factors (in Percentages)														
Debt Ratio	45	41.9	•	97.3	33.3	71.1	51.5	78.3	54.4	74.0	33.6	17.1	69.4	39.1
Return on Total Assets	46	8.4	•	123.6	54.7	38.6	16.2	20.4	13.7	11.0	8.3	16.9	7.3	7.2
Return on Equity Before Income Taxes	47	11.8	•	4427.7	81.7	130.2	32.2	85.3	28.6	38.9	12.1	19.7	18.9	9.3
Return on Equity After Income Taxes	48	8.5	•	4361.8	78.0	125.9	30.9	77.8	24.3	32.0	8.5	12.9	13.5	6.2
Profit Margin (Before Income Tax)	49	14.5	16.9	13.5	16.6	11.8	5.7	14.2	9.9	11.7	12.4	18.8	10.2	16.2
Profit Margin (After Income Tax)	50	10.5	16.2	13.3	15.9	11.4	5.4	13.0	8.4	9.6	8.6	12.3	7.3	10.8

Table I

Corporations with and without Net Income

CREDIT INTERMEDIATION

MONEY AMOUNTS AND SIZE OF ASSETS IN THOUSANDS OF DOLLARS

Item Description for Accounting Period 7/11 Through 6/12		Total	Zero Assets	Under 500	500 to 1,000	1,000 to 5,000	5,000 to 10,000	10,000 to 25,000	25,000 to 50,000	50,000 to 100,000	100,000 to 250,000	250,000 to 500,000	500,000 to 2,500,000	2,500,000 and over
Number of Enterprises	1	38788	7245	20017	2925	3906	722	844	601	687	901	420	393	127
Revenues ($ in Thousands)														
Net Sales	2	468971028	45940917	4004592	1267533	3439857	1806026	4253190	4804396	6821514	15039904	13692368	33188545	334712185
Interest	3	270583355	26780800	18435	13243	209546	46724	134116	476360	1285551	4524338	4697397	13933142	218463703
Rents	4	1233128	132970	1861	0	2404	3170	4510	1931	6126	17241	34122	81991	946802
Royalties	5	1197576	19703	76094	36	0	0	0	204	266	31604	9148	9360	1051160
Other Portfolio Income	6	17168018	2025041	3948	414	27272	132297	19576	41562	159800	508757	426664	1372956	12449726
Other Receipts	7	178788951	16982403	3904254	1253840	3200635	1623835	4094988	4284339	5369771	9957964	8525037	17791096	101800794
Total Receipts	8	468971028	45940917	4004592	1267533	3439857	1806026	4253190	4804396	6821514	15039904	13692368	33188545	334712185
Average Total Receipts	9	12091	6341	200	433	881	2501	5039	7994	9929	16692	32601	84449	2635529
Operating Costs/Operating Income (%)														
Cost of Operations	10	0.4	0.0	•	•	0.1	•	0.1	•	0.0	0.4	0.5	0.2	0.4
Salaries and Wages	11	9.3	9.2	24.0	11.8	25.9	26.9	25.7	24.8	20.9	18.4	19.5	16.6	6.6
Taxes Paid	12	1.6	3.4	3.9	2.3	3.8	3.3	3.1	3.0	2.7	3.0	2.9	2.3	1.0
Interest Paid	13	34.6	30.3	1.1	3.9	7.0	6.7	8.5	8.1	9.0	11.1	13.1	15.0	41.2
Depreciation	14	3.7	1.1	1.5	2.1	1.4	2.2	1.7	2.2	2.0	2.9	2.7	2.9	4.4
Amortization and Depletion	15	0.9	0.2	0.2	0.9	1.1	0.2	0.4	0.6	0.6	0.5	0.9	1.7	1.0
Pensions and Other Deferred Comp.	16	0.5	0.4	0.2	1.7	0.4	0.5	0.3	0.4	0.5	0.7	0.8	1.0	0.5
Employee Benefits	17	1.0	1.0	1.4	1.0	1.0	2.3	1.5	1.7	1.6	1.8	2.2	2.0	0.8
Advertising	18	1.4	0.1	2.2	1.6	3.6	2.1	2.3	2.8	1.4	1.2	2.2	1.6	1.5
Other Expenses	19	43.4	41.5	44.0	53.2	48.2	44.2	46.4	51.1	54.1	49.0	48.4	47.1	42.4
Officers' Compensation	20	1.3	1.7	20.1	10.8	8.2	7.4	8.0	4.8	4.5	4.7	3.3	2.0	0.4
Operating Margin	21	1.8	11.1	1.4	10.7	•	4.4	2.0	0.4	2.6	6.2	3.5	7.7	•
Operating Margin Before Officers' Comp.	22	3.1	12.8	21.5	21.5	7.6	11.7	10.0	5.2	7.1	10.9	6.7	9.7	0.1

Selected Average Balance Sheet ($ in Thousands)

Net Receivables 23	24428	0	11	186	868	2460	7036	13782	26972	59289	100126	247473	5638559
Inventories 24	•	•	•	•	•	•	•	•	•	•	•	•	•
Net Property, Plant and Equipment 25	1767	0	18	96	143	258	436	726	1381	3076	6135	15089	426122
Total Assets 26	218355	0	99	712	2420	7218	16303	36410	72481	159969	350627	1008864	60452766
Notes and Loans Payable 27	160782	0	60	527	1196	5678	8876	11608	11191	19238	46308	168320	48030071
All Other Liabilities 28	48489	0	14	90	430	1859	7060	23351	59007	135942	283743	749965	10081262
Net Worth 29	9084	0	26	96	794	-319	367	1451	2283	4788	20577	90580	2341432

Selected Financial Ratios (Times to 1)

Current Ratio 30	0.8	•	3.6	2.4	2.5	1.5	1.3	1.1	0.9	0.8	0.6	0.6	0.8
Quick Ratio 31	0.7	•	2.6	1.8	2.0	1.1	1.1	1.0	0.8	0.7	0.6	0.6	0.7
Net Sales to Working Capital 32	•	•	4.4	1.6	0.9	1.6	2.2	4.1	•	•	•	•	•
Coverage Ratio 33	1.0	1.3	2.3	3.8	0.9	1.7	1.2	1.0	1.2	1.5	1.2	1.5	1.0
Total Asset Turnover 34	0.1	•	2.0	0.6	0.4	0.3	0.3	0.2	0.1	0.1	0.1	0.1	0.0
Inventory Turnover 35	•	•	•	•	•	•	•	•	•	•	•	•	•
Receivables Turnover 36	•	•	•	•	•	•	•	•	•	•	•	•	•
Total Liabilities to Net Worth 37	23.0	•	2.9	6.4	2.0	•	43.4	24.1	30.8	32.4	16.0	10.1	24.8
Current Assets to Working Capital 38	•	•	1.4	1.7	1.6	2.9	4.4	11.7	•	•	•	•	•
Current Liabilities to Working Capital 39	•	•	0.4	0.7	0.6	1.9	3.4	10.7	•	•	•	•	•
Working Capital to Net Sales 40	•	•	0.2	0.6	1.2	0.6	0.5	0.2	•	•	•	•	•
Inventory to Working Capital 41	•	•	•	•	•	•	0.0	0.0	•	•	•	•	•
Total Receipts to Cash Flow 42	2.4	2.2	2.6	1.8	2.4	2.5	2.4	2.7	2.3	2.3	2.5	2.2	2.5
Cost of Goods to Cash Flow 43	0.0	0.0	•	•	0.0	•	0.0	•	0.0	0.0	0.0	0.0	0.0
Cash Flow to Total Debt 44	0.0	•	1.1	0.4	0.2	0.1	0.1	0.1	0.1	0.0	0.0	0.0	0.0

Selected Financial Factors (in Percentages)

Debt Ratio 45	95.8	•	74.0	86.5	67.2	104.4	97.7	96.0	96.9	97.0	94.1	91.0	96.1
Return on Total Assets 46	2.0	•	5.0	8.8	2.3	3.8	3.2	1.8	1.5	1.7	1.5	1.8	1.8
Return on Equity Before Income Taxes 47	2.2	•	10.9	48.0	•	•	26.8	0.8	8.0	18.5	4.6	6.6	•
Return on Equity After Income Taxes 48	•	•	8.0	45.6	•	•	17.3	•	3.2	11.7	•	2.6	•
Profit Margin (Before Income Tax) 49	1.6	9.8	1.4	10.7	•	4.4	2.0	0.1	1.8	5.3	2.9	7.1	•
Profit Margin (After Income Tax) 50	•	6.2	1.0	10.1	•	3.7	1.3	•	0.7	3.4	•	2.8	•

Table II

Corporations with Net Income

CREDIT INTERMEDIATION

MONEY AMOUNTS AND SIZE OF ASSETS IN THOUSANDS OF DOLLARS

Item Description for Accounting Period 7/11 Through 6/12		Total	Zero Assets	Under 500	500 to 1,000	1,000 to 5,000	5,000 to 10,000	10,000 to 25,000	25,000 to 50,000	50,000 to 100,000	100,000 to 250,000	250,000 to 500,000	500,000 to 2,500,000	2,500,000 and over
Number of Enterprises	1	19993	3452	9509	1498	2279	499	575	379	465	648	307	290	93
Revenues ($ in Thousands)														
Net Sales	2	246821433	31427598	3103259	1055448	2810609	1386187	3140732	3437675	4500960	11100968	10289275	25631314	148937409
Interest	3	99205769	18666014	17336	5478	80734	36609	89493	292202	853144	3328613	3419215	10559452	61857480
Rents	4	727032	67645	1861	0	1693	2513	4002	666	2786	9682	22012	51754	562418
Royalties	5	1196827	19668	76094	0	0	0	0	204	2	31519	9148	9315	1050876
Other Portfolio Income	6	8333709	1311718	2482	14	11926	132075	16970	27278	75792	410471	283395	1042028	5019557
Other Receipts	7	137358096	11362553	3005486	1049956	2716256	1214990	3030267	3117325	3569236	7320683	6555505	13968765	80447078
Total Receipts	8	246821433	31427598	3103259	1055448	2810609	1386187	3140732	3437675	4500960	11100968	10289275	25631314	148937409
Average Total Receipts	9	12345	9104	326	705	1233	2778	5462	9070	9679	17131	33516	88384	1601478
Operating Costs/Operating Income (%)														
Cost of Operations	10	0.3	0.0	•	•	0.1	•	0.1	•	0.1	0.4	0.3	0.2	0.4
Salaries and Wages	11	13.1	8.1	18.8	7.4	25.9	23.4	25.7	24.8	22.8	19.8	20.1	17.2	11.2
Taxes Paid	12	2.4	3.8	3.3	1.7	3.5	3.0	3.1	3.2	2.9	3.3	3.1	2.4	1.9
Interest Paid	13	15.7	27.1	0.7	1.5	4.8	6.3	6.6	8.0	9.5	10.5	12.0	14.0	15.5
Depreciation	14	3.3	0.8	1.2	1.8	1.3	1.9	1.2	1.2	1.7	2.1	3.0	2.7	4.3
Amortization and Depletion	15	1.2	0.2	0.2	•	0.1	0.1	0.4	0.4	0.6	0.5	0.5	1.7	1.5
Pensions and Other Deferred Comp.	16	0.8	0.4	0.3	1.9	0.4	0.4	0.3	0.4	0.7	0.8	0.8	1.1	0.9
Employee Benefits	17	1.3	0.9	1.2	0.2	0.9	2.1	1.4	1.4	1.7	1.8	2.3	2.0	1.2
Advertising	18	2.4	0.2	2.0	0.9	3.7	1.9	2.3	3.3	1.6	1.4	2.0	1.8	3.1
Other Expenses	19	37.8	32.7	32.7	51.8	31.2	30.9	31.4	32.0	35.9	35.7	34.0	35.6	40.2
Officers' Compensation	20	1.7	0.8	18.7	9.2	8.3	8.5	8.1	5.2	5.2	5.2	3.4	1.9	0.6
Operating Margin	21	20.0	25.1	20.9	23.6	19.8	21.6	19.4	20.2	17.4	18.5	18.5	19.5	19.3
Operating Margin Before Officers' Comp.	22	21.7	25.8	39.6	32.8	28.1	30.1	27.5	25.4	22.5	23.8	21.8	21.4	19.8

Selected Average Balance Sheet ($ in Thousands)

Net Receivables	23	35799	0	9	138	921	2789	8361	15924	28934	61958	107496	237057	5868432
Inventories	24	•	•	•	•	•	•	•	•	•	•	•	•	•
Net Property, Plant and Equipment	25	2131	0	20	58	148	234	299	673	1321	2957	6590	15085	349791
Total Assets	26	119756	0	114	717	2302	7061	16419	36332	72972	161403	350342	997045	19622735
Notes and Loans Payable	27	32045	0	29	324	1015	5993	7552	11303	12122	16610	44919	139579	5971226
All Other Liabilities	28	70185	0	7	97	380	2271	4381	18790	54056	125306	255763	707390	10767236
Net Worth	29	17525	0	77	296	908	-1202	4486	6239	6795	19487	49661	150076	2884272

Selected Financial Ratios (Times to 1)

Current Ratio	30	0.8	•	7.3	2.9	2.6	1.7	1.6	1.1	0.9	0.8	0.7	0.6	0.8
Quick Ratio	31	0.7	•	5.8	2.0	2.1	1.2	1.4	1.0	0.8	0.7	0.6	0.6	0.7
Net Sales to Working Capital	32	•	•	5.2	1.9	1.1	1.3	1.3	5.2	•	•	•	•	•
Coverage Ratio	33	2.2	1.9	31.5	17.2	5.2	4.4	3.9	3.5	2.7	2.7	2.5	2.3	2.2
Total Asset Turnover	34	0.1	•	2.9	1.0	0.5	0.4	0.3	0.2	0.1	0.1	0.1	0.1	0.1
Inventory Turnover	35	•	•	•	•	•	•	•	•	•	•	•	•	•
Receivables Turnover	36	•	•	•	•	•	•	•	•	•	•	•	•	•
Total Liabilities to Net Worth	37	5.8	•	0.5	1.4	1.5	•	2.7	4.8	9.7	7.3	6.1	5.6	5.8
Current Assets to Working Capital	38	•	•	1.2	1.5	1.6	2.4	2.6	13.9	•	•	•	•	•
Current Liabilities to Working Capital	39	•	•	0.2	0.5	0.6	1.4	1.6	12.9	•	•	•	•	•
Working Capital to Net Sales	40	•	•	0.2	0.5	0.9	0.8	0.8	0.2	•	•	•	•	•
Inventory to Working Capital	41	•	•	•	•	•	•	0.0	0.0	•	•	•	•	•
Total Receipts to Cash Flow	42	1.8	1.9	2.1	1.5	2.2	2.1	2.2	2.1	2.1	2.1	2.1	2.0	1.8
Cost of Goods to Cash Flow	43	0.0	0.0	•	•	0.0	•	0.0	•	0.0	0.0	0.0	0.0	0.0
Cash Flow to Total Debt	44	0.1	•	4.3	1.1	0.4	0.2	0.2	0.1	0.1	0.1	0.1	0.1	0.1

Selected Financial Factors (in Percentages)

Debt Ratio	45	85.4	•	32.1	58.7	60.6	117.0	72.7	82.8	90.7	87.9	85.8	84.9	85.3
Return on Total Assets	46	3.6	•	61.9	24.7	13.2	11.0	8.6	7.0	3.4	3.0	2.9	2.9	2.8
Return on Equity Before Income Taxes	47	13.8	•	88.2	56.2	26.9	•	23.5	29.0	23.5	15.4	12.0	11.0	10.6
Return on Equity After Income Taxes	48	10.2	•	86.1	54.6	25.8	•	22.4	26.6	21.1	13.1	9.2	7.8	7.4
Profit Margin (Before Income Tax)	49	19.6	24.2	20.9	23.6	19.8	21.6	19.3	19.9	16.5	17.5	17.8	18.8	19.0
Profit Margin (After Income Tax)	50	14.5	18.9	20.4	23.0	19.0	20.7	18.4	18.3	14.8	14.9	13.6	13.2	13.4

Table I

Corporations with and without Net Income

COMMERCIAL BANKING

MONEY AMOUNTS AND SIZE OF ASSETS IN THOUSANDS OF DOLLARS

Item Description for Accounting Period 7/11 Through 6/12		Total	Zero Assets	Under 500	500 to 1,000	1,000 to 5,000	5,000 to 10,000	10,000 to 25,000	25,000 to 50,000	50,000 to 100,000	100,000 to 250,000	250,000 to 500,000	500,000 to 2,500,000	2,500,000 and over
Number of Enterprises	1	1580	190	•	0	•	4	90	176	357	493	159	86	17
Revenues ($ in Thousands)														
Net Sales	2	78411934	43339855	•	0	•	26522	332535	911621	2151993	5720089	3419106	5818031	16657112
Interest	3	43704431	26032149	•	0	•	4409	41624	194693	649304	2257694	1629243	2519747	10373964
Rents	4	434869	128049	•	0	•	2	41	552	1714	5217	19606	6695	272993
Royalties	5	31482	19703	•	0	•	0	0	0	2	11637	31	0	109
Other Portfolio Income	6	4498915	1864595	•	0	•	5	2505	10909	111491	296937	196541	367818	1647518
Other Receipts	7	29742237	15295359	•	0	•	22106	288365	705467	1389482	3148604	1573685	2923771	4362528
Total Receipts	8	78411934	43339855	•	0	•	26522	332535	911621	2151993	5720089	3419106	5818031	16657112
Average Total Receipts	9	49628	228104	•	•	•	6630	3695	5180	6028	11603	21504	67652	979830
Operating Costs/Operating Income (%)														
Cost of Operations	10	0.1	•	•	•	•	•	•	•	•	•	0.6	•	0.2
Salaries and Wages	11	11.3	8.3	•	•	•	9.1	3.6	5.3	9.8	11.7	14.1	14.1	18.3
Taxes Paid	12	3.1	3.4	•	•	•	0.7	0.6	0.9	1.8	2.9	2.5	1.9	3.1
Interest Paid	13	23.2	30.7	•	•	•	6.3	3.4	5.7	10.0	11.8	13.6	14.6	15.9
Depreciation	14	2.3	1.1	•	•	•	0.3	0.5	0.8	1.8	1.9	2.3	2.0	5.6
Amortization and Depletion	15	0.7	0.2	•	•	•	0.1	0.1	0.4	0.2	0.5	0.4	0.7	2.5
Pensions and Other Deferred Comp.	16	0.7	0.4	•	•	•	0.1	0.1	0.2	0.4	0.5	0.5	0.8	1.5
Employee Benefits	17	1.3	0.9	•	•	•	0.5	1.0	1.1	1.9	1.8	2.1	1.7	1.9
Advertising	18	0.3	0.1	•	•	•	17.8	0.2	0.3	0.5	0.6	0.7	0.5	0.7
Other Expenses	19	46.6	41.6	•	•	•	267.7	99.8	91.7	77.4	61.4	64.9	66.5	35.5
Officers' Compensation	20	2.2	1.6	•	•	•	•	2.2	3.6	5.5	5.2	5.4	2.2	1.7
Operating Margin	21	8.1	11.7	•	•	•	•	•	•	•	1.8	•	•	13.0
Operating Margin Before Officers' Comp.	22	10.4	13.3	•	•	•	•	•	•	•	7.0	•	•	14.8

Selected Average Balance Sheet ($ in Thousands)

Net Receivables	23	197351	0	•	•	•	90	5842	14632	35712	84733	181970	466889	10888404
Inventories	24	•	•	•	•	•	•	•	•	•	•	•	•	•
Net Property, Plant and Equipment	25	4489	0	•	•	•	4	115	370	1168	2510	5339	12048	204561
Total Assets	26	384096	0	•	•	•	6883	18101	37497	72516	159236	340666	992147	20865859
Notes and Loans Payable	27	31262	0	•	•	•	0	1292	237	1432	4168	12119	40924	2424963
All Other Liabilities	28	313519	0	•	•	•	18102	25414	46988	74290	157196	338986	966115	14333746
Net Worth	29	39314	0	•	•	•	-11218	-8604	-9727	-3206	-2127	-10440	-14892	4107150

Selected Financial Ratios (Times to 1)

Current Ratio	30	1.0	•	•	•	•	0.5	1.0	1.1	1.0	1.0	0.9	0.9	1.0
Quick Ratio	31	1.0	•	•	•	•	0.5	0.9	1.0	0.9	0.9	0.9	0.9	1.0
Net Sales to Working Capital	32	•	•	•	•	•	•	20.0	1.7	•	•	•	•	4.6
Coverage Ratio	33	1.3	1.3	•	•	•	•	•	•	•	1.0	0.4	0.6	1.7
Total Asset Turnover	34	0.1	•	•	•	•	1.0	0.2	0.1	0.1	0.1	0.1	0.1	0.0
Inventory Turnover	35	•	•	•	•	•	•	•	•	•	•	•	•	•
Receivables Turnover	36	•	•	•	•	•	•	•	•	•	•	•	•	•
Total Liabilities to Net Worth	37	8.8	•	•	•	•	•	•	•	•	•	•	•	4.1
Current Assets to Working Capital	38	•	•	•	•	•	•	75.6	9.5	•	•	•	•	68.5
Current Liabilities to Working Capital	39	•	•	•	•	•	•	74.6	8.5	•	•	•	•	67.5
Working Capital to Net Sales	40	•	•	•	•	•	•	0.0	0.6	•	•	•	•	0.2
Inventory to Working Capital	41	•	•	•	•	•	•	•	•	•	•	•	•	0.0
Total Receipts to Cash Flow	42	2.3	2.2	•	•	•	•	2.1	3.7	2.6	2.5	2.8	2.4	2.2
Cost of Goods to Cash Flow	43	0.0	•	•	•	•	•	•	•	•	•	0.0	•	0.0
Cash Flow to Total Debt	44	0.1	•	•	•	•	•	0.1	0.0	0.0	0.0	0.0	0.0	0.0

Selected Financial Factors (in Percentages)

Debt Ratio	45	89.8	•	•	•	•	263.0	147.5	125.9	104.4	101.3	103.1	101.5	80.3
Return on Total Assets	46	3.8	•	•	•	•	•	•	•	•	0.9	0.3	0.6	1.3
Return on Equity Before Income Taxes	47	8.3	•	•	•	•	119.6	5.1	5.8	21.1	•	17.7	29.5	2.6
Return on Equity After Income Taxes	48	4.1	•	•	•	•	119.6	5.1	6.1	22.7	10.0	22.9	39.6	1.6
Profit Margin (Before Income Tax)	49	6.6	10.4	•	•	•	•	•	•	•	0.0	•	•	10.8
Profit Margin (After Income Tax)	50	3.2	6.7	•	•	•	•	•	•	•	•	•	•	6.8

Table II

Corporations with Net Income

COMMERCIAL BANKING

MONEY AMOUNTS AND SIZE OF ASSETS IN THOUSANDS OF DOLLARS

Item Description for Accounting Period 7/11 Through 6/12		Total	Zero Assets	Under 500	500 to 1,000	1,000 to 5,000	5,000 to 10,000	10,000 to 25,000	25,000 to 50,000	50,000 to 100,000	100,000 to 250,000	250,000 to 500,000	500,000 to 2,500,000	2,500,000 and over
Number of Enterprises	1	1013	113	0	0	•	0	•	93	225	342	110	62	14
Revenues ($ in Thousands)														
Net Sales	2	55260028	29725036	0	0	•	0	•	313031	938823	3263745	1931452	3390462	15634414
Interest	3	32540469	18129967	0	0	•	0	•	88659	372987	1550992	1091519	1705423	9578181
Rents	4	357108	63491	0	0	•	0	•	128	664	3493	11371	4939	272993
Royalties	5	31361	19668	0	0	•	0	•	0	2	11552	31	0	109
Other Portfolio Income	6	3491163	1177576	0	0	•	0	•	8187	46698	257634	101878	296210	1600945
Other Receipts	7	18839927	10334334	0	0	•	0	•	216057	518472	1440074	726653	1383890	4182186
Total Receipts	8	55260028	29725036	0	0	•	0	•	313031	938823	3263745	1931452	3390462	15634414
Average Total Receipts	9	54551	263053	•	•	•	•	•	3366	4173	9543	17559	54685	1116744
Operating Costs/Operating Income (%)														
Cost of Operations	10	0.1	•	•	•	•	•	•	•	•	•	1.1	•	0.2
Salaries and Wages	11	12.2	7.7	•	•	•	•	•	6.6	12.1	14.6	16.7	16.7	18.7
Taxes Paid	12	3.6	3.9	•	•	•	•	•	1.5	2.7	4.2	3.4	2.5	3.2
Interest Paid	13	21.7	26.9	•	•	•	•	•	7.6	13.8	14.4	15.9	18.1	15.4
Depreciation	14	2.5	0.8	•	•	•	•	•	1.1	2.3	2.3	2.8	2.7	5.9
Amortization and Depletion	15	0.9	0.2	•	•	•	•	•	0.3	0.2	0.6	0.5	0.7	2.5
Pensions and Other Deferred Comp.	16	0.8	0.4	•	•	•	•	•	0.5	0.7	0.8	0.8	1.2	1.6
Employee Benefits	17	1.4	0.9	•	•	•	•	•	1.9	3.0	2.3	2.9	2.2	1.9
Advertising	18	0.4	0.1	•	•	•	•	•	0.5	0.6	0.8	0.9	0.6	0.7
Other Expenses	19	32.9	33.1	•	•	•	•	•	27.1	37.0	32.6	26.2	31.9	33.4
Officers' Compensation	20	1.8	0.7	•	•	•	•	•	6.6	8.9	7.0	6.9	2.9	1.5
Operating Margin	21	21.7	25.3	•	•	•	•	•	46.3	18.5	20.3	22.1	20.6	15.0
Operating Margin Before Officers' Comp.	22	23.5	26.0	•	•	•	•	•	52.9	27.4	27.4	28.9	23.5	16.5

Selected Average Balance Sheet ($ in Thousands)													
Net Receivables **23**	269875	0	•	•	•	•	•	18015	39097	91105	205333	415406	13071782
Inventories **24**	•	•	•	•	•	•	•	•	•	•	•	•	•
Net Property, Plant and Equipment **25**	5731	0	•	•	•	•	•	386	1110	2585	5338	10773	240829
Total Assets **26**	503109	0	•	•	•	•	•	37445	73485	161092	339710	916228	24243896
Notes and Loans Payable **27**	43233	0	•	•	•	•	•	131	1395	4108	9693	32683	2775382
All Other Liabilities **28**	378302	0	•	•	•	•	•	38233	67179	142768	291440	805657	16633418
Net Worth **29**	81574	0	•	•	•	•	•	-919	4911	14216	38577	77888	4835096
Selected Financial Ratios (Times to 1)													
Current Ratio **30**	1.0	•	•	•	•	•	•	1.0	1.0	1.0	1.0	0.9	1.0
Quick Ratio **31**	1.0	•	•	•	•	•	•	1.0	1.0	1.0	0.9	0.9	1.0
Net Sales to Working Capital **32**	12.8	•	•	•	•	•	•	6.0	•	•	•	•	1.5
Coverage Ratio **33**	1.9	1.9	•	•	•	•	•	6.8	2.1	2.2	2.2	2.0	1.8
Total Asset Turnover **34**	0.1	•	•	•	•	•	•	0.1	0.1	0.1	0.1	0.1	0.0
Inventory Turnover **35**	•	•	•	•	•	•	•	•	•	•	•	•	•
Receivables Turnover **36**	•	•	•	•	•	•	•	•	•	•	•	•	•
Total Liabilities to Net Worth **37**	5.2	•	•	•	•	•	•	•	14.0	10.3	7.8	10.8	4.0
Current Assets to Working Capital **38**	88.9	•	•	•	•	•	•	58.7	•	•	•	•	23.9
Current Liabilities to Working Capital **39**	87.9	•	•	•	•	•	•	57.7	•	•	•	•	22.9
Working Capital to Net Sales **40**	0.1	•	•	•	•	•	•	0.2	•	•	•	•	0.7
Inventory to Working Capital **41**	0.0	•	•	•	•	•	•	•	•	•	•	•	0.0
Total Receipts to Cash Flow **42**	2.0	1.9	•	•	•	•	•	1.6	2.1	2.4	2.3	2.0	2.2
Cost of Goods to Cash Flow **43**	0.0	•	•	•	•	•	•	•	•	•	0.0	•	0.0
Cash Flow to Total Debt **44**	0.1	•	•	•	•	•	•	0.1	0.0	0.0	0.0	0.0	0.0
Selected Financial Factors (in Percentages)													
Debt Ratio **45**	83.8	•	•	•	•	•	•	102.5	93.3	91.2	88.6	91.5	80.1
Return on Total Assets **46**	4.5	•	•	•	•	•	•	4.6	1.6	1.9	1.8	2.2	1.3
Return on Equity Before Income Taxes **47**	13.4	•	•	•	•	•	•	•	12.8	11.9	8.9	12.9	2.9
Return on Equity After Income Taxes **48**	10.2	•	•	•	•	•	•	•	11.2	9.7	6.9	10.2	1.9
Profit Margin (Before Income Tax) **49**	20.0	24.3	•	•	•	•	•	44.1	15.1	17.8	19.7	18.4	12.5
Profit Margin (After Income Tax) **50**	15.3	19.0	•	•	•	•	•	42.7	13.2	14.5	15.2	14.6	8.2

Table I

Corporations with and without Net Income

SAVINGS INSTITUTIONS AND OTHER DEPOSITORY CREDIT

MONEY AMOUNTS AND SIZE OF ASSETS IN THOUSANDS OF DOLLARS

Item Description for Accounting Period 7/11 Through 6/12		Total	Zero Assets	Under 500	500 to 1,000	1,000 to 5,000	5,000 to 10,000	10,000 to 25,000	25,000 to 50,000	50,000 to 100,000	100,000 to 250,000	250,000 to 500,000	500,000 to 2,500,000	2,500,000 and over
Number of Enterprises	1	1306	246	0	•	•	0	20	93	141	260	194	224	52
Revenues ($ in Thousands)														
Net Sales	2	59106175	484049	0	•	•	0	11834	174067	694622	2562690	3619024	11829915	39649468
Interest	3	40425089	247480	0	•	•	0	9847	131918	414190	1644149	2602176	8040378	27325022
Rents	4	555108	989	0	•	•	0	122	736	2262	6987	10791	59930	473224
Royalties	5	1948	0	0	•	•	0	0	15	0	0	0	1280	653
Other Portfolio Income	6	2627278	27508	0	•	•	0	0	4404	20453	111380	165475	743974	1553319
Other Receipts	7	15496752	208072	0	•	•	0	1865	36994	257717	800174	840582	2984353	10297250
Total Receipts	8	59106175	484049	0	•	•	0	11834	174067	694622	2562690	3619024	11829915	39649468
Average Total Receipts	9	45257	1968	•	•	•	•	592	1872	4926	9856	18655	52812	762490
Operating Costs/Operating Income (%)														
Cost of Operations	10	0.0	•	•	•	•	•	•	•	•	1.0	•	•	•
Salaries and Wages	11	14.1	20.3	•	•	•	•	18.3	19.7	11.4	15.2	18.4	18.1	12.4
Taxes Paid	12	2.5	2.4	•	•	•	•	2.5	4.1	2.6	3.0	3.2	2.8	2.4
Interest Paid	13	21.9	12.0	•	•	•	•	26.8	20.0	17.7	17.6	21.3	19.5	23.1
Depreciation	14	2.8	1.2	•	•	•	•	2.8	2.6	1.9	4.4	2.7	2.9	2.7
Amortization and Depletion	15	1.2	0.1	•	•	•	•	•	0.2	0.1	0.3	0.2	0.6	1.6
Pensions and Other Deferred Comp.	16	1.4	0.5	•	•	•	•	1.3	2.6	1.6	1.7	2.1	1.9	1.2
Employee Benefits	17	2.2	2.9	•	•	•	•	3.0	4.1	2.4	2.7	3.3	2.8	1.9
Advertising	18	1.2	0.5	•	•	•	•	0.8	1.0	0.7	1.0	1.3	1.3	1.2
Other Expenses	19	42.4	50.8	•	•	•	•	1104.2	41.1	53.9	42.2	47.7	43.3	41.0
Officers' Compensation	20	1.8	7.4	•	•	•	•	4.3	10.7	6.2	4.9	4.4	2.6	0.9
Operating Margin	21	8.4	1.8	•	•	•	•	•	•	1.6	6.0	•	4.3	11.6
Operating Margin Before Officers' Comp.	22	10.2	9.2	•	•	•	•	•	4.6	7.8	10.8	•	6.8	12.5

Selected Average Balance Sheet ($ in Thousands)													
Net Receivables **23**	56749	0	•	•	•	•	753	2725	6831	15796	22846	65001	957194
Inventories **24**	•	•	•	•	•	•	•	•	•	•	•	•	•
Net Property, Plant and Equipment **25**	8131	0	•	•	•	•	216	611	1398	3280	6376	14995	94468
Total Assets **26**	813495	0	•	•	•	•	15354	38473	75976	163063	357542	972282	13811146
Notes and Loans Payable **27**	83722	0	•	•	•	•	348	1075	3482	9494	24421	58097	1702365
All Other Liabilities **28**	657626	0	•	•	•	•	30455	32104	68685	135813	303702	837440	10841072
Net Worth **29**	72148	0	•	•	•	•	-15449	5294	3809	17755	29419	76745	1267709
Selected Financial Ratios (Times to 1)													
Current Ratio **30**	0.3	•	•	•	•	•	0.4	0.4	0.4	0.3	0.3	0.3	0.3
Quick Ratio **31**	0.2	•	•	•	•	•	0.4	0.4	0.4	0.3	0.3	0.3	0.2
Net Sales to Working Capital **32**	•	•	•	•	•	•	•	•	•	•	•	•	•
Coverage Ratio **33**	1.3	1.1	•	•	•	•	•	0.7	1.0	1.3	0.7	1.2	1.5
Total Asset Turnover **34**	0.1	•	•	•	•	•	0.0	0.0	0.1	0.1	0.1	0.1	0.1
Inventory Turnover **35**	•	•	•	•	•	•	•	•	•	•	•	•	•
Receivables Turnover **36**	•	•	•	•	•	•	•	•	•	•	•	•	•
Total Liabilities to Net Worth **37**	10.3	•	•	•	•	•	•	6.3	18.9	8.2	11.2	11.7	9.9
Current Assets to Working Capital **38**	•	•	•	•	•	•	•	•	•	•	•	•	•
Current Liabilities to Working Capital **39**	•	•	•	•	•	•	•	•	•	•	•	•	•
Working Capital to Net Sales **40**	•	•	•	•	•	•	•	•	•	•	•	•	•
Inventory to Working Capital **41**	•	•	•	•	•	•	•	•	•	•	•	•	•
Total Receipts to Cash Flow **42**	2.3	2.2	•	•	•	•	2.9	3.4	2.6	2.5	3.4	2.6	2.1
Cost of Goods to Cash Flow **43**	0.0	•	•	•	•	•	•	•	•	0.0	•	•	•
Cash Flow to Total Debt **44**	0.0	•	•	•	•	•	0.0	0.0	0.0	0.0	0.0	0.0	0.0
Selected Financial Factors (in Percentages)													
Debt Ratio **45**	91.1	•	•	•	•	•	200.6	86.2	95.0	89.1	91.8	92.1	90.8
Return on Total Assets **46**	1.6	•	•	•	•	•	•	0.6	1.2	1.3	0.8	1.2	1.9
Return on Equity Before Income Taxes **47**	4.8	•	•	•	•	•	40.8	•	0.6	2.6	•	2.2	6.7
Return on Equity After Income Taxes **48**	2.4	•	•	•	•	•	40.8	•	•	1.1	•	•	4.2
Profit Margin (Before Income Tax) **49**	7.7	1.3	•	•	•	•	•	•	0.4	4.7	•	3.2	11.1
Profit Margin (After Income Tax) **50**	3.9	0.2	•	•	•	•	•	•	•	2.0	•	•	6.9

Table II

Corporations with Net Income

SAVINGS INSTITUTIONS AND OTHER DEPOSITORY CREDIT

MONEY AMOUNTS AND SIZE OF ASSETS IN THOUSANDS OF DOLLARS

Item Description for Accounting Period 7/11 Through 6/12		Total	Zero Assets	Under 500	500 to 1,000	1,000 to 5,000	5,000 to 10,000	10,000 to 25,000	25,000 to 50,000	50,000 to 100,000	100,000 to 250,000	250,000 to 500,000	500,000 to 2,500,000	2,500,000 and over
Number of Enterprises	1	762	16	0	0	•	0	•	55	100	202	144	167	43
Revenues ($ in Thousands)														
Net Sales	2	46427053	198594	0	0	•	0	•	104842	466524	2003295	2492725	8177109	32948384
Interest	3	32802200	117443	0	0	•	0	•	82292	295043	1309350	1936019	6005548	23049666
Rents	4	281843	510	0	0	•	0	•	137	1316	4280	7012	35235	233327
Royalties	5	1903	0	0	0	•	0	•	15	0	0	0	1235	653
Other Portfolio Income	6	1761792	25079	0	0	•	0	•	2144	13481	80511	120203	528146	992225
Other Receipts	7	11579315	55562	0	0	•	0	•	20254	156684	609154	429491	1606945	8672513
Total Receipts	8	46427053	198594	0	0	•	0	•	104842	466524	2003295	2492725	8177109	32948384
Average Total Receipts	9	60928	12412	•	•	•	•	•	1906	4665	9917	17311	48965	766241
Operating Costs/Operating Income (%)														
Cost of Operations	10	0.1	•	•	•	•	•	•	•	•	1.2	•	•	•
Salaries and Wages	11	13.8	17.8	•	•	•	•	•	12.8	10.7	15.0	17.6	19.1	12.2
Taxes Paid	12	2.7	2.3	•	•	•	•	•	3.8	2.6	3.1	3.5	3.1	2.5
Interest Paid	13	21.1	16.3	•	•	•	•	•	21.5	18.5	17.5	21.4	20.6	21.5
Depreciation	14	2.5	1.5	•	•	•	•	•	2.0	1.7	2.3	3.1	3.1	2.3
Amortization and Depletion	15	1.2	0.1	•	•	•	•	•	0.0	0.1	0.4	0.2	0.4	1.6
Pensions and Other Deferred Comp.	16	1.5	0.6	•	•	•	•	•	2.7	1.7	1.8	2.3	2.3	1.3
Employee Benefits	17	2.2	2.5	•	•	•	•	•	3.2	2.5	2.6	3.5	3.0	1.9
Advertising	18	1.3	0.8	•	•	•	•	•	0.9	0.7	1.0	1.2	1.4	1.3
Other Expenses	19	31.9	35.4	•	•	•	•	•	21.9	36.3	35.9	25.8	27.3	33.2
Officers' Compensation	20	1.7	2.2	•	•	•	•	•	10.8	6.3	4.9	5.0	2.7	0.9
Operating Margin	21	19.9	20.4	•	•	•	•	•	20.4	19.0	14.2	16.4	17.1	21.2
Operating Margin Before Officers' Comp.	22	21.6	22.6	•	•	•	•	•	31.2	25.3	19.1	21.4	19.8	22.1

Selected Average Balance Sheet ($ in Thousands)

Net Receivables 23	78036	0	•	•	•	•	•	1082	5842	15391	22839	70079	946867
Inventories 24	•	•	•	•	•	•	•	•	•	•	•	•	•
Net Property, Plant and Equipment 25	11018	0	•	•	•	•	•	561	1202	3246	6791	15023	95331
Total Assets 26	1128403	0	•	•	•	•	•	38128	76111	163366	355665	962450	14069467
Notes and Loans Payable 27	103231	0	•	•	•	•	•	1129	2974	8860	24247	49158	1507092
All Other Liabilities 28	894959	0	•	•	•	•	•	30971	68488	134735	286932	807170	10929052
Net Worth 29	130213	0	•	•	•	•	•	6028	4650	19772	44486	106122	1633322

Selected Financial Ratios (Times to 1)

Current Ratio 30	0.3	•	•	•	•	•	•	0.3	0.4	0.3	0.3	0.3	0.3
Quick Ratio 31	0.2	•	•	•	•	•	•	0.3	0.3	0.3	0.3	0.3	0.2
Net Sales to Working Capital 32	•	•	•	•	•	•	•	•	•	•	•	•	•
Coverage Ratio 33	1.9	2.2	•	•	•	•	•	1.9	2.0	1.7	1.7	1.8	2.0
Total Asset Turnover 34	0.1	•	•	•	•	•	•	0.0	0.1	0.1	0.0	0.1	0.1
Inventory Turnover 35	•	•	•	•	•	•	•	•	•	•	•	•	•
Receivables Turnover 36	•	•	•	•	•	•	•	•	•	•	•	•	•
Total Liabilities to Net Worth 37	7.7	•	•	•	•	•	•	5.3	15.4	7.3	7.0	8.1	7.6
Current Assets to Working Capital 38	•	•	•	•	•	•	•	•	•	•	•	•	•
Current Liabilities to Working Capital 39	•	•	•	•	•	•	•	•	•	•	•	•	•
Working Capital to Net Sales 40	•	•	•	•	•	•	•	•	•	•	•	•	•
Inventory to Working Capital 41	•	•	•	•	•	•	•	•	•	•	•	•	•
Total Receipts to Cash Flow 42	2.1	2.4	•	•	•	•	•	2.5	2.0	2.3	2.6	2.5	2.0
Cost of Goods to Cash Flow 43	0.0	•	•	•	•	•	•	•	•	0.0	•	•	•
Cash Flow to Total Debt 44	0.0	•	•	•	•	•	•	0.0	0.0	0.0	0.0	0.0	0.0

Selected Financial Factors (in Percentages)

Debt Ratio 45	88.5	•	•	•	•	•	•	84.2	93.9	87.9	87.5	89.0	88.4
Return on Total Assets 46	2.2	•	•	•	•	•	•	2.1	2.2	1.8	1.7	1.9	2.3
Return on Equity Before Income Taxes 47	8.9	•	•	•	•	•	•	6.2	17.7	6.5	5.7	7.3	9.7
Return on Equity After Income Taxes 48	6.7	•	•	•	•	•	•	4.9	14.6	4.7	3.9	5.1	7.4
Profit Margin (Before Income Tax) 49	19.1	20.1	•	•	•	•	•	19.8	17.6	12.9	14.5	15.9	20.6
Profit Margin (After Income Tax) 50	14.3	17.4	•	•	•	•	•	15.6	14.6	9.4	10.0	11.1	15.7

Table I

Corporations with and without Net Income

CREDIT CARD ISSUING AND OTHER CONSUMER CREDIT

MONEY AMOUNTS AND SIZE OF ASSETS IN THOUSANDS OF DOLLARS

Item Description for Accounting Period 7/11 Through 6/12		Total	Zero Assets	Under 500	500 to 1,000	1,000 to 5,000	5,000 to 10,000	10,000 to 25,000	25,000 to 50,000	50,000 to 100,000	100,000 to 250,000	250,000 to 500,000	500,000 to 2,500,000	2,500,000 and over
Number of Enterprises	1	6831	1421	2449	1141	1040	195	306	107	45	57	26	30	14
Revenues ($ in Thousands)														
Net Sales	2	102773538	829916	339720	225875	901041	412696	1707071	1110617	1067655	2710380	3498693	5433386	84536489
Interest	3	30878153	56506	12028	6725	32336	29870	25242	65590	111783	428576	226407	1741700	28141391
Rents	4	23339	292	0	0	342	306	474	99	0	724	2856	8666	9581
Royalties	5	581199	0	0	0	0	0	0	0	0	19966	9117	0	552115
Other Portfolio Income	6	4760707	95999	393	14	3452	888	1651	7675	11747	12639	8130	157987	4460131
Other Receipts	7	66530140	677119	327299	219136	864911	381632	1679704	1037253	944125	2248475	3252183	3525033	51373271
Total Receipts	8	102773538	829916	339720	225875	901041	412696	1707071	1110617	1067655	2710380	3498693	5433386	84536489
Average Total Receipts	9	15045	584	139	198	866	2116	5579	10380	23726	47551	134565	181113	6038321
Operating Costs/Operating Income (%)														
Cost of Operations	10	0.9	0.2	•	•	0.3	•	0.1	•	•	0.2	0.1	0.7	1.1
Salaries and Wages	11	9.1	17.6	16.1	12.7	22.0	19.5	20.4	17.6	21.5	19.1	17.0	13.5	7.3
Taxes Paid	12	1.4	3.7	3.0	2.9	3.4	2.7	2.5	2.4	2.8	2.5	2.8	2.3	1.2
Interest Paid	13	18.3	7.0	5.2	5.2	10.6	7.6	9.4	10.6	7.8	11.2	7.5	14.8	20.0
Depreciation	14	11.3	0.9	1.5	0.9	2.4	1.3	1.7	2.2	4.0	4.8	3.9	2.2	13.1
Amortization and Depletion	15	1.2	1.6	•	0.0	0.7	0.1	0.3	0.9	0.1	0.6	0.6	2.1	1.3
Pensions and Other Deferred Comp.	16	0.6	0.1	0.8	0.2	0.2	0.4	0.4	0.3	0.8	0.5	0.2	0.3	0.7
Employee Benefits	17	0.9	3.6	0.1	1.5	1.3	2.6	1.4	1.4	1.3	1.1	1.7	1.4	0.7
Advertising	18	3.1	1.5	2.9	3.6	1.5	1.5	2.3	1.4	1.8	1.6	2.6	1.6	3.4
Other Expenses	19	43.7	45.5	60.5	67.6	48.5	39.5	38.1	42.5	34.3	37.6	46.0	39.4	44.1
Officers' Compensation	20	0.8	0.9	19.6	7.8	9.7	3.5	9.1	5.7	3.4	2.9	1.3	1.2	0.2
Operating Margin	21	8.7	17.4	•	•	•	21.3	14.2	14.9	22.1	17.9	16.3	20.5	7.0
Operating Margin Before Officers' Comp.	22	9.4	18.4	9.8	5.4	9.1	24.8	23.3	20.6	25.6	20.8	17.6	21.7	7.2

Selected Average Balance Sheet ($ in Thousands)													
Net Receivables 23	54495	0	32	340	1585	3260	11482	26189	47889	79539	179679	712038	23604725
Inventories 24	•	•	•	•	•	•	•	•	•	•	•	•	•
Net Property, Plant and Equipment 25	5621	0	14	30	54	247	273	628	2543	3194	10146	8497	2661443
Total Assets 26	119176	0	153	713	2478	6929	16234	36389	68229	149979	378970	1123173	53210262
Notes and Loans Payable 27	54402	0	196	498	1033	3103	9641	23204	31577	84446	207401	703404	23623778
All Other Liabilities 28	47847	0	11	126	278	907	3055	6178	16072	34931	77039	256556	22299895
Net Worth 29	16926	0	-54	90	1167	2918	3537	7007	20580	30602	94530	163213	7286589

Selected Financial Ratios (Times to 1)													
Current Ratio 30	1.5	•	6.0	4.0	4.4	2.1	2.4	3.0	2.7	2.0	2.1	1.7	1.4
Quick Ratio 31	1.4	•	4.8	2.8	3.9	1.4	2.2	2.8	2.5	1.7	1.8	1.6	1.4
Net Sales to Working Capital 32	0.7	•	1.5	0.5	0.5	0.7	0.7	0.5	0.7	1.0	0.9	0.6	0.7
Coverage Ratio 33	1.5	3.5	•	0.6	0.9	3.8	2.5	2.4	3.8	2.6	3.2	2.4	1.4
Total Asset Turnover 34	0.1	•	0.9	0.3	0.3	0.3	0.3	0.3	0.3	0.3	0.4	0.2	0.1
Inventory Turnover 35	•	•	•	•	•	•	•	•	•	•	•	•	•
Receivables Turnover 36	•	•	•	•	•	•	•	•	•	•	•	•	•
Total Liabilities to Net Worth 37	6.0	•	•	7.0	1.1	1.4	3.6	4.2	2.3	3.9	3.0	5.9	6.3
Current Assets to Working Capital 38	3.1	•	1.2	1.3	1.3	1.9	1.7	1.5	1.6	2.1	1.9	2.5	3.3
Current Liabilities to Working Capital 39	2.1	•	0.2	0.3	0.3	0.9	0.7	0.5	0.6	1.1	0.9	1.5	2.3
Working Capital to Net Sales 40	1.5	•	0.7	2.0	1.9	1.4	1.4	2.0	1.5	1.0	1.1	1.8	1.5
Inventory to Working Capital 41	0.0	•	•	•	•	•	0.0	0.0	•	0.0	0.0	0.0	0.0
Total Receipts to Cash Flow 42	2.0	2.3	2.1	1.7	2.3	1.7	2.1	1.8	1.9	1.9	1.8	1.9	2.0
Cost of Goods to Cash Flow 43	0.0	0.0	•	•	0.0	•	0.0	•	•	0.0	0.0	0.0	0.0
Cash Flow to Total Debt 44	0.1	•	0.3	0.2	0.3	0.3	0.2	0.2	0.3	0.2	0.3	0.1	0.1

Selected Financial Factors (in Percentages)													
Debt Ratio 45	85.8	•	135.0	87.4	52.9	57.9	78.2	80.7	69.8	79.6	75.1	85.5	86.3
Return on Total Assets 46	3.5	•	•	0.8	3.5	8.8	8.1	7.3	10.4	9.2	8.5	5.7	3.2
Return on Equity Before Income Taxes 47	8.3	•	25.4	•	•	15.5	22.5	22.1	25.5	27.8	23.2	22.6	6.5
Return on Equity After Income Taxes 48	5.4	•	27.4	•	•	13.8	21.2	21.1	23.2	25.0	18.2	15.0	3.9
Profit Margin (Before Income Tax) 49	9.4	17.4	•	•	•	21.3	14.2	14.9	22.1	17.9	16.3	20.3	7.8
Profit Margin (After Income Tax) 50	6.1	10.7	•	•	•	19.0	13.4	14.3	20.2	16.1	12.8	13.5	4.7

Table II

Corporations with Net Income

CREDIT CARD ISSUING AND OTHER CONSUMER CREDIT

MONEY AMOUNTS AND SIZE OF ASSETS IN THOUSANDS OF DOLLARS

Item Description for Accounting Period 7/11 Through 6/12		Total	Zero Assets	Under 500	500 to 1,000	1,000 to 5,000	5,000 to 10,000	10,000 to 25,000	25,000 to 50,000	50,000 to 100,000	100,000 to 250,000	250,000 to 500,000	500,000 to 2,500,000	2,500,000 and over
Number of Enterprises	1	3720	955	825	580	779	135	243	70	38	41	23	20	11
Revenues ($ in Thousands)														
Net Sales	2	80186777	599964	307225	159799	802217	264496	1487102	972949	1027568	2373798	3405503	4945562	63840593
Interest	3	22295207	345	11049	23	24473	28688	15879	49239	102204	376595	169557	1476136	20041016
Rents	4	22840	4	0	0	342	306	262	99	0	724	2856	8666	9581
Royalties	5	581199	0	0	0	0	0	0	0	0	19966	9117	0	552115
Other Portfolio Income	6	968018	95999	0	14	2003	888	1239	3235	11496	9444	8130	138575	696993
Other Receipts	7	56319513	503616	296176	159762	775399	234614	1469722	920376	913868	1967069	3215843	3322185	42540888
Total Receipts	8	80186777	599964	307225	159799	802217	264496	1487102	972949	1027568	2373798	3405503	4945562	63840593
Average Total Receipts	9	21556	628	372	276	1030	1959	6120	13899	27041	57898	148065	247278	5803690
Operating Costs/Operating Income (%)														
Cost of Operations	10	0.7	0.3	•	•	0.3	•	0.2	•	•	•	0.1	0.8	0.8
Salaries and Wages	11	9.5	20.6	17.0	2.8	20.1	14.4	19.1	16.8	21.9	19.0	17.1	13.8	7.7
Taxes Paid	12	1.5	4.6	2.6	1.4	2.7	2.3	2.5	2.3	2.8	2.6	2.8	2.3	1.2
Interest Paid	13	12.4	2.4	3.3	1.3	8.6	6.8	8.0	9.3	7.5	7.7	6.3	9.7	13.6
Depreciation	14	5.1	1.1	0.8	0.6	1.9	0.4	0.9	0.7	2.1	2.6	4.0	1.8	5.8
Amortization and Depletion	15	1.4	0.9	•	•	0.1	0.0	0.3	0.2	0.1	0.4	0.6	2.1	1.5
Pensions and Other Deferred Comp.	16	0.5	0.2	0.9	•	0.2	0.2	0.3	0.3	0.8	0.5	0.2	0.3	0.5
Employee Benefits	17	0.8	2.9	0.0	0.1	1.1	1.3	1.2	1.2	1.2	1.1	1.7	1.4	0.7
Advertising	18	3.7	2.1	3.0	3.5	1.0	0.8	2.4	1.3	1.9	1.3	2.5	1.6	4.2
Other Expenses	19	47.6	33.0	28.4	67.1	39.4	34.1	36.0	39.4	33.7	36.3	44.8	38.8	49.9
Officers' Compensation	20	0.8	1.1	17.6	3.4	10.1	4.3	7.8	5.4	3.4	2.9	1.3	1.0	0.2
Operating Margin	21	15.9	30.9	26.5	19.7	14.2	35.4	21.3	23.2	24.6	25.7	18.5	26.4	14.0
Operating Margin Before Officers' Comp.	22	16.8	32.0	44.1	23.1	24.4	39.7	29.1	28.6	28.0	28.5	19.8	27.4	14.2

Selected Average Balance Sheet ($ in Thousands)

Net Receivables 23	70398	0	22	127	1600	2719	12176	27791	48785	91421	169524	756542	20967121
Inventories 24	•	•	•	•	•	•	•	•	•	•	•	•	•
Net Property, Plant and Equipment 25	6283	0	21	0	39	51	195	402	2828	3955	11444	12399	2041798
Total Assets 26	151552	0	74	692	2291	6385	16517	35707	68382	152027	375792	1193747	46618292
Notes and Loans Payable 27	57629	0	24	372	879	2982	9177	19869	32001	77649	187895	495027	17346762
All Other Liabilities 28	70136	0	8	157	313	1190	2982	7019	14392	32587	84386	354907	22569467
Net Worth 29	23787	0	41	163	1099	2214	4358	8818	21989	41791	103512	343812	6702062

Selected Financial Ratios (Times to 1)

Current Ratio 30	1.6	•	5.7	3.5	3.4	2.1	2.5	2.9	3.0	2.2	2.1	1.7	1.5
Quick Ratio 31	1.5	•	5.7	1.2	3.0	1.2	2.2	2.7	2.7	2.0	1.7	1.6	1.5
Net Sales to Working Capital 32	0.7	•	8.9	0.9	0.7	0.7	0.7	0.7	0.7	1.0	1.0	0.7	0.7
Coverage Ratio 33	2.3	13.7	9.1	15.8	2.6	6.2	3.7	3.5	4.3	4.3	3.9	3.7	2.0
Total Asset Turnover 34	0.1	•	5.0	0.4	0.4	0.3	0.4	0.4	0.4	0.4	0.4	0.2	0.1
Inventory Turnover 35	•	•	•	•	•	•	•	•	•	•	•	•	•
Receivables Turnover 36	•	•	•	•	•	•	•	•	•	•	•	•	•
Total Liabilities to Net Worth 37	5.4	•	0.8	3.2	1.1	1.9	2.8	3.0	2.1	2.6	2.6	2.5	6.0
Current Assets to Working Capital 38	2.8	•	1.2	1.4	1.4	1.9	1.7	1.5	1.5	1.9	1.9	2.4	2.9
Current Liabilities to Working Capital 39	1.8	•	0.2	0.4	0.4	0.9	0.7	0.5	0.5	0.9	0.9	1.4	1.9
Working Capital to Net Sales 40	1.5	•	0.1	1.1	1.4	1.4	1.4	1.5	1.4	1.0	1.0	1.4	1.5
Inventory to Working Capital 41	0.0	•	•	•	•	•	0.0	•	•	0.0	0.0	0.0	0.0
Total Receipts to Cash Flow 42	1.6	2.5	1.8	1.2	2.0	1.5	1.8	1.7	1.8	1.7	1.7	1.7	1.6
Cost of Goods to Cash Flow 43	0.0	0.0	•	•	0.0	•	0.0	•	•	•	0.0	0.0	0.0
Cash Flow to Total Debt 44	0.1	•	6.2	0.4	0.4	0.3	0.3	0.3	0.3	0.3	0.3	0.2	0.1

Selected Financial Factors (in Percentages)

Debt Ratio 45	84.3	•	44.2	76.4	52.0	65.3	73.6	75.3	67.8	72.5	72.5	71.2	85.6
Return on Total Assets 46	4.0	•	150.0	8.4	10.3	12.9	10.9	12.6	12.7	12.7	9.8	7.4	3.4
Return on Equity Before Income Taxes 47	14.4	•	239.2	33.1	13.3	31.3	30.0	36.6	30.2	35.5	26.5	18.9	12.1
Return on Equity After Income Taxes 48	10.7	•	231.7	31.9	12.9	28.2	28.6	35.4	27.7	32.6	21.3	13.5	8.5
Profit Margin (Before Income Tax) 49	15.9	30.8	26.5	19.7	14.2	35.4	21.3	23.2	24.5	25.6	18.5	26.2	14.0
Profit Margin (After Income Tax) 50	11.8	21.6	25.7	18.9	13.8	31.9	20.4	22.5	22.5	23.5	14.9	18.7	9.8

Table I

Corporations with and without Net Income

REAL ESTATE CREDIT INCL. MORTGAGE BANKERS AND ORIGINATORS

MONEY AMOUNTS AND SIZE OF ASSETS IN THOUSANDS OF DOLLARS

Item Description for Accounting Period 7/11 Through 6/12		Total	Zero Assets	Under 500	500 to 1,000	1,000 to 5,000	5,000 to 10,000	10,000 to 25,000	25,000 to 50,000	50,000 to 100,000	100,000 to 250,000	250,000 to 500,000	500,000 to 2,500,000	2,500,000 and over
Number of Enterprises	1	7205	1149	4184	206	996	178	246	96	72	47	15	9	7
Revenues ($ in Thousands)														
Net Sales	2	14878042	278583	954478	448935	548418	419300	1100636	922843	1338329	1796737	1326849	557524	5185410
Interest	3	1679849	24555	2056	1694	88872	6063	38867	30177	34957	97848	21815	182844	1150102
Rents	4	15850	0	1274	0	1960	63	3873	368	854	3381	7	3786	285
Royalties	5	51	0	0	0	0	0	0	0	51	0	0	0	0
Other Portfolio Income	6	1701498	32561	3513	0	12942	116207	2451	615	13970	73824	4683	2389	1438342
Other Receipts	7	11480794	221467	947635	447241	444644	296967	1055445	891683	1288497	1621684	1300344	368505	2596681
Total Receipts	8	14878042	278583	954478	448935	548418	419300	1100636	922843	1338329	1796737	1326849	557524	5185410
Average Total Receipts	9	2065	242	228	2179	551	2356	4474	9613	18588	38228	88457	61947	740773
Operating Costs/Operating Income (%)														
Cost of Operations	10	0.6	•	•	•	•	•	•	•	•	•	•	6.8	0.9
Salaries and Wages	11	28.2	33.5	30.5	11.7	16.7	26.6	39.0	42.2	42.3	38.5	43.9	26.4	14.3
Taxes Paid	12	3.3	7.4	4.2	1.5	5.2	3.2	4.4	4.3	4.1	4.3	4.2	3.1	1.8
Interest Paid	13	11.2	12.3	0.6	4.4	12.4	5.3	6.8	6.8	7.0	8.3	5.4	26.3	17.8
Depreciation	14	1.4	1.4	1.3	0.9	1.5	3.2	1.1	1.1	1.3	1.3	1.1	1.6	1.5
Amortization and Depletion	15	0.7	1.9	0.1	•	2.7	0.3	0.2	0.3	0.2	0.1	0.6	1.7	1.1
Pensions and Other Deferred Comp.	16	0.3	0.4	0.0	3.7	0.3	0.2	0.2	0.2	0.3	0.3	0.1	0.3	0.1
Employee Benefits	17	1.3	1.9	0.8	0.2	0.9	1.0	1.6	2.0	1.6	1.5	1.8	1.5	1.1
Advertising	18	3.5	0.9	2.3	0.2	10.5	0.5	3.6	2.7	2.0	3.3	7.7	1.1	3.3
Other Expenses	19	64.5	44.9	40.0	58.7	66.7	48.4	45.3	32.2	36.8	39.3	29.7	63.5	106.4
Officers' Compensation	20	4.9	1.6	23.1	9.6	7.1	9.8	6.4	5.3	3.8	8.5	2.0	1.7	0.3
Operating Margin	21	•	•	•	9.1	•	1.6	•	3.0	0.6	•	3.7	•	•
Operating Margin Before Officers' Comp.	22	•	•	20.2	18.7	•	11.3	•	8.3	4.4	3.1	5.7	•	•

Selected Average Balance Sheet ($ in Thousands)														
Net Receivables	23	2202	0	1	3	603	1204	3612	8468	13006	12999	39879	339228	1163826
Inventories	24	•	•	•	•	•	•	•	•	•	•	•	•	•
Net Property, Plant and Equipment	25	205	0	9	22	332	181	480	819	1416	5619	2942	6732	58021
Total Assets	26	11355	0	90	730	2750	6974	15643	34401	70260	174842	325084	1101979	6011464
Notes and Loans Payable	27	4421	0	46	1102	1213	5456	7835	21069	42843	117672	210448	718821	1008718
All Other Liabilities	28	4603	0	2	114	745	1610	5967	11303	17933	114379	84475	281313	2726454
Net Worth	29	2331	0	42	-486	793	-92	1840	2029	9484	-57209	30160	101844	2276292

Selected Financial Ratios (Times to 1)														
Current Ratio	30	0.7	•	1.8	0.5	1.6	0.6	0.6	0.8	0.5	0.3	0.4	0.7	0.9
Quick Ratio	31	0.6	•	1.7	0.4	1.3	0.6	0.5	0.6	0.4	0.2	0.2	0.6	0.9
Net Sales to Working Capital	32	•	•	12.1	•	1.3	•	•	•	•	•	•	•	•
Coverage Ratio	33	•	0.0	•	3.1	•	1.3	•	1.4	1.1	0.3	1.7	•	•
Total Asset Turnover	34	0.2	•	2.5	3.0	0.2	0.3	0.3	0.3	0.3	0.2	0.3	0.1	0.1
Inventory Turnover	35	•	•	•	•	•	•	•	•	•	•	•	•	•
Receivables Turnover	36	•	•	•	•	•	•	•	•	•	•	•	•	•
Total Liabilities to Net Worth	37	3.9	•	1.1	•	2.5	•	7.5	16.0	6.4	•	9.8	9.8	1.6
Current Assets to Working Capital	38	•	•	2.3	•	2.7	•	•	•	•	•	•	•	•
Current Liabilities to Working Capital	39	•	•	1.3	•	1.7	•	•	•	•	•	•	•	•
Working Capital to Net Sales	40	•	•	0.1	•	0.7	•	•	•	•	•	•	•	•
Inventory to Working Capital	41	•	•	•	•	•	•	•	•	•	•	•	•	•
Total Receipts to Cash Flow	42	2.5	3.1	3.3	1.5	2.9	2.1	3.0	3.2	3.4	3.3	3.5	4.2	1.8
Cost of Goods to Cash Flow	43	0.0	•	•	•	•	•	•	•	•	•	•	0.3	0.0
Cash Flow to Total Debt	44	0.1	•	1.4	1.2	0.1	0.2	0.1	0.1	0.1	0.0	0.1	0.0	0.1

Selected Financial Factors (in Percentages)														
Debt Ratio	45	79.5	•	53.0	166.6	71.2	101.3	88.2	94.1	86.5	132.7	90.7	90.8	62.1
Return on Total Assets	46	•	•	•	40.4	•	2.3	•	2.7	2.0	0.6	2.5	•	•
Return on Equity Before Income Taxes	47	•	•	•	•	•	•	•	14.0	1.0	3.6	10.8	•	•
Return on Equity After Income Taxes	48	•	•	•	•	•	•	•	8.1	0.2	3.9	8.0	•	•
Profit Margin (Before Income Tax)	49	•	•	•	9.1	•	1.6	•	3.0	0.5	•	3.7	•	•
Profit Margin (After Income Tax)	50	•	•	•	9.1	•	1.5	•	1.7	0.1	•	2.7	•	•

Table II

Corporations with Net Income

REAL ESTATE CREDIT INCL. MORTGAGE BANKERS AND ORIGINATORS

MONEY AMOUNTS AND SIZE OF ASSETS IN THOUSANDS OF DOLLARS

Item Description for Accounting Period 7/11 Through 6/12		Total	Zero Assets	Under 500	500 to 1,000	1,000 to 5,000	5,000 to 10,000	10,000 to 25,000	25,000 to 50,000	50,000 to 100,000	100,000 to 250,000	250,000 to 500,000	500,000 to 2,500,000	2,500,000 and over
Number of Enterprises	1	2825	264	1665	94	377	118	154	61	47	28	8	3	4
Revenues ($ in Thousands)														
Net Sales	2	8856908	203247	440407	372338	248669	342711	828025	691937	934138	1502236	942791	152823	2197586
Interest	3	660612	10376	2048	1655	205	5504	30699	23440	17451	28656	16487	67086	457005
Rents	4	7386	0	1274	0	1351	63	3685	127	451	253	0	0	183
Royalties	5	0	0	0	0	0	0	0	0	0	0	0	0	0
Other Portfolio Income	6	1225619	8691	2482	0	9033	116207	2094	131	2011	62359	1348	121	1021140
Other Receipts	7	6963291	184180	434603	370683	238080	220937	791547	668239	914225	1410968	924956	85616	719258
Total Receipts	8	8856908	203247	440407	372338	248669	342711	828025	691937	934138	1502236	942791	152823	2197586
Average Total Receipts	9	3135	770	265	3961	660	2904	5377	11343	19875	53651	117849	50941	549396
Operating Costs/Operating Income (%)														
Cost of Operations	10	•	•	•	•	•	•	•	•	•	•	•	•	•
Salaries and Wages	11	29.6	39.6	13.6	6.5	10.0	21.4	38.3	41.7	43.9	35.0	46.7	24.2	15.5
Taxes Paid	12	3.1	4.0	1.6	0.7	4.2	2.4	4.0	4.3	3.8	3.6	4.2	2.2	2.0
Interest Paid	13	9.6	7.6	0.2	0.5	8.2	4.3	5.6	5.9	5.5	5.7	5.1	27.5	22.0
Depreciation	14	1.3	1.1	0.2	0.6	2.2	3.9	1.2	1.1	0.8	0.7	0.9	0.9	1.9
Amortization and Depletion	15	0.1	1.5	0.1	•	0.0	0.4	0.3	0.4	0.1	0.1	0.0	0.0	0.0
Pensions and Other Deferred Comp.	16	0.4	0.6	•	4.1	•	0.1	0.2	0.1	0.3	0.3	0.1	0.0	0.2
Employee Benefits	17	1.2	2.3	0.5	0.1	0.8	0.4	1.5	1.9	1.2	1.1	2.0	0.1	1.2
Advertising	18	4.2	1.1	1.1	0.2	21.9	0.3	2.5	2.0	2.1	3.7	3.0	0.3	7.7
Other Expenses	19	29.5	34.2	46.3	64.5	25.5	41.9	26.7	25.2	28.5	27.8	25.7	26.1	24.0
Officers' Compensation	20	4.7	2.1	9.5	6.9	5.2	9.5	7.1	5.1	3.9	9.6	1.8	2.7	0.4
Operating Margin	21	16.3	6.0	26.8	16.0	22.1	15.4	12.7	12.3	9.8	12.5	10.7	16.1	25.0
Operating Margin Before Officers' Comp.	22	21.0	8.1	36.3	22.8	27.3	24.9	19.8	17.4	13.8	22.1	12.4	18.7	25.4

Selected Average Balance Sheet ($ in Thousands)													
Net Receivables 23	2827	0	0	0	568	1296	4134	11066	15405	5621	7763	235809	1164523
Inventories 24	•	•	•	•	•	•	•	•	•	•	•	•	•
Net Property, Plant and Equipment 25	170	0	4	26	368	209	386	786	1053	1820	3977	1492	15968
Total Assets 26	14069	0	159	870	2193	6810	15374	35233	71075	171874	351226	1000076	4822120
Notes and Loans Payable 27	3811	0	33	95	688	5259	6831	18161	41240	79934	248272	479396	15303
All Other Liabilities 28	4442	0	1	173	504	2290	3350	8585	18780	63854	60264	161068	1848585
Net Worth 29	5817	0	125	603	1000	-740	5193	8487	11055	28086	42689	359612	2958232

Selected Financial Ratios (Times to 1)													
Current Ratio 30	0.6	•	102.5	7.8	1.9	0.9	1.0	0.8	0.5	0.3	0.2	0.5	1.0
Quick Ratio 31	0.6	•	99.5	4.8	1.7	0.9	0.9	0.7	0.4	0.2	0.1	0.5	1.0
Net Sales to Working Capital 32	•	•	3.1	5.7	1.6	•	•	•	•	•	•	•	16.1
Coverage Ratio 33	2.7	1.8	172.7	35.5	3.7	4.6	3.3	3.1	2.8	3.2	3.1	1.6	2.1
Total Asset Turnover 34	0.2	•	1.7	4.6	0.3	0.4	0.3	0.3	0.3	0.3	0.3	0.1	0.1
Inventory Turnover 35	•	•	•	•	•	•	•	•	•	•	•	•	•
Receivables Turnover 36	•	•	•	•	•	•	•	•	•	•	•	•	•
Total Liabilities to Net Worth 37	1.4	•	0.3	0.4	1.2	•	2.0	3.2	5.4	5.1	7.2	1.8	0.6
Current Assets to Working Capital 38	•	•	1.0	1.1	2.1	•	•	•	•	•	•	•	37.5
Current Liabilities to Working Capital 39	•	•	0.0	0.1	1.1	•	•	•	•	•	•	•	36.5
Working Capital to Net Sales 40	•	•	0.3	0.2	0.6	•	•	•	•	•	•	•	0.1
Inventory to Working Capital 41	•	•	•	•	•	•	•	•	•	•	•	•	•
Total Receipts to Cash Flow 42	2.4	3.0	1.5	1.3	2.5	1.8	2.8	3.0	2.9	2.7	3.1	2.5	2.1
Cost of Goods to Cash Flow 43	•	•	•	•	•	•	•	•	•	•	•	•	•
Cash Flow to Total Debt 44	0.2	•	5.1	11.8	0.2	0.2	0.2	0.1	0.1	0.1	0.1	0.0	0.1

Selected Financial Factors (in Percentages)													
Debt Ratio 45	58.7	•	21.4	30.7	54.4	110.9	66.2	75.9	84.4	83.7	87.8	64.0	38.7
Return on Total Assets 46	5.8	•	44.7	74.8	9.1	8.4	6.4	5.9	4.2	5.7	5.3	2.2	5.4
Return on Equity Before Income Taxes 47	8.8	•	56.6	105.0	14.6	•	13.1	16.4	17.4	23.9	29.4	2.3	4.6
Return on Equity After Income Taxes 48	8.2	•	56.4	105.0	13.6	•	12.1	14.2	16.4	22.9	25.7	2.1	4.4
Profit Margin (Before Income Tax) 49	16.3	5.8	26.8	16.0	22.1	15.4	12.7	12.3	9.7	12.5	10.7	16.0	25.0
Profit Margin (After Income Tax) 50	15.3	5.1	26.7	16.0	20.6	15.3	11.6	10.6	9.1	12.0	9.3	14.6	23.6

Table I

Corporations with and without Net Income

INTL. TRADE, SECONDARY FINANCING, OTHER NONDEPOSITORY CREDIT

MONEY AMOUNTS AND SIZE OF ASSETS IN THOUSANDS OF DOLLARS

Item Description for Accounting Period 7/11 Through 6/12		Total	Zero Assets	Under 500	500 to 1,000	1,000 to 5,000	5,000 to 10,000	10,000 to 25,000	25,000 to 50,000	50,000 to 100,000	100,000 to 250,000	250,000 to 500,000	500,000 to 2,500,000	2,500,000 and over
Number of Enterprises	1	5944	1415	•	•	1049	178	107	56	28	19	15	24	25
Revenues ($ in Thousands)														
Net Sales	2	164322534	648141	•	•	592202	542667	599278	578131	408164	229753	746552	2482447	156689514
Interest	3	151581876	419307	•	•	69605	121	11258	43013	67399	65399	187630	1132836	149580497
Rents	4	47973	3640	•	•	0	2274	0	55	356	221	862	837	39726
Royalties	5	84400	0	•	•	0	0	0	189	0	1	0	8080	0
Other Portfolio Income	6	2822912	4375	•	•	9878	14058	11790	12544	1521	324	8562	14237	2745622
Other Receipts	7	9785373	220819	•	•	512719	526214	576230	522330	338888	163808	549498	1326457	4323669
Total Receipts	8	164322534	648141	•	•	592202	542667	599278	578131	408164	229753	746552	2482447	156689514
Average Total Receipts	9	27645	458	•	•	565	3049	5601	10324	14577	12092	49770	103435	6267581
Operating Costs/Operating Income (%)														
Cost of Operations	10	•	•	•	•	•	•	•	•	•	•	•	•	•
Salaries and Wages	11	2.1	8.1	•	•	23.0	23.2	21.6	19.2	16.8	9.6	11.3	13.9	1.4
Taxes Paid	12	0.2	0.6	•	•	5.1	3.4	3.5	3.1	2.2	1.6	2.9	2.3	0.1
Interest Paid	13	65.0	70.6	•	•	4.6	8.7	15.4	10.9	11.9	22.7	19.5	19.5	67.3
Depreciation	14	0.5	0.1	•	•	1.5	1.9	2.0	4.7	0.7	1.5	2.1	5.4	0.4
Amortization and Depletion	15	0.4	0.7	•	•	1.9	0.0	1.0	0.4	0.8	0.2	1.2	2.5	0.4
Pensions and Other Deferred Comp.	16	0.1	0.0	•	•	0.6	0.5	0.3	0.6	0.3	0.7	0.2	0.5	0.1
Employee Benefits	17	0.3	0.1	•	•	2.0	3.8	1.6	1.0	0.9	0.9	0.9	0.8	0.2
Advertising	18	0.1	1.9	•	•	2.9	2.7	2.6	1.9	0.5	0.3	1.3	3.3	0.0
Other Expenses	19	41.7	11.5	•	•	61.5	30.1	32.7	30.2	48.2	30.8	35.9	34.5	41.9
Officers' Compensation	20	0.4	3.1	•	•	4.9	10.0	9.4	4.8	3.5	3.6	2.3	1.8	0.2
Operating Margin	21	•	3.3	•	•	•	15.6	9.7	23.2	14.1	28.3	22.5	15.5	•
Operating Margin Before Officers' Comp.	22	•	6.4	•	•	•	25.6	19.1	28.0	17.5	31.8	24.8	17.3	•

Selected Average Balance Sheet ($ in Thousands)													
Net Receivables 23	25544	0	•	•	692	3002	6993	19882	45373	86009	186326	529773	5204015
Inventories 24	•	•	•	•	•	•	•	•	•	•	•	•	•
Net Property, Plant and Equipment 25	1055	0	•	•	126	461	841	1719	682	2495	5689	16243	209326
Total Assets 26	964537	0	•	•	1817	7426	16002	35198	76210	145239	327070	1230559	227448780
Notes and Loans Payable 27	942385	0	•	•	1149	4885	15920	18255	39115	89097	198586	685195	222972158
All Other Liabilities 28	18491	0	•	•	215	1726	3416	5635	18329	25542	85110	203038	4060463
Net Worth 29	3661	0	•	•	454	815	-3334	11308	18766	30600	43374	342326	416159
Selected Financial Ratios (Times to 1)													
Current Ratio 30	0.8	•	•	•	2.5	2.1	1.7	1.6	1.8	1.4	1.3	2.0	0.8
Quick Ratio 31	0.7	•	•	•	1.8	1.3	1.2	1.3	1.5	1.2	1.0	1.7	0.7
Net Sales to Working Capital 32	•	•	•	•	0.8	0.9	1.1	1.1	0.5	0.4	0.8	0.3	•
Coverage Ratio 33	0.8	1.0	•	•	•	2.8	1.6	3.1	2.2	2.2	2.2	1.8	0.8
Total Asset Turnover 34	0.0	•	•	•	0.3	0.4	0.4	0.3	0.2	0.1	0.2	0.1	0.0
Inventory Turnover 35	•	•	•	•	•	•	•	•	•	•	•	•	•
Receivables Turnover 36	•	•	•	•	•	•	•	•	•	•	•	•	•
Total Liabilities to Net Worth 37	262.5	•	•	•	3.0	8.1	•	2.1	3.1	3.7	6.5	2.6	545.5
Current Assets to Working Capital 38	•	•	•	•	1.7	1.9	2.4	2.8	2.2	3.4	4.0	2.0	•
Current Liabilities to Working Capital 39	•	•	•	•	0.7	0.9	1.4	1.8	1.2	2.4	3.0	1.0	•
Working Capital to Net Sales 40	•	•	•	•	1.3	1.1	0.9	0.9	1.9	2.6	1.3	3.9	•
Inventory to Working Capital 41	•	•	•	•	•	•	•	0.0	•	•	0.0	0.0	•
Total Receipts to Cash Flow 42	3.3	7.5	•	•	2.4	2.6	2.8	2.1	1.7	1.7	1.9	2.1	3.4
Cost of Goods to Cash Flow 43	•	•	•	•	•	•	•	•	•	•	•	•	•
Cash Flow to Total Debt 44	0.0	•	•	•	0.2	0.2	0.1	0.2	0.2	0.1	0.1	0.1	0.0
Selected Financial Factors (in Percentages)													
Debt Ratio 45	99.6	•	•	•	75.0	89.0	120.8	67.9	75.4	78.9	86.7	72.2	99.8
Return on Total Assets 46	1.5	•	•	•	•	10.0	8.8	10.0	5.0	4.2	6.4	2.9	1.5
Return on Equity Before Income Taxes 47	•	•	•	•	•	58.4	•	21.2	10.9	11.2	25.8	4.7	•
Return on Equity After Income Taxes 48	•	•	•	•	•	57.6	•	19.0	8.5	9.2	16.2	2.7	•
Profit Margin (Before Income Tax) 49	•	3.3	•	•	•	15.6	9.7	23.2	14.0	28.3	22.5	15.5	•
Profit Margin (After Income Tax) 50	•	1.8	•	•	•	15.4	9.4	20.8	11.0	23.3	14.1	8.9	•

Table II

Corporations with Net Income

INTL. TRADE, SECONDARY FINANCING, OTHER NONDEPOSITORY CREDIT

MONEY AMOUNTS AND SIZE OF ASSETS IN THOUSANDS OF DOLLARS

Item Description for Accounting Period 7/11 Through 6/12		Total	Zero Assets	Under 500	500 to 1,000	1,000 to 5,000	5,000 to 10,000	10,000 to 25,000	25,000 to 50,000	50,000 to 100,000	100,000 to 250,000	250,000 to 500,000	500,000 to 2,500,000	2,500,000 and over
Number of Enterprises	1	3518	762	1442	480	462	165	70	53	25	15	•	•	•
Revenues ($ in Thousands)														
Net Sales	2	14508258	614686	411844	234373	450477	531904	471105	518866	380534	210544	•	•	•
Interest	3	8655757	407882	556	3485	51370	9	8363	42703	58062	55126	•	•	•
Rents	4	47311	3640	0	0	0	1701	0	55	356	221	•	•	•
Royalties	5	84364	0	76094	0	0	0	0	189	0	1	•	•	•
Other Portfolio Income	6	172883	4375	0	0	340	14058	11790	8344	1521	324	•	•	•
Other Receipts	7	5547943	198789	335194	230888	398767	516136	450952	467575	320595	154872	•	•	•
Total Receipts	8	14508258	614686	411844	234373	450477	531904	471105	518866	380534	210544	•	•	•
Average Total Receipts	9	4124	807	286	488	975	3224	6730	9790	15221	14036	•	•	•
Operating Costs/Operating Income (%)														
Cost of Operations	10	•	•	•	•	•	•	•	•	•	•	•	•	•
Salaries and Wages	11	10.0	0.7	19.1	10.1	24.3	23.7	21.0	17.7	14.0	10.0	•	•	•
Taxes Paid	12	1.9	0.6	4.9	4.2	5.8	3.4	3.8	2.9	2.1	1.4	•	•	•
Interest Paid	13	29.3	72.2	0.3	2.1	3.1	8.8	4.2	11.0	11.6	20.0	•	•	•
Depreciation	14	1.9	0.1	0.6	3.1	1.8	1.9	2.0	1.9	0.7	1.6	•	•	•
Amortization and Depletion	15	0.9	0.1	•	•	0.2	0.1	0.1	0.3	0.9	0.2	•	•	•
Pensions and Other Deferred Comp.	16	0.4	•	•	2.0	0.8	0.5	0.4	0.7	0.4	0.7	•	•	•
Employee Benefits	17	0.9	•	1.8	•	2.4	3.8	1.3	1.0	0.9	0.9	•	•	•
Advertising	18	1.2	0.0	2.9	0.8	2.1	2.7	2.7	1.9	0.5	0.3	•	•	•
Other Expenses	19	27.8	8.9	41.7	31.4	31.4	23.9	28.8	30.8	47.8	27.0	•	•	•
Officers' Compensation	20	2.8	2.9	14.3	11.9	6.0	10.2	10.7	5.0	3.3	3.3	•	•	•
Operating Margin	21	22.6	14.5	14.2	34.4	22.2	20.8	24.8	26.6	17.8	34.7	•	•	•
Operating Margin Before Officers' Comp.	22	25.5	17.4	28.5	46.3	28.1	31.0	35.5	31.7	21.1	37.9	•	•	•

Selected Average Balance Sheet ($ in Thousands)													
Net Receivables 23	26448	0	43	253	506	3201	8954	20627	49868	82238	•	•	•
Inventories 24	•	•	•	•	•	•	•	•	•	•	•	•	•
Net Property, Plant and Equipment 25	353	0	10	133	280	480	519	1305	669	1679	•	•	•
Total Assets 26	83824	0	141	639	1804	7479	16649	35678	76295	152475	•	•	•
Notes and Loans Payable 27	70721	0	17	240	1141	3540	8364	17950	41241	95342	•	•	•
All Other Liabilities 28	6722	0	6	50	148	1787	1079	5640	18025	23822	•	•	•
Net Worth 29	6381	0	118	349	516	2152	7207	12087	17029	33311	•	•	•
Selected Financial Ratios (Times to 1)													
Current Ratio 30	1.4	•	50.1	3.8	3.8	2.4	2.6	1.5	2.0	1.5	•	•	•
Quick Ratio 31	1.3	•	31.2	3.0	2.0	1.6	1.9	1.3	1.6	1.2	•	•	•
Net Sales to Working Capital 32	0.4	•	2.3	1.3	0.9	0.8	0.8	1.0	0.5	0.4	•	•	•
Coverage Ratio 33	1.8	1.2	42.5	17.6	8.2	3.4	6.8	3.4	2.5	2.7	•	•	•
Total Asset Turnover 34	0.0	•	2.0	0.8	0.5	0.4	0.4	0.3	0.2	0.1	•	•	•
Inventory Turnover 35	•	•	•	•	•	•	•	•	•	•	•	•	•
Receivables Turnover 36	•	•	•	•	•	•	•	•	•	•	•	•	•
Total Liabilities to Net Worth 37	12.1	•	0.2	0.8	2.5	2.5	1.3	2.0	3.5	3.6	•	•	•
Current Assets to Working Capital 38	3.6	•	1.0	1.4	1.4	1.7	1.6	2.8	2.1	2.8	•	•	•
Current Liabilities to Working Capital 39	2.6	•	0.0	0.4	0.4	0.7	0.6	1.8	1.1	1.8	•	•	•
Working Capital to Net Sales 40	2.3	•	0.4	0.7	1.1	1.2	1.3	1.0	2.0	2.7	•	•	•
Inventory to Working Capital 41	0.0	•	•	•	•	•	•	•	•	•	•	•	•
Total Receipts to Cash Flow 42	2.1	4.4	2.1	1.6	2.3	2.6	2.2	1.9	1.6	1.7	•	•	•
Cost of Goods to Cash Flow 43	•	•	•	•	•	•	•	•	•	•	•	•	•
Cash Flow to Total Debt 44	0.0	•	6.0	1.0	0.3	0.2	0.3	0.2	0.2	0.1	•	•	•
Selected Financial Factors (in Percentages)													
Debt Ratio 45	92.4	•	16.4	45.4	71.4	71.2	56.7	66.1	77.7	78.2	•	•	•
Return on Total Assets 46	2.5	•	29.5	27.9	13.6	12.8	11.7	10.3	5.8	5.0	•	•	•
Return on Equity Before Income Taxes 47	14.2	•	34.4	48.2	41.9	31.2	23.2	21.6	15.8	14.6	•	•	•
Return on Equity After Income Taxes 48	10.4	•	32.6	47.6	36.2	30.9	22.8	19.4	13.0	12.4	•	•	•
Profit Margin (Before Income Tax) 49	22.0	14.5	14.2	34.4	22.2	20.8	24.8	26.6	17.7	34.7	•	•	•
Profit Margin (After Income Tax) 50	16.2	13.0	13.5	34.0	19.2	20.6	24.4	24.0	14.5	29.3	•	•	•

Table I

Corporations with and without Net Income

ACTIVITIES RELATED TO CREDIT INTERMEDIATION

MONEY AMOUNTS AND SIZE OF ASSETS IN THOUSANDS OF DOLLARS

Item Description for Accounting Period 7/11 Through 6/12		Total	Zero Assets	Under 500	500 to 1,000	1,000 to 5,000	5,000 to 10,000	10,000 to 25,000	25,000 to 50,000	50,000 to 100,000	100,000 to 250,000	250,000 to 500,000	500,000 to 2,500,000	2,500,000 and over
Number of Enterprises	1	15921	2823	10992	894	788	166	76	73	43	24	11	20	12
Revenues ($ in Thousands)														
Net Sales	2	49478804	360374	2172450	298198	1309400	404841	501837	1107118	1160751	2020256	1082144	7067242	31994192
Interest	3	2313956	802	3734	575	7256	6262	7278	10969	7918	30671	30126	315636	1892727
Rents	4	155988	0	588	0	38	525	0	119	940	711	0	2076	150992
Royalties	5	498497	0	0	0	0	0	0	0	213	0	0	0	498284
Other Portfolio Income	6	756707	0	43	30	8	1139	1180	5416	616	13653	43274	86549	604796
Other Receipts	7	45753656	359572	2168085	297593	1302098	396915	493379	1090614	1151064	1975221	1008744	6662981	28847393
Total Receipts	8	49478804	360374	2172450	298198	1309400	404841	501837	1107118	1160751	2020256	1082144	7067242	31994192
Average Total Receipts	9	3108	128	198	334	1662	2439	6603	15166	26994	84177	98377	353362	2666183
Operating Costs/Operating Income (%)														
Cost of Operations	10	1.2	•	•	•	•	•	•	•	0.2	1.7	3.9	0.0	1.6
Salaries and Wages	11	18.9	61.0	21.9	9.6	34.1	40.6	34.6	37.1	23.1	23.9	24.0	18.7	15.9
Taxes Paid	12	2.3	4.5	3.6	1.4	3.1	4.0	3.2	4.2	2.7	2.7	1.6	1.7	2.2
Interest Paid	13	7.6	0.9	0.8	2.6	2.8	4.6	3.9	5.5	4.6	2.0	7.7	5.4	9.5
Depreciation	14	3.1	1.4	1.6	3.1	0.7	2.6	3.4	3.0	2.0	2.8	2.8	3.5	3.3
Amortization and Depletion	15	2.1	0.5	0.3	3.6	0.4	0.3	0.8	1.0	2.6	1.0	6.4	3.8	1.9
Pensions and Other Deferred Comp.	16	0.7	•	0.3	•	0.4	0.8	0.3	0.4	0.2	0.7	0.1	0.4	0.8
Employee Benefits	17	1.7	0.6	1.8	0.8	0.3	1.6	1.7	2.3	1.4	2.0	2.1	1.7	1.7
Advertising	18	3.5	0.8	2.0	3.4	2.6	2.5	0.8	6.9	2.6	1.1	3.2	2.4	4.0
Other Expenses	19	38.4	64.0	41.6	49.6	27.9	48.7	33.3	54.7	51.3	48.3	38.3	46.5	34.8
Officers' Compensation	20	2.2	0.5	21.0	13.1	9.6	5.8	9.8	3.6	3.7	2.6	1.5	1.4	0.4
Operating Margin	21	18.4	•	5.0	12.9	18.0	•	8.2	•	5.5	11.0	8.3	14.7	23.9
Operating Margin Before Officers' Comp.	22	20.6	•	26.1	25.9	27.6	•	18.0	•	9.2	13.6	9.8	16.1	24.3

Selected Average Balance Sheet ($ in Thousands)

Net Receivables 23	1358	0	6	15	520	2357	3252	9941	10597	31700	56625	270778	1042223
Inventories 24	•	•	•	•	•	•	•	•	•	•	•	•	•
Net Property, Plant and Equipment 25	294	0	24	196	51	143	807	995	2313	7826	8848	41471	235674
Total Assets 26	10749	0	81	753	2739	7649	17048	34758	68154	154427	372636	1011071	10946554
Notes and Loans Payable 27	4564	0	42	657	1502	9963	10358	17909	25247	32217	114242	280011	4831157
All Other Liabilities 28	3559	0	18	73	477	3005	3864	9814	41946	75964	164393	448111	3342962
Net Worth 29	2626	0	21	24	760	-5319	2825	7036	961	46246	94001	282949	2772435

Selected Financial Ratios (Times to 1)

Current Ratio 30	1.2	•	3.1	2.4	2.2	1.5	0.9	1.0	1.0	1.1	0.7	1.4	1.1
Quick Ratio 31	0.7	•	2.5	2.3	1.7	1.2	0.7	0.7	0.8	0.8	0.6	1.3	0.6
Net Sales to Working Capital 32	5.4	•	6.5	1.5	1.3	1.9	•	•	44.3	21.0	•	3.2	5.5
Coverage Ratio 33	3.6	•	7.4	6.0	7.3	•	3.0	•	2.2	6.5	2.4	3.7	3.7
Total Asset Turnover 34	0.3	•	2.4	0.4	0.6	0.3	0.4	0.4	0.4	0.5	0.3	0.3	0.2
Inventory Turnover 35	•	•	•	•	•	•	•	•	•	•	•	•	•
Receivables Turnover 36	•	•	•	•	•	•	•	•	•	•	•	•	•
Total Liabilities to Net Worth 37	3.1	•	2.8	30.7	2.6	•	5.0	3.9	69.9	2.3	3.0	2.6	2.9
Current Assets to Working Capital 38	6.8	•	1.5	1.7	1.8	3.1	•	•	46.5	20.6	•	3.6	7.7
Current Liabilities to Working Capital 39	5.8	•	0.5	0.7	0.8	2.1	•	•	45.5	19.6	•	2.6	6.7
Working Capital to Net Sales 40	0.2	•	0.2	0.7	0.7	0.5	•	•	0.0	0.0	•	0.3	0.2
Inventory to Working Capital 41	0.0	•	•	•	•	•	•	•	0.5	0.0	•	0.0	0.0
Total Receipts to Cash Flow 42	1.9	4.2	2.5	2.4	2.4	3.2	2.7	3.7	1.9	1.9	2.3	1.8	1.8
Cost of Goods to Cash Flow 43	0.0	•	•	•	•	•	•	•	0.0	0.0	0.1	0.0	0.0
Cash Flow to Total Debt 44	0.2	•	1.3	0.2	0.4	0.1	0.2	0.1	0.2	0.4	0.2	0.3	0.2

Selected Financial Factors (in Percentages)

Debt Ratio 45	75.6	•	73.8	96.8	72.3	169.5	83.4	79.8	98.6	70.1	74.8	72.0	74.7
Return on Total Assets 46	7.8	•	14.2	6.8	12.7	•	4.6	•	4.0	7.1	4.9	7.0	8.5
Return on Equity Before Income Taxes 47	23.0	•	46.7	180.5	39.4	5.3	18.6	•	153.3	20.0	11.2	18.5	24.4
Return on Equity After Income Taxes 48	14.9	•	42.7	158.0	39.3	5.4	16.6	•	142.3	15.9	7.6	12.0	15.7
Profit Margin (Before Income Tax) 49	19.4	•	5.0	12.9	18.0	•	8.0	•	5.5	11.0	10.7	14.8	25.3
Profit Margin (After Income Tax) 50	12.6	•	4.6	11.3	18.0	•	7.1	•	5.1	8.7	7.3	9.6	16.4

Table II

Corporations with Net Income

ACTIVITIES RELATED TO CREDIT INTERMEDIATION

MONEY AMOUNTS AND SIZE OF ASSETS IN THOUSANDS OF DOLLARS

Item Description for Accounting Period 7/11 Through 6/12		Total	Zero Assets	Under 500	500 to 1,000	1,000 to 5,000	5,000 to 10,000	10,000 to 25,000	25,000 to 50,000	50,000 to 100,000	100,000 to 250,000	250,000 to 500,000	500,000 to 2,500,000	2,500,000 and over
Number of Enterprises	1	8156	1342	5576	344	632	80	47	47	29	20	•	•	•
Revenues ($ in Thousands)														
Net Sales	2	41582408	86071	1943783	288938	1278583	247076	286517	836049	753373	1747351	•	•	•
Interest	3	2251524	0	3682	314	4653	2407	5002	5870	7397	7893	•	•	•
Rents	4	10545	0	588	0	0	443	0	119	0	711	•	•	•
Royalties	5	498000	0	0	0	0	0	0	0	0	0	•	•	•
Other Portfolio Income	6	714235	0	0	0	8	922	351	5238	583	198	•	•	•
Other Receipts	7	38108104	86071	1939513	288624	1273922	243304	281164	824822	745393	1738549	•	•	•
Total Receipts	8	41582408	86071	1943783	288938	1278583	247076	286517	836049	753373	1747351	•	•	•
Average Total Receipts	9	5098	64	349	840	2023	3088	6096	17788	25978	87368	•	•	•
Operating Costs/Operating Income (%)														
Cost of Operations	10	0.2	•	•	•	•	•	•	•	0.3	0.8	•	•	•
Salaries and Wages	11	17.9	0.3	20.2	8.8	33.2	35.3	35.3	32.9	23.3	24.1	•	•	•
Taxes Paid	12	2.5	2.1	3.5	1.1	3.0	3.7	2.9	4.0	2.7	2.7	•	•	•
Interest Paid	13	4.5	2.4	0.5	2.3	2.3	3.0	4.5	4.7	5.1	2.1	•	•	•
Depreciation	14	2.6	3.0	1.6	2.8	0.6	0.5	1.4	1.4	1.9	2.3	•	•	•
Amortization and Depletion	15	1.5	•	0.3	•	0.2	•	1.4	0.8	2.8	0.9	•	•	•
Pensions and Other Deferred Comp.	16	0.7	•	0.3	•	0.4	0.5	0.5	0.3	0.3	0.5	•	•	•
Employee Benefits	17	1.3	•	1.4	0.7	0.2	1.3	1.7	0.9	1.4	1.4	•	•	•
Advertising	18	4.0	•	1.9	0.4	2.6	3.5	0.8	8.8	2.6	1.2	•	•	•
Other Expenses	19	37.1	39.8	28.4	43.7	26.6	27.2	23.1	32.8	40.6	48.1	•	•	•
Officers' Compensation	20	2.2	1.1	21.8	13.3	8.8	7.9	7.3	4.1	4.8	1.9	•	•	•
Operating Margin	21	25.6	51.3	20.1	26.9	22.2	17.1	21.1	9.3	14.2	13.8	•	•	•
Operating Margin Before Officers' Comp.	22	27.8	52.4	42.0	40.2	31.0	25.1	28.4	13.4	19.0	15.7	•	•	•

Selected Average Balance Sheet ($ in Thousands)													
Net Receivables 23	2450	0	0	33	636	4292	3842	12483	8580	37135	•	•	•
Inventories 24	•	•	•	•	•	•	•	•	•	•	•	•	•
Net Property, Plant and Equipment 25	407	0	26	61	62	77	373	918	2440	6905	•	•	•
Total Assets 26	15494	0	99	825	2763	7798	16960	35120	66909	158131	•	•	•
Notes and Loans Payable 27	5430	0	32	424	1331	17288	7493	16156	28964	35842	•	•	•
All Other Liabilities 28	5018	0	9	39	570	5092	5018	11667	44542	83689	•	•	•
Net Worth 29	5046	0	58	363	862	-14582	4450	7297	-6597	38600	•	•	•
Selected Financial Ratios (Times to 1)													
Current Ratio 30	1.2	•	3.9	1.9	1.9	1.2	0.9	1.0	1.0	1.0	•	•	•
Quick Ratio 31	0.8	•	3.0	1.8	1.7	1.1	0.6	0.8	0.8	0.8	•	•	•
Net Sales to Working Capital 32	4.7	•	8.2	2.3	1.9	2.7	•	21.2	•	•	•	•	•
Coverage Ratio 33	6.8	22.5	44.2	12.6	10.6	6.7	5.7	3.0	3.8	7.7	•	•	•
Total Asset Turnover 34	0.3	•	3.5	1.0	0.7	0.4	0.4	0.5	0.4	0.6	•	•	•
Inventory Turnover 35	•	•	•	•	•	•	•	•	•	•	•	•	•
Receivables Turnover 36	•	•	•	•	•	•	•	•	•	•	•	•	•
Total Liabilities to Net Worth 37	2.1	•	0.7	1.3	2.2	•	2.8	3.8	•	3.1	•	•	•
Current Assets to Working Capital 38	6.0	•	1.3	2.1	2.1	5.2	•	26.1	•	•	•	•	•
Current Liabilities to Working Capital 39	5.0	•	0.3	1.1	1.1	4.2	•	25.1	•	•	•	•	•
Working Capital to Net Sales 40	0.2	•	0.1	0.4	0.5	0.4	•	0.0	•	•	•	•	•
Inventory to Working Capital 41	0.0	•	•	•	•	•	•	0.0	•	•	•	•	•
Total Receipts to Cash Flow 42	1.7	1.1	2.3	2.0	2.2	2.4	2.5	2.7	1.9	1.8	•	•	•
Cost of Goods to Cash Flow 43	0.0	•	•	•	•	•	•	•	0.0	0.0	•	•	•
Cash Flow to Total Debt 44	0.3	•	3.6	0.9	0.5	0.1	0.2	0.2	0.2	0.4	•	•	•
Selected Financial Factors (in Percentages)													
Debt Ratio 45	67.4	•	41.6	56.0	68.8	287.0	73.8	79.2	109.9	75.6	•	•	•
Return on Total Assets 46	10.2	•	72.3	29.7	18.0	8.0	9.2	7.0	7.5	8.8	•	•	•
Return on Equity Before Income Taxes 47	26.8	•	121.0	62.3	52.2	•	28.8	22.5	•	31.2	•	•	•
Return on Equity After Income Taxes 48	18.6	•	118.1	58.4	52.0	•	26.7	18.1	•	25.3	•	•	•
Profit Margin (Before Income Tax) 49	26.5	51.3	20.1	26.9	22.2	17.1	21.0	9.2	14.2	13.8	•	•	•
Profit Margin (After Income Tax) 50	18.4	51.3	19.7	25.2	22.2	16.7	19.5	7.4	13.6	11.2	•	•	•

Table I

Corporations with and without Net Income

INVESTMENT BANKING AND SECURITIES DEALING

MONEY AMOUNTS AND SIZE OF ASSETS IN THOUSANDS OF DOLLARS

Item Description for Accounting Period 7/11 Through 6/12		Total	Zero Assets	Under 500	500 to 1,000	1,000 to 5,000	5,000 to 10,000	10,000 to 25,000	25,000 to 50,000	50,000 to 100,000	100,000 to 250,000	250,000 to 500,000	500,000 to 2,500,000	2,500,000 and over
Number of Enterprises	1	3847	1191	1916	339	233	23	47	42	18	11	6	10	13
Revenues ($ in Thousands)														
Net Sales	2	96050871	399288	124942	132788	369217	105723	141366	518577	369290	131409	427057	1329417	92001798
Interest	3	35379764	233492	1846	231	9090	3798	5625	13106	3970	33864	44171	190337	34840232
Rents	4	338112	0	0	0	661	0	0	16	0	0	2083	0	335352
Royalties	5	84657	0	0	0	3	0	0	0	0	10159	0	0	74495
Other Portfolio Income	6	3631506	33497	2180	406	3459	116	4198	45475	14986	30966	12	369176	3127033
Other Receipts	7	56616832	132299	120916	132151	356004	101809	131543	459980	350334	56420	380791	769904	53624686
Total Receipts	8	96050871	399288	124942	132788	369217	105723	141366	518577	369290	131409	427057	1329417	92001798
Average Total Receipts	9	24968	335	65	392	1585	4597	3008	12347	20516	11946	71176	132942	7077061
Operating Costs/Operating Income (%)														
Cost of Operations	10	174	•	•	•	•	•	•	•	•	•	4.7	•	18.1
Salaries and Wages	11	18.1	15.2	•	12.0	7.3	20.0	11.3	44.2	28.9	10.6	33.3	32.6	17.8
Taxes Paid	12	1.4	5.8	3.9	1.1	3.1	2.0	3.1	3.4	2.6	2.2	2.8	2.7	1.3
Interest Paid	13	28.1	24.9	0.3	•	0.6	3.0	2.9	1.9	1.5	22.2	2.1	8.8	29.0
Depreciation	14	1.0	0.1	0.1	1.6	0.5	0.4	0.3	1.1	0.9	0.8	2.6	1.8	1.0
Amortization and Depletion	15	0.6	•	1.6	•	0.5	•	0.2	0.1	0.1	1.2	0.8	4.7	0.6
Pensions and Other Deferred Comp.	16	0.8	•	3.5	0.3	0.6	1.8	0.3	0.4	1.0	0.1	8.1	0.1	0.7
Employee Benefits	17	0.7	0.3	1.0	0.3	1.3	0.7	1.5	1.3	1.6	0.3	2.0	1.3	0.7
Advertising	18	0.2	1.4	11.3	0.1	0.3	0.1	0.0	1.6	0.2	0.0	3.7	0.1	0.2
Other Expenses	19	41.7	43.7	63.4	72.9	70.1	21.4	42.4	33.5	49.5	51.7	50.4	44.0	41.5
Officers' Compensation	20	1.0	•	38.8	1.5	14.0	28.9	22.9	3.9	7.4	1.6	3.3	1.4	0.7
Operating Margin	21	•	8.6	•	10.2	1.7	21.6	15.1	8.8	6.3	9.1	•	2.5	•
Operating Margin Before Officers' Comp.	22	•	8.6	14.8	11.7	15.7	50.5	37.9	12.6	13.7	10.8	•	3.9	•

Selected Average Balance Sheet ($ in Thousands)														
Net Receivables	23	286529	0	3	10	228	3162	537	4652	10676	45136	18013	180676	84563090
Inventories	24	•	•	•	•	•	•	•	•	•	•	•	•	•
Net Property, Plant and Equipment	25	2817	0	0	8	178	79	127	668	750	1292	4200	9936	815589
Total Assets	26	1099521	0	74	681	2269	6666	16367	34478	69156	157119	344866	1149802	323849475
Notes and Loans Payable	27	165796	0	44	0	423	3070	2175	7734	13855	37747	122616	386025	48605952
All Other Liabilities	28	863384	0	4	15	319	1383	2026	8945	16224	31960	109895	485746	254976136
Net Worth	29	70340	0	26	666	1527	2214	12166	17800	39076	87412	112355	278032	20267387
Selected Financial Ratios (Times to 1)														
Current Ratio	30	1.1	•	13.6	29.6	2.2	4.0	5.7	2.4	1.7	2.0	1.8	0.8	1.1
Quick Ratio	31	0.7	•	6.5	4.7	1.9	4.0	2.8	1.7	1.2	1.9	0.8	0.4	0.7
Net Sales to Working Capital	32	0.7	•	1.3	0.9	3.4	1.1	0.4	1.1	1.5	0.4	0.8	•	0.6
Coverage Ratio	33	0.7	1.3	•	•	3.2	8.1	6.1	5.1	3.5	1.4	•	1.2	0.7
Total Asset Turnover	34	0.0	•	0.9	0.6	0.7	0.7	0.2	0.4	0.3	0.1	0.2	0.1	0.0
Inventory Turnover	35	•	•	•	•	•	•	•	•	•	•	•	•	•
Receivables Turnover	36	•	•	•	•	•	•	•	•	•	•	•	•	•
Total Liabilities to Net Worth	37	14.6	•	1.8	0.0	0.5	2.0	0.3	0.9	0.8	0.8	2.1	3.1	15.0
Current Assets to Working Capital	38	17.6	•	1.1	1.0	1.8	1.3	1.2	1.7	2.4	2.0	2.3	•	17.7
Current Liabilities to Working Capital	39	16.6	•	0.1	0.0	0.8	0.3	0.2	0.7	1.4	1.0	1.3	•	16.7
Working Capital to Net Sales	40	1.5	•	0.8	1.1	0.3	0.9	2.2	0.9	0.7	2.7	1.3	•	1.6
Inventory to Working Capital	41	0.0	•	•	•	•	•	•	•	•	•	0.0	•	0.0
Total Receipts to Cash Flow	42	3.7	2.6	2.8	1.3	1.5	2.5	2.7	3.3	2.0	2.5	3.6	2.4	3.8
Cost of Goods to Cash Flow	43	0.6	•	•	•	•	•	•	•	•	•	0.2	•	0.7
Cash Flow to Total Debt	44	0.0	•	0.5	19.7	1.4	0.4	0.3	0.2	0.3	0.1	0.1	0.1	0.0
Selected Financial Factors (in Percentages)														
Debt Ratio	45	93.6	•	64.9	2.2	32.7	66.8	25.7	48.4	43.5	44.4	67.4	75.8	93.7
Return on Total Assets	46	0.4	•	•	5.7	1.4	17.0	3.3	3.5	1.5	2.4	•	1.2	0.4
Return on Equity Before Income Taxes	47	•	•	•	5.8	1.5	44.8	3.7	5.5	1.9	1.2	•	0.9	•
Return on Equity After Income Taxes	48	•	•	•	4.4	0.9	42.0	2.7	2.4	1.6	0.7	•	0.2	•
Profit Margin (Before Income Tax)	49	•	8.6	•	9.9	1.4	21.6	14.8	7.9	3.7	9.0	•	1.8	•
Profit Margin (After Income Tax)	50	•	0.7	•	7.4	0.9	20.2	10.9	3.4	3.0	5.1	•	0.3	•

Table II

Corporations with Net Income

INVESTMENT BANKING AND SECURITIES DEALING

MONEY AMOUNTS AND SIZE OF ASSETS IN THOUSANDS OF DOLLARS

Item Description for Accounting Period 7/11 Through 6/12		Total	Zero Assets	Under 500	500 to 1,000	1,000 to 5,000	5,000 to 10,000	10,000 to 25,000	25,000 to 50,000	50,000 to 100,000	100,000 to 250,000	250,000 to 500,000	500,000 to 2,500,000	2,500,000 and over
Number of Enterprises	1	1076	245	591	54	88	14	25	30	8	•	0	•	•
Revenues ($ in Thousands)														
Net Sales	2	81442729	425654	82610	103029	173916	102547	140692	441105	228162	•	0	•	•
Interest	3	26336510	227989	15	0	1327	622	5625	13034	40	•	0	•	•
Rents	4	173621	0	0	0	0	0	0	16	0	•	0	•	•
Royalties	5	74525	0	0	0	0	0	0	0	0	•	0	•	•
Other Portfolio Income	6	3562878	33338	2180	0	84	116	3828	43547	6019	•	0	•	•
Other Receipts	7	51295195	164327	80415	103029	172505	101809	131239	384508	222103	•	0	•	•
Total Receipts	8	81442723	425654	82610	103029	173916	102547	140692	441105	228162	•	0	•	•
Average Total Receipts	9	75690	1737	140	1908	1976	7325	5628	14704	28520	•	•	•	•
Operating Costs/Operating Income (%)														
Cost of Operations	10	20.5	•	•	•	•	•	•	•	•	•	•	•	•
Salaries and Wages	11	16.1	13.5	•	6.8	4.3	20.7	11.4	39.1	24.8	•	•	•	•
Taxes Paid	12	1.0	5.4	4.0	0.2	1.5	2.0	3.0	2.9	1.8	•	•	•	•
Interest Paid	13	26.0	22.9	•	•	•	0.0	2.8	1.4	1.1	•	•	•	•
Depreciation	14	1.0	0.1	•	1.7	0.9	0.4	0.3	0.7	0.5	•	•	•	•
Amortization and Depletion	15	0.6	•	2.5	•	1.1	•	0.2	0.0	0.0	•	•	•	•
Pensions and Other Deferred Comp.	16	0.6	•	5.3	0.4	1.2	1.9	0.3	0.4	1.4	•	•	•	•
Employee Benefits	17	0.6	0.3	1.5	0.1	0.3	0.7	1.5	1.1	1.2	•	•	•	•
Advertising	18	0.2	1.3	•	0.1	0.4	0.1	0.0	1.8	0.1	•	•	•	•
Other Expenses	19	26.6	38.9	12.6	53.2	53.3	22.0	24.8	27.6	42.8	•	•	•	•
Officers' Compensation	20	0.8	•	58.2	0.2	19.2	29.8	23.0	4.1	9.1	•	•	•	•
Operating Margin	21	6.1	17.7	15.8	37.2	17.9	22.3	32.8	20.9	17.2	•	•	•	•
Operating Margin Before Officers' Comp.	22	6.9	17.7	74.1	37.4	37.1	52.1	55.8	25.0	26.3	•	•	•	•

Selected Average Balance Sheet ($ in Thousands)													
Net Receivables **23**	395000	0	9	0	427	151	742	1125	7266	•	•	•	•
Inventories **24**	•	•	•	•	•	•	•	•	•	•	•	•	•
Net Property, Plant and Equipment **25**	7295	0	0	0	19	131	191	671	460	•	•	•	•
Total Assets **26**	2792282	0	124	551	1750	5908	15252	34390	67152	•	•	•	•
Notes and Loans Payable **27**	461909	0	0	0	0	0	3729	2670	15610	•	•	•	•
All Other Liabilities **28**	1907282	0	8	7	691	2271	3795	11329	15239	•	•	•	•
Net Worth **29**	423091	0	117	544	1059	3637	7729	20392	36302	•	•	•	•
Selected Financial Ratios (Times to 1)													
Current Ratio **30**	1.1	•	10.5	27.8	2.1	1.8	3.2	2.1	1.6	•	•	•	•
Quick Ratio **31**	0.6	•	5.0	27.8	1.7	1.8	2.6	1.3	1.3	•	•	•	•
Net Sales to Working Capital **32**	0.4	•	1.9	9.8	2.7	4.2	1.1	1.6	2.8	•	•	•	•
Coverage Ratio **33**	1.3	1.8	•	•	•	586.4	12.6	15.8	13.9	•	•	•	•
Total Asset Turnover **34**	0.0	•	1.1	3.5	1.1	1.2	0.4	0.4	0.4	•	•	•	•
Inventory Turnover **35**	•	•	•	•	•	•	•	•	•	•	•	•	•
Receivables Turnover **36**	•	•	•	•	•	•	•	•	•	•	•	•	•
Total Liabilities to Net Worth **37**	5.6	•	0.1	0.0	0.7	0.6	1.0	0.7	0.8	•	•	•	•
Current Assets to Working Capital **38**	8.0	•	1.1	1.0	1.9	2.3	1.5	1.9	2.7	•	•	•	•
Current Liabilities to Working Capital **39**	7.0	•	0.1	0.0	0.9	1.3	0.5	0.9	1.7	•	•	•	•
Working Capital to Net Sales **40**	2.6	•	0.5	0.1	0.4	0.2	0.9	0.6	0.4	•	•	•	•
Inventory to Working Capital **41**	0.0	•	•	•	•	•	•	•	•	•	•	•	•
Total Receipts to Cash Flow **42**	3.4	2.3	3.7	1.1	1.5	2.4	1.9	2.8	1.8	•	•	•	•
Cost of Goods to Cash Flow **43**	0.7	•	•	•	•	•	•	•	•	•	•	•	•
Cash Flow to Total Debt **44**	0.0	•	5.0	236.0	2.0	1.3	0.4	0.4	0.5	•	•	•	•
Selected Financial Factors (in Percentages)													
Debt Ratio **45**	84.8	•	6.1	1.3	39.5	38.4	49.3	40.7	45.9	•	•	•	•
Return on Total Assets **46**	0.9	•	17.5	128.6	20.2	27.7	13.2	9.1	6.7	•	•	•	•
Return on Equity Before Income Taxes **47**	1.4	•	18.6	130.4	33.4	44.8	23.9	14.5	11.5	•	•	•	•
Return on Equity After Income Taxes **48**	1.0	•	18.4	119.2	31.3	42.0	21.0	10.7	10.7	•	•	•	•
Profit Margin (Before Income Tax) **49**	7.8	17.7	15.6	37.2	17.9	22.3	32.8	20.0	14.6	•	•	•	•
Profit Margin (After Income Tax) **50**	5.4	10.2	15.4	34.0	16.8	20.8	28.8	14.8	13.6	•	•	•	•

Table I

Corporations with and without Net Income

SECURITIES BROKERAGE

Item Description for Accounting Period 7/11 Through 6/12		Total	Zero Assets	Under 500	500 to 1,000	1,000 to 5,000	5,000 to 10,000	10,000 to 25,000	25,000 to 50,000	50,000 to 100,000	100,000 to 250,000	250,000 to 500,000	500,000 to 2,500,000	2,500,000 and over
		Money Amounts and Size of Assets in Thousands of Dollars												
Number of Enterprises	1	7073	1239	4494	392	651	94	69	33	23	22	9	17	29
		Revenues ($ in Thousands)												
Net Sales	2	94210571	384519	1973483	1408941	2256688	464441	2262840	952829	1165521	2059975	1892764	3000998	76387574
Interest	3	36145737	55763	34	10732	3712	1189	6226	1630	13550	54902	10035	134072	35853891
Rents	4	192748	0	0	0	0	4798	725	0	0	636	3347	0	183242
Royalties	5	10208	411	0	0	0	0	7211	0	0	0	0	2149	438
Other Portfolio Income	6	1351098	52049	2513	1	460	12530	10178	21781	57003	22714	5442	40340	1126088
Other Receipts	7	56510780	276296	1970936	1398208	2252516	445924	2238500	929418	1094968	1981723	1873940	2824437	39223915
Total Receipts	8	94210571	384519	1973483	1408941	2256688	464441	2262840	952829	1165521	2059975	1892764	3000998	76387574
Average Total Receipts	9	13320	310	439	3594	3466	4941	32795	28874	50675	93635	210307	176529	2634054
		Operating Costs/Operating Income (%)												
Cost of Operations	10	0.1	•	•	•	•	•	3.1	•	•	0.0	•	•	0.0
Salaries and Wages	11	22.7	11.8	20.2	40.5	40.0	36.9	13.4	36.8	32.5	30.2	31.1	40.9	20.7
Taxes Paid	12	2.1	2.5	3.5	1.6	3.3	3.0	1.7	4.4	3.7	2.5	3.1	3.3	2.0
Interest Paid	13	24.1	8.2	0.6	0.0	0.4	2.1	0.7	0.3	1.2	1.6	3.0	7.0	29.2
Depreciation	14	1.1	1.5	1.9	0.1	0.3	1.5	0.5	0.6	0.8	1.2	1.6	1.9	1.1
Amortization and Depletion	15	0.6	0.9	0.1	0.0	•	0.0	0.3	0.0	0.9	1.1	0.2	1.3	0.7
Pensions and Other Deferred Comp.	16	0.6	0.1	1.3	0.1	0.1	0.4	0.2	1.1	0.2	0.1	0.9	3.0	0.5
Employee Benefits	17	2.1	0.6	0.4	0.9	1.8	4.0	1.3	1.2	2.0	1.1	2.0	1.8	2.2
Advertising	18	0.9	5.0	1.8	0.1	0.1	0.9	0.3	0.6	0.7	0.4	0.6	0.5	0.9
Other Expenses	19	37.7	41.0	33.6	44.9	38.8	44.3	73.3	36.0	44.7	58.1	51.5	38.5	35.5
Officers' Compensation	20	4.5	4.1	22.1	10.1	12.2	12.4	3.5	7.0	5.3	2.1	1.1	2.5	3.9
Operating Margin	21	3.6	24.1	14.6	1.8	3.0	•	1.9	12.0	7.9	1.7	5.1	•	3.4
Operating Margin Before Officers' Comp.	22	8.1	28.3	36.6	11.9	15.1	6.8	5.3	19.0	13.2	3.8	6.2	1.8	7.3

Selected Average Balance Sheet ($ in Thousands)

Net Receivables 23	37690	0	3	158	80	407	1873	2678	8132	17575	105643	95601	9070621
Inventories 24	•	•	•	•	•	•	•	•	•	•	•	•	•
Net Property, Plant and Equipment 25	532	0	11	18	55	543	742	509	1203	3250	9435	28225	99482
Total Assets 26	218055	0	91	631	2124	8022	15328	37410	68851	157651	360906	1132146	52057565
Notes and Loans Payable 27	31101	0	46	37	104	675	3107	1554	10350	20608	69625	146342	7432789
All Other Liabilities 28	172552	0	15	244	641	2820	6708	13200	19295	59295	113038	663686	41540258
Net Worth 29	14402	0	30	350	1378	4527	5514	22656	39205	77748	178243	322117	3084519

Selected Financial Ratios (Times to 1)

Current Ratio 30	1.2	•	1.6	2.4	3.0	6.3	1.5	2.0	2.2	1.4	2.8	0.9	1.2
Quick Ratio 31	0.4	•	1.0	2.2	1.8	5.7	1.1	1.4	1.5	0.9	2.5	0.5	0.4
Net Sales to Working Capital 32	0.5	•	37.0	10.5	4.2	1.2	7.8	2.6	2.5	3.8	1.2	•	0.4
Coverage Ratio 33	1.2	4.6	24.0	979.8	8.7	•	3.3	45.2	6.9	1.8	2.7	0.9	1.1
Total Asset Turnover 34	0.1	•	4.8	5.7	1.6	0.6	2.1	0.8	0.7	0.6	0.6	0.2	0.1
Inventory Turnover 35	•	•	•	•	•	•	•	•	•	•	•	•	•
Receivables Turnover 36	•	•	•	•	•	•	•	•	•	•	•	•	•
Total Liabilities to Net Worth 37	14.1	•	2.0	0.8	0.5	0.8	1.8	0.7	0.8	1.0	1.0	2.5	15.9
Current Assets to Working Capital 38	6.5	•	2.6	1.7	1.5	1.2	2.8	2.0	1.8	3.6	1.6	•	6.5
Current Liabilities to Working Capital 39	5.5	•	1.6	0.7	0.5	0.2	1.8	1.0	0.8	2.6	0.6	•	5.5
Working Capital to Net Sales 40	1.9	•	0.0	0.1	0.2	0.8	0.1	0.4	0.4	0.3	0.8	•	2.3
Inventory to Working Capital 41	0.0	•	•	•	•	•	•	•	•	0.0	•	•	0.0
Total Receipts to Cash Flow 42	2.7	1.9	2.9	2.3	2.7	3.1	1.4	2.3	2.0	1.8	1.9	3.0	2.9
Cost of Goods to Cash Flow 43	0.0	•	•	•	•	•	0.0	•	•	0.0	•	•	0.0
Cash Flow to Total Debt 44	0.0	•	2.5	5.6	1.7	0.5	2.4	0.9	0.8	0.7	0.6	0.1	0.0

Selected Financial Factors (in Percentages)

Debt Ratio 45	93.4	•	66.7	44.5	35.1	43.6	64.0	39.4	43.1	50.7	50.6	71.5	94.1
Return on Total Assets 46	1.7	•	73.4	10.3	5.5	•	5.0	9.4	6.3	1.7	4.7	1.0	1.7
Return on Equity Before Income Taxes 47	3.4	•	211.4	18.5	7.5	•	9.6	15.1	9.5	1.5	6.0	•	2.9
Return on Equity After Income Taxes 48	1.9	•	209.9	15.3	7.2	•	5.7	11.7	5.6	0.0	3.7	•	1.6
Profit Margin (Before Income Tax) 49	3.6	29.3	14.6	1.8	3.0	•	1.6	11.9	7.3	1.2	5.0	•	3.4
Profit Margin (After Income Tax) 50	2.1	22.1	14.4	1.5	2.9	•	1.0	9.2	4.3	0.0	3.1	•	1.9

Table II

Corporations with Net Income

SECURITIES BROKERAGE

MONEY AMOUNTS AND SIZE OF ASSETS IN THOUSANDS OF DOLLARS

Item Description for Accounting Period 7/11 Through 6/12		Total	Zero Assets	Under 500	500 to 1,000	1,000 to 5,000	5,000 to 10,000	10,000 to 25,000	25,000 to 50,000	50,000 to 100,000	100,000 to 250,000	250,000 to 500,000	500,000 to 2,500,000	2,500,000 and over
Number of Enterprises	1	5068	•	3518	336	404	65	43	23	17	•	•	11	20
Revenues ($ in Thousands)														
Net Sales	2	50461983	•	1644836	1291228	1206042	210210	1475670	633425	618461	•	•	1714437	37999195
Interest	3	11857347	•	23	10630	2544	578	5966	1329	7506	•	•	84119	11671833
Rents	4	127309	•	0	0	0	4681	0	0	0	•	•	0	119280
Royalties	5	7848	•	0	0	0	0	7211	0	0	•	•	0	239
Other Portfolio Income	6	499745	•	49	1	454	11642	95	21336	50721	•	•	10453	325500
Other Receipts	7	37969734	•	1644764	1280597	1203044	193309	1462398	610760	560234	•	•	1619865	25882343
Total Receipts	8	50461983	•	1644836	1291228	1206042	210210	1475670	633425	618461	•	•	1714437	37999195
Average Total Receipts	9	9957	•	468	3843	2985	3234	34318	27540	36380	•	•	155858	1899960
Operating Costs/Operating Income (%)														
Cost of Operations	10	0.1	•	•	•	•	•	4.7	•	•	•	•	•	0.0
Salaries and Wages	11	25.8	•	18.5	41.6	22.8	25.0	11.6	33.5	40.1	•	•	29.0	26.0
Taxes Paid	12	2.5	•	3.7	1.5	2.8	2.5	1.3	3.7	4.3	•	•	3.3	2.4
Interest Paid	13	10.0	•	0.2	0.0	0.3	0.2	0.2	0.3	1.2	•	•	8.9	12.7
Depreciation	14	1.5	•	1.7	0.0	0.3	1.0	0.3	0.6	0.7	•	•	1.6	1.6
Amortization and Depletion	15	0.4	•	0.0	•	•	0.0	0.0	0.0	1.0	•	•	1.4	0.4
Pensions and Other Deferred Comp.	16	0.6	•	1.5	0.1	0.2	0.6	0.2	1.4	0.3	•	•	0.4	0.7
Employee Benefits	17	1.3	•	0.3	0.9	1.2	3.6	1.1	0.9	2.4	•	•	1.3	1.3
Advertising	18	1.5	•	1.6	0.1	0.2	0.3	0.3	0.1	0.5	•	•	0.2	1.8
Other Expenses	19	42.3	•	31.8	43.4	40.1	20.1	72.0	31.5	21.6	•	•	39.6	41.2
Officers' Compensation	20	2.3	•	18.5	9.3	17.3	22.0	3.1	7.2	7.2	•	•	0.6	0.7
Operating Margin	21	11.6	•	22.2	3.1	14.8	24.7	5.4	20.7	20.5	•	•	13.7	11.2
Operating Margin Before Officers' Comp.	22	13.9	•	40.6	12.4	32.0	46.6	8.5	27.9	27.7	•	•	14.4	11.9

Selected Average Balance Sheet ($ in Thousands)

Net Receivables 23	45218	•	1	183	89	315	2057	2319	9399	•	•	129915	11333628
Inventories 24	•	•	•	•	•	•	•	•	•	•	•	•	•
Net Property, Plant and Equipment 25	472	•	11	19	63	620	804	473	1059	•	•	30866	87350
Total Assets 26	138677	•	90	573	2003	8429	15980	35979	66658	•	•	1147051	34063737
Notes and Loans Payable 27	26603	•	41	0	144	61	1672	923	9322	•	•	137152	6617382
All Other Liabilities 28	102284	•	9	252	649	2896	5893	9073	18176	•	•	668767	25416085
Net Worth 29	9790	•	41	321	1210	5472	8415	25982	39159	•	•	341132	2030271

Selected Financial Ratios (Times to 1)

Current Ratio 30	1.7	•	1.9	2.1	4.4	12.8	2.0	2.2	2.2	•	•	0.8	1.7
Quick Ratio 31	1.3	•	1.1	2.0	2.5	12.6	1.5	1.9	1.5	•	•	0.5	1.3
Net Sales to Working Capital 32	0.2	•	30.2	13.4	2.5	0.7	5.2	2.7	1.6	•	•	•	0.2
Coverage Ratio 33	2.2	•	122.9	1548.3	48.7	104.6	32.8	63.5	16.9	•	•	2.5	1.9
Total Asset Turnover 34	0.1	•	5.2	6.7	1.5	0.4	2.1	0.8	0.5	•	•	0.1	0.1
Inventory Turnover 35	•	•	•	•	•	•	•	•	•	•	•	•	•
Receivables Turnover 36	•	•	•	•	•	•	•	•	•	•	•	•	•
Total Liabilities to Net Worth 37	13.2	•	1.2	0.8	0.7	0.5	0.9	0.4	0.7	•	•	2.4	15.8
Current Assets to Working Capital 38	2.4	•	2.1	1.9	1.3	1.1	2.0	1.8	1.8	•	•	•	2.3
Current Liabilities to Working Capital 39	1.4	•	1.1	0.9	0.3	0.1	1.0	0.8	0.8	•	•	•	1.3
Working Capital to Net Sales 40	4.1	•	0.0	0.1	0.4	1.4	0.2	0.4	0.6	•	•	•	5.4
Inventory to Working Capital 41	0.0	•	•	•	•	•	•	•	•	•	•	•	0.0
Total Receipts to Cash Flow 42	2.0	•	2.4	2.3	2.0	2.6	1.3	2.1	2.6	•	•	1.9	2.0
Cost of Goods to Cash Flow 43	0.0	•	•	•	•	•	0.1	•	•	•	•	•	0.0
Cash Flow to Total Debt 44	0.0	•	4.0	6.7	1.9	0.4	3.5	1.3	0.5	•	•	0.1	0.0

Selected Financial Factors (in Percentages)

Debt Ratio 45	92.9	•	54.4	44.0	39.6	35.1	47.3	27.8	41.3	•	•	70.3	94.0
Return on Total Assets 46	1.6	•	116.0	20.9	22.4	8.4	11.9	15.9	11.4	•	•	3.1	1.3
Return on Equity Before Income Taxes 47	12.0	•	252.5	37.3	36.4	12.9	21.9	21.7	18.2	•	•	6.2	10.7
Return on Equity After Income Taxes 48	9.1	•	251.1	33.1	35.9	11.6	17.7	17.4	12.9	•	•	4.4	7.8
Profit Margin (Before Income Tax) 49	11.8	•	22.2	3.1	14.8	21.8	5.4	20.5	19.6	•	•	13.5	11.4
Profit Margin (After Income Tax) 50	8.9	•	22.1	2.8	14.5	19.7	4.3	16.4	13.9	•	•	9.6	8.3

Table I

Corporations with and without Net Income

COMMODITY CONTRACTS DEALING AND BROKERAGE

Item Description for Accounting Period 7/11 Through 6/12		MONEY AMOUNTS AND SIZE OF ASSETS IN THOUSANDS OF DOLLARS												
		Total	Zero Assets	Under 500	500 to 1,000	1,000 to 5,000	5,000 to 10,000	10,000 to 25,000	25,000 to 50,000	50,000 to 100,000	100,000 to 250,000	250,000 to 500,000	500,000 to 2,500,000	2,500,000 and over
Number of Enterprises	1	2445	792	928	451	168	11	49	10	15	4	6	5	6
Revenues ($ in Thousands)														
Net Sales	2	5965181	207148	131324	96244	206153	109831	292928	19203	138171	67980	311464	163966	4220769
Interest	3	311519	568	365	45	451	73	2330	171	1653	1213	13909	11580	279160
Rents	4	76933	0	0	0	0	0	0	0	184	0	206	0	76544
Royalties	5	3622	0	0	0	0	0	0	0	0	0	3622	0	0
Other Portfolio Income	6	399556	185	1211	0	1104	0	4451	0	23392	203	78146	868	289995
Other Receipts	7	5173551	206395	129748	96199	204598	109758	286147	19032	112942	66564	215581	151518	3575070
Total Receipts	8	5965181	207148	131324	96244	206153	109831	292928	19203	138171	67980	311464	163966	4220769
Average Total Receipts	9	2440	262	142	213	1227	9985	5978	1920	9211	16995	51911	32793	703462
Operating Costs/Operating Income (%)														
Cost of Operations	10	2.2	•	•	•	•	•	•	•	•	•	•	•	3.2
Salaries and Wages	11	15.9	8.2	19.0	7.6	21.1	44.2	47.2	67.6	28.5	7.1	29.1	10.2	11.9
Taxes Paid	12	2.2	3.3	2.9	1.9	3.6	3.5	4.9	7.9	3.5	2.6	1.2	3.2	1.8
Interest Paid	13	6.4	20.3	3.3	0.6	7.8	0.0	5.6	14.2	3.7	7.4	2.3	10.6	6.3
Depreciation	14	5.4	0.4	0.7	7.2	1.3	1.6	1.9	2.1	0.6	0.1	0.9	0.6	7.1
Amortization and Depletion	15	1.4	•	•	•	5.5	0.4	•	10.6	1.7	0.0	3.9	3.9	1.2
Pensions and Other Deferred Comp.	16	0.4	0.1	•	4.7	0.6	2.8	0.1	•	0.9	•	0.1	0.5	0.3
Employee Benefits	17	1.5	•	3.4	1.1	0.8	2.3	3.9	6.1	1.8	1.0	2.5	0.9	1.4
Advertising	18	0.3	•	0.2	0.5	0.2	1.6	2.5	1.0	0.2	0.0	1.5	0.0	0.1
Other Expenses	19	55.1	21.6	59.3	52.6	36.7	13.5	45.7	128.2	60.1	37.1	33.6	52.4	60.8
Officers' Compensation	20	3.1	•	18.5	16.7	2.8	18.1	6.9	12.7	6.7	5.6	4.7	11.9	1.1
Operating Margin	21	6.0	46.1	•	7.1	19.5	11.9	•	•	•	39.0	20.3	5.7	4.9
Operating Margin Before Officers' Comp.	22	9.1	46.1	11.2	23.8	22.3	30.0	•	•	•	44.6	25.0	17.6	6.0

Selected Average Balance Sheet ($ in Thousands)													
Net Receivables 23	5762	0	0	7	670	510	3517	772	29277	59317	7580	216723	1996754
Inventories 24	•	•	•	•	•	•	•	•	•	•	•	•	•
Net Property, Plant and Equipment 25	836	0	6	71	16	980	1132	244	270	153	2128	2507	317514
Total Assets 26	29963	0	120	645	2174	7133	17679	31780	66240	182346	359363	686341	10653081
Notes and Loans Payable 27	3954	0	35	242	672	2569	8121	5124	12456	32198	67398	237711	1171368
All Other Liabilities 28	23249	0	10	46	1420	617	9380	6856	31211	113868	171910	454590	8635313
Net Worth 29	2760	0	75	356	81	3946	178	19800	22573	36281	120054	-5960	846400

Selected Financial Ratios (Times to 1)													
Current Ratio 30	1.8	•	8.8	1.4	1.5	11.1	1.7	1.7	1.2	1.0	0.7	1.3	1.9
Quick Ratio 31	1.1	•	8.1	1.4	1.4	10.9	0.8	1.0	0.9	0.5	0.6	0.8	1.2
Net Sales to Working Capital 32	0.2	•	2.2	5.1	3.0	1.8	1.5	0.4	1.0	2.5	•	0.4	0.2
Coverage Ratio 33	1.9	3.3	•	12.6	3.5	272.7	•	•	•	6.3	9.9	1.6	1.8
Total Asset Turnover 34	0.1	•	1.2	0.3	0.6	1.4	0.3	0.1	0.1	0.1	0.1	0.0	0.1
Inventory Turnover 35	•	•	•	•	•	•	•	•	•	•	•	•	•
Receivables Turnover 36	•	•	•	•	•	•	•	•	•	•	•	•	•
Total Liabilities to Net Worth 37	9.9	•	0.6	0.8	25.8	0.8	98.2	0.6	1.9	4.0	2.0	•	11.6
Current Assets to Working Capital 38	2.3	•	1.1	3.5	3.2	1.1	2.5	2.3	5.1	22.3	•	4.9	2.1
Current Liabilities to Working Capital 39	1.3	•	0.1	2.5	2.2	0.1	1.5	1.3	4.1	21.3	•	3.9	1.1
Working Capital to Net Sales 40	4.6	•	0.5	0.2	0.3	0.6	0.7	2.3	1.0	0.4	•	2.4	6.3
Inventory to Working Capital 41	0.0	•	•	•	•	•	•	•	•	•	•	•	0.0
Total Receipts to Cash Flow 42	1.8	1.5	2.3	1.9	2.0	4.3	6.6	•	2.7	1.3	4.4	1.8	1.6
Cost of Goods to Cash Flow 43	0.0	•	•	•	•	•	•	•	•	•	•	•	0.1
Cash Flow to Total Debt 44	0.0	•	1.4	0.4	0.3	0.7	0.1	•	0.1	0.1	0.0	0.0	0.0

Selected Financial Factors (in Percentages)													
Debt Ratio 45	90.8	•	37.0	44.7	96.3	44.7	99.0	37.7	65.9	80.1	66.6	100.9	92.1
Return on Total Assets 46	1.0	•	•	2.6	15.4	16.7	•	•	•	4.3	3.3	0.8	0.7
Return on Equity Before Income Taxes 47	5.3	•	•	4.3	295.2	30.0	•	•	•	18.3	8.8	•	4.1
Return on Equity After Income Taxes 48	2.3	•	•	3.9	294.4	30.0	•	•	•	13.2	5.8	•	1.7
Profit Margin (Before Income Tax) 49	6.0	46.1	•	7.1	19.5	11.9	•	•	•	39.0	20.3	5.9	5.0
Profit Margin (After Income Tax) 50	2.6	31.4	•	6.5	19.5	11.9	•	•	•	28.2	13.4	0.5	2.1

Table II

Corporations with Net Income

COMMODITY CONTRACTS DEALING AND BROKERAGE

MONEY AMOUNTS AND SIZE OF ASSETS IN THOUSANDS OF DOLLARS

Item Description for Accounting Period 7/11 Through 6/12		Total	Zero Assets	Under 500	500 to 1,000	1,000 to 5,000	5,000 to 10,000	10,000 to 25,000	25,000 to 50,000	50,000 to 100,000	100,000 to 250,000	250,000 to 500,000	500,000 to 2,500,000	2,500,000 and over
Number of Enterprises	1	1854	•	788	64	156	8	20	3	10	0	•	•	•
Revenues ($ in Thousands)														
Net Sales	2	5429168	•	154986	75778	189578	105580	109642	52297	174270	0	•	•	•
Interest	3	295744	•	4	4	0	0	2313	97	1324	0	•	•	•
Rents	4	76915	•	0	0	0	0	0	0	184	0	•	•	•
Royalties	5	3622	•	0	0	0	0	0	0	0	0	•	•	•
Other Portfolio Income	6	391843	•	1211	0	0	0	4398	0	17657	0	•	•	•
Other Receipts	7	4661044	•	153771	75774	189578	105580	102931	52200	155105	0	•	•	•
Total Receipts	8	5429168	•	154986	75778	189578	105580	109642	52297	174270	0	•	•	•
Average Total Receipts	9	2928	•	197	1184	1215	13198	5482	17432	17427	•	•	•	•
Operating Costs/Operating Income (%)														
Cost of Operations	10	2.5	•	•	•	•	•	•	•	•	•	•	•	•
Salaries and Wages	11	13.3	•	10.2	5.5	21.0	33.2	26.4	21.4	15.2	•	•	•	•
Taxes Paid	12	2.0	•	1.7	1.9	3.6	2.5	2.5	2.6	3.1	•	•	•	•
Interest Paid	13	6.3	•	2.6	•	7.7	0.0	4.7	0.2	4.4	•	•	•	•
Depreciation	14	5.6	•	0.1	•	1.4	0.7	0.7	0.6	0.3	•	•	•	•
Amortization and Depletion	15	0.9	•	•	•	6.0	•	•	3.9	1.3	•	•	•	•
Pensions and Other Deferred Comp.	16	0.4	•	•	6.0	0.3	2.7	0.2	•	0.7	•	•	•	•
Employee Benefits	17	1.3	•	2.5	0.5	0.3	2.0	1.6	2.2	0.9	•	•	•	•
Advertising	18	0.2	•	0.2	•	0.2	1.0	0.1	0.4	0.2	•	•	•	•
Other Expenses	19	49.8	•	34.5	12.0	32.9	8.8	13.3	35.3	27.6	•	•	•	•
Officers' Compensation	20	2.6	•	15.6	21.2	1.4	13.8	1.9	4.6	5.7	•	•	•	•
Operating Margin	21	15.2	•	32.6	52.9	25.2	35.4	48.5	28.9	40.5	•	•	•	•
Operating Margin Before Officers' Comp.	22	17.8	•	48.1	74.1	26.6	49.1	50.5	33.6	46.2	•	•	•	•

Selected Average Balance Sheet ($ in Thousands)

Net Receivables 23	6159	•	0	48	710	692	4414	2573	36203	•	•	•	•
Inventories 24	•	•	•	•	•	•	•	•	•	•	•	•	•
Net Property, Plant and Equipment 25	1034	•	0	0	17	421	100	760	327	•	•	•	•
Total Assets 26	35218	•	88	715	2135	6678	18519	29909	96265	•	•	•	•
Notes and Loans Payable 27	4206	•	38	0	660	60	3402	3500	22030	•	•	•	•
All Other Liabilities 28	27791	•	2	67	1470	519	7415	4551	49443	•	•	•	•
Net Worth 29	3221	•	48	648	4	6099	7702	21858	24791	•	•	•	•

Selected Financial Ratios (Times to 1)

Current Ratio 30	2.0	•	12.8	10.2	1.4	11.1	1.3	1.5	1.0	•	•	•	•
Quick Ratio 31	1.2	•	12.6	10.2	1.4	11.1	0.8	1.5	0.6	•	•	•	•
Net Sales to Working Capital 32	0.2	•	2.9	1.9	3.4	2.3	2.7	5.3	5.2	•	•	•	•
Coverage Ratio 33	3.4	•	13.7	•	4.3	12450.7	11.3	152.3	10.3	•	•	•	•
Total Asset Turnover 34	0.1	•	2.2	1.7	0.6	2.0	0.3	0.6	0.2	•	•	•	•
Inventory Turnover 35	•	•	•	•	•	•	•	•	•	•	•	•	•
Receivables Turnover 36	•	•	•	•	•	•	•	•	•	•	•	•	•
Total Liabilities to Net Worth 37	9.9	•	0.8	0.1	489.5	0.1	1.4	0.4	2.9	•	•	•	•
Current Assets to Working Capital 38	2.0	•	1.1	1.1	3.6	1.1	4.1	2.9	21.5	•	•	•	•
Current Liabilities to Working Capital 39	1.0	•	0.1	0.1	2.6	0.1	3.1	1.9	20.5	•	•	•	•
Working Capital to Net Sales 40	5.3	•	0.3	0.5	0.3	0.4	0.4	0.2	0.2	•	•	•	•
Inventory to Working Capital 41	0.0	•	•	•	•	•	•	•	•	•	•	•	•
Total Receipts to Cash Flow 42	1.7	•	1.7	1.5	1.9	2.3	1.7	1.6	1.8	•	•	•	•
Cost of Goods to Cash Flow 43	0.0	•	•	•	•	•	•	•	•	•	•	•	•
Cash Flow to Total Debt 44	0.1	•	3.0	11.4	0.3	10.0	0.3	1.3	0.1	•	•	•	•

Selected Financial Factors (in Percentages)

Debt Ratio 45	90.9	•	45.5	9.4	99.8	8.7	58.4	26.9	74.2	•	•	•	•
Return on Total Assets 46	1.8	•	78.5	87.6	18.8	69.9	15.7	17.0	8.1	•	•	•	•
Return on Equity Before Income Taxes 47	13.9	•	133.6	96.7	7049.2	76.5	34.5	23.1	28.5	•	•	•	•
Return on Equity After Income Taxes 48	10.4	•	133.6	95.3	7032.5	76.5	31.5	22.9	20.4	•	•	•	•
Profit Margin (Before Income Tax) 49	15.3	•	32.6	52.9	25.2	35.4	48.5	28.9	40.5	•	•	•	•
Profit Margin (After Income Tax) 50	11.5	•	32.6	52.2	25.2	35.4	44.3	28.8	29.0	•	•	•	•

Table I

Corporations with and without Net Income

SECURITIES & COMMODITY EXCHANGES, OTHER FINANCIAL INVESTMENT

MONEY AMOUNTS AND SIZE OF ASSETS IN THOUSANDS OF DOLLARS

Item Description for Accounting Period 7/11 Through 6/12		Total	Zero Assets	Under 500	500 to 1,000	1,000 to 5,000	5,000 to 10,000	10,000 to 25,000	25,000 to 50,000	50,000 to 100,000	100,000 to 250,000	250,000 to 500,000	500,000 to 2,500,000	2,500,000 and over
Number of Enterprises	1	47479	8843	32436	1840	2485	691	538	252	154	106	45	53	35
Revenues ($ in Thousands)														
Net Sales	2	122675501	4392144	9797840	983686	5593687	4534639	4562393	3461368	5485801	6456492	3375637	13135262	60896554
Interest	3	4939640	694214	15937	3778	53250	10649	41265	38152	72240	70143	166394	286847	3486770
Rents	4	496758	339136	0	0	184	0	927	4347	5601	12364	2116	36694	95391
Royalties	5	108131	214	24	1	64	2	12327	1837	16005	12953	876	129	63699
Other Portfolio Income	6	3409151	515456	92816	30559	229905	87038	156919	274225	89105	124935	205139	356797	1246258
Other Receipts	7	113721821	2843124	9689063	949348	5310284	4436950	4350955	3142807	5302850	6236097	3001112	12454795	56004436
Total Receipts	8	122675501	4392144	9797840	983686	5593687	4534639	4562393	3461368	5485801	6456492	3375637	13135262	60896554
Average Total Receipts	9	2584	497	302	535	2251	6562	8480	13736	35622	60910	75014	247835	1739902
Operating Costs/Operating Income (%)														
Cost of Operations	10	0.3	1.6	0.0	•	•	•	•	0.2	0.1	0.2	•	0.7	0.2
Salaries and Wages	11	23.2	12.2	17.5	14.2	28.7	38.9	41.0	26.4	15.5	30.2	20.8	17.8	23.0
Taxes Paid	12	2.8	1.4	3.2	2.2	3.0	3.0	5.1	3.0	1.7	2.9	2.7	2.2	2.8
Interest Paid	13	5.3	17.5	1.3	0.6	0.7	0.9	1.1	2.9	2.1	3.6	6.3	5.6	6.7
Depreciation	14	2.2	6.9	0.9	0.9	1.2	1.0	1.9	2.1	1.3	2.5	2.0	1.7	2.6
Amortization and Depletion	15	2.1	1.8	0.1	0.3	0.6	0.8	0.6	0.8	0.9	1.2	7.8	4.3	2.4
Pensions and Other Deferred Comp.	16	1.7	1.1	3.6	0.6	1.6	0.3	0.9	2.0	0.6	1.5	0.4	0.6	2.0
Employee Benefits	17	1.8	1.0	2.1	2.4	2.6	2.4	2.4	2.3	1.1	2.1	2.5	1.2	1.7
Advertising	18	1.4	0.9	0.8	0.2	0.6	0.2	0.4	0.4	0.3	2.2	0.4	0.6	2.0
Other Expenses	19	35.3	50.8	33.7	40.9	28.2	28.7	25.6	35.9	29.3	28.3	40.4	51.0	33.8
Officers' Compensation	20	7.1	3.7	22.0	12.7	18.0	20.4	7.5	9.3	7.3	9.4	4.2	5.2	3.1
Operating Margin	21	16.8	1.1	15.0	25.0	14.7	3.4	13.5	14.7	39.8	15.9	12.4	9.2	19.6
Operating Margin Before Officers' Comp.	22	24.0	4.8	37.0	37.7	32.8	23.8	20.9	24.0	47.1	25.3	16.6	14.4	22.7

Selected Average Balance Sheet ($ in Thousands)													
Net Receivables 23	1156	0	5	109	180	886	1604	3732	8800	17365	38584	132796	1133845
Inventories 24	•	•	•	•	•	•	•	•	•	•	•	•	•
Net Property, Plant and Equipment 25	333	0	9	65	177	342	811	1643	3204	10700	4417	22300	309987
Total Assets 26	14794	0	75	745	2219	7011	14974	35041	70522	152845	365224	1035687	16370237
Notes and Loans Payable 27	4203	0	41	341	534	1250	4177	6803	17628	38968	93574	334166	4648079
All Other Liabilities 28	6112	0	38	70	405	1305	2063	6049	14385	43951	80182	278302	7401561
Net Worth 29	4479	0	-4	335	1279	4456	8734	22189	38509	69926	191468	423219	4320596

Selected Financial Ratios (Times to 1)													
Current Ratio 30	0.8	•	2.1	2.3	2.7	2.6	1.8	2.2	1.3	1.4	1.9	1.3	0.8
Quick Ratio 31	0.5	•	1.8	2.1	1.9	2.1	1.3	1.5	1.0	1.2	1.2	0.8	0.4
Net Sales to Working Capital 32	•	•	11.7	2.8	4.2	5.0	4.0	1.8	7.0	3.8	1.4	3.2	•
Coverage Ratio 33	4.3	1.1	12.6	45.8	20.8	4.9	12.6	6.0	19.6	5.4	3.1	2.6	4.1
Total Asset Turnover 34	0.2	•	4.0	0.7	1.0	0.9	0.6	0.4	0.5	0.4	0.2	0.2	0.1
Inventory Turnover 35	•	•	•	•	•	•	•	•	•	•	•	•	•
Receivables Turnover 36	•	•	•	•	•	•	•	•	•	•	•	•	•
Total Liabilities to Net Worth 37	2.3	•	•	1.2	0.7	0.6	0.7	0.6	0.8	1.2	0.9	1.4	2.8
Current Assets to Working Capital 38	•	•	1.9	1.7	1.6	1.6	2.2	1.8	4.6	3.4	2.2	4.5	•
Current Liabilities to Working Capital 39	•	•	0.9	0.7	0.6	0.6	1.2	0.8	3.6	2.4	1.2	3.5	•
Working Capital to Net Sales 40	•	•	0.1	0.4	0.2	0.2	0.3	0.5	0.1	0.3	0.7	0.3	•
Inventory to Working Capital 41	•	•	•	•	•	•	•	0.0	0.0	0.0	•	0.0	•
Total Receipts to Cash Flow 42	2.1	2.4	2.4	1.7	2.8	3.8	3.1	2.6	1.5	2.5	2.3	1.8	2.0
Cost of Goods to Cash Flow 43	0.0	0.0	0.0	•	•	•	•	0.0	0.0	0.0	•	0.0	0.0
Cash Flow to Total Debt 44	0.1	•	1.6	0.7	0.9	0.7	0.4	0.4	0.7	0.3	0.2	0.2	0.1

Selected Financial Factors (in Percentages)													
Debt Ratio 45	69.7	•	105.4	55.0	42.3	36.4	41.7	36.7	45.4	54.3	47.6	59.1	73.6
Return on Total Assets 46	4.0	•	65.5	18.2	15.6	4.0	8.2	6.9	21.1	7.7	4.0	3.5	3.0
Return on Equity Before Income Taxes 47	10.1	•	•	39.7	25.8	5.0	13.0	9.1	36.7	13.7	5.2	5.4	8.5
Return on Equity After Income Taxes 48	7.4	•	•	37.6	23.9	4.0	11.4	6.5	35.4	11.3	3.5	1.4	5.8
Profit Margin (Before Income Tax) 49	17.5	1.0	15.0	24.9	14.6	3.4	13.4	14.6	39.7	15.8	13.3	9.2	21.1
Profit Margin (After Income Tax) 50	12.9	•	14.9	23.6	13.6	2.7	11.7	10.5	38.2	12.9	8.9	2.4	14.5

Table II

Corporations with Net Income

SECURITIES & COMMODITY EXCHANGES, OTHER FINANCIAL INVESTMENT

Item Description for Accounting Period 7/11 Through 6/12		MONEY AMOUNTS AND SIZE OF ASSETS IN THOUSANDS OF DOLLARS Total	Zero Assets	Under 500	500 to 1,000	1,000 to 5,000	5,000 to 10,000	10,000 to 25,000	25,000 to 50,000	50,000 to 100,000	100,000 to 250,000	250,000 to 500,000	500,000 to 2,500,000	2,500,000 and over
Number of Enterprises	1	27879	3812	20310	1233	1521	390	267	139	71	50	25	37	23
Revenues ($ in Thousands)														
Net Sales	2	108810136	4161865	7931858	886155	4799612	3984440	3739365	2758613	4807315	4939380	2771416	13151024	54879091
Interest	3	3995828	687077	15762	3439	22823	8702	33058	21055	37654	34736	151944	195747	2783831
Rents	4	477280	339107	0	0	172	0	859	1562	1243	6458	2116	35530	90233
Royalties	5	79992	184	0	1	64	2	12327	106	15945	7988	833	0	42543
Other Portfolio Income	6	3071580	505369	90317	30557	204992	31007	152547	268151	70542	90673	159940	321607	1145874
Other Receipts	7	101185456	2630128	7825779	852158	4571561	3944729	3540574	2467739	4681931	4799525	2456583	12598140	50816610
Total Receipts	8	108810136	4161865	7931858	886155	4799612	3984440	3739365	2758613	4807315	4939380	2771416	13151024	54879091
Average Total Receipts	9	3903	1092	391	719	3156	10217	14005	19846	67709	98788	110857	355433	2386047
Operating Costs/Operating Income (%)														
Cost of Operations	10	0.2	1.7	0.1	•	•	•	•	0.2	0.1	0.2	•	0.7	0.0
Salaries and Wages	11	21.0	10.7	14.6	15.7	25.7	36.4	34.9	26.5	11.3	27.7	18.7	15.1	21.8
Taxes Paid	12	2.7	1.2	2.9	2.3	2.8	2.5	5.5	2.9	1.5	2.9	2.9	1.9	2.9
Interest Paid	13	4.6	17.0	1.3	0.3	0.5	0.4	0.7	1.3	0.7	2.6	5.0	3.0	6.1
Depreciation	14	2.1	6.4	0.6	0.5	0.9	0.7	1.1	1.3	0.6	1.7	2.1	1.4	2.6
Amortization and Depletion	15	1.5	1.7	0.1	0.3	0.5	0.2	0.7	0.5	0.4	1.0	6.3	2.0	1.7
Pensions and Other Deferred Comp.	16	1.7	1.1	3.9	0.7	1.8	0.3	1.0	1.0	0.5	1.7	0.5	0.5	2.1
Employee Benefits	17	1.6	0.8	1.9	2.7	2.4	2.1	1.1	2.2	0.8	1.4	2.5	0.9	1.8
Advertising	18	1.4	0.8	0.6	0.2	0.7	0.2	0.4	0.2	0.3	2.6	0.4	0.5	2.1
Other Expenses	19	31.2	39.2	30.1	24.5	19.2	20.1	18.3	26.6	22.2	21.1	33.3	47.2	31.7
Officers' Compensation	20	6.7	3.0	19.3	13.6	17.6	21.5	8.2	7.5	7.5	10.2	4.5	4.9	3.0
Operating Margin	21	25.3	16.3	24.7	39.1	27.9	15.7	28.1	30.0	54.2	26.9	23.9	21.8	24.2
Operating Margin Before Officers' Comp.	22	32.0	19.3	44.0	52.7	45.6	37.2	36.3	37.4	61.7	37.1	28.4	26.8	27.2

Selected Average Balance Sheet ($ in Thousands)													
Net Receivables 23	1744	0	7	162	149	1037	2495	3033	10891	18330	47839	136885	1678533
Inventories 24	•	•	•	•	•	•	•	•	•	•	•	•	•
Net Property, Plant and Equipment 25	473	0	13	31	226	504	668	1848	2517	10040	6684	22019	446386
Total Assets 26	20401	0	78	707	2163	6750	15219	34429	71046	154828	368253	1034721	21359114
Notes and Loans Payable 27	5503	0	26	79	425	1077	3894	5323	13275	36240	99602	307440	5797190
All Other Liabilities 28	9022	0	51	74	288	1404	1832	7704	12635	53501	82556	296763	10054003
Net Worth 29	5876	0	2	554	1449	4269	9492	21401	45136	65087	186095	430517	5507921
Selected Financial Ratios (Times to 1)													
Current Ratio 30	0.9	•	2.1	3.7	4.3	2.7	2.3	1.8	2.2	1.2	2.0	1.1	0.8
Quick Ratio 31	0.5	•	1.8	3.5	3.3	2.3	1.9	1.2	1.7	1.0	1.3	0.8	0.5
Net Sales to Working Capital 32	•	•	13.5	2.4	4.8	7.1	4.2	3.2	4.7	9.6	1.6	10.7	•
Coverage Ratio 33	6.7	2.0	20.0	129.5	54.1	44.7	38.9	24.3	73.6	11.5	6.0	8.3	5.2
Total Asset Turnover 34	0.2	•	5.0	1.0	1.5	1.5	0.9	0.6	1.0	0.6	0.3	0.3	0.1
Inventory Turnover 35	•	•	•	•	•	•	•	•	•	•	•	•	•
Receivables Turnover 36	•	•	•	•	•	•	•	•	•	•	•	•	•
Total Liabilities to Net Worth 37	2.5	•	39.5	0.3	0.5	0.6	0.6	0.6	0.6	1.4	1.0	1.4	2.9
Current Assets to Working Capital 38	•	•	1.9	1.4	1.3	1.6	1.7	2.2	1.8	5.7	2.0	11.4	•
Current Liabilities to Working Capital 39	•	•	0.9	0.4	0.3	0.6	0.7	1.2	0.8	4.7	1.0	10.4	•
Working Capital to Net Sales 40	•	•	0.1	0.4	0.2	0.1	0.2	0.3	0.2	0.1	0.6	0.1	•
Inventory to Working Capital 41	•	•	•	•	•	•	•	0.0	0.0	0.0	•	0.0	•
Total Receipts to Cash Flow 42	1.9	2.1	2.1	1.7	2.4	3.1	2.5	2.2	1.3	2.2	2.1	1.5	1.9
Cost of Goods to Cash Flow 43	0.0	0.0	0.0	•	•	•	•	0.0	0.0	0.0	•	0.0	0.0
Cash Flow to Total Debt 44	0.1	•	2.5	2.7	1.8	1.3	1.0	0.7	1.9	0.5	0.3	0.4	0.1
Selected Financial Factors (in Percentages)													
Debt Ratio 45	71.2	•	97.5	21.6	33.0	36.8	37.6	37.8	36.5	58.0	49.5	58.4	74.2
Return on Total Assets 46	5.9	•	130.0	39.9	41.4	24.3	26.4	18.0	52.3	18.7	9.1	8.5	3.5
Return on Equity Before Income Taxes 47	17.3	•	5003.7	50.5	60.7	37.5	41.3	27.8	81.3	40.7	14.9	18.0	11.1
Return on Equity After Income Taxes 48	13.8	•	4973.2	48.6	58.0	35.6	38.3	22.9	78.7	35.1	11.7	12.4	8.0
Profit Margin (Before Income Tax) 49	26.1	16.3	24.7	39.0	27.9	15.7	28.0	30.0	54.2	26.8	25.1	21.8	25.6
Profit Margin (After Income Tax) 50	20.8	14.3	24.5	37.5	26.6	14.9	26.0	24.7	52.5	23.1	19.7	15.0	18.4

Table I

Corporations with and without Net Income

LIFE INSURANCE

Item Description for Accounting Period 7/11 Through 6/12		MONEY AMOUNTS AND SIZE OF ASSETS IN THOUSANDS OF DOLLARS												
		Total	Zero Assets	Under 500	500 to 1,000	1,000 to 5,000	5,000 to 10,000	10,000 to 25,000	25,000 to 50,000	50,000 to 100,000	100,000 to 250,000	250,000 to 500,000	500,000 to 2,500,000	2,500,000 and over
Number of Enterprises	1	752	19	153	65	85	61	61	42	37	32	41	68	87
Revenues ($ in Thousands)														
Net Sales	2	943384142	79885	26106	91057	59894	101063	2290433	498593	1417131	1593317	4812929	33146648	899267085
Interest	3	164336795	10043	202	463	4539	11654	28844	45686	76991	158402	627653	2927464	160444855
Rents	4	6970436	0	0	0	76	527	1492	3057	14159	1295	7978	20777	6921074
Royalties	5	13536	0	0	0	0	0	0	0	32	819	22	278	12386
Other Portfolio Income	6	27334893	398	951	261	1859	5674	5180	7145	10992	18097	105021	340333	26838983
Other Receipts	7	744728482	69444	24953	90333	53420	83208	2254917	442705	1314957	1414704	4072255	29857796	705049787
Total Receipts	8	943384142	79885	26106	91057	59894	101063	2290433	498593	1417131	1593317	4812929	33146648	899267085
Average Total Receipts	9	1254500	4204	171	1401	705	1657	37548	11871	38301	49791	117389	487451	10336403
Operating Costs/Operating Income (%)														
Cost of Operations	10	49.8	18.1	53.3	5.1	14.8	24.7	9.1	47.7	34.0	38.4	48.6	42.0	50.3
Salaries and Wages	11	2.0	•	•	•	•	•	0.0	0.0	2.8	0.2	0.6	0.5	2.0
Taxes Paid	12	0.7	0.9	0.8	0.3	1.8	3.0	0.4	1.3	2.2	1.1	1.3	0.7	0.7
Interest Paid	13	2.4	0.2	0.2	0.1	0.2	0.1	0.0	1.1	0.1	0.5	0.8	0.2	2.5
Depreciation	14	0.7	0.0	•	0.0	0.5	1.1	0.1	0.5	0.6	0.2	0.3	0.3	0.7
Amortization and Depletion	15	1.2	2.2	0.3	0.1	1.7	1.7	0.5	2.0	1.5	2.6	2.2	1.4	1.2
Pensions and Other Deferred Comp.	16	0.5	0.0	•	0.0	0.0	0.7	0.1	0.5	1.4	0.4	0.6	0.5	0.5
Employee Benefits	17	0.3	0.0	•	•	0.0	0.7	0.1	0.5	1.3	0.2	0.2	0.2	0.3
Advertising	18	0.2	1.5	•	•	0.1	2.8	0.0	0.1	0.3	0.1	0.6	0.4	0.2
Other Expenses	19	40.0	65.0	32.3	88.6	66.9	52.5	88.7	33.7	51.4	52.5	37.8	53.0	39.4
Officers' Compensation	20	0.1	•	0.0	•	•	•	0.0	•	0.2	0.1	0.4	0.1	0.1
Operating Margin	21	2.0	12.0	13.1	5.8	14.1	12.7	1.0	12.8	4.4	3.8	6.6	0.7	2.0
Operating Margin Before Officers' Comp.	22	2.1	12.0	13.1	5.8	14.1	12.7	1.0	12.8	4.6	3.8	7.0	0.7	2.1

Selected Average Balance Sheet ($ in Thousands)													
Net Receivables **23**	132836	0	7	6	38	172	902	1818	765	4346	3634	3499	1140139
Inventories **24**	•	•	•	•	•	•	•	•	•	•	•	•	•
Net Property, Plant and Equipment **25**	65788	0	0	0	4	84	102	389	1247	245	1790	4223	563564
Total Assets **26**	8106500	0	168	769	2625	7407	16621	36082	71964	163314	369368	1255925	68785889
Notes and Loans Payable **27**	251989	0	0	0	0	0	22	163	195	86	1589	4292	2173802
All Other Liabilities **28**	6664893	0	174	343	1370	3662	8847	22405	53773	144070	350067	1071256	56509560
Net Worth **29**	1189618	0	-7	426	1255	3745	7753	13514	17995	19158	17712	180377	10102527
Selected Financial Ratios (Times to 1)													
Current Ratio **30**	0.4	•	5.7	12.3	8.0	6.6	2.7	4.0	1.6	1.4	1.1	0.7	0.4
Quick Ratio **31**	0.3	•	4.7	8.9	5.9	5.5	1.9	3.1	1.1	1.1	0.7	0.5	0.3
Net Sales to Working Capital **32**	•	•	1.4	2.9	0.4	0.5	6.7	1.1	4.1	2.9	7.4	•	•
Coverage Ratio **33**	1.8	53.9	66.8	69.4	91.8	111.4	55.3	12.9	60.6	8.7	9.3	4.8	1.7
Total Asset Turnover **34**	0.2	•	1.0	1.8	0.3	0.2	2.3	0.3	0.5	0.3	0.3	0.4	0.2
Inventory Turnover **35**	•	•	•	•	•	•	•	•	•	•	•	•	•
Receivables Turnover **36**	•	•	•	•	•	•	•	•	•	•	•	•	•
Total Liabilities to Net Worth **37**	5.8	•	•	0.8	1.1	1.0	1.1	1.7	3.0	7.5	19.9	6.0	5.8
Current Assets to Working Capital **38**	•	•	1.2	1.1	1.1	1.2	1.6	1.3	2.8	3.3	8.3	•	•
Current Liabilities to Working Capital **39**	•	•	0.2	0.1	0.1	0.2	0.6	0.3	1.8	2.3	7.3	•	•
Working Capital to Net Sales **40**	•	•	0.7	0.3	2.4	1.9	0.1	0.9	0.2	0.4	0.1	•	•
Inventory to Working Capital **41**	•	•	•	•	•	•	•	•	•	•	•	•	•
Total Receipts to Cash Flow **42**	2.5	1.3	2.4	1.1	1.3	1.6	1.1	2.2	1.8	1.8	2.3	1.9	2.6
Cost of Goods to Cash Flow **43**	1.2	0.2	1.3	0.1	0.2	0.4	0.1	1.1	0.6	0.7	1.1	0.8	1.3
Cash Flow to Total Debt **44**	0.1	•	0.4	3.9	0.4	0.3	3.8	0.2	0.4	0.2	0.1	0.2	0.1
Selected Financial Factors (in Percentages)													
Debt Ratio **45**	85.3	•	103.9	44.6	52.2	49.4	53.4	62.5	75.0	88.3	95.2	85.6	85.3
Return on Total Assets **46**	0.7	•	13.5	10.6	3.8	2.7	2.3	4.5	2.3	1.2	2.3	0.3	0.7
Return on Equity Before Income Taxes **47**	2.0	•	•	18.8	7.8	5.4	4.9	11.0	9.1	9.4	43.7	1.6	1.9
Return on Equity After Income Taxes **48**	1.2	•	•	16.9	6.4	4.1	2.6	7.5	6.5	7.0	32.2	•	1.2
Profit Margin (Before Income Tax) **49**	1.9	12.0	13.1	5.7	13.9	12.1	1.0	12.5	4.3	3.6	6.6	0.6	1.9
Profit Margin (After Income Tax) **50**	1.2	7.9	12.4	5.1	11.4	9.4	0.5	8.5	3.1	2.7	4.9	•	1.2

Table II

Corporations with Net Income

LIFE INSURANCE

MONEY AMOUNTS AND SIZE OF ASSETS IN THOUSANDS OF DOLLARS

Item Description for Accounting Period 7/11 Through 6/12		Total	Zero Assets	Under 500	500 to 1,000	1,000 to 5,000	5,000 to 10,000	10,000 to 25,000	25,000 to 50,000	50,000 to 100,000	100,000 to 250,000	250,000 to 500,000	500,000 to 2,500,000	2,500,000 and over
Number of Enterprises	1	551	8	103	53	52	49	49	33	27	19	38	53	67
Revenues ($ in Thousands)														
Net Sales	2	730551688	79574	15490	90342	27114	81606	522031	378814	1077444	1059020	4460137	29610496	693149619
Interest	3	129200499	10040	150	400	2325	8737	27743	35928	56534	99264	594526	2526789	125838062
Rents	4	2446090	0	0	0	0	527	1231	1198	9880	39	7978	20473	2404764
Royalties	5	9074	0	0	0	0	0	0	0	32	0	22	276	8745
Other Portfolio Income	6	16870427	398	61	128	974	5099	5452	6570	10522	14479	86729	307767	16432246
Other Receipts	7	582025598	69136	15279	89814	23815	67243	487605	335118	1000476	945238	3770882	26755191	548465802
Total Receipts	8	730551688	79574	15490	90342	27114	81606	522031	378814	1077444	1059020	4460137	29610496	693149619
Average Total Receipts	9	1325865	9947	150	1705	521	1665	10654	11479	39905	55738	117372	558689	10345517
Operating Costs/Operating Income (%)														
Cost of Operations	10	47.8	17.8	31.5	4.8	16.3	20.2	41.8	44.8	31.2	34.6	47.5	41.6	48.1
Salaries and Wages	11	1.6	•	•	•	•	•	0.1	•	3.7	•	0.6	0.5	1.7
Taxes Paid	12	0.7	0.9	0.9	0.2	1.6	1.5	1.7	1.0	2.3	0.8	1.4	0.7	0.7
Interest Paid	13	1.9	0.2	0.2	0.0	0.3	0.0	0.1	1.3	0.1	0.7	0.9	0.2	2.0
Depreciation	14	0.4	0.0	•	0.0	0.0	0.3	0.4	0.1	0.6	0.1	0.4	0.3	0.4
Amortization and Depletion	15	1.3	2.2	0.3	0.1	1.2	1.2	1.5	1.6	1.5	2.1	2.3	1.3	1.3
Pensions and Other Deferred Comp.	16	0.5	0.0	•	0.0	•	0.2	0.4	0.2	1.6	0.2	0.6	0.5	0.5
Employee Benefits	17	0.3	0.0	•	•	•	0.7	0.3	0.2	1.5	0.1	0.2	0.2	0.3
Advertising	18	0.2	1.5	•	•	0.1	0.4	0.1	0.1	0.4	0.1	0.6	0.4	0.2
Other Expenses	19	41.5	65.2	39.4	89.0	40.9	48.9	44.3	31.0	50.5	53.2	37.5	50.0	41.1
Officers' Compensation	20	0.1	•	•	•	•	•	•	•	0.3	•	0.4	0.1	0.1
Operating Margin	21	3.7	12.2	27.7	5.9	39.5	26.4	9.4	19.7	6.3	8.0	7.7	4.1	3.6
Operating Margin Before Officers' Comp.	22	3.8	12.2	27.7	5.9	39.5	26.4	9.4	19.7	6.6	8.0	8.1	4.2	3.7

Selected Average Balance Sheet ($ in Thousands)

Net Receivables 23	56119	0	9	7	48	214	899	2272	716	6862	2877	3342	453019
Inventories 24	•	•	•	•	•	•	•	•	•	•	•	•	•
Net Property, Plant and Equipment 25	12775	0	0	0	0	103	95	126	1233	168	1931	5197	99105
Total Assets 26	7889780	0	180	767	2235	7379	20812	34347	73164	158764	371992	1283936	63543317
Notes and Loans Payable 27	153691	0	0	0	0	0	27	13	268	144	1714	5365	1258542
All Other Liabilities 28	6723894	0	215	385	850	3652	12499	19212	52726	136404	351167	1061462	54175172
Net Worth 29	1012195	0	-35	382	1385	3727	8286	15122	20170	22216	19110	217108	8109603

Selected Financial Ratios (Times to 1)

Current Ratio 30	0.4	•	5.4	11.6	12.4	9.1	3.3	6.3	1.4	1.3	1.3	0.9	0.4
Quick Ratio 31	0.3	•	4.3	8.5	9.5	7.4	2.2	4.9	1.1	1.0	0.9	0.7	0.3
Net Sales to Working Capital 32	•	•	1.1	3.2	0.3	0.6	1.7	1.0	5.8	3.0	3.8	•	•
Coverage Ratio 33	3.0	54.4	117.1	1765.7	117.6	553.3	116.5	16.1	73.9	12.7	10.0	27.3	2.9
Total Asset Turnover 34	0.2	•	0.8	2.2	0.2	0.2	0.5	0.3	0.5	0.4	0.3	0.4	0.2
Inventory Turnover 35	•	•	•	•	•	•	•	•	•	•	•	•	•
Receivables Turnover 36	•	•	•	•	•	•	•	•	•	•	•	•	•
Total Liabilities to Net Worth 37	6.8	•	•	1.0	0.6	1.0	1.5	1.3	2.6	6.1	18.5	4.9	6.8
Current Assets to Working Capital 38	•	•	1.2	1.1	1.1	1.1	1.4	1.2	3.6	3.9	4.3	•	•
Current Liabilities to Working Capital 39	•	•	0.2	0.1	0.1	0.1	0.4	0.2	2.6	2.9	3.3	•	•
Working Capital to Net Sales 40	•	•	0.9	0.3	3.0	1.8	0.6	1.0	0.2	0.3	0.3	•	•
Inventory to Working Capital 41	•	•	•	•	•	•	•	•	•	•	•	•	•
Total Receipts to Cash Flow 42	2.3	1.3	1.5	1.1	1.3	1.4	1.9	2.0	1.8	1.7	2.3	1.9	2.3
Cost of Goods to Cash Flow 43	1.1	0.2	0.5	0.1	0.2	0.3	0.8	0.9	0.6	0.6	1.1	0.8	1.1
Cash Flow to Total Debt 44	0.1	•	0.5	4.2	0.5	0.3	0.4	0.3	0.4	0.2	0.1	0.3	0.1

Selected Financial Factors (in Percentages)

Debt Ratio 45	87.2	•	119.5	50.2	38.0	49.5	60.2	56.0	72.4	86.0	94.9	83.1	87.2
Return on Total Assets 46	0.9	•	23.3	13.0	9.3	5.8	4.8	6.9	3.4	3.0	2.7	1.8	0.9
Return on Equity Before Income Taxes 47	4.9	•	•	26.1	14.9	11.5	12.0	14.7	12.3	20.0	47.0	10.4	4.6
Return on Equity After Income Taxes 48	3.6	•	•	23.6	13.1	10.0	9.3	10.7	9.2	16.7	35.5	7.3	3.5
Profit Margin (Before Income Tax) 49	3.7	12.2	27.7	5.9	39.5	25.7	9.3	19.4	6.2	8.0	7.7	4.1	3.6
Profit Margin (After Income Tax) 50	2.8	8.1	26.6	5.3	34.7	22.3	7.2	14.2	4.6	6.7	5.8	2.8	2.7

Table I

Corporations with and without Net Income

LIFE INSURANCE, STOCK COMPANIES (FORM 1120L)

Item Description for Accounting Period 7/11 Through 6/12		MONEY AMOUNTS AND SIZE OF ASSETS IN THOUSANDS OF DOLLARS Total	Zero Assets	Under 500	500 to 1,000	1,000 to 5,000	5,000 to 10,000	10,000 to 25,000	25,000 to 50,000	50,000 to 100,000	100,000 to 250,000	250,000 to 500,000	500,000 to 2,500,000	2,500,000 and over
Number of Enterprises	1	706	17	147	62	78	61	61	38	37	29	37	60	78
Revenues ($ in Thousands)														
Net Sales	2	821706807	79824	26066	90973	39059	101063	2290433	437598	1417131	1478106	4238881	31249025	780258648
Interest	3	139510255	10043	186	444	3135	11654	28844	38031	76991	131999	564918	2405891	136238121
Rents	4	6441694	0	0	0	0	527	1492	2051	14159	374	7641	18547	6396902
Royalties	5	12512	0	0	0	0	0	0	0	32	0	22	272	12186
Other Portfolio Income	6	23382758	398	951	203	1079	5674	5180	6932	10992	17355	94832	315852	22923310
Other Receipts	7	652359588	69383	24929	90326	34845	83208	2254917	390584	1314957	1328378	3571468	28508463	614688129
Total Receipts	8	821706807	79824	26066	90973	39059	101063	2290433	437598	1417131	1478106	4238881	31249025	780258648
Average Total Receipts	9	1163891	4696	177	1467	501	1657	37548	11516	38301	50969	114564	520817	10003316
Operating Costs/Operating Income (%)														
Cost of Operations	10	50.1	18.0	53.3	5.0	15.8	24.7	9.1	45.1	34.0	37.6	49.0	41.6	50.6
Salaries and Wages	11	2.1	•	•	•	•	•	0.0	0.0	2.8	0.2	0.7	0.5	2.2
Taxes Paid	12	0.7	0.9	0.8	0.3	1.4	3.0	0.4	1.2	2.2	1.0	1.3	0.7	0.7
Interest Paid	13	2.7	0.2	0.2	0.0	0.2	0.1	0.0	1.2	0.1	0.5	0.9	0.1	2.8
Depreciation	14	0.8	0.0	•	0.0	0.0	1.1	0.1	0.2	0.6	0.2	0.3	0.3	0.8
Amortization and Depletion	15	1.2	2.2	0.3	0.1	1.4	1.7	0.5	2.0	1.5	2.5	2.2	1.3	1.2
Pensions and Other Deferred Comp.	16	0.4	0.0	•	0.0	•	0.7	0.1	0.2	1.4	0.4	0.6	0.5	0.4
Employee Benefits	17	0.3	0.0	•	•	0.0	0.7	0.1	0.4	1.3	0.1	0.2	0.2	0.3
Advertising	18	0.2	1.5	•	•	0.1	2.8	0.0	0.1	0.3	0.1	0.7	0.4	0.2
Other Expenses	19	39.6	65.1	32.2	88.7	60.9	52.5	88.7	34.9	51.4	53.2	36.9	54.0	38.8
Officers' Compensation	20	0.1	•	•	•	•	•	0.0	•	0.2	0.1	0.4	0.1	0.1
Operating Margin	21	1.8	12.1	13.1	5.8	20.1	12.7	1.0	14.7	4.4	4.1	6.8	0.4	1.8
Operating Margin Before Officers' Comp.	22	1.9	12.1	13.1	5.8	20.1	12.7	1.0	14.7	4.6	4.2	7.3	0.5	1.9

Selected Average Balance Sheet ($ in Thousands)													
Net Receivables 23	139719	0	7	6	41	172	902	2003	765	4653	3338	3724	1256218
Inventories 24	•	•	•	•	•	•	•	•	•	•	•	•	•
Net Property, Plant and Equipment 25	67982	0	0	0	4	84	102	407	1247	187	1892	4410	610023
Total Assets 26	7641182	0	165	769	2240	7407	16621	34925	71964	159503	370455	1236935	67902866
Notes and Loans Payable 27	265839	0	0	0	0	0	22	180	195	94	1760	4739	2401472
All Other Liabilities 28	6216072	0	172	354	970	3662	8847	20976	53773	139362	355235	1055126	55184380
Net Worth 29	1159270	0	-7	415	1269	3745	7753	13769	17995	20047	13459	177069	10317014
Selected Financial Ratios (Times to 1)													
Current Ratio 30	0.4	•	5.4	12.4	8.9	6.6	2.7	3.8	1.6	1.4	1.1	0.7	0.4
Quick Ratio 31	0.3	•	4.4	9.0	6.9	5.5	1.9	2.8	1.1	1.0	0.7	0.4	0.3
Net Sales to Working Capital 32	•	•	1.4	2.9	0.3	0.5	6.7	1.1	4.1	3.2	11.4	•	•
Coverage Ratio 33	1.6	54.2	66.9	1749.0	86.0	111.4	55.3	13.0	60.6	8.8	8.6	3.9	1.6
Total Asset Turnover 34	0.2	•	1.1	1.9	0.2	0.2	2.3	0.3	0.5	0.3	0.3	0.4	0.1
Inventory Turnover 35	•	•	•	•	•	•	•	•	•	•	•	•	•
Receivables Turnover 36	•	•	•	•	•	•	•	•	•	•	•	•	•
Total Liabilities to Net Worth 37	5.6	•	•	0.9	0.8	1.0	1.1	1.5	3.0	7.0	26.5	6.0	5.6
Current Assets to Working Capital 38	•	•	1.2	1.1	1.1	1.2	1.6	1.4	2.8	3.7	13.2	•	•
Current Liabilities to Working Capital 39	•	•	0.2	0.1	0.1	0.2	0.6	0.4	1.8	2.7	12.2	•	•
Working Capital to Net Sales 40	•	•	0.7	0.3	3.1	1.9	0.1	0.9	0.2	0.3	0.1	•	•
Inventory to Working Capital 41	•	•	•	•	•	•	•	•	•	•	•	•	•
Total Receipts to Cash Flow 42	2.5	1.3	2.4	1.1	1.3	1.6	1.1	2.1	1.8	1.8	2.4	1.9	2.6
Cost of Goods to Cash Flow 43	1.3	0.2	1.3	0.1	0.2	0.4	0.1	0.9	0.6	0.7	1.2	0.8	1.3
Cash Flow to Total Debt 44	0.1	•	0.4	3.9	0.4	0.3	3.8	0.3	0.4	0.2	0.1	0.3	0.1
Selected Financial Factors (in Percentages)													
Debt Ratio 45	84.8	•	104.1	46.0	43.3	49.4	53.4	60.6	75.0	87.4	96.4	85.7	84.8
Return on Total Assets 46	0.7	•	14.3	11.0	4.5	2.7	2.3	5.2	2.3	1.4	2.4	0.2	0.7
Return on Equity Before Income Taxes 47	1.7	•	•	20.4	7.9	5.4	4.9	12.1	9.1	10.0	57.9	1.0	1.6
Return on Equity After Income Taxes 48	1.0	•	•	18.4	6.6	4.1	2.6	8.3	6.5	7.6	42.6	•	1.0
Profit Margin (Before Income Tax) 49	1.7	12.1	13.1	5.8	20.0	12.1	1.0	14.4	4.3	3.9	6.8	0.3	1.7
Profit Margin (After Income Tax) 50	1.0	8.0	12.5	5.2	16.7	9.4	0.5	9.9	3.1	3.0	5.0	•	1.1

Table II

Corporations with Net Income

LIFE INSURANCE, STOCK COMPANIES (FORM 1120L)

MONEY AMOUNTS AND SIZE OF ASSETS IN THOUSANDS OF DOLLARS

Item Description for Accounting Period 7/11 Through 6/12		Total	Zero Assets	Under 500	500 to 1,000	1,000 to 5,000	5,000 to 10,000	10,000 to 25,000	25,000 to 50,000	50,000 to 100,000	100,000 to 250,000	250,000 to 500,000	500,000 to 2,500,000	2,500,000 and over
Number of Enterprises	1	528	8	•	53	52	49	•	•	27	•	34	•	•
Revenues ($ in Thousands)														
Net Sales	2	612578283	79574	•	90342	27114	81606	•	•	1077444	•	3886089	•	•
Interest	3	104970131	10040	•	400	2325	8737	•	•	56534	•	531791	•	•
Rents	4	1919232	0	•	0	0	527	•	•	9880	•	7641	•	•
Royalties	5	8871	0	•	0	0	0	•	•	32	•	22	•	•
Other Portfolio Income	6	12981034	398	•	128	974	5099	•	•	10522	•	76541	•	•
Other Receipts	7	492699015	69136	•	89814	23815	67243	•	•	1000476	•	3270094	•	•
Total Receipts	8	612578283	79574	•	90342	27114	81606	•	•	1077444	•	3886089	•	•
Average Total Receipts	9	1160186	9947	•	1705	521	1665	•	•	39905	•	114297	•	•
Operating Costs/Operating Income (%)														
Cost of Operations	10	47.7	17.8	•	4.8	16.3	20.2	•	•	31.2	•	47.7	•	•
Salaries and Wages	11	1.8	•	•	•	•	•	•	•	3.7	•	0.7	•	•
Taxes Paid	12	0.7	0.9	•	0.2	1.6	1.5	•	•	2.3	•	1.4	•	•
Interest Paid	13	2.1	0.2	•	0.0	0.3	0.0	•	•	0.1	•	1.0	•	•
Depreciation	14	0.4	0.0	•	0.0	0.0	0.3	•	•	0.6	•	0.4	•	•
Amortization and Depletion	15	1.2	2.2	•	0.1	1.2	1.2	•	•	1.5	•	2.2	•	•
Pensions and Other Deferred Comp.	16	0.4	0.0	•	0.0	•	0.2	•	•	1.6	•	0.6	•	•
Employee Benefits	17	0.3	0.0	•	•	•	0.7	•	•	1.5	•	0.2	•	•
Advertising	18	0.2	1.5	•	•	0.1	0.4	•	•	0.4	•	0.7	•	•
Other Expenses	19	41.3	65.2	•	89.0	40.9	48.9	•	•	50.5	•	36.4	•	•
Officers' Compensation	20	0.1	•	•	•	•	•	•	•	0.3	•	0.5	•	•
Operating Margin	21	3.8	12.2	•	5.9	39.5	26.4	•	•	6.3	•	8.1	•	•
Operating Margin Before Officers' Comp.	22	3.8	12.2	•	5.9	39.5	26.4	•	•	6.6	•	8.6	•	•

Selected Average Balance Sheet ($ in Thousands)													
Net Receivables 23	56264	0	•	7	48	214	•	•	716	•	2465	•	•
Inventories 24	•	•	•	•	•	•	•	•	•	•	•	•	•
Net Property, Plant and Equipment 25	10590	0	•	0	0	103	•	•	1233	•	2059	•	•
Total Assets 26	6939067	0	•	767	2235	7379	•	•	73164	•	373483	•	•
Notes and Loans Payable 27	156965	0	•	0	0	0	•	•	268	•	1916	•	•
All Other Liabilities 28	5864823	0	•	385	850	3652	•	•	52726	•	356921	•	•
Net Worth 29	917279	0	•	382	1385	3727	•	•	20170	•	14647	•	•
Selected Financial Ratios (Times to 1)													
Current Ratio 30	0.4	•	•	11.6	12.4	9.1	•	•	1.4	•	1.2	•	•
Quick Ratio 31	0.3	•	•	8.5	9.5	7.4	•	•	1.1	•	0.8	•	•
Net Sales to Working Capital 32	•	•	•	3.2	0.3	0.6	•	•	5.8	•	4.3	•	•
Coverage Ratio 33	2.8	54.4	•	1765.7	117.6	553.3	•	•	73.9	•	9.2	•	•
Total Asset Turnover 34	0.2	•	•	2.2	0.2	0.2	•	•	0.5	•	0.3	•	•
Inventory Turnover 35	•	•	•	•	•	•	•	•	•	•	•	•	•
Receivables Turnover 36	•	•	•	•	•	•	•	•	•	•	•	•	•
Total Liabilities to Net Worth 37	6.6	•	•	1.0	0.6	1.0	•	•	2.6	•	24.5	•	•
Current Assets to Working Capital 38	•	•	•	1.1	1.1	1.1	•	•	3.6	•	5.0	•	•
Current Liabilities to Working Capital 39	•	•	•	0.1	0.1	0.1	•	•	2.6	•	4.0	•	•
Working Capital to Net Sales 40	•	•	•	0.3	3.0	1.8	•	•	0.2	•	0.2	•	•
Inventory to Working Capital 41	•	•	•	•	•	•	•	•	•	•	•	•	•
Total Receipts to Cash Flow 42	2.3	1.3	•	1.1	1.3	1.4	•	•	1.8	•	2.3	•	•
Cost of Goods to Cash Flow 43	1.1	0.2	•	0.1	0.2	0.3	•	•	0.6	•	1.1	•	•
Cash Flow to Total Debt 44	0.1	•	•	4.2	0.5	0.3	•	•	0.4	•	0.1	•	•
Selected Financial Factors (in Percentages)													
Debt Ratio 45	86.8	•	•	50.2	38.0	49.5	•	•	72.4	•	96.1	•	•
Return on Total Assets 46	1.0	•	•	13.0	9.3	5.8	•	•	3.4	•	2.8	•	•
Return on Equity Before Income Taxes 47	4.8	•	•	26.1	14.9	11.5	•	•	12.3	•	62.8	•	•
Return on Equity After Income Taxes 48	3.7	•	•	23.6	13.1	10.0	•	•	9.2	•	47.5	•	•
Profit Margin (Before Income Tax) 49	3.8	12.2	•	5.9	39.5	25.7	•	•	6.2	•	8.0	•	•
Profit Margin (After Income Tax) 50	2.9	8.1	•	5.3	34.7	22.3	•	•	4.6	•	6.1	•	•

Table I

Corporations with and without Net Income

LIFE INSURANCE, MUTUAL COMPANIES (FORM 1120L)

MONEY AMOUNTS AND SIZE OF ASSETS IN THOUSANDS OF DOLLARS

Item Description for Accounting Period 7/11 Through 6/12		Total	Zero Assets	Under 500	500 to 1,000	1,000 to 5,000	5,000 to 10,000	10,000 to 25,000	25,000 to 50,000	50,000 to 100,000	100,000 to 250,000	250,000 to 500,000	500,000 to 2,500,000	2,500,000 and over
Number of Enterprises	1	46	3	5	3	7	0	0	4	0	3	4	8	9
Revenues ($ in Thousands)														
Net Sales	2	121677335	61	40	84	20835	0	0	60995	0	115211	574048	1897623	119008437
Interest	3	24826540	0	16	19	1404	0	0	7655	0	26403	62735	521573	24206735
Rents	4	528742	0	0	0	76	0	0	1006	0	921	337	2230	524172
Royalties	5	1024	0	0	0	0	0	0	0	0	819	0	6	200
Other Portfolio Income	6	3952136	0	0	58	779	0	0	213	0	744	10190	24480	3915673
Other Receipts	7	92368893	61	24	7	18576	0	0	52121	0	86324	500786	1349334	90361657
Total Receipts	8	121677335	61	40	84	20835	0	0	60995	0	115211	574048	1897623	119008437
Average Total Receipts	9	2645159	20	8	28	2976	•	•	15249	•	38404	143512	237203	13223160
Operating Costs/Operating Income (%)														
Cost of Operations	10	48.2	177.0	42.5	25.0	13.0	•	•	66.7	•	49.5	45.7	48.6	48.2
Salaries and Wages	11	0.7	•	•	•	•	•	•	•	•	•	•	0.8	0.8
Taxes Paid	12	0.8	•	2.5	16.7	2.6	•	•	2.0	•	1.5	1.2	1.9	0.7
Interest Paid	13	0.8	•	•	85.7	•	•	•	•	•	0.0	0.0	0.6	0.8
Depreciation	14	0.4	•	•	•	1.3	•	•	1.9	•	0.2	0.4	0.3	0.4
Amortization and Depletion	15	1.5	•	•	•	2.3	•	•	1.6	•	3.4	2.5	3.2	1.4
Pensions and Other Deferred Comp.	16	1.1	•	•	•	0.0	•	•	2.4	•	1.3	0.4	1.2	1.1
Employee Benefits	17	0.1	•	•	•	0.0	•	•	1.5	•	0.9	0.4	0.3	0.1
Advertising	18	0.2	•	•	•	•	•	•	0.0	•	0.1	0.0	0.6	0.2
Other Expenses	19	42.9	11.5	55.0	23.8	78.1	•	•	24.7	•	43.8	44.3	38.0	43.0
Officers' Compensation	20	0.1	•	10.0	•	•	•	•	•	•	•	•	•	0.1
Operating Margin	21	3.3	•	•	•	2.7	•	•	•	•	•	5.0	4.5	3.2
Operating Margin Before Officers' Comp.	22	3.4	•	2.5	•	2.7	•	•	•	•	•	5.0	4.5	3.3

Selected Average Balance Sheet ($ in Thousands)													
Net Receivables 23	27206	0	0	0	0	•	•	61	•	1376	6376	1811	134123
Inventories 24	•	•	•	•	•	•	•	•	•	•	•	•	•
Net Property, Plant and Equipment 25	32119	0	0	0	0	•	•	220	•	806	842	2817	160921
Total Assets 26	15248124	0	268	766	6920	•	•	47079	•	200149	359316	1398355	76438749
Notes and Loans Payable 27	39424	0	0	0	0	•	•	0	•	0	0	938	200668
All Other Liabilities 28	13553307	0	268	125	5823	•	•	35984	•	189587	302262	1192232	67994449
Net Worth 29	1655392	0	0	641	1097	•	•	11095	•	10562	57054	205185	8243632
Selected Financial Ratios (Times to 1)													
Current Ratio 30	0.8	•	•	2.6	5.1	•	•	8.4	•	8.2	2.2	1.1	0.7
Quick Ratio 31	0.6	•	•	•	2.6	•	•	8.0	•	6.5	1.7	1.0	0.6
Net Sales to Working Capital 32	•	•	0.0	1.5	1.1	•	•	0.9	•	1.3	2.1	5.9	•
Coverage Ratio 33	5.1	•	•	0.4	•	•	•	•	•	•	1918.1	7.7	5.1
Total Asset Turnover 34	0.2	•	0.0	0.0	0.4	•	•	0.3	•	0.2	0.4	0.2	0.2
Inventory Turnover 35	•	•	•	•	•	•	•	•	•	•	•	•	•
Receivables Turnover 36	•	•	•	•	•	•	•	•	•	•	•	•	•
Total Liabilities to Net Worth 37	8.2	•	•	0.2	5.3	•	•	3.2	•	17.9	5.3	5.8	8.3
Current Assets to Working Capital 38	•	•	1.0	1.6	1.2	•	•	1.1	•	1.1	1.9	12.3	•
Current Liabilities to Working Capital 39	•	•	•	0.6	0.2	•	•	0.1	•	0.1	0.9	11.3	•
Working Capital to Net Sales 40	•	•	28.8	0.7	0.9	•	•	1.1	•	0.8	0.5	0.2	•
Inventory to Working Capital 41	•	•	•	•	•	•	•	•	•	•	•	0.0	•
Total Receipts to Cash Flow 42	2.3	•	2.5	•	1.3	•	•	4.3	•	2.4	2.1	2.4	2.3
Cost of Goods to Cash Flow 43	1.1	•	1.1	•	0.2	•	•	2.9	•	1.2	1.0	1.2	1.1
Cash Flow to Total Debt 44	0.1	•	0.0	•	0.4	•	•	0.1	•	0.1	0.2	0.1	0.1
Selected Financial Factors (in Percentages)													
Debt Ratio 45	89.1	•	100.0	16.3	84.1	•	•	76.4	•	94.7	84.1	85.3	89.2
Return on Total Assets 46	0.7	•	•	1.3	1.1	•	•	•	•	•	2.0	0.8	0.7
Return on Equity Before Income Taxes 47	5.3	•	•	•	6.9	•	•	•	•	•	12.6	5.0	5.3
Return on Equity After Income Taxes 48	3.3	•	•	•	4.0	•	•	•	•	•	9.6	2.9	3.3
Profit Margin (Before Income Tax) 49	3.3	•	•	•	2.6	•	•	•	•	•	5.0	4.3	3.3
Profit Margin (After Income Tax) 50	2.1	•	•	•	1.5	•	•	•	•	•	3.8	2.5	2.1

Table II

Corporations with Net Income

LIFE INSURANCE, MUTUAL COMPANIES (FORM 1120L)

MONEY AMOUNTS AND SIZE OF ASSETS IN THOUSANDS OF DOLLARS

Item Description for Accounting Period 7/11 Through 6/12		Total	Zero Assets	Under 500	500 to 1000	1,000 to 5,000	5,000 to 10,000	10,000 to 25,000	25,000 to 50,000	50,000 to 100,000	100,000 to 250,000	250,000 to 500,000	500,000 to 2,500,000	2,500,000 and over
Number of Enterprises	1	24	0	•	0	0	0	•	•	0	•	4	•	•
Revenues ($ in Thousands)														
Net Sales	2	117973405	0	•	0	0	0	•	•	0	•	574048	•	•
Interest	3	24230368	0	•	0	0	0	•	•	0	•	62735	•	•
Rents	4	526858	0	•	0	0	0	•	•	0	•	337	•	•
Royalties	5	203	0	•	0	0	0	•	•	0	•	0	•	•
Other Portfolio Income	6	3889393	0	•	0	0	0	•	•	0	•	10190	•	•
Other Receipts	7	89326583	0	•	0	0	0	•	•	0	•	500786	•	•
Total Receipts	8	117973405	0	•	0	0	0	•	•	0	•	574048	•	•
Average Total Receipts	9	4915559	•	•	•	•	•	•	•	•	•	143512	•	•
Operating Costs/Operating Income (%)														
Cost of Operations	10	48.3	•	•	•	•	•	•	•	•	•	45.7	•	•
Salaries and Wages	11	0.8	•	•	•	•	•	•	•	•	•	•	•	•
Taxes Paid	12	0.8	•	•	•	•	•	•	•	•	•	1.2	•	•
Interest Paid	13	0.8	•	•	•	•	•	•	•	•	•	0.0	•	•
Depreciation	14	0.4	•	•	•	•	•	•	•	•	•	0.4	•	•
Amortization and Depletion	15	1.5	•	•	•	•	•	•	•	•	•	2.5	•	•
Pensions and Other Deferred Comp.	16	1.1	•	•	•	•	•	•	•	•	•	0.4	•	•
Employee Benefits	17	0.1	•	•	•	•	•	•	•	•	•	0.4	•	•
Advertising	18	0.2	•	•	•	•	•	•	•	•	•	0.0	•	•
Other Expenses	19	42.6	•	•	•	•	•	•	•	•	•	44.3	•	•
Officers' Compensation	20	0.1	•	•	•	•	•	•	•	•	•	•	•	•
Operating Margin	21	3.4	•	•	•	•	•	•	•	•	•	5.0	•	•
Operating Margin Before Officers' Comp.	22	3.5	•	•	•	•	•	•	•	•	•	5.0	•	•

Selected Average Balance Sheet ($ in Thousands)													
Net Receivables 23	50603	•	•	•	•	•	•	•	•	•	6376	•	•
Inventories 24	•	•	•	•	•	•	•	•	•	•	•	•	•
Net Property, Plant and Equipment 25	60309	•	•	•	•	•	•	•	•	•	842	•	•
Total Assets 26	28476722	•	•	•	•	•	•	•	•	•	359316	•	•
Notes and Loans Payable 27	75251	•	•	•	•	•	•	•	•	•	0	•	•
All Other Liabilities 28	25343296	•	•	•	•	•	•	•	•	•	302262	•	•
Net Worth 29	3058175	•	•	•	•	•	•	•	•	•	57054	•	•

Selected Financial Ratios (Times to 1)													
Current Ratio 30	0.8	•	•	•	•	•	•	•	•	•	2.2	•	•
Quick Ratio 31	0.6	•	•	•	•	•	•	•	•	•	1.7	•	•
Net Sales to Working Capital 32	•	•	•	•	•	•	•	•	•	•	2.1	•	•
Coverage Ratio 33	5.3	•	•	•	•	•	•	•	•	•	1918.1	•	•
Total Asset Turnover 34	0.2	•	•	•	•	•	•	•	•	•	0.4	•	•
Inventory Turnover 35	•	•	•	•	•	•	•	•	•	•	•	•	•
Receivables Turnover 36	•	•	•	•	•	•	•	•	•	•	•	•	•
Total Liabilities to Net Worth 37	8.3	•	•	•	•	•	•	•	•	•	5.3	•	•
Current Assets to Working Capital 38	•	•	•	•	•	•	•	•	•	•	1.9	•	•
Current Liabilities to Working Capital 39	•	•	•	•	•	•	•	•	•	•	0.9	•	•
Working Capital to Net Sales 40	•	•	•	•	•	•	•	•	•	•	0.5	•	•
Inventory to Working Capital 41	•	•	•	•	•	•	•	•	•	•	•	•	•
Total Receipts to Cash Flow 42	2.3	•	•	•	•	•	•	•	•	•	2.1	•	•
Cost of Goods to Cash Flow 43	1.1	•	•	•	•	•	•	•	•	•	1.0	•	•
Cash Flow to Total Debt 44	0.1	•	•	•	•	•	•	•	•	•	0.2	•	•

Selected Financial Factors (in Percentages)													
Debt Ratio 45	89.3	•	•	•	•	•	•	•	•	•	84.1	•	•
Return on Total Assets 46	0.7	•	•	•	•	•	•	•	•	•	2.0	•	•
Return on Equity Before Income Taxes 47	5.6	•	•	•	•	•	•	•	•	•	12.6	•	•
Return on Equity After Income Taxes 48	3.5	•	•	•	•	•	•	•	•	•	9.6	•	•
Profit Margin (Before Income Tax) 49	3.5	•	•	•	•	•	•	•	•	•	5.0	•	•
Profit Margin (After Income Tax) 50	2.2	•	•	•	•	•	•	•	•	•	3.8	•	•

Table I

Corporations with and without Net Income

MUTUAL PROPERTY AND CASUALTY COMPANIES (FORM 1120-PC)

MONEY AMOUNTS AND SIZE OF ASSETS IN THOUSANDS OF DOLLARS

Item Description for Accounting Period 7/11 Through 6/12		Total	Zero Assets	Under 500	500 to 1,000	1,000 to 5,000	5,000 to 10,000	10,000 to 25,000	25,000 to 50,000	50,000 to 100,000	100,000 to 250,000	250,000 to 500,000	500,000 to 2,500,000	2,500,000 and over
Number of Enterprises	1	1427	34	63	0	543	160	203	107	92	74	52	69	28
Revenues ($ in Thousands)														
Net Sales	2	281147657	199136	984	0	556515	448457	1129507	1831604	2494289	5548328	7867876	44816980	216253982
Interest	3	14409335	10825	1	0	26958	20908	58419	66401	125064	257361	376364	1495896	11971137
Rents	4	541544	647	56	0	1628	491	2664	2025	3270	5027	15201	54127	456409
Royalties	5	1099	0	0	0	0	0	0	1	1	8	1	267	820
Other Portfolio Income	6	9521910	11127	0	0	8431	15015	33618	43806	100511	222350	280758	1425124	7381170
Other Receipts	7	256673769	176537	927	0	519498	412043	1034806	1719371	2265443	5063582	7195552	41841566	196444446
Total Receipts	8	281147657	199136	984	0	556515	448457	1129507	1831604	2494289	5548328	7867876	44816980	216253982
Average Total Receipts	9	197020	5857	16	•	1025	2803	5564	17118	27112	74977	151305	649521	7723356
Operating Costs/Operating Income (%)														
Cost of Operations	10	63.2	54.8	85.6	•	65.4	59.2	59.4	69.9	55.4	65.3	61.4	72.3	61.4
Salaries and Wages	11	14.6	9.0	•	•	13.2	14.2	10.4	9.9	17.1	17.5	14.9	13.2	14.8
Taxes Paid	12	2.5	2.4	•	•	2.8	2.3	2.8	2.1	3.2	2.7	2.5	1.8	2.6
Interest Paid	13	0.6	•	•	•	0.1	0.0	0.2	0.1	0.3	0.3	0.2	0.2	0.8
Depreciation	14	1.3	0.2	0.5	•	0.3	0.3	0.6	0.8	0.9	1.5	1.7	1.2	1.4
Amortization and Depletion	15	0.2	•	•	•	0.0	0.0	1.5	0.0	0.0	0.0	0.1	0.1	0.3
Pensions and Other Deferred Comp.	16	1.3	3.0	•	•	0.1	0.3	0.8	0.2	0.3	0.3	0.7	0.6	1.5
Employee Benefits	17	1.4	1.6	•	•	1.7	0.9	1.4	0.8	1.6	2.5	3.8	1.4	1.3
Advertising	18	1.1	0.1	•	•	0.2	0.3	0.3	0.3	0.6	0.8	0.4	0.3	1.4
Other Expenses	19	13.6	22.0	27.4	•	22.6	23.3	25.3	16.3	19.2	14.2	13.5	8.5	14.4
Officers' Compensation	20	0.3	0.3	•	•	2.4	1.9	1.2	0.9	1.1	0.7	0.8	0.4	0.2
Operating Margin	21	•	6.6	•	•	•	•	•	•	0.4	•	0.0	•	•
Operating Margin Before Officers' Comp.	22	0.1	6.9	•	•	•	•	•	•	1.6	•	0.8	0.3	0.2

Selected Average Balance Sheet ($ in Thousands)													
Net Receivables 23	42601	0	3	•	107	202	1107	2687	5746	15746	38987	116188	1730359
Inventories 24	•	•	•	•	•	•	•	•	•	•	•	•	•
Net Property, Plant and Equipment 25	6511	0	2	•	55	94	250	417	989	2744	5129	23278	249433
Total Assets 26	496163	0	116	•	2737	7690	16327	34660	70803	166805	348667	1158273	20763153
Notes and Loans Payable 27	9078	0	25	•	16	23	211	233	293	970	3057	4699	438935
All Other Liabilities 28	287120	0	84	•	1109	3959	10970	22493	44324	105671	209045	682375	11928340
Net Worth 29	199965	0	7	•	1612	3708	5146	11934	26186	60164	136565	471200	8395878
Selected Financial Ratios (Times to 1)													
Current Ratio 30	1.0	•	1.4	•	1.7	1.8	1.0	0.9	1.0	0.8	1.0	0.9	1.0
Quick Ratio 31	0.9	•	1.3	•	1.5	1.5	0.8	0.8	0.8	0.7	0.9	0.9	0.9
Net Sales to Working Capital 32	•	•	0.5	•	1.5	1.0	•	•	•	•	203.6	•	•
Coverage Ratio 33	•	•	•	•	•	•	•	•	•	•	•	•	•
Total Asset Turnover 34	0.4	•	0.1	•	0.4	0.4	0.3	0.5	0.4	0.4	0.4	0.6	0.4
Inventory Turnover 35	•	•	•	•	•	•	•	•	•	•	•	•	•
Receivables Turnover 36	•	•	•	•	•	•	•	•	•	•	•	•	•
Total Liabilities to Net Worth 37	1.5	•	15.7	•	0.7	1.1	2.2	1.9	1.7	1.8	1.6	1.5	1.5
Current Assets to Working Capital 38	•	•	3.8	•	2.5	2.2	•	•	•	•	258.5	•	•
Current Liabilities to Working Capital 39	•	•	2.8	•	1.5	1.2	•	•	•	•	257.5	•	•
Working Capital to Net Sales 40	•	•	1.9	•	0.7	1.0	•	•	•	•	0.0	•	•
Inventory to Working Capital 41	•	•	•	•	•	•	•	•	•	•	•	•	•
Total Receipts to Cash Flow 42	8.7	4.3	7.1	•	7.9	5.2	5.0	7.6	6.1	17.2	9.3	15.4	8.0
Cost of Goods to Cash Flow 43	5.5	2.3	6.1	•	5.2	3.1	3.0	5.3	3.4	11.3	5.7	11.2	4.9
Cash Flow to Total Debt 44	0.1	•	0.0	•	0.1	0.1	0.1	0.1	0.1	0.0	0.1	0.1	0.1
Selected Financial Factors (in Percentages)													
Debt Ratio 45	59.7	•	94.0	•	41.1	51.8	68.5	65.6	63.0	63.9	60.8	59.3	59.6
Return on Total Assets 46	•	•	•	•	•	•	•	•	•	•	•	•	•
Return on Equity Before Income Taxes 47	•	•	•	•	•	•	•	•	•	•	•	•	•
Return on Equity After Income Taxes 48	•	•	•	•	•	•	•	•	•	•	•	•	•
Profit Margin (Before Income Tax) 49	•	5.7	•	•	•	•	•	•	•	•	•	•	•
Profit Margin (After Income Tax) 50	•	1.0	•	•	•	•	•	•	•	•	•	•	•

Table II

Corporations with Net Income

MUTUAL PROPERTY AND CASUALTY COMPANIES (FORM 1120-PC)

MONEY AMOUNTS AND SIZE OF ASSETS IN THOUSANDS OF DOLLARS

Item Description for Accounting Period 7/11 Through 6/12		Total	Zero Assets	Under 500	500 to 1,000	1,000 to 5,000	5,000 to 10,000	10,000 to 25,000	25,000 to 50,000	50,000 to 100,000	100,000 to 250,000	250,000 to 500,000	500,000 to 2,500,000	2,500,000 and over
Number of Enterprises	1	727	23	31	0	295	70	96	51	52	35	23	37	14
Revenues ($ in Thousands)														
Net Sales	2	96587721	53606	984	0	154223	168671	548748	814474	1457290	2050236	4054518	28721853	58563119
Interest	3	3585156	6296	0	0	14644	6714	26505	29641	67667	132735	159416	778488	2363051
Rents	4	132752	647	56	0	407	199	1136	1675	1323	1687	8844	20514	96264
Royalties	5	1048	0	0	0	0	0	0	0	1	0	0	267	780
Other Portfolio Income	6	3264968	5500	0	0	5037	6274	17452	23068	66418	90369	140692	728709	2181447
Other Receipts	7	89603797	41163	928	0	134135	155484	503655	760090	1321881	1825445	3745566	27193875	53921577
Total Receipts	8	96587721	53606	984	0	154223	168671	548748	814474	1457290	2050236	4054518	28721853	58563119
Average Total Receipts	9	132858	2331	32	•	523	2410	5716	15970	28025	58578	176283	776266	4183080
Operating Costs/Operating Income (%)														
Cost of Operations	10	64.8	56.8	85.6	•	37.3	43.0	45.1	59.4	46.0	39.7	55.9	72.9	63.3
Salaries and Wages	11	12.5	12.1	•	•	14.8	13.7	9.4	10.8	17.7	22.0	12.8	10.8	12.9
Taxes Paid	12	2.3	2.5	•	•	3.1	1.3	3.0	2.2	2.9	3.2	2.1	1.6	2.7
Interest Paid	13	0.2	•	•	•	0.2	0.0	0.2	0.1	0.2	0.5	0.1	0.1	0.3
Depreciation	14	1.4	0.6	0.5	•	0.5	0.4	0.7	0.5	0.8	2.1	2.2	1.1	1.4
Amortization and Depletion	15	0.1	•	•	•	0.0	0.0	0.0	0.0	0.0	0.0	0.1	0.1	0.2
Pensions and Other Deferred Comp.	16	0.6	•	•	•	0.1	0.3	0.2	0.2	0.3	0.3	0.7	0.6	0.6
Employee Benefits	17	2.1	0.3	•	•	0.7	0.8	2.1	0.6	1.6	4.2	5.7	1.1	2.3
Advertising	18	1.2	0.3	•	•	0.4	0.2	0.2	0.3	0.4	1.3	0.4	0.3	1.7
Other Expenses	19	9.2	3.9	3.2	•	22.2	18.5	20.2	14.8	17.6	12.3	12.8	6.8	9.6
Officers' Compensation	20	0.3	0.1	•	•	2.7	2.4	1.1	0.9	1.2	1.0	0.8	0.3	0.2
Operating Margin	21	5.3	23.5	10.9	•	18.0	19.4	17.9	10.2	11.2	13.5	6.5	4.4	4.9
Operating Margin Before Officers' Comp.	22	5.6	23.5	10.9	•	20.7	21.8	18.9	11.2	12.4	14.5	7.3	4.7	5.1

Selected Average Balance Sheet ($ in Thousands)														
Net Receivables	23	24025	0	6	•	44	262	898	2370	5773	15578	28855	112289	825982
Inventories	24	•	•	•	•	•	•	•	•	•	•	•	•	•
Net Property, Plant and Equipment	25	4630	0	4	•	43	134	149	363	784	1342	5781	30398	140375
Total Assets	26	256137	0	202	•	2619	7137	16101	34324	70456	165248	353094	1161770	8648756
Notes and Loans Payable	27	1066	0	51	•	11	1	172	7	280	674	837	5500	35169
All Other Liabilities	28	144812	0	129	•	620	2483	9446	20445	39426	106148	199046	669482	4846732
Net Worth	29	110258	0	22	•	1988	4652	6483	13872	30750	58426	153211	486788	3766854

Selected Financial Ratios (Times to 1)														
Current Ratio	30	1.1	•	1.5	•	2.6	3.1	1.2	1.0	1.1	0.8	1.1	1.0	1.1
Quick Ratio	31	1.0	•	1.5	•	2.4	2.6	1.0	0.9	0.9	0.7	0.9	0.9	1.0
Net Sales to Working Capital	32	21.8	•	0.5	•	0.6	0.6	3.8	•	10.0	•	10.3	•	15.1
Coverage Ratio	33	18.0	•	•	•	100.1	3270.4	100.5	68.3	49.3	24.3	55.2	26.4	13.2
Total Asset Turnover	34	0.5	•	0.2	•	0.2	0.3	0.4	0.5	0.4	0.4	0.5	0.7	0.5
Inventory Turnover	35	•	•	•	•	•	•	•	•	•	•	•	•	•
Receivables Turnover	36	•	•	•	•	•	•	•	•	•	•	•	•	•
Total Liabilities to Net Worth	37	1.3	•	8.1	•	0.3	0.5	1.5	1.5	1.3	1.8	1.3	1.4	1.3
Current Assets to Working Capital	38	20.5	•	2.9	•	1.6	1.5	6.8	•	14.1	•	11.4	•	14.8
Current Liabilities to Working Capital	39	19.5	•	1.9	•	0.6	0.5	5.8	•	13.1	•	10.4	•	13.8
Working Capital to Net Sales	40	0.0	•	2.2	•	1.8	1.6	0.3	•	0.1	•	0.1	•	0.1
Inventory to Working Capital	41	0.0	•	•	•	•	•	•	•	•	•	•	•	0.0
Total Receipts to Cash Flow	42	8.3	6.1	7.1	•	2.6	2.7	2.8	4.3	3.9	4.5	5.8	10.6	8.6
Cost of Goods to Cash Flow	43	5.4	3.4	6.1	•	1.0	1.2	1.2	2.6	1.8	1.8	3.2	7.7	5.4
Cash Flow to Total Debt	44	0.1	•	0.0	•	0.3	0.4	0.2	0.2	0.2	0.1	0.2	0.1	0.1

Selected Financial Factors (in Percentages)														
Debt Ratio	45	57.0	•	89.0	•	24.1	34.8	59.7	59.6	56.4	64.6	56.6	58.1	56.4
Return on Total Assets	46	2.3	•	1.7	•	3.4	5.9	6.0	4.4	4.0	4.3	2.5	2.5	1.9
Return on Equity Before Income Taxes	47	5.0	•	15.6	•	4.4	9.0	14.7	10.7	9.0	11.7	5.7	5.6	4.1
Return on Equity After Income Taxes	48	3.4	•	15.0	•	3.6	7.2	12.3	9.0	6.9	9.3	4.0	3.6	2.8
Profit Margin (Before Income Tax)	49	4.1	23.5	10.9	•	16.8	17.4	16.7	9.3	9.9	11.7	5.0	3.5	3.7
Profit Margin (After Income Tax)	50	2.8	6.0	10.5	•	13.6	13.8	13.9	7.8	7.6	9.2	3.5	2.3	2.5

Table I

Corporations with and without Net Income

STOCK PROPERTY AND CASUALTY COMPANIES (FORM 1120-PC)

MONEY AMOUNTS AND SIZE OF ASSETS IN THOUSANDS OF DOLLARS

Item Description for Accounting Period 7/11 Through 6/12		Total	Zero Assets	Under 500	500 to 1,000	1,000 to 5,000	5,000 to 10,000	10,000 to 25,000	25,000 to 50,000	50,000 to 100,000	100,000 to 250,000	250,000 to 500,000	500,000 to 2,500,000	2,500,000 and over
Number of Enterprises	1	7396	316	2437	1118	2185	385	271	188	129	124	59	102	83
Revenues ($ in Thousands)														
Net Sales	2	780694760	3840477	61738	74618	493740	578179	2305171	4703245	6808358	15593837	16360633	68301604	661573158
Interest	3	35019841	79351	6109	10507	47267	31054	57971	102743	171068	302339	435341	2159105	31616986
Rents	4	963099	1650	0	0	599	3178	645	3181	3438	16890	12368	59567	861583
Royalties	5	28634	522	0	0	0	1	42	0	0	2866	11309	2093	11800
Other Portfolio Income	6	16126871	94972	1789	4223	24178	21784	33977	49882	65257	164331	206952	1282510	14177018
Other Receipts	7	728556315	3663982	53840	59888	421696	522162	2212536	4547439	6568595	15107411	15694663	64798329	614905771
Total Receipts	8	780694760	3840477	61738	74618	493740	578179	2305171	4703245	6808358	15593837	16360633	68301604	661573158
Average Total Receipts	9	105556	12153	25	67	226	1502	8506	25017	52778	125757	277299	669624	7970761
Operating Costs/Operating Income (%)														
Cost of Operations	10	63.7	56.6	68.4	70.1	63.5	44.5	66.0	68.5	64.2	66.3	67.2	65.2	63.4
Salaries and Wages	11	11.0	19.9	4.0	9.3	9.8	21.1	13.3	12.3	12.1	12.1	11.2	12.5	10.7
Taxes Paid	12	1.9	2.1	0.7	0.5	2.6	2.2	2.0	2.1	1.9	2.6	2.2	2.2	1.9
Interest Paid	13	1.3	0.8	1.2	0.0	0.5	0.8	0.3	0.2	0.6	0.4	0.2	0.9	1.4
Depreciation	14	0.9	0.8	0.0	•	0.3	0.4	0.7	0.4	0.9	0.8	0.9	1.0	0.9
Amortization and Depletion	15	0.3	0.2	0.5	•	0.2	0.1	0.1	0.1	0.1	0.1	0.2	0.3	0.3
Pensions and Other Deferred Comp.	16	0.3	0.1	•	•	0.0	0.1	0.0	0.1	0.1	0.1	0.2	0.4	0.3
Employee Benefits	17	1.0	0.8	0.0	•	1.1	0.5	0.4	0.5	1.1	0.6	0.8	1.2	1.0
Advertising	18	0.6	2.0	•	0.1	0.1	0.1	0.3	0.4	0.7	0.3	0.9	0.3	0.6
Other Expenses	19	15.3	21.0	11.8	17.0	22.8	20.7	20.8	12.7	16.4	13.9	15.8	14.9	15.3
Officers' Compensation	20	0.2	1.1	•	•	0.8	0.7	0.7	0.6	0.6	0.5	0.4	0.5	0.2
Operating Margin	21	3.4	•	13.4	3.1	•	8.6	•	2.2	1.4	2.1	0.0	0.5	4.0
Operating Margin Before Officers' Comp.	22	3.7	•	13.4	3.1	•	9.3	•	2.7	2.0	2.6	0.4	1.0	4.2

Selected Average Balance Sheet ($ in Thousands)														
Net Receivables	23	16382	0	6	22	111	186	1398	3086	6849	11973	36887	108341	1256068
Inventories	24	•	•	•	•	•	•	•	•	•	•	•	•	•
Net Property, Plant and Equipment	25	3588	0	0	0	10	118	145	357	519	2173	5312	19306	286120
Total Assets	26	284850	0	219	737	2222	6796	16024	36117	71917	161694	350542	1194550	23071487
Notes and Loans Payable	27	22689	0	1	3	24	119	558	1147	1595	7962	8625	71259	1908070
All Other Liabilities	28	165436	0	169	507	1851	3549	15286	58687	58585	103783	250801	773487	13107019
Net Worth	29	96724	0	50	228	347	3128	180	-23716	11736	49948	91116	349805	8056399
Selected Financial Ratios (Times to 1)														
Current Ratio	30	0.7	•	0.8	0.7	1.3	1.1	0.8	0.4	1.0	1.0	0.8	0.9	0.7
Quick Ratio	31	0.6	•	0.7	0.7	1.1	0.8	0.6	0.3	0.9	0.9	0.7	0.8	0.5
Net Sales to Working Capital	32	•	•	•	•	0.6	6.4	•	•	121.0	•	•	•	•
Coverage Ratio	33	3.1	•	12.1	98.7	•	10.1	•	9.5	2.8	5.8	•	0.7	3.3
Total Asset Turnover	34	0.4	•	0.1	0.1	0.1	0.2	0.5	0.7	0.7	0.8	0.8	0.6	0.3
Inventory Turnover	35	•	•	•	•	•	•	•	•	•	•	•	•	•
Receivables Turnover	36	•	•	•	•	•	•	•	•	•	•	•	•	•
Total Liabilities to Net Worth	37	1.9	•	3.4	2.2	5.4	1.2	87.9	•	5.1	2.2	2.8	2.4	1.9
Current Assets to Working Capital	38	•	•	•	•	3.9	14.8	•	•	105.3	•	•	•	•
Current Liabilities to Working Capital	39	•	•	•	•	2.9	13.8	•	•	104.3	•	•	•	•
Working Capital to Net Sales	40	•	•	•	•	1.6	0.2	•	•	0.0	•	•	•	•
Inventory to Working Capital	41	•	•	•	•	•	•	•	•	0.1	•	•	•	•
Total Receipts to Cash Flow	42	5.8	7.0	4.5	6.0	5.8	3.7	6.7	7.3	6.0	6.8	6.8	7.3	5.6
Cost of Goods to Cash Flow	43	3.7	4.0	3.1	4.2	3.7	1.6	4.4	5.0	3.9	4.5	4.6	4.8	3.6
Cash Flow to Total Debt	44	0.1	•	0.0	0.0	0.0	0.1	0.1	0.1	0.1	0.2	0.2	0.1	0.1
Selected Financial Factors (in Percentages)														
Debt Ratio	45	66.0	•	77.3	69.1	84.4	54.0	98.9	165.7	83.7	69.1	74.0	70.7	65.1
Return on Total Assets	46	1.4	•	1.7	0.3	•	1.9	•	1.4	1.2	1.7	•	0.4	1.6
Return on Equity Before Income Taxes	47	2.9	•	6.7	0.8	•	3.7	•	•	4.6	4.5	•	•	3.1
Return on Equity After Income Taxes	48	1.4	•	5.5	0.1	•	2.2	•	•	0.1	0.9	•	•	1.7
Profit Margin (Before Income Tax)	49	2.7	•	13.2	2.9	•	7.8	•	1.8	1.0	1.8	•	•	3.1
Profit Margin (After Income Tax)	50	1.3	•	10.8	0.2	•	4.5	•	0.1	0.0	0.4	•	•	1.7

Table II

Corporations with Net Income

STOCK PROPERTY AND CASUALTY COMPANIES (FORM 1120-PC)

MONEY AMOUNTS AND SIZE OF ASSETS IN THOUSANDS OF DOLLARS

Item Description for Accounting Period 7/11 Through 6/12		Total	Zero Assets	Under 500	500 to 1,000	1,000 to 5,000	5,000 to 10,000	10,000 to 25,000	25,000 to 50,000	50,000 to 100,000	100,000 to 250,000	250,000 to 500,000	500,000 to 2,500,000	2,500,000 and over
Number of Enterprises	1	5520	166	1777	951	1740	292	162	119	77	82	37	60	56
Revenues ($ in Thousands)														
Net Sales	2	613081420	1380675	23912	50531	313921	362782	1156252	3205765	3578411	12209881	10737268	41885243	538176779
Interest	3	25505854	38139	5990	10418	41641	26480	33716	61785	115976	206179	254691	1383103	23327737
Rents	4	686083	193	0	0	44	2452	280	922	2453	5755	8385	35912	629686
Royalties	5	23608	522	0	0	0	1	42	0	0	0	11309	22	11712
Other Portfolio Income	6	9471384	24974	1731	4186	22949	17324	16233	31476	41146	124339	137611	768027	8281386
Other Receipts	7	577394491	1316847	16191	35927	249287	316525	1105981	3111582	3418836	11873608	10325272	39698179	505926258
Total Receipts	8	613081420	1380675	23912	50531	313921	362782	1156252	3205765	3578411	12209881	10737268	41885243	538176779
Average Total Receipts	9	111065	8317	13	53	180	1242	7137	26939	46473	148901	290196	698087	9610300
Operating Costs/Operating Income (%)														
Cost of Operations	10	64.2	37.3	32.4	55.1	45.6	36.3	57.5	61.8	53.3	68.3	69.8	60.5	64.4
Salaries and Wages	11	9.5	28.1	0.6	•	6.3	15.8	10.6	13.3	13.1	10.9	8.7	12.4	9.1
Taxes Paid	12	1.8	3.3	0.2	0.4	1.8	1.8	1.6	2.3	2.2	2.6	2.0	2.4	1.8
Interest Paid	13	1.0	0.8	3.1	0.0	0.2	1.3	0.1	0.2	1.0	0.2	0.1	0.5	1.1
Depreciation	14	0.8	0.9	•	•	0.2	0.4	0.2	0.3	0.6	0.6	0.5	1.0	0.9
Amortization and Depletion	15	0.3	0.2	0.0	•	0.0	0.1	0.1	0.0	0.1	0.0	0.1	0.2	0.3
Pensions and Other Deferred Comp.	16	0.3	0.1	•	•	0.0	0.2	0.0	0.1	0.1	0.1	0.2	0.4	0.3
Employee Benefits	17	1.0	1.3	•	•	0.5	0.4	0.2	0.4	1.4	0.4	0.7	1.2	1.0
Advertising	18	0.6	4.7	•	•	0.0	0.1	0.1	0.5	0.8	0.3	0.7	0.2	0.6
Other Expenses	19	14.5	15.1	7.0	17.0	13.7	17.3	13.7	11.2	19.1	10.3	12.0	14.1	14.7
Officers' Compensation	20	0.2	1.9	•	•	1.0	0.9	0.5	0.6	0.6	0.4	0.3	0.6	0.2
Operating Margin	21	5.8	6.3	56.7	27.5	30.7	25.4	15.2	9.1	7.7	5.8	4.9	6.4	5.7
Operating Margin Before Officers' Comp.	22	6.0	8.2	56.7	27.5	31.7	26.3	15.7	9.7	8.3	6.3	5.1	7.0	5.8

Selected Average Balance Sheet ($ in Thousands)

Net Receivables	23	15079	0	5	25	92	119	1133	2771	6544	10810	28173	118993	1302180
Inventories	24	•	•	•	•	•	•	•	•	•	•	•	•	•
Net Property, Plant and Equipment	25	4042	0	0	0	8	82	148	312	366	1363	4967	16438	373282
Total Assets	26	238560	0	236	733	2226	6956	15647	35928	71474	167422	338526	1243944	21368332
Notes and Loans Payable	27	21414	0	0	3	17	123	233	709	1231	4693	4231	70303	2020708
All Other Liabilities	28	130388	0	168	487	1087	3772	8996	23160	43395	97038	201972	695425	11629942
Net Worth	29	86758	0	68	244	1122	3061	6418	12058	26847	65691	132322	478216	7717682

Selected Financial Ratios (Times to 1)

Current Ratio	30	0.7	•	0.8	0.7	1.2	0.9	1.3	1.0	1.2	1.1	1.0	1.0	0.6
Quick Ratio	31	0.6	•	0.7	0.6	1.0	0.7	1.0	0.8	1.0	0.9	0.9	0.9	0.5
Net Sales to Working Capital	32	•	•	•	•	0.7	•	3.4	•	5.7	26.6	•	•	•
Coverage Ratio	33	6.1	7.1	19.4	624.5	128.4	19.6	204.8	58.4	8.5	32.0	44.2	11.7	5.6
Total Asset Turnover	34	0.5	•	0.1	0.1	0.1	0.2	0.5	0.7	0.7	0.9	0.9	0.6	0.4
Inventory Turnover	35	•	•	•	•	•	•	•	•	•	•	•	•	•
Receivables Turnover	36	•	•	•	•	•	•	•	•	•	•	•	•	•
Total Liabilities to Net Worth	37	1.7	•	2.5	2.0	1.0	1.3	1.4	2.0	1.7	1.5	1.6	1.6	1.8
Current Assets to Working Capital	38	•	•	•	•	5.0	•	5.0	•	5.7	16.9	•	•	•
Current Liabilities to Working Capital	39	•	•	•	•	4.0	•	4.0	•	4.7	15.9	•	•	•
Working Capital to Net Sales	40	•	•	•	•	1.5	•	0.3	•	0.2	0.0	•	•	•
Inventory to Working Capital	41	•	•	•	•	•	•	•	•	0.0	0.0	•	•	•
Total Receipts to Cash Flow	42	5.3	5.0	1.7	2.5	2.5	2.5	3.6	5.2	3.9	6.6	6.3	5.3	5.2
Cost of Goods to Cash Flow	43	3.4	1.9	0.5	1.4	1.1	0.9	2.0	3.2	2.1	4.5	4.4	3.2	3.4
Cash Flow to Total Debt	44	0.1	•	0.0	0.0	0.1	0.1	0.2	0.2	0.3	0.2	0.2	0.2	0.1

Selected Financial Factors (in Percentages)

Debt Ratio	45	63.6	•	71.2	66.8	49.6	56.0	59.0	66.4	62.4	60.8	60.9	61.6	63.9
Return on Total Assets	46	3.0	•	3.4	2.0	2.4	4.6	6.7	6.7	5.3	5.0	3.9	3.5	2.9
Return on Equity Before Income Taxes	47	6.8	•	11.1	5.9	4.8	9.9	16.3	19.6	12.5	12.4	9.6	8.4	6.5
Return on Equity After Income Taxes	48	4.6	•	9.9	5.1	3.8	7.8	12.2	14.2	9.2	8.3	6.8	6.0	4.4
Profit Margin (Before Income Tax)	49	5.3	4.9	56.1	27.1	29.7	24.3	14.7	8.8	7.2	5.5	4.4	5.8	5.2
Profit Margin (After Income Tax)	50	3.6	3.8	50.1	23.2	23.7	19.1	11.0	6.3	5.3	3.6	3.1	4.1	3.5

Table I

Corporations with and without Net Income

INSURANCE AGENCIES AND BROKERAGES

MONEY AMOUNTS AND SIZE OF ASSETS IN THOUSANDS OF DOLLARS

Item Description for Accounting Period 7/11 Through 6/12		Total	Zero Assets	Under 500	500 to 1,000	1,000 to 5,000	5,000 to 10,000	10,000 to 25,000	25,000 to 50,000	50,000 to 100,000	100,000 to 250,000	250,000 to 500,000	500,000 to 2,500,000	2,500,000 and over
Number of Enterprises	1	95382	16498	69094	5733	3050	621	223	75	40	24	10	7	7
Revenues ($ in Thousands)														
Net Sales	2	78374405	1882699	22866866	5486335	7240242	8423158	3944699	1562468	2574981	2091544	2255586	3452790	16593037
Interest	3	366200	3113	8752	3049	7401	9058	12727	4629	6870	18792	5520	14234	272056
Rents	4	59241	0	4743	20	8708	10762	15504	2306	894	1101	303	9238	5661
Royalties	5	91137	0	0	35	2360	4	0	0	43	0	0	795	87899
Other Portfolio Income	6	907225	89306	18199	4518	14202	7592	21216	6151	4359	8102	4374	90281	638928
Other Receipts	7	76950602	1790280	22835172	5478713	7207571	8395742	3895252	1549382	2562815	2063549	2245389	3338242	15588493
Total Receipts	8	78374405	1882699	22866866	5486335	7240242	8423158	3944699	1562468	2574981	2091544	2255586	3452790	16593037
Average Total Receipts	9	822	114	331	957	2374	13564	17689	20833	64375	87148	225559	493256	2370434
Operating Costs/Operating Income (%)														
Cost of Operations	10	1.7	0.0	•	•	5.1	0.1	1.7	6.4	19.5	5.4	1.8	4.2	0.2
Salaries and Wages	11	31.2	22.7	25.2	27.6	32.9	24.4	35.7	33.7	31.2	31.0	17.4	31.8	44.7
Taxes Paid	12	3.4	3.1	3.6	3.5	3.8	2.3	3.4	3.6	3.2	3.1	2.9	2.8	3.8
Interest Paid	13	2.6	2.8	0.8	2.0	1.1	0.9	1.0	2.4	0.7	3.8	2.9	4.2	7.1
Depreciation	14	1.3	1.6	0.9	0.8	0.9	0.9	1.4	1.3	1.5	1.3	1.1	2.1	2.0
Amortization and Depletion	15	1.8	0.7	0.7	2.9	1.1	0.7	0.7	2.2	1.2	3.1	1.5	4.9	3.4
Pensions and Other Deferred Comp.	16	1.5	0.4	0.9	1.1	1.2	0.4	1.3	1.5	1.3	0.8	0.3	0.7	3.9
Employee Benefits	17	2.3	1.2	1.9	2.2	3.0	1.9	2.6	3.2	2.7	2.4	1.5	2.6	2.9
Advertising	18	1.5	3.8	2.2	1.2	0.9	1.4	1.1	0.9	1.0	1.0	2.1	2.7	0.6
Other Expenses	19	32.9	42.9	30.8	28.2	25.4	55.2	33.0	28.7	25.8	42.9	61.9	35.5	24.0
Officers' Compensation	20	10.9	9.8	18.5	16.0	14.6	7.2	11.8	10.5	4.7	3.8	1.4	2.6	3.7
Operating Margin	21	8.8	10.8	14.5	14.4	10.2	4.6	6.2	5.5	7.1	1.4	5.3	5.9	3.7
Operating Margin Before Officers' Comp.	22	19.7	20.6	33.0	30.4	24.8	11.8	17.9	16.0	11.8	5.2	6.7	8.5	7.5

Selected Average Balance Sheet ($ in Thousands)													
Net Receivables 23	254	0	4	37	375	1113	3434	8024	14158	23596	23808	218025	2517731
Inventories 24	•	•	•	•	•	•	•	•	•	•	•	•	•
Net Property, Plant and Equipment 25	47	0	14	86	97	808	1068	1192	3369	4751	7726	31519	195389
Total Assets 26	1291	0	85	730	2086	6590	15157	36259	68263	170258	330123	1161455	11173916
Notes and Loans Payable 27	269	0	49	355	476	2272	3055	10278	11939	51341	100856	318333	1558187
All Other Liabilities 28	515	0	19	124	999	2764	8368	18800	38327	71975	147222	418936	4484603
Net Worth 29	507	0	17	251	610	1554	3734	7180	17998	46942	82045	424187	5131126
Selected Financial Ratios (Times to 1)													
Current Ratio 30	1.1	•	1.6	1.6	1.3	1.3	1.2	1.3	1.1	0.9	1.1	1.1	1.0
Quick Ratio 31	0.9	•	1.5	1.4	1.1	1.1	1.1	1.1	0.9	0.7	0.9	1.0	0.8
Net Sales to Working Capital 32	27.6	•	22.6	11.5	8.4	16.2	9.9	4.1	27.1	•	35.7	13.0	•
Coverage Ratio 33	4.7	4.8	18.4	8.2	10.2	5.9	6.9	3.3	11.8	1.3	2.8	2.4	2.2
Total Asset Turnover 34	0.6	•	3.9	1.3	1.1	2.1	1.2	0.6	0.9	0.5	0.7	0.4	0.2
Inventory Turnover 35	•	•	•	•	•	•	•	•	•	•	•	•	•
Receivables Turnover 36	•	•	•	•	•	•	•	•	•	•	•	•	•
Total Liabilities to Net Worth 37	1.5	•	4.0	1.9	2.4	3.2	3.1	4.0	2.8	2.6	3.0	1.7	1.2
Current Assets to Working Capital 38	16.1	•	2.6	2.7	4.6	4.5	5.7	4.3	17.0	•	18.5	9.9	•
Current Liabilities to Working Capital 39	15.1	•	1.6	1.7	3.6	3.5	4.7	3.3	16.0	•	17.5	8.9	•
Working Capital to Net Sales 40	0.0	•	0.0	0.1	0.1	0.1	0.1	0.2	0.0	•	0.0	0.1	•
Inventory to Working Capital 41	0.0	•	•	•	•	•	0.0	0.0	0.0	•	•	0.0	•
Total Receipts to Cash Flow 42	2.8	2.5	2.6	2.9	3.2	1.8	2.8	3.3	3.4	2.5	1.6	2.8	4.3
Cost of Goods to Cash Flow 43	0.0	0.0	•	•	0.2	0.0	0.0	0.2	0.7	0.1	0.0	0.1	0.0
Cash Flow to Total Debt 44	0.4	•	1.8	0.7	0.5	1.5	0.5	0.2	0.4	0.3	0.6	0.2	0.1
Selected Financial Factors (in Percentages)													
Debt Ratio 45	60.7	•	80.1	65.6	70.7	76.4	75.4	80.2	73.6	72.4	75.1	63.5	54.1
Return on Total Assets 46	7.9	•	59.3	21.5	12.8	11.4	8.4	4.5	7.3	2.6	5.5	4.4	3.2
Return on Equity Before Income Taxes 47	15.8	•	281.4	54.9	39.5	40.3	29.1	15.8	25.2	2.2	14.0	7.0	3.8
Return on Equity After Income Taxes 48	14.4	•	279.1	54.6	38.6	37.9	26.3	11.9	22.4	0.8	10.3	5.2	2.6
Profit Margin (Before Income Tax) 49	9.8	10.8	14.5	14.4	10.2	4.6	6.1	5.4	7.1	1.2	5.1	6.0	8.2
Profit Margin (After Income Tax) 50	8.9	9.7	14.4	14.3	9.9	4.3	5.6	4.1	6.3	0.4	3.7	4.5	5.6

Table II

Corporations with Net Income

INSURANCE AGENCIES AND BROKERAGES

MONEY AMOUNTS AND SIZE OF ASSETS IN THOUSANDS OF DOLLARS

Item Description for Accounting Period 7/11 Through 6/12		Total	Zero Assets	Under 500	500 to 1,000	1,000 to 5,000	5,000 to 10,000	10,000 to 25,000	25,000 to 50,000	50,000 to 100,000	100,000 to 250,000	250,000 to 500,000	500,000 to 2,500,000	2,500,000 and over
Number of Enterprises	1	71749	9642	55088	3768	2400	564	160	60	34	14	•	•	•
Revenues ($ in Thousands)														
Net Sales	2	67226608	1240429	19947832	4150703	6300047	8199795	3428466	1251414	2435395	1405212	•	•	•
Interest	3	251142	2517	6898	1826	5164	5903	4762	4234	5714	17058	•	•	•
Rents	4	48667	0	4442	20	7851	9024	11720	2287	891	1101	•	•	•
Royalties	5	91135	0	0	35	2360	2	0	0	43	0	•	•	•
Other Portfolio Income	6	887933	89182	17621	3403	11190	4609	17943	4809	3484	7964	•	•	•
Other Receipts	7	65947731	1148730	19918871	4145419	6273482	8180257	3394041	1240084	2425263	1379089	•	•	•
Total Receipts	8	67226608	1240429	19947832	4150703	6300047	8199795	3428466	1251414	2435395	1405212	•	•	•
Average Total Receipts	9	937	129	362	1102	2625	14539	21428	20857	71629	100372	•	•	•
Operating Costs/Operating Income (%)														
Cost of Operations	10	1.7	0.0	•	•	5.8	•	1.8	0.7	20.6	0.7	•	•	•
Salaries and Wages	11	30.6	15.3	24.8	25.0	31.9	23.8	33.1	32.7	30.5	28.6	•	•	•
Taxes Paid	12	3.3	2.5	3.4	3.3	3.6	2.2	3.3	3.8	3.2	3.0	•	•	•
Interest Paid	13	2.3	3.5	0.8	2.1	0.8	0.9	0.8	1.9	0.6	1.9	•	•	•
Depreciation	14	1.1	0.7	0.9	0.6	0.7	0.8	1.1	1.5	1.3	1.5	•	•	•
Amortization and Depletion	15	1.6	0.6	0.5	2.9	1.0	0.7	0.7	1.6	1.1	1.3	•	•	•
Pensions and Other Deferred Comp.	16	1.6	0.2	0.9	1.1	1.1	0.4	1.2	1.9	1.1	1.2	•	•	•
Employee Benefits	17	2.3	1.3	1.8	2.0	3.1	1.9	2.6	3.2	2.7	2.4	•	•	•
Advertising	18	1.4	1.2	2.2	1.1	0.7	1.1	0.7	0.6	1.0	0.4	•	•	•
Other Expenses	19	32.0	35.7	28.7	25.1	22.7	55.7	32.4	29.0	25.2	46.4	•	•	•
Officers' Compensation	20	10.2	9.3	18.0	14.5	14.9	7.0	12.9	12.6	4.6	4.0	•	•	•
Operating Margin	21	12.0	29.6	18.1	22.1	13.8	5.5	9.4	10.5	8.0	8.7	•	•	•
Operating Margin Before Officers' Comp.	22	22.1	38.9	36.0	36.6	28.7	12.5	22.3	23.1	12.6	12.6	•	•	•

Selected Average Balance Sheet ($ in Thousands)														
Net Receivables	23	244	0	5	24	400	1121	3207	8982	13818	26170	•	•	•
Inventories	24	•	•	•	•	•	•	•	•	•	•	•	•	•
Net Property, Plant and Equipment	25	49	0	15	53	81	848	1019	1322	3625	6097	•	•	•
Total Assets	26	1415	0	88	761	2074	6580	15368	35805	66947	175737	•	•	•
Notes and Loans Payable	27	264	0	41	392	379	2370	2914	9559	10441	37739	•	•	•
All Other Liabilities	28	516	0	17	81	1094	2749	8674	18715	38189	76497	•	•	•
Net Worth	29	635	0	31	287	601	1461	3780	7531	18316	61501	•	•	•

Selected Financial Ratios (Times to 1)														
Current Ratio	30	1.1	•	2.0	2.0	1.3	1.3	1.3	1.5	1.1	1.0	•	•	•
Quick Ratio	31	0.9	•	1.9	1.8	1.1	1.1	1.1	1.3	0.9	0.8	•	•	•
Net Sales to Working Capital	32	15.7	•	18.6	9.9	9.3	19.9	9.8	2.8	18.6	•	•	•	•
Coverage Ratio	33	6.7	9.6	24.0	11.5	18.4	6.9	13.5	6.5	15.4	5.4	•	•	•
Total Asset Turnover	34	0.7	•	4.1	1.4	1.3	2.2	1.4	0.6	1.1	0.6	•	•	•
Inventory Turnover	35	•	•	•	•	•	•	•	•	•	•	•	•	•
Receivables Turnover	36	•	•	•	•	•	•	•	•	•	•	•	•	•
Total Liabilities to Net Worth	37	1.2	•	1.8	1.6	2.4	3.5	3.1	3.8	2.7	1.9	•	•	•
Current Assets to Working Capital	38	8.3	•	2.0	2.0	4.8	4.9	4.9	3.1	11.0	•	•	•	•
Current Liabilities to Working Capital	39	7.3	•	1.0	1.0	3.8	3.9	3.9	2.1	10.0	•	•	•	•
Working Capital to Net Sales	40	0.1	•	0.1	0.1	0.1	0.1	0.1	0.4	0.1	•	•	•	•
Inventory to Working Capital	41	0.0	•	•	•	•	•	0.0	0.0	0.0	•	•	•	•
Total Receipts to Cash Flow	42	2.6	1.9	2.5	2.5	3.1	1.7	2.6	2.8	3.3	2.0	•	•	•
Cost of Goods to Cash Flow	43	0.0	0.0	•	•	0.2	•	0.0	0.0	0.7	0.0	•	•	•
Cash Flow to Total Debt	44	0.5	•	2.5	0.9	0.6	1.6	0.7	0.3	0.4	0.4	•	•	•

Selected Financial Factors (in Percentages)														
Debt Ratio	45	55.1	•	64.9	62.2	71.0	77.8	75.4	79.0	72.6	65.0	•	•	•
Return on Total Assets	46	10.2	•	77.1	35.1	18.4	14.2	14.2	7.2	9.1	5.9	•	•	•
Return on Equity Before Income Taxes	47	19.3	•	210.6	84.7	60.1	54.8	53.4	28.9	31.2	13.7	•	•	•
Return on Equity After Income Taxes	48	17.8	•	209.0	84.3	58.9	52.0	49.6	24.3	27.9	11.8	•	•	•
Profit Margin (Before Income Tax)	49	13.1	29.6	18.1	22.1	13.8	5.5	9.4	10.5	8.0	8.4	•	•	•
Profit Margin (After Income Tax)	50	12.0	28.0	17.9	22.0	13.5	5.2	8.8	8.8	7.1	7.3	•	•	•

Table I

Corporations with and without Net Income

OTHER INSURANCE RELATED ACTIVITIES

MONEY AMOUNTS AND SIZE OF ASSETS IN THOUSANDS OF DOLLARS

Item Description for Accounting Period 7/11 Through 6/12		Total	Zero Assets	Under 500	500 to 1,000	1,000 to 5,000	5,000 to 10,000	10,000 to 25,000	25,000 to 50,000	50,000 to 100,000	100,000 to 250,000	250,000 to 500,000	500,000 to 2,500,000	2,500,000 and over
Number of Enterprises	1	14819	2080	11153	664	498	149	135	41	33	30	14	17	5
Revenues ($ in Thousands)														
Net Sales	2	51884243	211999	2666643	550490	3824036	1109855	2474883	1700449	1539426	3949091	2723261	9452275	21681834
Interest	3	682020	1379	555	1209	2516	7790	5518	4385	12551	34530	8052	114797	488739
Rents	4	351526	0	0	0	2933	2168	245531	2841	2191	2431	18376	6725	68330
Royalties	5	39622	7	0	0	0	0	23117	0	14	0	0	16384	99
Other Portfolio Income	6	475464	1115	1614	0	42917	1936	43220	23943	5629	16643	124095	103855	110495
Other Receipts	7	50335611	209498	2664474	549281	3775670	1097961	2157497	1669280	1519041	3895487	2572738	9210514	21014171
Total Receipts	8	51884243	211999	2666643	550490	3824036	1109855	2474883	1700449	1539426	3949091	2723261	9452275	21681834
Average Total Receipts	9	3501	102	239	829	7679	7449	18332	41474	46649	131636	194519	556016	4336367
Operating Costs/Operating Income (%)														
Cost of Operations	10	11.9	•	•	•	•	2.5	0.1	8.3	21.3	4.1	15.9	19.3	14.9
Salaries and Wages	11	18.6	7.2	12.5	20.0	32.9	30.6	40.1	24.0	25.9	24.1	20.1	20.8	10.7
Taxes Paid	12	2.2	2.3	2.7	3.0	3.5	3.3	3.8	3.6	3.0	2.5	1.8	2.7	1.3
Interest Paid	13	2.5	0.4	1.1	1.3	0.2	0.5	0.6	1.4	0.6	1.6	3.5	3.9	3.2
Depreciation	14	1.5	0.5	0.5	0.8	0.9	2.1	1.0	2.8	2.1	1.8	1.8	2.2	1.2
Amortization and Depletion	15	1.1	0.6	0.0	0.8	0.1	0.2	0.2	1.3	1.6	1.1	3.5	1.9	0.9
Pensions and Other Deferred Comp.	16	0.5	0.1	0.0	0.6	0.5	1.7	0.3	1.5	0.3	1.0	0.3	0.7	0.4
Employee Benefits	17	2.2	0.8	1.2	2.9	3.9	4.9	2.4	3.6	2.7	2.0	2.7	3.0	1.3
Advertising	18	0.6	1.7	1.2	2.1	1.0	0.3	0.4	2.0	0.9	0.4	0.3	0.7	0.2
Other Expenses	19	48.5	57.3	54.6	33.5	43.8	49.5	37.6	47.0	36.1	57.0	43.6	35.6	55.8
Officers' Compensation	20	2.6	17.7	10.8	13.9	6.2	7.1	6.4	2.2	1.4	1.7	1.7	2.5	0.4
Operating Margin	21	7.8	11.3	15.4	21.2	7.1	•	7.2	2.2	4.3	2.8	4.8	6.8	9.6
Operating Margin Before Officers' Comp.	22	10.4	29.0	26.3	35.0	13.3	4.3	13.6	4.5	5.7	4.5	6.5	9.2	10.0

Selected Average Balance Sheet ($ in Thousands)													
Net Receivables 23	669	0	11	121	387	1120	3243	4463	10626	22631	75196	232389	539208
Inventories 24	•	•	•	•	•	•	•	•	•	•	•	•	•
Net Property, Plant and Equipment 25	185	0	8	15	300	671	962	3727	3565	8148	16538	51065	128868
Total Assets 26	5222	0	47	745	2129	6415	15916	36868	70176	156169	358457	1140233	7859213
Notes and Loans Payable 27	1346	0	29	308	444	1671	2097	10106	9456	32624	99983	382964	1809840
All Other Liabilities 28	2071	0	-5	255	1172	6306	7098	15511	34848	79732	167439	461007	2747520
Net Worth 29	1805	0	22	182	514	-1562	6722	11251	25872	43814	91036	296261	3301853

Selected Financial Ratios (Times to 1)													
Current Ratio 30	1.0	•	2.3	1.7	1.2	1.1	2.0	1.4	1.1	1.6	0.8	1.0	0.9
Quick Ratio 31	0.8	•	2.1	1.1	0.7	0.9	1.6	1.0	0.9	1.1	0.7	0.8	0.7
Net Sales to Working Capital 32	485.0	•	14.5	4.5	25.2	28.2	3.6	8.8	14.0	5.4	•	•	•
Coverage Ratio 33	4.2	29.3	15.2	16.9	33.7	•	13.7	2.4	8.7	2.7	2.4	2.7	4.2
Total Asset Turnover 34	0.7	•	5.1	1.1	3.6	1.2	1.2	1.1	0.7	0.8	0.5	0.5	0.6
Inventory Turnover 35	•	•	•	•	•	•	•	•	•	•	•	•	•
Receivables Turnover 36	•	•	•	•	•	•	•	•	•	•	•	•	•
Total Liabilities to Net Worth 37	1.9	•	1.1	3.1	3.1	•	1.4	2.3	1.7	2.6	2.9	2.8	1.4
Current Assets to Working Capital 38	235.9	•	1.8	2.5	5.5	17.6	2.0	3.5	9.2	2.6	•	•	•
Current Liabilities to Working Capital 39	234.9	•	0.8	1.5	4.5	16.6	1.0	2.5	8.2	1.6	•	•	•
Working Capital to Net Sales 40	0.0	•	0.1	0.2	0.0	0.0	0.3	0.1	0.1	0.2	•	•	•
Inventory to Working Capital 41	1.6	•	•	•	•	•	•	0.0	0.0	0.0	•	•	•
Total Receipts to Cash Flow 42	1.9	1.6	1.5	2.0	2.1	2.8	2.4	2.1	2.7	1.8	2.2	2.5	1.6
Cost of Goods to Cash Flow 43	0.2	•	•	•	•	0.1	0.0	0.2	0.6	0.1	0.4	0.5	0.2
Cash Flow to Total Debt 44	0.6	•	6.4	0.7	2.3	0.3	0.8	0.8	0.4	0.7	0.3	0.3	0.6

Selected Financial Factors (in Percentages)													
Debt Ratio 45	65.4	•	52.6	75.6	75.9	124.3	57.8	69.5	63.1	71.9	74.6	74.0	58.0
Return on Total Assets 46	7.1	•	84.6	25.0	26.4	•	8.9	4.0	3.2	3.6	4.5	5.1	7.6
Return on Equity Before Income Taxes 47	15.7	•	166.9	96.5	106.1	14.2	19.4	7.7	7.7	8.1	10.2	12.3	13.7
Return on Equity After Income Taxes 48	11.2	•	166.3	94.9	96.6	20.9	17.6	3.8	5.7	4.6	8.3	7.6	9.0
Profit Margin (Before Income Tax) 49	8.1	11.3	15.4	21.2	7.1	•	7.1	2.1	4.3	2.7	4.8	6.6	10.5
Profit Margin (After Income Tax) 50	5.8	9.3	15.4	20.8	6.5	•	6.4	1.0	3.2	1.5	3.9	4.0	6.8

Table II

Corporations with Net Income

OTHER INSURANCE RELATED ACTIVITIES

MONEY AMOUNTS AND SIZE OF ASSETS IN THOUSANDS OF DOLLARS

Item Description for Accounting Period 7/11 Through 6/12		Total	Zero Assets	Under 500	500 to 1,000	1,000 to 5,000	5,000 to 10,000	10,000 to 25,000	25,000 to 50,000	50,000 to 100,000	100,000 to 250,000	250,000 to 500,000	500,000 to 2,500,000	2,500,000 and over
Number of Enterprises	1	10569	694	8672	547	368	110	89	25	24	20	•	•	•
Revenues ($ in Thousands)														
Net Sales	2	45737497	145578	2509176	463186	3672655	965648	2082243	1341788	1245496	3400223	•	•	•
Interest	3	559170	333	542	1209	2390	2653	3159	2718	9170	27306	•	•	•
Rents	4	324965	0	0	0	328	1671	245363	2339	2191	1851	•	•	•
Royalties	5	38132	7	0	0	0	0	23117	0	0	0	•	•	•
Other Portfolio Income	6	447730	128	1614	0	42899	1936	40380	20925	5492	13418	•	•	•
Other Receipts	7	44367500	145110	2507020	461977	3627038	959388	1770224	1315806	1228643	3357648	•	•	•
Total Receipts	8	45737497	145578	2509176	463186	3672655	965648	2082243	1341788	1245496	3400223	•	•	•
Average Total Receipts	9	4328	210	289	847	9980	8779	23396	53672	51896	170011	•	•	•
Operating Costs/Operating Income (%)														
Cost of Operations	10	12.5	•	•	•	•	•	0.1	5.8	18.0	4.8	•	•	•
Salaries and Wages	11	16.8	6.4	11.8	21.6	32.7	27.9	38.1	19.7	27.5	22.8	•	•	•
Taxes Paid	12	2.1	1.5	2.1	3.0	3.4	3.0	3.7	2.8	2.8	2.2	•	•	•
Interest Paid	13	2.2	0.1	0.8	1.6	0.2	0.3	0.3	0.7	0.5	1.3	•	•	•
Depreciation	14	1.3	0.1	0.5	0.9	0.8	1.5	1.0	1.4	2.2	1.7	•	•	•
Amortization and Depletion	15	0.9	0.7	0.0	1.0	0.1	0.2	0.2	0.3	0.8	1.1	•	•	•
Pensions and Other Deferred Comp.	16	0.5	•	•	0.7	0.4	1.8	0.3	1.6	0.3	0.6	•	•	•
Employee Benefits	17	1.9	•	1.3	3.5	3.9	4.8	2.1	4.0	2.7	1.8	•	•	•
Advertising	18	0.5	1.9	1.2	2.5	1.0	0.2	0.2	2.5	0.4	0.3	•	•	•
Other Expenses	19	48.6	57.8	54.4	20.7	44.0	44.8	37.1	49.1	34.5	57.9	•	•	•
Officers' Compensation	20	2.5	6.7	10.8	16.5	5.2	7.8	6.1	1.6	1.4	1.4	•	•	•
Operating Margin	21	10.1	24.7	17.2	28.1	8.3	7.7	10.8	10.6	8.9	4.2	•	•	•
Operating Margin Before Officers' Comp.	22	12.6	31.4	28.1	44.6	13.4	15.5	16.9	12.2	10.3	5.6	•	•	•

Selected Average Balance Sheet ($ in Thousands)													
Net Receivables 23	842	0	14	132	277	1094	3427	5495	11819	32258	•	•	•
Inventories 24	•	•	•	•	•	•	•	•	•	•	•	•	•
Net Property, Plant and Equipment 25	184	0	9	18	382	700	1266	2165	4105	7610	•	•	•
Total Assets 26	5695	0	49	753	2074	6428	16834	36560	70440	153230	•	•	•
Notes and Loans Payable 27	1472	0	30	374	454	883	2188	5652	5798	34245	•	•	•
All Other Liabilities 28	2380	0	-9	287	1132	5164	8486	17065	38778	71044	•	•	•
Net Worth 29	1843	0	28	92	487	382	6160	13843	25864	47940	•	•	•
Selected Financial Ratios (Times to 1)													
Current Ratio 30	1.0	•	3.4	1.3	1.1	2.0	2.1	1.6	1.1	1.4	•	•	•
Quick Ratio 31	0.9	•	3.0	1.0	0.6	1.7	1.8	1.3	0.9	1.1	•	•	•
Net Sales to Working Capital 32	132.0	•	14.0	9.1	123.7	3.6	3.5	7.0	12.8	7.7	•	•	•
Coverage Ratio 33	5.8	384.0	22.9	18.8	44.7	26.7	35.0	16.8	18.0	4.2	•	•	•
Total Asset Turnover 34	0.8	•	5.9	1.1	4.8	1.4	1.4	1.5	0.7	1.1	•	•	•
Inventory Turnover 35	•	•	•	•	•	•	•	•	•	•	•	•	•
Receivables Turnover 36	•	•	•	•	•	•	•	•	•	•	•	•	•
Total Liabilities to Net Worth 37	2.1	•	0.8	7.2	3.3	15.8	1.7	1.6	1.7	2.2	•	•	•
Current Assets to Working Capital 38	61.0	•	1.4	4.4	18.7	2.0	1.9	2.6	8.5	3.3	•	•	•
Current Liabilities to Working Capital 39	60.0	•	0.4	3.4	17.7	1.0	0.9	1.6	7.5	2.3	•	•	•
Working Capital to Net Sales 40	0.0	•	0.1	0.1	0.0	0.3	0.3	0.1	0.1	0.1	•	•	•
Inventory to Working Capital 41	0.4	•	•	•	•	•	•	0.0	0.0	0.0	•	•	•
Total Receipts to Cash Flow 42	1.8	1.2	1.5	2.3	2.0	2.1	2.3	1.7	2.5	1.7	•	•	•
Cost of Goods to Cash Flow 43	0.2	•	•	•	•	•	0.0	0.1	0.4	0.1	•	•	•
Cash Flow to Total Debt 44	0.6	•	9.1	0.6	3.1	0.7	1.0	1.4	0.5	1.0	•	•	•
Selected Financial Factors (in Percentages)													
Debt Ratio 45	67.6	•	43.6	87.8	76.5	94.1	63.4	62.1	63.3	68.7	•	•	•
Return on Total Assets 46	9.6	•	105.6	33.4	40.7	10.7	15.3	16.5	6.9	6.0	•	•	•
Return on Equity Before Income Taxes 47	24.6	•	179.2	259.5	169.3	174.1	40.7	41.1	17.9	14.5	•	•	•
Return on Equity After Income Taxes 48	18.5	•	178.6	255.5	155.7	136.7	37.7	35.9	15.1	9.8	•	•	•
Profit Margin (Before Income Tax) 49	10.5	24.7	17.2	28.1	8.3	7.6	10.7	10.6	8.9	4.1	•	•	•
Profit Margin (After Income Tax) 50	7.9	21.8	17.2	27.7	7.6	5.9	9.9	9.3	7.5	2.8	•	•	•

Table I

Corporations with and without Net Income

OPEN-END INVESTMENT FUNDS (FORM 1120-RIC)

MONEY AMOUNTS AND SIZE OF ASSETS IN THOUSANDS OF DOLLARS

Item Description for Accounting Period 7/11 Through 6/12		Total	Zero Assets	Under 500	500 to 1,000	1,000 to 5,000	5,000 to 10,000	10,000 to 25,000	25,000 to 50,000	50,000 to 100,000	100,000 to 250,000	250,000 to 500,000	500,000 to 2,500,000	2,500,000 and over
Number of Enterprises	1	14120	715	67	80	948	1048	1468	1291	1270	1991	1525	2635	1082
Revenues ($ in Thousands)														
Net Sales	2	366920228	1154713	2145	3034	106845	237451	670961	1249610	2591500	9307747	16182113	83729733	251684378
Interest	3	138052613	78495	81	855	30122	68810	180023	307905	631933	2502872	4934058	28226903	101090556
Rents	4	0	0	0	0	0	0	0	0	0	0	0	0	0
Royalties	5	0	0	0	0	0	0	0	0	0	0	0	0	0
Other Portfolio Income	6	44333911	273242	1687	444	40124	55335	154486	269785	598188	2404971	3526013	15819152	21190483
Other Receipts	7	184533704	802976	377	1735	36599	113306	336452	671920	1361379	4399904	7722042	39683678	129403339
Total Receipts	8	366920228	1154713	2145	3034	106845	237451	670961	1249610	2591500	9307747	16182113	83729733	251684378
Average Total Receipts	9	25986	1615	32	38	113	227	457	968	2041	4675	10611	31776	232610
Operating Costs/Operating Income (%)														
Cost of Operations	10	•	•	•	•	•	•	•	•	•	•	•	•	•
Salaries and Wages	11	0.0	0.0	•	1.4	0.1	0.0	0.2	0.1	0.1	0.1	0.1	0.1	0.0
Taxes Paid	12	0.4	0.2	0.1	0.3	0.9	0.4	0.5	0.6	0.6	0.6	0.6	0.6	0.3
Interest Paid	13	0.3	0.0	0.8	•	0.1	0.1	0.7	0.7	0.4	0.5	0.5	0.6	0.1
Depreciation	14	0.0	•	•	•	•	•	0.0	•	0.0	0.0	0.0	0.0	0.0
Amortization and Depletion	15	0.0	1.4	4.1	9.7	3.4	3.0	1.8	0.6	0.2	0.1	0.0	0.0	0.0
Pensions and Other Deferred Comp.	16	•	•	•	•	•	•	•	•	•	•	•	•	•
Employee Benefits	17	•	•	•	•	•	•	•	•	•	•	•	•	•
Advertising	18	0.0	•	•	•	•	•	0.0	•	0.0	0.0	0.0	0.0	0.0
Other Expenses	19	22.2	31.4	40.6	39.2	11.7	18.4	27.0	33.4	31.4	28.4	26.8	25.7	20.4
Officers' Compensation	20	0.0	•	•	•	•	•	0.5	0.3	0.1	0.0	0.0	0.0	0.0
Operating Margin	21	77.0	67.0	54.4	49.4	83.8	78.0	69.3	64.1	67.2	70.3	72.0	73.1	79.1
Operating Margin Before Officers' Comp.	22	77.0	67.0	54.4	49.4	83.8	78.0	69.8	64.5	67.3	70.3	72.0	73.1	79.1

Selected Average Balance Sheet ($ in Thousands)

Net Receivables	23	12131	0	0	3	18	42	136	447	973	1924	4503	16602	106074
Inventories	24	•	•	•	•	•	•	•	•	•	•	•	•	•
Net Property, Plant and Equipment	25	1	0	0	0	0	0	0	0	0	0	0	1	8
Total Assets	26	1057503	0	161	787	2942	7004	16163	36265	72438	163878	357795	1118372	10111244
Notes and Loans Payable	27	1140	0	0	0	0	1	77	16	153	620	1346	3467	3090
All Other Liabilities	28	53441	0	39	39	67	138	389	1123	3421	7812	19071	63384	495704
Net Worth	29	1002922	0	122	748	2875	6865	15697	35126	68865	155447	337377	1051521	9612451

Selected Financial Ratios (Times to 1)

Current Ratio	30	3.3	•	1.3	3.5	3.4	8.2	8.7	7.9	4.6	4.2	3.3	2.9	3.3
Quick Ratio	31	3.0	•	0.2	1.0	1.1	2.2	3.0	3.8	3.4	3.6	2.9	2.6	3.1
Net Sales to Working Capital	32	0.2	•	2.7	0.4	0.7	0.2	0.1	0.1	0.2	0.2	0.3	0.3	0.2
Coverage Ratio	33	254.0	2267.7	65.8	•	674.7	540.7	75.0	73.5	124.4	116.6	105.8	104.3	517.1
Total Asset Turnover	34	0.0	•	0.2	0.0	0.0	0.0	0.0	0.0	0.0	0.0	0.0	0.0	0.0
Inventory Turnover	35	•	•	•	•	•	•	•	•	•	•	•	•	•
Receivables Turnover	36	•	•	•	•	•	•	•	•	•	•	•	•	•
Total Liabilities to Net Worth	37	0.1	•	0.3	0.1	0.0	0.0	0.0	0.0	0.1	0.1	0.1	0.1	0.1
Current Assets to Working Capital	38	1.4	•	4.2	1.4	1.4	1.1	1.1	1.1	1.3	1.3	1.4	1.5	1.4
Current Liabilities to Working Capital	39	0.4	•	3.2	0.4	0.4	0.1	0.1	0.1	0.3	0.3	0.4	0.5	0.4
Working Capital to Net Sales	40	4.6	•	0.4	2.4	1.3	4.4	7.0	6.7	5.1	5.1	3.9	3.8	4.9
Inventory to Working Capital	41	•	•	•	•	•	•	•	•	•	•	•	•	•
Total Receipts to Cash Flow	42	1.1	1.2	6.1	1.4	1.2	1.1	1.1	1.2	1.1	1.1	1.1	1.1	1.0
Cost of Goods to Cash Flow	43	•	•	•	•	•	•	•	•	•	•	•	•	•
Cash Flow to Total Debt	44	0.4	•	0.1	0.7	1.4	1.5	0.9	0.7	0.5	0.5	0.5	0.4	0.4

Selected Financial Factors (in Percentages)

Debt Ratio	45	5.2	•	24.4	4.9	2.3	2.0	2.9	3.1	4.9	5.1	5.7	6.0	4.9
Return on Total Assets	46	1.7	•	11.0	2.4	2.3	1.9	1.5	1.4	1.4	1.5	1.7	1.8	1.7
Return on Equity Before Income Taxes	47	1.8	•	14.3	2.5	2.4	2.0	1.5	1.5	1.5	1.6	1.8	1.8	1.8
Return on Equity After Income Taxes	48	1.8	•	14.3	2.5	2.4	2.0	1.5	1.5	1.5	1.6	1.8	1.8	1.8
Profit Margin (Before Income Tax)	49	70.0	58.1	54.4	49.4	61.2	59.3	53.1	53.0	50.8	52.0	56.9	61.1	74.8
Profit Margin (After Income Tax)	50	70.0	58.1	54.4	49.4	60.9	59.3	53.1	53.0	50.8	52.0	56.9	61.1	74.8

Table II

Corporations with Net Income

OPEN-END INVESTMENT FUNDS (FORM 1120-RIC)

MONEY AMOUNTS AND SIZE OF ASSETS IN THOUSANDS OF DOLLARS

Item Description for Accounting Period 7/11 Through 6/12		Total	Zero Assets	Under 500	500 to 1,000	1,000 to 5,000	5,000 to 10,000	10,000 to 25,000	25,000 to 50,000	50,000 to 100,000	100,000 to 250,000	250,000 to 500,000	500,000 to 2,500,000	2,500,000 and over
Number of Enterprises	1	11424	455	33	60	701	808	1093	993	1029	1632	1315	2295	1010
Revenues ($ in Thousands)														
Net Sales	2	356293157	1096357	2027	2146	86310	199751	552168	1133640	2367246	8602215	15275494	79706882	247268923
Interest	3	137574825	77339	0	855	30046	67558	179067	304259	627102	2484739	4904293	28123006	100776562
Rents	4	0	0	0	0	0	0	0	0	0	0	0	0	0
Royalties	5	0	0	0	0	0	0	0	0	0	0	0	0	0
Other Portfolio Income	6	39053404	233910	1684	409	20954	25912	72626	217083	486023	2063540	3074394	14087581	18769289
Other Receipts	7	179664928	785108	343	882	35310	106281	300475	612298	1254121	4053936	7296807	37496295	127723072
Total Receipts	8	356293157	1096357	2027	2146	86310	199751	552168	1133640	2367246	8602215	15275494	79706882	247268923
Average Total Receipts	9	31188	2410	61	36	123	247	505	1142	2301	5271	11616	34731	244821
Operating Costs/Operating Income (%)														
Cost of Operations	10	•	•	•	•	•	•	•	•	•	•	•	•	•
Salaries and Wages	11	0.0	0.0	•	2.0	0.0	0.0	0.0	0.1	0.1	0.1	0.1	0.1	0.0
Taxes Paid	12	0.4	0.2	0.1	0.1	0.3	0.2	0.4	0.5	0.5	0.6	0.6	0.5	0.3
Interest Paid	13	0.3	0.0	0.9	•	0.1	0.0	0.0	0.0	0.4	0.5	0.5	0.6	0.1
Depreciation	14	0.0	•	•	•	•	•	•	•	0.0	0.0	0.0	0.0	0.0
Amortization and Depletion	15	0.0	1.3	3.1	10.9	4.0	3.1	2.1	0.7	0.2	0.1	0.0	0.0	0.0
Pensions and Other Deferred Comp.	16	•	•	•	•	•	•	•	•	•	•	•	•	•
Employee Benefits	17	•	•	•	•	•	•	•	•	•	•	•	•	•
Advertising	18	0.0	•	•	•	•	•	•	•	•	0.0	0.0	0.0	0.0
Other Expenses	19	20.4	28.2	15.2	14.5	10.8	13.8	19.7	22.3	25.0	23.8	23.3	22.2	19.4
Officers' Compensation	20	0.0	•	•	•	•	•	•	0.0	0.1	0.0	0.0	0.0	0.0
Operating Margin	21	78.9	70.3	80.7	72.5	84.8	82.9	77.7	76.4	73.7	74.9	75.5	76.5	80.1
Operating Margin Before Officers' Comp.	22	78.9	70.3	80.7	72.5	84.8	82.9	77.7	76.4	73.8	74.9	75.5	76.6	80.1

Selected Average Balance Sheet ($ in Thousands)

Net Receivables 23	13796	0	0	2	9	31	119	390	996	1887	4426	16383	108445
Inventories 24	•	•	•	•	•	•	•	•	•	•	•	•	•
Net Property, Plant and Equipment 25	1	0	0	0	0	0	0	0	0	0	0	1	8
Total Assets 26	1224670	0	166	815	2860	6959	16274	36382	72422	165225	357757	1123065	10432656
Notes and Loans Payable 27	1273	0	0	0	0	1	1	0	189	702	1539	3414	3309
All Other Liabilities 28	62255	0	60	22	63	108	393	890	3176	7981	19205	64081	515984
Net Worth 29	1161142	0	107	793	2797	6850	15880	35492	69058	156543	337013	1055571	9913363

Selected Financial Ratios (Times to 1)

Current Ratio 30	3.2	•	1.3	6.2	3.5	12.1	10.5	9.5	4.5	3.9	3.1	3.0	3.3
Quick Ratio 31	3.0	•	0.2	1.5	0.7	2.4	2.7	3.5	3.2	3.3	2.7	2.7	3.0
Net Sales to Working Capital 32	0.2	•	3.1	0.3	0.8	0.2	0.1	0.2	0.2	0.2	0.3	0.3	0.2
Coverage Ratio 33	272.4	14049.6	91.8	•	709.5	21414.0	1644.6	3874.9	165.7	123.6	118.5	114.6	521.5
Total Asset Turnover 34	0.0	•	0.4	0.0	0.0	0.0	0.0	0.0	0.0	0.0	0.0	0.0	0.0
Inventory Turnover 35	•	•	•	•	•	•	•	•	•	•	•	•	•
Receivables Turnover 36	•	•	•	•	•	•	•	•	•	•	•	•	•
Total Liabilities to Net Worth 37	0.1	•	0.6	0.0	0.0	0.0	0.0	0.0	0.0	0.1	0.1	0.1	0.1
Current Assets to Working Capital 38	1.4	•	4.0	1.2	1.4	1.1	1.1	1.1	1.3	1.3	1.5	1.5	1.4
Current Liabilities to Working Capital 39	0.4	•	3.0	0.2	0.4	0.1	0.1	0.1	0.3	0.3	0.5	0.5	0.4
Working Capital to Net Sales 40	4.4	•	0.3	3.2	1.3	4.8	7.4	5.9	4.3	4.3	3.4	3.5	4.8
Inventory to Working Capital 41	•	•	•	•	•	•	•	•	•	•	•	•	•
Total Receipts to Cash Flow 42	1.1	1.2	7.8	1.5	1.3	1.1	1.1	1.1	1.1	1.1	1.1	1.1	1.0
Cost of Goods to Cash Flow 43	•	•	•	•	•	•	•	•	•	•	•	•	•
Cash Flow to Total Debt 44	0.5	•	0.1	1.1	1.5	2.1	1.1	1.1	0.6	0.6	0.5	0.5	0.4

Selected Financial Factors (in Percentages)

Debt Ratio 45	5.2	•	36.0	2.7	2.2	1.6	2.4	2.4	4.6	5.3	5.8	6.0	5.0
Return on Total Assets 46	1.9	•	30.1	3.2	3.4	2.7	2.3	2.2	1.9	1.9	2.0	2.1	1.8
Return on Equity Before Income Taxes 47	2.0	•	46.5	3.3	3.5	2.7	2.3	2.2	2.0	2.0	2.2	2.2	1.9
Return on Equity After Income Taxes 48	2.0	•	46.5	3.3	3.5	2.7	2.3	2.2	2.0	2.0	2.2	2.2	1.9
Profit Margin (Before Income Tax) 49	73.0	64.1	80.7	72.5	78.8	75.0	72.9	68.7	60.2	59.1	62.4	66.0	76.6
Profit Margin (After Income Tax) 50	73.0	64.0	80.7	72.5	78.5	75.0	72.9	68.7	60.2	59.1	62.4	66.0	76.6

Table I

Corporations with and without Net Income

OTHER FINANCIAL VEHICLES

MONEY AMOUNTS AND SIZE OF ASSETS IN THOUSANDS OF DOLLARS

Item Description for Accounting Period 7/11 Through 6/12		Total	Zero Assets	Under 500	500 to 1,000	1,000 to 5,000	5,000 to 10,000	10,000 to 25,000	25,000 to 50,000	50,000 to 100,000	100,000 to 250,000	250,000 to 500,000	500,000 to 2,500,000	2,500,000 and over
Number of Enterprises	1	8078	1935	4002	140	932	243	201	136	115	106	65	128	75
Revenues ($ in Thousands)														
Net Sales	2	39307080	1310696	513737	-27639	105355	246613	635295	538835	1443975	1011949	1980317	6254155	25293793
Interest	3	29513053	803402	483972	5039	25991	23107	194313	82993	442014	661778	1404955	4615334	20770155
Rents	4	1550365	377	1798	0	0	0	5572	21995	82425	89182	73745	206508	1068761
Royalties	5	23999	378	0	82	0	7180	223	5379	0	14	65	10678	0
Other Portfolio Income	6	2544958	217703	1028	4724	45513	5045	135637	161115	61917	107758	327870	500767	975880
Other Receipts	7	5674705	288836	26939	-37484	33851	211281	299550	267353	857619	153217	173682	920868	2478997
Total Receipts	8	39307080	1310696	513737	-27639	105355	246613	635295	538835	1443975	1011949	1980317	6254155	25293793
Average Total Receipts	9	4866	677	128	-197	113	1015	3161	3962	12556	9547	30466	48861	337251
Operating Costs/Operating Income (%)														
Cost of Operations	10	0.2	•	•	•	•	•	•	0.1	4.7	•	•	•	•
Salaries and Wages	11	1.0	0.6	2.5	•	10.1	10.0	3.9	8.8	2.9	0.8	0.1	0.8	0.6
Taxes Paid	12	0.7	0.8	1.0	•	4.7	1.5	1.0	1.7	1.6	2.0	0.2	0.8	0.6
Interest Paid	13	17.8	8.2	8.9	•	9.9	3.1	11.4	10.3	13.6	25.1	40.9	23.0	15.7
Depreciation	14	0.9	0.1	0.3	•	0.1	0.1	0.8	1.8	3.8	1.1	0.0	0.9	0.8
Amortization and Depletion	15	0.6	0.4	0.1	•	2.0	5.5	0.2	0.3	0.8	0.5	0.9	0.4	0.7
Pensions and Other Deferred Comp.	16	0.0	0.0	•	•	1.4	2.0	0.4	0.9	0.2	•	0.0	0.0	•
Employee Benefits	17	0.5	•	0.1	•	0.8	0.5	0.5	2.7	0.3	0.1	0.0	0.0	0.6
Advertising	18	0.1	•	0.0	•	0.4	0.0	0.2	0.0	0.4	0.0	•	0.1	0.0
Other Expenses	19	38.1	89.6	115.5	•	136.3	32.0	89.1	91.6	44.4	31.1	25.1	40.9	31.3
Officers' Compensation	20	0.4	0.0	0.2	•	18.4	1.7	1.6	1.8	0.8	0.2	0.0	0.1	0.3
Operating Margin	21	39.8	0.4	•	162.9	•	43.4	•	•	26.4	39.0	32.8	33.0	49.4
Operating Margin Before Officers' Comp.	22	40.2	0.4	•	162.9	•	45.1	•	•	27.2	39.3	32.9	33.1	49.7

Selected Average Balance Sheet ($ in Thousands)

Net Receivables 23	9748	0	4	0	214	299	151	1956	4059	10411	30808	74802	866780
Inventories 24	•	•	•	•	•	•	•	•	•	•	•	•	•
Net Property, Plant and Equipment 25	1701	0	2	23	1	199	1104	472	1248	6793	1489	23349	125945
Total Assets 26	112101	0	113	838	2054	7378	16349	34363	70841	166544	350477	1203272	9209499
Notes and Loans Payable 27	31774	0	1623	830	884	1772	4783	9502	12233	35217	62733	374604	2525117
All Other Liabilities 28	23320	0	81	11	1065	88	2920	4456	9772	32577	49964	140044	2134620
Net Worth 29	57007	0	-1591	-3	105	5518	8647	20405	48836	98750	237780	688624	4549762

Selected Financial Ratios (Times to 1)

Current Ratio 30	0.8	•	0.0	27.7	2.2	7.5	1.4	2.1	2.6	1.2	1.9	1.0	0.7
Quick Ratio 31	0.6	•	0.0	14.0	2.0	3.4	1.0	1.6	1.8	1.1	1.6	0.7	0.6
Net Sales to Working Capital 32	•	•	•	•	0.4	0.4	2.8	1.2	1.1	1.6	0.9	•	•
Coverage Ratio 33	3.2	1.0	•	•	•	15.0	0.1	•	2.9	2.5	1.8	2.4	4.1
Total Asset Turnover 34	0.0	•	1.1	•	0.1	0.1	0.2	0.1	0.2	0.1	0.1	0.0	0.0
Inventory Turnover 35	•	•	•	•	•	•	•	•	•	•	•	•	•
Receivables Turnover 36	•	•	•	•	•	•	•	•	•	•	•	•	•
Total Liabilities to Net Worth 37	1.0	•	•	•	18.6	0.3	0.9	0.7	0.5	0.7	0.5	0.7	1.0
Current Assets to Working Capital 38	•	•	•	1.0	1.8	1.2	3.5	1.9	1.6	5.5	2.1	•	•
Current Liabilities to Working Capital 39	•	•	•	0.0	0.8	0.2	2.5	0.9	0.6	4.5	1.1	•	•
Working Capital to Net Sales 40	•	•	•	•	2.5	2.4	0.4	0.9	0.9	0.6	1.1	•	•
Inventory to Working Capital 41	•	•	•	•	•	•	•	•	0.0	•	•	•	•
Total Receipts to Cash Flow 42	1.4	1.4	1.2	0.7	5.3	1.4	1.8	2.6	1.5	1.7	2.4	1.5	1.3
Cost of Goods to Cash Flow 43	0.0	•	•	•	•	•	•	0.0	0.1	•	•	•	•
Cash Flow to Total Debt 44	0.1	•	0.1	•	0.0	0.4	0.2	0.1	0.4	0.1	0.1	0.1	0.1

Selected Financial Factors (in Percentages)

Debt Ratio 45	49.1	•	1504.0	100.3	94.9	25.2	47.1	40.6	31.1	40.7	32.2	42.8	50.6
Return on Total Assets 46	2.5	•	•	•	•	6.4	0.3	•	7.1	3.7	6.4	2.3	2.4
Return on Equity Before Income Taxes 47	3.4	•	2.3	11033.1	•	8.0	•	•	6.8	3.7	4.2	2.3	3.7
Return on Equity After Income Taxes 48	3.3	•	2.3	11100.5	•	7.7	•	•	6.0	3.2	3.7	2.2	3.6
Profit Margin (Before Income Tax) 49	39.7	•	•	162.9	•	43.3	•	•	26.4	38.6	32.8	32.8	49.4
Profit Margin (After Income Tax) 50	38.1	•	•	163.9	•	41.7	•	•	23.3	33.0	29.0	31.4	48.5

Table II

Corporations with Net Income

OTHER FINANCIAL VEHICLES

MONEY AMOUNTS AND SIZE OF ASSETS IN THOUSANDS OF DOLLARS

Item Description for Accounting Period 7/11 Through 6/12		Total	Zero Assets	Under 500	500 to 1,000	1,000 to 5,000	5,000 to 10,000	10,000 to 25,000	25,000 to 50,000	50,000 to 100,000	100,000 to 250,000	250,000 to 500,000	500,000 to 2,500,000	2,500,000 and over
Number of Enterprises	1	2778	682	1210	137	196	94	68	62	63	63	47	95	60
Revenues ($ in Thousands)														
Net Sales	2	31485928	627889	506257	5396	128813	211461	203437	324880	1305076	719104	1233712	5016794	21203109
Interest	3	24385442	119692	476962	361	12931	8770	41590	62495	395441	484885	679312	4030826	18072176
Rents	4	771239	85	0	0	0	0	0	1794	42454	21272	73745	110914	520975
Royalties	5	10804	57	0	82	0	0	0	16	0	0	65	10584	0
Other Portfolio Income	6	2258250	197031	675	4724	35657	5045	105047	150729	56514	85566	325292	372797	919170
Other Receipts	7	4060193	311024	28620	229	80225	197646	56800	109846	810667	127381	155298	491673	1690788
Total Receipts	8	31485928	627889	506257	5396	128813	211461	203437	324880	1305076	719104	1233712	5016794	21203109
Average Total Receipts	9	11334	921	418	39	657	2250	2992	5240	20715	11414	26249	52808	353385
Operating Costs/Operating Income (%)														
Cost of Operations	10	0.2	•	•	•	•	•	•	•	3.9	•	•	•	•
Salaries and Wages	11	0.6	1.2	0.0	•	7.2	8.8	0.1	1.7	2.4	1.0	0.1	0.3	0.5
Taxes Paid	12	0.5	1.3	0.0	0.2	1.8	0.6	1.3	0.4	1.6	1.9	0.3	0.7	0.4
Interest Paid	13	14.5	10.9	2.5	32.3	0.8	1.3	5.8	9.7	11.1	6.6	11.4	18.2	15.0
Depreciation	14	0.6	0.0	0.0	0.3	0.1	0.0	0.1	0.3	2.1	0.7	0.0	0.5	0.6
Amortization and Depletion	15	0.2	0.5	0.1	0.5	1.7	0.0	0.1	0.4	0.3	0.3	0.7	0.2	0.1
Pensions and Other Deferred Comp.	16	0.0	0.0	•	•	1.1	2.4	•	0.0	0.3	•	•	0.0	•
Employee Benefits	17	0.0	•	0.0	•	0.7	0.2	0.0	0.2	0.3	0.1	•	0.0	•
Advertising	18	0.0	•	0.0	•	0.4	0.0	0.0	0.0	0.4	0.0	•	0.0	0.0
Other Expenses	19	19.8	18.0	89.3	28.2	13.1	15.4	19.3	20.6	29.5	12.4	22.3	18.8	18.0
Officers' Compensation	20	0.3	0.0	0.1	•	15.1	1.3	0.2	2.0	0.7	0.2	0.0	0.1	0.2
Operating Margin	21	63.3	68.0	8.0	38.4	58.0	70.0	73.2	64.6	47.4	76.8	65.2	61.1	65.2
Operating Margin Before Officers' Comp.	22	63.6	68.0	8.1	38.4	73.1	71.3	73.4	66.7	48.1	77.0	65.2	61.2	65.5

Selected Average Balance Sheet ($ in Thousands)														
Net Receivables	23	26287	0	5	0	13	1	219	1102	5289	9076	33989	71948	1059946
Inventories	24	•	•	•	•	•	•	•	•	•	•	•	•	•
Net Property, Plant and Equipment	25	2869	0	0	23	4	2	0	57	1189	3868	1934	22617	90073
Total Assets	26	257843	0	167	841	1918	7477	17317	35140	73310	168797	346844	1203339	9427717
Notes and Loans Payable	27	61407	0	38	848	75	990	3293	8665	7615	16014	45685	318451	2261165
All Other Liabilities	28	61158	0	37	0	317	-13	1344	2922	7485	15880	34142	154720	2529070
Net Worth	29	135277	0	92	-7	1526	6500	12680	23553	58211	136903	267016	730168	4637482
Selected Financial Ratios (Times to 1)														
Current Ratio	30	0.9	•	1.3	1666.7	1.4	238.7	1.8	1.7	3.3	2.9	3.0	0.9	0.8
Quick Ratio	31	0.7	•	1.2	800.9	1.2	197.5	1.1	1.5	2.5	2.6	2.7	0.7	0.7
Net Sales to Working Capital	32	•	•	50.7	0.1	4.6	0.9	1.9	3.0	1.4	0.5	0.5	•	•
Coverage Ratio	33	5.4	7.2	4.2	2.2	72.9	54.5	13.7	7.6	5.3	12.7	6.7	4.3	5.3
Total Asset Turnover	34	0.0	•	2.5	0.0	0.3	0.3	0.2	0.1	0.3	0.1	0.1	0.0	0.0
Inventory Turnover	35	•	•	•	•	•	•	•	•	•	•	•	•	•
Receivables Turnover	36	•	•	•	•	•	•	•	•	•	•	•	•	•
Total Liabilities to Net Worth	37	0.9	•	0.8	•	0.3	0.2	0.4	0.5	0.3	0.2	0.3	0.6	1.0
Current Assets to Working Capital	38	•	•	5.0	1.0	3.5	1.0	2.3	2.5	1.4	1.5	1.5	•	•
Current Liabilities to Working Capital	39	•	•	4.0	0.0	2.5	0.0	1.3	1.5	0.4	0.5	0.5	•	•
Working Capital to Net Sales	40	•	•	0.0	7.7	0.2	1.1	0.5	0.3	0.7	1.9	1.9	•	•
Inventory to Working Capital	41	•	•	•	•	•	•	•	•	0.0	•	•	•	•
Total Receipts to Cash Flow	42	1.3	1.8	1.0	•	1.8	1.2	2.5	2.6	1.4	1.3	1.6	1.3	1.3
Cost of Goods to Cash Flow	43	0.0	•	•	•	•	•	•	•	0.1	•	•	•	•
Cash Flow to Total Debt	44	0.1	•	5.5	•	0.9	1.9	0.3	0.2	1.0	0.3	0.2	0.1	0.1
Selected Financial Factors (in Percentages)														
Debt Ratio	45	47.5	•	44.7	100.8	20.4	13.1	26.8	33.0	20.6	18.9	23.0	39.3	50.8
Return on Total Assets	46	3.4	•	26.1	3.3	20.1	21.4	13.7	11.1	16.5	5.6	5.8	3.5	3.0
Return on Equity Before Income Taxes	47	5.3	•	36.1	•	25.0	24.2	17.3	14.4	16.9	6.4	6.4	4.4	5.0
Return on Equity After Income Taxes	48	5.1	•	36.1	•	22.9	23.6	14.1	13.7	15.7	5.7	5.8	4.3	4.9
Profit Margin (Before Income Tax)	49	63.2	68.0	8.0	38.4	58.0	69.9	73.2	64.6	47.4	76.8	65.2	60.9	65.2
Profit Margin (After Income Tax)	50	61.2	53.1	8.0	33.3	53.2	68.1	59.6	61.6	44.0	69.0	59.0	59.1	64.2

Table I

Corporations with and without Net Income

LESSORS OF BUILDINGS

Item Description for Accounting Period 7/11 Through 6/12		MONEY AMOUNTS AND SIZE OF ASSETS IN THOUSANDS OF DOLLARS												
		Total	Zero Assets	Under 500	500 to 1,000	1,000 to 5,000	5,000 to 10,000	10,000 to 25,000	25,000 to 50,000	50,000 to 100,000	100,000 to 250,000	250,000 to 500,000	500,000 to 2,500,000	2,500,000 and over
Number of Enterprises	1	224996	24528	115341	37240	39830	4296	2220	615	375	236	105	143	66
Revenues ($ in Thousands)														
Net Sales	2	87534534	5054660	2657127	2396388	5810994	2520375	2963910	2086613	3955591	3487078	5268504	15459339	35873956
Interest	3	2687861	23995	18882	15440	45707	36310	38377	14426	61158	71152	121992	661048	1579374
Rents	4	38555951	329160	6963	18861	101156	101264	306624	326946	652601	1580083	1815017	9591849	23725426
Royalties	5	25800	45	1739	223	6534	3190	2519	253	340	345	93	10518	0
Other Portfolio Income	6	10250138	3400412	235957	101665	271368	293173	200863	139445	312778	247481	778296	1208679	3060015
Other Receipts	7	36014784	1301048	2393586	2260199	5386229	2086438	2415527	1605543	2928714	1588017	2553106	3987245	7509141
Total Receipts	8	87534534	5054660	2657127	2396388	5810994	2520375	2963910	2086613	3955591	3487078	5268504	15459339	35873956
Average Total Receipts	9	389	206	23	64	146	587	1335	3393	10548	14776	50176	108107	543545
Operating Costs/Operating Income (%)														
Cost of Operations	10	3.8	1.9	7.8	4.0	14.1	1.5	8.2	6.3	14.2	2.9	15.2	1.3	0.2
Salaries and Wages	11	5.1	1.3	5.6	8.4	8.4	14.5	6.8	12.4	10.7	3.4	5.1	3.8	3.7
Taxes Paid	12	6.8	4.7	14.0	12.2	12.2	9.3	9.3	8.8	6.7	9.4	5.8	6.0	5.0
Interest Paid	13	13.1	7.2	7.8	8.8	11.2	12.9	14.0	15.9	10.8	20.9	11.8	14.1	14.1
Depreciation	14	12.0	5.1	8.9	11.9	11.0	11.0	12.1	13.5	10.1	17.2	9.4	12.8	13.1
Amortization and Depletion	15	1.1	0.7	0.3	0.5	0.6	0.5	0.9	0.9	1.0	1.6	1.9	1.4	1.2
Pensions and Other Deferred Comp.	16	0.1	0.0	•	0.3	0.5	0.6	0.2	0.4	0.3	0.1	0.1	0.0	0.0
Employee Benefits	17	0.4	0.0	0.5	0.9	0.9	2.0	0.9	1.2	1.6	0.3	0.6	0.2	0.0
Advertising	18	0.4	0.1	0.9	0.3	0.2	1.1	0.6	0.6	1.3	0.3	0.7	0.3	0.2
Other Expenses	19	34.0	59.5	46.3	46.5	32.4	29.6	42.1	38.0	41.2	36.0	38.5	45.0	21.9
Officers' Compensation	20	1.4	0.2	2.8	4.7	5.0	7.7	2.7	3.0	1.4	1.1	0.4	0.9	0.5
Operating Margin	21	21.8	19.5	5.1	1.5	3.5	9.3	2.1	•	0.8	6.8	10.5	14.3	40.1
Operating Margin Before Officers' Comp.	22	23.2	19.6	7.9	6.2	8.5	17.1	4.8	2.0	2.2	7.9	10.9	15.1	40.6

Selected Average Balance Sheet ($ in Thousands)													
Net Receivables 23	66	0	3	17	34	273	437	646	1935	3174	9309	22439	64211
Inventories 24	•	•	•	•	•	•	•	•	•	•	•	•	•
Net Property, Plant and Equipment 25	2418	0	149	514	1444	4608	9282	20899	41595	98491	172021	568455	3920588
Total Assets 26	3942	0	192	719	2123	6977	14678	35114	70023	155740	346775	1158543	6123547
Notes and Loans Payable 27	1776	0	134	460	1434	4694	9117	19993	33376	77098	147181	407704	2312883
All Other Liabilities 28	287	0	7	46	181	593	1478	2424	5842	10996	22073	100517	394105
Net Worth 29	1879	0	51	213	508	1691	4083	12698	30805	67646	177522	650321	3416558
Selected Financial Ratios (Times to 1)													
Current Ratio 30	1.3	•	2.3	2.5	2.1	1.8	1.7	2.6	2.0	1.7	1.0	1.2	0.8
Quick Ratio 31	0.9	•	1.9	1.8	1.3	1.2	1.2	1.6	1.4	1.1	0.7	0.9	0.6
Net Sales to Working Capital 32	5.3	•	1.6	1.0	0.9	1.4	1.6	1.1	2.3	2.4	409.2	7.8	•
Coverage Ratio 33	2.7	3.7	1.6	1.2	1.3	1.7	1.1	0.9	1.1	1.3	1.9	2.0	3.9
Total Asset Turnover 34	0.1	•	0.1	0.1	0.1	0.1	0.1	0.1	0.2	0.1	0.1	0.1	0.1
Inventory Turnover 35	•	•	•	•	•	•	•	•	•	•	•	•	•
Receivables Turnover 36	•	•	•	•	•	•	•	•	•	•	•	•	•
Total Liabilities to Net Worth 37	1.1	•	2.8	2.4	3.2	3.1	2.6	1.8	1.3	1.3	1.0	0.8	0.8
Current Assets to Working Capital 38	4.3	•	1.8	1.7	1.9	2.3	2.5	1.6	2.0	2.5	209.2	5.7	•
Current Liabilities to Working Capital 39	3.3	•	0.8	0.7	0.9	1.3	1.5	0.6	1.0	1.5	208.2	4.7	•
Working Capital to Net Sales 40	0.2	•	0.6	1.0	1.2	0.7	0.6	0.9	0.4	0.4	0.0	0.1	•
Inventory to Working Capital 41	0.0	•	•	•	0.0	0.0	0.0	0.0	0.0	0.0	1.1	0.0	•
Total Receipts to Cash Flow 42	2.8	•	3.2	3.0	4.2	4.5	3.6	3.9	4.4	3.3	5.1	2.5	2.0
Cost of Goods to Cash Flow 43	0.1	•	0.3	0.1	0.6	0.1	0.3	0.2	0.6	0.1	0.8	0.0	0.0
Cash Flow to Total Debt 44	0.1	•	0.1	0.0	0.0	0.0	0.0	0.0	0.1	0.1	0.1	0.1	0.1
Selected Financial Factors (in Percentages)													
Debt Ratio 45	52.3	•	73.5	70.4	76.1	75.8	72.2	63.8	56.0	56.6	48.8	43.9	44.2
Return on Total Assets 46	3.4	•	1.5	0.9	1.0	1.9	1.4	1.4	1.7	2.6	3.2	2.6	4.8
Return on Equity Before Income Taxes 47	4.5	•	2.3	0.5	0.9	3.2	0.6	•	0.2	1.5	3.0	2.4	6.4
Return on Equity After Income Taxes 48	4.3	•	1.5	0.0	0.5	1.9	•	•	•	1.1	2.7	2.4	6.4
Profit Margin (Before Income Tax) 49	21.7	19.4	5.1	1.5	3.3	9.1	1.7	•	0.6	6.6	10.5	14.3	40.1
Profit Margin (After Income Tax) 50	20.9	17.1	3.4	0.0	1.7	5.4	•	•	•	4.9	9.5	14.2	40.1

Table II

Corporations with Net Income

LESSORS OF BUILDINGS

MONEY AMOUNTS AND SIZE OF ASSETS IN THOUSANDS OF DOLLARS

Item Description for Accounting Period 7/11 Through 6/12		Total	Zero Assets	Under 500	500 to 1,000	1,000 to 5,000	5,000 to 10,000	10,000 to 25,000	25,000 to 50,000	50,000 to 100,000	100,000 to 250,000	250,000 to 500,000	500,000 to 2,500,000	2,500,000 and over
Number of Enterprises	1	45135	6025	19963	8185	8356	1234	712	186	146	115	59	93	60
Revenues ($ in Thousands)														
Net Sales	2	69165565	4743047	1795443	1699760	3667638	1508018	1709034	1143105	1537988	2234808	3446070	10993310	34687345
Interest	3	2307554	17388	11388	10959	28423	29556	18263	8324	39535	45366	95304	480293	1522754
Rents	4	33169969	327618	4801	13715	32270	41470	158789	118956	348580	1056298	1173557	7069880	22824034
Royalties	5	10149	0	0	223	6534	325	2519	48	306	195	0	0	0
Other Portfolio Income	6	9323360	3278514	228102	89351	239135	266097	189341	105755	227426	195425	741182	1000485	2762547
Other Receipts	7	24354533	1119527	1551152	1585512	3361276	1170570	1340122	910022	922141	937524	1436027	2442652	7578010
Total Receipts	8	69165565	4743047	1795443	1699760	3667638	1508018	1709034	1143105	1537988	2234808	3446070	10993310	34687345
Average Total Receipts	9	1532	787	90	208	439	1222	2400	6146	10534	19433	58408	118208	578122
Operating Costs/Operating Income (%)														
Cost of Operations	10	3.0	0.4	7.8	3.6	14.8	0.6	5.6	3.9	15.1	2.4	21.9	0.5	0.2
Salaries and Wages	11	4.1	0.4	5.8	8.8	7.3	8.3	6.1	14.3	3.1	3.5	3.1	3.3	3.8
Taxes Paid	12	6.0	3.0	11.7	8.4	8.6	8.7	10.1	8.6	8.1	8.7	5.3	6.2	5.1
Interest Paid	13	11.2	3.8	6.9	5.2	6.8	10.3	9.1	9.1	11.3	15.3	7.8	11.3	13.5
Depreciation	14	11.0	2.9	4.8	6.7	6.8	8.5	9.7	10.1	9.7	14.5	6.6	12.7	13.1
Amortization and Depletion	15	1.0	0.7	0.1	0.4	0.3	0.3	0.7	0.8	1.1	1.4	1.0	1.1	1.1
Pensions and Other Deferred Comp.	16	0.1	0.0	•	0.2	0.3	0.2	0.2	0.4	0.1	0.1	0.0	0.0	0.0
Employee Benefits	17	0.2	0.0	0.3	0.6	0.7	0.6	0.9	0.8	0.2	0.2	0.5	0.1	0.0
Advertising	18	0.3	0.0	0.9	0.4	0.2	1.3	0.2	0.4	0.3	0.3	0.4	0.2	0.2
Other Expenses	19	22.1	10.4	31.5	39.2	24.0	21.1	24.1	26.4	22.1	25.5	16.4	29.4	20.1
Officers' Compensation	20	1.0	0.1	1.8	4.6	6.0	3.5	2.5	2.2	1.3	1.0	0.4	0.5	0.5
Operating Margin	21	40.0	78.5	28.4	21.9	24.2	36.5	30.7	23.0	27.7	27.2	36.8	34.6	42.4
Operating Margin Before Officers' Comp.	22	41.0	78.5	30.3	26.5	30.2	40.0	33.3	25.1	29.0	28.1	37.1	35.1	42.9

Selected Average Balance Sheet ($ in Thousands)

Net Receivables 23	201	0	5	23	68	395	667	1084	2869	2352	9151	18394	68633
Inventories 24	•	•	•	•	•	•	•	•	•	•	•	•	•
Net Property, Plant and Equipment 25	7905	0	116	442	1205	4497	8800	20215	41299	103526	162672	555636	4099931
Total Assets 26	13322	0	186	704	2096	7084	14971	35958	71531	157976	353788	1217640	6424476
Notes and Loans Payable 27	4870	0	147	374	972	3881	7238	13876	29532	70862	112719	336270	2379426
All Other Liabilities 28	937	0	10	72	245	516	1190	2345	6193	8056	16505	98689	425706
Net Worth 29	7515	0	28	258	879	2686	6543	19736	35806	79058	224564	782681	3619344

Selected Financial Ratios (Times to 1)

Current Ratio 30	1.1	•	3.4	2.1	2.4	2.8	2.9	2.6	3.2	2.3	1.3	1.2	0.8
Quick Ratio 31	0.8	•	3.1	1.7	1.8	2.0	2.2	1.9	2.4	1.7	0.9	0.8	0.6
Net Sales to Working Capital 32	15.8	•	3.0	3.1	1.6	1.4	1.3	1.7	1.6	2.3	9.8	11.6	•
Coverage Ratio 33	4.6	21.4	5.1	5.2	4.5	4.5	4.3	3.5	3.4	2.8	5.7	4.1	4.1
Total Asset Turnover 34	0.1	•	0.5	0.3	0.2	0.2	0.2	0.2	0.1	0.1	0.2	0.1	0.1
Inventory Turnover 35	•	•	•	•	•	•	•	•	•	•	•	•	•
Receivables Turnover 36	•	•	•	•	•	•	•	•	•	•	•	•	•
Total Liabilities to Net Worth 37	0.8	•	5.5	1.7	1.4	1.6	1.3	0.8	1.0	1.0	0.6	0.6	0.8
Current Assets to Working Capital 38	9.2	•	1.4	1.9	1.7	1.5	1.5	1.6	1.5	1.8	4.3	7.3	•
Current Liabilities to Working Capital 39	8.2	•	0.4	0.9	0.7	0.5	0.5	0.6	0.5	0.8	3.3	6.3	•
Working Capital to Net Sales 40	0.1	•	0.3	0.3	0.6	0.7	0.8	0.6	0.6	0.4	0.1	0.1	•
Inventory to Working Capital 41	0.0	•	•	•	0.0	0.0	•	0.0	0.0	0.0	0.0	0.0	•
Total Receipts to Cash Flow 42	2.2	4.9	2.2	2.0	2.8	2.8	2.5	2.6	3.1	2.5	3.3	2.1	2.0
Cost of Goods to Cash Flow 43	0.1	0.0	0.2	0.1	0.4	0.0	0.1	0.1	0.5	0.1	0.7	0.0	0.0
Cash Flow to Total Debt 44	0.1	•	0.3	0.2	0.1	0.1	0.1	0.1	0.1	0.1	0.1	0.1	0.1

Selected Financial Factors (in Percentages)

Debt Ratio 45	43.6	•	84.7	63.4	58.1	62.1	56.3	45.1	49.9	50.0	36.5	35.7	43.7
Return on Total Assets 46	5.9	•	17.1	8.0	6.5	8.0	6.3	5.4	5.7	5.2	7.4	4.5	5.0
Return on Equity Before Income Taxes 47	8.1	•	89.9	17.6	12.0	16.5	11.1	7.1	8.1	6.6	9.6	5.2	6.8
Return on Equity After Income Taxes 48	7.9	•	82.1	15.9	10.7	13.7	9.5	5.9	6.5	6.0	9.2	5.2	6.8
Profit Margin (Before Income Tax) 49	39.9	78.4	28.4	21.9	24.0	36.3	30.3	22.7	27.5	27.0	36.7	34.6	42.4
Profit Margin (After Income Tax) 50	38.9	75.9	25.9	19.7	21.5	30.0	25.9	18.9	22.2	24.3	35.2	34.5	42.4

Table I

Corporations with and without Net Income

LESSORS OF MINIWAREHOUSES, SELF-STORAGE, OTHER REAL ESTATE

MONEY AMOUNTS AND SIZE OF ASSETS IN THOUSANDS OF DOLLARS

Item Description for Accounting Period 7/11 Through 6/12		Total	Zero Assets	Under 500	500 to 1,000	1,000 to 5,000	5,000 to 10,000	10,000 to 25,000	25,000 to 50,000	50,000 to 100,000	100,000 to 250,000	250,000 to 500,000	500,000 to 2,500,000	2,500,000 and over
Number of Enterprises	1	82159	13872	43277	9886	11781	1447	941	372	209	196	77	85	15
Revenues ($ in Thousands)														
Net Sales	2	32579350	1411917	4109899	1172002	2239891	715178	1370559	1193179	1333635	2935606	2321844	6428006	7347634
Interest	3	1180279	66986	14537	20381	62225	15333	56639	52790	38763	96661	137395	322350	296219
Rents	4	10709770	72578	56988	1803	18666	52725	301792	326292	620971	1227605	1050446	4152446	2827458
Royalties	5	126150	12	3659	13540	22140	33967	19034	4237	1494	8177	19890	0	0
Other Portfolio Income	6	4864276	435111	146796	27645	323102	76762	143535	217964	140940	363678	586158	1159100	1243484
Other Receipts	7	15698875	837230	3887919	1108633	1813758	536391	849559	591896	531467	1239485	527955	794110	2980473
Total Receipts	8	32579350	1411917	4109899	1172002	2239891	715178	1370559	1193179	1333635	2935606	2321844	6428006	7347634
Average Total Receipts	9	397	102	95	119	190	494	1456	3207	6381	14978	30154	75624	489842
Operating Costs/Operating Income (%)														
Cost of Operations	10	0.9	0.0	•	•	4.1	0.3	•	0.1	0.4	0.6	5.6	0.3	0.5
Salaries and Wages	11	7.2	3.6	27.0	11.2	8.9	9.7	8.7	4.1	4.3	4.9	3.1	1.1	3.6
Taxes Paid	12	6.0	4.3	6.5	9.1	8.5	8.5	6.3	5.3	6.1	4.9	3.7	6.6	5.1
Interest Paid	13	12.8	26.1	1.8	4.7	11.7	20.8	16.2	14.6	21.2	15.3	12.8	14.8	12.0
Depreciation	14	9.0	3.9	2.2	4.7	14.1	12.4	7.7	10.5	10.4	11.0	7.8	13.5	8.0
Amortization and Depletion	15	1.3	0.7	0.1	0.2	0.5	1.4	0.7	0.7	1.1	1.4	1.0	1.5	2.6
Pensions and Other Deferred Comp.	16	0.1	0.1	0.5	0.5	0.1	0.2	0.2	0.2	0.0	0.3	0.0	•	•
Employee Benefits	17	0.7	0.3	3.9	0.4	0.8	1.3	0.5	0.5	0.4	0.2	0.3	0.0	0.1
Advertising	18	0.7	0.5	3.2	0.3	0.5	0.4	0.6	0.6	0.4	0.3	0.4	0.2	0.4
Other Expenses	19	50.4	74.8	40.2	64.9	41.5	61.7	64.6	65.2	63.5	63.1	58.5	43.5	41.7
Officers' Compensation	20	2.8	0.9	11.2	5.8	4.3	7.8	2.6	3.2	1.6	0.8	1.3	0.4	0.7
Operating Margin	21	8.0	•	3.3	•	5.0	•	•	•	•	•	5.5	18.0	25.4
Operating Margin Before Officers' Comp.	22	10.8	•	14.5	4.0	9.4	•	•	•	•	•	6.8	18.4	26.1

Selected Average Balance Sheet ($ in Thousands)													
Net Receivables 23	85	0	7	20	106	132	787	1221	1897	3503	11927	9608	67796
Inventories 24	•	•	•	•	•	•	•	•	•	•	•	•	•
Net Property, Plant and Equipment 25	1807	0	73	343	1126	2983	5408	10830	23653	52026	115255	455972	3497185
Total Assets 26	3891	0	149	695	2088	6935	15588	35088	70776	159098	351314	981666	5833302
Notes and Loans Payable 27	1330	0	68	314	1265	3448	6597	13153	25574	44781	94249	277932	1812643
All Other Liabilities 28	400	0	29	68	230	660	2132	5488	6348	12606	28272	48331	876108
Net Worth 29	2161	0	52	313	593	2826	6859	16447	38854	101711	228793	655403	3144551

Selected Financial Ratios (Times to 1)													
Current Ratio 30	1.5	•	1.5	2.7	2.0	3.7	2.0	1.5	1.8	2.7	3.0	1.7	0.5
Quick Ratio 31	1.0	•	1.2	1.9	1.3	1.4	1.2	0.9	1.2	1.8	2.1	1.2	0.5
Net Sales to Working Capital 32	3.1	•	8.4	1.2	1.0	0.5	0.9	1.4	1.4	1.5	1.2	4.6	•
Coverage Ratio 33	1.6	0.4	2.9	0.6	1.4	•	0.5	0.7	0.6	0.8	1.4	2.2	3.1
Total Asset Turnover 34	0.1	•	0.6	0.2	0.1	0.1	0.1	0.1	0.1	0.1	0.1	0.1	0.1
Inventory Turnover 35	•	•	•	•	•	•	•	•	•	•	•	•	•
Receivables Turnover 36	•	•	•	•	•	•	•	•	•	•	•	•	•
Total Liabilities to Net Worth 37	0.8	•	1.9	1.2	2.5	1.5	1.3	1.1	0.8	0.6	0.5	0.5	0.9
Current Assets to Working Capital 38	2.8	•	3.1	1.6	2.0	1.4	2.0	2.8	2.2	1.6	1.5	2.5	•
Current Liabilities to Working Capital 39	1.8	•	2.1	0.6	1.0	0.4	1.0	1.8	1.2	0.6	0.5	1.5	•
Working Capital to Net Sales 40	0.3	•	0.1	0.8	1.0	2.2	1.1	0.7	0.7	0.7	0.8	0.2	•
Inventory to Working Capital 41	0.0	•	•	•	0.0	0.0	0.0	0.0	0.0	0.0	0.0	0.0	•
Total Receipts to Cash Flow 42	2.7	5.6	4.2	2.1	3.3	6.1	3.2	2.5	2.8	2.3	3.9	2.3	2.1
Cost of Goods to Cash Flow 43	0.0	0.0	•	•	0.1	0.0	•	0.0	0.0	0.0	0.2	0.0	0.0
Cash Flow to Total Debt 44	0.1	•	0.2	0.1	0.0	0.0	0.1	0.1	0.1	0.1	0.1	0.1	0.1

Selected Financial Factors (in Percentages)													
Debt Ratio 45	44.5	•	65.1	54.9	71.6	59.2	56.0	53.1	45.1	36.1	34.9	33.2	46.1
Return on Total Assets 46	2.1	•	3.2	0.5	1.5	•	0.8	0.9	1.1	1.2	1.6	2.5	3.1
Return on Equity Before Income Taxes 47	1.5	•	6.0	•	1.6	•	•	•	•	•	0.7	2.1	4.0
Return on Equity After Income Taxes 48	1.3	•	5.1	•	0.5	•	•	•	•	•	0.7	2.0	4.0
Profit Margin (Before Income Tax) 49	8.0	•	3.3	•	4.9	•	•	•	•	•	5.5	18.1	25.4
Profit Margin (After Income Tax) 50	6.9	•	2.8	•	1.6	•	•	•	•	•	5.1	17.6	25.4

Table II

Corporations with Net Income

LESSORS OF MINIWAREHOUSES, SELF-STORAGE, OTHER REAL ESTATE

Item Description for Accounting Period 7/11 Through 6/12		MONEY AMOUNTS AND SIZE OF ASSETS IN THOUSANDS OF DOLLARS												
		Total	Zero Assets	Under 500	500 to 1,000	1,000 to 5,000	5,000 to 10,000	10,000 to 25,000	25,000 to 50,000	50,000 to 100,000	100,000 to 250,000	250,000 to 500,000	500,000 to 2,500,000	2,500,000 and over
Number of Enterprises	1	24291	4296	13018	2991	2729	552	310	135	86	85	28	50	11
Revenues ($ in Thousands)														
Net Sales	2	23783805	1094845	3558868	730918	1407372	501335	974528	739502	746487	1865327	1273944	4129057	6761622
Interest	3	796774	14405	9445	15579	39171	5486	46153	27678	28264	42931	47693	228451	291518
Rents	4	7015007	52097	1597	1797	3386	25273	163014	152984	314483	634359	512115	2342340	2811561
Royalties	5	97805	0	3659	13537	22108	33967	13083	3880	1493	6077	0	0	0
Other Portfolio Income	6	4481175	400519	141212	20489	289902	71503	132605	201513	133515	264911	549391	1054283	1221331
Other Receipts	7	11393044	627824	3402955	679516	1052805	365106	619673	353447	268732	917049	164745	503983	2437212
Total Receipts	8	23783805	1094845	3558868	730918	1407372	501335	974528	739502	746487	1865327	1273944	4129057	6761622
Average Total Receipts	9	979	255	273	244	516	908	3144	5478	8680	21945	45498	82581	614693
Operating Costs/Operating Income (%)														
Cost of Operations	10	0.0	0.0	•	•	•	0.4	•	•	•	0.3	•	0.0	•
Salaries and Wages	11	7.1	3.0	24.8	15.8	5.7	7.6	9.0	3.1	2.3	6.0	1.4	1.0	3.7
Taxes Paid	12	5.4	3.2	5.2	9.2	7.0	7.4	4.2	5.3	5.0	5.4	2.4	5.8	5.4
Interest Paid	13	7.9	8.7	1.0	3.7	10.4	9.4	6.5	9.4	12.5	10.3	5.7	9.7	9.6
Depreciation	14	6.2	1.9	1.5	3.9	6.6	7.7	5.1	6.9	8.5	10.8	3.9	9.7	6.4
Amortization and Depletion	15	0.7	0.8	0.1	0.3	0.6	1.4	0.3	0.6	0.8	1.4	0.4	1.2	0.6
Pensions and Other Deferred Comp.	16	0.2	0.1	0.6	0.7	0.0	0.0	0.2	0.1	0.0	0.5	0.1	•	•
Employee Benefits	17	0.6	0.2	3.5	0.4	0.4	0.6	0.4	0.3	0.2	0.3	•	0.0	•
Advertising	18	0.9	0.5	3.6	0.4	0.3	0.4	0.6	0.7	0.4	0.3	0.0	0.2	0.5
Other Expenses	19	35.4	36.6	35.5	30.6	19.8	26.4	37.9	23.2	35.3	34.7	42.0	30.4	42.7
Officers' Compensation	20	2.4	0.5	8.5	8.6	3.0	4.0	1.5	4.2	0.7	1.1	0.8	0.6	0.5
Operating Margin	21	33.1	44.5	15.7	26.3	46.2	34.7	34.3	46.3	34.2	29.0	43.2	41.5	30.6
Operating Margin Before Officers' Comp.	22	35.5	45.0	24.2	35.0	49.2	38.7	35.8	50.5	34.9	30.1	44.0	42.1	31.1

Selected Average Balance Sheet ($ in Thousands)														
Net Receivables	23	131	0	6	45	109	92	965	1926	1675	2045	3198	14944	82325
Inventories	24	•	•	•	•	•	•	•	•	•	•	•	•	•
Net Property, Plant and Equipment	25	3594	0	56	225	1181	3056	4942	11660	25607	62238	96425	462397	4053317
Total Assets	26	7260	0	138	680	2114	6388	15246	35325	69951	163720	353426	1045751	6510120
Notes and Loans Payable	27	1925	0	57	172	1247	1890	4509	12320	19621	50001	72990	221458	1722077
All Other Liabilities	28	629	0	25	87	263	772	1697	3495	4843	10689	23959	28788	830218
Net Worth	29	4705	0	56	421	604	3726	9040	19511	45487	103030	256477	795505	3957825
Selected Financial Ratios (Times to 1)														
Current Ratio	30	1.9	•	1.9	5.2	3.6	4.2	4.5	2.0	2.2	2.6	2.9	2.4	0.8
Quick Ratio	31	1.4	•	1.5	4.0	1.9	2.4	2.7	1.5	1.7	1.8	1.9	1.7	0.8
Net Sales to Working Capital	32	3.7	•	10.2	1.1	1.4	0.9	1.1	1.5	1.7	2.8	1.7	3.2	•
Coverage Ratio	33	5.2	6.2	17.1	8.0	5.4	4.6	6.2	6.0	3.7	3.8	8.6	5.3	4.2
Total Asset Turnover	34	0.1	•	2.0	0.4	0.2	0.1	0.2	0.2	0.1	0.1	0.1	0.1	0.1
Inventory Turnover	35	•	•	•	•	•	•	•	•	•	•	•	•	•
Receivables Turnover	36	•	•	•	•	•	•	•	•	•	•	•	•	•
Total Liabilities to Net Worth	37	0.5	•	1.5	0.6	2.5	0.7	0.7	0.8	0.5	0.6	0.4	0.3	0.6
Current Assets to Working Capital	38	2.2	•	2.1	1.2	1.4	1.3	1.3	2.1	1.8	1.6	1.5	1.7	•
Current Liabilities to Working Capital	39	1.2	•	1.1	0.2	0.4	0.3	0.3	1.1	0.8	0.6	0.5	0.7	•
Working Capital to Net Sales	40	0.3	•	0.1	0.9	0.7	1.2	0.9	0.6	0.6	0.4	0.6	0.3	•
Inventory to Working Capital	41	0.0	•	•	•	•	0.0	•	•	0.0	0.0	•	•	•
Total Receipts to Cash Flow	42	2.2	2.3	3.2	2.1	2.1	2.0	2.0	2.1	2.0	2.0	4.0	2.0	1.9
Cost of Goods to Cash Flow	43	0.0	0.0	•	•	•	0.0	•	•	•	0.0	•	0.0	•
Cash Flow to Total Debt	44	0.2	•	1.0	0.4	0.2	0.2	0.3	0.2	0.2	0.2	0.1	0.2	0.1
Selected Financial Factors (in Percentages)														
Debt Ratio	45	35.2	•	59.6	38.1	71.5	41.7	40.7	44.8	35.0	37.1	27.4	23.9	39.2
Return on Total Assets	46	5.5	•	33.1	10.8	13.8	6.2	8.4	8.7	5.8	5.3	6.3	4.1	3.8
Return on Equity Before Income Taxes	47	6.9	•	77.1	15.2	39.4	8.3	11.9	13.0	6.5	6.2	7.7	4.3	4.8
Return on Equity After Income Taxes	48	6.6	•	74.2	13.5	35.0	6.5	10.6	11.8	6.1	5.9	7.5	4.3	4.7
Profit Margin (Before Income Tax)	49	33.1	45.4	15.7	26.2	46.1	34.0	34.2	46.4	34.1	29.0	43.2	41.6	30.6
Profit Margin (After Income Tax)	50	31.5	38.1	15.1	23.2	41.0	26.7	30.5	42.2	31.8	27.8	42.4	41.0	30.6

Table I

Corporations with and without Net Income

OFFICES OF REAL ESTATE AGENTS AND BROKERS

MONEY AMOUNTS AND SIZE OF ASSETS IN THOUSANDS OF DOLLARS

Item Description for Accounting Period 7/11 Through 6/12		Total	Zero Assets	Under 500	500 to 1,000	1,000 to 5,000	5,000 to 10,000	10,000 to 25,000	25,000 to 50,000	50,000 to 100,000	100,000 to 250,000	250,000 to 500,000	500,000 to 2,500,000	2,500,000 and over
Number of Enterprises	1	124972	31754	87523	3249	1969	292	119	28	15	10	3	9	0
Revenues ($ in Thousands)														
Net Sales	2	37383095	2952587	17596062	2099734	1494140	1343640	1045067	474201	434939	550266	1678102	7714357	0
Interest	3	230421	67	14007	2242	18752	5202	1907	7804	3035	20171	18141	139093	0
Rents	4	219587	6101	33186	11188	23195	14496	4755	663	16754	15347	16602	77299	0
Royalties	5	526122	0	0	0	4	32	128	0	0	0	616	525343	0
Other Portfolio Income	6	232984	21507	2715	2907	11741	7316	1259	13046	14879	39248	28181	90187	0
Other Receipts	7	36173981	2924912	17546154	2083397	1440448	1316594	1037018	452688	400271	475500	1614562	6882435	0
Total Receipts	8	37383095	2952587	17596062	2099734	1494140	1343640	1045067	474201	434939	550266	1678102	7714357	0
Average Total Receipts	9	299	93	201	646	759	4602	8782	16936	28996	55027	559367	857151	•
Operating Costs/Operating Income (%)														
Cost of Operations	10	0.2	•	•	•	•	•	2.0	•	0.4	3.1	•	0.5	•
Salaries and Wages	11	32.2	9.3	26.8	22.0	57.0	59.7	47.0	23.9	29.4	26.4	9.2	50.7	•
Taxes Paid	12	2.9	2.0	2.7	3.7	2.8	3.3	2.3	3.7	4.3	3.7	1.0	3.9	•
Interest Paid	13	3.5	1.2	0.6	1.4	4.5	1.2	2.2	3.4	2.7	5.0	1.2	12.2	•
Depreciation	14	1.6	0.4	1.2	2.0	2.3	1.6	3.2	2.4	3.3	3.3	0.9	2.4	•
Amortization and Depletion	15	0.8	0.0	0.1	0.7	0.2	0.0	0.3	0.4	1.1	3.1	0.3	2.8	•
Pensions and Other Deferred Comp.	16	0.6	0.4	0.7	2.5	0.1	0.1	0.2	0.3	0.4	0.2	0.1	0.3	•
Employee Benefits	17	1.2	0.4	0.7	1.0	1.2	1.0	1.3	1.7	1.5	2.1	0.2	2.9	•
Advertising	18	3.3	2.4	3.8	5.0	3.1	3.8	4.8	3.0	3.5	2.2	0.4	2.5	•
Other Expenses	19	37.3	63.7	37.1	32.1	32.7	22.4	22.5	48.4	37.5	37.1	88.0	22.6	•
Officers' Compensation	20	8.2	6.9	11.8	19.8	4.0	2.3	7.1	5.8	4.7	5.9	0.4	1.3	•
Operating Margin	21	8.3	13.4	14.4	9.8	•	4.6	7.0	7.0	11.3	7.7	•	•	•
Operating Margin Before Officers' Comp.	22	16.4	20.3	26.2	29.6	•	6.9	14.1	12.9	16.0	13.6	•	•	•

Selected Average Balance Sheet ($ in Thousands)													
Net Receivables 23	29	0	2	50	290	470	339	4408	1716	15463	42877	231376	•
Inventories 24	•	•	•	•	•	•	•	•	•	•	•	•	•
Net Property, Plant and Equipment 25	58	0	15	340	553	1690	5191	7448	21456	19525	23869	203551	•
Total Assets 26	330	0	64	707	1874	6661	14743	33004	76879	159145	307096	2377317	•
Notes and Loans Payable 27	183	0	33	428	1127	3066	8577	11938	33115	24119	134678	1441276	•
All Other Liabilities 28	90	0	18	182	188	1444	2915	8565	8846	44816	138428	743490	•
Net Worth 29	57	0	13	97	559	2151	3251	12501	34918	90210	33990	192551	•
Selected Financial Ratios (Times to 1)													
Current Ratio 30	1.3	•	1.8	1.4	2.3	1.5	1.4	1.7	1.9	1.7	5.1	0.9	•
Quick Ratio 31	1.0	•	1.4	1.0	1.6	1.1	0.6	1.1	1.1	1.0	4.2	0.7	•
Net Sales to Working Capital 32	11.9	•	13.6	10.3	1.9	7.7	8.1	2.6	2.8	1.8	6.5	•	•
Coverage Ratio 33	3.4	12.1	25.7	8.1	•	4.8	4.2	3.0	5.2	2.5	•	0.8	•
Total Asset Turnover 34	0.9	•	3.1	0.9	0.4	0.7	0.6	0.5	0.4	0.3	1.8	0.4	•
Inventory Turnover 35	•	•	•	•	•	•	•	•	•	•	•	•	•
Receivables Turnover 36	•	•	•	•	•	•	•	•	•	•	•	•	•
Total Liabilities to Net Worth 37	4.8	•	4.0	6.3	2.4	2.1	3.5	1.6	1.2	0.8	8.0	11.3	•
Current Assets to Working Capital 38	4.0	•	2.3	3.5	1.7	3.0	3.5	2.4	2.1	2.4	1.2	•	•
Current Liabilities to Working Capital 39	3.0	•	1.3	2.5	0.7	2.0	2.5	1.4	1.1	1.4	0.2	•	•
Working Capital to Net Sales 40	0.1	•	0.1	0.1	0.5	0.1	0.1	0.4	0.4	0.6	0.2	•	•
Inventory to Working Capital 41	0.0	•	•	•	•	•	0.0	•	0.1	0.3	•	•	•
Total Receipts to Cash Flow 42	2.8	1.4	2.2	2.9	7.3	4.6	4.6	2.1	2.7	4.1	12.8	7.1	•
Cost of Goods to Cash Flow 43	0.0	•	•	•	•	•	0.1	•	0.0	0.1	•	0.0	•
Cash Flow to Total Debt 44	0.4	•	1.8	0.4	0.1	0.2	0.2	0.4	0.3	0.2	0.2	0.1	•
Selected Financial Factors (in Percentages)													
Debt Ratio 45	82.6	•	79.8	86.3	70.2	67.7	78.0	62.1	54.6	43.3	88.9	91.9	•
Return on Total Assets 46	10.6	•	46.8	10.2	•	4.0	5.5	5.4	5.2	4.4	•	3.7	•
Return on Equity Before Income Taxes 47	43.1	•	222.8	65.7	•	9.8	19.0	9.5	9.3	4.7	•	•	•
Return on Equity After Income Taxes 48	41.3	•	221.6	65.4	•	9.4	18.1	8.8	8.9	4.3	•	•	•
Profit Margin (Before Income Tax) 49	8.3	13.4	14.4	9.8	•	4.6	7.0	7.0	11.2	7.7	•	•	•
Profit Margin (After Income Tax) 50	7.9	13.2	14.3	9.8	•	4.4	6.7	6.5	10.8	7.0	•	•	•

Table II

Corporations with Net Income

Offices of Real Estate Agents and Brokers

Money Amounts and Size of Assets in Thousands of Dollars

Item Description for Accounting Period 7/11 Through 6/12		Total	Zero Assets	Under 500	500 to 1,000	1,000 to 5,000	5,000 to 10,000	10,000 to 25,000	25,000 to 50,000	50,000 to 100,000	100,000 to 250,000	250,000 to 500,000	500,000 to 2,500,000	2,500,000 and over
Number of Enterprises	1	77791	15752	59286	1739	724	180	68	•	9	•	0	4	0
Revenues ($ in Thousands)														
Net Sales	2	28095461	2632310	14228225	1568929	1382320	1263718	965178	•	279221	•	0	5096427	0
Interest	3	164936	55	328	117	12086	1744	973	•	2380	•	0	114496	0
Rents	4	134359	3302	19498	3899	11233	1814	4755	•	16649	•	0	40969	0
Royalties	5	66868	0	0	0	4	32	128	•	0	•	0	66089	0
Other Portfolio Income	6	183644	21507	1936	76	9905	1107	1240	•	3	•	0	79300	0
Other Receipts	7	27545654	2607446	14206463	1564837	1349092	1259021	958082	•	260189	•	0	4795573	0
Total Receipts	8	28095461	2632310	14228225	1568929	1382320	1263718	965178	•	279221	•	0	5096427	0
Average Total Receipts	9	361	167	240	902	1909	7021	14194	•	31025	•	•	1274107	•
Operating Costs/Operating Income (%)														
Cost of Operations	10	0.2	•	•	•	•	•	2.2	•	0.0	•	•	0.5	•
Salaries and Wages	11	32.7	6.7	23.9	19.5	56.7	61.1	46.9	•	30.7	•	•	60.6	•
Taxes Paid	12	2.8	1.6	2.6	3.0	1.7	3.1	2.1	•	3.9	•	•	4.3	•
Interest Paid	13	1.4	0.2	0.5	0.5	1.1	0.6	1.7	•	2.8	•	•	4.0	•
Depreciation	14	1.3	0.2	1.0	1.8	0.9	1.3	3.2	•	2.8	•	•	2.3	•
Amortization and Depletion	15	0.3	0.0	0.1	0.9	0.2	0.0	0.4	•	1.6	•	•	1.1	•
Pensions and Other Deferred Comp.	16	0.6	0.5	0.9	1.3	0.1	0.1	0.1	•	0.6	•	•	0.2	•
Employee Benefits	17	1.2	0.4	0.7	1.3	1.1	0.9	1.3	•	1.6	•	•	3.0	•
Advertising	18	3.1	2.4	3.9	3.2	2.5	4.0	5.0	•	2.9	•	•	0.9	•
Other Expenses	19	31.4	61.9	34.3	28.2	25.1	18.8	21.0	•	26.3	•	•	15.0	•
Officers' Compensation	20	8.6	6.9	11.3	24.6	3.0	1.6	6.8	•	2.7	•	•	1.3	•
Operating Margin	21	16.2	19.1	20.9	15.7	7.7	8.5	9.3	•	24.1	•	•	6.9	•
Operating Margin Before Officers' Comp.	22	24.8	26.0	32.2	40.3	10.6	10.0	16.1	•	26.8	•	•	8.1	•

Selected Average Balance Sheet ($ in Thousands)														
Net Receivables	**23**	26	0	2	37	241	667	208	•	956	•	•	313602	•
Inventories	**24**	•	•	•	•	•	•	•	•	•	•	•	•	•
Net Property, Plant and Equipment	**25**	43	0	13	364	442	510	3528	•	31599	•	•	168392	•
Total Assets	**26**	283	0	69	746	1736	6748	15300	•	81678	•	•	2566790	•
Notes and Loans Payable	**27**	102	0	24	230	597	2884	5654	•	41942	•	•	951612	•
All Other Liabilities	**28**	84	0	15	157	219	1497	4643	•	10951	•	•	973405	•
Net Worth	**29**	96	0	30	359	919	2368	5003	•	28785	•	•	641772	•
Selected Financial Ratios (Times to 1)														
Current Ratio	**30**	1.4	•	2.4	2.5	3.0	1.6	1.4	•	1.2	•	•	0.8	•
Quick Ratio	**31**	1.0	•	1.9	1.8	2.1	1.3	0.6	•	1.1	•	•	0.7	•
Net Sales to Working Capital	**32**	13.5	•	10.4	5.8	3.4	8.2	9.4	•	12.0	•	•	•	•
Coverage Ratio	**33**	12.6	80.0	39.6	33.0	8.1	14.2	6.5	•	9.5	•	•	2.7	•
Total Asset Turnover	**34**	1.3	•	3.5	1.2	1.1	1.0	0.9	•	0.4	•	•	0.5	•
Inventory Turnover	**35**	•	•	•	•	•	•	•	•	•	•	•	•	•
Receivables Turnover	**36**	•	•	•	•	•	•	•	•	•	•	•	•	•
Total Liabilities to Net Worth	**37**	1.9	•	1.3	1.1	0.9	1.9	2.1	•	1.8	•	•	3.0	•
Current Assets to Working Capital	**38**	3.8	•	1.7	1.7	1.5	2.6	3.4	•	5.7	•	•	•	•
Current Liabilities to Working Capital	**39**	2.8	•	0.7	0.7	0.5	1.6	2.4	•	4.7	•	•	•	•
Working Capital to Net Sales	**40**	0.1	•	0.1	0.2	0.3	0.1	0.1	•	0.1	•	•	•	•
Inventory to Working Capital	**41**	0.0	•	•	•	•	•	0.0	•	0.1	•	•	•	•
Total Receipts to Cash Flow	**42**	2.4	1.3	2.0	2.5	4.0	4.5	4.5	•	2.5	•	•	5.9	•
Cost of Goods to Cash Flow	**43**	0.0	•	•	•	•	•	0.1	•	0.0	•	•	0.0	•
Cash Flow to Total Debt	**44**	0.8	•	3.0	0.9	0.6	0.4	0.3	•	0.2	•	•	0.1	•
Selected Financial Factors (in Percentages)														
Debt Ratio	**45**	65.9	•	56.7	51.8	47.0	64.9	67.3	•	64.8	•	•	75.0	•
Return on Total Assets	**46**	22.5	•	74.8	19.6	9.6	9.5	10.2	•	10.2	•	•	5.4	•
Return on Equity Before Income Taxes	**47**	60.8	•	168.5	39.4	15.9	25.1	26.4	•	26.0	•	•	13.7	•
Return on Equity After Income Taxes	**48**	59.1	•	167.8	39.3	15.2	24.6	25.4	•	25.2	•	•	10.2	•
Profit Margin (Before Income Tax)	**49**	16.2	19.1	20.9	15.7	7.7	8.5	9.3	•	24.1	•	•	6.9	•
Profit Margin (After Income Tax)	**50**	15.8	19.0	20.8	15.6	7.3	8.3	8.9	•	23.4	•	•	5.1	•

Table I

Corporations with and without Net Income

OTHER REAL ESTATE ACTIVITIES

MONEY AMOUNTS AND SIZE OF ASSETS IN THOUSANDS OF DOLLARS

Item Description for Accounting Period 7/11 Through 6/12		Total	Zero Assets	Under 500	500 to 1,000	1,000 to 5,000	5,000 to 10,000	10,000 to 25,000	25,000 to 50,000	50,000 to 100,000	100,000 to 250,000	250,000 to 500,000	500,000 to 2,500,000	2,500,000 and over
Number of Enterprises	1	158187	33464	102587	8470	10727	1507	922	259	151	70	19	11	0
Revenues ($ in Thousands)														
Net Sales	2	52004102	1795025	19450397	4386604	9471904	1954784	2036182	1965020	1707585	2466994	1604230	5165377	0
Interest	3	1122424	9451	7834	8982	26041	34338	36941	40237	34775	68003	78770	777053	0
Rents	4	1592338	112137	122698	78761	140012	114290	134927	137645	168486	125756	255325	202302	0
Royalties	5	465825	1	0	29	93	424	18343	0	654	44314	14	401954	0
Other Portfolio Income	6	2441549	79116	133777	49132	151646	51876	118652	83181	66732	151733	125488	1430214	0
Other Receipts	7	46381966	1594320	19186088	4249700	9154112	1753856	1727319	1703957	1436938	2077188	1144633	2353854	0
Total Receipts	8	52004102	1795025	19450397	4386604	9471904	1954784	2036182	1965020	1707585	2466994	1604230	5165377	0
Average Total Receipts	9	329	54	190	518	883	1297	2208	7587	11309	35243	84433	469580	•
Operating Costs/Operating Income (%)														
Cost of Operations	10	0.1	1.4	•	•	•	0.3	0.0	0.9	0.3	•	0.1	0.1	•
Salaries and Wages	11	33.5	4.8	31.3	50.9	43.4	40.8	31.4	22.2	23.9	30.1	36.5	24.6	•
Taxes Paid	12	4.2	3.2	3.9	4.7	5.3	6.4	6.0	4.0	4.8	3.4	3.9	2.4	•
Interest Paid	13	4.1	3.5	0.8	1.6	2.6	6.9	7.4	7.1	10.7	9.1	10.3	11.3	•
Depreciation	14	2.7	2.6	1.6	0.9	2.4	4.0	5.7	3.1	6.4	4.4	7.3	3.5	•
Amortization and Depletion	15	0.4	0.1	0.2	0.1	0.5	0.1	0.4	0.7	0.6	1.3	0.8	1.3	•
Pensions and Other Deferred Comp.	16	0.8	0.5	1.1	0.3	1.2	0.4	0.6	0.2	0.8	0.3	0.1	0.8	•
Employee Benefits	17	2.6	0.5	1.7	8.4	2.1	4.7	2.6	1.9	1.9	2.3	1.4	2.7	•
Advertising	18	1.1	0.4	1.4	0.2	0.7	1.6	0.9	1.0	1.2	0.7	0.8	1.7	•
Other Expenses	19	40.6	82.9	38.3	22.1	35.1	47.0	33.4	65.1	54.2	50.5	38.3	42.4	•
Officers' Compensation	20	8.8	8.4	15.6	4.6	6.8	8.8	5.8	2.8	4.1	3.4	0.6	0.6	•
Operating Margin	21	1.2	•	4.2	6.1	•	•	5.8	•	•	•	•	8.5	•
Operating Margin Before Officers' Comp.	22	10.0	0.2	19.8	10.7	6.8	•	11.6	•	•	•	0.4	9.1	•

Selected Average Balance Sheet ($ in Thousands)														
Net Receivables	23	67	0	3	27	148	614	927	1874	2636	12225	17452	411379	•
Inventories	24	•	•	•	•	•	•	•	•	•	•	•	•	•
Net Property, Plant and Equipment	25	231	0	25	262	782	2238	5155	10558	23518	37058	163741	299582	•
Total Assets	26	760	0	81	718	2038	7193	15025	33587	71028	151736	337544	2080133	•
Notes and Loans Payable	27	383	0	59	349	1103	3555	6457	18970	27505	65116	173481	1050292	•
All Other Liabilities	28	160	0	20	99	366	1606	2947	7372	13078	22788	127904	484505	•
Net Worth	29	218	0	1	270	570	2033	5622	7246	30445	63832	36160	545337	•
Selected Financial Ratios (Times to 1)														
Current Ratio	30	2.3	•	1.4	3.0	2.4	1.8	1.9	1.5	1.6	1.9	1.0	5.2	•
Quick Ratio	31	1.2	•	1.0	1.7	1.5	1.0	1.0	0.8	0.9	1.3	0.6	2.2	•
Net Sales to Working Capital	32	2.2	•	20.1	2.7	2.2	1.3	1.0	2.2	1.8	2.0	•	0.5	•
Coverage Ratio	33	1.3	•	6.1	4.6	1.0	•	1.8	•	0.2	0.4	1.0	1.8	•
Total Asset Turnover	34	0.4	•	2.4	0.7	0.4	0.2	0.1	0.2	0.2	0.2	0.3	0.2	•
Inventory Turnover	35	•	•	•	•	•	•	•	•	•	•	•	•	•
Receivables Turnover	36	•	•	•	•	•	•	•	•	•	•	•	•	•
Total Liabilities to Net Worth	37	2.5	•	60.0	1.7	2.6	2.5	1.7	3.6	1.3	1.4	8.3	2.8	•
Current Assets to Working Capital	38	1.8	•	3.5	1.5	1.7	2.3	2.1	2.9	2.6	2.1	•	1.2	•
Current Liabilities to Working Capital	39	0.8	•	2.5	0.5	0.7	1.3	1.1	1.9	1.6	1.1	•	0.2	•
Working Capital to Net Sales	40	0.5	•	0.0	0.4	0.5	0.8	1.0	0.5	0.6	0.5	•	2.0	•
Inventory to Working Capital	41	0.0	•	•	•	0.0	0.0	0.0	0.0	0.0	0.0	•	0.0	•
Total Receipts to Cash Flow	42	3.1	1.7	2.8	5.9	3.5	5.5	3.4	3.7	3.6	3.0	3.6	2.3	•
Cost of Goods to Cash Flow	43	0.0	0.0	•	•	•	0.0	0.0	0.0	0.0	•	0.0	0.0	•
Cash Flow to Total Debt	44	0.2	•	0.9	0.2	0.2	0.0	0.1	0.1	0.1	0.1	0.1	0.1	•
Selected Financial Factors (in Percentages)														
Debt Ratio	45	71.4	•	98.4	62.3	72.1	71.7	62.6	78.4	57.1	57.9	89.3	73.8	•
Return on Total Assets	46	2.3	•	11.7	5.4	1.1	•	1.9	•	0.3	0.8	2.6	4.5	•
Return on Equity Before Income Taxes	47	1.7	•	596.9	11.2	•	•	2.2	•	•	•	0.3	7.5	•
Return on Equity After Income Taxes	48	0.6	•	576.3	10.9	•	•	1.5	•	•	•	•	5.3	•
Profit Margin (Before Income Tax)	49	1.2	•	4.2	5.9	•	•	5.7	•	•	•	0.1	8.7	•
Profit Margin (After Income Tax)	50	0.4	•	4.0	5.7	•	•	3.9	•	•	•	•	6.1	•

OTHER REAL ESTATE ACTIVITIES

MONEY AMOUNTS AND SIZE OF ASSETS IN THOUSANDS OF DOLLARS

Item Description for Accounting Period 7/11 Through 6/12		Total	Zero Assets	Under 500	500 to 1,000	1,000 to 5,000	5,000 to 10,000	10,000 to 25,000	25,000 to 50,000	50,000 to 100,000	100,000 to 250,000	250,000 to 500,000	500,000 to 2,500,000	2,500,000 and over
Number of Enterprises	1	74824	15441	51411	2927	3875	650	342	•	60	•	10	6	0
Revenues ($ in Thousands)														
Net Sales	2	36259355	1544817	15232600	1532149	5679469	1376599	1292648	•	809612	•	1345076	4942615	0
Interest	3	966834	7005	4993	5478	17158	21762	27053	•	22302	•	53408	768702	0
Rents	4	865936	60022	88687	40382	51378	48261	52619	•	108779	•	153644	179324	0
Royalties	5	462490	1	0	29	0	424	18343	•	104	•	14	399273	0
Other Portfolio Income	6	2210545	72385	37397	28729	141474	39171	117477	•	23120	•	122236	1429843	0
Other Receipts	7	31753550	1405404	15101523	1457531	5469459	1266981	1077156	•	655307	•	1015774	2165473	0
Total Receipts	8	36259355	1544817	15232600	1532149	5679469	1376599	1292648	•	809612	•	1345076	4942615	0
Average Total Receipts	9	485	100	296	523	1466	2118	3780	•	13494	•	134508	823769	•
Operating Costs/Operating Income (%)														
Cost of Operations	10	0.1	0.1	•	•	•	0.5	0.1	•	•	•	0.1	0.1	•
Salaries and Wages	11	29.7	2.0	31.0	17.6	43.3	31.2	20.2	•	25.0	•	39.9	24.6	•
Taxes Paid	12	3.4	1.8	3.3	2.2	4.5	3.7	4.7	•	5.3	•	2.9	2.3	•
Interest Paid	13	3.1	2.4	0.5	1.2	1.9	2.3	4.1	•	7.0	•	7.1	11.5	•
Depreciation	14	2.1	1.8	1.4	1.0	1.9	1.3	4.0	•	4.5	•	5.1	3.5	•
Amortization and Depletion	15	0.4	0.1	0.1	0.1	0.2	0.1	0.4	•	0.2	•	0.7	1.3	•
Pensions and Other Deferred Comp.	16	0.7	0.6	0.5	0.6	1.8	0.2	0.4	•	0.6	•	0.1	0.8	•
Employee Benefits	17	1.6	0.2	1.1	1.3	2.4	2.9	1.3	•	1.8	•	1.3	2.6	•
Advertising	18	1.1	0.2	1.3	0.4	0.6	0.4	1.0	•	0.8	•	0.7	1.7	•
Other Expenses	19	34.4	50.1	34.7	44.0	21.3	28.3	27.8	•	23.2	•	32.3	41.3	•
Officers' Compensation	20	7.5	7.8	12.8	4.5	5.3	6.1	6.1	•	5.9	•	0.2	0.4	•
Operating Margin	21	16.0	33.0	13.2	27.0	16.8	23.1	29.9	•	25.6	•	9.8	10.0	•
Operating Margin Before Officers' Comp.	22	23.5	40.8	26.0	31.5	22.1	29.1	36.0	•	31.6	•	10.0	10.3	•

Selected Average Balance Sheet ($ in Thousands)													
Net Receivables 23	91	0	2	38	176	421	1279	•	4442	•	24708	689560	•
Inventories 24	•	•	•	•	•	•	•	•	•	•	•	•	•
Net Property, Plant and Equipment 25	156	0	16	129	515	1388	3520	•	17397	•	184466	351990	•
Total Assets 26	754	0	73	666	2004	6926	15052	•	69556	•	312645	3245000	•
Notes and Loans Payable 27	317	0	18	237	1043	3015	5482	•	19817	•	91286	1671002	•
All Other Liabilities 28	168	0	18	120	387	893	2987	•	13583	•	158611	710151	•
Net Worth 29	270	0	37	308	574	3018	6584	•	36156	•	62748	863846	•
Selected Financial Ratios (Times to 1)													
Current Ratio 30	3.1	•	2.0	4.4	2.6	3.2	2.0	•	1.8	•	1.2	6.6	•
Quick Ratio 31	1.6	•	1.6	3.0	1.5	1.7	1.2	•	1.1	•	0.8	2.6	•
Net Sales to Working Capital 32	2.1	•	17.2	2.1	2.5	1.1	1.3	•	1.4	•	12.2	0.5	•
Coverage Ratio 33	6.1	14.8	27.7	23.7	9.8	10.8	8.3	•	4.6	•	2.4	1.9	•
Total Asset Turnover 34	0.6	•	4.1	0.8	0.7	0.3	0.3	•	0.2	•	0.4	0.3	•
Inventory Turnover 35	•	•	•	•	•	•	•	•	•	•	•	•	•
Receivables Turnover 36	•	•	•	•	•	•	•	•	•	•	•	•	•
Total Liabilities to Net Worth 37	1.8	•	1.0	1.2	2.5	1.3	1.3	•	0.9	•	4.0	2.8	•
Current Assets to Working Capital 38	1.5	•	2.0	1.3	1.6	1.5	2.0	•	2.3	•	5.4	1.2	•
Current Liabilities to Working Capital 39	0.5	•	1.0	0.3	0.6	0.5	1.0	•	1.3	•	4.4	0.2	•
Working Capital to Net Sales 40	0.5	•	0.1	0.5	0.4	0.9	0.7	•	0.7	•	0.1	2.0	•
Inventory to Working Capital 41	0.0	•	•	•	0.0	0.0	0.0	•	0.0	•	0.0	0.0	•
Total Receipts to Cash Flow 42	2.4	1.4	2.4	2.4	3.0	2.2	2.1	•	2.4	•	3.2	2.3	•
Cost of Goods to Cash Flow 43	0.0	0.0	•	•	•	0.0	0.0	•	•	•	0.0	0.0	•
Cash Flow to Total Debt 44	0.4	•	3.5	0.6	0.3	0.3	0.2	•	0.2	•	0.2	0.2	•
Selected Financial Factors (in Percentages)													
Debt Ratio 45	64.3	•	49.0	53.7	71.4	56.4	56.3	•	48.0	•	79.9	73.4	•
Return on Total Assets 46	12.3	•	55.7	22.2	13.6	7.8	8.5	•	6.3	•	7.4	5.5	•
Return on Equity Before Income Taxes 47	28.7	•	105.4	45.9	42.8	16.1	17.1	•	9.5	•	21.9	9.7	•
Return on Equity After Income Taxes 48	26.7	•	103.9	45.1	41.4	14.4	15.5	•	8.6	•	18.0	7.1	•
Profit Margin (Before Income Tax) 49	16.0	33.0	13.2	27.0	16.7	23.0	29.8	•	25.4	•	10.2	10.2	•
Profit Margin (After Income Tax) 50	14.9	31.6	13.1	26.5	16.2	20.5	27.0	•	23.1	•	8.4	7.5	•

Table I

Corporations with and without Net Income

AUTOMOTIVE EQUIPMENT RENTAL AND LEASING

MONEY AMOUNTS AND SIZE OF ASSETS IN THOUSANDS OF DOLLARS

Item Description for Accounting Period 7/11 Through 6/12		Total	Zero Assets	Under 500	500 to 1,000	1,000 to 5,000	5,000 to 10,000	10,000 to 25,000	25,000 to 50,000	50,000 to 100,000	100,000 to 250,000	250,000 to 500,000	500,000 to 2,500,000	2,500,000 and over
Number of Enterprises	1	6711	•	3889	•	924	•	153	58	26	16	0	3	7
Revenues ($ in Thousands)														
Net Sales	2	54321703	•	1507458	•	1533837	•	2454872	1052624	1483590	1637486	0	1828575	41596745
Interest	3	500994	•	42	•	1866	•	823	3118	787	4891	0	19839	468996
Rents	4	135105	•	0	•	0	•	2034	15	1344	27	0	0	131685
Royalties	5	224305	•	0	•	239	•	42	0	0	0	0	0	224024
Other Portfolio Income	6	4796284	•	13467	•	69337	•	231962	173758	157433	121907	0	23884	3919765
Other Receipts	7	48665015	•	1493949	•	1462395	•	2220011	875733	1324026	1510661	0	1784852	36852275
Total Receipts	8	54321703	•	1507458	•	1533837	•	2454872	1052624	1483590	1637486	0	1828575	41596745
Average Total Receipts	9	8094	•	388	•	1660	•	16045	18149	57061	102343	•	609525	5942392
Operating Costs/Operating Income (%)														
Cost of Operations	10	17.5	•	6.3	•	36.1	•	40.5	20.1	45.6	31.8	•	0.8	14.0
Salaries and Wages	11	12.3	•	4.3	•	4.0	•	7.0	7.1	8.0	6.1	•	8.0	14.1
Taxes Paid	12	3.1	•	2.1	•	1.4	•	2.0	1.5	2.0	2.1	•	0.3	3.6
Interest Paid	13	4.2	•	0.3	•	6.8	•	2.7	4.0	2.6	4.0	•	3.8	4.4
Depreciation	14	42.9	•	4.2	•	23.8	•	27.0	66.2	41.3	46.4	•	77.9	44.5
Amortization and Depletion	15	0.4	•	•	•	0.0	•	0.1	0.0	0.0	0.1	•	0.2	0.5
Pensions and Other Deferred Comp.	16	0.7	•	0.1	•	0.0	•	0.1	0.2	0.1	0.1	•	0.1	0.8
Employee Benefits	17	1.7	•	0.5	•	0.3	•	0.5	0.5	0.7	0.8	•	0.5	2.1
Advertising	18	1.3	•	0.3	•	0.4	•	0.8	0.2	0.7	0.4	•	0.1	1.5
Other Expenses	19	29.5	•	79.5	•	27.1	•	16.3	15.1	9.8	17.4	•	3.7	31.7
Officers' Compensation	20	1.0	•	3.6	•	2.6	•	1.3	1.5	0.9	1.4	•	0.3	0.8
Operating Margin	21	•	•	•	•	•	•	1.7	•	•	•	•	4.3	•
Operating Margin Before Officers' Comp.	22	•	•	2.5	•	0.0	•	3.0	•	•	•	•	4.6	•

Selected Average Balance Sheet ($ in Thousands)

Net Receivables 23	1338	•	5	•	246	•	2164	2720	4593	11068	•	108694	1069806
Inventories 24	•	•	•	•	•	•	•	•	•	•	•	•	•
Net Property, Plant and Equipment 25	7071	•	27	•	1343	•	8856	20823	35255	111950	•	726015	5437268
Total Assets 26	12187	•	65	•	2414	•	15396	35222	65532	171647	•	1453116	9203284
Notes and Loans Payable 27	7176	•	92	•	1796	•	10256	21533	41623	94314	•	1340702	5129587
All Other Liabilities 28	2902	•	5	•	235	•	1893	3533	7044	27898	•	287882	2452580
Net Worth 29	2109	•	-32	•	384	•	3247	10156	16865	49436	•	-175467	1621117

Selected Financial Ratios (Times to 1)

Current Ratio 30	0.6	•	1.1	•	2.0	•	1.0	1.1	1.1	0.5	•	0.2	0.6
Quick Ratio 31	0.5	•	0.6	•	1.1	•	0.7	0.7	0.6	0.4	•	0.1	0.5
Net Sales to Working Capital 32	•	•	138.2	•	4.0	•	84.3	20.2	55.8	•	•	•	•
Coverage Ratio 33	•	•	•	•	0.6	•	1.6	•	•	•	•	2.1	•
Total Asset Turnover 34	0.7	•	6.0	•	0.7	•	1.0	0.5	0.9	0.6	•	0.4	0.6
Inventory Turnover 35	•	•	•	•	•	•	•	•	•	•	•	•	•
Receivables Turnover 36	•	•	•	•	•	•	•	•	•	•	•	•	•
Total Liabilities to Net Worth 37	4.8	•	•	•	5.3	•	3.7	2.5	2.9	2.5	•	•	4.7
Current Assets to Working Capital 38	•	•	8.8	•	2.0	•	24.9	11.5	18.9	•	•	•	•
Current Liabilities to Working Capital 39	•	•	7.8	•	1.0	•	23.9	10.5	17.9	•	•	•	•
Working Capital to Net Sales 40	•	•	0.0	•	0.2	•	0.0	0.0	0.0	•	•	•	•
Inventory to Working Capital 41	•	•	1.5	•	0.2	•	3.6	0.5	3.8	•	•	•	•
Total Receipts to Cash Flow 42	13.7	•	1.5	•	13.6	•	8.8	•	•	•	•	13.1	16.6
Cost of Goods to Cash Flow 43	2.4	•	0.1	•	4.9	•	3.5	•	•	•	•	0.1	2.3
Cash Flow to Total Debt 44	0.1	•	2.6	•	0.1	•	0.2	•	•	•	•	0.0	0.0

Selected Financial Factors (in Percentages)

Debt Ratio 45	82.7	•	148.9	•	84.1	•	78.9	71.2	74.3	71.2	•	112.1	82.4
Return on Total Assets 46	•	•	•	•	2.9	•	4.5	•	•	•	•	3.4	•
Return on Equity Before Income Taxes 47	•	•	13.7	•	•	•	8.2	•	•	•	•	•	•
Return on Equity After Income Taxes 48	•	•	13.7	•	•	•	7.8	•	•	•	•	•	•
Profit Margin (Before Income Tax) 49	•	•	•	•	•	•	1.7	•	•	•	•	4.3	•
Profit Margin (After Income Tax) 50	•	•	•	•	•	•	1.6	•	•	•	•	4.2	•

Table II

Corporations with Net Income

AUTOMOTIVE EQUIPMENT RENTAL AND LEASING

MONEY AMOUNTS AND SIZE OF ASSETS IN THOUSANDS OF DOLLARS

Item Description for Accounting Period 7/11 Through 6/12		Total	Zero Assets	Under 500	500 to 1,000	1,000 to 5,000	5,000 to 10,000	10,000 to 25,000	25,000 to 50,000	50,000 to 100,000	100,000 to 250,000	250,000 to 500,000	500,000 to 2,500,000	2,500,000 and over
Number of Enterprises	1	2917	•	992	791	522	57	76	32	•	•	0	•	0
Revenues ($ in Thousands)														
Net Sales	2	9582320	•	269492	234523	971398	605980	1364022	371893	•	•	0	•	0
Interest	3	309417	•	0	0	1780	82	58	93	•	•	0	•	0
Rents	4	100318	•	0	0	0	0	2034	0	•	•	0	•	0
Royalties	5	239	•	0	0	239	0	0	0	•	•	0	•	0
Other Portfolio Income	6	361247	•	10076	3051	26334	18759	95698	26076	•	•	0	•	0
Other Receipts	7	8811099	•	259416	231472	943045	587139	1266232	345724	•	•	0	•	0
Total Receipts	8	9582320	•	269492	234523	971398	605980	1364022	371893	•	•	0	•	0
Average Total Receipts	9	3285	•	272	296	1861	10631	17948	11622	•	•	•	•	•
Operating Costs/Operating Income (%)														
Cost of Operations	10	28.6	•	•	•	34.7	77.8	36.0	31.2	•	•	•	•	•
Salaries and Wages	11	7.7	•	12.6	9.4	2.3	4.2	7.0	5.5	•	•	•	•	•
Taxes Paid	12	2.1	•	2.6	2.7	1.0	1.0	2.2	1.1	•	•	•	•	•
Interest Paid	13	5.4	•	0.4	7.7	5.3	1.5	2.5	4.5	•	•	•	•	•
Depreciation	14	25.4	•	10.4	17.5	14.4	3.0	22.4	22.7	•	•	•	•	•
Amortization and Depletion	15	0.1	•	•	0.1	0.0	0.1	0.0	0.0	•	•	•	•	•
Pensions and Other Deferred Comp.	16	0.1	•	0.4	•	•	0.0	0.2	0.5	•	•	•	•	•
Employee Benefits	17	1.0	•	2.8	•	0.2	0.7	0.5	1.0	•	•	•	•	•
Advertising	18	0.3	•	0.4	1.4	0.4	0.6	0.3	0.2	•	•	•	•	•
Other Expenses	19	21.6	•	40.2	33.9	31.9	6.7	16.0	11.3	•	•	•	•	•
Officers' Compensation	20	1.5	•	19.9	6.8	2.2	0.4	1.5	1.4	•	•	•	•	•
Operating Margin	21	6.3	•	10.1	20.5	7.8	4.0	11.3	20.6	•	•	•	•	•
Operating Margin Before Officers' Comp.	22	7.8	•	30.0	27.3	10.0	4.5	12.8	22.0	•	•	•	•	•

Selected Average Balance Sheet ($ in Thousands)													
Net Receivables 23	1474	•	0	86	334	710	2482	3556	•	•	•	•	•
Inventories 24	•	•	•	•	•	•	•	•	•	•	•	•	•
Net Property, Plant and Equipment 25	2418	•	31	261	917	1034	8335	18600	•	•	•	•	•
Total Assets 26	5590	•	76	791	2092	7334	15320	32978	•	•	•	•	•
Notes and Loans Payable 27	3752	•	35	448	1243	3927	10339	19181	•	•	•	•	•
All Other Liabilities 28	1186	•	3	18	197	647	1943	3298	•	•	•	•	•
Net Worth 29	651	•	37	324	651	2759	3039	10499	•	•	•	•	•
Selected Financial Ratios (Times to 1)													
Current Ratio 30	1.2	•	0.5	10.6	5.3	2.0	1.5	1.7	•	•	•	•	•
Quick Ratio 31	0.9	•	0.4	10.4	3.2	0.8	1.3	1.0	•	•	•	•	•
Net Sales to Working Capital 32	9.8	•	•	1.7	2.2	6.7	10.4	2.1	•	•	•	•	•
Coverage Ratio 33	2.2	•	24.0	3.6	2.5	3.7	5.5	5.6	•	•	•	•	•
Total Asset Turnover 34	0.6	•	3.6	0.4	0.9	1.4	1.2	0.4	•	•	•	•	•
Inventory Turnover 35	•	•	•	•	•	•	•	•	•	•	•	•	•
Receivables Turnover 36	•	•	•	•	•	•	•	•	•	•	•	•	•
Total Liabilities to Net Worth 37	7.6	•	1.0	1.4	2.2	1.7	4.0	2.1	•	•	•	•	•
Current Assets to Working Capital 38	6.8	•	•	1.1	1.2	2.0	2.8	2.4	•	•	•	•	•
Current Liabilities to Working Capital 39	5.8	•	•	0.1	0.2	1.0	1.8	1.4	•	•	•	•	•
Working Capital to Net Sales 40	0.1	•	•	0.6	0.4	0.2	0.1	0.5	•	•	•	•	•
Inventory to Working Capital 41	0.4	•	•	•	0.2	1.2	0.1	0.1	•	•	•	•	•
Total Receipts to Cash Flow 42	6.3	•	2.5	3.3	6.4	11.8	5.1	3.6	•	•	•	•	•
Cost of Goods to Cash Flow 43	1.8	•	•	•	2.2	9.1	1.8	1.1	•	•	•	•	•
Cash Flow to Total Debt 44	0.1	•	2.9	0.2	0.2	0.2	0.3	0.1	•	•	•	•	•
Selected Financial Factors (in Percentages)													
Debt Ratio 45	88.3	•	50.6	59.1	68.9	62.4	80.2	68.2	•	•	•	•	•
Return on Total Assets 46	6.9	•	37.9	10.6	11.6	8.0	16.2	8.8	•	•	•	•	•
Return on Equity Before Income Taxes 47	31.7	•	73.6	18.7	22.2	15.5	66.6	22.7	•	•	•	•	•
Return on Equity After Income Taxes 48	30.7	•	73.6	18.7	21.2	14.9	65.7	22.6	•	•	•	•	•
Profit Margin (Before Income Tax) 49	6.3	•	10.1	20.5	7.8	4.0	11.3	20.5	•	•	•	•	•
Profit Margin (After Income Tax) 50	6.1	•	10.1	20.5	7.4	3.9	11.1	20.5	•	•	•	•	•

Table I

Corporations with and without Net Income

OTHER CONSUMER GOODS AND GENERAL RENTAL CENTERS

MONEY AMOUNTS AND SIZE OF ASSETS IN THOUSANDS OF DOLLARS

Item Description for Accounting Period 7/11 Through 6/12		Total	Zero Assets	Under 500	500 to 1,000	1,000 to 5,000	5,000 to 10,000	10,000 to 25,000	25,000 to 50,000	50,000 to 100,000	100,000 to 250,000	250,000 to 500,000	500,000 to 2,500,000	2,500,000 and over
Number of Enterprises	1	10283	658	8138	574	630	230	23	14	5	7	0	3	0
Revenues ($ in Thousands)														
Net Sales	2	18123914	109172	2942212	758806	1417384	1728146	428880	1218794	310628	1221066	0	7988825	0
Interest	3	24528	63	2	521	126	0	52	19	117	8782	0	14846	0
Rents	4	9624	0	0	0	3058	0	0	0	1030	5537	0	0	0
Royalties	5	77568	0	0	0	0	0	0	9756	0	0	0	67812	0
Other Portfolio Income	6	272642	15227	11831	8866	105582	13855	10778	6539	2660	13604	0	83698	0
Other Receipts	7	17739552	93882	2930379	749419	1308618	1714291	418050	1202480	306821	1193143	0	7822469	0
Total Receipts	8	18123914	109172	2942212	758806	1417384	1728146	428880	1218794	310628	1221066	0	7988825	0
Average Total Receipts	9	1763	166	362	1322	2250	7514	18647	87057	62126	174438	•	2662942	•
Operating Costs/Operating Income (%)														
Cost of Operations	10	27.4	7.5	23.3	39.5	20.1	32.2	32.8	42.3	4.9	25.6	•	27.0	•
Salaries and Wages	11	17.7	22.9	19.0	17.0	21.0	11.9	20.6	16.3	25.3	19.1	•	17.5	•
Taxes Paid	12	3.4	2.8	4.4	3.1	4.7	3.7	2.8	2.8	2.8	3.8	•	2.8	•
Interest Paid	13	1.3	5.5	1.0	0.7	2.7	0.3	1.3	1.6	1.8	5.0	•	0.8	•
Depreciation	14	19.2	14.5	6.1	12.0	13.9	25.9	9.5	15.3	17.5	15.9	•	25.8	•
Amortization and Depletion	15	1.2	0.2	0.4	•	0.3	0.1	0.0	0.4	1.2	9.6	•	0.9	•
Pensions and Other Deferred Comp.	16	0.2	•	0.0	0.2	0.1	0.3	0.1	0.0	0.1	0.0	•	0.4	•
Employee Benefits	17	1.3	0.8	1.0	1.6	1.2	1.3	1.1	2.6	2.7	1.1	•	1.2	•
Advertising	18	3.8	1.8	2.0	2.0	2.1	1.8	1.7	1.4	11.4	1.8	•	5.8	•
Other Expenses	19	25.7	46.5	33.9	18.5	24.1	14.1	20.1	99.4	30.3	21.7	•	15.3	•
Officers' Compensation	20	2.2	1.9	3.6	4.6	3.2	3.3	2.1	0.5	1.9	1.0	•	1.4	•
Operating Margin	21	•	•	5.3	0.7	6.5	5.1	7.8	•	0.1	•	•	1.1	•
Operating Margin Before Officers' Comp.	22	•	•	8.9	5.3	9.7	8.5	9.9	•	2.0	•	•	2.6	•

Selected Average Balance Sheet ($ in Thousands)

Net Receivables 23	80	0	8	34	225	309	4815	2444	5885	20886	•	69604	•
Inventories 24	•	•	•	•	•	•	•	•	•	•	•	•	•
Net Property, Plant and Equipment 25	524	0	53	362	903	2398	6120	21040	17843	82557	•	840162	•
Total Assets 26	1548	0	134	774	1566	6902	14340	37935	68332	190446	•	3091833	•
Notes and Loans Payable 27	583	0	104	273	1229	720	6136	82715	12641	120951	•	613559	•
All Other Liabilities 28	819	0	15	96	189	6553	2316	134024	16177	39402	•	1443531	•
Net Worth 29	147	0	15	405	148	-371	5887	-178803	39514	30093	•	1034743	•

Selected Financial Ratios (Times to 1)

Current Ratio 30	0.6	•	2.6	3.7	2.1	2.5	2.6	0.1	0.9	0.8	•	0.4	•
Quick Ratio 31	0.4	•	1.2	1.6	1.4	1.1	2.1	0.0	0.8	0.7	•	0.3	•
Net Sales to Working Capital 32	•	•	11.1	4.6	7.9	4.3	3.9	•	•	•	•	•	•
Coverage Ratio 33	•	0.2	6.1	2.0	3.4	20.8	7.0	•	1.0	0.1	•	2.4	•
Total Asset Turnover 34	1.1	•	2.7	1.7	1.4	1.1	1.3	2.3	0.9	0.9	•	0.9	•
Inventory Turnover 35	•	•	•	•	•	•	•	•	•	•	•	•	•
Receivables Turnover 36	•	•	•	•	•	•	•	•	•	•	•	•	•
Total Liabilities to Net Worth 37	9.5	•	7.8	0.9	9.6	•	1.4	•	0.7	5.3	•	2.0	•
Current Assets to Working Capital 38	•	•	1.6	1.4	1.9	1.7	1.6	•	•	•	•	•	•
Current Liabilities to Working Capital 39	•	•	0.6	0.4	0.9	0.7	0.6	•	•	•	•	•	•
Working Capital to Net Sales 40	•	•	0.1	0.2	0.1	0.2	0.3	•	•	•	•	•	•
Inventory to Working Capital 41	•	•	0.7	0.5	0.5	0.6	0.0	•	•	•	•	•	•
Total Receipts to Cash Flow 42	9.9	4.8	3.6	8.1	4.8	6.3	4.8	•	4.1	9.8	•	8.8	•
Cost of Goods to Cash Flow 43	2.7	0.4	0.8	3.2	1.0	2.0	1.6	•	0.2	2.5	•	2.4	•
Cash Flow to Total Debt 44	0.1	•	0.8	0.4	0.3	0.2	0.5	•	0.5	0.1	•	0.1	•

Selected Financial Factors (in Percentages)

Debt Ratio 45	90.5	•	88.6	47.7	90.5	105.4	58.9	571.3	42.2	84.2	•	66.5	•
Return on Total Assets 46	•	•	17.2	2.5	13.3	5.9	11.7	•	1.7	0.3	•	1.6	•
Return on Equity Before Income Taxes 47	•	•	126.0	2.4	98.7	•	24.5	40.2	0.1	•	•	2.9	•
Return on Equity After Income Taxes 48	•	•	125.6	2.1	95.7	•	24.5	40.3	0.0	•	•	0.0	•
Profit Margin (Before Income Tax) 49	•	•	5.3	0.7	6.5	5.1	7.7	•	0.1	•	•	1.1	•
Profit Margin (After Income Tax) 50	•	•	5.3	0.6	6.3	5.1	7.7	•	0.0	•	•	0.0	•

Table II

Corporations with Net Income

OTHER CONSUMER GOODS AND GENERAL RENTAL CENTERS

MONEY AMOUNTS AND SIZE OF ASSETS IN THOUSANDS OF DOLLARS

Item Description for Accounting Period 7/11 Through 6/12		Total	Zero Assets	Under 500	500 to 1,000	1,000 to 5,000	5,000 to 10,000	10,000 to 25,000	25,000 to 50,000	50,000 to 100,000	100,000 to 250,000	250,000 to 500,000	500,000 to 2,500,000	2,500,000 and over
Number of Enterprises	1	6009	•	4760	327	423	127	14	3	•	•	•	0	•
Revenues ($ in Thousands)														
Net Sales	2	9602151	•	2063485	709847	1088297	1087451	370465	234315	•	•	•	0	•
Interest	3	3067	•	2	200	126	0	0	19	•	•	•	0	•
Rents	4	9500	•	0	0	3058	0	0	0	•	•	•	0	•
Royalties	5	0	•	0	0	0	0	0	0	•	•	•	0	•
Other Portfolio Income	6	164029	•	6288	8759	105375	13855	10778	415	•	•	•	0	•
Other Receipts	7	9425555	•	2057195	700888	979738	1073596	359687	233881	•	•	•	0	•
Total Receipts	8	9602151	•	2063485	709847	1088297	1087451	370465	234315	•	•	•	0	•
Average Total Receipts	9	1598	•	434	2171	2573	8563	26462	78105	•	•	•	•	•
Operating Costs/Operating Income (%)														
Cost of Operations	10	37.5	•	24.3	41.5	25.5	44.8	32.2	78.7	•	•	•	•	•
Salaries and Wages	11	14.3	•	17.5	16.8	20.3	8.4	23.5	6.7	•	•	•	•	•
Taxes Paid	12	2.7	•	3.5	3.0	4.3	2.9	2.8	1.3	•	•	•	•	•
Interest Paid	13	1.0	•	1.0	0.6	1.4	0.3	1.3	1.9	•	•	•	•	•
Depreciation	14	7.9	•	4.3	11.7	11.3	16.8	9.1	0.5	•	•	•	•	•
Amortization and Depletion	15	1.3	•	0.5	•	0.3	•	0.0	0.2	•	•	•	•	•
Pensions and Other Deferred Comp.	16	0.1	•	0.0	0.2	0.1	0.5	0.1	•	•	•	•	•	•
Employee Benefits	17	0.7	•	0.8	1.5	0.7	0.6	1.3	0.7	•	•	•	•	•
Advertising	18	5.2	•	2.3	2.1	2.2	1.4	1.1	0.7	•	•	•	•	•
Other Expenses	19	17.8	•	31.8	16.2	19.6	9.7	14.4	7.1	•	•	•	•	•
Officers' Compensation	20	2.7	•	3.1	4.7	3.1	3.4	1.9	1.1	•	•	•	•	•
Operating Margin	21	8.8	•	10.9	1.8	11.2	11.1	12.5	1.0	•	•	•	•	•
Operating Margin Before Officers' Comp.	22	11.5	•	14.0	6.5	14.3	14.5	14.3	2.2	•	•	•	•	•

Selected Average Balance Sheet ($ in Thousands)

Net Receivables	23	75	•	11	40	321	560	7870	10195	•	•	•	•	•
Inventories	24	•	•	•	•	•	•	•	•	•	•	•	•	•
Net Property, Plant and Equipment	25	235	•	22	221	630	2287	4172	4440	•	•	•	•	•
Total Assets	26	1050	•	117	695	1470	6758	14589	31513	•	•	•	•	•
Notes and Loans Payable	27	277	•	81	319	637	852	8444	21466	•	•	•	•	•
All Other Liabilities	28	434	•	15	76	210	1304	2334	8282	•	•	•	•	•
Net Worth	29	339	•	21	300	623	4602	3811	1766	•	•	•	•	•

Selected Financial Ratios (Times to 1)

Current Ratio	30	1.1	•	2.6	5.8	3.5	2.8	2.3	2.4	•	•	•	•	•
Quick Ratio	31	0.7	•	1.4	3.0	2.4	1.1	2.1	1.2	•	•	•	•	•
Net Sales to Working Capital	32	38.3	•	13.3	5.9	4.7	3.0	4.8	6.1	•	•	•	•	•
Coverage Ratio	33	9.8	•	11.7	4.2	8.8	35.2	10.6	1.5	•	•	•	•	•
Total Asset Turnover	34	1.5	•	3.7	3.1	1.8	1.3	1.8	2.5	•	•	•	•	•
Inventory Turnover	35	•	•	•	•	•	•	•	•	•	•	•	•	•
Receivables Turnover	36	•	•	•	•	•	•	•	•	•	•	•	•	•
Total Liabilities to Net Worth	37	2.1	•	4.5	1.3	1.4	0.5	2.8	16.8	•	•	•	•	•
Current Assets to Working Capital	38	8.7	•	1.6	1.2	1.4	1.6	1.8	1.7	•	•	•	•	•
Current Liabilities to Working Capital	39	7.7	•	0.6	0.2	0.4	0.6	0.8	0.7	•	•	•	•	•
Working Capital to Net Sales	40	0.0	•	0.1	0.2	0.2	0.3	0.2	0.2	•	•	•	•	•
Inventory to Working Capital	41	2.0	•	0.6	0.5	0.4	0.6	0.0	0.7	•	•	•	•	•
Total Receipts to Cash Flow	42	4.7	•	3.1	7.9	4.6	5.1	5.1	17.7	•	•	•	•	•
Cost of Goods to Cash Flow	43	1.8	•	0.8	3.3	1.2	2.3	1.6	13.9	•	•	•	•	•
Cash Flow to Total Debt	44	0.5	•	1.4	0.7	0.7	0.8	0.5	0.1	•	•	•	•	•

Selected Financial Factors (in Percentages)

Debt Ratio	45	67.7	•	81.9	56.8	57.6	31.9	73.9	94.4	•	•	•	•	•
Return on Total Assets	46	14.9	•	44.1	7.6	22.1	14.5	24.8	7.4	•	•	•	•	•
Return on Equity Before Income Taxes	47	41.5	•	223.2	13.3	46.2	20.7	86.0	46.4	•	•	•	•	•
Return on Equity After Income Taxes	48	36.1	•	222.6	12.6	45.2	20.7	86.0	39.5	•	•	•	•	•
Profit Margin (Before Income Tax)	49	8.8	•	10.9	1.8	11.2	11.1	12.4	1.0	•	•	•	•	•
Profit Margin (After Income Tax)	50	7.7	•	10.9	1.7	10.9	11.1	12.4	0.9	•	•	•	•	•

Table I

Corporations with and without Net Income

COMMERCIAL AND INDUSTRIAL MACHINERY AND EQUIPMENT RENTAL

MONEY AMOUNTS AND SIZE OF ASSETS IN THOUSANDS OF DOLLARS

Item Description for Accounting Period 7/11 Through 6/12		Total	Zero Assets	Under 500	500 to 1,000	1,000 to 5,000	5,000 to 10,000	10,000 to 25,000	25,000 to 50,000	50,000 to 100,000	100,000 to 250,000	250,000 to 500,000	500,000 to 2,500,000	2,500,000 and over
Number of Enterprises	1	23497	2803	13793	3078	2869	318	349	117	68	45	22	26	9
Revenues ($ in Thousands)														
Net Sales	2	46368175	1289788	2855602	1811025	5036517	2304687	3411812	2058434	2926361	2986106	3053830	8522210	10111806
Interest	3	919439	28668	2132	4284	2286	9569	22864	24876	37844	55113	146217	210187	375398
Rents	4	130226	0	0	1347	32157	985	972	517	180	20095	0	73973	0
Royalties	5	3850	0	0	0	0	0	0	0	0	936	0	2914	0
Other Portfolio Income	6	2142941	296899	193860	29028	221627	89597	123076	72082	110454	93759	134462	312821	465274
Other Receipts	7	43171719	964221	2659610	1776366	4780447	2204536	3264900	1960959	2777883	2816203	2773151	7922315	9271134
Total Receipts	8	46368175	1289788	2855602	1811025	5036517	2304687	3411812	2058434	2926361	2986106	3053830	8522210	10111806
Average Total Receipts	9	1973	460	207	588	1755	7247	9776	17593	43035	66358	138810	327777	1123534
Operating Costs/Operating Income (%)														
Cost of Operations	10	27.0	7.1	20.0	27.9	33.6	44.2	35.6	35.8	31.0	31.4	31.3	34.0	9.6
Salaries and Wages	11	11.6	13.7	13.6	13.2	9.6	11.5	12.6	11.2	12.1	10.1	11.5	9.9	13.0
Taxes Paid	12	2.2	2.7	3.3	2.7	3.4	2.3	2.4	2.0	2.2	1.8	2.5	1.5	1.8
Interest Paid	13	7.7	19.8	3.3	3.0	1.9	2.3	2.9	3.8	3.8	8.8	9.8	9.4	13.4
Depreciation	14	27.9	18.7	13.6	16.6	14.6	12.1	19.8	24.7	22.5	35.6	28.2	30.8	45.7
Amortization and Depletion	15	0.9	2.5	0.1	1.3	0.1	0.1	0.2	0.5	0.7	1.9	0.9	1.2	1.4
Pensions and Other Deferred Comp.	16	0.3	0.4	0.4	0.4	0.2	0.2	0.2	0.4	0.3	0.3	0.3	0.3	0.2
Employee Benefits	17	1.5	2.1	0.6	1.9	0.9	1.2	1.2	1.7	1.5	1.3	1.2	1.9	2.1
Advertising	18	0.3	0.2	0.4	0.6	0.3	0.5	0.4	0.3	0.5	0.2	0.3	0.3	0.1
Other Expenses	19	21.6	30.2	29.5	35.8	21.7	15.1	24.2	18.5	20.5	20.5	20.6	14.9	23.6
Officers' Compensation	20	2.8	2.6	12.2	4.1	5.8	3.8	2.2	2.4	3.6	1.1	1.6	0.9	0.6
Operating Margin	21	•	0.1	3.0	•	7.9	6.8	•	•	1.5	•	•	•	•
Operating Margin Before Officers' Comp.	22	•	2.7	15.2	•	13.7	10.6	0.5	1.0	5.1	•	•	•	•

Selected Average Balance Sheet ($ in Thousands)													
Net Receivables **23**	820	0	6	52	326	1280	1866	4437	11014	28965	76376	93046	1152534
Inventories **24**	•	•	•	•	•	•	•	•	•	•	•	•	•
Net Property, Plant and Equipment **25**	2244	0	62	285	944	2475	6326	14812	27631	83803	153393	455318	2521244
Total Assets **26**	4751	0	131	717	2027	7485	14519	35583	70974	167556	354551	1096275	4614815
Notes and Loans Payable **27**	2817	0	139	495	1324	3029	5898	15086	29763	75953	233987	627078	3030193
All Other Liabilities **28**	968	0	20	82	386	2493	2438	4745	18195	28287	64396	242533	963637
Net Worth **29**	966	0	-28	140	317	1963	6183	15753	23016	63316	56168	226664	620985
Selected Financial Ratios (Times to 1)													
Current Ratio **30**	1.6	•	0.8	2.0	1.4	3.1	1.4	2.1	1.4	1.5	1.7	1.4	1.9
Quick Ratio **31**	1.2	•	0.6	1.2	1.0	1.6	0.8	1.3	0.7	1.1	1.5	0.8	1.8
Net Sales to Working Capital **32**	3.6	•	•	4.4	7.4	2.7	6.9	2.9	5.2	4.6	3.2	4.7	1.8
Coverage Ratio **33**	0.5	1.0	1.9	•	5.2	4.0	0.4	0.6	1.5	•	0.2	0.5	0.1
Total Asset Turnover **34**	0.4	•	1.6	0.8	0.9	1.0	0.7	0.5	0.6	0.4	0.4	0.3	0.2
Inventory Turnover **35**	•	•	•	•	•	•	•	•	•	•	•	•	•
Receivables Turnover **36**	•	•	•	•	•	•	•	•	•	•	•	•	•
Total Liabilities to Net Worth **37**	3.9	•	•	4.1	5.4	2.8	1.3	1.3	2.1	1.6	5.3	3.8	6.4
Current Assets to Working Capital **38**	2.6	•	•	2.0	3.2	1.5	3.6	1.9	3.4	3.0	2.5	3.6	2.1
Current Liabilities to Working Capital **39**	1.6	•	•	1.0	2.2	0.5	2.6	0.9	2.4	2.0	1.5	2.6	1.1
Working Capital to Net Sales **40**	0.3	•	•	0.2	0.1	0.4	0.1	0.3	0.2	0.2	0.3	0.2	0.6
Inventory to Working Capital **41**	0.2	•	•	0.2	0.2	0.2	0.8	0.3	0.5	0.3	0.1	0.7	0.0
Total Receipts to Cash Flow **42**	13.1	4.7	4.9	7.3	4.9	6.9	10.4	11.0	7.6	•	18.3	37.1	•
Cost of Goods to Cash Flow **43**	3.5	0.3	1.0	2.0	1.6	3.1	3.7	3.9	2.3	•	5.7	12.6	•
Cash Flow to Total Debt **44**	0.0	•	0.3	0.1	0.2	0.2	0.1	0.1	0.1	•	0.0	0.0	•
Selected Financial Factors (in Percentages)													
Debt Ratio **45**	79.7	•	121.6	80.5	84.4	73.8	57.4	55.7	67.6	62.2	84.2	79.3	86.5
Return on Total Assets **46**	1.6	•	9.9	•	8.5	8.8	0.8	1.2	3.4	•	0.7	1.3	0.4
Return on Equity Before Income Taxes **47**	•	•	•	•	43.8	25.1	•	•	3.5	•	•	•	•
Return on Equity After Income Taxes **48**	•	•	•	•	41.5	23.8	•	•	2.4	•	•	•	•
Profit Margin (Before Income Tax) **49**	•	0.1	3.0	•	7.9	6.8	•	•	1.9	•	•	•	•
Profit Margin (After Income Tax) **50**	•	•	2.7	•	7.5	6.4	•	•	1.3	•	•	•	•

Table II

Corporations with Net Income

COMMERCIAL AND INDUSTRIAL MACHINERY AND EQUIPMENT RENTAL

MONEY AMOUNTS AND SIZE OF ASSETS IN THOUSANDS OF DOLLARS

Item Description for Accounting Period 7/11 Through 6/12		Total	Zero Assets	Under 500	500 to 1,000	1,000 to 5,000	5,000 to 10,000	10,000 to 25,000	25,000 to 50,000	50,000 to 100,000	100,000 to 250,000	250,000 to 500,000	500,000 to 2,500,000	2,500,000 and over
Number of Enterprises	1	10459	1256	5707	1172	1843	185	183	50	35	14	5	10	0
Revenues ($ in Thousands)														
Net Sales	2	18663527	393407	1271884	678345	4275414	1809332	2182089	1074505	1763899	883832	619405	3711415	0
Interest	3	243819	205	1350	1669	749	2319	17871	4498	15422	8331	92350	99055	0
Rents	4	50706	0	0	1	32156	255	972	49	0	9170	0	8103	0
Royalties	5	936	0	0	0	0	0	0	0	0	936	0	0	0
Other Portfolio Income	6	1168717	211775	123608	12034	206940	79373	80133	28256	81108	56160	74768	214561	0
Other Receipts	7	17199349	181427	1146926	664641	4035569	1727385	2083113	1041702	1667369	809235	452287	3389696	0
Total Receipts	8	18663527	393407	1271884	678345	4275414	1809332	2182089	1074505	1763899	883832	619405	3711415	0
Average Total Receipts	9	1784	313	223	579	2320	9780	11924	21490	50397	63131	123881	371142	•
Operating Costs/Operating Income (%)														
Cost of Operations	10	28.8	8.9	10.4	28.8	38.0	41.4	33.1	37.3	28.9	29.8	11.3	18.2	•
Salaries and Wages	11	9.8	1.1	10.9	10.5	8.3	11.9	14.4	13.7	11.1	10.0	7.4	6.8	•
Taxes Paid	12	2.3	1.0	2.8	2.5	3.5	2.3	2.4	2.3	2.1	1.6	1.7	1.4	•
Interest Paid	13	4.0	5.8	2.0	2.9	1.4	1.5	2.2	2.0	3.3	4.2	6.7	10.2	•
Depreciation	14	16.2	14.8	7.9	11.2	9.3	10.5	16.6	15.3	17.7	20.4	29.6	26.7	•
Amortization and Depletion	15	0.3	0.4	0.1	3.4	0.0	0.1	0.3	0.2	0.3	0.3	0.6	0.5	•
Pensions and Other Deferred Comp.	16	0.3	0.0	0.9	0.0	0.1	0.2	0.3	0.6	0.4	0.4	•	0.5	•
Employee Benefits	17	1.2	0.1	0.2	1.6	1.0	1.0	1.5	1.6	1.6	2.2	1.0	1.3	•
Advertising	18	0.3	0.1	0.7	0.2	0.4	0.3	0.5	0.4	0.5	0.2	0.2	0.1	•
Other Expenses	19	19.7	12.6	28.2	23.4	18.7	16.1	17.9	14.2	18.5	15.0	22.7	23.4	•
Officers' Compensation	20	3.9	0.2	10.3	3.4	6.3	4.1	2.4	2.6	4.7	1.4	1.8	1.1	•
Operating Margin	21	13.2	55.0	25.8	12.2	13.0	10.6	8.4	9.6	11.0	14.4	17.0	9.9	•
Operating Margin Before Officers' Comp.	22	17.0	55.2	36.1	15.5	19.2	14.7	10.9	12.2	15.7	15.8	18.8	11.0	•

Selected Average Balance Sheet ($ in Thousands)													
Net Receivables **23**	480	0	3	96	436	1719	1949	3425	11384	40412	86179	184496	•
Inventories **24**	•	•	•	•	•	•	•	•	•	•	•	•	•
Net Property, Plant and Equipment **25**	1518	0	51	268	802	2786	6009	12920	25935	57856	124823	918953	•
Total Assets **26**	3182	0	141	730	1937	7395	14041	34763	70838	149000	376799	1592824	•
Notes and Loans Payable **27**	1498	0	161	364	1106	2871	5051	10785	24277	42393	163540	802458	•
All Other Liabilities **28**	662	0	12	122	207	1249	2512	5767	20897	32338	95208	369301	•
Net Worth **29**	1022	0	-33	244	624	3276	6478	18211	25664	74269	118051	421065	•
Selected Financial Ratios (Times to 1)													
Current Ratio **30**	1.6	•	1.0	2.1	1.7	2.3	1.6	1.6	1.3	2.2	1.5	1.7	•
Quick Ratio **31**	1.2	•	0.7	1.2	1.4	1.6	1.0	0.7	0.7	1.7	1.4	1.2	•
Net Sales to Working Capital **32**	4.4	•	•	3.5	6.8	4.5	6.5	4.7	8.1	2.1	2.6	2.3	•
Coverage Ratio **33**	4.3	10.5	14.1	5.2	10.3	7.9	4.8	5.7	4.5	4.4	3.6	2.0	•
Total Asset Turnover **34**	0.6	•	1.6	0.8	1.2	1.3	0.8	0.6	0.7	0.4	0.3	0.2	•
Inventory Turnover **35**	•	•	•	•	•	•	•	•	•	•	•	•	•
Receivables Turnover **36**	•	•	•	•	•	•	•	•	•	•	•	•	•
Total Liabilities to Net Worth **37**	2.1	•	•	2.0	2.1	1.3	1.2	0.9	1.8	1.0	2.2	2.8	•
Current Assets to Working Capital **38**	2.6	•	•	1.9	2.5	1.7	2.7	2.7	5.0	1.9	2.8	2.5	•
Current Liabilities to Working Capital **39**	1.6	•	•	0.9	1.5	0.7	1.7	1.7	4.0	0.9	1.8	1.5	•
Working Capital to Net Sales **40**	0.2	•	•	0.3	0.1	0.2	0.2	0.2	0.1	0.5	0.4	0.4	•
Inventory to Working Capital **41**	0.3	•	•	0.1	0.1	0.3	0.7	0.9	0.7	0.2	0.0	0.4	•
Total Receipts to Cash Flow **42**	4.5	1.6	2.6	3.6	4.4	5.4	5.9	5.1	4.5	4.2	2.7	6.9	•
Cost of Goods to Cash Flow **43**	1.3	0.1	0.3	1.1	1.7	2.2	2.0	1.9	1.3	1.3	0.3	1.3	•
Cash Flow to Total Debt **44**	0.2	•	0.5	0.3	0.4	0.4	0.3	0.3	0.2	0.2	0.2	0.0	•
Selected Financial Factors (in Percentages)													
Debt Ratio **45**	67.9	•	123.3	66.6	67.8	55.7	53.9	47.6	63.8	50.2	68.7	73.6	•
Return on Total Assets **46**	9.6	•	44.0	11.9	17.2	16.0	9.0	7.2	10.5	7.9	7.8	4.7	•
Return on Equity Before Income Taxes **47**	23.1	•	•	28.7	48.3	31.6	15.5	11.3	22.7	12.2	18.0	8.8	•
Return on Equity After Income Taxes **48**	20.8	•	•	26.1	46.5	30.3	14.8	9.9	20.7	9.4	12.2	6.7	•
Profit Margin (Before Income Tax) **49**	13.2	55.0	25.8	12.1	13.0	10.6	8.4	9.6	11.5	14.4	17.1	10.0	•
Profit Margin (After Income Tax) **50**	11.9	51.5	25.3	11.0	12.5	10.1	8.0	8.4	10.5	11.1	11.7	7.6	•

Table I

Corporations with and without Net Income

LESSORS OF NONFINAN. INTANGIBLE ASSETS (EX. COPYRIGHTED WORKS)

MONEY AMOUNTS AND SIZE OF ASSETS IN THOUSANDS OF DOLLARS

Item Description for Accounting Period 7/11 Through 6/12		Total	Zero Assets	Under 500	500 to 1,000	1,000 to 5,000	5,000 to 10,000	10,000 to 25,000	25,000 to 50,000	50,000 to 100,000	100,000 to 250,000	250,000 to 500,000	500,000 to 2,500,000	2,500,000 and over
Number of Enterprises	1	3396	•	2599	•	191	•	28	0	8	11	4	8	3
Revenues ($ in Thousands)														
Net Sales	2	8084258	•	231203	•	434134	•	443603	0	98829	683313	668840	2555611	2055882
Interest	3	118068	•	0	•	125	•	393	0	5381	13540	4967	87859	4148
Rents	4	16433	•	0	•	0	•	0	0	119	4916	0	11398	0
Royalties	5	2830318	•	28425	•	6883	•	1480	0	47952	83910	480957	1521785	386513
Other Portfolio Income	6	69555	•	0	•	20882	•	282	0	909	393	0	15755	31335
Other Receipts	7	5049884	•	202778	•	406244	•	441448	0	44468	580554	182916	918814	1633886
Total Receipts	8	8084258	•	231203	•	434134	•	443603	0	98829	683313	668840	2555611	2055882
Average Total Receipts	9	2381	•	89	•	2273	•	15843	•	12354	62119	167210	319451	685294
Operating Costs/Operating Income (%)														
Cost of Operations	10	10.0	•	7.1	•	16.0	•	19.3	•	16.2	13.0	1.1	13.5	7.7
Salaries and Wages	11	18.5	•	3.9	•	45.3	•	18.0	•	12.2	21.7	4.4	14.1	25.7
Taxes Paid	12	2.6	•	1.6	•	2.9	•	3.1	•	3.1	3.4	0.3	2.5	2.2
Interest Paid	13	5.0	•	0.3	•	0.4	•	5.5	•	8.6	2.5	5.4	4.6	9.0
Depreciation	14	3.8	•	2.7	•	0.7	•	2.6	•	1.1	4.2	12.2	4.2	3.1
Amortization and Depletion	15	3.7	•	0.3	•	1.1	•	1.8	•	4.2	2.3	0.9	5.4	5.3
Pensions and Other Deferred Comp.	16	0.4	•	•	•	0.5	•	0.6	•	0.1	0.8	•	0.4	0.3
Employee Benefits	17	1.3	•	•	•	0.6	•	1.1	•	0.9	2.3	0.4	1.0	2.1
Advertising	18	1.8	•	4.1	•	3.8	•	2.6	•	1.6	2.9	0.1	1.5	0.5
Other Expenses	19	31.0	•	40.3	•	21.3	•	22.1	•	44.9	30.6	14.7	25.6	28.9
Officers' Compensation	20	3.7	•	5.9	•	11.2	•	3.7	•	6.8	5.3	0.8	2.0	3.4
Operating Margin	21	18.3	•	33.8	•	•	•	19.7	•	0.2	11.0	59.5	25.2	11.8
Operating Margin Before Officers' Comp.	22	22.0	•	39.7	•	7.4	•	23.4	•	7.0	16.3	60.3	27.2	15.1

Selected Average Balance Sheet ($ in Thousands)													
Net Receivables 23	423	•	2	•	374	•	1796	•	1149	13190	109117	39712	126542
Inventories 24	•	•	•	•	•	•	•	•	•	•	•	•	•
Net Property, Plant and Equipment 25	336	•	11	•	101	•	2004	•	1278	16266	2728	69549	91653
Total Assets 26	8399	•	65	•	1496	•	17527	•	70142	142041	344127	1221177	4587216
Notes and Loans Payable 27	2191	•	26	•	815	•	7098	•	14476	28017	121185	207877	1415525
All Other Liabilities 28	1250	•	2	•	422	•	3318	•	11922	45944	42344	175423	609576
Net Worth 29	4958	•	36	•	260	•	7111	•	43744	68081	180598	837876	2562115

Selected Financial Ratios (Times to 1)													
Current Ratio 30	1.8	•	1.5	•	1.4	•	2.3	•	4.7	1.6	2.3	3.4	1.0
Quick Ratio 31	0.9	•	0.7	•	1.2	•	1.9	•	0.4	1.0	1.9	2.1	0.3
Net Sales to Working Capital 32	2.5	•	7.8	•	10.2	•	4.6	•	0.7	3.2	1.4	1.3	168.5
Coverage Ratio 33	4.7	•	119.9	•	•	•	4.6	•	1.0	5.4	12.2	6.5	2.4
Total Asset Turnover 34	0.3	•	1.4	•	1.5	•	0.9	•	0.2	0.4	0.5	0.3	0.1
Inventory Turnover 35	•	•	•	•	•	•	•	•	•	•	•	•	•
Receivables Turnover 36	•	•	•	•	•	•	•	•	•	•	•	•	•
Total Liabilities to Net Worth 37	0.7	•	0.8	•	4.8	•	1.5	•	0.6	1.1	0.9	0.5	0.8
Current Assets to Working Capital 38	2.3	•	3.0	•	3.7	•	1.8	•	1.3	2.6	1.8	1.4	195.0
Current Liabilities to Working Capital 39	1.3	•	2.0	•	2.7	•	0.8	•	0.3	1.6	0.8	0.4	194.0
Working Capital to Net Sales 40	0.4	•	0.1	•	0.1	•	0.2	•	1.4	0.3	0.7	0.8	0.0
Inventory to Working Capital 41	0.0	•	•	•	•	•	0.1	•	0.0	0.0	0.2	0.0	0.1
Total Receipts to Cash Flow 42	2.2	•	1.4	•	15.9	•	2.6	•	2.4	2.6	1.4	2.1	3.1
Cost of Goods to Cash Flow 43	0.2	•	0.1	•	2.5	•	0.5	•	0.4	0.3	0.0	0.3	0.2
Cash Flow to Total Debt 44	0.3	•	2.3	•	0.1	•	0.6	•	0.2	0.3	0.8	0.4	0.1

Selected Financial Factors (in Percentages)													
Debt Ratio 45	41.0	•	44.1	•	82.6	•	59.4	•	37.6	52.1	47.5	31.4	44.1
Return on Total Assets 46	6.7	•	46.7	•	•	•	22.8	•	1.5	5.9	31.9	7.9	3.2
Return on Equity Before Income Taxes 47	9.0	•	82.9	•	•	•	43.9	•	0.0	10.0	55.8	9.7	3.3
Return on Equity After Income Taxes 48	6.2	•	82.9	•	•	•	42.0	•	•	7.8	36.1	6.3	2.6
Profit Margin (Before Income Tax) 49	18.6	•	33.8	•	•	•	19.7	•	0.2	11.0	60.3	25.6	12.4
Profit Margin (After Income Tax) 50	12.9	•	33.8	•	•	•	18.9	•	•	8.5	39.0	16.6	9.6

Table II

Corporations with Net Income

LESSORS OF NONFINAN. INTANGIBLE ASSETS (EX. COPYRIGHTED WORKS)

MONEY AMOUNTS AND SIZE OF ASSETS IN THOUSANDS OF DOLLARS

Item Description for Accounting Period 7/11 Through 6/12	Total	Zero Assets	Under 500	500 to 1,000	1,000 to 5,000	5,000 to 10,000	10,000 to 25,000	25,000 to 50,000	50,000 to 100,000	100,000 to 250,000	250,000 to 500,000	500,000 to 2,500,000	2,500,000 and over
Number of Enterprises 1	1537	0	1094	330	58	9	21	0	4	8	•	•	•
Revenues ($ in Thousands)													
Net Sales 2	6730795	0	216183	291036	73420	55144	315842	0	70883	637557	•	•	•
Interest 3	87141	0	0	0	125	252	251	0	992	12951	•	•	•
Rents 4	16180	0	0	0	0	0	0	0	45	4737	•	•	•
Royalties 5	2494137	0	28425	0	6883	0	0	0	43928	79555	•	•	•
Other Portfolio Income 6	64486	0	0	0	20882	0	130	0	16	267	•	•	•
Other Receipts 7	4068851	0	187758	291036	45530	54892	315461	0	25902	540047	•	•	•
Total Receipts 8	6730795	0	216183	291036	73420	55144	315842	0	70883	637557	•	•	•
Average Total Receipts 9	4379	•	198	882	1266	6127	15040	•	17721	79695	•	•	•
Operating Costs/Operating Income (%)													
Cost of Operations 10	8.8	•	•	•	14.0	•	2.1	•	18.1	13.9	•	•	•
Salaries and Wages 11	16.9	•	4.2	3.0	20.0	20.1	20.7	•	2.8	20.6	•	•	•
Taxes Paid 12	2.5	•	0.7	9.3	4.5	1.2	2.6	•	2.8	3.2	•	•	•
Interest Paid 13	4.7	•	0.3	0.1	0.8	0.2	2.6	•	6.7	2.7	•	•	•
Depreciation 14	4.2	•	0.6	0.0	1.4	1.9	1.4	•	0.1	4.1	•	•	•
Amortization and Depletion 15	3.9	•	0.4	0.0	1.9	0.1	0.6	•	1.7	1.0	•	•	•
Pensions and Other Deferred Comp. 16	0.4	•	•	0.2	•	2.5	0.8	•	•	0.7	•	•	•
Employee Benefits 17	1.3	•	•	0.2	•	2.8	1.2	•	0.2	1.5	•	•	•
Advertising 18	1.7	•	4.4	11.3	0.2	•	3.3	•	0.2	3.0	•	•	•
Other Expenses 19	25.6	•	40.8	20.7	•	58.8	21.0	•	39.4	30.3	•	•	•
Officers' Compensation 20	3.1	•	•	0.4	52.2	4.6	4.2	•	2.0	4.9	•	•	•
Operating Margin 21	27.0	•	48.7	54.9	25.5	7.7	39.4	•	25.9	14.1	•	•	•
Operating Margin Before Officers' Comp. 22	30.1	•	48.7	55.3	77.7	12.3	43.6	•	27.9	19.0	•	•	•

Selected Average Balance Sheet ($ in Thousands)													
Net Receivables 23	812	•	3	1	86	1129	1264	•	586	16321	•	•	•
Inventories 24	•	•	•	•	•	•	•	•	•	•	•	•	•
Net Property, Plant and Equipment 25	658	•	2	1	35	114	1606	•	1496	18538	•	•	•
Total Assets 26	17036	•	108	662	1525	7168	15612	•	64694	150700	•	•	•
Notes and Loans Payable 27	4227	•	57	0	523	0	3529	•	10051	38523	•	•	•
All Other Liabilities 28	2345	•	3	12	218	1597	2929	•	7490	62607	•	•	•
Net Worth 29	10465	•	49	650	784	5571	9153	•	47153	49570	•	•	•
Selected Financial Ratios (Times to 1)													
Current Ratio 30	1.8	•	1.2	18.2	1.1	1.8	1.6	•	7.2	1.4	•	•	•
Quick Ratio 31	0.9	•	0.4	18.2	0.9	1.7	1.3	•	0.7	0.9	•	•	•
Net Sales to Working Capital 32	2.3	•	21.8	4.2	24.3	4.7	11.6	•	1.4	4.4	•	•	•
Coverage Ratio 33	6.8	•	164.9	963.1	34.7	38.8	16.2	•	4.9	6.3	•	•	•
Total Asset Turnover 34	0.3	•	1.8	1.3	0.8	0.9	1.0	•	0.3	0.5	•	•	•
Inventory Turnover 35	•	•	•	•	•	•	•	•	•	•	•	•	•
Receivables Turnover 36	•	•	•	•	•	•	•	•	•	•	•	•	•
Total Liabilities to Net Worth 37	0.6	•	1.2	0.0	0.9	0.3	0.7	•	0.4	2.0	•	•	•
Current Assets to Working Capital 38	2.3	•	6.6	1.1	15.1	2.2	2.7	•	1.2	3.4	•	•	•
Current Liabilities to Working Capital 39	1.3	•	5.6	0.1	14.1	1.2	1.7	•	0.2	2.4	•	•	•
Working Capital to Net Sales 40	0.4	•	0.0	0.2	0.0	0.2	0.1	•	0.7	0.2	•	•	•
Inventory to Working Capital 41	0.0	•	•	•	•	•	0.0	•	0.0	0.0	•	•	•
Total Receipts to Cash Flow 42	2.1	•	1.1	1.3	•	1.8	1.7	•	1.5	2.4	•	•	•
Cost of Goods to Cash Flow 43	0.2	•	•	•	•	•	0.0	•	0.3	0.3	•	•	•
Cash Flow to Total Debt 44	0.3	•	3.0	54.1	•	2.2	1.4	•	0.7	0.3	•	•	•
Selected Financial Factors (in Percentages)													
Debt Ratio 45	38.6	•	55.1	1.9	48.6	22.3	41.4	•	27.1	67.1	•	•	•
Return on Total Assets 46	8.2	•	89.5	73.2	21.8	6.7	40.5	•	8.9	8.9	•	•	•
Return on Equity Before Income Taxes 47	11.5	•	198.2	74.5	41.2	8.4	64.8	•	9.7	22.7	•	•	•
Return on Equity After Income Taxes 48	8.6	•	198.2	74.5	29.4	5.6	62.8	•	6.4	18.5	•	•	•
Profit Margin (Before Income Tax) 49	27.4	•	48.7	54.9	25.5	7.7	39.4	•	25.9	14.1	•	•	•
Profit Margin (After Income Tax) 50	20.5	•	48.7	54.9	18.2	5.1	38.2	•	17.1	11.5	•	•	•

LEGAL SERVICES

MONEY AMOUNTS AND SIZE OF ASSETS IN THOUSANDS OF DOLLARS

Item Description for Accounting Period 7/11 Through 6/12		Total	Zero Assets	Under 500	500 to 1,000	1,000 to 5,000	5,000 to 10,000	10,000 to 25,000	25,000 to 50,000	50,000 to 100,000	100,000 to 250,000	250,000 to 500,000	500,000 to 2,500,000	2,500,000 and over
Number of Enterprises	1	122667	24895	•	4203	3613	235	119	41	21	•	•	4	0
Revenues ($ in Thousands)														
Net Sales	2	96948130	3417252	•	9755742	16193529	5054373	5389233	5203627	3175196	•	•	3420830	0
Interest	3	39915	3018	•	8223	3538	2998	893	2066	3306	•	•	11626	0
Rents	4	42540	83	•	13617	266	3058	2490	10724	1429	•	•	6792	0
Royalties	5	4054	1958	•	0	0	0	135	26	86	•	•	0	0
Other Portfolio Income	6	36147	1432	•	677	13435	406	1279	1757	1474	•	•	6871	0
Other Receipts	7	3275775	175354	•	436624	366632	218745	46822	95106	38645	•	•	-3002	0
Total Receipts	8	100346561	3599097	•	10214883	16577400	5279580	5440852	5313306	3220136	•	•	3443117	0
Average Total Receipts	9	818	145	•	2430	4588	22466	45721	129593	153340	•	•	860779	•
Operating Costs/Operating Income (%)														
Cost of Operations	10	5.2	1.3	•	2.1	7.3	0.5	2.4	0.6	4.6	•	•	19.3	•
Salaries and Wages	11	29.3	16.3	•	31.9	31.3	42.3	47.9	55.4	52.3	•	•	3.6	•
Taxes Paid	12	3.4	2.9	•	4.0	3.4	3.5	3.1	3.5	3.1	•	•	1.5	•
Interest Paid	13	0.5	0.4	•	0.7	0.5	0.5	0.4	0.3	1.4	•	•	2.5	•
Depreciation	14	1.2	1.8	•	1.0	0.9	1.4	1.2	1.6	1.7	•	•	2.3	•
Amortization and Depletion	15	0.2	•	•	0.0	0.0	0.0	0.0	0.1	0.2	•	•	3.8	•
Pensions and Other Deferred Comp.	16	1.8	1.0	•	2.1	1.5	2.8	2.3	2.9	2.2	•	•	0.4	•
Employee Benefits	17	2.1	1.0	•	1.8	2.4	2.0	2.7	2.7	2.5	•	•	1.9	•
Advertising	18	2.3	2.9	•	3.0	2.9	1.2	1.2	0.6	3.0	•	•	0.4	•
Other Expenses	19	27.0	40.7	•	25.0	22.0	18.6	21.6	22.5	26.6	•	•	54.6	•
Officers' Compensation	20	20.0	18.5	•	22.9	18.1	26.3	10.4	9.2	2.3	•	•	0.4	•
Operating Margin	21	7.0	13.2	•	5.3	9.7	0.7	6.7	0.5	0.0	•	•	9.3	•
Operating Margin Before Officers' Comp.	22	27.0	31.7	•	28.2	27.8	27.0	17.1	9.7	2.3	•	•	9.7	•

Selected Average Balance Sheet ($ in Thousands)													
Net Receivables 23	17	0	•	67	117	273	1330	4600	8650	•	•	114646	•
Inventories 24	1	0	•	0	7	0	264	123	346	•	•	44	•
Net Property, Plant and Equipment 25	33	0	•	143	282	1293	2412	9081	9274	•	•	83462	•
Total Assets 26	229	0	•	696	1810	6939	15980	35932	64312	•	•	1123240	•
Notes and Loans Payable 27	81	0	•	308	456	2027	4430	9278	19992	•	•	541102	•
All Other Liabilities 28	92	0	•	206	847	3556	5627	14996	19572	•	•	283593	•
Net Worth 29	56	0	•	182	508	1357	5923	11658	24748	•	•	298546	•
Selected Financial Ratios (Times to 1)													
Current Ratio 30	1.4	•	•	1.3	1.5	1.3	1.5	1.3	1.8	•	•	0.7	•
Quick Ratio 31	0.9	•	•	0.8	1.0	0.6	0.8	0.8	1.0	•	•	0.6	•
Net Sales to Working Capital 32	22.7	•	•	26.0	11.4	20.8	12.4	26.6	9.6	•	•	•	•
Coverage Ratio 33	20.4	43.3	•	15.8	25.7	11.9	21.4	8.9	2.0	•	•	5.0	•
Total Asset Turnover 34	3.5	•	•	3.3	2.5	3.1	2.8	3.5	2.4	•	•	0.8	•
Inventory Turnover 35	73.2	•	•	•	48.4	•	4.2	6.3	20.1	•	•	3728.4	•
Receivables Turnover 36	48.6	•	•	46.0	35.2	113.5	32.4	32.7	24.8	•	•	14.9	•
Total Liabilities to Net Worth 37	3.1	•	•	2.8	2.6	4.1	1.7	2.1	1.6	•	•	2.8	•
Current Assets to Working Capital 38	3.7	•	•	4.1	3.1	4.4	2.8	4.7	2.3	•	•	•	•
Current Liabilities to Working Capital 39	2.7	•	•	3.1	2.1	3.4	1.8	3.7	1.3	•	•	•	•
Working Capital to Net Sales 40	0.0	•	•	0.0	0.1	0.0	0.1	0.0	0.1	•	•	•	•
Inventory to Working Capital 41	0.0	•	•	•	0.0	•	0.1	0.0	0.0	•	•	•	•
Total Receipts to Cash Flow 42	3.2	1.9	•	3.5	3.5	5.6	4.3	5.7	4.5	•	•	1.6	•
Cost of Goods to Cash Flow 43	0.2	0.0	•	0.1	0.3	0.0	0.1	0.0	0.2	•	•	0.3	•
Cash Flow to Total Debt 44	1.4	•	•	1.3	1.0	0.7	1.1	0.9	0.8	•	•	0.6	•
Selected Financial Factors (in Percentages)													
Debt Ratio 45	75.6	•	•	73.9	72.0	80.4	62.9	67.6	61.5	•	•	73.4	•
Return on Total Assets 46	38.3	•	•	35.6	31.1	17.5	22.8	10.6	6.7	•	•	9.5	•
Return on Equity Before Income Taxes 47	149.4	•	•	127.7	106.7	81.9	58.7	29.0	8.7	•	•	28.6	•
Return on Equity After Income Taxes 48	146.0	•	•	125.6	104.6	78.9	56.8	26.3	6.8	•	•	21.9	•
Profit Margin (Before Income Tax) 49	10.5	18.5	•	10.0	12.1	5.2	7.7	2.7	1.4	•	•	10.0	•
Profit Margin (After Income Tax) 50	10.3	18.2	•	9.8	11.8	5.0	7.4	2.4	1.1	•	•	7.6	•

Table II

Corporations with Net Income

LEGAL SERVICES

MONEY AMOUNTS AND SIZE OF ASSETS IN THOUSANDS OF DOLLARS

Item Description for Accounting Period 7/11 Through 6/12		Total	Zero Assets	Under 500	500 to 1,000	1,000 to 5,000	5,000 to 10,000	10,000 to 25,000	25,000 to 50,000	50,000 to 100,000	100,000 to 250,000	250,000 to 500,000	500,000 to 2,500,000	2,500,000 and over
Number of Enterprises	1	93231	16981	69505	3432	2993	170	107	25	•	•	•	4	0
Revenues ($ in Thousands)														
Net Sales	2	80697888	2697637	36985104	7415542	14251332	3444230	5041858	4418715	•	•	•	3420830	0
Interest	3	26801	2804	2594	2115	1950	2416	516	1881	•	•	•	11626	0
Rents	4	35099	83	3524	13265	0	1	37	10724	•	•	•	6792	0
Royalties	5	2209	1958	5	0	0	0	135	26	•	•	•	0	0
Other Portfolio Income	6	32058	1432	6667	595	12807	189	1279	1757	•	•	•	6871	0
Other Receipts	7	2931884	168859	1622417	417285	233829	236604	46570	90587	•	•	•	-3002	0
Total Receipts	8	83725939	2872773	38620311	7848802	14499918	3683440	5090395	4523690	•	•	•	3443117	0
Average Total Receipts	9	898	169	556	2287	4845	21667	47574	180948	•	•	•	860779	•
Operating Costs/Operating Income (%)														
Cost of Operations	10	5.9	1.7	6.5	2.6	7.9	0.7	2.6	0.1	•	•	•	19.3	•
Salaries and Wages	11	28.5	15.4	21.6	29.6	30.0	42.0	47.5	56.0	•	•	•	3.6	•
Taxes Paid	12	3.2	2.7	3.2	4.0	3.3	3.4	3.1	3.6	•	•	•	1.5	•
Interest Paid	13	0.5	0.4	0.4	0.6	0.4	0.6	0.3	0.3	•	•	•	2.5	•
Depreciation	14	1.0	1.5	0.9	1.0	0.7	1.1	1.2	1.3	•	•	•	2.3	•
Amortization and Depletion	15	0.2	•	0.0	0.0	0.0	0.0	0.0	0.0	•	•	•	3.8	•
Pensions and Other Deferred Comp.	16	1.7	0.8	1.6	1.8	1.4	2.5	2.4	3.1	•	•	•	0.4	•
Employee Benefits	17	2.0	0.6	1.9	1.3	2.3	2.1	2.9	2.9	•	•	•	1.9	•
Advertising	18	2.3	3.3	2.8	2.2	2.4	1.4	1.2	0.4	•	•	•	0.4	•
Other Expenses	19	26.4	37.4	26.9	26.8	21.8	17.2	21.3	20.1	•	•	•	54.6	•
Officers' Compensation	20	18.4	15.6	22.5	22.0	17.3	26.3	10.2	10.5	•	•	•	0.4	•
Operating Margin	21	10.0	20.5	11.7	8.1	12.3	2.6	7.4	1.9	•	•	•	9.3	•
Operating Margin Before Officers' Comp.	22	28.4	36.2	34.2	30.1	29.6	29.0	17.6	12.4	•	•	•	9.7	•

Selected Average Balance Sheet ($ in Thousands)

Net Receivables 23	18	0	3	81	107	102	1479	2890	•	•	•	114646	•
Inventories 24	1	0	0	0	8	0	283	0	•	•	•	44	•
Net Property, Plant and Equipment 25	32	0	11	121	233	994	2126	7962	•	•	•	83462	•
Total Assets 26	251	0	88	688	1821	7038	15829	35098	•	•	•	1123240	•
Notes and Loans Payable 27	82	0	32	247	417	1872	3940	9141	•	•	•	541102	•
All Other Liabilities 28	100	0	36	180	902	3839	5931	17225	•	•	•	283593	•
Net Worth 29	69	0	20	261	501	1327	5958	8733	•	•	•	298546	•

Selected Financial Ratios (Times to 1)

Current Ratio 30	1.4	•	1.5	1.5	1.5	1.4	1.5	1.2	•	•	•	0.7	•
Quick Ratio 31	0.9	•	1.2	0.9	0.9	0.5	0.8	0.9	•	•	•	0.6	•
Net Sales to Working Capital 32	20.2	•	24.8	17.6	11.3	13.2	12.8	39.3	•	•	•	•	•
Coverage Ratio 33	29.1	69.8	44.4	24.8	32.3	17.9	26.6	17.7	•	•	•	5.0	•
Total Asset Turnover 34	3.5	•	6.0	3.1	2.6	2.9	3.0	5.0	•	•	•	0.8	•
Inventory Turnover 35	70.7	•	621.2	•	46.0	•	4.3	•	•	•	•	3728.4	•
Receivables Turnover 36	47.2	•	124.7	35.0	35.3	313.2	30.6	•	•	•	•	14.9	•
Total Liabilities to Net Worth 37	2.6	•	3.4	1.6	2.6	4.3	1.7	3.0	•	•	•	2.8	•
Current Assets to Working Capital 38	3.4	•	2.8	3.1	3.0	3.3	2.9	5.3	•	•	•	•	•
Current Liabilities to Working Capital 39	2.4	•	1.8	2.1	2.0	2.3	1.9	4.3	•	•	•	•	•
Working Capital to Net Sales 40	0.0	•	0.0	0.1	0.1	0.1	0.1	0.0	•	•	•	•	•
Inventory to Working Capital 41	0.0	•	•	•	0.0	•	0.1	•	•	•	•	•	•
Total Receipts to Cash Flow 42	2.9	1.7	2.7	2.9	3.3	4.7	4.2	6.0	•	•	•	1.6	•
Cost of Goods to Cash Flow 43	0.2	0.0	0.2	0.1	0.3	0.0	0.1	0.0	•	•	•	0.3	•
Cash Flow to Total Debt 44	1.6	•	2.9	1.7	1.1	0.8	1.1	1.1	•	•	•	0.6	•

Selected Financial Factors (in Percentages)

Debt Ratio 45	72.5	•	77.2	62.0	72.5	81.2	62.4	75.1	•	•	•	73.4	•
Return on Total Assets 46	49.2	•	99.0	45.8	37.9	29.2	25.8	22.9	•	•	•	9.5	•
Return on Equity Before Income Taxes 47	172.6	•	423.8	115.7	133.4	146.4	66.0	86.7	•	•	•	28.6	•
Return on Equity After Income Taxes 48	168.9	•	420.4	114.0	130.8	142.2	63.9	80.8	•	•	•	21.9	•
Profit Margin (Before Income Tax) 49	13.8	27.0	16.1	14.0	14.0	9.6	8.3	4.3	•	•	•	10.0	•
Profit Margin (After Income Tax) 50	13.5	26.7	15.9	13.8	13.8	9.3	8.1	4.0	•	•	•	7.6	•

Table I

Corporations with and without Net Income

ACCOUNTING, TAX PREPARATION, BOOKKEEPING, AND PAYROLL SERVICES

MONEY AMOUNTS AND SIZE OF ASSETS IN THOUSANDS OF DOLLARS

Item Description for Accounting Period 7/11 Through 6/12		Total	Zero Assets	Under 500	500 to 1,000	1,000 to 5,000	5,000 to 10,000	10,000 to 25,000	25,000 to 50,000	50,000 to 100,000	100,000 to 250,000	250,000 to 500,000	500,000 to 2,500,000	2,500,000 and over
Number of Enterprises	1	84135	17630	64175	1388	785	36	69	31	9	•	•	0	3
Revenues ($ in Thousands)														
Net Sales	2	53474741	1207084	20624008	4368911	7486203	822513	1563975	1598270	1484813	•	•	0	13478000
Interest	3	727781	3861	13731	1433	2884	618	302	821	432	•	•	0	697596
Rents	4	64697	0	13018	874	0	0	1740	725	0	•	•	0	48340
Royalties	5	339771	0	0	0	0	0	0	0	0	•	•	0	280272
Other Portfolio Income	6	221043	2797	23997	70	3824	2213	4443	18	256	•	•	0	182110
Other Receipts	7	1630174	87699	379079	139497	14371	1580	13924	141912	274	•	•	0	652273
Total Receipts	8	56458207	1301441	21053833	4510785	7507282	826924	1584384	1741746	1485775	•	•	0	15338591
Average Total Receipts	9	671	74	328	3250	9563	22970	22962	56185	165086	•	•	•	5112864
Operating Costs/Operating Income (%)														
Cost of Operations	10	10.2	0.4	0.9	17.8	19.5	32.7	50.2	40.1	76.9	•	•	•	1.3
Salaries and Wages	11	33.5	14.5	30.8	31.8	55.2	32.4	16.8	14.2	14.8	•	•	•	34.2
Taxes Paid	12	4.6	4.4	4.5	4.4	5.0	2.7	6.5	6.2	0.5	•	•	•	4.7
Interest Paid	13	1.2	2.7	0.5	0.5	0.3	0.5	0.8	1.3	0.7	•	•	•	2.6
Depreciation	14	1.4	1.1	0.8	1.6	0.5	0.5	1.5	1.4	0.5	•	•	•	2.6
Amortization and Depletion	15	0.9	1.3	0.3	0.8	0.3	0.5	0.4	0.3	0.1	•	•	•	2.0
Pensions and Other Deferred Comp.	16	1.3	0.3	1.5	0.5	0.7	0.7	0.4	0.2	0.0	•	•	•	2.0
Employee Benefits	17	2.0	1.7	2.1	2.6	1.2	1.5	3.5	1.3	0.3	•	•	•	2.3
Advertising	18	0.8	1.4	0.8	0.5	0.2	1.2	0.3	0.1	0.2	•	•	•	1.6
Other Expenses	19	29.2	54.1	26.5	18.3	13.0	16.0	13.6	39.5	4.1	•	•	•	45.8
Officers' Compensation	20	10.9	17.2	22.1	15.8	2.4	5.5	3.6	1.0	0.3	•	•	•	0.3
Operating Margin	21	4.1	0.9	9.2	5.4	1.6	5.6	2.4	•	1.6	•	•	•	0.8
Operating Margin Before Officers' Comp.	22	15.0	18.1	31.4	21.2	4.1	11.1	6.0	•	1.8	•	•	•	1.1

Selected Average Balance Sheet ($ in Thousands)													
Net Receivables	23	49	0	3	163	114	892	2814	6788	9825	•	•	• 984112
Inventories	24	0	0	0	0	0	31	9	58	254	•	•	• 3943
Net Property, Plant and Equipment	25	27	0	12	179	245	277	1155	1554	1555	•	•	• 297266
Total Assets	26	968	0	55	738	1793	6880	15652	36807	68577	•	•	• 23424267
Notes and Loans Payable	27	107	0	23	242	678	2915	1999	7231	13700	•	•	• 1754303
All Other Liabilities	28	629	0	16	203	649	1753	10299	25548	37423	•	•	• 16118542
Net Worth	29	233	0	16	292	466	2212	3354	4028	17453	•	•	• 5551421
Selected Financial Ratios (Times to 1)													
Current Ratio	30	1.2	•	1.6	1.6	0.8	1.0	1.2	1.3	1.2	•	•	• 1.1
Quick Ratio	31	0.3	•	1.3	1.3	0.7	0.8	0.7	0.8	0.6	•	•	• 0.2
Net Sales to Working Capital	32	12.8	•	29.7	24.3	•	673.1	15.2	7.5	25.0	•	•	• 4.5
Coverage Ratio	33	9.2	4.2	25.8	17.6	7.8	13.0	5.6	3.6	3.2	•	•	• 6.9
Total Asset Turnover	34	0.7	•	5.9	4.3	5.3	3.3	1.4	1.4	2.4	•	•	• 0.2
Inventory Turnover	35	278.4	•	245.0	5283.4	13773.0	241.7	1214.7	359.3	498.6	•	•	• 14.3
Receivables Turnover	36	10.2	•	70.9	26.2	82.6	6.9	11.3	9.4	9.4	•	•	• 3.7
Total Liabilities to Net Worth	37	3.2	•	2.5	1.5	2.8	2.1	3.7	8.1	2.9	•	•	• 3.2
Current Assets to Working Capital	38	7.7	•	2.7	2.8	•	84.8	6.8	3.9	6.7	•	•	• 8.6
Current Liabilities to Working Capital	39	6.7	•	1.7	1.8	•	83.8	5.8	2.9	5.7	•	•	• 7.6
Working Capital to Net Sales	40	0.1	•	0.0	0.0	•	0.0	0.1	0.1	0.0	•	•	• 0.2
Inventory to Working Capital	41	0.0	•	0.0	0.0	•	0.9	0.0	0.0	0.0	•	•	• 0.0
Total Receipts to Cash Flow	42	3.0	1.9	3.2	4.3	8.1	5.2	6.7	2.4	19.3	•	•	• 1.9
Cost of Goods to Cash Flow	43	0.3	0.0	0.0	0.8	1.6	1.7	3.4	1.0	14.8	•	•	• 0.0
Cash Flow to Total Debt	44	0.3	•	2.6	1.6	0.9	0.9	0.3	0.6	0.2	•	•	• 0.1
Selected Financial Factors (in Percentages)													
Debt Ratio	45	76.0	•	71.6	60.4	74.0	67.8	78.6	89.1	74.5	•	•	• 76.3
Return on Total Assets	46	7.2	•	69.3	39.3	11.7	22.1	6.5	6.5	5.6	•	•	• 3.4
Return on Equity Before Income Taxes	47	26.7	•	234.3	93.7	39.3	63.5	24.9	43.2	15.2	•	•	• 12.3
Return on Equity After Income Taxes	48	22.8	•	233.1	93.6	39.0	63.2	21.3	39.7	12.9	•	•	• 8.0
Profit Margin (Before Income Tax)	49	9.8	8.7	11.3	8.7	1.9	6.1	3.7	3.4	1.6	•	•	• 15.2
Profit Margin (After Income Tax)	50	8.3	8.3	11.3	8.7	1.9	6.1	3.1	3.1	1.4	•	•	• 9.8

Table II

Corporations with Net Income

ACCOUNTING, TAX PREPARATION, BOOKKEEPING, AND PAYROLL SERVICES

MONEY AMOUNTS AND SIZE OF ASSETS IN THOUSANDS OF DOLLARS

Item Description for Accounting Period 7/11 Through 6/12		Total	Zero Assets	Under 500	500 to 1,000	1,000 to 5,000	5,000 to 10,000	10,000 to 25,000	25,000 to 50,000	50,000 to 100,000	100,000 to 250,000	250,000 to 500,000	500,000 to 2,500,000	2,500,000 and over
Number of Enterprises	1	59925	10019	48085	1055	648	33	44	25	•	•	3	0	0
Revenues ($ in Thousands)														
Net Sales	2	40994767	790660	16673388	2948807	3595267	776610	575999	1354064	•	•	12398306	0	0
Interest	3	707628	3842	5528	16	2047	618	261	668	•	•	694273	0	0
Rents	4	63343	0	13018	0	0	0	1740	244	•	•	48340	0	0
Royalties	5	280148	0	0	0	0	0	0	0	•	•	280148	0	0
Other Portfolio Income	6	213045	2795	19960	5	3824	2213	550	18	•	•	182114	0	0
Other Receipts	7	1284254	49651	328353	138441	11850	1558	8303	97035	•	•	649944	0	0
Total Receipts	8	43543185	846948	17040247	3087269	3612988	780999	586853	1452029	•	•	14253125	0	0
Average Total Receipts	9	727	85	354	2926	5576	23667	13338	58081	•	•	4751042	•	•
Operating Costs/Operating Income (%)														
Cost of Operations	10	10.0	0.4	1.0	10.0	40.3	29.0	12.2	46.4	•	•	0.9	•	•
Salaries and Wages	11	28.8	11.2	28.2	36.5	20.3	34.1	32.7	6.9	•	•	34.7	•	•
Taxes Paid	12	4.4	3.1	4.4	3.5	5.1	2.9	4.0	6.0	•	•	4.8	•	•
Interest Paid	13	0.7	3.3	0.5	0.6	0.5	0.5	1.0	0.7	•	•	0.9	•	•
Depreciation	14	1.4	1.3	0.7	1.1	0.7	0.6	2.8	0.3	•	•	2.7	•	•
Amortization and Depletion	15	1.0	1.7	0.3	1.1	0.4	0.6	0.4	0.0	•	•	2.1	•	•
Pensions and Other Deferred Comp.	16	1.2	0.4	1.5	0.3	0.4	0.8	0.5	0.2	•	•	1.8	•	•
Employee Benefits	17	1.9	1.1	2.1	2.4	1.4	1.6	2.3	1.0	•	•	2.1	•	•
Advertising	18	1.0	1.1	0.8	0.5	0.4	1.3	0.6	0.1	•	•	1.7	•	•
Other Expenses	19	31.0	48.8	25.1	20.2	21.6	15.7	22.0	39.5	•	•	46.9	•	•
Officers' Compensation	20	11.4	12.7	22.9	15.3	3.5	5.5	7.4	0.6	•	•	0.2	•	•
Operating Margin	21	7.3	14.8	12.6	8.4	5.3	7.6	14.1	•	•	•	1.3	•	•
Operating Margin Before Officers' Comp.	22	18.7	27.5	35.6	23.7	8.8	13.1	21.5	•	•	•	1.5	•	•

Selected Average Balance Sheet ($ in Thousands)														
Net Receivables	**23**	51	0	4	178	123	844	3548	4422	•	•	719777	•	•
Inventories	**24**	0	0	0	0	0	34	2	42	•	•	2658	•	•
Net Property, Plant and Equipment	**25**	32	0	12	203	219	298	1245	1110	•	•	284458	•	•
Total Assets	**26**	1160	0	59	777	1810	6936	16540	35781	•	•	20575089	•	•
Notes and Loans Payable	**27**	69	0	21	229	603	3100	1805	5557	•	•	592828	•	•
All Other Liabilities	**28**	787	0	16	169	573	982	10839	24430	•	•	14779432	•	•
Net Worth	**29**	304	0	22	379	634	2854	3896	5794	•	•	5202829	•	•
Selected Financial Ratios (Times to 1)														
Current Ratio	**30**	1.1	•	1.6	2.4	0.9	1.4	1.3	1.5	•	•	1.1	•	•
Quick Ratio	**31**	0.3	•	1.4	2.2	0.8	1.1	0.6	0.8	•	•	0.2	•	•
Net Sales to Working Capital	**32**	10.7	•	31.9	13.1	•	26.5	4.8	5.8	•	•	4.5	•	•
Coverage Ratio	**33**	20.3	7.6	33.1	23.1	12.9	17.6	17.4	8.3	•	•	19.8	•	•
Total Asset Turnover	**34**	0.6	•	5.9	3.6	3.1	3.4	0.8	1.5	•	•	0.2	•	•
Inventory Turnover	**35**	294.9	•	6764.9	2007.1	35319.1	202.3	997.4	601.4	•	•	14.0	•	•
Receivables Turnover	**36**	11.7	•	62.9	23.3	44.8	6.9	5.4	•	•	•	•	•	•
Total Liabilities to Net Worth	**37**	2.8	•	1.7	1.1	1.9	1.4	3.2	5.2	•	•	3.0	•	•
Current Assets to Working Capital	**38**	7.7	•	2.8	1.7	•	3.4	4.0	3.0	•	•	9.2	•	•
Current Liabilities to Working Capital	**39**	6.7	•	1.8	0.7	•	2.4	3.0	2.0	•	•	8.2	•	•
Working Capital to Net Sales	**40**	0.1	•	0.0	0.1	•	0.0	0.2	0.2	•	•	0.2	•	•
Inventory to Working Capital	**41**	0.0	•	0.0	0.0	•	0.0	0.0	0.0	•	•	0.0	•	•
Total Receipts to Cash Flow	**42**	2.6	1.6	3.0	3.4	4.4	4.8	2.9	2.3	•	•	1.8	•	•
Cost of Goods to Cash Flow	**43**	0.3	0.0	0.0	0.3	1.8	1.4	0.4	1.0	•	•	0.0	•	•
Cash Flow to Total Debt	**44**	0.3	•	3.2	2.1	1.1	1.2	0.4	0.8	•	•	0.1	•	•
Selected Financial Factors (in Percentages)														
Debt Ratio	**45**	73.8	•	63.1	51.2	65.0	58.9	76.4	83.8	•	•	74.7	•	•
Return on Total Assets	**46**	8.5	•	90.6	49.3	19.3	29.5	13.4	9.4	•	•	3.6	•	•
Return on Equity Before Income Taxes	**47**	31.0	•	237.9	96.8	50.9	67.6	53.6	50.9	•	•	13.4	•	•
Return on Equity After Income Taxes	**48**	26.7	•	236.8	96.8	50.6	67.4	48.8	47.9	•	•	8.8	•	•
Profit Margin (Before Income Tax)	**49**	13.8	22.0	14.8	13.1	5.8	8.2	16.0	5.4	•	•	16.9	•	•
Profit Margin (After Income Tax)	**50**	11.9	21.3	14.8	13.1	5.8	8.2	14.5	5.1	•	•	11.1	•	•

Table I

Corporations with and without Net Income

ARCHITECTURAL, ENGINEERING, AND RELATED SERVICES

MONEY AMOUNTS AND SIZE OF ASSETS IN THOUSANDS OF DOLLARS

Item Description for Accounting Period 7/11 Through 6/12		Total	Zero Assets	Under 500	500 to 1,000	1,000 to 5,000	5,000 to 10,000	10,000 to 25,000	25,000 to 50,000	50,000 to 100,000	100,000 to 250,000	250,000 to 500,000	500,000 to 2,500,000	2,500,000 and over
Number of Enterprises	1	103924	17612	78260	2607	3968	653	497	115	83	58	26	33	11
Revenues ($ in Thousands)														
Net Sales	2	213928684	2402114	41659704	5404091	25626316	9362913	15448845	6345331	8966201	11301633	10662103	26979176	49770257
Interest	3	377033	3302	5437	1775	9157	4844	16734	4724	12165	10406	106199	112648	89640
Rents	4	232351	10639	8430	7214	3028	6109	1519	1979	10208	10239	22697	7523	142768
Royalties	5	81369	612	18	0	2808	1178	0	81	4317	8527	13096	12676	38055
Other Portfolio Income	6	1104665	43379	70764	41688	103919	47385	13154	2688	125150	74964	35439	64568	481569
Other Receipts	7	4067594	53518	146056	152204	92574	154365	293218	84102	136398	145138	160453	297496	2352071
Total Receipts	8	219791696	2513564	41890409	5606972	25837802	9576794	15773470	6438905	9254439	11550907	10999987	27474087	52874360
Average Total Receipts	9	2115	143	535	2151	6512	14666	31737	55990	111499	199154	423076	832548	4806760
Operating Costs/Operating Income (%)														
Cost of Operations	10	47.0	31.3	21.0	26.5	42.3	36.8	33.0	42.8	49.4	44.4	56.1	47.4	78.8
Salaries and Wages	11	18.5	16.6	21.2	23.3	20.2	23.7	26.0	23.2	19.2	20.7	15.2	15.7	12.7
Taxes Paid	12	2.9	2.5	4.0	3.6	3.1	3.5	3.5	3.1	3.3	2.7	2.5	2.2	1.7
Interest Paid	13	0.9	1.6	0.6	0.5	0.5	0.7	0.6	0.6	0.7	1.2	1.7	2.2	0.6
Depreciation	14	1.9	1.7	1.2	1.8	1.6	1.9	2.0	2.0	2.6	2.6	5.2	2.6	1.4
Amortization and Depletion	15	0.5	0.3	0.1	0.3	0.1	0.1	0.2	0.6	0.6	0.7	0.9	1.3	0.6
Pensions and Other Deferred Comp.	16	1.0	1.2	1.0	1.0	0.9	1.0	1.6	1.1	1.2	0.8	1.0	0.7	1.1
Employee Benefits	17	2.5	1.6	2.1	2.7	2.1	2.8	3.3	2.7	2.8	3.3	2.9	2.6	2.3
Advertising	18	0.3	0.2	0.4	0.3	0.4	0.3	0.3	0.4	0.3	0.2	0.2	0.2	0.0
Other Expenses	19	18.0	28.9	29.7	25.3	16.8	19.9	22.8	18.5	18.0	21.6	13.2	22.7	3.1
Officers' Compensation	20	5.5	7.3	13.5	11.2	9.1	6.8	4.9	3.7	2.7	1.9	1.2	1.4	0.8
Operating Margin	21	1.1	6.8	5.1	3.5	3.0	2.5	2.0	1.3	•	•	•	1.1	•
Operating Margin Before Officers' Comp.	22	6.6	14.0	18.6	14.7	12.1	9.3	6.9	5.0	1.9	1.8	1.0	2.4	•

Selected Average Balance Sheet ($ in Thousands)													
Net Receivables 23	304	0	8	157	673	2610	5537	12118	20880	39520	90035	225217	744659
Inventories 24	41	0	1	19	142	367	760	1669	1596	7059	18785	26591	81216
Net Property, Plant and Equipment 25	141	0	18	116	433	1227	2234	4152	8529	16232	40525	91966	279264
Total Assets 26	1345	0	71	693	2169	6682	15903	35649	70762	162080	373066	1013448	4459146
Notes and Loans Payable 27	344	0	55	293	696	1438	4078	7194	15739	40470	95088	276357	804418
All Other Liabilities 28	499	0	22	534	617	2193	5559	13089	32135	64771	120099	380486	1679339
Net Worth 29	502	0	-7	-134	856	3051	6266	15366	22888	56839	157880	356606	1975390

Selected Financial Ratios (Times to 1)													
Current Ratio 30	1.4	•	1.1	0.9	2.1	2.0	1.6	1.6	1.4	1.5	1.6	1.7	1.2
Quick Ratio 31	1.0	•	1.0	0.7	1.7	1.6	1.3	1.3	1.0	0.9	1.1	1.3	0.7
Net Sales to Working Capital 32	10.0	•	148.5	•	9.1	6.3	7.9	6.1	9.6	7.0	5.6	5.0	11.9
Coverage Ratio 33	5.6	8.2	11.1	14.6	8.6	8.2	8.3	5.7	4.4	3.2	2.8	2.4	7.4
Total Asset Turnover 34	1.5	•	7.5	3.0	3.0	2.1	2.0	1.5	1.5	1.2	1.1	0.8	1.0
Inventory Turnover 35	23.3	•	100.5	29.2	19.3	14.3	13.5	14.1	33.4	12.3	12.3	14.6	43.9
Receivables Turnover 36	6.7	•	71.7	9.0	9.6	6.1	5.9	4.6	5.6	4.8	4.3	3.6	5.7
Total Liabilities to Net Worth 37	1.7	•	•	•	1.5	1.2	1.5	1.3	2.1	1.9	1.4	1.8	1.3
Current Assets to Working Capital 38	3.2	•	10.5	•	1.9	2.0	2.6	2.6	3.7	3.2	2.6	2.5	5.3
Current Liabilities to Working Capital 39	2.2	•	9.5	•	0.9	1.0	1.6	1.6	2.7	2.2	1.6	1.5	4.3
Working Capital to Net Sales 40	0.1	•	0.0	•	0.1	0.2	0.1	0.2	0.1	0.1	0.2	0.2	0.1
Inventory to Working Capital 41	0.2	•	0.3	•	0.2	0.2	0.2	0.2	0.2	0.3	0.3	0.2	0.2
Total Receipts to Cash Flow 42	5.6	2.7	3.3	3.7	6.0	4.9	4.4	5.7	6.6	5.1	8.1	4.5	28.7
Cost of Goods to Cash Flow 43	2.6	0.9	0.7	1.0	2.5	1.8	1.5	2.4	3.2	2.3	4.5	2.1	22.6
Cash Flow to Total Debt 44	0.4	•	2.1	0.7	0.8	0.8	0.7	0.5	0.3	0.4	0.2	0.3	0.1

Selected Financial Factors (in Percentages)													
Debt Ratio 45	62.7	•	109.6	119.4	60.5	54.3	60.6	56.9	67.7	64.9	57.7	64.8	55.7
Return on Total Assets 46	7.6	•	46.4	23.2	12.7	11.6	9.3	5.1	4.9	4.7	5.4	4.2	4.2
Return on Equity Before Income Taxes 47	16.6	•	•	•	28.4	22.3	20.7	9.8	11.7	9.1	8.3	6.8	8.2
Return on Equity After Income Taxes 48	13.6	•	•	•	26.7	19.6	18.2	7.2	7.1	5.9	3.7	5.2	5.0
Profit Margin (Before Income Tax) 49	4.1	11.4	5.6	7.2	3.8	4.8	4.2	2.7	2.5	2.7	3.2	3.0	3.6
Profit Margin (After Income Tax) 50	3.3	9.0	5.5	6.9	3.5	4.2	3.7	2.0	1.5	1.7	1.4	2.3	2.2

Table II

Corporations with Net Income

ARCHITECTURAL, ENGINEERING, AND RELATED SERVICES

MONEY AMOUNTS AND SIZE OF ASSETS IN THOUSANDS OF DOLLARS

Item Description for Accounting Period 7/11 Through 6/12		Total	Zero Assets	Under 500	500 to 1,000	1,000 to 5,000	5,000 to 10,000	10,000 to 25,000	25,000 to 50,000	50,000 to 100,000	100,000 to 250,000	250,000 to 500,000	500,000 to 2,500,000	2,500,000 and over
Number of Enterprises	1	69241	12211	51306	1988	2644	514	358	73	60	39	19	20	8
Revenues ($ in Thousands)														
Net Sales	2	168477306	1865293	33441939	3571138	20354697	7875514	12038456	4146348	7212384	8649125	9446872	20894996	38980545
Interest	3	216532	1729	3826	683	2804	2546	5187	3623	9763	7144	41655	71873	65699
Rents	4	159314	10469	2286	6454	2986	6	1324	1061	8194	7874	18289	6128	94242
Royalties	5	64633	82	18	0	0	0	0	81	374	8033	12763	5226	38055
Other Portfolio Income	6	830197	42600	69208	1368	29806	44936	10060	607	61880	64224	22797	36631	446082
Other Receipts	7	1942705	63431	135654	141448	92554	129814	274063	63667	116106	98084	83089	257040	487754
Total Receipts	8	171690687	1983604	33652931	3721091	20482847	8052816	12329090	4215387	7408701	8834484	9625465	21271894	40112377
Average Total Receipts	9	2480	162	656	1872	7747	15667	34439	57745	123478	226525	506603	1063595	5014047
Operating Costs/Operating Income (%)														
Cost of Operations	10	45.9	29.9	22.3	17.5	45.2	39.8	33.5	38.5	46.0	45.4	55.9	47.8	72.6
Salaries and Wages	11	18.3	14.1	20.5	25.0	17.7	21.7	25.8	24.1	19.6	19.7	15.1	15.3	14.4
Taxes Paid	12	2.8	2.3	3.8	3.5	2.7	3.4	3.6	3.3	3.3	2.5	2.5	2.1	2.1
Interest Paid	13	0.6	0.7	0.5	0.5	0.3	0.4	0.4	0.4	0.6	0.7	0.5	1.3	0.5
Depreciation	14	1.5	1.5	1.2	1.9	1.2	1.7	1.7	2.1	2.2	2.3	1.8	1.5	1.6
Amortization and Depletion	15	0.4	0.4	0.0	0.2	0.1	0.1	0.1	0.2	0.3	0.4	0.9	0.9	0.6
Pensions and Other Deferred Comp.	16	1.1	1.2	1.0	1.0	0.8	1.0	1.4	1.3	1.4	0.7	1.1	0.8	1.3
Employee Benefits	17	2.3	1.4	2.2	2.3	1.9	2.9	3.2	2.9	2.8	2.9	2.8	2.0	2.1
Advertising	18	0.2	0.2	0.3	0.4	0.3	0.3	0.2	0.4	0.3	0.2	0.2	0.2	0.0
Other Expenses	19	16.8	23.8	27.6	26.4	14.8	16.9	20.3	19.0	16.7	20.5	14.0	23.3	2.3
Officers' Compensation	20	5.3	7.4	12.6	12.2	8.8	7.0	5.1	3.2	2.6	2.1	1.1	1.5	0.6
Operating Margin	21	4.7	17.3	8.1	9.1	6.2	4.8	4.6	4.6	4.2	2.4	4.0	3.3	1.7
Operating Margin Before Officers' Comp.	22	10.0	24.6	20.7	21.3	15.0	11.8	9.8	7.8	6.9	4.6	5.1	4.8	2.3

Selected Average Balance Sheet ($ in Thousands)													
Net Receivables 23	342	0	10	151	738	2720	5744	11345	22381	43013	103126	280658	760492
Inventories 24	42	0	1	11	165	303	745	1596	1191	9678	21154	16865	85686
Net Property, Plant and Equipment 25	122	0	18	123	395	965	1727	3606	7565	15622	35558	54293	250339
Total Assets 26	1401	0	78	718	2121	6528	16093	35605	70973	167428	364949	1058746	4418444
Notes and Loans Payable 27	290	0	55	331	436	1302	3217	5188	12599	31747	92680	196932	694291
All Other Liabilities 28	515	0	26	195	510	1897	5173	13806	29546	67222	109880	468146	1617692
Net Worth 29	595	0	-3	192	1174	3330	7703	16611	28827	68460	162389	393669	2106460

Selected Financial Ratios (Times to 1)													
Current Ratio 30	1.6	•	1.2	1.8	2.6	2.3	1.9	1.7	1.6	1.5	1.6	1.7	1.3
Quick Ratio 31	1.1	•	1.1	1.4	2.2	1.9	1.5	1.4	1.3	1.0	1.2	1.3	0.8
Net Sales to Working Capital 32	9.7	•	95.0	8.6	8.5	6.0	6.4	5.6	7.4	7.4	6.3	5.7	12.9
Coverage Ratio 33	12.9	36.5	18.5	27.5	23.5	19.2	19.8	15.0	13.2	8.5	12.6	5.0	11.9
Total Asset Turnover 34	1.7	•	8.4	2.5	3.6	2.3	2.1	1.6	1.7	1.3	1.4	1.0	1.1
Inventory Turnover 35	26.5	•	181.6	27.5	21.0	20.1	15.1	13.7	46.4	10.4	13.1	29.6	41.3
Receivables Turnover 36	6.6	•	81.3	8.5	10.0	6.5	5.9	4.2	5.7	4.9	•	3.6	•
Total Liabilities to Net Worth 37	1.4	•	•	2.7	0.8	1.0	1.1	1.1	1.5	1.4	1.2	1.7	1.1
Current Assets to Working Capital 38	2.8	•	6.5	2.3	1.6	1.8	2.1	2.4	2.7	3.1	2.6	2.5	4.7
Current Liabilities to Working Capital 39	1.8	•	5.5	1.3	0.6	0.8	1.1	1.4	1.7	2.1	1.6	1.5	3.7
Working Capital to Net Sales 40	0.1	•	0.0	0.1	0.1	0.2	0.2	0.2	0.1	0.1	0.2	0.2	0.1
Inventory to Working Capital 41	0.2	•	0.2	0.1	0.1	0.2	0.2	0.1	0.1	0.3	0.3	0.1	0.2
Total Receipts to Cash Flow 42	5.0	2.3	3.2	2.8	5.4	5.0	4.2	4.7	5.2	4.7	6.1	3.9	22.8
Cost of Goods to Cash Flow 43	2.3	0.7	0.7	0.5	2.4	2.0	1.4	1.8	2.4	2.1	3.4	1.9	16.6
Cash Flow to Total Debt 44	0.6	•	2.5	1.2	1.5	1.0	0.9	0.6	0.5	0.5	0.4	0.4	0.1

Selected Financial Factors (in Percentages)													
Debt Ratio 45	57.5	•	103.9	73.2	44.6	49.0	52.1	53.3	59.4	59.1	55.5	62.8	52.3
Return on Total Assets 46	12.9	•	77.2	34.7	25.8	17.5	15.8	10.7	12.8	8.1	8.9	6.4	6.3
Return on Equity Before Income Taxes 47	28.0	•	•	124.7	44.6	32.4	31.3	21.4	29.1	17.4	18.3	13.8	12.1
Return on Equity After Income Taxes 48	24.2	•	•	120.4	42.7	29.3	28.5	17.6	24.2	13.5	12.2	11.4	8.1
Profit Margin (Before Income Tax) 49	6.9	23.6	8.7	13.3	6.8	7.0	7.2	6.3	7.0	5.4	6.0	5.2	5.2
Profit Margin (After Income Tax) 50	5.9	20.6	8.6	12.9	6.5	6.4	6.5	5.1	5.8	4.2	4.0	4.3	3.5

Table I

Corporations with and without Net Income

SPECIALIZED DESIGN SERVICES

MONEY AMOUNTS AND SIZE OF ASSETS IN THOUSANDS OF DOLLARS

Item Description for Accounting Period 7/11 Through 6/12		Total	Zero Assets	Under 500	500 to 1,000	1,000 to 5,000	5,000 to 10,000	10,000 to 25,000	25,000 to 50,000	50,000 to 100,000	100,000 to 250,000	250,000 to 500,000	500,000 to 2,500,000	2,500,000 and over
Number of Enterprises	1	40094	10243	28559	668	547	42	15	17	0	0	0	3	0
Revenues ($ in Thousands)														
Net Sales	2	18074241	525590	11311674	826638	2576490	31101	183666	750387	0	0	0	1868696	0
Interest	3	2930	1	2304	1	208	0	21	203	0	0	0	192	0
Rents	4	52	0	0	0	52	0	0	0	0	0	0	0	0
Royalties	5	13088	0	0	0	0	0	0	0	0	0	0	13088	0
Other Portfolio Income	6	14654	287	6242	0	7968	0	30	106	0	0	0	20	0
Other Receipts	7	98814	62025	5198	34	2483	-248	699	-75	0	0	0	28698	0
Total Receipts	8	18203779	587903	11325418	826673	2587201	30853	184416	750621	0	0	0	1910694	0
Average Total Receipts	9	454	57	397	1238	4730	735	12294	44154	•	•	•	636898	•
Operating Costs/Operating Income (%)														
Cost of Operations	10	37.2	14.9	38.8	40.0	51.1	•	44.7	50.2	•	•	•	7.5	•
Salaries and Wages	11	14.8	0.4	11.9	20.5	12.8	0.2	22.7	14.4	•	•	•	36.2	•
Taxes Paid	12	2.7	2.9	2.7	2.4	1.9	1.1	3.9	1.6	•	•	•	3.5	•
Interest Paid	13	0.5	0.5	0.4	0.6	0.4	•	0.0	0.4	•	•	•	1.0	•
Depreciation	14	1.5	4.0	1.0	1.0	1.8	0.0	4.8	1.7	•	•	•	3.5	•
Amortization and Depletion	15	0.2	0.0	0.0	0.2	0.2	0.0	0.0	0.3	•	•	•	1.1	•
Pensions and Other Deferred Comp.	16	0.5	1.1	0.4	0.9	0.3	•	0.8	0.5	•	•	•	0.5	•
Employee Benefits	17	1.2	•	0.8	0.5	1.0	•	3.1	2.5	•	•	•	4.2	•
Advertising	18	1.0	0.5	0.8	2.0	1.2	•	0.3	0.4	•	•	•	1.6	•
Other Expenses	19	27.6	44.1	27.2	25.0	23.4	22.5	10.5	15.0	•	•	•	39.7	•
Officers' Compensation	20	7.9	21.3	9.4	6.6	5.2	3.9	1.7	4.0	•	•	•	1.2	•
Operating Margin	21	5.0	10.3	6.4	0.2	0.8	72.3	7.4	8.9	•	•	•	0.1	•
Operating Margin Before Officers' Comp.	22	12.9	31.6	15.8	6.8	6.0	76.1	9.1	13.0	•	•	•	1.3	•

Selected Average Balance Sheet ($ in Thousands)													
Net Receivables 23	22	0	10	118	311	0	2032	6704	•	•	•	69060	•
Inventories 24	13	0	3	147	107	520	429	7621	•	•	•	55913	•
Net Property, Plant and Equipment 25	41	0	13	47	394	1	2125	3572	•	•	•	315762	•
Total Assets 26	162	0	74	563	1779	9367	12400	33609	•	•	•	619170	•
Notes and Loans Payable 27	86	0	77	112	955	0	270	2294	•	•	•	192907	•
All Other Liabilities 28	74	0	20	258	834	7635	1822	21565	•	•	•	353968	•
Net Worth 29	2	0	-23	193	-11	1732	10307	9750	•	•	•	72295	•
Selected Financial Ratios (Times to 1)													
Current Ratio 30	1.6	•	2.0	2.2	0.8	•	5.0	1.5	•	•	•	2.0	•
Quick Ratio 31	1.1	•	1.8	1.1	0.5	•	4.0	0.9	•	•	•	1.1	•
Net Sales to Working Capital 32	14.2	•	16.8	4.7	•	7.5	2.6	5.3	•	•	•	6.3	•
Coverage Ratio 33	13.7	42.9	18.4	1.4	4.4	•	180.4	22.6	•	•	•	3.4	•
Total Asset Turnover 34	2.8	•	5.3	2.2	2.6	0.1	1.0	1.3	•	•	•	1.0	•
Inventory Turnover 35	12.8	•	48.5	3.4	22.5	•	12.8	2.9	•	•	•	0.8	•
Receivables Turnover 36	22.9	•	47.7	8.5	23.9	1.8	3.7	6.7	•	•	•	18.0	•
Total Liabilities to Net Worth 37	91.9	•	•	1.9	•	4.4	0.2	2.4	•	•	•	7.6	•
Current Assets to Working Capital 38	2.5	•	2.0	1.8	•	1.0	1.3	2.9	•	•	•	2.0	•
Current Liabilities to Working Capital 39	1.5	•	1.0	0.8	•	•	0.3	1.9	•	•	•	1.0	•
Working Capital to Net Sales 40	0.1	•	0.1	0.2	•	0.1	0.4	0.2	•	•	•	0.2	•
Inventory to Working Capital 41	0.5	•	0.1	0.6	•	•	0.0	0.9	•	•	•	0.6	•
Total Receipts to Cash Flow 42	3.5	1.7	3.6	4.4	4.5	1.1	6.6	4.9	•	•	•	2.7	•
Cost of Goods to Cash Flow 43	1.3	0.3	1.4	1.8	2.3	•	3.0	2.5	•	•	•	0.2	•
Cash Flow to Total Debt 44	0.8	•	1.1	0.8	0.6	0.1	0.9	0.4	•	•	•	0.4	•
Selected Financial Factors (in Percentages)													
Debt Ratio 45	98.9	•	131.3	65.7	100.6	81.5	16.9	71.0	•	•	•	88.3	•
Return on Total Assets 46	17.3	•	36.9	1.9	4.2	5.7	7.8	12.3	•	•	•	3.4	•
Return on Equity Before Income Taxes 47	1488.3	•	•	1.6	•	30.6	9.3	40.5	•	•	•	20.4	•
Return on Equity After Income Taxes 48	1468.0	•	•	1.6	•	30.6	7.4	38.1	•	•	•	20.4	•
Profit Margin (Before Income Tax) 49	5.7	22.1	6.5	0.3	1.2	71.5	7.8	8.9	•	•	•	2.4	•
Profit Margin (After Income Tax) 50	5.7	21.8	6.5	0.3	1.1	71.5	6.2	8.4	•	•	•	2.4	•

Table II

Corporations with Net Income

SPECIALIZED DESIGN SERVICES

Item Description for Accounting Period 7/11 Through 6/12		MONEY AMOUNTS AND SIZE OF ASSETS IN THOUSANDS OF DOLLARS Total	Zero Assets	Under 500	500 to 1,000	1,000 to 5,000	5,000 to 10,000	10,000 to 25,000	25,000 to 50,000	50,000 to 100,000	100,000 to 250,000	250,000 to 500,000	500,000 to 2,500,000	2,500,000 and over
Number of Enterprises	1	24130	5141	18127	422	411	0	15	14	0	0	0	0	0
Revenues ($ in Thousands)														
Net Sales	2	14030663	410667	9054964	519846	1705980	0	183666	2155540	0	0	0	0	0
Interest	3	2523	1	2103	0	131	0	21	266	0	0	0	0	0
Rents	4	52	0	0	0	52	0	0	0	0	0	0	0	0
Royalties	5	0	0	0	0	0	0	0	0	0	0	0	0	0
Other Portfolio Income	6	7989	287	0	0	7549	0	30	123	0	0	0	0	0
Other Receipts	7	88884	61572	2774	34	2069	0	699	21738	0	0	0	0	0
Total Receipts	8	14130111	472527	9059841	519880	1715781	0	184416	2177667	0	0	0	0	0
Average Total Receipts	9	586	92	500	1232	4175	•	12294	155548	•	•	•	•	•
Operating Costs/Operating Income (%)														
Cost of Operations	10	33.7	5.8	38.0	36.6	40.9	•	44.7	13.4	•	•	•	•	•
Salaries and Wages	11	14.6	•	11.3	21.9	11.8	•	22.7	30.7	•	•	•	•	•
Taxes Paid	12	2.6	3.1	2.6	2.5	2.0	•	3.9	3.1	•	•	•	•	•
Interest Paid	13	0.4	0.5	0.3	0.4	0.5	•	0.0	0.8	•	•	•	•	•
Depreciation	14	1.5	3.0	0.9	0.1	2.4	•	4.8	3.1	•	•	•	•	•
Amortization and Depletion	15	0.2	•	0.0	0.3	0.2	•	0.0	0.9	•	•	•	•	•
Pensions and Other Deferred Comp.	16	0.5	1.4	0.3	1.4	0.4	•	0.8	0.6	•	•	•	•	•
Employee Benefits	17	1.4	•	0.7	0.8	1.3	•	3.1	4.3	•	•	•	•	•
Advertising	18	0.7	0.5	0.7	3.0	0.6	•	0.3	0.3	•	•	•	•	•
Other Expenses	19	28.0	34.5	26.2	16.5	31.0	•	10.5	36.3	•	•	•	•	•
Officers' Compensation	20	7.2	26.0	8.1	7.4	4.7	•	1.7	2.1	•	•	•	•	•
Operating Margin	21	9.3	25.4	10.8	9.1	4.3	•	7.4	4.3	•	•	•	•	•
Operating Margin Before Officers' Comp.	22	16.5	51.3	18.9	16.5	9.1	•	9.1	6.4	•	•	•	•	•

Selected Average Balance Sheet ($ in Thousands)													
Net Receivables **23**	23	0	10	90	296	•	2032	13263	•	•	•	•	•
Inventories **24**	9	0	3	88	81	•	429	1515	•	•	•	•	•
Net Property, Plant and Equipment **25**	57	0	16	12	464	•	2125	62274	•	•	•	•	•
Total Assets **26**	177	0	78	550	1799	•	12400	121441	•	•	•	•	•
Notes and Loans Payable **27**	61	0	48	73	1196	•	270	5448	•	•	•	•	•
All Other Liabilities **28**	71	0	12	303	656	•	1822	77029	•	•	•	•	•
Net Worth **29**	45	0	19	174	-53	•	10307	38964	•	•	•	•	•
Selected Financial Ratios (Times to 1)													
Current Ratio **30**	1.5	•	2.1	1.7	0.8	•	5.0	1.3	•	•	•	•	•
Quick Ratio **31**	1.2	•	1.9	0.8	0.6	•	4.0	0.9	•	•	•	•	•
Net Sales to Working Capital **32**	20.6	•	18.0	5.8	•	•	2.6	19.7	•	•	•	•	•
Coverage Ratio **33**	26.5	82.4	39.3	25.4	11.2	•	180.4	7.7	•	•	•	•	•
Total Asset Turnover **34**	3.3	•	6.4	2.2	2.3	•	1.0	1.3	•	•	•	•	•
Inventory Turnover **35**	21.0	•	63.8	5.1	21.0	•	12.8	13.6	•	•	•	•	•
Receivables Turnover **36**	27.3	•	58.4	7.8	23.1	•	4.2	•	•	•	•	•	•
Total Liabilities to Net Worth **37**	2.9	•	3.1	2.2	•	•	0.2	2.1	•	•	•	•	•
Current Assets to Working Capital **38**	3.0	•	1.9	2.5	•	•	1.3	4.2	•	•	•	•	•
Current Liabilities to Working Capital **39**	2.0	•	0.9	1.5	•	•	0.3	3.2	•	•	•	•	•
Working Capital to Net Sales **40**	0.0	•	0.1	0.2	•	•	0.4	0.1	•	•	•	•	•
Inventory to Working Capital **41**	0.3	•	0.1	0.8	•	•	0.0	0.2	•	•	•	•	•
Total Receipts to Cash Flow **42**	3.0	1.4	3.1	4.1	3.0	•	6.6	2.7	•	•	•	•	•
Cost of Goods to Cash Flow **43**	1.0	0.1	1.2	1.5	1.2	•	3.0	0.4	•	•	•	•	•
Cash Flow to Total Debt **44**	1.5	•	2.7	0.8	0.8	•	0.9	0.7	•	•	•	•	•
Selected Financial Factors (in Percentages)													
Debt Ratio **45**	74.4	•	75.7	68.4	103.0	•	16.9	67.9	•	•	•	•	•
Return on Total Assets **46**	34.2	•	70.8	21.3	12.5	•	7.8	7.8	•	•	•	•	•
Return on Equity Before Income Taxes **47**	128.3	•	283.8	64.7	•	•	9.3	21.0	•	•	•	•	•
Return on Equity After Income Taxes **48**	127.0	•	282.8	64.7	•	•	7.4	20.3	•	•	•	•	•
Profit Margin (Before Income Tax) **49**	10.0	40.4	10.8	9.1	4.9	•	7.8	5.3	•	•	•	•	•
Profit Margin (After Income Tax) **50**	9.9	40.0	10.8	9.1	4.8	•	6.2	5.1	•	•	•	•	•

Table I

Corporations with and without Net Income

Computer Systems Design and Related Services

Item Description for Accounting Period 7/11 Through 6/12		Money Amounts and Size of Assets in Thousands of Dollars												
		Total	Zero Assets	Under 500	500 to 1,000	1,000 to 5,000	5,000 to 10,000	10,000 to 25,000	25,000 to 50,000	50,000 to 100,000	100,000 to 250,000	250,000 to 500,000	500,000 to 2,500,000	2,500,000 and over
Number of Enterprises	1	139225	31815	93929	5028	5986	960	842	294	157	112	41	48	13
Revenues ($ in Thousands)														
Net Sales	2	262134754	13372649	33214587	11267661	29123328	15682054	21028777	13071959	12845223	15828475	10250748	42677820	43771473
Interest	3	709771	9974	15835	3127	10621	12966	10311	13531	15823	37729	24418	94624	460812
Rents	4	141108	54	43214	26	196	97	1580	102	5154	9227	1177	74512	5769
Royalties	5	1245633	30439	58	1463	7257	202	7510	71834	69695	94168	150773	166299	645936
Other Portfolio Income	6	1222463	325984	55896	1496	112892	39446	51612	23241	46653	20200	112732	75691	356618
Other Receipts	7	3264321	111795	242672	150315	311792	265077	333042	140178	339570	342144	124346	471524	431866
Total Receipts	8	268718050	13850895	33572262	11424088	29566086	15999842	21432832	13320845	13322118	16331943	10664194	43560470	45672474
Average Total Receipts	9	1930	435	357	2272	4939	16667	25455	45309	84854	145821	260102	907510	3513267
Operating Costs/Operating Income (%)														
Cost of Operations	10	30.4	17.6	23.6	23.6	31.8	40.0	42.7	37.0	42.4	40.3	32.5	46.6	5.9
Salaries and Wages	11	24.9	37.5	19.7	34.4	27.4	20.6	25.5	26.4	23.2	25.7	25.1	14.8	31.9
Taxes Paid	12	3.5	3.8	3.2	3.9	3.2	2.6	3.1	3.7	2.9	2.4	2.6	1.8	6.7
Interest Paid	13	1.8	1.1	0.4	0.9	0.8	0.5	0.6	1.0	0.8	1.3	1.9	2.6	4.9
Depreciation	14	2.0	1.8	0.9	0.8	1.2	1.1	1.7	1.9	2.5	2.2	1.9	2.6	3.6
Amortization and Depletion	15	1.2	0.8	0.1	0.5	0.4	0.7	0.7	0.9	1.0	1.5	2.2	2.1	2.1
Pensions and Other Deferred Comp.	16	0.8	0.3	1.0	0.5	0.8	0.5	0.6	0.7	0.3	0.3	0.4	0.6	1.7
Employee Benefits	17	2.6	2.0	1.6	1.8	2.7	2.3	2.2	2.7	2.0	1.9	2.3	2.8	4.3
Advertising	18	1.1	0.9	0.7	0.4	0.9	1.0	1.5	3.2	2.2	1.4	1.1	1.1	0.3
Other Expenses	19	27.4	32.9	27.9	25.4	23.8	27.6	21.9	23.7	23.2	22.8	30.5	22.2	39.3
Officers' Compensation	20	4.4	3.9	14.6	7.4	8.0	3.6	3.1	2.5	2.1	2.3	1.9	0.9	0.6
Operating Margin	21	•	•	6.4	0.5	•	•	•	•	•	•	•	1.7	•
Operating Margin Before Officers' Comp.	22	4.3	1.1	21.0	7.9	7.1	3.2	•	•	•	0.2	•	2.6	•

Selected Average Balance Sheet ($ in Thousands)

Net Receivables	23	450	0	10	192	742	2261	5143	9528	18441	33855	70091	166435	2262681
Inventories	24	15	0	2	18	50	168	285	558	1037	1269	3565	6623	15910
Net Property, Plant and Equipment	25	97	0	8	44	136	376	1104	2036	4395	7085	9996	66372	365855
Total Assets	26	1819	0	60	686	2128	7193	15339	33662	69745	159805	340246	1096927	8174632
Notes and Loans Payable	27	562	0	43	319	800	1200	2681	6047	13386	27210	85820	273686	3133775
All Other Liabilities	28	632	0	21	262	1029	3490	8405	17787	28153	57787	123703	348172	2324809
Net Worth	29	625	0	-4	104	299	2503	4253	9828	28206	74808	130723	475070	2716049

Selected Financial Ratios (Times to 1)

Current Ratio	30	1.3	•	1.5	1.8	1.6	1.7	1.4	1.4	1.5	1.5	1.1	1.6	1.0
Quick Ratio	31	1.1	•	1.3	1.5	1.3	1.5	1.2	1.1	1.2	1.2	0.9	1.3	0.9
Net Sales to Working Capital	32	10.5	•	24.8	10.1	8.3	7.0	8.6	8.2	6.4	5.5	23.4	7.0	31.7
Coverage Ratio	33	2.5	1.8	20.5	3.1	1.8	4.6	•	•	3.0	2.2	2.0	2.5	1.8
Total Asset Turnover	34	1.0	•	5.9	3.3	2.3	2.3	1.6	1.3	1.2	0.9	0.7	0.8	0.4
Inventory Turnover	35	38.3	•	51.7	29.4	30.9	39.0	37.5	29.5	33.4	44.8	22.8	62.6	12.4
Receivables Turnover	36	4.3	•	32.5	13.2	6.9	7.3	5.1	4.8	4.5	4.5	4.4	5.5	1.5
Total Liabilities to Net Worth	37	1.9	•	•	5.6	6.1	1.9	2.6	2.4	1.5	1.1	1.6	1.3	2.0
Current Assets to Working Capital	38	4.4	•	3.0	2.3	2.7	2.3	3.7	3.8	3.0	2.9	14.0	2.7	27.6
Current Liabilities to Working Capital	39	3.4	•	2.0	1.3	1.7	1.3	2.7	2.8	2.0	1.9	13.0	1.7	26.6
Working Capital to Net Sales	40	0.1	•	0.0	0.1	0.1	0.1	0.1	0.1	0.2	0.2	0.0	0.1	0.0
Inventory to Working Capital	41	0.1	•	0.1	0.1	0.1	0.1	0.1	0.1	0.1	0.1	0.4	0.1	0.3
Total Receipts to Cash Flow	42	3.7	3.4	3.1	4.0	4.7	3.7	5.6	5.0	4.5	4.6	3.5	4.2	2.5
Cost of Goods to Cash Flow	43	1.1	0.6	0.7	0.9	1.5	1.5	2.4	1.8	1.9	1.9	1.1	1.9	0.1
Cash Flow to Total Debt	44	0.4	•	1.8	1.0	0.6	0.9	0.4	0.4	0.4	0.4	0.3	0.3	0.2

Selected Financial Factors (in Percentages)

Debt Ratio	45	65.6	•	106.8	84.8	86.0	65.2	72.3	70.8	59.6	53.2	61.6	56.7	66.8
Return on Total Assets	46	4.6	•	46.3	9.3	3.3	4.8	•	•	2.7	2.5	2.7	5.4	3.7
Return on Equity Before Income Taxes	47	7.9	•	•	41.3	10.8	10.8	•	•	4.5	2.9	3.6	7.5	5.1
Return on Equity After Income Taxes	48	5.0	•	•	38.3	4.3	6.2	•	•	1.5	1.3	1.4	4.0	3.0
Profit Margin (Before Income Tax)	49	2.6	0.9	7.4	1.9	0.7	1.7	•	•	1.5	1.5	1.9	4.0	4.1
Profit Margin (After Income Tax)	50	1.6	•	7.3	1.8	0.3	1.0	•	•	0.5	0.7	0.8	2.1	2.4

Table II

Corporations with Net Income

COMPUTER SYSTEMS DESIGN AND RELATED SERVICES

MONEY AMOUNTS AND SIZE OF ASSETS IN THOUSANDS OF DOLLARS

Item Description for Accounting Period 7/11 Through 6/12		Total	Zero Assets	Under 500	500 to 1,000	1,000 to 5,000	5,000 to 10,000	10,000 to 25,000	25,000 to 50,000	50,000 to 100,000	100,000 to 250,000	250,000 to 500,000	500,000 to 2,500,000	2,500,000 and over
Number of Enterprises	1	86417	15053	62672	3603	3603	648	452	155	93	64	33	31	10
Revenues ($ in Thousands)														
Net Sales	2	206881597	9818804	28614943	9382207	22037860	12099441	14742285	9204078	9164068	10713157	7683629	34023478	39397647
Interest	3	228119	2119	9902	2582	3331	8745	3836	6011	6131	20356	19706	71796	73604
Rents	4	87316	3	1033	18	0	0	720	56	4792	6605	1079	70615	2396
Royalties	5	935246	28168	0	1463	0	0	3488	56040	10739	26308	150773	150043	508225
Other Portfolio Income	6	1016229	298752	50607	898	99910	39428	29752	18236	23558	14050	112655	73271	255112
Other Receipts	7	2429694	64697	210941	130470	182169	257620	300930	85674	310904	260269	80112	270384	275522
Total Receipts	8	211578201	10212543	28887426	9517638	22323270	12405234	15081011	9370095	9520192	11040745	8047954	34659587	40512506
Average Total Receipts	9	2448	678	461	2642	6196	19144	33365	60452	102368	172512	243877	1118051	4051251
Operating Costs/Operating Income (%)														
Cost of Operations	10	29.0	13.6	23.3	23.9	32.2	44.5	45.7	41.7	41.0	41.7	25.0	45.5	2.8
Salaries and Wages	11	23.4	37.9	18.7	33.7	23.6	19.9	19.7	22.6	20.1	22.1	24.9	13.5	32.8
Taxes Paid	12	3.6	4.0	2.9	3.8	2.9	2.6	2.8	3.0	2.8	2.2	2.8	1.8	7.2
Interest Paid	13	1.3	0.4	0.2	0.7	0.4	0.2	0.4	0.4	0.6	1.1	2.1	1.3	3.6
Depreciation	14	1.9	1.2	0.7	0.5	0.8	0.8	1.3	1.1	2.2	2.0	1.8	2.5	3.8
Amortization and Depletion	15	0.9	0.5	0.0	0.3	0.3	0.4	0.2	0.5	0.7	0.9	2.2	1.5	1.9
Pensions and Other Deferred Comp.	16	0.9	0.2	0.9	0.5	0.9	0.6	0.7	0.9	0.3	0.2	0.5	0.7	1.7
Employee Benefits	17	2.4	1.7	1.5	1.6	2.2	2.3	1.7	2.5	1.8	1.4	2.5	2.5	4.3
Advertising	18	0.7	0.7	0.5	0.3	0.7	0.8	1.1	1.8	2.2	1.2	1.1	0.4	0.3
Other Expenses	19	25.7	29.4	25.7	20.8	19.0	17.0	18.1	18.6	22.4	20.6	33.5	24.0	38.8
Officers' Compensation	20	4.2	3.0	13.8	7.2	8.2	3.4	2.8	2.1	2.0	1.4	1.5	0.8	0.6
Operating Margin	21	6.1	7.3	11.7	6.7	8.7	7.4	5.5	4.8	3.7	5.0	2.1	5.6	2.2
Operating Margin Before Officers' Comp.	22	10.3	10.4	25.5	13.9	16.9	10.8	8.3	6.9	5.7	6.5	3.6	6.4	2.8

Selected Average Balance Sheet ($ in Thousands)													
Net Receivables **23**	506	0	10	187	861	2656	6337	11595	20308	35033	67141	204962	2026913
Inventories **24**	17	0	2	17	62	161	293	790	1285	1517	2228	8216	29799
Net Property, Plant and Equipment **25**	117	0	9	45	85	350	985	1770	4988	6052	8932	78280	454548
Total Assets **26**	2011	0	69	691	2097	7158	15558	33688	71734	166024	340307	1196946	7688290
Notes and Loans Payable **27**	481	0	27	181	467	733	1919	5115	12361	31153	59199	270607	2191818
All Other Liabilities **28**	692	0	18	171	931	2967	7654	16039	25780	50399	116374	329730	2714783
Net Worth **29**	838	0	24	340	698	3458	5985	12534	33593	84472	164734	596609	2781689
Selected Financial Ratios (Times to 1)													
Current Ratio **30**	1.4	•	2.4	2.4	2.0	2.1	1.5	1.5	1.6	1.6	1.3	1.6	1.1
Quick Ratio **31**	1.2	•	2.1	2.1	1.7	1.8	1.4	1.3	1.2	1.2	1.1	1.3	0.9
Net Sales to Working Capital **32**	9.6	•	15.5	8.7	7.3	5.9	8.2	7.7	6.4	5.4	6.6	8.0	22.2
Coverage Ratio **33**	7.8	32.2	52.0	12.9	25.1	46.6	18.7	17.1	14.2	9.1	4.3	7.0	2.6
Total Asset Turnover **34**	1.2	•	6.7	3.8	2.9	2.6	2.1	1.8	1.4	1.0	0.7	0.9	0.5
Inventory Turnover **35**	40.9	•	49.3	36.1	32.0	51.6	50.9	31.3	31.5	46.0	26.1	60.7	3.7
Receivables Turnover **36**	4.7	•	50.2	15.5	7.3	7.4	5.3	•	4.7	4.8	4.7	5.3	•
Total Liabilities to Net Worth **37**	1.4	•	1.9	1.0	2.0	1.1	1.6	1.7	1.1	1.0	1.1	1.0	1.8
Current Assets to Working Capital **38**	3.5	•	1.7	1.7	2.0	1.9	2.9	2.8	2.7	2.6	4.0	2.8	15.4
Current Liabilities to Working Capital **39**	2.5	•	0.7	0.7	1.0	0.9	1.9	1.8	1.7	1.6	3.0	1.8	14.4
Working Capital to Net Sales **40**	0.1	•	0.1	0.1	0.1	0.2	0.1	0.1	0.2	0.2	0.2	0.1	0.0
Inventory to Working Capital **41**	0.1	•	0.1	0.1	0.1	0.1	0.1	0.1	0.1	0.1	0.1	0.1	0.2
Total Receipts to Cash Flow **42**	3.2	2.7	2.8	3.7	3.8	4.0	4.2	4.2	3.6	3.8	2.8	3.4	2.5
Cost of Goods to Cash Flow **43**	0.9	0.4	0.7	0.9	1.2	1.8	1.9	1.8	1.5	1.6	0.7	1.5	0.1
Cash Flow to Total Debt **44**	0.6	•	3.6	2.0	1.2	1.3	0.8	0.7	0.7	0.5	0.5	0.5	0.3
Selected Financial Factors (in Percentages)													
Debt Ratio **45**	58.3	•	65.2	50.8	66.7	51.7	61.5	62.8	53.2	49.1	51.6	50.2	63.8
Return on Total Assets **46**	11.7	•	85.9	33.5	30.4	26.6	17.3	12.5	11.7	9.7	6.3	8.3	4.8
Return on Equity Before Income Taxes **47**	24.5	•	242.0	62.8	87.7	53.9	42.5	31.6	23.3	16.9	9.9	14.3	8.0
Return on Equity After Income Taxes **48**	21.0	•	239.6	61.5	83.1	49.0	38.4	27.9	19.1	14.5	7.8	9.9	5.4
Profit Margin (Before Income Tax) **49**	8.6	11.3	12.6	8.2	10.0	10.0	7.8	6.7	7.9	8.5	7.0	7.8	5.7
Profit Margin (After Income Tax) **50**	7.3	9.5	12.5	8.0	9.5	9.1	7.0	5.9	6.5	7.3	5.5	5.4	3.8

Table I

Corporations with and without Net Income

MANAGEMENT, SCIENTIFIC, AND TECHNICAL CONSULTING SERVICES

Item Description for Accounting Period 7/11 Through 6/12		MONEY AMOUNTS AND SIZE OF ASSETS IN THOUSANDS OF DOLLARS												
		Total	Zero Assets	Under 500	500 to 1,000	1,000 to 5,000	5,000 to 10,000	10,000 to 25,000	25,000 to 50,000	50,000 to 100,000	100,000 to 250,000	250,000 to 500,000	500,000 to 2,500,000	2,500,000 and over
Number of Enterprises	1	226814	54110	158458	6647	5958	715	492	199	90	80	37	21	6
Revenues ($ in Thousands)														
Net Sales	2	210726235	4761258	51422191	23153746	27153969	8220437	9974876	9595629	5079565	10885833	17300791	16820023	26357919
Interest	3	351296	1026	6958	6365	27349	10079	26215	12963	10910	25317	38627	100986	84501
Rents	4	53356	541	1240	0	4874	2254	159	890	1585	15273	1088	4044	21407
Royalties	5	144783	0	1427	309	0	0	251	1	11	82725	9353	28315	22391
Other Portfolio Income	6	1108431	164773	35375	21961	50531	55433	50551	58675	63682	38648	200106	112625	256072
Other Receipts	7	4198998	113918	785544	417628	593390	216824	371178	120393	373090	324693	150024	388376	343937
Total Receipts	8	216583099	5041516	52252735	23600009	27830113	8505027	10423230	9788551	5528843	11372489	17699989	17454369	27086227
Average Total Receipts	9	955	93	330	3550	4671	11895	21185	49189	61432	142156	478378	831160	4514371
Operating Costs/Operating Income (%)														
Cost of Operations	10	30.3	11.1	21.1	49.0	29.4	24.9	46.2	26.7	21.8	39.2	54.6	26.7	17.8
Salaries and Wages	11	24.3	24.1	18.3	12.6	25.1	33.1	22.0	25.5	31.9	22.7	16.5	34.1	41.2
Taxes Paid	12	3.1	4.1	2.8	2.2	2.7	3.6	2.9	2.7	3.2	2.5	4.2	3.7	3.8
Interest Paid	13	0.8	0.7	0.4	0.2	0.5	0.3	0.9	1.0	1.6	1.7	1.2	2.0	0.8
Depreciation	14	1.4	2.9	1.0	0.5	1.2	1.0	1.4	1.9	4.1	2.7	1.4	1.8	1.5
Amortization and Depletion	15	0.4	0.3	0.0	0.1	0.5	0.1	0.6	0.9	0.7	1.3	0.7	1.4	0.3
Pensions and Other Deferred Comp.	16	1.4	3.6	1.3	1.1	0.7	1.1	1.2	0.4	1.6	0.8	0.7	1.4	3.4
Employee Benefits	17	2.1	2.6	1.6	0.6	1.6	2.9	2.1	3.0	8.2	2.7	3.6	3.0	1.4
Advertising	18	0.5	0.8	1.0	0.3	0.5	0.4	0.5	0.3	0.7	0.5	0.7	0.3	0.1
Other Expenses	19	24.3	31.2	29.3	21.7	25.8	20.8	16.6	24.1	28.0	24.4	14.5	24.4	23.9
Officers' Compensation	20	7.0	16.2	15.1	7.4	8.5	8.5	3.0	3.8	4.6	1.8	0.8	0.7	0.4
Operating Margin	21	4.3	2.5	8.0	4.5	3.4	3.4	2.6	9.6	•	•	1.0	0.6	5.5
Operating Margin Before Officers' Comp.	22	11.3	18.6	23.1	11.9	11.9	11.9	5.6	13.4	•	1.5	1.8	1.3	5.8

Selected Average Balance Sheet ($ in Thousands)														
Net Receivables	23	122	0	6	82	569	2147	3643	8789	12372	32944	46658	272438	1092964
Inventories	24	11	0	1	17	31	61	380	587	1185	1527	2145	52012	39383
Net Property, Plant and Equipment	25	47	0	8	174	233	834	1384	4378	7591	14619	20853	51389	160132
Total Assets	26	562	0	57	706	2119	7134	15846	35406	69919	151894	349480	1056339	4597915
Notes and Loans Payable	27	170	0	48	240	942	2307	3697	9974	21176	42034	78845	240260	819800
All Other Liabilities	28	222	0	17	176	550	2652	6173	10683	20631	51459	109256	404387	2948966
Net Worth	29	170	0	-9	289	627	2174	5975	14750	28112	58400	161380	411692	829149
Selected Financial Ratios (Times to 1)														
Current Ratio	30	1.5	•	1.7	2.3	1.8	1.9	1.4	1.7	1.5	1.3	1.8	1.5	1.0
Quick Ratio	31	1.1	•	1.5	2.0	1.5	1.4	1.1	1.3	1.1	1.1	1.1	1.1	0.9
Net Sales to Working Capital	32	11.0	•	21.4	16.4	8.2	5.5	8.9	6.9	5.7	8.3	6.9	5.4	128.3
Coverage Ratio	33	10.3	12.6	25.3	38.3	12.1	21.0	9.1	12.3	2.5	3.4	5.0	3.4	12.2
Total Asset Turnover	34	1.7	•	5.7	4.9	2.2	1.6	1.3	1.4	0.8	0.9	1.3	0.8	1.0
Inventory Turnover	35	26.1	•	65.7	100.6	42.7	46.6	24.7	21.9	10.4	34.9	118.9	4.1	19.9
Receivables Turnover	36	7.5	•	64.1	38.8	8.3	5.2	5.2	5.8	3.9	4.1	8.9	3.0	3.9
Total Liabilities to Net Worth	37	2.3	•	•	1.4	2.4	2.3	1.7	1.4	1.5	1.6	1.2	1.6	4.5
Current Assets to Working Capital	38	3.2	•	2.4	1.8	2.2	2.2	3.6	2.5	3.2	4.0	2.3	3.1	57.1
Current Liabilities to Working Capital	39	2.2	•	1.4	0.8	1.2	1.2	2.6	1.5	2.2	3.0	1.3	2.1	56.1
Working Capital to Net Sales	40	0.1	•	0.0	0.1	0.1	0.2	0.1	0.1	0.2	0.1	0.1	0.2	0.0
Inventory to Working Capital	41	0.1	•	0.1	0.1	0.1	0.0	0.2	0.1	0.1	0.1	0.0	0.4	0.8
Total Receipts to Cash Flow	42	3.6	3.0	2.8	4.0	3.8	4.2	4.7	3.1	4.1	4.0	6.2	4.1	3.5
Cost of Goods to Cash Flow	43	1.1	0.3	0.6	1.9	1.1	1.0	2.2	0.8	0.9	1.6	3.4	1.1	0.6
Cash Flow to Total Debt	44	0.7	•	1.7	2.1	0.8	0.6	0.4	0.7	0.3	0.4	0.4	0.3	0.3
Selected Financial Factors (in Percentages)														
Debt Ratio	45	69.8	•	115.3	59.0	70.4	69.5	62.3	58.3	59.8	61.6	53.8	61.0	82.0
Return on Total Assets	46	13.2	•	57.0	32.5	13.9	11.5	10.2	17.2	3.3	5.3	7.7	5.1	8.8
Return on Equity Before Income Taxes	47	39.5	•	•	77.1	43.0	36.0	24.1	38.0	4.8	9.7	13.3	9.2	44.6
Return on Equity After Income Taxes	48	34.7	•	•	75.6	40.7	32.9	22.1	35.4	2.2	7.8	8.5	6.1	30.2
Profit Margin (Before Income Tax)	49	7.2	8.3	9.6	6.4	5.9	6.8	7.1	11.6	2.4	4.2	4.6	4.7	8.4
Profit Margin (After Income Tax)	50	6.3	6.5	9.5	6.3	5.6	6.2	6.5	10.8	1.1	3.3	2.9	3.1	5.7

Table II

Corporations with Net Income

MANAGEMENT, SCIENTIFIC, AND TECHNICAL CONSULTING SERVICES

MONEY AMOUNTS AND SIZE OF ASSETS IN THOUSANDS OF DOLLARS

Item Description for Accounting Period 7/11 Through 6/12		Total	Zero Assets	Under 500	500 to 1,000	1,000 to 5,000	5,000 to 10,000	10,000 to 25,000	25,000 to 50,000	50,000 to 100,000	100,000 to 250,000	250,000 to 500,000	500,000 to 2,500,000	2,500,000 and over
Number of Enterprises	1	140250	22423	107462	4794	4505	486	297	124	49	59	•	17	•
Revenues ($ in Thousands)														
Net Sales	2	183814793	3494836	43051169	21865010	23306808	6789510	8157501	7339641	3710058	8879887	•	14923940	•
Interest	3	245120	240	1370	5866	22046	7398	22675	8637	2742	20281	•	95922	•
Rents	4	39095	372	9	0	2905	1177	140	872	1414	7081	•	2631	•
Royalties	5	121542	0	0	0	0	0	251	1	11	61762	•	27772	•
Other Portfolio Income	6	1043285	163014	24682	21681	47032	55301	42080	49767	54641	35623	•	105306	•
Other Receipts	7	3849013	203104	587671	404542	543956	196971	384161	116706	230343	305562	•	386698	•
Total Receipts	8	189112848	3861566	43664901	22297099	23922747	7050357	8606808	7515624	3999209	9310196	•	15542269	•
Average Total Receipts	9	1348	172	406	4651	5310	14507	28979	60610	81617	157800	•	914251	•
Operating Costs/Operating Income (%)														
Cost of Operations	10	31.2	6.8	21.3	51.5	27.4	17.7	50.7	27.4	23.1	44.0	•	28.7	•
Salaries and Wages	11	23.6	21.5	17.8	11.6	25.1	35.6	19.5	23.4	28.1	19.8	•	33.6	•
Taxes Paid	12	3.0	3.3	2.7	2.0	2.7	3.6	2.6	2.5	2.9	2.3	•	3.7	•
Interest Paid	13	0.6	0.4	0.3	0.1	0.4	0.2	0.6	0.6	1.0	1.4	•	1.7	•
Depreciation	14	1.1	0.7	0.8	0.4	1.0	0.6	1.1	1.2	2.1	2.5	•	1.6	•
Amortization and Depletion	15	0.3	0.0	0.0	0.0	0.2	0.0	0.3	0.5	0.7	1.1	•	1.2	•
Pensions and Other Deferred Comp.	16	1.4	4.1	1.0	1.0	0.7	1.2	1.2	0.5	2.0	0.9	•	1.1	•
Employee Benefits	17	2.0	1.4	1.5	0.5	1.5	2.8	1.7	3.0	10.3	2.4	•	2.6	•
Advertising	18	0.4	0.8	0.6	0.2	0.3	0.4	0.3	0.2	0.6	0.5	•	0.2	•
Other Expenses	19	22.3	24.6	26.9	20.1	24.5	20.5	12.6	19.0	22.0	21.6	•	23.7	•
Officers' Compensation	20	6.3	15.5	13.3	7.0	8.7	9.6	2.5	4.3	4.8	1.9	•	0.6	•
Operating Margin	21	7.7	20.9	13.9	5.6	7.4	7.8	6.9	17.5	2.4	1.5	•	1.3	•
Operating Margin Before Officers' Comp.	22	14.1	36.5	27.2	12.6	16.0	17.4	9.4	21.8	7.2	3.5	•	1.9	•

Selected Average Balance Sheet ($ in Thousands)

Net Receivables 23	166	0	5	86	579	2335	4206	9276	15655	33397	•	317929	•
Inventories 24	14	0	1	19	29	73	361	456	457	1523	•	60546	•
Net Property, Plant and Equipment 25	54	0	9	120	208	888	1451	4912	5078	15206	•	53534	•
Total Assets 26	683	0	59	707	2081	7499	16013	34653	69427	156100	•	1088538	•
Notes and Loans Payable 27	158	0	21	136	572	1521	3241	8620	13744	41978	•	224317	•
All Other Liabilities 28	240	0	13	165	569	2319	5758	10251	23005	51982	•	452638	•
Net Worth 29	284	0	25	406	940	3658	7013	15782	32678	62139	•	411582	•

Selected Financial Ratios (Times to 1)

Current Ratio 30	1.7	•	2.4	2.9	1.9	1.9	1.4	2.0	1.7	1.4	•	1.5	•
Quick Ratio 31	1.4	•	2.2	2.6	1.5	1.6	1.2	1.6	1.3	1.1	•	1.2	•
Net Sales to Working Capital 32	9.1	•	18.5	16.0	8.6	6.4	9.8	6.4	5.2	7.8	•	4.5	•
Coverage Ratio 33	18.6	73.0	61.2	89.7	25.7	63.7	22.1	34.0	11.4	5.5	•	4.4	•
Total Asset Turnover 34	1.9	•	6.8	6.5	2.5	1.9	1.7	1.7	1.1	1.0	•	0.8	•
Inventory Turnover 35	29.4	•	121.7	120.6	49.3	33.9	38.6	35.5	38.3	43.5	•	4.2	•
Receivables Turnover 36	8.0	•	80.6	53.4	11.0	5.5	5.6	6.3	4.0	4.5	•	3.0	•
Total Liabilities to Net Worth 37	1.4	•	1.4	0.7	1.2	1.0	1.3	1.2	1.1	1.5	•	1.6	•
Current Assets to Working Capital 38	2.5	•	1.7	1.5	2.1	2.1	3.2	2.0	2.5	3.7	•	2.8	•
Current Liabilities to Working Capital 39	1.5	•	0.7	0.5	1.1	1.1	2.2	1.0	1.5	2.7	•	1.8	•
Working Capital to Net Sales 40	0.1	•	0.1	0.1	0.1	0.2	0.1	0.2	0.2	0.1	•	0.2	•
Inventory to Working Capital 41	0.1	•	0.0	0.1	0.1	0.0	0.2	0.1	0.0	0.1	•	0.4	•
Total Receipts to Cash Flow 42	3.4	2.0	2.5	3.9	3.4	3.5	4.4	2.8	3.7	4.1	•	3.9	•
Cost of Goods to Cash Flow 43	1.1	0.1	0.5	2.0	0.9	0.6	2.2	0.8	0.9	1.8	•	1.1	•
Cash Flow to Total Debt 44	1.0	•	4.6	3.8	1.3	1.0	0.7	1.1	0.6	0.4	•	0.3	•

Selected Financial Factors (in Percentages)

Debt Ratio 45	58.4	•	57.8	42.6	54.8	51.2	56.2	54.5	52.9	60.2	•	62.2	•
Return on Total Assets 46	21.9	•	105.3	49.3	25.8	21.9	22.3	35.1	12.2	7.5	•	6.1	•
Return on Equity Before Income Taxes 47	49.8	•	245.6	85.0	54.9	44.3	48.6	74.8	23.7	15.5	•	12.4	•
Return on Equity After Income Taxes 48	45.2	•	244.0	83.5	52.9	41.5	45.8	71.0	19.5	13.1	•	8.7	•
Profit Margin (Before Income Tax) 49	10.8	31.4	15.3	7.6	10.0	11.6	12.4	19.9	10.2	6.4	•	5.8	•
Profit Margin (After Income Tax) 50	9.8	28.9	15.2	7.4	9.6	10.9	11.7	18.9	8.4	5.4	•	4.1	•

Table I

Corporations with and without Net Income

SCIENTIFIC RESEARCH AND DEVELOPMENT SERVICES

MONEY AMOUNTS AND SIZE OF ASSETS IN THOUSANDS OF DOLLARS

Item Description for Accounting Period 7/11 Through 6/12		Total	Zero Assets	Under 500	500 to 1,000	1,000 to 5,000	5,000 to 10,000	10,000 to 25,000	25,000 to 50,000	50,000 to 100,000	100,000 to 250,000	250,000 to 500,000	500,000 to 2,500,000	2,500,000 and over
Number of Enterprises	1	18345	4255	10201	871	1698	484	456	131	105	81	33	25	4
Revenues ($ in Thousands)														
Net Sales	2	48810506	1464739	3644298	1343204	3901848	2744746	3016878	2413255	2870368	3954821	4752809	14075494	4628047
Interest	3	215203	4861	2314	3228	5336	3937	16557	7586	16450	26764	33331	74220	20618
Rents	4	15607	536	6	0	2726	89	1928	1257	1193	4096	1995	1774	7
Royalties	5	1816116	29557	1111	0	5174	1784	16857	1995	150123	290906	56626	551665	710317
Other Portfolio Income	6	1195046	320106	16185	0	74968	97529	67228	7025	96969	80744	28439	369386	36471
Other Receipts	7	4014960	51269	168792	142503	238732	37784	329707	158024	427624	429863	206821	1568370	255468
Total Receipts	8	56067438	1871068	3832706	1488935	4228784	2885869	3449155	2589142	3562727	4787194	5080021	16640909	5650928
Average Total Receipts	9	3056	440	376	1709	2490	5963	7564	19764	33931	59101	153940	665636	1412732
Operating Costs/Operating Income (%)														
Cost of Operations	10	28.9	14.9	9.2	20.0	30.7	36.1	27.5	30.4	20.8	33.1	26.3	32.1	39.8
Salaries and Wages	11	31.3	76.4	24.1	35.1	35.9	31.3	45.5	36.6	37.2	38.8	31.7	21.1	26.5
Taxes Paid	12	3.3	4.9	2.8	4.6	4.1	4.5	5.4	4.4	4.6	3.7	2.9	2.0	2.3
Interest Paid	13	2.9	2.8	1.2	2.3	2.5	2.1	4.2	2.9	3.5	3.3	3.2	3.2	2.7
Depreciation	14	4.2	6.5	1.5	1.6	4.4	3.9	9.2	6.1	4.8	4.6	3.8	3.3	4.1
Amortization and Depletion	15	3.0	6.0	0.6	1.3	2.5	1.8	3.4	3.7	5.5	6.8	2.4	2.0	3.5
Pensions and Other Deferred Comp.	16	0.9	0.9	1.7	2.1	1.2	1.5	0.7	1.3	0.4	1.0	0.6	0.7	0.3
Employee Benefits	17	3.6	3.6	2.1	2.1	5.0	4.3	6.0	4.0	4.0	3.8	3.9	2.9	2.7
Advertising	18	1.8	0.9	3.8	1.7	0.7	1.0	1.5	1.0	3.0	2.0	1.9	1.9	1.7
Other Expenses	19	50.0	51.0	49.3	52.5	49.1	52.2	85.0	65.4	65.4	58.0	51.8	41.8	25.3
Officers' Compensation	20	5.8	25.0	9.9	15.3	12.6	7.2	9.8	6.8	5.5	5.6	3.2	1.3	0.7
Operating Margin	21	•	•	•	•	•	•	•	•	•	•	•	•	•
Operating Margin Before Officers' Comp.	22	•	•	3.9	•	•	•	•	•	•	•	•	•	•

Selected Average Balance Sheet ($ in Thousands)													
Net Receivables 23	625	0	22	112	333	779	1328	3002	6244	13982	32495	193837	375728
Inventories 24	181	0	2	26	116	510	427	1233	1688	2762	11106	37419	193028
Net Property, Plant and Equipment 25	550	0	20	97	324	872	2011	4726	4777	12477	33748	135685	319142
Total Assets 26	5522	0	102	782	2291	6915	15707	35552	68904	147980	350580	1141608	5300078
Notes and Loans Payable 27	1510	0	144	842	993	2457	3384	6692	12199	21407	87093	396933	1098098
All Other Liabilities 28	1848	0	69	384	986	2496	5965	12362	23465	45083	103357	354893	1811256
Net Worth 29	2164	0	-111	-444	312	1962	6357	16498	33240	81490	160130	389782	2390724

Selected Financial Ratios (Times to 1)													
Current Ratio 30	2.0	•	0.6	0.8	1.9	2.0	2.3	2.4	2.5	2.5	2.7	1.8	1.4
Quick Ratio 31	1.4	•	0.5	0.6	1.6	1.6	1.9	1.9	1.9	1.8	1.7	1.3	0.9
Net Sales to Working Capital 32	2.0	•	•	•	3.6	2.5	1.1	1.4	1.1	0.9	1.1	2.5	3.9
Coverage Ratio 33	•	•	0.3	•	•	•	•	•	•	•	•	3.5	6.3
Total Asset Turnover 34	0.5	•	3.5	2.0	1.0	0.8	0.4	0.5	0.4	0.3	0.4	0.5	0.2
Inventory Turnover 35	4.2	•	16.8	11.9	6.1	4.0	4.3	4.5	3.4	5.9	3.4	4.8	2.4
Receivables Turnover 36	4.9	•	27.9	11.2	6.4	6.6	5.5	4.9	4.7	3.9	5.5	3.5	4.0
Total Liabilities to Net Worth 37	1.6	•	•	•	6.3	2.5	1.5	1.2	1.1	0.8	1.2	1.9	1.2
Current Assets to Working Capital 38	2.0	•	•	•	2.2	2.0	1.7	1.7	1.6	1.7	1.6	2.2	3.3
Current Liabilities to Working Capital 39	1.0	•	•	•	1.2	1.0	0.7	0.7	0.6	0.7	0.6	1.2	2.3
Working Capital to Net Sales 40	0.5	•	•	•	0.3	0.4	0.9	0.7	0.9	1.1	0.9	0.4	0.3
Inventory to Working Capital 41	0.1	•	•	•	0.1	0.2	0.1	0.1	0.1	0.1	0.1	0.2	0.6
Total Receipts to Cash Flow 42	4.7	•	2.4	5.7	7711.2	93.5	•	42.3	4.0	9.8	4.8	2.4	3.1
Cost of Goods to Cash Flow 43	1.4	•	0.2	1.1	2369.6	33.7	•	12.8	0.8	3.2	1.3	0.8	1.2
Cash Flow to Total Debt 44	0.2	•	0.7	0.2	0.0	0.0	•	0.0	0.2	0.1	0.2	0.3	0.1

Selected Financial Factors (in Percentages)													
Debt Ratio 45	60.8	•	209.2	156.8	86.4	71.6	59.5	53.6	51.8	44.9	54.3	65.9	54.9
Return on Total Assets 46	•	•	1.4	•	•	•	•	•	•	•	•	5.5	3.8
Return on Equity Before Income Taxes 47	•	•	2.5	96.7	•	•	•	•	•	•	•	11.6	7.0
Return on Equity After Income Taxes 48	•	•	2.5	96.7	•	•	•	•	•	•	•	5.3	5.9
Profit Margin (Before Income Tax) 49	•	•	•	•	•	•	•	•	•	•	•	8.0	14.6
Profit Margin (After Income Tax) 50	•	•	•	•	•	•	•	•	•	•	•	3.7	12.1

Table II

Corporations with Net Income

SCIENTIFIC RESEARCH AND DEVELOPMENT SERVICES

MONEY AMOUNTS AND SIZE OF ASSETS IN THOUSANDS OF DOLLARS

Item Description for Accounting Period 7/11 Through 6/12		Total	Zero Assets	Under 500	500 to 1,000	1,000 to 5,000	5,000 to 10,000	10,000 to 25,000	25,000 to 50,000	50,000 to 100,000	100,000 to 250,000	250,000 to 500,000	500,000 to 2,500,000	2,500,000 and over
Number of Enterprises	1	7455	487	5774	226	602	149	99	39	28	21	12	16	0
Revenues ($ in Thousands)														
Net Sales	2	35085743	978420	3587621	403451	2486438	1841830	1617985	1890234	1551991	2001537	3084966	15641269	0
Interest	3	94377	2283	1688	51	1420	734	6994	2698	7038	4481	11111	55879	0
Rents	4	9175	536	0	0	2726	8	756	1035	0	2498	0	1615	0
Royalties	5	1492467	9037	0	0	2203	0	1112	1560	124128	134493	6770	1213163	0
Other Portfolio Income	6	1071347	305420	16185	0	72711	87462	17827	5924	91318	68454	5042	401005	0
Other Receipts	7	3055093	31755	162796	116747	158765	12288	125898	41495	369457	244475	14722	1776699	0
Total Receipts	8	40808202	1327451	3768290	520249	2724263	1942322	1770572	1942946	2143932	2455938	3122611	19089630	0
Average Total Receipts	9	5474	2726	653	2302	4525	13036	17885	49819	76569	116949	260218	1193102	•
Operating Costs/Operating Income (%)														
Cost of Operations	10	29.0	5.2	8.8	8.8	34.7	27.4	26.3	28.4	18.4	43.6	18.3	36.6	•
Salaries and Wages	11	22.0	56.9	21.9	30.8	20.7	18.2	26.8	22.2	27.1	19.5	23.2	19.4	•
Taxes Paid	12	2.5	4.3	2.4	3.7	2.9	3.4	3.2	2.9	3.1	2.7	2.5	2.0	•
Interest Paid	13	1.4	1.4	0.7	•	1.3	0.5	0.4	0.5	3.3	0.5	1.3	1.8	•
Depreciation	14	2.7	7.2	1.1	0.6	1.2	1.5	3.7	3.6	2.8	3.0	2.2	3.1	•
Amortization and Depletion	15	1.2	1.9	0.0	0.0	0.3	0.1	0.3	0.2	1.7	1.2	0.8	2.0	•
Pensions and Other Deferred Comp.	16	1.0	1.3	1.8	6.8	1.0	2.1	0.8	1.5	0.4	1.7	0.8	0.5	•
Employee Benefits	17	2.7	3.8	2.0	4.0	3.0	3.4	4.0	2.6	2.6	2.2	2.5	2.6	•
Advertising	18	1.6	0.3	3.8	0.2	0.4	0.5	0.5	0.7	0.7	1.2	1.9	1.7	•
Other Expenses	19	32.1	26.9	40.9	14.7	22.1	26.0	26.9	25.6	42.9	23.5	29.6	34.9	•
Officers' Compensation	20	3.5	0.6	9.5	17.9	10.6	4.3	4.0	3.5	3.0	2.7	1.8	1.1	•
Operating Margin	21	0.4	•	7.2	12.5	1.7	12.6	3.2	8.4	•	•	15.2	•	•
Operating Margin Before Officers' Comp.	22	3.9	•	16.8	30.3	12.3	17.0	7.1	11.8	•	0.8	17.0	•	•

Selected Average Balance Sheet ($ in Thousands)														
Net Receivables	23	877	0	30	88	547	1452	3016	7217	9344	21930	40036	251159	•
Inventories	24	276	0	3	0	125	1031	353	1859	2610	7290	10399	84397	•
Net Property, Plant and Equipment	25	574	0	29	83	329	1042	2244	7074	4787	15654	21669	157593	•
Total Assets	26	5874	0	129	909	2126	6995	15938	35619	69122	151440	374973	1745959	•
Notes and Loans Payable	27	1149	0	55	0	852	1058	1127	3909	8304	15909	62083	375052	•
All Other Liabilities	28	1993	0	12	56	838	2179	5840	11780	29626	39719	112008	618619	•
Net Worth	29	2733	0	62	852	437	3759	8971	19929	31192	95812	200883	752288	•

Selected Financial Ratios (Times to 1)														
Current Ratio	30	2.0	•	2.0	13.4	3.3	2.3	3.0	2.0	2.1	2.8	3.0	1.6	•
Quick Ratio	31	1.4	•	1.7	13.4	2.9	1.6	2.4	1.6	1.5	2.0	2.0	1.1	•
Net Sales to Working Capital	32	3.4	•	13.8	2.6	4.1	4.3	2.3	4.4	2.6	1.8	1.9	3.6	•
Coverage Ratio	33	14.1	20.1	19.4	•	9.8	41.2	31.5	23.6	10.9	43.1	13.7	11.3	•
Total Asset Turnover	34	0.8	•	4.8	2.0	1.9	1.8	1.0	1.4	0.8	0.6	0.7	0.6	•
Inventory Turnover	35	4.9	•	15.9	•	11.5	3.3	12.2	7.4	3.9	5.7	4.5	4.2	•
Receivables Turnover	36	6.0	•	38.6	6.3	7.1	7.6	6.0	6.6	6.5	3.7	10.4	4.6	•
Total Liabilities to Net Worth	37	1.1	•	1.1	0.1	3.9	0.9	0.8	0.8	1.2	0.6	0.9	1.3	•
Current Assets to Working Capital	38	2.0	•	2.0	1.1	1.4	1.7	1.5	2.0	1.9	1.6	1.5	2.6	•
Current Liabilities to Working Capital	39	1.0	•	1.0	0.1	0.4	0.7	0.5	1.0	0.9	0.6	0.5	1.6	•
Working Capital to Net Sales	40	0.3	•	0.1	0.4	0.2	0.2	0.4	0.2	0.4	0.6	0.5	0.3	•
Inventory to Working Capital	41	0.2	•	0.1	•	0.1	0.4	0.1	0.2	0.2	0.1	0.0	0.3	•
Total Receipts to Cash Flow	42	2.4	4.9	2.1	1.9	3.8	2.9	2.9	3.2	1.5	2.6	2.4	2.1	•
Cost of Goods to Cash Flow	43	0.7	0.3	0.2	0.2	1.3	0.8	0.8	0.9	0.3	1.1	0.4	0.8	•
Cash Flow to Total Debt	44	0.6	•	4.3	16.3	0.6	1.3	0.8	1.0	0.9	0.7	0.6	0.5	•

Selected Financial Factors (in Percentages)														
Debt Ratio	45	53.5	•	51.9	6.2	79.5	46.3	43.7	44.0	54.9	36.7	46.4	56.9	•
Return on Total Assets	46	15.4	•	62.3	81.4	24.3	32.8	13.3	15.9	28.5	13.4	12.6	11.5	•
Return on Equity Before Income Taxes	47	30.7	•	122.9	86.7	106.1	59.5	22.9	27.1	57.4	20.7	21.7	24.2	•
Return on Equity After Income Taxes	48	25.9	•	122.8	86.7	101.6	54.6	20.2	22.1	50.0	19.0	20.1	18.2	•
Profit Margin (Before Income Tax)	49	17.8	26.5	12.3	41.4	11.2	18.1	12.6	11.2	32.3	20.8	17.0	18.7	•
Profit Margin (After Income Tax)	50	15.0	24.6	12.3	41.4	10.7	16.6	11.1	9.1	28.1	19.1	15.7	14.0	•

Table I

Corporations with and without Net Income

ADVERTISING AND RELATED SERVICES

Item Description for Accounting Period 7/11 Through 6/12		MONEY AMOUNTS AND SIZE OF ASSETS IN THOUSANDS OF DOLLARS												
		Total	Zero Assets	Under 500	500 to 1,000	1,000 to 5,000	5,000 to 10,000	10,000 to 25,000	25,000 to 50,000	50,000 to 100,000	100,000 to 250,000	250,000 to 500,000	500,000 to 2,500,000	2,500,000 and over
Number of Enterprises	1	49740	10800	34880	1325	2010	359	191	65	44	32	12	14	6
Revenues ($ in Thousands)														
Net Sales	2	91904628	714015	17485785	4023726	10124251	8006024	4648039	3529070	3118625	7174990	3038561	8674008	21367533
Interest	3	881654	997	4025	53	3531	4251	3091	2929	1651	5544	6931	28886	819765
Rents	4	126020	0	2485	1886	343	0	68	654	96	13259	339	5023	101867
Royalties	5	89136	0	0	0	0	0	0	38793	22361	65	5074	19704	3138
Other Portfolio Income	6	457113	0	4833	8	4272	836	6176	2758	16963	2651	730	15470	402417
Other Receipts	7	1677114	21823	43422	12062	85584	90471	42707	179113	50410	135542	12167	472521	531293
Total Receipts	8	95135665	736835	17540550	4037735	10217981	8101582	4700081	3753317	3210106	7332051	3063802	9215612	23226013
Average Total Receipts	9	1913	68	503	3047	5084	22567	24608	57743	72957	229127	255317	658258	3871002
Operating Costs/Operating Income (%)														
Cost of Operations	10	37.6	32.7	33.8	61.9	40.4	63.7	62.0	60.9	51.8	64.2	51.4	30.3	6.1
Salaries and Wages	11	21.1	13.3	10.3	7.2	18.2	5.9	17.2	17.1	21.2	13.8	19.4	22.3	43.3
Taxes Paid	12	2.4	2.5	1.9	1.6	2.5	0.8	1.8	2.1	1.8	1.4	2.1	3.0	4.0
Interest Paid	13	3.3	0.5	0.3	0.5	0.5	0.2	0.7	0.9	1.3	0.9	2.3	6.7	9.8
Depreciation	14	1.8	2.9	0.9	0.9	0.9	0.4	0.8	1.7	2.0	1.6	2.1	3.7	3.2
Amortization and Depletion	15	1.4	0.4	0.1	0.1	0.3	0.2	0.6	1.3	1.8	1.2	1.2	4.2	2.8
Pensions and Other Deferred Comp.	16	0.6	0.2	0.9	0.3	0.6	0.2	0.4	0.3	0.2	0.3	0.5	0.3	1.0
Employee Benefits	17	1.4	0.6	0.7	0.6	1.3	0.4	1.3	1.2	1.1	0.9	1.3	2.4	2.3
Advertising	18	4.0	3.7	6.6	3.9	1.6	15.6	1.5	5.6	1.2	0.7	0.5	5.3	0.3
Other Expenses	19	22.2	47.0	25.3	15.4	27.8	8.7	12.1	11.2	19.1	15.7	16.8	23.5	29.5
Officers' Compensation	20	5.0	4.9	13.5	6.4	5.5	2.5	3.3	2.5	2.6	1.1	1.6	1.2	3.2
Operating Margin	21	•	•	5.6	1.0	0.4	1.5	•	•	•	•	0.8	•	•
Operating Margin Before Officers' Comp.	22	4.1	•	19.1	7.4	5.9	3.9	1.6	•	•	•	2.4	•	•

Selected Average Balance Sheet ($ in Thousands)

Net Receivables	23	428	0	12	162	841	2713	6398	10146	19875	31769	55814	181172	1840521
Inventories	24	36	0	1	25	149	394	286	794	475	2633	3960	8910	145651
Net Property, Plant and Equipment	25	133	0	13	197	291	282	1263	6276	3459	9765	20981	84615	445804
Total Assets	26	2471	0	59	663	2250	7114	15282	37629	69754	149023	326777	1295117	12935804
Notes and Loans Payable	27	606	0	75	284	1059	882	2099	11207	10628	33367	77513	615474	2079614
All Other Liabilities	28	1100	0	22	225	1333	4636	9564	13953	35102	59534	126986	396256	6007223
Net Worth	29	765	0	-37	154	-143	1596	3620	12468	24023	56122	122277	283388	4848967

Selected Financial Ratios (Times to 1)

Current Ratio	30	0.9	•	1.2	1.3	1.5	1.4	1.3	1.5	1.3	1.3	0.9	1.1	0.7
Quick Ratio	31	0.7	•	1.1	1.2	1.3	1.2	1.2	1.2	1.0	1.0	0.7	0.7	0.5
Net Sales to Working Capital	32	•	•	86.4	36.5	9.2	13.3	9.3	7.8	6.6	15.6	•	21.6	•
Coverage Ratio	33	1.8	•	18.6	3.7	3.6	16.0	0.2	2.7	0.1	1.2	1.9	1.5	1.4
Total Asset Turnover	34	0.7	•	8.5	4.6	2.2	3.1	1.6	1.4	1.0	1.5	0.8	0.5	0.3
Inventory Turnover	35	19.5	•	142.9	76.6	13.6	36.0	52.8	41.7	77.2	54.6	32.9	21.0	1.5
Receivables Turnover	36	4.8	•	39.9	24.8	7.0	8.1	4.3	5.2	4.0	7.1	5.3	4.0	2.1
Total Liabilities to Net Worth	37	2.2	•	•	3.3	•	3.5	3.2	2.0	1.9	1.7	1.7	3.6	1.7
Current Assets to Working Capital	38	•	•	5.9	4.4	3.0	3.6	4.6	3.1	4.3	4.9	•	12.6	•
Current Liabilities to Working Capital	39	•	•	4.9	3.4	2.0	2.6	3.6	2.1	3.3	3.9	•	11.6	•
Working Capital to Net Sales	40	•	•	0.0	0.0	0.1	0.1	0.1	0.1	0.2	0.1	•	0.0	•
Inventory to Working Capital	41	•	•	0.2	0.1	0.3	0.2	0.2	0.1	0.0	0.2	•	0.3	•
Total Receipts to Cash Flow	42	4.8	3.0	3.7	8.0	4.0	10.6	11.5	10.2	6.4	6.9	6.3	4.1	3.9
Cost of Goods to Cash Flow	43	1.8	1.0	1.3	4.9	1.6	6.7	7.1	6.2	3.3	4.4	3.2	1.2	0.2
Cash Flow to Total Debt	44	0.2	•	1.4	0.7	0.5	0.4	0.2	0.2	0.2	0.3	0.2	0.1	0.1

Selected Financial Factors (in Percentages)

Debt Ratio	45	69.0	•	163.0	76.8	106.3	77.6	76.3	66.9	65.6	62.3	62.6	78.1	62.5
Return on Total Assets	46	4.6	•	53.0	8.8	4.0	8.8	0.2	3.4	0.2	1.7	3.3	4.8	3.8
Return on Equity Before Income Taxes	47	6.8	•	•	27.5	•	36.9	•	6.5	•	0.8	4.2	7.4	2.9
Return on Equity After Income Taxes	48	5.2	•	•	18.6	•	34.3	•	5.4	•	•	3.2	4.0	1.7
Profit Margin (Before Income Tax)	49	2.8	•	5.9	1.4	1.3	2.6	•	1.5	•	0.2	2.0	3.4	3.9
Profit Margin (After Income Tax)	50	2.1	•	5.9	0.9	1.1	2.5	•	1.2	•	•	1.5	1.8	2.3

Table II

Corporations with Net Income

ADVERTISING AND RELATED SERVICES

MONEY AMOUNTS AND SIZE OF ASSETS IN THOUSANDS OF DOLLARS

Item Description for Accounting Period 7/11 Through 6/12		Total	Zero Assets	Under 500	500 to 1,000	1,000 to 5,000	5,000 to 10,000	10,000 to 25,000	25,000 to 50,000	50,000 to 100,000	100,000 to 250,000	250,000 to 500,000	500,000 to 2,500,000	2,500,000 and over
Number of Enterprises	1	29843	4320	23158	742	1132	286	107	40	23	15	•	8	•
Revenues ($ in Thousands)														
Net Sales	2	68118844	302095	12786696	3423457	6364146	7498151	2656326	2361866	1596786	5444807	•	4393653	•
Interest	3	835685	19	1260	22	2743	3242	2333	721	721	2022	•	16760	•
Rents	4	112420	0	2485	1886	123	0	0	0	53	1707	•	5023	•
Royalties	5	69601	0	0	0	0	0	0	38793	19736	6	•	4368	•
Other Portfolio Income	6	418004	0	3086	8	4271	584	1809	274	179	1706	•	3175	•
Other Receipts	7	1345041	19733	10247	18497	61623	88066	27051	176595	36369	26386	•	373627	•
Total Receipts	8	70899595	321847	12803774	3443870	6432906	7590043	2687519	2578249	1653844	5476634	•	4796606	•
Average Total Receipts	9	2376	75	553	4641	5683	26539	25117	64456	71906	365109	•	599576	•
Operating Costs/Operating Income (%)														
Cost of Operations	10	39.5	30.7	39.8	68.2	41.4	63.9	59.3	71.3	51.0	71.8	•	34.8	•
Salaries and Wages	11	22.0	6.7	12.2	6.0	17.5	4.6	16.5	9.5	22.7	10.0	•	29.3	•
Taxes Paid	12	2.5	1.6	2.1	1.2	2.6	0.7	1.9	1.3	1.9	1.1	•	3.8	•
Interest Paid	13	3.2	0.0	0.4	0.1	0.2	0.1	0.2	0.8	1.0	0.5	•	4.2	•
Depreciation	14	1.2	3.1	0.6	0.4	0.6	0.2	0.6	0.8	1.9	0.6	•	2.5	•
Amortization and Depletion	15	0.9	0.0	0.1	0.0	0.1	0.0	0.2	0.5	0.5	0.7	•	2.7	•
Pensions and Other Deferred Comp.	16	0.6	•	0.3	0.2	0.8	0.2	0.6	0.4	0.3	0.4	•	0.4	•
Employee Benefits	17	1.3	0.4	0.7	0.3	1.4	0.3	1.3	0.9	1.2	0.7	•	3.1	•
Advertising	18	2.9	0.1	1.3	2.8	1.8	16.6	1.5	7.9	0.2	0.2	•	1.5	•
Other Expenses	19	18.8	29.7	24.5	10.7	18.0	7.5	7.4	5.8	12.3	10.4	•	14.2	•
Officers' Compensation	20	4.0	3.5	7.7	4.4	7.0	2.5	3.5	2.2	2.8	0.7	•	1.2	•
Operating Margin	21	3.1	24.3	10.4	5.7	8.6	3.4	7.1	•	4.2	2.8	•	2.3	•
Operating Margin Before Officers' Comp.	22	7.1	27.7	18.1	10.1	15.6	5.9	10.6	0.7	7.0	3.6	•	3.5	•

Selected Average Balance Sheet ($ in Thousands)													
Net Receivables **23**	588	0	8	231	1059	2877	5972	9595	22577	40011	•	230663	•
Inventories **24**	49	0	1	27	154	458	80	1138	702	5309	•	9636	•
Net Property, Plant and Equipment **25**	100	0	13	56	167	273	1231	5338	2881	7900	•	33635	•
Total Assets **26**	3283	0	59	622	2240	7188	14836	34919	68045	141152	•	1375520	•
Notes and Loans Payable **27**	533	0	71	132	173	684	577	9383	9452	23923	•	475612	•
All Other Liabilities **28**	1566	0	19	284	1138	4193	9892	12996	38678	78359	•	453914	•
Net Worth **29**	1185	0	-31	207	929	2311	4367	12540	19915	38869	•	445995	•
Selected Financial Ratios (Times to 1)													
Current Ratio **30**	0.9	•	1.2	1.6	1.6	1.5	1.2	1.5	1.3	1.0	•	1.2	•
Quick Ratio **31**	0.7	•	1.1	1.6	1.4	1.3	1.2	1.2	0.9	0.7	•	0.8	•
Net Sales to Working Capital **32**	•	•	84.5	24.5	8.3	13.7	11.1	7.8	6.0	•	•	8.4	•
Coverage Ratio **33**	3.3	2216.5	29.4	58.7	43.8	49.9	53.2	10.1	8.4	7.7	•	3.7	•
Total Asset Turnover **34**	0.7	•	9.4	7.4	2.5	3.6	1.7	1.7	1.0	2.6	•	0.4	•
Inventory Turnover **35**	18.4	•	399.9	115.3	15.1	36.5	184.2	37.0	50.4	49.1	•	19.8	•
Receivables Turnover **36**	4.2	•	68.8	27.6	6.3	10.1	4.3	6.1	2.9	•	•	2.7	•
Total Liabilities to Net Worth **37**	1.8	•	•	2.0	1.4	2.1	2.4	1.8	2.4	2.6	•	2.1	•
Current Assets to Working Capital **38**	•	•	5.5	2.6	2.7	3.2	5.1	2.9	4.4	•	•	7.0	•
Current Liabilities to Working Capital **39**	•	•	4.5	1.6	1.7	2.2	4.1	1.9	3.4	•	•	6.0	•
Working Capital to Net Sales **40**	•	•	0.0	0.0	0.1	0.1	0.1	0.1	0.2	•	•	0.1	•
Inventory to Working Capital **41**	•	•	0.1	0.0	0.2	0.2	0.0	0.2	0.1	•	•	0.1	•
Total Receipts to Cash Flow **42**	4.6	2.0	3.3	7.1	4.1	9.7	8.0	8.7	5.7	7.8	•	4.4	•
Cost of Goods to Cash Flow **43**	1.8	0.6	1.3	4.9	1.7	6.2	4.7	6.2	2.9	5.6	•	1.5	•
Cash Flow to Total Debt **44**	0.2	•	1.8	1.6	1.0	0.6	0.3	0.3	0.3	0.5	•	0.1	•
Selected Financial Factors (in Percentages)													
Debt Ratio **45**	63.9	•	153.6	66.7	58.5	67.9	70.6	64.1	70.7	72.5	•	67.6	•
Return on Total Assets **46**	7.4	•	102.1	47.2	24.8	17.2	14.0	14.4	9.0	10.0	•	6.3	•
Return on Equity Before Income Taxes **47**	14.3	•	•	139.5	58.4	52.4	46.8	36.0	27.0	31.5	•	14.2	•
Return on Equity After Income Taxes **48**	12.5	•	•	127.7	56.8	50.1	45.8	34.2	23.2	24.2	•	10.4	•
Profit Margin (Before Income Tax) **49**	7.4	30.8	10.5	6.3	9.7	4.6	8.2	7.7	7.7	3.4	•	11.5	•
Profit Margin (After Income Tax) **50**	6.5	30.5	10.4	5.7	9.4	4.4	8.0	7.3	6.7	2.6	•	8.4	•

OTHER PROFESSIONAL, SCIENTIFIC, AND TECHNICAL SERVICES

Item Description for Accounting Period 7/11 Through 6/12		MONEY AMOUNTS AND SIZE OF ASSETS IN THOUSANDS OF DOLLARS												
		Total	Zero Assets	Under 500	500 to 1,000	1,000 to 5,000	5,000 to 10,000	10,000 to 25,000	25,000 to 50,000	50,000 to 100,000	100,000 to 250,000	250,000 to 500,000	500,000 to 2,500,000	2,500,000 and over
Number of Enterprises	1	98673	16822	75105	3665	2403	257	221	78	60	28	13	16	3
Revenues ($ in Thousands)														
Net Sales	2	90927053	2142125	33825678	6791945	6582978	2509006	5922557	3924934	4512571	3401249	3469837	14332337	3511837
Interest	3	110893	1011	5129	774	5944	3161	2516	5639	6317	11466	3521	25926	39489
Rents	4	44032	0	2028	0	288	328	153	54	1244	53	0	39884	0
Royalties	5	871156	1	14152	0	0	0	18	34043	104	685	998	221281	599875
Other Portfolio Income	6	163712	52932	16812	5708	1911	23280	1329	10121	7129	7860	3785	9999	22849
Other Receipts	7	1133695	100559	222478	-21512	31718	64195	290140	53871	83107	62532	3235	223641	19725
Total Receipts	8	93250541	2296628	34086277	6776915	6622839	2599970	6216713	4028662	4610472	3483845	3481376	14853068	4193775
Average Total Receipts	9	945	137	454	1849	2756	10117	28130	51650	76841	124423	267798	928317	1397925
Operating Costs/Operating Income (%)														
Cost of Operations	10	26.5	14.6	19.7	39.4	30.1	46.5	44.9	56.8	36.8	23.8	31.1	19.9	1.3
Salaries and Wages	11	21.3	20.9	19.2	16.2	21.1	14.9	19.6	16.5	24.2	29.5	18.7	27.3	31.5
Taxes Paid	12	3.1	3.0	3.4	3.8	2.4	2.2	2.7	2.4	3.1	3.2	2.4	3.1	2.6
Interest Paid	13	2.0	1.4	0.6	0.6	1.2	0.8	0.8	0.7	2.3	2.2	1.9	2.9	18.7
Depreciation	14	2.2	2.2	1.7	2.0	1.1	2.0	2.7	1.9	2.9	4.4	1.6	2.1	6.6
Amortization and Depletion	15	1.2	0.4	0.3	0.5	0.5	0.3	0.4	0.4	1.2	2.8	4.3	3.5	2.9
Pensions and Other Deferred Comp.	16	0.9	0.4	0.8	1.0	1.4	0.4	0.6	1.0	0.9	0.7	1.0	1.3	1.6
Employee Benefits	17	2.4	2.0	1.1	1.3	1.2	5.5	1.5	1.6	2.6	1.6	3.5	6.5	2.8
Advertising	18	0.8	0.8	1.0	0.3	0.8	1.3	0.5	0.6	1.1	1.3	0.3	0.5	0.2
Other Expenses	19	29.5	37.1	30.7	21.0	27.3	21.9	21.6	16.1	23.9	30.3	29.5	32.7	60.5
Officers' Compensation	20	6.8	12.7	11.2	8.3	10.0	5.1	4.0	2.0	3.0	1.9	1.6	1.2	0.6
Operating Margin	21	3.3	4.3	10.3	5.5	2.7	•	0.8	0.1	•	•	4.2	•	•
Operating Margin Before Officers' Comp.	22	10.1	17.0	21.5	13.8	12.7	4.2	4.9	2.1	1.0	0.2	5.7	0.2	•

Selected Average Balance Sheet ($ in Thousands)													
Net Receivables 23	111	0	8	133	401	1432	3470	9663	13264	33631	77831	178017	465880
Inventories 24	12	0	4	17	31	164	612	667	1274	6356	6190	7992	7000
Net Property, Plant and Equipment 25	69	0	23	196	222	582	1942	5023	7181	15238	21773	76921	170290
Total Assets 26	797	0	96	720	1957	7609	15176	34751	70759	165756	365763	1068520	8450697
Notes and Loans Payable 27	226	0	46	271	484	4320	3672	6985	21383	66167	74413	364229	1443032
All Other Liabilities 28	316	0	29	168	902	2213	5309	12338	19963	50438	105773	423217	4255387
Net Worth 29	256	0	22	281	571	1076	6195	15427	29413	49151	185576	281074	2752279
Selected Financial Ratios (Times to 1)													
Current Ratio 30	1.2	•	1.7	1.2	1.7	0.9	1.6	1.6	1.3	0.8	2.4	1.1	0.6
Quick Ratio 31	0.9	•	1.4	1.0	1.4	0.7	1.2	1.3	1.0	0.6	2.0	0.8	0.3
Net Sales to Working Capital 32	23.5	•	22.6	37.1	6.0	•	7.9	6.5	10.0	•	2.9	24.2	•
Coverage Ratio 33	4.1	9.0	18.4	9.2	3.9	4.2	8.3	4.9	1.1	1.5	3.4	1.9	0.6
Total Asset Turnover 34	1.2	•	4.7	2.6	1.4	1.3	1.8	1.4	1.1	0.7	0.7	0.8	0.1
Inventory Turnover 35	20.8	•	21.6	43.7	26.3	27.7	19.7	42.9	21.7	4.6	13.4	22.3	2.2
Receivables Turnover 36	8.6	•	56.6	18.3	5.8	8.0	7.7	5.3	6.2	3.4	3.2	5.8	2.6
Total Liabilities to Net Worth 37	2.1	•	3.4	1.6	2.4	6.1	1.4	1.3	1.4	2.4	1.0	2.8	2.1
Current Assets to Working Capital 38	6.8	•	2.5	6.2	2.4	•	2.6	2.6	4.0	•	1.7	9.8	•
Current Liabilities to Working Capital 39	5.8	•	1.5	5.2	1.4	•	1.6	1.6	3.0	•	0.7	8.8	•
Working Capital to Net Sales 40	0.0	•	0.0	0.0	0.2	•	0.1	0.2	0.1	•	0.4	0.0	•
Inventory to Working Capital 41	0.3	•	0.2	0.6	0.0	•	0.2	0.1	0.1	•	0.1	0.3	•
Total Receipts to Cash Flow 42	3.3	2.3	2.8	4.7	3.7	4.8	4.7	6.0	4.8	3.7	3.2	3.1	2.2
Cost of Goods to Cash Flow 43	0.9	0.3	0.6	1.9	1.1	2.2	2.1	3.4	1.8	0.9	1.0	0.6	0.0
Cash Flow to Total Debt 44	0.5	•	2.1	0.9	0.5	0.3	0.6	0.4	0.4	0.3	0.5	0.4	0.1
Selected Financial Factors (in Percentages)													
Debt Ratio 45	68.0	•	77.2	60.9	70.8	85.9	59.2	55.6	58.4	70.3	49.3	73.7	67.4
Return on Total Assets 46	9.2	•	54.6	15.2	6.2	4.5	11.6	4.9	2.8	2.3	4.7	4.7	1.7
Return on Equity Before Income Taxes 47	21.6	•	226.4	34.6	15.8	24.6	25.1	8.7	0.9	2.4	6.5	8.7	•
Return on Equity After Income Taxes 48	19.7	•	224.5	33.6	14.9	19.4	23.0	5.6	•	•	6.0	5.0	•
Profit Margin (Before Income Tax) 49	6.0	11.5	11.1	5.2	3.3	2.7	5.8	2.7	0.3	1.0	4.5	2.7	•
Profit Margin (After Income Tax) 50	5.5	11.0	11.0	5.1	3.1	2.1	5.3	1.7	•	•	4.2	1.6	•

Table II

Corporations with Net Income

OTHER PROFESSIONAL, SCIENTIFIC, AND TECHNICAL SERVICES

MONEY AMOUNTS AND SIZE OF ASSETS IN THOUSANDS OF DOLLARS

Item Description for Accounting Period 7/11 Through 6/12		Total	Zero Assets	Under 500	500 to 1,000	1,000 to 5,000	5,000 to 10,000	10,000 to 25,000	25,000 to 50,000	50,000 to 100,000	100,000 to 250,000	250,000 to 500,000	500,000 to 2,500,000	2,500,000 and over
Number of Enterprises	1	63529	7764	51620	2374	1367	143	137	50	36	•	•	13	0
Revenues ($ in Thousands)														
Net Sales	2	71402458	1513653	28090348	5274697	4921876	1683054	4896210	3017544	2880567	•	•	14123499	0
Interest	3	77314	199	1452	576	2988	2941	2009	1122	4170	•	•	54444	0
Rents	4	35720	0	1174	0	288	328	70	0	1147	•	•	32661	0
Royalties	5	265582	0	14152	0	0	0	18	34043	104	•	•	215787	0
Other Portfolio Income	6	127579	52932	7346	5564	1297	15341	736	6501	4232	•	•	27020	0
Other Receipts	7	848940	2698	170008	21822	31014	82921	216398	45856	71014	•	•	179686	0
Total Receipts	8	72757593	1569482	28284480	5302659	4957463	1784585	5115441	3105066	2961234	•	•	14633097	0
Average Total Receipts	9	1145	202	548	2234	3627	12480	37339	62101	82256	•	•	1125623	•
Operating Costs/Operating Income (%)														
Cost of Operations	10	24.2	11.0	19.0	36.8	34.0	34.9	48.4	59.7	23.9	•	•	11.3	•
Salaries and Wages	11	20.6	17.4	18.5	16.6	17.6	15.8	18.1	14.4	25.1	•	•	28.5	•
Taxes Paid	12	2.9	3.0	3.1	3.8	2.1	2.1	2.5	2.2	3.2	•	•	3.1	•
Interest Paid	13	1.7	0.3	0.5	0.7	0.6	0.3	0.5	0.4	2.7	•	•	5.6	•
Depreciation	14	1.9	1.2	1.2	1.4	0.9	1.3	2.1	1.0	2.5	•	•	3.3	•
Amortization and Depletion	15	0.8	0.0	0.3	0.2	0.3	0.2	0.4	0.2	0.9	•	•	2.2	•
Pensions and Other Deferred Comp.	16	0.9	0.5	0.9	1.3	1.0	0.5	0.5	1.0	1.1	•	•	1.0	•
Employee Benefits	17	2.5	1.7	1.0	1.5	1.4	6.9	1.4	1.3	2.5	•	•	6.6	•
Advertising	18	0.7	0.7	0.9	0.3	0.6	1.7	0.2	0.6	1.5	•	•	0.5	•
Other Expenses	19	28.0	25.9	29.2	23.3	23.8	22.4	15.6	12.4	28.3	•	•	36.3	•
Officers' Compensation	20	6.4	15.2	11.1	5.7	5.8	5.9	3.7	1.3	2.9	•	•	1.1	•
Operating Margin	21	9.3	23.1	14.2	8.6	11.9	8.0	6.7	5.5	5.5	•	•	0.4	•
Operating Margin Before Officers' Comp.	22	15.7	38.3	25.4	14.3	17.8	13.9	10.3	6.7	8.4	•	•	1.5	•

Selected Average Balance Sheet ($ in Thousands)													
Net Receivables	23	109	0	10	192	395	1070	4512	10683	13545	•	•	173256	•
Inventories	24	11	0	5	24	28	266	608	479	1512	•	•	9608	•
Net Property, Plant and Equipment	25	76	0	25	225	210	535	2183	3151	6946	•	•	112280	•
Total Assets	26	719	0	106	734	1818	7673	15224	34310	70173	•	•	1718382	•
Notes and Loans Payable	27	200	0	44	256	363	3737	2400	5730	23743	•	•	490749	•
All Other Liabilities	28	305	0	34	239	737	1416	4799	12163	18501	•	•	920431	•
Net Worth	29	213	0	28	240	718	2520	8025	16416	27929	•	•	307201	•
Selected Financial Ratios (Times to 1)													
Current Ratio	30	1.5	•	1.7	1.1	2.0	1.0	2.0	1.6	1.3	•	•	1.2	•
Quick Ratio	31	1.2	•	1.5	0.9	2.0	0.6	1.6	1.3	1.0	•	•	0.9	•
Net Sales to Working Capital	32	13.1	•	23.5	66.1	6.1	•	7.2	7.2	10.2	•	•	23.2	•
Coverage Ratio	33	7.7	85.9	28.4	14.7	23.0	47.2	24.2	24.2	4.1	•	•	1.8	•
Total Asset Turnover	34	1.6	•	5.1	3.0	2.0	1.5	2.3	1.8	1.1	•	•	0.6	•
Inventory Turnover	35	24.4	•	22.8	33.8	44.0	15.4	28.4	75.2	12.6	•	•	12.8	•
Receivables Turnover	36	11.3	•	62.5	16.6	10.1	•	8.2	6.9	5.8	•	•	6.7	•
Total Liabilities to Net Worth	37	2.4	•	2.7	2.1	1.5	2.0	0.9	1.1	1.5	•	•	4.6	•
Current Assets to Working Capital	38	3.0	•	2.4	11.0	2.0	•	2.0	2.6	3.9	•	•	6.8	•
Current Liabilities to Working Capital	39	2.0	•	1.4	10.0	1.0	•	1.0	1.6	2.9	•	•	5.8	•
Working Capital to Net Sales	40	0.1	•	0.0	0.0	0.2	•	0.1	0.1	0.1	•	•	0.0	•
Inventory to Working Capital	41	0.1	•	0.2	1.2	0.1	•	0.1	0.1	0.1	•	•	0.2	•
Total Receipts to Cash Flow	42	2.9	2.1	2.6	3.7	2.9	3.1	4.8	5.1	3.0	•	•	2.7	•
Cost of Goods to Cash Flow	43	0.7	0.2	0.5	1.4	1.0	1.1	2.3	3.1	0.7	•	•	0.3	•
Cash Flow to Total Debt	44	0.8	•	2.7	1.2	1.1	0.7	1.0	0.7	0.6	•	•	0.3	•
Selected Financial Factors (in Percentages)													
Debt Ratio	45	70.4	•	73.3	67.4	60.5	67.2	47.3	52.2	60.2	•	•	82.1	•
Return on Total Assets	46	20.2	•	79.4	29.6	26.2	22.0	27.3	15.2	12.7	•	•	6.3	•
Return on Equity Before Income Taxes	47	59.4	•	287.0	84.7	63.5	65.6	49.6	30.5	24.2	•	•	15.4	•
Return on Equity After Income Taxes	48	56.0	•	284.9	83.0	62.2	61.7	46.9	25.9	18.9	•	•	11.1	•
Profit Margin (Before Income Tax)	49	11.3	26.8	14.9	9.1	12.7	14.0	11.1	8.3	8.4	•	•	4.3	•
Profit Margin (After Income Tax)	50	10.6	26.0	14.8	8.9	12.4	13.2	10.5	7.0	6.6	•	•	3.2	•

Table I

Corporations with and without Net Income

OFFICES OF BANK HOLDING COMPANIES

MONEY AMOUNTS AND SIZE OF ASSETS IN THOUSANDS OF DOLLARS

Item Description for Accounting Period 7/11 Through 6/12		Total	Zero Assets	Under 500	500 to 1,000	1,000 to 5,000	5,000 to 10,000	10,000 to 25,000	25,000 to 50,000	50,000 to 100,000	100,000 to 250,000	250,000 to 500,000	500,000 to 2,500,000	2,500,000 and over
Number of Enterprises	1	5274	157	386	0	119	21	142	415	841	1491	829	713	160
Revenues ($ in Thousands)														
Net Sales	2	180167266	436430	5958	0	476711	8051	20977	214194	798284	3250874	3232483	8425440	163297864
Interest	3	402152941	1319279	1083	0	31076	3123	78229	256910	1176799	5511094	7561829	21782121	364431398
Rents	4	16954560	68470	0	0	94	0	423	2914	6347	27990	42053	196626	16609644
Royalties	5	254385	29	0	0	0	0	0	1291	99	150	223	4775	247818
Other Portfolio Income	6	42927573	149255	21	0	5579	3303	6084	54041	176065	739346	822615	2090485	38880779
Other Receipts	7	122554694	384314	71615	0	54242	58721	156891	517387	1609944	4375318	4618008	7235853	103472401
Total Receipts	8	765011419	2357777	78677	0	567702	73198	262604	1046737	3767538	13904772	16277211	39735300	686939904
Average Total Receipts	9	145053	15018	204	•	4771	3486	1849	2522	4480	9326	19635	55730	4293374
Operating Costs/Operating Income (%)														
Cost of Operations	10	1.5	•	•	•	•	•	•	•	0.2	0.0	0.0	0.0	1.6
Salaries and Wages	11	75.9	110.4	83.9	•	5.7	86.7	95.6	52.4	61.7	66.4	82.8	90.6	75.4
Taxes Paid	12	8.1	14.0	4.0	•	0.9	35.2	20.2	11.8	12.9	12.6	14.7	14.4	7.5
Interest Paid	13	65.4	101.3	61.3	•	4.0	559.0	98.3	65.8	70.3	70.2	83.1	79.2	64.3
Depreciation	14	19.2	20.4	1.2	•	0.3	2.3	14.6	9.8	11.3	12.3	14.1	16.7	19.7
Amortization and Depletion	15	4.7	2.4	0.5	•	0.2	1.8	2.4	1.5	1.4	1.4	1.9	2.8	4.9
Pensions and Other Deferred Comp.	16	3.1	6.6	0.3	•	0.1	1.6	4.3	3.4	3.5	4.1	4.7	5.4	3.0
Employee Benefits	17	9.4	8.8	3.7	•	1.3	8.0	27.7	13.5	13.8	12.4	13.1	11.8	9.2
Advertising	18	6.3	3.8	0.5	•	0.2	1.8	3.7	3.4	3.5	4.3	4.1	4.6	6.5
Other Expenses	19	172.9	361.3	1617.5	•	58.2	659.0	1191.9	282.8	239.6	170.9	216.5	184.1	170.6
Officers' Compensation	20	5.4	17.5	7.4	•	3.1	28.8	94.6	49.4	42.5	32.5	28.3	19.7	3.4
Operating Margin	21	•	•	•	•	26.2	•	•	•	•	•	•	•	•
Operating Margin Before Officers' Comp.	22	•	•	•	•	29.3	•	•	•	•	•	•	•	•

Selected Average Balance Sheet ($ in Thousands)

Net Receivables 23	1079590	0	0	•	1194	0	9669	19597	40784	94114	200671	555540	30918920
Inventories 24	6	0	0	•	71	0	0	0	0	0	7	4	119
Net Property, Plant and Equipment 25	21615	0	0	•	803	0	158	562	1306	3260	6694	19296	552363
Total Assets 26	2733386	0	16	•	3410	6318	19007	38045	73918	163482	347703	1001617	81803320
Notes and Loans Payable 27	434490	0	57	•	1729	5845	434	934	2539	6439	15181	48186	13950141
All Other Liabilities 28	1880197	0	40	•	777	4574	20329	35644	67091	144546	310312	862605	54712812
Net Worth 29	418699	0	-82	•	904	-4101	-1756	1467	4289	12497	22209	90826	13140366

Selected Financial Ratios (Times to 1)

Current Ratio 30	0.9	•	2.5	•	3.2	0.3	0.8	1.0	1.0	1.0	0.9	0.9	0.9
Quick Ratio 31	0.8	•	2.5	•	2.9	0.2	0.8	1.0	1.0	1.0	0.9	0.9	0.8
Net Sales to Working Capital 32	•	•	10.4	•	2.7	•	•	1.5	•	•	•	•	•
Coverage Ratio 33	1.8	•	•	•	12.3	0.1	•	0.7	0.9	1.4	1.3	1.4	1.8
Total Asset Turnover 34	0.0	•	1.0	•	1.2	0.1	0.0	0.0	0.0	0.0	0.0	0.0	0.0
Inventory Turnover 35	83.6	•	•	•	•	•	•	•	15.9	0.3	0.1	0.8	141.6
Receivables Turnover 36	0.0	•	•	•	3.5	64.9	0.0	0.0	0.0	0.0	0.0	0.0	0.0
Total Liabilities to Net Worth 37	5.5	•	•	•	2.8	•	•	24.9	16.2	12.1	14.7	10.0	5.2
Current Assets to Working Capital 38	•	•	1.7	•	1.5	•	•	92.5	•	•	•	•	•
Current Liabilities to Working Capital 39	•	•	0.7	•	0.5	•	•	91.5	•	•	•	•	•
Working Capital to Net Sales 40	•	•	0.1	•	0.4	•	•	0.7	•	•	•	•	•
Inventory to Working Capital 41	•	•	•	•	0.0	•	•	•	•	•	•	•	•
Total Receipts to Cash Flow 42	0.5	0.5	•	•	1.5	•	0.4	0.6	0.6	0.6	0.5	0.5	0.5
Cost of Goods to Cash Flow 43	0.0	•	•	•	•	•	•	•	0.0	0.0	0.0	0.0	0.0
Cash Flow to Total Debt 44	0.0	•	•	•	1.0	•	0.0	0.0	0.0	0.0	0.0	0.0	0.0

Selected Financial Factors (in Percentages)

Debt Ratio 45	84.7	•	626.6	•	73.5	164.9	109.2	96.1	94.2	92.4	93.6	90.9	83.9
Return on Total Assets 46	1.4	•	•	•	57.5	4.6	•	0.6	0.8	1.3	1.2	1.3	1.5
Return on Equity Before Income Taxes 47	4.1	•	86.4	•	199.3	45.1	26.9	•	•	4.5	4.2	3.7	4.1
Return on Equity After Income Taxes 48	3.0	•	86.4	•	199.1	45.1	27.6	•	•	3.1	2.1	2.0	3.0
Profit Margin (Before Income Tax) 49	49.7	•	•	•	45.0	•	•	•	•	25.7	23.7	28.7	52.7
Profit Margin (After Income Tax) 50	36.2	•	•	•	44.9	•	•	•	•	18.1	12.1	15.0	38.9

Table II

Corporations with Net Income

OFFICES OF BANK HOLDING COMPANIES

MONEY AMOUNTS AND SIZE OF ASSETS IN THOUSANDS OF DOLLARS

Item Description for Accounting Period 7/11 Through 6/12		Total	Zero Assets	Under 500	500 to 1,000	1,000 to 5,000	5,000 to 10,000	10,000 to 25,000	25,000 to 50,000	50,000 to 100,000	100,000 to 250,000	250,000 to 500,000	500,000 to 2,500,000	2,500,000 and over
Number of Enterprises	1	3551	19	•	0	96	•	80	317	612	1138	617	530	137
Revenues ($ in Thousands)														
Net Sales	2	171790367	82259	•	0	467883	•	8204	165538	631919	2634313	2703828	6523667	158567382
Interest	3	377069712	228049	•	0	3290	•	51832	158773	792836	3837410	5424942	15882838	350689742
Rents	4	15763657	1816	•	0	10	•	225	524	3175	16377	25103	132414	15584015
Royalties	5	251564	0	•	0	0	•	0	1291	47	148	223	2037	247818
Other Portfolio Income	6	41053235	71137	•	0	3790	•	4817	43175	139855	585516	664044	1608626	37929587
Other Receipts	7	113934554	35042	•	0	12127	•	16006	325743	810927	2926197	2661156	4935285	102206494
Total Receipts	8	719863089	418303	•	0	487100	•	81084	695044	2378759	9999961	11479296	29084867	665225038
Average Total Receipts	9	202721	22016	•	•	5074	•	1014	2193	3887	8787	18605	54877	4855657
Operating Costs/Operating Income (%)														
Cost of Operations	10	1.6	•	•	•	•	•	•	•	0.3	0.0	0.0	0.0	1.7
Salaries and Wages	11	74.6	78.1	•	•	4.1	•	116.0	47.3	52.1	59.0	72.0	84.6	74.8
Taxes Paid	12	7.8	13.2	•	•	0.6	•	33.5	11.2	11.9	11.9	13.4	14.0	7.4
Interest Paid	13	64.2	70.6	•	•	0.5	•	152.9	58.1	61.7	62.3	71.8	70.3	64.0
Depreciation	14	18.5	10.8	•	•	0.1	•	16.8	8.4	9.6	11.7	12.5	16.0	18.9
Amortization and Depletion	15	4.6	1.4	•	•	•	•	1.1	1.1	1.0	1.2	1.6	2.6	4.8
Pensions and Other Deferred Comp.	16	3.0	3.6	•	•	0.0	•	5.6	3.4	3.5	4.2	4.5	6.0	2.8
Employee Benefits	17	9.2	7.6	•	•	0.9	•	46.5	13.9	13.1	11.6	11.9	11.1	9.1
Advertising	18	6.3	6.6	•	•	0.1	•	6.1	3.5	3.3	4.2	3.8	4.5	6.5
Other Expenses	19	164.1	143.6	•	•	9.5	•	241.9	151.1	100.2	102.0	117.0	127.9	168.2
Officers' Compensation	20	4.9	29.3	•	•	2.2	•	180.1	47.9	39.6	31.2	26.3	20.1	3.3
Operating Margin	21	•	•	•	•	82.0	•	•	•	•	•	•	•	•
Operating Margin Before Officers' Comp.	22	•	•	•	•	84.2	•	•	•	•	•	•	•	•

Selected Average Balance Sheet ($ in Thousands)

Net Receivables 23	1484204	0	•	•	1270	•	12051	20430	42215	95086	204159	557559	34360077
Inventories 24	5	0	•	•	0	•	0	0	0	0	0	5	115
Net Property, Plant and Equipment 25	28513	0	•	•	963	•	126	446	1149	3056	6398	18527	606263
Total Assets 26	3831929	0	•	•	3437	•	20384	38451	74171	161853	349332	996338	92115583
Notes and Loans Payable 27	626197	0	•	•	1247	•	231	698	1802	5768	13819	45568	15933737
All Other Liabilities 28	2603330	0	•	•	681	•	17141	35435	64419	139956	303372	851821	61273088
Net Worth 29	602402	0	•	•	1508	•	3012	2318	7950	16128	32140	98949	14908758

Selected Financial Ratios (Times to 1)

Current Ratio 30	0.9	•	•	•	3.3	•	1.1	1.0	1.0	1.0	1.0	0.9	0.9
Quick Ratio 31	0.8	•	•	•	3.2	•	1.0	1.0	1.0	1.0	0.9	0.9	0.8
Net Sales to Working Capital 32	•	•	•	•	3.1	•	0.1	0.7	0.9	•	•	•	•
Coverage Ratio 33	1.9	2.9	•	•	160.6	•	2.0	2.0	2.0	2.0	2.0	2.1	1.9
Total Asset Turnover 34	0.0	•	•	•	1.4	•	0.0	0.0	0.0	0.0	0.0	0.0	0.0
Inventory Turnover 35	144.4	•	•	•	•	•	•	•	15.9	0.3	18.1	0.8	171.1
Receivables Turnover 36	0.0	•	•	•	4.7	•	0.0	0.0	0.0	0.0	0.0	0.0	0.0
Total Liabilities to Net Worth 37	5.4	•	•	•	1.3	•	5.8	15.6	8.3	9.0	9.9	9.1	5.2
Current Assets to Working Capital 38	•	•	•	•	1.4	•	18.4	45.6	56.4	•	•	•	•
Current Liabilities to Working Capital 39	•	•	•	•	0.4	•	17.4	44.6	55.4	•	•	•	•
Working Capital to Net Sales 40	•	•	•	•	0.3	•	9.7	1.4	1.1	•	•	•	•
Inventory to Working Capital 41	•	•	•	•	•	•	•	•	0.0	•	•	•	•
Total Receipts to Cash Flow 42	0.5	0.4	•	•	1.1	•	0.2	0.5	0.6	0.6	0.5	0.5	0.5
Cost of Goods to Cash Flow 43	0.0	•	•	•	•	•	•	•	0.0	0.0	0.0	0.0	0.0
Cash Flow to Total Debt 44	0.0	•	•	•	2.4	•	0.0	0.0	0.0	0.0	0.0	0.0	0.0

Selected Financial Factors (in Percentages)

Debt Ratio 45	84.3	•	•	•	56.1	•	85.2	94.0	89.3	90.0	90.8	90.1	83.8
Return on Total Assets 46	1.5	•	•	•	122.7	•	1.6	1.6	1.7	1.8	1.8	1.8	1.5
Return on Equity Before Income Taxes 47	4.6	•	•	•	277.9	•	5.3	13.1	8.3	9.3	9.9	9.2	4.4
Return on Equity After Income Taxes 48	3.5	•	•	•	277.7	•	4.6	12.1	7.4	7.9	8.1	7.0	3.3
Profit Margin (Before Income Tax) 49	57.5	132.1	•	•	86.0	•	155.8	58.2	63.8	64.8	72.9	74.0	56.3
Profit Margin (After Income Tax) 50	43.4	90.1	•	•	85.9	•	134.7	53.6	57.0	55.3	59.2	56.4	42.1

Table I

Corporations with and without Net Income

OFFICES OF OTHER HOLDING COMPANIES

MONEY AMOUNTS AND SIZE OF ASSETS IN THOUSANDS OF DOLLARS

Item Description for Accounting Period 7/11 Through 6/12		Total	Zero Assets	Under 500	500 to 1,000	1,000 to 5,000	5,000 to 10,000	10,000 to 25,000	25,000 to 50,000	50,000 to 100,000	100,000 to 250,000	250,000 to 500,000	500,000 to 2,500,000	2,500,000 and over
Number of Enterprises	1	45097	12055	19155	3642	5584	1533	1398	746	440	298	119	95	32
Revenues ($ in Thousands)														
Net Sales	2	1489716	30313	1029	0	12774	22014	10554	12372	173294	51487	35932	130761	1009186
Interest	3	5308714	207011	32279	10658	74853	412434	105009	159990	199755	292714	368449	1106865	2338697
Rents	4	471586	227774	5197	44069	13799	36133	44130	16259	31902	31636	2266	3727	14694
Royalties	5	2151076	41222	3042	1744	26722	16209	3198	42320	11482	32161	11016	6022	1955937
Other Portfolio Income	6	12961620	1144495	217659	155862	332690	185915	344108	386685	468806	1134426	1462442	2145855	4982678
Other Receipts	7	25332867	3110413	291504	110784	1139021	676111	941095	1177512	1252303	1870184	943185	2913278	10907477
Total Receipts	8	47715579	4761228	550710	323117	1599859	1348816	1448094	1795138	2137542	3412608	2823290	6306508	21208669
Average Total Receipts	9	1058	395	29	89	287	880	1036	2406	4858	11452	23725	66384	662771
Operating Costs/Operating Income (%)														
Cost of Operations	10	27.9	73.1	0.6	•	•	12.4	19.7	•	29.7	15.6	67.4	35.3	25.6
Salaries and Wages	11	79.6	853.3	197.7	•	689.3	157.1	504.9	226.6	107.0	79.9	118.9	74.0	34.0
Taxes Paid	12	90.3	242.3	1619.6	•	261.8	144.0	417.4	354.1	29.2	283.3	257.7	86.3	68.1
Interest Paid	13	711.6	1990.4	7638.2	•	743.9	2173.3	1554.7	1661.5	189.9	1119.6	1635.5	1052.3	602.1
Depreciation	14	36.0	64.4	823.3	•	127.2	78.4	205.0	165.1	18.6	44.6	43.7	20.1	31.9
Amortization and Depletion	15	133.1	1841.5	1277.4	•	100.9	65.6	720.8	303.4	35.7	214.3	104.8	207.3	78.1
Pensions and Other Deferred Comp.	16	8.1	0.4	•	•	7.1	11.9	28.2	34.1	0.8	3.1	36.2	5.1	8.6
Employee Benefits	17	8.3	63.4	356.5	•	50.3	20.2	28.6	28.8	2.8	5.9	11.1	13.1	5.2
Advertising	18	14.8	1.6	8.1	•	2.0	0.7	2.0	7.7	1.3	0.9	0.7	1.6	21.0
Other Expenses	19	1166.4	10512.0	49670.6	•	5791.1	2334.8	9838.5	8415.1	690.0	4029.1	4334.3	2245.1	233.4
Officers' Compensation	20	28.1	86.5	688.2	•	452.8	155.2	171.6	288.6	16.2	53.6	36.6	56.2	8.7
Operating Margin	21	•	•	•	•	•	•	•	•	•	•	•	•	•
Operating Margin Before Officers' Comp.	22	•	•	•	•	•	•	•	•	•	•	•	•	•

Selected Average Balance Sheet ($ in Thousands)

Net Receivables 23	695	0	4	14	105	190	429	606	2336	3905	17874	20755	719494
Inventories 24	9	0	0	0	0	0	2	40	47	536	400	855	1991
Net Property, Plant and Equipment 25	219	0	2	69	80	296	326	1082	1528	2930	7368	6837	136175
Total Assets 26	13295	0	118	733	2241	7064	16112	34657	70459	154659	338432	1021910	9639599
Notes and Loans Payable 27	4232	0	47	156	664	1821	3327	5538	10387	26681	68513	258556	4026198
All Other Liabilities 28	1873	0	29	121	327	818	1779	3948	10605	19607	44570	99085	1554923
Net Worth 29	7190	0	41	456	1250	4425	11006	25171	49467	108371	225348	664269	4058478

Selected Financial Ratios (Times to 1)

Current Ratio 30	1.2	•	2.3	1.2	2.8	2.1	1.7	2.3	1.9	1.4	2.3	1.5	0.9
Quick Ratio 31	0.7	•	1.8	0.9	1.6	1.5	1.1	1.2	1.1	0.8	1.5	1.0	0.5
Net Sales to Working Capital 32	0.1	•	0.0	•	0.0	0.0	0.0	0.0	0.1	0.0	0.0	0.0	•
Coverage Ratio 33	3.2	1.2	•	1.3	7.0	1.4	1.0	3.0	1.6	1.8	2.0	2.1	4.2
Total Asset Turnover 34	0.0	•	0.0	•	0.0	0.0	0.0	0.0	0.0	0.0	0.0	0.0	0.0
Inventory Turnover 35	1.1	•	•	0.3	•	6.3	1.0	•	2.5	0.1	0.5	0.6	4.1
Receivables Turnover 36	0.1	•	0.0	•	0.0	0.1	0.0	0.0	0.2	0.0	0.0	0.1	0.1
Total Liabilities to Net Worth 37	0.8	•	1.8	0.6	0.8	0.6	0.5	0.4	0.4	0.4	0.5	0.5	1.4
Current Assets to Working Capital 38	6.4	•	1.7	6.8	1.6	1.9	2.4	1.8	2.1	3.4	1.8	3.0	•
Current Liabilities to Working Capital 39	5.4	•	0.7	5.8	0.6	0.9	1.4	0.8	1.1	2.4	0.8	2.0	•
Working Capital to Net Sales 40	11.0	•	469.0	•	136.0	41.6	158.1	202.8	12.9	36.1	116.1	34.1	•
Inventory to Working Capital 41	0.0	•	•	0.0	0.0	•	0.0	0.0	0.0	0.1	0.0	0.0	•
Total Receipts to Cash Flow 42	0.1	0.0	0.0	•	0.0	0.0	0.0	0.0	0.2	0.0	0.0	0.1	0.1
Cost of Goods to Cash Flow 43	0.0	0.0	0.0	0.0	•	0.0	0.0	•	0.1	0.0	0.0	0.0	0.0
Cash Flow to Total Debt 44	0.1	•	0.1	0.1	0.2	0.1	0.1	0.2	0.1	0.1	0.1	0.1	0.1

Selected Financial Factors (in Percentages)

Debt Ratio 45	45.9	•	64.7	37.8	44.2	37.4	31.7	27.4	29.8	29.9	33.4	35.0	57.9
Return on Total Assets 46	5.6	•	•	1.5	5.3	6.4	0.7	2.4	1.7	2.3	2.9	3.0	8.2
Return on Equity Before Income Taxes 47	7.2	•	•	0.5	8.2	3.1	0.0	2.2	0.9	1.5	2.1	2.5	14.8
Return on Equity After Income Taxes 48	4.1	•	•	•	6.7	1.9	•	1.1	0.0	•	0.1	0.7	9.9
Profit Margin (Before Income Tax) 49	1556.3	340.8	•	•	4488.4	954.8	17.1	3281.9	109.6	927.0	1594.3	1187.1	1901.0
Profit Margin (After Income Tax) 50	883.0	•	•	•	3642.9	590.7	•	1657.8	4.3	•	86.2	321.2	1279.0

Table II

Corporations with Net Income

OFFICES OF OTHER HOLDING COMPANIES

MONEY AMOUNTS AND SIZE OF ASSETS IN THOUSANDS OF DOLLARS

Item Description for Accounting Period 7/11 Through 6/12		Total	Zero Assets	Under 500	500 to 1000	1,000 to 5,000	5,000 to 10,000	10,000 to 25,000	25,000 to 50,000	50,000 to 100,000	100,000 to 250,000	250,000 to 500,000	500,000 to 2,500,000	2,500,000 and over
Number of Enterprises	1	14841	3253	•	1668	2628	•	531	325	172	137	49	48	23
Revenues ($ in Thousands)														
Net Sales	2	1183652	9174	•	0	2046	•	8558	12060	34988	38662	31699	52492	981714
Interest	3	3253846	160278	•	6336	22316	•	44876	114032	92460	153371	144172	685565	1773925
Rents	4	304913	209598	•	0	11952	•	12365	13571	22677	16490	8	827	286
Royalties	5	2086128	372	•	6	21220	•	3103	40283	9762	31965	0	4508	1955660
Other Portfolio Income	6	11722290	1081519	•	98004	297126	•	306025	347454	398734	1071916	1347793	1658819	4751229
Other Receipts	7	25597275	3081416	•	148838	1165781	•	1078625	1291948	1425447	2282586	1181346	2485499	10234006
Total Receipts	8	44148104	4542357	•	253184	1520441	•	1453552	1819348	1984068	3594990	2705018	4887710	19696820
Average Total Receipts	9	2975	1396	•	152	579	•	2737	5598	11535	26241	55204	101827	856383
Operating Costs/Operating Income (%)														
Cost of Operations	10	27.9	61.6	•	•	•	•	10.6	•	21.8	20.7	76.0	46.5	26.2
Salaries and Wages	11	37.2	172.4	•	•	324.3	•	57.1	61.6	309.4	65.2	109.7	115.9	16.0
Taxes Paid	12	94.2	654.4	•	•	1185.4	•	361.4	281.6	73.4	325.0	187.3	165.6	65.1
Interest Paid	13	547.3	3675.4	•	•	1322.5	•	574.1	735.0	284.5	515.5	727.5	834.5	507.1
Depreciation	14	9.6	49.0	•	•	166.6	•	103.8	85.0	30.4	18.8	44.4	22.8	3.4
Amortization and Depletion	15	91.3	5582.1	•	•	12.0	•	277.0	114.7	108.4	172.3	53.6	80.3	37.1
Pensions and Other Deferred Comp.	16	8.9	1.2	•	•	12.4	•	5.6	33.5	2.1	2.8	29.1	7.1	8.7
Employee Benefits	17	4.8	26.8	•	•	92.5	•	3.9	9.2	5.6	4.6	10.2	13.1	3.4
Advertising	18	15.6	0.2	•	•	11.9	•	1.8	7.5	1.0	0.9	0.2	1.4	18.5
Other Expenses	19	402.2	9414.4	•	•	3994.6	•	2488.2	2197.8	922.8	961.5	1022.9	918.4	169.7
Officers' Compensation	20	25.7	284.6	•	•	2155.4	•	92.5	184.8	39.3	53.8	23.9	89.1	8.9
Operating Margin	21	•	•	•	•	•	•	•	•	•	•	•	•	•
Operating Margin Before Officers' Comp.	22	•	•	•	•	•	•	•	•	•	•	•	•	•

Selected Average Balance Sheet ($ in Thousands)													
Net Receivables	23	1774	0	•	20	39	•	556	755	2096	4631	19471	13034	998034
Inventories	24	10	0	•	0	0	•	3	0	73	111	40	1238	2767
Net Property, Plant and Equipment	25	188	0	•	1	27	•	197	629	1347	3510	1870	4892	53998
Total Assets	26	27198	0	•	731	2043	•	16640	34771	69116	159146	333975	1042365	11830244
Notes and Loans Payable	27	9437	0	•	48	366	•	2310	3962	9709	20260	50668	240636	5097676
All Other Liabilities	28	3178	0	•	87	123	•	1933	2790	10169	19034	39943	113648	1410186
Net Worth	29	14584	0	•	596	1554	•	12397	28018	49238	119852	243364	688081	5322383
Selected Financial Ratios (Times to 1)													
Current Ratio	30	1.2	•	•	1.8	5.9	•	1.8	3.1	1.8	1.5	4.2	1.3	1.1
Quick Ratio	31	0.8	•	•	1.5	3.3	•	1.2	1.6	1.1	0.9	2.9	1.1	0.7
Net Sales to Working Capital	32	0.1	•	•	•	0.0	•	0.0	0.0	0.0	0.0	0.0	0.0	0.2
Coverage Ratio	33	7.0	9.4	•	69.6	51.2	•	23.7	16.9	14.7	15.3	10.2	9.9	5.1
Total Asset Turnover	34	0.0	•	•	•	0.0	•	0.0	0.0	0.0	0.0	0.0	0.0	0.0
Inventory Turnover	35	2.1	•	•	•	•	•	0.6	•	0.6	0.5	12.4	0.4	4.0
Receivables Turnover	36	0.1	•	•	•	0.0	•	0.0	0.0	0.1	0.1	0.0	0.1	0.1
Total Liabilities to Net Worth	37	0.9	•	•	0.2	0.3	•	0.3	0.2	0.4	0.3	0.4	0.5	1.2
Current Assets to Working Capital	38	5.5	•	•	2.2	1.2	•	2.3	1.5	2.3	2.9	1.3	3.9	13.5
Current Liabilities to Working Capital	39	4.5	•	•	1.2	0.2	•	1.3	0.5	1.3	1.9	0.3	2.9	12.5
Working Capital to Net Sales	40	11.8	•	•	•	512.1	•	76.8	114.2	23.7	27.6	81.3	35.6	4.1
Inventory to Working Capital	41	0.0	•	•	•	•	•	0.0	•	0.0	0.0	0.0	0.0	0.0
Total Receipts to Cash Flow	42	0.0	0.0	•	•	0.0	•	0.0	0.0	0.0	0.0	0.0	0.0	0.1
Cost of Goods to Cash Flow	43	0.0	0.0	•	•	•	•	0.0	•	0.0	0.0	0.0	0.0	0.0
Cash Flow to Total Debt	44	0.1	•	•	0.8	0.9	•	0.5	0.6	0.4	0.4	0.3	0.2	0.1
Selected Financial Factors (in Percentages)													
Debt Ratio	45	46.4	•	•	18.5	23.9	•	25.5	19.4	28.8	24.7	27.1	34.0	55.0
Return on Total Assets	46	11.3	•	•	18.7	25.8	•	13.2	13.3	12.3	14.0	14.4	8.6	9.3
Return on Equity Before Income Taxes	47	18.0	•	•	22.6	33.2	•	16.9	15.5	16.1	17.4	17.8	11.7	16.7
Return on Equity After Income Taxes	48	13.4	•	•	20.7	30.6	•	14.2	13.4	13.9	14.0	13.2	8.3	11.6
Profit Margin (Before Income Tax)	49	3298.5	31018.7	•	•	66373.5	•	13003.5	11686.5	3889.6	7381.1	6686.6	7388.2	2084.3
Profit Margin (After Income Tax)	50	2452.7	23336.6	•	•	61112.1	•	10920.0	10138.0	3372.9	5953.6	4977.1	5231.2	1444.8

Table I

Corporations with and without Net Income

EMPLOYMENT SERVICES

MONEY AMOUNTS AND SIZE OF ASSETS IN THOUSANDS OF DOLLARS

Item Description for Accounting Period 7/11 Through 6/12		Total	Zero Assets	Under 500	500 to 1,000	1,000 to 5,000	5,000 to 10,000	10,000 to 25,000	25,000 to 50,000	50,000 to 100,000	100,000 to 250,000	250,000 to 500,000	500,000 to 2,500,000	2,500,000 and over
Number of Enterprises	1	24437	4821	16292	1605	1213	256	147	38	19	14	14	17	0
Revenues ($ in Thousands)														
Net Sales	2	170261350	3091949	36697601	12441821	13025470	10105396	9818979	6293295	6139641	7443496	12687505	52516197	0
Interest	3	158563	1497	1785	1033	4022	147	653	1052	587	3924	6595	137270	0
Rents	4	11225	0	4310	0	315	0	2	1417	41	2166	1349	1625	0
Royalties	5	306818	0	0	0	0	0	0	0	586	0	38061	268172	0
Other Portfolio Income	6	216049	18153	358	3132	55886	12795	9057	1053	56	7989	110	107459	0
Other Receipts	7	999135	22761	84044	7353	66720	43216	16886	17130	8075	2559	25883	704504	0
Total Receipts	8	171953140	3134360	36788098	12453339	13152413	10161554	9845577	6313947	6148986	7460134	12759503	53735227	0
Average Total Receipts	9	7037	650	2258	7759	10843	39694	66977	166156	323631	532867	911393	3160896	•
Operating Costs/Operating Income (%)														
Cost of Operations	10	52.9	59.7	40.2	69.3	49.4	36.1	56.5	55.7	36.5	44.6	69.6	59.7	•
Salaries and Wages	11	22.4	17.6	21.0	9.5	23.2	41.0	21.2	28.8	48.7	40.2	11.3	19.4	•
Taxes Paid	12	6.8	5.4	7.8	6.9	7.4	7.2	6.7	4.8	6.3	7.5	5.6	6.3	•
Interest Paid	13	0.4	0.6	0.1	0.1	0.3	0.5	0.3	0.8	0.1	0.4	0.7	0.5	•
Depreciation	14	0.3	0.2	0.1	0.1	0.4	0.2	0.4	0.2	0.3	0.2	0.5	0.5	•
Amortization and Depletion	15	0.4	0.6	0.1	0.1	0.0	0.0	0.4	0.4	0.1	0.7	1.0	0.6	•
Pensions and Other Deferred Comp.	16	0.2	0.7	0.1	1.2	0.2	0.0	0.1	0.0	0.1	0.1	0.1	0.1	•
Employee Benefits	17	2.1	1.9	0.7	1.6	3.3	3.1	2.7	1.3	2.6	1.3	1.2	2.8	•
Advertising	18	0.3	0.2	0.2	0.1	0.3	0.1	1.2	0.2	0.1	0.1	0.4	0.3	•
Other Expenses	19	11.9	11.6	24.6	8.4	12.2	8.5	8.9	6.9	4.1	3.8	7.9	8.5	•
Officers' Compensation	20	1.6	1.4	4.2	2.0	1.6	1.3	1.5	0.4	0.4	0.3	0.7	0.5	•
Operating Margin	21	0.8	0.0	0.7	0.6	1.6	1.8	0.2	0.6	0.6	0.7	1.0	0.8	•
Operating Margin Before Officers' Comp.	22	2.4	1.4	4.9	2.5	3.2	3.2	1.7	0.9	1.0	1.0	1.8	1.2	•

Selected Average Balance Sheet ($ in Thousands)

Net Receivables 23	542	0	9	276	965	2050	7131	14994	21496	47282	106089	400145	•
Inventories 24	1	0	0	0	1	4	2	27	50	609	102	636	•
Net Property, Plant and Equipment 25	74	0	15	26	154	191	765	1476	2303	4244	14928	46945	•
Total Assets 26	1796	0	99	730	1940	7082	15119	36369	64694	159579	372431	1450554	•
Notes and Loans Payable 27	381	0	54	96	439	2822	4354	16065	20246	44797	78394	215074	•
All Other Liabilities 28	700	0	49	435	814	2996	7206	15183	28754	75594	117716	527421	•
Net Worth 29	715	0	-4	198	687	1263	3558	5122	15694	39188	176322	708060	•

Selected Financial Ratios (Times to 1)

Current Ratio 30	1.4	•	0.8	1.6	2.4	1.2	1.5	1.3	1.1	1.2	1.8	1.3	•
Quick Ratio 31	1.2	•	0.7	1.4	2.1	0.8	1.3	1.1	0.9	0.8	1.6	1.1	•
Net Sales to Working Capital 32	29.1	•	•	33.0	11.3	50.8	16.7	29.6	57.8	42.4	12.3	23.8	•
Coverage Ratio 33	5.8	3.4	8.4	5.9	9.4	5.8	2.6	2.2	7.3	3.0	3.2	7.2	•
Total Asset Turnover 34	3.9	•	22.7	10.6	5.5	5.6	4.4	4.6	5.0	3.3	2.4	2.1	•
Inventory Turnover 35	3635.2	•	202333.5	•	5313.2	3945.1	18318.4	3403.5	2361.2	389.1	6169.3	2898.7	•
Receivables Turnover 36	14.2	•	175.9	33.7	13.1	20.2	11.2	13.5	15.1	8.7	9.9	8.7	•
Total Liabilities to Net Worth 37	1.5	•	•	2.7	1.8	4.6	3.2	6.1	3.1	3.1	1.1	1.0	•
Current Assets to Working Capital 38	3.7	•	•	2.6	1.7	6.2	2.8	4.2	8.2	6.7	2.2	4.5	•
Current Liabilities to Working Capital 39	2.7	•	•	1.6	0.7	5.2	1.8	3.2	7.2	5.7	1.2	3.5	•
Working Capital to Net Sales 40	0.0	•	•	0.0	0.1	0.0	0.1	0.0	0.0	0.0	0.1	0.0	•
Inventory to Working Capital 41	0.0	•	•	•	0.0	0.0	0.0	0.0	0.0	0.1	0.0	0.0	•
Total Receipts to Cash Flow 42	8.0	8.9	4.1	12.1	7.4	10.3	12.4	14.8	22.9	23.7	12.0	9.7	•
Cost of Goods to Cash Flow 43	4.2	5.3	1.6	8.4	3.6	3.7	7.0	8.3	8.4	10.6	8.3	5.8	•
Cash Flow to Total Debt 44	0.8	•	5.4	1.2	1.2	0.7	0.5	0.4	0.3	0.2	0.4	0.4	•

Selected Financial Factors (in Percentages)

Debt Ratio 45	60.2	•	103.9	72.9	64.6	82.2	76.5	85.9	75.7	75.4	52.7	51.2	•
Return on Total Assets 46	8.8	•	24.9	8.2	16.1	16.1	3.6	7.5	4.4	4.4	5.6	8.1	•
Return on Equity Before Income Taxes 47	18.3	•	•	25.2	40.5	74.6	9.4	28.6	15.7	11.9	8.2	14.3	•
Return on Equity After Income Taxes 48	14.7	•	•	23.3	39.0	71.6	6.8	27.8	14.6	8.7	5.3	10.3	•
Profit Margin (Before Income Tax) 49	1.9	1.4	1.0	0.6	2.6	2.4	0.5	0.9	0.8	0.9	1.6	3.3	•
Profit Margin (After Income Tax) 50	1.5	1.4	0.9	0.6	2.5	2.3	0.4	0.9	0.7	0.6	1.0	2.4	•

Table II

Corporations with Net Income

EMPLOYMENT SERVICES

MONEY AMOUNTS AND SIZE OF ASSETS IN THOUSANDS OF DOLLARS

Item Description for Accounting Period 7/11 Through 6/12		Total	Zero Assets	Under 500	500 to 1,000	1,000 to 5,000	5,000 to 10,000	10,000 to 25,000	25,000 to 50,000	50,000 to 100,000	100,000 to 250,000	250,000 to 500,000	500,000 to 2,500,000	2,500,000 and over
Number of Enterprises	1	12510	2016	8693	•	783	250	93	24	11	9	11	•	0
Revenues ($ in Thousands)														
Net Sales	2	130810367	1060954	30373343	•	11322382	10088530	6752542	5067181	2965645	4360877	11817922	•	0
Interest	3	125793	2	1229	•	3973	62	230	594	87	2971	1760	•	0
Rents	4	9006	0	4310	•	315	0	2	1417	41	1541	609	•	0
Royalties	5	301391	0	0	•	0	0	0	0	586	0	38061	•	0
Other Portfolio Income	6	201314	18152	358	•	55814	12359	32	704	56	7761	26	•	0
Other Receipts	7	900667	21035	50418	•	59353	43200	11639	11436	3709	2060	23151	•	0
Total Receipts	8	132348538	1100143	30429658	•	11441837	10144151	6764445	5081332	2970124	4375210	11881529	•	0
Average Total Receipts	9	10579	546	3500	•	14613	40577	72736	211722	270011	486134	1080139	•	•
Operating Costs/Operating Income (%)														
Cost of Operations	10	51.2	35.9	39.3	•	50.0	36.2	66.2	59.3	59.7	23.3	73.8	•	•
Salaries and Wages	11	22.3	18.3	17.5	•	25.5	40.9	11.7	26.8	23.8	59.3	8.7	•	•
Taxes Paid	12	7.0	6.0	9.0	•	8.2	7.2	7.1	4.3	5.4	7.4	5.7	•	•
Interest Paid	13	0.3	0.2	0.1	•	0.3	0.4	0.2	0.3	0.1	0.5	0.6	•	•
Depreciation	14	0.3	0.0	0.1	•	0.2	0.2	0.3	0.1	0.3	0.3	0.4	•	•
Amortization and Depletion	15	0.2	0.0	0.1	•	0.0	0.0	0.1	0.1	0.0	0.2	0.4	•	•
Pensions and Other Deferred Comp.	16	0.2	0.3	0.1	•	0.2	0.0	0.0	0.0	0.1	0.2	0.1	•	•
Employee Benefits	17	2.2	0.7	0.8	•	3.8	3.1	2.9	0.8	1.5	1.7	1.1	•	•
Advertising	18	0.2	0.1	0.2	•	0.3	0.1	0.3	0.2	0.1	0.1	0.3	•	•
Other Expenses	19	12.5	25.7	27.2	•	7.1	8.4	7.2	6.5	6.1	4.4	6.5	•	•
Officers' Compensation	20	1.7	3.3	4.2	•	1.6	1.3	1.4	0.3	0.8	0.4	0.7	•	•
Operating Margin	21	1.9	9.3	1.5	•	2.8	2.1	2.7	1.1	2.0	2.2	1.6	•	•
Operating Margin Before Officers' Comp.	22	3.6	12.7	5.7	•	4.4	3.4	4.1	1.4	2.8	2.5	2.3	•	•

Selected Average Balance Sheet ($ in Thousands)													
Net Receivables 23	753	0	10	•	767	2097	7599	17341	22219	48114	121135	•	•
Inventories 24	1	0	0	•	0	5	2	26	0	1139	138	•	•
Net Property, Plant and Equipment 25	105	0	23	•	95	194	616	1822	2480	4285	14186	•	•
Total Assets 26	2720	0	110	•	1863	7096	15055	35729	64383	167414	389670	•	•
Notes and Loans Payable 27	403	0	46	•	353	2655	2512	9887	17776	39358	78804	•	•
All Other Liabilities 28	1021	0	59	•	766	2986	6310	13956	26655	88476	131972	•	•
Net Worth 29	1296	0	5	•	744	1455	6233	11886	19951	39580	178893	•	•
Selected Financial Ratios (Times to 1)													
Current Ratio 30	1.4	•	0.7	•	1.9	1.2	1.7	1.6	1.4	1.1	1.8	•	•
Quick Ratio 31	1.2	•	0.6	•	1.7	0.8	1.5	1.4	1.1	0.7	1.6	•	•
Net Sales to Working Capital 32	31.2	•	•	•	18.7	56.1	14.5	21.1	19.2	39.8	13.4	•	•
Coverage Ratio 33	11.2	57.5	14.3	•	16.1	7.0	14.1	4.9	17.5	6.3	4.8	•	•
Total Asset Turnover 34	3.8	•	31.8	•	7.8	5.7	4.8	5.9	4.2	2.9	2.8	•	•
Inventory Turnover 35	5176.6	•	163340.3	•	111086.0	2910.7	28285.2	4800.9	•	99.3	5736.3	•	•
Receivables Turnover 36	15.1	•	335.5	•	21.6	•	11.2	15.8	10.5	8.1	•	•	•
Total Liabilities to Net Worth 37	1.1	•	21.3	•	1.5	3.9	1.4	2.0	2.2	3.2	1.2	•	•
Current Assets to Working Capital 38	3.8	•	•	•	2.1	6.6	2.4	2.7	3.7	7.8	2.2	•	•
Current Liabilities to Working Capital 39	2.8	•	•	•	1.1	5.6	1.4	1.7	2.7	6.8	1.2	•	•
Working Capital to Net Sales 40	0.0	•	•	•	0.1	0.0	0.1	0.0	0.1	0.0	0.1	•	•
Inventory to Working Capital 41	0.0	•	•	•	0.0	0.0	0.0	0.0	•	0.1	0.0	•	•
Total Receipts to Cash Flow 42	6.9	2.8	3.6	•	10.1	10.1	11.0	14.2	13.3	15.7	12.7	•	•
Cost of Goods to Cash Flow 43	3.5	1.0	1.4	•	5.1	3.7	7.3	8.4	7.9	3.7	9.4	•	•
Cash Flow to Total Debt 44	1.1	•	9.2	•	1.3	0.7	0.7	0.6	0.5	0.2	0.4	•	•
Selected Financial Factors (in Percentages)													
Debt Ratio 45	52.4	•	95.5	•	60.1	79.5	58.6	66.7	69.0	76.4	54.1	•	•
Return on Total Assets 46	13.3	•	56.4	•	31.5	17.4	14.8	10.1	9.6	8.5	7.4	•	•
Return on Equity Before Income Taxes 47	25.5	•	1167.0	•	73.9	72.8	33.3	24.0	29.2	30.4	12.8	•	•
Return on Equity After Income Taxes 48	21.6	•	1142.5	•	71.7	70.2	31.0	23.4	27.8	25.5	9.2	•	•
Profit Margin (Before Income Tax) 49	3.2	13.0	1.7	•	3.8	2.6	2.9	1.4	2.2	2.5	2.1	•	•
Profit Margin (After Income Tax) 50	2.7	13.0	1.6	•	3.7	2.5	2.7	1.3	2.1	2.1	1.5	•	•

Table I

Corporations with and without Net Income

Travel Arrangement and Reservation Services

Money Amounts and Size of Assets in Thousands of Dollars

Item Description for Accounting Period 7/11 Through 6/12		Total	Zero Assets	Under 500	500 to 1,000	1,000 to 5,000	5,000 to 10,000	10,000 to 25,000	25,000 to 50,000	50,000 to 100,000	100,000 to 250,000	250,000 to 500,000	500,000 to 2,500,000	2,500,000 and over
Number of Enterprises	1	17034	3111	12276	751	661	65	68	39	21	17	14	9	0
Revenues ($ in Thousands)														
Net Sales	2	36645575	1134517	7601449	2841363	4335993	1363650	2316922	2435733	1830341	2660946	3988037	6136624	0
Interest	3	116964	7005	76	708	673	43	8287	2727	9902	14405	24274	48864	0
Rents	4	33438	42	3	0	70	13	437	234	1521	5072	4493	21553	0
Royalties	5	181200	8	0	0	0	0	0	1	415	343	0	180433	0
Other Portfolio Income	6	177502	51842	0	0	9231	6	14178	20557	5639	36775	25499	13774	0
Other Receipts	7	3019741	902746	17854	396	-1184	1976	37170	120417	158566	227883	827085	726833	0
Total Receipts	8	40174420	2096160	7619382	2842467	4344783	1365688	2376994	2579669	2006384	2945424	4869388	7128081	0
Average Total Receipts	9	2358	674	621	3785	6573	21011	34956	66145	95542	173260	347813	792009	•
Operating Costs/Operating Income (%)														
Cost of Operations	10	53.0	81.8	77.7	57.2	60.9	8.8	57.6	75.1	51.5	39.8	48.2	18.2	•
Salaries and Wages	11	13.4	1.2	5.2	8.9	6.6	11.2	15.9	8.9	17.3	18.8	20.9	25.6	•
Taxes Paid	12	1.8	0.1	0.7	1.4	2.1	1.2	1.7	1.0	2.2	2.3	2.2	3.3	•
Interest Paid	13	1.2	6.5	0.1	0.2	0.2	0.1	0.1	0.0	1.0	1.0	1.2	4.0	•
Depreciation	14	1.4	0.3	0.1	0.6	1.8	1.3	0.6	0.5	1.9	2.4	2.5	2.6	•
Amortization and Depletion	15	0.6	0.2	0.1	0.0	0.2	0.1	0.1	0.1	0.7	0.9	0.9	2.2	•
Pensions and Other Deferred Comp.	16	3.3	85.5	0.3	0.3	0.3	0.1	0.2	0.4	0.4	0.9	1.3	1.5	•
Employee Benefits	17	1.6	1.0	0.7	1.3	0.4	0.7	1.5	0.8	2.2	2.1	3.1	2.9	•
Advertising	18	4.5	11.8	0.4	0.4	0.9	2.0	5.8	2.2	4.7	1.6	3.1	15.5	•
Other Expenses	19	25.0	13.6	10.4	23.6	22.3	70.8	13.5	12.9	22.8	37.3	36.2	35.0	•
Officers' Compensation	20	1.8	0.6	2.5	3.9	3.0	1.3	1.5	0.9	1.8	0.6	0.7	1.3	•
Operating Margin	21	•	•	1.8	2.2	1.3	2.5	1.5	•	•	•	•	•	•
Operating Margin Before Officers' Comp.	22	•	•	4.3	6.1	4.3	3.8	3.0	•	•	•	•	•	•

Selected Average Balance Sheet ($ in Thousands)													
Net Receivables 23	219	0	2	72	528	1886	3043	8626	11666	15106	48571	160787	•
Inventories 24	12	0	0	0	95	39	542	525	777	922	1366	3747	•
Net Property, Plant and Equipment 25	119	0	5	69	223	190	1102	1484	12305	22010	23184	74540	•
Total Assets 26	1689	0	42	614	2095	6450	15657	40540	71201	146919	356522	1594955	•
Notes and Loans Payable 27	317	0	27	100	208	65	1211	1004	15903	31368	66486	324555	•
All Other Liabilities 28	742	0	23	132	1567	5419	9848	27421	32926	52339	163237	583455	•
Net Worth 29	631	0	-9	382	321	966	4598	12114	22372	63212	126800	686945	•
Selected Financial Ratios (Times to 1)													
Current Ratio 30	1.0	•	1.5	3.1	1.5	2.6	1.3	0.9	1.1	1.2	0.9	0.9	•
Quick Ratio 31	0.7	•	1.2	2.8	1.2	2.2	0.8	0.6	0.8	0.8	0.6	0.6	•
Net Sales to Working Capital 32	95.6	•	54.1	12.0	10.9	6.1	16.2	•	43.5	16.7	•	•	•
Coverage Ratio 33	2.8	•	34.6	13.3	9.7	42.4	39.5	86.5	4.1	4.2	2.9	2.1	•
Total Asset Turnover 34	1.3	•	14.7	6.2	3.1	3.3	2.2	1.5	1.2	1.1	0.8	0.4	•
Inventory Turnover 35	92.9	•	3968.9	•	42.0	46.8	36.2	89.4	57.8	67.5	100.5	33.1	•
Receivables Turnover 36	9.2	•	160.8	60.1	11.2	16.2	11.4	8.2	8.7	6.3	7.6	3.5	•
Total Liabilities to Net Worth 37	1.7	•	•	0.6	5.5	5.7	2.4	2.3	2.2	1.3	1.8	1.3	•
Current Assets to Working Capital 38	27.0	•	3.1	1.5	2.9	1.6	4.9	•	16.0	5.3	•	•	•
Current Liabilities to Working Capital 39	26.0	•	2.1	0.5	1.9	0.6	3.9	•	15.0	4.3	•	•	•
Working Capital to Net Sales 40	0.0	•	0.0	0.1	0.1	0.2	0.1	•	0.0	0.1	•	•	•
Inventory to Working Capital 41	0.7	•	0.0	•	0.2	0.0	0.3	•	0.3	0.2	•	•	•
Total Receipts to Cash Flow 42	4.1	•	9.5	4.0	4.7	1.4	6.3	6.8	4.4	2.6	2.9	2.8	•
Cost of Goods to Cash Flow 43	2.2	•	7.4	2.3	2.8	0.1	3.6	5.1	2.3	1.0	1.4	0.5	•
Cash Flow to Total Debt 44	0.5	•	1.3	4.0	0.8	2.8	0.5	0.3	0.4	0.7	0.4	0.3	•
Selected Financial Factors (in Percentages)													
Debt Ratio 45	62.7	•	120.9	37.8	84.7	85.0	70.6	70.1	68.6	57.0	64.4	56.9	•
Return on Total Assets 46	4.2	•	30.7	14.9	5.3	8.7	9.2	5.0	5.1	4.3	2.7	3.6	•
Return on Equity Before Income Taxes 47	7.3	•	•	22.2	31.1	56.6	30.6	16.6	12.2	7.7	5.0	4.4	•
Return on Equity After Income Taxes 48	5.6	•	•	21.7	25.1	56.6	26.2	13.9	7.3	6.6	3.3	3.1	•
Profit Margin (Before Income Tax) 49	2.1	•	2.0	2.2	1.5	2.6	4.1	3.2	3.1	3.1	2.2	4.4	•
Profit Margin (After Income Tax) 50	1.7	•	2.0	2.2	1.2	2.6	3.5	2.7	1.9	2.7	1.5	3.2	•

Table II

Corporations with Net Income

TRAVEL ARRANGEMENT AND RESERVATION SERVICES

MONEY AMOUNTS AND SIZE OF ASSETS IN THOUSANDS OF DOLLARS

Item Description for Accounting Period 7/11 Through 6/12		Total	Zero Assets	Under 500	500 to 1,000	1,000 to 5,000	5,000 to 10,000	10,000 to 25,000	25,000 to 50,000	50,000 to 100,000	100,000 to 250,000	250,000 to 500,000	500,000 to 2,500,000	2,500,000 and over
Number of Enterprises	1	9844	1567	7031	•	499	12	58	29	13	12	8	•	0
Revenues ($ in Thousands)														
Net Sales	2	27047678	97278	4154622	•	2772827	313271	2288264	2256288	1362069	2091417	3072654	•	0
Interest	3	87844	0	55	•	559	0	8284	1817	3768	13838	10305	•	0
Rents	4	30839	0	3	•	0	0	437	7	1436	4971	2432	•	0
Royalties	5	181192	0	0	•	0	0	0	1	415	343	0	•	0
Other Portfolio Income	6	128430	43375	0	•	9216	0	14178	16224	4836	8378	18445	•	0
Other Receipts	7	1654240	3617	6392	•	-7845	1954	36142	116782	142546	201276	426245	•	0
Total Receipts	8	29130223	144270	4161072	•	2774757	315225	2347305	2391119	1515070	2320223	3530081	•	0
Average Total Receipts	9	2959	92	592	•	5561	26269	40471	82452	116544	193352	441260	•	•
Operating Costs/Operating Income (%)														
Cost of Operations	10	49.4	•	75.5	•	60.2	5.0	57.7	76.5	52.2	33.3	44.3	•	•
Salaries and Wages	11	15.2	•	4.0	•	9.1	42.4	15.8	8.6	16.9	19.6	19.9	•	•
Taxes Paid	12	2.0	1.4	0.9	•	1.9	4.3	1.6	0.9	2.4	2.4	2.1	•	•
Interest Paid	13	1.1	0.1	0.1	•	0.2	•	0.1	0.0	0.5	0.7	0.9	•	•
Depreciation	14	1.4	2.3	0.2	•	1.9	0.8	0.6	0.5	1.7	2.5	1.4	•	•
Amortization and Depletion	15	0.7	•	0.1	•	0.1	0.1	0.1	0.1	0.3	0.6	0.8	•	•
Pensions and Other Deferred Comp.	16	0.6	•	0.1	•	0.5	0.3	0.2	0.3	0.3	0.8	0.8	•	•
Employee Benefits	17	1.7	•	0.4	•	0.5	2.3	1.4	0.5	2.2	2.2	2.8	•	•
Advertising	18	5.0	0.2	0.5	•	1.0	7.3	5.9	2.0	4.8	0.9	2.7	•	•
Other Expenses	19	23.7	55.5	9.3	•	16.5	22.8	13.3	11.8	21.3	41.9	35.2	•	•
Officers' Compensation	20	2.2	•	4.2	•	4.1	1.4	1.5	0.9	1.9	0.7	0.6	•	•
Operating Margin	21	•	40.5	4.7	•	4.0	13.2	1.7	•	•	•	•	•	•
Operating Margin Before Officers' Comp.	22	•	40.5	8.9	•	8.1	14.6	3.3	•	•	•	•	•	•

Selected Average Balance Sheet ($ in Thousands)													
Net Receivables 23	287	0	0	•	440	1785	2888	11365	12952	11593	36766	•	•
Inventories 24	16	0	0	•	117	0	535	699	172	483	600	•	•
Net Property, Plant and Equipment 25	165	0	6	•	280	387	1262	1503	15172	18887	25294	•	•
Total Assets 26	2384	0	58	•	2202	8232	15811	39537	72012	151723	363299	•	•
Notes and Loans Payable 27	403	0	28	•	252	0	1400	1185	7026	8845	44478	•	•
All Other Liabilities 28	1039	0	28	•	1336	3697	8919	33356	36478	56749	166154	•	•
Net Worth 29	943	0	2	•	613	4535	5493	4995	28508	86128	152668	•	•
Selected Financial Ratios (Times to 1)													
Current Ratio 30	1.0	•	1.7	•	2.4	1.9	1.3	0.9	1.2	1.1	0.8	•	•
Quick Ratio 31	0.7	•	1.4	•	1.8	1.4	0.9	0.6	1.0	0.7	0.7	•	•
Net Sales to Working Capital 32	90.1	•	28.7	•	5.3	8.0	16.2	•	23.6	46.1	•	•	•
Coverage Ratio 33	5.4	823.3	48.1	•	18.5	•	43.0	105.0	13.2	8.3	5.5	•	•
Total Asset Turnover 34	1.2	•	10.1	•	2.5	3.2	2.5	2.0	1.5	1.1	1.1	•	•
Inventory Turnover 35	83.0	•	2109.3	•	28.7	•	42.5	85.0	318.6	120.1	283.6	•	•
Receivables Turnover 36	9.8	•	401.6	•	9.0	•	13.4	7.9	11.1	7.3	•	•	•
Total Liabilities to Net Worth 37	1.5	•	28.4	•	2.6	0.8	1.9	6.9	1.5	0.8	1.4	•	•
Current Assets to Working Capital 38	26.8	•	2.4	•	1.7	2.1	4.0	•	7.4	12.7	•	•	•
Current Liabilities to Working Capital 39	25.8	•	1.4	•	0.7	1.1	3.0	•	6.4	11.7	•	•	•
Working Capital to Net Sales 40	0.0	•	0.0	•	0.2	0.1	0.1	•	0.0	0.0	•	•	•
Inventory to Working Capital 41	0.6	•	0.0	•	0.1	•	0.3	•	0.1	0.1	•	•	•
Total Receipts to Cash Flow 42	3.9	1.2	8.0	•	5.5	3.0	6.3	6.9	4.0	2.2	2.8	•	•
Cost of Goods to Cash Flow 43	1.9	•	6.0	•	3.3	0.1	3.6	5.3	2.1	0.7	1.2	•	•
Cash Flow to Total Debt 44	0.5	•	1.3	•	0.6	2.4	0.6	0.3	0.6	1.2	0.7	•	•
Selected Financial Factors (in Percentages)													
Debt Ratio 45	60.4	•	96.6	•	72.1	44.9	65.3	87.4	60.4	43.2	58.0	•	•
Return on Total Assets 46	6.8	•	49.6	•	10.9	43.9	11.1	8.0	10.6	6.9	5.2	•	•
Return on Equity Before Income Taxes 47	14.1	•	1428.1	•	37.1	79.7	31.2	62.6	24.7	10.7	10.1	•	•
Return on Equity After Income Taxes 48	12.2	•	1418.1	•	33.0	79.7	26.9	53.8	18.5	9.5	7.8	•	•
Profit Margin (Before Income Tax) 49	4.8	88.8	4.8	•	4.1	13.8	4.3	4.0	6.7	5.3	4.0	•	•
Profit Margin (After Income Tax) 50	4.2	88.8	4.8	•	3.6	13.8	3.7	3.5	5.0	4.7	3.1	•	•

Table I

Corporations with and without Net Income

OTHER ADMINISTRATIVE AND SUPPORT SERVICES

MONEY AMOUNTS AND SIZE OF ASSETS IN THOUSANDS OF DOLLARS

Item Description for Accounting Period 7/11 Through 6/12		Total	Zero Assets	Under 500	500 to 1,000	1,000 to 5,000	5,000 to 10,000	10,000 to 25,000	25,000 to 50,000	50,000 to 100,000	100,000 to 250,000	250,000 to 500,000	500,000 to 2,500,000	2,500,000 and over
Number of Enterprises	1	220027	53647	151134	8134	5610	790	322	149	100	57	27	48	8
Revenues ($ in Thousands)														
Net Sales	2	230247058	6412190	65239395	15318927	28524214	12610861	11075778	6223563	9304919	9075195	7235463	42612202	16614352
Interest	3	455685	6580	8914	4075	9805	5596	8909	7736	7476	23142	13310	257262	102880
Rents	4	49456	2350	749	3266	7389	340	1529	1452	1460	417	3264	23869	3372
Royalties	5	361528	5510	0	0	0	455	881	0	29095	753	10345	191549	122940
Other Portfolio Income	6	1229404	98417	76907	25943	47995	20854	56877	7407	13968	59241	18885	441479	361427
Other Receipts	7	4448995	273301	235690	142115	222625	452816	306597	128659	195838	507728	191183	1679673	112772
Total Receipts	8	236792126	6798348	65561655	15494326	28812028	13090922	11450571	6368817	9552756	9666476	7472450	45206034	17317743
Average Total Receipts	9	1076	127	434	1905	5136	16571	35561	42744	95528	169587	276757	941792	2164718
Operating Costs/Operating Income (%)														
Cost of Operations	10	35.9	29.0	34.3	45.6	44.4	47.1	49.2	31.8	44.9	29.7	39.9	32.8	10.0
Salaries and Wages	11	22.0	12.0	20.6	16.2	18.2	20.6	20.5	23.1	20.9	20.4	29.1	28.1	27.0
Taxes Paid	12	3.6	3.3	3.6	3.8	3.8	2.7	3.8	3.3	3.5	3.2	3.7	4.2	3.2
Interest Paid	13	2.1	1.3	0.6	0.6	0.9	0.6	0.7	1.1	1.3	2.3	3.4	2.9	11.8
Depreciation	14	2.3	2.4	1.7	2.6	1.9	2.1	1.4	3.1	2.8	2.1	3.3	2.7	4.5
Amortization and Depletion	15	1.1	0.5	0.2	0.1	0.3	0.1	0.4	1.0	1.2	1.8	2.0	1.9	5.5
Pensions and Other Deferred Comp.	16	0.6	0.2	0.6	0.6	0.2	0.4	0.5	0.4	0.5	0.3	0.2	0.8	1.0
Employee Benefits	17	2.4	1.2	1.1	1.3	1.5	2.6	2.1	2.4	3.3	10.0	3.5	3.2	2.8
Advertising	18	1.3	0.8	1.4	1.5	1.4	1.6	0.3	3.1	2.3	1.0	0.7	0.6	1.6
Other Expenses	19	23.0	40.3	23.6	15.8	19.4	19.6	19.2	28.9	18.6	31.2	18.1	23.7	28.5
Officers' Compensation	20	4.0	7.9	7.4	7.0	4.2	3.0	1.8	2.5	1.7	1.4	0.7	0.9	0.7
Operating Margin	21	1.8	1.1	5.1	4.7	3.9	•	0.3	•	•	•	•	•	3.4
Operating Margin Before Officers' Comp.	22	5.8	9.0	12.4	11.7	8.1	2.6	2.1	1.9	0.6	•	•	•	4.1

Selected Average Balance Sheet ($ in Thousands)														
Net Receivables	23	115	0	9	100	486	1507	5086	7309	20230	26213	48884	192236	298588
Inventories	24	11	0	2	36	52	235	516	1045	2012	2205	3871	5851	20868
Net Property, Plant and Equipment	25	114	0	21	206	427	1931	2078	5708	9989	12617	55077	85063	944172
Total Assets	26	712	0	74	700	2018	7171	15395	34910	69444	158700	349055	932200	5303539
Notes and Loans Payable	27	325	0	56	290	876	2684	4293	10999	25012	57861	139673	337592	3120189
All Other Liabilities	28	176	0	17	176	636	2293	5386	10675	24011	43068	84264	218107	1054582
Net Worth	29	210	0	1	234	506	2194	5716	13236	20421	57771	125119	376501	1128768

Selected Financial Ratios (Times to 1)														
Current Ratio	30	1.5	•	1.4	1.9	1.5	1.3	1.4	1.5	1.4	1.4	1.7	1.5	1.7
Quick Ratio	31	1.1	•	1.1	1.4	1.2	0.9	1.1	1.0	1.1	1.0	1.0	1.2	0.9
Net Sales to Working Capital	32	12.6	•	44.2	10.9	13.5	15.7	12.6	6.8	9.4	8.8	5.6	8.4	7.5
Coverage Ratio	33	3.3	6.6	10.8	10.3	6.6	6.8	6.6	2.6	2.2	2.3	0.6	2.6	1.7
Total Asset Turnover	34	1.5	•	5.9	2.7	2.5	2.2	2.2	1.2	1.3	1.0	0.8	1.0	0.4
Inventory Turnover	35	35.3	•	59.6	24.0	43.7	32.0	32.8	12.7	20.8	21.5	27.6	49.7	9.9
Receivables Turnover	36	9.4	•	47.3	19.3	10.5	10.7	7.5	5.8	4.9	7.0	4.0	5.1	6.6
Total Liabilities to Net Worth	37	2.4	•	84.5	2.0	3.0	2.3	1.7	1.6	2.4	1.7	1.8	1.5	3.7
Current Assets to Working Capital	38	3.0	•	3.6	2.1	3.0	4.0	3.3	3.0	3.5	3.4	2.5	2.9	2.5
Current Liabilities to Working Capital	39	2.0	•	2.6	1.1	2.0	3.0	2.3	2.0	2.5	2.4	1.5	1.9	1.5
Working Capital to Net Sales	40	0.1	•	0.0	0.1	0.1	0.1	0.1	0.1	0.1	0.1	0.2	0.1	0.1
Inventory to Working Capital	41	0.1	•	0.3	0.2	0.1	0.3	0.2	0.1	0.2	0.1	0.1	0.1	0.1
Total Receipts to Cash Flow	42	4.2	2.5	4.1	5.7	5.0	5.1	5.1	3.7	5.8	3.2	6.8	4.1	3.1
Cost of Goods to Cash Flow	43	1.5	0.7	1.4	2.6	2.2	2.4	2.5	1.2	2.6	1.0	2.7	1.4	0.3
Cash Flow to Total Debt	44	0.5	•	1.4	0.7	0.7	0.6	0.7	0.5	0.3	0.5	0.2	0.4	0.2

Selected Financial Factors (in Percentages)														
Debt Ratio	45	70.5	•	98.8	66.6	74.9	69.4	62.9	62.1	70.6	63.6	64.2	59.6	78.7
Return on Total Assets	46	10.1	•	35.8	17.5	14.6	8.8	9.7	3.3	3.9	5.4	1.4	7.2	8.0
Return on Equity Before Income Taxes	47	23.9	•	2776.7	47.4	49.4	24.5	22.0	5.4	7.3	8.4	•	11.0	15.9
Return on Equity After Income Taxes	48	20.7	•	2752.3	46.8	47.8	22.7	19.7	4.6	5.3	5.6	•	7.5	11.1
Profit Margin (Before Income Tax)	49	4.8	7.1	5.5	5.9	4.9	3.4	3.7	1.7	1.6	3.1	•	4.7	8.7
Profit Margin (After Income Tax)	50	4.2	6.5	5.5	5.8	4.8	3.1	3.3	1.5	1.2	2.0	•	3.2	6.1

Table II

Corporations with Net Income

OTHER ADMINISTRATIVE AND SUPPORT SERVICES

MONEY AMOUNTS AND SIZE OF ASSETS IN THOUSANDS OF DOLLARS

Item Description for Accounting Period 7/11 Through 6/12		Total	Zero Assets	Under 500	500 to 1,000	1,000 to 5,000	5,000 to 10,000	10,000 to 25,000	25,000 to 50,000	50,000 to 100,000	100,000 to 250,000	250,000 to 500,000	500,000 to 2,500,000	2,500,000 and over
Number of Enterprises	1	137215	28538	97979	5568	4179	502	234	73	54	32	13	34	8
Revenues ($ in Thousands)														
Net Sales	2	175583500	4318986	47715861	11744735	23584329	8786728	8944541	3432031	5320127	6440689	4313610	34367511	16614352
Interest	3	386677	3214	1301	3788	5642	4448	7803	3155	4545	21958	5292	222652	102880
Rents	4	40828	1976	0	1118	7285	196	1479	1429	642	404	3101	19827	3372
Royalties	5	315942	5510	0	0	0	0	6	0	29093	751	0	157641	122940
Other Portfolio Income	6	1125553	97974	58657	24115	24467	17386	56169	5289	5287	51584	11563	411635	361427
Other Receipts	7	3883114	163541	138399	143739	191056	342548	290948	133839	91222	518090	180990	1575970	112772
Total Receipts	8	181335614	4591201	47914218	11917495	23812779	9151306	9300946	3575743	5450916	7033476	4514556	36755236	17317743
Average Total Receipts	9	1322	161	489	2140	5698	18230	39748	48983	100943	219796	347274	1081036	2164718
Operating Costs/Operating Income (%)														
Cost of Operations	10	34.7	32.3	33.2	42.2	43.6	43.6	48.2	37.2	36.5	25.9	37.6	35.2	10.0
Salaries and Wages	11	22.0	9.0	19.5	17.0	17.2	23.7	19.1	21.7	24.1	18.2	34.0	28.8	27.0
Taxes Paid	12	3.7	3.0	3.3	3.9	3.6	3.4	3.8	4.1	3.8	2.6	4.7	4.4	3.2
Interest Paid	13	2.0	1.1	0.5	0.5	0.6	0.5	0.5	0.6	1.0	1.4	1.2	1.9	11.8
Depreciation	14	2.2	1.6	1.5	2.6	1.8	2.5	1.3	2.4	2.0	1.6	2.9	2.6	4.5
Amortization and Depletion	15	1.0	0.3	0.2	0.1	0.2	0.0	0.3	0.7	0.7	0.8	1.0	1.3	5.5
Pensions and Other Deferred Comp.	16	0.6	0.2	0.4	0.8	0.2	0.2	0.6	0.5	0.5	0.3	0.3	1.0	1.0
Employee Benefits	17	2.4	1.0	0.9	1.2	1.4	2.9	1.9	2.7	3.5	13.2	3.5	3.3	2.8
Advertising	18	1.2	0.9	1.2	1.3	1.5	1.0	0.3	0.6	3.8	1.3	0.3	0.6	1.6
Other Expenses	19	21.5	32.4	22.5	15.1	18.5	15.9	19.8	23.6	17.8	34.8	13.1	20.3	28.5
Officers' Compensation	20	3.8	5.9	7.3	7.1	4.2	3.1	1.8	2.1	1.6	1.3	0.7	0.9	0.7
Operating Margin	21	5.1	12.2	9.5	8.3	7.1	3.2	2.5	3.8	4.7	•	0.6	•	3.4
Operating Margin Before Officers' Comp.	22	8.9	18.1	16.7	15.4	11.3	6.3	4.2	5.9	6.3	0.1	1.4	0.6	4.1

Selected Average Balance Sheet ($ in Thousands)														
Net Receivables	23	139	0	9	99	508	1171	5412	6438	21626	34436	73437	226060	298588
Inventories	24	11	0	2	34	52	198	402	1407	2161	2956	4914	3921	21874
Net Property, Plant and Equipment	25	140	0	22	204	419	2235	2169	4170	10206	14028	51198	89945	944172
Total Assets	26	855	0	79	710	2059	7143	15258	34647	69378	160407	337003	933798	5303539
Notes and Loans Payable	27	365	0	45	243	841	2783	3828	8292	21496	53350	99291	258805	3120189
All Other Liabilities	28	202	0	14	145	598	1499	5385	10220	24172	47981	80767	235109	1054582
Net Worth	29	288	0	19	323	619	2861	6045	16135	23711	59076	156945	439884	1128768

Selected Financial Ratios (Times to 1)														
Current Ratio	30	1.7	•	1.6	2.3	1.7	1.7	1.5	1.8	1.5	1.6	2.5	1.6	1.7
Quick Ratio	31	1.3	•	1.4	1.9	1.4	1.1	1.2	1.2	1.2	1.2	1.6	1.3	0.9
Net Sales to Working Capital	32	10.8	•	33.8	9.2	11.2	11.9	11.6	5.2	8.1	8.0	3.7	7.7	7.5
Coverage Ratio	33	5.4	18.5	19.5	20.5	13.8	17.0	14.1	15.2	8.2	6.7	5.2	4.6	1.7
Total Asset Turnover	34	1.5	•	6.2	3.0	2.7	2.5	2.5	1.4	1.4	1.3	1.0	1.1	0.4
Inventory Turnover	35	40.6	•	69.1	25.9	47.4	38.6	45.8	12.5	16.6	17.6	25.4	90.7	9.5
Receivables Turnover	36	9.8	•	59.6	20.6	11.2	•	8.2	5.5	4.4	6.8	2.9	5.4	•
Total Liabilities to Net Worth	37	2.0	•	3.1	1.2	2.3	1.5	1.5	1.1	1.9	1.7	1.1	1.1	3.7
Current Assets to Working Capital	38	2.5	•	2.6	1.8	2.4	2.5	2.9	2.2	3.1	2.8	1.7	2.6	2.5
Current Liabilities to Working Capital	39	1.5	•	1.6	0.8	1.4	1.5	1.9	1.2	2.1	1.8	0.7	1.6	1.5
Working Capital to Net Sales	40	0.1	•	0.0	0.1	0.1	0.1	0.1	0.2	0.1	0.1	0.3	0.1	0.1
Inventory to Working Capital	41	0.1	•	0.2	0.2	0.1	0.1	0.1	0.1	0.2	0.1	0.1	0.0	0.1
Total Receipts to Cash Flow	42	3.9	2.3	3.6	4.8	4.5	5.1	4.3	3.4	4.6	2.5	6.0	4.4	3.1
Cost of Goods to Cash Flow	43	1.3	0.7	1.2	2.0	1.9	2.2	2.1	1.3	1.7	0.6	2.2	1.5	0.3
Cash Flow to Total Debt	44	0.6	•	2.3	1.1	0.9	0.8	1.0	0.7	0.5	0.8	0.3	0.5	0.2

Selected Financial Factors (in Percentages)														
Debt Ratio	45	66.4	•	75.7	54.6	69.9	59.9	60.4	53.4	65.8	63.2	53.4	52.9	78.7
Return on Total Assets	46	15.8	•	64.6	30.5	23.8	19.2	17.4	11.6	11.6	11.8	6.3	9.8	8.0
Return on Equity Before Income Taxes	47	38.1	•	251.8	64.0	73.3	45.2	40.8	23.3	29.7	27.2	11.0	16.2	15.9
Return on Equity After Income Taxes	48	34.4	•	250.1	63.2	71.6	43.1	37.8	22.0	26.6	22.3	8.1	12.0	11.1
Profit Margin (Before Income Tax)	49	8.6	18.5	9.9	9.8	8.0	7.4	6.5	8.0	7.1	8.0	5.2	7.1	8.7
Profit Margin (After Income Tax)	50	7.7	17.7	9.8	9.7	7.9	7.0	6.0	7.6	6.4	6.5	3.8	5.2	6.1

Table I

Corporations with and without Net Income

WASTE MANAGEMENT AND REMEDIATION SERVICES

MONEY AMOUNTS AND SIZE OF ASSETS IN THOUSANDS OF DOLLARS

Item Description for Accounting Period 7/11 Through 6/12		Total	Zero Assets	Under 500	500 to 1,000	1,000 to 5,000	5,000 to 10,000	10,000 to 25,000	25,000 to 50,000	50,000 to 100,000	100,000 to 250,000	250,000 to 500,000	500,000 to 2,500,000	2,500,000 and over
Number of Enterprises	1	14445	1853	9376	875	1684	337	162	66	33	32	13	9	7
Revenues ($ in Thousands)														
Net Sales	2	75471972	1241275	6071541	1970752	9143108	5834292	4025442	2566498	2572272	3920525	3663793	5877337	28585137
Interest	3	494874	6	376	59	1612	1238	3696	2229	685	1915	507	38953	443598
Rents	4	77770	3	0	0	2924	307	639	535	2504	2476	3201	5910	59273
Royalties	5	9832	0	0	0	0	0	0	5	373	151	5	7973	1324
Other Portfolio Income	6	595775	145402	16820	71266	42112	14699	5861	30592	4931	8693	32762	127027	95607
Other Receipts	7	614174	21303	-42144	2755	29133	32518	27660	47380	23811	48369	12941	15060	395388
Total Receipts	8	77264397	1407989	6046593	2044832	9218889	5883054	4063298	2647239	2604576	3982129	3713209	6072260	29580327
Average Total Receipts	9	5349	760	645	2337	5474	17457	25082	40110	78927	124442	285631	674696	4225761
Operating Costs/Operating Income (%)														
Cost of Operations	10	41.7	58.5	35.4	53.1	46.1	67.0	47.3	56.6	63.3	45.2	29.3	28.2	34.7
Salaries and Wages	11	15.3	15.0	13.7	7.5	9.1	7.9	13.6	6.8	6.8	11.9	19.8	17.6	21.0
Taxes Paid	12	2.7	2.7	3.5	2.3	2.7	1.7	2.5	1.4	1.9	2.6	2.9	3.3	3.0
Interest Paid	13	3.3	2.6	0.3	0.8	0.9	1.1	1.1	1.5	2.5	2.5	4.2	4.3	5.8
Depreciation	14	7.1	2.1	2.0	3.9	4.9	3.9	6.4	7.3	5.8	8.9	8.7	9.5	9.3
Amortization and Depletion	15	2.0	1.3	0.0	0.0	0.1	0.4	0.3	0.6	0.7	1.8	2.6	3.1	3.6
Pensions and Other Deferred Comp.	16	0.3	0.3	0.1	0.3	0.2	0.4	0.7	0.2	0.2	0.4	0.2	1.1	0.3
Employee Benefits	17	2.0	1.0	1.9	1.2	1.4	1.0	2.1	4.6	2.2	2.7	1.5	2.3	2.0
Advertising	18	0.3	0.2	0.9	0.3	0.4	0.3	0.5	0.2	0.3	0.2	0.2	0.3	0.3
Other Expenses	19	21.6	15.8	28.3	16.7	29.3	13.1	19.5	18.8	15.3	21.3	32.2	31.3	17.7
Officers' Compensation	20	1.7	3.8	7.4	5.8	2.2	2.0	2.7	2.1	1.4	1.6	0.8	0.5	0.2
Operating Margin	21	1.9	•	6.4	8.2	2.8	1.2	3.4	•	•	0.9	•	•	2.2
Operating Margin Before Officers' Comp.	22	3.7	0.5	13.9	14.0	5.0	3.2	6.0	1.9	1.0	2.5	•	•	2.4

Selected Average Balance Sheet ($ in Thousands)

Net Receivables 23	649	0	23	68	593	2213	2871	4971	13057	27728	40350	88436	559829
Inventories 24	68	0	2	70	39	452	467	696	1364	2697	6315	12135	34914
Net Property, Plant and Equipment 25	2345	0	35	327	993	2302	6618	12233	24101	39686	134379	402757	3071197
Total Assets 26	6189	0	120	724	2171	6896	15838	35027	69980	154954	352616	1085967	7880056
Notes and Loans Payable 27	2420	0	50	499	899	3017	6059	14154	27855	57901	151381	374717	3070344
All Other Liabilities 28	1842	0	33	40	820	1382	4312	10373	16152	44796	68299	262874	2543188
Net Worth 29	1928	0	37	185	453	2497	5467	10499	25974	52257	132936	448375	2266524

Selected Financial Ratios (Times to 1)

Current Ratio 30	1.2	•	1.9	3.1	1.3	1.7	1.6	1.5	1.7	1.4	1.2	1.3	1.0
Quick Ratio 31	0.9	•	1.7	2.2	1.1	1.3	1.4	1.1	1.4	1.1	0.9	0.9	0.7
Net Sales to Working Capital 32	21.6	•	19.7	9.7	24.4	10.0	9.6	9.9	8.4	8.2	23.1	15.7	1087.7
Coverage Ratio 33	2.3	4.9	22.2	16.1	5.2	2.9	5.0	3.0	1.3	2.0	0.8	1.5	2.0
Total Asset Turnover 34	0.8	•	5.4	3.1	2.5	2.5	1.6	1.1	1.1	0.8	0.8	0.6	0.5
Inventory Turnover 35	32.0	•	146.7	17.2	64.0	25.7	25.2	31.6	36.2	20.6	13.1	15.2	40.5
Receivables Turnover 36	8.2	•	32.7	40.5	9.0	7.8	8.4	6.6	5.9	4.9	8.5	6.2	7.7
Total Liabilities to Net Worth 37	2.2	•	2.3	2.9	3.8	1.8	1.9	2.3	1.7	2.0	1.7	1.4	2.5
Current Assets to Working Capital 38	5.3	•	2.2	1.5	4.5	2.4	2.7	2.9	2.5	3.4	6.0	4.7	290.4
Current Liabilities to Working Capital 39	4.3	•	1.2	0.5	3.5	1.4	1.7	1.9	1.5	2.4	5.0	3.7	289.4
Working Capital to Net Sales 40	0.0	•	0.1	0.1	0.0	0.1	0.1	0.1	0.1	0.1	0.0	0.1	0.0
Inventory to Working Capital 41	0.3	•	0.1	0.4	0.1	0.3	0.1	0.3	0.2	0.2	1.0	0.3	7.8
Total Receipts to Cash Flow 42	4.9	5.0	3.5	4.3	3.7	8.5	5.1	5.9	7.9	5.3	3.9	3.5	5.7
Cost of Goods to Cash Flow 43	2.0	2.9	1.3	2.3	1.7	5.7	2.4	3.3	5.0	2.4	1.1	1.0	2.0
Cash Flow to Total Debt 44	0.3	•	2.2	1.0	0.9	0.5	0.5	0.3	0.2	0.2	0.3	0.3	0.1

Selected Financial Factors (in Percentages)

Debt Ratio 45	68.9	•	69.5	74.4	79.1	63.8	65.5	70.0	62.9	66.3	62.3	58.7	71.2
Return on Total Assets 46	6.5	•	33.9	39.6	11.2	8.0	8.4	4.9	3.7	3.9	2.5	3.9	5.9
Return on Equity Before Income Taxes 47	11.7	•	106.1	145.3	43.6	14.4	19.4	10.8	2.5	5.7	•	3.2	10.3
Return on Equity After Income Taxes 48	9.3	•	104.2	145.2	41.5	13.7	17.2	9.3	1.2	3.5	•	2.5	6.9
Profit Margin (Before Income Tax) 49	4.3	10.1	6.0	12.0	3.6	2.1	4.3	2.9	0.8	2.4	•	2.2	5.7
Profit Margin (After Income Tax) 50	3.4	9.9	5.9	12.0	3.5	2.0	3.8	2.5	0.4	1.5	•	1.7	3.9

Table II

Corporations with Net Income

WASTE MANAGEMENT AND REMEDIATION SERVICES

MONEY AMOUNTS AND SIZE OF ASSETS IN THOUSANDS OF DOLLARS

Item Description for Accounting Period 7/11 Through 6/12		Total	Zero Assets	Under 500	500 to 1,000	1,000 to 5,000	5,000 to 10,000	10,000 to 25,000	25,000 to 50,000	50,000 to 100,000	100,000 to 250,000	250,000 to 500,000	500,000 to 2,500,000	2,500,000 and over
Number of Enterprises	1	9133	1216	5749	486	1227	228	133	40	19	19	5	•	•
Revenues ($ in Thousands)														
Net Sales	2	62105288	850488	4445393	1382680	6962300	5076410	3380900	1880909	1498001	2642119	1620989	•	•
Interest	3	484015	2	191	59	1444	1065	2881	2118	222	589	351	•	•
Rents	4	67752	0	0	0	423	78	639	532	406	190	754	•	•
Royalties	5	9300	0	0	0	0	0	0	0	0	0	5	•	•
Other Portfolio Income	6	463554	90562	16820	70716	28099	13077	5495	28134	2253	6267	2824	•	•
Other Receipts	7	456626	21008	13894	2738	25103	32427	25303	28771	11751	16382	1188	•	•
Total Receipts	8	63586535	962060	4476298	1456193	7017369	5123057	3415218	1940464	1512633	2665547	1626111	•	•
Average Total Receipts	9	6962	791	779	2996	5719	22470	25678	48512	79612	140292	325222	•	•
Operating Costs/Operating Income (%)														
Cost of Operations	10	42.2	63.5	39.1	63.0	38.6	69.6	45.2	63.3	65.1	46.8	43.2	•	•
Salaries and Wages	11	15.3	10.2	12.2	5.0	10.1	5.6	14.0	6.9	6.0	11.2	11.8	•	•
Taxes Paid	12	2.6	2.5	3.1	1.6	2.5	1.4	2.5	1.1	1.8	2.7	2.2	•	•
Interest Paid	13	3.1	2.3	0.3	0.4	0.8	0.4	0.9	0.9	1.4	1.3	3.1	•	•
Depreciation	14	6.8	1.8	1.5	2.4	5.0	3.4	5.5	5.1	4.7	6.1	5.8	•	•
Amortization and Depletion	15	1.9	0.2	0.0	•	0.1	0.1	0.3	0.4	0.6	1.0	1.4	•	•
Pensions and Other Deferred Comp.	16	0.4	0.5	0.2	0.4	0.2	0.3	0.7	0.3	0.3	0.5	0.1	•	•
Employee Benefits	17	1.7	0.9	1.4	0.4	1.7	0.9	2.2	0.7	2.5	2.0	1.8	•	•
Advertising	18	0.3	0.2	0.9	0.1	0.5	0.3	0.3	0.1	0.1	0.2	0.1	•	•
Other Expenses	19	19.7	13.0	22.4	8.7	32.9	11.7	19.9	15.9	10.2	19.2	27.4	•	•
Officers' Compensation	20	1.5	2.7	7.8	5.7	2.4	1.9	2.7	0.8	1.8	1.5	0.4	•	•
Operating Margin	21	4.3	2.2	11.1	12.4	5.3	4.5	5.9	4.6	5.5	7.6	2.8	•	•
Operating Margin Before Officers' Comp.	22	5.9	5.0	18.9	18.1	7.6	6.4	8.6	5.4	7.3	9.1	3.2	•	•

Selected Average Balance Sheet ($ in Thousands)													
Net Receivables 23	824	0	27	57	587	2113	2647	5653	16171	33618	48788	•	•
Inventories 24	86	0	1	80	32	664	481	692	1391	2182	18248	•	•
Net Property, Plant and Equipment 25	3154	0	26	232	1091	2234	6770	11259	20413	34536	94384	•	•
Total Assets 26	8054	0	127	736	2295	7078	15694	34422	67672	159423	312049	•	•
Notes and Loans Payable 27	2991	0	54	364	874	1609	5608	11499	20735	50272	124364	•	•
All Other Liabilities 28	2369	0	49	14	835	1638	3489	10289	15853	48514	64409	•	•
Net Worth 29	2694	0	23	358	587	3831	6597	12634	31084	60636	123276	•	•
Selected Financial Ratios (Times to 1)													
Current Ratio 30	1.2	•	1.5	9.2	1.3	2.3	1.7	1.9	2.0	1.5	2.1	•	•
Quick Ratio 31	1.0	•	1.4	6.2	1.1	1.6	1.4	1.3	1.8	1.2	1.5	•	•
Net Sales to Working Capital 32	23.9	•	24.9	6.4	22.5	8.8	8.9	8.2	6.2	6.3	7.1	•	•
Coverage Ratio 33	3.2	7.7	39.3	50.6	8.9	13.8	8.8	10.0	5.7	7.4	2.0	•	•
Total Asset Turnover 34	0.8	•	6.1	3.9	2.5	3.1	1.6	1.4	1.2	0.9	1.0	•	•
Inventory Turnover 35	33.2	•	448.8	22.4	68.9	23.3	23.9	43.0	36.9	29.8	7.7	•	•
Receivables Turnover 36	8.3	•	31.3	42.7	8.7	12.0	9.1	6.6	4.6	4.5	•	•	•
Total Liabilities to Net Worth 37	2.0	•	4.5	1.1	2.9	0.8	1.4	1.7	1.2	1.6	1.5	•	•
Current Assets to Working Capital 38	5.4	•	2.8	1.1	4.2	1.8	2.4	2.2	2.0	2.9	1.9	•	•
Current Liabilities to Working Capital 39	4.4	•	1.8	0.1	3.2	0.8	1.4	1.2	1.0	1.9	0.9	•	•
Working Capital to Net Sales 40	0.0	•	0.0	0.2	0.0	0.1	0.1	0.1	0.2	0.2	0.1	•	•
Inventory to Working Capital 41	0.3	•	0.0	0.4	0.0	0.3	0.1	0.2	0.1	0.1	0.4	•	•
Total Receipts to Cash Flow 42	4.7	4.2	3.4	4.2	3.0	7.0	4.4	5.3	7.3	4.3	3.8	•	•
Cost of Goods to Cash Flow 43	2.0	2.6	1.3	2.6	1.1	4.9	2.0	3.4	4.7	2.0	1.6	•	•
Cash Flow to Total Debt 44	0.3	•	2.2	1.8	1.1	1.0	0.6	0.4	0.3	0.3	0.5	•	•
Selected Financial Factors (in Percentages)													
Debt Ratio 45	66.6	•	81.9	51.3	74.4	45.9	58.0	63.3	54.1	62.0	60.5	•	•
Return on Total Assets 46	8.3	•	73.9	70.0	16.9	18.2	12.7	11.7	9.2	8.6	6.4	•	•
Return on Equity Before Income Taxes 47	17.0	•	397.3	141.1	58.7	31.2	26.7	28.7	16.5	19.5	8.1	•	•
Return on Equity After Income Taxes 48	14.2	•	392.3	141.0	56.5	30.6	24.4	26.6	14.6	16.3	5.4	•	•
Profit Margin (Before Income Tax) 49	6.7	15.3	11.8	17.8	6.1	5.4	6.9	7.7	6.5	8.5	3.1	•	•
Profit Margin (After Income Tax) 50	5.6	15.0	11.6	17.8	5.8	5.3	6.3	7.1	5.8	7.1	2.1	•	•

Table I

Corporations with and without Net Income

EDUCATIONAL SERVICES

Item Description for Accounting Period 7/11 Through 6/12		MONEY AMOUNTS AND SIZE OF ASSETS IN THOUSANDS OF DOLLARS												
		Total	Zero Assets	Under 500	500 to 1,000	1,000 to 5,000	5,000 to 10,000	10,000 to 25,000	25,000 to 50,000	50,000 to 100,000	100,000 to 250,000	250,000 to 500,000	500,000 to 2,500,000	2,500,000 and over
Number of Enterprises	1	60627	16130	40719	1185	1892	363	183	55	30	43	13	•	•
Revenues ($ in Thousands)														
Net Sales	2	64962081	1459425	9859582	2360057	7734252	3257575	3712173	3230287	2367525	6571735	3108810	•	•
Interest	3	124583	625	1272	137	2745	4802	3795	3076	6169	7714	6158	•	•
Rents	4	38059	0	30	12	90	152	0	2677	4839	9975	8422	•	•
Royalties	5	127443	1540	0	0	0	28913	0	4836	136	25908	1018	•	•
Other Portfolio Income	6	231830	109622	8810	175	1660	1178	5347	22456	36715	5048	4030	•	•
Other Receipts	7	535848	5679	45875	28651	82685	39521	8791	66818	40315	112058	31273	•	•
Total Receipts	8	66019844	1576891	9915569	2389032	7821432	3332141	3730106	3330150	2455699	6732438	3159711	•	•
Average Total Receipts	9	1089	98	244	2016	4134	9179	20383	60548	81857	156568	243055	•	•
Operating Costs/Operating Income (%)														
Cost of Operations	10	10.8	11.6	10.2	14.7	14.4	5.6	12.1	27.3	13.5	11.0	2.4	•	•
Salaries and Wages	11	30.8	18.9	24.8	35.9	29.2	37.7	30.7	30.6	28.4	32.5	34.1	•	•
Taxes Paid	12	3.5	2.4	4.2	3.5	3.7	4.8	3.3	3.4	3.6	3.8	4.7	•	•
Interest Paid	13	1.6	1.8	0.8	0.6	0.5	0.5	0.7	1.7	4.6	2.8	1.8	•	•
Depreciation	14	3.5	2.1	2.0	1.5	1.8	1.7	3.2	3.8	6.1	3.9	6.7	•	•
Amortization and Depletion	15	0.9	0.2	0.2	0.0	0.3	0.2	0.6	1.3	1.1	1.9	1.6	•	•
Pensions and Other Deferred Comp.	16	0.4	0.4	0.5	0.2	0.5	0.9	0.5	0.4	0.4	0.5	0.4	•	•
Employee Benefits	17	2.5	1.4	1.7	2.3	1.3	1.7	2.0	2.6	2.5	2.4	4.1	•	•
Advertising	18	6.0	3.4	2.3	0.9	2.1	3.3	6.7	6.0	5.6	6.9	6.1	•	•
Other Expenses	19	30.7	58.3	41.8	29.3	31.6	34.6	32.2	20.0	28.8	29.5	34.5	•	•
Officers' Compensation	20	3.9	9.0	10.6	4.3	7.5	4.4	3.0	1.4	1.8	2.1	1.0	•	•
Operating Margin	21	5.4	•	1.0	6.9	7.0	4.6	5.1	1.5	3.5	2.8	2.7	•	•
Operating Margin Before Officers' Comp.	22	9.3	•	11.6	11.2	14.6	9.0	8.1	2.8	5.3	4.9	3.7	•	•

Selected Average Balance Sheet ($ in Thousands)													
Net Receivables 23	93	0	4	102	434	1222	3329	5778	10879	16792	29031	•	•
Inventories 24	9	0	1	11	51	26	276	1602	688	1515	1217	•	•
Net Property, Plant and Equipment 25	165	0	14	258	534	1183	3168	7683	16676	31223	94781	•	•
Total Assets 26	904	0	61	669	2002	6574	15483	37601	69752	156739	343956	•	•
Notes and Loans Payable 27	286	0	48	156	650	771	3023	17049	25211	51634	74610	•	•
All Other Liabilities 28	286	0	27	206	753	3323	5193	13680	23689	47007	88231	•	•
Net Worth 29	332	0	-13	308	598	2480	7268	6872	20852	58098	181114	•	•

Selected Financial Ratios (Times to 1)													
Current Ratio 30	1.3	•	1.1	1.8	1.4	1.2	1.9	1.2	0.9	1.2	1.1	•	•
Quick Ratio 31	1.0	•	0.8	1.6	1.2	1.1	1.6	0.9	0.8	1.0	0.8	•	•
Net Sales to Working Capital 32	12.4	•	70.8	12.6	10.5	20.5	4.7	20.9	•	15.0	54.6	•	•
Coverage Ratio 33	5.3	0.2	3.0	15.5	16.6	14.4	8.7	3.6	2.6	2.9	3.4	•	•
Total Asset Turnover 34	1.2	•	4.0	3.0	2.0	1.4	1.3	1.6	1.1	1.0	0.7	•	•
Inventory Turnover 35	12.9	•	18.4	26.7	11.6	19.0	8.9	10.0	15.5	11.1	4.7	•	•
Receivables Turnover 36	11.1	•	51.3	15.8	10.1	6.8	6.0	10.4	6.6	•	6.0	•	•
Total Liabilities to Net Worth 37	1.7	•	•	1.2	2.3	1.7	1.1	4.5	2.3	1.7	0.9	•	•
Current Assets to Working Capital 38	4.0	•	9.0	2.2	3.2	6.6	2.2	6.8	•	5.0	17.1	•	•
Current Liabilities to Working Capital 39	3.0	•	8.0	1.2	2.2	5.6	1.2	5.8	•	4.0	16.1	•	•
Working Capital to Net Sales 40	0.1	•	0.0	0.1	0.1	0.0	0.2	0.0	•	0.1	0.0	•	•
Inventory to Working Capital 41	0.1	•	0.3	0.1	0.1	0.1	0.1	0.6	•	0.1	0.2	•	•
Total Receipts to Cash Flow 42	3.4	2.2	3.2	3.5	3.2	3.0	3.3	5.8	3.6	3.6	3.1	•	•
Cost of Goods to Cash Flow 43	0.4	0.3	0.3	0.5	0.5	0.2	0.4	1.6	0.5	0.4	0.1	•	•
Cash Flow to Total Debt 44	0.6	•	1.0	1.6	0.9	0.7	0.8	0.3	0.5	0.4	0.5	•	•

Selected Financial Factors (in Percentages)													
Debt Ratio 45	63.3	•	120.8	54.0	70.1	62.3	53.1	81.7	70.1	62.9	47.3	•	•
Return on Total Assets 46	10.2	•	9.5	25.8	17.7	10.2	8.2	9.8	13.5	7.8	4.2	•	•
Return on Equity Before Income Taxes 47	22.6	•	•	52.5	55.8	25.0	15.4	38.8	27.7	13.7	5.7	•	•
Return on Equity After Income Taxes 48	16.7	•	•	49.0	54.2	23.9	14.4	32.7	21.0	8.0	3.9	•	•
Profit Margin (Before Income Tax) 49	7.0	•	1.6	8.1	8.2	6.9	5.5	4.5	7.3	5.2	4.3	•	•
Profit Margin (After Income Tax) 50	5.2	•	1.5	7.6	7.9	6.6	5.2	3.8	5.5	3.1	3.0	•	•

Table II

Corporations with Net Income

EDUCATIONAL SERVICES

MONEY AMOUNTS AND SIZE OF ASSETS IN THOUSANDS OF DOLLARS

Item Description for Accounting Period 7/11 Through 6/12		Total	Zero Assets	Under 500	500 to 1,000	1,000 to 5,000	5,000 to 10,000	10,000 to 25,000	25,000 to 50,000	50,000 to 100,000	100,000 to 250,000	250,000 to 500,000	500,000 to 2,500,000	2,500,000 and over
Number of Enterprises	1	33191	6993	23321	767	1605	285	113	38	20	26	•	•	•
Revenues ($ in Thousands)														
Net Sales	2	52748208	755364	5701225	1648146	6776519	2712888	2999191	2498285	1875797	4791543	•	•	•
Interest	3	50046	7	196	122	2589	4608	2524	2925	3251	2398	•	•	•
Rents	4	23926	0	30	0	81	152	0	2677	410	490	•	•	•
Royalties	5	97267	0	0	0	0	28913	0	2927	136	2078	•	•	•
Other Portfolio Income	6	195892	108288	8745	175	1660	1178	4719	22456	4543	3320	•	•	•
Other Receipts	7	437750	1367	72729	1747	80715	32836	-7292	30541	38216	77971	•	•	•
Total Receipts	8	53553089	865026	5782925	1650190	6861564	2780575	2999142	2559811	1922353	4877800	•	•	•
Average Total Receipts	9	1613	124	248	2151	4275	9756	26541	67363	96118	187608	•	•	•
Operating Costs/Operating Income (%)														
Cost of Operations	10	11.0	6.6	10.6	16.6	14.9	4.0	14.1	29.4	12.5	13.8	•	•	•
Salaries and Wages	11	29.1	10.2	17.4	26.7	28.0	38.5	26.3	27.2	27.7	30.1	•	•	•
Taxes Paid	12	3.2	1.6	3.5	2.4	3.8	4.6	3.0	3.0	3.9	3.7	•	•	•
Interest Paid	13	0.9	0.4	0.5	0.6	0.5	0.3	0.4	1.4	1.3	1.4	•	•	•
Depreciation	14	3.3	1.7	1.4	1.3	1.5	1.4	2.8	2.2	6.2	3.8	•	•	•
Amortization and Depletion	15	0.7	0.0	0.2	0.0	0.1	0.1	0.2	0.3	0.5	1.2	•	•	•
Pensions and Other Deferred Comp.	16	0.4	0.6	0.7	0.2	0.5	1.1	0.6	0.4	0.5	0.3	•	•	•
Employee Benefits	17	2.3	0.9	0.9	1.2	1.1	1.4	1.6	2.3	2.4	1.8	•	•	•
Advertising	18	6.4	1.8	2.5	1.1	1.8	2.9	6.1	6.2	5.5	7.5	•	•	•
Other Expenses	19	28.8	65.2	40.3	31.7	30.1	32.3	30.9	18.6	27.7	24.6	•	•	•
Officers' Compensation	20	3.8	8.7	12.1	4.8	8.3	4.8	3.1	1.4	1.6	2.3	•	•	•
Operating Margin	21	10.0	2.3	10.0	13.5	9.5	8.7	11.1	7.8	10.2	9.4	•	•	•
Operating Margin Before Officers' Comp.	22	13.8	11.0	22.1	18.3	17.7	13.6	14.1	9.2	11.9	11.7	•	•	•

Selected Average Balance Sheet ($ in Thousands)													
Net Receivables 23	133	0	2	50	453	1185	3746	5887	12417	17175	•	•	•
Inventories 24	11	0	1	9	37	24	339	2227	959	814	•	•	•
Net Property, Plant and Equipment 25	242	0	15	334	510	846	3220	7536	19411	35665	•	•	•
Total Assets 26	1209	0	56	703	1896	6696	15476	37534	72800	153020	•	•	•
Notes and Loans Payable 27	283	0	33	144	470	321	2216	17214	15652	40205	•	•	•
All Other Liabilities 28	395	0	13	116	645	3583	6535	13045	25014	47791	•	•	•
Net Worth 29	530	0	10	444	781	2793	6725	7274	32134	65024	•	•	•
Selected Financial Ratios (Times to 1)													
Current Ratio 30	1.5	•	3.1	2.5	1.6	1.1	1.7	1.5	1.3	1.2	•	•	•
Quick Ratio 31	1.0	•	2.4	2.3	1.3	1.0	1.4	1.1	1.1	1.0	•	•	•
Net Sales to Working Capital 32	9.5	•	11.4	12.6	9.3	30.6	6.0	9.7	14.8	18.1	•	•	•
Coverage Ratio 33	13.5	46.4	25.8	23.6	23.5	42.1	30.3	8.5	10.7	9.0	•	•	•
Total Asset Turnover 34	1.3	•	4.3	3.1	2.2	1.4	1.7	1.8	1.3	1.2	•	•	•
Inventory Turnover 35	15.5	•	18.6	38.2	17.2	15.8	11.0	8.7	12.2	31.3	•	•	•
Receivables Turnover 36	11.6	•	92.5	17.4	10.7	8.7	6.3	10.1	6.5	9.8	•	•	•
Total Liabilities to Net Worth 37	1.3	•	4.8	0.6	1.4	1.4	1.3	4.2	1.3	1.4	•	•	•
Current Assets to Working Capital 38	3.1	•	1.5	1.6	2.7	9.4	2.4	3.1	4.6	5.6	•	•	•
Current Liabilities to Working Capital 39	2.1	•	0.5	0.6	1.7	8.4	1.4	2.1	3.6	4.6	•	•	•
Working Capital to Net Sales 40	0.1	•	0.1	0.1	0.1	0.0	0.2	0.1	0.1	0.1	•	•	•
Inventory to Working Capital 41	0.1	•	0.1	0.1	0.1	0.1	0.1	0.3	0.1	0.1	•	•	•
Total Receipts to Cash Flow 42	3.0	1.4	2.5	2.8	3.1	2.7	2.8	4.4	3.1	3.4	•	•	•
Cost of Goods to Cash Flow 43	0.3	0.1	0.3	0.5	0.5	0.1	0.4	1.3	0.4	0.5	•	•	•
Cash Flow to Total Debt 44	0.8	•	2.1	2.9	1.2	0.9	1.1	0.5	0.7	0.6	•	•	•
Selected Financial Factors (in Percentages)													
Debt Ratio 45	56.1	•	82.8	36.9	58.8	58.3	56.5	80.6	55.9	57.5	•	•	•
Return on Total Assets 46	16.4	•	51.8	43.5	25.0	16.3	19.6	20.4	18.2	15.2	•	•	•
Return on Equity Before Income Taxes 47	34.5	•	290.1	66.0	58.0	38.3	43.6	92.9	37.4	31.7	•	•	•
Return on Equity After Income Taxes 48	27.8	•	287.4	62.3	56.5	37.0	41.9	84.5	30.9	23.3	•	•	•
Profit Margin (Before Income Tax) 49	11.5	16.8	11.5	13.6	10.7	11.2	11.0	10.3	12.8	11.2	•	•	•
Profit Margin (After Income Tax) 50	9.3	16.6	11.4	12.9	10.5	10.9	10.6	9.3	10.6	8.2	•	•	•

Table I

Corporations with and without Net Income

OFFICES OF PHYSICIANS

Item Description for Accounting Period 7/11 Through 6/12		MONEY AMOUNTS AND SIZE OF ASSETS IN THOUSANDS OF DOLLARS												
		Total	Zero Assets	Under 500	500 to 1,000	1,000 to 5,000	5,000 to 10,000	10,000 to 25,000	25,000 to 50,000	50,000 to 100,000	100,000 to 250,000	250,000 to 500,000	500,000 to 2,500,000	2,500,000 and over
Number of Enterprises	1	161581	19165	130687	6769	4258	417	171	53	33	24	0	4	0
Revenues ($ in Thousands)														
Net Sales	2	251029993	6757164	130333627	23849058	45440250	9703453	8843884	5897352	3663140	5606058	0	10936006	0
Interest	3	61447	163	12539	810	7502	1072	4126	3902	3722	13964	0	13647	0
Rents	4	120157	491	33088	14622	15359	7713	2122	17802	6029	20449	0	2482	0
Royalties	5	37697	0	7545	0	0	0	295	0	2100	0	0	27758	0
Other Portfolio Income	6	424711	30274	136648	7245	76928	123023	13000	8029	1525	8254	0	19784	0
Other Receipts	7	8971687	377304	4495478	601767	1971717	561019	224445	201824	173079	139467	0	225588	0
Total Receipts	8	260645692	7165396	135018925	24473502	47511756	10396280	9087872	6128909	3849595	5788192	0	11225265	0
Average Total Receipts	9	1613	374	1033	3616	11158	24931	53145	115640	116654	241175	•	2806316	•
Operating Costs/Operating Income (%)														
Cost of Operations	10	4.1	0.3	2.8	5.9	5.4	4.2	9.1	4.7	10.0	8.5	•	3.7	•
Salaries and Wages	11	31.3	50.1	26.1	26.6	33.5	42.0	39.9	48.0	45.9	42.6	•	46.0	•
Taxes Paid	12	3.2	3.8	3.3	3.1	3.1	3.4	3.4	2.7	3.0	2.8	•	2.7	•
Interest Paid	13	0.4	0.3	0.2	0.3	0.4	0.6	0.4	0.6	1.0	1.7	•	1.0	•
Depreciation	14	1.4	0.7	1.0	1.8	1.8	2.5	1.9	1.5	2.7	2.8	•	0.9	•
Amortization and Depletion	15	0.1	0.1	0.0	0.0	0.1	0.1	0.1	0.3	0.4	0.7	•	0.4	•
Pensions and Other Deferred Comp.	16	3.6	2.7	3.8	2.7	3.4	2.6	3.0	2.9	2.4	1.9	•	7.6	•
Employee Benefits	17	2.5	3.0	1.9	1.4	2.3	2.9	3.4	8.0	4.1	3.7	•	6.2	•
Advertising	18	0.5	0.2	0.4	0.6	0.6	0.3	0.5	0.2	1.3	0.2	•	0.1	•
Other Expenses	19	31.5	18.7	29.4	34.7	33.3	38.6	39.6	34.3	31.0	36.2	•	32.5	•
Officers' Compensation	20	19.8	21.5	26.9	17.9	17.0	7.5	2.8	1.3	3.8	0.6	•	0.3	•
Operating Margin	21	1.8	•	4.1	5.1	•	•	•	•	•	•	•	•	•
Operating Margin Before Officers' Comp.	22	21.6	20.2	31.0	23.0	16.2	2.8	•	•	•	•	•	•	•

Selected Average Balance Sheet ($ in Thousands)

Net Receivables 23	27	0	2	48	175	805	3438	7494	13515	30821	•	127631	•
Inventories 24	2	0	0	5	4	40	109	205	261	638	•	27430	•
Net Property, Plant and Equipment 25	63	0	21	165	557	2285	4162	11168	15202	34882	•	93232	•
Total Assets 26	284	0	90	693	1782	6705	14805	39541	68448	176007	•	1992182	•
Notes and Loans Payable 27	116	0	48	245	880	2483	7696	13819	24125	53505	•	467137	•
All Other Liabilities 28	156	0	34	205	806	3919	6750	15070	21319	65813	•	2539300	•
Net Worth 29	12	0	8	243	97	303	358	10652	23005	56688	•	-1014254	•

Selected Financial Ratios (Times to 1)

Current Ratio 30	1.2	•	1.2	1.6	1.0	0.8	1.1	1.0	1.1	1.5	•	1.4	•
Quick Ratio 31	1.0	•	1.1	1.3	0.8	0.5	0.9	0.7	0.8	1.2	•	1.2	•
Net Sales to Working Capital 32	83.8	•	115.7	25.8	640.3	•	92.6	290.9	35.6	12.1	•	22.1	•
Coverage Ratio 33	16.5	16.1	36.8	26.8	10.7	5.4	•	•	0.7	1.9	•	2.0	•
Total Asset Turnover 34	5.5	•	11.1	5.1	6.0	3.5	3.5	2.8	1.6	1.3	•	1.4	•
Inventory Turnover 35	37.0	•	77.3	43.8	147.8	24.2	43.0	25.7	42.4	31.2	•	3.7	•
Receivables Turnover 36	58.2	•	438.9	77.1	57.9	22.8	15.9	17.0	8.6	9.0	•	21.6	•
Total Liabilities to Net Worth 37	22.6	•	10.0	1.9	17.4	21.1	40.3	2.7	2.0	2.1	•	•	•
Current Assets to Working Capital 38	6.6	•	5.6	2.7	52.4	•	13.4	39.6	9.2	2.9	•	3.6	•
Current Liabilities to Working Capital 39	5.6	•	4.6	1.7	51.4	•	12.4	38.6	8.2	1.9	•	2.6	•
Working Capital to Net Sales 40	0.0	•	0.0	0.0	0.0	•	0.0	0.0	0.0	0.1	•	0.0	•
Inventory to Working Capital 41	0.1	•	0.0	0.0	0.2	•	0.2	0.6	0.1	0.0	•	0.2	•
Total Receipts to Cash Flow 42	3.2	4.9	3.2	2.8	3.2	3.0	3.1	3.3	3.8	3.0	•	3.4	•
Cost of Goods to Cash Flow 43	0.1	0.0	0.1	0.2	0.2	0.1	0.3	0.2	0.4	0.3	•	0.1	•
Cash Flow to Total Debt 44	1.8	•	3.9	2.8	2.0	1.2	1.2	1.2	0.6	0.7	•	0.3	•

Selected Financial Factors (in Percentages)

Debt Ratio 45	95.8	•	90.9	65.0	94.6	95.5	97.6	73.1	66.4	67.8	•	150.9	•
Return on Total Assets 46	32.8	•	88.0	40.7	24.6	10.5	•	•	1.0	4.2	•	2.8	•
Return on Equity Before Income Taxes 47	729.2	•	937.8	111.7	409.1	189.6	•	•	•	6.2	•	•	•
Return on Equity After Income Taxes 48	714.4	•	930.5	110.7	401.4	184.1	•	•	•	1.5	•	•	•
Profit Margin (Before Income Tax) 49	5.6	4.8	7.7	7.7	3.7	2.5	•	•	•	1.5	•	1.0	•
Profit Margin (After Income Tax) 50	5.5	4.6	7.6	7.6	3.6	2.4	•	•	•	0.4	•	0.6	•

Table II

Corporations with Net Income

OFFICES OF PHYSICIANS

MONEY AMOUNTS AND SIZE OF ASSETS IN THOUSANDS OF DOLLARS

Item Description for Accounting Period 7/11 Through 6/12		Total	Zero Assets	Under 500	500 to 1,000	1,000 to 5,000	5,000 to 10,000	10,000 to 25,000	25,000 to 50,000	50,000 to 100,000	100,000 to 250,000	250,000 to 500,000	500,000 to 2,500,000	2,500,000 and over
Number of Enterprises	1	108360	8447	90928	5527	3045	272	•	25	18	•	0	•	•
Revenues ($ in Thousands)														
Net Sales	2	179748373	1625692	97536142	19733603	30284617	6263669	•	3659025	2448309	•	0	•	•
Interest	3	31833	157	4783	700	2929	524	•	1727	1553	•	0	•	•
Rents	4	32093	0	10778	13403	1174	401	•	1001	2536	•	0	•	•
Royalties	5	7840	0	7545	0	0	0	•	0	0	•	0	•	•
Other Portfolio Income	6	358905	29910	95139	6489	74706	120639	•	1672	1075	•	0	•	•
Other Receipts	7	7011773	321340	3428786	562562	1625391	429445	•	139109	147986	•	0	•	•
Total Receipts	8	187190817	1977099	101083173	20316757	31988817	6814678	•	3802534	2601459	•	0	•	•
Average Total Receipts	9	1727	234	1112	3676	10505	25054	•	152101	144526	•	•	•	•
Operating Costs/Operating Income (%)														
Cost of Operations	10	4.2	0.4	2.8	7.0	6.0	4.0	•	2.6	12.9	•	•	•	•
Salaries and Wages	11	28.2	31.1	23.8	25.3	29.1	38.4	•	46.5	44.0	•	•	•	•
Taxes Paid	12	3.1	4.1	3.2	2.8	3.1	3.5	•	2.5	2.6	•	•	•	•
Interest Paid	13	0.3	0.8	0.2	0.3	0.4	0.5	•	0.3	0.9	•	•	•	•
Depreciation	14	1.1	0.6	0.7	1.7	1.7	2.3	•	0.9	1.5	•	•	•	•
Amortization and Depletion	15	0.1	0.2	0.0	0.1	0.1	0.1	•	0.3	0.4	•	•	•	•
Pensions and Other Deferred Comp.	16	3.7	2.3	3.8	2.6	3.1	3.0	•	3.8	2.1	•	•	•	•
Employee Benefits	17	2.3	1.1	1.7	1.3	2.1	2.7	•	10.3	4.3	•	•	•	•
Advertising	18	0.5	0.7	0.4	0.6	0.6	0.4	•	0.1	0.4	•	•	•	•
Other Expenses	19	32.0	36.9	29.6	35.0	35.7	36.3	•	31.0	32.9	•	•	•	•
Officers' Compensation	20	19.2	15.2	25.9	16.0	16.3	10.0	•	1.5	0.8	•	•	•	•
Operating Margin	21	5.4	6.5	7.7	7.5	1.7	•	•	0.2	•	•	•	•	•
Operating Margin Before Officers' Comp.	22	24.6	21.7	33.6	23.5	18.0	8.8	•	1.7	•	•	•	•	•

Selected Average Balance Sheet ($ in Thousands)														
Net Receivables	23	24	0	3	39	115	606	•	7039	16896	•	•	•	•
Inventories	24	2	0	0	6	2	27	•	252	356	•	•	•	•
Net Property, Plant and Equipment	25	60	0	22	159	538	2882	•	9773	14021	•	•	•	•
Total Assets	26	289	0	94	687	1749	6875	•	39235	67789	•	•	•	•
Notes and Loans Payable	27	90	0	34	223	689	3254	•	15111	25918	•	•	•	•
All Other Liabilities	28	162	0	31	162	435	2294	•	14438	21725	•	•	•	•
Net Worth	29	37	0	28	303	626	1326	•	9686	20146	•	•	•	•
Selected Financial Ratios (Times to 1)														
Current Ratio	30	1.5	•	1.5	2.1	1.4	1.1	•	0.9	1.2	•	•	•	•
Quick Ratio	31	1.3	•	1.4	1.6	1.3	0.8	•	0.8	1.0	•	•	•	•
Net Sales to Working Capital	32	39.8	•	64.3	18.4	38.6	183.3	•	•	22.8	•	•	•	•
Coverage Ratio	33	34.0	34.9	61.3	37.5	21.0	15.3	•	13.5	4.7	•	•	•	•
Total Asset Turnover	34	5.7	•	11.4	5.2	5.7	3.3	•	3.7	2.0	•	•	•	•
Inventory Turnover	35	34.2	•	73.5	43.8	246.4	34.0	•	15.4	49.4	•	•	•	•
Receivables Turnover	36	73.2	•	378.3	82.6	77.9	33.8	•	28.9	9.5	•	•	•	•
Total Liabilities to Net Worth	37	6.7	•	2.4	1.3	1.8	4.2	•	3.1	2.4	•	•	•	•
Current Assets to Working Capital	38	3.0	•	3.0	1.9	3.3	15.2	•	•	5.1	•	•	•	•
Current Liabilities to Working Capital	39	2.0	•	2.0	0.9	2.3	14.2	•	•	4.1	•	•	•	•
Working Capital to Net Sales	40	0.0	•	0.0	0.1	0.0	0.0	•	•	0.0	•	•	•	•
Inventory to Working Capital	41	0.1	•	0.0	0.0	0.0	0.2	•	•	0.0	•	•	•	•
Total Receipts to Cash Flow	42	2.8	1.7	2.8	2.6	2.7	2.7	•	3.1	3.0	•	•	•	•
Cost of Goods to Cash Flow	43	0.1	0.0	0.1	0.2	0.2	0.1	•	0.1	0.4	•	•	•	•
Cash Flow to Total Debt	44	2.4	•	5.8	3.6	3.2	1.5	•	1.6	1.0	•	•	•	•
Selected Financial Factors (in Percentages)														
Debt Ratio	45	87.0	•	70.2	55.9	64.2	80.7	•	75.3	70.3	•	•	•	•
Return on Total Assets	46	56.1	•	132.2	55.9	43.5	27.2	•	16.5	8.7	•	•	•	•
Return on Equity Before Income Taxes	47	420.5	•	436.6	123.2	115.9	131.8	•	61.9	23.0	•	•	•	•
Return on Equity After Income Taxes	48	413.4	•	433.6	122.2	114.2	129.8	•	56.4	20.0	•	•	•	•
Profit Margin (Before Income Tax)	49	9.5	28.1	11.4	10.5	7.3	7.6	•	4.1	3.4	•	•	•	•
Profit Margin (After Income Tax)	50	9.3	27.3	11.3	10.4	7.2	7.5	•	3.7	3.0	•	•	•	•

Table I

Corporations with and without Net Income

OFFICES OF DENTISTS

MONEY AMOUNTS AND SIZE OF ASSETS IN THOUSANDS OF DOLLARS

Item Description for Accounting Period 7/11 Through 6/12		Total	Zero Assets	Under 500	500 to 1,000	1,000 to 5,000	5,000 to 10,000	10,000 to 25,000	25,000 to 50,000	50,000 to 100,000	100,000 to 250,000	250,000 to 500,000	500,000 to 2,500,000	2,500,000 and over
Number of Enterprises	1	75246	4406	62344	6976	1483	18	7	0	3	4	5	0	0
Revenues ($ in Thousands)														
Net Sales	2	62453843	2651732	43061868	10563035	3348986	366643	298543	0	64297	458884	1639855	0	0
Interest	3	5692	74	1898	1221	185	78	109	0	3	76	2048	0	0
Rents	4	562	0	0	1	0	0	0	0	0	561	0	0	0
Royalties	5	0	0	0	0	0	0	0	0	0	0	0	0	0
Other Portfolio Income	6	105091	2314	70904	5153	11815	0	14770	0	0	0	135	0	0
Other Receipts	7	1625978	865	1376756	151800	49168	192	36962	0	2086	530	7619	0	0
Total Receipts	8	64191166	2654985	44511426	10721210	3410154	366913	350384	0	66386	460051	1649657	0	0
Average Total Receipts	9	853	603	714	1537	2299	20384	50055	•	22129	115013	329931	•	•
Operating Costs/Operating Income (%)														
Cost of Operations	10	5.6	0.0	5.3	5.9	11.4	•	16.2	•	41.6	13.7	3.2	•	•
Salaries and Wages	11	25.2	47.1	23.3	22.4	27.8	35.5	50.4	•	16.6	26.8	43.5	•	•
Taxes Paid	12	3.9	5.2	3.9	3.4	3.6	2.9	3.1	•	1.9	2.7	4.5	•	•
Interest Paid	13	1.2	1.0	0.8	2.0	1.6	0.1	8.9	•	1.5	5.1	3.9	•	•
Depreciation	14	2.7	1.2	2.6	3.0	3.2	0.3	0.9	•	4.2	3.6	6.9	•	•
Amortization and Depletion	15	0.6	0.6	0.4	1.0	0.9	•	0.4	•	1.6	4.5	3.3	•	•
Pensions and Other Deferred Comp.	16	2.0	1.0	2.1	2.5	0.8	0.3	7.0	•	•	•	1.1	•	•
Employee Benefits	17	1.1	1.4	1.0	1.1	0.8	0.5	4.5	•	5.1	1.9	0.7	•	•
Advertising	18	1.4	5.1	1.3	1.1	0.9	2.3	0.8	•	3.2	0.5	2.7	•	•
Other Expenses	19	32.7	40.0	33.0	27.6	37.7	51.5	23.8	•	24.9	42.3	31.6	•	•
Officers' Compensation	20	17.5	2.4	19.9	19.6	5.7	6.1	0.8	•	0.3	0.5	0.6	•	•
Operating Margin	21	6.1	•	6.3	10.6	5.6	0.6	•	•	•	•	•	•	•
Operating Margin Before Officers' Comp.	22	23.5	•	26.2	30.2	11.3	6.7	•	•	•	•	•	•	•

Selected Average Balance Sheet ($ in Thousands)												
Net Receivables 23	11	0	2	25	97	4404	4857	•	6901	5891	42096	•	•
Inventories 24	1	0	1	1	0	0	66	•	1045	1695	425	•	•
Net Property, Plant and Equipment 25	83	0	53	228	594	239	639	•	5868	11719	70041	•	•
Total Assets 26	260	0	145	672	1549	5116	25827	•	76151	179179	464937	•	•
Notes and Loans Payable 27	160	0	94	494	892	269	11828	•	12118	65532	205016	•	•
All Other Liabilities 28	53	0	37	75	145	3948	36018	•	12325	42552	82457	•	•
Net Worth 29	47	0	14	103	512	899	-22019	•	51708	71095	177464	•	•
Selected Financial Ratios (Times to 1)												
Current Ratio 30	1.3	•	1.1	1.7	1.9	1.2	0.4	•	2.7	1.0	1.6	•	•
Quick Ratio 31	1.1	•	1.0	1.4	1.9	1.1	0.3	•	0.7	0.7	1.0	•	•
Net Sales to Working Capital 32	46.5	•	114.4	17.9	11.8	29.5	•	•	1.2	142.6	10.5	•	•
Coverage Ratio 33	8.1	•	12.4	7.0	5.5	11.7	1.1	•	2.6	0.7	0.6	•	•
Total Asset Turnover 34	3.2	•	4.8	2.3	1.5	4.0	1.7	•	0.3	0.6	0.7	•	•
Inventory Turnover 35	63.7	•	59.4	171.1	•	•	104.5	•	8.5	9.3	24.7	•	•
Receivables Turnover 36	70.8	•	259.3	43.9	33.1	4.3	12.5	•	1.9	15.0	8.5	•	•
Total Liabilities to Net Worth 37	4.5	•	9.4	5.5	2.0	4.7	•	•	0.5	1.5	1.6	•	•
Current Assets to Working Capital 38	4.2	•	7.8	2.4	2.1	7.1	•	•	1.6	21.6	2.6	•	•
Current Liabilities to Working Capital 39	3.2	•	6.8	1.4	1.1	6.1	•	•	0.6	20.6	1.6	•	•
Working Capital to Net Sales 40	0.0	•	0.0	0.1	0.1	0.0	•	•	0.9	0.0	0.1	•	•
Inventory to Working Capital 41	0.0	•	0.1	0.0	•	•	•	•	0.0	1.9	0.0	•	•
Total Receipts to Cash Flow 42	2.9	3.5	2.9	3.0	2.5	2.0	8.7	•	4.9	2.7	4.4	•	•
Cost of Goods to Cash Flow 43	0.2	0.0	0.2	0.2	0.3	•	1.4	•	2.0	0.4	0.1	•	•
Cash Flow to Total Debt 44	1.3	•	1.8	0.9	0.9	2.4	0.1	•	0.2	0.4	0.3	•	•
Selected Financial Factors (in Percentages)												
Debt Ratio 45	81.9	•	90.4	84.7	66.9	82.4	185.3	•	32.1	60.3	61.8	•	•
Return on Total Assets 46	32.2	•	49.9	31.8	13.2	2.8	15.5	•	1.1	2.4	1.8	•	•
Return on Equity Before Income Taxes 47	156.2	•	478.1	178.0	32.6	14.7	•	•	1.0	•	•	•	•
Return on Equity After Income Taxes 48	155.4	•	476.8	176.1	32.6	13.9	•	•	0.8	•	•	•	•
Profit Margin (Before Income Tax) 49	8.8	•	9.6	12.1	7.4	0.6	0.5	•	2.4	•	•	•	•
Profit Margin (After Income Tax) 50	8.8	•	9.6	12.0	7.4	0.6	0.5	•	1.8	•	•	•	•

Table II

Corporations with Net Income

OFFICES OF DENTISTS

MONEY AMOUNTS AND SIZE OF ASSETS IN THOUSANDS OF DOLLARS

Item Description for Accounting Period 7/11 Through 6/12		Total	Zero Assets	Under 500	500 to 1,000	1,000 to 5,000	5,000 to 10,000	10,000 to 25,000	25,000 to 50,000	50,000 to 100,000	100,000 to 250,000	250,000 to 500,000	500,000 to 2,500,000	2,500,000 and over
Number of Enterprises	1	54528	1448	46087	5870	1099	•	•	0	3	0	0	0	0
Revenues ($ in Thousands)														
Net Sales	2	47905487	2174656	33778256	9158928	2127981	•	•	0	78936	0	0	0	0
Interest	3	1773	67	372	1114	35	•	•	0	3	0	0	0	0
Rents	4	1	0	0	1	0	•	•	0	0	0	0	0	0
Royalties	5	0	0	0	0	0	•	•	0	0	0	0	0	0
Other Portfolio Income	6	59543	1642	54040	3815	45	•	•	0	0	0	0	0	0
Other Receipts	7	1163204	635	959421	149837	49029	•	•	0	2226	0	0	0	0
Total Receipts	8	49130008	2177000	34792089	9313695	2177090	•	•	0	81165	0	0	0	0
Average Total Receipts	9	901	1503	755	1587	1981	•	•	•	27055	•	•	•	•
Operating Costs/Operating Income (%)														
Cost of Operations	10	5.6	•	5.9	4.9	7.8	•	•	•	42.1	•	•	•	•
Salaries and Wages	11	24.0	49.0	22.6	22.5	23.5	•	•	•	17.0	•	•	•	•
Taxes Paid	12	3.8	4.5	3.9	3.3	3.0	•	•	•	4.2	•	•	•	•
Interest Paid	13	1.1	0.1	0.9	1.8	2.1	•	•	•	8.1	•	•	•	•
Depreciation	14	2.2	0.1	2.0	2.9	4.2	•	•	•	4.1	•	•	•	•
Amortization and Depletion	15	0.5	0.1	0.4	0.8	1.2	•	•	•	3.4	•	•	•	•
Pensions and Other Deferred Comp.	16	2.0	1.2	2.0	2.6	1.0	•	•	•	•	•	•	•	•
Employee Benefits	17	1.0	1.4	0.9	1.1	0.8	•	•	•	0.8	•	•	•	•
Advertising	18	1.4	5.8	1.3	0.9	1.0	•	•	•	1.5	•	•	•	•
Other Expenses	19	30.7	35.1	31.0	26.7	36.8	•	•	•	16.2	•	•	•	•
Officers' Compensation	20	17.3	2.3	18.6	19.6	6.7	•	•	•	1.0	•	•	•	•
Operating Margin	21	10.5	0.5	10.5	12.8	11.9	•	•	•	1.7	•	•	•	•
Operating Margin Before Officers' Comp.	22	27.7	2.8	29.1	32.4	18.6	•	•	•	2.7	•	•	•	•

Selected Average Balance Sheet ($ in Thousands)													
Net Receivables 23	8	0	3	17	81	•	•	•	7342	•	•	•	•
Inventories 24	1	0	1	1	0	•	•	•	0	•	•	•	•
Net Property, Plant and Equipment 25	85	0	56	226	639	•	•	•	5823	•	•	•	•
Total Assets 26	250	0	160	681	1569	•	•	•	117853	•	•	•	•
Notes and Loans Payable 27	151	0	95	455	948	•	•	•	40432	•	•	•	•
All Other Liabilities 28	35	0	26	79	91	•	•	•	15457	•	•	•	•
Net Worth 29	64	0	40	146	530	•	•	•	61965	•	•	•	•
Selected Financial Ratios (Times to 1)													
Current Ratio 30	1.8	•	1.6	2.2	1.9	•	•	•	1.0	•	•	•	•
Quick Ratio 31	1.6	•	1.5	1.8	1.9	•	•	•	0.9	•	•	•	•
Net Sales to Working Capital 32	25.7	•	36.8	13.1	9.4	•	•	•	99.7	•	•	•	•
Coverage Ratio 33	12.5	10.7	15.3	8.9	7.8	•	•	•	1.6	•	•	•	•
Total Asset Turnover 34	3.5	•	4.6	2.3	1.2	•	•	•	0.2	•	•	•	•
Inventory Turnover 35	83.2	•	80.5	133.7	•	•	•	•	•	•	•	•	•
Receivables Turnover 36	86.7	•	231.0	51.7	29.5	•	•	•	7.2	•	•	•	•
Total Liabilities to Net Worth 37	2.9	•	3.1	3.7	2.0	•	•	•	0.9	•	•	•	•
Current Assets to Working Capital 38	2.3	•	2.6	1.8	2.1	•	•	•	38.4	•	•	•	•
Current Liabilities to Working Capital 39	1.3	•	1.6	0.8	1.1	•	•	•	37.4	•	•	•	•
Working Capital to Net Sales 40	0.0	•	0.0	0.1	0.1	•	•	•	0.0	•	•	•	•
Inventory to Working Capital 41	0.0	•	0.0	0.0	•	•	•	•	•	•	•	•	•
Total Receipts to Cash Flow 42	2.7	3.4	2.7	2.8	2.2	•	•	•	6.4	•	•	•	•
Cost of Goods to Cash Flow 43	0.2	•	0.2	0.1	0.2	•	•	•	2.7	•	•	•	•
Cash Flow to Total Debt 44	1.7	•	2.2	1.0	0.9	•	•	•	0.1	•	•	•	•
Selected Financial Factors (in Percentages)													
Debt Ratio 45	74.3	•	75.3	78.5	66.2	•	•	•	47.4	•	•	•	•
Return on Total Assets 46	49.7	•	66.1	37.5	20.1	•	•	•	2.8	•	•	•	•
Return on Equity Before Income Taxes 47	178.0	•	250.6	154.6	51.9	•	•	•	1.9	•	•	•	•
Return on Equity After Income Taxes 48	177.1	•	250.0	153.1	51.9	•	•	•	1.4	•	•	•	•
Profit Margin (Before Income Tax) 49	13.0	0.6	13.5	14.5	14.2	•	•	•	4.6	•	•	•	•
Profit Margin (After Income Tax) 50	13.0	0.6	13.5	14.4	14.2	•	•	•	3.3	•	•	•	•

Table I

Corporations with and without Net Income

OFFICES OF OTHER HEALTH PRACTITIONERS

Item Description for Accounting Period 7/11 Through 6/12		MONEY AMOUNTS AND SIZE OF ASSETS IN THOUSANDS OF DOLLARS												
		Total	Zero Assets	Under 500	500 to 1,000	1,000 to 5,000	5,000 to 10,000	10,000 to 25,000	25,000 to 50,000	50,000 to 100,000	100,000 to 250,000	250,000 to 500,000	500,000 to 2,500,000	2,500,000 and over
Number of Enterprises	1	111802	19227	89054	2606	711	52	83	31	17	11	6	4	0
Revenues ($ in Thousands)														
Net Sales	2	70289705	2495453	39727539	4743060	3120926	2033472	3204619	1048085	2105078	3121437	1590493	7099543	0
Interest	3	94259	7840	567	494	22	186	2223	3048	2167	11569	20241	45901	0
Rents	4	28189	0	11030	0	16	434	226	4762	4152	3537	4032	0	0
Royalties	5	0	0	0	0	0	0	0	0	0	0	0	0	0
Other Portfolio Income	6	174579	8921	4806	11258	1168	14225	621	46166	62693	8889	11778	4054	0
Other Receipts	7	1622466	25022	234307	3174	9652	23796	82861	30394	536443	177878	65503	433437	0
Total Receipts	8	72209198	2537236	39978249	4757986	3131784	2072113	3290550	1132455	2710533	3323310	1692047	7582935	0
Average Total Receipts	9	646	132	449	1826	4405	39848	39645	36531	159443	302119	282008	1895734	•
Operating Costs/Operating Income (%)														
Cost of Operations	10	14.5	4.4	11.3	9.2	14.0	18.1	36.2	9.8	34.0	53.8	7.0	8.2	•
Salaries and Wages	11	21.8	19.5	19.0	38.5	31.5	44.9	26.1	44.5	17.5	19.5	18.9	14.0	•
Taxes Paid	12	3.0	3.6	3.3	3.8	3.0	3.2	2.2	3.1	1.8	1.8	2.2	1.4	•
Interest Paid	13	0.7	0.8	0.5	1.0	0.5	0.5	0.3	1.4	1.0	0.2	3.7	1.4	•
Depreciation	14	1.5	2.7	1.3	1.4	2.2	1.2	1.4	2.5	1.2	1.2	1.3	2.3	•
Amortization and Depletion	15	0.4	0.3	0.1	1.2	0.3	0.1	0.2	0.2	1.1	0.2	1.0	1.4	•
Pensions and Other Deferred Comp.	16	0.9	0.2	1.0	2.1	1.2	0.1	0.2	0.7	0.2	0.3	0.0	0.4	•
Employee Benefits	17	1.5	1.6	1.3	1.6	1.0	2.7	2.8	4.2	1.7	2.0	1.2	1.3	•
Advertising	18	1.3	0.5	1.5	0.8	0.9	0.6	5.4	0.1	0.2	0.5	1.3	0.5	•
Other Expenses	19	41.2	38.6	39.7	21.6	32.7	27.2	25.8	35.5	67.6	25.1	57.6	74.4	•
Officers' Compensation	20	9.2	17.5	12.8	11.5	8.7	1.2	1.4	2.6	0.3	0.2	0.7	0.3	•
Operating Margin	21	4.1	10.3	8.3	7.5	4.0	•	•	•	•	•	5.3	•	•
Operating Margin Before Officers' Comp.	22	13.3	27.8	21.1	18.9	12.6	1.2	•	•	•	•	6.0	•	•

Selected Average Balance Sheet ($ in Thousands)													
Net Receivables 23	27	0	3	54	290	2204	2818	5309	10080	18288	36299	311500	•
Inventories 24	4	0	2	11	56	76	333	216	1236	920	5506	21985	•
Net Property, Plant and Equipment 25	32	0	20	103	436	771	2554	3409	9173	16557	21375	82362	•
Total Assets 26	182	0	71	675	1520	7440	15430	34732	66286	140931	334014	940670	•
Notes and Loans Payable 27	65	0	31	312	557	4030	4735	13274	19793	16125	111734	279781	•
All Other Liabilities 28	58	0	15	76	368	3060	7696	11927	23585	61478	199733	302884	•
Net Worth 29	59	0	24	287	595	350	2999	9531	22909	63329	22546	358006	•
Selected Financial Ratios (Times to 1)													
Current Ratio 30	1.4	•	1.7	2.5	1.6	1.3	0.8	1.5	1.0	1.2	0.9	1.3	•
Quick Ratio 31	1.1	•	1.5	2.3	1.2	1.2	0.5	0.8	0.8	0.7	0.5	1.2	•
Net Sales to Working Capital 32	28.4	•	30.4	12.2	18.2	29.3	•	5.6	298.5	34.4	•	16.5	•
Coverage Ratio 33	10.8	16.4	20.1	9.0	10.4	4.5	2.5	3.5	3.1	7.8	4.2	1.9	•
Total Asset Turnover 34	3.5	•	6.3	2.7	2.9	5.3	2.5	1.0	1.9	2.0	0.8	1.9	•
Inventory Turnover 35	25.3	•	23.9	15.5	11.0	93.3	42.1	15.3	34.1	165.8	3.4	6.6	•
Receivables Turnover 36	25.5	•	115.4	42.3	12.3	19.8	17.6	4.6	13.1	13.2	3.1	11.4	•
Total Liabilities to Net Worth 37	2.1	•	1.9	1.3	1.6	20.2	4.1	2.6	1.9	1.2	13.8	1.6	•
Current Assets to Working Capital 38	3.7	•	2.3	1.7	2.7	4.3	•	3.1	68.7	7.6	•	4.0	•
Current Liabilities to Working Capital 39	2.7	•	1.3	0.7	1.7	3.3	•	2.1	67.7	6.6	•	3.0	•
Working Capital to Net Sales 40	0.0	•	0.0	0.1	0.1	0.0	•	0.2	0.0	0.0	•	0.1	•
Inventory to Working Capital 41	0.2	•	0.2	0.1	0.2	0.1	•	0.0	2.7	0.1	•	0.2	•
Total Receipts to Cash Flow 42	2.4	2.4	2.5	4.2	3.3	4.5	4.3	3.1	1.6	4.2	1.5	1.3	•
Cost of Goods to Cash Flow 43	0.3	0.1	0.3	0.4	0.5	0.8	1.6	0.3	0.5	2.2	0.1	0.1	•
Cash Flow to Total Debt 44	2.1	•	3.9	1.1	1.4	1.2	0.7	0.4	1.8	0.9	0.6	2.3	•
Selected Financial Factors (in Percentages)													
Debt Ratio 45	67.7	•	65.4	57.4	60.9	95.3	80.6	72.6	65.4	55.1	93.2	61.9	•
Return on Total Assets 46	26.0	•	59.1	23.6	13.7	12.6	2.2	4.8	6.0	3.8	12.2	5.1	•
Return on Equity Before Income Taxes 47	73.1	•	162.2	49.3	31.7	207.9	6.6	12.5	11.8	7.3	137.6	6.3	•
Return on Equity After Income Taxes 48	70.3	•	161.2	49.2	31.0	165.0	1.4	5.3	10.9	5.6	88.6	3.9	•
Profit Margin (Before Income Tax) 49	6.8	12.0	8.9	7.8	4.3	1.9	0.5	3.5	2.2	1.6	11.7	1.3	•
Profit Margin (After Income Tax) 50	6.6	11.9	8.8	7.8	4.2	1.5	0.1	1.5	2.0	1.2	7.5	0.8	•

Table II

Corporations with Net Income

OFFICES OF OTHER HEALTH PRACTITIONERS

Item Description for Accounting Period 7/11 Through 6/12		MONEY AMOUNTS AND SIZE OF ASSETS IN THOUSANDS OF DOLLARS												
		Total	Zero Assets	Under 500	500 to 1,000	1,000 to 5,000	5,000 to 10,000	10,000 to 25,000	25,000 to 50,000	50,000 to 100,000	100,000 to 250,000	250,000 to 500,000	500,000 to 2,500,000	2,500,000 and over
Number of Enterprises	1	84830	11794	69918	2427	573	•	58	15	8	•	•	•	0
Revenues ($ in Thousands)														
Net Sales	2	50121323	1942716	29234740	4312020	2309433	•	1748869	677161	839988	•	•	•	0
Interest	3	80503	7838	502	494	14	•	2207	3038	1523	•	•	•	0
Rents	4	18686	0	11030	0	0	•	85	3601	209	•	•	•	0
Royalties	5	0	0	0	0	0	•	0	0	0	•	•	•	0
Other Portfolio Income	6	171904	8763	4665	11258	1168	•	569	45996	62682	•	•	•	0
Other Receipts	7	1156135	25022	206419	1097	7337	•	76137	26500	517631	•	•	•	0
Total Receipts	8	51548551	1984339	29457356	4324869	2317952	•	1827867	756296	1422033	•	•	•	0
Average Total Receipts	9	608	168	421	1782	4045	•	31515	50420	177754	•	•	•	•
Operating Costs/Operating Income (%)														
Cost of Operations	10	12.3	4.1	9.3	7.8	19.0	•	37.9	7.3	1.5	•	•	•	•
Salaries and Wages	11	22.1	21.8	19.8	39.4	24.6	•	30.6	44.5	15.7	•	•	•	•
Taxes Paid	12	3.0	3.9	3.2	3.8	2.7	•	3.4	3.1	2.2	•	•	•	•
Interest Paid	13	0.8	1.0	0.5	1.0	0.5	•	0.5	1.7	1.3	•	•	•	•
Depreciation	14	1.3	1.6	1.4	1.3	2.1	•	2.1	0.7	0.6	•	•	•	•
Amortization and Depletion	15	0.4	0.4	0.1	1.2	0.5	•	0.2	0.2	1.1	•	•	•	•
Pensions and Other Deferred Comp.	16	0.8	0.3	0.9	2.2	1.0	•	0.3	1.0	0.0	•	•	•	•
Employee Benefits	17	1.2	1.9	0.9	1.4	0.8	•	2.9	4.9	0.5	•	•	•	•
Advertising	18	1.2	0.3	1.6	0.7	1.0	•	1.5	0.0	0.4	•	•	•	•
Other Expenses	19	39.5	32.8	37.5	21.8	35.0	•	15.9	32.9	138.2	•	•	•	•
Officers' Compensation	20	9.1	16.2	12.4	10.7	4.3	•	2.2	1.4	0.3	•	•	•	•
Operating Margin	21	8.2	15.8	12.4	8.7	8.7	•	2.5	2.3	•	•	•	•	•
Operating Margin Before Officers' Comp.	22	17.3	32.0	24.7	19.4	13.0	•	4.7	3.7	•	•	•	•	•

Selected Average Balance Sheet ($ in Thousands)													
Net Receivables 23	24	0	2	38	241	•	3058	6502	8080	•	•	•	•
Inventories 24	3	0	2	7	69	•	445	397	206	•	•	•	•
Net Property, Plant and Equipment 25	30	0	22	99	352	•	3000	3329	6494	•	•	•	•
Total Assets 26	170	0	73	683	1492	•	14957	34163	61132	•	•	•	•
Notes and Loans Payable 27	62	0	28	288	566	•	3560	8916	15122	•	•	•	•
All Other Liabilities 28	46	0	11	71	241	•	5528	13710	28363	•	•	•	•
Net Worth 29	63	0	33	324	685	•	5868	11538	17647	•	•	•	•

Selected Financial Ratios (Times to 1)													
Current Ratio 30	1.7	•	2.3	2.5	2.7	•	1.0	1.9	1.0	•	•	•	•
Quick Ratio 31	1.4	•	1.9	2.3	1.9	•	0.8	1.6	0.8	•	•	•	•
Net Sales to Working Capital 32	19.6	•	21.1	12.5	9.2	•	168.5	5.5	103.8	•	•	•	•
Coverage Ratio 33	14.6	19.0	26.8	10.0	20.1	•	15.7	9.1	7.1	•	•	•	•
Total Asset Turnover 34	3.5	•	5.8	2.6	2.7	•	2.0	1.3	1.7	•	•	•	•
Inventory Turnover 35	21.1	•	16.8	18.7	11.0	•	25.7	8.3	7.8	•	•	•	•
Receivables Turnover 36	24.7	•	193.2	51.1	11.7	•	14.3	4.5	10.4	•	•	•	•
Total Liabilities to Net Worth 37	1.7	•	1.2	1.1	1.2	•	1.5	2.0	2.5	•	•	•	•
Current Assets to Working Capital 38	2.5	•	1.7	1.7	1.6	•	37.8	2.2	31.3	•	•	•	•
Current Liabilities to Working Capital 39	1.5	•	0.7	0.7	0.6	•	36.8	1.2	30.3	•	•	•	•
Working Capital to Net Sales 40	0.1	•	0.0	0.1	0.1	•	0.0	0.2	0.0	•	•	•	•
Inventory to Working Capital 41	0.1	•	0.1	0.0	0.2	•	2.9	0.0	0.0	•	•	•	•
Total Receipts to Cash Flow 42	2.3	2.3	2.3	3.9	2.7	•	5.5	2.6	0.7	•	•	•	•
Cost of Goods to Cash Flow 43	0.3	0.1	0.2	0.3	0.5	•	2.1	0.2	0.0	•	•	•	•
Cash Flow to Total Debt 44	2.4	•	4.5	1.3	1.9	•	0.6	0.8	3.3	•	•	•	•

Selected Financial Factors (in Percentages)													
Debt Ratio 45	63.2	•	53.9	52.5	54.1	•	60.8	66.2	71.1	•	•	•	•
Return on Total Assets 46	41.1	•	78.5	26.0	25.8	•	15.1	20.8	15.3	•	•	•	•
Return on Equity Before Income Taxes 47	104.3	•	164.0	49.3	53.4	•	36.0	54.7	45.6	•	•	•	•
Return on Equity After Income Taxes 48	100.7	•	163.1	49.2	52.6	•	32.2	42.5	43.2	•	•	•	•
Profit Margin (Before Income Tax) 49	11.0	18.0	13.1	9.0	9.1	•	7.0	14.0	7.7	•	•	•	•
Profit Margin (After Income Tax) 50	10.7	17.8	13.0	9.0	8.9	•	6.3	10.9	7.3	•	•	•	•

Table I

Corporations with and without Net Income

OUTPATIENT CARE CENTERS

Item Description for Accounting Period 7/11 Through 6/12		MONEY AMOUNTS AND SIZE OF ASSETS IN THOUSANDS OF DOLLARS Total	Zero Assets	Under 500	500 to 1,000	1,000 to 5,000	5,000 to 10,000	10,000 to 25,000	25,000 to 50,000	50,000 to 100,000	100,000 to 250,000	250,000 to 500,000	500,000 to 2,500,000	2,500,000 and over
Number of Enterprises	1	7867	1765	5151	300	496	43	49	22	13	10	6	13	0
Revenues ($ in Thousands)														
Net Sales	2	36681905	977030	3221804	891967	5651299	1188247	1660397	1753401	2704987	1405684	1154609	16072480	0
Interest	3	117836	2926	285	806	3600	689	4714	248	2683	940	1405	99540	0
Rents	4	14446	217	0	0	93	687	929	0	0	2064	210	10245	0
Royalties	5	0	0	0	0	0	0	0	0	0	0	0	0	0
Other Portfolio Income	6	210144	10262	112	78102	12	7335	2484	731	510	4	1264	109329	0
Other Receipts	7	2527667	14898	3727	7648	26496	15147	35697	36011	46951	12074	101154	2227865	0
Total Receipts	8	39551998	1005333	3225928	978523	5681500	1212105	1704221	1790391	2755131	1420766	1258642	18519459	0
Average Total Receipts	9	5028	570	626	3262	11455	28188	34780	81381	211933	142077	209774	1424574	•
Operating Costs/Operating Income (%)														
Cost of Operations	10	21.7	32.0	3.2	30.2	5.0	2.2	0.1	28.6	40.6	20.3	10.2	30.8	•
Salaries and Wages	11	21.4	22.8	17.9	25.8	27.2	6.2	26.4	19.8	3.7	25.0	25.7	22.9	•
Taxes Paid	12	2.9	2.7	3.4	2.8	2.5	0.7	2.2	2.1	0.5	2.8	3.4	3.6	•
Interest Paid	13	3.3	5.0	0.1	0.5	0.2	0.9	0.7	1.0	0.5	1.9	6.9	6.0	•
Depreciation	14	2.8	2.5	0.6	2.7	0.6	0.3	1.7	0.6	0.9	2.2	2.4	4.9	•
Amortization and Depletion	15	1.6	3.7	0.0	0.0	0.1	0.0	0.1	0.5	0.4	1.0	1.8	3.1	•
Pensions and Other Deferred Comp.	16	0.7	0.3	0.4	0.2	2.0	0.0	0.7	0.2	0.0	0.3	0.3	0.5	•
Employee Benefits	17	4.2	1.2	1.1	2.7	2.5	0.5	2.2	27.0	0.4	1.2	2.1	4.8	•
Advertising	18	0.4	0.8	0.9	0.1	0.4	0.2	0.9	0.4	0.5	0.5	0.2	0.2	•
Other Expenses	19	39.9	33.2	48.5	27.5	49.6	87.1	65.6	18.3	54.2	43.8	52.4	28.4	•
Officers' Compensation	20	1.8	2.5	6.2	1.5	4.6	0.3	1.5	0.8	0.3	0.8	1.2	0.6	•
Operating Margin	21	•	•	17.5	6.0	5.3	1.5	•	0.8	•	0.2	•	•	•
Operating Margin Before Officers' Comp.	22	1.2	•	23.7	7.4	9.9	1.8	•	1.6	•	0.9	•	•	•

Selected Average Balance Sheet ($ in Thousands)														
Net Receivables	23	782	0	14	49	912	827	3401	11459	10280	15033	28251	361599	•
Inventories	24	62	0	2	8	38	370	6	139	524	1314	1108	17666	•
Net Property, Plant and Equipment	25	546	0	13	359	313	463	1947	1920	10282	30072	27482	246933	•
Total Assets	26	5015	0	91	757	2482	7084	13932	33939	66738	153017	394176	2386573	•
Notes and Loans Payable	27	2421	0	104	244	1300	60	4328	11458	13148	44218	265242	1163228	•
All Other Liabilities	28	1219	0	46	245	663	4004	6835	14323	26531	40318	41006	548766	•
Net Worth	29	1374	0	-59	269	519	3020	2770	8158	27059	68481	87928	674579	•
Selected Financial Ratios (Times to 1)														
Current Ratio	30	1.3	•	0.6	1.0	1.4	1.6	1.4	1.2	1.6	1.1	2.1	1.4	•
Quick Ratio	31	1.0	•	0.5	0.5	1.1	0.9	1.1	1.1	1.1	1.0	1.5	1.0	•
Net Sales to Working Capital	32	12.8	•	•	•	23.7	13.7	11.6	22.3	15.0	29.8	5.5	7.7	•
Coverage Ratio	33	3.2	0.2	150.4	30.9	29.5	5.0	1.7	3.8	0.4	1.7	1.3	2.5	•
Total Asset Turnover	34	0.9	•	6.9	3.9	4.6	3.9	2.4	2.3	3.1	0.9	0.5	0.5	•
Inventory Turnover	35	16.2	•	9.3	105.9	15.1	1.6	5.9	163.9	161.3	21.7	17.7	21.5	•
Receivables Turnover	36	6.6	•	59.5	119.3	13.2	14.9	10.6	8.8	29.3	6.5	6.2	6.0	•
Total Liabilities to Net Worth	37	2.6	•	•	1.8	3.8	1.3	4.0	3.2	1.5	1.2	3.5	2.5	•
Current Assets to Working Capital	38	3.9	•	•	•	3.7	2.6	3.4	5.6	2.7	8.7	1.9	3.6	•
Current Liabilities to Working Capital	39	2.9	•	•	•	2.7	1.6	2.4	4.6	1.7	7.7	0.9	2.6	•
Working Capital to Net Sales	40	0.1	•	•	•	0.0	0.1	0.1	0.0	0.1	0.0	0.2	0.1	•
Inventory to Working Capital	41	0.2	•	•	•	0.0	0.0	0.0	0.0	0.0	0.3	0.1	0.2	•
Total Receipts to Cash Flow	42	2.4	4.1	1.8	2.7	1.9	1.1	1.6	5.1	1.9	2.4	1.9	3.2	•
Cost of Goods to Cash Flow	43	0.5	1.3	0.1	0.8	0.1	0.0	0.0	1.5	0.8	0.5	0.2	1.0	•
Cash Flow to Total Debt	44	0.5	•	2.4	2.3	3.1	6.0	1.9	0.6	2.8	0.7	0.3	0.2	•
Selected Financial Factors (in Percentages)														
Debt Ratio	45	72.6	•	165.0	64.5	79.1	57.4	80.1	76.0	59.5	55.2	77.7	71.7	•
Return on Total Assets	46	9.7	•	122.0	63.6	27.8	17.1	2.9	9.2	0.6	2.9	4.5	7.9	•
Return on Equity Before Income Taxes	47	24.4	•	•	173.7	128.2	32.2	5.8	28.2	•	2.5	5.0	17.1	•
Return on Equity After Income Taxes	48	19.7	•	•	170.1	124.8	25.8	3.4	23.1	•	1.2	1.0	12.2	•
Profit Margin (Before Income Tax)	49	7.2	•	17.7	15.7	5.8	3.5	0.5	2.9	•	1.2	2.3	9.3	•
Profit Margin (After Income Tax)	50	5.8	•	17.7	15.4	5.7	2.8	0.3	2.4	•	0.6	0.5	6.6	•

Table II

Corporations with Net Income

OUTPATIENT CARE CENTERS

MONEY AMOUNTS AND SIZE OF ASSETS IN THOUSANDS OF DOLLARS

Item Description for Accounting Period 7/11 Through 6/12		Total	Zero Assets	Under 500	500 to 1,000	1,000 to 5,000	5,000 to 10,000	10,000 to 25,000	25,000 to 50,000	50,000 to 100,000	100,000 to 250,000	250,000 to 500,000	500,000 to 2,500,000	2,500,000 and over
Number of Enterprises	1	4333	61	3448	259	467	25	36	14	8	6	0	8	0
Revenues ($ in Thousands)														
Net Sales	2	29864934	587548	2854406	773759	5610539	687659	916036	1313265	1077061	1242197	0	14802464	0
Interest	3	90877	82	141	806	3559	647	4334	144	2028	1290	0	77846	0
Rents	4	7356	0	0	0	93	687	650	0	0	194	0	5732	0
Royalties	5	0	0	0	0	0	0	0	0	0	0	0	0	0
Other Portfolio Income	6	196595	23	20	78102	12	7335	30	15	510	1219	0	109329	0
Other Receipts	7	2228580	2022	3686	5678	26165	15138	28704	29060	19729	48471	0	2049927	0
Total Receipts	8	32388342	589675	2858253	858345	5640368	711466	949754	1342484	1099328	1293371	0	17045298	0
Average Total Receipts	9	7475	9667	829	3314	12078	28459	26382	95892	137416	215562	•	2130662	•
Operating Costs/Operating Income (%)														
Cost of Operations	10	22.9	41.8	3.6	27.0	4.7	3.2	0.2	30.3	49.5	22.0	•	32.4	•
Salaries and Wages	11	21.1	19.5	17.2	22.2	27.3	9.8	31.8	19.7	4.6	16.6	•	21.1	•
Taxes Paid	12	2.9	2.3	3.1	2.4	2.5	1.2	2.5	1.6	0.8	2.1	•	3.6	•
Interest Paid	13	2.7	0.4	0.1	0.4	0.2	1.5	1.2	0.5	0.3	3.2	•	4.8	•
Depreciation	14	2.9	2.8	0.6	3.0	0.5	0.2	1.7	0.3	0.6	2.2	•	4.8	•
Amortization and Depletion	15	1.5	1.1	0.0	0.0	0.1	0.1	0.1	0.1	0.2	0.9	•	2.9	•
Pensions and Other Deferred Comp.	16	0.7	0.3	0.5	0.0	2.0	0.0	0.6	0.1	0.1	0.1	•	0.6	•
Employee Benefits	17	4.8	0.4	1.2	2.3	2.5	0.7	2.3	35.5	0.7	0.9	•	4.9	•
Advertising	18	0.3	0.5	0.6	0.1	0.3	0.4	1.7	0.3	0.5	0.4	•	0.2	•
Other Expenses	19	36.1	19.1	45.5	25.8	49.5	78.9	54.4	7.3	42.4	44.2	•	28.6	•
Officers' Compensation	20	2.0	2.2	6.3	1.0	4.6	0.5	1.8	0.4	0.5	0.9	•	0.6	•
Operating Margin	21	2.1	9.6	21.1	15.8	5.8	3.4	1.7	4.0	0.0	6.5	•	•	•
Operating Margin Before Officers' Comp.	22	4.1	11.8	27.3	16.8	10.4	3.9	3.5	4.4	0.5	7.4	•	•	•

Selected Average Balance Sheet ($ in Thousands)

Net Receivables 23	1229	0	20	1	968	571	3088	11345	4796	15688	•	548239	•
Inventories 24	100	0	3	1	40	23	6	160	83	940	•	26411	•
Net Property, Plant and Equipment 25	856	0	16	406	301	675	1725	1750	11000	41532	•	370565	•
Total Assets 26	7213	0	130	783	2438	6774	13702	33575	64139	244886	•	3293990	•
Notes and Loans Payable 27	3346	0	149	126	1272	104	4760	7256	7722	142602	•	1520824	•
All Other Liabilities 28	1765	0	45	47	626	3832	5540	17155	16988	48416	•	778379	•
Net Worth 29	2102	0	-64	609	540	2838	3402	9164	39429	53868	•	994786	•

Selected Financial Ratios (Times to 1)

Current Ratio 30	1.4	•	0.7	13.6	1.4	2.0	1.5	1.4	2.5	1.8	•	1.3	•
Quick Ratio 31	1.0	•	0.6	6.2	1.2	1.4	1.1	1.3	1.8	1.2	•	1.0	•
Net Sales to Working Capital 32	11.8	•	•	11.8	23.8	10.2	8.2	13.7	6.0	9.5	•	8.4	•
Coverage Ratio 33	5.0	28.8	183.1	68.0	33.4	5.6	5.5	14.7	8.9	4.3	•	3.3	•
Total Asset Turnover 34	1.0	•	6.4	3.8	4.9	4.1	1.9	2.8	2.1	0.8	•	0.6	•
Inventory Turnover 35	15.7	•	9.3	1487.9	14.0	38.4	8.3	177.5	805.9	48.4	•	22.7	•
Receivables Turnover 36	6.3	•	57.5	2829.1	13.1	10.5	•	8.8	30.5	•	•	6.6	•
Total Liabilities to Net Worth 37	2.4	•	•	0.3	3.5	1.4	3.0	2.7	0.6	3.5	•	2.3	•
Current Assets to Working Capital 38	3.8	•	•	1.1	3.6	2.0	3.1	3.4	1.7	2.3	•	3.9	•
Current Liabilities to Working Capital 39	2.8	•	•	0.1	2.6	1.0	2.1	2.4	0.7	1.3	•	2.9	•
Working Capital to Net Sales 40	0.1	•	•	0.1	0.0	0.1	0.1	0.1	0.2	0.1	•	0.1	•
Inventory to Working Capital 41	0.2	•	•	•	0.0	•	0.0	0.0	0.0	0.0	•	0.2	•
Total Receipts to Cash Flow 42	2.4	3.6	1.7	2.1	1.9	1.2	1.8	7.8	2.3	1.9	•	3.0	•
Cost of Goods to Cash Flow 43	0.5	1.5	0.1	0.6	0.1	0.0	0.0	2.4	1.1	0.4	•	1.0	•
Cash Flow to Total Debt 44	0.6	•	2.5	8.0	3.4	5.8	1.4	0.5	2.4	0.6	•	0.3	•

Selected Financial Factors (in Percentages)

Debt Ratio 45	70.9	•	149.1	22.2	77.8	58.1	75.2	72.7	38.5	78.0	•	69.8	•
Return on Total Assets 46	12.7	•	136.1	103.7	31.9	34.2	12.2	18.5	4.9	11.6	•	8.8	•
Return on Equity Before Income Taxes 47	34.7	•	•	131.3	139.7	67.0	40.2	63.3	7.1	40.4	•	20.2	•
Return on Equity After Income Taxes 48	29.2	•	•	129.4	136.3	55.3	37.6	56.1	5.3	31.0	•	14.8	•
Profit Margin (Before Income Tax) 49	10.6	10.0	21.2	26.8	6.3	6.9	5.4	6.2	2.1	10.5	•	10.8	•
Profit Margin (After Income Tax) 50	8.9	8.8	21.2	26.4	6.1	5.7	5.0	5.5	1.5	8.1	•	7.9	•

Table I

Corporations with and without Net Income

MISC. HEALTH CARE AND SOCIAL ASSISTANCE

MONEY AMOUNTS AND SIZE OF ASSETS IN THOUSANDS OF DOLLARS

Item Description for Accounting Period 7/11 Through 6/12		Total	Zero Assets	Under 500	500 to 1,000	1,000 to 5,000	5,000 to 10,000	10,000 to 25,000	25,000 to 50,000	50,000 to 100,000	100,000 to 250,000	250,000 to 500,000	500,000 to 2,500,000	2,500,000 and over
Number of Enterprises	1	68303	14396	48436	2736	2153	210	161	78	48	39	19	23	3
Revenues ($ in Thousands)														
Net Sales	2	116308294	6051796	30196691	6311345	9093234	2866260	5394898	4144261	4531128	5877758	7714820	20352587	13773515
Interest	3	154915	4007	1781	197	2158	858	4203	5818	2098	10684	3009	56680	63422
Rents	4	44812	0	2809	38	6631	1505	3554	1542	3817	9767	235	14679	234
Royalties	5	83396	0	0	0	0	0	1061	0	41175	31288	1926	6897	1048
Other Portfolio Income	6	404343	53843	30026	247	45326	27029	28090	12321	13406	13331	2888	114326	63508
Other Receipts	7	1902239	120431	622866	198246	123842	63928	32817	62896	-45630	44466	173906	268857	235618
Total Receipts	8	118897999	6230077	30854173	6510073	9271191	2959580	5464623	4226838	4545994	5987294	7896784	20814026	14137345
Average Total Receipts	9	1741	433	637	2379	4306	14093	33942	54190	94708	153520	415620	904958	4712448
Operating Costs/Operating Income (%)														
Cost of Operations	10	15.8	3.3	8.5	8.0	17.1	21.1	32.4	31.8	31.9	20.0	14.3	16.9	19.6
Salaries and Wages	11	32.6	30.5	35.7	41.1	34.1	36.6	24.4	29.6	27.9	28.5	40.6	33.5	22.3
Taxes Paid	12	4.2	3.3	5.0	4.2	4.6	3.8	3.1	4.6	3.7	4.1	4.6	4.4	2.5
Interest Paid	13	2.0	0.8	0.3	1.1	0.9	1.1	0.9	1.1	1.9	3.1	3.6	4.9	2.9
Depreciation	14	2.4	1.1	1.1	1.6	1.8	2.0	2.2	2.2	2.5	3.3	3.0	4.3	3.1
Amortization and Depletion	15	0.9	0.7	0.2	0.3	0.1	0.2	0.5	0.5	1.3	1.7	1.6	1.7	1.5
Pensions and Other Deferred Comp.	16	0.3	0.2	0.3	0.2	0.5	0.3	0.2	0.4	0.4	0.3	0.2	0.2	0.5
Employee Benefits	17	2.7	2.4	1.5	1.7	2.7	3.9	1.3	2.9	2.7	2.6	2.4	3.4	5.5
Advertising	18	0.5	0.6	0.6	0.6	0.4	0.9	0.7	0.5	0.4	0.7	0.5	0.6	0.3
Other Expenses	19	32.9	55.8	32.2	31.4	31.7	28.3	32.5	26.4	26.0	33.4	32.5	30.8	33.8
Officers' Compensation	20	4.4	2.3	11.8	3.7	4.9	2.1	1.7	1.7	1.2	1.2	0.6	0.6	1.1
Operating Margin	21	1.4	•	2.8	6.2	1.3	•	•	•	0.1	1.0	•	•	6.9
Operating Margin Before Officers' Comp.	22	5.8	1.3	14.6	9.9	6.2	1.7	1.6	0.0	1.3	2.3	•	•	8.0

Selected Average Balance Sheet ($ in Thousands)														
Net Receivables	23	161	0	10	86	368	1311	3747	9459	15655	23916	68007	129261	650563
Inventories	24	11	0	1	3	9	292	287	562	1093	1897	6317	10298	27859
Net Property, Plant and Equipment	25	181	0	27	228	703	2118	2667	6146	7453	20936	44518	177146	488480
Total Assets	26	1173	0	88	739	2095	6705	16353	35746	73019	147455	326581	1064307	7535336
Notes and Loans Payable	27	564	0	51	322	1067	3235	4634	7818	25178	71341	158687	552250	3722636
All Other Liabilities	28	277	0	32	199	347	1690	5729	13159	23786	35042	83110	218265	1548455
Net Worth	29	332	0	5	218	680	1780	5990	14769	24055	41073	84785	293793	2264246

Selected Financial Ratios (Times to 1)														
Current Ratio	30	1.5	•	1.4	1.3	2.3	1.8	1.5	1.7	1.2	1.4	2.1	1.3	1.7
Quick Ratio	31	1.1	•	1.2	1.0	1.9	1.5	1.2	1.2	0.9	1.2	1.6	1.0	0.6
Net Sales to Working Capital	32	13.5	•	56.7	34.7	7.3	9.2	11.3	6.3	25.4	11.0	7.0	18.9	6.0
Coverage Ratio	33	2.8	4.8	16.0	9.2	4.5	3.5	2.2	1.3	1.2	1.9	0.6	1.2	4.3
Total Asset Turnover	34	1.5	•	7.1	3.1	2.0	2.0	2.0	1.5	1.3	1.0	1.2	0.8	0.6
Inventory Turnover	35	24.9	•	80.0	55.0	83.5	9.9	37.9	30.1	27.5	15.9	9.2	14.5	32.4
Receivables Turnover	36	10.9	•	69.2	21.4	13.2	8.3	9.6	5.8	5.9	5.8	5.6	5.9	14.1
Total Liabilities to Net Worth	37	2.5	•	16.7	2.4	2.1	2.8	1.7	1.4	2.0	2.6	2.9	2.6	2.3
Current Assets to Working Capital	38	2.9	•	3.6	4.7	1.8	2.2	3.0	2.5	7.6	3.4	2.0	4.5	2.5
Current Liabilities to Working Capital	39	1.9	•	2.6	3.7	0.8	1.2	2.0	1.5	6.6	2.4	1.0	3.5	1.5
Working Capital to Net Sales	40	0.1	•	0.0	0.0	0.1	0.1	0.1	0.2	0.0	0.1	0.1	0.1	0.2
Inventory to Working Capital	41	0.1	•	0.1	0.0	0.0	0.0	0.1	0.1	0.3	0.1	0.1	0.2	0.0
Total Receipts to Cash Flow	42	3.2	1.9	3.2	3.0	3.3	3.9	3.4	4.5	4.3	3.1	3.7	4.0	2.6
Cost of Goods to Cash Flow	43	0.5	0.1	0.3	0.2	0.6	0.8	1.1	1.4	1.4	0.6	0.5	0.7	0.5
Cash Flow to Total Debt	44	0.6	•	2.3	1.5	0.9	0.7	0.9	0.6	0.5	0.5	0.5	0.3	0.3

Selected Financial Factors (in Percentages)														
Debt Ratio	45	71.7	•	94.3	70.4	67.5	73.5	63.4	58.7	67.1	72.1	74.0	72.4	70.0
Return on Total Assets	46	8.3	•	37.8	32.7	8.4	8.1	4.3	2.1	3.0	6.1	2.6	4.9	7.6
Return on Equity Before Income Taxes	47	18.9	•	625.3	98.8	20.0	21.6	6.5	1.2	1.6	10.6	•	2.9	19.4
Return on Equity After Income Taxes	48	14.9	•	619.0	98.7	18.9	17.5	4.1	0.1	•	7.0	•	0.3	12.1
Profit Margin (Before Income Tax)	49	3.7	2.9	5.0	9.4	3.2	2.8	1.2	0.3	0.4	2.9	•	1.0	9.6
Profit Margin (After Income Tax)	50	2.9	2.6	4.9	9.3	3.0	2.3	0.7	0.0	•	1.9	•	0.1	6.0

Table II

Corporations with Net Income

MISC. HEALTH CARE AND SOCIAL ASSISTANCE

MONEY AMOUNTS AND SIZE OF ASSETS IN THOUSANDS OF DOLLARS

Item Description for Accounting Period 7/11 Through 6/12		Total	Zero Assets	Under 500	500 to 1,000	1,000 to 5,000	5,000 to 10,000	10,000 to 25,000	25,000 to 50,000	50,000 to 100,000	100,000 to 250,000	250,000 to 500,000	500,000 to 2,500,000	2,500,000 and over
Number of Enterprises	1	43541	7404	32478	1962	1333	159	95	41	25	24	8	12	0
Revenues ($ in Thousands)														
Net Sales	2	78464092	4531684	20709474	5010758	5887013	1943107	4184565	2590356	2824969	4596938	3389473	22795755	0
Interest	3	133697	2440	1464	62	1184	643	3264	1279	766	9745	1293	111556	0
Rents	4	39455	0	0	0	6539	1505	3554	74	3817	9353	82	14531	0
Royalties	5	67094	0	0	0	0	0	0	0	40216	23906	1909	1063	0
Other Portfolio Income	6	326345	51452	30026	247	44556	539	8994	8146	457	3430	1451	177046	0
Other Receipts	7	1007251	114940	96828	167949	161642	48968	7843	28763	10667	20068	45988	303598	0
Total Receipts	8	80037934	4700516	20837792	5179016	6100934	1994762	4208220	2628618	2880892	4663440	3440196	23403549	0
Average Total Receipts	9	1838	635	642	2640	4577	12546	44297	64113	115236	194310	430024	1950296	•
Operating Costs/Operating Income (%)														
Cost of Operations	10	19.1	1.5	11.2	7.5	23.4	23.0	39.6	34.5	34.3	19.9	20.7	23.0	•
Salaries and Wages	11	28.8	30.0	33.2	39.2	27.8	34.4	22.2	31.2	22.7	28.0	19.6	25.3	•
Taxes Paid	12	4.0	3.4	4.9	4.3	4.4	4.0	3.2	4.8	3.2	4.3	3.0	3.2	•
Interest Paid	13	1.4	0.3	0.2	1.1	0.7	0.8	0.5	0.9	1.3	2.1	1.2	3.1	•
Depreciation	14	2.0	0.9	1.1	1.7	1.7	1.7	1.7	1.5	2.4	2.6	1.4	3.4	•
Amortization and Depletion	15	0.7	0.3	0.1	0.0	0.1	0.2	0.3	0.6	0.7	1.3	1.4	1.5	•
Pensions and Other Deferred Comp.	16	0.4	0.2	0.4	0.3	0.6	0.5	0.2	0.5	0.6	0.3	0.1	0.4	•
Employee Benefits	17	2.8	2.8	1.5	2.0	2.4	3.1	1.1	2.5	2.6	2.4	1.8	4.7	•
Advertising	18	0.5	0.6	0.7	0.6	0.3	0.5	0.7	0.3	0.3	0.3	0.8	0.5	•
Other Expenses	19	29.1	52.2	27.3	30.0	23.7	23.6	23.3	14.8	25.3	33.0	44.1	27.8	•
Officers' Compensation	20	4.0	2.6	10.4	3.0	4.8	1.9	1.7	1.7	1.2	1.0	0.6	0.9	•
Operating Margin	21	7.3	5.2	9.0	10.4	10.2	6.6	5.4	6.7	5.6	4.6	5.0	6.2	•
Operating Margin Before Officers' Comp.	22	11.3	7.8	19.4	13.4	15.0	8.4	7.1	8.5	6.7	5.6	5.7	7.1	•

Selected Average Balance Sheet ($ in Thousands)													
Net Receivables 23	161	0	10	102	269	1182	3782	9813	15349	29419	83698	284448	•
Inventories 24	10	0	1	5	6	122	416	583	1319	1499	6859	14762	•
Net Property, Plant and Equipment 25	162	0	26	258	623	2502	3077	5261	6871	15688	19664	271312	•
Total Assets 26	1070	0	85	768	2074	6423	16507	36347	69856	148816	314463	2306413	•
Notes and Loans Payable 27	425	0	30	222	576	3179	4028	8352	21558	60915	63043	1047766	•
All Other Liabilities 28	232	0	24	136	324	1061	5042	10536	22372	40850	80876	446608	•
Net Worth 29	414	0	31	410	1174	2183	7436	17458	25926	47051	170544	812039	•

Selected Financial Ratios (Times to 1)													
Current Ratio 30	1.4	•	2.1	2.0	3.4	2.4	1.5	2.0	1.2	1.8	2.1	1.0	•
Quick Ratio 31	1.2	•	2.0	1.7	2.9	1.9	1.3	1.4	1.0	1.5	1.8	0.8	•
Net Sales to Working Capital 32	18.2	•	27.6	14.9	5.6	7.7	15.1	6.1	20.7	8.5	6.1	•	•
Coverage Ratio 33	7.7	34.1	41.6	13.8	21.1	12.4	12.2	10.3	6.9	3.8	6.3	3.9	•
Total Asset Turnover 34	1.7	•	7.5	3.3	2.1	1.9	2.7	1.7	1.6	1.3	1.3	0.8	•
Inventory Turnover 35	34.9	•	81.1	42.1	184.0	23.0	42.0	37.3	29.4	25.4	12.8	29.6	•
Receivables Turnover 36	10.8	•	65.4	18.9	15.1	7.7	13.3	6.3	6.9	6.0	4.1	6.8	•
Total Liabilities to Net Worth 37	1.6	•	1.8	0.9	0.8	1.9	1.2	1.1	1.7	2.2	0.8	1.8	•
Current Assets to Working Capital 38	3.2	•	1.9	2.0	1.4	1.7	3.0	2.0	5.3	2.3	1.9	•	•
Current Liabilities to Working Capital 39	2.2	•	0.9	1.0	0.4	0.7	2.0	1.0	4.3	1.3	0.9	•	•
Working Capital to Net Sales 40	0.1	•	0.0	0.1	0.2	0.1	0.1	0.2	0.0	0.1	0.2	•	•
Inventory to Working Capital 41	0.1	•	0.0	0.0	0.0	0.0	0.1	0.1	0.3	0.0	0.1	•	•
Total Receipts to Cash Flow 42	3.0	1.8	3.2	2.7	3.0	3.7	3.9	5.2	3.3	2.7	2.1	3.1	•
Cost of Goods to Cash Flow 43	0.6	0.0	0.4	0.2	0.7	0.8	1.6	1.8	1.1	0.5	0.4	0.7	•
Cash Flow to Total Debt 44	0.9	•	3.7	2.7	1.6	0.8	1.2	0.6	0.8	0.7	1.4	0.4	•

Selected Financial Factors (in Percentages)													
Debt Ratio 45	61.3	•	63.9	46.6	43.4	66.0	55.0	52.0	62.9	68.4	45.8	64.8	•
Return on Total Assets 46	18.1	•	74.2	49.4	30.9	19.1	17.5	15.8	14.3	10.5	10.5	9.9	•
Return on Equity Before Income Taxes 47	40.7	•	200.5	85.9	52.0	51.7	35.6	29.7	32.9	24.5	16.3	20.8	•
Return on Equity After Income Taxes 48	35.6	•	199.0	85.8	50.9	47.3	32.3	27.9	28.1	19.3	12.5	13.9	•
Profit Margin (Before Income Tax) 49	9.3	10.2	9.6	13.8	13.8	9.2	6.0	8.2	7.5	6.0	6.5	8.9	•
Profit Margin (After Income Tax) 50	8.2	9.8	9.5	13.8	13.5	8.4	5.5	7.7	6.4	4.8	5.0	5.9	•

Table I

Corporations with and without Net Income

HOSPITALS, NURSING, AND RESIDENTIAL CARE FACILITIES

MONEY AMOUNTS AND SIZE OF ASSETS IN THOUSANDS OF DOLLARS

Item Description for Accounting Period 7/11 Through 6/12		Total	Zero Assets	Under 500	500 to 1,000	1,000 to 5,000	5,000 to 10,000	10,000 to 25,000	25,000 to 50,000	50,000 to 100,000	100,000 to 250,000	250,000 to 500,000	500,000 to 2,500,000	2,500,000 and over
Number of Enterprises	1	19149	824	13088	1797	2743	272	228	82	41	32	8	21	13
Revenues ($ in Thousands)														
Net Sales	2	146053896	226060	11708451	3812313	15577949	4043255	5845291	4961769	4649012	8343145	2600389	13332272	70953989
Interest	3	1321951	431	93	726	2959	921	2570	5285	3258	11042	9543	52874	1232250
Rents	4	545635	20	492	0	776	694	10005	20670	3158	23221	4426	25090	457083
Royalties	5	772	0	0	0	0	0	0	0	0	772	0	0	0
Other Portfolio Income	6	588902	2606	185	326	7293	11698	16060	14252	2965	28392	16001	211671	277453
Other Receipts	7	9356208	-20780	57320	23694	764118	31133	80954	80965	133372	515087	127946	568984	6993416
Total Receipts	8	157867364	208337	11766541	3837059	16353095	4087701	5954880	5082941	4791765	8921659	2758305	14190891	79914191
Average Total Receipts	9	8244	253	899	2135	5962	15028	26118	61987	116872	278802	344788	675757	6147245
Operating Costs/Operating Income (%)														
Cost of Operations	10	5.1	0.1	8.6	5.5	5.3	23.1	11.7	9.3	6.5	6.0	2.4	6.4	2.3
Salaries and Wages	11	40.9	33.1	40.9	37.4	41.9	24.8	30.7	38.3	41.4	41.7	47.1	42.6	42.2
Taxes Paid	12	5.3	4.4	5.5	5.2	6.7	6.4	5.7	6.0	5.8	5.9	7.1	5.7	4.6
Interest Paid	13	4.4	10.0	0.5	1.0	0.7	1.0	1.4	1.5	1.6	1.4	3.3	3.9	7.3
Depreciation	14	3.4	2.1	1.0	1.1	1.1	1.2	1.7	2.5	2.7	2.8	2.4	4.2	4.7
Amortization and Depletion	15	0.7	1.1	0.0	0.3	0.1	0.2	0.3	0.1	0.5	0.4	0.6	1.1	1.0
Pensions and Other Deferred Comp.	16	0.5	•	0.2	0.1	0.2	0.8	0.4	0.1	0.3	0.4	0.1	0.1	0.7
Employee Benefits	17	4.7	6.2	1.7	2.0	3.2	6.5	4.5	4.3	4.1	3.6	5.4	5.9	5.6
Advertising	18	0.3	0.2	0.7	0.7	0.2	0.1	0.4	0.3	0.3	0.3	0.4	0.3	0.3
Other Expenses	19	39.2	64.2	34.2	37.6	39.4	29.7	41.6	35.6	38.8	42.5	34.5	32.6	41.6
Officers' Compensation	20	1.3	3.1	6.8	4.4	1.6	3.6	1.0	0.8	0.8	0.7	0.4	0.3	0.3
Operating Margin	21	•	•	0.0	4.7	•	2.7	0.8	1.2	•	•	•	•	•
Operating Margin Before Officers' Comp.	22	•	•	6.8	9.1	1.2	6.3	1.8	2.0	•	•	•	•	•

Selected Average Balance Sheet ($ in Thousands)													
Net Receivables 23	838	0	14	119	543	1569	3091	6718	14086	29386	68963	67545	691561
Inventories 24	12	0	0	1	2	20	55	249	443	1310	1835	2252	4902
Net Property, Plant and Equipment 25	2695	0	64	216	625	2612	4940	16139	28631	66285	128122	382440	2550522
Total Assets 26	7652	0	117	688	2162	6930	14968	34420	69008	171088	358029	902352	7661924
Notes and Loans Payable 27	4749	0	134	319	1091	3002	8679	18796	33202	77116	165290	417255	5183035
All Other Liabilities 28	1831	0	74	114	755	3480	5214	11151	21266	67217	145217	237420	1507773
Net Worth 29	1072	0	-91	254	316	448	1075	4473	14540	26756	47522	247677	971116
Selected Financial Ratios (Times to 1)													
Current Ratio 30	1.3	•	0.3	2.5	1.7	0.9	1.4	1.3	1.3	1.6	1.6	1.4	1.3
Quick Ratio 31	1.0	•	0.3	2.2	1.4	0.7	1.1	1.1	1.1	1.2	1.4	1.2	0.9
Net Sales to Working Capital 32	20.8	•	•	10.6	11.4	•	15.6	22.7	18.5	12.2	9.1	11.7	20.6
Coverage Ratio 33	1.5	•	2.0	6.4	7.5	4.7	2.9	3.4	1.2	1.8	1.7	1.9	1.3
Total Asset Turnover 34	1.0	•	7.7	3.1	2.6	2.1	1.7	1.8	1.6	1.5	0.9	0.7	0.7
Inventory Turnover 35	31.9	•	1208.5	97.8	127.7	175.6	54.4	22.6	16.5	12.0	4.2	18.1	25.3
Receivables Turnover 36	9.5	•	61.1	15.3	11.7	9.2	8.6	8.4	8.8	8.8	4.3	8.3	8.6
Total Liabilities to Net Worth 37	6.1	•	•	1.7	5.8	14.5	12.9	6.7	3.7	5.4	6.5	2.6	6.9
Current Assets to Working Capital 38	4.3	•	•	1.7	2.5	•	3.7	4.9	4.4	2.8	2.7	3.2	4.4
Current Liabilities to Working Capital 39	3.3	•	•	0.7	1.5	•	2.7	3.9	3.4	1.8	1.7	2.2	3.4
Working Capital to Net Sales 40	0.0	•	•	0.1	0.1	•	0.1	0.0	0.1	0.1	0.1	0.1	0.0
Inventory to Working Capital 41	0.0	•	•	0.0	0.0	•	0.0	0.1	0.1	0.1	0.0	0.1	0.0
Total Receipts to Cash Flow 42	2.9	3.7	4.8	3.1	2.8	3.6	2.9	3.0	3.1	2.9	3.2	3.7	2.6
Cost of Goods to Cash Flow 43	0.1	0.0	0.4	0.2	0.1	0.8	0.3	0.3	0.2	0.2	0.1	0.2	0.1
Cash Flow to Total Debt 44	0.4	•	0.9	1.6	1.1	0.6	0.6	0.7	0.7	0.6	0.3	0.3	0.3
Selected Financial Factors (in Percentages)													
Debt Ratio 45	86.0	•	177.9	63.0	85.4	93.5	92.8	87.0	78.9	84.4	86.7	72.6	87.3
Return on Total Assets 46	6.7	•	7.6	19.5	13.7	10.4	6.8	9.1	3.2	4.0	5.1	5.1	6.6
Return on Equity Before Income Taxes 47	16.7	•	•	44.6	81.2	126.7	62.6	48.9	2.8	11.4	15.8	8.8	11.2
Return on Equity After Income Taxes 48	13.3	•	•	41.7	79.8	126.6	59.4	44.8	1.5	8.5	6.3	6.3	7.6
Profit Margin (Before Income Tax) 49	2.3	•	0.5	5.3	4.5	3.8	2.6	3.6	0.4	1.2	2.3	3.4	2.0
Profit Margin (After Income Tax) 50	1.9	•	0.5	5.0	4.4	3.8	2.5	3.3	0.2	0.9	0.9	2.5	1.4

Table II

Corporations with Net Income

HOSPITALS, NURSING, AND RESIDENTIAL CARE FACILITIES

MONEY AMOUNTS AND SIZE OF ASSETS IN THOUSANDS OF DOLLARS

Item Description for Accounting Period 7/11 Through 6/12		Total	Zero Assets	Under 500	500 to 1,000	1,000 to 5,000	5,000 to 10,000	10,000 to 25,000	25,000 to 50,000	50,000 to 100,000	100,000 to 250,000	250,000 to 500,000	500,000 to 2,500,000	2,500,000 and over
Number of Enterprises	1	10978	39	7477	1211	1847	123	155	56	21	22	•	•	•
Revenues ($ in Thousands)														
Net Sales	2	88084323	33776	6676333	2337182	10961451	2479886	3619458	3090733	2682995	6032228	•	•	•
Interest	3	1154603	274	62	363	2767	43	1390	4570	220	10331	•	•	•
Rents	4	344904	3	492	0	776	694	0	18817	2996	14315	•	•	•
Royalties	5	772	0	0	0	0	0	0	0	0	772	•	•	•
Other Portfolio Income	6	398112	957	44	326	6077	11454	3449	14134	2574	21935	•	•	•
Other Receipts	7	4413551	305	34211	23693	687697	23773	50294	62973	126387	466737	•	•	•
Total Receipts	8	94396265	35315	6711142	2361564	11658768	2515850	3674591	3191227	2815172	6546318	•	•	•
Average Total Receipts	9	8599	906	898	1950	6312	20454	23707	56986	134056	297560	•	•	•
Operating Costs/Operating Income (%)														
Cost of Operations	10	5.4	•	6.2	7.4	2.3	19.2	12.2	13.1	5.7	6.7	•	•	•
Salaries and Wages	11	40.2	37.3	36.1	32.3	44.5	31.8	34.1	33.3	42.8	43.1	•	•	•
Taxes Paid	12	5.5	4.8	4.9	5.2	7.2	7.2	6.4	5.8	5.4	6.2	•	•	•
Interest Paid	13	3.7	10.3	0.6	1.1	0.7	0.5	1.2	1.7	0.8	1.5	•	•	•
Depreciation	14	3.0	4.3	1.0	1.3	0.9	0.7	1.8	2.6	2.3	3.0	•	•	•
Amortization and Depletion	15	0.6	1.4	0.0	0.2	0.0	0.3	0.2	0.1	0.2	0.4	•	•	•
Pensions and Other Deferred Comp.	16	0.3	•	0.3	0.2	0.2	1.2	0.2	0.1	0.5	0.5	•	•	•
Employee Benefits	17	4.5	2.0	1.7	1.2	3.3	4.3	4.9	2.7	4.0	3.4	•	•	•
Advertising	18	0.3	0.3	0.7	0.9	0.2	0.2	0.3	0.4	0.3	0.4	•	•	•
Other Expenses	19	36.9	36.3	35.2	37.0	36.2	27.1	31.6	35.5	38.5	39.4	•	•	•
Officers' Compensation	20	1.4	1.0	7.2	5.1	2.2	1.0	1.4	1.0	1.0	0.7	•	•	•
Operating Margin	21	•	2.4	6.0	8.1	2.4	6.6	5.5	3.7	•	•	•	•	•
Operating Margin Before Officers' Comp.	22	•	3.4	13.2	13.3	4.6	7.6	6.9	4.7	•	•	•	•	•

Selected Average Balance Sheet ($ in Thousands)

Net Receivables 23	852	0	18	112	455	1709	3007	5764	14247	32595	•	•	•
Inventories 24	15	0	0	1	2	29	49	311	381	1567	•	•	•
Net Property, Plant and Equipment 25	2571	0	63	248	677	1247	5367	17326	19816	71153	•	•	•
Total Assets 26	7769	0	126	675	2248	6310	14689	35429	64792	176535	•	•	•
Notes and Loans Payable 27	4210	0	103	305	765	1453	8376	20495	21379	67390	•	•	•
All Other Liabilities 28	1821	0	27	112	643	2915	3623	10788	18542	58242	•	•	•
Net Worth 29	1738	0	-4	258	840	1942	2690	4146	24871	50903	•	•	•

Selected Financial Ratios (Times to 1)

Current Ratio 30	1.5	•	1.6	2.4	2.2	1.4	1.6	1.4	1.6	1.7	•	•	•
Quick Ratio 31	1.2	•	1.5	2.1	1.9	1.3	1.3	1.2	1.3	1.4	•	•	•
Net Sales to Working Capital 32	14.5	•	50.5	11.2	8.3	16.9	10.9	14.6	11.7	10.9	•	•	•
Coverage Ratio 33	2.5	1.7	12.4	9.7	12.7	18.0	6.6	5.2	5.4	3.3	•	•	•
Total Asset Turnover 34	1.0	•	7.1	2.9	2.6	3.2	1.6	1.6	2.0	1.6	•	•	•
Inventory Turnover 35	29.2	•	•	163.9	58.4	131.0	58.6	23.2	19.2	11.8	•	•	•
Receivables Turnover 36	7.8	•	54.2	12.5	12.8	8.7	7.2	7.1	8.9	7.8	•	•	•
Total Liabilities to Net Worth 37	3.5	•	•	1.6	1.7	2.2	4.5	7.5	1.6	2.5	•	•	•
Current Assets to Working Capital 38	3.1	•	2.7	1.7	1.9	3.4	2.7	3.6	2.7	2.5	•	•	•
Current Liabilities to Working Capital 39	2.1	•	1.7	0.7	0.9	2.4	1.7	2.6	1.7	1.5	•	•	•
Working Capital to Net Sales 40	0.1	•	0.0	0.1	0.1	0.1	0.1	0.1	0.1	0.1	•	•	•
Inventory to Working Capital 41	0.0	•	•	0.0	0.0	0.0	0.0	0.1	0.0	0.1	•	•	•
Total Receipts to Cash Flow 42	2.8	2.8	3.4	3.1	2.7	3.8	3.1	2.7	2.8	2.8	•	•	•
Cost of Goods to Cash Flow 43	0.2	•	0.2	0.2	0.1	0.7	0.4	0.4	0.2	0.2	•	•	•
Cash Flow to Total Debt 44	0.5	•	2.0	1.5	1.6	1.2	0.6	0.7	1.2	0.8	•	•	•

Selected Financial Factors (in Percentages)

Debt Ratio 45	77.6	•	102.9	61.8	62.6	69.2	81.7	88.3	61.6	71.2	•	•	•
Return on Total Assets 46	9.4	•	50.4	29.2	25.0	27.3	13.1	13.4	8.7	7.5	•	•	•
Return on Equity Before Income Taxes 47	25.0	•	•	68.6	61.7	83.8	60.7	92.6	18.4	18.2	•	•	•
Return on Equity After Income Taxes 48	21.3	•	•	64.3	60.9	83.7	58.8	86.1	16.9	16.0	•	•	•
Profit Margin (Before Income Tax) 49	5.4	7.0	6.6	9.2	8.7	8.1	7.0	7.0	3.6	3.4	•	•	•
Profit Margin (After Income Tax) 50	4.6	6.1	6.5	8.6	8.6	8.1	6.8	6.5	3.3	3.0	•	•	•

Table I

Corporations with and without Net Income

OTHER ARTS, ENTERTAINMENT, AND RECREATION

MONEY AMOUNTS AND SIZE OF ASSETS IN THOUSANDS OF DOLLARS

Item Description for Accounting Period 7/11 Through 6/12		Total	Zero Assets	Under 500	500 to 1,000	1,000 to 5,000	5,000 to 10,000	10,000 to 25,000	25,000 to 50,000	50,000 to 100,000	100,000 to 250,000	250,000 to 500,000	500,000 to 2,500,000	2,500,000 and over
Number of Enterprises	1	75651	16416	55411	2050	1365	201	83	44	29	21	16	15	0
Revenues ($ in Thousands)														
Net Sales	2	49251895	1247822	17111009	4746267	5411713	1142808	1565140	887789	1232705	2508002	3454377	9944264	0
Interest	3	165035	3083	2918	936	2196	216	2264	2736	1342	1529	8097	139719	0
Rents	4	76740	0	617	0	2342	0	285	5822	383	898	28276	38117	0
Royalties	5	52742	0	221	0	0	0	926	7582	120	17315	14604	11974	0
Other Portfolio Income	6	135821	24693	23661	12	3763	5854	637	372	216	4229	8686	63697	0
Other Receipts	7	2607991	77604	371272	32223	173204	119767	38844	174716	272323	310007	571060	466970	0
Total Receipts	8	52290224	1353202	17509698	4779438	5593218	1268645	1608096	1079017	1507089	2841980	4085100	10664741	0
Average Total Receipts	9	691	82	316	2331	4098	6312	19375	24523	51969	135332	255319	710983	•
Operating Costs/Operating Income (%)														
Cost of Operations	10	19.2	7.0	8.9	10.0	17.2	23.5	51.9	20.9	32.6	22.0	20.1	35.6	•
Salaries and Wages	11	15.2	8.2	11.8	5.9	12.7	14.9	13.3	19.6	31.1	41.1	31.5	13.6	•
Taxes Paid	12	3.7	2.1	2.3	2.7	2.4	2.1	2.2	3.0	3.2	3.4	7.5	6.8	•
Interest Paid	13	1.7	3.4	0.4	0.5	0.5	0.9	0.3	1.2	1.7	3.0	2.0	4.8	•
Depreciation	14	2.7	2.4	0.8	0.8	1.8	4.3	1.0	4.7	3.7	3.2	5.1	5.9	•
Amortization and Depletion	15	1.3	1.7	0.0	0.1	0.4	0.5	0.4	0.6	1.8	3.1	4.6	3.3	•
Pensions and Other Deferred Comp.	16	1.6	0.6	2.6	0.7	0.9	0.8	0.4	0.5	1.5	2.0	2.2	0.8	•
Employee Benefits	17	1.1	0.8	0.7	0.1	0.7	0.7	1.2	1.0	3.4	1.8	4.3	1.1	•
Advertising	18	2.2	5.9	1.1	2.2	3.3	1.3	1.2	1.4	3.0	5.2	1.6	2.6	•
Other Expenses	19	32.3	86.4	34.9	18.8	33.8	33.9	13.8	47.9	36.6	25.6	31.6	29.1	•
Officers' Compensation	20	18.8	4.9	32.6	52.8	12.7	7.6	4.2	1.8	2.6	1.9	2.7	0.9	•
Operating Margin	21	0.3	•	3.9	5.3	13.6	9.4	10.1	•	•	•	•	•	•
Operating Margin Before Officers' Comp.	22	19.1	•	36.5	58.2	26.3	17.0	14.3	•	•	•	•	•	•

Selected Average Balance Sheet ($ in Thousands)

Net Receivables 23	41	0	2	24	106	366	1373	3192	8162	15316	23982	100642	•
Inventories 24	10	0	1	10	243	95	79	895	1236	1985	2561	11175	•
Net Property, Plant and Equipment 25	140	0	8	321	389	618	2512	9086	13561	40411	92127	368283	•
Total Assets 26	604	0	48	675	1953	7752	15021	32731	72333	155961	356735	1580234	•
Notes and Loans Payable 27	238	0	46	319	1099	2480	1567	11985	17287	59052	109419	577867	•
All Other Liabilities 28	209	0	16	111	690	630	3455	15130	43527	71088	135124	516042	•
Net Worth 29	158	0	-14	244	165	4642	9999	5615	11519	25822	112192	486324	•

Selected Financial Ratios (Times to 1)

Current Ratio 30	1.3	•	1.9	3.0	1.3	5.2	2.3	1.5	1.7	0.9	1.2	1.2	•
Quick Ratio 31	0.8	•	1.6	2.5	0.7	4.8	1.9	0.8	1.1	0.6	0.8	0.6	•
Net Sales to Working Capital 32	11.1	•	19.6	11.8	15.6	2.0	5.2	4.5	3.4	•	13.4	8.4	•
Coverage Ratio 33	4.9	•	18.2	13.9	32.0	22.5	37.7	17.2	1.7	1.4	3.4	1.6	•
Total Asset Turnover 34	1.1	•	6.5	3.4	2.0	0.7	1.3	0.6	0.6	0.8	0.6	0.4	•
Inventory Turnover 35	12.1	•	20.0	22.5	2.8	14.0	124.1	4.7	11.2	13.2	16.9	21.1	•
Receivables Turnover 36	17.3	•	189.1	102.0	41.5	11.1	11.4	5.2	5.9	7.7	8.2	8.2	•
Total Liabilities to Net Worth 37	2.8	•	•	1.8	10.9	0.7	0.5	4.8	5.3	5.0	2.2	2.2	•
Current Assets to Working Capital 38	4.1	•	2.1	1.5	4.3	1.2	1.8	2.9	2.5	•	7.5	7.3	•
Current Liabilities to Working Capital 39	3.1	•	1.1	0.5	3.3	0.2	0.8	1.9	1.5	•	6.5	6.3	•
Working Capital to Net Sales 40	0.1	•	0.1	0.1	0.1	0.5	0.2	0.2	0.3	•	0.1	0.1	•
Inventory to Working Capital 41	0.2	•	0.0	0.1	1.1	0.0	0.0	0.0	0.1	•	0.1	0.3	•
Total Receipts to Cash Flow 42	2.9	1.6	2.7	4.6	2.2	2.0	4.1	1.6	3.2	4.7	3.0	3.6	•
Cost of Goods to Cash Flow 43	0.6	0.1	0.2	0.5	0.4	0.5	2.1	0.3	1.0	1.0	0.6	1.3	•
Cash Flow to Total Debt 44	0.5	•	1.9	1.2	1.0	0.9	0.9	0.5	0.2	0.2	0.3	0.2	•

Selected Financial Factors (in Percentages)

Debt Ratio 45	73.9	•	128.9	63.8	91.6	40.1	33.4	82.8	84.1	83.4	68.6	69.2	•
Return on Total Assets 46	8.8	•	42.5	22.3	35.6	15.3	16.5	12.4	1.8	3.2	4.2	3.2	•
Return on Equity Before Income Taxes 47	26.7	•	•	57.2	408.5	24.4	24.2	68.3	4.7	5.6	9.4	4.0	•
Return on Equity After Income Taxes 48	25.2	•	•	55.3	404.5	23.9	22.9	63.9	2.7	4.6	6.6	3.4	•
Profit Margin (Before Income Tax) 49	6.5	•	6.2	6.0	17.0	19.9	12.8	19.0	1.3	1.2	4.9	3.0	•
Profit Margin (After Income Tax) 50	6.1	•	6.2	5.8	16.8	19.5	12.2	17.8	0.7	1.0	3.4	2.5	•

Table II

Corporations with Net Income

OTHER ARTS, ENTERTAINMENT, AND RECREATION

MONEY AMOUNTS AND SIZE OF ASSETS IN THOUSANDS OF DOLLARS

Item Description for Accounting Period 7/11 Through 6/12		Total	Zero Assets	Under 500	500 to 1,000	1,000 to 5,000	5,000 to 10,000	10,000 to 25,000	25,000 to 50,000	50,000 to 100,000	100,000 to 250,000	250,000 to 500,000	500,000 to 2,500,000	2,500,000 and over
Number of Enterprises	1	40745	6723	31627	1268	836	167	50	23	18	10	12	10	0
Revenues ($ in Thousands)														
Net Sales	2	35685295	695944	12785270	4014988	4884391	982519	1335538	715136	654650	1193136	2958948	5464775	0
Interest	3	123480	1969	1423	922	1757	126	486	253	1276	776	5894	108596	0
Rents	4	47506	0	0	0	1972	0	285	5143	0	894	16254	22958	0
Royalties	5	16764	0	0	0	0	0	93	13	120	5032	191	11314	0
Other Portfolio Income	6	90890	23344	23661	12	3763	5703	629	217	29	449	8370	24711	0
Other Receipts	7	2055842	126774	254047	32212	188031	124230	45080	166331	145214	297629	320106	356193	0
Total Receipts	8	38019777	848031	13064401	4048134	5079914	1112578	1382111	887093	801289	1497916	3309763	5988547	0
Average Total Receipts	9	933	126	413	3193	6076	6662	27642	38569	44516	149792	275814	598855	•
Operating Costs/Operating Income (%)														
Cost of Operations	10	13.7	1.0	6.5	4.4	16.5	16.1	54.9	14.6	32.2	9.8	17.6	22.3	•
Salaries and Wages	11	15.2	9.0	11.7	5.0	12.1	15.3	10.0	21.8	19.9	52.5	32.8	16.6	•
Taxes Paid	12	3.7	2.2	2.0	2.8	2.2	2.1	2.0	2.5	3.0	4.7	8.4	8.1	•
Interest Paid	13	1.0	0.7	0.3	0.2	0.2	0.9	0.2	0.9	1.2	3.0	1.6	3.8	•
Depreciation	14	1.9	0.5	0.5	0.4	1.1	4.6	0.7	4.1	3.5	2.7	2.6	5.8	•
Amortization and Depletion	15	1.0	1.3	0.0	0.1	0.2	0.2	0.0	0.4	1.0	4.0	5.1	2.2	•
Pensions and Other Deferred Comp.	16	1.7	0.8	2.6	0.8	0.9	1.0	0.4	0.5	0.6	2.5	2.3	1.3	•
Employee Benefits	17	1.0	1.1	0.5	0.1	0.6	0.5	1.0	0.8	1.5	1.2	3.8	1.4	•
Advertising	18	1.7	0.8	1.2	2.4	3.5	0.5	0.6	0.4	2.9	2.9	0.8	1.4	•
Other Expenses	19	29.7	72.2	31.7	15.0	30.6	32.5	10.5	43.7	29.0	27.2	21.0	37.1	•
Officers' Compensation	20	21.5	8.1	32.2	62.0	13.8	8.3	4.0	1.5	2.7	2.7	3.1	0.9	•
Operating Margin	21	7.9	2.4	10.7	6.7	18.2	18.0	15.8	8.9	2.3	•	0.9	•	•
Operating Margin Before Officers' Comp.	22	29.5	10.4	43.0	68.8	32.0	26.3	19.8	10.4	5.1	•	3.9	0.1	•

Selected Average Balance Sheet ($ in Thousands)													
Net Receivables 23	48	0	2	26	120	403	1731	2456	5328	12930	24066	104422	•
Inventories 24	9	0	2	2	76	60	39	4	923	1056	2654	14076	•
Net Property, Plant and Equipment 25	145	0	5	208	277	600	2758	7427	11516	42845	88012	314689	•
Total Assets 26	704	0	48	667	1912	7980	14998	33965	69673	157774	350015	1483637	•
Notes and Loans Payable 27	219	0	22	201	168	1847	873	8973	10709	75424	90306	526684	•
All Other Liabilities 28	235	0	15	145	500	479	3060	12909	35831	70345	151548	478223	•
Net Worth 29	250	0	11	321	1244	5654	11066	12083	23133	12005	108161	478730	•
Selected Financial Ratios (Times to 1)													
Current Ratio 30	1.4	•	1.7	3.1	2.5	7.2	3.6	1.2	3.1	0.9	1.0	1.2	•
Quick Ratio 31	0.8	•	1.5	2.7	1.8	6.8	3.3	0.8	1.8	0.6	0.6	0.6	•
Net Sales to Working Capital 32	9.8	•	28.7	12.3	8.0	1.7	5.1	15.1	1.5	•	80.1	5.5	•
Coverage Ratio 33	14.9	35.1	48.6	31.9	118.6	33.4	105.8	38.0	21.3	5.1	9.1	3.4	•
Total Asset Turnover 34	1.2	•	8.4	4.7	3.1	0.7	1.8	0.9	0.5	0.8	0.7	0.4	•
Inventory Turnover 35	14.1	•	12.0	91.2	12.7	15.9	372.0	1098.4	12.7	11.1	16.3	8.6	•
Receivables Turnover 36	23.7	•	256.4	103.0	60.1	22.0	16.8	18.3	7.8	7.7	9.0	9.0	•
Total Liabilities to Net Worth 37	1.8	•	3.4	1.1	0.5	0.4	0.4	1.8	2.0	12.1	2.2	2.1	•
Current Assets to Working Capital 38	3.6	•	2.3	1.5	1.7	1.2	1.4	6.1	1.5	•	39.3	6.7	•
Current Liabilities to Working Capital 39	2.6	•	1.3	0.5	0.7	0.2	0.4	5.1	0.5	•	38.3	5.7	•
Working Capital to Net Sales 40	0.1	•	0.0	0.1	0.1	0.6	0.2	0.1	0.7	•	0.0	0.2	•
Inventory to Working Capital 41	0.1	•	0.1	0.0	0.1	0.0	0.0	0.0	0.0	•	0.9	0.3	•
Total Receipts to Cash Flow 42	2.5	1.1	2.5	4.9	2.1	1.7	3.5	1.4	2.1	2.8	3.2	2.3	•
Cost of Goods to Cash Flow 43	0.3	0.0	0.2	0.2	0.4	0.3	1.9	0.2	0.7	0.3	0.6	0.5	•
Cash Flow to Total Debt 44	0.8	•	4.4	1.9	4.1	1.5	1.9	1.0	0.4	0.3	0.3	0.2	•
Selected Financial Factors (in Percentages)													
Debt Ratio 45	64.5	•	77.1	51.9	34.9	29.2	26.2	64.4	66.8	92.4	69.1	67.7	•
Return on Total Assets 46	19.3	•	111.0	37.0	68.3	23.3	34.6	30.9	13.6	11.6	10.0	4.7	•
Return on Equity Before Income Taxes 47	50.7	•	474.3	74.5	104.1	31.9	46.4	84.7	38.9	122.7	28.8	10.2	•
Return on Equity After Income Taxes 48	49.0	•	471.5	72.1	103.3	31.4	44.6	80.8	37.3	118.3	25.0	9.1	•
Profit Margin (Before Income Tax) 49	14.5	24.1	12.9	7.5	22.2	30.7	19.2	32.9	24.7	12.3	12.7	8.9	•
Profit Margin (After Income Tax) 50	14.0	22.1	12.8	7.3	22.0	30.1	18.5	31.4	23.7	11.9	11.0	8.0	•

Table I

Corporations with and without Net Income

AMUSEMENT, GAMBLING, AND RECREATION INDUSTRIES

MONEY AMOUNTS AND SIZE OF ASSETS IN THOUSANDS OF DOLLARS

Item Description for Accounting Period 7/11 Through 6/12		Total	Zero Assets	Under 500	500 to 1,000	1,000 to 5,000	5,000 to 10,000	10,000 to 25,000	25,000 to 50,000	50,000 to 100,000	100,000 to 250,000	250,000 to 500,000	500,000 to 2,500,000	2,500,000 and over
Number of Enterprises	1	47596	9792	30267	3309	3152	536	295	132	60	24	11	15	4
Revenues ($ in Thousands)														
Net Sales	2	49569110	616536	11372101	3217982	7233444	2876871	2495256	2619665	2734683	2033182	2101187	6821352	5446852
Interest	3	475957	335	1679	2322	30392	5226	6263	5972	19430	7228	7977	24526	364607
Rents	4	142379	1213	3795	6768	3773	13050	3232	7656	9173	878	17953	42755	32133
Royalties	5	123318	0	0	12	24778	1449	0	801	945	29646	1987	0	63699
Other Portfolio Income	6	372059	25448	21821	19318	18858	48102	14619	85406	40710	1197	11087	36795	48699
Other Receipts	7	3985406	133979	303265	286028	414311	337930	497901	142006	180647	214057	448126	868356	158801
Total Receipts	8	54668229	777511	11702661	3532430	7725556	3282628	3017271	2861506	2985588	2286188	2588317	7793784	6114791
Average Total Receipts	9	1149	79	387	1068	2451	6124	10228	21678	49760	95258	235302	519586	1528698
Operating Costs/Operating Income (%)														
Cost of Operations	10	21.2	37.1	29.4	14.9	27.7	26.7	21.5	30.8	12.2	14.9	17.4	6.7	16.0
Salaries and Wages	11	22.5	13.4	13.7	30.9	19.2	27.7	35.8	25.2	27.7	23.9	28.6	27.7	19.2
Taxes Paid	12	8.4	6.9	3.3	6.9	7.6	8.1	7.4	5.3	8.4	6.9	8.1	13.7	17.5
Interest Paid	13	5.1	7.1	0.6	1.6	3.2	5.8	3.1	2.9	2.8	5.5	11.1	10.3	12.6
Depreciation	14	8.7	6.0	3.2	8.6	6.4	7.1	10.3	9.6	8.8	10.2	12.1	13.8	15.2
Amortization and Depletion	15	0.9	1.2	0.1	0.3	0.3	2.5	0.8	1.0	1.2	1.5	1.5	1.1	1.8
Pensions and Other Deferred Comp.	16	0.2	0.3	0.0	0.2	0.5	0.3	0.2	0.1	0.3	0.3	0.5	0.1	0.2
Employee Benefits	17	1.7	0.7	0.8	1.5	1.6	2.1	2.4	1.4	2.8	2.9	2.4	1.7	1.9
Advertising	18	2.6	2.8	1.8	2.8	2.0	2.5	2.4	1.8	2.5	3.2	3.0	3.2	4.1
Other Expenses	19	36.1	45.5	41.0	40.8	33.2	37.4	30.9	28.6	42.5	47.5	38.7	37.8	20.1
Officers' Compensation	20	3.2	7.3	6.6	4.5	3.6	3.8	2.7	0.9	1.1	1.5	1.0	0.8	0.8
Operating Margin	21	•	•	•	•	•	•	•	•	•	•	•	•	•
Operating Margin Before Officers' Comp.	22	•	•	6.0	•	•	•	•	•	•	•	•	•	•

Selected Average Balance Sheet ($ in Thousands)													
Net Receivables 23	48	0	2	25	116	416	687	1017	4037	8652	14874	22699	62937
Inventories 24	26	0	4	10	72	269	375	914	1491	2830	2952	13233	19872
Net Property, Plant and Equipment 25	782	0	60	382	1347	4513	10015	20383	43852	76228	177069	647280	1430385
Total Assets 26	1396	0	102	681	2133	7078	15708	34234	70027	159697	347987	1089628	3309496
Notes and Loans Payable 27	764	0	76	480	1351	5010	6765	11370	27013	76850	220545	676528	1498943
All Other Liabilities 28	317	0	20	167	447	1292	3145	9690	28784	57500	72394	281529	370618
Net Worth 29	315	0	6	34	335	775	5798	13174	14230	25346	55048	131571	1439935
Selected Financial Ratios (Times to 1)													
Current Ratio 30	1.0	•	1.0	1.0	1.1	1.0	1.7	1.1	0.8	1.1	0.9	0.7	0.9
Quick Ratio 31	0.7	•	0.7	0.8	0.8	0.6	1.1	0.7	0.6	0.8	0.6	0.4	0.7
Net Sales to Working Capital 32	•	•	•	•	48.9	•	6.2	65.3	•	20.2	•	•	•
Coverage Ratio 33	1.0	0.7	4.7	•	1.5	•	2.1	1.5	0.6	•	0.9	0.7	1.3
Total Asset Turnover 34	0.7	•	3.7	1.4	1.1	0.8	0.5	0.6	0.7	0.5	0.5	0.4	0.4
Inventory Turnover 35	8.6	•	27.7	13.9	8.9	5.3	4.9	6.7	3.7	4.4	11.2	2.3	10.9
Receivables Turnover 36	21.2	•	205.4	37.7	19.4	14.4	10.5	13.6	14.0	9.3	13.2	17.7	23.4
Total Liabilities to Net Worth 37	3.4	•	16.5	19.0	5.4	8.1	1.7	1.6	3.9	5.3	5.3	7.3	1.3
Current Assets to Working Capital 38	•	•	•	•	11.5	•	2.5	19.9	•	8.4	•	•	•
Current Liabilities to Working Capital 39	•	•	•	•	10.5	•	1.5	18.9	•	7.4	•	•	•
Working Capital to Net Sales 40	•	•	•	•	0.0	•	0.2	0.0	•	0.0	•	•	•
Inventory to Working Capital 41	•	•	•	•	1.3	•	0.3	3.2	•	0.6	•	•	•
Total Receipts to Cash Flow 42	4.3	3.0	3.6	4.1	4.1	7.6	3.8	4.9	3.8	4.3	4.4	4.4	5.7
Cost of Goods to Cash Flow 43	0.9	1.1	1.0	0.6	1.1	2.0	0.8	1.5	0.5	0.6	0.8	0.3	0.9
Cash Flow to Total Debt 44	0.2	•	1.1	0.4	0.3	0.1	0.2	0.2	0.2	0.1	0.1	0.1	0.1
Selected Financial Factors (in Percentages)													
Debt Ratio 45	77.4	•	94.3	95.0	84.3	89.0	63.1	61.5	79.7	84.1	84.2	87.9	56.5
Return on Total Assets 46	3.7	•	11.0	•	5.1	•	3.5	2.6	1.0	•	5.5	3.1	6.5
Return on Equity Before Income Taxes 47	•	•	152.0	•	11.1	•	4.8	2.4	•	•	•	•	3.1
Return on Equity After Income Taxes 48	•	•	145.0	•	10.3	•	4.5	1.8	•	•	•	•	1.5
Profit Margin (Before Income Tax) 49	•	•	2.4	•	1.6	•	3.3	1.6	•	•	•	•	3.2
Profit Margin (After Income Tax) 50	•	•	2.2	•	1.5	•	3.1	1.2	•	•	•	•	1.6

Table II

Corporations with Net Income

AMUSEMENT, GAMBLING, AND RECREATION INDUSTRIES

MONEY AMOUNTS AND SIZE OF ASSETS IN THOUSANDS OF DOLLARS

Item Description for Accounting Period 7/11 Through 6/12		Total	Zero Assets	Under 500	500 to 1,000	1,000 to 5,000	5,000 to 10,000	10,000 to 25,000	25,000 to 50,000	50,000 to 100,000	100,000 to 250,000	250,000 to 500,000	500,000 to 2,500,000	2,500,000 and over
Number of Enterprises	1	22496	3378	16327	1123	1265	156	147	58	21	7	5	8	0
Revenues ($ in Thousands)														
Net Sales	2	25709975	215704	7643901	984183	4132334	1193319	1603305	1360551	1115625	767026	543355	6150671	0
Interest	3	364010	313	1090	130	28260	3072	4788	2137	1674	1077	253	321214	0
Rents	4	50947	1213	5	1908	2751	10907	2624	4906	3368	560	200	22504	0
Royalties	5	54682	0	0	0	24778	1449	0	0	907	27547	0	0	0
Other Portfolio Income	6	231009	17287	21064	334	17651	1821	13412	84349	14252	254	4919	55664	0
Other Receipts	7	2038692	130149	84902	32612	298618	132136	399904	42559	39957	43976	367560	466326	0
Total Receipts	8	28449315	364666	7750962	1019167	4504392	1342704	2024033	1494502	1175783	840440	916287	7016379	0
Average Total Receipts	9	1265	108	475	908	3561	8607	13769	25767	55990	120063	183257	877047	•
Operating Costs/Operating Income (%)														
Cost of Operations	10	23.7	9.4	34.0	24.7	27.7	48.3	21.7	33.3	15.2	9.9	20.1	5.7	•
Salaries and Wages	11	19.1	14.0	11.4	20.6	16.6	16.4	38.0	26.9	24.2	25.9	30.4	21.3	•
Taxes Paid	12	9.1	3.5	2.5	5.3	8.0	3.6	7.1	5.0	10.3	8.4	7.4	21.1	•
Interest Paid	13	4.0	1.7	0.3	0.8	1.7	1.7	2.4	1.3	1.6	1.5	13.6	12.0	•
Depreciation	14	5.8	11.0	1.9	2.7	3.9	3.9	7.9	8.7	8.4	8.1	15.9	9.8	•
Amortization and Depletion	15	0.6	0.0	0.1	0.3	0.2	0.3	0.9	0.5	0.2	1.3	2.0	1.5	•
Pensions and Other Deferred Comp.	16	0.3	0.0	0.0	0.3	0.7	0.4	0.2	0.1	0.4	0.6	1.0	0.2	•
Employee Benefits	17	1.5	0.9	0.6	0.9	1.4	1.1	2.0	1.3	1.9	5.1	3.7	2.1	•
Advertising	18	2.3	3.1	1.4	2.0	2.0	1.5	2.0	1.8	2.8	3.4	5.8	3.6	•
Other Expenses	19	30.4	60.3	36.1	24.6	30.7	20.4	29.6	18.9	27.4	31.9	47.2	26.6	•
Officers' Compensation	20	3.3	8.2	5.5	4.6	4.1	3.7	2.1	0.8	1.9	2.2	1.2	1.0	•
Operating Margin	21	•	•	6.1	13.1	3.0	•	•	1.4	5.7	1.8	•	•	•
Operating Margin Before Officers' Comp.	22	3.2	•	11.6	17.7	7.2	2.4	•	2.3	7.6	4.0	•	•	•

Selected Average Balance Sheet ($ in Thousands)													
Net Receivables 23	35	0	3	11	127	557	773	900	3318	8654	5557	19270	•
Inventories 24	27	0	4	19	120	638	395	965	1723	3867	2821	10275	•
Net Property, Plant and Equipment 25	670	0	51	319	1031	2554	8255	16724	43162	88711	146647	966495	•
Total Assets 26	1281	0	105	645	2107	6479	15710	35288	75517	156394	330678	1753088	•
Notes and Loans Payable 27	553	0	55	200	684	2437	6270	9388	17707	41732	162852	891278	•
All Other Liabilities 28	204	0	22	68	264	1489	3638	5442	14141	37399	46902	243165	•
Net Worth 29	524	0	28	378	1158	2552	5802	20458	43669	77263	120924	618644	•

Selected Financial Ratios (Times to 1)													
Current Ratio 30	1.4	•	0.9	2.1	2.0	2.0	2.3	1.1	1.8	1.1	1.0	1.1	•
Quick Ratio 31	0.9	•	0.7	1.5	1.4	1.0	1.4	0.7	1.4	1.0	0.7	0.7	•
Net Sales to Working Capital 32	17.4	•	•	7.3	8.8	5.4	4.3	31.4	6.5	23.7	•	42.9	•
Coverage Ratio 33	3.6	35.3	22.8	20.8	8.0	7.4	6.2	9.9	7.9	8.6	2.5	1.7	•
Total Asset Turnover 34	0.9	•	4.5	1.4	1.6	1.2	0.7	0.7	0.7	0.7	0.3	0.4	•
Inventory Turnover 35	9.9	•	35.7	11.5	7.6	5.8	6.0	8.1	4.7	2.8	7.7	4.3	•
Receivables Turnover 36	28.3	•	218.7	47.8	22.6	17.4	14.2	15.1	19.6	9.5	20.0	26.1	•
Total Liabilities to Net Worth 37	1.4	•	2.8	0.7	0.8	1.5	1.7	0.7	0.7	1.0	1.7	1.8	•
Current Assets to Working Capital 38	3.7	•	•	1.9	2.0	2.0	1.7	10.6	2.2	8.0	•	8.2	•
Current Liabilities to Working Capital 39	2.7	•	•	0.9	1.0	1.0	0.7	9.6	1.2	7.0	•	7.2	•
Working Capital to Net Sales 40	0.1	•	•	0.1	0.1	0.2	0.2	0.0	0.2	0.0	•	0.0	•
Inventory to Working Capital 41	0.5	•	•	0.1	0.2	0.9	0.2	1.9	0.2	0.4	•	0.6	•
Total Receipts to Cash Flow 42	3.1	1.0	3.1	3.1	2.7	4.0	3.0	4.5	3.0	3.1	1.8	3.4	•
Cost of Goods to Cash Flow 43	0.7	0.1	1.1	0.8	0.8	1.9	0.6	1.5	0.5	0.3	0.4	0.2	•
Cash Flow to Total Debt 44	0.5	•	1.9	1.1	1.3	0.5	0.4	0.3	0.6	0.5	0.3	0.2	•

Selected Financial Factors (in Percentages)													
Debt Ratio 45	59.1	•	73.5	41.4	45.0	60.6	63.1	42.0	42.2	50.6	63.4	64.7	•
Return on Total Assets 46	12.9	•	35.1	23.8	21.3	15.1	10.2	8.2	8.9	9.0	11.1	9.1	•
Return on Equity Before Income Taxes 47	22.9	•	126.6	38.7	33.9	33.2	23.1	12.8	13.5	16.1	18.2	10.9	•
Return on Equity After Income Taxes 48	21.0	•	123.9	38.0	33.4	32.9	22.5	11.9	12.4	15.7	12.7	8.2	•
Profit Margin (Before Income Tax) 49	10.5	56.9	7.5	16.7	12.0	11.1	12.3	11.1	11.1	11.4	20.3	8.8	•
Profit Margin (After Income Tax) 50	9.6	56.7	7.3	16.4	11.8	11.0	12.0	10.4	10.2	11.1	14.2	6.6	•

Table I

Corporations with and without Net Income

ACCOMMODATION

MONEY AMOUNTS AND SIZE OF ASSETS IN THOUSANDS OF DOLLARS

Item Description for Accounting Period 7/11 Through 6/12		Total	Zero Assets	Under 500	500 to 1,000	1,000 to 5,000	5,000 to 10,000	10,000 to 25,000	25,000 to 50,000	50,000 to 100,000	100,000 to 250,000	250,000 to 500,000	500,000 to 2,500,000	2,500,000 and over
Number of Enterprises	1	31154	5200	13796	3550	6937	956	434	116	63	42	26	21	13
Revenues ($ in Thousands)														
Net Sales	2	81038533	3158906	3639564	1640012	7927676	3133532	3585930	2246408	1944565	8841414	4003148	6056798	34860578
Interest	3	1349460	45850	723	379	10087	1075	4727	6491	14930	53843	22200	199464	989691
Rents	4	578390	45117	2775	1072	6806	1351	7533	7857	17283	12759	18866	150521	306450
Royalties	5	2634733	7825	0	0	0	0	862	0	0	35926	234501	36	2355583
Other Portfolio Income	6	1704043	529417	26630	115	5037	7171	3025	36291	43032	101749	41392	30647	879536
Other Receipts	7	11197125	2101217	117019	33193	102160	121327	138644	47977	-266448	324773	72865	234931	8169470
Total Receipts	8	98502284	5888332	3786711	1674771	8051766	3264456	3740721	2345024	1753362	9370464	4392972	6672397	47561308
Average Total Receipts	9	3162	1132	274	472	1161	3415	8619	20216	27831	223106	168960	317733	3658562
Operating Costs/Operating Income (%)														
Cost of Operations	10	15.6	4.0	12.2	5.1	16.7	15.0	35.0	21.9	23.0	23.1	17.1	16.1	12.4
Salaries and Wages	11	27.8	9.4	18.4	15.0	14.8	17.0	13.2	15.8	18.1	11.5	19.3	23.6	43.5
Taxes Paid	12	7.8	4.4	7.4	9.6	6.6	6.7	6.0	5.8	7.6	3.2	4.5	12.0	9.5
Interest Paid	13	9.1	8.0	1.7	6.9	8.2	7.4	5.0	5.2	5.7	1.2	2.6	11.2	13.7
Depreciation	14	7.1	4.9	3.0	7.7	9.1	9.1	7.0	7.3	8.9	2.4	8.9	12.2	7.1
Amortization and Depletion	15	0.9	0.6	0.3	0.3	0.7	0.4	0.2	0.8	0.4	0.3	0.9	1.3	1.2
Pensions and Other Deferred Comp.	16	0.5	0.2	0.0	0.0	0.0	0.3	0.1	0.2	0.3	0.1	0.2	0.3	1.0
Employee Benefits	17	2.8	1.2	2.1	0.3	0.8	1.4	1.1	1.1	3.0	1.1	2.3	2.9	4.4
Advertising	18	2.7	0.9	2.1	2.0	1.4	1.2	2.3	1.9	2.5	3.1	3.0	3.2	3.2
Other Expenses	19	49.1	166.3	56.6	57.6	38.8	39.1	35.0	43.1	34.4	59.2	52.6	29.3	43.6
Officers' Compensation	20	1.2	0.9	2.3	2.8	2.6	3.2	1.7	1.0	1.4	0.3	1.4	0.6	0.8
Operating Margin	21	•	•	•	•	0.3	•	•	•	•	•	•	•	•
Operating Margin Before Officers' Comp.	22	•	•	•	•	2.9	2.4	•	•	•	•	•	•	•

Selected Average Balance Sheet ($ in Thousands)													
Net Receivables 23	300	0	3	11	71	133	800	1197	2820	10887	15268	78449	422057
Inventories 24	104	0	2	7	17	29	92	212	555	1848	2295	17739	188489
Net Property, Plant and Equipment 25	3355	0	113	590	1670	4914	10067	21539	44618	70179	172538	531695	4330151
Total Assets 26	7556	0	163	712	2198	6463	15016	34031	72936	154568	327062	878903	12360454
Notes and Loans Payable 27	3958	0	131	606	1883	5261	9971	21332	38864	42301	112413	512653	5888656
All Other Liabilities 28	2156	0	19	44	186	565	1521	4895	9698	71889	58102	106846	4329824
Net Worth 29	1442	0	13	62	128	637	3523	7805	24373	40378	156547	259403	2141974
Selected Financial Ratios (Times to 1)													
Current Ratio 30	1.3	•	1.0	1.2	1.6	0.8	1.9	1.4	1.4	0.8	1.4	1.9	1.2
Quick Ratio 31	0.9	•	0.7	1.1	1.2	0.6	1.4	0.9	1.1	0.6	1.0	1.4	0.9
Net Sales to Working Capital 32	12.9	•	•	40.3	11.6	•	5.8	13.9	6.8	•	7.9	3.5	12.1
Coverage Ratio 33	0.9	•	•	0.3	1.2	1.4	0.5	1.0	•	1.3	•	0.8	1.0
Total Asset Turnover 34	0.3	•	1.6	0.6	0.5	0.5	0.6	0.6	0.4	1.4	0.5	0.3	0.2
Inventory Turnover 35	3.9	•	21.1	3.4	11.2	17.0	31.6	20.1	12.8	26.3	11.5	2.6	1.8
Receivables Turnover 36	9.1	•	71.9	32.8	17.6	25.1	10.1	14.5	9.5	23.8	8.3	3.8	6.8
Total Liabilities to Net Worth 37	4.2	•	11.9	10.5	16.2	9.1	3.3	3.4	2.0	2.8	1.1	2.4	4.8
Current Assets to Working Capital 38	4.8	•	•	5.9	2.7	•	2.1	3.9	3.2	•	3.8	2.1	6.0
Current Liabilities to Working Capital 39	3.8	•	•	4.9	1.7	•	1.1	2.9	2.2	•	2.8	1.1	5.0
Working Capital to Net Sales 40	0.1	•	•	0.0	0.1	•	0.2	0.1	0.1	•	0.1	0.3	0.1
Inventory to Working Capital 41	0.5	•	•	0.1	0.2	•	0.1	0.1	0.1	•	0.1	0.2	0.8
Total Receipts to Cash Flow 42	3.1	1.1	3.3	3.2	3.2	3.8	4.5	3.8	11.4	3.2	3.0	5.0	3.1
Cost of Goods to Cash Flow 43	0.5	0.0	0.4	0.2	0.5	0.6	1.6	0.8	2.6	0.8	0.5	0.8	0.4
Cash Flow to Total Debt 44	0.1	•	0.5	0.2	0.2	0.1	0.2	0.2	0.1	0.6	0.3	0.1	0.1
Selected Financial Factors (in Percentages)													
Debt Ratio 45	80.9	•	92.2	91.3	94.2	90.1	76.5	77.1	66.6	73.9	52.1	70.5	82.7
Return on Total Assets 46	2.8	•	•	1.1	5.3	5.5	1.5	3.1	•	2.2	•	2.8	3.0
Return on Equity Before Income Taxes 47	•	•	•	•	16.9	17.2	•	0.6	•	2.1	•	•	0.3
Return on Equity After Income Taxes 48	•	•	•	•	16.1	15.7	•	•	•	1.1	•	•	•
Profit Margin (Before Income Tax) 49	•	•	•	•	1.9	3.3	•	0.3	•	0.4	•	•	0.2
Profit Margin (After Income Tax) 50	•	•	•	•	1.8	3.0	•	•	•	0.2	•	•	•

Table II

Corporations with Net Income

ACCOMMODATION

MONEY AMOUNTS AND SIZE OF ASSETS IN THOUSANDS OF DOLLARS

Item Description for Accounting Period 7/11 Through 6/12		Total	Zero Assets	Under 500	500 to 1,000	1,000 to 5,000	5,000 to 10,000	10,000 to 25,000	25,000 to 50,000	50,000 to 100,000	100,000 to 250,000	250,000 to 500,000	500,000 to 2,500,000	2,500,000 and over
Number of Enterprises	1	13331	1642	5884	1252	3690	549	175	63	28	22	•	8	•
Revenues ($ in Thousands)														
Net Sales	2	33082762	940869	1644332	683118	4431566	1895258	1578559	1169961	877719	4857970	•	1628011	•
Interest	3	634870	1388	38	282	10048	409	2723	3082	8535	11147	•	38374	•
Rents	4	325022	44825	2736	0	2011	1042	6911	5986	11790	2251	•	56112	•
Royalties	5	1917408	4227	0	0	0	0	255	0	0	33558	•	0	•
Other Portfolio Income	6	1249187	327618	26464	0	5037	7032	2571	16417	42916	100926	•	5637	•
Other Receipts	7	5731145	42659	88910	4037	63885	74811	43103	44701	36605	267111	•	79630	•
Total Receipts	8	42940394	1361586	1762480	687437	4512547	1978552	1634122	1240147	977565	5272963	•	1807764	•
Average Total Receipts	9	3221	829	300	549	1223	3604	9338	19685	34913	239680	•	225970	•
Operating Costs/Operating Income (%)														
Cost of Operations	10	18.5	4.4	11.1	4.3	13.5	17.9	25.2	20.2	15.1	22.4	•	9.6	•
Salaries and Wages	11	25.9	9.6	18.5	10.6	13.4	16.0	14.3	15.0	20.3	8.6	•	23.6	•
Taxes Paid	12	6.6	6.0	7.3	9.2	6.3	7.4	5.4	7.1	8.7	3.4	•	8.7	•
Interest Paid	13	7.4	15.0	2.5	5.9	7.5	6.9	4.1	4.3	6.5	1.1	•	8.6	•
Depreciation	14	7.0	5.9	2.8	7.2	8.1	6.9	6.0	7.2	8.9	2.5	•	10.0	•
Amortization and Depletion	15	0.8	0.5	0.3	0.3	0.7	0.3	0.2	0.5	0.5	0.2	•	0.2	•
Pensions and Other Deferred Comp.	16	0.8	0.7	0.1	•	0.1	0.3	0.1	0.3	0.4	0.1	•	0.1	•
Employee Benefits	17	2.2	1.1	4.0	0.3	0.7	1.8	1.1	1.3	3.0	1.3	•	2.2	•
Advertising	18	2.5	1.6	1.9	2.5	1.2	1.1	1.1	1.4	2.8	2.5	•	2.8	•
Other Expenses	19	46.1	70.4	44.6	45.2	34.5	28.2	32.8	39.8	30.6	62.3	•	35.6	•
Officers' Compensation	20	1.8	0.8	3.8	3.4	3.2	5.0	2.4	0.7	1.4	0.2	•	0.4	•
Operating Margin	21	•	•	3.2	11.0	10.8	8.2	7.4	2.1	1.7	•	•	•	•
Operating Margin Before Officers' Comp.	22	•	•	7.0	14.5	14.0	13.3	9.8	2.9	3.1	•	•	•	•

Selected Average Balance Sheet ($ in Thousands)														
Net Receivables	23	339	0	3	20	94	127	1593	1683	3253	12137	•	25411	•
Inventories	24	168	0	1	2	22	42	105	196	198	1036	•	35249	•
Net Property, Plant and Equipment	25	2962	0	136	710	1606	4555	9230	23435	38774	63021	•	426718	•
Total Assets	26	8056	0	182	810	2270	6660	15186	33860	71543	153702	•	697140	•
Notes and Loans Payable	27	4088	0	151	582	1587	4984	8946	19239	32508	38474	•	377951	•
All Other Liabilities	28	2035	0	25	38	114	246	1089	4712	11704	42676	•	59917	•
Net Worth	29	1933	0	6	190	570	1430	5151	9910	27331	72552	•	259272	•
Selected Financial Ratios (Times to 1)														
Current Ratio	30	1.7	•	1.3	1.5	3.4	2.2	2.6	1.3	1.9	1.3	•	2.2	•
Quick Ratio	31	1.1	•	0.9	1.4	2.8	1.5	2.1	0.9	1.3	0.9	•	1.0	•
Net Sales to Working Capital	32	5.1	•	46.0	30.0	4.8	9.6	3.8	13.6	4.2	20.2	•	2.7	•
Coverage Ratio	33	2.9	2.9	5.2	3.0	2.7	2.8	3.7	2.9	3.0	4.6	•	2.1	•
Total Asset Turnover	34	0.3	•	1.5	0.7	0.5	0.5	0.6	0.5	0.4	1.4	•	0.3	•
Inventory Turnover	35	2.7	•	25.8	12.5	7.4	14.6	21.6	19.1	24.0	47.8	•	0.6	•
Receivables Turnover	36	7.1	•	56.4	26.5	13.8	22.1	5.7	12.3	10.6	•	•	2.3	•
Total Liabilities to Net Worth	37	3.2	•	31.7	3.3	3.0	3.7	1.9	2.4	1.6	1.1	•	1.7	•
Current Assets to Working Capital	38	2.5	•	4.4	3.1	1.4	1.8	1.6	4.6	2.2	4.3	•	1.8	•
Current Liabilities to Working Capital	39	1.5	•	3.4	2.1	0.4	0.8	0.6	3.6	1.2	3.3	•	0.8	•
Working Capital to Net Sales	40	0.2	•	0.0	0.0	0.2	0.1	0.3	0.1	0.2	0.0	•	0.4	•
Inventory to Working Capital	41	0.4	•	0.1	0.0	0.1	0.1	0.0	0.1	0.0	0.1	•	0.4	•
Total Receipts to Cash Flow	42	2.3	1.3	2.8	2.3	2.5	2.9	2.7	2.9	2.9	2.9	•	2.7	•
Cost of Goods to Cash Flow	43	0.4	0.1	0.3	0.1	0.3	0.5	0.7	0.6	0.4	0.6	•	0.3	•
Cash Flow to Total Debt	44	0.2	•	0.6	0.4	0.3	0.2	0.3	0.3	0.2	1.0	•	0.2	•
Selected Financial Factors (in Percentages)														
Debt Ratio	45	76.0	•	96.9	76.5	74.9	78.5	66.1	70.7	61.8	52.8	•	62.8	•
Return on Total Assets	46	6.7	•	19.8	11.8	10.6	10.1	8.9	6.8	8.6	7.2	•	5.2	•
Return on Equity Before Income Taxes	47	18.6	•	523.4	33.5	26.6	30.5	19.0	15.2	15.0	11.9	•	7.2	•
Return on Equity After Income Taxes	48	15.3	•	522.6	32.0	26.3	29.3	17.8	13.9	12.2	10.8	•	6.2	•
Profit Margin (Before Income Tax)	49	14.5	28.6	10.4	11.7	12.6	12.6	10.8	8.1	13.0	3.9	•	9.2	•
Profit Margin (After Income Tax)	50	11.9	26.9	10.4	11.1	12.5	12.1	10.2	7.4	10.6	3.6	•	7.9	•

Table I

Corporations with and without Net Income

FOOD SERVICES AND DRINKING PLACES

MONEY AMOUNTS AND SIZE OF ASSETS IN THOUSANDS OF DOLLARS

Item Description for Accounting Period 7/11 Through 6/12		Total	Zero Assets	Under 500	500 to 1,000	1,000 to 5,000	5,000 to 10,000	10,000 to 25,000	25,000 to 50,000	50,000 to 100,000	100,000 to 250,000	250,000 to 500,000	500,000 to 2,500,000	2,500,000 and over
Number of Enterprises	1	268049	36748	206128	13339	9875	1222	439	119	59	52	20	36	•
Revenues ($ in Thousands)														
Net Sales	2	363847089	7084536	115880727	26055393	41540909	17648127	12652315	5937450	7000706	13177121	10169449	35499868	•
Interest	3	389498	1445	7323	4375	8180	6432	2609	5694	765	5900	9313	96039	•
Rents	4	725968	1713	15816	592	6469	2348	3029	7739	10473	31655	11029	341526	•
Royalties	5	4636804	18040	0	19	3451	5787	42781	26603	71441	208726	660010	847134	•
Other Portfolio Income	6	3199870	379896	78404	8915	42633	59625	14719	7466	80188	27160	34798	595795	•
Other Receipts	7	8484231	206149	583629	173608	287572	207655	411638	105577	79812	141958	-45734	1139612	•
Total Receipts	8	381283460	7691779	116565899	26242902	41889214	17929974	13127091	6090529	7243385	13592520	10838865	38519974	•
Average Total Receipts	9	1422	209	566	1967	4242	14673	29902	51181	122769	261395	541943	1069999	•
Operating Costs/Operating Income (%)														
Cost of Operations	10	42.1	42.3	42.2	39.2	44.2	37.4	45.3	43.2	43.6	37.1	43.8	40.8	•
Salaries and Wages	11	18.9	17.1	17.5	20.3	15.8	21.7	19.2	17.5	19.2	19.8	23.2	23.5	•
Taxes Paid	12	4.1	5.0	4.3	4.5	3.8	3.6	4.0	4.2	4.0	3.8	3.7	3.9	•
Interest Paid	13	1.6	1.4	0.5	0.8	1.0	1.1	1.6	1.4	1.6	1.8	2.9	2.2	•
Depreciation	14	3.3	3.9	1.9	2.5	3.2	3.3	3.8	4.6	4.3	4.5	5.3	6.0	•
Amortization and Depletion	15	0.6	0.9	0.3	0.3	0.5	0.6	0.8	0.6	0.5	0.8	1.2	0.6	•
Pensions and Other Deferred Comp.	16	0.2	0.0	0.0	0.1	0.1	0.0	0.3	0.2	0.1	0.2	0.2	0.3	•
Employee Benefits	17	1.2	0.5	0.5	0.6	0.9	0.7	1.0	1.8	0.9	1.4	2.1	1.4	•
Advertising	18	2.2	1.6	1.7	1.9	2.9	3.4	3.1	2.9	2.7	2.3	2.4	2.7	•
Other Expenses	19	24.2	38.4	24.9	24.8	22.9	25.9	21.3	22.7	22.8	30.3	19.8	21.2	•
Officers' Compensation	20	2.4	2.5	4.6	3.2	2.4	0.9	1.3	1.3	0.9	0.8	0.6	0.9	•
Operating Margin	21	•	•	1.6	1.8	2.4	1.0	•	•	•	•	•	•	•
Operating Margin Before Officers' Comp.	22	1.6	•	6.2	5.0	4.7	2.0	•	0.9	0.3	•	•	•	•

Selected Average Balance Sheet ($ in Thousands)													
Net Receivables 23	45	0	3	25	110	205	994	2069	3680	9715	12783	41921	•
Inventories 24	21	0	7	27	45	175	456	752	2169	3405	11539	18109	•
Net Property, Plant and Equipment 25	290	0	59	326	833	3034	6719	15088	33235	74446	130568	429117	•
Total Assets 26	889	0	123	683	1863	6677	15166	34582	71482	165006	353886	904039	•
Notes and Loans Payable 27	387	0	92	392	1080	3432	7744	14901	29426	67183	189077	299722	•
All Other Liabilities 28	291	0	26	135	336	1676	3094	8495	21516	49124	117140	287408	•
Net Worth 29	211	0	4	157	448	1569	4329	11185	20540	48699	47668	316909	•
Selected Financial Ratios (Times to 1)													
Current Ratio 30	1.0	•	1.3	1.2	1.4	0.9	1.3	1.2	0.8	0.8	0.9	1.0	•
Quick Ratio 31	0.7	•	0.8	0.9	0.9	0.6	1.0	0.8	0.5	0.5	0.6	0.7	•
Net Sales to Working Capital 32	187.9	•	71.5	53.7	24.4	•	26.7	42.5	•	•	•	•	•
Coverage Ratio 33	3.8	•	5.1	4.3	4.2	3.3	2.2	2.6	2.8	1.2	1.5	3.6	•
Total Asset Turnover 34	1.5	•	4.6	2.9	2.3	2.2	1.9	1.4	1.7	1.5	1.4	1.1	•
Inventory Turnover 35	26.9	•	33.3	28.6	41.6	30.8	28.7	28.7	23.8	27.6	19.3	22.2	•
Receivables Turnover 36	30.3	•	202.7	83.8	31.9	80.2	31.4	25.8	29.3	30.5	23.4	25.3	•
Total Liabilities to Net Worth 37	3.2	•	27.0	3.4	3.2	3.3	2.5	2.1	2.5	2.4	6.4	1.9	•
Current Assets to Working Capital 38	24.0	•	4.6	5.4	3.7	•	4.0	7.4	•	•	•	•	•
Current Liabilities to Working Capital 39	23.0	•	3.6	4.4	2.7	•	3.0	6.4	•	•	•	•	•
Working Capital to Net Sales 40	0.0	•	0.0	0.0	0.0	•	0.0	0.0	•	•	•	•	•
Inventory to Working Capital 41	3.1	•	0.9	0.8	0.3	•	0.5	0.6	•	•	•	•	•
Total Receipts to Cash Flow 42	5.4	8.1	6.0	5.4	5.8	5.3	6.5	5.7	6.2	4.5	7.2	5.7	•
Cost of Goods to Cash Flow 43	2.3	3.4	2.5	2.1	2.6	2.0	3.0	2.5	2.7	1.7	3.1	2.3	•
Cash Flow to Total Debt 44	0.4	•	0.8	0.7	0.5	0.5	0.4	0.4	0.4	0.5	0.2	0.3	•
Selected Financial Factors (in Percentages)													
Debt Ratio 45	76.3	•	96.4	77.0	76.0	76.5	71.5	67.7	71.3	70.5	86.5	64.9	•
Return on Total Assets 46	9.3	•	12.3	9.4	9.5	8.1	6.8	5.2	7.5	3.4	6.2	8.3	•
Return on Equity Before Income Taxes 47	29.0	•	276.3	31.2	30.0	24.2	13.1	9.9	16.7	2.2	14.8	17.1	•
Return on Equity After Income Taxes 48	21.6	•	269.9	30.2	29.2	23.5	12.2	8.5	15.2	0.1	7.3	11.6	•
Profit Margin (Before Income Tax) 49	4.5	•	2.2	2.5	3.2	2.6	2.0	2.2	2.9	0.4	1.4	5.5	•
Profit Margin (After Income Tax) 50	3.4	•	2.1	2.4	3.1	2.5	1.8	1.9	2.6	0.0	0.7	3.7	•

Table II

Corporations with Net Income

FOOD SERVICES AND DRINKING PLACES

MONEY AMOUNTS AND SIZE OF ASSETS IN THOUSANDS OF DOLLARS

Item Description for Accounting Period 7/11 Through 6/12		Total	Zero Assets	Under 500	500 to 1,000	1,000 to 5,000	5,000 to 10,000	10,000 to 25,000	25,000 to 50,000	50,000 to 100,000	100,000 to 250,000	250,000 to 500,000	500,000 to 2,500,000	2,500,000 and over
Number of Enterprises	1	•	14122	109325	8940	6701	1026	305	80	40	30	•	25	•
Revenues ($ in Thousands)														
Net Sales	2	•	2580380	79187942	18951289	31012360	15473919	8683244	4351499	4889982	8352968	•	28654493	•
Interest	3	•	608	6656	2176	3689	5090	1919	3179	544	2984	•	35597	•
Rents	4	•	81	5879	29	5176	2011	1906	6886	6357	22189	•	262766	•
Royalties	5	•	11342	0	19	1065	11	30250	22439	59332	143218	•	506163	•
Other Portfolio Income	6	•	289894	50669	7030	23587	56514	5754	7167	80081	26645	•	539525	•
Other Receipts	7	•	151776	431337	107417	220868	189918	357014	89397	61941	104839	•	1082285	•
Total Receipts	8	•	3034081	79682483	19067960	31266745	15727463	9080087	4480567	5098237	8652843	•	31080829	•
Average Total Receipts	9	•	215	729	2133	4666	15329	29771	56007	127456	288428	•	1243233	•
Operating Costs/Operating Income (%)														
Cost of Operations	10	•	47.5	40.5	39.0	43.7	35.8	42.5	40.8	48.1	34.7	•	41.8	•
Salaries and Wages	11	•	11.2	17.5	20.5	14.9	22.8	20.4	18.5	16.3	18.1	•	22.3	•
Taxes Paid	12	•	4.4	4.1	4.4	3.7	3.6	4.1	4.3	3.7	3.4	•	3.9	•
Interest Paid	13	•	1.6	0.4	0.7	0.9	1.0	1.3	1.3	1.4	1.4	•	1.5	•
Depreciation	14	•	2.2	1.4	1.8	2.5	3.4	3.3	3.4	3.9	4.2	•	6.6	•
Amortization and Depletion	15	•	0.3	0.2	0.2	0.5	0.7	0.7	0.5	0.4	0.7	•	0.3	•
Pensions and Other Deferred Comp.	16	•	0.0	0.0	0.1	0.1	0.0	0.3	0.2	0.1	0.2	•	0.3	•
Employee Benefits	17	•	0.1	0.5	0.7	0.9	0.7	1.0	1.7	0.9	1.4	•	1.2	•
Advertising	18	•	1.2	1.8	1.4	2.8	3.5	2.9	3.2	2.9	2.4	•	2.5	•
Other Expenses	19	•	31.0	23.4	23.1	22.0	25.3	20.8	22.5	19.8	33.5	•	20.4	•
Officers' Compensation	20	•	1.8	4.3	2.9	2.4	0.9	1.7	1.3	0.9	0.8	•	0.9	•
Operating Margin	21	•	•	5.8	5.2	5.7	2.3	1.1	2.3	1.6	•	•	•	•
Operating Margin Before Officers' Comp.	22	•	0.4	10.1	8.0	8.1	3.3	2.8	3.6	2.5	•	•	•	•

Selected Average Balance Sheet ($ in Thousands)

Net Receivables 23	•	0	4	29	144	214	1100	2338	2883	10923	•	40493	•
Inventories 24	•	0	8	28	48	182	463	606	2254	3658	•	21464	•
Net Property, Plant and Equipment 25	•	0	60	309	764	3141	6622	16141	33664	80749	•	525983	•
Total Assets 26	•	0	138	676	1856	6770	15570	34890	68798	170500	•	967183	•
Notes and Loans Payable 27	•	0	66	324	930	3381	7171	16213	27907	62791	•	298730	•
All Other Liabilities 28	•	0	26	106	308	1198	2716	8042	17966	51104	•	285898	•
Net Worth 29	•	0	46	247	617	2192	5683	10635	22925	56605	•	382555	•

Selected Financial Ratios (Times to 1)

Current Ratio 30	•	•	1.5	1.5	1.6	1.0	1.6	1.0	0.9	0.9	•	1.0	•
Quick Ratio 31	•	•	1.0	1.1	1.1	0.7	1.3	0.7	0.5	0.6	•	0.7	•
Net Sales to Working Capital 32	•	•	45.9	27.5	16.4	433.3	15.6	470.0	•	•	•	824.4	•
Coverage Ratio 33	•	11.0	15.9	9.1	8.4	4.8	5.4	4.9	5.3	3.0	•	6.0	•
Total Asset Turnover 34	•	•	5.2	3.1	2.5	2.2	1.8	1.6	1.8	1.6	•	1.2	•
Inventory Turnover 35	•	•	35.5	29.1	41.9	29.7	26.1	36.6	26.1	26.4	•	22.3	•
Receivables Turnover 36	•	•	224.6	75.4	28.4	81.5	28.5	31.7	35.8	•	•	27.3	•
Total Liabilities to Net Worth 37	•	•	2.0	1.7	2.0	2.1	1.7	2.3	2.0	2.0	•	1.5	•
Current Assets to Working Capital 38	•	•	2.9	2.9	2.6	47.1	2.6	73.5	•	•	•	126.5	•
Current Liabilities to Working Capital 39	•	•	1.9	1.9	1.6	46.1	1.6	72.5	•	•	•	125.5	•
Working Capital to Net Sales 40	•	•	0.0	0.0	0.1	0.0	0.1	0.0	•	•	•	0.0	•
Inventory to Working Capital 41	•	•	0.5	0.3	0.2	5.6	0.3	5.8	•	•	•	16.0	•
Total Receipts to Cash Flow 42	•	3.5	5.0	4.9	5.0	5.2	5.4	4.9	5.8	3.4	•	5.5	•
Cost of Goods to Cash Flow 43	•	1.7	2.0	1.9	2.2	1.8	2.3	2.0	2.8	1.2	•	2.3	•
Cash Flow to Total Debt 44	•	•	1.6	1.0	0.7	0.6	0.5	0.5	0.5	0.7	•	0.4	•

Selected Financial Factors (in Percentages)

Debt Ratio 45	•	•	66.6	63.5	66.7	67.6	63.5	69.5	66.7	66.8	•	60.4	•
Return on Total Assets 46	•	•	35.6	20.3	18.5	11.2	12.7	10.3	12.8	6.7	•	10.5	•
Return on Equity Before Income Taxes 47	•	•	99.9	49.5	49.0	27.3	28.3	26.9	31.2	13.4	•	22.2	•
Return on Equity After Income Taxes 48	•	•	98.8	48.5	48.2	26.7	27.4	24.7	29.2	10.3	•	15.7	•
Profit Margin (Before Income Tax) 49	•	16.2	6.4	5.8	6.5	4.0	5.6	5.3	5.9	2.7	•	7.4	•
Profit Margin (After Income Tax) 50	•	15.6	6.3	5.6	6.4	3.9	5.5	4.8	5.5	2.1	•	5.2	•

Table I

Corporations with and without Net Income

AUTOMOTIVE REPAIR AND MAINTENANCE

MONEY AMOUNTS AND SIZE OF ASSETS IN THOUSANDS OF DOLLARS

Item Description for Accounting Period 7/11 Through 6/12		Total	Zero Assets	Under 500	500 to 1,000	1,000 to 5,000	5,000 to 10,000	10,000 to 25,000	25,000 to 50,000	50,000 to 100,000	100,000 to 250,000	250,000 to 500,000	500,000 to 2,500,000	2,500,000 and over
Number of Enterprises	1	109761	17412	82902	6107	3106	150	45	17	5	•	•	•	0
Revenues ($ in Thousands)														
Net Sales	2	69006879	2923986	38914221	9111657	10075881	1472898	1164918	748765	451170	•	•	•	0
Interest	3	22166	4	3034	4919	1064	157	688	1152	90	•	•	•	0
Rents	4	39887	365	7935	1234	2775	35	442	233	2294	•	•	•	0
Royalties	5	107827	2036	0	0	0	0	0	0	0	•	•	•	0
Other Portfolio Income	6	107042	8679	24004	10458	10690	303	2841	39235	2132	•	•	•	0
Other Receipts	7	447053	114275	139269	22419	52867	27501	30068	9180	1827	•	•	•	0
Total Receipts	8	69730854	3049345	39088463	9150687	10143277	1500894	1198957	798565	457513	•	•	•	0
Average Total Receipts	9	635	175	472	1498	3266	10006	26643	46974	91503	•	•	•	•
Operating Costs/Operating Income (%)														
Cost of Operations	10	49.5	33.3	47.5	54.0	53.8	59.8	66.9	27.4	36.8	•	•	•	•
Salaries and Wages	11	13.4	19.8	13.1	9.7	15.1	10.6	11.1	31.5	19.2	•	•	•	•
Taxes Paid	12	3.5	5.7	3.5	3.3	3.7	1.8	2.5	5.4	2.9	•	•	•	•
Interest Paid	13	1.2	1.1	0.8	1.7	1.3	1.5	0.3	1.9	3.2	•	•	•	•
Depreciation	14	2.0	1.7	1.6	2.3	2.3	2.2	3.0	6.1	3.0	•	•	•	•
Amortization and Depletion	15	0.5	0.4	0.2	0.3	0.7	0.3	0.1	1.0	1.3	•	•	•	•
Pensions and Other Deferred Comp.	16	0.2	0.0	0.1	0.8	0.1	0.1	0.2	0.2	0.6	•	•	•	•
Employee Benefits	17	1.2	0.5	1.2	1.5	0.9	0.5	1.6	1.7	4.1	•	•	•	•
Advertising	18	1.4	0.7	1.3	1.4	1.3	1.6	0.7	1.3	0.3	•	•	•	•
Other Expenses	19	19.5	35.8	20.7	16.4	14.5	15.8	11.2	21.4	28.0	•	•	•	•
Officers' Compensation	20	5.7	4.1	7.4	5.0	3.3	2.7	2.2	1.5	1.2	•	•	•	•
Operating Margin	21	2.0	•	2.5	3.6	2.9	3.1	0.2	0.6	•	•	•	•	•
Operating Margin Before Officers' Comp.	22	7.7	0.9	10.0	8.5	6.2	5.7	2.4	2.1	0.7	•	•	•	•

Selected Average Balance Sheet ($ in Thousands)													
Net Receivables **23**	17	0	8	52	107	798	1549	2491	18980	•	•	•	•
Inventories **24**	21	0	11	62	155	732	1340	1615	2645	•	•	•	•
Net Property, Plant and Equipment **25**	80	0	33	302	754	2534	5321	12084	16633	•	•	•	•
Total Assets **26**	211	0	88	663	1651	6971	13649	31604	82049	•	•	•	•
Notes and Loans Payable **27**	136	0	76	447	915	3005	5023	13838	25506	•	•	•	•
All Other Liabilities **28**	53	0	26	130	268	1143	146	5210	27695	•	•	•	•
Net Worth **29**	22	0	-14	87	469	2823	8480	12557	28847	•	•	•	•
Selected Financial Ratios (Times to 1)													
Current Ratio **30**	1.4	•	1.4	1.8	2.3	1.7	1.3	1.4	1.3	•	•	•	•
Quick Ratio **31**	0.9	•	1.0	1.0	1.3	0.9	0.6	1.0	1.1	•	•	•	•
Net Sales to Working Capital **32**	26.8	•	43.4	13.6	9.8	10.1	20.5	18.1	13.6	•	•	•	•
Coverage Ratio **33**	3.6	2.1	5.0	3.3	3.7	4.4	10.2	4.8	1.3	•	•	•	•
Total Asset Turnover **34**	3.0	•	5.3	2.2	2.0	1.4	1.9	1.4	1.1	•	•	•	•
Inventory Turnover **35**	15.1	•	19.6	13.0	11.3	8.0	12.9	7.5	12.6	•	•	•	•
Receivables Turnover **36**	38.7	•	58.7	29.4	31.0	13.2	16.8	18.6	4.5	•	•	•	•
Total Liabilities to Net Worth **37**	8.5	•	•	6.7	2.5	1.5	0.6	1.5	1.8	•	•	•	•
Current Assets to Working Capital **38**	3.3	•	3.8	2.3	1.8	2.5	4.5	3.6	4.2	•	•	•	•
Current Liabilities to Working Capital **39**	2.3	•	2.8	1.3	0.8	1.5	3.5	2.6	3.2	•	•	•	•
Working Capital to Net Sales **40**	0.0	•	0.0	0.1	0.1	0.1	0.0	0.1	0.1	•	•	•	•
Inventory to Working Capital **41**	0.9	•	1.0	0.6	0.5	0.8	1.1	0.8	0.2	•	•	•	•
Total Receipts to Cash Flow **42**	6.4	3.7	6.2	6.8	7.8	6.2	9.7	5.0	4.8	•	•	•	•
Cost of Goods to Cash Flow **43**	3.2	1.2	3.0	3.7	4.2	3.7	6.5	1.4	1.8	•	•	•	•
Cash Flow to Total Debt **44**	0.5	•	0.7	0.4	0.4	0.4	0.5	0.5	0.4	•	•	•	•
Selected Financial Factors (in Percentages)													
Debt Ratio **45**	89.4	•	115.6	87.0	71.6	59.5	37.9	60.3	64.8	•	•	•	•
Return on Total Assets **46**	12.7	•	19.8	12.9	9.5	9.1	6.5	12.7	4.5	•	•	•	•
Return on Equity Before Income Taxes **47**	86.9	•	•	68.9	24.6	17.3	9.4	25.3	2.7	•	•	•	•
Return on Equity After Income Taxes **48**	84.6	•	•	67.1	23.9	16.7	9.2	25.0	1.9	•	•	•	•
Profit Margin (Before Income Tax) **49**	3.1	1.2	3.0	4.0	3.6	5.0	3.1	7.2	0.9	•	•	•	•
Profit Margin (After Income Tax) **50**	3.0	1.1	3.0	3.9	3.5	4.8	3.0	7.1	0.6	•	•	•	•

Table II

Corporations with Net Income

AUTOMOTIVE REPAIR AND MAINTENANCE

MONEY AMOUNTS AND SIZE OF ASSETS IN THOUSANDS OF DOLLARS

Item Description for Accounting Period 7/11 Through 6/12		Total	Zero Assets	Under 500	500 to 1,000	1,000 to 5,000	5,000 to 10,000	10,000 to 25,000	25,000 to 50,000	50,000 to 100,000	100,000 to 250,000	250,000 to 500,000	500,000 to 2,500,000	2,500,000 and over
Number of Enterprises	1	70891	9620	54181	4564	2345	127	31	10	•	•	•	•	0
Revenues ($ in Thousands)														
Net Sales	2	53867120	1930403	29022500	7747182	9411852	1130428	1075377	498714	•	•	•	•	0
Interest	3	9765	4	1637	4809	1018	47	663	1152	•	•	•	•	0
Rents	4	9014	0	4007	1234	2775	35	25	233	•	•	•	•	0
Royalties	5	2351	2036	0	0	0	0	0	0	•	•	•	•	0
Other Portfolio Income	6	92548	7976	23303	7038	10588	303	2841	36879	•	•	•	•	0
Other Receipts	7	357613	94796	124134	21195	42280	26154	26686	9609	•	•	•	•	0
Total Receipts	8	54338411	2035215	29175581	7781458	9468513	1156967	1105592	546587	•	•	•	•	0
Average Total Receipts	9	767	212	538	1705	4038	9110	35664	54659	•	•	•	•	•
Operating Costs/Operating Income (%)														
Cost of Operations	10	49.0	24.1	46.7	54.3	54.6	55.5	66.6	12.4	•	•	•	•	•
Salaries and Wages	11	13.6	21.0	12.9	10.2	15.2	11.4	11.0	45.7	•	•	•	•	•
Taxes Paid	12	3.3	4.5	3.2	3.2	3.7	1.8	2.5	6.1	•	•	•	•	•
Interest Paid	13	0.9	1.3	0.6	1.5	1.0	1.5	0.2	2.0	•	•	•	•	•
Depreciation	14	1.5	1.3	1.2	1.6	1.8	1.5	2.6	2.1	•	•	•	•	•
Amortization and Depletion	15	0.4	0.2	0.2	0.4	0.4	0.4	0.1	1.4	•	•	•	•	•
Pensions and Other Deferred Comp.	16	0.3	0.0	0.1	0.9	0.2	0.0	0.2	0.1	•	•	•	•	•
Employee Benefits	17	1.2	0.5	1.1	1.6	0.9	0.4	1.8	1.2	•	•	•	•	•
Advertising	18	1.2	0.9	1.2	1.1	1.3	2.1	0.7	1.2	•	•	•	•	•
Other Expenses	19	17.7	35.0	19.2	14.2	13.5	17.9	10.1	23.6	•	•	•	•	•
Officers' Compensation	20	5.6	4.7	7.4	4.9	3.4	3.1	2.4	1.4	•	•	•	•	•
Operating Margin	21	5.4	6.5	6.1	6.1	4.0	4.3	1.8	2.6	•	•	•	•	•
Operating Margin Before Officers' Comp.	22	11.0	11.1	13.4	11.0	7.4	7.5	4.2	4.1	•	•	•	•	•

Selected Average Balance Sheet ($ in Thousands)													
Net Receivables **23**	19	0	9	56	138	651	2016	2801	•	•	•	•	•
Inventories **24**	21	0	10	57	158	636	1702	1336	•	•	•	•	•
Net Property, Plant and Equipment **25**	74	0	27	258	656	2335	4910	7443	•	•	•	•	•
Total Assets **26**	212	0	83	648	1600	6829	12538	33848	•	•	•	•	•
Notes and Loans Payable **27**	109	0	51	380	768	2703	3121	15831	•	•	•	•	•
All Other Liabilities **28**	51	0	26	128	227	1079	3915	7626	•	•	•	•	•
Net Worth **29**	52	0	6	140	606	3047	5502	10390	•	•	•	•	•
Selected Financial Ratios (Times to 1)													
Current Ratio **30**	1.7	•	1.6	1.8	2.5	2.2	1.2	1.6	•	•	•	•	•
Quick Ratio **31**	1.1	•	1.2	1.0	1.5	1.2	0.8	1.2	•	•	•	•	•
Net Sales to Working Capital **32**	21.7	•	31.6	15.2	9.7	7.7	38.8	13.6	•	•	•	•	•
Coverage Ratio **33**	7.7	10.2	12.2	5.3	5.4	5.4	25.1	7.0	•	•	•	•	•
Total Asset Turnover **34**	3.6	•	6.4	2.6	2.5	1.3	2.8	1.5	•	•	•	•	•
Inventory Turnover **35**	17.6	•	25.6	16.3	13.9	7.8	13.6	4.6	•	•	•	•	•
Receivables Turnover **36**	40.0	•	62.6	31.7	31.9	15.3	17.0	19.7	•	•	•	•	•
Total Liabilities to Net Worth **37**	3.1	•	12.0	3.6	1.6	1.2	1.3	2.3	•	•	•	•	•
Current Assets to Working Capital **38**	2.5	•	2.6	2.3	1.7	1.8	6.3	2.7	•	•	•	•	•
Current Liabilities to Working Capital **39**	1.5	•	1.6	1.3	0.7	0.8	5.3	1.7	•	•	•	•	•
Working Capital to Net Sales **40**	0.0	•	0.0	0.1	0.1	0.1	0.0	0.1	•	•	•	•	•
Inventory to Working Capital **41**	0.6	•	0.6	0.5	0.5	0.5	2.0	0.4	•	•	•	•	•
Total Receipts to Cash Flow **42**	5.8	2.6	5.5	6.5	7.5	5.2	9.5	3.6	•	•	•	•	•
Cost of Goods to Cash Flow **43**	2.8	0.6	2.6	3.5	4.1	2.9	6.3	0.4	•	•	•	•	•
Cash Flow to Total Debt **44**	0.8	•	1.3	0.5	0.5	0.5	0.5	0.6	•	•	•	•	•
Selected Financial Factors (in Percentages)													
Debt Ratio **45**	75.4	•	92.3	78.4	62.1	55.4	56.1	69.3	•	•	•	•	•
Return on Total Assets **46**	25.8	•	46.0	21.2	14.1	10.7	13.4	21.0	•	•	•	•	•
Return on Equity Before Income Taxes **47**	91.2	•	548.0	79.7	30.2	19.5	29.4	58.7	•	•	•	•	•
Return on Equity After Income Taxes **48**	89.7	•	546.0	78.2	29.5	18.8	28.8	57.9	•	•	•	•	•
Profit Margin (Before Income Tax) **49**	6.3	11.9	6.6	6.6	4.6	6.7	4.7	12.2	•	•	•	•	•
Profit Margin (After Income Tax) **50**	6.2	11.8	6.6	6.4	4.5	6.4	4.6	12.1	•	•	•	•	•

Table I

Corporations with and without Net Income

OTHER REPAIR AND MAINTENANCE

MONEY AMOUNTS AND SIZE OF ASSETS IN THOUSANDS OF DOLLARS

Item Description for Accounting Period 7/11 Through 6/12		Total	Zero Assets	Under 500	500 to 1,000	1,000 to 5,000	5,000 to 10,000	10,000 to 25,000	25,000 to 50,000	50,000 to 100,000	100,000 to 250,000	250,000 to 500,000	500,000 to 2,500,000	2,500,000 and over
Number of Enterprises	1	59209	12316	42590	2120	1806	171	135	44	16	•	•	•	•
Revenues ($ in Thousands)														
Net Sales	2	41954146	1171596	14790895	4257819	8218449	2681640	3276473	2821159	1624164	•	•	•	•
Interest	3	112634	7	2166	3300	6271	1493	1787	1305	1017	•	•	•	•
Rents	4	11533	0	2105	1427	2750	2602	2021	461	0	•	•	•	•
Royalties	5	165062	0	0	0	0	0	307	0	145	•	•	•	•
Other Portfolio Income	6	249525	11104	12668	5	23321	3676	6326	3837	13583	•	•	•	•
Other Receipts	7	458403	27060	12325	122897	9042	13408	16411	12295	13796	•	•	•	•
Total Receipts	8	42951303	1209767	14820159	4385448	8259833	2702819	3303325	2839057	1652705	•	•	•	•
Average Total Receipts	9	725	98	348	2069	4574	15806	24469	64524	103294	•	•	•	•
Operating Costs/Operating Income (%)														
Cost of Operations	10	53.6	39.9	44.5	57.0	54.0	62.6	60.9	63.9	69.4	•	•	•	•
Salaries and Wages	11	12.6	8.7	14.3	12.1	13.2	12.7	9.9	10.0	7.9	•	•	•	•
Taxes Paid	12	2.7	3.3	2.6	3.3	3.0	2.8	1.7	2.7	1.6	•	•	•	•
Interest Paid	13	1.5	0.7	0.5	0.5	0.8	0.5	0.5	1.0	1.5	•	•	•	•
Depreciation	14	2.1	1.6	1.9	1.4	1.9	1.2	3.8	2.6	5.1	•	•	•	•
Amortization and Depletion	15	0.4	0.3	0.0	0.0	0.4	0.0	0.1	0.4	0.8	•	•	•	•
Pensions and Other Deferred Comp.	16	0.4	0.1	0.3	0.3	0.2	0.5	0.5	0.5	0.7	•	•	•	•
Employee Benefits	17	1.6	1.1	0.6	2.9	1.6	2.0	2.9	1.8	2.9	•	•	•	•
Advertising	18	0.6	1.0	0.7	0.4	0.6	0.1	0.3	0.3	0.2	•	•	•	•
Other Expenses	19	17.2	32.7	21.0	18.6	13.9	8.6	16.5	11.9	11.2	•	•	•	•
Officers' Compensation	20	5.1	13.6	7.4	5.8	4.3	4.1	2.1	1.8	0.8	•	•	•	•
Operating Margin	21	2.3	•	6.2	•	6.0	4.7	0.7	3.2	•	•	•	•	•
Operating Margin Before Officers' Comp.	22	7.4	10.7	13.6	3.5	10.3	8.8	2.8	5.0	•	•	•	•	•

Selected Average Balance Sheet ($ in Thousands)														
Net Receivables	23	83	0	14	249	472	2052	3074	9117	20011	•	•	•	•
Inventories	24	42	0	11	110	229	1164	3278	7534	12234	•	•	•	•
Net Property, Plant and Equipment	25	49	0	17	101	279	1269	3126	5976	10803	•	•	•	•
Total Assets	26	391	0	73	663	1709	6828	14799	34322	68488	•	•	•	•
Notes and Loans Payable	27	181	0	35	234	754	2336	3448	8672	23183	•	•	•	•
All Other Liabilities	28	95	0	27	144	410	1748	4341	10174	25895	•	•	•	•
Net Worth	29	114	0	12	284	545	2744	7010	15476	19410	•	•	•	•

Selected Financial Ratios (Times to 1)														
Current Ratio	30	1.9	•	1.7	2.2	2.6	1.7	2.0	2.0	1.3	•	•	•	•
Quick Ratio	31	1.3	•	1.2	1.4	1.8	1.1	1.2	1.1	0.7	•	•	•	•
Net Sales to Working Capital	32	8.0	•	18.4	7.5	6.7	9.0	4.9	5.9	11.0	•	•	•	•
Coverage Ratio	33	4.1	1.5	13.0	2.6	9.0	11.0	4.1	4.7	0.8	•	•	•	•
Total Asset Turnover	34	1.8	•	4.8	3.0	2.7	2.3	1.6	1.9	1.5	•	•	•	•
Inventory Turnover	35	9.0	•	13.5	10.4	10.7	8.4	4.5	5.4	5.8	•	•	•	•
Receivables Turnover	36	8.4	•	25.7	9.9	10.6	9.7	7.9	7.2	5.6	•	•	•	•
Total Liabilities to Net Worth	37	2.4	•	5.3	1.3	2.1	1.5	1.1	1.2	2.5	•	•	•	•
Current Assets to Working Capital	38	2.1	•	2.4	1.8	1.6	2.5	2.0	2.0	4.6	•	•	•	•
Current Liabilities to Working Capital	39	1.1	•	1.4	0.8	0.6	1.5	1.0	1.0	3.6	•	•	•	•
Working Capital to Net Sales	40	0.1	•	0.1	0.1	0.1	0.1	0.2	0.2	0.1	•	•	•	•
Inventory to Working Capital	41	0.5	•	0.7	0.4	0.4	0.7	0.7	0.8	1.6	•	•	•	•
Total Receipts to Cash Flow	42	5.7	3.7	4.5	8.2	5.8	8.7	6.8	7.7	13.6	•	•	•	•
Cost of Goods to Cash Flow	43	3.1	1.5	2.0	4.7	3.1	5.4	4.1	4.9	9.4	•	•	•	•
Cash Flow to Total Debt	44	0.4	•	1.3	0.6	0.7	0.4	0.5	0.4	0.2	•	•	•	•

Selected Financial Factors (in Percentages)														
Debt Ratio	45	70.7	•	84.1	57.1	68.1	59.8	52.6	54.9	71.7	•	•	•	•
Return on Total Assets	46	11.2	•	32.9	3.7	19.6	13.8	3.3	9.0	1.8	•	•	•	•
Return on Equity Before Income Taxes	47	28.9	•	191.6	5.3	54.7	31.3	5.3	15.7	•	•	•	•	•
Return on Equity After Income Taxes	48	26.9	•	191.0	3.9	52.4	28.4	4.3	11.7	•	•	•	•	•
Profit Margin (Before Income Tax)	49	4.7	0.4	6.4	0.8	6.5	5.5	1.5	3.8	•	•	•	•	•
Profit Margin (After Income Tax)	50	4.3	•	6.4	0.6	6.3	5.0	1.2	2.8	•	•	•	•	•

Table II

Corporations with Net Income

OTHER REPAIR AND MAINTENANCE

MONEY AMOUNTS AND SIZE OF ASSETS IN THOUSANDS OF DOLLARS

Item Description for Accounting Period 7/11 Through 6/12		Total	Zero Assets	Under 500	500 to 1,000	1,000 to 5,000	5,000 to 10,000	10,000 to 25,000	25,000 to 50,000	50,000 to 100,000	100,000 to 250,000	250,000 to 500,000	500,000 to 2,500,000	2,500,000 and over
Number of Enterprises	1	38454	6092	29118	1570	1381	156	85	37	7	•	•	•	•
Revenues ($ in Thousands)														
Net Sales	2	32892251	564853	10743635	3373588	6984482	2611682	2453184	2620270	720287	•	•	•	•
Interest	3	107524	0	546	3078	5277	1343	1050	947	13	•	•	•	•
Rents	4	5167	0	1170	1427	23	1502	548	461	0	•	•	•	•
Royalties	5	164917	0	0	0	0	0	307	0	0	•	•	•	•
Other Portfolio Income	6	226782	10563	5233	5	23091	3334	5448	3837	1569	•	•	•	•
Other Receipts	7	428581	24493	9215	121108	5191	13035	6095	10862	5466	•	•	•	•
Total Receipts	8	33825222	599909	10759799	3499206	7018064	2630896	2466632	2636377	727335	•	•	•	•
Average Total Receipts	9	880	98	370	2229	5082	16865	29019	71253	103905	•	•	•	•
Operating Costs/Operating Income (%)														
Cost of Operations	10	52.7	23.1	40.5	59.3	53.3	62.0	61.6	65.2	76.3	•	•	•	•
Salaries and Wages	11	12.1	7.0	13.7	9.7	13.2	12.6	9.0	9.4	6.7	•	•	•	•
Taxes Paid	12	2.6	2.0	2.6	3.1	2.8	2.8	1.7	2.6	1.6	•	•	•	•
Interest Paid	13	1.5	0.4	0.5	0.3	0.6	0.5	0.4	0.9	0.5	•	•	•	•
Depreciation	14	1.8	0.5	1.8	1.0	1.6	1.2	3.3	2.5	1.5	•	•	•	•
Amortization and Depletion	15	0.3	0.1	0.0	0.1	0.3	0.0	0.1	0.3	0.1	•	•	•	•
Pensions and Other Deferred Comp.	16	0.4	0.0	0.3	0.3	0.2	0.5	0.6	0.5	1.2	•	•	•	•
Employee Benefits	17	1.7	0.0	0.6	3.1	1.5	2.0	3.7	1.8	1.4	•	•	•	•
Advertising	18	0.6	1.1	0.7	0.3	0.7	0.1	0.3	0.2	0.2	•	•	•	•
Other Expenses	19	16.0	40.5	20.6	18.0	13.4	8.4	12.1	9.8	5.2	•	•	•	•
Officers' Compensation	20	5.2	11.5	8.2	6.1	4.0	4.2	2.2	1.8	0.9	•	•	•	•
Operating Margin	21	5.2	13.9	10.5	•	8.4	5.6	4.9	4.9	4.6	•	•	•	•
Operating Margin Before Officers' Comp.	22	10.3	25.4	18.7	4.7	12.4	9.8	7.1	6.7	5.5	•	•	•	•

Selected Average Balance Sheet ($ in Thousands)													
Net Receivables 23	101	0	11	246	432	2203	3366	9818	23568	•	•	•	•
Inventories 24	48	0	11	62	240	1162	4488	7515	14261	•	•	•	•
Net Property, Plant and Equipment 25	47	0	15	117	261	1109	2345	5930	6052	•	•	•	•
Total Assets 26	478	0	70	655	1706	6870	14367	35364	64412	•	•	•	•
Notes and Loans Payable 27	222	0	37	137	629	2319	2392	8315	17106	•	•	•	•
All Other Liabilities 28	111	0	23	151	377	1892	4441	10967	21802	•	•	•	•
Net Worth 29	146	0	9	367	699	2658	7534	16081	25504	•	•	•	•
Selected Financial Ratios (Times to 1)													
Current Ratio 30	2.0	•	1.7	2.5	2.7	1.6	2.3	2.1	1.4	•	•	•	•
Quick Ratio 31	1.3	•	1.2	1.6	1.9	1.1	1.3	1.1	0.8	•	•	•	•
Net Sales to Working Capital 32	7.5	•	19.1	8.1	7.0	9.6	4.6	5.8	7.2	•	•	•	•
Coverage Ratio 33	6.3	54.1	22.1	8.0	14.8	14.4	14.5	7.2	12.6	•	•	•	•
Total Asset Turnover 34	1.8	•	5.3	3.3	3.0	2.4	2.0	2.0	1.6	•	•	•	•
Inventory Turnover 35	9.4	•	14.1	20.5	11.2	8.9	4.0	6.1	5.5	•	•	•	•
Receivables Turnover 36	8.5	•	31.5	14.0	11.8	10.9	7.3	8.2	4.5	•	•	•	•
Total Liabilities to Net Worth 37	2.3	•	6.6	0.8	1.4	1.6	0.9	1.2	1.5	•	•	•	•
Current Assets to Working Capital 38	2.0	•	2.4	1.7	1.6	2.6	1.7	1.9	3.5	•	•	•	•
Current Liabilities to Working Capital 39	1.0	•	1.4	0.7	0.6	1.6	0.7	0.9	2.5	•	•	•	•
Working Capital to Net Sales 40	0.1	•	0.1	0.1	0.1	0.1	0.2	0.2	0.1	•	•	•	•
Inventory to Working Capital 41	0.5	•	0.7	0.2	0.4	0.7	0.7	0.8	1.3	•	•	•	•
Total Receipts to Cash Flow 42	5.1	1.8	3.8	7.9	5.1	8.2	7.1	8.0	10.0	•	•	•	•
Cost of Goods to Cash Flow 43	2.7	0.4	1.5	4.7	2.7	5.1	4.4	5.2	7.6	•	•	•	•
Cash Flow to Total Debt 44	0.5	•	1.6	0.9	1.0	0.5	0.6	0.5	0.3	•	•	•	•
Selected Financial Factors (in Percentages)													
Debt Ratio 45	69.5	•	86.8	44.0	59.0	61.3	47.6	54.5	60.4	•	•	•	•
Return on Total Assets 46	17.1	•	58.9	8.8	28.1	16.7	11.8	12.7	9.7	•	•	•	•
Return on Equity Before Income Taxes 47	47.1	•	425.1	13.7	64.0	40.2	20.9	24.1	22.5	•	•	•	•
Return on Equity After Income Taxes 48	44.7	•	423.9	12.3	61.7	37.0	19.4	19.4	21.6	•	•	•	•
Profit Margin (Before Income Tax) 49	8.0	20.1	10.6	2.3	8.8	6.4	5.5	5.5	5.6	•	•	•	•
Profit Margin (After Income Tax) 50	7.6	19.0	10.6	2.1	8.5	5.9	5.1	4.4	5.3	•	•	•	•

Table I

Corporations with and without Net Income

PERSONAL AND LAUNDRY SERVICES

Item Description for Accounting Period 7/11 Through 6/12		MONEY AMOUNTS AND SIZE OF ASSETS IN THOUSANDS OF DOLLARS												
		Total	Zero Assets	Under 500	500 to 1,000	1,000 to 5,000	5,000 to 10,000	10,000 to 25,000	25,000 to 50,000	50,000 to 100,000	100,000 to 250,000	250,000 to 500,000	500,000 to 2,500,000	2,500,000 and over
Number of Enterprises	1	167182	38735	115826	7148	4973	272	138	40	21	•	4	•	0
Revenues ($ in Thousands)														
Net Sales	2	77307289	3038075	27174744	10278149	11504824	4158069	2036837	1363766	1777498	•	1018606	•	0
Interest	3	104735	55	4055	2599	15609	3211	2050	4613	1112	•	5112	•	0
Rents	4	64681	1	4567	5032	3461	1365	5608	2043	412	•	7110	•	0
Royalties	5	195405	0	29583	779	1205	3	1560	0	455	•	0	•	0
Other Portfolio Income	6	320709	37522	45807	36504	17455	13342	3112	3369	253	•	2316	•	0
Other Receipts	7	2113587	13232	1416328	42425	161038	47533	66871	62657	17189	•	5021	•	0
Total Receipts	8	80106406	3088885	28675084	10365488	11703592	4223523	2116038	1436448	1796919	•	1038165	•	0
Average Total Receipts	9	479	80	248	1450	2353	15528	15334	35911	85568	•	259541	•	•
Operating Costs/Operating Income (%)														
Cost of Operations	10	26.7	19.5	18.1	29.7	31.9	53.8	32.0	21.3	37.2	•	29.0	•	•
Salaries and Wages	11	21.9	13.6	26.2	18.9	21.5	12.6	18.0	22.9	18.4	•	28.1	•	•
Taxes Paid	12	4.2	3.6	4.3	4.5	3.7	4.2	3.0	2.8	3.5	•	3.5	•	•
Interest Paid	13	1.6	0.8	0.8	1.2	1.9	0.7	1.8	1.7	1.4	•	2.3	•	•
Depreciation	14	3.6	3.3	2.5	3.4	3.8	3.2	5.0	4.8	4.4	•	8.2	•	•
Amortization and Depletion	15	1.1	0.6	0.5	0.6	0.6	0.3	0.4	0.6	1.0	•	2.8	•	•
Pensions and Other Deferred Comp.	16	0.4	0.0	0.1	0.4	0.3	0.3	0.4	0.7	0.3	•	2.2	•	•
Employee Benefits	17	1.2	0.3	0.7	0.9	1.5	0.5	2.7	4.3	1.8	•	3.3	•	•
Advertising	18	1.6	1.5	1.5	1.9	1.7	1.1	3.5	1.9	1.6	•	1.1	•	•
Other Expenses	19	31.1	50.7	36.2	26.9	29.8	18.2	31.2	38.7	26.0	•	22.6	•	•
Officers' Compensation	20	5.6	6.4	9.3	8.2	3.9	1.4	2.4	1.8	2.1	•	1.5	•	•
Operating Margin	21	1.0	•	•	3.4	•	3.6	•	•	2.4	•	•	•	•
Operating Margin Before Officers' Comp.	22	6.6	6.1	9.0	11.6	3.2	5.1	2.0	0.3	4.4	•	•	•	•

Selected Average Balance Sheet ($ in Thousands)													
Net Receivables 23	25	0	3	47	208	983	2030	3232	9505	•	20457	•	•
Inventories 24	14	0	3	32	56	385	355	1937	1382	•	7294	•	•
Net Property, Plant and Equipment 25	107	0	23	323	787	2250	4182	8899	25086	•	158064	•	•
Total Assets 26	342	0	69	705	1824	6554	14053	34912	77439	•	406698	•	•
Notes and Loans Payable 27	142	0	53	332	1104	1511	4871	8787	22534	•	160354	•	•
All Other Liabilities 28	122	0	13	135	478	2491	4471	19280	19936	•	118870	•	•
Net Worth 29	78	0	3	238	243	2552	4710	6845	34970	•	127474	•	•

Selected Financial Ratios (Times to 1)													
Current Ratio 30	1.4	•	1.4	1.6	1.8	1.2	1.4	1.5	1.4	•	0.5	•	•
Quick Ratio 31	0.9	•	1.0	1.3	1.3	0.8	1.2	0.7	1.1	•	0.4	•	•
Net Sales to Working Capital 32	17.3	•	38.7	16.9	7.9	28.6	9.9	6.3	15.2	•	•	•	•
Coverage Ratio 33	3.9	2.8	7.3	4.6	1.5	8.0	2.9	3.2	3.5	•	•	•	•
Total Asset Turnover 34	1.4	•	3.4	2.0	1.3	2.3	1.1	1.0	1.1	•	0.6	•	•
Inventory Turnover 35	8.7	•	15.7	13.3	13.1	21.4	13.3	3.7	22.8	•	10.1	•	•
Receivables Turnover 36	18.7	•	87.5	29.9	10.7	13.9	7.8	8.9	9.0	•	•	•	•
Total Liabilities to Net Worth 37	3.4	•	23.4	2.0	6.5	1.6	2.0	4.1	1.2	•	2.2	•	•
Current Assets to Working Capital 38	3.3	•	3.7	2.6	2.2	5.4	3.3	3.1	3.9	•	•	•	•
Current Liabilities to Working Capital 39	2.3	•	2.7	1.6	1.2	4.4	2.3	2.1	2.9	•	•	•	•
Working Capital to Net Sales 40	0.1	•	0.0	0.1	0.1	0.0	0.1	0.2	0.1	•	•	•	•
Inventory to Working Capital 41	0.5	•	0.3	0.4	0.2	1.1	0.2	0.3	0.2	•	•	•	•
Total Receipts to Cash Flow 42	4.1	3.2	3.7	4.9	4.2	5.6	4.8	4.2	4.4	•	8.3	•	•
Cost of Goods to Cash Flow 43	1.1	0.6	0.7	1.5	1.3	3.0	1.5	0.9	1.6	•	2.4	•	•
Cash Flow to Total Debt 44	0.4	•	1.0	0.6	0.3	0.7	0.3	0.3	0.5	•	0.1	•	•

Selected Financial Factors (in Percentages)													
Debt Ratio 45	77.3	•	95.9	66.2	86.7	61.1	66.5	80.4	54.8	•	68.7	•	•
Return on Total Assets 46	8.7	•	20.5	11.1	3.7	13.8	5.5	5.4	5.3	•	•	•	•
Return on Equity Before Income Taxes 47	28.4	•	432.9	25.6	9.8	31.0	10.7	18.7	8.4	•	•	•	•
Return on Equity After Income Taxes 48	24.6	•	428.1	25.0	7.7	29.5	9.5	18.0	6.0	•	•	•	•
Profit Margin (Before Income Tax) 49	4.8	1.4	5.2	4.2	1.0	5.2	3.4	3.8	3.5	•	•	•	•
Profit Margin (After Income Tax) 50	4.1	1.2	5.1	4.1	0.8	4.9	3.0	3.6	2.5	•	•	•	•

Table II

Corporations with Net Income

PERSONAL AND LAUNDRY SERVICES

MONEY AMOUNTS AND SIZE OF ASSETS IN THOUSANDS OF DOLLARS

Item Description for Accounting Period 7/11 Through 6/12		Total	Zero Assets	Under 500	500 to 1,000	1,000 to 5,000	5,000 to 10,000	10,000 to 25,000	25,000 to 50,000	50,000 to 100,000	100,000 to 250,000	250,000 to 500,000	500,000 to 2,500,000	2,500,000 and over
Number of Enterprises	1	95901	19054	69008	4724	2762	213	82	28	•	6	0	•	0
Revenues ($ in Thousands)														
Net Sales	2	58106936	1937584	21142185	6948602	7754320	3726986	1540846	955833	•	722304	0	•	0
Interest	3	83952	54	1598	2246	11895	1217	694	4312	•	1455	0	•	0
Rents	4	32736	1	491	4765	3027	882	5581	922	•	121	0	•	0
Royalties	5	163390	0	0	0	0	3	1496	0	•	0	0	•	0
Other Portfolio Income	6	293530	28943	38766	33056	15066	11954	1359	3369	•	4084	0	•	0
Other Receipts	7	1973439	2127	1437827	27909	121267	38823	39345	50318	•	42662	0	•	0
Total Receipts	8	60653983	1968709	22620867	7016578	7905575	3779865	1589321	1014754	•	770626	0	•	0
Average Total Receipts	9	632	103	328	1485	2862	17746	19382	36241	•	128438	•	•	•
Operating Costs/Operating Income (%)														
Cost of Operations	10	27.5	24.6	18.7	32.4	29.1	54.7	26.3	23.7	•	22.6	•	•	•
Salaries and Wages	11	21.8	10.9	27.3	16.5	20.9	12.2	18.9	17.5	•	17.2	•	•	•
Taxes Paid	12	4.0	3.2	4.2	3.6	3.4	4.1	2.7	2.5	•	3.2	•	•	•
Interest Paid	13	1.4	0.4	0.7	0.9	1.5	0.4	1.0	2.2	•	2.0	•	•	•
Depreciation	14	2.9	1.7	2.1	2.5	2.3	3.0	4.4	5.4	•	4.1	•	•	•
Amortization and Depletion	15	1.0	0.2	0.3	0.5	0.6	0.3	0.2	0.5	•	1.7	•	•	•
Pensions and Other Deferred Comp.	16	0.4	•	0.1	0.5	0.5	0.2	0.4	0.8	•	0.5	•	•	•
Employee Benefits	17	1.1	0.4	0.8	0.7	1.2	0.2	2.4	3.6	•	0.9	•	•	•
Advertising	18	1.5	1.5	1.5	1.9	1.5	0.9	2.7	0.5	•	0.3	•	•	•
Other Expenses	19	28.1	38.4	32.6	24.3	30.3	17.6	34.5	39.3	•	44.7	•	•	•
Officers' Compensation	20	5.4	5.5	8.7	8.6	4.3	1.3	1.7	2.0	•	2.5	•	•	•
Operating Margin	21	4.8	13.3	3.1	7.3	4.5	5.0	4.5	2.1	•	0.2	•	•	•
Operating Margin Before Officers' Comp.	22	10.2	18.8	11.8	15.9	8.8	6.3	6.3	4.1	•	2.7	•	•	•

Selected Average Balance Sheet ($ in Thousands)

Net Receivables 23	30	0	3	51	207	1117	1595	3310	•	23312	•	•	•
Inventories 24	20	0	3	41	47	432	359	1627	•	1062	•	•	•
Net Property, Plant and Equipment 25	124	0	26	278	633	1728	4551	10396	•	14224	•	•	•
Total Assets 26	424	0	75	711	1730	6343	14678	36371	•	152936	•	•	•
Notes and Loans Payable 27	137	0	47	240	670	1034	3856	10763	•	33416	•	•	•
All Other Liabilities 28	153	0	11	86	493	2259	5272	20786	•	65354	•	•	•
Net Worth 29	134	0	17	385	566	3050	5550	4822	•	54165	•	•	•

Selected Financial Ratios (Times to 1)

Current Ratio 30	1.7	•	1.9	2.8	2.1	1.6	1.4	1.3	•	1.0	•	•	•
Quick Ratio 31	1.1	•	1.5	2.2	1.5	1.0	1.1	0.5	•	0.9	•	•	•
Net Sales to Working Capital 32	12.7	•	23.7	8.4	7.0	14.7	13.1	8.4	•	513.0	•	•	•
Coverage Ratio 33	7.7	40.8	16.5	10.2	5.4	18.3	8.3	4.8	•	4.6	•	•	•
Total Asset Turnover 34	1.4	•	4.1	2.1	1.6	2.8	1.3	0.9	•	0.8	•	•	•
Inventory Turnover 35	8.2	•	17.4	11.7	17.2	22.1	13.8	5.0	•	25.6	•	•	•
Receivables Turnover 36	20.5	•	95.3	27.2	13.7	13.9	9.1	9.2	•	•	•	•	•
Total Liabilities to Net Worth 37	2.2	•	3.4	0.8	2.1	1.1	1.6	6.5	•	1.8	•	•	•
Current Assets to Working Capital 38	2.4	•	2.1	1.6	1.9	2.7	3.4	4.3	•	180.3	•	•	•
Current Liabilities to Working Capital 39	1.4	•	1.1	0.6	0.9	1.7	2.4	3.3	•	179.3	•	•	•
Working Capital to Net Sales 40	0.1	•	0.0	0.1	0.1	0.1	0.1	0.1	•	0.0	•	•	•
Inventory to Working Capital 41	0.4	•	0.2	0.2	0.1	0.6	0.2	0.4	•	4.5	•	•	•
Total Receipts to Cash Flow 42	3.7	2.6	3.4	4.1	3.4	5.4	4.0	4.3	•	6.2	•	•	•
Cost of Goods to Cash Flow 43	1.0	0.6	0.6	1.3	1.0	2.9	1.1	1.0	•	1.4	•	•	•
Cash Flow to Total Debt 44	0.6	•	1.6	1.1	0.7	1.0	0.5	0.3	•	0.2	•	•	•

Selected Financial Factors (in Percentages)

Debt Ratio 45	68.4	•	77.1	45.8	67.3	51.9	62.2	86.7	•	64.6	•	•	•
Return on Total Assets 46	15.4	•	43.6	19.1	12.8	18.9	11.1	9.8	•	7.2	•	•	•
Return on Equity Before Income Taxes 47	42.4	•	178.8	31.7	31.9	37.1	25.9	58.5	•	15.8	•	•	•
Return on Equity After Income Taxes 48	38.6	•	177.5	31.2	30.3	35.5	24.2	56.9	•	12.7	•	•	•
Profit Margin (Before Income Tax) 49	9.4	14.9	10.1	8.3	6.4	6.5	7.6	8.3	•	7.1	•	•	•
Profit Margin (After Income Tax) 50	8.5	14.6	10.0	8.2	6.1	6.2	7.1	8.0	•	5.7	•	•	•

Table I

Corporations with and without Net Income

RELIGIOUS, GRANTMAKING, CIVIC AND PROFESSIONAL ORGANIZATIONS

MONEY AMOUNTS AND SIZE OF ASSETS IN THOUSANDS OF DOLLARS

Item Description for Accounting Period 7/11 Through 6/12		Total	Zero Assets	Under 500	500 to 1,000	1,000 to 5,000	5,000 to 10,000	10,000 to 25,000	25,000 to 50,000	50,000 to 100,000	100,000 to 250,000	250,000 to 500,000	500,000 to 2,500,000	2,500,000 and over
Number of Enterprises	1	45808	5957	34133	3054	2354	184	94	18	12	•	•	0	•
Revenues ($ in Thousands)														
Net Sales	2	9379674	373748	3069159	1341162	2727974	384487	670788	294491	423780	•	•	0	•
Interest	3	73752	917	15743	10617	31536	4821	3660	2626	3038	•	•	0	•
Rents	4	33988	0	14882	1360	8666	782	383	0	2042	•	•	0	•
Royalties	5	28725	0	4580	1630	0	0	0	0	22350	•	•	0	•
Other Portfolio Income	6	115052	27206	57432	1067	12556	1678	12366	325	1940	•	•	0	•
Other Receipts	7	3102352	8046	972390	310522	329603	83491	186046	79796	40175	•	•	0	•
Total Receipts	8	12733543	409917	4134186	1666358	3110335	475259	873243	377238	493325	•	•	0	•
Average Total Receipts	9	278	69	121	546	1321	2583	9290	20958	41110	•	•	•	•
Operating Costs/Operating Income (%)														
Cost of Operations	10	17.3	8.6	9.7	20.3	16.4	15.7	32.0	5.9	52.7	•	•	•	•
Salaries and Wages	11	13.4	12.3	7.5	12.0	15.1	24.8	19.8	26.1	17.3	•	•	•	•
Taxes Paid	12	2.7	3.5	2.5	1.7	2.5	3.5	3.9	3.6	3.0	•	•	•	•
Interest Paid	13	0.9	0.5	1.0	0.5	0.4	2.4	1.7	2.8	0.6	•	•	•	•
Depreciation	14	2.4	1.6	1.3	1.2	1.8	7.9	6.2	5.4	3.7	•	•	•	•
Amortization and Depletion	15	0.3	0.9	0.0	0.1	0.0	0.1	0.0	2.3	1.1	•	•	•	•
Pensions and Other Deferred Comp.	16	0.2	•	0.1	0.1	0.1	0.7	0.2	0.2	1.1	•	•	•	•
Employee Benefits	17	2.0	1.1	0.8	1.5	2.2	3.6	5.0	2.7	1.9	•	•	•	•
Advertising	18	2.3	6.5	4.2	3.3	0.3	0.3	0.5	0.3	0.7	•	•	•	•
Other Expenses	19	91.2	65.2	103.5	84.8	73.6	59.4	51.4	74.4	24.6	•	•	•	•
Officers' Compensation	20	1.2	9.1	0.9	0.5	0.5	1.9	1.3	1.4	1.6	•	•	•	•
Operating Margin	21	•	•	•	•	•	•	•	•	•	•	•	•	•
Operating Margin Before Officers' Comp.	22	•	•	•	•	•	•	•	•	•	•	•	•	•

Selected Average Balance Sheet ($ in Thousands)													
Net Receivables 23	24	0	5	36	94	372	1187	6790	13896	•	•	•	•
Inventories 24	1	0	0	1	7	33	48	131	250	•	•	•	•
Net Property, Plant and Equipment 25	71	0	8	66	349	2750	9672	10832	17943	•	•	•	•
Total Assets 26	467	0	83	710	2002	6500	16765	37643	75779	•	•	•	•
Notes and Loans Payable 27	32	0	13	41	171	819	1683	4878	6232	•	•	•	•
All Other Liabilities 28	219	0	13	150	323	1088	4225	17585	23734	•	•	•	•
Net Worth 29	216	0	56	519	1507	4593	10857	15181	45813	•	•	•	•

Selected Financial Ratios (Times to 1)													
Current Ratio 30	2.0	•	4.8	6.5	5.7	2.8	1.7	1.2	1.5	•	•	•	•
Quick Ratio 31	1.3	•	4.5	6.1	5.4	2.3	1.3	0.9	1.3	•	•	•	•
Net Sales to Working Capital 32	1.4	•	1.6	0.9	1.0	1.1	3.7	4.6	4.1	•	•	•	•
Coverage Ratio 33	3.2	1.4	3.9	•	3.2	2.4	5.9	2.1	15.7	•	•	•	•
Total Asset Turnover 34	0.4	•	1.1	0.6	0.6	0.3	0.4	0.4	0.5	•	•	•	•
Inventory Turnover 35	40.7	•	153.0	96.3	28.4	10.0	47.6	7.4	74.4	•	•	•	•
Receivables Turnover 36	8.8	•	18.7	13.0	12.3	7.5	5.2	2.8	2.9	•	•	•	•
Total Liabilities to Net Worth 37	1.2	•	0.5	0.4	0.3	0.4	0.5	1.5	0.7	•	•	•	•
Current Assets to Working Capital 38	2.0	•	1.3	1.2	1.2	1.5	2.4	5.5	3.1	•	•	•	•
Current Liabilities to Working Capital 39	1.0	•	0.3	0.2	0.2	0.5	1.4	4.5	2.1	•	•	•	•
Working Capital to Net Sales 40	0.7	•	0.6	1.1	1.0	0.9	0.3	0.2	0.2	•	•	•	•
Inventory to Working Capital 41	0.0	•	0.0	0.0	0.0	0.0	0.0	0.0	0.0	•	•	•	•
Total Receipts to Cash Flow 42	1.3	1.9	1.2	1.5	1.5	1.8	2.0	1.4	3.5	•	•	•	•
Cost of Goods to Cash Flow 43	0.2	0.2	0.1	0.3	0.2	0.3	0.7	0.1	1.8	•	•	•	•
Cash Flow to Total Debt 44	0.6	•	2.8	1.5	1.6	0.6	0.6	0.5	0.3	•	•	•	•

Selected Financial Factors (in Percentages)													
Debt Ratio 45	53.7	•	31.8	27.0	24.7	29.3	35.2	59.7	39.5	•	•	•	•
Return on Total Assets 46	1.3	•	4.4	•	0.8	1.9	4.1	2.5	4.1	•	•	•	•
Return on Equity Before Income Taxes 47	1.9	•	4.8	•	0.7	1.6	5.3	3.2	6.3	•	•	•	•
Return on Equity After Income Taxes 48	1.3	•	3.8	•	0.5	0.8	4.7	2.5	3.8	•	•	•	•
Profit Margin (Before Income Tax) 49	2.0	0.2	3.0	•	1.0	3.4	8.1	3.0	8.1	•	•	•	•
Profit Margin (After Income Tax) 50	1.3	•	2.4	•	0.7	1.7	7.2	2.3	4.9	•	•	•	•

Table II

Corporations with Net Income

RELIGIOUS, GRANTMAKING, CIVIC AND PROFESSIONAL ORGANIZATIONS

Item Description for Accounting Period 7/11 Through 6/12		MONEY AMOUNTS AND SIZE OF ASSETS IN THOUSANDS OF DOLLARS												
		Total	Zero Assets	Under 500	500 to 1,000	1,000 to 5,000	5,000 to 10,000	10,000 to 25,000	25,000 to 50,000	50,000 to 100,000	100,000 to 250,000	250,000 to 500,000	500,000 to 2,500,000	2,500,000 and over
Number of Enterprises	1	20128	2202	14243	1825	1712	82	45	10	9	0	0	0	0
Revenues ($ in Thousands)														
Net Sales	2	5311254	256506	1335343	653386	1887105	242524	440228	154329	341833	0	0	0	0
Interest	3	57442	3	12723	8715	27376	3805	1709	1856	1256	0	0	0	0
Rents	4	13733	0	2097	641	8448	212	383	0	1951	0	0	0	0
Royalties	5	22349	0	0	0	0	0	0	0	22349	0	0	0	0
Other Portfolio Income	6	110721	27206	55910	1018	11860	1299	11288	325	1814	0	0	0	0
Other Receipts	7	1893049	240	420970	112233	194949	-260	112078	33202	1019639	0	0	0	0
Total Receipts	8	7408548	283955	1827043	775993	2129738	247580	565686	189712	1388842	0	0	0	0
Average Total Receipts	9	368	129	128	425	1244	3019	12571	18971	154316	•	•	•	•
Operating Costs/Operating Income (%)														
Cost of Operations	10	19.6	7.0	14.8	25.1	16.2	11.3	36.7	4.7	47.0	•	•	•	•
Salaries and Wages	11	11.2	10.6	6.7	8.2	10.8	20.2	15.9	25.1	19.1	•	•	•	•
Taxes Paid	12	2.4	3.9	2.9	1.0	1.7	2.6	3.5	3.0	3.5	•	•	•	•
Interest Paid	13	0.5	0.1	0.2	0.3	0.5	0.2	0.9	3.9	0.7	•	•	•	•
Depreciation	14	1.6	0.1	1.2	0.3	1.5	2.1	4.2	2.6	3.0	•	•	•	•
Amortization and Depletion	15	0.2	•	•	0.0	0.0	0.1	0.0	4.4	1.3	•	•	•	•
Pensions and Other Deferred Comp.	16	0.2	•	•	0.0	0.1	1.0	0.3	0.3	1.4	•	•	•	•
Employee Benefits	17	1.7	1.6	0.1	0.9	1.8	4.0	5.5	2.3	2.0	•	•	•	•
Advertising	18	0.9	9.5	1.0	0.0	0.4	0.2	0.3	0.2	0.8	•	•	•	•
Other Expenses	19	91.1	58.1	93.8	80.9	76.5	48.2	41.0	67.9	310.8	•	•	•	•
Officers' Compensation	20	1.2	11.1	0.0	0.0	0.6	3.0	1.8	1.2	1.8	•	•	•	•
Operating Margin	21	•	•	•	•	•	7.1	•	•	•	•	•	•	•
Operating Margin Before Officers' Comp.	22	•	9.2	•	•	•	10.1	•	•	•	•	•	•	•

Selected Average Balance Sheet ($ in Thousands)														
Net Receivables	23	37	0	6	16	81	499	2173	8409	29544	•	•	•	•
Inventories	24	1	0	0	0	6	45	59	83	174	•	•	•	•
Net Property, Plant and Equipment	25	64	0	8	43	276	610	7519	3634	21135	•	•	•	•
Total Assets	26	444	0	108	696	1953	6493	16736	40183	120966	•	•	•	•
Notes and Loans Payable	27	26	0	3	31	134	121	1484	4989	6869	•	•	•	•
All Other Liabilities	28	102	0	10	74	277	1531	4912	21923	81054	•	•	•	•
Net Worth	29	316	0	95	590	1542	4841	10340	13272	33043	•	•	•	•
Selected Financial Ratios (Times to 1)														
Current Ratio	30	3.6	•	9.4	8.6	5.6	3.1	2.6	1.3	1.0	•	•	•	•
Quick Ratio	31	3.2	•	9.0	8.3	5.4	2.7	1.9	0.9	0.6	•	•	•	•
Net Sales to Working Capital	32	1.1	•	1.1	0.7	1.0	1.0	2.2	2.7	•	•	•	•	•
Coverage Ratio	33	17.6	173.8	88.6	6.7	5.9	44.6	20.1	2.9	22.8	•	•	•	•
Total Asset Turnover	34	0.6	•	0.9	0.5	0.6	0.5	0.6	0.4	0.3	•	•	•	•
Inventory Turnover	35	47.5	•	174.6	3418.9	27.6	7.4	60.8	8.8	102.2	•	•	•	•
Receivables Turnover	36	7.2	•	16.4	20.1	14.6	8.6	3.7	2.0	•	•	•	•	•
Total Liabilities to Net Worth	37	0.4	•	0.1	0.2	0.3	0.3	0.6	2.0	2.7	•	•	•	•
Current Assets to Working Capital	38	1.4	•	1.1	1.1	1.2	1.5	1.6	4.6	•	•	•	•	•
Current Liabilities to Working Capital	39	0.4	•	0.1	0.1	0.2	0.5	0.6	3.6	•	•	•	•	•
Working Capital to Net Sales	40	0.9	•	0.9	1.5	1.0	1.0	0.5	0.4	•	•	•	•	•
Inventory to Working Capital	41	0.0	•	0.0	0.0	0.0	0.0	0.0	0.0	•	•	•	•	•
Total Receipts to Cash Flow	42	1.1	1.7	1.1	1.6	1.4	1.9	2.0	1.4	0.3	•	•	•	•
Cost of Goods to Cash Flow	43	0.2	0.1	0.2	0.4	0.2	0.2	0.7	0.1	0.1	•	•	•	•
Cash Flow to Total Debt	44	1.8	•	6.4	2.1	1.9	1.0	0.8	0.4	1.4	•	•	•	•
Selected Financial Factors (in Percentages)														
Debt Ratio	45	28.7	•	12.2	15.2	21.0	25.4	38.2	67.0	72.7	•	•	•	•
Return on Total Assets	46	5.5	•	14.1	1.2	1.7	4.3	11.1	4.3	4.9	•	•	•	•
Return on Equity Before Income Taxes	47	7.3	•	15.8	1.2	1.8	5.6	17.1	8.5	17.0	•	•	•	•
Return on Equity After Income Taxes	48	6.3	•	14.4	1.0	1.6	3.9	15.8	7.0	12.4	•	•	•	•
Profit Margin (Before Income Tax)	49	8.7	8.8	16.1	2.0	2.6	9.1	18.1	7.3	14.8	•	•	•	•
Profit Margin (After Income Tax)	50	7.6	8.3	14.6	1.7	2.2	6.4	16.7	6.0	10.8	•	•	•	•

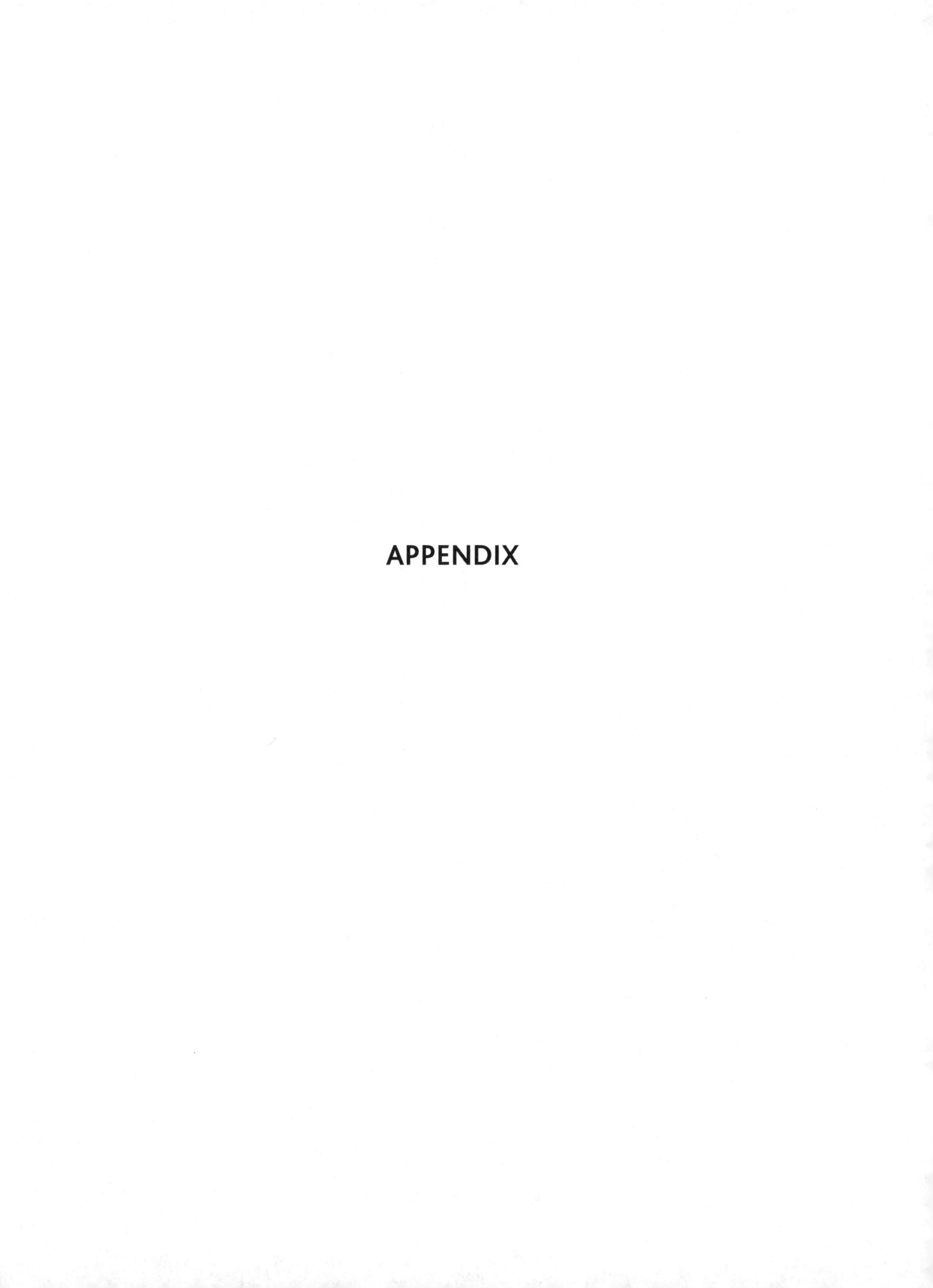

APPENDIX

APPENDIX

NAICS To Published Industry Codes

SOI Published Code	PBA Code	NAICS Code	Industry

AGRICULTURE, FORESTRY, FISHING AND HUNTING

Crop Production

SOI Published Code	PBA Code	NAICS Code	Industry
111005	**111100**		**Oilseed and Grain Farming**
		111150	Corn Farming
		111130	Dry Pea and Bean Farming
		111199	Grain Farming, NEC
		111120	Oilseed (except Soybean) Farming
		111191	Oilseed and Grain Comination Farming
		111160	Rice Farming
		111110	Soybean Farming
		111140	Wheat Farming
111005	**111210**		**Vegetable and Melon Farming**
		111211	Potato Farming
		111219	Vegetable (except Potato) and Melon Farming
111005	**111300**		**Fruit & Tree Nut Farming**
		111331	Apple Orchards
		111334	Berry (except Strawberry) Farming
		111320	Citrus (except Orange) Groves
		111336	Fruit and Nut Combination Farming
		111332	Grape Vineyards
		111310	Orange Groves
		111339	Other Noncitrus Fruit Farming
		111333	Strawberry Farming
		111335	Tree Nut Farming

SOI Published Code	PBA Code	NAICS Code	Industry
111005	**111400**		**Greenhouse, Nursery & Floriculture Production**
		111422	Floriculture Production
		111411	Mushroom Production
		111421	Nursery and Tree Production
		111419	Other Food Crops Grown Under Cover
111005	**111900**		**Other Crop Farming**
		111920	Cotton Farming
		111998	Crop Farming, NEC
		111940	Hay Farming
		111992	Peanut Farming
		111991	Sugar Beet Farming
		111930	Sugarcane Farming
		111910	Tobacco Farming
Animal Production			
111005	**112111**		**Beef Cattle Ranching and Farming**
111005	**112112**		**Cattle Feedlots**
111005	**112120**		**Dairy Cattle and Milk Production**
111005	**112210**		**Hog and Pig Farming**
111005	**112300**		**Poultry and Egg Production**
		112320	Broilers & Other Meat Type Chicken Production
		112310	Chicken Egg Production
		112340	Poultry Hatcheries
		112390	Poultry Production, NEC
		112330	Turkey Production

SOI Published Code	PBA Code	NAICS Code	Industry
111005	**112400**		**Sheep and Goat Farming**
		112420	Goat Farming
		112410	Sheep Farming
111005	**112510**		**Animal Aquaculture (including shellfish, finfish farms & hatcheries)**
		112511	Finfish Farming and Fish Hatcheries
		112519	Other Animal Aquaculture
		112512	Shellfish Farming
111005	**112900**		**Other Animal Production**
		112990	Animal Production, NEC
		112910	Apiculture
		112390	Fur-Bearing Animal and Rabbit Production
		112920	Horse and Other Equine Production (breeding horses)
Forestry and Logging			
113005	**113110**		**Timber Tract Operations**
113005	**113210**		**Forest Nuseries and Gathering of Forest Products**
113005	**113310**		**Logging**
Fishing and Trapping			
114005	**114110**		**Fishing**
		114111	Finfish Fishing
		114119	Marine Fishing, NEC
		114112	Shellfish Fishing

SOI Published Code	PBA Code	NAICS Code	Industry
114005	**114210**		**Hunting and Trapping**

Support Activities for Agricultre and Forestry

SOI Published Code	PBA Code	NAICS Code	Industry
114005	**115110**		**Support Activities for Crop Production**
		115111	Cotton Ginning
		115113	Crop Harvesting, Primarily by Machine
		115115	Garm Labor Contractors and Crew Leaders
		115116	Farm Management Services
		115114	Postharvest Crop Activities (except Cotton Ginning)
		115112	Soil Preparation, Planting and Cultivating
114005	**115210**		**Support Activities for Animal Production**
114005	**115310**		**Support Activities for Forestry**

MINING

Mining

SOI Published Code	PBA Code	NAICS Code	Industry
211110	**211110**		**Oil and Gas Extraction**
		211111	Crude Petroleum and Natural Gas Extraction
		211112	Natural Gas Liquid Extraction
212110	**212110**		**Coal Mining**
		212113	Anthracite Mining
		212112	Bituminous Coal Underground Mining
		212111	Bituminous Coal and Lignite Surface Mining
212200	**212200**		**Metal Ore Mining**
		212234	Copper Ore and Nickel Ore Mining
		212221	Gold Ore Mining

SOI Published Code	PBA Code	NAICS Code	Industry
		212210	Iron Ore Mining
		212231	Lead Ore and Zinc Ore Mining
		212299	Metal Ore Mining, NEC
		212222	Silver Ore Mining
		212291	Uranium-Radium-Vanadium Ore Mining
212315	**212310**		**Stone Mining and Quarrying**
		212313	Crushed and Broken Granite Mining and Quarrying
		212312	Crushed and Broken Limestone Mining and Quarrying
		212319	Crushed and Broken Stone Mining and Quarrying, NEC
		212311	Dimension Stone Mining and Quarrying
212315	**212320**		**Sand, Gravel, Clay & Ceramic & Refactory Minerals, Mining & Quarrying**
		212325	Clay and Ceramic and Refactory Minerals Mining
		212321	Construction Sand and Gravel Mining
		212322	Industrial Sand Mining
		212324	Kaolin and Ball Clay Mining
212315	**212390**		**Other Nonmetallic Mineral Mining and Quarrying**
		212399	Nonmetallic Mineral Mining, NEC
		212393	Other Chemical and Fertilizer Mineral Mining
		212392	Phosphate Rock Mining
		212391	Potash, Soda, and Borate Mineral Mining
213110	**213110**		**Support Activities for Mining**
		213111	Driling Oil and Gas Wells
		213113	Support Activities for Coal Mining
		213114	Support Activities for Metal Mining
		213115	Support Activities for Nonmetallic Minerals (except Fuels)
		213112	support Activities for Oil and Gas Operations

SOI Published Code	PBA Code	NAICS Code	Industry

UTILITIES

Utilities

SOI Published Code	PBA Code	NAICS Code	Industry
221100	**221100**		**Electric Power Generation, Transmission & Distribution**
		221121	Electric Bulk Power Transmission and Control
		221122	Electric Power Distribution
		221112	Fossil Fuel Electric Power Generation
		221111	Hydroelectric Power Generation
		221113	Nuclear Electric Power Generation
		221119	Other Electric Power Generation
221210	**221210**		**Natural Gas Distribution**
221300	**221300**		**Water, Sewage, & Other Systems**
		221320	Sewage Treatment Facilities
		221330	Steam and Air-Conditioning Supply
		221310	Water Supply and Irrigation Systems
221500	**221500**		**Combination Electric and Gas Services**

CONSTRUCTION

Construction

SOI Published Code	PBA Code	NAICS Code	Industry
236115	**236110**		**Residential Building Construction**
		236115	New Sinlge-Family Housing Construction (except Operative Builders)
		236116	New Multifamily Housing Construction (except Operative Builders)
		236117	New Housing Operative Builders
		236118	Residential Remodelers
236115	**236200**		**Nonresidential Building Construction**
		236210	Industrial Building Construction
		236220	Commerical and Industrial Building Contruction

SOI Published Code	PBA Code	NAICS Code	Industry
Heavy and Civil Engineering Construction			
237105	**237100**		**Utility System Construction**
		237110	Water and Sewer Line and Related Structure Construction
		237120	Oil and Gas Pipeline and Structures Construction
		237130	Power & Communication Line and Related Structure Construction
237210	**237210**		**Land Subdivision**
237105	**237310**		**Highway, Street, and Bridge Construction**
237105	**237990**		**Other Heavy and Civil Engineering Construction**
Specialty Trade Contractors			
238905	**238100**		**Foundation, Structure & Building Exterior Contractors (including framing, carpentry, masonry, glass, roofing, and siding)**
		238110	Poured Concrete Foundation and Structure Contractors
		238120	Structural Steel and Precast Concrete Contractors
		238130	Framing Contractors
		238140	Masonry Contractors
		238150	Glass and Glazing Contractors
		238160	Roofing Contractors
		238170	Siding Contractors
		238190	Other Foundation, Structure, and Building Exterior Contractors
238210	**238210**		**Electrical Contractors**
238220	**238220**		**Plumbing, Heating, and Air-Conditioning Contractors**
238905	**238290**		**Other Building Equipment Contractors**

SOI Published Code	PBA Code	NAICS Code	Industry
238905	**238300**		**Building Finishing Contractors (including drywall, insulation, paiting, wallcovering, flooring, tile and finish carpentry)**
		238310	Drywall and Insulation Contractors
		238320	Painting and Wall Covering Contractors
		238330	Floor Contractors
		238340	Tile and Terrazzo Contractors
		238350	Finish Carpentry Contractors
		238390	Other Building Finishing Contractors
238905	**238900**		**Other Specialty Trade Contractors (including site preparation)**
		238910	Site Preparation Contractors
		238990	All Other Specialty Trade Contractors

MANUFACTURING

Food Manufacturing

SOI Published Code	PBA Code	NAICS Code	Industry
311115	**311110**		**Animal Food Manufacturing**
		311111	Dog and Cat Food Manufacturing
		311119	Other Animal Food Manufacturing
311115	**311200**		**Grain and Oilseed Milling**
		311230	Breakfast Cereal Manufacturing
		311225	Fats and Oils Refining and Blending
		311211	Flour Milling
		311213	Malt Manufacturing
		311212	Rice Milling
		311222	Soybean Processing
		311221	West Corn Milling
311300	**311300**		**Sugar & Confectionery Product Manufacturing**
		311313	Beet Sugar Manufacturing
		311312	Cane Sugar Refining

SOI Published Code	PBA Code	NAICS Code	Industry
		311320	Chocolate and Confectionery Manufacturing from Cacao Beans
		311330	Confectionery Manufacturing from Purchased Chocolate
		311340	Noncholocate Confectionary Manufacturing
		311311	Sugarcane Mills
311400	**311400**		**Fruit & Vegetable Preserving & Specialty Food Manufacturing**
		311423	Dried and Dehydrated Food Manufacturing
		311411	Frozen Fruit, Juice and Vegetable Manufacturing
		311412	Frozen Specialty Food Manufacturing
		311421	Fruit and Vegetable Canning
		311422	Specialty Canning
311500	**311500**		**Dairy Product Manufacturing**
		311513	Cheese Manufacturing
		311512	Creamery Butter Manufacturing
		311514	Dry, Condensed, and Evaporated Dairy Product Manufacturing
		311511	Fluid Milk Manufacturing
		311520	Ice Cream and Frozen Dessert Manufacturing
311615	**311610**		**Animal Slaughtering & Processing**
		311611	Animal (except Poultry) Slaughtering
		311612	Meat Processed for Carcasses
		311615	Poultry Processing
		311613	Rendering and Meat Byproduct Processing
311615	**311710**		**Seafood Product Preparation & Packaging**
		311712	Fresh and Frozen Seafood Processing
		311711	Seafood Canning
311800	**311800**		**Bakeries & Tortilla Manufacturing**
		311812	Commerical Bakeries

SOI Published Code	PBA Code	NAICS Code	Industry
		311821	Cookie and Cracker Manufacturing
		311823	Dry Pasta Manufacturing
		311822	Flour Mixes and Dough Manufacturing from Purchased Flour
		311813	Frozen Cakes, Pies, and other Pastries Manufacturing
		311811	Retail Bakeries
		311830	Toritilla Manufacturing
311900	**311900**		**Other Food Manufacturing (including coffee, tea, flavorings & seasonings)**
		311920	Coffee and Tea Manufacturing
		311930	Flavoring Syrup and Concentrate Manufacturing
		311999	Flood Manufacturing, NEC
		311941	Mayonnaise, Dressing and Other Prepared Sauce Manufacturing
		311919	Other Snack Food Manufacturing
		311991	Perishable Prepared Food Manufacturing
		311911	Roasted Nuts and Peanut Butter Manufacturing
		311942	Spice and Extract Manufacturing
Beverage & Tobacco Product Manufacturing			
312110	**312110**		**Soft Drink & Ice Manufacturing**
		312112	Bottled Water Manufacturing
		312113	Ice Manufacuring
		312111	Soft Drink Manufacturing
312120	**312120**		**Breweries**
312135	**312130**		**Wineries**
312135	**312140**		**Distilleries**

SOI PUBLISHED CODE	PBA CODE	NAICS CODE	INDUSTRY
312200	**312200**		**Tobacco Manufacturing**
		312221	Cigarette Manufacturing
		312229	Tobacco Product Manufacturing, NEC
		312210	Tobacco Stemming and Redrying

Textile Mills & Textile Product Mills

SOI PUBLISHED CODE	PBA CODE	NAICS CODE	INDUSTRY
313000	**313000**		**Textile Mills**
		313311	Broadwoven Fabric Finishing Mills
		313210	Broadwoven Fabric Mills
		313320	Fabric Coating Mills
		313221	Narrow Fabric Mills
		313230	Nonwoven Fabric Mills
		313249	Other Knit Fabric and Lace Mills
		313222	Schiffli Machine Embroidery
		313312	Textile and Fabric Finishing (except Broadwoven Fabric) Mills
		313113	Thread Mills
		313241	Weft Knit Fabric Mills
		313111	Yarn Spinning Mills
		313112	Yarn Texturing, Throwing, and Twisting Mills
314000	**314000**		**Textile Product Mills**
		314912	Canvas and Related Product Mills
		314110	Carpet and Rug Mills
		314121	Curtain and Drapery Mills
		314129	Other Household Textile Product Mills
		314991	Rope, Cordage, and Twine Mills
		314911	Textile Bag Mills
		314999	Textile Product Mills, NEC
		314992	Tire Cord and Tire Fabric Mills

SOI Published Code	PBA Code	NAICS Code	Industry
Apparel Manufacturing			
315100	**315100**		**Apparel Knitting Mills**
		315119	Other Hosiery and Sock Mills
		315191	Outerwear Knitting Mills
		315111	Sheer Hosiery Mills
		315192	Underwear and Nightwear Knitting Mills
315215	**315210**		**Cut and Sew Apparel Contractors**
		315211	Men's and Boy's Cut and Sew Apparel Contractors
		315212	Women's, Girls and Infants Cuts and Sew Apparel Contractors
315215	**315220**		**Men's and Boy's Cut and Sew Apparel Manufacturing**
		315228	Men's and Boys' Cut and Sew Other Outerwear Manufacturing
		315223	Men's and Boys' Cut and Sew Shirt (except Work Shirt) Manufacturing
		315222	Men's and Boys' Cut and Sew Suit, Coat, and Overcoat Manufacturing
		315224	Men's and Boys' Cut and Sew Trouser, Slack and Jean Manufacturing
		315221	Men's and Boys' Cut and Sew Underwear and Nightware
		315225	Men's and Boys' Cut and Sew Work Clothing Manufacturing
315215	**315230**		**Women's and Girls' Cut and Sew Apparel Manufacturing**
		315232	Women's and Girls' Cut and Sew Blouse and Shirt Manufacturing
		315233	Women's and Girls' Cut and Sew Dress Manufacturing
		315231	Women's and Girls' Cut and Sew Lingerie, Loungwear, & Nightgown Manufacturing
		315239	Women's and Girls' Cut and Sew Other Outerwear Manufacturing
		315234	Women's and Girls' Cut and Sew Suit, Coat, Tailored Jackt and Skirt Manufacturing
315215	**315290**		**Other Cut and Sew Apparel**
		315299	All Other Cut and Sew Apparel Manufacturing
		315292	Fur and Leather Apparel Manufacturing
		315291	Infants' Cut and Sew Apparel Manufacturing

SOI Published Code	PBA Code	NAICS Code	Industry
315990	**315990**		**Apparel Accessories and Other Apparel Manufacturing**
		315992	Glove and Mitten Manufacturing
		315991	Hat, Cap, and Millinery Manufacturing
		315993	Men's and Boy's Neckwear Manufacturing
		315999	Other Apparel Accessories and Other Apparel Manufacturing
Leather and Allied Products Manufacturing			
316115	**316110**		**Leather and Hide Tanning and Finishing**
316115	**316210**		**Footwear Manufacturing (including Rubber and Plastics)**
		316212	House Slipper Manufacturing
		316213	Men's Footwear (except Athletic) Manufacturing
		316219	Other Footwear Manufacturing
		316211	Rubber and Plastics Footwear Manufacturing
		316214	Women's Footwear (except Athletic) Manufacturing
316115	**316990**		**Other Leather & Allied Product Manufacturing**
		316999	Leather Good Manufacturing, NEC
		316991	Luggage Manufacturing
		316993	Personal Leather Good (except Women's Handbag and Purse) Manufacturing
		316992	Women's Handbag and Purse Manufacturing
Wood Product Manufacturing			
321115	**321110**		**Sawmills and Wood Preservation**
		321113	Sawmills
		321114	Wood Preservation
32115	**321210**		**Veneer, Plywood & Engineered Wood Product Manufacturing**
		321213	Engineered Wood Member (except Truss) Manufacturing
		321211	Hardwood Veneer and Plywood Manufacturing
		321219	Reconstituted Wood Product Manufacturing

SOI Published Code	PBA Code	NAICS Code	Industry
		321212	Softwood Veneer and Plywood Manufacturing
		321214	Truss Manufacturing
321115	**321900**		**Other Wood Product Manufacturing**
		321999	All Other Miscellaneous Wood Product Manufacturing
		321912	Cut Stock, Resawing Lumber, and Planing
		321991	Manufactured Home (Mobile Home) Manufacturing
		321918	Other Millwork (including Flooring)
		321992	Prefabricated Wood Building Manufacturing
		321920	Wood Container and Pallet Manufacturing
		321911	Wood Window and Door Manufacturing
Paper Manufacturing			
322100	**322100**		**Pulp, Paper and Paperboard Mills**
		322122	Newsprint Mills
		322121	Paper (except Newsprint) Mills
		322130	Paperboard Mills
		322110	Pulp Mills
322200	**322200**		**Converted Paper Product Manufacturing**
		322299	All Other Converted Paper Product Manufacturing
		322221	Coated and Laminated Packaging Paper and Plastics Film Manufacturing
		322222	Coated and Laminated Paper Manufacturing
		322211	Corrugated and Solid Fiber Box Manufacturing
		322231	Die-Cut Paper and Paperboard Office Supplies Manufacturing
		322232	Envelope Manufacturing
		322214	Fiber Can, Tube, Drum, and Similar Products Manufacturing
		322212	Folding Paperboard Box Manufacturing
		322225	Laminated Aluminum Foil Manufacturing for Felxible Pacakaging Uses
		322215	Nonfolding Sanitary Food Container Manufacturing
		322223	Plastics, Foil and Coated Paper Bag Manufacturing
		322291	Sanitary Paper Product Manufacturing
		322213	Setup Paperboard Box Manufacturing

SOI Published Code	PBA Code	NAICS Code	Industry
		322233	Satationery, Tablet, and Related Product Manufacturing
		322226	Surface-Coated Paperboard Manufacturing
		322224	Uncoated Paper and Multiwall Bag Manufacturing
Printing and Related Support Activites			
323100	**323100**		**Printing and Related Support Activites**
		323118	Blankbood, Looseleaf Binders, and Devices Manufacturing
		323117	Books Printing
		323112	Commerical Flexographic Printing
		323111	Commerical Gravure Printing
		323110	Commercial Lithographic Printing
		323113	Commerical Screen Printing
		323115	Digital Printing
		323116	Manifold Business Forms Printing
		323119	Other Commerical Printing
		323122	Prepress Services
		323114	Quick Printing
		323121	Tradebinding and Related Work
Petroleum and Coal Products Manufacturing			
324110	**324110**		**Petroleum Refineries (including Integrated)**
324115	**324120**		**Asphalt Paving, Roofing & Saturated Materials Manufacturing**
		324121	Asphalt Paving, Mixture and Block Manufacturing
		324122	Asphalt Shingle and Coating Materials Manufacturing
324125	**324190**		**Other Petroleum and Coal Products**
		324199	All Other Petroleum and Coal Products Manufacturing
		324191	Petroleum Lubricating Oil and Grease Manufacturing

SOI Published Code	PBA Code	NAICS Code	Industry
Chemical Manufacturing			
325100	**325100**		**Basic Chemical Manufacturing**
		325181	Alkalies and Chlorine Manufacturing
		325188	All Other Basic Inorganic Chemical Manufacturing
		325199	All Other Basic Organic Chemical Manufacturing
		325182	Carbon Black Manufacturing
		325192	Cyclic Crude and Intermediate Manufacturing
		325193	Ethyl Alcohol Manufacturing
		325191	Gum and Wood Chemical Manufacturing
		325120	Industrial Gas Manufacturing
		325131	Inorganic Dye and Pigment Manufacturing
		325110	Petrochemical Manufacturing
		325132	Synthetic Organic Dye and Pigment Manufacturing
325200	**325200**		**Resin, Synthetic Rubber & Artificial & Synthetic Fibers & Filaments Manufacturing**
		325221	Cellulosic Organic Fiber Manufacturing
		325222	Noncellulosic Organic Fiber Manufacturing
		325211	Plastics Material and Resin Manufacturing
		325212	Synthetic Rubber Manufacturing
325905	**325300**		**Pesticide, Fertilizer, & Other Agricultural Chemical Manufacturing**
		325314	Fertilizer (Mixing Only) Manufacturing
		325311	Nitrogenous Fetilizer Manufacturing
		325320	Pesticide and Other Agricultural Chemical Manufacturing
		325312	Phosphatic Fertilizer Manufacturing
325410	**325410**		**Pharmaceutical & Medicine Manufacturing**
		325414	Biological Product (except Diagnostic) Manufacturing
		325413	In-Vitro Diagnostic Sustance Manufacturing
		325411	Medicinal and Botanical Manufacturing
		325412	Pharmaceutical Preparation Manufacturing

SOI Published Code	PBA Code	NAICS Code	Industry
325500	**325500**		**Paint, Coating and Adhesive Manufacturing**
		325520	Adhesive Manufacturing
		325510	Paint and Coating Manufacturing
325600	**325600**		**Soap, Cleaning Compound & Toilet Preparation Manufacturing**
		325612	Polish and Other Sanitation Good Manufacturing
		325611	Soap and Other Detergent Manufacturing
		325613	Surface Active Agent Manufacturing
		325620	Toilet Preparation Manufacturing
325905	**325900**		**Other Chemical Products & Preparation Manufacturing**
		325998	Chemical Product and Preparation Manufacturing, NEC
		325991	Custom Compounding of Purchased Resins
		325920	Explosives Manufacturing
		325992	Photographic Film, Paper, Plate, and Chemical Manufacturing
		325910	Printing Ink Manufacturing
Plastics and Rubber Products Manufacturing			
326100	**326100**		**Plastics Product Manufacturing**
		326130	Laminated Plastics Plate, Sheet and Shape Manufacturing
		326160	Plastics Bottle Manufacturing
		326122	Plastics Pipe and Pipe Fitting Manufacturing
		326191	Plastics Plumbing Fixture Manufacturing
		326199	Plastics Product Manufacturing, NEC
		326140	Polystyrene Foam Product Manufacturing
		326192	Resilient Floor Covering Manufacturing
		326111	Unsupported Plastics Bag Manufacturing
		326113	Unsupported Plastics Film and Sheet (except Packaging) Manufacturing
		326112	Unsupported Plastics Packaging Film and Sheet Manufacturing
		326121	Unsupported Plastics Profile Shape Manufacturing
		326150	Urethane and Other Foam Product (except Polystyrene) Manufacturing

SOI Published Code	PBA Code	NAICS Code	Industry
326200	**326200**		**Rubber Product Manufacturing**
		326299	All Other Rubber Product Manufacturing
		326291	Rubber Product Manufacturing for Mechanical Use
		326220	Rubber and Plastics Hoses and Belting Manufacturing
		326211	Tire Manufacturing (except Retreading)
		326212	Tire Retreading

Nonmetallic Mineral Product Manufacturing

SOI Published Code	PBA Code	NAICS Code	Industry
327105	**327100**		**Clay Product & Refactory Manufacturing**
		327121	Brick and Structural Clay Tile Manufacturing
		327122	Ceramic Wall and Floor Tile Manufacturing
		327124	Clay Refactory Manufacturing
		327125	Nonclay Refactory Manufacturing
		327123	Other Structual Clay Product Manufacturing
		327113	Porcelain Electrical Supply Manufacturing
		327111	Vitreous China Plumbing Fixture and China and Earthenware Bathroom Accessories Manufacturing
		321112	Vitreous China, Fine Earthenware, and Other Pottery Product Manufacturing
327210	**327210**		**Glass and Glass Product Manufacturing**
		327211	Flat Glass Manufacturing
		327213	Glass Container Manufacturing
		327215	Glass Product Manufactuing Made of Purchased Glass
		327212	Other Pressed and Blown Glass and Glassware Manufacturing
327305	**327300**		**Cement and Concrete Products Manufacturing**
		327310	Cement Manufacturing
		328331	Concrete Block and Brick Manufacturing
		327332	Concrete Pipe Manufacturing
		327390	Other Concrete Product Manufacturing
		327320	Ready-Mix Concrete Manufacturing

SOI Published Code	PBA Code	NAICS Code	Industry
327305	**327400**		**Lime & Gypsum Product Manufacturing**
		327420	Gypsum Product Manufacturing
		327410	Lime Manufacturing
327105	**327900**		**Other Nonmetallic Mineral Product Manufacturing**
		327910	Abrasive Product Manufacturing
		327991	Cut Stone and Stone Product Manufacturing
		327992	Ground or Treated Mineral and Earth Manufacturing
		327993	Mineral Wood Manufacturing
		327999	Nonmetallic Mineral Product Manufacturing, NEC
Primary Metal Manufacturing			
331115	**331110**		**Iron and Steel Mills and Ferroalloy Manufacturing**
		331112	Electometallurgical Ferroalloy Product Manufacturing
		331111	Iron and Steel Mills
331115	**331200**		**Steel Product Manufacturing from Purchased Steel**
		331210	Iron and Steel Pipe Tube Manufacturing from Purchased Steel
		331221	Rolled Steel Shape Manufacturing
		331222	Steel Wire Drawing
331315	**331310**		**Alumina & Aluminum Production and Processing**
		331311	Alumina Refining
		331316	Aluminum Extruded Product Manufacturing
		331315	Aluminum Sheet, Plate, and Foil Manufacturing
		331319	Other Aluminum Rolling and Drawing
		331312	Primary Aluminum Production
		331314	Secondary Smelting and Alloying of Aluminum

SOI Published Code	PBA Code	NAICS Code	Industry
331315	**331400**		**Nonferrous Metal (except Aluminum) Production and Processing**
		331421	Copper Rolling, Drawing and Extruding
		331422	Copper Wire (except Mechanical) Drawing
		331491	Nonferrous Metal (except Copper and Aluminum) Rolling, Drawing Extrudinga and Alloying
		331411	Primary Smelting and Refining of Copper
		331419	Primary Smelting and Refining of Nonferrous Metal (except Copper and Aluminum)
		331423	Secondary Smelting and Refining, and Alloying of Copper
		331492	Secondary Smelting and Refining, and Alloying of Nonferrous Metal (except copper and aluminum)
331500	**331500**		**Foundries**
		331521	Aluminum Die-Casting Foundries
		331524	Aluminum Foundries (except Die-Casting)
		331525	Copper Foundries (except Die-Casting)
		331511	Iron Foundries
		331522	Nonferrous (except Aluminum) Die-Casting Foundries
		331528	Other Nonferrous Foundries (except Die-Casting)
		331513	Steel Foundries (except Investment)
		331512	Steel Investment Foundries
Fabricated Metal Product Manufacturing			
332110	**332110**		**Forging and Stamping**
		332115	Crown and Closure Manufacturing
		332114	Custom Roll Forming
		332111	Iron and Steel Forging
		332116	Metal Stamping
		332112	Nonferrous Forging
		332117	Powder Metallurgy Part Manufacturing
332215	**332210**		**Cutlery and Handtool Manufacturing**
		332211	Cutlery and Flatware (except Precious) Manufacturing

SOI Published Code	PBA Code	NAICS Code	Industry
		332212	Hand and Edge Tool Manufacturing
		332214	Kitchen Utensil, Pot and Pan Manufacturing
		332213	Saw Blade and Handsaw Manufacturing
332300	**332300**		**Architectural and Structural Metals Manufacturing**
		332312	Fabricated Structural Metal Manufacturing
		332321	Metal Window and Door Manufacturing
		332323	Ornamental and Architectural Metal Work Manufacturing
		332313	Plate Work Manufacturing
		332311	Prefabricated Metal Building and Component Manufacturing
		332322	Sheet Metal Work Manufacturing
332400	**332400**		**Boiler, Tank and Shipping Container Manufacturing**
		332431	Metal Can Manufacturing
		332420	Metal Tank (Heavy Gauge) Manufacturing
		332439	Other Metal Container Manufacturing
		332410	Power Boiler and Heat Exchanger Manufacturing
332215	**332510**		**Hardware Manufacturing**
332215	**332610**		**Spring and Wire Product Manufacturing**
		332618	Other Fabricated Wire Product Manufacturing
		332611	Spring (Heavy Gauge) Manufacturing
		332612	Spring (Light Gauge) Manufacturing
332215	**332700**		**Machine Shops, Turned Product, and Sew, Nut and Bold Manufacturing**
		332722	Bolt, Nut, Screw, Rivet and Washer Manufacturing
		332710	Machine Shops
		332721	Precision Turned Product Manufacturing

SOI Published Code	PBA Code	NAICS Code	Industry
332810	**332810**		**Coating, Engraving, Heat Treating and Allied Activites**
		332813	Electoplating, Plating, Polishing, Anodizing and Coloring
		332812	Metal Coating, Engraving (except Jewelry and Silverware), and Allied Services to Manufacturers
		332811	Metal Head Treating
332900	**332900**		**Other Fabricated Metal Product Manufacturing**
		332999	All Other Miscellaneous Fabricated Metal Product Manufacturing
		332993	Ammunition (except Small Arms) Manufacturing
		332991	Ball and Roller Bearing Manufacturing
		332998	Enameled Iron and Metal Sanitary Ware Manufacturing
		332996	Fabricated Pipe and Pipe Fitting Manufacturing
		332912	Fluid Power Valve and Hose Fitting Manufacturing
		332997	Industrial Pattern Manufacturing
		332911	Industrial Valve Manufacturing
		332919	Other Metal Valve and Pipe Fitting Manufacturing
		332995	Other Ordnance and Accessories Manufacturing
		332913	Plumbing Fixture Fitting and Trim Manufacturing
		332992	Small Arms Ammunition Manufacturing
		332994	Small Arms Manufacturing
Machinery Manufacturing			
333100	**333100**		**Agriculture, Construction and Mining Machinery Manufacturing**
		333120	Construction Machinery Manufacturing
		333111	Farm Machinery and Equipmetn Manufacturing
		333112	Lawn and Garden Tractor and Home Lawn and Garden Equipment Manufacturing
		333131	Mining Machinery and Equipment Manufacturing
		333132	Oil and Gas Field Machinery and Equipment Manufacturing
333200	**333200**		**Industrial Machinery Manufacturing**
		333298	All Other Industrial Machinery Manufacturing
		333294	Food Product Machinery Manufacturing

SOI Published Code	PBA Code	NAICS Code	Industry
		333291	Paper Industry Machinery Manufacturing
		333220	Plastics and Rubber Industry Machinery Manufacturing
		333293	Printing Machinery and Equipment Manufacturing
		333210	Sawmill and Woodworking Machinery Manufacturing
		333295	Semiconductor Machinery Manufacturing
		333292	Textile Machinery Manufacturing
333310	**333310**		**Commerical and Service Industry Machinery Manufacturing**
		333311	Automatic Vending Machine Manufacturing
		333312	Commerical Laundry, Drycleaning, and Pressing Machine Manufacturing
		333313	Office Machinery Manufacturing
		333314	Optical Instrument and Lens Manufacturing
		333319	Other Commerical and Service Industry Machinery Manufacturing
		333315	Photographic and Photocopying Equipment Manufacturing
333410	**333410**		**Ventilation, Heating, Air Conditioning, and Commerical Refrigeration Equipment Manufacturing**
		333411	Air Purification Equipment Manufacturing
		333415	Air-Conditiong and warm Air Heating Equipment and Commerical Industrial Refrigeration Equipment Manufacturing
		333414	Heating Equipment (except Warm Air Furnaces) Manufacturing
		333412	Industrial and Commerical Fan and Blower Manufacturing
333510	**333510**		**Metalworking Machinery Manufacturing**
		333511	Industrial Mold Manufacturing
		333512	Machine Tool (Metal Cutting Types) Manufacturing
		333513	Machine Tool (Metal Forming Types) Manufacturing
		333518	Other Metalworking Machinery Manufacturing
		333516	Rolling Mill Machinery and Equipment Manufacturing
		333514	Special Die and Tool, Die Set, Jig and Fixture Manufacturing
		333515	Cutting Tool and Machine Tool Accessory Manufacturing

SOI Published Code	PBA Code	NAICS Code	Industry
333610	**333610**		**Engine, Turbine and Power Transmission Equipment Manufacturing**
		333613	Mechanical Power Transmission Equipment Manufacturing
		333618	Other Engine Equipment Manufacturing
		333612	Speed Changer, Industrial High-Speed Drive, and Gear Manufacturing
		333611	Turbine and Turbine Generator Set Units Manufacturing
333900	**333900**		**Other General Purpose Machinery Manufacturing**
		333912	Air and Gas Compressor Manufacturing
		333999	All Other Miscellaneous General Purpose Machinery Manufacturing
		333922	Conveyor and Conveying Equipment Manufacturing
		333921	Elevator and Moving Stairway Manufacturing
		333995	Fluid Power Cylinder and Actuator Manufacturing
		333996	Fluid Power Pump and Motor Manufacturing
		333994	Industrial Process Furnace and Oven Manufacturing
		333924	Industrial Truck, Tractor, Trailer and Stacker Machinery Manufacturing
		333913	Measuring and Dispensing Pump Manufacturing
		333923	Overhead Traveling Crane, Hoist, and Monorail System Maufacturing
		333993	Packaging Machinery Manufacturing
		333991	Power-Driven Handtool Manufacturing
		333911	Pump and Pumping Equipment Manufacturing
		333997	Scale and Balance (except Laboratory) Manufacturing
		333992	Welding and Soldering Equipment Manufacturing
Computer & Electronic Product Manufacturing			
334110	**334110**		**Computer and Periphery Equipment Manufacturing**
		334112	Computer Storage Device Manufacturing
		334113	Computer Terminal Manufacturing
		334111	Electronic Computer Manufacturing
		334119	Other Computer Peripheral Equipmemt Manufacturing
334200	**334200**		**Communications Equipment Manufacturing**
		334290	Communcations Equipment Manufacturing, NEC

SOI Published Code	PBA Code	NAICS Code	Industry
		334220	Radio and Television Broadcasting and Wireless Communication Equipment Manufacturing
		334210	Telephone Apparatus Manufacturing
334315	**334310**		**Audio and Visual Equipment Manufacturing**
334410	**334410**		**Semiconductor & Other Electronic Components Manufacturing**
		334412	Bare Printed Circuit Board Manufacturing
		334411	Electorn Tube Manufacturing
		334414	Electronic Capacitor Manufacturing
		334416	Electronic Coil, Transformer, and Other Inductor Manufacturing
		334417	Electronic Connector Manufacturing
		334415	Electronic Resistor Manufacturing
		334419	Other Electric Component Manufacturing
		334418	Printed Circuit Assembly (Electronic Aseembly) Manufacturing
		334413	Semiconductor and Related Device Manufacturing
334500	**334500**		**Navigational, Measuring, Electromedical & Control Instruments Manufacturing**
		334516	Analytical Laboratory Instrument Manufacturing
		334512	Automatic Enviromental Control Manufacturing for Residential, Commerical and Appliance Use
		334510	Electromedical and Electrotherapeutic Apparatus Manufacturing
		334515	Instrument Manufacturing for Measuring and Testing Electricity and Electrical Signals
		334513	Instruments and Related Prodcuts Manufacturing for Measuring, Displaying and Controlling Industrial Process Variables
		334517	Irradiation Apparatus Manufacturing
		334519	Other Measuring and Controlling Device Manufacturing
		334511	Search, Detection, Navigationk Guidance, Aeronautical, and Nautical System and Instrument Manufacturing
		334514	Totalizing Fluid Meter and Counting Device Manufacturing
		334518	Watch, Clock and Part Manufacturing

SOI Published Code	PBA Code	NAICS Code	Industry
334315	**334610**		**Manufactuing and Reproducing Magnetic and Optical Media**
		334613	Magnetic and Optical Recording Media Manufacturing
		334612	Prerecorded Compact Disc (except Software) Tape, and Record Reproduction
		334611	Software Reproducing

Electrical Equipment, Appliance and Component Manufacturing

SOI Published Code	PBA Code	NAICS Code	Industry
335105	**335100**		**Electical Lighting Equipment Manufacturing**
		335122	Commercial, Industrial, and Institutional Electric Lighting Fixture Manufacturing
		335110	Electric Lamp Bulb and Part Manufacturing
		335129	Other Lighting Equipment Manufacturing
		335121	Residential Electric Lighting Fixture Manufacturing
335105	**335200**		**Household Appliance Manufacturing**
		335211	Electric Housewares and Household Fan Manufacturing
		335221	Household Cooking Appliance Manufacturing
		335224	Household Laundry Equipment Manufacturing
		335222	Household Refrigerator and Home Freezer Manufacturing
		335212	Household Vacuum Cleaner Manufacturing
		335228	Other Major Household Appliance Manufacturing
335310	**335310**		**Electrical Equipment Manufacturing**
		335312	Motor and Genrator Manufacturing
		335311	Power, Distribution, and Specialty Transformer Manufacturing
		335314	Relay and Industrial Control Manufacturing
		335313	Switchgear and Switchboard Apparatus Manufacturing
335900	**335900**		**Other Electrical Equipment and Component Manufacturing**
		335991	Carbon and Graphite Product Manufacturing
		335931	Current-Carrying Wiring Device Manufacturing
		335999	All Other Miscellaneous Electrical Equipment and Component Manufacturing

SOI Published Code	PBA Code	NAICS Code	Industry
		335921	Fiber Optic Cable Manufacturing
		335932	Noncurrent-Carrying Wiring Device Manufacturing
		335929	Other Communication and Energy Wire Manufacturing
		335912	Primary Battery Manufacturing
		335911	Storage Battery Manufacturing
Transportation Equipment Manufacturing			
336105	**336100**		**Motor Vehicle Manufacturing**
		336111	Automobile Manufacturing
		336120	Heavy Duty Truck Manufacturing
		336112	Light Truck and Utility Vehicle Manufacturing
336105	**336210**		**Motor Vehicle Body and Trailer Manufacturing**
		336213	Motor Home Manufacturing
		336211	Motor Vehicle Body Manufacturing
		336214	Travel Trailer and Camper Manufacturing
		336212	Truck Trailer Manufacturing
336105	**336300**		**Motor Vehicle Parts Manufacturing**
		336399	All Other Motor Vehicle Parts Manufacturing
		336311	Carburetor, Piston, Piston Ring and Valve Manufacturing
		336312	Gasoline Engine and Engine Parts Manufacturing
		336391	Motor Vehicle Air-Conditioning Manufacturing
		336340	Motor Vehicle Brake System Manufacturing
		336370	Motor Vehicle Metal Stamping
		336360	Motor Vehicle Seating and Interior Trim Manufacturing
		336330	Motor Vehicle Steering and Suspension Component (except Spring) Manufacturing
		336350	Motor Vehicle Transmission and Power Train Parts Manufacturing
		336322	Other Motor Vehicle Electrical and Electronic Equipment Manufacturing
		336321	Vehicular Lighting Equipment Manufacturing

SOI Published Code	PBA Code	NAICS Code	Industry
336410	**336410**		**Aerospace Product and Parts Manufacturing**
		336412	Aircraft Engine and Engine Parts Manufacturing
		336411	Aircraft Manufacturing
		336414	Guided Missile and Space Vehicle Manufacturing
		336415	Guided Missile and Space Vehicle Propulsion Unit and Propulsion Unit Parts Manufacturing
		336413	Other Aircraft Parts and Auxillary Equipment Manufacturing
		336419	Other Guided Missile and Space Vehicle Parts and Auxillary Equipment Manufacturing
336995	**336510**		**Railroad Rolling Stock Manufacturing**
336610	**336610**		**Ship and Boat Building**
		336612	Boat Building
		336611	Ship Building and Repairing
336995	**336990**		**Other Transportation Equipment Manufacturing**
		336992	Military Armored Vehicle, Tank and Tank Component Manufacturing
		336991	Motorcycle, Bicycle and Parts Manufacturing
		336999	Transportation Equipment Manufacturing, NEC
Furniture and Related Product Manufacturing			
337000	**337000**		**Furniture and Related Product Manufacturing**
		337920	Blind and Shade Manufacturing
		337212	Custom Architectural Woodwork and Millwork Manufacturing
		337125	Household Furniture (except Wood and Metal) Manufacturing
		337127	Institutional Furniture Manufacturing
		337910	Mattress Manufacturing
		337124	Metal Household Furniture Manufacturing
		337122	Nonupholstered Wood Household Furniture Manufacturing
		337214	Office Furniture (Except Wood) Manufacturing
		337215	Showcase, Partition, Shelving, and Locker Manufacturing

SOI Published Code	PBA Code	NAICS Code	Industry
		337121	Upholstered Household Furniture Manufacturing
		337110	Wood Kitchen Cabinet and Countertop Manufacturing
		337211	Wood Office Furniture Manufacturing
		337129	Wood Television, Radio and Sewing Machine Cabinet Manufacturing
Miscellaneous Manufacturing			
339110	**339110**		**Medical Equipment and Supplies Manufacturing**
		339114	Dental Equipment and Supplies Manufacturing
		339116	Dental Laboratories
		339111	Laboratory Apparatus and Furniture Manufacturing
		339115	Ophthalmic Goods Manufacturing
		339113	Surgical Appliance and Supplies Manufacturing
		339112	Surgical and Medical Instrument Manufacturing
339900	**339900**		**Other Miscellaneous Manufacturing**
		339994	Broom, Brush and Mop Manufacturing
		339995	Burial Casket Manufacturing
		339944	Carbon Paper and Inked Ribbon Manufacturing
		339914	Costume Jewelry and Novelty Manufacturing
		339931	Doll and Stuff Toy manufacturing
		339993	Fastener, Button, Needle, and Pin Manufacturing
		339932	Game, Toy, and Children's Vehicle Manufacturing
		339991	Gasket, Packing, and Sealing Device Manufacturing
		339913	Jewelers' Material and Lapidary Work Manufacturing
		339911	Jewelry (except Costume) Manufacturing
		339942	Lead Pencil and Art Good Manufacturing
		339943	Marking Device Manufacturing
		339999	Miscellaneous Manufacturing, NEC
		339992	Musical Instrument Manufacturing
		339941	Pen and Mechanical Pencil Manufacturing
		339950	Sign Manufacturing
		339912	Silverware and Holloware Manufacturing
		339920	Sporting and Athletic Goods Manufacturing

SOI Published Code	PBA Code	NAICS Code	Industry
			WHOLESALE TRADE
Merchant Wholesalers, Durable Goods			
423100	**423100**		**Motor Vehicle & Motor Vehicle Parts & Supplies**
		423110	Automobile and Other Motor Vehicle Merchant Wholesalers
		423120	Motor Vehicle Supplies and New Parts Merchant Wholesalers
		423130	Tire and Tube Merchant Wholesalers
		423140	Motor Vehicle Parts (Used) Merchant Wholesalers
423905	**423200**		**Furniture and Home Furninshings**
		423210	Furniture Merchant Wholesalers
		423220	Home Funishings Merchant Wholesalers
423300	**423300**		**Lumber and Other Construction Materials**
		423310	Lumber, Plywood, Millwork, and Wood Panel Merchant Wholesalers
		423320	Brick, Stone, and Related Construction Material Merchant Wholesalers
		423330	Roofing, siding and Insulation Material Merchant Wholesalers
		423390	Other Construction Material Merchant Wholesalers
423400	**423400**		**Professional and Commerical Equipment and Supplies**
		423410	Photographic Equipment and Supplies Merchant Wholesalers
		423420	Office Equipment Merchant Wholesalers
		423430	Computer and Computer Peripheral Equipment and Software Merchant Wholesalers
		423440	Other Commerical Equipment Merchant Wholesalers
		423450	Medical, Dental, and Hospital Equipment and Supplies Merchant Wholesalers
		423460	Ophthalmic Goods Merchant Wholesalers
		423490	Other Professional Equipment and Supplies Merchant Wholesaler
423500	**423500**		**Metal and Mineral (Except Petroleum)**
		423510	Metal Service Centers and Other Metal Merchant Wholesalers
		423520	Coal and Other Minearl and Ore Merchant Wholesalers

SOI Published Code	PBA Code	NAICS Code	Industry
423600	**423600**		**Electrical and Electronic Goods**
		423610	Electrical Apparatus and Equipment, Wiring Supplies, and Related Equipment Merchant Wholesalers
		423620	Electrical and Electronic Appliance, Television and Radio Set Merchant Wholesalers
		423690	Other Electronic Parts and Equipment Merchant Wholesalers
423700	**423700**		**Hardware & Plumbing & Heating Equipment & Supplies**
		423710	Hardware Merchant Wholesales
		423720	Plumbing and Heating Equipment and Supplies (Hydronics) Merchant Wholesalers
		423730	Warm Air Heating and Air-Conditioning Equipment and Supplies Merchant Wholesalers
		423740	Refrigeration Equipment and Supplies Merchant Wholesalers
423800	**423800**		**Machinery, Equipment and Supplies Wholesalers**
		423810	Construction and Mining (except Oil Well) Machinery and Merchant Equipment
		423820	Farm and Garden Machinery and Equipment Merchant Wholesalers
		423890	Industrial Machinery and Equipment Merchant Wholesalers
		423840	Industrial Supplies Merchant Wholesalers
		423850	Service Establishment Equipment and Supplies Merchant Wholesalers
		423860	Transporation Equipment and Supplies (except Motor Vehicles) Merchant Wholesalers
423905	**423910**		**Sporting and Recreational Goods and Supplies**
423905	**423920**		**Toy and Hobby Goods and Supplies**
423905	**423930**		**Recyclable Materials**

SOI Published Code	PBA Code	NAICS Code	Industry
423905	**423940**		**Jewelry, Watch, Precious Stone, and Precious Metals**
423905	**423990**		**Other Miscellaneous Durable Goods**
Merchant Wholesalers, Nondurable Goods			
424100	**424100**		**Paper and Paper Products**
		424110	Printing and Writing Paper Merchant Wholesalers
		424120	Stationery and Office Supplies Merchant Wholesalers
		424130	Industrial and Personal Service Paper Merchant Wholesalers
424210	**424210**		**Drug and Druggists' Sundries**
424300	**424300**		**Apparel, Piece Goods and Notions**
		424310	Piece Goods, Notions, and Other Dry Goods Merchant Wholesalers
		424320	Men's and Boys' Clothing and Furnishings Merchant Wholesalers
		424330	Women's Children's and Infant's Clothing and Accessories Merchant Wholesalers
		424340	Footwear Wholesalers
424400	**424400**		**Grocery and Related Products**
		424450	Confectionary Merchant Wholesalers
		424430	Dairy Product (except Dried or Canned) Merchant Wholesalers
		424460	Fish and Seafood Merchant Wholesalers
		424480	Fresh Fruit and Vegetable Merchant Wholesalers (tomatoes, produce)
		424410	General Line Grocery Merchant Wholesalers
		424470	Meat and Meat Product Merchant Wholesalers
		424490	Other Grocery and Related Products Merchant Wholesalers
		424420	Packaged Frozen Food Merchant Wholesalers
		424440	Poultry and Poultry Product Merchant Wholesalers

SOI Published Code	PBA Code	NAICS Code	Industry
424500	**424500**		**Farm Product Raw Materials**
		424510	Grain and Field Bean Merchant Wholesalers
		424520	Livestock Merchant Wholesalers
		424590	Other Farm Product Raw Material Merchant Wholesalers
424600	**424600**		**Chemical and Allied Products**
		424690	Other Chemical and Allied Products Merchant Wholesalers
		424610	Plastics Materials and Basic Forms and Shapes Merchant Wholesalers
424700	**424700**		**Petroleum and Petroleum Products**
		424710	Petroleum Bulk Stations and Terminals
		424720	Petroleum and Petroleum Products Merchant Wholesalers (except Bulk Stations and Terminals)
424800	**424800**		**Beer, Wine and Distilled Alcoholic Beverages**
		424810	Beer and Ale Merchant Wholesalers
		424820	Wine and Distilled Alcoholic Beverage Merchant Wholesalers
424915	**424910**		**Farm Supplies**
424915	**424920**		**Book, Periodical, and Newspapers**
424915	**424930**		**Flower, Nursery Stock, Florists' Supplies**
424915	**424940**		**Tobacco and Tobacco Products**
424915	**424950**		**Paint, Varnish and Supplies**

SOI Published Code	PBA Code	NAICS Code	Industry
424915	424990		Other Miscellaneous Nondurable Goods

Wholesale Electronic Markets & Agents & Brokers

SOI Published Code	PBA Code	NAICS Code	Industry
425115	425110		Busines to Business Electronic Markets
425115	425120		Wholesale Trade Agents and Brokers

RETAIL TRADE

Motor Vehicle and Parts Dealers

SOI Published Code	PBA Code	NAICS Code	Industry
441115	441110		New Car Dealers
441115	441120		Used Car Dealers
441215	441210		Recrational Vehicle Dealers
441215	441221		Motorcycle Dealers
441215	441222		Boat Dealers
441215	441229		All Other Motor Vehicle Dealers
441215	441300		Automotive Parts, Accessories
		441310	Automotive Parts and Accessories Stores
		441320	Tire Dealers

SOI Published Code	PBA Code	NAICS Code	Industry
Furniture and Home Furnishings Stores			
442115	442110		Furniture Stores
442115	442210		Floor Covering Stores
442115	442291		Window Treatment Stores
442115	442299		All Other Home Furnishings Stores
Electronics and Appliance Stores			
443115	443111		Household Appliance Stores
443115	443112		Radio, Television, and Other Electronics Stores
443115	443120		Computer and Software Stores
443115	443130		Camera and Photographic Supplies Store
444115	444110		Home Centers
444115	444120		Paint and Wallpaper Stores
444130	444130		Hardware Stores
444190	444190		Other Building Material Dealers

SOI Published Code	PBA Code	NAICS Code	Industry
444200	**444200**		**Law and Garden Equipment and Supplies Stores**
		444210	Outdoor Power Equipment Stores
Food and Beverage Stores			
445115	**445110**		**Supermarkets and Other Grocery (except Convience) Stores**
445115	**445120**		**Convience Stores**
445115	**445210**		**Meat Markets**
445115	**445220**		**Fish and Seafood Markets**
445115	**445230**		**Fruit and Vegetables Markets**
445115	**445291**		**Baked Good Stores**
445115	**445292**		**Confectionery and Nut Store**
445115	**445299**		**All Other Specialty Food Stores**
445310	**445310**		**Beer, Wine and Liquor Stores**
Health and Personal Care Stores			
446115	**446110**		**Pharmacies and Drug Stores**

SOI Published Code	PBA Code	NAICS Code	Industry
446115	**446120**		**Cosmetics, Beauty Supplies and Perfume Stores**
446115	**446130**		**Optical Goods Stores**
446115	**446190**		**Other Health and Person Care Stores**
		446199	All Other Health and Personal Care Stores
		446191	Food (Health) Supplement Stores
447100	**447100**		**Gasoline Stations**
		447110	Gasoline Stations with Convience Stores
		447190	Other Gasoline Stations
Clothing and Clothing Acessories Stores			
448115	**448110**		**Men's Clothing Stores**
448115	**448120**		**Women's Clothing Stores**
448115	**448130**		**Children's and Infant's Clothing Stores**
448115	**448140**		**Family Clothing Stores**
448115	**448150**		**Clothing Acessories Stores**
448115	**448190**		**Other Clothing Stores**
448115	**448210**		**Shoe Stores**

SOI Published Code	PBA Code	NAICS Code	Industry
448115	448310		Jewelry Stores
448115	448320		Luggage and Leather Goods Stores
Sporting Goods, Hobby, Book & Music Stores			
451115	451110		Sporting Goods Stores
451115	451120		Hobby, Toy, and Game Stores
451115	451130		Sewing, Needlework, and Piece Goods Stores
451115	451140		Musical Instrument and Supplies Stores
451115	451211		Book Stores
451115	451212		News Dealers and Newsstands
451115	451220		Prerecorded Tape, Compact Disc, and Record Stores
General Merchandise Stores			
452115	452110		Department Stores
452115	452900		General Merchandise Stores
		452990	All Other General Merchandise Stores
		452910	Warehouse Clubs and Superstores

SOI Published Code	PBA Code	NAICS Code	Industry
Miscellaneous Store Retailers			
453115	453110		Florists
453115	453210		Office Supplies and Stationary Stores
453115	453220		Gift, Novelty and Souvenir Stores
453115	453310		Used Merchandise Stores
453115	453910		Pet and Pet Supplies Stores
453115	453920		Art Dealers
453115	453930		Manufactured (Mobile) Home Dealers
453115	453990		All Other Miscellaneous Store Retailers (including Tobacco, Candle & Trophy Shops)
		453998	Miscellaneous Store Retailers (except Tobacco Stores)
		453991	Tobacco Stores
Nonstore Retailers			
454115	454110		Electronic Shopping and Mail-Order Houses
454115	454210		Vending Machine Operators

SOI Published Code	PBA Code	NAICS Code	Industry
454115	**454311**		**Heating Oil Dealers**
454115	**454312**		**Liquified Petroleum Gas (Bottled Gas) Dealers**
454115	**454319**		**Other Fuel Dealers**
454115	**454390**		**Other Direct Selling Establishments**

WHOLESALE/RETAIL NON-ALLOCABLE

SOI Published Code	PBA Code	NAICS Code	Industry
460000	**460000**		**Wholesale/Retail Non-Allocable**

TRANSPORTATION AND WAREHOUSING

Air, Rail and Water Transportation

SOI Published Code	PBA Code	NAICS Code	Industry
481000	**481000**		**Air Transportation**
		481212	Nonscheduled Chartered Freight Air Transportation
		481211	Nonscheduled Chartered Passenger Air Transportation
		481219	Other Nonscheduled Air Transportation
		481112	Scheduled Freight Air Transportation
		481111	Scheduled Passenger Air Transportation
482110	**482110**		**Rail Transportation**
		482111	Line-Haul Railroads
		482112	Short Line Railroads
483000	**483000**		**Water Transportation**
		483113	Coastal and Great Lakes Freight Transportation
		483114	Coastal and Great Lakes Passenger Transportation

SOI Published Code	PBA Code	NAICS Code	Industry
		483111	Deep Sea Freight Transportation
		483112	Deep Sea Passenger Transportation
		483211	Inland Water Freight Transportation
		483212	Inland Water Passenger Transportation
Truck Transportation			
484115	**484110**		**General Freight Trucking, Local**
484115	**484120**		**General Freight Trucking, Long Distance**
		484122	General Freight Trucking, Long Distance, Less Than Truckload
		484121	General Freight Trucking, Long Distance,Truckload
484115	**484190**		**General Freight Trucking Non Allocable**
484200	**484200**		**Specialized Freight Trucking**
		484220	Specialized Freight (except Used Goods) Trucking, Local
		484230	Specialized Freight (except Used Goods)Trucking, Long-Distance
		484210	Used Household and Office Goods Moving
Transit and Ground Passenger Transportation			
485115	**485110**		**Urban Transit Systems**
		485113	Bus and Other Motor Vehicle Transit Systems
		485112	Commuter Rail Systems
		485111	Mixed Mode Transit Systems
		485119	Other Urban Transit Systems
485115	**485210**		**Interurban & Rural Bus Transportation**
485115	**485310**		**Taxi Service**

SOI Published Code	PBA Code	NAICS Code	Industry
485115	**485320**		**Limousine Service**
485115	**485410**		**School and Employee Bus Transportation**
485115	**485510**		**Charter Bus Industry**
485115	**485990**		**Other Transit & Ground Passenger Transportation**
		485991	Special Needs Transportation
		485999	Transit and Ground Passenger Transportation, NEC
Pipeline Transportation			
486000	**486000**		**Pipeline Transportation**
		486990	All Other Pipeline Transportation
		486110	Pipeline Transportation of Cruide Oil
		486210	Pipeline Transportation of Natural Gas
		486910	Pipeline Transportation of Refined Petroleum Products
Scenic & Sightseeing Transportation			
487005	**487000**		**Scenic & Sightseeing Transportation**
		487110	Scenic & Sightseeing Transportation, Land
		487990	Scenic & Sightseeing Transportation, Other
		487210	Scenic & Sightseeing Transportation, Water
Support Activities for Transportation			
487005	**488100**		**Support Activities for Air Transportation**
		488111	Air Traffic Control
		488119	Other Airport Operations
		488190	Support Activities for Air Transportation, NEC

SOI Published Code	PBA Code	NAICS Code	Industry
487005	**488210**		**Support Activities for Rail Transportation**
487005	**488300**		**Support Activities for Water Transportation**
		488330	Navigational Services to Shipping
		488310	Port and Harbor Operations
		488390	Support Activities for Water Transportation, NEC
487005	**488410**		**Motor Vehicle Towing**
487005	**488490**		**Other Support Activities for Road Transportation**
487005	**488510**		**Freight Transportation Arrangement**
487005	**488990**		**Other Support Activities for Transportation**
		488991	Packing and Crating
		488999	Support Activities for Transportation, NEC
Couriers and Messengers			
487005	**492110**		**Couriers**
487005	**492210**		**Local Messengers and Local Delivery**
Warehousing and Storage			
493100	**493100**		**Warehousign & Storage (excluding lessor or miniwarehouses & Self Storage)**
		493130	Farm Product Warehousing and Storage
		493110	General Warehousing and Storage
		493190	Other Warehousing and Storage
		493120	Refigerated Warehousing and Storage

SOI Published Code	PBA Code	NAICS Code	Industry
			INFORMATION
Publishing Industries (except Internet)			
511110	**511110**		**Newspaper Publishing**
511120	**511120**		**Periodical Publishers**
511130	**511130**		**Book Publishers**
511145	**511140**		**Directory & Mailing List Publishers**
511145	**511190**		**Other Publishers**
		511191	Greeting Card Publishers
		511199	All Other Publishers
511210	**511210**		**Software Publishers**
Motion Picture & Sound Recording Industries			
512100	**512100**		**Motion Picture & Video Industries (except Video Rental)**
		512132	Drive-In Motion Picture Theaters
		512131	Motion Picture Teathers (except Drive-Ins)
		512120	Motion Picture and Video Distribution
		512199	Other Motion Picture and Video Industries
		512110	Motion Picture and Video Production
		512191	Teleproduction and Other Postproduction Services
512200	**512200**		**Sound Recording Industries**
		512220	Integrated Record Production/Distribution
		512230	Music Publishers

SOI Published Code	PBA Code	NAICS Code	Industry
		512290	Other Sound Recoring Industries
		512210	Record Production
		512240	Sound Recording Studios
Broadcasting (except Internet)			
515105	**515100**		**Radio & Television Broadcasting**
		513111	Radio Networks
		513112	Radio Stations
		513120	Television Broadcasting
515105	**515210**		**Cable & Other Subscription Programming**
Telecommunications			
517000	**517000**		**Telecommunications (including paging, cellular, satellite, cable & other program distribution, resellers & other telecommunications**
		517110	Wired Telecommunications Carriers
		517210	Wireless Telecommunication Carriers (except Satellite)
		517410	Statelitte Telecommunications
		517911	Telecommunication Resellers
		517919	All Other Telecommunications
Internet Service Providers, Web Search Portals & Data Processing Services			
518210	**518210**		**Data Processing, Hosting & Related Services**
Other Information Services			
519100	**519100**		**Other Information Services (including new syndicates & libraries)**
		519110	News Syndicates
		519130	Internet Publishing and Broadcasting and Web Search Portals
		519120	Libraries and Archives
		519190	All Other Information Services

SOI Published Code	PBA Code	NAICS Code	Industry
			FINANCE & INSURANCE
Depository Credit Intermediation			
522110	522110		Commerical Banking
522125	522120		Savings Institutions
522125	522130		Credit Unions
522125	522190		Other Depository Credit Intermediation
Nondepository Credit Intermediation			
522215	522210		Credit Card Issuing
522215	522220		Sales Financing
522215	522291		Consumer Lending
522292	522292		Real Estate Credit (including Mortgage Bankers, and Originators)
522295	522293		International Trade Financing
522295	522294		Secondary Market Financing
522295	522298		All Other Nondepository Credit Intermediation

SOI Published Code	PBA Code	NAICS Code	Industry
Activities Related to Credit Intermediation			
522300	**522300**		**Activities Related to Credit Intermediation (including loan brokers, check clearing & money transmitting)**
		522320	Financial Transactions Processing, Reserve and Clearninghouse Activities (AutomatedClearinghouse, Electronic Funds Transfer Services)
		522310	Mortgage and Nonmortgage Loan Brokers
		522390	Other Activities Related to Credit Intermediation
Securities, Commodity Contracts, and Other Finanical Investment Activities			
523110	**523110**		**Investment Banking and Securities Dealing**
523120	**523120**		**Securities Brokerage**
523135	**523130**		**Commodity Contracts Dealings**
523135	**523140**		**Commodity Contracts Brokerage**
523905	**523210**		**Securities and Commodity Exchanges**
523905	**523900**		**Other Financial Investment Activities (including portfolio management & investment advice)**
		523999	Finanical Investment Advice (Securities/Commondities Exchange Clearinghouses, Stock Quotation Services)
		523930	Investment Advice (Finanical Advice, Advisory, Counseling, or Investment Services, Finanical Planner/Consultant, Management Group)
		523910	Miscellaneous Intermediation (Investment Clubs, Venture Capital Cos.)
		523920	Portfolio Management (Investment or Financial Management, Commodity Trading Advisor (CTA)
		523991	Trust, Fiduciary and Custody Activities

SOI Published Code	PBA Code	NAICS Code	Industry
Insurance Carriers & Related Activities			
524142	**524142**		**Life Insurance, Stock Companies (Form 1120L)**
524143	**524143**		**Life Insurance, Mutual Companies (Form 1120L)**
524156	**524156**		**Mutual Property and Casualty Companies (Form 1120PC)**
524159	**524159**		**Stock Property and Casualty Companies (Form 1120PC)**
524210	**524210**		**Insurance Agencies and Brokerages**
524290	**524290**		**Other Insurance Realted Activities (including third-party administration or insurance and pension funds)**
		524298	All Other Insurance Related Activities
		524291	Claims Adjusting
		524292	Third Party Adminstration of Insurance and Pension Funds
Funds, Trusts & Other Finanical Variables			
525995	**525100**		**Insurance & Other Employee Benefits**
		525120	Health and Welfare Funds
		525190	Other Insurance Funds
		525110	Pension Funds
525910	**525910**		**Open-End Investment Funds (Form 1120-RIC)**
525995	**525920**		**Trust, Estates, and Agency Accounts**
525995	**525990**		**Other Financial Vehicles**

SOI Published Code	PBA Code	NAICS Code	Industry
REAL ESTATE AND RENTAL AND LEASING			
Real Estate			
531115	531110		Lessor of Residential Buildings and Dwellings (Form 1120-REIT, Equity Only)
531115	531114		Cooperative Housing (Form 1120-REIT, Equity Only)
531115	531120		Lessor of Nonresidential Buildings (except Miniwarehouses) (Form 1120-REIT Equity Only)
531135	531130		Lessor of Miniwarehouses & Self-Storage Units (Form 1120-REIT Equity Only)
531135	531190		Lessor of Other Real Estate Property (Form 1120-REIT Equity Only)
531210	531210		Offices of Real Estate Agents and Brokers
531315	531310		Real Estate Property Managers
		531312	Nonresidential Property Managers
		531311	Residential Property Managers (condominium management)
531315	531320		Offics of Real Estate Appraisers
531315	531390		Other Activities Related to Real Estate

SOI Published Code	PBA Code	NAICS Code	Industry
Rental and Leasing Services			
532100	**532100**		**Automotive Equipment Rental and Leasing**
		532112	Passenger Car Leasing
		532111	Passenger Car Rental
		532120	Truck, Utility Trailer and RV (Recreation Vehicle) Rental and Leasing
532215	**532210**		**Consumer Electronics & Appliances Rental**
532215	**532220**		**Formal Wear and Costume Rental**
532215	**532230**		**Video Tape and Disc Rental**
532215	**532290**		**Other Consumer Goods Rental**
		532299	Consumer Goods Rental, NEC
		532291	Home Health Equipment Rental
		532292	Recreational Goods Rental
532215	**532310**		**General Rental Centers**
532400	**532400**		**Commerical and Industrial Machinery & Equipment Rental**
		532411	Commerical Air, Rail and Water Transportation Equipment Rental & Leasing
		532412	Construction, Mining and Forestry Machinery & Equipment Rental & Leasing
		532420	Office Machinery and Equipment Rental & Leasing
		432490	Other Commerical and Industrial Machinery & Equipment Rental & Leasing

SOI Published Code	PBA Code	NAICS Code	Industry
Lessor of Nonfinanical Intangible Assets (except copyrighted work)			
533110	533110		Lessor of Nonfinanical Intangible Assets (except Copyrighted Work)

PROFESSIONAL, SCIENTIFIC AND TECHNICAL SERVICES

SOI Published Code	PBA Code	NAICS Code	Industry
Legal Services			
541115	541110		Office of Lawyers
541115	541190		Other Legal Services
		541199 Legal Services, NEC	
		541191 Title Abstract and Settlement Offices	
Accounting, Tax Preparation, Bookkeping & Payroll Services			
541215	541211		Offices of Certified Public Accoutants
541215	541213		Tax Preparation Services
541215	541214		Payroll Services
541215	541219		Other Accounting Services
Architectual, Engineering & Related Services			
541315	541310		Architectural Services
541315	541320		Landscape Architectural Services

SOI Published Code	PBA Code	NAICS Code	Industry
541315	**541330**		**Engineering Services**
541315	**541340**		**Drafting Services**
541315	**541350**		**Building Inspection Services**
541315	**541360**		**Geophysical Surveying and Mapping Services**
541315	**541370**		**Surveying and Mapping (except Geophysical) Services**
541315	**541380**		**Testing Laboratories**
Specialized Design Services			
541400	**541400**		**Specialied Design Services (including interior, industrial, graphic & fashion design)**
		541430 Graphic Design Services	
		541420 Industrial Design Services	
		541410 Inerior Design Services	
		541490 Other Specialized Design Services	
Computer Systems Design & Related Services			
541515	**541511**		**Custom Computer Programming Services**
541515	**541512**		**Computer Systems Design Services**
541515	**541513**		**Computer Facilities Management Services**

SOI Published Code	PBA Code	NAICS Code	Industry
541515	**541519**		**Other Computer Related Services**

Other Professional, Scientific & Technical Services

SOI Published Code	PBA Code	NAICS Code	Industry
541600	**541600**		**Management, Scientific & Technical Consulting Services**
		541611	Administrative Management and General Management Consulting Services
		541620	Environmental Consulting Services
		541612	Human Resources Consulting Services
		541613	Marketing Consulting Services
		541618	Other Management Consulting Services
		541690	Other Scientific and Technical Consulting Services
		541614	Process, Physical Distribution and Logistics Consulting Services
541700	**541700**		**Scientific Research & Development Services**
		541711	Research and Development in Biotechnology
		541712	Research and Development in Physical, Engineering & Life Sciences (except Biotechnology)
		541720	Research and Development in the Social Sciences and Humanities
541800	**541800**		**Advertising & Related Services**
		541810	Advertising Agencies
		541870	Advertising Material Distribution Services
		541860	Direct Mail Advertising
		541850	Display Advertising
		541830	Media Buying Agencies
		541840	Media Representatives
		541890	Other Services Related to Advertising
		541820	Public Relations Agencies
541915	**541910**		**Marketing Research & Public Opinion Polling**

SOI Published Code	PBA Code	NAICS Code	Industry
541915	**541920**		**Photographic Services**
		541922	Commercial Photography
		541921	Photography Studios, Portrait
541915	**541930**		**Translation and Interpretation Services**
541915	**541940**		**Veterinary Services**
541915	**541990**		**All Other Professional, Scientific, and Technical Services**

MANAGEMENT OF COMPANIES (HOLDING COMPANIES)

SOI Published Code	PBA Code	NAICS Code	Industry
551111	**551111**		**Offices of Bank Holding Companies**
551112	**551112**		**Office of Other Holding Companies (personal holding companies, investments)**

ADMINISTRATIVE AND SUPPORT & WASTE MANAGEMENT & REMEDIATION SERVICES

Administrative and Support Services

SOI Published Code	PBA Code	NAICS Code	Industry
561905	**561110**		**Office Administrative Services**
561905	**561210**		**Facilities Support Services**
561300	**561300**		**Employment Services**
		561330	Professional Employer Organizations
		561311	Employment Placement Agencies

SOI Published Code	PBA Code	NAICS Code	Industry
		561312	Executive Search Services
		561320	Temporary Help Services
561905	**561410**		**Document Preparation Services**
561905	**561420**		**Telephone Call Centers**
		561421	Telephone Answering Services
		561422	Telemarketing Bureaus and Other Contact Centers
561905	**561430**		**Business Services Centers (including private mail centers & copy shops)**
		561439	Other Business Service Centers (including Copy Shops)
		461431	Private Mail Centers
561905	**561430**		**Business Services Centers (Including private mail center & copy shops)**
		561439	Other Business Service Centers (including Copy Shops)
		461431	Private Mail Centers
561905	**561440**		**Collection Agencies**
561905	**561450**		**Credit Bureaus**
561905	**561490**		**Other Business Support Services (including reposession services, court reporting & stenotype services)**
		561492	Court Reporting and Stenotype Services
		561499	Business Support Services, NEC
		561491	Repossession Services

SOI Published Code	PBA Code	NAICS Code	Industry
561500	**561500**		**Travel Arrangement and Reservation Services**
		561591	Convention and Visitors Bureaus
		561520	Tour Operators
		561510	Travel Agencies
		561599	Travel Arrangement and Reservation Services, NEC
561905	**561600**		**Investigation & Sercurity Services**
		561613	Armored Car Services
		561611	Investigation Services
		561622	Locksmiths
		561612	Security Guards and Patrol Services
		561621	Security Systems Services (except Locksmiths)
561905	**561710**		**Extermination & Pest Control Services**
561905	**561720**		**Janitorial Services**
561905	**561730**		**Landscaping Services**
561905	**561740**		**Carpet & Upholstery Cleaning Services**
561905	**561790**		**Other Services to Buildings and Dwellings**
561905	**561900**		**Other Support Services**
		561920	Convention and Trade Show Organizers
		561910	Packaging and Labeling Services
		561990	All Other Support Services

SOI Published Code	PBA Code	NAICS Code	Industry
Waste Management & Remediation Services			
562000	**562000**		**Waste Management & Remediation Services**
		562998	All other Miscellaneous Waste Management Services
		562112	Hazardous Waste Collection
		562211	Hazardous Waste Treatment and Disposal
		562920	Materials Recovery Facilities
		562219	Other Nonhazardous Waste Treatment and Disposal
		562119	Other Waste Collection
		562910	Remediation Services
		562991	Spetic Tank and Related Services
		562111	Solid Waste Collection
		562213	Solid Waste Combustors and Incinerators
		562212	Solid Waste Landfill

EDUCATIONAL SERVICES

SOI Published Code	PBA Code	NAICS Code	Industry
611000	**611000**		**Educational Services (including schools, colleges & universities)**
		611699	All Other Miscellaneous Schools and Instruction
		611513	Apprenticeship Training
		611692	Automobile Driving Schools
		611410	Business and Secretarial Schools
		611310	Colleges, Universities and Professional Schools
		611420	Computer Training
		611511	Cosmetology and Barber Schools
		611710	Educational Support Services
		611110	Elementary and Secondary Schools
		611691	Exam Preparation and Tutoring
		611610	Fine Arts Schools
		611512	Flight Training
		611210	Junior Colleges
		611630	Language Schools
		611519	Other Technical and Trade Schools
		611430	Professional and Management Development Training
		611620	Sports and Recreation Instruction

SOI Published Code	PBA Code	NAICS Code	Industry
HEALTH CARE AND SOCIAL ASSISTANCE			
Offices & Physicians & Dentists			
621115	621111		Offices of Physicians (except Mental Health Specialist)
621115	621112		Offices of Physicians, Mental Health Specialist
621210	621210		Offices of Dentists
Offices of Other Health Practitioners			
621315	621310		Offices of Chiropractors
621315	621320		Offices of Optometrists
621315	621330		Office of Mental Health Practitioners (except Physicians)
621315	621340		Offices of Physical, Occupational and Speech Therapists & Audiologist
621315	621391		Offices of Podiatrists
621315	621399		Offices of All Other Miscellaneous Health Practitioners
Outpatient Care Centers			
621415	621410		Family Planning Centers

SOI Published Code	PBA Code	NAICS Code	Industry
621415	**621420**		**Outpatient Mental Health and Substance Abuse Centers**
621415	**621491**		**HMO Medical Centers**
621415	**621492**		**Kidney Dialysis Centers**
621415	**621493**		**Freestanding Ambulatory Surgical & Emergency Centers**
621415	**621498**		**All Other Outpatient Care Centers**
Medical and Diagnostic Laboratories			
621515	**621510**		**Medical and Diagnostic Laboratories**
		621512	Diagnostic Imaging Centers
		621511	Medical Laboratories
Home Health Care Services			
621515	**621610**		**Home Health Care Services**
Other Ambulatory Health Care Services			
621515	**621900**		**All Other Miscellaneous Ambulatory Health Care Services**
		621910	Ambulance Services
		621991	Blood and Organ Banks
Hospitals			
622005	**622000**		**Hospitals**
		622110	General Medical and Surgical Hospitals
		622210	Psychiatric and Substance Abuse Hospitals
		622310	Specialty (except Psychiatric and Substance Abuse) Hosptials

SOI Published Code	PBA Code	NAICS Code	Industry
Nursing & Residential Care Facilities			
622005	**623000**		**Nursing & Residential Care Facilities**
		623311	Continuing Care Retirement Communities
		623312	Homes for the Elderly
		623110	Nursing Care Facilities
		623990	Other Residential Care Facilities
		623220	Residential Mental Health and Substance Abuse Facilities
		623210	Residential Mental Health Retardation Facilities
Social Assistance			
621515	**624100**		**Individual and Family**
		624110	Child and Youth Services
		624190	Other Individual and Family Services
		624120	Service for the Elderly and Persons with Disabilities
621515	**624200**		**Community Food & Housing & Emergency & Other Relief Services**
		624210	Community Food Services
		624230	Emergency and Other Relief Services
		624229	Other Community Housing Services
		624221	Temporary Services
621515	**624310**		**Vocational Rehibilitation Services**
621515	**624410**		**Child Day Care Services**

ARTS, ENTERTAINMENT AND RECREATION

SOI Published Code	PBA Code	NAICS Code	Industry
Performing Arts, Spectator Sports & Related Industries			
711105	**711100**		**Performing Arts Companies**
		711120	Dance Companies

SOI Published Code	PBA Code	NAICS Code	Industry
		711130	Musical Groups and Artists
		711190	Other Performing Arts Companies
		711110	Theater Companies and Dinner Theaters
711105	**711210**		**Spectator Sports (Including Sports Clubs and Racetracks)**
		711219	Other Spectator Sports
		711212	Racetracks
		711211	Sports Teams and Clubs
711105	**711300**		**Promoters of Performing Arts, Sports, and Similar Events**
		711310	Promoters of Performing Arts, Sports, and Similar Events with Facilities
		711320	Promoters of Performing Arts, Sports, and Similar Events without Facilities
711105	**711410**		**Agents & Managers for Artists, Athletes, Entertainers & Other Public Figures**
711105	**711510**		**Independent Artists, Writers and Performers**
Museums, Historical Sites & Similar Institutions			
711105	**712100**		**Museums, Historical Sites & Other Similar Institutions**
		712120	Historical Sites
		712110	Museums, Historical Sites & Other Similar Institutions
		712190	Nature Parks and Other Similar Institutions
		712130	Zoos and Botanical Gardens
Amusement, Gambling and Recreational Activities			
713105	**713100**		**Amusement Parks and Arcades**
		713120	Amusement Arcades
		713110	Amusement and Theme Parks

SOI Published Code	PBA Code	NAICS Code	Industry
713105	**713200**		**Gambling Industry**
		713210	Casinos (except Casino Hotels)
		713290	Other Gambling Industries
713105	**713900**		**Other Amusement & Recreation Industries (including golf courses, skiing facilities, marinas, fitness centers & bowling centers)**
		713990	All Other Amusement and Recreation Industries
		713950	Bowling Centers
		713940	Fitness and Recreational Sports Centers
		713910	Gold Courses and Country Clubs
		713930	Marinas
		713920	Skiing Facilities

ACCOMMODATION & FOOD SERVICES

Accommodation

SOI Published Code	PBA Code	NAICS Code	Industry
721115	**721110**		**Hotels (except Casino Hotels) and Motels**
721115	**721120**		**Casino Hotels**
721115	**721191**		**Bed-and-Breakfast Inns**
721115	**721199**		**All Other Traveler Accomodation**
721115	**721210**		**RV (Recreational Vehicle) Parks and Recreational Parks**
		721211	RV (Recreational Vehicle) Parks and Campgrounds
		721214	Recreational and Vacation Camps (except Campgrounds)

SOI Published Code	PBA Code	NAICS Code	Industry
721115	**721310**		**Rooming and Boarding Houses**
Food Services and Drinking Places			
722115	**722110**		**Full-Service Restaurants**
722115	**722210**		**Limited Service Eating Place**
		722212 Cafeterias	
		722211 Limited-Service Restaurants	
		722213 Snack and Nonalcoholic Beverage Bars	
722115	**722300**		**Special Food Services (including food service contractors & caterers)**
		722320 Caterers	
		722310 Food Service Contractors	
		722330 Mobile Food Services	
722115	**722410**		**Drinking Places (Alcoholic Beverages)**

OTHER SERVICES

SOI Published Code	PBA Code	NAICS Code	Industry
Repair and Maintenance			
811115	**811110**		**Automotive Mechanical and Electrical Repair and Maintenance**
		811112 Automotive Exhaust System Repair	
		811113 Automotive Transmission Repair	
		811111 General Automotive Repair Maintenance	
		811118 Other Automotive Mechanical and Electrical Repair and Maintenance	
811115	**811120**		**Automotive Body, Paint, Interior & Glass Repair**
		811121 Automotive Body, Paint, and Interior Repair and Maintenance	
		811122 Automotive Glass Replacement Shops	

SOI Published Code	PBA Code	NAICS Code	Industry
811115	**811190**		**Other Automotive Repair & Maintenance (including oil change & lubrication shops & car washes)**
		811198	All Other Automotive Repair and Maintenance
		811191	Automotive Oil Change and Lubrication Shops
		811192	Car Washes
811215	**811210**		**Electronic & Precision Equipment Repair & Maintenance**
		811213	Communication Equipment Repair and Maintenance
		811212	Computer and Office Machine Repair and Maintenance
		811211	Consumer Electronics Repair and Maintenance
		811219	Other Electronic & Precision Equipment Repair & Maintenance except Automotive
811215	**811310**		**Commerical & Industrial Machinery & Equipment (except Automotive & Electronic) Repair & Maintenance**
811215	**811410**		**Home & Garden Equipment & Appliance Repair & Maintenance**
		811412	Appliance Repair and Maintenance
		811411	Home and Garden Equipment Repair and Maintenance
811215	**811420**		**Reupholstery & Furniture Repair**
811215	**811430**		**Footware and Leather Goods Repair**
811215	**811490**		**Other Personal and Household Goods Repair & Maintenance**
Personal and Laundry Services			
812115	**812111**		**Barber Shops**

SOI Published Code	PBA Code	NAICS Code	Industry
812115	**812112**		**Beauty Salons**
812115	**812113**		**Nail Salons**
812115	**812190**		**Other Personal Care Services (including diet & weight reducing centers)**
		812191	Diet and Weight Reducing Centers
		812199	Other Personal Care Services
812115	**812210**		**Funeral Homes and Funeral Services**
812115	**812220**		**Cemeteries and Crematories**
812115	**812310**		**Coin-Operated Laundries and Drycleaners**
812115	**812320**		**Drycleaning and Laundry Services (except Coin-Operated)**
812115	**812330**		**Linen and Uniform Supply**
		812332	Industrial Launderers
		812331	Linen Supply
812115	**812910**		**Pet Care (except Veterinary) Services**
812115	**812920**		**Photofinishing**
		812992	One-Hour Photofinishing
		812921	Photofinishing Laboratories (except One-Hour)

SOI PUBLISHED CODE	PBA CODE	NAICS CODE	INDUSTRY
812115	**812930**		**Parking Lots and Garages**
812115	**812990**		**All Other Personal Services**

Religious, Grantmaking, Civic, Professional and Similar Organizations

SOI PUBLISHED CODE	PBA CODE	NAICS CODE	INDUSTRY
813000	**813000**		**Religious, Grantmaking, Civic, Professional and Similar Organizations**
		813910	Business Activities
		813410	Civic and Social Organizations
		813312	Environment, Conservation and Wildlife Organizations
		813211	Grantmaking Foundations
		813311	Human Rights Organization
		813930	Labor Unions and Similar Labor Organizations
		813219	Other Grantmaking and Giving Services
		813990	Other Similar Organizations (except Business, Professional, Labor and Political Organizations)
		813319	Other Social Advocacy Organizations
		813940	Political Organizations
		813920	Professional Organizations
		813110	Religious Oraganizations
		813212	Voluntary Health Organizations

NATURE OF BUSINESS NOT ALLOCABLE

SOI PUBLISHED CODE	PBA CODE	NAICS CODE	INDUSTRY
900000	**900000**		**Nature of Business Not Allocable**

INDEX

INDEX

A

Accommodation, 379, 380
Accommodation and food services, 379–382
Accounting, tax preparation, bookkeeping, and payroll services, 333, 334
Activities related to credit intermediation, 287, 288
Administrative and support and waste management and remediation services, 353–354
Administrative and support services, 353–358
Advertising and related services, 345, 346
Aerospace product and parts, 155, 156
Agricultural production, 1, 2
Agriculture, construction, and mining machinery manufacturing, 123, 124
Agriculture, forestry, fishing and hunting, 1–6
Air, rail, and water transportation, 237–242
Air transportation, 237, 238
Amusement, gambling, and recreation industries, 377, 378
Animal food and grain and oilseed milling, 37, 38
Apparel accessories and other apparel manufacturing, 67, 68
Apparel knitting mills, 63, 64
Apparel manufacturing, 63–72
Apparel, piece goods, and notions, 187, 188
Architectural and structural metals manufacturing, 115, 116
Architectural, engineering, and related services, 335, 336
Arts, entertainment, and recreation, 375–378
Asphalt paving, roofing, other petroleum and coal product manufacturing, 81, 82
Audio & video equip., reproducing magnetic and optical media, 141, 142
Automotive equipment rental and leasing, 324, 325
Automotive repair and maintenance, 383, 384

B

Bakeries and tortilla, 47, 48
Basic chemical, 83, 84
Beer, wine and distilled alcoholic beverage, 197, 198
Beer, wine, and liquor stores, 221, 222
Beverage and tobacco product manufacturing, 51–58
Boiler, tank, and shipping container manufacturing, 117, 118
Book publishers, 257, 258
Breweries, 53, 54
Broadcasting (except internet), 267, 268
Building material and garden equipment and supplies dealers, 211–218

C

Cement, concrete, lime and gypsum product manufacturing, 103, 104
Chemical and allied products, 193, 194
Chemical manufacturing, 83–94
Chemical product and preparation manufacturing, 93, 94
Clay, refractory, and other nonmetallic mineral products, 99, 100
Clothing and clothing accessories stores, 227, 228
Coal mining, 9–10
Coating, engraving, heat treating, and allied activities, 119, 120
Combination gas and electric, 23, 24
Commercial and industrial machinery and equipment rental, 327, 328
Commercial and service industry machinery manufacturing, 127, 128
Commercial banking, 277, 278
Commodity contracts dealing and brokerage, 293, 294
Communications equipment, 139, 140
Computer and electronic product manufacturing, 137–146
Computer and peripheral equipment manufacturing, 137, 138
Computer systems design and related services, 339, 340
Construction, 25–30
Construction of buildings, 25, 26
Converted paper product manufacturing, 75, 76

Credit card issuing and other consumer credit, 281, 282
Credit Intermediation, 275, 276
Cut and sew apparel contractors and mftrs., 65, 66
Cutlery, hardware, spring and wire, machine shops, nut, bolt, 113, 114

D

Dairy products, 43, 44
Data processing, hosting, and related services, 271, 272
Database, directory, and other publishers, 259, 260
Depository credit intermediation, 277–280
Drugs and druggists' sundries, 185, 186

E

Educational services, 361, 362
Electric power generation, transmission, and distribution, 17, 18
Electrical contractors, 31, 32
Electrical equipment, appliance, and component manufacturing, 147–152
Electrical equipment, 149, 150
Electrical goods, 175, 176
Electrical lighting equipment and household appliance, 147, 148
Electronics and appliance stores, 209, 210
Employment services, 353, 354
Engine, turbine, and power transmission equipment, 133, 134

F

Fabricated metal product manufacturing, 111–122
Farm product raw material, 191, 192
Finance and insurance, 275–316
Food and beverage stores, 219, 220
Food, beverage, and liquor stores, 219–236
Food manufacturing, 37–50
Food services and drinking places, 381, 382
Forestry and logging, 3, 4
Forging and stamping, 111, 112
Foundries, 109, 110
Fruit and vegetable preserving and specialty food, 41, 42
Furniture and home furnishing stores, 207, 208
Furniture and related product manufacturing, 161, 162
Furniture, sports, toys, jewelry, other durable goods, 181, 182

G

Gasoline stations, 225, 226
General merchandise stores, 231, 232
Glass and glass product manufacturing, 101, 102
Grocery and related product, 189, 190

H

Hardware, plumbing, heating equipment, and supplies, 177, 178
Hardware stores, 213, 214
Health and personal care stores, 223, 224
Health care and social assistance, 363–374
Heavy and civil engineering construction, 27, 28
Home centers; paint and wallpaper stores, 211, 212
Hospitals, nursing and residential care facilities, 373, 374

I

Industrial machinery 125, 126
Information, 253–276
Insurance agencies and brokerages, 305, 306
Insurance carriers and related activities, 297–310
Intl. trade, secondary financing, other nondepository credit, 285, 286
Investment banking and securities dealing, 289, 290
Iron, steel mills, and steel product, 105, 106

L

Land subdivision, 29, 30
Lawn and garden equipment and supplies stores, 217, 218
Leather and allied product manufacturing, 69, 70
Legal services, 331, 332
Lessors of buildings, 315, 316

Lessors of miniwarehouses, self-storage, other real estate, 317, 318
Lessors of nonfinan. intangible assets (ex. Copyrighted works), 329, 330
Life insurance, 297, 398
Life insurance, mutual companies (Form 1120L), 300, 301
Life insurance, stock companies (Form 1120L), 299, 300
Lumber and other construction materials wholesalers, 169, 170

M

Machinery, equipment, and supplies, 179, 180
Machinery manufacturing, 123–136
Management of companies (holding companies), 349–352
Management, scientific, and technical consulting services, 341, 342
Manufacturing, 37–166
Meat and seafood processing, 45, 46
Medical equipment and supplies, 163, 164
Metal and mineral (except petroleum), 173, 174
Metal ore mining, 11, 12
Metalworking machinery, 131, 132
Mining, 7–16
Misc. health care and social assistance, 371, 372
Miscellaneous manufacturing, 163–166
Miscellaneous nondurable goods, 199, 200
Miscellaneous store retailers, 233, 234
Motion picture and sound recording industries, 263–266
Motion picture and video industries (except video rental), 263, 264
Motor vehicle and motor vehicle parts and supplies, 167, 168
Motor vehicle and parts manufacturing, 153, 154
Motor vehicle dealers and parts dealers, 203–206
Mutual property and casualty companies (Form 1120-PC), 303, 304

N

Natural gas distribution, 19, 20
Navigational, measuring, electromedical, and control instruments, 145, 146
New and used car dealers, 203, 204
Newspaper publishers, 253, 254
Nondepository credit intermediation, 281–288
Nonferrous metal production and processing, 107, 108
Nonmetallic mineral mining and quarrying, 13, 14
Nonmetallic mineral product manufacturing, 99–104
Nonstore retailers, 235, 236

O

Offices of bank holding companies, 349, 350
Offices of dentists, 365, 366
Offices of other bank holding companies, 351, 352
Offices of other health practitioners, 367, 368
Offices of physicians, 363, 364
Offices of real estate agents and brokers, 319, 320
Oil and gas extraction, 7, 8
Open-end investment funds (Form 1120-RIC), 311, 312
Other administrative and support services, 357, 358
Other arts, entertainment, and recreation, 375, 379
Other building material dealers, 215, 216
Other consumer goods and general rental centers, 325, 326
Other electrical equipment and component manufacturing, 151, 152
Other fabricated metal product, 121, 122
Other financial vehicles, 313, 314
Other financial vehicles and other investment companies, 313–314
Other food, 49, 50
Other general purpose machinery, 135, 136
Other information services, internet publishing, web portals, 273, 275
Other insurance related activities, 309, 310
Other miscellaneous manufacturing, 165, 166

Other motor vehicle and parts dealers, 205, 206
Other professional, scientific, and technical services, 347, 348
Other real estate activities, 321, 322
Other repair and maintenance, 385, 386
Other services, 383–390
Other special trade contractors, 35, 36
Other transportation and support activities, 249, 250
Other transportation equipment and railroad rolling stock manufacturing, 159, 160
Outpatient care centers, 369, 370

P

Paint, coating, and adhesive, 89, 90
Paper and paper product, 183, 184
Paper manufacturing, 73–76
Periodical publishers, 255, 256
Personal and laundry services, 387, 388
Petroleum and coal products manufacturing, 79–82
Petroleum and petroleum products, 195, 196
Petroleum refineries (including integrated), 79, 80
Pharmaceutical and medicine, 87, 88
Pipeline transportation, 247, 248
Plastics and rubber product manufacturing, 95–98
Plastics product, 95, 96
Plumbing, heating, and air conditioning contractors, 33, 34
Primary metal manufacturing, 105–110
Printing and related support activities, 77, 78
Professional and commercial equipment and supplies 171, 172
Professional, scientific, and technical services, 331–348
Publishing industries, 253–262
Pulp, paper, and paperboard mills, 73, 74

R

Rail transportation, 239, 240
Real estate, 315–322
Real estate and rental leasing, 315–330
Real estate credit Incl. Mortgage Bankers and Originators, 283, 284
Religious, grantmaking, civic, professional organizations, 389, 390
Rental and leasing services, 323–330
Repair and maintenance, 383–384
Resin, synthetic rubber, and fibers and filaments, 85, 86
Retail trade, 203–236
Rubber product, 97, 98

S

Savings institutions, credit unions, and other depository credit intermediation, 279, 280
Scientific research and development services, 343, 344
Securities brokerage, 291, 292
Securities, commodity contracts, and other financial investments, 289–296
Security and commodity exchanges and other financial investment, 295, 296
Semiconductor and other electronic component,143, 144
Ship and boat building, 157, 158
Soap, cleaning compound, and toilet preparation, 91, 92
Soft drink and ice, 51, 52
Software publishers, 261, 262
Sound recording industries, 265, 266
Special trade contractors, 31–36
Specialized design services, 337, 338
Sporting goods, hobby, book, and music stores, 229, 230
Stock property and casualty companies (Form 1120-PC), 305, 306
Sugar and confectionery products, 39, 40
Support activities and fishing, hunting, and trapping, 5, 6
Support activities for mining, 15, 16

T

Telecommunications (wired, wireless, satellite, internet providers), 269, 270
Textile mills, 59, 60
Textile mills and textile product mills, 59–62
Textile product mills, 61, 62
Tobacco manufacturing, 57, 58

Transit and ground passenger transportation, 245, 246
Transportation and warehousing, 237–252
Transportation equipment manufacturing, 153–162
Travel arrangement and reservation services, 355, 356
Truck transportation, 243, 244

U

Utilities, 17–24

V

Ventilation, heating, A.C. & commercial refrigeration equip., 129, 130

W

Warehousing and storage, 251, 252
Waste management and remediation services, 359, 360
Water, sewage, and other systems, 21, 22
Water transportation, 241, 242
Wholesale electronic markets and agents and brokers, 201, 202
Wholesale trade, 167–202
Wholesale trade, durable goods, 167–182
Wholesale trade, nondurable goods, 183–202
Wineries and distilleries, 55, 56
Wood product manufacturing, 71, 72